HBR Guide to **Getting the Right Work Done**

Harvard Business Review Guides

Arm yourself with the advice you need to succeed on the job, from the most trusted brand in business. Packed with how-to essentials from leading experts, the HBR Guides provide smart answers to your most pressing work challenges.

The titles include:

HBR Guide to Better Business Writing

HBR Guide to Finance Basics for Managers

HBR Guide to Getting the Mentoring You Need

HBR Guide to Getting the Right Job

HBR Guide to Getting the Right Work Done

HBR Guide to Giving Effective Feedback

HBR Guide to Making Every Meeting Matter

HBR Guide to Managing Stress at Work

HBR Guide to Managing Up and Across

HBR Guide to Persuasive Presentations

HBR Guide to Project Management

HBR Guide to **Getting the Right Work Done**

HARVARD BUSINESS REVIEW PRESS

Boston, Massachusetts

Printed in the United States of America

20 19 18 17 16

Library of Congress Cataloging-in-Publication Data

HBR guide to getting the right work done.
p. cm.
ISBN 978-1-4221-8711-1 (alk. paper)
1. Time management. 2. Decision making. I. Harvard Business Review Press. II. Title: Harvard Business Review guide to getting the right work done. III. Title: Guide to getting the right work done.
HD69.T54.H374 2012
650.1'1—dc23

2012012383

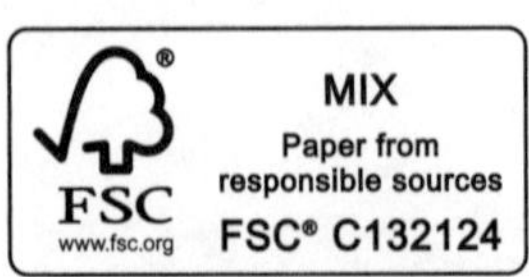

What You'll Learn

Are you paralyzed by the pile of projects on your plate? Has fear of delegation buried you in administrivia? Is your focus destroyed by the incessant call of e-mail and Twitter? Do you leave work exhausted—but with little to show for it? Are promotions passing you by because your peers are more productive?

You can't possibly tackle every task that awaits you. But here's the good news: You can learn to get the *right* work done, focusing your time and energy where it'll yield the greatest reward—for you and your organization. This guide will help by offering a range of accessible tools so you can sample them and see what works for you.

You'll get better at:

- Prioritizing
- Staying focused
- Working less but accomplishing more
- Stopping bad habits and developing good ones
- Writing to-do lists that work

- Breaking overwhelming projects into manageable pieces
- Thwarting e-mail overload
- Refueling your energy

Contents

Section 8: MAINTAIN YOUR NEW APPROACH

Section 9: EXPLORE FURTHER

Section 1
Get Started

Chapter 1
You Can't Get It *All* Done

by Peter Bregman

Brad is as hard a worker as anyone I know. (Names and some details have been changed.) He's not just busy, he's keenly focused on getting the right things done. And it pays off—he is the largest single revenue generator at his well-known professional services firm. A few days before Thanksgiving, Brad flew from Boston to Los Angeles with his family. During the five-hour flight, he decided not to use the plane's Internet access, choosing to play with his children instead. A five-hour digital vacation.

When they landed, Brad turned on his BlackBerry and discovered that a crisis had developed while he was in the air. He had close to five hundred new e-mail messages.

So much for a digital vacation.

The truth is, we can't really get away from it. There's no escaping the nonstop surge of e-mail, text, voice mail, Twitter, Facebook, LinkedIn—and that's just the technology-based stream. How can we ever catch up?

We can't.

The idea that we can get it all done is the biggest myth in time management. There's no way Brad can meaningfully go through all his e-mail, and there's no way any of us are going to accomplish everything we want to.

Face it: You're a limited resource.

On the one hand, that's depressing. On the other hand, acknowledging it can be tremendously empowering. Once we admit that we aren't going to get it *all* done, we're in a much better position to make explicit choices about what we *are* going to do. Instead of letting things haphazardly fall through the cracks, we can intentionally push the unimportant things aside and focus our energy on the things that matter most.

That's what this guide is all about.

There are two main challenges in doing the right things: identifying what they are and then doing them.

To determine the "right things," we need to make choices that will move us toward the outcomes we most want. Which, of course, means we need to know what our priorities are.

In terms of the second challenge—the "doing" or follow-through—we need tools. Rituals. To-do lists. Delegation skills.

But which tools will work best for you? Which rituals will help you follow through? You might be the kind of person who can read through a book like this, full of great advice, and implement it all at once. I am not. I get overwhelmed and end up not changing anything.

So, here's one way to use this guide:

1. **Identify your time management challenges.** Do you leave the office with a nagging feeling that you worked all day but didn't get your most important work done? Are you distracted by little things? Avoiding big, hairy projects? Take this three-minute quiz (see "How well do you manage distraction?") to discover where you're distracting yourself the most.

2. **Find one piece of advice you think will have the greatest impact on your work.** Once you've identified your biggest challenges, read through this guide and find a tip that speaks to you. Maybe you're not clear on your "right things." Maybe the rituals you're using aren't working. Maybe you procrastinate. Choose one tactic you think will help you the most. Then do that *one* thing.

3. **Do it again.** Once that tactic has had an impact on your work, repeat the process. Return to this guide and select another tip.

Because Brad is a paragon of productivity, he decided to put his BlackBerry away and wait to reply to the messages until he was in his hotel room. Then, using his laptop, he attacked the crisis: called his client to allay their concerns, delegated tasks to his team, and sent an e-mail to his team and his client detailing the plan. Within an hour, he had finished, shut his laptop, left his BlackBerry in his room, and enjoyed a fun, chaos-filled dinner with

TABLE 1-1

How well do you manage distraction?

1.	Even though it feels like I work nonstop all day, I still don't get the most important things done.	Never	Occasionally	Often	Always
2.	No matter what I intend to focus on at the beginning of the day, as soon as I start working (checking e-mail, etc.), I seem to get derailed and lose my focus.	Never	Occasionally	Often	Always
3.	When I have something important and challenging I want to accomplish, I spend my time doing lots of little things and avoiding the big one.	Never	Occasionally	Often	Always
4.	When my work gets challenging, I somehow keep interrupting myself by surfing the Web, doing e-mail, and other distractions.	Never	Occasionally	Often	Always
5.	When I'm on a conference call, I get bored and start multitasking until I miss something important; then I try to recover without making it obvious that I wasn't paying attention.	Never	Occasionally	Often	Always
6.	I'm late for meetings and appointments because I try to get one more thing done instead of leaving enough time for preparation and/or travel.	Never	Occasionally	Often	Always
7.	I feel overwhelmed and stressed out by the number of things I have to do.	Never	Occasionally	Often	Always
8.	My work day ends in frustration as I think about all the things I intended to accomplish but didn't.	Never	Occasionally	Often	Always
9.	When I try to make space for my own work, I get interrupted by others and I find it hard to protect my time.	Never	Occasionally	Often	Always
10.	I don't spend enough time at work in my "sweet spot" (doing work I'm really good at and enjoy the most).	Never	Occasionally	Often	Always

Score yourself

Number of checks in:

Never _____

Occasionally _____

Often _____

Always _____

Guide to scores

If you selected mostly "Never," congratulations! You're already doing a great job of focusing on the work that will give you—and your organization—the highest reward. You likely already have rituals and tactics that make you productive. Look to this guide for some new tips and ideas to expand your collection of productivity tools.

If you selected mostly "Occasionally," you're doing pretty well. Perhaps willpower or delegating is helping you focus on getting the right work done. But there's even more you could be doing to boost your productivity. Perhaps you haven't experimented with rituals. Perhaps your obsession with e-mail is derailing you. Read on to discover new ideas about how you can get even more of the right work done.

If you selected mostly "Often," you could use a process to help you get and stay focused on the right work. Resist the allure of "urgent" projects to focus on the work with the greatest long-term rewards. Learn how to craft the most useful to-do lists so that you can power through them and leave work feeling a sense of accomplishment.

If you selected mostly "Always," you need help. But you know that, because you bought this guide, so you're already on the path to productivity. Pick your biggest pain point and start there, then return to the Guide as often as you need to.

This quiz is derived from Peter's book, *18 Minutes: Find Your Focus, Master Distractions, and Get the Right Things Done*. For free *18 Minutes* tools and resources (including an online version of this quiz offering more detailed results and feedback), visit http://www.peterbregman.com.

his family—which, at that time, was precisely the right thing for him to do.

Peter Bregman is a strategic adviser to CEOs and their leadership teams. His latest book is *18 Minutes: Find Your Focus, Master Distraction, and Get the Right Things Done.*

Chapter 2

Nine Things Successful People Do Differently

by Heidi Grant Halvorson

Why have you been so successful in reaching some of your goals, but not others? If you aren't sure, you're far from alone. Even brilliant, highly accomplished people are pretty lousy when it comes to understanding why they succeed or fail. The intuitive answer—that you're born predisposed to certain talents and lacking in others—is really just one small piece of the puzzle. In fact, decades of research on achievement suggest that successful people reach their personal and professional goals not

---

Excerpted with permission from *Nine Things Successful People Do Differently* (product #11065).

simply because of who they are, but more often because of what they do.

What follows are the nine things that successful people do—the strategies they use to set and pursue goals (sometimes without consciously realizing it) that have the biggest impact on performance.

1. Get Specific

When you set a goal, be as specific as possible. "Lose five pounds" is a better goal than "lose some weight," because it gives you a clear idea of what success looks like. Knowing exactly what you want to achieve keeps you motivated until you get there. Also, consider the specific actions you'll need to take to reach your goal. Promising you'll "eat less" or "sleep more" is too vague. "I'll be in bed by 10 PM on weeknights" leaves no doubt about what you need to do, and whether or not you've actually done it.

Spelling out exactly what you want to achieve removes the possibility of settling for less—of telling yourself that what you've done is "good enough." It also makes your course of action clearer.

Instead of "getting ahead at work," make your goal more concrete, such as "a pay raise of at least $ _____" or "a promotion to at least the _____ level."

To be successful, you also need to get specific about the obstacles you may encounter. In fact, what you really need to do is go back and forth, thinking about the success you want to achieve and the steps it will take to get there. This strategy is called **mental contrasting,** and it's a remarkably effective way to set goals and strengthen your commitment.

To use the mental contrasting technique, first imagine how you'll feel attaining your goal. Picture it as vividly as you can—really consider the details. Next, think about the obstacles in your way. For instance, if you wanted to get a better, higher-paying job, you would start by imagining the sense of pride and excitement you would feel accepting a lucrative offer at a top firm. Then you would think about what stands between you and that offer—namely, all the other really outstanding candidates. Kind of makes you want to polish up your résumé a bit, doesn't it?

That's called **experiencing the necessity to act;** it's a state that's critical for reaching your goal, because it gets the psychological wheels in motion. Mental contrasting turns wishes and desires into reality by bringing attention and clarity to what you will need to do to make them happen.

2. Seize the Moment to Act on Your Goals

Given how busy most of us are and how many things we're juggling at once, it's not surprising that we routinely miss opportunities to act on a goal. Did you really have no time to work out today? No chance at any point to return that phone call?

To seize the moment, decide when and where you'll take action, in advance. Be specific ("If it's Monday, Wednesday, or Friday, I'll work out for thirty minutes before work"). Studies show that this **if-then planning** helps your brain to detect and take advantage of the opportunity when it arises, increasing your chances of success by roughly 300 percent. (For more on planning when and where you'll perform tasks, see "How to Tackle Your To-Do List," later in this guide.)

Deciding in advance when and where you will take specific actions to reach your goal (or how you will address obstacles you might encounter) is probably the most effective single thing you can do to ensure your success.

If-then plans take the form:

> If X happens, then I will do Y.

For example:

> If I'm getting too distracted by colleagues, then I'll stick to a five-minute chat limit and return to work.

Why are these plans so effective? Because they're written in the language of your brain—the language of contingencies. Humans are particularly good at encoding and remembering information in "if X, then Y" terms, and using these contingencies to guide their behavior, often below their level of awareness.

Once you've formulated your if-then plan, your unconscious brain will start scanning the environment, searching for the situation in the "if" part of your plan. This enables you to seize the critical moment ("Oh, it's 4 PM! I'd better return those calls!"), even when you're busy doing other things.

Since you've already decided exactly what you need to do, you can execute the plan without having to consciously think about it.

3. Know Exactly How Far You Have Left to Go

Achieving any goal also requires honest and regular monitoring of your progress—if not by others, then by you yourself. If you don't know how well you're doing, you can't adjust your behavior or your strategies accordingly. Check your progress frequently—weekly, or even daily, depending on the goal.

Feedback helps motivate us because we subconsciously tune in to the presence of a discrepancy between where we are now and where we want to be. When your brain detects a discrepancy, it reacts by throwing resources at it: attention, effort, deeper processing of information, and willpower.

If self-monitoring and seeking out feedback are so important, you may be wondering why we don't always do it. The first and most obvious reason is that it's effortful; you need to stop whatever else you're doing and really focus on assessment. And of course, the news isn't always positive; sometimes we avoid checking in on our progress because we don't want to acknowledge how little progress we've made. Self-monitoring requires a lot of willpower, but you can make it easier by using if-then planning to schedule your self-assessments.

Done the right way, assessing your progress will keep you motivated from start to finish. Done the wrong way, it may actually lower your motivation. Recent research by University of Chicago psychologists Minjung Koo and Ayelet Fishbach examined how people pursuing goals were affected by focusing on either how far they had already come (**to-date thinking**) or what was left to be accomplished (**to-go thinking**).

Koo and Fishbach's studies consistently show that when we're pursuing a goal and consider how far we've already come, we feel a premature sense of accomplishment and begin to slack off.

When we focus on progress made, we're also more likely to try to achieve a sense of "balance" by making progress on other important goals. As a result, we wind up with lots of pots on the stove, but nothing is ever ready to eat.

If, instead, we focus on how far we have left to go (to-go thinking), motivation is not only sustained, it's heightened. So when you're assessing your progress, stay focused on the goal and never congratulate yourself too much on a job half-done. Save it for a job well—and completely—done.

4. Be a Realistic Optimist

When you're setting a goal, by all means engage in positive thinking about how likely you are to achieve it. Believing in your ability to succeed is enormously helpful for creating and sustaining your motivation. But don't underestimate the time, planning, effort, and persistence it will take to reach your goal. Thinking things will come to you easily and effortlessly leaves you ill prepared for the journey ahead and can significantly increase the odds of failure.

This is the difference between being a realistic optimist and an unrealistic optimist.

Realistic optimists believe they will succeed, but also believe they have to make success happen—through things like planning, persistence, and choosing the right strategies. They recognize the need for considering how they'll deal with obstacles.

Unrealistic optimists, on the other hand, believe that success will happen to them—that the universe will reward them for their positive thinking.

Cultivate your realistic optimism by combining a positive attitude with an honest assessment of the challenges that await you. Don't just visualize success; visualize the steps you will take in order to make success happen. If your first strategy doesn't work, what's plan B? (This is another great time to use your if-then plans.) Remember, it's not "negative" to think about the problems you are likely to face—it's foolish not to.

5. Focus on Getting Better, Rather Than Being Good

Believing you have the ability to reach your goals is important, but so is believing you can *get* the ability. Many of us believe that our intelligence, personality, and physical aptitudes are fixed—that no matter what we do, we won't improve. As a result, we focus on goals that are all about proving ourselves, rather than developing and acquiring new skills.

Fortunately, **abilities of all kinds are profoundly malleable.** Embracing the fact that you can change will allow you to make better choices and reach your fullest potential. People whose goals are about getting better, rather than being good, take difficulty in stride and appreciate the journey as much as the destination.

How can you motivate yourself to approach new responsibilities with confidence and energy? The answer is simple, though perhaps a little surprising: **give yourself permission to screw up.**

I know this may not be something you're thrilled to hear, because you're probably thinking, if you screw up you'll be the one to pay for it. But you needn't worry, because when people feel they're allowed to make mistakes, they're significantly less likely to actually make them!

People approach any task with one of two types of goals: what I call **be-good goals,** where the focus is on proving that you have a lot of ability and already know what you're doing, and **get-better goals,** where the focus is on developing ability and learning to master a new skill.

The problem with be-good goals is that they tend to backfire when we're faced with something unfamiliar or difficult. We quickly start feeling that we don't actually know what we're doing, that we lack ability—and this creates a lot of anxiety. And nothing interferes with performance quite like anxiety does; it is *the* productivity killer.

Get-better goals, on the other hand, are practically bulletproof. When we think about what we're doing in terms of learning and mastering—accepting that we may make some mistakes along the way—we stay motivated despite setbacks that might occur.

A focus on getting better also enhances the experience of working; we naturally find what we do more interesting and enjoyable when we think about it in terms of progress, rather than perfection. Finding what you do interesting and believing it has inherent value is one of the most effective ways to stay motivated despite unexpected roadblocks. In fact, interest doesn't just keep you going despite fatigue; it actually replenishes your energy.

6. Have Grit

Grit is a willingness to commit to long-term goals and to persist in the face of difficulty. Gritty people obtain more education in their lifetimes and earn higher college GPAs. Grit predicts which cadets will stick out their first grueling year at West Point. In fact, grit even predicts how far contestants at the Scripps National Spelling Bee will go.

The good news is that if you aren't particularly gritty now, you can do something about it. People who lack grit often believe that they just don't have the innate abilities successful people have. If that describes your own thinking, you're wrong. As I mentioned earlier, effort, planning, persistence, and good strategies are what it really takes to succeed. Embracing this knowledge will not only help you see yourself and your goals more accurately, but also do wonders for your grit.

Study after study of successful people, whether they are athletes, musicians, or mathematicians, shows that the key to success and enhanced ability is deliberate practice—thousands of hours spent mastering the necessary skills and knowledge.

Grit is all about not giving up in the face of difficulty, even when you're tired or discouraged. And the best predictor of not giving up is how we explain that difficulty in the first place. When you're having a hard time, what do you blame?

Entity theorists, who are convinced that ability is fixed, tend to **blame setbacks on a lack of ability.** If this is hard for me, I must not be good at it. As a result, they lack grit; they give up on themselves way too soon, inadvertently reinforcing their misconception that they can't improve.

Incremental theorists, on the other hand, tend to **blame setbacks on more controllable factors**—insufficient effort, using the wrong strategy, poor planning. When faced with difficulty, they try harder, armed with the belief that improvement is always possible. This gritty attitude leads to far greater long-term accomplishments.

Change really is always possible, and the science here is crystal clear. There is no ability that can't be developed with experience. The next time you find yourself thinking, "But I'm just not good at this," remember: You're just not good at it *yet.*

7. Build Your Willpower Muscle

Our self-control "muscle" is just like others in your body; when it doesn't get much exercise, it becomes weaker over time. But when you give it regular workouts, it will grow stronger and help you reach your goals.

To build willpower, take on a challenge that requires you to do something you'd rather not do. Give up high-fat snacks, do a hundred sit-ups a day, try to learn a new skill. When you find yourself wanting to give in or give up—don't. Start with just one activity and make a plan for how you'll deal with troubles when they occur ("If I want a snack, I'll eat one piece of fresh or three pieces of dried fruit"). It will be hard in the beginning, but it will get easier, and that's the whole point. As your strength grows, you can take on more challenges and step up your self-control workout.

Like biceps or triceps, willpower can vary in its strength, not only from person to person, but from moment to moment.

The good news is that willpower depletion is only temporary. Give your muscle time to bounce back, and you'll be back in fighting form. When rest is not an option, you can accelerate your recovery simply by thinking about people you know who have a lot of self-control.

Or, you can try giving yourself a pick-me-up. Anything that lifts your spirits—listening to a favorite song, calling a good friend, or reflecting on a past success—should also help restore your self-control when you're looking for a quick fix.

8. Don't Tempt Fate

No matter how strong your willpower muscle becomes, it's important to always respect the fact that it's limited, and if you overtax it, you will temporarily run out of steam. Don't try to take on two challenging goals at once, if you can help it (like quitting smoking *and* dieting). And make achieving your goal easier by keeping yourself out of harm's way. Many people are overly confident in their ability to resist temptation, and as a result they put themselves in situations where temptations abound. Successful people know not to make reaching a goal harder than it already is.

Resisting temptation is a key part of successfully reaching just about any goal. What we want to do is often the very opposite of what we need to do. This may sound a bit counterintuitive, but the very first thing you're going to want to do if you're serious about resisting temptation is **make peace with the fact that your willpower is limited.**

Even if you've built up large reserves of willpower, you won't have much left for sticking to your resolutions at the end of a long day of putting out fires at work. That's why it's so important to give some thought to when you're most likely to feel drained and vulnerable and make an if-then plan to keep yourself out of harm's way.

It's far easier to abstain from doing something all together than it is to give in just a little and then stop. And you need more and more self-control to stop a behavior the longer it goes on. If you don't want to eat the entire slice of cake, don't take "just one bite."

9. Focus on What You Will Do, Not What You Won't Do

Do you want to get promoted, quit smoking, or put a lid on your bad temper? Then plan how you'll replace counterproductive behaviors with more constructive ones. Too often, people concentrate all their efforts on what they want to stop doing and fail to consider how they will fill the void. Trying to avoid a thought can make it more active in your mind ("Don't think about white bears!"). The same holds true when it comes to behavior; by trying not to do something, you strengthen rather than diminish the impulse.

If you want to change your ways, ask yourself, "What will I do instead?" For example, if you're trying to gain control of your temper, you might make a plan such as, "If I'm starting to feel angry, then I'll take three deep breaths to calm down." By using deep breathing as a replacement for giving in to your anger, your success-sabotaging impulse will get worn away over time until it disappears completely.

Once you've decided to make an if-then plan to help you reach your goal, the next thing you need to do is figure out how to construct it.

There are three types of if-then plans:

- **"Replacement" if-then plans** do just what the name suggests—replace a negative behavior with a more positive one (as in the anger management strategy just described).
- **"Ignore" if-then plans** are focused on blocking out unwanted feelings, like cravings, performance anxiety, or self-doubts. ("If I have the urge to smoke, then I'll ignore it.")
- Finally, **"negation" if-then plans** involve spelling out the actions you won't be taking in the future. With these plans, if there is a behavior you want to avoid, you simply plan not to perform this behavior. ("If I am at the mall, then I won't buy anything.")

Of all three types, replacement plans are most successful. When it comes to reaching your goals, focusing on what you *will* do, not what you *won't* do, is the most effective way to achieve them.

Heidi Grant Halvorson, PhD, is a motivational psychologist and author of the HBR Single *Nine Things Successful People Do Differently* (Harvard Business Press, 2011) and the book *Succeed: How We Can Reach Our Goals* (Hudson Street Press, 2011). Her personal blog, *The Science of Success,* can be found at http://www.heidigranthalvorson.com/.

Chapter 3

Being More Productive

An Interview with David Allen and Tony Schwartz

by Daniel McGinn

David Allen is a productivity consultant and the author of the best seller *Getting Things Done,* which outlines the list-driven efficiency system adherents call by its acronym: GTD. Tony Schwartz, the author of the best-seller *Be Excellent at Anything,* is the CEO of The Energy Project, which helps people and organizations fuel engagement and productivity by drawing on the science of high performance.

Excerpted from *Harvard Business Review,* May 2011 (product # R1105D).

In this edited conversation with HBR, they discuss the distractive pull of e-mail, how they've been influenced by each other, and why you should do your most important task first thing in the morning (even though only one of them does).

HBR: Let's start with something simple. How does each of you define what you do?

Allen: I help people and organizations produce more with less input. I teach a set of best practices and a methodology that produce a greater sense of concentration and control.

Schwartz: We teach individuals and organizations how to manage energy more skillfully in order to get more work done in less time, more sustainably. That requires a new way of working—one that balances periods of high focus with intermittent renewal.

Both of you have written several books describing your techniques, but give me a quick summary.

Allen: I call what I've uncovered "the strategic value of clear space." Say you're going to cook dinner for people, it's 5:00 PM, and they're coming at 6:00. You want to have all the right ingredients. You want to have the right tools. You want the kitchen to be nice and clear. You need the freedom to make a creative mess. I teach people to achieve that freedom by taking very immediate, concrete steps: downloading all your commitments and projects into lists, focusing on "next actions," and thinking about the context—work that needs to be done in your office, or on the phone, or on the computer. You don't need to change who you are. You just need some simple but very powerful techniques.

Schwartz: We focus on the four primary dimensions of energy that we all need to perform at our best. The ground level is physical—fitness, sleep, nutrition, and rest. At the emotional level, it's about cultivating positive emotions—and as a leader, communicating them to others. At the mental level, it's about gaining more control of your attention—both by increasing [your] ability to focus on one thing at a time and by learning to shift into the right hemisphere to do more-creative work. And at the spiritual level, it's about defining purpose, because when something really matters, you bring far more energy to it. Very few [managers and] leaders I've met fully appreciate how meeting these needs—in themselves and for others—is absolutely critical to sustainable high performance. They're good at doing things, and they've been rewarded by being given more things to do. But increasingly, demand is outrunning their capacity. They're overloaded with e-mail and texts and all the information that comes in. We have to teach them to step back and say, "What do I actually want to do? What are the right choices? What are the costs of this choice?"

Let's talk about some of the concrete principles you teach. Tony, explain why you think people should

approach work as a series of short sprints, not an all-day marathon.

Schwartz: There's a fundamental misunderstanding about how human beings operate at their best. Most of us mistakenly assume we're meant to run like computers—at high speeds, continuously, for long periods of time, running multiple programs simultaneously. It's just not true. Human beings are designed to be *rhythmic.* The heart pulses; muscles contract and relax. We're at our best when we're moving rhythmically between spending energy and renewing it. We need to recognize the insight of athletes, who manage their work-rest ratios. We encourage people to work intensely for 90 minutes and then take a break to recover. We teach them to eat small, energy-rich meals every few hours, rather than three big meals a day. We believe napping drives productivity, although that remains a tough sell in most companies. Still, the reality is that if a person works continuously all through the day, she'll produce less than a person of equal talent who works very intensely for short periods and then recovers before working intensely again. (To learn more, see "Power Through Your Day in 90-Minute Cycles" and "Manage Your Energy, Not Your Time," later in this guide.)

Allen: It's also an issue of choosing the right work. Peter Drucker said that the toughest job for knowledge workers is defining the work. A century ago, 80% of the world made and moved things. You worked as long as you could, and then you slept, and then you got up and worked again. You didn't have to triage or make executive decisions. It's harder to be productive today because the work has become much more complex.

David, what's the biggest roadblock to productivity that you typically observe when you go into an organization for the first time?

Allen: People don't capture stuff that has their attention. They don't acknowledge it or objectify it. And it keeps rolling around in the organizational psyche as well as the personal psyche, draining energy and creating incredible psychic residue. People say, "I'll do that," but they don't write it down, and it goes into a black hole. That would be fine if it were just one thing, but it's hundreds of things. And people don't determine exactly what their commitment to that stuff is—what's the outcome they want to achieve, what's the next action required to move it forward. Your head is for having ideas, not holding them. Just dumping everything out of your head and externalizing it is a huge step, and it can have a significant effect.

The devil's advocate position is that this results in gigantic to-do lists, which are overwhelming in themselves.

Allen: You need lists because your brain isn't good at keeping them. Your mind is this dumb little computer that will wake you up at 3:00 AM and beat you bloody over stuff you can't do spit about while you're lying there. All it's doing is repeating stuff in open loops, and it sucks your energy like crazy.

Schwartz: There's a process of humility that's required here. It's a little bit of a turn on the 12-step notion of admitting that you're powerless over your addictions. In this case, the addiction is to e-mail and information. The problem is that our willpower and self-discipline are wildly overrated. We think the way to make a change is to push harder—to resist that chocolate-chip cookie, or wake up early and get to the gym. It doesn't work. It's humbling to discover that we're creatures of habit, and what we did yesterday is what we're going to do today. You want to co-opt the process by which negative habits arise without your intention, and substitute what we call "positive rituals," or deliberate practices. (See Section 5: Create Rituals.)

How much do you know about each other's work—and how much do you use each other's strategies?

Schwartz: I always kept lists, but until I connected with David's work, I didn't realize that anything I didn't download would potentially create distractions—so now I keep lists of *everything*. Another ritual I have that aligns with David's work is to always do the most important task of the day first thing in the morning, when I'm most rested and least distracted. Ninety percent of people check their e-mail as soon as they get to work. That turns their agenda over to someone else.

David, how has Tony's thinking influenced the way you work?

Allen: The piece that's made the biggest difference is his work on energy cycles. I actually brought a pillow into work. I work in a glass office, and now people can see me lying on my floor taking a nap for 20 minutes. That's directly from Tony's work. I wish I had the discipline Tony does to tackle the hardest tasks first thing in the morning, but I don't.

Schwartz: It's not that you don't have the discipline—it's that you don't have the ritual. If you built that ritual, I have zero doubt that you could do it.

Allen: Part of the way to attack that problem is to break big tasks down and focus on smaller "next actions," which can seem more manageable. What most people put on a to-do list are vague things like "Mom." Great! So Tony will write down "Mom," signifying that he has to decide whether to get his mother a birthday present, and what to buy, and how to deliver it. He'll resist looking at the list, because he knows there's a lot of work in that simple notation. Instead the list should specify a smaller next action—say, "Call sister re: Mom's birthday." Oh, look—I can do that! There's actually a part of us that loves to produce, that loves to be complete. Now I've created motivation: I see a desired result, I have the confidence I can get there, and I see the path. A lot of what GTD does is set it up so that you only have to think about things once. The problem is that everybody is multitasking and getting distracted by the latest and loudest. They fail because they haven't captured, clarified, organized, or built in a regular review system they trust.

Schwartz: Let me beg to differ a little. Say you're working on a primary task and you get an e-mail. You hear that little Pavlovian beep, and you cannot resist it. So you turn to the e-mail and lose track of the initial task, and it takes you time to reconnect to it afterward. Researchers have found that over time and with practice, people get better at task shifting, but they never get remotely as good as they'd be if they did one thing at a time. (For more on effective to-do lists and multitasking, see Section 3: Organize Your Time.)

Allen: Let's take it a step further. Why do people get disturbed by that e-mail beep? It's because they don't trust that they've emptied their e-mail every 24 hours. Most people are living in an emergency scan mode. They never deal with their e-mail, so they're afraid there's still something sitting in there, and they're constantly allowing themselves to get distracted by it. (See Section 7: Take Control of Your E-mail.)

Last question: If people could take just one thing away from your work, what should it be?

Schwartz: [We] need to recognize that human beings are basically organisms containing energy. And that energy is either being renewed or being dissipated over time. An organization has to realize that part of its responsibility, whether it wants it or not, is to ensure that people have full tanks of energy. This is one of the big variables that will determine which organizations thrive in the next 10 or 20 years. [And until organizations do so, we need to take on that responsibility for ourselves.]

Allen: Think about it this way: While we've been sitting here talking, stuff has been piling up in our in-boxes and our voice mails. Some of it has the potential to meaningfully shift our priorities. When we turn to this accumulated stuff, we'll need to eliminate old business that is pulling on us, that's taking our attention, and reallocate our resources to these new priorities. You can only do one thing at a time, and you only have so many resources. You either feel OK about sitting here talking to us, or you feel bad about the 9,000 other things you're not doing. Everybody needs a system to make those choices wisely.

Daniel McGinn is a senior editor at *Harvard Business Review*.

Section 2
Prioritize Your Work

Chapter 4
Get a Raise by Getting the Right Work Done

by Peter Bregman

My friend Dave is notorious for eating fried food. (Names and some details changed.) Yet recently he was surprised to learn that his cholesterol was high because, as he put it, "The day before the test, I ate really well."

The idea of immediate results is alluring. But whether it's managing our diet or prioritizing our workload, there are no quick fixes.

I was reminded of this when a reporter asked me what advice I would give to someone who wanted to ask for a raise at a time when most wages are stagnating or falling. My answer? Don't ask.

It's not that I think people can't get raises right now. But if you haven't spent the last year laying the groundwork, it's highly unlikely that you'll be successful now. There's no formula—no perfect words or spinning of events—that will magically deliver a raise with a day or two of preparation.

But there is a formula for getting more money over time. And it starts with your ability to prioritize.

The formula is based on one simple premise: We can get more money when we demonstrate that we've added more value. And we can add more value when we spend the majority of our time focusing on the work that the most senior leaders in our organization *consider* valuable, which is almost always work that increases revenue or profits, either short-term or long-term.

But when we're not clear about what work is most important to our organization, one of two things can happen: Either we put the same amount of energy and effort into everything or we let the wrong things fall through the cracks.

Making more intentional and strategic choices about where to spend our time can mean the difference between a stagnant salary and a growing one. We can be more productive when we know which initiatives deserve our highest priority.

Here's my formula for getting a raise:

1. During this year's compensation conversation, take whatever is given to you without negotiation and with appreciation. Then explain that you're less interested in a raise right now and more interested in **how you can add tremendous value to the organization.**

2. Think like a shareholder of the company. Ask lots of questions about the strategy and what's keeping the top leaders awake at night. Understand how your department affects revenue or profitability and what's important to your direct manager. With your manager, identify the top two or three things you can work on that will drive revenue or profitability. Once you've had that conversation, **you'll have your raiseworthy work focus.**

3. Now **keep those two or three revenue and/or profitability drivers at the top of your to-do list.** Approach your daily work so that the majority of your effort moves the organization further in those areas. Share your to-do list with your manager, to keep you on the same page about your priorities and how your work affects the bigger picture. Quantify the impact you're making. If your manager asks you to do things outside of your top priorities, push back and discuss the possible trade-offs you could make. Sure, you'll need to work on some things that aren't important. But make a strategic choice to shortchange those.

After about six months of this laser focus, you'll be ready to talk about how you've added tremendous value on the things that matter most.

During that discussion you'll also be ready to talk about a real raise. That's good timing, since most organizations are beginning to think through their departmental budgets and promotions around the six-month mark.

Here's why this formula works: It's not a trick. If you focus on your highest-priority work—even if it requires that you push back when your manager asks you to work on other tasks—ultimately you and your manager will be more productive, and the organization will benefit. That's money in the bank. It will make your job more secure and you more promotable.

"So," I asked Dave. "Now that you know you have high cholesterol, are you going to change the way you eat?"

"No," Dave answered, true to form, "I'm taking a pill. My cholesterol will be lower in a few days and I can still eat everything."

Maybe I like doing things the hard way. But as far as I know, there's no pill for getting a raise.

Peter Bregman is a strategic adviser to CEOs and their leadership teams. His latest book is *18 Minutes: Find Your Focus, Master Distraction, and Get the Right Things Done*.

Chapter 5
The Worth-Your-Time Test

by Peter Bregman

Nate Eisman recently started working for a large consulting firm after many years as an independent consultant. (Some details changed to protect privacy.) He called me for some advice.

"I'm wasting a tremendous amount of time," he complained. "I'm in meetings all day. The only way I can get any real work done is by coming in super early and staying super late."

Nate had gone from an organization of one to an organization of several thousand and was drowning in the time suck of collaboration. He is not alone.

Working with people takes time. And different people have different priorities. Someone may need your per-

Adapted from content posted on hbr.org on April 1, 2010.

spective on an issue that's critical to him but not to you. Still, if he's a colleague, it's important to help. And often, we want to help.

On the other hand, we've all felt Nate's pain: How can we spend time where we add the most value and let go of the rest?

We need a way to quickly and confidently identify and reduce our extraneous commitments, to know for sure whether we need to deal with something or delegate it, and to manage our desire to be available to others. I propose a brief test that every commitment should pass before you agree to it. When someone comes to you with a request, ask yourself:

1. Am I the right person?
2. Is this the right time?
3. Do I have enough information?

If the request fails the test—if the answer to any one of these questions is "no"—then don't do it. Pass it to someone else (the right person), schedule it for another time (the right time), or wait until you have the information you need (either you or someone else needs to get it).

Sometimes it's impossible or inappropriate to wall yourself off completely. For example, what if your boss is the person who interrupts you? Or what if you're on vacation and an important client reaches out with a time-sensitive and crucial question?

The three test questions offer a clear, easy, and consistent way of knowing how to respond—and help us avoid the tendency to say yes to everything.

If your boss asks you to do something and her request fails the test, it's not just okay, it's *useful* to push back on or redirect her so the work is completed productively. It's not helpful to you, your boss, or your organization if you waste your time on the wrong work.

That's the irony. We try to be available because we want to be helpful. And yet being overwhelmed with tasks—especially those we consider to be a waste of our time—is exactly what will make us unhelpful.

When we get a meeting request that doesn't pass the test, we should decline it. When we're cc'd on an e-mail that doesn't require our attention, we need to delete it. And a 50-page presentation needs to pass the test before we read it—and even then, it's worth an e-mail asking which are the critical pages to review.

A few weeks after sharing the three questions with Nate, I called him at his office at around 6 PM to see how it was going. I guess it was going well, because I never reached him. He had already gone home.

Peter Bregman is a strategic adviser to CEOs and their leadership teams. His latest book is *18 Minutes: Find Your Focus, Master Distraction, and Get the Right Things Done.*

Chapter 6

Say Yes to Saying No

by Alexandra Samuel

If your e-mail in-box looks like mine, it's full of requests and invitations that promise challenging new projects, clients, and commitments. Sure, you enjoy the stimulation and excitement that come with these offers, but it's a fine line. You have to be selective about what you take on—and disciplined about retiring long-standing activities to make room for new ones. You have to be able to say no. Frequently, politely, and effectively.

The good news is that the same technologies that threaten to overload you with things to say yes to can also help you say no. Here's how:

Adapted from content posted on hbr.org on January 8, 2010.

Set your intentions

Before you say no, make it clear to yourself what you want to say yes to. Sites like 43Things.com and SuperViva .com can help you create lists of what you want to accomplish and experiences you want to have. Writing down your goals will help you clarify what's important, identify what you want to eliminate, and get the community support to achieve it.

Prioritize your commitments

A simple Excel spreadsheet can help you evaluate what's on your plate before you agree to take on more. Capture every project you're working on—even ones you've only thought about—and list these in column A, one row per task. Use column B to assign a priority to each project, ranking items from 1–5. In column C, capture the name of anyone who could take over or help with certain projects. Sort your projects according to priority.

For high-priority tasks you've noted could be delegated, e-mail or meet with everyone to whom you hope to transfer projects.

Review with your boss the list of high-priority tasks that only you can handle. Are they aligned with her and your unit's goals? If not, reevaluate to see if you should: shift priorities; delegate more of the projects; or defer some to a later date. (To download a sample Excel spreadsheet, visit my website at http://www.alexandrasamuel .com/career-work/excel-template-7-steps-to-achieving-your-goals.)

Make it easy to say "no"

When my in-box piles up with unanswered messages, you can bet that it's full of e-mails that require a no—ones that I can't bring myself to write. To make it easier, I've created a few different signature files in my e-mail client, with polite "no" messages for different circumstances: *I'd love to join you, but my schedule is really booked for the next month;* or *Thanks for thinking of us, but we're only taking on XYZ type of client right now;* or *That sounds like a great project, but my pro bono work is already committed for this quarter.* Using these removes the burden of working up the energy to let someone down.

Make "no" your default answer

Say no to the majority of invitations and project offers you receive unless they meet a short set of criteria. For example, I look for conferences that combine business development (getting clients), professional development (improving skills or knowledge), and personal development (regeneration or personal growth), and attend only events that promise meaningful value on at least two of those fronts. Write down your criteria and stick them to your computer monitor, or put them on a digital sticky note.

None of these practices will eliminate the anxiety that comes from saying no or the fear that you may be passing up a fantastic opportunity. But it's because saying no is so difficult that we need tools and systems to make it a little easier and a little more habitual. The more you say no, the better you'll be able to focus on your most important work.

Alexandra Samuel is the Director of the Social + Interactive Media Centre at Emily Carr University, and the co-founder of Social Signal, a Vancouver-based social media agency. You can follow Alex on Twitter at @awsamuel or her blog at alexandrasamuel.com.

Section 3
Organize Your Time

Chapter 7

A Practical Plan for When You Feel Overwhelmed

by Peter Bregman

We've all experienced it: that feeling that we've got so much to do that there's no chance we'll get it all done. And certainly not done on time. Right now, I'm feeling completely overwhelmed by my to-do list.

Here's the crazy part. I just spent the last two days *trying* to work without actually working. I start something but get distracted by the Internet. Or a phone call. Or an e-mail. At a time when I need to be most efficient, I've become less efficient than ever.

You'd think it would be the opposite—that when we have a lot to do, we'd become very productive in order to get it done. Sometimes that happens.

Adapted from content posted on hbr.org on September 23, 2010.

But often, when there's so much competing for our attention, we don't know where to begin—so we don't begin anywhere.

Next time you find yourself in this situation, try this approach:

1. **Write down everything you have to do on a piece of paper.** Resist the urge to use technology for this task. Why? I'm not sure, but somehow writing on paper—and then crossing things out—creates momentum.

2. **Spend 15 minutes completing as many of the easiest, fastest tasks on your list as you can.** Make your quick phone calls. Send your short e-mails. Don't worry about whether these are the most important tasks on your list. You're moving. The goal is to cross off as many tasks as possible in the shortest time. Use a timer to keep you focused.

3. **Work on the most daunting task for the next 35 minutes without interruption.** Turn off your phone, close all the unnecessary windows on your computer, and choose the most challenging task on your list, the one that instills the most stress or is the highest priority. *Then work on it and only it*—without hesitation or distraction—for 35 minutes.

4. **Take a break for 10 minutes, then begin the cycle again.** After 35 minutes of focused work, take

a break. Then start the hourlong process over again, beginning with the 15 minutes of quick actions.

"Thirty years ago," Anne Lamott writes in her book *Bird by Bird*, "my older brother, who was ten years old at the time, was trying to get a report on birds written that he'd had three months to write. It was due the next day. We were out at our family cabin in Bolinas, and he was at the kitchen table close to tears, surrounded by binder paper and pencils and unopened books on birds, immobilized by the hugeness of the task ahead. Then my father sat down beside him, put his arm around my brother's shoulder, and said, 'Bird by bird, buddy. Just take it bird by bird.'"

That's it. *Bird by bird, starting with a bunch of easy birds to help you feel accomplished and then tackling a hard one to gain serious traction and reduce your stress level.* All timed.

Working within a specific and limited time frame is important because the **race against time keeps you focused.** When stress is generalized and diffuse, it's hard to manage. Using a short time frame actually increases the pressure but keeps your effort specific and particular to a single task. That increases good, motivating stress while reducing negative, disconcerting stress. So the fog of feeling overwhelmed dissipates, and forward movement becomes possible.

In practice, I'm finding that although I make myself work at least the full 35 minutes, I don't *always* stop when the 35 minutes of hard work are over, because I'm in the middle of something and I have traction. On the other hand, though it's tempting, I don't exceed the 15 minutes of easy, fast work. When the timer stops, so do I, immediately transitioning to the hard work.

Maybe this method has been working simply because it's novel for me and, like a new diet, offers some structure to motivate my effort. Today, though, it doesn't matter, because it's a useful tool for me. And I'll keep using it until I don't need it or it stops working.

Am I still stressed? Sure. But overwhelmed? Much less so. Because I'm crossing things off my list and getting somewhere on my little tasks as well as my big ones, bird by bird.

Peter Bregman is a strategic adviser to CEOs and their leadership teams. His latest book is *18 Minutes: Find Your Focus, Master Distraction, and Get the Right Things Done.*

Chapter 8

Stop Procrastinating—Now

by Amy Gallo

It seems that no one is immune to procrastination. When someone asked Ernest Hemingway how to write a novel, he replied, "First you defrost the refrigerator." But putting off tasks takes a big toll on our productivity and our psyche.

Here are five principles to follow the next time you find yourself procrastinating:

1. Figure Out What's Holding You Back

When you find yourself ignoring or delaying a task, ask yourself why. Psychiatrist Ned Hallowell says there are two types of tasks we most often defer:

Adapted from content posted on hbr.org on October 11, 2011.

- **Something you don't like to do.** This is the most common one. As Hallowell says, "You don't put off eating your favorite dessert."
- **Something you don't know how to do.** When you lack the necessary knowledge or are unsure of how to start a job, you're more likely to avoid it.

Once you've identified why you've put something off, you can break the cycle and prevent future bouts of procrastination.

2. Set Deadlines

One of the simplest things to do is create a schedule with clear due dates for each task. "As soon as you get the project, chunk it down into a few manageable segments," advises Teresa Amabile, coauthor of *The Progress Principle.* Then, assign deadlines for each task. "Put an appointment in your calendar to work on a small piece of the next segment each day to allow yourself to get it done a bit at a time," she says. These "small wins" make the work more manageable and contribute to your sense of progress. And achieving them is much easier than trying to barrel through a complex project.

Use whatever visual cues work for you: Set reminders in your calendar, add items to your to-do list, or put a sticky note on your computer screen.

3. Increase the Rewards

We often dally because the reward for doing an assignment is too far off. To make a task feel more urgent, focus on short-term rewards. If you always procrastinate on filing your taxes, for example, focus on getting a refund by a certain date. And if there aren't any obvious rewards, create your own. Treat yourself to a coffee break or a quick chat with a coworker once you've finished a task. Embed the reward into the work by making it more fun to do, like partnering with a colleague on a particularly difficult project.

4. Involve Others

One of the principles Hallowell emphasizes is "Never worry alone." If you don't know how to do something, ask for help. Turn to a trusted colleague or a friend for advice. Asking people to review your work can also help spur you to get started, because you know they're expecting it.

5. Get in the Habit

"People throw up a hand and say 'I'm such a procrastinator' as if they have no control," says Hallowell. "You do have control over this, and you'll be very proud when you change it." There are immediate benefits when you start getting things done right away, and it's a habit you can cultivate. Amabile suggests tracking your improvement. "Spend just five minutes a day to note the progress you made, any setbacks you encountered, and what you might do the next day to enable further progress," she says. She recommends you do this in a work diary (see "Use a 10-Minute Diary to Stay on Track," later in this guide). Then see yourself—and talk about yourself with others—as someone who gets things done. "The most powerful event for maintaining positive inner work life is making progress in meaningful work," says Amabile.

Amy Gallo is a contributing editor at *Harvard Business Review*. Follow her on Twitter at @amyegallo.

Chapter 9

Don't Let Long-Term Projects Become Last-Minute Panic

by Peter Bregman

I want to write a screenplay.

Actually, I wanted to write one last year, but then other work took more time than I expected, and I kept pushing "Write screenplay" off my to-do list.

I know I'm not alone in struggling to make incremental progress on long-term projects or goals. How *do* you get started when you have "all the time in the world"?

Maybe you have no due date, like my screenplay. Or maybe you have a deadline that's months away—like preparing a speech, developing a business plan, or designing a training program. Perhaps you tend to procrastinate on projects with generous schedules—until "next month" becomes "next week" and then "next day," and suddenly your long-term project has morphed into a short-term, panic-filled nightmare.

Accomplishing something big and important is rarely as simple as just getting it done. Often we don't know how to start and, even when we do, we rarely have all the knowledge and skills we need to see it through. Also, we always have more urgent things to do and so we push off long-term goals. (See the previous article, "Stop Procrastinating—Now," for more ideas about overcoming the temptation to postpone work.)

We all know the basic advice: Break the work into smaller, more manageable chunks; focus on the next small step; set intermediate deadlines.

It's good advice. But, in my experience, it's not enough.

The reason we procrastinate on a big, long-term project is because it's important. So important, we're too scared to work on it.

I've never written a screenplay. I don't know how to format it. I don't know how to structure the story. I don't even know the story I want to tell.

I'm afraid that I'll fail. That I'll spend a lot of time on it—while other more immediate things don't get done—and that it'll be terrible, anyway.

My screenplay is work I care about deeply. Almost all big projects fit into that category—including the competitive analysis your boss asked for. Because a big project is a mirror. Even if you think you don't care about it, a big project reflects your smarts, effort, and character. It has your signature on it. Failure in a long-term project isn't just a work issue, it's an identity issue.

So what's the antidote?

Acknowledge your fear

As soon as you know you're going to give that speech or design that training program, take a quiet moment and feel the fear that comes with the importance—and unknowns—of the project. Maybe you're afraid of getting in front of all those people to give your speech. Maybe you're afraid that your training design will expose how much you *don't* know. Maybe you're afraid of letting other people down.

Share your fear

Some people may think you're a wimp, but that hasn't been my experience. Telling others you're intimidated by something you have to do gives them permission to feel—and maybe express—their own fear. I find that people are gracious, supportive, and empathic.

Round up the tools you need

Acknowledging your fear also serves another, crucial purpose: it *informs* you. By recognizing that you don't have everything you need to see the project through, you're identifying your next, manageable step: gathering the necessary tools, information, skills, and support.

Lower your expectations

You're scared because you expect a lot from yourself and you're afraid you'll underperform. When you acknowledge that fear, you recognize that you might not have all that it takes to meet your expectations. Admitting that, in turn, reduces your expectation of getting it perfect right off the bat. And lowering your expectation of getting it right is key to getting started.

Make it a priority

Even if the long-term project isn't your choice—commit yourself to it fully. Make it one of your top five priorities. This forces you to also identify what's *not* a priority. If you have too many important goals, you'll never get to the big long-term ones. So slash your list until you're left with only five.

I use a six-box to-do list—each box represents one of my top five priorities and the sixth box, labeled "The Other 5%," is for everything else. (See figure 9-1, "Sample *18 Minutes* daily to-do list.") That last box shouldn't take more than 5% of your time. One of my five boxes always represents a long-term priority, which, for this year, contains my screenplay. Having a long-term project on my daily to-do list means every day I make incremental progress toward my big goal.

Break the work into smaller pieces, and set deadlines

Now you're ready for the standard advice. Break the work into manageable chunks and make sure you know how to do the first chunk. Set an intermediate deadline. If you need other people's help, get them involved early. Finally, decide when and where you're going to accomplish the

FIGURE 9-1

Sample *18 Minutes* daily to-do list

Date: ____________________

Do great work with current clients	**Develop new business opportunities**
- Follow-up meetings with Anycorp and Bigorg GMs - Mary appt for next week - Jason—on-boarding docs - Set up flight to SF - E-mail request to clients for Howie to call - Speak with Luisa about 360 - Ideas for General Corporation leadership team	- Abigail—M&A work? - Referrals from Tom - Talk to Fernanda about real estate opportunity - Lunch with Joe
Speak and write about my ideas - Next HBR article - Review changes to WSJ article - Speaking engagement call with Loretta - Rich—ideas for future management guides - Slides for keynote speech	**Express myself creatively** - Talk with Alice about screenplay
Nurture myself and my family - Write in journal 30 minutes/day - Type with Isabelle - Book flights to Bahamas - Exercise 60 minutes/day - Make reservation for dinner with Eleanor	**The other 5%** - Dr. Clancy—confirm Wed CT scan - Call Tim - Lunch with Kathy to talk about job search - Andrew—Amex card - Research new running sneakers - Buy bathing suit - Get exact numbers from Kristin

Download a blank six-box to-do list at http://peterbregman.com/18minutes/.

first chunk and make an appointment with yourself in your calendar.

When you sit down to start your work, you may feel the resistance—fear—come up again. But now you know what it is. Acknowledge it, and it'll be easier to move into the work.

Peter Bregman is a strategic adviser to CEOs and their leadership teams. His latest book is *18 Minutes: Find Your Focus, Master Distraction, and Get the Right Things Done.*

Chapter 10
Stop Multitasking

by Peter Bregman

During a conference call with the executive committee of a nonprofit board on which I sit, I decided to send an e-mail to a client.

I know—multitasking is dangerous.

But I wasn't texting while driving. I was safe at my desk. What could go wrong?

Well, I sent the client the message. Then I had to send him another one, this time with the attachment I'd forgotten to append. Finally, my third e-mail to him explained why that attachment wasn't what he was expecting. When I eventually refocused on the call, I realized I hadn't heard a question the board's chair had asked me.

I swear I wasn't sleep-deprived or smoking anything. But I might as well have been. A study showed that people distracted by incoming e-mail and phone calls saw a 10-point drop in their IQs. What's the impact of

---

Adapted from content posted on hbr.org on May 20, 2009.

10 points? The same as losing a night of sleep. More than twice the effect of smoking marijuana.

Doing several things at once is a trick we play on ourselves, thinking we're getting more done. In reality, our productivity decreases by as much as 40%. We don't actually multitask. We switch-task, shifting rapidly from one thing to another, interrupting ourselves, and losing time in the process.

You might think you're different, that you've done it so much you've become good at it.

But research shows that heavy multitaskers are less competent at doing several things at once than light multitaskers. Unlike most things, the more you multitask, the worse you are at it. Practice, in this case, works against you.

I decided to try an experiment. For one week I would do no multitasking and see what happened. What techniques would help? Could I sustain a focus on one thing at a time for that long?

For the most part, I succeeded. If I was on the phone, I did nothing but participate in the conversation. In meetings, I was fully focused on the presentation or discussion at hand. And when I was working at my desk, I held off any interruptions—e-mail, a knock on the door—until I finished my task.

I discovered six things:

1. **It was delightful.** When I shut off my cell phone I was much more deeply engaged and present. While it may seem that thumbing out a text under the table during a meeting takes only a

split second, it's a longer distraction than that. First you think about your text, then you type it out, then you think about how the other person might respond, then you check for her response, etc. Before you know it, you've missed the whole meeting.

2. **I made significant progress on challenging projects.** Activities like writing or strategy work require thought and persistence. They're the kind I usually try to distract myself from. I stayed with each project when it got hard, and I experienced a number of breakthroughs.

3. **My stress level dropped dramatically.** Multitasking isn't just inefficient, it's stressful. It was a relief to focus on only one thing at a time. It felt reassuring to completely finish a task before moving to the next.

4. **I had no patience for wasted time.** I became laser-focused on getting things done. An hour-long meeting seemed interminable. A meandering conversation was excruciating.

5. **I had tremendous patience for useful and enjoyable things.** When I was on a call with a client, I closed my computer, shut my eyes, and focused completely. I was able to pick up nuance and subtle emotion. And when I was brainstorming about a difficult problem, I stuck with it. Nothing else was competing for my attention, so I was able to settle into the one thing I was doing.

6. **There was no downside.** I lost nothing by not multitasking. No projects were left unfinished. No one became frustrated with me for not answering a call or failing to return an e-mail the second I received it.

So how do we resist the temptation to multitask?

Turn off interruptions

Often I write at 6 AM, when there's nothing to distract me. I shut down my computer's wireless connection and turn off my phone. In my car, I leave my phone in the trunk. Drastic? Maybe. But most of us shouldn't trust ourselves.

Prioritize

Say you're the only person with information that your team needs in order to move forward with a time-sensitive project, but you're on an important conference call. What do you do? Decide which task is more important to focus on and ask the other one to wait. Making a conscious choice to interrupt one task for another is better than trying to do them at the same time. So either excuse yourself from the conference call for a moment, or tell your team to wait until you're done.

Use your loss of patience to your advantage

Create unrealistically short deadlines. Cut all meetings in half. Give yourself a third of the time you think you need to accomplish something.

There's nothing like a deadline to keep things moving. And when things are moving fast, we can't help but focus on them. If it turns out you only have 30 minutes to finish a presentation you thought would take an hour, are you really going to answer your cell phone?

Because multitasking is so stressful, single-tasking to meet a tight deadline will actually reduce your stress. And giving yourself less time to do things may make you even more productive and relaxed.

Peter Bregman is a strategic adviser to CEOs and their leadership teams. His latest book is *18 Minutes: Find Your Focus, Master Distraction, and Get the Right Things Done.*

Chapter 11

How to Stay Focused on What's Important

by Gina Trapani

Most of us spend our workdays in one of two ways: reacting to urgent demands, or proactively focusing on what we decided ahead of time are our most critical tasks to accomplish. The best way to be productive is to mitigate the urgent to work on the important.

What's the difference between urgent and important? "Urgent" tasks include things like:

- Frantic e-mails that need a response "right now"
- Sudden requests that seem like they'll take only two minutes but instead take an hour

Adapted from content posted on hbr.org on February 18, 2009.

- Putting out fires—especially others'
- Fixing the day's crisis rather than stepping back to consider what will solve the chronic problem
- Tasks you'd rather do first because they're less intimidating than your priorities

We're drawn to these seemingly "urgent" tasks because they keep us busy and make us feel needed and essential. If we label projects as urgent, it justifies the time and attention we throw at them.

But dealing with a constant stream of "urgent" tasks leaves you wrung out at the end of the day, wondering where all your time went, staring at the important work you've yet to start, much less complete.

On the flip side, important work:

- Moves you and your business toward long-term goals
- Can be hard work that feels scary because you're not confident you can actually do it
- May not give you that same shot of adrenaline that "urgent" requests do

If your workplace encourages constant, frantic headless-chicken running, it can feel impossible to focus on what's actually important versus what seems urgent. Still, an awareness of the difference and a few simple techniques can help. Here are three.

Choose three important tasks to complete each day

Write them down on a slip of paper and keep it visible on your desk. If, for example, you're tempted to respond to an e-mail notification, check your list and remember that that "ding" probably has nothing to do with your most critical work. When you have an unexpected hour thanks to a canceled meeting, move forward on those three important tasks.

Turn off your e-mail

Shut down Outlook, turn off e-mail notifications on your mobile, and do whatever else you have to do to muffle e-mail interruptions. When you decide to work on one of your important tasks, give yourself at least an hour of uninterrupted time to complete it. If the Web is too much of a temptation, disconnect your computer from the Internet for that hour.

Set up a weekly 20-minute meeting with yourself

Put it on your calendar, and don't book over it—treat it with the same respect you'd treat a meeting with your boss. If you don't have an office door or you work in a busy open area, book a conference room. Go there to be alone. Bring your project list, to-do list, and calendar, and spend the time reviewing what you finished in the past week and what you want to get done next week. This is a great time to choose your daily three important tasks. Productivity author David Allen refers to this as the "weekly review," and it's one of the most effective ways to be mindful of how you're spending your time.

For other ideas on how to tackle your day, see "Power Through Your Day in 90-Minute Cycles" (later in this guide) and "A Practical Plan for When You Feel Overwhelmed" (earlier in this guide).

Gina Trapani is the founding editor of the personal productivity blog Lifehacker.com.

Chapter 12
To-Do Lists That Work

by Gina Trapani

Here's how to write to-do lists that work:

1. **Break it down.** Take a task and carve it into bite-sized chunks. Then break it down some more. Don't confuse to-do's with goals or projects. A to-do is a single, specific action that will move a project toward completion. It's just one step. For example, "Plan the committee lunch" is a project. "E-mail Karen to get catering contact" is a to-do.

   Breaking down your task into the smallest possible actions forces you to think through each step up front. With the thinking out of the way, it's easy to dash off that e-mail, make

Adapted from content posted on hbr.org on January 13, 2009.

that call, or file that report, and move your work along with much less resistance.

2. **Use specific action verbs and include details** You're overdue for a check-in with your mentor, but the "Lunch with Judy" to-do just hasn't gotten done. When you write down that task, use an action verb (call? e-mail?) and include whatever details your future self needs to check it off. "Call Judy at 555–4567 for lunch on January 17, 18, or 19" is a specific, detailed to-do.

Make your to-do's small and specific to set yourself up for that glorious moment when you can cross them off your list as *DONE.*

Here are some more tips for effective to-do lists from the hbr.org community.

- Bucket your work in any way that makes sense for you (for example, work/home/freelance); by area of responsibility (Smith account/Culver account/web team); by difficulty level (group all of your "easy" five-minute tasks together so when you have spare time, you can quickly spot them and knock a few off). Give each bucket its own column.

- Deliberately use a small-trim book or paper (6″ × 9″) to keep your list short or a distinctive size (like an 8.5″ × 11″ piece of paper folded in half) that makes it stand out from other papers you carry.

- Make a two-view list. Two lists, with the same to-do's, but one organized by buckets, one by week. Bonus: You get the joy of crossing off one task in *TWO* places.
- Pick a medium that works for you: a notebook you love (for example, Moleskine); a web-based app that syncs on your mobile and computer, wherever you are; your mobile's voice-memo function.
- Make notes in the margin or beside an item to mark when it's due (M or 2/16).
- Highlight your top-priority items or put a bright-colored sticky with your top three things to do for the day on top of your longer list/buckets.
- Build in rewards. For example, for every three things you cross off your work list, allow yourself to do one home/personal task; or for every one difficult work task you accomplish, reward yourself with three easy or fun work ones.
- Rewrite your list every other day or so to help you reprioritize.
- When a task is done, check off a box or cross off the item with a fat marker—whatever gives you the most satisfaction.

Gina Trapani is the founding editor of the personal productivity blog Lifehacker.com.

Chapter 13

How to Tackle Your To-Do List

by Peter Bregman

For many of us, our to-do list has become more of a guilt list: an inventory of everything we want to do and really should do, but never get to. And the longer the list, the less likely we'll get to everything on it, and the more stressed we become.

So how do we turn *intention* into *action*?

It's the power of when and where.

Decide when and where you'll do something, and the likelihood that you'll follow through increases dramatically. The reason we're always left with unfinished items on our to-do lists is because they're the wrong tool to drive our accomplishments. A list is useful as a *collection* tool—to ensure we know the pool of things that we need to do.

Adapted from content posted on hbr.org on March 2, 2011.

A calendar, on the other hand, is the perfect tool to guide our daily accomplishments. A calendar is finite; there are only so many available hours. This becomes clear the instant we try to cram an unrealistic number of things into any one day.

Once you have your to-do list, open your calendar and decide when and where you're going to do each item. Schedule each task for a specific time, placing the most challenging and important items at the beginning of the day—before even checking your e-mail.

Since your entire to-do list won't fit into your calendar, prioritize. What do you really need to do today? What important items have you been ignoring? Where can you slot them into your schedule? Once you schedule an item, cross it off your list.

Transferring items from your to-do list to your calendar will help you make strategic choices about where you spend your time, but it will also leave you with a long list of items that didn't fit into your calendar for the day.

What do you do with those things?

I created a three-day rule to prevent items from haunting me indefinitely.

Here's what I do: After I've filled my calendar for the day, I review what's left on the list. I leave new items, those I just added that day or in the previous two days, on the list to see if they make it onto my calendar the following day.

But for everything else—anything that's been on my calendar for three days—I do one of four things:

1. **Do it immediately.** I'm often amazed at how many things have been sitting on my list for

days that, when I finally decide to do them, take no time at all. Often they turn out to be 30-second voice mails or two-minute e-mails.

2. **Schedule it.** For those things that I don't do immediately, I look for a time to slot them into my calendar, even if it's six months away. If it's important enough for me to have on my list, then I need to commit to doing it at a specific time and day. I can always change my plan when I review my calendar for that day, but if I want to do it, I need to schedule it.

3. **Let it go.** That's a nice way of saying delete the to-do. If I'm not willing to do something immediately or schedule it for a specific time and day, I won't ever do it. I face the reality that while I might like these things to be priorities, they currently aren't.

4. **Add it to a someday/maybe list.** Sometimes it's too hard to delete something. I don't want to admit that I'm not going to do it. And I want to remember that I think, someday, maybe it would be a good idea. So I put those items in a someday/maybe list, which I learned about from David Allen, author of *Getting Things Done.* It's where I put things to slowly die. I rarely, if ever, do things on this list. I look at it occasionally, get rid of the items that are no longer relevant, and then put the list away for another month. I probably could delete everything on this list, but I sleep a little better

knowing I can put things on it when I'm not courageous or guilt-free enough to do away with them right off the bat. And who knows? Perhaps someday, maybe, I'll do something on that list.

Peter Bregman is a strategic adviser to CEOs and their leadership teams. His latest book is *18 Minutes: Find Your Focus, Master Distraction, and Get the Right Things Done.*

Chapter 14
Reward Yourself for Doing Dreaded Tasks

by Alexandra Samuel

For some of us, checking off each item on our to-do lists provides the endorphin rush we need to make task completion an intrinsic joy. But most of us need a little extra motivation, especially for boring work like recording billable hours, uncomfortable tasks like facing awkward conversations with dissatisfied clients, or major projects like writing a complex case study. Setting up a compelling reward system can help you power through your to-dos.

Here are some types of rewards to consider:

Regenerative

By rewarding yourself in a way that recharges your body and brain, you'll give yourself more energy to tackle your next task or project. Use these brief rewards midmorning, midafternoon, or midproject to help maintain your momentum. Examples of regenerative rewards include:

- Meditating for 20 minutes in a secluded spot
- Using your lunch hour to treat yourself to a yoga class, run, or walk
- Doing 5 to 10 minutes of stretches in your office, guided by a video on your computer or iPad
- Talking with a good friend for 5 or 10 minutes
- Treating yourself to a second cup of coffee or a snack after an hour of focused work

Productive

Often—hopefully—work is rewarding in and of itself: meeting with colleagues you respect and enjoy or crafting a PowerPoint deck that incorporates self-deprecating humor or favorite photographs. Use these aspects of your job as rewards for completing something more difficult or tedious. Other examples of productive rewards include:

- Reading a popular business book or article
- Taking a working meeting to a good restaurant
- Installing or tweaking a piece of software you've been eager to use
- Reading/posting an article you think your colleagues/clients would enjoy to Twitter, LinkedIn, or Google+
- Cleaning your desk

Concurrent

Some tasks are so odious or boring that even the prospect of a pint of ice cream can't help you face them. These tasks call for a concurrent reward: something you do *while* working so that you can bear to plow through your in-box backlog or complete your quarterly budget report.

This type of reward works especially well for tasks that are time-consuming but not concentration-intensive. You can make even difficult tasks that require your full concentration more pleasant in the right setting. Some concurrent rewards include:

- Setting up camp in a Wi-Fi-enabled restaurant so you can eat while you work
- Making a work date with a friend so you can chat while you purge your e-mail in-boxes
- Storing up mindless tasks to complete while watching your favorite TV show at home
- Downloading some new music to listen to while you purge your files
- Making arrangements to work from home for the day

Cumulative

Establish a special-purpose account to pay into every time you complete an especially challenging or large project. Set different dollar values depending on the size and unpleasantness of the task. Examples include:

- An iTunes account
- A replenishable gift card to your favorite coffee shop or store
- A PayPal account you can refill with quick micropayments to treat yourself to some online shopping
- A discretionary savings account that you use to fund something significant like tickets to a sports or arts event

You'll know your reward system is working when your to-do list no longer includes tasks you've been avoiding for weeks, or when you find yourself racing to complete your least-favorite work so that you can get to that delicious brownie, fantastic concert, or backlog of *Mad Men* episodes.

Alexandra Samuel is the Director of the Social + Interactive Media Centre at Emily Carr University, and the cofounder of Social Signal, a Vancouver-based social media agency. You can follow Alex on Twitter at @awsamuel or her blog at alexandrasamuel.com.

Section 4
Delegate Effectively

Chapter 15
Management Time
Who's Got the Monkey?

A summary of the full-length HBR article by **William Oncken, Jr.,** *and* **Donald L. Wass,** *highlighting key ideas, with commentary by* **Stephen R. Covey.**

THE IDEA IN BRIEF

You're racing down the hall. An employee stops you and says, "We've got a problem." You assume you should get involved but can't make an on-the-spot decision. You say, "Let me think about it."

You've just allowed a "monkey" to leap from your employee's back to yours. You're now working for the person who works for you. Take on enough monkeys, and you won't have time to focus on your own priorities.

Reprint #99609

How do you avoid accumulating monkeys? Develop your employees' initiative. For example, when one of your people tries to hand you a problem, clarify whether he should: recommend and then implement a solution; take action, then brief you immediately; or act and report the outcome at a regular update.

When you encourage your employees to handle their own monkeys, they acquire new skills—and you gain time to do your own job.

THE IDEA IN PRACTICE

How do you return monkeys to their proper owners? Try these tactics:

Make Appointments to Deal with Monkeys

Avoid discussing any monkey on an ad hoc basis—for example, when you pass an employee in the hall. You won't convey the proper seriousness. Instead, have your employee schedule an appointment to discuss the issue.

Specify Level of Initiative

Your employees can exercise five levels of initiative in handling on-the-job problems. From lowest to highest, the levels are:

1. Wait until told what to do.
2. Ask what to do.

3. Recommend an action, then with your approval, implement it.
4. Take independent action but advise you at once.
5. Take independent action and update you at an agreed-on time; for example, your weekly meeting.

When an employee brings a problem to you, outlaw use of level 1 or 2. Agree on and assign level 3, 4, or 5 to the monkey. Take no more than 15 minutes to discuss the problem.

Agree on a Status Update

After deciding how to proceed, agree on a time and place when the employee will give you a progress report.

Develop Employees' Skills

Employees try to hand off monkeys when they lack the desire or ability to handle them. Help employees develop needed problem-solving skills. It's initially more time-consuming than tackling problems yourself—but it saves time in the long run.

Foster Trust

Developing employees' initiative requires a trusting relationship. If they're afraid of failing, they'll keep bringing their monkeys to you rather than working to solve their own problems. To promote trust, reassure them that it's safe to make mistakes.

Why is it that managers are typically running out of time while their subordinates are typically running out of work? Here we shall explore the meaning of management time as it relates to the interaction between managers and their bosses, their peers, and their subordinates.

Specifically, we shall deal with three kinds of management time:

Boss-imposed time—used to accomplish those activities that the boss requires and that the manager cannot disregard without direct and swift penalty.

System-imposed time—used to accommodate requests from peers for active support. Neglecting these requests will also result in penalties, though not always as direct or swift.

Self-imposed time—used to do those things that the manager originates or agrees to do. A certain portion of this kind of time, however, will be taken by subordinates and is called subordinate-imposed time. The remaining portion will be the manager's own and is called discretionary time. Self-imposed time is not subject to penalty since neither the boss nor the system can discipline the manager for not doing what they didn't know he had intended to do in the first place.

To accommodate those demands, managers need to control the timing and the content of what they do. Since what their bosses and the system impose on them are subject to penalty, managers cannot tamper with those requirements. Thus their self-imposed time becomes their major area of concern.

Managers should try to increase the discretionary component of their self-imposed time by minimizing or doing away with the subordinate component. They will then use the added increment to get better control over their boss-imposed and system-imposed activities. Most managers spend much more time dealing with subordinates' problems than they even faintly realize. Hence we shall use the monkey-on-the-back metaphor to examine how subordinate-imposed time comes into being and what the superior can do about it.

Where Is the Monkey?

Let us imagine that a manager is walking down the hall and that he notices one of his subordinates, Jones, coming his way. When the two meet, Jones greets the manager with, "Good morning. By the way, we've got a problem. You see . . . ." As Jones continues, the manager recognizes in this problem the two characteristics common to all the problems his subordinates gratuitously bring to his attention. Namely, the manager knows (a) enough to get involved, but (b) not enough to make the on-the-spot decision expected of him. Eventually, the manager says, "So glad you brought this up. I'm in a rush right now. Meanwhile, let me think about it, and I'll let you know." Then he and Jones part company.

Let us analyze what just happened. Before the two of them met, on whose back was the "monkey"? The subordinate's. After they parted, on whose back was it? The manager's. Subordinate-imposed time begins the moment a monkey successfully leaps from the back of a subordinate to the back of his or her superior and does not end until the monkey is returned to its proper owner for care and feeding. In accepting the monkey, the manager has voluntarily assumed a position subordinate to his subordinate. That is, he has allowed Jones to make him her subordinate by doing two things a subordinate is generally expected to do for a boss—the manager has accepted a responsibility from his subordinate, and the manager has promised her a progress report.

The subordinate, to make sure the manager does not miss this point, will later stick her head in the manager's office and cheerily query, "How's it coming?" (This is called supervision.)

Or let us imagine in concluding a conference with Johnson, another subordinate, the manager's parting words are, "Fine. Send me a memo on that."

Let us analyze this one. The monkey is now on the subordinate's back because the next move is his, but it is poised for a leap. Watch that monkey. Johnson dutifully writes the requested memo and drops it in his out-basket. Shortly thereafter, the manager plucks it from his in-basket and reads it. Whose move is it now? The manager's. If he does not make that move soon, he will get a follow-up memo from the subordinate. (This is another form of supervision.) The longer the manager delays, the more frustrated the subordinate will become (he'll be spinning his wheels) and the more guilty the manager will feel (his backlog of subordinate-imposed time will be mounting).

Or suppose once again that at a meeting with a third subordinate, Smith, the manager agrees to provide all the necessary backing for a public relations proposal he has just asked Smith to develop. The manager's parting words to her are, "Just let me know how I can help."

Now let us analyze this. Again the monkey is initially on the subordinate's back. But for how long? Smith realizes that she cannot let the manager "know" until her proposal has the manager's approval. And from experience, she also realizes that her proposal will likely be sitting in the manager's briefcase for weeks before he eventually gets to it. Who's really got the monkey? Who will be checking up on whom? Wheel spinning and bottlenecking are well on their way again.

A fourth subordinate, Reed, has just been transferred from another part of the company so that he can launch and eventually manage a newly created business venture. The manager has said they should get together soon to hammer out a set of objectives for the new job, adding, "I will draw up an initial draft for discussion with you."

Let us analyze this one, too. The subordinate has the new job (by formal assignment) and the full responsibility (by formal delegation), but the manager has the next move. Until he makes it, he will have the monkey, and the subordinate will be immobilized.

Why does all of this happen? Because in each instance the manager and the subordinate assume at the outset, wittingly or unwittingly, that the matter under consideration is a joint problem. The monkey in each case begins its career astride both their backs. All it has to do is

MAKING TIME FOR GORILLAS

by Stephen R. Covey

When Bill Oncken wrote this article in 1974, managers were in a terrible bind. They were desperate for a way to free up their time, but command and control was the status quo. Managers felt they weren't allowed to empower their subordinates to make decisions. Too dangerous. Too risky. That's why Oncken's message—give the monkey back to its rightful owner—involved a critically important paradigm shift. Many managers working today owe him a debt of gratitude.

It is something of an understatement, however, to observe that much has changed since Oncken's radical recommendation. Command and control as a management philosophy is all but dead, and "empowerment" is the word of the day in most organizations trying to thrive in global, intensely competitive markets. But command and control stubbornly remains a common practice. Management thinkers and executives have discovered in the last decade that bosses cannot just give a monkey back to their subordinates and then merrily get on with their own business. Empowering subordinates is hard and complicated work.

The reason: when you give problems back to subordinates to solve themselves, you have to be sure that they have both the desire and the ability to do so. As every executive knows, that isn't always the case. Enter a whole new set of problems. Empowerment often means you have to develop people, which is initially much more time consuming than solving the problem on your own.

Just as important, empowerment can only thrive when the whole organization buys into it—when formal systems and the informal culture support it. Managers need to be rewarded for delegating decisions and developing people. Otherwise, the degree of real empowerment in an organization will vary according to the beliefs and practices of individual managers.

But perhaps the most important lesson about empowerment is that effective delegation—the kind Oncken advocated—depends on a trusting relationship between a manager and his subordinate. Oncken's message may have been ahead of his time, but what he suggested was still a fairly dictatorial solution. He basically told bosses, "Give the problem back!" Today, we know that this approach by itself is too authoritarian. To delegate effectively, executives need to establish a running dialogue with subordinates. They need to establish a partnership. After all, if subordinates are afraid of failing in front of their boss, they'll keep coming back for help rather than truly take initiative.

Oncken's article also doesn't address an aspect of delegation that has greatly interested me during the past two decades—that many managers are actually *eager* to take on their subordinates' monkeys. Nearly all the managers I talk with agree that their people are underutilized in their present jobs. But even some of the most success-

(*continued*)

(*continued*)

ful, seemingly self-assured executives have talked about how hard it is to give up control to their subordinates.

I've come to attribute that eagerness for control to a common, deep-seated belief that rewards in life are scarce and fragile. Whether they learn it from their family, school, or athletics, many people establish an identity by comparing themselves with others. When they see others gain power, information, money, or recognition, for instance, they experience what the psychologist Abraham Maslow called "a feeling of deficiency"—a sense that something is being taken from them. That makes it hard for them to be genuinely happy about the success of others—even of their loved ones. Oncken implies that managers can easily give back or refuse monkeys, but many managers may subconsciously fear that a subordinate taking the initiative will make them appear a little less strong and a little more vulnerable.

How, then, do managers develop the inward security, the mentality of "abundance," that would enable them to relinquish control and seek the growth and development of those around them? The work I've done with numerous organizations suggests that managers who live with integrity according to a principle-based value system are most likely to sustain an empowering style of leadership.

Given the times in which he wrote, it was no wonder that Oncken's message resonated with managers. But it was reinforced by Oncken's wonderful gift for storytelling. I got to know Oncken on the speaker's circuit in the 1970s, and I was always impressed by how he dramatized his ideas in colorful detail. Like the Dilbert comic strip, Oncken had a tongue-in-cheek style that got to the core of managers' frustrations and made them want to take back control of their time. And the monkey on your back wasn't just a metaphor for Oncken—it was his personal symbol. I saw him several times walking through airports with a stuffed monkey on his shoulder.

I'm not surprised that his article is one of the two best-selling HBR articles ever. Even with all we know about empowerment, its vivid message is even more important and relevant now than it was 25 years ago. Indeed, Oncken's insight is a basis for my own work on time management, in which I have people categorize their activities according to urgency and importance. I've heard from executives again and again that half or more of their time is spent on matters that are urgent but not important. They're trapped in an endless cycle of dealing with other people's monkeys, yet they're reluctant to help those people take their own initiative. As a result, they're often too busy to spend the time they need on the real gorillas in their organization. Oncken's article remains a powerful wake-up call for managers who need to delegate effectively.

Stephen R. Covey is vice chairman of the Franklin Covey Company, a global provider of leadership development and productivity services and products. He is the author of *The 7 Habits of Highly Effective People* (Simon & Schuster, 1989) and *First Things First* (Simon & Schuster, 1994).

move the wrong leg, and—presto!—the subordinate deftly disappears.

The manager is thus left with another acquisition for his menagerie. Of course, monkeys can be trained not to move the wrong leg. But it is easier to prevent them from straddling backs in the first place.

Who Is Working for Whom?

Let us suppose that these same four subordinates are so thoughtful and considerate of their superior's time that they take pains to allow no more than three monkeys to leap from each of their backs to his in any one day. In a five-day week, the manager will have picked up 60 screaming monkeys—far too many to do anything about them individually. So he spends his subordinate-imposed time juggling his "priorities."

Late Friday afternoon, the manager is in his office with the door closed for privacy so he can contemplate the situation, while his subordinates are waiting outside to get their last chance before the weekend to remind him that he will have to "fish or cut bait." Imagine what they are saying to one another about the manager as they wait: "What a bottleneck. He just can't make up his mind. How anyone ever got that high up in our company without being able to make a decision we'll never know."

Worst of all, the reason the manager cannot make any of these "next moves" is that his time is almost entirely eaten up by meeting his own boss-imposed and system-imposed requirements. To control those tasks, he needs discretionary time that is in turn denied him when he is preoccupied with all these monkeys. The manager is caught in a vicious circle. But time is a-wasting (an understatement). The manager calls his secretary on the intercom and instructs her to tell his subordinates that he won't be able to see them until Monday morning. At 7 PM, he drives home, intending with firm resolve to return to the office tomorrow to get caught up over the weekend. He returns bright and early the next day only to see, on the nearest green of the golf course across from his office window, a foursome. Guess who?

That does it. He now knows who is really working for whom. Moreover, he now sees that if he actually accomplishes during this weekend what he came to accomplish, his subordinates' morale will go up so sharply that they will each raise the limit on the number of monkeys they will let jump from their backs to his. In short, he now sees, with the clarity of a revelation on a mountaintop, that the more he gets caught up, the more he will fall behind.

He leaves the office with the speed of a person running away from a plague. His plan? To get caught up on something else he hasn't had time for in years: a weekend with his family. (This is one of the many varieties of discretionary time.)

Sunday night he enjoys ten hours of sweet, untroubled slumber, because he has clear-cut plans for Monday. He is going to get rid of his subordinate-imposed time. In exchange, he will get an equal amount of discretionary time, part of which he will spend with his subordinates to make sure that they learn the difficult but rewarding managerial art called "The Care and Feeding of Monkeys."

The manager will also have plenty of discretionary time left over for getting control of the timing and the content not only of his boss-imposed time but also of his system-imposed time. It may take months, but compared with the way things have been, the rewards will be enormous. His ultimate objective is to manage his time.

Getting Rid of the Monkeys

The manager returns to the office Monday morning just late enough so that his four subordinates have collected outside his office waiting to see him about their monkeys. He calls them in one by one. The purpose of each interview is to take a monkey, place it on the desk between them, and figure out together how the next move might conceivably be the subordinate's. For certain monkeys, that will take some doing. The subordinate's next move may be so elusive that the manager may decide—just for now—merely to let the monkey sleep on the subordinate's back overnight and have him or her return with it at an appointed time the next morning to continue the joint quest for a more substantive move by the subordinate. (Monkeys sleep just as soundly overnight on subordinates' backs as they do on superiors'.)

As each subordinate leaves the office, the manager is rewarded by the sight of a monkey leaving his office on the subordinate's back. For the next 24 hours, the subordinate will not be waiting for the manager; instead, the manager will be waiting for the subordinate.

Later, as if to remind himself that there is no law against his engaging in a constructive exercise in the interim, the manager strolls by the subordinate's office, sticks his head in the door, and cheerily asks, "How's it coming?" (The time consumed in doing this is discretionary for the manager and boss imposed for the subordinate.)

When the subordinate (with the monkey on his or her back) and the manager meet at the appointed hour the next day, the manager explains the ground rules in words to this effect:

> *At no time while I am helping you with this or any other problem will your problem become my problem. The instant your problem becomes mine, you no longer have a problem. I cannot help a person who hasn't got a problem.*
>
> *When this meeting is over, the problem will leave this office exactly the way it came in—on your back. You may ask my help at any appointed time, and we will make a joint determination of what the next move will be and which of us will make it.*
>
> *In those rare instances where the next move turns out to be mine, you and I will determine it together. I will not make any move alone.*

The manager follows this same line of thought with each subordinate until about 11 AM, when he realizes that he doesn't have to close his door. His monkeys are gone. They will return—but by appointment only. His calendar will assure this.

Transferring the Initiative

What we have been driving at in this monkey-on-the-back analogy is that managers can transfer initiative back

THE DELEGATION CHECKLIST

by Peter Bregman

When it comes to delegating effectively, communication is key. Most of us think we communicate well, which is why we often inadvertently leave out important information. Sometimes we assume that the people to whom we're delegating share our understanding. Or we resist clarifying something because we don't want to insult the person.

Thankfully, there's a simple solution to ensure projects you delegate will transfer well: Create a checklist and use it during every handoff.

Before you pass off a project, complete the delegation checklist with the person who'll be taking on the responsibility. Reviewing the list together ensures that you transfer all important information. With the following questions as a starting point, add or delete some to suit your particular situation. It takes no longer than 10 minutes to complete the checklist, but it could save you countless dropped balls and service failures.

to their subordinates and keep it there. We have tried to highlight a truism as obvious as it is subtle: namely, before developing initiative in subordinates, the manager must see to it that they *have* the initiative. Once the manager takes it back, he will no longer have it and he can kiss his discretionary time good-bye. It will all revert to subordinate-imposed time.

Delegation Checklist

- What do you understand the priorities of this project to be?
- What are your next key steps, and by when do you plan to accomplish them?
- What key contingencies should you plan for now?
- When will you next check in with me on progress/issues?
- Who else needs to know our plans, and how will you communicate them?
- What concerns or ideas do you have that we haven't already discussed?

Adapted from content posted on hbr.org on January 25, 2011.
Peter Bregman is a strategic adviser to CEOs and their leadership teams. His latest book is *18 Minutes: Find Your Focus, Master Distraction, and Get the Right Things Done*.

Nor can the manager and the subordinate effectively have the same initiative at the same time. The opener, "Boss, we've got a problem," implies this duality and represents, as noted earlier, a monkey astride two backs, which is a very bad way to start a monkey on its career. Let us, therefore, take a few moments to examine what we call "The Anatomy of Managerial Initiative."

There are five degrees of initiative that the manager can exercise in relation to the boss and to the system:

1. wait until told (lowest initiative);
2. ask what to do;
3. recommend, then take resulting action;
4. act, but advise at once;
5. and act on own, then routinely report (highest initiative).

Clearly, the manager should be professional enough not to indulge in initiatives 1 and 2 in relation either to

TIPS FOR DELEGATING EFFECTIVELY

- Recognize the capabilities of your employees and trust their ability to get the job done.
- Consider delegation a development opportunity—a way to broaden your people's skills.
- Focus on results and let go of your need to get involved in *how* tasks are accomplished.
- Explain assignments clearly and provide resources needed for successful completion.
- Always delegate to the lowest possible level to make the best use of staff resources.

Adapted from *Pocket Mentor: Managing Projects* (product #1878), Harvard Business Review Press, 2006.

the boss or to the system. A manager who uses initiative 1 has no control over either the timing or the content of boss-imposed or system-imposed time and thereby forfeits any right to complain about what he or she is told to do or when. The manager who uses initiative 2 has control over the timing but not over the content. Initiatives 3, 4, and 5 leave the manager in control of both, with the greatest amount of control being exercised at level 5.

In relation to subordinates, the manager's job is twofold. First, to outlaw the use of initiatives 1 and 2, thus giving subordinates no choice but to learn and master "Completed Staff Work." Second, to see that for each problem leaving his or her office there is an agreed-upon level of initiative assigned to it, in addition to an agreed-upon time and place for the next manager-subordinate conference. The latter should be duly noted on the manager's calendar.

The Care and Feeding of Monkeys

To further clarify our analogy between the monkey on the back and the processes of assigning and controlling, we shall refer briefly to the manager's appointment schedule, which calls for five hard-and-fast rules governing the "Care and Feeding of Monkeys." (Violation of these rules will cost discretionary time.)

Rule 1

Monkeys should be fed or shot. Otherwise, they will starve to death, and the manager will waste valuable time on postmortems or attempted resurrections.

Rule 2

The monkey population should be kept below the maximum number the manager has time to feed. Subordinates will find time to work as many monkeys as he or she finds time to feed, but no more. It shouldn't take more than five to 15 minutes to feed a properly maintained monkey.

Rule 3

Monkeys should be fed by appointment only. The manager should not have to hunt down starving monkeys and feed them on a catch-as-catch-can basis.

Rule 4

Monkeys should be fed face to face or by telephone, but never by mail. (Remember—with mail, the next move will be the manager's.) Documentation may add to the feeding process, but it cannot take the place of feeding.

Rule 5

Every monkey should have an assigned next feeding time and degree of initiative. These may be revised at any time by mutual consent but never allowed to become vague or indefinite. Otherwise, the monkey will either starve to death or wind up on the manager's back.

"Get control over the timing and content of what you do" is appropriate advice for managing time. The first order of business is for the manager to enlarge his or her discretionary time by eliminating subordinate-imposed time.

The second is for the manager to use a portion of this newfound discretionary time to see to it that each subordinate actually has the initiative and applies it. The third is for the manager to use another portion of the increased discretionary time to get and keep control of the timing and content of both boss-imposed and system-imposed time. All these steps will increase the manager's leverage and enable the value of each hour spent in managing management time to multiply without theoretical limit.

William Oncken, Jr., was chairman of the William Oncken Corporation until his death in 1988. His son, William Oncken III, now heads the company. **Donald L. Wass** was president of the William Oncken Company of Texas when the article first appeared. He now heads the Dallas–Fort Worth region of The Executive Committee (TEC), an international organization for presidents and CEOs.

Chapter 16

Levels of Delegation

by Linda A. Hill and Kent Lineback

If you think that delegation is appropriate only for employees who've already demonstrated complete competence in an area, then you may be trapped in this vicious cycle: Until your employee has the opportunity to perform an activity by herself, she'll never develop the necessary skill and experience to do it well. But until she does it well, you'll continue to believe that you must be involved—either by performing the task yourself or by micromanaging her so closely she never learns to do it independently.

Here's a way to think about delegation as three levels corresponding to your direct reports' increasing levels of competence:

Delegation level 1 **Low delegation—high control**	**Delegation level 2** **Moderate delegation—moderate control**	**Delegation level 3** **High delegation—low control**
Use with someone about to do work he's never or rarely done before	**Use with** someone who has some experience, perhaps someone who's observed others and should be ready to act on her own	**Use with** someone who has actually demonstrated competence
Prep: Here the problem is more likely one of skill versus will, so describe how to do the work and coach him through the steps involved. Make clear the boundaries: budget, strategy, policy, and so on. If appropriate, take him through practice runs. If the problem is also one of will, set the activity in the context of the team's work and its purpose and goals. Make sure he understands the consequences of possible outcomes.	***Prep:*** Ask her to describe her plan for doing the work and the various "What . . . ?" questions. Satisfy yourself that she's well prepared and ready. Explain constraints or boundaries. Agree on what constitutes success. Coach as necessary. Make sure she understands the reason for doing the work and why it's important. See whether she can link to team purpose and goals.	***Prep:*** Leave the prep to him. Involve yourself only if the work—say, a discussion he will have with an important prospective customer—is unusually important to team purpose and goals. If it is, ask for his preparatory thinking. Provide clear direction and boundaries. Agree on success. Here the issue may be more one of will than skill, so make sure he understands the importance and consequences of the action.
Do: At first, you do the work as he observes. If the consequences of failure are low, you could observe while he performs the task.	***Do:*** Let her do the work, perhaps with you present observing, perhaps alone, depending on the situation and your judgment of her readiness.	***Do:*** He conducts the discussion without your involvement or presence.
Review: Walk through what you (or he) did. Answer questions. Identify lessons. Have him describe how he would do it next time.	***Review:*** Ask for her self-assessment of how it went, in terms of both skill and will. What went well and what could be improved? Then, if you were present, give your assessment and discuss any differences. Identify lessons. Focus on tangible outcomes and specific behaviors. If you couldn't be present, ask others who were there. Reach agreement with her about what should be different or better next time.	***Review:*** If this was routine work and it had a good or expected outcome, you won't have a review discussion except as part of a periodic general performance review. If it was more than routine work or the outcome was unexpected, ask for his self-assessment of what happened and what might be learned from it.

Source: Reprinted with permission from *Being the Boss: The 3 Imperatives for Becoming a Great Leader* by Linda A. Hill and Kent Lineback. Harvard Business Review Press, 2011.

Section 5
Create Rituals

Chapter 17
Ritual
How to Get Important Work Done

by Tony Schwartz

Most of us feel pulled in more directions than ever, expected to work longer hours, and asked to get more done, often with fewer resources. But we also know people who get lots done, including the important stuff, and still manage to have lives.

What have they figured out that the rest of us haven't?

The answer, surprisingly, isn't that they have more will or discipline than we do. The counterintuitive secret to getting things done is to make them more automatic, so they require less energy.

How do we do that? By developing **rituals—highly specific behaviors, done at precise times, so they**

Adapted from content posted on hbr.org on May 24, 2011.

eventually become automatic and no longer require conscious will or discipline. Decide what behavior you want to change, design the ritual you'll undertake, and then get out of your own way.

Over the past decade, I've built a series of rituals into my daily schedule to make sure that I get to the most important things—and that I don't get derailed by the endlessly alluring trivia of everyday life.

Here are four of the rituals that have made the biggest difference to me:

1. **Going to bed at the same time every night.** This ritual ensures that I get eight hours of sleep. Nothing is more critical to the way I feel every day. If I'm flying somewhere and know I'll arrive too late to get my eight hours, I make it a priority to make up the hours I need on the plane.

2. **Working out as soon as I wake up.** Since exercise has a huge impact on how I feel all day long, this ritual ensures that I work out even when I don't feel like it.

3. **Launching my workday by focusing first on whatever I've decided the night before is my most important activity.** Then I take a break after 90 minutes to refuel. Today—which happens to be a Sunday—this blog was my priority. My break was playing tennis for an hour. During the week it might be chatting with a colleague for a few minutes or getting a snack. (Working

in 90-minute segments throughout your day can be another useful ritual to develop. See the next article, "Power Through Your Day in 90-Minute Cycles," to learn more.)

4. **Immediately writing down on a list any idea or task that occurs to me over the course of the day.** Once it's on paper, it means I don't walk around feeling preoccupied by it—or risk forgetting it.

Obviously, I'm human and fallible, so I don't perform every one of these rituals every day. But when I do miss one, I pay the price, and feel even more pulled to it the next day.

Tony Schwartz is the president and CEO of The Energy Project and the author of *Be Excellent at Anything*. Become a fan of The Energy Project and connect with Tony on Twitter at @tonyschwartz and @energy_project.

Chapter 18

Power Through Your Day in 90-Minute Cycles

by Tony Schwartz

For nearly a decade, I've begun my workdays by focusing for 90 minutes, uninterrupted, on the task I decide the night before is the most important to tackle the following day. After 90 minutes, I take a break. When my break is up, I begin the cycle again.

To make this possible, I turn off my e-mail while I'm working, close unnecessary windows on my computer, and let the phone go to voice mail.

I typically get more work done and feel more satisfied than I do for any comparable period of time the rest of the day. It can be tough on some days to fully focus

Adapted from content posted on hbr.org on May 24, 2011.

for 90 minutes, but I always have a clear stopping time, which makes it easier.

I launched this practice because my energy, will, and capacity for intense focus diminish as the day wears on. Anything really challenging that I put off tends not to get done, and it's the most difficult work that generally produces the greatest value. Usually, that means a challenge that is "important but not urgent," to use Steven Covey's language. These are precisely the types of activities we most often postpone in favor of those that are more urgent, easier to accomplish, or provide more immediate gratification. (See "How to Stay Focused on What's Important," earlier in this guide.)

I first made this discovery while writing a book. At the time, I'd written three previous books. For each one, I'd dutifully sit down at my desk at 7 AM and I'd often stay there until 7 PM.

I never finished a book in less than a year. Looking back, I probably spent more time avoiding writing than I did actually writing. I made lists, responded to e-mail, answered the phone, and kept my desk clean and my files well organized. There were days I never got to writing at all. It was incredibly frustrating.

For my new book, *The Way We're Working Isn't Working*, I wrote without interruptions for three 90-minute periods and took a break between each one. I had breakfast after the first session, went for a run after the second, and had lunch after the third. I wrote no more than 4 ½ hours a day, and finished the book in fewer than six months. By writing in several cycles of 90 minutes each and building in periods of renewal, I was able to focus far more intensely and get more done in less time.

What made me so productive? Creating the ritual of tackling the most important work at the start of the day and working with my body's natural rhythms. At the heart of making this work is to build highly precise, deliberate rituals, done at specific times, so they eventually become automatic and don't require much expenditure of energy or self-discipline, akin to brushing your teeth at night.

Pioneering sleep researcher Nathaniel Kleitman observed that our bodies operate by the same 90-minute "basic rest-activity" cycle during the day that we do when we sleep. When we're awake, we move from higher to lower alertness every 90 minutes. This "ultradian rhythm," researcher Peretz Lavie and others have found, governs our energy levels. The human body is hardwired to pulse, and requires renewal at regular intervals, not just physically, but also mentally and emotionally.

Many of us unwittingly train ourselves to ignore signals from our body that we need a rest—difficulty concentrating, physical restlessness, irritability. Instead, we find ways to override this need with caffeine, sugar, and our own stress hormones—adrenalin, noradrenalin, and cortisol—all of which provide short bursts of energy but impair our ability to consistently focus on our work for a significant period of time.

By intentionally aligning with my body's natural rhythms, I've learned to listen to its signals. When I notice them, it usually means I've hit the 90-minute mark.

At that point, I take a break, even if I'm on a roll, because I've learned that if I don't, I'll pay the price later in the day.

When I'm not working on a book, I still choose the next day's most important work the night before, because I don't want to squander energy thinking about what to do during the time I've set aside to actually work. I start at a very specific time, because when I don't, I give myself license to procrastinate.

Ideally you'll be able to divide up your day into several 90-minute focused work segments, with brief periods of renewal in between each. However, it's not always possible to structure your days this way. So make it a high priority to find at least one time a day to focus single-mindedly on your most challenging and important task.

Tony Schwartz is the president and CEO of The Energy Project and the author of *Be Excellent at Anything*. Become a fan of The Energy Project on Facebook and connect with Tony on Twitter at @tonyschwartz and @energy_project.

Chapter 19

An 18-Minute Plan for Managing Your Day

by Peter Bregman

I began my day yesterday with the best intentions. I walked into my office in the morning with a vague sense of what I wanted to accomplish. Then I sat down, turned on my computer, and checked my e-mail. Two hours later, after fighting several fires, solving other people's problems, and dealing with whatever happened to be thrown at me through my computer and phone, I could hardly remember what I had originally set out to do.

Most of us start every day knowing we're not going to get it all done. So how we spend our time is a key strategic decision. That's why it's a good idea to create both a to-do list and a *to-don't* list.

But even with those lists, the challenge—as always—is execution. How can you stick to a plan when so many things threaten to derail it? How can you focus on just a few important tasks when so many others require your attention?

We need a trick.

Jack LaLanne, the fitness guru, knew all about tricks. He had one trick that I believe was his real secret power.

Ritual.

At the age of 94, he still spent the first two hours of his day exercising. Ninety minutes lifting weights and 30 minutes swimming or walking. Every morning. He needed to do so to achieve his goals: on his 95th birthday he planned to swim from the coast of California to Santa Catalina Island—a distance of 20 miles.

So he worked consistently and deliberately. He did the same things day in and day out. He cared about his fitness and he built it into his schedule.

Managing our time needs to become a ritual, too. Not simply a list or a vague sense of our priorities. That's not consistent or deliberate. It needs to be an ongoing process we follow, no matter what, to keep us focused on our priorities throughout the day.

We can do it in three steps that take fewer than 18 minutes over an eight-hour workday:

1. **(5 minutes): Set Your Plan for the Day.** Before turning on your computer, sit down with a blank piece of paper and decide what will make this day highly successful. What can you real-

istically accomplish that will further your goals and allow you to leave at the end of the day feeling productive? Write those things down. Now, most important, take your calendar and schedule those things into time slots, placing the hardest and most important items at the beginning of the day—before checking your e-mail. If your entire list doesn't fit into your calendar, reprioritize your list. There is tremendous power in deciding when you're going to do something. (See "How to Tackle Your To-Do List," earlier in this guide.)

2. **(1 minute every hour): Refocus.** Set your watch, phone, or computer to ring every hour. When it rings, take a deep breath, look at your list, and ask yourself: *Am I doing what I most need to be doing right now?* Then look at your calendar and deliberately recommit to how you're going to use the next hour. Manage your day hour by hour. Don't let the hours—or the inevitable interruptions—manage you.

3. **(5 minutes at end of day): Review.** Shut off your computer and review your day. What worked? Where did you focus? Where did you get distracted? What did you learn that will help you be more productive tomorrow?

The power of rituals is their predictability: You do the same thing in the same way over and over again. And the outcome of a ritual is predictable, too. If you choose your focus deliberately and wisely and consistently remind yourself of that focus, you will *stay* focused.

This particular ritual may not help you swim 20 miles through the ocean or live to be 100. But it may just help you leave your office feeling productive and successful. And, at the end of the day, isn't that a higher priority?

Peter Bregman is a strategic adviser to CEOs and their leadership teams. His latest book is *18 Minutes: Find Your Focus, Master Distraction, and Get the Right Things Done.*

Chapter 20

Use a 10-Minute Diary to Stay on Track

by Teresa Amabile and Steven Kramer

What's the best way to use the last 10 minutes of your day? Many productivity gurus recommend an end-of-the-day meeting with yourself to review your to-do list, check how you're doing against short- and long-term goals, or select the most challenging project you'll tackle the following day. Our research suggests that not only should you do an end-of-day review, but you'll reap the greatest benefits for your productivity and personal well-being if you actually record your thoughts in a "mini-diary." A work diary will improve your focus, track your progress, and make you more satisfied with your work—which will help you be even more productive.

No question: This reflective time is often the first thing that we drop when we're feeling overloaded. Adding a daily writing assignment—the word "diary" conjures up a long-term commitment—seems counterproductive to making headway on "real" work. So **try it for just one month,** focusing on just one short-term project (for example, developing a departmental staffing plan), or just one area of professional development (improving your presentation skills).

Take 10 minutes at the end of each workday, write no more than 100 words, and see what you've learned after four weeks. You may be surprised.

You'll get five benefits from keeping a work diary. You:

1. **Track your progress.** The diary is a record of your "small wins," incremental steps toward meaningful goals, that can boost your motivation—if only you take a moment to reflect on them.

2. **Plan.** You use the diary as a tool for drafting your next steps.

3. **Fuel personal growth.** The diary gives you a way of working through your difficult—even traumatic—events, gaining new perspectives on them.

4. **Sharpen your focus.** You identify your strengths, passions, and challenges by looking at patterns in your entries over time. For example, your diary may reveal that you've been spending a lot of time on low-priority issues. Reviewing your diary and identifying

this pattern can help you recommit to focusing your time and energy on your most important work.

5. **Develop patience.** The diary serves as a reminder during frustrating days that, in the past, you've persevered through days that, at the time, seemed even worse.

Our research shows that, of all these benefits, using a work diary to track your progress may be the most important one for your productivity and psychological well-being. As part of a massive study on the psychology of everyday work life, we collected nearly 12,000 diary entries from 238 professionals working on complex, creative projects. Our analyses revealed a big surprise. Of all the things that could make people feel both happy and highly motivated to dig into their work, the single most important event was simply making progress in work they cared about. We call this *the progress principle,* and it applies even when the progress is an incremental small win. When we see we're making progress, we're motivated to keep going, and it's easier to keep our focus—even when we encounter setbacks. Witness this example, from the diary of a software engineer in our study:

> *Today, when I started work [. . .] there was a note from a user regarding some work I had done for him. It was very complimentary and it made me feel pretty good. Also in the note was a request to go ahead with an enhancement to the database analysis package. I was able to code and load this request today in less than the*

estimated time, which makes me feel good. And I know it will please our user when he comes in tomorrow.

That entry probably took fewer than five minutes to write. Yet, at the end of the day, that engineer was quite happy—and seems motivated toward high productivity the next day, too. Making progress, and noting it, can provide a real lift—and give you the boost you need to keep working on the projects that will yield the greatest benefit for your organization and its customers.

Daily writing and review helps in negative situations, too. In the following entry, an employee struggles to gain a sense of control during a traumatic event in her company—a downsizing. Even though her own job might still be in jeopardy, her work diary helps her shape a healthy perspective; it enables her to focus on her work, amid swirling gossip and uncertainty. Her personal growth is almost palpable in this entry:

This morning, my project manager came over and sat next to me and asked me if I was okay after all the layoffs that went on yesterday. I thought that was really nice. We all had a very rough day yesterday, but I feel better today. In 45 days, we will all know our fate, and then we can get on with our lives one way or the other. The outcome of all this is really out of our control. I'm trying to concentrate on what IS in my control, by doing my job.

And here, in his final entry for our study, a professional tells us directly how valuable it was for him to fill out the diary questionnaire that we sent every day during his project:

> *I did find value in doing the questionnaires, especially when I was disciplined enough to do them at the end of the day, when everything was still fresh in my mind. It helped me to reflect on the day, my accomplishments, the team's work, and how I was feeling in general. When you're working at a hectic pace, reflection time is rare, but [it's] really beneficial.*

Don't dismiss the idea of trying a work diary because you think you have to create finely-crafted entries for posterity. We've found that if you avoid making a big commitment to it, you'll be more successful. Don't worry about how to express yourself. Simply describe one event or insight from the day. In our study, the average length of the entries was a mere 54 words.

To get started:

- **Pick a time.** Consider when you're most likely to have ten minutes to yourself. Ideally, this will be the same time each day, because it's much easier to get into the habit that way. For some of us, that will be the very end of the day, just before bed. For others, it's at the end of the workday, or on the train ride home.

- **Create a memory trigger.** Choose something you'll see or hear at the designated writing time. For example, if you want to do the diary before you leave the office at 5:00, set a repeating alarm in your calendar for 4:50. If you choose bedtime, put your diary notebook and a pen on your bedside table.

- **Select a medium.** Find something you enjoy using. People have very different preferences for diarykeeping. Some love a leather-bound, monogrammed, silk-bookmarked, five-year diary, with just a few pre-ruled lines for each day. Others like online journaling programs (like iDoneThis). Whether it's a Word doc, a note app, a spiral-bound notebook to an Excel spreadsheet, use whatever works for you.

- **Reflect on your day.** Some people discover what they think as they write, but most of us need a bit of time to collect our thoughts. Use the first three minutes to let your mind go to any one of these types of events from the day:

  - Progress . . . and what led to it. (Congratulate yourself!)
  - Setbacks . . . and what might have caused them. (Learn from them!)
  - Something good. (Feel grateful!)
  - Something difficult. (Get it off your chest!)
  - One thing you can do tomorrow to make your work go better. (Then plan how to do it!)
  - Anything else that dominates your reflection time.

- **Write.** Use the remaining seven minutes to jot down your thoughts. Don't give a thought to grammar, proper sentence construction, style, etc. Focus on the event.
- **Review.** Once in a while, take a few minutes to sit down with your journal and a favorite beverage in a comfy chair. Much of the value in a diary comes from periodically reviewing the past few days (or more).

Keep a diary for just one project, for just a few weeks, and you might find it's a productivity tool you don't want to give up.

Teresa Amabile is the Edsel Bryant Ford Professor of Business Administration at Harvard Business School. She researches what makes people creative, productive, happy, and motivated at work. **Steven Kramer** is a psychologist and independent researcher. They are coauthors of *The Progress Principle* (Harvard Business Review Press, 2011).

Section 6
Renew Your Energy

Chapter 21

How to Accomplish More by Doing Less

by Tony Schwartz

We know that it's not just the number of hours we sit at our desks that determines the value we generate. It's the energy and focus we bring to those hours. Human beings are designed to pulse rhythmically between spending and renewing energy. That's how we operate at our best. Maintaining a steady reservoir of energy—physically, mentally, emotionally, and even spiritually—requires refueling intermittently.

Take for example, two people of equal skill—Bill and Nick—who work in the same office. Each day they arrive at work at 9:00 AM and leave at 7:00 PM.

Adapted from content posted on hbr.org on December 13, 2011.

Bill works for 10 hours—essentially without stopping—juggling tasks at his desk and running between meetings all day long. He even eats lunch at his desk. By 1:00 PM, Bill's feeling tired and beginning to lose focus. Between 4:00 and 7:00 PM, he's really dragging and easily distracted.

It's the **law of diminishing returns.** Because he doesn't take breaks to renew his energy, Bill effectively delivers about 6 hours of productive work over his 10-hour day—about 60% of his capacity.

Now contrast that with Nick. He puts in the same 10 hours as Bill. But rather than working essentially without stopping, Nick paces himself: he works intensely for approximately 90 minutes at a stretch, and then takes a 15-minute break before resuming work. At 12:15, he goes out for lunch for 45 minutes or works out in a nearby gym. At 3:00 PM, he goes out to his car and takes a brief rest. Sometimes it turns into a 15- or 20-minute nap. Finally, between 4:30 and 5:00, he takes a 15-minute walk outside.

Nick takes off a total of two hours during his 10 at work, so he "only" puts in 8 hours. But because he's building in periods of renewal with scheduled breaks, he's able to work at 80% percent of his full capacity over the course of the whole day—**20% more than Bill.**

Cycling through periods of work and rest allows Nick to be more focused and alert than Bill, to make fewer mistakes, and to return home at night with more energy left for his family.

Work the way Nick does, and you'll get more done, in less time, at a higher level of quality, more sustainably.

Learn how to **manage your energy, not your time,** in the next article.

Tony Schwartz is the president and CEO of The Energy Project and the author of *Be Excellent at Anything*. Become a fan of The Energy Project on Facebook and connect with Tony on Twitter at @tonyschwartz and @energy_project.

Chapter 22

Manage Your Energy, Not Your Time

A summary of the full-length HBR article by **Tony Schwartz** *and* **Catherine McCarthy**, *highlighting key ideas.*

THE IDEA IN BRIEF

Is your job demanding more from you than ever before? Do you feel as if you're working additional hours but rarely getting ahead? Is your mobile device leashing you to your job 24/7? Do you feel exhausted, disengaged, sick?

Spending longer days at the office and putting in extra hours at home doesn't work because your time is a limited resource. But your personal energy is renewable. By fostering deceptively simple **rituals** that will help you regularly replenish your energy, you can strengthen your physical, emotional, mental, and spiritual resilience. These rituals include taking brief breaks at specific intervals, expressing appreciation to others, reducing interruptions, and spending more time on the activities you do best and enjoy most.

THE IDEA IN PRACTICE

Try these practices to renew the four dimensions of your personal energy:

Physical Energy

- Enhance your sleep by setting an earlier bedtime and reducing alcohol use.
- Reduce stress by engaging in cardiovascular activity at least three times a week and strength training at least once a week.
- Eat small meals and light snacks every three hours.
- Learn to notice signs of imminent flagging energy, including restlessness, yawning, hunger, and difficulty concentrating.
- Take brief but regular breaks away from your desk at 90- to 120-minute intervals throughout the day.

Emotional Energy

- Defuse negative emotions—irritability, impatience, anxiety, insecurity—through deep abdominal breathing.

- Fuel positive emotions in yourself and others by regularly expressing appreciation to people in detailed, specific terms through notes, e-mails, calls, or conversations.
- Look at upsetting situations through new lenses. Adopt a **reverse lens** to ask, "What would the other person in this conflict say, and how might he be right?" Use a **long lens** to ask, "How will I likely view this situation in six months?" Employ a **wide lens** to ask, "How can I grow and learn from this situation?"

Mental Energy

- Reduce interruptions by performing high-concentration tasks away from phones and e-mail.
- Respond to voice mails and e-mails at designated times during the day.
- Select the most important challenge for the next day the night before. Then make that challenge your first priority when you arrive at work in the morning.

Spiritual Energy

- Identify your "sweet spot" activities—those that give you feelings of effectiveness, effortless absorption, and fulfillment. Find ways to do more of these. One executive who hated doing sales reports delegated them to someone who loved that activity.

- Allocate time and energy to what you consider most important. For example, spend the last 20 minutes of your evening commute relaxing, so you can connect with your family once you're home.

- Live your core values. For instance, if being considerate is important to you but you're perpetually late for meetings, practice intentionally showing up five minutes early for meetings.

Are You Headed for an Energy Crisis?

Take the following quiz to identify which areas of your life could benefit from energy-renewing rituals.

Please check the statements below that are true for you:

Body

- ☐ I don't regularly get at least seven to eight hours of sleep, and I often wake up feeling tired.

- ☐ I frequently skip breakfast, or I settle for something that isn't nutritious.

- ☐ I don't work out enough (meaning cardiovascular training at least three times a week and strength training at least once a week).

- ☐ I don't take regular breaks during the day to renew and recharge, or I often eat lunch at my desk, if I eat it at all.

Emotions

- ☐ I frequently find myself feeling irritable, impatient, or anxious at work, especially when work is demanding.
- ☐ I don't have enough time with my family and loved ones, and when I'm with them, I'm not always *really* with them.
- ☐ I have too little time for the activities that I most deeply enjoy.
- ☐ I don't stop frequently enough to express my appreciation to others or to savor my accomplishments and blessings.

Mind

- ☐ I have difficulty focusing on one thing at a time, and I am easily distracted during the day, especially by e-mail.
- ☐ I spend much of my day reacting to immediate crises and demands rather than focusing on activities with longer-term value and high leverage.
- ☐ I don't take enough time for reflection, strategizing, and creative thinking.
- ☐ I often work in the evenings or on weekends, and I almost never take an e-mail–free vacation.

Spirit

- ☐ I don't spend enough time at work doing what I do best and enjoy most.

- ☐ There are significant gaps between what I say is most important to me and how I actually allocate my time and energy.
- ☐ My decisions at work are more often influenced by external demands than by a strong, clear sense of my own purpose.
- ☐ I don't invest enough time and energy in making a positive difference to others or to the world.

How Is Your Overall Energy?

Total number of statements checked: ____

Guide to energy scores

0–3: Excellent energy management skills

4–6: Reasonable energy management skills

7–10: Significant energy management deficits

11–16: A full-fledged energy management crisis

What Do You Need to Work On?

Number of checks in each category:

Body ____

Mind ____

Emotions ____

Spirit ____

Guide to category scores

0: Excellent energy management skills

1: Strong energy management skills

2: Significant deficits

3: Poor energy management skills

4: A full-fledged energy crisis

Tony Schwartz (tony@theenergyproject.com) is the president and CEO of The Energy Project in New York City, and a coauthor of *The Power of Full Engagement: Managing Energy, Not Time, Is the Key to High Performance and Personal Renewal* (Free Press, 2003).

Catherine McCarthy (catherine@theenergyproject.com) is a senior vice president at The Energy Project.

Chapter 23

Why Great Performers Sleep More

by Tony Schwartz

Why is sleep one of the first things we're willing to sacrifice as the demands in our lives keep rising? We continue to live by a remarkably durable myth: Sleeping one hour less will give us one more hour of productivity. In reality, even small amounts of sleep deprivation take a significant toll on our health, mood, cognitive capacity, and productivity.

How Much Sleep Do You Need?

When researchers put test subjects into environments without clocks or windows and ask them to sleep any

Adapted from content posted on hbr.org on March 3, 2011.

time they feel tired, 95% sleep between seven and eight hours out of every 24. Another 2.5% sleep more than eight hours. That means just 2.5% of us require fewer than seven hours of sleep a night to feel fully rested. That's one out of every 40 people.

In my talks, when I ask who has had fewer than seven hours of sleep several nights during the past week, the majority raise their hands. That's true whether it's an audience of corporate executives, teachers, cops, or government workers.

Great performers are an exception. Typically, they sleep significantly *more* than the rest of us. In Anders Ericsson's famous study of violinists, the top performers slept an average of eight and a half hours out of every 24, including a 20- to 30-minute midafternoon nap—some two hours a day more than the average American.

The top violinists also reported that except for practice itself, sleep was the most important factor in improving their skills.

As I gathered research about sleep, I felt increasingly compelled to give it higher priority in my own life. Today, I go to great lengths to ensure that I get at least eight hours every night, and ideally between eight and a half and nine hours, even when I'm traveling.

I still take the overnight redeye from California to New York, but I'm asleep by takeoff—even if I have to take a sleeping aid. When I get home at 6:00 or 7:00 AM, I go right to bed until I've had my eight hours. What I've learned about those days is that I'd rather work at 100% for five or six hours than at 60% for eight or nine hours.

With sufficient sleep, I feel better, I work with more focus, and I manage my emotions better, which is good for

WHAT PEOPLE ARE SAYING ON HBR.ORG

Try the coffee nap—Lifehacker had a great article about [naps]. I'm a paramedic and I've used this trick for ages. Fix a cup of coffee so you can drink it quickly. Set up the spot where you'll nap and then drink the coffee. Set a timer for 20 minutes and make sure you get up when it goes off. Any longer and you'll feel worn out. I know this has saved my life on many late-night, long-distance transports. —Posted by John

everyone around me. I dislike enduring even a single day when I haven't had enough sleep because the impact is immediate and unavoidable. On the rare days that I don't get enough, I try hard to get at least a 20- to 30-minute nap in the afternoon. That's a big help.

How to Get More Sleep

Here are three other tips to improve the quantity and quality of your sleep:

- **Write down what's on your mind before you get into bed.** If you leave items such as unfinished to-do's and unresolved issues in your working memory, they'll make it harder to fall asleep, and you'll end up ruminating about them if you wake up during the night.

- **Go to bed earlier—and at a set time.** Sounds obvious, right? The problem is there's no alternative. You're already waking up at the latest possible time you can. If you don't ritualize a specific bedtime, you'll find ways to stay up later, just the way you do now.

- **Start winding down at least 45 minutes before you turn out the light.** You won't fall asleep if you're all wound up from answering e-mail or doing other work. Create a ritual around drinking a cup of herbal tea, listening to music that helps you relax, or reading a dull book.

Tony Schwartz is the president and CEO of The Energy Project and the author of *Be Excellent at Anything*. Become a fan of The Energy Project on Facebook and connect with Tony on Twitter at @tonyschwartz and @energy_project.

Section 7:
Take Control of Your E-mail

Chapter 24
Simplify Your E-mail

by Gina Trapani

If you spend more time dealing with e-mail than getting the right work done, it's time for an e-mail makeover.

Clear Out Your In-Box

Computer scientists developed e-mail based on the paradigm of postal mail, so think of your in-box like your physical mailbox. You wouldn't keep bills you have to pay and the invitation to that birthday party in there forever, right? Sort by sender, date, or subject line to clear out your messages as efficiently as possible. Then delete the junk; unsubscribe from newsletters you never read or websites you no longer visit. If you have thousands of messages in your main folder, business writer Amy Gallo

Adapted from content posted on hbr.org on June 9, 2009.

suggests creating a new subfolder in your Archive folder called "Old In-box" and putting all of your messages in there. You'll still have access to them if you need them, but you'll be able to jump-start your new e-mail process without the drudgery of actually reviewing every old message.

Set Up Just Three Folders

Sometimes it's not just the sheer volume of messages that makes e-mail management a time-sink, it's the complicated folder system we've concocted. Streamline your in-box by creating these three folders:

Follow-up: For messages you have to respond to or act on that will take longer than a couple of minutes. (Put a corresponding item on your to-do list for each of these messages.)

Hold: For messages where you're waiting for something to happen, like a package shipment or event invitation. (Put a corresponding item on your calendar for each of these messages.)

Archive: For messages you're done with but want to keep for reference.

Maintain Your New System

Once you've cleaned out your in-box, you'll want to keep it organized and manageable, so you can focus your attention on your most important work.

Here are some techniques to keep your e-mail under control:

- **Process your e-mail in batches.** Most of us are on e-mail all day, scanning for anything urgent and ignoring everything else, which is how backlog accumulates in your in-box. Instead of checking every time you hear the incoming message "ding," process your e-mail in batches. Completely shut down your e-mail or set it and your handheld to check for messages only every few hours. Then, when you have time or are in between tasks, fully commit yourself to processing new messages. Alexandra Samuel, cofounder of Social Signal, recommends selecting specific times when you'll process e-mail (for example, 8:00 to 10:00 AM and 4:00 to 6:00 PM). Notify correspondents and colleagues of your schedule through your e-mail signature or a note on your blog (and clear this approach with your supervisor, if applicable). Assume that if it's an emergency, people will call you—but refrain from actually suggesting that, since you don't want to encourage a constantly ringing phone.

- **Use the "two-minute" rule.** As you process your e-mail in batches, reply to any messages that will take fewer than two minutes on the spot. Don't delay and leave them in your in-box marked as read, thinking you'll get back to them; don't even file them away in "Follow-up." Just take care of them immediately. To help keep you within the two-minute mark, try answering all e-mails in three sentences or fewer (visit **Three.Sentenc.es**), says Dave Kerpen, CEO of Likeable Media. Anything that takes more text probably requires a quick call instead. Have your team or department try this as a group experiment, and watch your collective e-mail–processing time shrink.

- **End "Reply all."** Kerpen also recommends using internal social networking tools instead of e-mail to chat with your coworkers, facilitate collaboration and passive listening, and eliminate the dreaded "Reply all" e-mail chains. Try a private, closed Facebook group. Or explore proprietary tools such as **Jive** and **Yammer**, which allow organizations to set up private social networking platforms. Jive is best for large enterprises, while Yammer is suitable for departments or smaller organizations. Get an on-the-spot answer and get on with your work.

- **Stop spamming people.** Samuel notes that a major contributor to e-mail overload is the widely held expectation that every e-mail must get a reply, even if it's just "OK" or "Thanks." Don't do it.

For more suggestions on keeping your e-mail under control, see the next article, "Eight E-mail Overload Experiments."

Gina Trapani is the founding editor of the personal productivity blog Lifehacker.com.

Chapter 25

Eight E-mail Overload Experiments

by Alexandra Samuel

If you've tried all of the basic ways to structure and manage your e-mail, but are still feeling overwhelmed, here are eight road-tested experiments for battling e-mail overload that range from reasonable to radical. Try each one, or a couple at a time—but push yourself to the very limits of your comfort zone, because the tactics that seem most inconceivable may be just the ones that help you discover a new way to work more effectively with e-mail.

If your company's culture includes expecting instant replies to every message, e-mail your colleagues and regular correspondents to let them know about your experiment. This will help avoid ruffled feathers over some of the more radical suggestions.

1. **Reject the mandatory reply.** Set up an autoresponder that lets all correspondents know that you're only replying to selected e-mail, depending on your availability and priorities—and make it clear you don't expect a reply to every e-mail you send them, either.

   Here's one version:

   SUBJECT: Limited e-mail means I may not reply to the message you sent

   Thank you for getting in touch. I'm experimenting with a new approach to e-mail: I'm sending and replying to a smaller number of messages. I still check e-mail regularly, so if you don't get a reply within 72 hours please assume I have reviewed and filed your message. This approach should help me focus my attention on my current priorities. Thank you for your understanding.

   For a less extreme solution, add a polite line to your standard e-mail signature. Here's mine:

   Alexandra Samuel, PhD
   Director, Social + Interactive Media Centre,
   Emily Carr University
   alex@alexandrasamuel.com |
   Twitter @awsamuel
   Join the fight against e-mail overload:
   - Focus on *your* priorities; I'll understand if you don't reply.
   - Sorry if I don't reply; I'm trying to focus, too.
   - If it's urgent, reach me by Twitter or SMS.

2. **Set message quotas.** For outbound messages, limit the number of e-mail threads you initiate each day. Assume that every e-mail you send will generate 4–10 responses, so you're creating work for yourself with each message. Send fewer, and you'll get fewer. For incoming messages, guesstimate the number and make that your daily quota. Use filters in your e-mail software to sort incoming mail and keep all but the most crucial messages out of your in-box. Auto-file other messages in alternative folders. Keep adding rules until your daily in-box volume falls below the quota you've set.

   For example, I automatically direct e-mails into different folders for internal mail, messages I'm cc'd on, social network notifications, and more. My closest colleagues know that any e-mail marked "URGENT" still comes directly to my in-box; you might set your rules to ensure that all messages from your boss come through marked as high priority or color coded in a way that makes them stand out. The filters thin the incoming messages to a manageable level and ensure that e-mails from current or prospective clients don't get lost in a sea of spam.

3. **Reply by phone.** You can eliminate dozens of e-mails a day with quick calls. A five-minute chat about a landmine your project just stumbled on may be more efficient than crafting an

e-mail that adequately explains the situation. Also, thank people in person or by phone, even if that means leaving a voice mail (detailed thanks for project work, however, should always go by e-mail, so the recipient can file it for performance reviews). Most crucially, switch to phone or in-person communication whenever you get a message that angers or hurts you, because e-mail exchanges tend to escalate and solidify grievances.

4. **Do not copy.** Refuse to send, read, or reply to cc'ed messages. As blogging entrepreneur Anil Dash puts it, including someone as a cc on an e-mail is like saying "This is important enough for me to interrupt you [with] but not to write to you [about directly]." If a message you're sending requires a recipient's attention, include that person in the "to" field; if not, leave them off entirely. Tell colleagues they should address messages to you directly if they need you to reply.

5. **Don't touch that phone!** When you have a few minutes between meetings or while waiting for a plane, don't use that time to respond to e-mail on your mobile's tiny keyboard. Rather than send a rash or typo-ridden reply, wait until you're back at your desk or with your laptop or tablet, when you can craft a better response in less time.

6. **Take an e-mail vacation:** Try a two-week vacation, a six-month sabbatical, or something in between. But it's not much of a break if you come back to an overflowing in-box, so before you tune out, turn on the vacation autoresponder with a message like this:

   Thanks for your message. I'm taking an e-mail vacation until the new year. The message you've just sent me has been filed, so it's not lost forever, but if you need a reply it would be great if you could e-mail me sometime on or after January 4. If you need to reach me urgently, I'll be available by Twitter or mobile phone.

   Set your e-mail program to file everything in a folder labeled "Vacation," and when you return, take a quick look for any truly life-changing messages you may have missed and actively ignore the rest. If someone really wants to reach you, they'll e-mail again.

7. **Reply to *every* e-mail:** If ignoring e-mail makes your palms sweat, maybe it's time to give into its primacy. For two weeks, make your *entire morning* an e-mail processing zone. (If three hours isn't enough, block as big a chunk of time as you think you'll need.) See whether your commitment to a 100% response rate makes you more effective. This will help you make some conscious decisions about how

to better allocate your time and triage your in-box.

8. **Give up e-mail altogether:** For the ultimate in in-box liberation, give it up. Yes, you really can—especially if you're comfortable with social media tools. Use your blog to post updates on your work instead of sending an e-mail to a big distribution list; Basecamp or another project management tool to communicate with project teams; Google Docs to circulate drafts; Skype for a quick conversation instead of a 14-message exchange; and Twitter DMs, chat, and SMS for tight, efficient, and confidential messaging. Take your e-mail address off your business card and Web page, and encourage anyone who needs to reach you to pick up the phone.

Alexandra Samuel is the Director of the Social + Interactive Media Centre at Emily Carr University, and the cofounder of Social Signal, a Vancouver-based social media agency. You can follow Alex on Twitter at @awsamuel or her blog at alexandrasamuel.com.

Section 8
Maintain Your New Approach

Chapter 26
Sustaining Your Productivity System

by Alexandra Samuel

A productivity system is like any other faith: It works for as long as you continue to believe in it. Let a hint of skepticism creep in—about the discipline required, the rewards promised, or the potential superiority of other ideologies—and the threat of disorder quickly returns.

If you can accept that your system is a work in progress, it's a lot easier to keep that threat at bay. Here are some tips for sustaining your productivity system:

1. **Focus on outcomes.** Many productivity methodologies are so specific about their recommended processes that your zeal for maintaining your folders, sorting your communications,

or acquiring snazzy storage bins can easily eclipse the problems or benefits that motivated you in the first place. Remember that adherence to a system is a false god: Don't stick to it just because you bought the book or the software. If you're working effectively and meeting your deadlines, it doesn't matter if you no longer geocode your task list.

2. **Make micro commitments.** When you embrace a new productivity religion, adopt its minor practices as well as its major ones. Sometimes the smaller commitments are the most sustainable. For example, two years after I got serious about In-box Zero, I no longer process my in-box to empty *every day*. But my e-mail is still dramatically easier to manage, thanks to the various filters I initially set up as part of my in-box zero approach.

3. **Find fellow adherents.** One of my big stumbling blocks with David Allen's book *Getting Things Done* was Allen's denunciation of hanging folders; my file cabinet *only* worked with hanging files. Happily, I thought to Google "GTD hanging files," and discovered a community of enthusiasts discussing the merits of various folder styles—and even brands—with the seriousness of Talmudic scholars. Reading about how other people implemented and adjusted the system liberated me from my slavish

adherence to every detail. You can also *make* your own adherents: Marnie Webb, the CEO of nonprofit tech resource CompuMentor/TechSoup, keeps a shelf full of copies of *Getting Things Done*. "When one of my team members complains about not being able to manage their lists or having too much to do, I pull a book off my shelf," Webb says. "I tell them to complain again after they've implemented [GTD] for three months."

4. **Schedule routine maintenance.** A few years ago I sorted all the junk in our home office into beautifully labeled boxes. Six months later, a friend observed that whether you opened a box labeled "Bills to Pay" or "Pens and Highlighters," you were guaranteed to find a pad of Post-its, an iPod adapter, a handful of batteries, and 37 cents in change. Now I know that *getting* organized isn't enough—to *stay* organized, I have to set aside a couple of days every 4–6 months so that I can reestablish order and update my systems. (This is one of my favorite ways to make productive use of the few days after a major trip or project wrap-up, when I'm too brain-dead to do anything more demanding.)

5. **Anticipate obsolescence.** Even the best productivity systems and tips may not survive the passage of time and the advent of new

technologies. So stick with software tools that provide options for exporting your data to .csv, iCal, or other standard formats, so you don't get trapped by any one platform.

6. **Embrace eclecticism.** Troy Angrignon, vice president of sales and marketing at Cloudscaling, is religious about tracking his tasks and goals using a single, two-column document whose structure borrows from just about every productivity guru out there—Brian Tracy, David Allen, Robert Fritz. While combining approaches might amount to apostasy in the eyes of any one system's adherents, it's allowed Angrignon to develop a customized method that's served him well for 15 years, even as he continues to make adjustments and sample new tools. You may also find that tweaking your productivity system, whether it's trying out a new calendaring approach or sorting your paper files, is part of your creative process—a way of preparing yourself for a new year or project.

Alexandra Samuel is the Director of the Social + Interactive Media Centre at Emily Carr University, and the cofounder of Social Signal, a Vancouver-based social media agency. You can follow Alex on Twitter at @awsamuel or her blog at alexandrasamuel.com.

Section 9

Explore Further

Chapter 27
More Productivity Books to Explore

by Ilan Mochari

This guide provides a wide range of tactics and tips for improving your productivity. If you wish to explore further, we've summarized the approaches of three other experts: Stephen Covey, Julie Morgenstern, and David Allen.

The Seven Habits of Highly Effective People, **by Stephen R. Covey**

The Basic Idea: This is a guide to changing your life, not just the way you manage your day. To zero in on the best ways to spend your time and energy, focus on things you can control, keep your desired outcomes (for both individual projects and your life overall) in mind, improve your personal and professional relationships, nurture yourself, and classify your tasks as urgent or important.

Ideal if you:

- Want to transform how you live. For example, you *can* break old habits like procrastination, but it will require work on your character, not just your productivity practices.
- Have spiritual leanings and want to develop mission statements for different areas of your life ("I want to raise two self-confident children" or "I'm here to deliver smart and media-savvy public relations services to my customers. I will draw on my industry knowledge, my understanding of my clients and their challenges, and a genuine passion for what I do.").
- Enjoy a longer read, rich with personal anecdotes and scholarly references.

Not ideal if you:

- Are happy with your life outside work and simply want a nuts-and-bolts system for managing workflow.
- Will roll your eyes at phrases like "opening the gate of change," "emotional bank account," and "abundance mentality."
- Are looking for advice that addresses modern worklife and gadgets. Covey's advice transcends trends, but his book predates smartphones and social networking.
- Are looking for advice on organizing your physical workspace.

Additional resources: franklincovey.com, stephencovey.com, the3rdalternative.com.

Organizing from the Inside Out, by Julie Morgenstern

The Basic Idea: This book will help you organize your physical spaces depending on your personality, needs, and goals. Identify the root cause of your clutter (Is your current system too complex? Are you by nature a packrat?). Find homes for your most important things by using the Kindergarten approach: Divide your space into specific activity zones that have everything necessary to do whatever type of work you've assigned to that area, with appropriate supplies and storage units to keep them contained. For example, set up a bill-paying area with everything you need—even if it means duplicates (like postage stamps) in multiple zones.

Ideal if you:	Not ideal if you:
• Literally have trouble finding things. • Want advice about organizing physical spaces (desks, offices, filing systems). • Prefer lists and tips in clearly signposted sections.	• Aren't a fan of self-reflection. • Are looking for more advice about productivity or time management. • Are looking for a quick fix or an excuse to purge everything. Morgenstern recommends a three-step approach (analyzye, strategize, attack), with a five-step process for the attack phase.

Additional resources: juliemorgenstern.com, oprah.com/home/More-with-Organizing-Expert-Julie-Morgenstern, amazon.com/Julie-Morgenstern/e/B001IGQY78

Getting Things Done, by David Allen

The Basic Idea: This book will help you gather, evaluate, and make progress on all of your tasks. Don't rely on your brain to remember everything you have to do. Instead, write it all down in a calendar and series of lists (projects, next actions, waiting for, maybe/someday). Review each task and determine if you should: do it, delegate it, or defer it. When you're ready to start a new task, use four criteria to decide what to do: context, time available, energy available, priority. Once a week, gather your lists and calendar to review your system, update your lists, and check in with yourself about where you are relative to your workload and schedule.

Ideal if you:	Not ideal if you:
• Want a nuts-and-bolts guide to determining priorities and mastering workflow. • Prefer bulleted lists, diagrams, scattered inspirational quotes, and flowcharts. • Have the authority or resources to delegate. • Are looking for advice on setting up physical work spaces, as well as productivity in general.	• Seek spiritual guidance, too. • Enjoy storytelling or personal anecdotes in your business reading. • Are overwhelmed by setting up elaborate physical file-folder systems. • Aren't comfortable delegating.

Additional resources: davidco.com, gtdtimes.com, youtube.com/watch?v=Qo7vUdKTlhk

---

Ilan Mochari is chief writer for *The Build Network* and a contributor to the *MIT Sloan Management Review*.

Chapter 28
Productivity Apps and Tools

Here are some apps and websites to further fuel your interest in making the most of your time and energy. This is by no means an exhaustive list—we've compiled favorites from some of the most productive members of our hbr.org community: Joshua Gans, Skoll Chair in Innovation and Entrepreneurship, Rotman School of Management, University of Toronto; Heidi Grant Halvorson, PhD, author of *Nine Things Successful People Do Differently*; Whitney Johnson, author of *Dare Dream Do*; Dave Kerpen, author of *Likeable Social Media*; and Andrew McAfee, author of *Enterprise 2.0*. Since technology is ever-evolving, consider this an inspiration list. For example, if Longer Days is no longer available when you look for it, try a search for virtual assistant to see what new offerings exist.

Manage Your Schedule

- **Longer Days, Brickwork,** and **Uassist.ME** are just three of dozens of virtual assistant companies that provide online access to people to help with administrative tasks, such as scheduling meetings and calls, researching individuals' backgrounds for networking opportunities, marketing research (such as company information or revenue data); other professional functions, such as copywriting and managing event RSVPs; and even personal tasks like scheduling doctor's appointments. Virtual assistants add extra hands without adding extra headcount. The programs are relatively inexpensive: Longerdays.com offers 20 hours for $350 and Uassist.ME charges $650 per month for about 40 hours/month's worth of work. *—Dave Kerpen*

- **Tungle.Me** and **Doodle** will end those long, painful e-mail chains that often result when you're trying to set up a meeting with multiple people inside and outside of your organization. **Tungle .Me** allows people to see your calendar availability and easily schedule meetings and phone calls, and it syncs with most Web and mobile calendar applications. **Doodle** allows multiple parties to share their availability via poll and quickly find a mutually convenient date and time for an event. *—Dave Kerpen*

Make Your Lists

- **Workflowy** is an online tool and app that allows you to better organize yourself by mimicking the way you naturally think. It helps you make a list of high-level ideas and tasks and then breaks them into smaller pieces. For example, I've started with Personal and Work as my two broad categories. Under "Work," I've created sublists such as Rose Park Advisors, Book launch, and HBR blog. You can subdivide lists like this almost infinitely. *—Whitney Johnson*

- **Remember The Milk** is an online task manager that allows you to easily track your to-do list from your smartphone. You can add items to your to-do list, set location tags to help you remember to take care of things when you're out and about, organize tasks by priority, schedule tasks by integrating with popular calendar tools (including Outlook and Google Calendar), and sync everything so that you can see your updated, prioritized list whether you're at your desk or on the go. *—Dave Kerpen*
- **Evernote** allows you to capture notes, files, and images and later access them from your tablet, mobile, or computer through a robust search feature. Save favorite Web pages with notes about them, take a picture of a potential location for a future launch party, record your thoughts on your next product idea and add to it whenever and wherever inspiration strikes, or keep your scanned itineraries and travel docs all in one place. Evernote also makes it easy to share notes and documents with friends, classmates, and colleagues. *—Dave Kerpen*

Manage Your Reminders

- **Due** is an iPhone app that repeatedly reminds you to do something at a certain time—until you do it. Here's how it works: You need to remember to write an e-mail to someone but can't do it right now. With Due, you set your phone to alert you to write the e-mail at a certain time (30 minutes from now, 4 PM). I used to leave myself notes or write on my hand. With Due, I can do the same thing but with more precision. It will continue to beep until I accept the reminder or change the time I want to be reminded. *—Joshua Gans*

- **Nudge-mail** helps you remember what you need to do when you need to do it. Whether your spouse asks you to pick up milk on your way home or a client requests a draft proposal, Nudge-mail reminds you of the task at the right time. Just forward an e-mail to addresses like "tomorrow@nudge-mail.com" or "2hours@nudge-mail.com" and free your mind to focus on your next important task.

  —Dave Kerpen

Manage Your Files

- If you use multiple computers, work on several projects, and/or have multiple colleagues, try **Dropbox.** It's a cloud-based storage utility that eliminates file-related hassles. It puts your files in one folder that all of your devices can access, and synchronizes them in the background without your having to lift a finger. It also allows you to share different folders with collaborators. How many times have you tried to send a file via e-mail, only to have a server reject it because it was too big? Just create a Dropbox folder, invite the recipient(s) to share it, and your problems are past tense. *—Andrew McAfee*

- **JotNot** is an iPhone app that allows you to take a photo of any image or document and instantly turn it into a .pdf—for example, you can sign and fax back a contract in seconds, on the go. *—Dave Kerpen*

Manage Your Social Media

- I don't know what I would do without **HootSuite.** It's a social media dashboard that allows you to monitor and post to all your networks simultaneously. If you blog or use social media for your work, this is a *huge* timesaver. When I've written something new or read something I want to share on my networks, I can let everyone know with a single entry, rather than having to log on to each network separately. I use it to manage my Facebook, Twitter, LinkedIn, and Google+ accounts, and you can also use it with Tumblr, WordPress, and Foursquare. *—Heidi Grant Halvorson, PhD*

- **Buffer** allows you to schedule Tweets and Facebook messages (and soon, LinkedIn posts) ahead of time, and automatically spaces them out. In five minutes, you can find interesting articles worth sharing with colleagues and prospective clients, and be tweeting all day, without actually going to Twitter again. *—Dave Kerpen*

- **Rapportive** is a browser add-on for Gmail that transforms Gmail's bland sidebar into a time-saver. Instead of ads, you'll see social media information about the sender of the e-mail: his picture, links to his profile, recent Tweets, etc. The add-on is available for Firefox, Chrome, and Safari, is free to use, and integrates smoothly with Gmail. This tool obviates the need for a separate search to find out more about new contacts or clients. *—Dave Kerpen*

- **Dragon Dictation** is a voice-recognition application that allows you to easily dictate text or e-mail messages. Speak into the program and instantly see the transcription. Faster and safer than typing while on the go, you can dictate everything from Tweets to longer e-mail messages. *—Dave Kerpen*

- **NutshellMail** eliminates the need for multiple visits to your social network accounts. It sends you a daily summary and includes only important information such as Facebook likes, posts, and comments; and Twitter mentions, new followers, and Tweets. *—Dave Kerpen*

Index

Notes

Notes

Notes

Notes

Notes

Notes

Notes

Notes

Notes

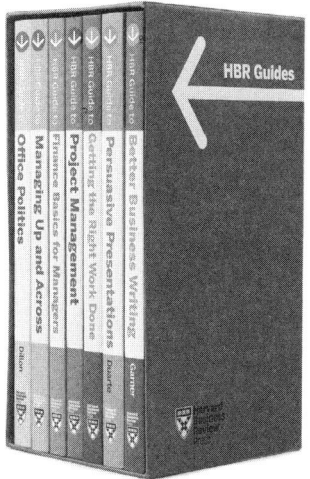

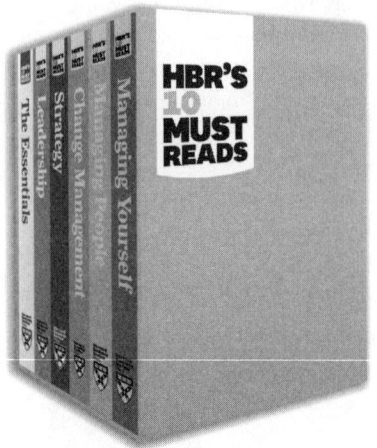

HBR Guide to **Coaching Employees**

Harvard Business Review Guides

Arm yourself with the advice you need to succeed on the job, from the most trusted brand in business. Packed with how-to essentials from leading experts, the HBR Guides provide smart answers to your most pressing work challenges.

The titles include:

HBR Guide to Better Business Writing

HBR Guide to Coaching Employees

HBR Guide to Finance Basics for Managers

HBR Guide to Getting the Mentoring You Need

HBR Guide to Getting the Right Job

HBR Guide to Getting the Right Work Done

HBR Guide to Giving Effective Feedback

HBR Guide to Leading Teams

HBR Guide to Making Every Meeting Matter

HBR Guide to Managing Stress at Work

HBR Guide to Managing Up and Across

HBR Guide to Negotiating

HBR Guide to Networking

HBR Guide to Office Politics

HBR Guide to Persuasive Presentations

HBR Guide to Project Management

HBR Guide to **Coaching Employees**

HARVARD BUSINESS REVIEW PRESS

Boston, Massachusetts

HBR Press Quantity Sales Discounts

Harvard Business Review Press titles are available at significant quantity discounts when purchased in bulk for client gifts, sales promotions, and premiums. Special editions, including books with corporate logos, customized covers, and letters from the company or CEO printed in the front matter, as well as excerpts of existing books, can also be created in large quantities for special needs.

For details and discount information for both print and ebook formats, contact booksales@harvardbusiness.org, tel. 800-988-0886, or www.hbr.org/bulksales.

Printed in the United States of America
10

The web addresses referenced in this book were live and correct at the time of the book's publication but may be subject to change.

Library-of-Congress cataloging information forthcoming
ISBN: 978-1-62527-533-2
eISBN: 978-1-62527-538-7

The paper used in this publication meets the requirements of the American National Standard for Permanence of Paper for Publications and Documents in Libraries and Archives Z39.48-1992.

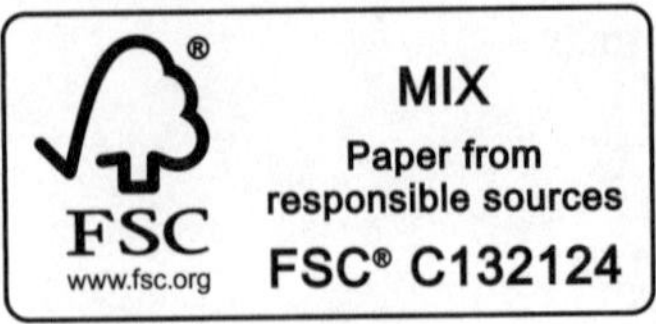

What You'll Learn

When you're swamped with work, it's hard to make time to coach your employees—and do it *well.* But if you don't help them build their skills, they'll keep coming to you for answers instead of finding their own solutions. That kind of hand-holding kills productivity and creativity, and you can't sustain it. In the long run, it eats up a lot more time and energy than investing in people's development.

So you really must coach to be an effective manager. Got a star on your team who's eager to advance? An underperformer who's dragging the group down? A steady contributor who feels bored and neglected? With all of them, you'll need to agree on goals for growth, motivate them to achieve those goals, support their efforts, and measure their progress. This guide gives you the tools to do that.

You'll get better at:

- Asking the right questions before you dispense advice
- Creating realistic but inspiring plans for growth

- Providing the support employees need to achieve peak performance
- Tapping their learning styles to make greater progress
- Giving them feedback they'll actually apply
- Giving them room to grapple with problems and discover solutions
- Engaging your employees and fostering independence
- Matching people's skills with your organization's needs
- Customizing your approach

Contents

Section 2: COACHING YOUR EMPLOYEES

Section 3: CUSTOMIZE YOUR COACHING

Introduction: Why Coach?

by Ed Batista

After graduating from business school, I was hired by a founding board of directors to launch a new organization, the Nonprofit Technology Enterprise Network. I had shared a leadership position before, but this was my first time as a solo chief executive, and I believed it was my responsibility to come up with the best ideas myself and champion them aggressively.

This approach led to a number of conflicts with my directors. A mentor of mine on the board took me aside and said, "We think you're a talented young guy, but you have some rough edges. We'd like you to invest in yourself and get a coach." One of my former professors had a coaching practice, and I asked her to take me on as a client. That was one of the best things I've ever done.

Although few coaching clients ultimately decide to become coaches, as I did, my positive experience of coaching is typical. The tremendous growth in the field over the past 20 years has been driven by consistent reports from clients who feel more effective and fulfilled as a result of the coaching they've received. And it doesn't help only at the individual level. Although researchers can't yet precisely measure coaching's effect on organizational performance, numerous studies (published in the *Journal of Management, Consulting Psychology Journal,* and other publications) show a positive impact.

Being coached helped me understand that I could make the biggest difference as a leader not by doing more than everyone else but by empowering other people to do more and motivating them to do their best. This meant letting go of certain responsibilities and recognizing the limits of my expertise. I didn't need to have all the answers; I just needed to ask the right questions. In short, I came to realize that effective leadership looks a lot like coaching.

But what do we mean by *coaching* in the first place? The simplest definition is "asking questions that help people discover the answers that are right for them." A more specific definition that applies to you as a leader and manager is "a style of management primarily characterized by asking employees questions in order to help them fulfill their immediate responsibilities more effectively and advance their development as professionals over time." The emphasis on *asking questions* is noteworthy when we consider that conventional leadership roles typically position the leader as the expert, someone who *provides answers* and whose domain knowledge is one of the foundations of her authority. In contrast, when a leader acts as a coach, she needs to adopt a different mind-set and add value in different ways.

It's no coincidence that the increased demand for coaching has accompanied the shift from command-and-control hierarchies to flatter, more distributed organizations. In the 1950s, management thinker Peter Drucker coined the term *knowledge worker* to describe a newly emerging cohort among the white-collar ranks; today most professionals fall into this category. Because they require (and desire) little or no direct supervision and often know more about their tasks than their managers do, knowledge workers usually respond well to coaching. Unlike directive, top-down management, coaching allows them to make the most of their expertise while compelling them to stretch and grow. As their manager, you set overall direction for them—but you let them figure out how best to get there.

Many senior managers and HR executives have come to view coaching as an investment in high potentials or as a perk for stars. Others still see coaching mainly as a corrective measure for underperformers. Daniel Goleman noted in his classic *Harvard Business Review* (HBR) article "Leadership That Gets Results" (March–April 2000) that despite coaching's merits, it was used least often among the management styles he studied. Leaders told Goleman that they didn't have time to coach their employees, and you may feel the same way. But coaching is broadly applicable, and managers at all levels can benefit from working with their direct reports in this way. You may need to encourage those around you to participate—and you may need to be persuaded yourself.

If so, I urge you to give it a try and gauge the return on your investment. Although external coaches like me will always play an important role in supporting leaders and their teams, coaching shouldn't be our exclusive domain. It's an essential management tool, and there are circumstances when a "coaching manager" can be more useful than a professional coach. I often help clients reflect on difficult experiences in order to make sense of what happened and extract some learning, but these conversations occur days or even weeks after the event. A leader who has coaching skills can help team members begin to reflect on a difficult experience immediately. Highly skilled leaders can even facilitate these discussions with their entire team present, allowing everyone to learn simultaneously. When leaders view coaching as the sole purview of external professionals like me, they miss countless opportunities to add value.

My experience as a coaching client, as someone who teaches coaching to MBA students, and as a professional coach has shown me the value of coaching as a management technique, and a large and growing body of research reinforces this conclusion. It takes time and effort, but the material in this guide will help you integrate coaching methods and processes into your own management style.

There's no "right" way to coach, so you'll have to decide for yourself which approaches described in the chapters that follow work best for you and your direct reports. Like any new skill, coaching requires practice, and you'll need to step outside your comfort zone as you experiment. Don't be too quick to write off a technique just because it feels awkward at first.

Coaching presents every manager with challenges. You may have to reconsider your leadership style and the ways in which you add value. You may feel reluctant to surrender control or to give people room to make mistakes, and you'll almost certainly be tempted to jump in with solutions when they're struggling with a problem. But those challenges get easier the more you coach, and the payoff is enormous: You'll tap your employees' full potential while leading more strategically.

Last year a client who'd founded a successful company concluded that his management style was holding back the firm. He and his senior managers had so many tactical responsibilities that they weren't truly leading. They were putting out fires, with a limited capacity to take a longer view and make the systemic changes the business needed.

So my client decided to restructure his role, delegating some tasks to his senior managers. He coached them as they assumed these duties, prompting them with questions to solve problems in creative new ways rather than simply telling them what had worked in the past. They, in turn, took the same approach with their direct reports.

As a result, the company's management team raised its sights and focused on more-strategic issues, which had a positive impact on the business. And my client found that he was actually more productive while spending less time in the office. When he sold the company and stepped down from his leadership role, he left with confidence that the management team would adjust seamlessly, and the business has continued to thrive.

That's what's possible when you coach your employees. That's why it's absolutely worth your time. And that's why you'll find this guide an invaluable addition to your leadership reading.

Ed Batista is an executive coach and an instructor at the Stanford Graduate School of Business. He writes regularly on issues related to coaching and professional development at www.edbatista.com, and he is currently writing a book on self-coaching for Harvard Business Review Press.

Section 1
Preparing to Coach Your Employees

Chapter 1
Shift Your Thinking to Coach Effectively

by Candice Frankovelgia

Do you ever say to yourself (or others), "This person just doesn't get it" or "This person will never have what it takes"? If so, you may have what Stanford psychologist Carol Dweck calls a *fixed mind-set*, which will severely limit your ability to make a difference as a coach. Low expectations rarely yield growth and often lead to frustration on both sides. You may occasionally encounter someone who truly can't develop, but the real barrier is most often *the belief that the person won't make progress.*

Adapted from the Center for Creative Leadership's course "Coaching for Greater Effectiveness." For further information, visit www.ccl.org.

It's easy to fall into this trap. After you've acquired a lot of experience and knowledge in your field, doing things yourself may seem simpler and faster than helping your direct reports improve their critical thinking, technical, or organizational skills. But that's a short-term solution that leads to long-term problems. If you keep providing all the answers, people will keep lining up at your door looking for them.

Shifting Your Mind-Set

In the end, it's actually less time-consuming to embrace a *growth mind-set*—one that assumes your people can learn. If you invest in their coaching and development early on, you'll reap benefits later: They'll start solving more of their own day-to-day problems, freeing you to focus on strategic issues and developing more leaders.

Shifting to a growth mind-set takes effort. In the coaching workshops I teach to managers, participants talk about how hard it can be at first—but once they make the switch, they start seeing better outcomes.

An R&D director at a manufacturing company had an employee who struggled to give clear, concise, organized presentations. When that person asked for input on a draft slide deck, the manager's impulse was to mark it up with suggestions to reorganize the information and cut down on the length. But then she caught herself. She called the employee in for a conversation and asked clarifying questions: What are the key points you want to convey? How much does your audience already know? What points will be difficult for people to grasp? If you were in their place, would this presentation help you reach your goals? What can you do to bring it more in line with what your stakeholders are hoping to achieve? With renewed energy and focus, the employee went back to work and improved the presentation without heavy-handed intervention from the manager.

A growth mind-set can feel risky because it forces you, the coach, to develop skills of your own that go beyond subject-matter expertise. You must ask questions and really listen without jumping in to provide what you believe is the "right" answer. And you must be honest about the performance you expect and where your employee stands, to make sure you're on the same page about the development work that needs to be done. Otherwise, you're resigning yourself to the status quo—so why even bother to coach?

Sharpening Your Coaching Skills

Here are the key skills you'll need to hone before you can help others learn and grow:

Reconciling intent and impact

You can gauge an employee's impact on the organization by observing him in action and using performance metrics such as satisfaction surveys and sales figures. But you won't know his intent—the driving force behind his behavior—unless he shares it with you.

When employees underperform, there's often a gap between intent and impact, and that can lead to great misunderstanding and frustration. Coaching them effectively involves clarifying their intent so that you can close that gap. How? By asking them what impact they *meant* to have. For instance, you might say to someone, "You were quiet at the last sales meeting—can we talk about why?" You and others may have viewed his silence as resistance or disengagement, but perhaps he was just trying to cede the floor for a change, knowing that he can be domineering in group discussions.

Once you've asked the question, listen closely to the answer. (See the sidebar "Active Listening Tactics.") Discuss behaviors that confuse or surprise you, especially those that don't match the intent he describes.

ACTIVE LISTENING TACTICS

Pay attention. Build rapport by giving your full attention. Maintain comfortable eye contact and an open posture (avoid hunching, crossing your legs, or hunkering behind a desk). Be genuinely curious. Allow time and opportunity for the other person to think and speak. Avoid distractions such as e-mail.

Notice nonverbal cues. "Hear" the speaker's nonverbal messages and body language. Do the tone of voice and facial expression match what's being said? If not, comment on what you notice and ask your employee to tell you more about it.

Affirm what you hear. Indicate understanding: "I hear what you are saying" or "I'm following you. Could you say more?" This simply means that you are listening closely—not that you agree.

You're likely to miss out on critical information if you find yourself:

- Talking more than listening
- Suggesting solutions before the employee has the chance to do so
- Interrupting
- Thinking about what you want to say next instead of focusing on what your employee is saying

Reflect what you see and hear. Reflect (like a mirror) the other person's emotions without agreeing or disagreeing: "You seem worried about . . ." This encourages the speaker to express feelings and deepen exploration.

Paraphrase what you hear. Periodically restate basic ideas to check your grasp of key points: "If I understand, your idea is . . . Did I get the essence of it? If not, please tell me more."

Summarize key themes. Briefly sum up the other person's point of view to show you've listened and to check your understanding: "It sounds like your main concern is . . ." or "These seem to be your main points . . . Is that right?"

- Using body language that signals impatience or distraction—checking your e-mail, accepting phone calls, leaning back in your chair
- Saying what you would have done differently in the same situation

As a rule of thumb, ask more than you tell—aim for a ratio of about 4:1. If you flip that ratio, you're teaching, not coaching. Though teaching plays an important role in developing others, it's limited to what you know. Coaching is an interactive opportunity to discover and create previously unknown solutions. (See the sidebar "Teaching Versus Coaching.")

Always assume positive intent, even when dealing with difficult behavior. People usually mean well—and if you give them the benefit of the doubt, they'll be more forthcoming about their intent and more receptive to feedback.

Recognizing your biases

Your own preferences can get in the way of discovering others' intent. Maybe you have a gut reaction against certain personality types or struggle to identify with colleagues whose work styles differ from yours. Whatever your biases, recognizing them allows you to move past them by inquiring about intent rather than jumping to conclusions or filling in the blanks.

To spot your biases, use frustration as your guide. Think about what gets on your nerves at work and then ask a few trusted colleagues for feedback. What do they think your bugbears are? Compare their thoughts with yours—look for similarities and patterns.

TEACHING VERSUS COACHING

To develop employees' skills, you must first decide whether to teach or coach. Are you working with an inexperienced colleague or one who requires immediate improvement? If so, you'll want to teach, which means showing or telling her what to do. Otherwise, you're probably better off coaching—asking questions that prompt her to think and solve problems on her own. That way, your employee will gain the independence and confidence she needs to grow, whether she's trying to achieve greater mastery in her role or take on new responsibilities.

Approach:	Used for:	Example:
Teaching: a *directive* approach	Instructing	Having an employee shadow you on a task or project, such as a joint sales call, so that she can learn by observing you
	Providing answers	Explaining the business strategy to a new hire
Coaching: a *supportive* approach	Encouraging independence	Allowing someone to learn on the job, even if it means risking mistakes
	Serving as a resource	Providing helpful contacts so that your employee can learn from others, not just you

Adapted from *Harvard Business Essentials: Coaching and Mentoring* (Harvard Business School Press, 2004)

That exercise helped one manager recognize her tendency to jump right into action rather than spend time defining and aligning processes. She noticed how impatient she became when team members kept pulling conversations back to "process" instead of "just getting the work done." When she asked them for candid feedback on this, they explained that her impatience actually slowed them down (the last thing she wanted to do) because they often had to loop back to clarify expectations with her. So her impact—as well as her team's—didn't match her intent. She met her employees halfway by doing a better job of clarifying expectations up front. She also encouraged them to make more adjustments on the fly so they wouldn't get paralyzed by planning and slavish adherence to process. As the general level of impatience and frustration dropped, the group began to operate more efficiently and enjoyed the work more.

Matching people's skills with big-picture needs

As a coach to your employees, you're not just helping them grow for their own sake—noble as that is. You're also boosting their ability to support the company's mission and goals. By explicitly connecting their skills with big-picture needs, you'll give them a sense of purpose and belonging, which will motivate them to grow. If you explain how improving their communication skills will make the team more efficient, for example, or increase sales to clients, they'll be more likely to take their development in that area as seriously as you do.

How can you get better at connecting the dots between their skills and the organization's needs? There's no magic here—again, you'll get a wealth of information simply by asking. Where do they feel their skills are best used? What excites them about their work? What areas do they struggle with? What would they like to do more of? Less of? How do they see all that fitting into the organization's objectives? (For more on channeling employees' passions and strengths, see chapter 2, "Set the Stage to Stimulate Growth.")

Make it clear that you're looking out for their interests as well as the company's. They'll be eager to help you figure out how they can best serve the organization—and how the organization (and you) can best serve them.

Developing a growth mind-set means you're learning right along with your employees. The more coaching practice you get, the sharper your skills will become—but give yourself a running start by favoring inquiry over advocacy. Ask questions about others' intent, your own biases, and individuals' place in the big picture. And resist the temptation to coach by explaining how *you* do things. With prompting, not lecturing, your employees will discover solutions of their own and make greater, more lasting progress toward their developmental goals.

Candice Frankovelgia is a coaching portfolio manager and a senior faculty member at the Center for Creative Leadership.

Chapter 2

Set the Stage to Stimulate Growth

by Edward M. Hallowell, MD

Editor's note: Before you begin coaching your employees, set the stage for success. Make sure they're doing the right jobs to begin with, they feel connected to their work and to one another, they're receptive, and they're capable of mastering the skills and tasks their roles require. Using basic principles from brain science, you can address each of those issues and help people achieve peak performance.

The brain is remarkably *plastic*: It grows and adapts throughout life.

That means you're never stuck with who you are or who your employees are. We used to think only young

---

Adapted from *Shine: Using Brain Science to Get the Best from Your People* (product #9238), by Edward M. Hallowell, MD, Harvard Business Review Press, 2011

brains could change and develop. We now know that adult brains do, too. We can all get smarter and wiser and happier. The conventional, dreary wisdom that people can't change is scientifically incorrect.

We've also discovered many of the forces that make the brain change for better or worse. For example, challenging a person in an area where she is skilled makes her brain grow, much like a muscle. But overwhelming her with more than she can cope with is bad for her brain. Instilling confidence in someone leads to improved performance. But an atmosphere of chronic fear disables the brain and makes performance worse.

So, what about the guy down the hall who keeps failing in his role? With proper care, he can learn to perform at higher levels—he can continue to grow for decades. And you, as his manager, can help him do so.

Achieving Peak Performance

Drawing on what we know about neuroplasticity, I've outlined a practical plan for achieving peak performance. By *peak performance,* I don't mean taking on every task and embracing every opportunity. When people try to do more than they can handle, they fall short. Instead, I'm talking about *consistent excellence, with improvement over time at a specific task or set of tasks.*

How can people pull that off? By following these five steps, with your guidance and support.

Step 1: Select

Before your employees do anything, it's important to figure out what they *should* do. Help them achieve peak performance by selecting tasks (1) that they are good at; (2) that they like to do; and (3) that add value to the project or organization. The intersection of those three elements creates the magical field in which consistent excellence can happen.

This first step influences everything that follows, yet it is often overlooked. Millions of employees underachieve simply because they stumbled into the wrong job and never got out of it. It is critical that you know your employees well enough to help them get into the right slots in the organization.

Consider Mary Ann, a customer service associate at a large financial services firm. After five years of answering customer calls, there wasn't a problem she hadn't heard or solved. Even so, she never felt 100% comfortable in her role. She got flustered when customers became irritated, and she dreaded fielding the calls. As a result, she took a bit longer than she should answering calls in the queue, which meant that she served fewer customers. Customer reviews were OK but not great. In general, Mary Ann seemed to lack enthusiasm, to merely go through the motions.

One night, while chatting with her at a company-sponsored happy hour, her manager discovered that Mary Ann trained volunteers at a local nonprofit every weekend. She loved the work and looked forward to it. What she enjoyed most was helping the young volunteers develop their skills.

The next day, the manager reassigned Mary Ann. Rather than taking calls, she became responsible for training new customer service associates. Suddenly Mary Ann started to thrive. She was excited to come to work and brimming with new ideas for training associates and improving customer service. Younger associates began to look up to her. The number of calls answered by the department increased; customer reviews improved.

With her manager's assistance, Mary Ann found the right match for herself in the organization. She took on the kind of work she enjoyed most, used skills that set her apart from others, and began adding more value to the organization—all of which allowed her to deliver peak performance.

As Mary Ann's manager did, look for the telltale signs of a wrong fit: You can tell that someone is not in the right role if he never gets excited about his job, for example, or if he chronically complains. This doesn't mean he's dull or that the line of work he's in is intrinsically dull—just that he's not assigned to the right tasks.

Investigate your employees' skills and interests so that you can deploy people to their (and your) best advantage. How? By using the most powerful assessment tool ever invented: the one-on-one conversation.

It astonishes me how few managers do this. Clients often tell me, "No one has ever asked me what I like to do or what I do best." They say they don't volunteer that information because they don't want to make waves. While I always encourage them to speak up anyway—it is in everyone's best interest—it's simpler if managers take the initiative.

A structured interview (see the sidebar at the end of this chapter) can help you unearth your direct reports' strengths and passions. Ask each employee to take a few days to think carefully about their replies to each question and write down their answers. Then have a conversation to review the answers in person.

As you talk face-to-face, you'll develop understanding and trust. You'll also be able to ask follow-up questions and give employees the wonderful—and in some organizations, rare—experience of feeling heard. That alone will boost their motivation and performance.

Step 2: Connect

People who feel connected to others, to their tasks, and to the organization's mission perform at the highest levels. They're loyal, excited to contribute, and even willing to make sacrifices to preserve that sense of attachment. As a manager, you can foster it by creating an environment where it's safe for people to be themselves and forge ties. You'll inspire them to do far more than they thought they could.

The modern workplace tends to leave people *disconnected*—emotionally alone, isolated, exhausted, anxious, and afraid—with no idea how they got that way or what to do about it. Often, they're too mentally overloaded or too stressed to converse and connect. This kind of disengagement short-circuits performance more quickly than anything else.

One of the greatest disconnectors is fear. People may fear disapproval, a poor result, criticism, looking stupid, going beyond their comfort zone, or making others look bad. Whatever the cause, if they're afraid, they underachieve.

Here again, brain science shows us why. As fear mounts, the brain's deep centers take over. Areas like the amygdala, the hypothalamus, and the locus coeruleus light up. Higher cortical thinking—concocting new ideas, seeing shades of gray—ceases because the brain must devote its full attention to the perceived threat. If there were a saber-toothed tiger about to jump out at you, this would be good. You would not want to be concocting new ideas and seeing shades of gray. You'd want to be fleeing or killing the tiger. But a saber-toothed manager—or, more generally, a culture of fear at work—can elicit the same response. Excessive fear renders peak performance neurologically impossible.

So make it a priority to promote positive connections for employees—and to rein in fear.

As human beings, we are wired to connect. When we see another person in distress, for example, our "mirror neurons" create an imagined version of that distress within us. This is the biological basis for empathy, and it is common to us all.

Why, then, do so many people struggle to connect with others? We're all too busy. We do not spend enough time together, face-to-face. We overrely on electronic connections and so don't develop the trust required for candid exchanges. But you can help your employees overcome those forces. Try the following techniques:

1. **Noticing and acknowledging your employees.** People feel good when they are acknowledged—and bad when they're not. You do not need to have deep conversations to promote connection. Just saying hi or even smiling works wonders. To walk past someone as if that person were not

there—which happens *all the time*—is a surefire disconnector.

2. **Allowing for idiosyncrasies and peccadilloes.** Encourage your employees to be who they are. We're all a little strange. When you are relaxed about yourself as a manager, you give others permission to be the same.

3. **Encouraging conversation.** Agree as a group not to send e-mails without first considering whether it's better to communicate in person or over the phone. And never use e-mail to work out emotionally laden issues. Simple changes like these will reset people's attentional systems. Employees will become less ravenous for distraction and less likely to look to e-mails or text messages for a "fix." They'll train their brains to wait while they do more important work. And they will be more likely to communicate with others in person, which fosters connection.

4. **Encouraging breaks.** When you can see that people are starting to feel stressed, urge them to stop what they're doing. Even switching to something else can help. Many "disconnecting" episodes—flare-ups, arguments, and the like—occur as a direct result of stress.

5. **Offering food and drink.** Food is a symbolic form of nurturing. Stock up on fruits, nuts, and bottles of sparkling water.

6. **Fostering impromptu get-togethers.** Planned parties are fine, but they are often command performances and can feel stilted. Impromptu gatherings—grabbing lunch, going out for coffee, catching a ball game after work—all promote connectedness.

Step 3: Play

Not enough managers recognize the importance of *play* in catalyzing peak performance. By play, I mean *any activity that involves imagination.* So defined, it constitutes the most advanced, productive activity the human brain can engage in. When workers seem dull or apathetic, it is usually because they are not engaged in imaginative, creative problem solving.

By valuing and promoting play, you can transform your employees' performance. Here are some ways to encourage people to leap from the humdrum to the exceptional:

1. **Ask open-ended questions.** The Socratic method remains one of the best ways to teach. Instead of giving answers, ask questions that engage the imagination, invite people to brainstorm and reflect, and help them make discoveries. For example:

   - What can we learn from what just happened?
   - Where did we go wrong?
   - What are we doing right?
   - What else could we do?

- What changes could we make to the prototype?
- Why are we spending so much time on this topic?
- What are we avoiding?

2. **Model a questioning attitude.** Show people that it is safe to disagree with the party line and with the boss—that it is in fact *good* to bring up opposing points of view. You need to model this. Your employees aren't likely to initiate such behavior on their own.

3. **Decorate and arrange your workspace with an eye toward facilitating play.** You might choose lively color schemes, for example, or rearrange work areas to increase opportunities for interaction, as the Atlanta Housing Authority did when it revamped its cubicle system. It lowered cubicle walls to improve sight lines between employees and set up "teaming tables" where employees could conveniently share ideas and their work.

4. **Try what organic chemists call "retrograde synthesis."** In chemistry, you work backward from the molecule you are trying to synthesize. You can use the same approach to jump-start play and creativity. Simply envision your goal and work your way back, step-by-step, until you get to where you are now.

Step 4: Grapple and Grow

This step is about mastering challenging tasks that *matter.* People who do this feel a sense of well-being and accomplishment—and their success makes them want to work even harder.

But before you ask more of people, consider the following:

- Are they operating at the intersection of what they like, what they're good at, and what adds value to the organization?
- Do they feel safe at work, comfortable enough to be candid and open, connected enough to look forward to coming in?
- Are they imaginatively engaged with their work?

Only when you can say yes to all those questions—that is, after you've helped people select, connect, and play—will hard work lead to growth. Otherwise it leads to stress, frustration, mistakes, depression, absenteeism, and inferior performance. Just as achieving mastery can instill confidence and motivation, failing to make progress can damage self-esteem and *de*motivate people.

So be on the lookout for frustration or a lack of progress. When you see a logjam, break it by redirecting employees to other tasks or providing coaching to help them overcome obstacles. And encourage people to ask for help when they need it. Let them know it is not only OK but desirable to do so.

Step 5: Shine

As your employees work hard and advance, they'll gain recognition—which affirms the value of what they've accomplished. Help them shine by praising and rewarding them for a job well executed. People who shine are motivated. They feel connected and extremely loyal to the team, the group, and the organization. They want to keep shining, and they want to help others shine, too.

Edward M. Hallowell, MD, a psychiatrist, served as an instructor at Harvard Medical School for 20 years. He is the director of the Hallowell Centers in New York City, San Francisco, and Sudbury, Massachusetts.

STRUCTURED INTERVIEW: ARE YOUR EMPLOYEES DOING THE RIGHT TASKS?

Give this questionnaire to your direct reports. Lay out the ground rules and let everyone know exactly how the information will be used, who will have access to it, and where it will be stored. Only after you've dispelled people's fears will they open up and give you useful information.

This questionnaire is a tool for putting what you already know about yourself into words. As you fill it out, you will be generating what amounts to a neuropsychological assessment—not the kind that a doctor would conduct, but one that is in many ways more useful.

(continued)

STRUCTURED INTERVIEW: ARE YOUR EMPLOYEES DOING THE RIGHT TASKS?

(*continued*)

Once you have answered these questions, you and your manager will be better able to find the right tasks for you at work because you will have a clearer idea of what your skills and preferences are, how you work best in the organization, and under what conditions you feel most comfortable and motivated.

1. What are you best at doing? (Can you think of ways to incorporate more of what you do best into your job?)

2. What do you most like to do? (This is not always the same as what you do best. Unless it is illegal or bad for you, you ought to preserve sizable chunks of time for what you most like to do.)

3. What do you wish you were better at? (This may be a skill you can develop through coaching or a task you should delegate.)

4. What talents do you have that you haven't developed? (Don't say "none." Everyone has bundles of them. Pick a few. Just because you name them doesn't mean you have to develop them.)

5. What skills are you most proud of? (This may reflect obstacles you have overcome.)

6. What do others say are your greatest strengths? (This question is designed to help you identify skills you may not value because they seem easy to you.)
7. What have you gotten better at that you used to be bad at? (This gives you an idea of where putting in additional effort can pay off.)
8. What are you just not getting better at, no matter how hard you try? (This tells you where you shouldn't waste more time.)
9. What do you most dislike doing? (Your answer here suggests what tasks you might want to delegate or hire out.)
10. The lack of which skills most gets in your way? (If you lack a skill required in your current job and you can't delegate it, then that is getting in your way. Your answer to this question might lead you to take a course, read a book, or work with a coach.)
11. What sorts of people do you work best and worst with? (Do you hate to work with highly organized analytic types, or do you love it? Do creative types drive you crazy, or do you work well with them? Make up your own categories.)

(*continued*)

STRUCTURED INTERVIEW:
ARE YOUR EMPLOYEES DOING THE RIGHT TASKS?

(*continued*)

12. What sort of organizational culture brings out the best in you? (It's amazing how many people won't leave a culture they are hideously unsuited to work in.)
13. What were you doing when you were happiest in your work life? (Could you find a way to incorporate that into what you're doing now?)
14. What regrets do you have about how you have run your career? (Could you make any changes based on those regrets?)
15. What are your most cherished hopes for the future, workwise? (What stands in the way of realizing those hopes?)
16. What are you most proud of in your work life? (Your answer here is another tip-off as to what you should be doing.)

17. What one lesson about managing a career would you pass along to the next generation? (This question is another way of getting at your thoughts on what you have done, what's worked, and what hasn't.)

18. What was the most important work-related lesson you learned from your parents? (As you reflect on this, you will get an idea of how attitudes are passed from generation to generation and shape how your mind works.)

19. What lesson did the best boss you ever had teach you about yourself? (Other people often know us better than we do.)

20. How could your time be better used in your current job to add value to the organization? (Your answer here gives your manager valuable input he or she may never have asked for.)

Adapted from the "Hallowell Self-Report Job-Fit Scale" in *Shine*

Chapter 3

Earn Your Employees' Trust

by Jim Dougherty

When I took over as CEO of Intralinks, a company that provides secure Web-based electronic deal rooms, the company was hemorrhaging so much cash that its survival was at stake. The service was going down three times per week; we were in violation of the contract with our largest client; our chief administrative officer had just been demoted, and so on.

So what did I do on my first day? I spent more than four hours listening to client support calls at the call center. I shared headsets with many of the team, moving from desk to desk to speak to the reps. To say they were surprised is an understatement: Many CEOs never visit the call center, and virtually none do it on their first afternoon on the job.

I made this my priority in part because I wanted to gain the trust of my team. I knew we had to make radical changes to behaviors, expectations, and attitudes. There was no time to be subtle. I needed to show I was different, that things were going to be different, and I needed to establish trust as quickly as possible.

As I've led various companies over the years, one of the most valuable lessons I've learned is that establishing trust is the top priority. Whether you are taking over a small department, an entire division, a company, or even a Boy Scout troop, the first thing you must get is the trust of the members. When asked, most leaders will agree to this notion, but few do anything to act on it.

Without trust, employees won't level with you; at best, you'll learn either untruths or partial truths about how they see themselves and their roles within the organization. They won't tell you what their own goals are, or their weaknesses, or how they want to grow—critical information if you're going to help them develop within the organization. Sometimes employees will go out of their way to hoard and distort the truth, especially if they fear that you will throw them under the bus if they make a mistake—or if *you* make a mistake. And if you don't have their trust, it will also make it harder for them to hear and react constructively to your feedback—whether positive or corrective—about the changes you want them to make. Finally, without trust, it is very unlikely that you as a leader will learn the truth about what is really going on in your organization and in the marketplace.

There are two elements to building trust: the actual meetings you have with your employees, building your relationship as you actively coach them; and the daily behaviors you exhibit as you go about your work with them.

Building Trust Through Listening

The best way to start building trust is to take the time to meet with your direct reports and hear what they have to say. If you are new to your role, you should do this as soon as you can; it should be one of your top priorities as you transition. It's important to start early on so that your team quickly learns to see you in this light; once you're categorized as an untrustworthy manager or leader, it's hard to build back that trust.

The key concept here is to consistently find focused time to spend with your individual team members. Set up a plan—make a promise—for how much time you'll spend and how often for your first six months. It's critical to do this slowly but surely rather than having a burst of meetings at first and then failing to follow through (a common pitfall). Make sure your plan is realistic so that you can actually meet it.

As in any relationship in life, it's important to focus on the person you are meeting with. The meetings can't be rushed. Bring a pad and take notes. Listen intently; these first meetings aren't about you telling your employees what you expect, or giving them feedback; instead, it's for them to tell you about themselves, how they want to grow, and how they see the organization.

These are the questions I ask as we begin our relationship.

- If you had my job, what would be the first three things you would do? Why?
- What are your career objectives? What skills do you want to add, experiences you want to have?
- How can we start you moving down that path? What can be done soon to help you move in that direction? (Brainstorm together on these items.)
- How do you think I could help you succeed?

Once you've identified steps that they could take, be sure to follow through. That's what makes you trustworthy.

For example, in my first manager role, I created something we called "value-added assignments." We'd have a sales representative who wanted to learn more about marketing, for example, join a team working on how to market to a new customer segment. The sales rep would provide a cross-discipline perspective for the team, and in turn she would get to see how marketing really worked. This idea came directly from the questions I had asked this employee about what she wanted to do and learn, and it helped her grow not only because of the experience, but also because she saw that I was listening and responding to her own thoughts, and that I was truly interested in helping her grow (and not just assigning her more work).

As you learn more about your direct reports, exchanging information about your personal lives is a way to build trust as well, but you don't want to be too invasive. That line is different for every person, and you'll need to feel it out. I usually start by asking where someone is from: then he'll share as much as he feels is appropriate. You should reciprocate with information about yourself.

Note that you need to have a legitimate interest in what is going on in his life. Don't fake it. For example, commit to memory how old his children are. I also keep a Word document for each of my employees to remind me about the things they've told me so that I'll remember about little Jimmy's recital or Laila's soccer game and can ask about how they went.

Building Trust Through Behaviors

Listening to your employees and acting on what you hear are one part of how you'll gain their trust, but your day-to-day behaviors also affect how much they believe you're authentically interested in their growth and development.

Here are some tips.

- **Give credit where credit's due.** In any situation in which you're describing your team's accomplishments, think and say "we" rather than "I." If one of your direct reports contributed to a project, go out of your way to credit her, especially as the project is presented to a wider group or to management levels higher than yours. This is a great way to show your employees that taking growth assignments will bring them rewards.

- **Set an example.** Your team members see everything you do. If you expect them to grow in certain ways, take feedback in certain ways, or shift their behavior in certain ways, you need to model those things for them. If you practice what you preach, they'll take you at your word on other things.

- **Take one for the team.** Accepting an occasional tedious assignment, or taking one off the plate of one of your team members—especially if it means that he's able to attend a concert or game he thought he'd have to miss—goes a long way toward showing your reports that you're on their side. It also models selfless behavior for them: They'll be more willing to take on the next assignment you delegate or help out when a colleague is in the same predicament.

- **Be transparent with tough decisions and feedback.** Just because you want to show you're on their side doesn't mean tough decisions will favor your team's whims or wishes or that you won't sometimes have strong constructive feedback. (And being known as a pushover doesn't help you become trusted.) When you have to convey tough news, be clear and transparent, and provide as much explanation as you can. Be open to questions and feedback.

By the end of my first year on the job we'd signed 150 new long-term contracts (up from zero), revenue was up by almost 600%, our burn rate was cut by 75%, and we'd positioned ourselves to raise a $50 million round of financing a few months later in the depth of the dot-com winter.

None of this could have happened without the team's amazing growth over the course of that year, and that couldn't have happened if team members didn't trust me when I pushed them, prodded them, and demanded the world of them. New leaders must remember that the key to success lies in the growth of their team. Creating a trusting, honest dialogue with these key personnel should be every new leader's top priority.

Jim Dougherty, a veteran software CEO and entrepreneur, is a senior lecturer at MIT Sloan School of Management.

Section 2
Coaching Your Employees

Chapter 4
Holding a Coaching Session

by Amy Jen Su

Coaching sessions are conversations between you and your employee in which you identify areas for growth, create development plans, perform exercises, and check in on progress. A coaching session can kick off a specific development process around a particular skill or behavior as needed; you can then hold further sessions to follow up and monitor progress. A coaching session can also be a regular, more general conversation about the employee's growth.

Coaching sessions are distinct from other types of conversations you may already be having with your employees, such as performance reviews or regular check-ins. Table 4-1 compares and contrasts the focus and time frames for each of these; you'll notice that of these three

TABLE 4-1

Types of direct report meetings

Meeting type	Time horizon	Focus
Performance review	Annual; retrospective	Assess performance of the employee retrospectively over a given time period against a set of objectives related to current job responsibilities. Formal.
One-on-one meeting	Typically weekly or biweekly; current	Discuss existing business projects, work plans, and objectives related to current job responsibilities. Informal.
Coaching sessions	Generally once per month; retrospective, current, and prospective	Discuss development and growth. Addresses both recent and current performance and future potential. Can be formal or informal.

types of conversations, the coaching session is the one that has the broadest time horizon and also looks the farthest forward to examine, plan, and work toward your direct report's future.

Coaching sessions typically range from 30 minutes to an hour, but they do not have to be long to be successful. In fact, research from the Corporate Executive Board shows that there is "no connection between time . . . and effectiveness at development."[1] Instead of adding more coaching time to your already full load as a manager, make the most of each session. You can do so by asking the right questions and engaging in dialogue to increase your direct report's awareness of her own choices, actions, and behaviors, along with their impact—as well as gain her buy in for the development plan.

Agree to Outcomes at the Start

As a first step in your coaching session, work together with your direct report to define what you're looking to achieve. Is there a particular skill she has been working on? A question she has about how to handle a particular colleague or type of assignment? A long-term goal she wants to work toward? And what kind of progress can you expect to make in your time together today?

Encourage your employee to take part in identifying a clear scope for the session by directly asking her what *she* hopes to achieve and what she wants to make sure to get to. You can offer ideas for further shaping the agenda based on your previous observations, but in most cases you'll want to start your coaching session by asking your direct report to share her own impressions. This might catch her off guard; more likely she will expect you to set the agenda. But by opening your session with a question, you begin as you'll hope to continue: with your employee talking, you listening, and with both of you then building solutions together.

There are many types of coaching sessions, but here are three of the most popular:

- **Long-term development help.** For example, "I want to increase my comfort around senior management and get better at presenting to this audience." This type of coaching focuses on a goal that takes time and practice, anywhere from six months to a year, with follow-up coaching sessions at least once per month. To keep focused on the development plan and to take the opportunity to build successively on the learning from each session, schedule these follow-ups in advance.

- **Debrief on an event or project.** For example, "The meeting with the other team did not go as well as planned. I would like to review what happened and determine what I could do differently next time." This type focuses on learning from recent events to identify new ideas, skills, and ways of handling similar situations in the future. This type of meeting often occurs in a follow-up coaching session embedded in long-term development help, but it may also be purely episodic: a chance to learn from a onetime mistake or an opportunity to praise and encourage a productive behavior.
- **Short-term problem solving.** For example, "Our colleague in another division has been making multiple requests with unreasonable deadlines. I would like your help on how to better respond and prioritize these." This is a highly focused coaching session: Your employee has something specific she needs help with in real time. It requires getting to the heart of the matter so that she leaves the session with actionable tasks she can use to address the problem immediately. Sometimes a short-term problem may help uncover a longer-term development need, but that is not always the case. These types of problems may come up in your regular one-on-one meetings as you delve into a project or other day-to-day work. Recognize these as oppor-

tunities to put on your coaching hat; many managers miss them.

Setting the explicit goals of your coaching session in this way allows you to plan how to proceed: what kinds of questions to ask and how to frame a solution.

Build a Baseline Understanding of the Issues

Once you understand what kind of coaching your direct report is looking for, you will probably feel tempted to "fix the problem" immediately—to share your wisdom about the topic, give her the advice you think she needs, or carefully explain your point of view about why things didn't go well. But don't do it! This is the place where coaching most often goes wrong.

Instead, at this stage you need to get more information to create a clear baseline understanding of the situation: Your employee very likely still knows more about it than you do. To help her develop effectively, you need to learn more about her point of view of the situation and any related situations in the past, and her level of development with the skill involved. Could she be struggling because she has an outdated mind-set that is repeatedly getting in the way? Does she lack a certain skill? Have her emotions been triggered by something in a way that is holding her back? Is she not preparing as well as she could? Collecting background information is critical to making an assessment of the root causes of your employee's challenge and thus identifying an effective development path.

Tell your employee that you would like to learn more about the situation and ask her questions that can help you understand her perspective. For example, for the employee with the long-term goal of becoming more comfortable around senior management, ask questions that probe her past experiences and their effects on her and others, as well as her current processes. These questions might include:

- How would you describe your current level of comfort around our senior team?
- When you have presented to this audience in the past, how would you describe your impact?
- How do you prepare for these interactions now?
- When have you been effective in these types of interactions? Ineffective?
- What was different or similar about the meetings when you were effective versus those when you weren't?

For an employee who is many coaching sessions in, a focused debrief of a particular event or project is more appropriate. In this case you can home in more closely on the details.

- How did the presentation you gave to this group go on Friday?
- How would you describe the impact you had?
- What worked well? What didn't?

Or, for an employee with a short-term problem, ask questions that give you a more concrete sense of the issue and its impact.

- Tell me more about the situation. What are the requests being made, and what are the deadlines involved?
- Which of these are tied to our highest department priorities?
- What trade-offs will we have to make in order to meet the high-priority requests?

Keep your questions open-ended; starting your questions with the words *what*, *how*, or *tell me more* tends to draw out an answer, whereas starting with *why* or asking a closed-ended question (in which the answer is a simple yes or no) can make the employee defensive. In answering your skillfully worded questions, your employee may already begin identifying some root causes and solutions she didn't see before. This self-awareness will increase her buy in for any actions or development plan that will come out of the session.

Hold Up the Mirror, Reframe, and Practice New Skills

Once you have a stronger understanding of the situation, it may again be tempting to simply offer a solution or hand down a piece of advice. Instead, now aim for an open, robust two-way dialogue in which you help the employee herself understand possible new choices, new strategies, or new skills she could develop. Here are several tactics for creating a productive dialogue:

- **Hold up the mirror.** What did you hear as your employee spoke that particularly struck you? Offer her a reflection that redescribes the situation she has outlined with your own perspective, and then ask for her response to that reflection. For example, you might say, "Based on what you have shared, it seems that two things may be creating your discomfort with senior management. First, a mind-set around positional authority may be leading you to be more deferential than necessary. Second, there may be an opportunity to increase your skill in preparing for these types of interactions to raise your comfort level. Do those things resonate?"

- **Frame or reframe the situation.** Help her see the situation differently. "Could I offer you a new way of thinking about the situation? Perhaps we could explore a broader range of what appropriate respect for senior management could look like. The frame you currently have focuses your attention on the differences in your age and experience with these individuals, which may be making you more nervous and tentative. Instead, consider what it would mean to focus on the shared conviction you feel for what we need to do for the business. As you hear me say these things, what resonates and what doesn't?"

- **Practice or role-play.** A coaching session is a great time to practice new skills or a new mind-set with your employee. In our example, you and your employee might role-play an upcoming interaction with senior management. You'll get to observe her behavior and offer real-time guidance about the way certain behaviors can be perceived. In addition to role-playing, you could review an ideal example of the type of behavior or skill you are working on. For example, review a presentation that has worked well for senior management; you could go over it together and discuss why this one was effective. You can also review your direct report's current processes together: She could show you how she prepares for these meetings now, and you can fine-tune her preparation techniques together.

As you offer assessments, introduce possible new frames, and practice exercises, continue to check in with your employee to make sure that what you are saying and doing is resonating for her. If not, take the opportunity to ask more questions and find out more about the situation before proceeding. The observations, suggestions, and practices that you offer are the core of your coaching session, but to be effective they need to be tailored to her particular situation.

Ensure an Actionable and Practical Close

As you near the end of the coaching session, ask your employee to articulate what she's learned and what her action items are, saying something like, "As we get to the last ten minutes here of our session, what are the top two or three things you are taking away from our conversation?" Your employee may highlight a-ha's that particularly struck her, or new ways of seeing things that have helped her think differently about her situation. Or she may share the things she is excited to practice or do differently. Having your direct report summarize her gains—rather than doing it yourself—helps with her buy in; it also allows you to sense what she's heard and what she might yet have to learn.

Consider the coaching session as a kickoff for the employee's actual development: The rubber will hit the road once she puts what she's learned to use. While you're both still in the room, agree on when to check in again, and identify any tasks to be completed before then. In this example, you and your employee might agree to meet again in a month; in the meantime she will get ready for another senior-level meeting using the preparation techniques you worked on together in the coaching session.

Continue to demonstrate openness and support as your time together draws to a close, asking questions like, "Is there anything else that you hoped we would get to today? Come by between now and our next session on this if you have questions or need to discuss something."

Over time, by asking so many questions of your employee as part of the coaching session, you will also help develop her own ability to coach herself—asking herself the questions that you've often teed up for her—so that she can continue to grow even without you by her side.

Amy Jen Su is a cofounder and managing partner of Paravis Partners, an executive coaching and leadership development firm. She is the author of the forthcoming book, *The Leader You Want to Be: Five Essential Principles for Bringing Out Your Best Self—Every Day*, and coauthor, with Muriel Maignan Wilkins, of *Own the Room: Discover Your Signature Voice to Master Your Leadership Presence*. Follow Amy on Twitter @amyjensu.

NOTE

1. Corporate Leadership Council Learning and Development, Manager-Led Development Effectiveness Survey, available at https://clc.executiveboard.com/Public/PDF/CLC_LD_Program_Brochure.pdf.

Chapter 5
Following Up After a Coaching Session

by Pam Krulitz and Nina Bowman

It is often said that the real work of coaching happens *after* a coaching session. That's when you and your direct report actually put your conversation into practice, after all. But as a manager, how do you make sure to follow up appropriately? And how do you know whether your coaching is working?

Align Expectations for Follow-Up

After a coaching meeting, your direct report can quickly become aware of how difficult it is to balance new coaching commitments with the hectic demands of normal day-to-day work. To keep the process on track, you need to work with him in advance to set up a thoughtful approach for maintaining momentum between sessions.

While still in the coaching meeting itself, set clear agreements about how you will move forward. Address the following.

- **Action items.** Agree on the specific actions that you and your direct report will take between sessions. For example, if he is working on developing peer relationships, he may agree to have lunch with some of those peers before your next meeting. He may agree to hold a difficult conversation with a direct report whom he's been avoiding. Coaching can provide an excellent accountability mechanism to hold your employees to task for the things they've said they want to do to develop—but only if you clearly define those actions and their deadlines up front.

- **Feedback.** Provide feedback after your initial coaching session either in the moment or, more likely, in additional formal coaching sessions. Agreeing on how you will proceed and being clear about the frequency of your involvement between sessions will prevent your direct reports from being unnecessarily stressed or frustrated by well-intentioned check-ins. You will also want to decide whether others in the organization will play a role in offering feedback throughout the coaching process. For example, a direct report who is struggling with speaking up in group settings may want to include a peer who can observe him in meetings and provide informal feedback.

- **Resource needs.** Ask your employee what tools or support may be helpful. He may need specific learning resources, such as articles, books, assessments, or training programs. He may also need you to connect him with others in the organization for mentoring, or to have him shadow you in meetings. Understanding his needs will let you know which resources you will need to identify and gather between coaching meetings.

As you discuss these items, ask your employee about his preferences. Don't just impose your way of doing things.

Capture what you've agreed upon after each meeting. Depending on the tools available and the process followed in your organization, you may ask your direct report to complete a coaching plan template or document the goals he's agreed to in a system that captures development plans. Or you may simply have him send a follow-up e-mail documenting your agreements and expectations. Table 5-1 shows an example of a coaching action plan.

Check In on Your Direct Report

With your expectations aligned, after each coaching session you can continue to support your employee's development in the following ways.

- **Follow up on agreements.** Because we naturally tend to focus on what's in front of us or what's due next, the longer-term agreements made in your coaching conversation can easily fall by the

TABLE 5-1

Goals and action plan

Goals ***What skills or competencies do I want to develop?***	**Action steps** ***What do I need to do to develop in these areas?***	**Measures of success** ***What will be the impact if I am successful:*** ***– On myself?*** ***– On my colleagues?*** ***– On my results?***
1. I want to better focus on my long-term priorities.	• Delegate more responsibility to team members and do so clearly, making them the point of contact to outside groups for their areas of responsibility. • Set up regular, one-on-one time with each team member to minimize responding to questions and issues throughout the day. • Put my top 3 goals for the month on my computer as my screen saver. • Take 15 minutes each morning to plan for the day, and make sure enough time is allocated toward my long-term priorities. • When I'm asked to do something, take a deep breath, reflect on the need behind the request, and consider my options rather than saying yes immediately. • Read David Allen's *Getting Things Done* and the HBR article "Manage Your Energy, Not Your Time" for additional ideas.	• I'll feel less frazzled when I arrive in the morning and when I'm heading home in the evening. • My team will feel more ownership for their areas of responsibility and will not ask as many questions. • I'll be able to check off some of my longer-term goals.

2. I want to be more clear and succinct in my communications.	• Before each meeting I attend, jot down the two or three points that I want to make or ideas I have about the topic. • Before sending an e-mail or speaking in a meeting, consider the most important message I want to send and focus on that, providing additional context only if it is relevant to my audience. • Reread each e-mail before sending to check for clear, strong, actionable tone and message. • Reduce use of qualifiers such as "I think . . .", "I'm not sure but . . .", "you know . . ." • Make strong requests: what I need, when I need it by, and whom I need it from. • Read Amy Jen Su and Muriel Maignan Wilkins's *Own the Room: Discover Your Signature Voice to Master Your Leadership Presence*.	• My voice and opinions will be heard and considered more often. • I'll feel more confident in my contribution and value. • My team will be less confused and I'll get fewer e-mail replies asking for explanations.

Source: ©Isis Associates 2004–2013.

wayside. If you don't follow up on those agreements, however, your direct report is less likely to take them seriously. Periodically reviewing the written plan will hold everyone accountable: You'll be more likely to stick to the agreed-upon check-in dates, provide your employee with the resources such as the articles and books you identified, and follow up with engaging others in his development.

- **Observe signs of growth.** Continually assess how your direct report is doing by keeping an eye on his performance, however informally. Are you seeing signs of progress in his behavior, his relationships, his attitude, or his results? Are others speaking about him differently? For example, if he is working on being a better listener in meetings, you may choose to carefully observe him in a few gatherings and jot down your own thoughts.

- **Check in directly.** Employees can get stuck between sessions; a new behavior may not work as hoped, or they may get frustrated with the ups and downs of the learning process. A simple check-in can get them unstuck and moving forward again. Initiate these as you've planned, but also consider instituting an open-door policy that encourages your direct reports to come to you if they have questions. During these check-ins, ask your employee about how things are changing and whether he himself is seeing any signs of development. Encourage him to jot down things that he's noticing or learning, and use this material as the basis for your next formal coaching meeting.

- **Communicate impact.** As you see your direct report begin to change and grow, communicate the impact of his growth to him explicitly: It may be harder for him to see. What impact is coaching making on him as an individual? Is he being included in more strategic discussions? What is the impact on your group or division? Has that group been able to achieve more of its goals? What is the impact on the organization? Helping your employee understand the full effect of the changes that he is working hard to achieve can increase his motivation and serve as a reminder that the coaching you are providing serves both him *and* the organization.
- **Focus on the relationship.** As you work with your direct report, continue to foster an environment of openness and willingness to learn. If you sense a shift in the relationship, a decline in trust, or hesitation toward openness, it may be time to check in explicitly on what he is thinking and feeling after your conversations.

In the meantime, stay attuned to the following signs that the coaching process may be going off track, and intervene early.

- Your direct report comes to coaching meetings without having completed agreed-upon assignments or practices.

- Your direct report blames others for his failures as he tries new things, or he doesn't feel comfortable talking about both successes and failures.
- Your direct report doesn't demonstrate ownership of the coaching process by pushing back on you when appropriate or suggesting new ideas and methods of his own.

What if you've been vigilant about thoughtful follow-up, but your direct report is still not progressing on a critical development need? You may need to enlist the help of someone outside your chain of command: A trusted colleague, a member of the HR team, or a professional external coach may have the objectivity, skills, and relationship to help your team member progress. Ultimately, you and your staff member may need to have a conversation about whether the role is the right fit for him.

Check In on Yourself

Although much of the follow-up process focuses on your direct report, the process also requires self-reflection on your part. As the manager and coach, you may want to ask yourself two questions.

1. **Am I meeting the needs of this employee?** The coaching process will look and feel different for each of your direct reports, and what works for one employee may not work for another. Approach the process with a trial-and-error mentality, and show openness in making ad-

justments along the way. Frequently ask your direct report what is working and what is not. Approaches that don't work for a person at one point in the process can succeed later, so if a new practice or exercise is proving difficult, you may need to either change the plan or encourage patience.

Meeting the needs of your employee during coaching may also mean having a conversation with him if you have differing views on how he is progressing. For example, he may share that he understood the lessons from the books you provided and found them useful, but if he doesn't appear to be putting the lessons into practice, it may mean that the approach isn't working despite his enthusiasm. It is important for you as the coach to use your own judgment in addition to the employee's feedback to determine whether his needs are really being met.

2. **Am I holding up my end of the bargain?** Assisting with the development of others can often expose your own strengths and weaknesses. For example, Lisa and her manager, Arya, agreed that Lisa needed to step up more and take more responsibility. However, when Lisa tried to take ownership of a particular project, Arya had trouble letting go, insisting on daily reviews of every detail. But when she took a moment to reflect on her role as a coach, Arya realized that developing Lisa on this particular goal would first mean

> changing her own approach. Coaching often requires you as a manager to hold up a mirror to yourself to see whether you're unknowingly getting in the way of your direct report's progress or whether you're acting in ways that send mixed messages about your expectations.

Coaching can be a challenging and yet uplifting process for both direct report and manager as you watch your employee grow and add value to the organization in new and different ways. By incorporating a follow-up process that includes aligning expectations up front, checking in with your direct report and checking in with yourself, you can see, encourage, and spur that growth, with results that can be well worth the time and attention you invest.

Pam Krulitz is a managing partner with Paravis Partners and is on the faculty of the Georgetown University Leadership Coaching program. She coaches entrepreneurs, senior executives, and high potentials to support their growth as leaders and achievement of their business goals. **Nina Bowman** is a senior partner with Paravis Partners and provides executive coaching, training, and leadership development consulting services to senior executives.

Chapter 6
Giving Feedback That Sticks

by Ed Batista

Although coaching is primarily about asking questions rather than providing answers, your employees will want your candid feedback on their performance. I've been involved in thousands of feedback conversations with clients and students over the years, and again and again I've heard people say, "Just give it to me straight."

But that simple request can be difficult to fulfill. When you say "Can I give you some feedback?" to your employees, their heart rate and blood pressure are almost certain to increase, and they may experience other signs of stress as well. These are symptoms of a "threat response," also known as "fight-or-flight": a cascade of neurological and physiological events that impair the ability to process complex information and react thoughtfully. When people are in the grip of a threat response, they're less capable of absorbing and applying feedback.

You've probably observed this dynamic in feedback conversations with employees that didn't go as well as you'd hoped. Some people respond with explanations, defensiveness, or even hostility, while others minimize eye contact, cross their arms, hunch over, and generally look as if they'd rather be doing anything but talking to you. These fight-or-flight behaviors suggest that your feedback probably won't have the desired impact.

How do you avoid triggering a threat response—and deliver feedback your people can digest and use? These guidelines will help.

Cultivate the Relationship

We lay the foundations for effective feedback by building relationships with others over time. When people feel connected to us, even difficult conversations with them are less likely to trigger a threat response. Social psychologist John Gottman, a leading expert on building relationships, has found from his research that success in difficult conversations depends on what he calls "the quality of the friendship." Gottman cites several steps we can take to develop high-quality relationships:

- **Make the other person feel "known."** Making people aware that you see them as individuals—and not merely as employees—is a critical step in the process, but it need not be overly time-consuming. Several years ago a coaching client of mine who ran a midsize company felt that he was too distant from his employees but didn't have the time to take someone to lunch every day. His efficient compromise was to view every interaction, no matter how fleeting, as an opportunity to get to know that person a little better. He made a habit of asking employees one question about their work or their personal lives each time he encountered them. "Whenever I can, I connect," he told me. Although at times this slowed his progress through the office, the result was worth it.

- **Respond to even small bids for attention.** We seek attention from those around us not only in obvious ways but also through countless subtle "bids." As Gottman writes in *The Relationship Cure,* "A bid can be a question, a gesture, a look, a touch—any single expression that says, 'I want to feel connected to you.' A response to a bid is just that—a positive or negative answer to somebody's request for emotional connection." But many of us miss bids from our employees. That's because we're less observant of social cues from people over whom we wield authority, according to research by Dacher Keltner of the University of California, Berkeley, and others. To connect more effectively with employees, take stock of how much you notice—or miss—their efforts to gain your attention. And solicit feedback from peers, friends, and family members on your listening skills and how often you interrupt.
- **Regularly express appreciation.** As Gottman's research shows, the ratio of positive to negative interactions in a successful relationship is 5:1, even

during periods of conflict. This ratio doesn't apply to a single conversation, and it doesn't mean that we're obligated to pay someone five compliments before we can offer critical feedback. But it does highlight the importance of providing positive feedback and expressing other forms of appreciation over time in order to strengthen the relationship. (See the sidebar "The Pitfalls of Positive Feedback.")

Manage Emotions

Although excessive negative feelings inhibit learning and communication, emotions play a vital role in feedback. They convey emphasis and let others know what we value. Emotional experiences stick with people, last longer in their memories, and are easier to recall. And extensive neuroscience research in recent decades makes clear that emotions are essential to our reasoning process: Strong emotions can pull us off course, but in general emotions support better decision making.

So while you'll want to avoid triggering a threat response, don't try to remove all emotion from your coaching. That can diminish the impact of your feedback and lead to a cycle of ineffective conversations. Instead, aim for a balance: Express *just enough* emotion to engage the other person but not so much that you provoke a hostile or defensive reaction, shut down the conversation, or damage the relationship.

The right amount of emotion depends on the issue you're addressing and varies from one relationship to another—and even from one day to the next. The key

THE PITFALLS OF POSITIVE FEEDBACK

Praise is supposed to make your employees feel good and motivate them, but often it does just the opposite. Here are three common problems and ways to avoid them:

1. ***People don't trust the praise.*** Before delivering unpleasant feedback to your direct reports, do you say something nice to soften the blow? Many of us do—and we unwittingly condition people to hear our positive feedback as a hollow preamble to the real message. Rather than feeling genuinely appreciated, they're waiting for the other shoe to drop. Though we've diminished our anxiety about bearing bad news, we haven't helped them receive it. We've actually undermined our ability to deliver any meaningful feedback, positive or negative.

   What to do: Instead of giving a spoonful of sugar before every dose of constructive criticism, lead off with your investment in the relationship and your reasons for having the conversation. For example: "It's important that we can be candid and direct with each other so we can work together effectively. I have some concerns for us to discuss, and I'm optimistic that we can resolve them."
2. ***People resent it.*** Managers also use positive feedback to overcome resistance to requests.

(*continued*)

THE PITFALLS OF POSITIVE FEEDBACK

(*continued*)

This age-old tactic can work in the moment but carries a long-term cost. It creates a sense of obligation, a "social debt" the recipient feels compelled to repay by acceding to your wishes. But if you train people to always expect requests after your praise, they'll eventually feel manipulated and resentful—and less inclined to help you out.

What to do: Motivate people over the long term by expanding your persuasive tool kit. As Jay Conger explains in his classic article "The Necessary Art of Persuasion" (HBR May–June 1998), you can gain lasting influence in four ways: establish credibility through expertise and work you've done in others' interests, frame goals around common ground and shared advantage, support your views with compelling data and examples, and connect emotionally with people so they'll be more receptive to your message.

3. **We praise the wrong things.** When aimed at the wrong targets, praise does more harm than good. As Stanford psychologist Carol Dweck notes in a January 2012 HBR IdeaCast interview, "The whole self-esteem movement taught us erroneously that praising intelligence, talent, and abilities would foster self-confidence and self-esteem, and everything great would follow. But we've found it

backfires. People who are praised for talent now worry about doing the next thing, about taking on the hard task, and not looking talented, tarnishing that reputation for brilliance. So they'll stick to their comfort zones and get really defensive when they hit setbacks."

What to do: Praise effort, not ability. Dweck suggests focusing on "the strategies, the doggedness and persistence, the grit and resilience" that people exhibit when facing challenges. And explain exactly what actions prompted your praise. If you're vague or generic, you'll fail to reinforce the desired behavior.

question is how responsive the other person will be to your emotions. A coaching client of mine who'd recently launched a company had some critical feedback for his cofounder, but previous conversations didn't have the desired effect. For the feedback to stick, my client needed to become fairly heated and more vocally and physically expressive. This worked because the two of them had a long-standing friendship. The cofounder didn't respond defensively—rather, the intensity got his attention. In contrast, when this same client of mine had some critical feedback for a subordinate, he reined in his emotions, modulated his expressiveness, and delivered the feedback in a matter-of-fact tone. The goal was to convey the importance of the issues without overwhelming the subordinate, and in this case my client's authority was sufficient on its own.

Of course, we may not know how another person will respond to our emotions, and when we're in the grip of strong feelings, it's hard to calibrate how we express them in conversation. The solution is to practice. By having more feedback conversations, we learn not only how specific individuals respond to us but also how we express our emotions in helpful and unhelpful ways.

Play Fair

You're sure to elicit a threat response if you provide feedback the other person views as unfair or inaccurate. But how do you avoid that, given how subjective perceptions of fairness and accuracy are?

David Bradford of the Stanford Graduate School of Business suggests "staying on our side of the net"—that is, focusing our feedback on our feelings about the behavior and avoiding references to the other person's motives. We're in safe territory on *our* side of the net; others may not like what we say when we describe how we feel, but they can't dispute its accuracy. However, when we make guesses about their motives, we cross over to *their* side of the net, and even minor inaccuracies can provoke a defensive reaction.

For example, when giving critical feedback to someone who's habitually late, it's tempting to say something like, "You don't value my time, and it's very disrespectful of you." But these are guesses about the other person's state of mind, not statements of fact. If we're even slightly off base, the employee will feel misunderstood and be less receptive to the feedback. A more effective way to make the same point is to say, "When you're late, I feel devalued and disrespected." It's a subtle distinction, but by focusing on the specific behavior and our internal response—by staying on our side of the net—we avoid making an inaccurate, disputable guess.

Because motives are often unclear, we constantly cross the net in an effort to make sense of others' behavior. While this is inevitable, it's good practice to notice when we're guessing someone's motives and get back on our side of the net before offering feedback.

Set the Stage

It's easy to take our surroundings for granted, but they have a big impact on any interaction. Paying attention to logistical details like these will help make your feedback conversations more productive:

- **Timing.** Although I encourage shorter, informal feedback conversations (see the end of this chapter), sometimes it's necessary to have a longer, in-depth discussion. When that's the case, be deliberate about scheduling. Instead of simply fitting it into an available slot on your calendar, choose a time when you and the other person will both be at your best, such as at the beginning of the day, before you're preoccupied with other issues, or at the end of the day, when you can spend more time in reflection. Think about the activities you and your employee will be engaged in just before and just after the conversation. If either of you are coming from (or heading to) a stressful experience, you'll be better off finding another time.

- **Duration.** We often put events on our calendars for a standard amount of time without considering what's needed for each interaction. Think about how much time a given feedback conversation is likely to take if it goes well—and if it goes poorly. You don't want to get into a meaningful discussion with an employee and suddenly find that you're late for your next meeting. Also, consider what you'll do if the conversation goes worse (or better) than expected. How bad (or good) will it have to be for you to ignore the next event on your calendar in order to continue the conversation?

- **Physical location.** Meeting in your office will reinforce hierarchical roles, which can be useful when you need to establish some distance between yourself and the other person—but this will also induce stress and increase the odds of a threat response. A less formal setting—such as a conference room, a restaurant, or even outdoors—will put you on a more even footing and reduce the likelihood of a threat response. Choose a location that suits the needs of the conversation, ensures sufficient privacy, and minimizes interruptions and distractions.

- **Proximity.** When meeting with an employee in an office or a conference room, sitting across from each other—with a desk or table in between—

creates physical distance, emphasizing your respective roles and reinforcing your authority. But you don't always want to do that. When you're trying to create a stronger connection with the other person or convey a greater sense of empathy, it's preferable to sit closer and on adjoining sides of the table or desk. Think about the optimal proximity between you and the other person at that moment. Perhaps even being seated is too formal, and you should go for a walk.

With a little practice, these guidelines will help you improve your feedback skills. As with any skill you're trying to master, experiment in low-risk situations before jumping into a high-stakes feedback conversation. Here are some ways to get started:

- **Have feedback conversations more often.** We associate feedback with performance reviews, but they're not good opportunities to improve our feedback skills because they're so infrequent and they tend to be stressful. Rather than saving up feedback for an employee on a wide range of topics, try offering smaller pieces of focused feedback on a regular basis. Even a two-minute debrief with an employee after a meeting or a presentation can be a useful learning opportunity for both of you.

- **Role-play difficult conversations.** With clients in my coaching practice and with my MBA students at Stanford, I've found that role-playing is a highly effective way to prepare to deliver challenging feedback. Conduct this exercise with a friendly colleague: Start by delivering your feedback while your colleague role-plays the recipient, which will allow you to try out different approaches. Then have your colleague give you the same feedback while you role-play the recipient. You'll learn from your colleague's approach, and you'll see the conversation from your employee's point of view. The preparation will help you refine your delivery and feel more relaxed in the actual conversation.

- **Ask for feedback yourself.** By asking employees to give you feedback on your effectiveness as a leader and manager, you'll benefit in three ways: You'll get valuable input, you'll understand what it's like to be on the receiving end, and your willingness to listen will make your own feedback mean more. If you sense that employees are reluctant to give you feedback, ask them to help you accomplish some specific goals, such as being more concise or interrupting less often. By acknowledging your own areas for improvement, you'll make it easier for them to speak up.

Ed Batista is an executive coach and an instructor at the Stanford Graduate School of Business. He writes regularly on issues related to coaching and professional development at www.edbatista.com, and he is currently writing a book on self-coaching for Harvard Business Review Press.

Chapter 7

Enlist Knowledge Coaches

A summary of the full-length HBR article "Deep Smarts," by **Dorothy Leonard** *and* **Walter Swap,** *highlighting key ideas.*

THE IDEA IN BRIEF

It takes years for your company's best people to acquire their expertise—but only seconds for them to walk out the door when opportunity beckons. And when they go, they take their deep smarts with them. Deeply smart people make intuitive decisions fast and spot problems and possibilities others miss. Informed by almost preternaturally sound judgment and a gut sense for

---

Adapted from *Harvard Business Review,* September 2004 (product #7731)

interrelationships, they see the big picture—rather than getting bogged down in details. Their wisdom is crucial to your company's survival.

How to capture the deep smarts residing in your organization? Turn your experts into knowledge coaches. Knowledge coaches use learn-by-doing techniques—guided practice, observation, problem solving, and experimentation—to help novices absorb long-acquired business wisdom.

Knowledge coaching not only spurs transfer and retention of vital wisdom, it yields breakthrough product ideas and more efficient business processes. Can your company afford *not* to invest in it?

THE IDEA IN PRACTICE

Consider these knowledge coaching techniques:

Guided practice

Novices practice skills under the watchful eye of knowledge coaches, who then provide feedback that allows them to refine their new capabilities.

> *Example:* At SAIC, new consultants learn their trade from seasoned colleagues through a "see one, lead one, teach one" process. First, they observe an expert helping a client solve a specific problem. Next, they practice their skills by leading a client session, receiving feedback from the knowledge coach. Then, they teach those skills to another consultant.

Guided observation

This technique takes two forms—shadowing and field trips. Through *shadowing*, novices absorb deep smarts by following experienced, skilled colleagues, and then discussing their observations with those colleagues. One junior consultant who sat in on client meetings and then analyzed his observations with an older colleague contended, "I learned more from those debriefs than in four years at my prior company and two years of business school."

During *field trips*, novices break out of rigid mental habits and expand their experience through exposure to novel ways of thinking and behaving.

> *Example:* On field trips to Mexico, Korea, and a U.S. specialty toy store, teams from retailer Best Buy observed young people engaged in communal play focused on a product (such as a doll) or technology (such as video games). These visits spurred ideas for providing socially oriented experiences in Best Buy stores. For instance, the company's engineers developed "PCBang," which enables teens and people in their early twenties—much younger than Best Buy's typical customer—to play computer games and socialize.

Guided problem solving

Knowledge coaches and protégés work on problems jointly, so protégés learn how to approach problems.

> *Example:* A senior engineer renowned for his ability to bring multiple perspectives to the design of complex products had his protégé spend several months on the assembly line tackling problems with a test

technician. The senior engineer joined many of these sessions, adding perspectives the technician lacked—such as customer preferences. The protégé acquired comprehensive know-how about the product, from design to production to fulfillment of customers' needs.

Guided experimentation

Knowledge coaches help novices set up modest experiments that speed learning.

Example: Start-up company ActivePhoto had developed a technology for instantly downloading and cataloging digital photographs. To determine its most profitable market, the firm conducted pilot studies with three promising customer bases: public emergency services, insurance-claims processing, and online auctioning. Through discussions of each experiment's results with knowledge coaches, ActivePhoto quickly eliminated the first market.

Dorothy Leonard is the William J. Abernathy Professor Emerita of Business Administration at Harvard Business School in Boston. **Walter Swap** is a professor emeritus of psychology at Tufts University in Medford, Massachusetts. They are the coauthors of *Deep Smarts: How to Cultivate and Transfer Enduring Business Wisdom* (Harvard Business School Publishing, 2005) and *Critical Knowledge Transfer: Tools for Managing Your Company's Deep Smarts* (Harvard Business Review Press, December 2014).

Chapter 8
Coaching Effectively in Less Time

by Daisy Wademan Dowling

Virtually all of the young executives I work with want to be good managers and mentors. They just don't have the time—or so they believe. "I could either bring in a new deal, or I could take one of my people out for lunch to talk about their career," a financial services leader told me recently. "In this industry and in this market, which one do you think I'm going to pick?"

Good question. It's not easy to help your employees develop even as you take advantage of every business opportunity, but you can make coaching easier on yourself in three ways: planning coaching time well, giving

---

Adapted from content posted on hbr.org on February 3, 2009

feedback efficiently, and making use of found time to coach when you can.

Plan Coaching Time Well

Set aside time to think about and pursue issues with your team. Keep each of these sessions brief, but make them regular: Put a 30-minute weekly recurring item on your calendar, for example, and don't let yourself slip into rescheduling or working through it.

Use this window to think about your team's actions over the past week. Who needs praise? Motivation? Better prioritization skills? Feedback on a lousy presentation? To be told to wear a tie to the office? You may notice these things in passing, but if you don't schedule time to focus on them, you'll find yourself worrying about them all week—on the way to the office, in meetings about other things—and never actually address them.

Also use this time to check in on your direct reports' progress and development more broadly. Do you have a new employee whose needs and interests you want to get to know better? A mentee who has asked for help developing a particular skill? A direct report you haven't really touched base with recently? Instead of having to find the time to plan their coaching, you can use the window you've already set aside.

Once you've identified the issues that need addressing, use the remainder of the time to drop a congratulatory e-mail, to walk over to your direct report and give her some quick feedback (more on this later), or, if the situation warrants, to set up time to hold a formal coaching session.

Your strategy here is containment: Scheduling windows to think about and address coaching issues lets you limit them to a manageable amount of time.

Give Feedback Efficiently

Once you've identified that you need to give feedback to a direct report, you can make that process more efficient in three ways.

- **Create a standard way in.** For the majority of managers, providing feedback—particularly constructive feedback—is stressful and requires significant forethought. How should you bring up the bungled analysis, the hurdles to promotion, or even the meeting that went unusually well? Like chess masters, we spend most of our time contemplating the first move. That's why the key to reducing the time you spend mulling over and preparing for each coaching conversation is to have a standard way in: a simple, routinized way to open discussions about performance. Keep it simple, and announce directly what's to come. A straightforward "I'm going to give you some feedback" or "Are you open to my coaching on this?" gets immediate attention and sets the right tone. It will make it easier to prepare for the game if you have your opener ready. Furthermore, your direct reports will become familiar with your opener, and that will help them be attuned to and hear the feedback more clearly.
- **Be blunt.** The number one mistake executives make in coaching and delivering feedback to their

people is being insufficiently candid—typically, because they don't want to be mean. If you've ever used the phrase "maybe you could . . ." in a coaching conversation or asked one of your people to "think about" a performance issue, there's a 99% probability you're not being blunt enough. But the more candid you are, the more likely your coachee is to hear your message, and thus the more likely you are to have impact, and quickly. The trick to being candid without feeling like an ogre? Be honest, be sincere, be personal—while addressing the issue head-on. The best feedback I ever received came a few years into my career, directly after a terrible meeting I had with senior management, in which I had been both unprepared and defensive. As we rode down in the elevator afterward, my boss said quietly, "Next time, I expect you to do better." Don't dance around the issues, and don't let the person you're coaching do so either.

- **Ask him to play it back.** If your feedback doesn't end up sticking, you'll need to deliver it a second time—and a third, and a fourth—all of which takes your valuable time and managerial energy. To avoid the need for encore performances, check to make sure you've made an impact on the first go-round by asking the person you're coaching to paraphrase what he heard. If your coachee can clearly explain to you—in his own words—what he needs to change or do next, that goes a long way to ensuring he's gotten the message. You'll then know that the conversation is over and you can get back to other things. If the message is muddled, you can correct it immediately. In either case, you've limited the need for future follow-up.

Use Found Time

If you plan and use your coaching time wisely, you'll find that you can maintain your coaching relationships and get your other work done as well. But what if you're in a crunch period or for some other reason just can't find the minutes to spare for your weekly check-in? If that's the case, use what I call the 3.1% coaching method: Limit your people-development activities to no more than 15 incremental minutes per day. That's 75 minutes a week, or 3.1% of a hypothetical 40-hour workweek. Here's how to find those 15 minutes.

- **Turn dead time into development time.** Walking back to your office after a meeting? Use those two minutes to give your direct report feedback on the presentation and on how he could do better next time. He didn't have a speaking role? Ask how he thought the meeting went and how he might have made certain points differently—and then offer feedback on that. Direct, in-the-moment feedback is your single best tool for developing people. Look for every two-minute stretch in your day during which you could be talking to someone else—most often, that's travel time—and convert those windows into coaching opportunities.

Walking down to the corner to get a cup of coffee? Ask one of your employees to come along—and talk about goals and priorities. Driving to the airport? Check in with an employee or two over the phone.

- **Make two calls per day.** On your way home from work, call (or e-mail) two people you met with that day and offer "feedforward": "I like what you've done with the Smithers account. Next time, let's try to keep marketing costs down. Thanks for your hard work." Always make "thank you" a part of the message. Employees who feel appreciated, and know that you're trying to develop their skills, stay engaged over the long run.

- **Show up in her work space.** Once per day, get up and walk over to the desk of one of your direct reports. Take two minutes to ask her what she's working on. Once she's finished answering, respond, "What do you need from me to make that project/transaction successful?" The goal is for her to hear you saying, "I know who you are, I've got high expectations—and I've got your back."

With consistent (read: daily) use, these strategies will pay off. Your employees will feel that you're not just their boss, but a coach. They'll sharpen their skills *and* stay motivated.

And for any manager, that's time well spent.

Daisy Wademan Dowling serves as managing director and head of talent development for the Blackstone Group, the global asset management firm. She is also the author of *Remember Who You Are* (Harvard Business Review Press, 2004) and a regular contributor to HBR.

Chapter 9

Help People Help Themselves

by Ed Batista

When I take on new clients in my executive coaching practice, I emphasize how much work they will be doing *without* me. That's because they typically spend just 1% of their working hours in coaching sessions; the other 99% of the time, they're managing interactions, making choices, and solving problems on their own. Although our conversations may influence my clients as they go about their day-to-day activities, most of the time they're *coaching themselves.* They're assessing what's working and what's not, deciding where to change course and where to hold steady, and repeating this process as they steer themselves through professional challenges.

The same holds true for your employees if you manage knowledge workers who operate with little, if any, direct supervision. You check in with them regularly to plan, prioritize, and assess progress toward goals, but you don't peer over their shoulders all day, telling them how to complete each task. You don't have time to provide such detailed guidance—and even if you did, they would perceive it as intrusive micromanagement.

This constraint actually presents a tremendous opportunity: You can be a more effective leader and manager by helping your employees coach themselves. To be clear, "self-coaching" is not a solitary process but, rather, a self-directed one. Your employees will continue to need your guidance and support, but their "coaching" shouldn't just be a series of formal discussions with you. It's a tool they can use on their own or in any conversation with anyone.

Here's how you can get them started.

Foster a Growth Mind-Set

As discussed earlier in this guide, people have two basic mind-sets about development: Those with a *fixed mind-set* view qualities such as intelligence and talent as predetermined and unchanging, while those with a *growth mind-set* believe that these qualities can be enhanced through dedication and effort. (See chapter 1, "Shift Your Thinking to Coach Effectively.") Research by Stanford psychologist Carol Dweck demonstrates not only the impact of mind-set on performance but also the relative ease with which people can shift mind-sets. As she has observed, "Just by knowing about the two mind-sets, you can start thinking and reacting in new ways."

A growth mind-set yields substantial benefits in a self-coaching context: When people view themselves as works in progress, they remain open to learning and change. They're more persistent in seeking solutions to problems, more resilient in the face of setbacks, and more receptive to critical feedback. They also learn more from their mistakes, as research by Michigan State psychologist Jason Moser indicates, in part because they don't get as upset by failures, and they spend more time assessing what went wrong.

Encouraging a growth mind-set doesn't mean simply offering praise and avoiding criticism; it means focusing your feedback—both positive and negative—on employees' efforts to accomplish their goals, not on their inherent abilities. When we praise people for their talents or criticize them for their inadequacies, they adopt a fixed mind-set, undermining their attempts to self-coach. But when we praise them for their determination and criticize flagging effort, they're more likely to adopt a growth mind-set, which makes self-coaching easier and more fruitful.

You can further support a growth mind-set by viewing setbacks as learning opportunities. While you should

SELF-COACHING TIP

High achievers are as likely as underperformers to have a fixed mind-set. Promote a growth mind-set by emphasizing the value of determination and persistence—not just strengths and achievements—when reviewing their performance. Encourage them to do the same in their self-assessments.

provide candid feedback when employees fail, emphasize the value of learning from the experience. Respond to failures with an attitude of curiosity and a commitment to understanding root causes, and highlight areas where greater determination or persistence might have resulted in success.

Ask Before You Advise

As longtime MIT management professor Edgar Schein cautions in *Helping,* dispensing wisdom prematurely is a trap for anyone seeking to help others, and it's particularly dangerous for a manager guiding a direct report. When an employee presents you with a problem, you probably feel an immediate urge to respond with a solution. That may seem like a logical and efficient way to provide support, but it comes at a price. You limit the range of possible solutions to your own ideas, diminish your employees' ownership of the situation, and increase their dependence on you. (Again, see chapter 1, "Shift Your Thinking to Coach Effectively.")

Resisting that urge is a critical step in helping your employees coach themselves. By backing off just a bit, you'll compel them to fully tap their own knowledge and expertise—which may be more extensive than yours—and encourage them to take greater responsibility and act more independently. So when an employee seeks your support, start by asking questions, not giving answers. Follow these guidelines:

- **Avoid questions that invite "Yes" or "No" answers.** These questions are direct, but that's not always an advantage. The downside in a self-coaching context is that they stop the conversation just when you want the other person to reflect more deeply on his or her experience.

- **Embrace questions that sound naive.** Although sophisticated questions may demonstrate your understanding of a situation's complexities, they also put the emphasis on your own expertise. Simple, open-ended questions such as "What will success look like?" and "What challenges will you face?" are more useful in challenging the other person to think creatively.
- **Use "Why . . ." questions with care.** Asking people why they did something can help them step back and reassess their approach, but it can also trigger defensive rationalization. That's less likely to

SELF-COACHING TIP

Emphasize your role as a questioner rather than a source of solutions, and encourage employees to engage others in the same way. They can turn any conversation into a self-coaching dialogue simply by asking their peers and colleagues to pose questions before offering advice. Note the questions that draw out the most meaningful answers, and suggest that your employees ask similar questions of themselves when facing a challenge or looking back on an experience.

> happen with "How . . ." and "What . . ." questions such as "How do you feel about what happened?" and "What would you do differently?"—which don't sound accusatory.

Of course, your employees sometimes need your advice—but wait for those moments and jump in as necessary, not as a first response to every problem they face. To reassure those who simply want to be given an answer, you might say, "I'll be happy to offer my opinion later, but, first, what do you think?"

Be Transparent

While your employees may pick up tips on self-coaching by observing how you coach them, you'll make it easier for them to replicate the process—both on their own and in coaching conversations with others—by talking openly about the techniques you're using. This transparency will also help them understand why you're behaving differ-

SELF-COACHING TIP

Leave a few minutes at the end of every coaching session to discuss the conversation itself. Talk about why it was helpful—and what might have made it even more helpful. Spell out which coaching techniques you used and ask for feedback. Encourage your employees to use the methods that worked best when they initiate coaching conversations with others.

ently if new coaching techniques involve a change in your management style.

For example, if your employees are accustomed to coming to you for answers—and you've readily supplied them—a sudden emphasis on asking questions may feel jarring or frustrating to them unless you provide context for it. Explain why you're asking the questions and what benefits you hope to obtain by doing so.

When your employees see what coaching techniques you're using, they can share with you what works best for them (not all techniques work equally well for everyone). And that understanding will feed their self-coaching efforts. They'll benefit more from individual reflection when they step back from their coaching with you and articulate its impact on their actions.

Then, by asking colleagues and friends to adopt the same techniques they've found effective in conversations with you, they can recruit new, supportive members of their self-coaching team. You'll continue to be a key member of that team, of course, but you won't need to be there for every coaching conversation or experience.

Ed Batista is an executive coach and an instructor at the Stanford Graduate School of Business. He writes regularly on issues related to coaching and professional development at www.edbatista.com, and he is currently writing a book on self-coaching for Harvard Business Review Press.

Chapter 10
Avoid Common Coaching Mistakes

by Muriel Maignan Wilkins

Managers learning to coach are often eager to use their newly honed skills with their staff. But even a few missteps can easily discourage managers from committing to coaching their employees over the long haul. Here are four common mistakes made by managers learning to coach, as well as guidance on how to avoid—and correct—them.

Common Mistake 1: Coaching the "Mini-Me"

Coaching is about helping your team member reach her own potential. Yet, time and time again, managers instead try to coach individuals into the managers' own image. Don't fall into the trap of trying to coach your team member into a replica of yourself, or she will become rapidly disengaged from the coaching process. Both your attempt to support her and her attempt to deliver will prove unsustainable in the long term.

One of my clients made this mistake early on. As a manager learning to coach, he enthusiastically provided his staff members with advice and individualized guidance for their professional development. But rather than letting them develop their own paths and learn from their own successes and mistakes, he typically began his coaching conversations with "Well, if it were me . . ." His coaching didn't stick, and he, as well as his direct reports, got frustrated with the efforts.

Remedy

Coaching is not about you—and it's certainly not about creating another you. Your team member has different strengths and weaknesses from you, and different interests and goals. To ensure that your coaching is centered on the employee and not on you, you have to meet him where he is in terms of skill, capability, and commitment to the assignment at hand. Before you craft advice to share with him, start by understanding his strengths and weaknesses and identify how they differ from yours. Take his understanding of the situation into account by asking questions. Consider how he looks at the situation. Then you can frame your suggestions and feedback based on realistic expectations.

Common Mistake 2: Thinking Coaching Is Special Time

Managers often overly mystify coaching and as a result make the perennial mistake of waiting for the right time to coach. And, unfortunately, that right time often never comes, because making coaching larger than life makes it unattainable and impractical even for the best of us. And so all our best-laid coaching plans never come to fruition.

Remedy

You do not need to wait for a special time to coach, and not every coaching conversation needs to be a big development discussion with a capital *D*. The best coaching is integrated into your and the employee's day-to-day work life. Make it a practice to coach in the moment. If your employee is about to prepare for something, proactively spend a few minutes coaching him on how he will approach the deliverable. If he has completed an assignment, debrief with some coaching questions that will help him learn from the experience and use the knowledge for the next time around.

Certainly you should still hold scheduled sit-down discussions with your direct reports to discuss their development goals and a plan of action, but don't wait for those meetings. If you do, you'll miss the opportunity to give feedback in real time, and you'll also put such weight on those bigger meetings that they will be emotionally fraught and less productive.

Common Mistake 3: Losing Your Patience

Coaching requires patience. It is not about pushing or pulling your team members directly to the specific results you want them to achieve; it's more like watching on the sidelines during game time, letting them find their own way.

For example, over her years as an analyst, Paula had carefully developed a very distinct way of analyzing her division's end-of-month reports. Now the division manager, she has become increasingly frustrated with the way the new analyst approaches the reports; it seems inefficient and imprecise. Rather than invest the time to walk the analyst through her approach, however, Paula simply takes over and does it herself, figuring that it will take less time to do it correctly. Little does Paula recognize that in the long run she is doing a disservice to the analyst, to herself, and even to the organization by not teaching her hard-earned skills to her next-level staff.

For the results- and action-oriented drivers among us, however, stepping back and letting your direct report make mistakes—or just different choices from those you would have made—can feel like a tortuous process. Especially when you're short on time, or when a project is particularly important, it is easy to lose your patience: You may look flustered, let frustration creep into your voice, or simply snatch the task away and do it yourself. But giving in to your impatience in this way counteracts all your previous efforts by making your employee want to throw up his hands (if you've given up on him, why shouldn't he?).

Remedy

Resist the urge to succumb to the tiny voice inside telling you, "Oh, it would just be easier to tell him exactly what to do, or better yet, just do it myself already!" To approach coaching with composure, follow these guidelines.

- **Embrace the idea that coaching is not a quick-fix proposition.** Coaching is a marathon, not a sprint. Don't expect your direct report to move the needle from 0 to 10 after one opportunity to practice the skill when he's been without it for years. You should expect him to stumble a few times before he gets it. Just reminding yourself that you shouldn't expect to see results right away can put you in a better frame of mind. It also allows you to see when to celebrate a direct report's successes—even if his work isn't perfect.

- **Set a time line.** Even if you know it will take some time before your direct report has mastered this new skill, it can help you to cite a specific target date by which point you expect her to be independent. It can be motivating to her to have a target date, and helpful to you to estimate when you can depend on her to perform the task proficiently.

- **Establish clear milestones.** Don't wait until that target date to check in with your direct report to see how she is doing on the task. Instead, do so over the duration of the project by breaking down the assignment into smaller chunks. This will enable you to coach her along the way rather than in retrospect; it will also satiate your need to see progress and movement on the assignment. Your direct report will also gain confidence as she accomplishes each milestone or corrects the course successfully.

- **Watch your tone.** In the moment, as with all professional communication, take a deep breath if you feel yourself getting flustered or about to make a snap decision because something just seems so easy for you and apparently hard for your direct report. And if you do slip into backseat-driver mode, be courageous enough to apologize.

Common Mistake 4: Assuming Everyone Is Coachable

Patience is important in coaching, but sometimes managers can be too patient.

John was frustrated and discouraged with one of his employees. He'd spent an inordinate amount of time coaching her on meeting deadlines on time, to no avail. She simply made no efforts to try doing anything differently. John kept trying new ways to engage her, but he wasn't getting anywhere.

No matter how much of an optimist you are, sometimes you need to be realistic: Like John, you may have an employee who is not coachable—or not coachable at this time. Many managers fail to recognize this situation, and subsequently they exert far more energy than needed, with little results.

Remedy

A person must want to be coached in order for it to work, because ultimately the responsibility and ownership of the effort are hers. Start by giving your team member the benefit of the doubt, but as you work with her, quickly assess her coachability. From what you've seen, does she want to learn? Is she trying (even if she's not succeeding)? Does she seem genuinely appreciative of the coaching?

If you're not sure, talk to her about it. Give some feedback on how you've seen her approach the coaching you've given; how she responds to such a conversation can be very telling about how much this is something she actually wants.

In the rare cases in which you discover that you really are dealing with someone who is not coachable, don't hesitate to try a strategy other than coaching rather than waste your energy. In certain situations, it may be appropriate to take a more directive stance. And in situations where performance is severely affected despite many attempts at coaching, you should consider whether your direct report is in the right role.

Learning to be an effective coach as a manager takes lots of practice. Over time, you will hone your skill and build your repertoire of tried-and-true strategies that help you effectively develop your employees. Although these remedies are meant to help you get there more efficiently, don't be concerned if you trip up every now and then on any of these pitfalls or others you might encounter. As with the staff members you are coaching, some of your best learning will often come through your mistakes.

Muriel Maignan Wilkins is the cofounder and managing partner of Paravis Partners, a Washington, D.C.–based leadership coaching and consulting firm. Previously, she held various advisory and leadership roles in marketing and strategy at Prudential, Accenture, and *U.S. News & World Report*. She is the coauthor with Amy Jen Su of *Own the Room: Discover Your Signature Voice to Master Your Leadership Presence* (Harvard Business Review Press, 2013).

Section 3
Customize Your Coaching

Chapter 11
Tailor Your Coaching to People's Learning Styles

by David A. Kolb and Kay Peterson

As you coach your employees to develop their skills or improve their performance, you can set them up for success by understanding how they learn best and adjusting your methods accordingly. They may prefer learning through intense experience, sustained reflection, analytical thinking, goal-directed action, or a combination of approaches (the basic steps in what we call the Experiential Learning Cycle—see figure 11-1). By tapping into their preferred styles, you will engage them more deeply and motivate them. As a result, they'll make greater—and faster—progress toward their goals.

FIGURE 11-1

The Experiential Learning Cycle

The people you coach learn through experience: They think about it, extrapolate lessons from it, and experiment with those lessons—which leads to new experiences and learning.

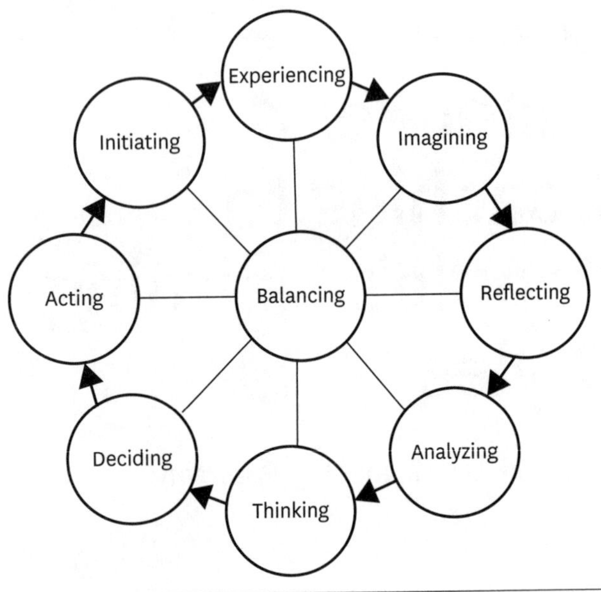

If the benefits of customized coaching are so clear, why don't more managers do it? Largely because we tend to favor our own learning preferences when we teach others (see table 11-1). We assume that what works for us will work for everyone else, but that's just not the case.

Take Marie, a vice president of operations for a national manufacturing company. She had a quick, decisive learning style—and struggled to coach direct reports whose styles differed from hers. Rather than let them

TABLE 11-1

Questions to help you coach more holistically

When coaching people whose learning styles don't match yours, you must communicate in a way that resonates with *them*. Try asking yourself the following questions as prompts for the different styles. They'll help you customize your coaching to your employees—whether they favor Reflecting, Initiating, or another approach entirely—instead of retreating to your own comfort zone.

INITIATING	EXPERIENCING	IMAGINING
How can I inspire my employee to learn? What questions can I ask to promote discovery? What experiments will help my employee apply the lessons learned? Can I provide opportunities to influence others? Am I bringing enough energy to our coaching sessions?	Am I fully present (without distractions) during each coaching session? Am I attending to the relationship? Am I connecting emotionally? Am I making my employee feel supported?	Am I listening and receptive? Should we explore more diverse sources of information? Am I helping my employee explore all possibilities? Have I judged too soon? Have I shown empathy?
REFLECTING	**ANALYZING**	**THINKING**
Have I asked thought-provoking questions? Am I allowing time for my employee to "struggle" and find answers? Can I slow things down? Have I considered other points of view? Have I observed and deliberated?	Have I articulated a thorough, precise coaching plan? Can I use a model or theory to explain it? Can I provide data or specialized knowledge to support it? Are my thoughts organized? Am I presenting ideas logically?	What is the larger plan for development or improvement? Have I been objective and logical, setting aside my emotions and self-interest? Am I stepping back to generalize and articulate lessons learned? How can I structure our sessions differently? Am I assessing costs and benefits?

(*continued*)

TABLE 11-1 (CONTINUED)

DECIDING	ACTING	BALANCING
What is the goal of the session? How will I know if we have reached it? What practical results can we achieve? Is it time to choose a course of action? Can I provide direct, immediate feedback?	What can we get done now? Are we considering both the task and the people it will affect? Am I encouraging my employee to take risks? What activities will support my employee's learning and help him or her apply it?	What are my employee's blind spots? Which skills does this situation call for—and which ones are missing? Are we considering all options when setting development goals and deciding how to meet them?

take the lead, she jumped in to help them solve each challenge as soon as they encountered it. Things got done her way, but people weren't really learning—and she became frustrated with their lack of growth.

But then she recognized how she'd contributed to the problem: She hadn't allowed people to take enough responsibility for their own development, nor had she considered their approaches to learning. She turned the situation around by taking the time to identify her employees' learning styles and changing her coaching tactics to suit them.

When coaching Tyler, for example, Marie discovered through observation and conversations with him that his preferred style was Experiencing, or learning through feelings and relationships. (See the following section "What Are Your Employees' Learning Styles?" for more on recognizing preferences.) So she resisted the urge to set goals and take action right away, as she usually did.

Instead, she connected with him emotionally first, asking how he felt about his team's relationships and revealing her own feelings about working on a team, which conveyed her support and established trust.

One of Tyler's goals was to overcome his fear of difficult conversations and handle them better. Together, he and Marie identified a way of conquering that fear: organizing his thoughts before trying to communicate them. Tyler then practiced by role-playing with Marie. (He felt comfortable doing so because of the personal connection they had established.) Because the learning process reflected his style, he became more invested in it—and his skills improved each time he practiced.

What Are Your Employees' Learning Styles?

Personality type, education, and cultural background all influence learning preferences. And once someone finds success with a certain style, she'll continue to rely on it, reinforcing the preference.

Here are the nine learning styles you may recognize in members of your team and the coaching tactics that complement them:

1. **Initiating: experimenting with new courses of action.** These learners enjoy networking, influencing others, thinking on their feet, and seeking opportunities. Encourage them to jump in and learn from trial and error. Use inspiring, energetic language to communicate with them (*set the pace, grab the chance, seize the opportunity*).

2. **Experiencing: finding meaning from deep involvement in experiences and relationships.** These learners focus on emotions and intuition. Connect with them on a personal level and encourage them to work with others. Use language that is sensitive and accepting (*touched, grounded, present, mindful*).

3. **Imagining: contemplating experiences and considering a range of solutions.** These learners seek and appreciate diverse input from many people. Listen to their many creative ideas before prompting them to focus on one. Encourage them to discover a course of action through a series of small decisions. Use words that convey open-mindedness, empathy, and trust (*value ideas, brainstorm, reach for the stars, create an ideal vision, consider other perspectives*).

4. **Reflecting: connecting experiences and ideas through sustained reflection.** These learners observe others, take multiple perspectives into account, and wait to act until they're confident about the outcome. Allow adequate time for them to watch, listen, and rehearse quietly on their own. Communicate with words that convey a slow and thoughtful approach (*take plenty of time, be cautious, pause, process the idea, watch a role model*).

5. **Analyzing: integrating and systematizing ideas.** These learners like to make plans, attend to de-

tails, and use theories to test assumptions. Provide conceptual models so they can process ideas before applying them. Use concise, logical language (*seek details, organize the facts, synthesize the data, do the research, make a plan*).

6. **Thinking: engaging in disciplined logic or mathematics.** These learners prefer quantitative analysis and abstract reasoning, and tend to focus on one objective at a time. Engage them by weighing costs and benefits. Communicate using the language of logic and reason (*see the point, just the facts, sharpen our focus, create a spreadsheet, examine the data*).

7. **Deciding: choosing a single course of action early on to achieve practical results.** These learners efficiently set goals and critically evaluate whatever solution they've chosen. Involve them in figuring out which problems to solve and setting standards, and allow them to measure their own success. Use language that's pragmatic and direct (*take a practical approach, measure success, critical feedback, strong direction, best practice*).

8. **Acting: taking assertive, goal-directed steps toward change.** These learners care about completing tasks *and* meeting people's needs, and they take risks to get things done faster and better. Encourage trial and error and on-the-job experiments. Choose words that

convey dynamism and speed (*take action, quick turnaround, achieve results, implement the plan*).

9. **Balancing: weighing the pros and cons of acting versus reflecting, and experiencing versus thinking.** These learners can flexibly assume any learning style to fill gaps in their knowledge. Tap their abilities to identify blind spots and to adapt. Communicate with language that reflects their flexibility (*balance the situation, include variety, adapt, take a holistic perspective*).

Do any of your direct reports, like Tyler, learn best through feelings and relationships (Experiencing or Imagining)? Which ones prefer watching role models from a safe distance and emulating their behavior (Reflecting)? Which are comfortable with trial and error (Initiating or Acting)? To find out, try asking employees whether they *generally* gravitate toward feeling, watching, thinking, or acting—and map their answers to the learning styles defined above.

But that's just a start. (You'll probably get uneven responses—many people haven't even thought about their learning preferences and may struggle to articulate them.) So add your own observations to the mix: What appears to interest and motivate each employee? Knowing that can shed light on learning preferences. For example, an employee who always emerges from your group's annual strategy off-site with renewed enthusiasm, rallying others to support the mission and business model, is likely to have an Initiating style. By contrast, someone who avoids deliberating but digs into every task with energy and commitment probably has an Acting style of learning.

Language cues can also be telling: Note whether employees favor expressions of feeling, believing, thinking, or doing. Someone who often talks in emotional-relational terms ("I loved the discussion we had" or "The financials are making me anxious") probably focuses on feelings and learns by Experiencing rather than Thinking or Deciding.

What If Their Styles Aren't Doing the Trick?

Knowing how people like to learn will accelerate their overall development—but using only their preferred styles won't help them tackle every challenge they face. They'll often need to try out new styles to meet their goals.

Consider Alex, an accountant who has been promoted to lead his department. His primary learning style is Analyzing; he also relies on Thinking and Deciding, though to a lesser extent. This approach has served him well as an individual contributor. But to thrive in his new leadership position, he'll need to expand his repertoire of backup styles to include Initiating, Experiencing, and Imagining.

Now suppose you are his manager. You can help him experiment with these learning styles and strengthen his use of them through practice. Ask him to facilitate a brainstorming session, for instance, to become better at Imagining as he envisions new possibilities for the group. Develop his capacity for Initiating by assigning him to a cross-functional project, where his success will depend in part on his ability to influence people who don't report to him. Work with him to build key relationships so he'll spend more time Experiencing—introduce him to colleagues whose styles differ from (and complement) his. During your regular check-ins, talk about these experiments in order to make the learning explicit and deliberate. Ask him what he's enjoying and what he finds challenging. See what lessons he can tease out on his own; if he struggles to do that, refer him back to the Learning Cycle—remind him which styles will help him succeed as a department head.

As he's trying out new styles, however, you will still want to use data, frameworks, theories, and goal setting to motivate him, given his natural preference for Analyzing, Thinking, and Deciding. To get him to sharpen his networking skills, for instance, make the interpersonal challenge more appealing to him by enhancing it with analysis: Ask him to map out his current network and identify which people's functions and expertise will help him most in his new role.

To do everything we're suggesting, you'll need to *really* know your employees—talk to them, observe them, analyze them, ask colleagues about them. Since individuals' learning preferences are so deeply ingrained, your coaching will be more efficient and fruitful if you meet people where they are in the Learning Cycle. Yet it's equally important to recognize when their styles aren't panning out. By playing to their preferences—while also encouraging them to become more flexible—you'll help them discover and reach their potential.

David A. Kolb, a psychologist and educational theorist, is the founder of Experience Based Learning Systems and a professor emeritus at Case Western Reserve University. His renowned Kolb Learning Style Inventory is outlined briefly in this chapter. **Kay Peterson,** a principal at Learning Partners Group, is an organizational development consultant and coach specializing in experiential learning and learning-style flexibility.

Chapter 12
Coaching Your Stars, Steadies, and Strugglers

by Jim Grinnell

Let's say you have three direct reports: Cindy always exceeds her numbers, rarely asks for your help, and often takes initiative on new projects. Performancewise, she's every manager's dream, although she can be abrasive and dismissive of her colleagues. Compare her with Ed, a pleasant colleague who gets the job done competently. His attitude is "a day's work for a day's pay," and for him that day ends at 5:00 PM. And then there's Sam. He's very likeable, but he can't seem to get things right. It's heartbreaking—he stays late every day and

Adapted from "The ABCs of Employee Coaching," posted on May 31, 2012, at businesslearningcoach.com

takes work home on the weekends just to perform at a subpar level.

How do you coach Cindy, Ed, and Sam? Should you give them equal time? Should you emphasize the same things?

This may sound unfair, but you cannot treat them the same way. You need to make some choices—place some bets on where your efforts will pay off.

The Stars

We often assume it's best to leave A players like Cindy alone. They've mastered their domain, and we don't want to muck things up, so we keep our distance as managers.

But that's a mistake. You should actually devote more coaching time to your stars than to anyone else because that's where you'll yield the greatest results. Plus, they need more support than you might think. As executive coach Steven Berglas points out in "How to Keep A Players Productive" (HBR September 2006), stars, "despite their veneer of self-satisfaction, smugness, and even bluster," are often insecure individuals in need of praise and nurturing. Many high performers grew up in an environment where great was never good enough. As a result, they often feel they're *masquerading* as successful.

When you coach A players, offset their insecurities with affirmation. Try the following suggestions, drawn from Berglas's article:

- **Praise your stars genuinely and frequently.** They'll immediately sniff out platitudes and empty accolades. When you praise them, focus on the skills and strengths they value in themselves. For instance, if a direct report says she gets charged up by landing high-margin sales deals, congratulate her when she does so. And if she responds well to public recognition, share the news in a department meeting or send out a group e-mail when she brings in a big account.

- **Rein them in.** Left to their own devices, A players will keep raising their own standards and over time will push themselves to performance they can't sustain. So act like a governor on an engine: Keep their expectations from revving to the point of breakdown. One way to do this is to discuss your concerns about their frenetic pace with them. They're self-focused, so they'll probably be receptive if you direct the conversation to *their* well-being.

- **Nudge them to play nicely.** A players tend to be hyper-judgmental of their colleagues. Unless you explicitly hold them accountable for collegiality and teamwork, they may create interpersonal turmoil, undermining their positive contributions. Sometimes they'll demonstrate annoyance when their teammates don't perform to their standards, or they'll act with contempt when asked to assist coworkers. When delivering constructive feedback to A players, comment on the behavior, not on the person (a lot of "you" statements may get their defenses up). And be specific about the impact of their behavior on the team's performance. That's something they'll care about.

High performers can be hard to take. It's tempting to bring them down a peg or two when they start acting up, but keep that impulse in check. You'll get much more out of them—and less grief—if you allow them to savor their accomplishments.

The Steadies

If A players are your lead singers and guitarists, B players such as Ed in the example earlier are your drummers and bass players. They certainly don't get top billing, but they hold everything together in the organization. B players make up the lion's share of the workforce—75% to 80%, by some estimates. And they dutifully get the job done with little fanfare or oversight.

Still, they need your attention. Here are some tips on coaching them effectively, based on insights from "Let's Hear It for B Players" (HBR June 2003), by Thomas J. DeLong and Vineeta Vijayaraghavan:

- **Accept them for who they are.** Some managers assume you should try to move your B players up to the A level. While this approach is intuitively appealing, it's not the best investment of your time, for a variety of reasons: Many B players have reached the limits of their abilities. Some have made a conscious life choice to occupy the meaty part of the performance curve because they're winding down their careers, for example, or seeking work/life balance. While a subset have A-level potential, the majority are entrenched at the B level. But these folks still bring tremendous value. They're often straight shooters who provide insights others are afraid to share. They are also less apt to leave—and thus disrupt—the organization.

- **Recognize and reward them.** Though they don't receive (or expect) the same financial rewards or promotions as A players, B players crave affirmation. If a B player puts in extra effort to respond to a customer complaint, acknowledge it. And deliver your praise however your employee likes to receive it. Some people prefer it one-on-one, while others seek public accolades.
- **Give them options.** B performers may not want to grow and develop as much as their A peers—but they don't want to stagnate, either. Provide opportunities for them to grow within their comfort zones. Invest in training that will help them shore up their strengths. Send them to conferences and seminars on topics they care about. Ask them to mentor junior employees. Solicit their input on decisions. B players have a lot to offer—but you need to make it relatively easy for them.

The Strugglers

Managers often devote most of their coaching to the employees who struggle the most, like Sam—and that's a losing proposition.

When we talk about C players, we're not referring to employees who are adjusting to the organization or to new roles; we're talking about individuals who *should be* performing at a higher level. Over time, they just don't carry their weight. They drag down their teams and sometimes even corrode their coworkers' attitudes. And to the extent that C players are taking up space, they block the advancement of stronger candidates.

So what do you do with them? In "A New Game Plan for C Players" (HBR January 2002), Beth Axelrod, Helen Handfield-Jones, and Ed Michaels suggest a tough but respectful approach: Give low performers a chance at redemption but set firm expectations to overcome procrastination and rationalization. Here's how:

- **Create a clear plan for improvement.** Employees won't improve in a vacuum. They need guidance on what to change and help changing it. Set concrete goals for them and have a well-defined end point. If C players don't meet agreed-upon standards within a specified amount of time, help them make a graceful, dignified exit. Make sure you've documented their progress, or lack thereof, so you don't take them by surprise or leave yourself open to any HR or legal battles.

- **Give candid, real-time feedback.** As difficult as it may be to provide critical feedback, you are doing C players no favors by withholding it. They need to understand if and how they're improving and where they're falling short. (See chapter 6, "Giving Feedback That Sticks.")

- **Provide a support network.** Don't invest a ton of your time coaching C players, but don't leave them to languish, either. You may want to rely on existing training programs or farm out the coaching, perhaps pairing the C player with a competent peer.

That's how to coach someone like Sam. If he doesn't make progress, don't let him stick around, no matter how nice he is and how hard he tries. The amount of time you give him will depend on the nature of his job and his commitment and capacity to improve. In most instances you'll know within a few months whether further investment will help. You need to move sensitively but swiftly in dealing with Sam. You owe it to Cindy and Ed—and to your organization—to focus your coaching efforts where they'll pan out.

Jim Grinnell is an associate professor of management at Merrimack College in North Andover, Massachusetts. His consulting firm, Grinnell Consulting, works with firms on leadership coaching and organizational change and development.

Chapter 13

Coaching Your Rookie Managers

by Carol A. Walker

Most organizations promote employees into managerial positions based on their technical competence. Very often, however, those people fail to grasp how their roles have changed—that their jobs are no longer about personal achievement but instead about enabling others to achieve, that sometimes driving the bus means taking a backseat, and that building a team is often more important than cutting a deal. Even the best employees can have trouble adjusting to these new realities. That trouble may be exacerbated by normal insecurities that make rookie managers hesitant to ask for help, even when they find themselves in thoroughly unfamiliar territory. As these new managers internalize their stress, their focus

---

Adapted from *Harvard Business Review*, April 2002 (product #R0204H)

becomes internal as well. They become insecure and self-focused and cannot properly support their teams. Inevitably, trust breaks down, staff members are alienated, and productivity suffers.

Many companies unwittingly support this downward spiral by assuming that their rookie managers will somehow learn critical management skills by osmosis. Some rookies do, to be sure, but in my experience they're the exceptions. Most need more help. In the absence of comprehensive training and intensive coaching—which most companies don't offer—the rookie manager's boss plays a key role. Of course, it's not possible for most senior managers to spend hours and hours every week overseeing a new manager's work, but if you know what typical challenges a rookie manager faces, you'll be able to anticipate some problems before they arise and nip others in the bud.

Delegating

Effective delegation may be one of the most difficult tasks for rookie managers. Senior managers bestow on them big responsibilities and tight deadlines, and they put a lot of pressure on them to produce results. The natural response of rookies when faced with such challenges is to "just do it," thinking that's what got them promoted in the first place. But their reluctance to delegate assignments also has its roots in some very real fears. First is the fear of losing stature: If I assign high-profile projects to my staff members, they'll get the credit. What kind of visibility will I be left with? Will it be clear to my boss and my staff what value I'm adding? Second is the fear of abdicating control: If I allow Frank to do this, how can

I be sure that he will do it correctly? In the face of this fear, the rookie manager may delegate tasks but supervise Frank so closely that he will never feel accountable. Finally, the rookie may be hesitant to delegate work because he's afraid of overburdening his staff. He may be uncomfortable assigning work to former peers for fear that they'll resent him. But the real resentment usually comes when staff members feel that lack of opportunity is blocking their advancement.

Signs that these fears may be playing out include new managers who work excessively long hours, are hesitant to take on new responsibilities, have staff members who seem unengaged, or have a tendency to answer on behalf of employees instead of encouraging them to communicate with you directly.

The first step toward helping young managers delegate effectively is to get them to understand their new role. Acknowledge that their job fundamentally differs from an individual contributor's. Clarify what you and the organization value in leaders. Developing talented, promotable staff is critical in any company. Let new managers know that they will be rewarded for these less tangible efforts in addition to hitting numerical goals. Understanding this new role is half the battle for rookie managers, and one that many companies mistakenly assume is evident from the start.

After clarifying how your rookie manager's role has changed, you can move on to tactics.

When a new manager grumbles about mounting workloads, seize the opportunity to discuss delegation. Encourage him to take small risks initially, playing to the obvious strengths of his staff members. Early successes will build the manager's confidence and willingness to take progressively larger risks in stretching each team member's capabilities. Reinforce to him that delegation does not mean abdication. Breaking a complex project into manageable chunks, each with clearly defined milestones, makes effective follow-up easier. It's also important to schedule regular meetings before the project even begins in order to ensure that the manager stays abreast of progress and that staff members feel accountable.

One young manager I worked with desperately needed to find time to train and supervise new employees. His firm had been recently acquired, and he had to deal with high staff turnover and new industrywide rules and regulations. The most senior person on his staff—a woman who had worked for the acquiring company—was about to return from an extended family leave, and he was convinced that he couldn't ask her for help. After all, she had a part-time schedule, and she'd asked to be assigned to the company's largest client. To complicate matters, he suspected that she resented his promotion. As we evaluated the situation, the manager was able to see that the senior staffer's number one priority was reestablishing herself as an important part of the team. Once he realized this, he asked her to take on critical supervisory responsibilities, balanced with a smaller client load, and she eagerly agreed. Indeed, she returned from leave excited about partnering with her manager to develop the team.

Getting Support from Above

Most first-time managers see their relationship with their boss more as one of servitude than of partnership. They will wait for you to initiate meetings, ask for reports, and question results. You may welcome this restraint, but generally it's a bad sign. For one thing, it puts undue pressure on you to keep the flow of communication going. Even more important, it prevents new managers from looking to you as a critical source of support. If they don't see you that way, it's unlikely that they will see themselves that way for their own people. The problem isn't only that your position intimidates them; it's also that they fear being vulnerable. A newly promoted manager doesn't want you to see weaknesses, lest you think you made a mistake in promoting her. When I ask rookie managers about their relationships with their bosses, they often admit that they are trying to "stay under the boss's radar" and are "careful about what [they] say to the boss."

Some inexperienced managers will not seek your help even when they start to founder. Seemingly capable rookie managers often try to cover up a failing project or relationship—just until they can get it back under control.

What's the boss of a rookie manager to do? You can begin by clarifying expectations. Explain the connection between the rookie's success and your success so that she understands that open communication is necessary for you to achieve your goals. Explain that you don't expect her to have all the answers. Introduce her to other managers within the company who may be helpful, and encourage her to contact them as needed. Let her know that mistakes happen but that the cover-up is always worse than the crime. Let her know that you like to receive occasional lunch invitations as much as you like to extend them.

Lunch and drop-by meetings are important, but they usually aren't enough. Consider meeting regularly with a new manager—perhaps weekly in the early stages of a new assignment, moving to biweekly or monthly as her confidence builds. These meetings will develop rapport, provide you with insight into how the person is approaching the job, and make the new manager organize her thoughts on a regular basis. Be clear that the meetings are her time and that it's up to her to plan the agenda. The message you send is that the individual's work is important to you and that you're a committed business partner. More subtly, you're modeling how to simultaneously empower and guide direct reports.

Projecting Confidence

Looking confident when you don't feel confident—it's a challenge we all face, and as senior managers we're usually conscious of the need when it arises. Rookie managers are often so internally focused that they are unaware of this need or the image they project. They are so focused on substance that they forget that form counts, too. The first weeks and months on the job are a critical time for new leaders to reach out to staff. If they don't project confidence, they are unlikely to inspire and energize their teams.

I routinely work with new managers who are unaware that their everyday demeanor is hurting their organizations. In one rapidly growing technology company, the service manager, Linda, faced high levels of stress. Service outages were all too common, and they were beyond her control. Customers were exacting, and they too were under great pressure. Her rapidly growing staff was generally inexperienced. Distraught customers and employees had her tied up in knots almost daily. She consistently appeared breathless, rushed, and fearful that the other shoe was about to drop. The challenge was perhaps too big for a first-time manager, but that's what happens in rapidly growing companies. On one level, Linda was doing an excellent job keeping the operation going. The client base was growing and retention was certainly high—largely as a result of her energy and resourcefulness. But on another level, she was doing a lot of damage.

Linda's frantic demeanor had two critical repercussions. First, she had unwittingly defined the standard for acceptable conduct in her department, and her inexperienced staff began to display the same behaviors. Before long, other departments were reluctant to communicate with Linda or her team, for fear of bothering them or eliciting an emotional reaction. But for the company to arrive at real solutions to the service problems, departments needed to openly exchange information, and that wasn't happening. Second, Linda was not portraying herself to senior managers as promotion material. They were pleased with her troubleshooting abilities, but they did not see a confident, thoughtful senior manager in the making. The image Linda was projecting would ultimately hold back both her career and her department.

Not all rookie managers display the problems that Linda did. Some appear excessively arrogant. Others wear their self-doubt on their sleeves. Whether your managers appear overwhelmed, arrogant, or insecure, honest feedback is your best tool. You can help rookie managers by telling them that it's always safe to let out their feelings—in your office, behind closed doors. Reinforce just how long a shadow they cast once they assume leadership positions. Their staff members watch them closely, and if they see professionalism and optimism, they are likely to demonstrate those characteristics as well. Preach the gospel of conscious comportment—a constant awareness of the image one is projecting to the world. If you observe a manager projecting a less-than-positive image, tell that person right away.

Just-in-time coaching is often the most effective method for showing rookie managers how to project confidence. For instance, the first time you ask a new manager to carry out an initiative, take a little extra time to walk her through the process. Impress upon her the cardinal rule of management: Your staff members don't necessarily have to like you, but they do need to trust you. Ensure that the new manager owns the message she's delivering.

Focusing on the Big Picture

Rookie managers have a real knack for allowing immediate tasks to overshadow overarching initiatives. This is particularly true for those promoted from within, because they've just come from the front lines where they're accustomed to constant firefighting. As a recent individual contributor armed with plenty of technical know-how, the rookie manager instinctively runs to the immediate rescue of any client or staff member in need. The sense of accomplishment rookies get from such rescues is seductive and far more exhilarating than rooting out the cause of all the firefighting. And what could be better for team spirit than having the boss jump into the trenches and fight the good fight?

Of course, a leader shows great team spirit if he joins the troops in emergencies. But are all those emergencies true emergencies? Are newer staff members being empowered to handle complex challenges? And if the rookie manager is busy fighting fires, who is thinking strategically for the department? If you're the senior manager and these questions are popping into your head, you may well have a rookie manager who doesn't fully understand his role or is afraid to seize it.

I recently worked with a young manager who had become so accustomed to responding to a steady flow of problems that he was reluctant to block off any time to work on the strategic initiatives we had identified. When I probed, he revealed that he felt a critical part of his role was to wait for crises to arise. "What if I schedule this time and something urgent comes up and I disappoint someone?" he asked. When I pointed out that he could always postpone his strategy sessions if a true emergency arose, he seemed relieved. But he saw the concept of making time to think about the business as self-indulgent—this, despite the fact that his group was going to be asked to raise productivity significantly in the following fiscal year, and he'd done nothing to prepare for that reality.

As a senior manager, you can help your rookies by explaining to them that strategic thinking is a necessary skill for career advancement: For first-time managers, 10% of the work might be strategic and 90% tactical. As executives climb the corporate ladder, however, those percentages will flip-flop. To be successful at the next level, managers must demonstrate that they can think and act strategically. You can use your regularly scheduled meetings to help your managers focus on the big picture. Don't allow them to simply review the latest results and move on. Ask probing questions about those results. For example, "What trends are you seeing in the marketplace that could affect you in two quarters? Tell me how your competition is responding to those same trends." Don't let them regale you with the wonderful training their staffs have been getting without asking, "What additional skills do we need to build in the staff to increase productivity by 25% next year?" If you aren't satisfied with your managers' responses, let them know that you expect them to think this way—not to have all the answers, but to be fully engaged in the strategic thought process.

Giving Constructive Feedback

It's human nature to avoid confrontations, and most people feel awkward when they have to correct others' behavior or actions. Rookie managers are no exception, and they often avoid addressing important issues with their staff.

You can help by creating an environment in which constructive feedback is perceived not as criticism but as a source of empowerment. This begins with the feedback you offer to your managers about their own development.

Often, brainstorming sessions can help rookie managers see that sticky personal issues can be broken down into straightforward business issues. Recommending a change in action is much easier than recommending a change in attitude. Never forget the old saw: You can't ask people to change their personalities, but you can ask them to change their behaviors.

Indeed, you should share your own techniques for dealing with difficult conversations. One manager I worked with became defensive whenever a staff member questioned her judgment. She didn't really need me to tell her that her behavior was undermining her image and effectiveness. She did need me to offer her some techniques that would enable her to respond differently in the heat of the moment. She trained herself to respond quickly and earnestly with a small repertoire of questions like, "Can you tell me more about what you mean by that?" This simple technique bought her the time she needed to gather her thoughts and engage in an interchange that was productive rather than defensive. She was too close to the situation to come up with the technique herself.

Delegating, thinking strategically, communicating—you may think this all sounds like Management 101. And you're right. The most basic elements of management are often what trip up managers early in their careers. And because they are the basics, the bosses of rookie managers often take them for granted. They shouldn't—an extraordinary number of people fail to develop these skills. I've maintained an illusion throughout this article—that only rookie managers suffer because they haven't mastered these core skills. But the truth is, managers at all levels make these mistakes. An organization that supports its new managers by helping them to develop these skills will have surprising advantages over the competition.

Carol A. Walker is the president of Prepared to Lead (www.preparedtolead.com), a management consulting firm devoted to helping organizations maximize the effectiveness of first-time managers. Before founding the company, she worked for 15 years as an executive in the insurance and technology industries.

Chapter 14

Coaching Rising Managers to Emotional Maturity

by Kerry A. Bunker, Kathy E. Kram, and Sharon Ting

In the past 10 years, we've met dozens of managers who have fallen victim to a harmful mix of their own ambition and their bosses' willingness to overlook a lack of people skills. Indeed, most executives seek out smart, aggressive people, paying more attention to their accomplishments than to their emotional maturity. What's more, they know that their strongest performers have options—if they don't get the job they want at one company, they're bound to get it somewhere else. Why risk losing them to a competitor by delaying a promotion?

Adapted from *Harvard Business Review,* December 2002 (product #R0212F)

The answer is that promoting them can be just as risky. Putting these unseasoned managers into positions of authority too quickly robs them of the opportunity to develop the emotional competencies that come with time and experience—competencies like the ability to negotiate with peers, regulate their emotions in times of crisis, or win support for change. You may be delighted with such managers' intelligence and passion—and may even see younger versions of themselves—but peers and subordinates are more likely to see them as arrogant and inconsiderate, or, at the very least, aloof. And therein lies the problem. At some point in a young manager's career, usually at the vice president level, raw talent and determined ambition become less important than the ability to influence and persuade. And unless senior executives appreciate this fact and make emotional competence a top priority, these high-potential managers will continue to fail, often at significant cost to the company.

Research has shown that the higher a manager rises in the ranks, the more important soft leadership skills are to his success.[1] Our colleagues at the Center for Creative Leadership have found that about a third of senior executives derail or plateau at some point, most often due to an emotional deficit such as the inability to build a team or regulate their own emotions in times of stress. And in our combined 55 years of coaching and teaching, we've seen firsthand how a young manager risks his career when he fails to develop emotional competencies. But the problem isn't youth per se. The problem is a lack of emotional maturity, which doesn't come easily or automatically and isn't something you learn from a book. It's one thing to understand the importance of relationships at an intellectual level and to learn techniques like active listening; it's another matter entirely to develop a full range of interpersonal competencies like patience, openness, and empathy. Emotional maturity involves a fundamental shift in self-awareness and behavior, and that change requires practice, diligence, and time.

This article will look at five strategies for boosting emotional competencies and redirecting managers who are paying a price for damaged or nonexistent relationships. The strategies aren't terribly complicated, but implementing them and getting people to change their entrenched behaviors can be very difficult. Many of these managers are accustomed to receiving accolades, and it often isn't easy for them to hear—or act on—difficult messages. You may have to satisfy yourself with small victories and accept occasional slipups. But perhaps the greatest challenge is having the discipline to resist the charm of the young and the clueless—to refrain from promoting them before they are ready and to stay the course even if they threaten to quit.

Deepen 360-Degree Feedback

With its questionnaires and standardized rating scales, 360-degree feedback as it is traditionally implemented may not be sufficiently specific or detailed to get the attention of inexperienced managers who excel at bottom-line measures but struggle with more subtle relationship challenges. These managers will benefit from a deeper and more thorough process that includes time for reflection and follow-up conversations. That means, for example, interviewing a wider range of the manager's peers and subordinates and giving her the opportunity to read verbatim responses to open-ended questions. Such detailed and extensive feedback can help a person see herself more as others do, a must for the young manager lacking the self-awareness to understand where she's falling short.

We witnessed this lack of self-awareness in Bill Miller, a 42-year-old vice president at a software company—an environment where technical ability is highly prized (as with all the examples in these pages, we've changed Miller's name and other identifying features to protect our clients' identities). Miller had gone far on pure intellect, but he never fully appreciated his own strengths. So year after year, in assignment after assignment, he worked doubly hard at learning the complexities of the business, neglecting his relationships with his colleagues as an unintended consequence. His coworkers considered his smarts and business acumen among the finest in the company, but they found him unapproachable and detached. As a result, top management questioned his ability to lead the type of strategic change that would require motivating staff at all levels. Not until Miller went through an in-depth 360-degree developmental review was he able to accept that he no longer needed to prove his intelligence—that he could relax in that respect and instead work on strengthening his personal connections. After months of working hard to cultivate stronger relationships with his employees, Miller began to notice that he felt more included in chance social encounters like hallway conversations.

Art Grainger, a 35-year-old senior manager at a cement and concrete company, was generally considered a champion by his direct reports. He was also known for becoming defensive whenever his peers or superiors questioned or even discussed his unit's performance. Through 360-degree reviews, he discovered that while everyone saw him as committed, results-oriented, and technically brilliant, they also saw him as overly protective, claiming he resisted any action or decision that might affect his department. Only when Grainger heard that his staff agreed with what his bosses had been telling him for years did he concede that he needed to change. Since then, he has come to see members of other departments as potential allies and has tried to redefine his team to include people from across the company.

It's worth noting that many of these smart young managers aren't used to hearing criticism. Consequently, they may discount negative feedback, either because the comments don't mesh with what they've heard in previous conversations or because their egos are so strong. Or they may conclude that they can "fix" the problem right away—after all, they've been able to fix most problems they've encountered in the past. But developing emotional competencies requires practice and ongoing personal interactions. The good news is that if you succeed in convincing them that these issues are career threatening, they may apply the same zeal to their emotional development that they bring to their other projects. And that's why 360-degree feedback is so valuable: When it comes from multiple sources and is ongoing, it's difficult to ignore.

Interrupt the Ascent

When people are continually promoted within their areas of expertise, they don't have to stray far from their comfort zones, so they seldom need to ask for help, especially if they're good problem solvers. Accordingly, they may become overly independent and fail to cultivate relationships with people who could be useful to them in the future. What's more, they may rely on the authority that comes with rank rather than learning how to influence people.

We sometimes counsel our clients to broaden young managers' skills by assigning them to cross-functional roles outside their expected career paths. This is distinct from traditional job rotation, which has employees spending time in different functional areas to enhance and broaden their knowledge of the business. Rather, the manager is assigned a role in which he doesn't have much direct authority. This will help him focus on developing other skills like negotiation and influencing peers.

Such cross-functional assignments—with no clear authority or obvious ties to a career path—can be a tough sell. It's not easy to convince young managers that these assignments are valuable, nor is it easy to help them extract relevant knowledge.

Act on Your Commitment

One of the reasons employees get stuck in the pattern we've described is that their bosses point out deficits in emotional competencies but don't follow through. They either neglect to articulate the consequences of continuing the destructive behavior or make empty threats but proceed with a promotion anyway. The hard-charging young executive can only conclude that these competencies are optional.

A cautionary tale comes from Mitchell Geller who, at 29, was on the verge of being named partner at a law firm. He had alienated many of his peers and subordinates over the years through his arrogance, a shortcoming duly noted on his yearly performance reviews, yet his keen legal mind had won him promotion after promotion. With Geller's review approaching, his boss, Larry Snow, pointed to heavy attrition among the up-and-coming lawyers who worked for Geller and warned him that further advancement would be contingent on a change in personal style. Geller didn't take the feedback to heart—he was confident that he'd get by, as he always had, on sheer talent. And true to form, Snow didn't stick to his guns. The promotion came through even though Geller's behavior hadn't changed. Two weeks later, Geller, by then a partner responsible for managing client relationships, led meetings with two key accounts. Afterward, the first client approached Snow and asked him to sit in on future meetings. Then the second client withdrew his business altogether, complaining that Geller had refused to listen to alternative points of view.

Contrast Geller's experience with that of 39-year-old Barry Kessler, a senior vice president at an insurance company. For years, Kessler had been heir apparent to the CEO due to his strong financial skills and vast knowledge of the business—that is, until John Mason, his boss and the current CEO, began to question the wisdom of promoting him.

While Kessler managed his own group exceptionally well, he avoided collaboration with other units, which was particularly important as the company began looking for new growth opportunities, including potential alliances with other organizations. The problem wasn't that Kessler was hostile, it was that he was passively disengaged—a flaw that hadn't seemed as important when he was responsible only for his own group. In coaching Kessler, we learned that he was extremely averse to conflict and that he avoided situations where he couldn't be the decision maker. His aversions sharply limited his ability to work with peers.

Mason sent a strong signal, not only to Kessler but to others in the organization, when he essentially demoted Kessler by taking away some of his responsibilities and temporarily pulling him from the succession plan. To give Kessler an opportunity to develop the skills he lacked, Mason asked him to lead a cross-functional team dedicated to finding strategic opportunities for growth. Success would require Kessler to devote more time to developing his interpersonal skills. He had no authority over the other team members, so he had to work through disputes and help the team arrive at a consensus. Two years later, Kessler reports that he is more comfortable with conflict and feedback, and he's worked his way back into the succession plan.

Institutionalize Personal Development

One of the most effective ways to build managers' emotional competencies is to weave interpersonal goals into the fabric of the organization, where everyone is expected to demonstrate a specific set of emotional skills and where criteria for promotion include behaviors as well as technical ability. A built-in process will make it easier to uncover potential problems early and reduce the chances that people identified as needing personal development will feel singled out or unfairly held back. Employees will know exactly what's expected of them and what it takes to advance in their careers.

At one company where the senior management team committed to developing the emotional competencies of the company's leaders, the team first provided extensive education on coaching to the HR department, which in turn supervised a program whereby top managers coached their younger and more inexperienced colleagues. The goal was to have both the experienced and inexperienced benefit: The junior managers provided feedback on the senior people's coaching skills, and the senior people helped foster emotional competencies in their less experienced colleagues.

The results were encouraging. Wes Burke, an otherwise high-performing manager, had recently been struggling to meet his business targets. After spending time with Burke and conferring with his subordinates and peers, his coach (internal to the organization) came to believe that, in his zest to achieve his goals, Burke was unable to slow down and listen to other people's ideas. Burke wasn't a boor: He had taken courses in communication and knew how to fake listening behaviors such as nodding his head and giving verbal acknowledgments, but he was often distracted and not really paying attention. He never accepted this feedback until one day, while he was walking purposefully through the large operations plant he managed, a floor supervisor stopped him to discuss his ideas for solving an ongoing production problem. Burke flipped on his active-listening mode. After uttering a few acknowledgments and saying, "Thanks, let's talk more about that," he moved on, leaving the supervisor feeling frustrated and at a loss for how to capture his boss's interest. As it happened, Burke's coach was watching. He pulled the young manager aside and said, "You didn't hear a word Karl just said. You weren't really listening." Burke admitted as much to himself and his coach. He then apologized to Karl, much to the supervisor's surprise. Keeping this incident in mind helped Burke remember the importance of his working relationships. His coach had also helped him realize that he shouldn't have assumed his sheer will and drive would somehow motivate his employees. Burke had been wearing people down, physically and psychologically. A year later, Burke's operation was hitting its targets, an accomplishment he partially attributes to the one-on-one coaching he received.

Cultivate Informal Networks

While institutionalized programs to build emotional competencies are critical, some managers will benefit more from an informal network of relationships that fall outside the company hierarchy. Mentoring, for example, can help both junior and senior managers further their emotional development through a new type of relationship. And when the mentoring experience is a positive one, it often acts as a springboard to a rich variety of relationships with others throughout the organization. In particular, it gives junior managers a chance to experience different leadership styles and exposes them to diverse viewpoints.

Sonia Greene, a 32-year-old manager at a consulting firm, was hoping to be promoted to principal, but she hadn't raised the issue with her boss because she assumed he didn't think she was ready, and she didn't want to create tension. She was a talented consultant with strong client relationships, but her internal relationships were weak due to a combination of shyness, an independent nature, and a distaste for conflict, which inhibited her from asking for feedback. When her company launched a mentoring program, Greene signed up, and through a series of lengthy conversations with Jessica Burnham, a partner at the firm, she developed new insights about her strengths and weaknesses. The support of an established player such as Burnham helped Greene become more confident and honest in her development discussions with her boss, who hadn't been aware that Greene was willing to receive and act on feedback. Today, Greene is armed with a precise understanding of what she needs to work on and is well on her way to being promoted. What's more, her relationship with Burnham has prompted her to seek out other connections, including a peer group of up-and-coming managers who meet monthly to share experiences and offer advice to one another.

Delaying a promotion can be difficult given the steadfast ambitions of the young executive and the hectic pace of organizational life, which makes personal learning seem like an extravagance. It requires a delicate balance of honesty and support, of patience and goading. It means going against the norm of promoting people almost exclusively on smarts, talent, and business results. It also means contending with the disappointment of an esteemed subordinate.

But taking the time to build people's emotional competencies isn't an extravagance; it's critical to developing effective leaders. Give in to the temptation to promote your finest before they're ready, and you're left with executives who may thrive on change and demonstrate excellent coping and survival skills but who lack the self-awareness, empathy, and social abilities required to foster and nurture those strengths in others. MBA programs and management books can't teach young executives everything they need to know about people skills. Indeed, there's no substitute for experience, reflection, feedback, and, above all, practice.

Kerry A. Bunker is president of the leadership learning firm Mangrove Leadership Solutions, LLC and a senior fellow at both the Center for Creative Leadership and The Conference Board. **Kathy E. Kram** is the R.C. Shipley Professor in Management and Professor of Organizational Behavior, Boston University. At the time of original publication, **Sharon Ting** was a manager of the Awareness Program for Executive Excellence at the Center for Creative Leadership in Greensboro, North Carolina.

NOTE

1. In his HBR articles "What Makes a Leader" (November–December 1998) and "Primal Leadership: The Hidden Driver of Great Performance" (with Richard Boyatzis and Annie McKee, December 2001), Daniel Goleman makes the case that emotional competence is the crucial driver of a leader's success.

Chapter 15
Coaching Teams

by J. Richard Hackman

Team coaching is about group processes. It involves direct interaction with a team that is intended to help members use their collective resources well in accomplishing work. Examples of coaching include leading a launch meeting before work begins (which can help members become oriented to and engaged with their task), providing the team feedback about its problem analysis (which can increase the quality of its analytic work), or asking a team reflective questions about why members made a particular decision (which can help them make better use of their knowledge and experience). By contrast, a leader who personally coordinates the work of a team or who negotiates outside resources for its use is doing things that can be quite helpful to the team—but he or she is

---

Adapted from *Leading Teams: Setting the Stage for Great Performances* (product #3332), by J. Richard Hackman, Harvard Business Review Press, 2002, pp. 165–196.

not coaching. Coaching is about building teamwork, not about doing the team's work.

Coaching can address any aspect of team interaction that is impeding members' ability to work well together or that shows promise of strengthening team functioning. In practice, however, a more focused approach brings better results. Research has identified three aspects of group interaction that have special leverage in shaping team effectiveness: the amount of effort members apply to their collective work, the appropriateness to the task and situation of the performance strategies they employ in carrying out the work, and the level of knowledge and skill they apply to the work.[1]

Process Losses and Gains

All task-performing teams encounter what psychologist Ivan Steiner calls "process losses," and can all potentially create synergistic process gains. Process losses are inefficiencies or internal breakdowns that keep a group from doing as well as it theoretically could, given its resources and member talents.[2] They develop when members interact in ways that depress the team's effort, the appropriateness of its strategy, or the utilization of member talent, and they waste or misapply member time, energy, and expertise. Process gains develop when members interact in ways that enhance collective effort, generate uniquely appropriate strategies for working together, or actively develop members' knowledge and skills. When this happens, the team has created new internal resources that can be used in its work, capabilities that did not exist be-

TABLE 15-1

Characteristic process losses and gains for each of the three performance processes

Effort

Process loss: "Social loafing" by team members
Process gain: Development of high shared commitment to the team and its work

Performance strategy

Process loss: Mindless reliance on habitual routines
Process gain: Invention of innovative, task-appropriate work procedures

Knowledge and skill

Process loss: Inappropriate weighting of member contributions
Process gain: Sharing of knowledge and development of member skills

fore the team created them. As seen in table 15-1, there are special kinds of process losses and process gains associated with each of the three performance processes we have identified.

What Coaches Do and When They Do It

A coaching intervention is any action that seeks to minimize process losses or to foster process gains for any of the three key performance processes. Coaching that addresses effort is motivational in character; its functions are to minimize free riding and to build shared commitment to the group and its work. Coaching that addresses performance strategy is consultative in character; its functions are to minimize thoughtless reliance on habitual routines and to foster the invention of ways of proceeding with the work that are especially well aligned with task and situational requirements and opportunities. Coaching that addresses knowledge and skill is educational in character; its functions are to minimize suboptimal weighting of members' contributions and to foster the development of members' knowledge and skill.

Coaching that succeeds in reducing losses or fostering gains for one or more of the three performance processes virtually always contributes to overall team effectiveness. This kind of coaching can be done by anyone (including rank-and-file team members, external managers, and outside consultants—not just a person officially designated as "team leader"), and it can be provided at any time in the course of a team's work. There are, nonetheless, three particular times in a team's life when members are likely to be especially receptive to each of the three types of coaching interventions. And, as we will see, there are other times in a team's life cycle when even competent coaching is unlikely to make much of a difference in how well members work together.

The findings of organizational psychologist Connie Gersick are especially useful in explaining why certain kinds of coaching interventions are uniquely helpful at different times in the team life cycle. In a field study of the life histories of a number of task-performing teams, Gersick found that each of the groups she tracked developed a distinctive approach toward its task as soon as it commenced work, and stayed with that approach until almost exactly halfway between its first meeting and its project deadline.[3] At the midpoint of their lives, all teams underwent a major transition. In a concentrated burst of changes, they dropped old patterns of behavior, reengaged with outside supervisors, and adopted new perspectives on their work. Following the midpoint transition, groups entered a period of focused task execution, which persisted until very near the project deadline, at which time a new set of issues having to do with termination processes arose and captured members' attention.

Gersick's findings suggest that when a team is just starting a new piece of work, members may be especially open to interventions that address their level of engagement with the team and its work. The midpoint, when half the allotted time has elapsed (or, perhaps, the work is half done), is a uniquely appropriate time for interventions that help members reflect on how well their performance strategies are working, and to change them if needed. And the end, when a work cycle has been completed, is the time when a team is ready to entertain interventions aimed at helping members learn from their experiences. The proper times for motivational, consultative, and educational interventions are summarized in figure 15-1.[4]

FIGURE 15-1

The temporal appropriateness of coaching interventions

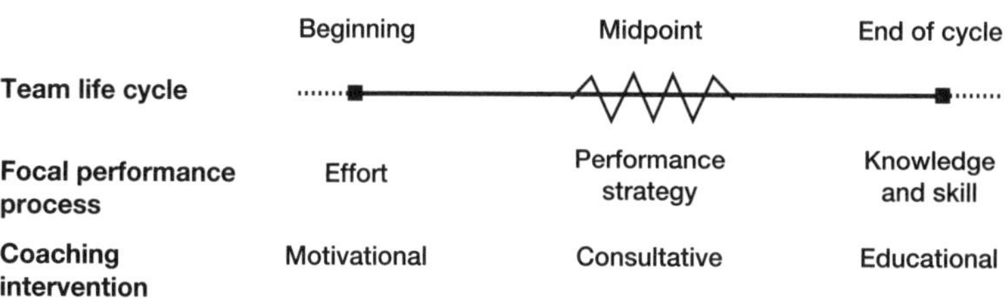

Beginnings

There is much on a team's plate when members first come together to perform a piece of work—establishing the boundary that distinguishes members from nonmembers, starting to formulate member roles and behavioral norms, and engaging with (and, inevitably, redefining) the group task. Members' decisions about such matters, whether made explicitly or implicitly, establish a track for the group on which members stay for a considerable time.[5] A coaching intervention that helps a team have a good launch increases the chances that the track will be one that enhances members' commitment to the team and motivation for its work.

The leader's behavior at the launch meeting of any type of work team serves to breathe life into the team's structural shell, no matter how rudimentary it may be, and thereby help the team start functioning on its own. If the launch meeting is successful, the team leader will have helped the team move from being just a list of names to being a real, bounded social system. The official task that the team was assigned will have been examined, assessed, and then redefined to become the slightly different task that members actually work on.[6] And the norms of conduct specified by those who created the team will have been assessed, tried out (sometimes explicitly but more often implicitly through members' behaviors), and gradually revised and made the team's own.

Midpoints

The midpoint of a team's life cycle, when a team is likely to experience a naturally occurring upheaval in how members are relating to one another and to their work, turns out to be an especially good time for a coaching intervention that invites them to reflect on the team's performance strategy. At such times (or at other natural breakpoints or low-workload periods), coaching interventions that encourage members to mindfully reflect on their work thus far and on the challenges they next will face can be quite helpful to them in revising and improving their plans for the next phase of their work.

Research by organizational psychologist Anita Woolley provides compelling support for this proposition. She devised an experimental version of an architectural task, involving construction of a college residence hall out of LEGO bricks. Groups were informed in advance how the structures they created would be evaluated, on dimensions that included sturdiness (assessed using a "drop test" unique in the annals of architecture), aesthetics, and technical indices involving floor space, number of floors, and so on. She devised two coaching-type interventions, one intended to improve members' interpersonal relations, and another that provided assistance to the team in developing a task-appropriate performance strategy. Each team received only one intervention, which was administered either at the beginning or at the midpoint of its work period.[7]

Woolley's findings, shown in figure 15-2, confirm that strategy interventions are especially helpful when they come near the midpoint of a team's work cycle. When the strategy intervention was administered at the beginning of the work period, before members had logged some experience with the task, it did not help. Note also that the intervention that addressed members' interpersonal

FIGURE 15-2

Coaching type and timing

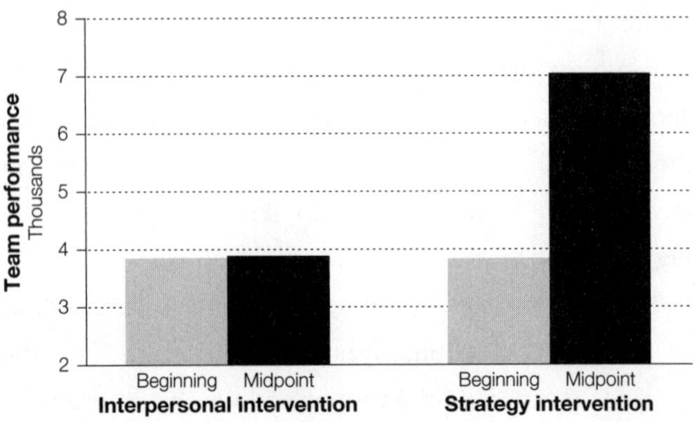

Source: Based on findings from Anita Woolley, "Effects of intervention content and timing on group task performance," *Journal of Applied Behavioral Science* 34, 1998.

relationships rather than their task processes made no difference whatever in team performance, regardless of when it was administered—an important finding to which we will return shortly.

Coaching about performance strategy helps team members stay closely in touch with changing demands and opportunities in their environment and encourages them to find ways to implement their chosen performance strategies mindfully and efficiently. Strategy-focused coaching can also help members find or invent new performance strategies that are more appropriate to the task and environment than those they had previously been using. It can even prompt a team to engage in some persuasion or political action to try to negotiate a change in organizational constraints that may be impeding their performance.

Endings

Because focus on the project dissipates somewhat once a piece of work is finished, postperformance periods offer an especially good time for coaching interventions aimed at helping members capture and internalize the lessons that can be learned from their work experiences. Even then, however, team members may be disinclined to exploit the learning opportunities that are available to them. When a team learns that it has performed splendidly—for example, an athletic team that has won the championship game or a task force whose project proposal has been approved—members may be much more disposed to celebrate their success than to explore what they can learn from their experience. Celebration is to be valued because it confirms that the team has done well and it fosters collective internal motivation. But if receiving positive performance feedback prompts nothing more than that, members may fail to notice those aspects of the feedback that could help them learn how to work together even more effectively in the future. It is fine for a basketball team to hoist the coach to members' shoulders to cut the net from the hoop; but in the locker room later, or at practice the next day, the team should also take a few moments to reflect on the lessons to be learned from its victory.

What Good Coaches Don't Do

Although I am agnostic about the particular behaviors or styles coaches should exhibit, that is decidedly not the case regarding the focus of coaches' activities. That focus should be on a team's task performance processes, not on members' social interactions or interpersonal relationships. The great majority of writing about team coaching posits (sometimes explicitly but more often implicitly) that coaching interventions should foster smooth or harmonious relationships among team members. This emphasis on harmony is misplaced and derives from a logical fallacy about the role of interpersonal processes in shaping team performance outcomes.

When we observe a team that is having performance problems, we often simultaneously see a group that is plagued with interpersonal difficulties—conflict among members, leadership struggles, communications breakdowns, and so on. It is natural to infer that these difficulties are causing the performance problems and, therefore, that the best way to improve team performance would be to fix them. As reasonable and as consistent with lay experience as this inference is, it is neither logical nor correct. In fact, the causal arrow often points in the opposite direction—how a group is performing shapes the character of members' interaction rather than vice versa. Or at least it shapes members' perceptions of their interaction. Social psychologist Barry Staw gave teams false feedback about their performance and then asked members to provide objective descriptions of how the team had functioned. Teams that had been led to believe that they had performed well reported that their interaction had been more harmonious and that they had communicated better (among other differences) than did groups whose members thought they had performed poorly.[8]

As tempting as it may be for coaches to jump in and try to make things better when they observe members enmeshed in interpersonal conflicts or leadership struggles, there is little reason to believe that such interventions will succeed in clearing out the interpersonal underbrush so task work can get back on track. More advisable, perhaps, would be to address the structural or contextual conditions that may have engendered the interpersonal difficulties, and to supplement those structural improvements with well-timed and task-focused coaching of the kind described in this chapter.

Yet even teams that are appropriately structured and supported inevitably encounter some rough interpersonal sledding. Despite the pain that members may feel while experiencing and trying to resolve such problems, they are not necessarily bad for a group or detrimental to its performance. On the contrary, research shows that certain patterns of interaction that are often experienced as problematic by team members and coded the same way by outside observers can actually promote team performance and member learning.[9] Task-based conflict is one such pattern, and the vocal presence of a member with "deviant" views is another. A skilled coach knows that it sometimes is best to leave things alone and let the tension remain high for a while, rather than to rush in and try to contain the problems or refocus their most negative manifestations.

Sharing Coaching

Throughout this chapter, I have discussed coaching as if it were done by one person, perhaps someone designated as “team leader” or “team advisor” or, for that matter, “coach.” In practice, coaching is often done by a number of individuals, sometimes different ones at different times or for different purposes—including, especially in mature self-managing teams, team members themselves. What is critical is that competent coaching be available to a team, regardless of who provides it or what formal positions those providers hold.

The potential benefits of sharing coaching among team members are wonderfully evidenced by the Orpheus Chamber Orchestra, a twenty-six-person ensemble that both rehearses and performs without a conductor. Although that orchestra has no leader on the podium, it has much more leadership than do orchestras known for their famous conductors.[10] For each piece of music the orchestra chooses to perform, one violinist is selected by his or her peers to serve as concertmaster. That person manages the rehearsal process for that piece—beginning each rehearsal, fielding suggestions from members about interpretive matters, deciding when spirited disagreements among members must be set aside to get on with the rehearsal, and taking the lead in figuring out how to handle transitions in the music that in a traditional orchestra would be signaled by a conductor’s baton.

There is abundant shared leadership and peer-to-peer coaching in this unusual orchestra, but it is far from a one-person, one-vote democracy.[11] Orpheus members are quite discriminating about who is invited to have special say in the preparation of each piece. Only some violinists are chosen to serve as concertmasters, for example, and it is clear to all which members have earned the right to be listened to especially carefully about which musical issues. Members are not treated as equals because in fact they are not equals: Each individual brings special talents and interests to the ensemble and has also some areas of relative disinterest and lesser strength. Orpheus members recognize that fact and exploit it relentlessly in the interest of collective excellence. The orchestra's willingness to acknowledge, to respect, and to exploit the individual differences among its members is one of its greatest strengths as a self-managing team. It is as fine an example of shared leadership and peer coaching as I have encountered.

One of the things that helps peer coaching work so well at the Orpheus Chamber Orchestra is that those who are coaching are also playing in the orchestra, and therefore they are always there. It is difficult, if not impossible, for any of the three kinds of coaching explored in this chapter—motivational, consultative, and educational coaching—to be accomplished by remote control. Good coaching helps team members practice and learn the skills and rewards of being superb self-managers, and that is highly unlikely to happen if the coach is rarely around.[12]

J. Richard Hackman was one of the world's leading experts on group and organizational behavior and was a professor of social and organizational psychology at Harvard University.

NOTES

1. For details, see J. R. Hackman and C. G. Morris, "Group Tasks, Group Interaction Process, and Group Performance Effectiveness: A Review and Proposed Integration," in *Advances in Experimental Social Psychology* 8: 45–99, ed. L. Berkowitz (New York: Academic Press, 1975); and J. R. Hackman and R. Wageman, *A Theory of Team Coaching,* manuscript submitted for publication (2001).

2. For additional details about the origins, dynamics, and consequences of process losses in groups, see I. D. Steiner, *Group Process and Productivity* (New York: Academic Press, 1972).

3. Since the groups' projects in the original study [C. J. G. Gersick, "Time and Transition in Work Teams: Toward a New Model of Group Development," *Academy of Management Journal* 31 (1988): 9–41] were of varying duration, these periods varied from several days to several weeks. A subsequent experimental study [C. J. G. Gersick, "Marking Time: Predictable Transitions in Task Groups," *Academy of Management Journal* 31 (1989): 9–41], in which all groups had the same amount of time to complete their task, found the same life-cycle dynamics as did the original field study.

4. For details, including discussion of conditions under which time-inappropriate motivational, educational, and consultative coaching interventions may nonetheless succeed, see J. R. Hackman and R. Wageman, *A Theory of Team Coaching,* manuscript submitted for publication (2001). Timing issues in coaching teams are also explored in a teaching case and video; see R. Wageman and J. R. Hackman, "The Overhead Reduction Task Force" [Case No. 9-400-026], [Videocassette No. 9-400- 501], [Teaching Note No. 5-400-027] (Boston: Harvard Business School Publishing, 1999).

5. It is a characteristic of all social systems, from small groups to large organizations, that decisions made early in a system's life have consequences over its entire life span. See P. David, "Understanding the Economics of QWERTY: The Necessity of History," in *Economic History and the Modern Historian,* ed. W. Parker (London: Blackwell, 1986), 30–59; W. R. Scott, "Unpacking Institutional Arguments," in *The New Institutionalism in Organizational Analysis,* ed. W. W. Powell and P. J. DiMaggio (Chicago: University of Chicago Press, 1991), 164–182.

6. Although I am aware of no systematic research on the process by which work teams revise and redefine their assigned tasks, the task redefinition process has been examined for individual performers (see J. R. Hackman, "Toward Understanding the Role of Tasks in Behavioral Research," *Acta Psychologica* 31 (1969): 97–128; and B. M. Staw and R. D. Boettger, "Task Revision: A Neglected Form of Work Performance," *Academy of Management Journal* 33 (1990): 534–559).

7. For details, see A. W. Woolley, "Effects of Intervention Content and Timing on Group Task Performance," *Journal of Applied Behavioral Science* 34 (1998): 30–49.

8. For details, see B. M. Staw, "Attribution of the 'Causes' of Performance: A General Alternative Interpretation of Cross-Sectional Research on Organizations," *Organizational Behavior and Human Performance* 13 (1975): 414–432.

9. Two findings are of special interest in the present context. Jehn (1995) found that task conflict could facilitate group performance for engaging tasks, but that it impaired group functioning for tasks that were highly routine. This finding further affirms the interdependence between team structure (here, the design of its task) and group interaction processes. Coaching interventions that help team members identify and address differences in their views about how the task ought to be performed can be helpful if the team task is motivationally well designed—but can backfire if the task is routine and repetitive [K. A. Jehn, "A Multimethod Examination of the Benefits and Detriments of Intragroup Conflict," *Administrative Science Quarterly* 40 (1995): 256–282]. Research by Jehn and Mannix (2001) highlights the role of timing in understanding and addressing conflict among members. Among other findings, these researchers observed that well-performing teams exhibited moderate levels of task conflict at the midpoint of the group interaction. And, as we have seen, the midpoint is exactly the time when teams are most open to coaching interventions intended to help members bring their task performance strategies into better alignment with task and situational demands. [K. A. Jehn and E. A. Mannix, "The Dynamic Nature of Conflict: A Longitudinal Study of Intragroup Conflict and Group Performance," *Academy of Management Journal* 44 (2001): 238–251].

10. For details, see E. V. Lehman and J. R. Hackman, "The Orpheus Chamber Orchestra: Case and Video," Boston: Kennedy School of Government, Harvard University (2001); H. Seifter and P. Economy, *Leadership Ensemble* (New York: Henry Holt, 2001); and J. Traub, "Passing the Baton: What C.E.O.s Could Learn from the Orpheus Chamber Orchestra," *The New Yorker* (Aug. 26/Sept. 2 1996): 100–105.

11. The idea of shared leadership is generally more attractive in theory than it is in practice. Not to have some single individual who is responsible for making sure things stay on track is to invite coordination problems ("Who *was* supposed to do that?") and unnecessary interpersonal conflict as those who are supposedly sharing leadership arrange themselves into a hierarchy. Ideas such as "Co-CEOs" and the "Office of the President" sound better than they actually work.

12. It also is possible, of course, for a coach to be *oppressively* present. If the coach takes over and handles personally all the problems he or she believes to be really serious, then members will be unlikely to ever develop their collective capabilities as a self-managing team.

Index

Index

Notes

Notes

Notes

Notes

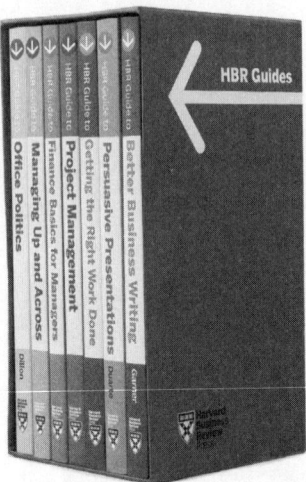

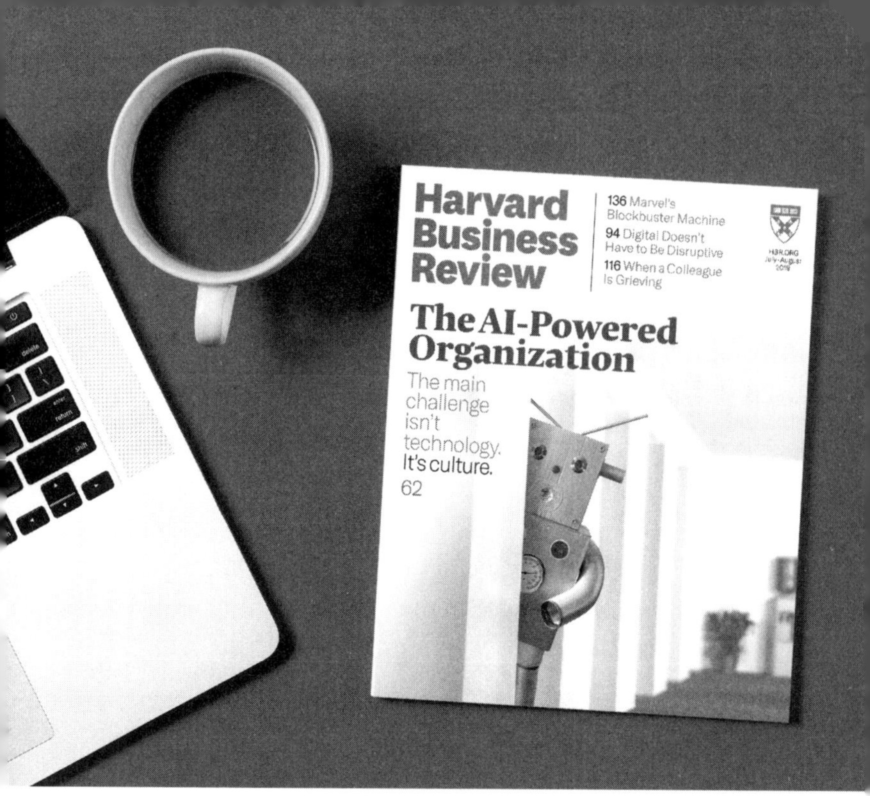
Harvard Business Review
136 Marvel's Blockbuster Machine
94 Digital Doesn't Have to Be Disruptive
116 When a Colleague Is Grieving
HBR.ORG
The AI-Powered Organization
The main challenge isn't technology. It's culture.
62

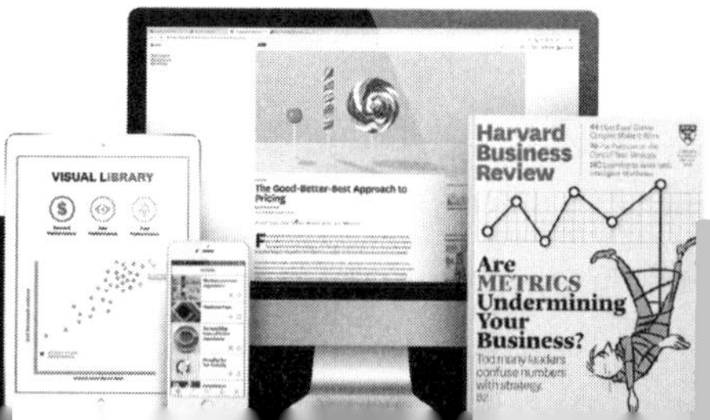
VISUAL LIBRARY
The Good-Better-Best Approach to Pricing
Harvard Business Review
Are METRICS Undermining Your Business?

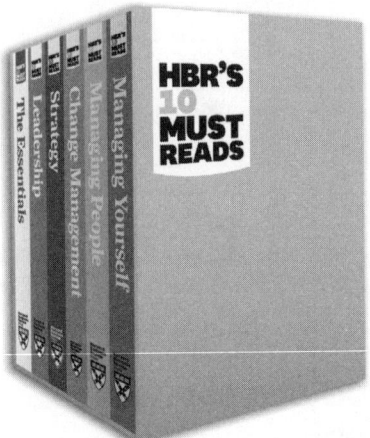

HBR Guide to **Delivering Effective Feedback**

Harvard Business Review Guides

Arm yourself with the advice you need to succeed on the job, from the most trusted brand in business. Packed with how-to essentials from leading experts, the HBR Guides provide smart answers to your most pressing work challenges.

The titles include:

HBR Guide to Better Business Writing

HBR Guide to Building Your Business Case

HBR Guide to Buying a Small Business

HBR Guide to Coaching Employees

HBR Guide to Delivering Effective Feedback

HBR Guide to Finance Basics for Managers

HBR Guide to Getting the Mentoring You Need

HBR Guide to Getting the Right Job

HBR Guide to Getting the Right Work Done

HBR Guide to Leading Teams

HBR Guide to Making Every Meeting Matter

HBR Guide to Managing Conflict at Work

HBR Guide to Managing Stress at Work

HBR Guide to Managing Up and Across

HBR Guide to Negotiating

HBR Guide to Networking

HBR Guide to Office Politics

HBR Guide to Persuasive Presentations

HBR Guide to Project Management

HBR Guide to **Delivering Effective Feedback**

HARVARD BUSINESS REVIEW PRESS

Boston, Massachusetts

Printed in the United States of America

10 9 8 7 6

Library of Congress Cataloging-in-Publication Data

Names: Harvard Business Review Press, issuing body.
Title: HBR guide to delivering effective feedback / Harvard Business Review Press.
Description: Boston, Massachusetts : Harvard Business Review Press, [2016]
Identifiers: LCCN 2015047167 | ISBN 9781633691643 (hardcover : alk. paper)
Subjects: LCSH: Employee retention. | Feedback (Psychology) | Employees—Rating of. | Personnel management.
Classification: LCC HF5549.5.R58 H424 2016 | DDC 658.3/14—dc23
LC record available at http://lccn.loc.gov/2015047167

The paper used in this publication meets the requirements of the American National Standard for Permanence of Paper for Publications and Documents in Libraries and Archives Z39.48–1992.

What You'll Learn

Are you worried about losing your star performer to greener pastures? Or struggling with a problem employee? Do you dread annual performance appraisals?

As a manager, you know it's important to give your employees the feedback they need to develop. But communicating it in a way that motivates them to improve can be a challenge. And the prospect of facing someone who may get emotional can seem overwhelming.

But whether you are discussing a formal performance assessment or addressing everyday behavior, you can transform these stressful encounters into productive conversations. Brimming with actionable advice on everything from delivering constructive comments to recognizing exceptional work, this guide will give you the tools and confidence you need to master giving effective feedback to your direct reports.

You'll learn how to:

- Incorporate ongoing feedback into your daily interactions with employees
- Transform annual appraisals into catalysts for growth

- Plan for a tense conversation with a combative recipient
- Provide a clear message that emphasizes improvement
- Identify the reasons behind performance issues—including your own role
- Motivate individuals by acknowledging accomplishments
- Coach your star to the next level
- Measure performance when results aren't easily quantified
- Establish goals that will help your people develop
- Communicate criticism effectively across global cultures
- Engage your team during feedback discussions

Contents

Section 1: ONGOING FEEDBACK

Section 1
Ongoing Feedback

Chapter 1

Giving Effective Feedback

If you're like most managers, the prospect of giving feedback to your employees can be nerve-racking. Perhaps you're worried about how your staff will react. Or maybe you're doubtful that your comments will make a difference in their work or behavior.

But feedback is a vital tool for ensuring that your employees are developing in your organization. A feedback discussion is an opportunity for you to share your observations with your employees about their job performance and elicit productive change. Without it, they will have no idea of how you see them. Avoid having a tough conversation with your underperformers early on, and their performance (and possibly your team's) plummets.

Adapted from *Giving Feedback* (product #348X), *Performance Appraisal* (product #12352), both from the Pocket Mentor series, and the 20-Minute Manager series books *Giving Effective Feedback* (product #13999) and *Performance Reviews* (product #15035)

Assume that your high performers know their value and will keep up the good work, and they may start "phoning it in" or leave your company altogether to advance their careers.

Feedback increases employees' self-awareness and fosters positive change throughout the organization. There are two main types: **Ongoing feedback** occurs on a regular or ad hoc basis; it can be delivered up (to your boss), down (to your employees), or across the organizational chart (to your peers). **Formal feedback**, typically shared during annual or semiannual performance reviews, tends to be between you and your direct report. This guide will prepare you to discuss both types with your employees.

Ongoing Feedback

Grounded in the goals you and your employees have set together at the beginning of the year, ongoing feedback provides opportunities for early intervention if someone is not hitting the mark. It also allows you to recognize and reinforce good work. Ongoing feedback includes on-the-spot conversations (for example, constructive comments about an employee's presentation delivery at a board meeting), the weekly check-in meetings you have with each member of your team to gauge progress on both little- and big-picture objectives, and career coaching sessions. Such frequent interactions not only help keep people on track but also make it easier for you to prepare your formal annual appraisal. By taking note of your observations and discussing your employees' progress throughout the year, you'll already know where your direct reports' strengths and weaknesses lie, and your employees will already be working on areas for improvement and development before the formal feedback session.

Formal Feedback

Formal feedback enables you to summarize all the evaluations and support you've provided throughout the year. Like ongoing feedback, these yearly assessments afford you the opportunity to identify what's going well with an employee's performance and to diagnose problems before they worsen. This discussion shouldn't contain any surprises: You'll have already talked about performance issues in your ongoing feedback sessions, as well as expectations that affect pay, merit increases, bonuses, and promotions. But the formal review also gives you the chance to plan for the future. It allows you and your direct reports to discuss where they might develop and collaborate on new goals for the upcoming year, so they can move forward in their job and career.

Think of both ongoing and formal feedback as part of a partnership with your employees, one that promotes trust and candid dialogue. For example, encourage them to pinpoint factors that support or impede their work; they can do this in the face-to-face discussion or in a written self-assessment in advance of the meeting. Perhaps solidifying relationships with team members through lunches or after-work drinks is helping them achieve important objectives. Or maybe difficulty controlling e-mail tone is alienating key IT project managers. Encourage them to also note achievements ("I closed two new deals worth $100,000 and established a weekly check-in with our new distributor") and identify resources they need for future development (such as training on a new sales-reporting system or a mentor to advise them in a new job function).

Given how widespread the fear of feedback is (on both sides of the exchange), you may think you can't possibly overcome your anxiety and have a meaningful conversation with your direct report. But you can—and the articles in this guide will help.

Chapter 2

Sometimes Negative Feedback Is Best

by Heidi Grant Halvorson

If I see one more article about how you should never be "critical" or "negative" when giving feedback to an employee or colleague, I think my head will explode. It's incredibly frustrating. This kind of advice is undoubtedly well meant, and it certainly *sounds* good. After all, you probably don't relish the thought of having to tell someone else what they are doing wrong—at minimum, it's a little embarrassing for both of you.

But avoiding negative feedback is both wrongheaded and dangerous. *Wrongheaded* because, when delivered the right way, at the right time, criticism is in fact highly motivating. *Dangerous* because without awareness of the

---

Adapted from content posted on hbr.org on January 28, 2013

mistakes they are making, no one can possibly improve. Staying "positive" when doling out feedback will only get you so far.

Hang on, you say. *Can't negative feedback be discouraging? Demotivating?*

That's perfectly true.

And don't people need encouragement to feel confident? Doesn't that help them stay motivated?

In many cases, yes.

Confusing, isn't it? Thankfully, brilliant research by Stacey Finkelstein from Columbia University and Ayelet Fishbach from the University of Chicago sheds light on the seemingly paradoxical nature of feedback by making it clear why, when, and for whom negative feedback is appropriate.

It's important to begin by understanding the function that positive and negative feedback serve. Praise (for instance, *Here's what you did really well . . .*) increases *commitment* to the work you do by enhancing both your experience and your confidence. A more critical assessment (for example, *Here's where you went wrong . . .*), on the other hand, is *informative*—it tells you where you need to spend your effort and offers insight into how you might improve.

Given these two different functions, positive and negative feedback should be more effective (and more motivating) for different people at different times. For instance, when you don't really know what you are doing, encouragement helps you to stay optimistic and feel more at ease with the challenges you are facing—something *novices* tend to need. But when you are an *expert* and you already more or less know what you are doing, it's constructive criticism that can help you do what it takes to get to the top of your game.

As Finkelstein and Fishbach show, novices and experts are indeed looking for, and motivated by, different kinds of information. In one of their studies, American students taking either beginner or advanced-level French classes were asked whether they would prefer an instructor who emphasized what they were doing right (focusing on their strengths) or what they were doing wrong (focusing on their mistakes and how to correct them). Beginners overwhelmingly preferred a cheerleading, strength-focused instructor. Advanced students, on the other hand, preferred a more critical instructor who would help them develop their weaker skills.

In a second study, the researchers looked at a very different behavior: engaging in environmentally friendly actions. Their "experts" were members of environmental organizations (for instance, Greenpeace), while their "novices" were nonmembers. Each participant in the study made a list of the actions they regularly took that helped the environment—things like recycling, avoiding bottled water, and taking shorter showers. They were offered feedback from an environmental consultant on the effectiveness of their actions, and were given a choice: Would you prefer to know more about the actions you take that *are* effective, or about the actions you take that are *not*? Experts were much more likely to choose the negative feedback—about ineffective actions—than novices.

Taken together, these studies show that people who are experienced in a given domain—people who already have developed some knowledge and skills—don't actually live in fear of negative feedback. If anything, they seek it out. Intuitively they realize that negative feedback offers the key to getting ahead, while positive feedback merely tells them what they already know.

But what about motivation? What kind of feedback makes you want to take action? When participants in the environmental study were *randomly* given either positive or negative feedback about their actions, and were then asked how much of their $25 study compensation they would like to donate to Greenpeace, the type of feedback they received had a dramatic effect on their motivation to give. When negative feedback was given, experts gave more on average to Greenpeace ($8.53) than novices ($1.24). But when positive feedback was given, novices ($8.31) gave far more than experts ($2.92).

I'm not suggesting that you never tell rookies about their mistakes, or that you never praise seasoned professionals for their outstanding work. And of course, negative feedback should always be accompanied by good advice and given with tact.

But I *am* suggesting that piling on praise is a more effective motivator for the rookie than the pro. And I'm saying, point blank, that you shouldn't worry so much when it comes to identifying mistakes with someone experienced. Negative feedback won't crush their confidence—it just might give them the information they need to take their performance to the next level.

Heidi Grant Halvorson, PhD, is associate director for the Motivation Science Center at the Columbia University Business School and author of *Nine Things Successful People Do Differently* and *No One Understands You and What to Do about It.*

Chapter 3
Giving Feedback That Sticks

by Ed Batista

"Can I give you some feedback?"

When you ask your employees this question, their heart rate and blood pressure are almost certain to increase, and they may experience other signs of stress as well. These are symptoms of a "threat response," also known as "fight-or-flight": a cascade of neurological and physiological events that impair the ability to process complex information and react thoughtfully. When people are in the grip of a threat response, they're less capable of absorbing and applying your observations.

You've probably noticed this dynamic in feedback conversations that didn't go as well as you'd hoped. Some

---

Adapted from the *HBR Guide to Coaching Employees* (product #13990), Harvard Business Review Press, 2015 people respond with explanations, defensiveness, or even hostility, while others minimize eye contact, cross their arms, hunch over, and generally look as if they'd rather be doing anything but talking to you. These fight-or-flight behaviors suggest that your comments probably won't have their desired impact.

How do you avoid triggering a threat response—and deliver feedback your people can digest and use? The guidelines that follow will help.

Cultivate the Relationship

We lay the foundations for effective feedback by building relationships with others over time. When people feel connected to us, even difficult conversations with them are less likely to trigger a threat response. Social psychologist John Gottman, a leading expert on building relationships, has found from his research that success in difficult conversations depends on what he calls "the quality of the friendship." Gottman cites several steps we can take to develop high-quality relationships:

- **Make the other person feel "known."** Making people aware that you see them as individuals—and not merely as employees—is a critical step in the process, but it need not be overly time-consuming. Several years ago, a coaching client of mine who ran a midsize company felt that he was too distant from his employees but didn't have the time to take someone to lunch every day. His efficient compromise was to view every interaction, no matter how fleeting, as an opportunity to get to know that person a little better. He made a habit of asking employees one question about their work or their personal lives each time he encountered them. "Whenever I can, I connect," he told me. Although at times this slowed his progress through the office, the result was worth it.

- **Respond to even small bids for attention.** We seek attention from those around us not only in obvious ways but also through countless subtle "bids." As Gottman writes in *The Relationship Cure,* "A bid can be a question, a gesture, a look, a touch—any single expression that says, 'I want to feel connected to you.' A response to a bid is just that—a positive or negative answer to somebody's request for emotional connection." But many of us miss bids from our employees. That's because we're less observant of social cues from people over whom we wield authority, according to research by Dacher Keltner of the University of California, Berkeley, and others. To connect more effectively with employees, take stock of how much you notice—or have missed previously—their efforts to gain your attention. And solicit feedback from peers, friends, and family members on your listening skills and how often you interrupt.

- **Regularly express appreciation.** As Gottman's research shows, the ratio of positive to negative interactions in a successful relationship is 5:1, even during periods of conflict. This ratio doesn't apply to a single conversation, and it doesn't mean that we're obligated to pay someone five compliments before we can offer critical feedback (in fact, doing so could confuse your message). But it does highlight the importance of providing positive feedback and expressing other forms of appreciation over time in order to strengthen the relationship. (See the sidebar "The Pitfalls of Positive Feedback.")

THE PITFALLS OF POSITIVE FEEDBACK

Praise is supposed to make your employees feel good and motivate them, but often it does just the opposite. Here are three common problems and ways to avoid them:

1. ***People don't trust the praise.*** Before delivering unpleasant feedback to your direct reports, do you say something nice to soften the blow? Many of us do—and thus unwittingly condition people to hear our positive feedback as a hollow preamble to the real message. Rather than feeling genuinely appreciated, they're waiting for the other shoe to drop. Though you've diminished your anxiety about bearing bad news, you haven't helped your direct reports receive it. You've actually undermined your ability to deliver any meaningful feedback, positive or negative.

   What to do: Instead of giving a spoonful of sugar before every dose of constructive criticism, lead off with your investment in the relationship and your reasons for having the conversation. For example: "It's important that we can be candid and direct with each other so we can work together effectively. I have some concerns for us to discuss, and I'm optimistic that we can resolve them."

2. ***People resent it.*** Managers also use positive feedback to overcome resistance to requests. This age-old tactic can work in the moment but carries a long-term cost. It creates a sense of obligation, a "social debt" the recipient feels compelled to repay by acceding to your wishes. But if you train people to always expect requests after your praise, they'll eventually feel manipulated and resentful—and less inclined to help you out.

   What to do: Motivate people over the long term by expanding your persuasive tool kit. As Jay Conger explains in his classic article "The Necessary Art of Persuasion" (HBR May–June 1998), you can gain lasting influence in four ways: establish credibility through expertise and work you've done in others' interests, frame goals around common ground and shared advantage, support your views with compelling data and examples, and connect emotionally with people so they'll be more receptive to your message.

(*continued*)

THE PITFALLS OF POSITIVE FEEDBACK

(*continued*)

3. ***We praise the wrong things.*** When aimed at the wrong targets, praise does more harm than good. As Stanford psychologist Carol Dweck notes in a January 2012 HBR IdeaCast interview, "The whole self-esteem movement taught us erroneously that praising intelligence, talent, and abilities would foster self-confidence and self-esteem, and everything great would follow. But we've found it backfires. People who are praised for talent now worry about doing the next thing, about taking on the hard task, and not looking talented, tarnishing that reputation for brilliance. So they'll stick to their comfort zones and get really defensive when they hit setbacks."

   What to do: Praise effort, not ability. Dweck suggests focusing on "the strategies, the doggedness and persistence, the grit and resilience" that people exhibit when facing challenges. And explain exactly what actions prompted your praise. If you're vague or generic, you'll fail to reinforce the desired behavior.

Set the Stage

Once you've laid the groundwork with your employee, prepare for a feedback discussion by considering logistics. It's easy to take our surroundings for granted, but they have a big impact on any interaction. Paying attention to details like these will help make your conversations more productive:

- **Timing.** Be deliberate about scheduling a feedback session, whether it is a shorter, informal conversation or a longer, in-depth discussion. Instead of simply fitting it into an available slot on your calendar, choose a time when you and the other person will both be at your best, such as at the beginning of the day, before you're preoccupied with other issues, or at the end of the day, when you can spend more time in reflection. Think about the activities you and your employee will be engaged in just before and just after you meet. If either of you are coming from (or heading to) a stressful experience, you'll be better off finding another time.

- **Duration.** We often put events on our calendars for a standard amount of time without considering what's really needed for each interaction. Think about how much time a given feedback conversation is likely to take if it goes well—and if it goes poorly. You don't want to get into a meaningful discussion with an employee and suddenly find that you're late for your next meeting. Also, consider what you'll do if the session goes worse (or better) than expected. How bad (or good) will it have to be for you to ignore the next event on your calendar in order to continue the conversation?

- **Physical location.** Meeting in your office will reinforce hierarchical roles, which can be useful when you need to establish some distance between yourself and the other person—but this will also induce stress and increase the odds of a threat response. A less formal setting—such as a conference room, a restaurant, or even outdoors—will put you on a more even footing and reduce the likelihood of a threat response. Choose a location that suits the needs of the conversation, ensures sufficient privacy, and minimizes interruptions and distractions.

- **Proximity.** When meeting with an employee in an office or a conference room, sitting across from each other over a desk or table creates physical distance, emphasizing your respective roles and reinforcing your authority. But you don't always want to do that. When you're trying to create a stronger connection with the other person or convey a greater sense of empathy, it's preferable to sit closer and on adjoining sides of the table or desk. Think about the optimal proximity between you and the other person at that moment. Perhaps even being seated is too formal, and you should go for a walk.

Focus on Facts, Not Assumptions

Next, concentrate on the message you want to convey. You're sure to elicit a threat response if you provide feedback the other person views as unfair or inaccurate. Your feedback should address their performance based on the goals and targets you set at the beginning of the year. But sometimes this assessment isn't black and white. How do you avoid a negative reaction, given how subjective perceptions of fairness and accuracy are?

David Bradford of the Stanford Graduate School of Business suggests "staying on our side of the net"—that is, focusing our feedback on our feelings about the behavior and avoiding references to the other person's motives. We're in safe territory on our side of the net; others may not like what we say when we describe how we feel, but they can't dispute its accuracy. However, when we make guesses about their motives, we cross over to their side of the net, and even minor inaccuracies can provoke a defensive reaction.

For example, when giving critical feedback to someone who's habitually late, it's tempting to say something like, "You don't value my time, and it's very disrespectful of you." But these are guesses about the other person's state of mind, not statements of fact. If we're even slightly off base, the employee will feel misunderstood and be less receptive to the feedback. A more effective way to make the same point is to say, "When you're late, I feel devalued and disrespected." It's a subtle distinction, but by focusing on the specific behavior and our internal response, we avoid making an inaccurate, disputable guess.

Because motives are often unclear, we constantly cross the net in an effort to make sense of others' behavior. While this is inevitable, it's good practice to notice when we're guessing someone's motives and get back on our side of the net before offering feedback. (For more on framing the feedback discussion, see the next chapter, "A Better Way to Deliver Bad News.")

Manage Emotions

Although excessive negative feelings inhibit learning and communication, emotions play a vital role in feedback. They convey emphasis and let others know what we value. Emotional experiences stick with people, last longer in their memories, and are easier to recall. And extensive neuroscience research in recent decades makes clear that emotions are essential to our reasoning process: Strong emotions can pull us off course, but in general emotions support better decision making.

So while you'll want to avoid triggering a threat response, don't remove all emotion from your discussion. That can diminish the impact of your feedback and lead to a cycle of ineffective conversations. Instead, aim for a balance: Express *just enough* emotion to engage the other person but not so much that you provoke a hostile or defensive reaction, shut down the conversation, or damage the relationship. (If you do anticipate a combative response, see chapter 15, "Delivering Criticism to a Defensive Employee.")

The right amount of emotion depends on the issue you're addressing and varies from one relationship to another—and even from one day to the next. The key question is how responsive the other person will be to your emotions. A coaching client of mine who'd recently launched a company had some critical feedback for his cofounder, but previous conversations didn't have the desired effect. For the feedback to stick, my client needed to become fairly heated and more vocally and physically expressive. This worked because the two of them had a long-standing friendship. The cofounder didn't respond defensively—rather, the intensity got his attention. In contrast, when this same client had some critical feedback for a subordinate, he reined in his emotions, modulated his expressiveness, and delivered the feedback in a matter-of-fact tone. The goal was to convey the importance of the issues without overwhelming the subordinate, and in this case, my client's authority was sufficient on its own.

Of course, we may not know how another person will respond to our emotions, and when we're in the grip of strong feelings, it's hard to calibrate how we express them in conversation. The solution is to practice. By having more feedback conversations, we learn not only how specific individuals respond to us but also how we express our emotions in helpful and unhelpful ways.

Rehearse and Repeat

With a little practice, these guidelines will help you improve your feedback skills. As with any skill you're trying to master, experiment in low-risk situations before jumping into a high-stakes feedback conversation. Here are a few ways to make feedback a habit and improve your skills:

- **Have feedback conversations more often.** Rather than saving up feedback for an employee on a wide range of topics during a performance review, offer smaller pieces of focused feedback on a regular basis. Even a two-minute debrief with an employee after a meeting or a presentation can be a useful learning opportunity for both of you. The sidebar, "When to Give Feedback," provides some recommendations for when feedback would be beneficial, as well as when it wouldn't.

- **Role-play difficult conversations.** With clients in my coaching practice and with my MBA students at Stanford, I've found that role-playing is a highly effective way to prepare to deliver challenging feedback. Conduct this exercise with a friendly colleague: Start by delivering your feedback while your colleague role-plays the recipient, which will allow you to try out different approaches. Then have your colleague give you the same feedback while you role-play the recipient. You'll learn from your colleague's approach, and you'll see the conversation from your employee's point of view. The preparation will help you refine your delivery and feel more relaxed in the actual conversation.

- **Ask for feedback yourself.** By asking employees to give you feedback on your effectiveness as a leader and manager, you'll benefit in three ways: You'll get valuable input; you'll understand what it's like to be on the receiving end; and your willingness to listen will make your own feedback mean more. If you sense that employees are reluctant to give you feedback, ask them to help you accomplish some specific goals, such as being more concise or interrupting less often. By acknowledging your own areas for improvement, you'll make it easier for them to speak up.

WHEN TO GIVE FEEDBACK

As you practice giving feedback more often, you'll learn when a behavior warrants immediate feedback. Until then, here are some suggestions as to when it is an opportune time to meet with your employee—and when you should avoid it.

Offering feedback can be most useful in the following instances:

- When good work, successful projects, and resourceful behavior deserve to be recognized
- When the likelihood of improving a person's skills is high, because the opportunity to use those skills again is imminent
- When the person is already expecting feedback, either because a feedback session was scheduled in advance or because she knows that you observed the behavior
- When a problem cannot be ignored, because the person's behavior is negatively affecting a colleague, the team, or the organization

In other cases, feedback can be detrimental to the situation. Avoid giving feedback in these circumstances:

- When you do not have all the information about a given incident

(*continued*)

WHEN TO GIVE FEEDBACK

(*continued*)

- When the only feedback you can offer concerns factors that the recipient cannot easily change or control
- When the person who needs the feedback appears to be highly emotional or especially vulnerable immediately after a difficult event
- When you do not have the time or the patience to deliver the feedback in a calm and thorough manner
- When the feedback is based on your personal preference, not a need for more effective behavior
- When you have not yet formulated a possible solution to help the feedback recipient move forward

Bear in mind that when you give positive feedback frequently, your negative feedback, when it is warranted, will seem more credible and less threatening. Offering input only when problems arise may cause people to see you as unappreciative or petty.

Adapted from *Giving Effective Feedback* (20-Minute Manager series) (product #13999), Harvard Business Review Press, 2014.

Ed Batista is an executive coach and an instructor at the Stanford Graduate School of Business. He writes regularly on issues related to coaching and professional development at www.edbatista.com, and he is currently writing a book on self-coaching for Harvard Business Review Press.

Chapter 4
A Better Way to Deliver Bad News

by Jean-François Manzoni

A summary of the full-length HBR article by Jean-François Manzoni, highlighting key ideas.

IDEA IN BRIEF

That dreaded moment has come: You're delivering critical feedback to an employee. Despite your best efforts, the conversation is a disaster: tempers flare, the employee gets defensive, your relationship grows strained.

What happened? Like most managers, you probably inadvertently sabotaged the meeting—preparing for it in

---

Reprinted from *Harvard Business Review*, September 2002 (product #R0209J)

a way that stifled honest discussion and prevented you from delivering feedback effectively.

In other words, you most likely engaged in restrictive framing—a *narrow, binary,* and *frozen* approach to feedback: You initiated the conversation without considering alternative explanations for the problem behavior, assumed a win-or-lose outcome, and rigidly maintained your assumptions during the conversation.

Delivering corrective feedback doesn't have to be so difficult—if you use a more open-minded, flexible approach that convinces employees the process is fair.

IDEA IN PRACTICE

Restrictive Framing

When preparing to give feedback, you may picture relevant events, decide which information to discuss, and define a solution—all *before* the conversation. This framing sets the stage for trouble.

> *Example:* Liam, a VP, hears complaints that Jeremy, a product manager, isn't delegating enough. Liam's framing—"Jeremy's too controlling"—is *narrow* (Liam excludes other possibilities; e.g., Jeremy wants to delegate but doesn't know how) and *binary* (he assumes Jeremy must delegate or his subordinates will leave and he'll burn out). During the conversation, Liam's framing is *frozen* (he neither hears nor addresses Jeremy's objections). Result? Neither Liam nor Jeremy learn from the meeting.

Two Biases

Why do we frame feedback narrowly—despite predictably poor results? Two biases color the feedback process. And the more stressed we are, the more powerful these biases become:

- **Fundamental attribution error.** We often attribute problems to subordinates' disposition ("Jeremy's too controlling") rather than their circumstances (e.g., perhaps Jeremy *is* delegating, but his subordinates have some other ax to grind). Too busy to identify all potential causes and solutions to a problem, we grab the first acceptable one.

- **False consensus effect.** We assume others see situations as we do, and fail to revise our framing during feedback sessions.

Reframing Feedback

To avoid the restrictive-feedback trap, watch for these biases. Consider alternative explanations for problems rather than leaping to conclusions.

> *Example:* Liam frames his concerns about Jeremy openly: "I've heard complaints that Jeremy isn't delegating—and some of his employees are feeling sufficiently frustrated that I'm afraid we'll start losing them. I'd like to find out if Jeremy knows about the complaints, and get his take."

This framing isn't *narrow* (Liam hasn't leapt to conclusions about the problem's causes) or *binary* (it avoids a win-or-lose outcome). And since Liam avoids a preconceived outcome, he has nothing on which to *freeze.* He initiates the conversation openly: "I don't know if you're aware of this—or if it's true—but I've heard that Frank and Joan are anxious to take on more responsibility. What do you think?"

Why Open Framing Works

Open framing shows you have good intentions, the feedback *development* process was fair (you collected all relevant information), and the *communication* process was fair (you listen to and respect employees).

When employees feel they're getting fair feedback, they accept it more willingly—and work to improve performance.

Giving feedback to your employees, particularly when their performances fall short of expectations, is one of the most critical roles you play as a manager. For most people, it's also one of the most dreaded. Such conversations can be very unpleasant—emotions can run high, tempers can flare. And so, fearing that an employee will become defensive and that the conversation will only strain the relationship, the boss all too often inadvertently sabotages the meeting by preparing for it in a way that stifles honest discussion. This is an unintentional—indeed, unconscious—habit that's a byproduct of stress and that makes it difficult to deliver corrective feedback effectively.

The good news is that these conversations don't have to be so hard. By changing the mind-set with which you develop and deliver negative feedback, you can greatly increase the odds that the process will be a success—that you will have productive conversations, that you won't damage relationships, and that your employees will make real improvements in performance. In the pages that follow, I'll describe what goes wrong during these meetings and why. I'll look in detail at how real-life conversations have unfolded and what the managers could have done differently to reach more satisfying outcomes. As a first step, let's look at the way bosses prepare feedback—that is, the way they frame issues in their own minds in advance of a discussion.

Framing Feedback

In an ideal world, a subordinate would accept corrective feedback with an open mind. He or she would ask a few clarifying questions, promise to work on the issues discussed, and show signs of improvement over time. But things don't always turn out this way.

Let's consider the following example. Liam, a vice president at a consumer products company, had heard some complaints about a product manager, Jeremy. (Names and other identifying information for the subjects mentioned in this article have been altered.) Jeremy consistently delivered high-quality work on time, but several of his subordinates had grumbled about his apparent unwillingness to delegate. They felt their contributions weren't valued and that they didn't have an opportunity to learn and grow. What's more, Liam worried that Jeremy's own career prospects would be limited if his focus on the day-to-day details of his subordinates' work kept him from taking on more strategic projects. As his boss,

Liam felt a responsibility to let Jeremy know about his concerns. Here's how the conversation unfolded:

> **Liam:** "I'd like to discuss your work with you. You're doing a great job, and we really value your contributions. But I think you do too much. You have some great people working for you; why not delegate a little more?"
>
> **Jeremy:** "I don't understand. I delegate when I think it's appropriate. But a lot of people in this company rely on quality work coming out of my department, so I need to stay involved."
>
> **Liam:** "Yes, and we all appreciate your attention to detail. But your job as a manager is to help your employees grow into new roles and take on more responsibility. Meanwhile, you're so focused on the details that you don't have time to think about the bigger picture, about the direction you're taking this product."
>
> **Jeremy:** "That's not true. I'm always thinking about the future."
>
> **Liam:** "I'm just saying, you'd have more time for strategic thinking if you weren't so mired in the day-to-day stuff."
>
> **Jeremy:** "Are you saying I'm not a strategic thinker?"
>
> **Liam:** "You're so busy dotting every *i* and crossing every *t* that I just don't know what kind of thinking you're capable of!"

This type of exchange is surprisingly common. Each side pushes his point of view more and more aggressively, and the conversation escalates until a relatively minor difference becomes much more dramatic. (For a visual representation of a deteriorating discussion, see the sidebar "Scripted Escalation.") Often, as Liam did in the preceding conversation, one person or the other unintentionally says something overly critical. Of course, it may not get to that point—one or both parties may choose to give in rather than fight. But either way, escalate or fold, the subordinate probably hasn't accepted the news the boss set out to deliver. Managers tend to attribute such nonacceptance to employees' pride or defensiveness. Indeed, it's not unusual for people to feel defensive about their work or, for that matter, to hold inflated views of their performance and capabilities. But more often than not, the boss is also to blame. Let's examine why.

Whenever we face a decision or situation, we frame it, consciously or not. At its simplest, a frame is the decision maker's image of a situation—that is, the way he or she pictures the circumstances and elements surrounding the decision. The frame defines the boundaries and dimensions of the decision or situation—for instance, which issues will be looked at, which components are in and which are out, how various bits of information will be weighed, how the problem might be solved or a successful outcome determined, and so on. Managers tend to frame difficult situations and decisions in a way that is *narrow* (alternatives aren't included or even considered) and *binary* (there are only two possible outcomes—win or lose). Then, during the feedback discussion, their framing remains *frozen*—unchanged, regardless of the direction the conversation takes.

In anticipation of the conversation with Jeremy, for example, Liam framed the problem in his mind as "Jeremy's too controlling." This is a narrow framing because it excludes many alternative explanations—for instance, "Jeremy would really like to hand off some responsibility but doesn't know how and is embarrassed to acknowledge that." Or "Jeremy is actually delegating as much as he can given his subordinates' current skill levels; they are frustrated but really cannot handle more than they do." Or maybe "Jeremy is delegating quite a lot, but Frank and Joan have some other ax to grind." Liam may be making matters worse without realizing it by sending Jeremy mixed signals: "Empower your subordinates, but make no mistakes." We don't know for sure; nor does Liam.

Operating from this narrow view, Liam also approached the discussion with a binary framing that leaves both parties with very little room to maneuver: "Jeremy must learn to delegate or we'll lose Frank and Joan—and meanwhile, he'll burn himself out." Last but not least, Liam's framing remained frozen throughout the exchange despite clear signals that Jeremy was not buying the feedback. At no point was Liam processing, let alone addressing, Jeremy's objections. It's no surprise that the meeting ended badly.

The Dangers of Easing In

After they've had a few bad experiences delivering narrowly framed feedback, managers tend to fall back on the

SCRIPTED ESCALATION

Take a look at how quickly a minor point of difference during a feedback discussion can turn into a major disagreement. Jerry starts the conversation by noting that he'd done a good job on his project. Beth, his boss, is not in violent disagreement with his assessment and acknowledges that "it wasn't bad." Jerry could reaffirm his opening bid but instead tries to pull Beth's view closer to his own by overstating his initial point. Beth disagrees with Jerry's inflated statement, and instead of reiterating her first comment, she yields to the temptation to pull Jerry closer to her point of view. Both present stronger and stronger positions, trying to convince the other, and a minor difference quickly becomes a major point of contention.

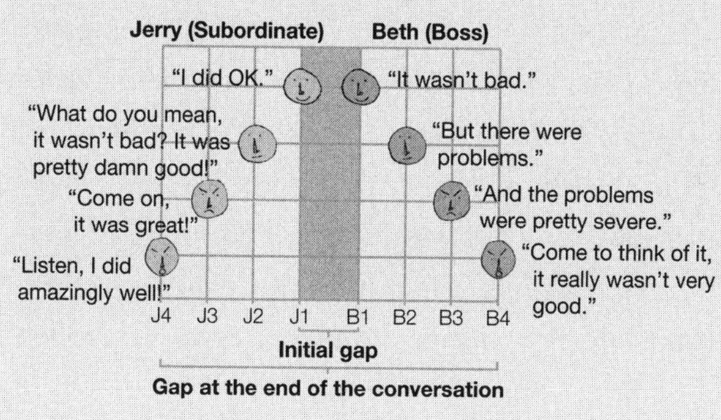
Jerry (Subordinate)
Beth (Boss)
"I did OK."
"It wasn't bad."
"What do you mean, it wasn't bad? It was pretty damn good!"
"But there were problems."
"Come on, it was great!"
"And the problems were pretty severe."
"Listen, I did amazingly well!"
"Come to think of it, it really wasn't very good."
J4
J3
J2
J1
B1
B2
B3
B4
Initial gap
Gap at the end of the conversation

conventional wisdom that it's better to soften bad news with some good.

They try to avoid uncomfortable confrontations by using an indirect approach: They make up their minds about an issue and then try to help their employees reach the same conclusions by asking a carefully designed set of questions.

At first glance, this type of "easing in" seems more open and fair than the forthright approach that Liam took, since the manager is involving the subordinate in a conversation, however scripted. But like the forthright approach, easing in reflects a narrow and binary framing that typically remains frozen throughout the process. Indeed, there would be no need to ease in if the manager were approaching the conversation with a truly open mind. And easing in carries an additional risk: The employee may not give you the answers you're looking for.

For example, Alex, an executive at a pharmaceuticals company, had some difficult news to communicate to one of his subordinates, Erin. She was a middle manager at the company and did an excellent job handling her department but was not contributing satisfactorily to a companywide task force chaired by Alex. Erin was remarkably silent during the meetings, which led Alex to conclude that she was too busy to participate fully and had little to offer the group. Alex's solution? Take her off the task force so she could focus on her primary responsibilities. But because he suspected Erin would be hurt or insulted if he suggested she step down, Alex hoped to prompt her to resign from the committee by asking her a series of questions that would make her see she was too busy to continue. Let's look at what happened.

Alex: "Do you sometimes feel as though you're wasting your time in the task force meetings?"

Erin: "No, I learn a lot from the meetings—and from watching the way you run them."

Alex: "But do you find that your mind is on your daily job when you're at committee meetings?"

Erin: "Not really. I hope I haven't given you the impression that I'm not fully committed. I think this is important work, and I'm excited to be a part of it, and I think I have some good ideas to offer."

Alex: "What if you could participate more informally? You could take yourself off the team as a permanent member, but you could continue to receive the agenda and minutes and contribute when your particular area of expertise is required."

Erin: "It sounds like you want me off the committee. Why? I don't think the committee work has undermined my commitment to my real work. I'm making my numbers. Plus, it's a learning opportunity."

Alex: "No, no, I just want to make sure it's something you really want to do."

Erin: "It is."

As you can see, Erin didn't play along. Alex was not ready for a confrontation, so he folded—and lost. He didn't get Erin off the committee, nor did he communicate his view that her committee work was subpar, so he has no way to help her improve her performance. What's more, he introduced a source of stress into their relationship: Erin is likely to have been unsettled by the interaction, as Alex implied some level of dissatisfaction with her performance without telling her what it is.

As in our previous example, Alex's framing of the issue was narrow: "Erin doesn't talk at the meetings, probably because she's overloaded, so the committee is a waste of her time." His framing was also binary; the interaction could be a success only if Erin agreed to get off the committee without losing her motivation for her regular work. And this framing remained frozen because Alex was concentrating on asking the "right" questions and couldn't process anything but the "right" answers.

Meanwhile, Erin may actually benefit from being on the committee, even if she doesn't say much. She learns a lot, and it gives her visibility. And if she can find a way to contribute more, the committee may well benefit from her membership. But by framing the issue the way he did, Alex excluded other possible solutions, any of which may have been more productive for all concerned: Maybe Erin would talk more in the meetings if Alex probed the reasons for her silence and helped her find a way to contribute what may be very valuable insights. And if overwork is indeed an issue, perhaps there are duties Erin might give up to gain more time and energy.

Easing in is a gamble. You might get lucky, but you have only half the cards. The subordinate may not give you the answers you're looking for, as we saw with Erin, either because she genuinely doesn't agree or because she sees that the game is rigged and refuses to play along. Or the subordinate may decide to stop resisting and pretend to go along but still fail to believe the feedback. And there's another risk, regardless of how the conversation ends: The employee may forever lose confidence in his or her boss. Erin may always wonder what Alex has up his sleeve, having caught him being disingenuous once.

Indeed, that's what happened to Mark, a marketing director at a large consulting firm. His boss, Rene, had called him into a meeting to discuss his role, and Mark left the meeting having relinquished control of his pet project, developing and implementing the company's first advertising campaign. Rene had asked him a series of seemingly innocuous questions, such as "Do you find endless meetings with different agencies to be a waste of your time?" and "Do you feel like your time would be better spent developing new communications materials?" Mark eventually accepted what was clearly the "right" conclusion from his boss's perspective—to surrender the project—even though he wanted to continue. Worse, he didn't know why Rene wanted him off the project, so as a learning opportunity, it was wasted. His relationship with his boss is now tainted; Mark can no longer take Rene's comments at face value.

Why Is It So Hard?

It's very clear from a distance what went wrong for Liam and Alex. Most managers today are well trained and well meaning; why can't they see what they're doing wrong? The tendency to frame threatening situations in narrow terms can be traced to the combination of several phenomena.

First, research shows that when analyzing others' behavior, most people tend to overestimate the effect of a person's stable characteristics—the individual's disposition and capabilities—and underestimate the impact of the specific conditions under which that person is operating. So, for instance, a manager will attribute a subordinate's performance problems to his or her disposition rather than to circumstances in the workplace, leading to a rather simplistic interpretation. This phenomenon is known as the *fundamental attribution error.*

Second, people are more prone to committing the fundamental attribution error when they operate under demanding conditions. We can better distinguish the impact of situational forces when we have time and energy to spare than when we face multiple demands on our attention. Unfortunately, managers tend to be busy. Facing huge workloads and tight deadlines, they have limited time and attention to engage in exhaustive analyses of all the potential causes of the situations they observe or of the many possible solutions to a given problem. So they settle on the first acceptable explanation. "Jeremy's too controlling" explained all the symptoms, so Liam did not go further.

Research can also give us some insight into why bosses tend to frame things in a binary way. In particular, Harvard Business School professor Chris Argyris's work over nearly five decades has established that under stressful circumstances, people behave in predictable ways. They design their behaviors, often unconsciously, to gain control of a situation and to win—which means, unfortunately, that the other side usually has to lose. That's binary framing.

And why is it so hard for bosses to revise their restrictive framing midstream? For several powerful reasons. First, bosses don't set out to frame situations in restrictive ways; they do so unconsciously, most of the time, and it's hard to question a constraint that we don't know we're imposing on ourselves. Second, humans tend to assume that other reasonable people will see the situation as they see it. That's called the *false consensus effect.* Our framing of an issue represents our view of reality, the facts as we see them. We are reasonable and competent people; why would others see the situation differently?

Bosses can get past these hurdles by recognizing them and becoming more conscious and careful when framing decisions. But then they have to beat another cause of frozen framing: a busy processor. For instance, Liam becomes increasingly stressed as Jeremy continues to push back against his version of the facts, and both devote so much energy to trying to control their growing irritation that they have few resources left to listen, process, and respond constructively.

Reframing Feedback

Let's be clear: I'm not suggesting that bosses systematically misdiagnose the causes of their subordinates' performance problems. Liam's and Alex's early diagnoses may well have been right. And even if their feedback discussions had been more productive, their subordinates may not have been able to sufficiently improve their performances to meet their bosses' expectations. But Jeremy and Erin will almost certainly fail to improve if they don't understand and accept the feedback. Restrictive framing not only makes feedback conversations more stressful than they need to be, it also increases the likelihood that subordinates won't believe what their bosses say. Indeed, subordinates are more likely to accept and act on their bosses' feedback if they feel it is developed and communicated fairly. (See the sidebar "Making Feedback More Acceptable.")

So, for instance, imagine how differently Liam and Jeremy's conversation might have gone had the manager framed his concerns more broadly: "I've heard complaints that Jeremy isn't delegating—and some of his employees are feeling sufficiently frustrated that I'm afraid we'll start losing them. I'd like to find out if Jeremy knows about the complaints and get his take on the situation."

This frame isn't narrow. Liam hasn't reached a conclusion about why Jeremy doesn't delegate or whether, indeed, Jeremy is refusing to delegate at all. Nor is the frame binary. Liam hasn't fixed on a win-or-lose outcome. And because Liam hasn't entered the conversation with a preconceived outcome in mind, he has nothing on which to freeze. Now, Liam can open the conversation in a much more open way. He might say, for instance, "Jeremy, I don't know if you're aware of this—or if it's true or not—but I've heard that Frank and Joan are anxious to take on a bit more responsibility. What do you think?" This can lead to a discussion of Frank's and Joan's capabilities, as well as Jeremy's own role and aspirations, without locking Jeremy and Liam into a test of wills.

As for Alex, instead of approaching the meeting with the goal of getting Erin off the committee with minimal

MAKING FEEDBACK MORE ACCEPTABLE

Research shows that people tend to be more willing to accept feedback when they have the feeling that:

- The person offering the feedback is reliable and has good intentions toward them.
- The feedback development process is fair—that is, the person giving the feedback collects all relevant information; allows the subordinate to clarify and explain matters; considers the subordinate's opinions; and applies consistent standards when delivering criticism.
- The feedback communication process is fair—that is, the person offering the feedback pays careful attention to the subordinate's ideas; shows respect for the subordinate; and supports the subordinate despite their disagreements.

This short list makes clear the negative impact of approaching a feedback discussion with restrictive framing: Narrow framing tells the employee that the feedback wasn't developed fairly. And a boss constrained by a binary and frozen frame comes across as biased, close-minded, and unsupportive—ensuring that the subordinate will feel as though the feedback hasn't been communicated fairly.

damage, he could have framed the interaction more broadly: "I have a great subordinate who doesn't say much on the committee. Let's sit down and talk about her work, the committee, her career plans, and how committee membership fits in with those plans." Because this framing doesn't fix on a win-or-lose outcome, Alex would have felt less need to control the discussion and hence less compelled to ease in.

While most managers can easily see what they're doing wrong when shown how they've developed and presented their feedback, restrictive framing remains a surprisingly persistent problem, even for seasoned managers who excel at other aspects of leadership. But giving feedback doesn't have to be stressful for you, demoralizing for your employees, or damaging to your professional relationships.

Offering more effective critiques requires that you learn to recognize the biases that color the development of feedback. It requires that you take the time to consider alternative explanations for behaviors you've witnessed rather than leaping to hasty conclusions that only serve to paint you and your subordinates into a corner. And it requires that you take into account the circumstances an employee is working under rather than attributing weak performance to the person's disposition.

In short, it requires a broad and flexible approach, one that will convince your employees that the process is fair and that you're ready for an honest conversation.

Jean-François Manzoni is Professor of Management Practice and the Shell Chaired Professor in Human Resources and Organisational Development at INSEAD (Singapore campus). He is a coauthor, along with Jean-Louis Barsoux, of *The Set-Up-to-Fail Syndrome: How Good Managers Cause Great People to Fail* (Harvard Business School Press, 2002).

Chapter 5
The Set-Up-to-Fail Syndrome

by Jean-François Manzoni and Jean-Louis Barsoux

A summary of the full-length HBR article by Jean-François Manzoni and Jean-Louis Barsoux, highlighting key ideas.

IDEA IN BRIEF

That darned employee! His performance keeps deteriorating—*despite* your close monitoring. What's going on?

Brace yourself: You may be at fault, by unknowingly triggering the set-up-to-fail syndrome. Employees whom you (perhaps falsely) view as weak performers live *down* to your expectations. Here's how:

Reprinted from *Harvard Business Review*, March–April 1998 (product #R98209)

1. You start with a positive relationship.
2. Something—a missed deadline, a lost client—makes you question the employee's performance. You begin micromanaging him.
3. Suspecting your reduced confidence, the employee starts doubting *himself*. He stops giving his best, responds mechanically to your controls, and avoids decisions.
4. You view his new behavior as additional proof of mediocrity—and tighten the screws further.

Why not just fire him? Because you're likely to repeat the pattern with others. Better to *reverse* the dynamic instead. Unwinding the set-up-to-fail spiral actually pays big dividends: Your company gets the best from your employees—and from you.

IDEA IN PRACTICE

How Set-Up-to-Fail Starts

A manager categorizes employees as "in" or "out," based on:

- Early *perceptions* of employees' motivation, initiative, creativity, strategic perspectives
- Previous bosses' impressions
- An early mishap
- Boss-subordinate incompatibility

The manager then notices *only* evidence supporting his categorization, while dismissing contradictory evidence. The boss also treats the groups differently:

- "In" groups get autonomy, feedback, and expressions of confidence.
- Members of "out" groups get controlling, formal management emphasizing rules.

The Costs of Set-Up-to-Fail

This syndrome hurts everyone:

- *Employees* stop volunteering ideas and information and asking for help, avoid contact with bosses, or grow defensive.
- The *organization* fails to get the most from employees.
- The *boss* loses energy to attend to other activities. His reputation suffers as other employees deem him unfair.
- *Team spirit* wilts as targeted performers are alienated and strong performers are overburdened.

How to Reverse Set-Up-to-Fail

If the syndrome hasn't started, prevent it:

- Establish expectations with new employees early. Loosen the reins as they master their jobs.
- Regularly challenge your own assumptions. Ask: "What are the *facts* regarding this employee's performance?" "Is he really that bad?"

- Convey openness, letting employees challenge your opinions. They'll feel comfortable discussing their performance and relationship with you.

If the syndrome has already erupted, discuss the dynamic with the employee:

1. Choose a neutral, nonthreatening location; use affirming language ("Let's discuss our relationship and roles"); and acknowledge your part in the tension.

2. Agree on the employee's weaknesses and strengths. Support assessments with facts, not feelings.

3. Unearth causes of the weaknesses. Do you disagree on priorities? Does your employee lack specific knowledge or skills? Ask: "How is my behavior making things worse for you?"

4. Identify ways to boost performance. Training? New experiences? Decide the quantity and type of supervision you'll provide. Affirm your desire to improve matters.

5. Agree to communicate more openly: "Next time I do something that communicates low expectations, can you let me know immediately?"

When an employee fails—or even just performs poorly—managers typically do not blame themselves. The employee doesn't understand the work, a manager might contend. Or the employee isn't driven to succeed, can't set priorities, or won't take direction. Whatever the reason, the problem is assumed to be the employee's fault—and the employee's responsibility.

But is it? Sometimes, of course, the answer is yes. Some employees are not up to their assigned tasks and never will be, for lack of knowledge, skill, or simple desire. But sometimes—and we would venture to say often—an employee's poor performance can be blamed largely on his boss.

Perhaps "blamed" is too strong a word, but it is directionally correct. In fact, our research strongly suggests that bosses—albeit accidentally and usually with the best intentions—are often complicit in an employee's lack of success. (See the sidebar "About the Research.") How? By creating and reinforcing a dynamic that essentially sets up perceived underperformers to fail. If the Pygmalion effect describes the dynamic in which an individual lives up to great expectations, the set-up-to-fail syndrome explains the opposite. It describes a dynamic in which employees perceived to be mediocre or weak performers live down to the low expectations their managers have for them. The result is that they often end up leaving the organization—either of their own volition or not.

The syndrome usually begins surreptitiously. The initial impetus can be performance related, such as when an employee loses a client, undershoots a target, or misses a deadline. Often, however, the trigger is less specific. An employee is transferred into a division with a lukewarm recommendation from a previous boss. Or perhaps the

ABOUT THE RESEARCH

This article is based on two studies designed to understand better the causal relationship between leadership style and subordinate performance—in other words, to explore how bosses and subordinates mutually influence each other's behavior. The first study, which comprised surveys, interviews, and observations, involved 50 boss-subordinate pairs in four manufacturing operations in *Fortune* 100 companies. The second study, involving an informal survey of about 850 senior managers attending INSEAD executive-development programs over the last three years, was done to test and refine the findings generated by the first study. The executives in the second study represented a wide diversity of nationalities, industries, and personal backgrounds.

boss and the employee don't really get along on a personal basis—several studies have indeed shown that compatibility between boss and subordinate, based on similarity of attitudes, values, or social characteristics, can have a significant impact on a boss's impressions. In any case, the syndrome is set in motion when the boss begins to worry that the employee's performance is not up to par.

The boss then takes what seems like the obvious action in light of the subordinate's perceived shortcomings: he increases the time and attention he focuses on the employee. He requires the employee to get approval before making decisions, asks to see more paperwork documenting those decisions, or watches the employee at meetings more closely and critiques his comments more intensely.

These actions are intended to boost performance and prevent the subordinate from making errors. Unfortunately, however, subordinates often interpret the heightened supervision as a lack of trust and confidence. In time, because of low expectations, they come to doubt their own thinking and ability, and they lose the motivation to make autonomous decisions or to take any action at all. The boss, they figure, will just question everything they do—or do it himself anyway.

Ironically, the boss sees the subordinate's withdrawal as proof that the subordinate is indeed a poor performer. The subordinate, after all, isn't contributing his ideas or energy to the organization. So what does the boss do? He increases his pressure and supervision again—watching, questioning, and double-checking everything the subordinate does. Eventually, the subordinate gives up on his dreams of making a meaningful contribution. Boss and subordinate typically settle into a routine that is not really satisfactory but, aside from periodic clashes, is otherwise bearable for them. In the worst-case scenario, the boss's intense intervention and scrutiny end up paralyzing the employee into inaction and consume so much of the boss's time that the employee quits or is fired.

Perhaps the most daunting aspect of the set-up-to-fail syndrome is that it is self-fulfilling and self-reinforcing—it is the quintessential vicious circle. The process is self-fulfilling because the boss's actions contribute to the very behavior that is expected from weak performers. It is self-reinforcing because the boss's low expectations, in being fulfilled by his subordinates, trigger more of the same behavior on his part, which in turn triggers more of the same behavior on the part of subordinates. And on and on, unintentionally, the relationship spirals downward.

A case in point is the story of Steve, a manufacturing supervisor for a *Fortune* 100 company. When we first met Steve, he came across as highly motivated, energetic, and enterprising. He was on top of his operation, monitoring problems and addressing them quickly. His boss expressed great confidence in him and gave him an excellent performance rating. Because of his high performance, Steve was chosen to lead a new production line considered essential to the plant's future.

In his new job, Steve reported to Jeff, who had just been promoted to a senior management position at the plant. In the first few weeks of the relationship, Jeff periodically asked Steve to write up short analyses of significant quality-control rejections. Although Jeff didn't really explain this to Steve at the time, his request had two major objectives: to generate information that would help both of them learn the new production process, and to help Steve develop the habit of systematically performing root cause analysis of quality-related problems. Also, being new on the job himself, Jeff wanted to show his own boss that he was on top of the operation.

Unaware of Jeff's motives, Steve balked. Why, he wondered, should he submit reports on information he understood and monitored himself? Partly due to lack of time, partly in response to what he considered interference from his boss, Steve invested little energy in the reports. Their tardiness and below-average quality annoyed Jeff, who began to suspect that Steve was not a particularly proactive manager. When he asked for the reports again, he was more forceful. For Steve, this merely confirmed that Jeff did not trust him. He withdrew more and more from interaction with him, meeting his demands with increased passive resistance. Before long, Jeff became convinced that Steve was not effective enough and couldn't handle his job without help. He started to supervise Steve's every move—to Steve's predictable dismay. One year after excitedly taking on the new production line, Steve was so dispirited he was thinking of quitting.

How can managers break the set-up-to-fail syndrome? Before answering that question, let's take a closer look at the dynamics that set the syndrome in motion and keep it going.

Deconstructing the Syndrome

We said earlier that the set-up-to-fail syndrome usually starts surreptitiously—that is, it is a dynamic that usually creeps up on the boss and the subordinate until suddenly both of them realize that the relationship has gone sour. But underlying the syndrome are several assumptions about weaker performers that bosses appear to accept uniformly. Our research shows, in fact, that executives typically compare weaker performers with stronger performers using the following descriptors:

- Less motivated, less energetic, and less likely to go beyond the call of duty

- More passive when it comes to taking charge of problems or projects
- Less aggressive about anticipating problems
- Less innovative and less likely to suggest ideas
- More parochial in their vision and strategic perspective
- More prone to hoard information and assert their authority, making them poor bosses to their own subordinates

It is not surprising that on the basis of these assumptions, bosses tend to treat weaker and stronger performers very differently. Indeed, numerous studies have shown that up to 90% of all managers treat some subordinates as though they were members of an in-group, while they consign others to membership in an out-group. Members of the in-group are considered the trusted collaborators and therefore receive more autonomy, feedback, and expressions of confidence from their bosses. The boss-subordinate relationship for this group is one of mutual trust and reciprocal influence. Members of the out-group, on the other hand, are regarded more as hired hands and are managed in a more formal, less personal way, with more emphasis on rules, policies, and authority. (For more on how bosses treat weaker and stronger performers differently, see the chart "In with the In Crowd, Out with the Out.")

Why do managers categorize subordinates into either in-groups or out-groups? For the same reason that we

In with the in crowd, out with the out

Boss's behavior toward perceived stronger performers	Boss's behavior toward perceived weaker performers
Discusses project objectives, with a limited focus on project implementation. Gives subordinate the freedom to choose his own approach to solving problems or reaching goals.	Is directive when discussing tasks and goals. Focuses on what needs get done as well as how it should get done.
Treats unfavorable variances, mistakes, or incorrect judgments as learning opportunities.	Pays close attention to unfavorable variances, mistakes, or incorrect judgments.
Makes himself available, as in "Let me know if I can help." Initiates casual and personal conversations.	Makes himself available to subordinate on a need-to-see basis. Bases conversations primarily on work-related topics.
Is open to subordinate's suggestions and discusses them with interest.	Pays little interest to subordinate's comments or suggestions about how and why work is done.
Gives subordinate interesting and challenging stretch assignments. Often allows subordinate to choose his own assignments.	Reluctantly gives subordinate anything but routine assignments. When handing out assignments, gives subordinate little choice. Monitors subordinate heavily.
Solicits opinions from subordinate on organizational strategy, execution, policy, and procedures.	Rarely asks subordinate for input about organizational or work-related matters.
Often defers to subordinate's opinion in disagreements.	Usually imposes own views in disagreements.
Praises subordinate for work well done.	Emphasizes what the subordinate is doing poorly.

tend to typecast our family, friends, and acquaintances: it makes life easier. Labeling is something we all do, because it allows us to function more efficiently. It saves time by providing rough-and-ready guides for interpreting events and interacting with others. Managers, for instance, use categorical thinking to figure out quickly who should get what tasks. That's the good news.

The downside of categorical thinking is that in organizations it leads to premature closure. Having made up his mind about a subordinate's limited ability and poor motivation, a manager is likely to notice supporting evidence while selectively dismissing contrary evidence. (For example, a manager might interpret a terrific new product idea from an out-group subordinate as a lucky onetime event.) Unfortunately for some subordinates, several studies show that bosses tend to make decisions about in-groups and out-groups even as early as five days into their relationships with employees.

Are bosses aware of this sorting process and of their different approaches to "in" and "out" employees? Definitely. In fact, the bosses we have studied, regardless of nationality, company, or personal background, were usually quite conscious of behaving in a more controlling way with perceived weaker performers. Some of them preferred to label this approach as "supportive and helpful." Many of them also acknowledged that—although they tried not to—they tended to become impatient with weaker performers more easily than with stronger performers. By and large, however, managers are aware of the controlling nature of their behavior toward perceived weaker performers. For them, this behavior is not an error in implementation; it is intentional.

What bosses typically do *not* realize is that their tight controls end up hurting subordinates' performance by undermining their motivation in two ways: first, by depriving subordinates of autonomy on the job and, second, by making them feel undervalued. Tight controls are an indication that the boss assumes the subordinate can't perform well without strict guidelines. When the subordinate senses these low expectations, it can undermine his self-confidence. This is particularly problematic because numerous studies confirm that people perform up or down to the levels their bosses expect from them or, indeed, to the levels they expect from themselves.[1]

Of course, executives often tell us, "Oh, but I'm very careful about this issue of expectations. I exert more control over my underperformers, but I make sure that it does not come across as a lack of trust or confidence in their ability." We believe what these executives tell us. That is, we believe that they do try hard to disguise their intentions. When we talk to their subordinates, however, we find that these efforts are for the most part futile. In fact, our research shows that most employees can—and do—"read their boss's mind." In particular, they know full well whether they fit into their boss's in-group or out-group. All they have to do is compare how they are treated with how their more highly regarded colleagues are treated.

Just as the boss's assumptions about weaker performers and the right way to manage them explains his complicity in the set-up-to-fail syndrome, the subordinate's assumptions about what the boss is thinking explain his own complicity. The reason? When people perceive disapproval, criticism, or simply a lack of confidence and appreciation, they tend to shut down—a behavioral phenomenon that manifests itself in several ways.

Primarily, shutting down means disconnecting intellectually and emotionally. Subordinates simply stop giving their best. They grow tired of being overruled, and they lose the will to fight for their ideas. As one subordinate put it, "My boss tells me how to execute every detail. Rather than arguing with him, I've ended up wanting to say, 'Come on, just tell me what you want me to do, and I'll go do it.' You become a robot." Another perceived weak performer explained, "When my boss tells me to do something, I just do it mechanically."

Shutting down also involves disengaging personally—essentially reducing contact with the boss. Partly, this disengagement is motivated by the nature of previous exchanges that have tended to be negative in tone. As one subordinate admitted, "I used to initiate much more contact with my boss until the only thing I received was negative feedback; then I started shying away."

Besides the risk of a negative reaction, perceived weaker performers are concerned with not tainting their images further. Following the often-heard aphorism "Better to keep quiet and look like a fool than to open your mouth and prove it," they avoid asking for help for fear of further exposing their limitations. They also tend to volunteer less information—a simple "heads up" from a perceived underperformer can cause the boss to overreact and jump into action when none is required. As one perceived weak performer recalled, "I just wanted to let my boss know about a small matter, only slightly out of the routine, but as soon as I mentioned it, he was all over my case. I should have kept my mouth closed. I do now."

Finally, shutting down can mean becoming defensive. Many perceived underperformers start devoting more energy to self-justification. Anticipating that they will be personally blamed for failures, they seek to find excuses early. They end up spending a lot of time looking in the rearview mirror and less time looking at the road ahead. In some cases—as in the case of Steve, the manufacturing supervisor described earlier—this defensiveness can lead to noncompliance or even systematic opposition to the boss's views. While this idea of a weak subordinate going head to head with his boss may seem irrational, it may reflect what Albert Camus once observed: "When deprived of choice, the only freedom left is the freedom to say no."

The Syndrome Is Costly

There are two obvious costs of the set-up-to-fail syndrome: the emotional cost paid by the subordinate and the organizational cost associated with the company's failure to get the best out of an employee. Yet there are other costs to consider, some of them indirect and long term.

The boss pays for the syndrome in several ways. First, uneasy relationships with perceived low performers often sap the boss's emotional and physical energy. It can be quite a strain to keep up a facade of courtesy and pretend everything is fine when both parties know it is not. In addition, the energy devoted to trying to fix these relationships or improve the subordinate's performance through increased supervision prevents the boss from attending to other activities—which often frustrates or even angers the boss.

Furthermore, the syndrome can take its toll on the boss's reputation, as other employees in the organization observe his behavior toward weaker performers. If the boss's treatment of a subordinate is deemed unfair or unsupportive, observers will be quick to draw their lessons. One outstanding performer commented on his boss's controlling and hypercritical behavior toward another subordinate: "It made us all feel like we're expendable." As organizations increasingly espouse the virtues of learning and empowerment, managers must cultivate their reputations as coaches, as well as get results.

The set-up-to-fail syndrome also has serious consequences for any team. A lack of faith in perceived weaker performers can tempt bosses to overload those whom they consider superior performers; bosses want to entrust critical assignments to those who can be counted on to deliver reliably and quickly and to those who will go beyond the call of duty because of their strong sense of shared fate. As one boss half-jokingly said, "Rule number one: if you want something done, give it to someone who's busy—there's a reason why that person is busy."

An increased workload may help perceived superior performers learn to manage their time better, especially as they start to delegate to their own subordinates more effectively. In many cases, however, these performers simply absorb the greater load and higher stress which, over time, takes a personal toll and decreases the attention they can devote to other dimensions of their jobs, particularly those yielding longer-term benefits. In the worst-case scenario, overburdening strong performers can lead to burnout.

Team spirit can also suffer from the progressive alienation of one or more perceived low performers. Great teams share a sense of enthusiasm and commitment to a common mission. Even when members of the boss's out-group try to keep their pain to themselves, other team members feel the strain. One manager recalled the discomfort experienced by the whole team as they watched their boss grill one of their peers every week. As he explained, "A team is like a functioning organism. If one member is suffering, the whole team feels that pain."

In addition, alienated subordinates often do not keep their suffering to themselves. In the corridors or over lunch, they seek out sympathetic ears to vent their recriminations and complaints, not only wasting their own time but also pulling their colleagues away from productive work. Instead of focusing on the team's mission, valuable time and energy is diverted to the discussion of internal politics and dynamics.

Finally, the set-up-to-fail syndrome has consequences for the subordinates of the perceived weak performers. Consider the weakest kid in the school yard who gets pummeled by a bully. The abused child often goes home and pummels his smaller, weaker siblings. So it is with the people who are in the boss's out-group. When they have to manage their own employees, they frequently replicate the behavior that their bosses show to them. They fail to recognize good results or, more often, supervise their employees excessively.

Breaking Out Is Hard to Do

The set-up-to-fail syndrome is not irreversible. Subordinates can break out of it, but we have found that to be rare. The subordinate must consistently deliver such superior results that the boss is forced to change the employee from out-group to in-group status—a phenomenon made difficult by the context in which these subordinates operate. It is hard for subordinates to impress their bosses when they must work on unchallenging tasks, with no autonomy and limited resources; it is also hard for them to persist and maintain high standards when they receive little encouragement from their bosses.

Furthermore, even if the subordinate achieves better results, it may take some time for them to register with the boss because of his selective observation and recall. Indeed, research shows that bosses tend to attribute the good things that happen to weaker performers to external factors rather than to their efforts and ability (while the opposite is true for perceived high performers: successes tend to be seen as theirs, and failures tend to be attributed to external uncontrollable factors). The subordinate will therefore need to achieve a string of successes in order to have the boss even contemplate revising the initial categorization. Clearly, it takes a special kind of courage, self-confidence, competence, and persistence on the part of the subordinate to break out of the syndrome.

Instead, what often happens is that members of the out-group set excessively ambitious goals for themselves to impress the boss quickly and powerfully—promising to hit a deadline three weeks early, for instance, or attacking six projects at the same time, or simply attempting to handle a large problem without help. Sadly, such superhuman efforts are usually just that. And in setting goals so high that they are bound to fail, the subordinates also come across as having had very poor judgment in the first place.

The set-up-to-fail syndrome is not restricted to incompetent bosses. We have seen it happen to people perceived within their organizations to be excellent bosses. Their mismanagement of some subordinates need not prevent them from achieving success, particularly when they and the perceived superior performers achieve high levels of individual performance. However, those bosses could be even more successful to the team, the organization, and themselves if they could break the syndrome.

Getting It Right

As a general rule, the first step in solving a problem is recognizing that one exists. This observation is especially relevant to the set-up-to-fail syndrome because of its self-fulfilling and self-reinforcing nature. Interrupting the syndrome requires that a manager understand the dynamic and, particularly, that he accept the possibility that his own behavior may be contributing to a subordinate's underperformance. The next step toward cracking the syndrome, however, is more difficult: it requires a carefully planned and structured intervention that takes the form of one (or several) candid conversations meant to bring to the surface and untangle the unhealthy dynamics that define the boss and the subordinate's relationship. The goal of such an intervention is to bring about a sustainable increase in the subordinate's performance while progressively reducing the boss's involvement.

It would be difficult—and indeed, detrimental—to provide a detailed script of what this kind of conversation should sound like. A boss who rigidly plans for this conversation with a subordinate will not be able to engage in real dialogue with him, because real dialogue requires flexibility. As a guiding framework, however, we offer five components that characterize effective interventions. Although they are not strictly sequential steps, all five components should be part of these interventions.

First, the boss must create the right context for the discussion

He must, for instance, select a time and place to conduct the meeting so that it presents as little threat as possible to the subordinate. A neutral location may be more conducive to open dialogue than an office where previous and perhaps unpleasant conversations have taken place. The boss must also use affirming language when asking the subordinate to meet with him. The session should not be billed as "feedback," because such terms may suggest baggage from the past. "Feedback" could also be taken to mean that the conversation will be one-directional, a monologue delivered by the boss to the subordinate. Instead, the intervention should be described as a meeting to discuss the performance of the subordinate, the role of the boss, and the relationship between the subordinate and the boss. The boss might even acknowledge that he feels tension in the relationship and wants to use the conversation as a way to decrease it.

Finally, in setting the context, the boss should tell the perceived weaker performer that he would genuinely like the interaction to be an open dialogue. In particular, he should acknowledge that he may be partially responsible for the situation and that his own behavior toward the subordinate is fair game for discussion.

Second, the boss and the subordinate must use the intervention process to come to an agreement on the symptoms of the problem

Few employees are ineffective in all aspects of their performance. And few—if any—employees desire to do poorly on the job. Therefore, it is critical that the intervention result in a mutual understanding of the specific job responsibilities in which the subordinate is weak. In the case of Steve and Jeff, for instance, an exhaustive sorting of the evidence might have led to an agreement that Steve's underperformance was not universal but instead largely confined to the quality of the reports he submitted (or failed to submit). In another situation, it might be agreed that a purchasing manager was weak when it came to finding offshore suppliers and to voicing his ideas in meetings. Or a new investment professional and his boss might come to agree that his performance was subpar when it came to timing the sales and purchase of stocks, but they might also agree that his financial analysis of stocks was quite strong. The idea here is that before working to improve performance or reduce tension in a relationship, an agreement must be reached about what areas of performance contribute to the contentiousness.

We used the word "evidence" earlier in discussing the case of Steve and Jeff. That is because a boss needs to back up his performance assessments with facts and data—that is, if the intervention is to be useful. They cannot be based on feelings—as in Jeff telling Steve, "I just have the feeling you're not putting enough energy into the reports." Instead, Jeff needs to describe what a good report should look like and the ways in which Steve's reports fall short. Likewise, the subordinate must be allowed—indeed, encouraged—to defend his performance, compare it with colleagues' work, and point out areas in which he is strong. After all, just because it is the boss's opinion does not make it a fact.

Third, the boss and the subordinate should arrive at a common understanding of what might be causing the weak performance in certain areas

Once the areas of weak performance have been identified, it is time to unearth the reasons for those weaknesses. Does the subordinate have limited skills in organizing work, managing his time, or working with others? Is he lacking knowledge or capabilities? Do the boss and the subordinate agree on their priorities? Maybe the subordinate has been paying less attention to a particular dimension of his work because he does not realize its importance to the boss. Does the subordinate become less effective under pressure? Does he have lower standards for performance than the boss does?

It is also critical in the intervention that the boss bring up the subject of his own behavior toward the subordinate and how this affects the subordinate's performance. The boss might even try to describe the dynamics of the set-up-to-fail syndrome. "Does my behavior toward you make things worse for you?" he might ask, or, "What am

I doing that is leading you to feel that I am putting too much pressure on you?"

This component of the discussion also needs to make explicit the assumptions that the boss and the subordinate have thus far been making about each other's intentions. Many misunderstandings start with untested assumptions. For example, Jeff might have said, "When you did not supply me with the reports I asked for, I came to the conclusion that you were not very proactive." That would have allowed Steve to bring his buried assumptions into the open. "No," he might have answered, "I just reacted negatively because you asked for the reports in writing, which I took as a sign of excessive control."

Fourth, the boss and the subordinate should arrive at an agreement about their performance objectives and on their desire to have the relationship move forward

In medicine, a course of treatment follows the diagnosis of an illness. Things are a bit more complex when repairing organizational dysfunction, since modifying behavior and developing complex skills can be more difficult than taking a few pills. Still, the principle that applies to medicine also applies to business: boss and subordinate must use the intervention to plot a course of treatment regarding the root problems they have jointly identified.

The contract between boss and subordinate should identify the ways they can improve on their skills, knowledge, experience, or personal relationship. It should also include an explicit discussion of how much and what type of future supervision the boss will have. No boss, of course, should suddenly abdicate his involvement; it is legitimate for bosses to monitor subordinates' work, particularly when a subordinate has shown limited abilities in one or more facets of his job. From the subordinate's point of view, however, such involvement by the boss is more likely to be accepted, and possibly even welcomed, if the goal is to help the subordinate develop and improve over time. Most subordinates can accept temporary involvement that is meant to decrease as their performance improves. The problem is intense monitoring that never seems to go away.

Fifth, the boss and the subordinate should agree to communicate more openly in the future

The boss could say, "Next time I do something that communicates low expectations, can you let me know immediately?" And the subordinate might say, or be encouraged to say, "Next time I do something that aggravates you or that you do not understand, can you also let me know right away?" Those simple requests can open the door to a more honest relationship almost instantly.

No Easy Answer

Our research suggests that interventions of this type do not take place very often. Face-to-face discussions about a subordinate's performance tend to come high on the list of workplace situations people would rather avoid, because such conversations have the potential to make both parties feel threatened or embarrassed. Subordinates are reluctant to trigger the discussion because they are worried about coming across as thin-skinned or whiny. Bosses tend to avoid initiating these talks because they are concerned about the way the subordinate might react; the discussion could force the boss to make explicit his lack of confidence in the subordinate, in turn putting the subordinate on the defensive and making the situation worse.[2]

As a result, bosses who observe the dynamics of the set-up-to-fail syndrome being played out may be tempted to avoid an explicit discussion. Instead, they will proceed tacitly by trying to encourage their perceived weak performers. That approach has the short-term benefit of bypassing the discomfort of an open discussion, but it has three major disadvantages.

First, a one-sided approach on the part of the boss is less likely to lead to lasting improvement because it focuses on only one symptom of the problem—the boss's behavior. It does not address the subordinate's role in the underperformance.

Second, even if the boss's encouragement were successful in improving the employee's performance, a unilateral approach would limit what both he and the subordinate could otherwise learn from a more up-front handling of the problem. The subordinate, in particular, would not have the benefit of observing and learning from how his boss handled the difficulties in their relationship—problems the subordinate may come across someday with the people he manages.

Finally, bosses trying to modify their behavior in a unilateral way often end up going overboard; they suddenly give the subordinate more autonomy and responsibility than he can handle productively. Predictably, the subordinate fails to deliver to the boss's satisfaction, which leaves the boss even more frustrated and convinced that the subordinate cannot function without intense supervision.

We are not saying that intervention is always the best course of action. Sometimes, intervention is not possible or desirable. There may be, for instance, overwhelming evidence that the subordinate is not capable of doing his job. He was a hiring or promotion mistake, which is best handled by removing him from the position. In other cases, the relationship between the boss and the subordinate is too far gone—too much damage has occurred to repair it. And finally, sometimes bosses are too busy and under too much pressure to invest the kind of resources that intervention involves.

Yet often the biggest obstacle to effective intervention is the boss's mind-set. When a boss believes that a subordinate is a weak performer and, on top of everything else, that person also aggravates him, he is not going to be able to cover up his feelings with words; his underlying convictions will come out in the meeting. That is why preparation for the intervention is crucial. Before even deciding to have a meeting, the boss must separate emotion from reality. Was the situation always as bad as it is now? Is the subordinate really as bad as I think he is? What is the hard evidence I have for that belief? Could there be other factors, aside from performance, that have led me to label this subordinate a weak performer? Aren't there a few things that he does well? He must have displayed above-average qualifications when we decided to hire him. Did these qualifications evaporate all of a sudden?

The boss might even want to mentally play out part of the conversation beforehand. If I say this to the subordinate, what might he answer? Yes, sure, he would say that it was not his fault and that the customer was unreasonable. Those excuses—are they really without merit? Could he have a point? Could it be that, under other circumstances, I might have looked more favorably upon them? And if I still believe I'm right, how can I help the subordinate see things more clearly?

The boss must also mentally prepare himself to be open to the subordinate's views, even if the subordinate challenges him about any evidence regarding his poor performance. It will be easier for the boss to be open if, when preparing for the meeting, he has already challenged his own preconceptions.

Even when well prepared, bosses typically experience some degree of discomfort during intervention meetings. That is not all bad. The subordinate will probably be somewhat uncomfortable as well, and it is reassuring for him to see that his boss is a human being, too.

Calculating Costs and Benefits

As we've said, an intervention is not always advisable. But when it is, it results in a range of outcomes that are uniformly better than the alternative—that is, continued underperformance and tension. After all, bosses who systematically choose either to ignore their subordinates' underperformance or to opt for the more expedient solution of simply removing perceived weak performers are condemned to keep repeating the same mistakes. Finding and training replacements for perceived weak performers is a costly and recurrent expense. So is monitoring and controlling the deteriorating performance of a disenchanted subordinate. Getting results *in spite of* one's staff is not a sustainable solution. In other words, it makes sense to think of the intervention as an investment, not an expense—with the payback likely to be high.

How high that payback will be and what form it will take obviously depend on the outcome of the intervention, which will itself depend not only on the quality of the intervention but also on several key contextual factors: How long has that relationship been spiraling downward? Does the subordinate have the intellectual and emotional resources to make the effort that will be required? Does the boss have enough time and energy to do his part?

We have observed outcomes that can be clustered into three categories. In the best-case scenario, the intervention leads to a mixture of coaching, training, job redesign, and a clearing of the air; as a result, the relationship and the subordinate's performance improve, and the costs associated with the syndrome go away or, at least, decrease measurably.

In the second-best scenario, the subordinate's performance improves only marginally, but because the subordinate received an honest and open hearing from the boss, the relationship between the two becomes more productive. Boss and subordinate develop a better understanding of those job dimensions the subordinate can do well and those he struggles with. This improved understanding leads the boss and the subordinate to explore *together* how they can develop a better fit between the job and the subordinate's strengths and weaknesses. That improved fit can be achieved by significantly modifying the subordinate's existing job or by transferring the subordinate to another job within the company. It may even result in the subordinate's choosing to leave the company.

While that outcome is not as successful as the first one, it is still productive; a more honest relationship eases the strain on both the boss and the subordinate, and in turn on the subordinate's subordinates. If the subordinate moves to a new job within the organization that better suits him, he will likely become a stronger performer. His relocation may also open up a spot in his old job for a better performer. The key point is that, having been treated fairly, the subordinate is much more likely to accept the outcome of the process. Indeed, recent studies show that the perceived fairness of a process has a major impact on employees' reactions to its outcomes. (See "Fair Process: Managing in the Knowledge Economy," by W. Chan Kim and Renée Mauborgne, HBR July–August 1997.)

Such fairness is a benefit even in the cases where, despite the boss's best efforts, neither the subordinate's performance nor his relationship with his boss improves significantly. Sometimes this happens: the subordinate truly lacks the ability to meet the job requirements, he has no interest in making the effort to improve, and the boss and the subordinate have both professional and personal differences that are irreconcilable. In those cases, however, the intervention still yields indirect benefits because, even if termination follows, other employees within the company are less likely to feel expendable or betrayed when they see that the subordinate received fair treatment.

Prevention Is the Best Medicine

The set-up-to-fail syndrome is not an organizational fait accompli. It can be unwound. The first step is for the boss to become aware of its existence and acknowledge the possibility that he might be part of the problem. The second step requires that the boss initiate a clear, focused intervention. Such an intervention demands an open exchange between the boss and the subordinate based on the evidence of poor performance, its underlying causes, and their joint responsibilities—culminating in a joint decision on how to work toward eliminating the syndrome itself.

Reversing the syndrome requires managers to challenge their own assumptions. It also demands that they have the courage to look within themselves for causes and solutions before placing the burden of responsibility where it does not fully belong. Prevention of the syndrome, however, is clearly the best option.

In our current research, we examine prevention directly. Our results are still preliminary, but it appears that bosses who manage to consistently avoid the set-up-to-fail syndrome have several traits in common. They do not, interestingly, behave the same way with all subordinates. They are more involved with some subordinates than others—they even monitor some subordinates more than others. However, they do so without disempowering and discouraging subordinates.

How? One answer is that those managers begin by being actively involved with all their employees, gradually reducing their involvement based on improved performance. Early guidance is not threatening to subordinates, because it is not triggered by performance shortcomings; it is systematic and meant to help set the conditions for future success. Frequent contact in the beginning of the relationship gives the boss ample opportunity to communicate with subordinates about priorities, performance measures, time allocation, and even expectations of the type and frequency of communication. That kind of clarity goes a long way toward preventing the dynamic of the set-up-to-fail syndrome, which is so often fueled by unstated expectations and a lack of clarity about priorities.

For example, in the case of Steve and Jeff, Jeff could have made explicit very early on that he wanted Steve to set up a system that would analyze the root causes of quality control rejections systematically. He could have explained the benefits of establishing such a system during the initial stages of setting up the new production line, and he might have expressed his intention to be actively involved in the system's design and early operation. His future involvement might then have decreased in such a way that could have been jointly agreed on at that stage.

Another way managers appear to avoid the set-up-to-fail syndrome is by challenging their own assumptions and attitudes about employees on an ongoing basis. They work hard at resisting the temptation to categorize employees in simplistic ways. They also monitor their own reasoning. For example, when feeling frustrated about a subordinate's performance, they ask themselves, "What are the facts?" They examine whether they are expecting things from the employee that have not been articulated, and they try to be objective about how often and to what extent the employee has really failed. In other words, these bosses delve into their own assumptions and behavior before they initiate a full-blown intervention.

Finally, managers avoid the set-up-to-fail syndrome by creating an environment in which employees feel comfortable discussing their performance and their relationships with the boss. Such an environment is a function of several factors: the boss's openness, his comfort level with having his own opinions challenged, even his sense of humor. The net result is that the boss and the subordinate feel free to communicate frequently and to ask one another questions about their respective behaviors before problems mushroom or ossify.

The methods used to head off the set-up-to-fail syndrome do, admittedly, involve a great deal of emotional investment from bosses—just as interventions do. We believe, however, that this higher emotional involvement is the key to getting subordinates to work to their full potential. As with most things in life, you can only expect to get a lot back if you put a lot in. As a senior executive once said to us, "The respect you give is the respect you get." We concur. If you want—indeed, need—the people in your organization to devote their whole hearts and minds to their work, then you must, too.

NOTES

1. The influence of expectations on performance has been observed in numerous experiments by Dov Eden and his colleagues. See Dov Eden, "Leadership and Expectations: Pygmalion Effects and Other Self-fulfilling Prophecies in Organizations," *Leadership Quarterly*, Winter 1992, vol. 3, no. 4, pp. 271–305.

2. Chris Argyris has written extensively on how and why people tend to behave unproductively in situations they see as threatening or embarrassing. See, for example, *Knowledge for Action: A Guide to Overcoming Barriers to Organizational Change* (San Francisco: Jossey-Bass, 1993).

Jean-François Manzoni is Professor of Management Practice and the Shell Chaired Professor in Human Resources and Organisational Development at INSEAD (Singapore campus). He is a coauthor, along with Jean-Louis Barsoux, of *The Set-Up-to-Fail Syndrome: How Good Managers Cause Great People to Fail* (Harvard Business School Press, 2002).

Jean-Louis Barsoux is a research fellow at INSEAD, where he specializes in organizational behavior. He is the coauthor with Susan C. Schneider of *Managing Across Cultures*.

Chapter 6
How to Give Feedback That Helps People Grow

by Monique Valcour

Over the years, I've asked hundreds of students in my executive education courses what skills they believe are essential for leaders. "The ability to give tough feedback" comes up frequently. But what exactly is "tough feedback"? The phrase connotes bad news, like when you have to tell a team member that they've screwed up on something important. "Tough" also signifies the way we think we need to *act* when giving negative feedback: firm, resolute, and unyielding.

But the word also points to the discomfort some of us experience when giving negative feedback, and to the

---

Adapted from content posted on hbr.org on August 11, 2015

challenge of doing so in a way that motivates change instead of making the other person feel defensive. Managers fall into a number of common traps. We might be angry at an employee and use the conversation to blow off steam rather than to coach. Or we may delay giving a needed critique because we anticipate that the employee will become argumentative and refuse to accept responsibility. We might try surrounding negative feedback with praise, like disguising a bitter-tasting pill in a spoonful of honey. But this approach is misguided, because we don't want the constructive message to slip by unnoticed. Instead, it's essential to create conditions in which the receiver can take in feedback, reflect on it, and learn from it.

To get a feel for what this looks like in practice, I juxtapose two feedback conversations that occurred following a workplace conflict. MJ Paulitz, a physical therapist in the Pacific Northwest, was treating a hospital patient one day when a fellow staff member paged her. Following procedure, she excused herself and stepped out of the treatment room to respond to the page. The colleague who sent it didn't answer her phone when MJ called, nor had she left a message describing the situation that warranted the page. This happened two more times during the same treatment session. The third time she left her patient to respond to the page, MJ lost her cool and left an angry voicemail message. Upset upon hearing the message, her colleague reported it to their supervisor as abusive.

MJ's first feedback session took place in her supervisor's office. She recalls, "When I went into his office, he had already decided that I was the person at fault, he had all the information he needed, and he wasn't interested in hearing my side of the story. He did not address the three times she pulled me out of patient care. He did not acknowledge that that might have been the fuse that set me off." Her supervisor referred MJ to the human resources department for corrective action. She left seething with a sense of injustice.

MJ describes the subsequent feedback conversation with human resources as transformative. "The woman in HR could see that I had a lot of just-under-the-surface feelings, and she acknowledged them. She said, 'I can only imagine what you're feeling right now. Here you are in my office, in corrective action. If it were me, I might be feeling angry, frustrated, embarrassed . . . Are any of these true for you?' That made a huge difference."

With trust established, MJ was ready to take responsibility for her behavior and commit to changing it. Next, the HR person said, "Now let's talk about how you reacted to those feelings in the moment." She created a space that opened up a genuine dialogue.

The subsequent conversation created powerful learning that has stuck with MJ to this day. "Oftentimes when we're feeling a strong emotion, we go down what the HR person called a 'cowpath,' because it's well worn, very narrow, and always leads to the same place. Let's say you're angry. What do you do? You blow up. It's okay that you feel those things; it's just not okay to blow up. She asked me to think about what I could do to get on a different path."

"The feedback from the HR person helped me learn to find the space between what I'm feeling and the next thing that slides out of my mouth. She gave me the opportunity to grow internally. What made it work was establishing a safe space, trust, and rapport, and then getting down to 'you need to change'—rather than starting with 'you need to change,' which is what my supervisor did. I did need to change; that was the whole point of the corrective action. But she couldn't start there, because I would have become defensive, shut down, and not taken responsibility. I still to this day think that my coworker should have been reprimanded. But I also own my part in it. I see that I went down that cowpath, and I know that I won't do it a second time."

WHAT PEOPLE ARE SAYING ON HBR.ORG

In any feedback session, **the intention of the giver determines how the message is delivered**—the approach, manner, tone, and words used. If there is trust between the giver and the receiver, and consideration and openness, with the giver's sole focus on the receiver's growth, the feedback may still be tough and but also positive.

—Posted by Cindy

When feedback is "tough," it means the giver is not yet ready to deliver it. It is "tough" because it involves behaviors and feelings the giver cannot understand and control.

Feedback should never be "tough" because it needs to be factual and constructive, based on the process that has led someone to act in a certain way. Asking open-ended questions is a sure way to make it more effective.

—Posted by Michel

One of my all-time workplace pet peeves is bosses who hear a complaint, jump to conclusions, and refuse to even entertain another side of the story.

It's one thing for a manager to have his or her own opinions on what's good performance and what's not and to refuse to debate them. And I can understand a boss taking action, under some circumstances, if multiple customers or coworkers have complained—without necessarily endorsing the substance of their complaints. But **it's flat-out wrong to conclude that someone had in fact done something wrong, just on someone else's say-so.**

—Posted by Jeffrey

The difference in the two sessions MJ described boils down to *coaching*, which deepens self-awareness and catalyzes growth, versus *reprimanding*, which sparks self-protection and avoidance of responsibility. To summarize, powerful, high-impact feedback conversations share the following elements:

- **An intention to help the employee grow.** The point of the discussion is not to simply tell them what they did wrong. The feedback should increase, not drain, the employee's motivation and resources for change. When preparing for a feedback conversation, reflect on what you hope to achieve and on what impact you'd like to have on them, perhaps by doing a short meditation just before the meeting.

- **Openness on the part of the feedback giver.** If you start off feeling uncomfortable and self-protective, your employee will match that energy, and you'll each leave the conversation frustrated with the other person. By remaining open to their point of view, you'll create a high-quality connection that facilitates change.

- **A collaborative mind-set.** Invite the employee into the problem-solving process. Ask questions such as: What ideas do you have? What are you taking away from this conversation? What steps will you take, by when, and how will I know?

Giving developmental feedback that sparks growth is a critical challenge to master, because it can make the difference between an employee who contributes powerfully and positively to the organization and one who feels diminished by the organization and contributes far less. A single conversation can switch an employee on—or shut them down. A true leader sees the raw material for brilliance in every employee and creates the conditions to let it shine, even when the challenge is tough.

Monique Valcour is an executive coach, keynote speaker, and faculty affiliate of ThirdPath Institute. Her coaching, research, and consulting help companies and individuals craft high-performance, meaningful jobs, careers, workplaces, and lives.

Chapter 7

Recognize Good Work in a Meaningful Way

by Christina Bielaszka-DuVernay

Recognition gets great lip service. Ask three managers if they consider it important to recognize the value their teams deliver, and chances are very good that you'll get three positive responses.

But probe a little bit, and you'll discover that the walk is leagues away from thc talk.

Manager 1 makes recognition a priority—when he has time to think about it. For Manager 2, recognizing her team means having sandwiches brought in once or twice a quarter for a conference room lunch. Manager 3 is fairly consistent in doling out praise and rewards—

Adapted from content posted on hbr.org on February 29, 2008

too consistent, in fact. The boilerplate language in his thank-you notes and the inevitable $25 gift certificate to a family-style chain restaurant have become an in-joke among his team members, generating eye rolls more than anything else.

For recognition to strengthen your team's performance, say Adrian Gostick and Chester Elton, authors of *The Carrot Principle: How the Best Managers Use Recognition to Engage Their People, Retain Talent, and Accelerate Performance*, it can't be haphazard, generalized to the group, or generic. So what characterizes recognition that actually works?

Deliver Recognition Frequently

Once or twice a quarter won't cut it, as Manager 2 has not yet realized. Research conducted by The Gallup Organization (Washington, DC) found that employees' engagement and motivation are strongly affected by how often they receive recognition for their work.

Three years after the US branch of accounting firm KPMG introduced its recognition program, Encore, the number of employees who agreed with the statement "Taking everything into account, this is a great place to work" rose 20%. In analyzing the program's effectiveness unit by unit, Sylvia Brandes, KPMG's US director of compensation, discovered that units offering their employees less frequent recognition suffered notably higher turnover than units in which recognition was a frequent occurrence.

So how frequently should you let your team members know you recognize and appreciate their efforts? At least once every other week.

We're not talking gold watches here, point out Gostick and Elton. "Managers who earn the most trust and dedication from their people do so with many simple but powerful actions," they write in *The Carrot Principle.* These can include sending them a sincere thank-you note, copying them on a memo praising their performance, or taking a moment in the weekly staff meeting to highlight their actions. To keep yourself on track, Gostick and Elton recommend maintaining a simple recognition scorecard for every employee that notes the date praise was given and for what.

Tie the Message to Organizational Values

If you want recognition to reinforce the sort of thinking and behavior you'd like to see more of, connect your praise explicitly to the values of the organization, whether that's the team, the unit, or the company as a whole. If you're making a connection to company values, keep in mind that they may be less than clear to the employee.

"So many companies' mission or values statements go wrong," says Gostick. "Either it's a laundry list or it lauds such feel-good but generic values as hard work, service, innovation, and so on. The result is that no one really knows what values or behaviors really matter."

And even when the values are clearly defined and kept to a manageable number, employees are notorious for ignoring or tuning out the various means by which a company seeks to communicate them. When's the last time you read the entire e-mail update from your CEO? Or resisted the urge to fiddle with your mobile device during a speech about the company's values?

But the moment of personal recognition is one time that the employee is not tuning out. And if this occasion is before a group of her peers, chances are that many of them—particularly if they like and respect her—are also paying attention. So when you single out an individual for praise, whether it's in a one-on-one meeting or before a group, link that person's behavior with the organization's values. For example:

- "Thank you, Peter, for going the extra mile to keep our client happy. As you know, our team is trying to improve its service-renewal scores and this client is one of our biggest accounts, so your actions really mean a lot."
- "That was a great idea to invite the special projects team to our staff meeting. We talk a lot around here about the value of cross-unit collaboration, but we don't always do such a good job of actually doing it! I really appreciate your efforts in this area—thanks."

Match the Award to the Achievement

Remember Manager 3 and his $25 restaurant gift certificates? His recognition efforts met with derision because he dispensed them without regard to the degree of the employee's effort or achievement. Someone who came in over the weekend to integrate the latest data into an important report would receive the same reward as someone whose three-month-long project unearthed an opportunity to eliminate $50,000 annually in unit expenses.

"It's demotivating to give someone a minor award for a major accomplishment," says Gostick. "It's a slap in the face."

But before you think in purely monetary terms about what would be appropriate for a certain level of achievement, consider the final quality of effective recognition.

Tailor Rewards to the Individual

What's meaningful to one employee versus another can vary significantly. A particularly ambitious employee might really value face time with the CEO or appointment to a high-level project team as recognition for her efforts. A very conscientious employee who always seems to have trouble leaving the office might get more out of an explicit directive to take a day off and take his family to the zoo, courtesy of the company.

Cash awards, say Gostick and Elton, tend not to be as worthwhile as thank-yous, unless they're quite substantial ($1,000 or more). Instead of using the money to buy something special and memorable, most employees just use it to pay bills and quickly forget about its significance.

Don't Forget Teams

Manager 2's mistake was to try to acknowledge individuals' efforts by giving blanket recognition to the group. It's a tactic that's next to useless.

But when your team as a whole achieves goals, recognizing its accomplishments is perfectly appropriate. And don't wait until the particular project is near completion.

"In sports, we don't wait for the team to win before we applaud; we celebrate each incremental step toward victory," says Gostick. "Yet in business, there's this tendency to wait until the project is clearly working well before we celebrate anything."

At the start of a project, "set short-term goals and articulate the reward the team will receive for reaching them," he advises. Each milestone reached presents an occasion to celebrate everyone's contribution to the group effort, reinforce the project's importance, and reignite the team's commitment to working together creatively and collaboratively in pursuit of the end goal.

Whether you're acknowledging the accomplishments of a team or an individual, recognition can be a key motivator toward pushing your direct reports to the next level.

Christina Bielaszka-DuVernay was the editor of *Harvard Management Update.*

Section 2

Formal Performance Appraisals

Chapter 8

Delivering an Effective Performance Review

by Rebecca Knight

When performance review season arrives, you know the drill. Drag each of your direct reports into a conference room for a one-on-one, hand them an official-looking document, and then start in with the same, tired conversation. Say some positive things about what the employee is good at, then some unpleasant things about what he's not good at, and end—wearing your most solicitous smile—some more ego strokes. The result: a mixed message that leaves even your best employees feeling disappointed.

Adapted from content posted on hbr.org on November 3, 2011

Your formal review sessions with your employees don't need to be so tiresome—or confusing. If you take the right approach, appraisals are an excellent opportunity to keep solid performers moving onward and upward and redirect the poor ones.

What the Experts Say

For many employees, a face-to-face performance review is the most stressful work conversation they'll have all year. For managers, the discussion is just as tense. "What a performance appraisal requires is for one person to stand in judgment of another. Deep down, it's uncomfortable," says Dick Grote, author of *How to Be Good at Performance Appraisals*. Evaluating an employee's job performance should consist of more than an annual chat, according to James Baron, the William S. Beinecke Professor of Management at Yale School of Management. Performance management is a process, he says: "Presumably, you're giving a tremendous amount of real-time feedback, and your employees are people you know well. Hopefully, your relationship can survive candid feedback." No matter what kind of appraisal system your company uses, here are several strategies to help you make performance review season less nerve-racking and more productive.

Set expectations early

The performance review doesn't start with a sit-down in the spare conference room. You must be clear from the outset how you'll evaluate your employees. Grote suggests holding "performance planning" sessions with each of your direct reports at the beginning of the year to discuss that person's goals and your expectations. (See chapter 11, "How to Set and Support Employee Goals.") "You'll see immediate improvement in performance because everyone knows what the boss expects," he says. "And it earns you the right to hold people accountable at the end of the year." Listen carefully to your employees' personal ambitions, as it will inform the way you assess their work. "Oftentimes, managers are evaluating performance without necessarily knowing what that person's career aspirations are. We often assume that everyone wants to be CEO. But that's not always the case," says Baron. Understanding what your direct reports want from their careers will help you figure out ways to broaden their professional experiences.

Lay the groundwork

About two weeks before the face-to-face review, ask your employee to jot down a few things he's done over the last year that he's proud of. This will both help refresh your memory and "put a positive focus on an event that is so often seen as negative," says Grote. Next, review other notes you've kept on him throughout the year: a well-executed project; a deadline missed; the deft handling of a difficult client. Finally, ask for feedback from others in the company who work closely with your employee. "The larger number of independent evaluations the better," says Baron. About an hour before the meeting, give your employee a copy of his appraisal. That way, he can have his initial emotional response—positive or negative—in the privacy of his own cubicle. "When people read someone's assessment of them, they are going to have all sorts of churning emotions," says Grote. "Let them have that on their own time, and give them a chance to think about it." Then with a calmer, cooler head, the employee can prepare for a rational and constructive business conversation.

Set the tone

Too often, the face-to-face conversation takes the form of a "feedback sandwich": compliments, criticism, more praise. But this approach demoralizes your stars and falsely encourages your poor performers. Instead, pick a side. "Most people are good solid workers, so for the vast majority, you should concentrate exclusively on things the person has done well," says Grote, adding that this method tends to motivate people who are already competent at their jobs. For your marginal workers, however, do not sugarcoat bad news. Performance reviews are your chance to confront poor performers and demand improvement. "People are resilient," says Grote. "As time goes on, that person is not going to get a promotion and not going to get a raise . . . You're not doing this person any favors by [avoiding their deficiencies]." (For more on dealing with those who are not meeting expectations, see chapter 14, "How to Help an Underperformer.")

Constructively coach

After discussing the strengths and achievements of your solid performers, ask them how they feel about how things are going. "In most cases, you're dealing with mature adults and you'll elicit their honest concerns," says Grote. For both solid and poor performers, frame feedback in terms of a "stop, start, and continue" model, suggests Baron. What is the employee doing now that is not working? What actions should they adopt to be more successful? What are they doing that is highly effective? Focusing on behaviors, not dispositions, takes the personal edge out of the conversation. Give specific advice and targeted praise. "Don't say things like: 'You need to be more proactive.' That doesn't mean anything. Say something like: 'You need to take more initiative in calling potential sales leads.'" Similarly, "Saying: 'You're an innovator' is nice but it's helpful to know exactly what they're doing that reflects that," says Baron.

Hold your ground

The hot-button issues associated with performance reviews are money and rank. If your company allows it, separate any talk of compensation from the performance review. "But if you must, do not save the salary information for the end of the conversation," says Grote, "otherwise there'll be an invisible parrot above the employee's head squawking: 'How much?' throughout the entire discussion." Rank is another place for potential bruised feelings. A majority of companies require managers to rate their employees—often on a scale of 1 to 5. Your goal is go over the data and make a judgment call. Remember: the 1–5 system is not analogous to the A–F grading scheme in school; most employees will get the middle rank, a 3. This might leave some employees feeling let down, thinking they're merely "average." Don't cave in. "In the corporate world, you're dealing with a highly selective group," says Grote. "The rules of the game have changed. In school, a C was mediocre, but a 3 in the working world means they're meeting expectations. They're shooting par." Conveying that message is a leadership challenge. "People can accept it rationally but it may be hard to accept viscerally," he says. "This is why it's so important to hold a performance planning meeting at the outset. If they hit their targets, they are a 3. It's a goal."

Principles to Remember

- Make it clear at the beginning of the year how you'll evaluate your employees with individual performance planning sessions.
- Give your employees a copy of their appraisal before the meeting so they can have their initial emotional response in private.
- Deliver a positive message to your good performers by concentrating mainly on their strengths and achievements during the conversation.
- Note specific behaviors you want your employee to stop, start, and continue.

Case Study #1: Understand Expectations and Set the Right Tone

Ben Snyder (not his real name), an expat working in London at a global media company, was new at his job. He'd inherited an employee, Jim, whose primary responsibility was to travel to Africa, the Middle East, and Russia to develop partnerships that would ultimately drive sales to Ben's business. But Jim wasn't delivering.

"During quarterly performance reviews, Jim and I had long conversations about his approaches and the great relationships he was developing. I would tell him how glad I was that people were talking to him, that he was forming these relationships. But I also told him that we needed tangible deals," says Ben.

This happened for three straight quarters: same conversation, no deals. Increasingly, Ben was under pressure: Jim was spending a lot of the company's money with nothing to show for it.

"I needed to scare him into action. At the next performance review, I gave Jim 90 days to close a deal."

Nothing changed, and Jim was dismissed. "Even when we sat down with HR and let him go, he was genuinely surprised," recalls Ben.

In retrospect, Ben says he went overboard in validating Jim's spadework, and didn't establish the right tone during their conversations. "The message wasn't clear—Jim only heard what he wanted to hear—the positive praise about the relationship building. He ignored the demand to close deals."

Ben also should have worked harder in the beginning to understand the specifics of Jim's job and set clear expectations. "It was a business I wasn't familiar with. I didn't know how to push him in the right direction because I wasn't exactly sure what he was doing. I had never really sat down with him and defined what success should look like."

Case Study #2: Be Clear and Specific

Lucy Orren (name has been changed) worked as a director of business development at a biotech start-up in New Jersey. She managed Peter, who was, according to Lucy, "a real star. He was smart, very conscientious, and good at everything he tried." One of Peter's biggest responsibilities was giving presentations.

"One of the vice presidents at my company brought it to my attention that Peter used a certain crutch phrase too often, and that while he was a good speaker, he was very deliberate in the way that he spoke, which was sometimes too slow. She thought it connoted a lack of energy. I thought it was a relatively minor problem, but I decided to bring it up in the performance appraisal."

During the face-to-face discussion, however, Lucy chickened out. "Peter was so good at his job, that I was reluctant to give him any criticism," she says. "I tried to couch the advice when we were discussing his strengths. He didn't get it."

At the very end of the conversation, Lucy highlighted areas of improvement. She told Peter to try to be more upbeat during his presentations. But the advice was too vague; Peter wasn't sure what to do with the recommendation.

"The next few presentations he gave were pretty rocky. He overcompensated," recalls Lucy.

After one of his presentations, Lucy realized she needed to be more specific with her coaching. She warned him of the crutch phrase and told him to try to speak faster.

"Peter came through, and improved on every level. He still uses the crutch phrase every so often, but there is more momentum to his presentations."

Rebecca Knight is a freelance journalist in Boston and a lecturer at Wesleyan University. Her work has been published in the *New York Times, USA Today,* and the *Financial Times.*

Chapter 9

Managing Performance When It's Hard to Measure

by Jim Whitehurst

Organizations of all kinds have long struggled to accurately measure the performance of individual members. The typical approach is to assess an individual's performance against a metric usually tied to whether or not they performed a task and the amount of output they generated by doing so. There's a lot riding on these assessments: everything from compensation increases and bonus payments to promotions. And as anyone who has ever given or received a traditional performance review

Adapted from content originally posted on hbr.org on May 11, 2015

knows, this process can be highly subjective—even in the most metrics-obsessed organizations.

But what about the kinds of jobs where measuring someone's "output" isn't about counting the number of widgets they produced, but rather it's about how they managed a team or influenced others or helped people collaborate better? While it might be easy to measure someone's output on an assembly line, how do we decide how well a manager manages or a leader leads?

In the case of an organization like Red Hat (where I am the CEO), which collaborates with many open source software communities like Linux and OpenStack, these questions are all the more difficult to answer—like how to measure someone's contribution to an external community—and traditional performance reviews just don't cut it for us. For example, building enterprise open source software, like we do at Red Hat, involves collaborating with people outside of the company who volunteer their efforts. That means you can't simply issue orders or direct what work gets done and when. What you can do is build influence and trust with other members of the community. But doing that can involve making contributions that offer no direct output or result. It's not quid pro quo, and it's not easy to track and measure.

Conventional performance reviews can also undermine a company's agility and lead to missed opportunities (see the sidebar "Deloitte's Performance Snapshot"). What happens when an individual's goals no longer make sense because the competitive landscape has changed, but their performance rating (and by extension, their compensation and advancement opportunities) is resting on the completion of those goals? That's not a system that promotes innovation.

How do you even begin to appraise someone's performance in these scenarios?

At Red Hat, we've developed a simpler, more flexible approach to performance reviews, one that doesn't limit managers to narrow measures of performance.

Agree on Employee Objectives

We've found that it's essential to ensure that associates and their managers are on the same page when it comes to the responsibilities and expectations for the role. We encourage people to track what's important and to set individual goals that contribute to our company's mission and strategy. We recommend a regular check-in process to keep managers and associates in sync. However, we've found it best to let managers and associates determine the frequency of those meetings. Some take place weekly, others happen on a monthly or quarterly basis.

Get Input from Others

When measuring against these goals, we rely not only on the manager's observations, but also on associates' peers and communities to informally assess how people perform. We pay attention to their reputations and how they are regarded by others. We look at the scope and quality of their influence. The result is that rather than "managing up" to their boss to get a good review, Red Hatters are accountable to the community as a whole.

Focus on Opportunities, Not Score-keeping

Our associates are incredibly talented, passionate people. We don't want them to fixate on a number or letter grade, so we don't hand them a bottom-line score to sum up last year's performance. Instead, we focus on developing their strengths and growing their capabilities. We advise managers to give continuous, real-time feedback throughout the year and to use the annual review as an opportunity to reflect back on everything their associates have achieved, what they've learned along the way, and what opportunities they will pursue in the coming months. Unlike many companies, we don't expect our managers to fit people to a bell curve with a maximum number of low and high performers. Instead, we tell them to pay attention to both performance and potential and to focus on connecting their people with opportunities for growth and development.

DELOITTE'S PERFORMANCE SNAPSHOT

by Marcus Buckingham and Ashley Goodall

At Deloitte we're redesigning our performance management system. Like many other companies, we realize that our current process for evaluating the work of our people—and then training them, promoting them, and paying them accordingly—is increasingly out of step with our objectives.

In a public survey Deloitte conducted recently, more than half the executives questioned (58%) believe that their current performance management approach drives neither employee engagement nor high performance. They, and we, are in need of something nimbler, real-time, and more individualized—something squarely focused on fueling performance in the future rather than assessing it in the past.

What might surprise you, however, is what we'll include in Deloitte's new system and what we won't. It will have no cascading objectives, no once-a-year reviews, and no 360-degree-feedback tools. We've arrived at a very different and much simpler design for managing people's performance. Its hallmarks are speed, agility, one-size-fits-one, and constant learning, and it's underpinned by a new way of collecting reliable performance data.

Rather than asking more people for their opinion of a team member (in a 360-degree or an upward-feedback survey, for example), we found that we will need to ask only the immediate team leader—but, critically, to ask a different kind of question. People may rate other people's skills inconsistently, but they are highly consistent when rating their own feelings and intentions. To see performance at the individual level, then, we will ask team leaders not about the *skills* of each team member

(*continued*)

(*continued*)

but about their *own future actions* with respect to that person.

At the end of every project (or once every quarter for long-term projects) we will ask team leaders to respond to four future-focused statements about each team member:

1. Given what I know of this person's performance, and if it were my money, I would award this person the highest possible compensation increase and bonus.
2. Given what I know of this person's performance, I would always want him or her on my team.
3. This person is at risk for low performance.
4. This person is ready for promotion today.

In effect, we are asking our team leaders what they would *do* with each team member rather than what they *think* of that individual. When we aggregate these data points over a year, weighting each according to the duration of a given project, we produce a rich stream of information for leaders' discussions of what they, in turn, will do—whether it's a question of succession planning, development paths, or performance-pattern analysis.

In addition to this consistent—and countable—data, when it comes to compensation, we want to factor in some uncountable things, such as the difficulty of project assignments in a given year and contributions to the organization other than formal projects. So the data will serve as the starting point for compensation, not the ending point. The final determination will be reached either by a leader who knows each individual personally or by a group of leaders looking at an entire segment of our practice and at many data points in parallel.

We could call this new evaluation a rating, but it bears no resemblance, in generation or in use, to the ratings of the past. Because it allows us to quickly capture performance at a single moment in time, we call it a *performance snapshot.*

Adapted from "Reinventing Performance Management" (*Harvard Business Review,* April 2015), reprint #R1504B.

Marcus Buckingham provides performance management tools and training to organizations. He is the author of several best-selling books and *StandOut 2.0: Assess Your Strengths, Find Your Edge, Win at Work* (Harvard Business Review Press, 2015).

Ashley Goodall is the director of leader development at Deloitte Services LP, based in New York.

Emphasize Achievement, Not Just Advancement

Finally, when it comes to promotions, raises, and bonuses, we don't force managers to apply a merit matrix or rigid formula. Instead, we give them the flexibility to make decisions that are right for their people. This means our managers don't have to enter inaccurate ratings to "game the system," a problem faced by many other companies.

The conventional way to reward top performers is to promote them into managerial roles. This often creates an army of ineffective and unengaged managers. But we have come to embrace the concept of a "career of achievement" in addition to a "career of advancement." Some of the most influential leaders in our organization do not have fancy titles or even people who directly report to them. They are expert individual contributors who help shape the direction and priorities of Red Hat and key open source communities through their contributions and thought leadership.

A great example is Máirín Duffy, one of our user interface designers. Máirín started working at Red Hat as an intern and later joined us full time in 2005, after she graduated from college. While Máirín has made exceptional contributions to our core Red Hat Enterprise Linux product, she has also earned a stellar reputation throughout the company (as well as open source communities) for her reasoned and intelligent contributions to mailing list conversations on everything from the creation of Red Hat's mission statement to contentious internal debates.

It was in a case involving the latter that led Red Hat's executive vice president and chief people officer DeLisa Alexander to approach Máirín to talk about a proposed project. In other words, a senior leader in the company went directly to someone working closer to the front lines to gather feedback on a fairly major corporatewide decision, simply because DeLisa knew that Máirín could help make or break the success of the final decision based on her level of influence throughout the company.

A traditional performance review rating could never capture the kind of influence Máirín has built inside our organization and the communities we participate in. Even a 360-degree review from her immediate peers or manager wouldn't reach far enough to show Máirín's impact. But everyone at Red Hat knows who Máirín is because her contributions shape many areas of the company. With a performance management process that emphasizes individual development, influence, and innovation, Red Hat is able to retain and grow passionate, talented associates like Máirín.

Jim Whitehurst is the president and CEO of Red Hat, the world's leading provider of open source enterprise IT products and solutions, and the author of the book *The Open Organization* (Harvard Business Review Press, 2015).

Chapter 10

Stop Worrying About Your Employee's Weaknesses

by Peter Bregman

Your son comes home one day, looks down at his feet, and gives you his report card. You smile at him as you open it up and look inside. Then your smile disappears when you see the F in math. You also see an A (English) and two Bs (history and science). You look down at him and ask, "What happened in math, Johnny? Why did you get this F?"

We want our kids to be successful at everything they do. And if they're not good at something, we ask why they failed. We tell them to work harder at it. Understand what went wrong, focus, and fix it.

Adapted from content posted on hbr.org on May 19, 2009

WHAT PEOPLE ARE SAYING ON HBR.ORG

A great manager recognizes the strengths of their people and then puts them in position to win. **A performance review would serve the company better if it were less a report card and more of a coaching session.** The manager should focus on providing the necessary resources to the employee (in your example, someone who loves spreadsheets) and removing the obstacles so that the employee can win. Given that the employee is in the right position, it is often the manager who is the obstacle to success.
—Posted by Ted

This is a terrific approach to managing and motivating employees. If you take it one step further and **share individual members' strengths with the whole team, they begin to see each other for the unique qualities they bring.** They even begin to rely on each other in new ways. And, focusing on strengths lets an employee's gifts shine and productivity climbs and confidence grows.
—Posted by Amy

Some respondents have criticized your example about the salesperson and the spreadsheet. However, **I find that I actually become more proficient in weak areas by partnering with an expert** who will do the work and also explain things to me in terms I can understand.
—Posted by Mary

I'm a presentation skills coach, [and] I always try to coach people to focus on their strengths and build on what they do well. **The more comfortable and confident people get, the more their "weaknesses" will disappear.** People often ask for constructive criticism and want know what they're doing wrong. They're not doing anything "wrong." They can be coached to do something "different" that might compensate for their (temporary) shortcomings.

—Posted by Steve

But that's a mistake. The wrong focus. If you dwell on Johnny's failure, on his weakness, you'll be setting him up for a life of struggle and low self-esteem while reducing his chances of reaching his full potential.

And you won't fix his weakness. You'll just reinforce it.

The problem with a report card is that it measures all students against the same criteria, which ignores that each student is different—with unique talents, distinct likes and dislikes, and particular aspirations. And when we see the F on Johnny's report card, it's easy for us to get distracted from our primary job: to help him deeply enjoy his life and fulfill his potential by developing and deriving pleasure from his unique talents.

Fast-forward 20 years. Johnny is now an adult. As he sits down for a performance review with his manager, she spends a few quiet minutes looking over his review and then raises her eyes to meet his.

"You've worked hard this year, John. Your client orientation is superb. You've met your sales goals, and you're a solid team player. But you have an area that needs development, specifically, your detail orientation. The spreadsheets we get from you are a mess. Let's talk about how you can get better in that."

An A, two Bs, and an F. And his manager handles it the same way his parent did. By focusing the conversation, and John's effort, on his least favorite and weakest area.

We have a report card problem in our companies, and it's costing us a tremendous amount of time, money, potential, and happiness. It's costing us talent.

Traditional management systems encourage mediocrity in everything and excellence in nothing. Most performance-review systems set an ideal picture of how we want everyone to act (standards, competencies, and so on) and then assess how closely people match that ideal, nudging them to improve their weaknesses so they "meet or exceed expectations" in every area.

But how will John add the most value to his organization? He's amazing with people, not spreadsheets. He'll work hardest, derive the most pleasure, and contribute his maximum potential with the greatest result if he is able to focus as much time as possible in his area of strength.

Which means taking his focus off developing the things in which he's weak. They're just a distraction.

Here's what his manager should say: "You've worked hard this year, John. Your client orientation is superb. You've met your sales goals, and you're a solid team player. But working on those spreadsheets isn't a good use of your time, and it's not your strength. I'm going to ask David to do those for you from now on. He loves spreadsheets and is great at them. I want to spend the rest of our time talking about how you can get even better at working with your clients. That's where you shine—where you add the most value to the company—and you seem to really enjoy it."

An organization should be a platform for unique talent. A performance-review system should be flexible enough to reflect and reward the successful contributions of diverse employees. Let's acknowledge that no one can possibly be great at everything—and place all our effort on developing their strengths further.

If it's impossible to take away the part of their job in which they're weak, then help them improve just enough so that it doesn't get in the way of their strength. If you can't take the spreadsheets away from John, help him get a C and move on. That would be preferable to spending the time and effort it would take for him to get an A or even a B.

Peter Bregman is CEO of Bregman Partners, a company that strengthens leadership in people and in organizations through programs (including the Bregman Leadership Intensive), coaching, and as a consultant to CEOs and their leadership teams. Best-selling author of *18 Minutes*, his most recent book is *Four Seconds*.

Chapter 11
How to Set and Support Employee Goals

by Amy Gallo

As you think about how employees should be developing and what their future looks like, you must also think about the goals they should be aspiring to. Employees want to see how their work contributes to larger corporate objectives, and setting the right targets makes this connection explicit for them and for you, their manager.

A performance planning meeting shortly after the review session affords you an opportunity to collaborate with your direct report on goals for the upcoming year, since where your employees need to improve will be fresh on your mind. Within this conversation, you can

---

Adapted from content posted on hbr.org on February 7, 2011

discuss not only your perception of where your employees should devote their time, but also what they want in their own career and how they're going to reach those milestones.

What the Experts Say

How involved should you be in helping employees establish and achieve their goals? Since failure to meet goals can have consequences for you, your employee, and your team, as well as the broader organization, you need to balance your involvement with the employee's ownership over the process. Linda Hill, coauthor of *Being the Boss: The 3 Imperatives for Becoming a Great Leader,* says, "A manager's job is to provide 'supportive autonomy' that's appropriate to the person's level of capability." The key is to be hands-on while giving your people the room they need to succeed on their own. Here are some principles to follow as you navigate how to best craft goals and support your people in reaching their objectives.

Connect employee goals to larger company goals

For goals to be meaningful and effective in motivating employees, they must be tied to larger organizational ambitions. Employees who don't understand the roles they play in their company's success are more likely to become disengaged. "Achieving goals is often about making trade-offs when things don't go as planned. [Employees] need to understand the bigger picture to make those trade-offs when things go wrong," says Hill. No matter what level the employee is at, they should be able to articulate exactly how their efforts feed into the broader company strategy.

Make goals attainable but challenging

Since employees are ultimately responsible for reaching their goals, they need to have a strong voice in setting them. However, you need to support them through this process by providing input and direction regarding what the company is trying to achieve. Ask your employee to draft goals that directly contribute to the organization's mission. Once they've suggested an initial list, discuss whether the targets are both realistic and challenging enough. "Stretch targets emerge as a process of negotiation between the employee and the manager," says Srikant M. Datar, the Arthur Lowes Dickinson Professor of Accounting at Harvard University. Be careful, though: Your team members are likely to resent you if you insist on goals that are too challenging to accomplish. Don't aim too low, either. If you are overly cautious, you will miss opportunities and settle for mediocrity. "When done well, stretch goals create a lot of energy and momentum in an organization," says Datar. But when done badly, they "do not achieve the goal of motivating employees and helping them achieve better performance as they were designed to do." Even worse, poorly set goals can undermine employees' morale and productivity, and the organization's performance overall.

Create a plan for success

Once a goal is set, ask your employee to explain how they plan to meet it. Have them break it down into tasks and set interim objectives, especially if it's a large or long-term project. Ask your employee: "What are the appropriate milestones?" "What are possible risks, and how do you plan to manage them?" Because targets are rarely pursued in a vacuum, Hill suggests that you "help your people understand who they are dependent on to achieve those goals." Then problem solve with them on how to best influence those people to get the job done.

Monitor progress

Staying on top of employee progress will help head off any troubles early on. "We often get problems because we don't signal that we are partners in achieving goals," says Hill. Don't wait for review time or the end of a project to check in. Review long-term and short-term goals on a weekly basis. Even your high-performing employees need ongoing feedback and coaching. Ask your employee what type of monitoring and feedback would be most helpful to them, especially if the task is particularly challenging or something they are doing for the first time.

Assist in problem solving

Very few of us reach our goals without some bumps along the way. Build relationships with employees so that they feel comfortable coming to you if and when problems arise. If your employee encounters an unforeseen obstacle, the goal may need reworking. First, however, ask them to bring a potential solution to you so you can give them coaching and advice. If their efforts to solve the problem fail, you will need to get further involved.

Sculpt for personal goals

Some managers neglect to think about what an employee is personally trying to accomplish in the context of work.

"If I account for the interests of the whole person, not just the work person, I'm going to get more value from them," says Stewart D. Friedman, author of *Total Leadership: Be a Better Leader, Have a Richer Life*. For example, if your employee has expressed an interest in teaching but that is not part of their job responsibilities, you may be able to find ways to sculpt that job to include opportunities to train peers or less-experienced colleagues. (See the sidebar "Job Sculpting.")

JOB SCULPTING

by Timothy Butler and James Waldroop

Job sculpting is the art of matching people to jobs through a customized career path that allow their deeply embedded life interests to be expressed—and increase the chance of retaining talented people. Since an effective performance review dedicates time to discussing past performance and plans for the future, it presents an opportune time to job sculpt.

Managers don't need special training to job sculpt. They just need to start listening more carefully when employees describe what they like and dislike about

(*continued*)

(continued)

their jobs. Consider the case of a pharmaceutical company executive who managed 30 salespeople. In a performance review, one of her people offhandedly mentioned that her favorite part of the past year had been helping their division find new office space and negotiating for its lease. In the past, the executive would have paid the comment little heed. After all, what did it have to do with the woman's performance in sales? But listening with the ears of a job sculptor, the executive probed further, asking, "What made the search for new office space fun for you?" and "How was that different from what you do day-to-day?" The conversation revealed that the saleswoman was actually very dissatisfied and bored with her current position and was considering leaving. In fact, the saleswoman yearned for work that met her deeply embedded life interests, which had to do with *influence through language and ideas* and *creative production.* Her sales job encompassed the former, but it was only when she had the chance to think about the location, design, and layout of the new office that her creativity could be fully expressed. The manager helped the woman move to a position where her primary responsibility was to design marketing and advertising materials.

Along with listening carefully and asking probing questions during the performance review, managers can ask employees to play an active role in job sculpting—before the meeting starts. In most corporate settings, the employee's preparation for a performance review includes a written assessment of accomplishments, goals for the upcoming review period, skill areas in need of development, and plans for accomplishing both goals and growth. During the review, this assessment is then compared to the supervisor's assessment.

But imagine what would happen if employees were also expected to write up their personal views of career satisfaction. Imagine if they were to prepare a few paragraphs on what kind of work they love or if they described their favorite activities on the job. Because so many people are unaware of their deeply embedded life interests—not to mention unaccustomed to discussing them with their managers—such exercises might not come easily at first. Yet they would be an excellent starting point for a discussion, ultimately allowing employees to speak more clearly about what they want from work, both in the short and long term. And that information would make even the best job-sculpting managers more effective.

Once managers and employees have discussed deeply embedded life interests, it's time to customize the next work assignment accordingly. In cases where the employee requires only a small change in his

(*continued*)

(continued)

activities, that might just mean adding a new responsibility. For example, an engineer who has a deeply embedded life interest in *counseling and mentoring* might be asked to plan and manage the orientation of new hires. Or a logistics planner with a deeply embedded life interest in *influence through language and ideas* could be given the task of working on recruitment at college campuses. The goals here would be to give some immediate gratification through an immediate and real change in the job and to begin the process of moving the individual to a role that more fully satisfies him.

Adapted from "Job Sculpting: The Art of Retaining Your Best People" (*Harvard Business Review*, September–October 1999), reprint #99502.

Timothy Butler is Director of Career Development Programs at Harvard Business School and author of *Getting Unstuck: How Dead Ends Become New Paths*.

James Waldroop is a founding principal of the consulting firm Peregrine Partners.

The first step is for you to understand what these goals are. Ask employees if they have any personal goals they want to share with you. Don't pressure them; they should share these aspirations only if they feel comfortable. Friedman suggests you then ask, "What adjustments might we try that would help you achieve your goals?"

This allows the employee to take ownership of the solution. Just as with work goals, you need to be sure personal goals contribute to your team, unit, or to the company. "It's got to be a shared commitment to experiment and mutual responsibility to check in on how it's going. It's got to be a win for both," says Friedman.

Hold people accountable—including yourself

There will be times, even with the best support, when employees fail to meet their targets. Hill advises, "Hold people accountable. You can't say 'Gee, that's too bad.' You need to figure out what went wrong and why." Discuss with your employee what happened and what each of you think went wrong. If the problem was within their control, ask them to apply the possible solutions you've discussed, take another stab at reaching the goal, and check in with you more frequently. If it was something that was outside their power or the goal was too ambitious, acknowledge the disappointment but don't dwell on it. "Do the diagnosis, get the learning, and move on," says Hill.

As discussed in chapter 5, "The Set-Up-to-Fail Syndrome," it's possible that you may have contributed to the problem. Be willing to reflect on your role in the failure. Were you too hands-off, and fail to check in frequently enough? Did you not review the work in a timely way? Have an open conversation about what you can do next time. "If you don't hold yourself accountable, they're going to have trouble with you," says Hill.

Principles to Remember

Do:

- Connect individuals' goals to broader organization objectives
- Show employees that you are a partner in achieving their goals
- Learn about and incorporate employees' personal interests into their professional goals

Don't:

- Allow employees to set goals alone
- Take a hands-off approach with high performers
- Ignore failures

Case Study: A Partner in Goal Attainment

Meghan Lantier is known at Bliss PR for being a natural people developer. As the vice president of the firm's financial services practice, Meghan manages several senior account executives, including Shauna Ellerson (not her real name). Meghan has overseen Shauna's work since Shauna started at Bliss four-and-a-half years ago. Since the beginning, they have set goals through a collaborative process: Shauna develops draft goals, Meghan comes up with goals she believes Shauna needs to focus on, and then they identify the overlap between them. "I want to make sure they are manageable but stretched, too," says Meghan. The two regularly check in on these goals. Meghan takes a hands-on approach, providing Shauna with regular input. They also sit down together at least four times a year to have a more formal discussion about Shauna's ambitions.

One of Shauna's goals is to become more of a thought leader on one of their largest financial services accounts. She has mastered the day-to-day work of managing the client and now needs to focus on the bigger picture. Shauna has been working on this goal for several months now by speaking up more in client meetings and providing more input into the content, not just the process, of their work. "We don't need a goal-review session. I give her constant feedback in the context of the work," says Meghan.

Meghan also knows that, ultimately, Shauna is responsible for her own achievements. "I'm fully invested in making it work, but I realized the limitations I have as a manager to make it happen," she says. It hasn't been necessary to talk about the consequences if Shauna fails to meet the goal—there are natural consequences in Bliss's high-performing culture. If you don't succeed, you don't get the better assignments.

Amy Gallo is a contributing editor at Harvard Business Review and the author of the *HBR Guide to Managing Conflict at Work.*

Chapter 12

When to Grant a Promotion or Raise

by Amy Gallo

Managers who want to recognize employees for good work have many tools at their disposal. One of the more traditional ways to reward a top performer is to give her a promotion or raise, or both. Even if you don't openly talk about this in your performance review session (as discussed in chapter 8, "Delivering an Effective Performance Review"), it's often something a manager will think about—or an employee will ask about—around formal appraisal time.

But how can you know whether someone is ready for the next challenge or deserving of that bump in pay? Human resource policies and company culture often dictate when and how people move up in a company. However,

---

Adapted from content posted on hbr.org on January 12, 2011

managers in most companies have a good deal of input into the decision and, in some cases, they are the ultimate decision makers. Whether you have this authority or not, you need to make promotions and raises part of an ongoing discussion with employees about their performance.

What the Experts Say

According to Herminia Ibarra, the Cora Chaired Professor of Leadership and Learning and Faculty Director of the INSEAD Leadership Initiative, "Many times a manager feels responsible for finding their people their next step in the organization." Managers should make these decisions about promotions and raises carefully. "I think who an organization promotes is a very strong index of their core culture," says Susan David, codirector of the Institute of Coaching, founding director of Evidence Based Psychology. Managers should recognize that who they reward sends a signal to the rest of the organization. Therefore, they need to be sure they are endorsing behavior that is in line with the organization's values. For example, an employee who exceeds his targets but treats his team members poorly should not be rewarded in an organization that values teamwork.

Similarly, the way an organization promotes people has implications for an individual's success. Organizations often assume that a promotion should involve giving star performers responsibility for managing more people and developing—rather than just executing—strategy. "Yet these are not areas of genius for all. Many organizations lose some of their best operational people because they create single pathways to organizational success," says David. It's possible to reward people in other ways. "Organizations [that] create multiple, flexible pathways to success will keep their best people, keep them engaged, and keep them for longer," she says. Next time you are trying to decide whether to recognize strong performance with a promotion or raise, follow these principles.

Assess current performance using multiple sources

As a first step, make sure the employee is able to do the job you are considering promoting her into. Take a look at her performance. "There will be markers even in the current job that show how they'll do in the new role," says David. She recommends you use multisource feedback: Draw not only on your own assessment but also on others'. It is especially important to seek input from people who interact with the employees in ways that you don't. Talk to peers, team members, and people she manages. In some cases, you may find that she's already doing parts of the new job. "Some people do their job as it is described and some enlarge their job; they innovate around the parameters of the job. That's the best evidence of all—when they're already doing the job," says Ibarra.

Consider the "competence-challenge balance"

"We all want to be and feel we are good at things. We also have the need to feel we are growing and learning," says David. A good indicator that you may need to promote someone is if he expresses a desire to learn more and take on a new challenge. Your goal-setting discussion will help you assess this. People who are particularly good at their jobs may quickly master them and need to be stretched. "If in their current jobs employees are reaching points where they are overqualified, this is a strong risk factor for disengagement and loss of those employees," says David. You need to constantly assess your people and be sure they are working at the edges of their abilities. If they are performing well but not learning anything new, a promotion or an alternative assignment may be best for both the individual and the organization.

Make sure it's a good match

Before promoting someone into a new role, consider whether it's something she will enjoy doing. Many managers fail to consider that just because someone is good at a job, doesn't mean she will take pleasure in it. "One of the greatest tools a manager can use is an authentic, honest conversation with the individual," explains David. Ask your employee whether she is interested in and excited about the new responsibilities. If not, consider creating an alternative role that stretches her, fulfills her, and fills a need in the organization.

Experiment before making the job permanent

Occasionally, you may need more information to judge the employee's expected performance in a new role. As Ibarra says, "It gets tricky when performance in a current role is not a good predictor of performance in a new role." In these cases, design an assignment that is similar to the tasks and challenges of the new job to test the employee's ability. Be transparent with the employee about this experiment. Make it short-term, and outline clear success criteria and an evaluation timeline. Be careful, though—you don't want to invisibly promote your people without recognizing their contributions. Providing more responsibility without a corresponding change in title or raise can sap motivation.

Determine fair compensation

With some promotions, it may be obvious how much of a raise you should give based on how much others doing the same job are paid. However, many job changes are not as clear cut. The employee may be retaining some of her former responsibilities while taking on new ones. Create a job description for the new role. Take a look at all her duties and try to benchmark them against other jobs in the company or in the broader employment market. If you don't have similar positions in the organization, look at increases that went with other promotions in the organization. If most promotions come with a particular increase in salary, stick with a similar percentage.

Know when to say no

"There are people who will ask for a promotion even if they're not ready," says Ibarra. Your job is to help calibrate those requests. If your employee raises the idea of a promotion but you worry he's not ready, have an open discussion to hear his reasoning and share your concerns. Be clear about what competencies or experiences he needs to gain to be promoted and create an action plan for how he can do that. Provide him with the tasks and assignments he needs to expand his skills.

Because of a limited budget, you may have to say no to someone who is deserving. Or there may not be the right opportunity. To promote, David says, "there needs to be a strategic need in the organization" that this person can meet. These can be tough conversations. Be honest and transparent. Explain the rationale, and be sure the employee understands that you value him. Give him stretch goals that help prepare him for the future when the company is better positioned to give him a promotion or raise.

Consider other ways to motivate

Most important, find other ways to keep the employee engaged. "Leaders are often comforted by their capacity to give a raise or a promotion because these strategies are seen as tangible and executable. However, while these extrinsic motivators are a useful and important part of keeping employees engaged, they are certainly not the only ones," says David. Instead, rely on intrinsic motivators, such as recognizing contributions, providing opportunities to gain new skills or experiences, and supporting autonomy and choice within a job (see chapter 7, "Recognize Good Work in a Meaningful Way"). For example, you may have leeway as a manager to make modifications to the employee's current position so that he is spending half of his time on his current job and the other half on new, more challenging responsibilities. Doing this may be more motivational in the long run and can often inspire loyalty. "Overreliance on pay and promotion as motivators leads to an organizational culture that is very transactional and disengaged," says David. Employees who feel valued are likely to wait out the hard times.

Principles to Remember

Do:

- Make sure your people are working at the edge of their abilities
- Create an assignment that helps you assess whether the employee will excel in a new role
- Find other ways beyond raises and promotions to motivate your people

Don't:

- Say no to a request for a raise or promotion without a clear explanation
- Rely solely on your assessment of the employee's performance without asking others for input
- Assume that a promotion alone will make the employee happy

WHAT PEOPLE ARE SAYING ON HBR.ORG

Employee turnover is thought to be one of the biggest upcoming costs and challenges for companies.

If that's the case, companies need to be proactive in keeping their top players around. Extrinsic motivators like money and promotions are great, but they're not enough to keep people engaged and motivated. In a

(*continued*)

(*continued*)

Towers Watson white paper "Turbocharging Employee Engagement: The Power of Recognition from Managers," a main finding is that "strong manager performance in recognizing employee performance increases engagement by almost 60%."

Real-time recognition for tasks well done and employees aligning themselves with company values is a powerful tool not to be overlooked. **Recognition (and rewards) are key to maintaining a motivated workforce.**

—Posted by Sarah

My current position is in a not-for-profit community healthcare facility. Funding is primarily through grants and Medicare or Medicaid. These sources have already been shrinking and more cuts are coming. There have been no bonuses for two years, and raises vanished before that. In addition, more responsibility is a growing burden for staff.

Combine that with the economic hardship of the employees' families and the need for other types of recognition and reward becomes imperative—otherwise, they will be off to find higher-paying jobs.

Your idea of an employee ". . . spending half of his time on his current job and the other half on new, more challenging responsibilities," then, for us, also **has an additional positive effect—more gets done by fewer staff and it helps to prevent burnout by providing variation in tasks, duties, and new coworkers.**

—Posted by Betty

Case Study 1: A New Role for the Firm and the Employee

Elise Giannasi was hired by a strategy consulting firm as the executive assistant to the managing partner. A year into the job, she was receiving glowing reviews and Shanti Nayak, the firm's director of people, says it was clear that she was a star performer. In particular, Shanti noted that Elise had done a great job of building relationships with clients. Her relationships had been instrumental in setting up key appointments and ensuring that bills got paid. The managing partner felt she was ready to move up. But according to Shanti, "there was no typical role for people to move into unless they were on the traditional consultant path."

At the time, the firm didn't have a staff member dedicated solely to business development. People throughout the firm were doing it as an "extracurricular" task. However, the tough economic climate forced the firm to develop a much more formalized process and needed someone to be responsible for it. Shanti explains that they had two debates going on simultaneously: Was this a role they needed? And, if so, was Elise the right person for the role? While Elise was doing small pieces of client development already, she had never filled a role like this before. Shanti knew that Elise had worked hard to develop the right relationships both inside and outside the firm, and she had confidence Elise could do it. When she talked to others in the firm, they endorsed her assessment. In the end, Shanti says, "It felt like a risk worth taking." Shanti explained that since this was a new position, it was difficult to decide how much to pay Elise once she was promoted.

They looked at what other promotions carried in terms of a raise—in particular, the percentage increase that associates received when they became senior associates. Elise was given a similar percentage increase and a new title: manager of business development.

Case Study 2: An Apprenticeship Model for On-the-Job Learning

When Sarah Vania joined the International Rescue Committee as the senior human resource partner, she was particularly impressed with Nicole Clemons, an HR administrator. Nicole was studying for her master's degree while working full time. She commuted two hours by bus to her job, using that time to study. Nicole had always received very good reviews. Sarah thought, "Here's a high-potential person who has earned her right to development." When Sarah sat down with her for their first review together, Nicole asked, "What's the path ahead for me?" She had applied for an open HR partner role, but because it was two steps up from her current role, the organization didn't feel she was ready. Without a logical next step, however, Nicole would be stuck in her current role. "As a manager, I owed her a career path, but I didn't have the budget to create a new role and hire a new admin," says Sarah.

Instead, she decided to create an alternative role for Nicole. Nicole would continue her duties as an HR administrator but also take on two of Sarah's client groups to manage. This apprentice model would allow Nicole to learn on the job what it means to be an HR partner, with Sarah providing her feedback and support. "It helps her learn in a manageable, supported way, rather than trial by fire," explains Sarah. Sarah spoke with the leaders of each client group. She made it clear that although Nicole was still learning the role, she would make their groups her first priority and Sarah would be there if any issues came up. "I asked for their help and explained the benefit," says Sarah. Nicole has since taken on more responsibility, and Sarah says she is well on her way to qualifying for the partner role.

Amy Gallo is a contributing editor at Harvard Business Review and the author of the *HBR Guide to Managing Conflict at Work*.

Chapter 13
Tips for Record Keeping

To prepare for annual reviews, many managers find it useful to keep a file (electronic or hard copy) on every employee's performance and update it throughout the year. Documenting employee performance entails special legal considerations, so consult your human resource manager or internal legal team. If you don't have either resource in your organization, consult a lawyer who specializes in employment law. This is especially advisable when a person's performance is beginning to suffer or if you may need to fire them.

Here are a few things to consider when preparing employee records:

- Record the date and specifics of what occurred: "Jane started sending detailed agendas prior to our weekly meeting with marketing, thereby allowing everyone time to prepare and send adjustments as necessary. This helped the team dive in and cover a large number of topics in a short period of time."

- Stick to the facts: Note the behaviors (for example, Joe's follow-up e-mail campaigns increased sales by 10%) rather than judgments (for example, Mary doesn't know how to manage her time).
- Whenever possible, make your notes on the same day that you've given someone feedback, while it's still fresh in your mind.
- Hang on to e-mails or notes that highlight the accomplishments of your employee, whether they're instances you've noticed yourself or praise from others.
- For performance issues, document the issue and the next steps, including timelines, action items, training, specific goals, and expected outcomes.
- Check in (via e-mail or a face-to-face meeting) with other people who are in a position to evaluate your employee's performance, such as direct reports, clients, vendors, and peers. Ask for feedback on qualities or behaviors, including specific examples that support their observations. Document their feedback, and add it to your file.
- Request regular informal progress reports from your employee that explain how their work is progressing, as well as any concerns or problems they may be having. This will tip you off if there are any issues brewing in your employee's performance

and give you the heads-up about what they plan to do next.

When it comes time to conduct your employee's annual review, the bulk of the work will already be done, since you'll have kept such good notes. Your task will then be merely to review and find common themes, rather than rack your brain for highlights or relying on only the most recent performance.

Section 3
Tough Topics

Chapter 14

How to Help an Underperformer

by Amy Gallo

As a manager, you can't accept underperformance. It's frustrating, it's time-consuming, and it can demoralize the other people on your team. But what do you do about an employee whose performance isn't up to snuff? How do you provide them with the feedback they need and help turn around the problematic behavior? And how long do you let it go on before you cut your losses? By facing the issue head-on and creating a correction plan with your employee, you can set your underperformer on the path for improvement.

What the Experts Say

Your company may have a prescribed way of handling an underperformer, but most of those recommended

---

Adapted from content posted on hbr.org on June 23, 2014

processes aren't that useful, says Jean-François Manzoni, INSEAD professor and coauthor of the book *The Set-Up-to-Fail Syndrome: How Good Managers Cause Great People to Fail.* "When you talk to senior executives, they'll usually acknowledge that those don't work," he says. So it's up to you as the manager to figure out what to do. "When people encounter an issue with underperformance, they really are on their own," says Joseph Weintraub, coauthor of *The Coaching Manager: Developing Top Talent in Business.*

Here's how to stage a productive intervention.

Don't ignore the problem

Too often, underperformance issues go unaddressed. "Most performance problems aren't dealt with directly," says Weintraub. "More often, instead of taking action, the manager will transfer the person somewhere else or let him stay put without doing anything." This is the wrong approach. Never allow underperformance to fester on your team. It's rare that these situations resolve themselves, and they will likely get worse. "You'll become more and more irritated and that's going to show and make the person uncomfortable," says Manzoni. If a problem arises, take steps toward solving it as soon as possible.

Consider what's causing the problem

Is the person a poor fit for the job? Do they lack the necessary skills? Or have they just misunderstood expectations? When it comes to performance, it's common to find mismatches between what managers and employees think is important, Weintraub explains. Consider the role you might be playing in the problem. "You may have contributed to the negative situation," says Manzoni. "After all, it's rare that it's all the subordinate's fault just as it's rare that it's all the boss's." Don't focus exclusively on what the underperformer needs to do to remedy the situation—think about what changes you can make as well.

Ask others what you might be missing

Before you act, look at the problem objectively. Talk to the person's previous boss or someone who's worked with them, or conduct a 360 review. When approaching other people, though, do it carefully and confidentially. Manzoni suggests you say something like: "I'm worried that my frustration may be clouding my judgment. All I can see are the mistakes he's making. I want to make an honest effort to see what I'm missing." Look for evidence that proves your assumptions wrong.

Talk to the underperformer

Once you've checked in with others, talk to the employee directly. Explain exactly what you're observing, point to ways the team's work is affected, and make clear that you want to help. Manzoni suggests the conversation go something like this: "I'm seeing issues with your performance. I believe that you can do better and I know that I may be contributing to the problem. So how do we get out of this? How do we improve?" It's important to engage the person in brainstorming solutions. "Ask them to come up with ideas," says Weintraub. Don't expect an immediate response though. They may need time to digest your feedback and come back later with some proposals.

Confirm that the person is coachable

In most cases, the next step would be to arrange ongoing feedback or coaching sessions. But you can't coach someone who doesn't agree that they need help. In the initial conversation—and throughout the intervention—the employee must acknowledge the problem. "If someone says, 'I am who I am' or implies that they're not going to change, then you've got to make a decision whether you can live with the issue and at what cost," says Weintraub. On the other hand, if you see a willingness to change and a genuine interest in improving, chances are you can work together to turn things around.

Make a plan

Once you've confirmed that the person is coachable, create a concrete plan for what both you and the employee are going to do differently, agreeing on measurable actions so you can mark progress. Write down the specific goals to be met and plan the execution of these tasks by assigning start and end dates. Then identify what resources the employee needs to accomplish those goals, whether time, equipment, or assistance or coaching from others. Once you've outlined everything on paper, ask them how they feel about the plan, answering any questions or clarifying any points as necessary. You don't want them to make promises they can't meet, and you want to make sure you're in agreement moving forward. Then, give them time. "Everyone needs time to change and maybe learn or acquire new skills," says Weintraub.

Regularly monitor progress

Once the conversation is over, the manager's work isn't done. You must follow up to make sure that the correction plan is being implemented. Ask the person to check in with you regularly, or set up specific dates in the future to check progress. It may be helpful to ask the employee if they have someone they'd like you to enlist in the effort. Weintraub suggests you ask: "Is there anyone you trust who can provide me with feedback about how well you're doing in making these changes?" Doing this sends a positive message: "It says I want this to work and I want you to feel comfortable; I'm not going to sneak around your back."

Respect confidentiality

Along the way, it's important to keep what's happening confidential—while also letting others know you're working on the underperformance problem. Manzoni admits that this is a tricky balancing act. Don't discuss the specific details with others, he says. But you might tell them something like: "Bill and I are working together on his output and lately we've had good discussions. I need your help in being as positive and supportive as you can."

Praise and reward positive change

If the person makes positive changes, say so. Make clear that you've noticed developments, and reward your employee accordingly. "At some point, if the nonperformer has improved, be sure to take them off the death spiral. You want a team that can make mistakes and learn from them," says Weintraub.

If there isn't improvement, take action

Of course, if things don't get better, change the tenor of the discussion. "At some point you leave coaching and get into the consequences speech. You might say, 'Let me be very clear that this is the third time this has happened, and since your behavior hasn't changed, I need to explain the consequences,'" says Weintraub. Disciplinary actions, particularly letting someone go, shouldn't be taken lightly. "When you fire somebody, it not only affects that person, but also you, the firm, and everybody around you," says Manzoni.

While it may be painful to fire someone, it may be the best option for your team. "It's disheartening if you see the person next to you not performing," says Weintraub. Manzoni elaborates: "The person you're asking to leave is only one of the stakeholders. The people left behind are the more important ones . . . When people feel the process is fair, they're willing to accept a negative outcome."

Principles to Remember

Do:

- Take action as soon as possible—the sooner you intervene the better
- Consider how you might be contributing to the performance issues

- Make a concrete, measurable plan for improvement

Don't:

- Assume the issue is resolved after one conversation
- Try to coach someone who is unwilling to admit that there's an issue
- Talk about specific performance issues with others on the team

Case Study 1: Commit to the Time Investment

Allie Rogovin managed a five-person team at Teach For America when she brought in Max (name has been changed) as a recruiting coordinator. The job had two main responsibilities: completing administrative duties that supported the recruiting team and managing special projects. Allie recognized that the administrative component wasn't that exciting, so she "let him know that the better and faster he completed these tasks, the more time he'd have for the fun projects." But before long, Max was struggling with the core part of his role. "I realized a couple months into the job he wasn't getting his administrative duties done in time," she admits.

Allie started by giving Max an action plan template. She asked him to take 20 minutes at the end of each day to enter and prioritize all of his tasks. She then reviewed his list every evening and gave him input on how he might shuffle his priorities for the next day. They also

WHAT PEOPLE ARE SAYING ON HBR.ORG

Yes, it's important to gauge whether the employee is coachable. It is equally important to **determine if the manager is competent to coach the employee through the process.** Too many managers lack the skill or patience to help the employee work their way through the performance issue. The best manager-teacher-coach will be flexible in helping the employee utilize skills and talents different from the manager's rather than using the old, stale, "Here, let me show you how it's done."
—Posted by Mike

Do you have the right person in the right position? And if so, have you translated the organization's vision to their position? **Too many times we put people in positions, thinking they are the right person, and then we don't help them succeed.** We don't translate the vision of the company into their specific area and set specific key performance indicators for that person or team.

So, when you address this problem, remember to go back to the basic, foundational reason for that person's position, and let them know how it helps achieve the overall vision.
—Posted by RJ

started meeting three times a week instead of just once a week.

"He was a very valuable team member, and I knew he could do a good job. That made me want to invest time in working with him," she says. She continued meeting with Max regularly and reviewing his priorities for three months: "I didn't think it was going to be that long but I wanted to see that he was building new habits." Max still occasionally missed deadlines but he was showing definite signs of improvement.

"We tweaked the plan along the way and he eventually got into the swing of things," she says. "I frankly wouldn't have done it if I didn't see huge potential in him."

Case Study 2: Recognize When Change Won't Happen

Bill Wright (not his real name), a business developer at a residential building company, hired a new project manager last summer. We'll call him Jack. Right from the start, Bill saw performance issues. One of Jack's primary responsibilities was to develop small projects. That meant defining the scope of the project, talking with homeowners, negotiating with subcontractors, and coordinating with design professionals. "He was taking too long to get things done. What should have taken days, was taking three to four weeks," Bill says. This was problematic for many reasons: "I was supposed to be billing his time to the client but I couldn't bill for the amount of time he was putting in. Plus, I had disgruntled homeowners who were wondering why things were taking so long."

Bill met with Jack weekly to review the current workload, prioritize tasks, and resolve any issues. "I wanted to help him move things forward, but eventually I got so frustrated that I started to take projects over," Bill says. At Jack's 90-day review, Bill had a frank conversation with his employee about the consequences of not being able to turn around his performance. "When I asked what he needed, Jack said that he wanted more than an hour of my time each week to get more input on his work. I said I was happy to do that and asked him to go ahead and schedule a regular meeting time," Bill says. But Jack never followed up or put any additional time on Bill's calendar.

"It was very clear that it wasn't working out. There were never signs of any progress." That's when Bill sat Jack down and made it clear that his job was on the line. Again, there was no change in behavior, so several weeks later, he let Jack go. "I look back on it and realize I made a bad hire. I recently hired his replacement and it's like night and day. He already gets the job."

Amy Gallo is a contributing editor at Harvard Business Review and the author of the *HBR Guide to Managing Conflict at Work.*

Chapter 15

Delivering Criticism to a Defensive Employee

by Holly Weeks

How do you handle giving unfavorable feedback to someone who will surely take it badly—and I mean *really* badly? Think shouting, tears, defensiveness, accusations, personal attacks, revising history, twisting words—pick your nightmare.

Consider the case of Melissa, who was the team leader on a recently concluded project that had been an unsatisfactory experience for the whole group. For most of the team, the project was a disappointment from the start:

Adapted from content posted on hbr.org on August 12, 2015

team members were assigned, not self-selected; it was not a high-profile project; and the deliverables were really important only for Melissa's mentor's research. Melissa's role was not a powerful one. She was first among equals and the liaison to management, but had more responsibility than actual authority. The carrot that management held out to members of the team was that this was a stepping-stone project: if the results were satisfactory, they could anticipate higher-profile projects going forward.

James, a team member working from a remote location, handled the situation by making the project a lower priority than his other work. He often finished his tasks late or failed to deliver at all, but he knew Melissa would pick up the slack because it was in her mentor's interest for someone to do so. He considered this a pragmatic solution—he had a lot of work to do. His miscalculation, however, was to assume that the team's work would be seen only as a whole. Instead, when the project ended, Melissa was asked to recommend individuals from the team for a new, more important project. James would not be one of them, and Melissa had scheduled a feedback session with him to let him know.

Melissa knew the conversation would not go well. James was known to shout at people, distort their words, accuse them of victimizing him, and more. Melissa's own temperament was unlike his, and the thought of giving James negative feedback was a nightmare.

How should Melissa handle the situation?

When we fear someone's reaction, most of us look for techniques to make the other person act differently.

But when they get disagreeable feedback, people generally repeat tactics that they've had success with in the past—that's why they use them. In the face of negative feedback, it's likely that James will be surprised and angry. He's likely to believe that Melissa misrepresented the project's outcome and is scapegoating him, robbing him of the only benefit of four months' work. In James' view, how he responds makes sense: Melissa is not reliable, not his boss, and intends to hurt him. Why would he act differently? He wants her to back off.

Melissa foresees that scenario, but her temperament makes her vulnerable to choosing what business theorist Chris Argyris calls "defensive strategies"—ambiguous, counterproductive behavior chosen to avoid interpersonal discomfort. Examples of this might be Melissa deferring to James, apologizing and agreeing that he is being misused, while stressing that she is just the messenger. Or she might e-mail the message, letting him simmer in solitude. Or she could ask someone else to tell him. Any of these would protect Melissa from immediate discomfort, but they also signal weak competence.

Defensive strategies become "skilled incompetence," Argyris says—we get really good at avoiding the difficult bits, but can't reach good outcomes and never really accomplish our goals. That can't be recommended as a feedback approach, even if it seems better than butting heads.

Yet if Melissa does try to toughen up and match James' confrontational style, even though she knows firsthand that won't be well received, it's sure to backfire. Emotions will rise, and the conversation will degenerate on both sides, destroying the relationship and potentially both of their reputations.

Melissa needs to try a different approach. One tactic is to focus on immunizing herself against her own vulnerability to James' difficult behavior. This is like a scientist who, when studying how a pathogen compromises a cell, focuses on the cell, not the bug.

How would Melissa self-immunize against James' outbursts? By recognizing that *she* has to react to the tactic for it to work. Instead of reacting, she can neutralize how she responds, without giving in or giving up what she has to say. To get there, she can use a blueprint that pulls together three attributes of speaking well in tough moments: clear content, neutral tone, and temperate phrasing.

> **Clear content:** Let your words do your work for you. Say what you mean. Imagine that you are a newscaster and that it's important that people understand the information. If your counterpart distorts what you say, repeat it just as you said it the first time.
>
> **Neutral tone:** Tone is the nonverbal part of the message you're delivering. It's the inflection in your voice, your facial expressions, and your conscious and unconscious body language. These all carry emotional weight in a difficult conversation. It's hard to use a neutral tone when your emotions are running high. That's why you need to practice it ahead of time, so you become accustomed to using it. Think of the

classic neutrality of NASA communications in tough situations: "Houston, we have a problem."

Temperate phrasing: There are lots of different ways to say what you have to say. Some are considered and nonconfrontational; some baldly provoke your counterpart with loaded language. If your counterpart dismisses, resists, or throws back your words, he's not likely to hold on to your content—so choose your words carefully. (See the sidebar "Phrases to Make Sure You're Heard.")

PHRASES TO MAKE SURE YOU'RE HEARD

By Amy Gallo

- "My perspective is based on the following assumptions . . ."
- "I came to this conclusion because . . ."
- "I'd love to hear your reaction to what I just said."
- "Do you see any flaws in my reasoning?"
- "Do you see the situation differently?"

Adapted from the *HBR Guide to Managing Conflict at Work* (product #15006), Harvard Business Review Press, 2015.

Amy Gallo is a contributing editor at Harvard Business Review and the author of the *HBR Guide to Managing Conflict at Work*.

Clear content, neutral tone, and temperate phrasing are a package deal. Melissa won't get good results if she uses temperate phrasing, but mixes her message with a lot of contradictory body language. Nor will it work well if she softens her content because she thinks it is too blunt. Being blunt is a characteristic of intemperate phrasing, not of content. So softening the content to fix a problem of phrasing won't get her where she wants to go.

If Melissa says to James, "In February, March, and April, the team didn't get the deliverables you committed to on the dates you agreed to," her content is clear and her phrasing is temperate. We have to imagine that her tone is neutral, but Melissa can do it. If she says, "With those omissions, I can't stand behind a recommendation for you," she is clear and temperate again. We do understand that the news is not good and James is still likely to dip into his arsenal of difficult tactics. But Melissa is on solid ground, neither altering her message nor responding to his tactics. With this blueprint in place, repetition can be a good friend: if James challenges her or distorts her message, Melissa can repeat what she has said, rather than following James down a rabbit hole. When it's time to end the meeting, she can say something simple such as: "Thank you for meeting with me. [Short pause.] I wish this had worked out differently."

Will James be happy with this conversation? I think not. Nobody likes unfavorable feedback. But remember, when delivering negative feedback to someone who's likely to get defensive, it's not your job to make the other person feel better. It's your job to convey the information in a clear, neutral, and temperate way—by sticking to the facts and to the blueprint.

Holly Weeks publishes, teaches, and consults on communications issues. She is Adjunct Lecturer in Public Policy at the Harvard Kennedy School and the author of *Failure to Communicate: How Conversations Go Wrong and What You Can Do to Right Them* (Harvard Business School Press, 2008).

Chapter 16

How to Give Star Performers Productive Feedback

by Amy Gallo

As counterintuitive as it may seem, giving feedback to a top performer can be even tougher than giving it to an underperformer or a combative employee. Top performers may not have obvious development needs, and in identifying those needs, you can feel like you're being nitpicky or overdemanding. In addition, top performers may not be used to hearing constructive feedback and may bristle at the slightest hint that they're not perfect.

But giving your stars good feedback is essential to keeping them engaged, focused, and motivated. Luckily,

Adapted from content posted on hbr.org on December 3, 2009

feedback discussions do not need to be unpleasant, especially with top performers. Instead of dreading your next conversation with them, think of it as an exciting opportunity to celebrate success and discuss what's next.

What the Experts Say

Don't be tempted to bend the rules for top performers. No matter who the receiver is, follow good feedback practice. Do your homework: Gather data and details to support your point of view. Always describe behaviors, not traits. Don't dwell on the past; focus on what the employee can change in the future. Check for understanding and clarify and agree on the next steps and a fair way to measure progress.

That said, feedback for your top performers does require special care. Don't assume your star is perfect. INSEAD professor Jean-François Manzoni says, "Everyone has some room for improvement, in this job or the next, within our current set of capabilities or a broader set that will likely come in handy in the future." You do your stars a disservice if you fail to help them figure out how they can continue to grow.

When conducting your research, remember that results don't always speak for themselves. High performers often have great results, yet it's important to understand *how* they achieve those results and at what cost. Unfortunately, they often get results by forgoing other things, such as caring for their people, building alliances with others, or maintaining a healthy work-life balance. In addition, top performers' strengths may often be their weaknesses. For instance, an employee who has the ability to stay out of workplace drama and focus on her work may be perceived by peers as unapproachable. Think carefully about the behaviors that have enabled your star to succeed—they may be the same behaviors holding her back.

To make the most of your feedback sessions, regularly discuss these three topics: current performance, the next performance frontier, and future goals and aspirations.

Express gratitude for current performance

Many managers make the mistake of assuming that their top performers already know how well they are doing. Always start your feedback session by specifically stating what your star has accomplished. Show gratitude for their contributions and successes. As Manzoni says, "Advice is more likely to be welcome if it builds on comments acknowledging and celebrating this year's performance and is clearly positioned at helping the subordinate continue to develop beyond the current role and capability set." Constructive feedback is more easily received if it is preceded by genuine appreciation for hard work. Given how valuable your star is to you and your organization, you can't express enough how much you value them.

WHAT PEOPLE ARE SAYING ON HBR.ORG

If you're not getting constructive feedback from your manager, you don't need to wait for review time to ask. Explain to your manager that you want feedback. After a project milestone or a particularly important meeting, ask your manager if she has any feedback for you.

(*continued*)

(*continued*)

You can ask questions such as, "Do you think I handled that OK?" or "Do you have any advice about how I might do better next time?" Be prepared to ask follow-up questions, especially if you are a star performer. Chances are you're doing great and your manager will need to be prompted to think about how you can improve. Many managers are inexperienced in giving feedback, and the more you can be clear about what you are looking for, the more helpful it will be to [your manager].

—Posted by Amy

I've seen star performers leave organizations because they are starved for constructive feedback from their managers. **They often assume that their manager doesn't care about their performance because of the lack of feedback they receive.**

—Posted by Gabrielle

What I find useful is to **give feedback that helps shape the person's personal goals as well as professional goals.** For example, I have one employee who is passionate about the Middle East and Arabic studies. So we found a way at UniversalGiving to let her find and

source NGOs (nongovernmental organizations) in that area. It fits her goals, and it fits ours. She moved from Executive Assistance (which she did very well) to NGO Marketing.
—Posted by Pamela

Research is clear on the importance of feedback—both positive and negative—on employee engagement. It's those employees who are ignored who just don't care to give their all. Gallup proved this in a study showing:

- Managers who focus on employee strengths have 61% engaged employees and 1% actively disengaged.
- Managers who focus on employee weaknesses have 45% engaged employees and 22% actively disengaged.
- Managers who ignore their employees have 2% engaged employees and 40% actively disengaged.

It's critical to note that it is the direct manager's behavior that has the most impact on engagement. Too many, however, prefer to just close the door and ignore their teams.
—Posted by Derek

Discuss obstacles to their development

Your top performer is likely committed to self-improvement—that's probably one of the ways he became a top performer. As a manager, it's your responsibility to help him determine how to keep improving. Tap into that commitment and engage your high performer in a discussion about how he might achieve the next level of performance, whether it is a new sales target or a promotion. Discussions should include acknowledging what might be standing in the way and how he can overcome those obstacles. These don't need to be negative conversations, however. Manzoni had a particularly good manager who adeptly helped him think about what was next and how he could get there. As Manzoni says, "I never felt criticized. Instead, I walked into his office six feet tall, and I came out of it nine feet tall."

Identify future goals and aspirations

Once you and your star have agreed on where she is headed, ask about her motivation and values. Ask prompting questions such as "What do you want to be known for?" or "What matters most to you?" This will give her a chance to reflect on her career path and how this current role and the next performance frontier fit in. It will give your high performer what Jamie Harris, a senior consultant at Interaction Associates, describes as a "window into greater awareness about what enables [your star] to succeed in the current situation and what she wants to achieve next." It will also allow you to figure out how you can align the person's motivations with those of the company. Harris says, "Some people perform well in any context, but people will almost always perform well when their own excellence is aligned with that of the organization."

As you give feedback to high performers, solicit their input on how you are doing as a manager. Ask questions such as "How can I continue to support your high performance?" or "What can we do as an organization to keep getting better and supporting your great work?" This is important because, as Harris says, it "shows that you're their ally in achieving what they want to achieve. This also helps cement their connection to the organization."

Frequency is key

In giving feedback to your stars, frequency is crucial. Harris warns that you shouldn't be tempted to leave your high performers alone. He says, "The higher the performer, the more frequently you should be providing feedback." Don't wait for review time. You and your company depend on retaining top performers. Therefore, it is a wise investment of your time and energy to support and develop them.

Principles to Remember

Do:

- Give both positive and constructive feedback to high performers regularly
- Identify development areas, even if there are only a few

- Focus on the future and ask about motivations and goals

Don't:

- Presume your stars have reached the limits of their performance
- Leave your top performers alone
- Assume your best workers know how appreciated they are

Case Study: Reframing Feedback in the Context of Long-Term Goals

Gretchen Anderson has worked with many young, ambitious professionals throughout her career. During her tenure at a strategy consulting firm, Gretchen managed a particularly ambitious consultant named Melissa. Melissa was an extremely hardworking associate—so hardworking that Gretchen and others at the firm were concerned she would not be able to sustain her accelerated pace. Her reviews consisted mostly of positive feedback about her performance. However, Gretchen felt she needed to address the pace of Melissa's work: "I didn't want her to be another burnout story."

Upon hearing the feedback, Melissa became very emotional. She didn't understand why Gretchen would thank her for her hard work and then tell her to stop working so hard. She felt she should be the judge of when she was working too much. In each of Melissa's feedback sessions, this issue became a source of intense emotion for Melissa and conflict with Gretchen. Melissa regularly asked for follow-up sessions to keep discussing the issue and grilling Gretchen about the fairness of the feedback.

After a half-dozen conversations, Gretchen decided she needed to find a way to reframe the issue so Melissa could understand what was at stake. Instead of starting the sessions focused on current performance, Gretchen began by asking Melissa about her long-term career goals. Gretchen said, "I knew I couldn't change her nature, but I could focus on helping her change her behavior as long as I could get her in the right frame of mind first."

Melissa said she wanted to be promoted to manager as soon as possible. With that goal as the backdrop, Gretchen was able to explain more clearly to Melissa the consequences of her work pace: As a manager, Melissa would need to set an example for her associates. Also, if she was constantly working at capacity, how would she handle a last-minute client request? Melissa needed to figure out how to build more spaces into her schedule so that when she became a manager, she'd be able to serve her clients well and treat her associates fairly. Melissa's drive to work hard was not going to go away, so instead of battling that, Gretchen gave her a reason she could relate to for modifying her behavior.

Amy Gallo is a contributing editor at Harvard Business Review and the author of the *HBR Guide to Managing Conflict at Work*.

Chapter 17
Prioritizing Feedback—Even When Time Is Short

by Daisy Wademan Dowling

Virtually all of the young executives I work with want to be good managers and mentors. They just don't have the time—or so they believe. "I could either bring in a new deal or I could take one of my people out for lunch to talk about their career," a financial services leader told me recently. "In this industry and in this market, which one do you think I'm going to pick?"

Good question. It's not easy to help your employees develop while you're trying to take advantage of every

---

Adapted from the *HBR Guide to Coaching Employees* (product #13990), Harvard Business Review Press, 2015 business opportunity, but you can make it easier on yourself, in part by giving feedback efficiently.

Once you've identified that you need to give feedback to a direct report, make that process more efficient in three ways.

Create a Standard Way In

For the majority of managers, providing feedback—particularly constructive feedback—is stressful and requires significant forethought. How should you bring up the bungled analysis, the hurdles to promotion, or even the meeting that went unusually well? Like chess masters, we spend most of our time contemplating the first move. That's why the key to reducing the time you spend mulling over and preparing for each conversation is to have a standard way in: a simple, routinized way to open discussions about performance.

Keep it simple, and announce directly what's to come. A straightforward "I'm going to give you some feedback" or "Are you open to my coaching on this?" gets immediate attention and sets the right tone. It will make it easier to prepare for the game if you have your opener ready. Furthermore, your direct reports will become familiar with your opener, and that will help them be attuned to and hear the feedback more clearly.

Be Blunt

The number-one mistake executives make in coaching and delivering feedback to their people is being insufficiently candid—typically, because they don't want to be mean. If you've ever used the phrase "Maybe you could . . ."

in a coaching conversation or asked one of your people to "think about" a performance issue, there's a 99% probability you're not being blunt enough. But the more candid you are, the more likely your direct report is to hear your message, and thus the more likely you are to have impact, and quickly. The trick to being candid without feeling like an ogre? Be honest, be sincere, be personal—while addressing the issue head-on.

The best feedback I ever received came a few years into my career, directly after a terrible meeting I had with senior management in which I had been both unprepared and defensive. As we rode down in the elevator afterward, my boss said quietly, "Next time, I expect you to do better." Don't dance around the issues, and don't let the recipient do so either.

Ask for Playback

If your feedback doesn't stick, you'll need to deliver it a second time—and a third, and a fourth—all of which takes your valuable time and managerial energy. To avoid the need for encore performances, make sure you've made an impact on the first go-round by asking the person to paraphrase what he heard. If he can clearly explain to you—in his own words—what he needs to change or do next, that goes a long way to ensuring he's gotten the message. Then you'll know that the conversation is over and you can get back to other things. If the message is muddled, you can correct it immediately. In either case, you've curtailed the need for future follow-up.

By doing these things regularly (perhaps even daily), you'll not only save yourself and your direct report time, but your employees will feel that you're not just their boss, but a coach. They'll sharpen their skills *and* stay motivated. And for any manager, that's time well spent.

Daisy Wademan Dowling serves as managing director and head of talent development for the Blackstone Group, the global asset management firm. She is also the author of *Remember Who You Are* (Harvard Business School Press, 2004) and a regular contributor to HBR.

Chapter 18
Navigating the Choppy Waters of Cross-Cultural Feedback

by Andy Molinsky

Although many of us don't like to do it, we know that critiquing others' work—ideally in a constructive, polite, empowering manner—is an essential part of our jobs. But does critical feedback work similarly across cultures? Do people in Shanghai provide critical feedback in the same way as people in Stuttgart, Strasbourg, and Stockholm?

Nein, non, and *nej.*

Instead, they confront situations where they do have to adjust their feedback style, and sometimes that's easier

---

Adapted from content posted on hbr.org on February 15, 2013

said than done. Take the case of Jens, a German executive who was sent by the German corporate headquarters of his company to improve efficiency at the company's manufacturing plant in Shanghai. All his efforts, however, seemed to be producing the exact opposite result. Employee productivity and effectiveness were both going down, and Jens could not figure out what was going wrong. He was using everything he knew that worked in Germany—especially in terms of performance feedback. In fact, he made doubly sure to be just as demanding and exacting with his Chinese employees as he would have been with German staff. If his Chinese employees failed to produce what he was looking for, Jens would be "on it," providing immediate critique to get the process moving back in the right direction. But this approach failed miserably. Rather than improving efficiency, Jens seemed to be reducing it, and his own bosses from corporate started to make calls. The entire situation was becoming a disaster.

It turns out that what worked in Germany in terms of tough, critical, to-the-point negative feedback was actually demotivating to Jens's new Chinese employees, who were used to a far gentler feedback style. In Germany, you typically don't single out specific accomplishments or offer praise unless the accomplishment is truly extraordinary. Employees are expected to do a particular job, and when they do that job, they do not need to be recognized. In China—at least at this particular plant—the culture was quite different. Employees expected more positive reinforcement rather than pure critique. Positive comments were what motivated them to increase productivity and put forth that extra, discretionary effort.

It took quite some time and effort on Jens's part to recognize this difference and to be willing to adapt his behavior to accommodate the Chinese approach because to him, this motivational style felt awkward and unnatural. He didn't feel like himself when he was "soft" with his employees, and he had serious doubts about the effectiveness of doing so. However, over time and through quite a bit of trial and error, Jens was able to develop a new feedback style that worked in the Chinese setting and also felt acceptable (or acceptable enough) to his German mind-set. It took time and effort, but in the end was quite effective.

Clearly, performance feedback can be very different across cultures, whether you're in Germany, China, the UK, or the US. Given that fact and our interest in becoming effective global managers, what can you do to ensure your style fits the new setting?

- **Learn the new cultural rules.** Many managers I speak with tell me how they had just assumed their style was universal, and that lack of awareness was what initially got them into trouble. How direct and to-the-point are you expected to be? How important is it to save face or protect the social standing of others when delivering feedback in group settings? Learning the cultural code by reading up on the culture and observing it in action is the very first step toward developing cultural fluency.

- **Find a cultural mentor.** In Jens's case, he had a Chinese-born cultural mentor to help guide him out of this quagmire. Although this particular consultant didn't share Jens's German culture, he was globally savvy, having worked in high-level positions in multinational companies for many years. A mentor who appreciates your position as well as the expectations of the new culture can help you craft a new style that fits where you are and that feels authentic to you.

- **Customize your behavior.** Don't assume you have to follow the other culture's behavior to the letter to be successful. You often can create a blend or a hybrid that feels comfortable (enough) for you that is effective in the new setting. Jens, for example, was able to adjust his feedback style to be somewhat less frank than his German approach, and it worked.

As organizations become more global, most of us will be face to face with colleagues of different cultural backgrounds, whether it's abroad or in our own offices. Learning how to navigate difficult conversations and to provide critique across cultures is certainly a challenge. But with these tips in mind, you can face this challenge head-on, no matter what part of the world you're in.

Andy Molinsky is a professor of International Management and Organizational Behavior at the Brandeis International Business School. He is the author of the book *Global Dexterity: How to Adapt Your Behavior across Cultures without Losing Yourself in the Process* (Harvard Business Review Press, 2013).

Chapter 19

How to Discuss Performance with Your Team

by Rebecca Knight

The majority of this book has been geared toward giving individuals feedback. But you're not always dealing with one person at a time. What if you're assessing a team's work? What type of constructive criticism is appropriate in a group setting? How much is too much? And how should your colleagues help?

Just because you're facing a group of employees, rather than just one, doesn't mean you must hold your tongue. There are a few ways that you can provide feedback to the entire team so that they all benefit.

Adapted from content posted on hbr.org on June 16, 2014

What the Experts Say

Providing feedback isn't solely the team leader's responsibility, according to Mary Shapiro, author of the *HBR Guide to Leading Teams*. For starters, that would be impractical. "You can't be the only one holding everyone accountable because you can't possibly observe everything that's going on," she says. Second, if you're the only one praising or critiquing, group dynamics suffer. "You want to give everyone the opportunity to say his piece," she says. Your job as manager is to ensure that team members are "providing regular constructive feedback," says Roger Schwarz, organizational psychologist and author of *Smart Leaders, Smarter Teams*. "There needs to be an expectation within the team that this is a shared leadership responsibility," he says. Here are some principles to help you lay the groundwork for ensuring and enhancing this effective team practice.

Set expectations early

"When a team works well together, it's because its members are operating from the same mind-set and are clear about their goals and their norms," says Schwarz. At the start of a new project, help your direct reports "decide how they're going to work together"—and importantly, how they will "hold each other accountable," says Shapiro. She recommends coming up with an "explicit agreement" about how the team will handle issues like the division of labor and deadlines. Stipulate, for example, that if a colleague knows he is going to miss an important deadline for his portion of a project, he must e-mail the team at least 24 hours in advance. "If someone doesn't follow through on the expectations the team created, he'll get feedback from the group about what happened because he fell short."

Create opportunities for regular check-ins

There's no hard-and-fast rule about how often your team should meet to review how things are going, but in general, "it's better to start out with more structure and relax it over time, than to start out with too little structure and have to impose it later," Shapiro says. When you're in the early stages of creating a project plan, schedule regular check-ins as part of the timeline. "If the team is running smoothly, you can always cancel the meeting."

Ask general questions

Giving and receiving feedback is a skill—and most people are not naturally good at it, says Shapiro. "One of your goals is to develop your team's capacity to give feedback and help people get used to articulating how they feel the team is doing." Take baby steps. At the second or third check-in, ask the group general questions such as, "On a scale of 1 to 5, how well is the team sharing the workload? What needs to change?" As the leader, you're the moderator of this conversation. Once team members have spoken, offer your view about "where the team excels and where it faces challenges," Schwarz adds.

Work your way up to structured reviews

As your team gets accustomed to working together and sharing feedback, "you need to do a deeper dive into how team members are doing at the individual level," says Shapiro. Ask each person to prepare specific reviews of colleagues to be read aloud at the next meeting. "Every team member should say one thing they appreciate about the other members and one thing that would be helpful if they did differently." The aim is to help "people understand how their behavior is impacting others," she says. "If they hear the same kind of feedback from multiple people, that is powerful." When it's your turn, Schwarz recommends validating your observations with others. "Ask: 'Are you seeing things the same way?' Get other people's reactions."

Keep performance issues out in the open

The management mantra for giving individuals feedback is: "Praise in public, criticize in private." But in team settings, this goes out the window, according to Schwarz. "In the traditional view, it's inappropriate to raise issues in a meeting that would make people uncomfortable or put people on the spot." But your job as a leader is not always to make people feel comfortable. When teams have problems, "it should all be out in the open," he says. "You alone can't help people improve; there needs to be a group plan." After you've "harnessed the power of the group" to prompt change, one-on-one conversations with struggling colleagues are then in order, says Shapiro. "Say to them: 'What did you hear from the team? How are you going to do things differently? And how can I help?'"

Foster team relationships

Conflicts between coworkers are inevitable. But, Schwarz says, "you can't just say, 'I'll handle it,' because [as the manager] you can't solve a problem to which you're not a primary stakeholder. You can coach people on how to have difficult conversations, and you can help facilitate those conversations, but team members need to address issues where the interdependencies lie." Help colleagues build trust before problems arise by encouraging open conversation. And, when there is conflict, make sure they understand, they need to "give feedback directly to each other," says Schwarz. Adds Shapiro: "The only way good work gets done is through good relationships—the better the relationship, the better the work."

Debrief every project

At the end of a project or when your team is disbanding, schedule a final check-in to discuss "what worked and what didn't, what should we bring forward and what should we do differently next time," says Schwarz. Take careful notes: the information gleaned in this session should not only be part of the organization's final project review, but also part of each team member's annual performance appraisal, says Shapiro. The objective is to "provide closure on the team and also determine what each member needs to do to further develop," she says.

Principles to Remember

Do:

- Make sure your team understands that feedback is a shared leadership responsibility
- Schedule routine check-in meetings

- Keep the tone positive by encouraging team members to say what they appreciate about others' contributions

Don't:

- Shy away from performance issues
- Deliver your own feedback to the team without asking them how they think they're doing first
- Put yourself in the middle of personality conflicts

Case Study 1: Create Opportunities for Team and Individual Reflection

Once every quarter, Laree Daniel—chief administrative officer of Aflac, the insurance company—assembles an ad hoc team around a particular customer incident for an in-depth feedback session. "I take a customer case study in which we either did very well or very poorly, and I gather everyone that touched the customer in some form," she says.

First, Laree makes sure everyone is up to speed. Team members are given an information packet that includes a write-up of the incident, transcripts of phone calls, copies of customer letters, and copies of the company's responses. Next, she poses a series of questions to the team: What worked well? Where were the gaps? What can we do better?

The goal, she says, is to get the team to reflect on the company's behavior from both the customer's perspective and shareholder's. "This isn't about blame, and I'm not scolding anyone," she says. "I am the facilitator and I make it a neutral environment."

During these feedback meetings, colleagues often have epiphanies. "They realize: 'I didn't know [my behavior] would have that impact,'" she says. "It becomes a dynamic learning experience."

The feedback and information she picks up from those meetings are used to make process improvements. "Often the best ideas come from those people who were closest to the work."

Case Study 2: Focus on Empowering Your Team

David S. Rose, the angel investor and CEO of Gust—a platform for the sourcing and management of early-stage investments—has a simple approach when it comes to giving group feedback. "The goal is not to depress the team," he says. "I try to keep everything upbeat and lay out our strengths and our challenges.

A few years ago, for instance, he was involved in leading a 15-person technical team at a software company. The group's biggest issue was its disappointing B2B product suite. "Customers were unhappy and the front-end salespeople were being yelled at," he says. "As a team, we had some good individual contributors but we needed to get better at working together. I couldn't just walk in and give feedback along the lines of: 'These products are terrible; you're all fired.' We needed to identify the organizational problems and come up with a prescription for a path forward."

He broke the team into subgroups of two or three people, and he tasked each with brainstorming how to manage a particular inter-team challenge. The subgroups then provided feedback to everyone else; based on that, the team developed a strategy to improve workflow and communication. "We came up with a plan and the whole team felt empowered," he says. "We knew what the problems were and we figured out how to solve them."

Within nine months, he says, the products were in far better shape.

Rebecca Knight is a freelance journalist in Boston and a lecturer at Wesleyan University. Her work has been published in the *New York Times, USA Today,* and the *Financial Times.*

Index

Notes

Notes

Notes

Notes

Notes

Notes

Notes

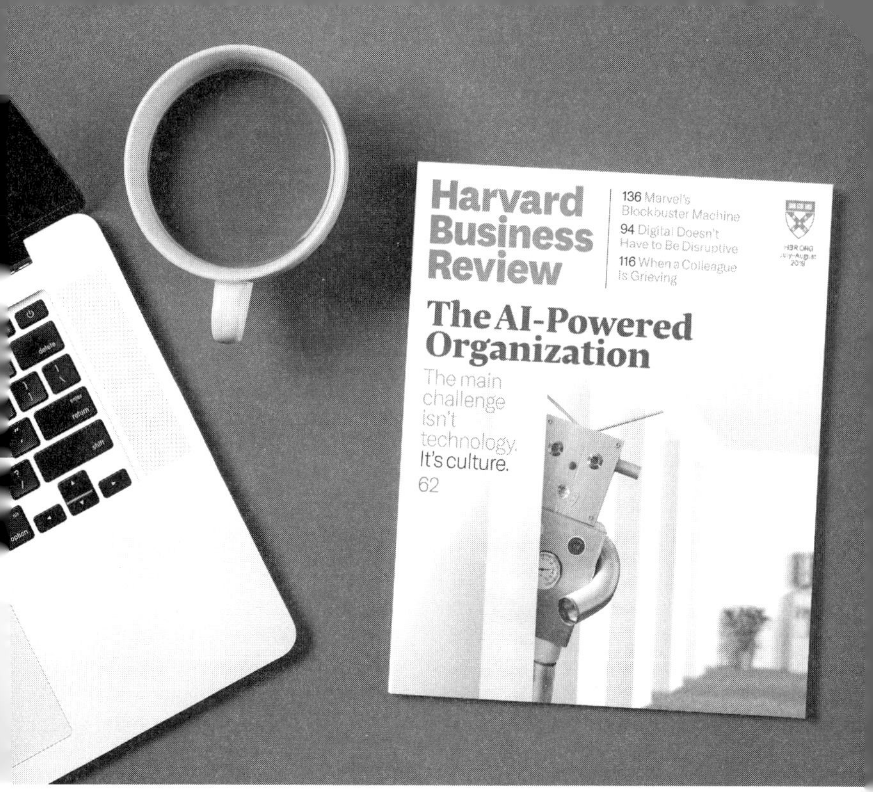
Harvard Business Review
136 Marvel's Blockbuster Machine
94 Digital Doesn't Have to Be Disruptive
116 When a Colleague is Grieving
The AI-Powered Organization
The main challenge isn't technology. It's culture.
62

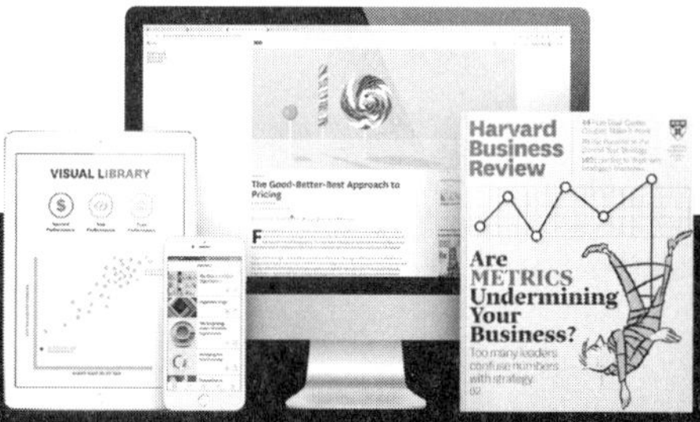
VISUAL LIBRARY
The Good-Better-Best Approach to Pricing
Harvard Business Review
Are METRICS Undermining Your Business?

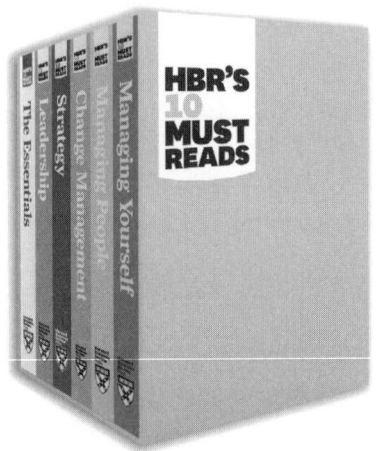

HBR Guide to **Negotiating**

Harvard Business Review Guides

Arm yourself with the advice you need to succeed on the job, from the most trusted brand in business. Packed with how-to essentials from leading experts, the HBR Guides provide smart answers to your most pressing work challenges.

The titles include:

HBR Guide to Better Business Writing

HBR Guide to Building Your Business Case

HBR Guide to Coaching Employees

HBR Guide to Finance Basics for Managers

HBR Guide to Getting the Mentoring You Need

HBR Guide to Getting the Right Job

HBR Guide to Getting the Right Work Done

HBR Guide to Giving Effective Feedback

HBR Guide to Leading Teams

HBR Guide to Making Every Meeting Matter

HBR Guide to Managing Stress at Work

HBR Guide to Managing Up and Across

HBR Guide to Negotiating

HBR Guide to Networking

HBR Guide to Office Politics

HBR Guide to Persuasive Presentations

HBR Guide to Project Management

HBR Guide to **Negotiating**

Jeff Weiss

HARVARD BUSINESS REVIEW PRESS

Boston, Massachusetts

Printed in the United States of America

10 9 8 7 6

Names: Weiss, Jeff A., author.
Title: HBR guide to negotiating / Jeff Weiss.
Other titles: Harvard Business Review guide to negotiating
Description: Boston, Massachusetts : Harvard Business Review Press, [2016]
Identifiers: LCCN 2015044110 (print) | LCCN 2015049476 (ebook) | ISBN 9781633690769 (hardcover : alk. paper) | ISBN 9781633690776 ()
Subjects: LCSH: Negotiation in business.
Classification: LCC HD58.6 .W45 2016 (print) | LCC HD58.6 (ebook) | DDC 658.4/052–dc23
LC record available at http://lccn.loc.gov/2015044110

ISBN: 9781633690769
eISBN: 9781633690776

The paper used in this publication meets the requirements of the American National Standard for Permanence of Paper for Publications and Documents in Libraries and Archives Z39.48-1992.

What You'll Learn

For many people, negotiating may be scary or unpleasant. You worry that you may not have the right skills to go head-to-head with someone and get what you deserve, or that you'll damage your relationship with your boss, customer, or colleague in the process. You fear that the negotiation will escalate into hard bargaining or a heated debate and that, in the end, one of you is going to have to give up something you want just to reach an agreement.

But negotiations don't need to be stressful. You can work with your counterpart to get what both of you want in a more productive, positive way. In this guide, you'll learn a collaborative and creative approach that results in better outcomes and stronger relationships. It works in any situation in which you and a counterpart need to come to terms despite competing interests—from formal multimillion-dollar sales agreements to informal conversations with colleagues about how you will tackle a quick project.

You'll get better at:

- Identifying the real issues at stake
- Overcoming your assumptions about the other party

- Preparing materials in advance
- Setting the right tone as you begin the conversation
- Coming up with potential solutions that work for both parties
- Narrowing down your options
- Handling emotions in the negotiating room
- Recovering when communications break down
- Taming the hard bargainer
- Knowing when to walk away—and how to strengthen your fallback plan beforehand
- Managing multiple-party negotiations
- Reality-proofing your agreement
- Learning from your negotiation

Contents

Introduction

Negotiation is about creativity, not compromise.

Whether you're aware of it or not, you're negotiating all the time. When you ask your boss for more resources, agree with a vendor on a price, deliver a performance evaluation, convince a business partner to join forces with your company, or even decide with your spouse where to go on your next vacation, you're taking a potentially conflict-filled conversation and working toward a joint solution. That's what a negotiation is—a situation in which two parties with potentially competing incentives and goals come together to create a solution that satisfies everyone.

It's not just high-stakes, months-long discussions that warrant a thoughtful approach. Improving your ability to handle all of these situations pays off. This means honing skills such as conflict management (as you'd expect) and creative thinking (which you might not), both of which are critical to reaching mutually beneficial decisions.

I've heard many people say that being a good negotiator is about thinking quickly on your feet or being a better orator or debater than your counterpart. Sure, those things are helpful. But the best negotiators—the ones who most often get what they want—are those who are the most prepared and the most creative.

This guide will help you develop the skills to negotiate like them so that you'll be more effective at work—and even get that trip to Maui on the calendar.

The advice in this guide is meant for professionals at all levels. You may have years of experience under your belt or be relatively new to negotiation. It is also applicable to negotiations of any size, whether you're the lone person at the table or have a team supporting you. Throughout the guide, I'll give examples of negotiations large and small to show you how the tactics I recommend play out.

Rethink Your Approach to Negotiations

There's a popular misconception that in a negotiation, you can either "win" or preserve your relationship with your counterpart—your boss, a customer, a business partner—but you can't do both. People assume they need to choose between getting good results by being hard and bargaining at all costs or developing a good relationship by being soft and making concessions.

That way of thinking causes the typical negotiation to go something like this:

Party 1: Here's what I want.

Party 2: Here's what I want.

Party 1: OK, I'll make this small concession to get closer to what you want. But just this one time.

Party 2: OK, since you did that, I'll also make a small concession. But just this one time.

Party 1: Well, that was the best I can do.

Party 2: Me, too.

Party 1: I guess I need to get my boss involved (or find someone else with whom to negotiate).

Party 2: I may need to walk away, too.

Party 1: Maybe there's something I can do. What if I make this additional concession?

Party 2: That would help.

Party 1: I'll need to get a concession from you then.

Party 2: OK. What if we agreed to split the difference?

Party 1: It's a deal.

Sound familiar? This is a common approach, often called "positional bargaining." People believe that if they go into the negotiation looking stern and unmovable, and then make small planned concessions and not-so-thinly veiled threats along the way, they'll have more influence and get the results they want. But in my view, that isn't a path toward negotiation that gets you what you want. It's simply a haggle, a concessions game that forces you (and your counterpart) to compromise.

Positional bargaining isn't all bad. It can be quick and efficient. It requires little preparation other than knowing what your opening offer is, what concessions you're willing to make, and any threats you might use. And in the end, it always feels as if you got something, because if your counterpart played his role, then he conceded as well. In fact, positional bargaining works well when you are negotiating simple transactions that have low stakes and you don't care about your ongoing relationship with the other party (think about agreeing on a price for that leather couch off Craigslist).

But this approach can be dangerous. In almost all business negotiations—requesting a raise with your boss, resolving a conflict with a customer, convincing others of a change in policy, agreeing on a budget for next year, for example—there is a lot more at stake, and chances are strong that you'll need to continue to work with the other party going forward. If you were to try to use positional bargaining in those situations, you wouldn't get impressive results. You have to be able to stand firm *and* maintain important relationships.

Positional bargaining rewards stubbornness and deception; it often yields arbitrary outcomes; and it risks doing damage to your relationships. Most importantly, it causes you to miss the opportunity to get more value out of the negotiation than you originally expected. In other words, you won't be creative and find ways to expand the pie because you'll be so focused on exactly how to divide it up.

Perhaps most dangerously, there is an underlying assumption in this approach that you're in a zero-sum game: If you gain something, the other party has to give up something in return. In the vast majority of negotia-

TABLE I-1

A critical shift in negotiations approach

From	To
What do you want?	Why do you want it?
Will you accept, or will you give up?	What are some different possible ways we might resolve this?
How about we just split it?	By what criteria/legitimate process can we evaluate (and defend) the best answer?
Saying, "I understand"	Showing I understand
Thinking my strength comes from knowing I am right, anchoring well, and effectively using threats	Thinking my strength comes from being open to learning and persuasion, being skilled at figuring out their motives, and being extremely creative

tions I've worked on, there is always more value to be created than originally thought. The pie is rarely—probably never—fixed.

To negotiate more effectively, you need to shift your approach away from this combative and compromising approach and toward a more collaborative one. Table I-1 shows how to reframe key questions about the negotiation with this approach in mind. For example, instead of asking yourself, "What am I willing to give up?" you might think more creatively and wonder, "What are different ways we can resolve this?" This helps ensure you aren't shrinking the pie but expanding it. Throughout this guide, I'll offer advice on how to make this critical shift.

The Circle of Value Approach

This shift is the foundation of what my colleagues and I call the *circle of value approach to negotiating*. This is where two parties come together to jointly solve a problem—decide on a contract, create the parameters of a new job, or delineate the conditions of a partnership. Together they dig to fully understand each other's underlying interests, invent options that will meet everyone's core interests (including those of people not even in the room), discuss rational precedent, and use external standards to evaluate the possibilities—all while actively managing communications and building a working relationship.

At first read, this may sound like a "soft" approach to negotiation. In fact, it is just the opposite: It takes discipline and toughness to truly get creative and to apply sound decision-making criteria. Taking a joint problem-solving approach does not require, or even condone, sacrificing your own interests. It is about being clear about *why* you want what you want (and why the other party wants what she wants)—and using that information to find a high-value solution that gets you both there.

This is a method that my partners and I have developed and refined over the past three decades since its origin in our work with Roger Fisher at the Harvard Negotiation Project. We apply it—along with the frameworks, checklists, and techniques shared in this guide—with corporate clients, government leaders, and students at Harvard, Dartmouth's Tuck School of Business, and West Point. It's grounded in research, but more importantly, it's based on what very successful negotiators do from the battlefields of Afghanistan to the boardrooms of Silicon Valley, from Tokyo to Johannesburg to Berlin, from complex sales and purchases to alliances and acquisitions.

The benefits of this approach include better solutions, improved working relationships, greater buy-in and commitment, and more successful implementation of solutions.

Of course, there are challenges as well. This approach requires more preparation, deeper skill, and real discipline. You'll likely need to set aside a significant amount of time in advance of your negotiation to think through your needs, your counterpart's needs, creative options, and more. Not every negotiation will wrap up in one sitting. Some may require multiple sessions with time in between to rethink, regroup with others, or revise your plan. It will take discipline to control your responses—to avoid reacting unthinkingly to what your counterpart might do or say, or to "change the game" when necessary—and to keep moving in the direction you desire. Even the simplest negotiations require thought before, during, and after as you enter and work within the circle of value.

You may feel uncomfortable at times as you use what may be an unconventional approach. Your counterpart might be uncomfortable as well. She might even interpret your openness to collaboration as weakness and think she can take advantage of you. But if you follow the advice here, she won't. In fact, you'll shape the negotiation and get the results you seek, and often much better ones than you ever expected.

Chapter 1
The Seven Elements Tool

Carefully define your measure of success.

How you define success in a negotiation will influence how you prepare and, in turn, how you negotiate. Think through what you want to achieve: What would a successful agreement look like? How do you want to feel when you've left the table? You want to identify specific criteria that will help guide your preparation, and you'll also use these measures to evaluate the agreement when it's complete.

Beware: There are a lot of common measures that are limiting, and even dangerous. Some professionals think they've negotiated well when they've extracted more concessions than they gave up or when they've pushed their counterpart past his bottom line. Others believe that success means they avoided confrontation or an uncomfortable situation. Still others are happy if they simply reached any agreement at all.

These measures focus on the wrong things, and they can undermine your effectiveness. Using them may limit your approach, hinder creativity, and most importantly, lead you to leave value on the table because you haven't considered a better solution. It's tempting to use these measures, especially when you sense your counterpart or your boss is doing the same, but don't. Instead, use a more robust definition of success, one that meets seven criteria.

Define Success with Seven Elements

Aim for an agreement that:

- Satisfies everyone's core **interests** (yours and theirs)
- Is the best of many **options**
- Meets legitimate, fair **standards**
- Is better than your **alternatives**
- Is comprised of clear, realistic **commitments**
- Is the result of effective **communication**
- Helps build the kind of **relationship** you want

We call these bolded terms the *seven elements*. Not only do they form a helpful checklist for determining whether your negotiation was successful, they can also guide the entire circle of value approach. We'll use them throughout the book, but for now, let's focus on how they define a successful negotiation.

Satisfies everyone's core interests

By *interests*, we do not mean the preconceived demands or positions that you or the other party may have, but rather the underlying needs, aims, fears, and concerns that shape what you want.

For example, when negotiating a job offer, you may say to yourself that you want no less than $75K and a 15% bonus. But those are demands, rather than statements that explain *why* you want what you want. Do you want that money to pay off short-term debt, cover increased living expenses, travel, create long-term security, or something else? These are your motivating interests. They're important to identify because you may be able to satisfy them in many other ways, some of which might be even more valuable to you than $75K plus 15%.

Aim for an outcome that satisfies your full range of interests *and* your counterpart's; this will go a long way toward ensuring that your agreement sticks.

Is the best of many options

Options are the solutions you generate that could meet your and your counterpart's interests. During the course of a productive negotiation, the two of you will develop many options to discuss.

Your final agreement should be the best of those many options. A good negotiator leaves the discussion thinking that she and her counterpart created real value; if the outcome feels like it was the only solution possible, it's probably not a good one.

Meets legitimate, fair standards

Standards are external, objective measures that can be applied to an agreement to assess its fairness. These might be formal guidelines, such as market prices or rules and regulations; they could be common practices or precedents in your industry; or they might be a third party's informal assessment. Those evaluating the agreement—you and your counterpart, your boss, leaders at the other company, outside regulators—are going to want to know it is fair and will want to compare it against objective criteria or external principles. You can't simply have ceded to a lower price because your counterpart begged and pleaded, or won a key concession because you outnegotiated him.

In research we conducted with close to 1,000 negotiators all over the world, we found that what the vast majority of people wanted most from a negotiation was to leave feeling that they were fairly treated and that they could defend the outcome to stakeholders and critics. Most reported this as more important than thinking they got a "great deal." Aim for an agreement that would be considered fair by those in the room and outside of it.

Is better than your alternatives

An *alternative* is something you would do to fulfill your interests if you couldn't reach an agreement with your counterpart, something that would not require the other party's consent.

Typically when thinking ahead to situations in which they are unable to come to an agreement, most people simply say, "I'm not willing to go below $120K" or "My boss told us to abandon the discussion if we can't get these terms." Unfortunately, while this "bottom line" might be your desired threshold, it's often arbitrary. Instead, consider what your alternatives truly are: What would you do if you were unable to reach an agreement with your counterpart? Would you find another vendor? Could your company make the part? Or would you stop manufacturing the product altogether? And what would all of this cost you in terms of time, quality, and money?

Once you've identified these alternatives, consider which is the best one. (This is sometimes referred to as your BATNA—your best alternative to a negotiated agreement. I'll refer to it as your *best alternative.*)

Any outcome you agree to needs to be better than what you would do if you walked away from the negotiating table. If the best option that your counterpart will consider is worth less than your best alternative, by definition you're better off resorting to that alternative.

Is comprised of clear, realistic commitments

Each party ultimately makes *commitments* to do or not do certain things, to do them in a certain way, by a certain date, and so on. These promises—to provide a service, pay a fee, deliver a product, provide resources—need to be operational, sufficiently detailed, and realistic. They also need to be made by someone with the correct authority and with the approval of necessary stakeholders.

It's not just the final agreement that is comprised of commitments: Each party will likely make promises during the process of negotiating as well (to research standards, to vet an option with people back at the home office). It's important that each of these commitments, including the final one, is made by someone with the authority to do so, on both sides of the table.

After all, structuring unrealistic agreements is a waste of time. It might feel good to think you "got them," but when the agreement unravels a week, a month, or even a year later because, for example, your supplier can't realistically produce the parts you desperately need, you will likely end up wishing you had never agreed to those terms in the first place. For an agreement to be successful, it needs to be clear that each side can hold up its end of the bargain.

Is the result of effective communication

Many negotiators make the mistake of focusing only on the substance of the negotiation (interests, options, standards, and so on). How you *communicate* about that substance, however, can make all the difference. The language you use and the way that you build understanding, jointly solve problems, and together determine the process of the negotiation with your counterpart make your negotiation more efficient, yield clear agreements that each party understands, and help you build better relationships.

Open lines of communication between parties make for an effective negotiation and will make it easier to negotiate with this party the next time as well.

Helps build the kind of relationship you want

Another critical factor in the success of your negotiation is how you manage your *relationship* with your counterpart. You may want to establish a new connection or repair a damaged one; in any case, you want to build a strong working relationship built on mutual respect, well-established trust, and a side-by-side problem-solving approach.

Using All Seven Elements

Some elements have more to do with the process, or the "how" of negotiation, and some are more relevant to the substance, or the "what." You can see all seven elements and how they are used in figure 1-1.

Some clients have asked me whether it's acceptable to simply do better than their best alternative and to call it a successful negotiation if only that element of success is reached. My response is almost always the same: Aim to

FIGURE 1-1

The seven elements of negotiation

Substance	① Interests ② Options ③ Standards ④ Alternatives
Process	⑤ Commitments ⑥ Communication ⑦ Relationship

satisfy the requirements of *all* seven elements, both the substantive ones and the process ones. Each is important to ensuring you've gotten the most you can out of the agreement. You wouldn't cut down your checklist for assessing the safety of a product, reviewing a contract, or purchasing a key piece of equipment, so why do it here? Begin with this structured approach, and stay disciplined throughout your negotiation.

The seven elements provide a useful framework to define your measure of success, and as you'll see in the chapters to come, you can use these elements to help you prepare, determine your approach in the room, diagnose and handle difficult situations, and capture what you've learned afterward. To help you with this, use the Seven Elements Tool (figure 1-2) to document information about each of the seven elements during your prep work and the negotiation itself. Think expansively, and write down as many responses as you can for each prompt. When you learn something new before or during the negotiation, or something happens that you didn't anticipate, return to this tool and update it. This valuable worksheet will guide you throughout the entire negotiation process.

Keep in mind, you won't always use the elements in the exact same order; nor will this tool remain static throughout your negotiation. You'll likely use it iteratively, coming back to the elements over and over as you gather more information.

Now that you have a good understanding of what success looks like and the tool to get you started, it's time to prepare for the negotiation.

FIGURE 1-2

Seven Elements Tool

Related Parties	Interests
	Our interests
Core Issues	*The other party's interests*
	Third-party interests

(*continued*)

(*continued*)

Options	**Standards**
Issue #1:	*Issue #1:*
Issue #2:	*Issue #2:*
Issue #3:	*Issue #3:*

<table>
<tr><th>Alternatives</th><th colspan="4">Commitments</th><th colspan="2">Relationship</th></tr>
<tr><td rowspan="2">Our alternatives to a negotiated agreement with this party (highlight the best one)</td><td colspan="4">Elements of a framework for agreement</td><td>Current</td><td>Preferred</td></tr>
<tr><td colspan="4">What authority do we have?</td><td colspan="2">Possible diagnoses for any gap</td></tr>
<tr><td>Ways to improve our best alternative</td><td colspan="4">What authority does our counterpart have?</td><td colspan="2" rowspan="7">Possible ways to bridge the gap</td></tr>
<tr><td rowspan="3">The other party’s alternatives (highlight the best one)</td><td>What level of commitment do we want?</td><td>This meeting</td><td>Next meeting</td><td>End of negotiation</td></tr>
<tr><td>Expressing views</td><td>☐</td><td>☐</td><td>☐</td></tr>
<tr><td>Generating options</td><td>☐</td><td>☐</td><td>☐</td></tr>
<tr><td rowspan="3">Ways to weaken their best alternative</td><td>Joint recommendations</td><td>☐</td><td>☐</td><td>☐</td></tr>
<tr><td>Tentative agreement</td><td>☐</td><td>☐</td><td>☐</td></tr>
<tr><td>Firm, signed deal</td><td>☐</td><td>☐</td><td>☐</td></tr>
</table>

(continued)

(continued)

Communication	
Meeting purpose	*Questions to ask/things to listen for*
Desired outputs	*Information to disclose*
Who should be there?	*Assumptions to test*
Appropriate process	*How to handle conflicts?*

Section 1

Before You Get in the Room

The best negotiator is the most prepared one.

Preparation is the key to any successful negotiation, but few people spend enough time on it. I've had sales leaders tell me that they prepare in accordance with how long it takes to get to their customer's office. That's fine if your meeting is in Tokyo and you live in Manhattan. But it's abysmal if you're meeting the customer in Brooklyn.

Prepare as far in advance of the negotiation as possible. Take time to:

- Question your assumptions about the negotiation
- Think through what you want from the negotiation and why—and what the other party wants and why

- Get creative about your options
- Consider objective standards to apply to your options
- Assess your best alternative (and theirs)
- Plan how you'll manage communication and your relationship with your counterpart
- Lay the groundwork for a successful negotiation by reaching out to the other party in advance

Doing all of this ahead of time gives you the advantage in the room. You'll be able to better control the process and shape the outcome.

In the next chapter, I'll discuss how to overcome some of the more common negative assumptions that you may hold as you go into conversations with your counterpart. Then, in the rest of this section, I'll address how to prepare for both the substance and the logistics of your negotiation.

Chapter 2

Question Your Assumptions About the Negotiation

Develop new, more empowering expectations.

As you launch into the preparation process, you may already have a lot of assumptions about how your negotiation will go, many of them negative. You may suspect that there is only one option the other party will agree to (because your counterpart has never budged from his stated policy) or that the negotiation itself will be unpleasantly contentious (because that's always been your experience).

But assumptions like this can be dangerous and limiting: They hinder your creativity. For example, if you think the other party is going to cling to a specific policy, you'll be focused on combating it directly and unlikely to throw out more-inventive options that may actually get you and your counterpart something *better.* Or if you assume the other party is going to push hard, you might send signals that you're going to do the same, without even realizing it.

Take, for example, a salesperson working with a procurement manager. The salesperson might think, "Well, the procurement manager has never gone for a risk-sharing deal in the past, so let's not even bring that up this time." This assumption will cause him to hold back what might be a viable solution for both sides, and if the purchaser learns he's holding something back because he's underestimated him, he risks damaging the relationship. Perhaps most dangerously, the salesperson could be leaving value on the table by not mentioning the option he's hiding. A relatively simple shift in thinking—from "He'll never go for that" to "If I never try, I'll never know if he might go for some new, creative options"—can positively change the negotiation.

As you begin preparing, take a closer look at the assumptions you've already made and how they might be holding you back. Then challenge them, and see if you can shift them. Continue this process for the entire negotiation, checking to see what assumptions you've made and recasting them if necessary.

The salesperson in the example might, after all, offer risk sharing as an option: "I know you haven't been interested in the past, but we've changed how we structure these deals to address the accounting issues you raised. It might solve the pricing issue, so I wanted to test this out again and see if we might be able to make it appealing for both of us."

Even if the purchaser says no, the salesperson has demonstrated his understanding of his counterpart's interests and his willingness to be collaborative and open to creative solutions.

Be Aware of the Assumptions You Often Make

In order to go into a negotiation with an open mind, you must first become cognizant that you hold particular assumptions that may be limiting your perspective. That's not as easy as it sounds, because these notions are often deeply embedded; they often feel like objective truths rather than subjective beliefs.

Common negative assumptions fall into two categories: premature judgments about your counterpart, and those about the negotiation more generally:

About the other party

- As in the example with the salesperson, you may expect your counterpart to do certain things based on prior experience with her: "She'll never go for an equal partnership" or "She always acts nice until the very end."
- Even if you've never negotiated with the person, you guess how she's going to behave based on

where she's from or her role: "People from the Northeast are aggressive; those from the West Coast are laid back" or "People in procurement care only about the bottom-line price; engineers care only about the quality of the product and are pushovers when it comes to actual cost."

About how the negotiation will go

- You may assume that business negotiations are always formal, protracted, and overly focused on terms and conditions, or that certain kinds of personal negotiations are always contentious or zero sum, such as those about asking for a raise, purchasing a car, or buying a house.

As you're preparing for your negotiation, think back to past negotiations, or other types of work situations, and list assumptions you made that turned out to be false. Try to spot patterns and identify the kinds of assumptions you typically make.

Then review the list and ask yourself which of these are pertinent to the current situation. As you do, add any other assumptions that come to mind about the negotiation at hand.

Shift Your Assumptions

Once you have a list of your assumptions, for each item, ask yourself whether it's possible that the assumption is not true and then what it would take to disprove it. Depending on how you answer, there are a number of ways to change your thinking.

Shifting your assumptions about the other party

Hard data is one of the best ways to refute a myth. Find people who know the person or organization with whom you're going to negotiate. Talk to others who have worked with him. You might even find people who have a similar job as your counterpart and can give you a sense of what the person might care about, what pressures he may be under, or what his interests might be. Gather as many facts as you can that might disprove, or at least challenge, what you're given to believe.

If you don't have access to those facts, invite some of your trusted colleagues to a meeting where you can explain what your assumptions are and ask that *they* systematically challenge them. Give them permission to poke holes in your theories, and they can help you see things from a different perspective.

Shifting your assumptions about how the negotiation will go

To address your negative ideas about how the negotiation will go, reframe them into "enabling" assumptions—ones that support a more positive outcome. (If you aren't able to disprove myths about the other party, this approach can work for her as well.)

To do so, imagine how you would act if your belief *weren't* true. This is what the salesperson did in the example earlier: Realizing his possibly faulty and debilitating assumption—that his counterpart was likely to be "yet another unimaginative procurement manager" who would never even consider discussing a risk-sharing deal, and therefore that it wasn't worth even raising the idea—he jotted down a few ways in which risk sharing *could* work (both for him and his counterpart). Armed with this list, he is ready to share this information with the procurement manager in the negotiation itself in order to both test his openness to the idea and persuade him how it could benefit each of them.

In table 2-1, I've listed some other limiting assumptions and their more enabling partners.

TABLE 2-1

Shifting your assumptions about the negotiation

Limiting	Enabling
Our interests are opposed, so we can't both get what we want.	While some interests conflict, others are shared or just different.
These negotiations are always contentious. There's no other way to handle this except to haggle and eventually compromise.	There are many ways to negotiate, and with a little discipline, I can lead the way to a more collaborative negotiation.
The other party makes poor decisions.	The other party, like all people, will do what she believes is in her best interest.
I should behave as badly as he does.	I should do what moves us in the right direction no matter how the other party behaves.
We have no choice but to go with this solution.	There are always other options, and nothing is settled unless I agree.
These people are impossible to deal with.	With the right tools and approach, I can understand what motivates them and craft an agreement that works.

Look to Be Surprised

Throughout your interactions with your counterpart, continue to look for data that challenges your assumptions. Consider assigning someone on your team to be a watchdog; his job is to keep an eye out for any evidence that proves your expectations wrong. Maybe you presumed that the other party was going to be unbending, but you notice a willingness to involve new people in the discussion or to share information that you never thought she'd reveal: It looks like it's time to revisit your beliefs about her.

Also question your assumptions anytime you get stuck in the negotiation. Go back to your list and see which of the thoughts you wrote down might be holding you back at this particular moment. If you could disprove or reframe any of them, would it help you move the process forward?

Finally, review your assumptions after the negotiation is over. Look over the list and determine what you've learned. Record the new lessons so that you don't make the same mistakes next time. (I'll go into more detail on learning from your negotiation in section 4.)

Keep in mind that many of your assumptions, even negative ones, will be proven correct once you're in the room. After all, you made many of them based on past experience, and that can be a good guide. Perhaps the other party *does* make poor decisions or *is* particularly stubborn. But shifting to a more positive belief anyway will get you beyond those limitations. If you assume that you or the other party cannot get creative, change the course of the negotiation, fix the relationship, or trust each other, you never will.

Chapter 3
Prepare the Substance

Understand interests, brainstorm options, research standards, and consider alternatives.

To be agile and creative in a negotiation, you need to prepare for both the substance and the process—*what* you will say and do and also *how* you say and do it. You've been introduced to the seven elements and used them to define what success looks like. Now you'll use the same elements to prepare. In this chapter, we'll focus on the first four—interests, options, standards, and alternatives—which outline the content of your conversation. The other three—commitments, communication, and relationships—are more about process, and we'll cover those in the next chapter.

One note: While I lay out the elements here in a logical order, it's important to remember that, in practice, things are much more fluid; you'll iterate between them throughout the negotiation. For example, it's helpful to brainstorm interests to lay the foundation so you can then generate options, but thinking about options may help you uncover interests you hadn't yet thought about. When you're actually in the negotiating room, you'll be returning to your prep work and updating it as well.

Reserve Time for Preparation

Negotiations—of any size—require time, commitment, and careful preparation. You should devote the same amount of time to getting ready as you think the negotiation will take—at a minimum. This is true for even seemingly straightforward discussions. If you've scheduled a two-hour conversation, spend at least two hours getting ready. And the more complex the issues at hand, the more you need to prepare, at least double or triple the length of time you'll spend at the table.

There are times, of course, when you won't be able to thoroughly prepare: You see your boss on your way into a meeting, for example, and you have to agree on a deadline for an upcoming report; a vendor shows up unexpectedly and wants to negotiate a new volume purchase; or a customer calls demanding a price cut. Discussions like these still require some quick prep work—or, in the worst case, just running through the seven elements in your head as you're walking down the hall—so you can understand how you'll view success and understand your and your counterpart's point of view.

Identify Whom to Involve in Your Preparation

While you may do most of your prep work on your own, it's helpful to get others involved, if not to actively assist you, then at least to provide useful information.

As you work on each element in your preparation, reach out to colleagues both inside and outside your organization who have been in similar negotiations, either with similar issues or with the same party. Invite them to a brainstorming session to talk about the other party's interests and alternatives, for example, or just to pick their brains for five minutes: "Carol, I'm doing a limited liability agreement with a new customer, and we're trying to agree on the terms. Here are the constraints; how have you done this in the past?"

Also think broadly about who will be affected by the results of the negotiation. It might be your peers, who have to implement the decision you come to; your spouse, who cares about how your salary negotiation turns out; and, in high-stakes cases, your company's CEO or the board. These folks don't need to be included in every preparation session, but it can be helpful to review your work on the seven elements with them before you go into the room; you don't want to find out after the fact that an option you've proposed isn't feasible or doesn't account for an important interest of theirs. Most people remember to do this with their boss but neglect to do it adequately with other stakeholders.

Even if no one else is affected by the outcome of your negotiation, it's always helpful to have someone else involved during preparation to challenge your thinking and ask tough questions. Find a trusted coworker to review your work with you and play devil's advocate.

Set the Stage for Your Preparations

To begin, think again about all of the parties involved in your negotiation—the stakeholders you just identified, as well as anyone else who is involved directly (the negotiators and those to whom they will need to defend the agreement) and indirectly (end users, senior management, legal, finance, regulators). Draw a map that shows roughly how all of these players are interconnected—who reports to whom, who influences whom. Once you've connected with your counterpart, you'll dive deeper into this list of people and how they'll influence the negotiation (see chapter 5), but for now, capture a quick snapshot of the players.

Then identify the core issues—the discrete points that the negotiation needs to resolve. For example, in a sales negotiation, you may need to agree on price, service, delivery date, and so forth. Thinking through each issue will help as you think about your interests, the other party's interests, and a wide range of different options.

Keep these two things—who the parties are and what the issues are—in mind as you prepare for the negotiation using each of the seven elements.

Interests: Identify Underlying Aims and Needs

Begin going through the elements by understanding your interests. This often takes more work than you might think. You may have broad desires like "make as much money as I can" or "get it done quickly" or "maintain control of the project." Or you may have an idea of what you want in your head—the $75K plus 15% bonus discussed in chapter 1. But you need to get beyond *what* you want to *why* you want it. Why do you want that particular salary and bonus? What are you going to do with the money? What is driving your desire to want to structure it with a bonus? What are your deep-down needs, aims, fears, and concerns in this negotiation? You want to be sure to identify not just one or two of them, but all of your relevant motivations.

Write down every interest you can think of. Then take each one in turn and ask why it's important. Continue this line of questioning by asking why *that* reason is important and then again why *that* reason is important. Keep asking *why, why, why*. By digging deeper, you'll get a better understanding of what you really want from the negotiation, so you can be more creative about finding solutions that yield better outcomes overall.

Consider the other party

Think about what the other party's interests might be. Your first guess may be just that, a guess. That's OK, but seek to back it up with evidence. Look at past negotiations with this particular person or organization. What was driving your counterpart in these situations? If you haven't participated in those discussions yourself, ask colleagues who have.

Talk to people who know your counterpart outside the context of a negotiation. What do they think he cares about most? Look at similar negotiations with other companies or people. What did those people care about that might inform your estimate of the current party's interests?

Think of these initial ideas as hypotheses that you can test as you gather more data, before and during the negotiation; after all, you want to be careful that you're not just making assumptions. And, as with your own interests, get more specific by asking yourself *why* your counterpart might care about each of these interests.

Consider other stakeholders

Think, too, about your list of the other individuals directly or indirectly involved in the negotiation. For example, consider why HR might care about the compensation package you are negotiating with your future boss; think about what concerns regulators who are monitoring your company's R&D alliance might have; or reflect on what the finance department might worry about in the sale you're negotiating with a customer.

Identify areas of conflict and common ground

Once you have each individual's interests listed, note where your interests overlap, which are different but complementary, and which conflict. Thinking in advance about what drives your behavior and theirs on similar issues will help you brainstorm options that take advantage of interests that complement one another or bridge the gap between those that conflict.

Options: Imagine Potential Solutions

When brainstorming options, your goal is to develop possible solutions that meet the interests of everyone involved in the negotiation.

Write down as many good, bad, and crazy ideas as you can; don't settle for one or two options. Aim for at least seven or eight, even in a simple negotiation, and many more in a complex one. Allow yourself to come up with solutions that seem unrealistic; often from those impossible options, you'll see a path toward a more viable one. Those solutions may not address every interest listed, but each should meet at least one interest from each stakeholder.

During this portion of your prep, you might come up with an option that you feel is perfect—it meets everyone's needs. But don't become too wedded to a single idea here or even worry about prioritizing your ideas yet. You want to develop as many as you can so that you can go into the room fully armed with a range of solutions. That way you'll have a backup if your perfect idea doesn't actually end up working, and you will have your eyes and ears open if your counterpart shares something new about her interests or tosses out an even better plan.

At this point, don't worry about whether you'll divulge these options to the other party when you get into the room; just be creative. If you run out of steam, go back and look at your lists of interests, pick conflicting ones from each party's list, and ask, "What can I do about these?"

Focusing on those deeper underlying interests you identified earlier is the key to this exercise. For example, when imagining the options for your raise negotiation with your boss, avoid thinking, "I want $75K and she just doesn't want to increase my salary." (There don't seem to be many options that would meet both of those broad statements of interest.) Instead, consider that you want this raise primarily to pay for the online classes you're taking at night and the increased child-care costs involved. She may be worried about keeping salary levels consistent and having cash on hand to fund the new hire she keeps talking about, too. Once you're thinking this way, you can see that one option might be to have the company pay for your courses, especially if they make you a more valuable employee—even more so if your newly earned skills would mean your boss wouldn't have to make the new hire at all.

Make smarter trade-offs

Some options you create may be simple trades: For example, you may consider that you will accept a vendor's increase in price if he provides a higher level of service.

However, push yourself as much as you can to be more sophisticated. Invent high-gain and low-cost trade-off options. Think about what kind of options would be valuable to the other party, but don't take much away from you, and vice versa.

For example, imagine you're negotiating with a customer who is buying a new piece of equipment worth several million dollars. You know that he's deeply concerned about ensuring that the new equipment will work with his company's existing equipment. If you have plenty of engineers available at that time, you might offer to have your engineers do a pre-inspection to certify compatibility, free of charge. This doesn't cost you much (since the engineers' other projects aren't taking all their time), and it meets the customer's interest—confidence in his company's ability to use the expensive new equipment.

Get some help

If you think you've come up with all the options you can, share the interests you've identified with a colleague who *isn't* familiar with the negotiation. Ask her: "What have I missed?" "What could you imagine working here?" "Is there something else I should consider putting on the table?" She may provide you with a different perspective that can lead to more creative options.

Review your list

When you think you're done, review your list of options against the interests you identified earlier and consider whether there are ways to improve them; can you revise or add to what you have so that the options better satisfy your and your counterpart's goals?

Standards: Find Objective Criteria to Assess Fairness

Next, think about what standards might apply to the situation. Standards help you ascertain what would be considered fair if someone outside was looking in on your negotiation. They can be formal, written guidelines; common practices or precedents; or a third party's informal assessment.

Consider what objective criteria you and your counterpart might apply to determine acceptable prices, volumes, payment conditions, quality standards, cancellation terms, or other stipulations of your agreement. What standard might help you select one of your options over another?

Research written standards that might legitimize your eventual agreement. You might simply search the web, or you may need to purchase industry reports, attend conferences, or perform other forms of market research. It may take a little sleuthing, but more often than not you'll find something that will help.

For example, in a sales meeting, you might use publicly available information about what other companies have paid for similar products and services. In an alliance negotiation in which you are deciding who has rights to newly developed intellectual property, you might look at other situations in your industry where each partner is making similar investments and taking similar risks. For a conversation about your salary, look for data on what other people make who have the same level of experience and work in the same industry and region as you. If you can find that data from a reliable source, both you and your manager will likely see this as a helpful standard.

If you're unable to find existing criteria, set up a process to assess fairness, such as asking a disinterested third party to look at the agreement. For example, if you're negotiating the price for a portion of your business, approach an investment banker whom you and the buyer both trust to review the deal.

Alternatives: Consider Fallback Solutions

Now it's time to think about your alternatives, or what you would do if you're unable to reach an agreement with your counterpart. Go back to your list of interests and ask yourself what you might do to meet them if you cannot come to an agreement. Jot down all the possibilities that come to mind.

For example, if you and a supplier aren't able to settle on terms, you could go to another supplier. You could stay with this supplier, but escalate the negotiation to his boss. Or you could hold out a few months and see if the deal gets better with time. In a raise negotiation, if you aren't able to agree on an arrangement that meets your range of interests, you could look for a different job, go freelance, or—in the previous example—decide not to take those classes after all.

Consider alternatives that you or your organization might simply pursue on your own (manufacturing a part yourself) as well as those that involve other parties (finding another supplier). In either case, research each alternative you identify: Get bids and understand costs and benefits so that you can understand how each alternative reflects your interests.

Strengthen your best alternative

Once you've created a list of five or more alternatives, ask yourself which best meets your interests. This is your *best alternative* and sets the bar for any agreement: Never agree to an option that is worth less to you than your best alternative.

Now ask yourself what you can do to make this alternative more valuable to you. As a simple example, if you're a manager negotiating a revised agreement with a longtime vendor, you might decide that your best alternative would be to switch to a different supplier. You've done research and identified potential alternatives and even solicited bids. But if you've identified this as your best alternative, find a way to improve those bids. You might negotiate the price with one supplier or send some of your engineers to work with her to improve her product. Doing this work up front improves your ability to resort to your best alternative: You're poised to take that option if necessary.

Weaken the other party's alternatives

Also think about what the other party's alternatives might be. You won't know for sure, but come up with some hypotheses. Perhaps you've heard he's working with another supplier, or you assume that he has another job candidate in the interview process.

Assess how you can weaken the other party's best alternative. Can you change your counterpart's perception of how strong that alternative is? Can you show him that it wouldn't be easy to change to a new supplier by demonstrating the switching costs? Or can you show that you are more valuable than the other job candidates because you're likely the only one who knows the organization as well as you do?

Here's another example: If you're getting ready to discuss an agreement with a colleague from another department and you assume his best alternative is to go to your boss instead, you might go to your manager preemptively and explain the situation: "I just want to give you a heads-up that you might get a phone call. When you do, do what you think is best, but I'd prefer you refer him back to me." If your boss agrees, then in that one easy move, you've eliminated your counterpart's ability to get a better deal by escalating the issue.

Push as Far as You Can

As you prepare each of these four elements, push yourself: Don't settle for two or three interests; find seven or eight. Come up with a whole range of relevant standards. Develop options that might seem crazy at first. Ask yourself hard questions, and if you're unable to, bring someone in to help. The harder you push and the deeper you go in your preparation, the more power you'll have at the table.

You may not be able to answer all of these questions during your preparation. If you've never interacted with the other party before, you may not know her specific interests or have a way to find out. You may not be able to uncover relevant standards. That's OK. Identifying these holes as you prepare is just as important as completing what you know. These gaps help you decide where to start when you walk in the room: You'll want to open the first meeting by asking about the other party's interests, for example, or probing about her best alternative.

Don't skip out on portions of your preparation, even if you think, for example, that it's highly unlikely that you'll need to resort to your alternative. Even if you don't end up using it, your preparation will help you make the right decisions in the negotiation. Prepare every element using the questions in the box "Questions to Answer While Preparing for the Substance of Your Negotiation" at the end of this chapter so that you are ready for anything that comes your way.

Preparing When You're Short on Time

Even if you find yourself with limited time to prepare—you're facing an immediate discussion or a customer calls you for a spur-of-the-moment chat—it's important to consider each element carefully before your negotiation. You'll need to understand the full range of solutions available to you in order to best meet your interests, even if that means looking elsewhere. In a case such as this, run through each of the elements in your mind and list all that time will allow.

For example, Annie is walking down the hall and spots a colleague, Raj, whose help she needs in staffing a new strategic project. Raj has 15 people on his team and lots of projects to which they are assigned, and Annie has the same. Unfortunately, Annie cannot get one of her priority projects done on time without the expertise of two of Raj's team members.

Annie waves to Raj, asking if she can set up a time with him later in the week to talk about the possibility of borrowing some of his people for the project. He tells her he'll be out of the office, but if she can wait five minutes, he'll be happy to discuss it today. He ducks into a conference room and says he'll be right out.

Annie didn't expect to have the discussion immediately, but she takes what time she has to prepare. She asks herself the following:

What are my interests?

- To get the new strategic project done well and on time
- To ensure my team's other projects remain on track
- To stay within a small hiring budget
- To keep up the morale of my team
- To solve the staffing problem quickly

What might Raj's interests be?

- To ensure his team's projects are not derailed
- To keep control over his resources, so he can plan ahead and have the flexibility to adjust his people's projects
- To finish some lingering projects on which his team is behind
- To avoid setting a precedent of loaning out his people, particularly during busy times

What are some creative joint options?

- Raj loans me the two experts I need for three weeks, and I loan him three people afterward to help finish up the projects on which he is behind.

- His experts agree to provide training and supervision for some of my team members and help him and his people look like heroes to the executive team.

- He and I pool our limited hiring budgets and jointly hire another person who has the expertise we both need.

- He loans me the experts, but he can pull them back any time for his own projects with two days' notice.

- We jointly make the case to our managers to extend the schedule on one or more of Raj's projects, so we can tackle my new one together.

What are some persuasive standards to apply?

- Previous instances of resource sharing when working together in the past

- How other departments or functions within our company determine resource sharing

- What we believe our managers consider are the most important projects to get done in the near term, given strategic importance, revenue-generating opportunities, and the cost of delay

- How much of the expertise I think I need tends to be required on similar projects in our industry

What are my alternatives if we can't reach an agreement?

- Negotiate with a different colleague who may have the same kinds of expert resources on her team
- Escalate the issue to my boss for help in securing the expertise needed or for additional funds to hire from the outside
- Hire someone part-time who can train my team
- Negotiate to delay the start of this project until experts are free

What are Raj's alternatives if we can't reach an agreement?

- Simply say no and focus on his own projects
- Delay the decision by saying, "I'll get back to you in a few days"
- Negotiate with others for resources that will help him get his projects back on track
- Bury his experts in his more strategic projects, so I can't make the case to management to lend those people to me

By quickly asking herself these questions and coming up with even just a few answers for each, Annie is better equipped to have a successful negotiation and knows what alternatives she can leverage if she and Raj have trouble reaching an agreement, even though time is short.

Now that you've gone through the first four elements of success, let's move on to the next three: commitments, communication, and relationship.

QUESTIONS TO ANSWER WHILE PREPARING FOR THE SUBSTANCE OF YOUR NEGOTIATION

Interests:

- What are your interests and *why*?
- What might the other party's interests be and *why*?
- Are there any third parties whose interests should be considered?
- Which interests are shared, which are just different, and which conflict?

Options:

- List a range of options that might meet different combinations of both parties' interests.
- How can you build upon these options to even better meet your interests and theirs?

Standards:

- What external criteria might be relevant?
- What standards might a third party apply to evaluate the fairness of the agreement?
- What other objective standards might be relevant to apply here?

QUESTIONS TO ANSWER WHILE PREPARING FOR THE SUBSTANCE OF YOUR NEGOTIATION

Alternatives:

- How can you satisfy your interests without the other party?
- How might the other party satisfy their interests without you?
- How can you improve your alternatives?
- How can you weaken the other party's alternatives?

Chapter 4

Prepare the Process

Plan how you will work and communicate with the other party.

Once you have a grasp of the substance of your negotiation, it's time to think about the process. Imagine that the interests, alternatives, options, and standards you've just formulated are the "what" of your negotiation. Now, plan the "how."

Commitments: Identify Milestones and Consider Who Has Authority

Think about the smaller commitments each side will make throughout the process and determine who has authority to make each of those commitments. You'll have an agreement at the end that represents the total package you've shaped, but along the way you will also make more-discrete promises, and each of those need to be realistic. Take time now to prepare how and when those commitments will be fulfilled.

Identify milestones

Start by thinking about the negotiation from start to finish. Maybe it will be one meeting, or perhaps you'll need to get together multiple times. Roughly estimate how many sessions it will take and identify a smaller goal or set of goals for each one. Even for smaller negotiations or quick hallway discussions, you'll want to delineate your plan for each touch point.

Start with the first meeting you've envisioned. What's its purpose, and what do you want to achieve? Maybe all you want from this initial discussion is to build the relationship, showing your counterpart that you're trustworthy and committed to coming up with a joint solution. Or maybe you want to walk out with a solid understanding of his interests. Perhaps you want to lay out some options for the other party to consider or take back to his boss.

Do this for each subsequent session, too, identifying what you hope to achieve at each milestone. When do you hope to have a joint recommendation? When do you want to have a signed agreement in place?

In a simple negotiation, you might plan to make the following commitments (and ask your counterpart to do the same):

Meeting 1. Generate a range of options to mull over

Meeting 2. Create a draft agreement

Meeting 3. Reach a final agreement

In a more complex negotiation, the commitments might look like this:

Meeting 1. Agree on what the core issues are and the timeline for addressing them

Meeting 2. Come to a clear understanding of interests around each key issue

Meeting 3. Create a framework for the agreement and brainstorm options for filling the framework

Meeting 4. Decide on options to review internally

Meeting 5. Define standards to apply and use them to narrow down options to a select few for you to each review individually

Meeting 6. Agree on a joint recommendation to share with stakeholders

There are two primary reasons to map out milestones in advance. First, it helps you plan for each session adequately: Walking into a meeting to define the issues to eventually resolve requires a different kind of preparation from going into a meeting to develop a full agreement. Second, it identifies set times to go back to your stakeholders during the negotiation and get their input or approval so that you can make sure that they are available at those times.

Know who has authority to make commitments

You and your colleague may be planning to discuss what resources each of your teams can give to a new cross-functional project, but before you meet, consider whether either of you has the authority to make the final call on these allocations—and if not, who does. Similarly, think about the authority of your counterpart. From whom will she be getting approval?

If you need to get approval from others, keep that in mind as you set milestones and build in time to go back and huddle with your team. Similarly, if your counterpart has a low level of authority, you need to be prepared to give her the time and evidence she needs to get the agreement approved.

Lastly, if you don't yet have enough information about your counterpart to make this assessment, note that so you can ask about the structure of who can make what commitments once you are face-to-face with her.

Communication: Plan Messaging and Process

As you prepare to reach out to the other party to begin the negotiation, think about what and how you are communicating. You'll want to think about what messages you want to send, identify what information you need, and create an agenda to send to your counterpart.

Plan your messaging

Whether oral or written, verbal or nonverbal, the messages you convey during your interaction—and how and when you do it—can have great impact on the course of the negotiation, so it pays to be deliberate. Equally important to consider are the messages you *don't* want to send.

First, think through what you want the other party to understand and how you'll convey it. You might want to express how seriously you take the negotiation, your desire to move quickly (or slowly), your level of authority, or your wish to repair a damaged relationship.

Take this example: A sales team has been working with a prospective customer for months, and they have a solution they think will work. They need to agree on details such as price and precise configuration. The team has determined the messages they want to send in the next session:

- There's tremendous value for the customer in this solution.
- The customer should focus on the total cost of ownership for this product, not simply the price.
- The product configured as discussed is $4 million apiece, but each machine will save the customer $2.5 million in increased volume and reduction in defects.
- There are other product configurations, which could bring down the price.
- Given what the customer has said about his interest in cutting costs, increasing volume, and reducing defects, the team believes this solution best meets his needs.

Now that the team knows what they want to get across, they can think about the best way to deliver those messages. They'll decide who on the team will say what, in what order, and at what points during the next session.

Know what information you need

Equally important to knowing the messages you want to send is identifying what you want to learn from your counterpart. There are likely to be holes in your preparation—things you need to confirm about her interests, her alternatives, her authority, and so forth. You'll also want to learn about how she views you, your relationship, and any past history you have. Craft a set of questions to ask in the room to uncover critical information and test any hypotheses you made.

In the earlier example, because the sales team is trying to better understand the buyer's interests and his ability to make a commitment, they might ask questions like "We talked before about downtime for this piece of equipment. How much is that costing you every day now?" or "You said there are some folks in your organization whom you need to convince. Who are they, and what are their interests?"

The team may prepare questions to query the other party for feedback on the messages they plan to present. To keep the lines of communication open, they can ask things like "Are there other interests that this solution doesn't meet?" and "Do our calculations seem right? If not, what are we missing?"

Draft an agenda

The last piece you'll need is an agenda to share with your counterpart. Use the milestones you laid out when preparing commitments and the communication goals you have for each session, and create a draft agenda. This tentative plan will help you communicate with the other party about how you expect the negotiation will go. If you plan to develop a series of options by the end of the first meeting, for example, draft an agenda that includes exploring her interests, sharing some of yours, jointly brainstorming possible options, and narrowing down to a few ideas for further consideration. Also consider who needs to be in the session. Can you and your counterpart be the only ones in the room? Do you need someone with a particular expertise, perspective, or level of authority? Include the appropriate individuals on the attendee list in your agenda.

Relationship: Plan How You Will Work Together

Whether your relationship with your counterpart is ongoing or you expect it to last for only the duration of the negotiation, it pays to invest in it. It creates the foundation for the best possible outcome of your negotiation.

Identify any gaps in the relationship

Start by assessing the relationship as it stands now. Is there one? If there is, is it based on trust? Has it ever involved creative, joint problem solving? How about risk taking? Are you able to deal with differences? Has there been damage to the relationship that needs to be repaired? You may have done some of this as you questioned your assumptions about the negotiation, but take a moment to think about with whom you'll be interacting.

Then think about the relationship you want to have. Do you want to deepen trust? Encourage an equal partnership? Do you want to express emotions more openly? Or are you happy with the way the relationship is and just want to maintain it?

Examine any gaps between how you see the current state and the ideal you've described. First, assess why the gaps exist. What caused a breakdown in trust or a lack of respect? What happened to make the relationship a transactional one? Why can't you solve problems together or take risks? Why do you feel unable to share your emotions about the state of the agreement?

Take action on the gaps

Next, ask yourself what you can do to address the situation. For example, perhaps you've identified that the lack of trust a customer has expressed stems from the time you broke a key commitment. Now that you're negotiating a contract renewal, you'll know that you need to talk early on about what happened, why, and how you can ensure it won't happen again.

Or perhaps you need to agree on a plan for sharing resources with your fellow manager in an overseas office, and any communication between the two of you—never mind negotiations over touchy subjects—is awkward. This may be because you've mostly communicated over late-night e-mails and met in person only once. For this negotiation, you might decide to meet face-to-face, or at least via video conference. Leave time before you dive into the negotiation to get to know each other, discuss the pressures you're each under, and perhaps even show a little empathy for the amount of work your counterpart has taken on after hours.

When the relationship is broken

If your relationship with your counterpart is truly damaged, you need to take further steps. Focus on fixing the relationship before you address the substance of the negotiation. Take time to understand your counterpart's story about past interactions, share your own story, and try to build understanding. If the situation calls for it, actively show your empathy or plan an apology. If the problem is big, you're unlikely to solve all of the relationship challenges in just a few conversations, but aim to get the relationship to a point where you can work together in the negotiation without strong emotions getting in the way. (We'll go into more detail on how to fix a damaged relationship in chapter 6.)

When the relationship is threatened

Alternatively, you may be negotiating with someone with whom you have a perfectly good relationship, but you don't expect to see eye to eye on the issue up for discussion and worry this might strain the relationship. For example, imagine you're the head of HR and a long-standing, valued employee requests a more flexible schedule, which your company's policy doesn't provide.

Don't plan to jump in with a hard line, sharing that the policy is the policy and it applies to everyone. Instead, define an approach that respects your existing relationship, demonstrates openness and creativity, and sets a strong precedent for future dealings.

This is where the communication and relationship elements intersect: Send the right messages to keep the relationship strong. Here are some of the messages you may want to plan to send:

- You're a valuable employee.
- We want to treat you fairly and with respect.
- We are willing to be creative.
- Here is our policy and why.
- Here is how it compares with flextime policies at other organizations (including researched standards).

You may also want to ask questions:

- "Why is flextime important to you?" and "How would you use this time?" (getting to the person's interests)
- "What are your other alternatives if we can't make this work?" (the person's alternatives)
- "Are there any other ideas you have, beyond giving you flextime, for how we together might meet your interests?" (the person's options)

Instead of angering the employee by shutting him down before you have a chance to discuss the issue, you tee up a respectful conversation in which you are firm, but listen; are open to persuasion; and aim to be creative.

With a little hard work, you will find a solution: perhaps more vacation time for reduced compensation, allowing him to work at home on Mondays and Fridays, delegating some of his work to other employees, or helping him find child-care options.

On the off chance that you two cannot come to a clever solution, at least the relationship is preserved by the way you approached the discussion.

When you don't yet have a relationship

Sometimes you're negotiating with someone with whom you've never worked. Your goal in these cases is to bring the other party to trust or respect you. Think about how you might forge a connection once you're in the room. Do you know someone in common or have a shared interest? To prepare, research the person's background, using Google or LinkedIn, to identify potential connections. Also think about situations in which you've had a strong relationship with your counterpart and what contributed to that dynamic. If you're selling a product, plan to talk about other customers who were satisfied or a specific problem you solved for a client.

As you think about what kind of relationship you want to have (or avoid) with your counterpart, you'll inevitably come up with additional things on which to prepare under communication—a message you want to send, a piece of information you need. With all of the elements, approach them iteratively and return to previous ones as needed.

Anticipate Surprises

At this point, take a step back and ask yourself: What might I be overlooking? What faulty assumptions am

I making? Am I being overly positive or confident about certain elements? Am I being overly negative or concerned about others? What have I assumed is not likely that might very well happen? Review and revise your preparation based on the answers to these questions.

Then think through any external factors that might alter the negotiation. Will a competitor show up with an equally or more attractive offer? Will your counterpart get pulled from the negotiation, leaving you to interact with someone else entirely? Will someone at the counterpart's company raise a concern about working with your company? Will your counterpart's company get acquired? Might regulations change and create new risks or dictate the need for new terms?

Plan for these risks ahead of time. Write down everything that could go wrong (or differently than expected) and what action you can take in each scenario. You can't get rid of surprises altogether, but you can minimize their impact.

Some negotiators are tempted to map out tactical steps they'll take to make the negotiation go exactly as they plan. As my mentor, Roger Fisher, used to say, "It's better to have a map of the terrain than to have planned one path through the woods." Be prepared, but be flexible. You want to drive the negotiation while also listening and learning.

Most importantly, be ready and willing to be surprised, because chances are, you will be. If you prepare well, making sure to answer all the questions in the box "Questions to Answer While Preparing the Process of

Your Negotiation," you will learn from those surprises—an unexpected interest, a creative option, a persuasive standard—and the things you learn along the way can make all the difference in your negotiation.

QUESTIONS TO ANSWER WHILE PREPARING THE PROCESS OF YOUR NEGOTIATION

Commitments:

- What do you want to accomplish in your first meeting?
- What level of commitment do you want to have by the end of the upcoming session?
- What type of commitment do you want when the issue is fully resolved?
- What kind of authority do you have to make commitments?
- What is your counterpart's level of authority?

Communication:

- What is the best agenda for the upcoming session?
- What messages do you want to send?
- What do you want to learn from the other party?
- How does the other party perceive you, and how might you change that perception?

QUESTIONS TO ANSWER WHILE PREPARING THE PROCESS OF YOUR NEGOTIATION

- What did your preparation about interests reveal that you need to test?
- What other questions do you want to make sure to ask the other party?

Relationship:

- How is the relationship now?
- What kind of working relationship do you want to build?
- What are the reasons for that gap? How can you bridge it?
- What do you want to do—or avoid—in the upcoming session to develop this kind of relationship?

Chapter 5
Connect in Advance

Agree on the process and who's involved.

The final step in preparing for your negotiation is to actually connect with your counterpart. You'll want to agree on the process, decide where and when the negotiation will take place, become familiar with the players in both parties, help your counterpart prepare, and set the right tone for the negotiation as a whole.

Agree on the Process

Before you tackle the substance, talk to your counterpart about *how* you want to negotiate. This will entail some sort of conversation in advance of the negotiation itself. Negotiating over the negotiation is important and often forgotten: People like to get down to business and skip advance discussion, but if you discover deep into the process that you disagree on what the core issues are, both sides will be frustrated.

Your preparation will help you and your counterpart begin to answer the following questions. As you go, explain that you want to work together to find a solution, that you believe there are solutions that will get you both what you want, and that you want to work together using a joint problem-solving approach.

- What issues do we need to cover?
- What process do we want to use?
- Are there any other parties we need to include? When and how?
- Do we want to establish any ground rules?
- Do we want to set a timeline?
- How will we resolve conflict?
- What will we do if the negotiation begins to break down?
- Are there any specific ways we both should prepare before we begin? What are the topics around which we should prepare?

In most situations, this prenegotiation activity involves just a few e-mail exchanges or a short conversation. Sometimes this is as simple as calling your colleague and saying that before you meet next week to talk about resource sharing, you wanted to discuss who should attend the meeting and whether there are some key issues on which you and they should prepare ahead of time. Or if you're meeting with your boss to advocate for taking on additional responsibilities, this might entail sending the draft agenda you've prepared for your next check-in and asking for feedback before you meet.

In complex alliance, sales, purchasing, or acquisition negotiations, however, this initial process should be more robust. In those cases, hold a more formal "negotiation launch" to discuss these questions in detail over the course of a series of prenegotiation meetings.

Treat these initial interactions as your chance to influence how the negotiation will go, setting a collaborative and creative tone from the get-go. In our surveys of hundreds of people over time, we've seen that well over 50% of people choose an approach based on how their counterpart negotiates. Rather than leaving your negotiation up to the other person—who may well choose a poor approach—jointly shape the process before it begins.

Choose a Time and Place

After you've established what the process will be, carefully select the time and place to meet. Issues of location and timing may seem trivial, but they're not: When and where you negotiate has a large influence on how the negotiation goes and, often, what the outcome will be.

Think about the larger context for the discussion. What will have happened before, and what will come after, both for you and your counterpart? For example, you don't want to engage in negotiations with your boss about increasing your sales team's travel budget just after he's returned from a meeting with the CFO about controlling costs. Pay attention to the broader timing as well: What's happening that day, week, or quarter for your counterpart, his company, or his stakeholders?

Think about the location, too. Will you meet at his headquarters or your office? If you're having a sensitive conversation with your boss, does it make sense to discuss it behind closed doors rather than in the hallway? If you need to build or rebuild the relationship, might the initial meetings be better off somewhere friendlier than a conference room? If there are cultural or language barriers, you may want to host a video conference, rather than have a long conference call, so that everyone can see gestures and facial expressions. If you sense that the biggest barrier to an agreement will be to convince the other party of the value of your product, consider giving your counterpart a tour of another customer's site and then beginning negotiations at a nearby hotel.

Jointly choosing the time and location with your counterpart can model the approach for the rest of your discussions. Think of it as a mini-negotiation. If you force a location or time upon him, your counterpart may try to reciprocate that forceful behavior in the actual negotiation. If you tee up the logistics as a draft plan, share your reasoning, and ask for his feedback, you set the right tone going forward.

Identify the Players

It's easy to assume that if you're meeting with John, you'll be negotiating with John, but just as you have numerous constituents who care about the negotiation, so does your counterpart. Beyond John are a number of people who influence what options he can entertain, have a say in what he can commit to, and can otherwise alter the course of the negotiation. Understand who these people are and how they influence the person with whom you're negotiating.

Create a relationship map

You created a rough map of these relationships in your preparation, but now that you are in contact with your counterpart, ask who is involved in this negotiation both directly and indirectly. Build on the map you created by adding any individuals you may have missed and including all those on your counterpart's side. Figure 5-1 provides an illustration of your counterpart's stakeholders as you follow these steps:

1. Identify all the people from your party and the other party who need to buy into any agreed-upon course of action or decision. Who are the stakeholders? Don't just focus on who has the authority to approve a decision or make it go more smoothly, but think also about who can veto or derail it (step A).

2. Estimate each individual's biases. Who is likely to be supportive, and who might be opposed to the kinds of options that you've brainstormed? Think about the consequences of a decision for each stakeholder to understand where he or she might stand.

FIGURE 5-1

Relationship map

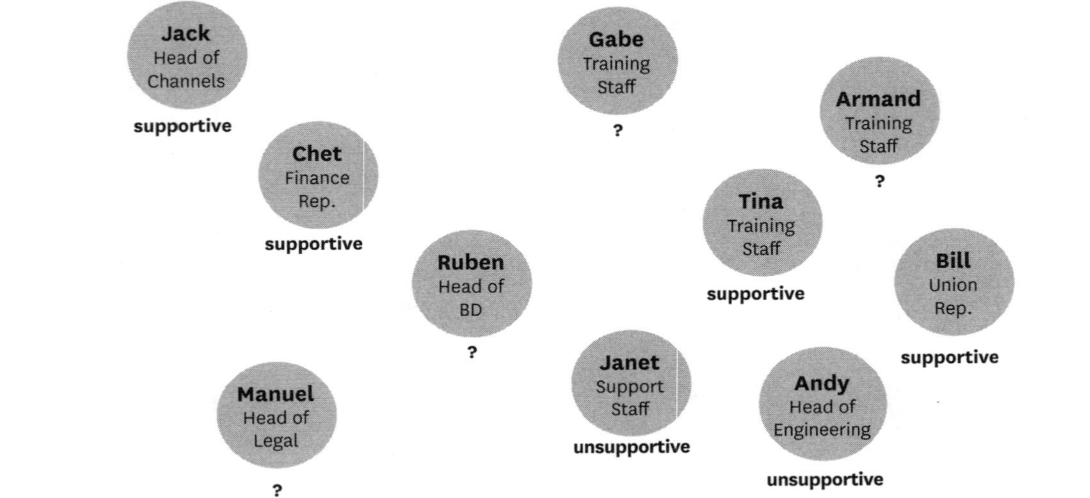

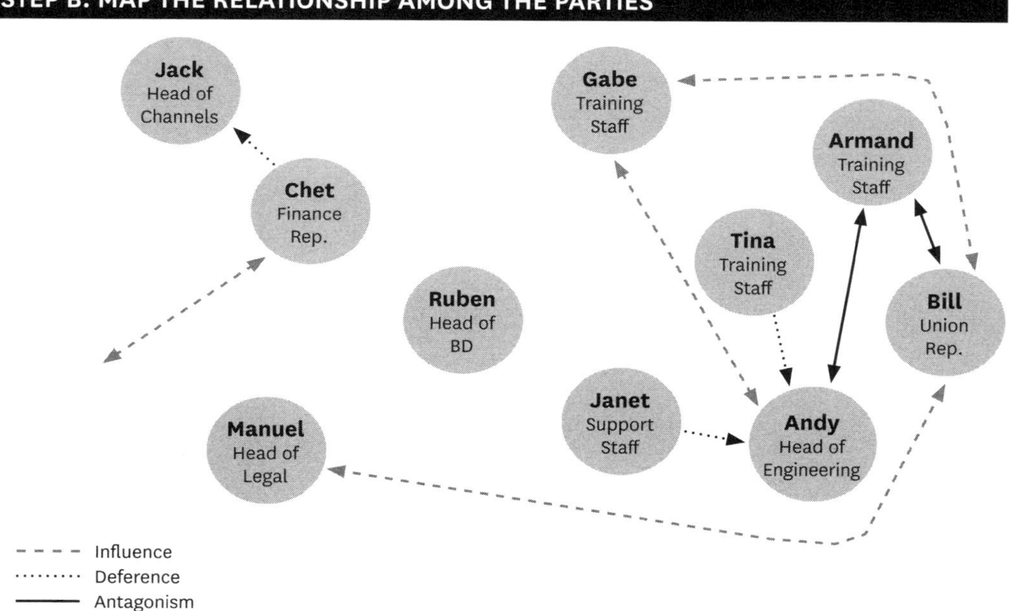

STEP C: DETERMINE THE BEST SEQUENCE

1. **First go to:**
   Jack
   Chet
2. **Then approach:**
   Armand
   Bill
   Ruben
   Manuel
3. **Next go to:**
   Gabe
   Andy
   Tina
4. **Finally, approach:**
   Janet

3. If you are not negotiating with the decision maker herself—and you can't change the process so that you are—then you will also want to identify the "influence relationships" between the parties (step B). Is there antagonism between two people such that if Jim supports the agreement, then Heather is likely to oppose it? Who has influence over others and can sway them to support a decision? Is there anyone who defers to others and will simply support (or reject) an agreement if she knows a certain person has already accepted (or rejected) it?

You may not be able to gather all this intelligence about the other party from your counterpart. Consider other avenues for getting the information: Think back to your past experiences working with the other party, consult colleagues who have worked with them in the past, and approach mutual acquaintances who can help clarify these connections.

Use the map to influence decision makers

This map will help you get buy-in and build support, especially as you get close to an agreement. Here are three ways to put it to use:

1. **Bridge gaps in your influence.** Look for critical decision makers and influencers in the other party with whom you currently have no relationship. Create a strategy to connect with these people. Start by seeking out people who are likely to support the agreement and can help

influence pivotal but potentially unsympathetic parties.

2. **Note which relationships are antagonistic.** Determine if any of the existing relationships may be detrimental to the outcome of the negotiation and create strategies for managing those risks (you already did some of this in step B). Figure out how to mitigate any potential damage these negative relationships can cause. Laying the groundwork to influence a key stakeholder may take extra time, but it will also increase the odds of getting him on board.

3. **Determine a sequence for getting buy-in.** Think about the most efficient path to getting approval for the final decision, perhaps focusing your efforts on getting those whose support would lead others to follow suit. If you can't get the attention of a pivotal party or it will take three weeks to set up a meeting, enlist the assistance of those who have access to that person.

Help Your Counterpart Prepare

As you begin your conversations with your counterpart, help her think about how to prepare. Negotiations go more smoothly if the other party is equally equipped, and helping her along will encourage collaboration. This may seem like a radical idea (you're helping the other side!), but think about it: If your counterpart shows up not knowing what her interests are or unsure of what her best alternative may be, you may have the upper hand, but the negotiation is going to be slow and laborious while she works through what she wants.

Don't share all of your preparation with the other party, but ask questions in advance of the first meeting, either in an e-mail or in person, that prompt your counterpart to contemplate the seven elements on her own. It's much better if you both come to the table with this information in hand.

Set the Right Tone

As I've pointed out throughout this chapter, your first interactions are your opportunity to set the right tone for the negotiation. Consider the key messages you've defined in your prep work as you think about how to convey them.

You can communicate some of the softer messages about the process (for example, "I want to work collaboratively") by jointly agreeing on the time and place, asking about who else is involved, and helping your counterpart prepare. The substantive messages about the content of the negotiation require separate communications. If the messages you want to send are particularly nuanced or complex, have a face-to-face conversation.

However you choose to communicate, be deliberate so that you don't accidentally convey the wrong message. For example, if you want the other party to be put on his toes, share the fact that you have three other good job offers and that you have to decide by Monday. But if what you really want to convey is that you like the role but are interested in a better compensation package, say that.

Neither of these approaches is wrong, but you should know what tone you're setting.

Once you've agreed on the logistics and identified the relevant parties, you're ready to turn to the negotiation itself. In the next section, I'll explain how to put all of your preparation into action when you walk into the room.

Section 2
In the Room

Power comes from negotiating with discipline.

Typically, when negotiation parties have differing interests and concerns, they each start by putting a proposal on the table. Then they engage in a concessionary haggle between these opening positions. This leads to arbitrary, often lowest-common-denominator outcomes and, far too frequently, damaged relationships. Most important, it leaves value on the table.

But with the circle of value approach, negotiation needn't be a zero-sum game. We use an image of a *circle* because rather than a linear back-and-forth between you and your counterpart, you're creating a space to productively explore interests, options, and standards. With this method, you develop—and distribute—value together and work to reach an agreement that benefits both sides.

This section will help you take a more disciplined approach while you're in the discussion. You'll learn to:

1. Use communication and relationships to get into the circle of value
2. Maximize your time in the circle by exploring interests, brainstorming options, and agreeing on fair standards
3. Make a good choice by assessing your alternatives and making thoughtful commitments

In the next chapter, I'll focus on how to communicate and how to build your relationship with the other party. Then, in the following two chapters, I'll explain how and when to employ the other elements. Finally, I'll conclude this section with suggestions about how to continuously adapt your approach throughout the negotiation so that you can respond to whatever comes your way.

Chapter 6

Begin the Negotiation

Establish how you'll work together.

Budding negotiators often wonder whether they should open the conversation at the first meeting. Should I make the first move, or should they?

Most people choose a negotiation approach based on what the other party does: They wait to see how their counterpart is going to negotiate, and then follow suit. Instead of sitting back and waiting for your counterpart to make an opening move, lead the way.

Similarly, if your counterpart takes charge, but does so in a way that you don't feel is helpful, there is no need to follow. If he opens your conversation by tossing out a position, or perhaps making a subtle threat, take a deep breath and ignore it. Explain that you'd rather work in a different way, by developing—and distributing—value together and working to reach an agreement that benefits both sides.

So what should your first move be?

Instead of laying a preferred option or demand on the table and waiting for a reaction from the other party, start by establishing *how* you will work together, invoking the elements of communication and relationship. You'll focus on these throughout the negotiation, but they're a particularly useful starting point.

Establish Effective Communication

Use this first experience in the room together to establish how you'll interact during the course of the negotiation. You laid the groundwork for this in your preparatory interactions with your counterpart, but now that you're in the room, show her how you'll work with her throughout your time together:

1. Use questions and listening skills to learn as much as possible and demonstrate understanding to the other party.

2. Make your own messages clear, confirm that you are being understood, and manage any obstacles that get in the way of your being understood.

Ask questions and listen

As your negotiation session opens, leverage what you have prepared: review the agenda, and discuss the desired goals for this meeting and what you want to have at the end of it. As you begin, ask good questions and demonstrate that you are truly listening to your counterpart.

Let's say you begin to query him about his interests. You can do this directly by saying something like, "Based on our past discussions, it sounds like what matters to you is reducing overall costs, improving quality, and decreasing downtime. Is that accurate? What am I missing?"

Then listen carefully to what he shares (and note what he doesn't). Summarize his points back to him. People want to feel heard. Check for understanding so that you have the right information and to make him feel he got his point across.

As you listen, avoid reacting to what you hear ("Oh, that couldn't possibly be that important to you" or "Wow, I want just the opposite."). Instead, absorb it and use it. You might say something like, "You really care about paying off debt and getting better training? Got it. We'll need to figure out a solution that meets those interests *and* some that I have. Are there other interests you haven't shared yet?"

Make your messages clear

Set a good example by sharing information yourself; that will go a long way to keeping the lines of communications open. Whenever you suggest an option or offer a standard, share your reasoning. But don't give speeches, either. Brevity is important. Share your ideas in consumable chunks, giving your counterpart time to absorb them and ask questions. For example, if you say too much all at once, the great point you made about needing to use a standard that your boss would find persuasive will get lost.

If you find yourself giving mini-speeches, stop yourself and ask questions instead. Test to see if you have been understood. Solicit your counterpart's reactions. See if she has some new ideas sparked by what you just shared.

Watch out for situations in which you may have misunderstood each other. If you find that you view things differently (you disagree on whether a standard is valid, for example), slow down and explore the issue together. Instead of debating who's right and who's wrong, share the reasoning behind your perspective and ask for hers. You may not see eye to eye, but reaching an understanding of why you see the issues differently will allow the negotiation to move forward.

Make sure you're engaged in a discussion, not a debate. The more your counterpart feels listened to, the more open to persuasion she'll be. If you get to a point where you can make her case as well as (or even better than) she can, you know you're headed in the right direction.

Continue to use these questioning and listening tactics throughout the negotiation.

Build the Working Relationship

Early in the negotiation is also the right time to focus on your relationship by separating it from the essence of what's being discussed in the negotiation. We call this *negotiating on two tracks.*

Negotiate on two tracks

People often believe they need to make concessions or forgo their interests for the sake of "the relationship." We've heard people say things like:

- "Well, I really like my boss, and if I act like she's not paying me well, she might feel that I disrespected her, so I'm going to just let the bonus idea drop."
- "This company is my biggest customer, and they're just asking for an extra three weeks of work, so I'm not going to risk rattling the cage by bringing up that this is out of scope and that they should pay an additional fee."
- "My customer said that he wants us to be a better partner, that we lost his trust because of how we reacted to the outage six months ago, and now he's demanding a 15% discount on the renewed contract to demonstrate that we care about him. That feels like a small concession to keep this half-billion-dollar contract."

Conceding like this in an attempt to make the other party happy is a mistake. You're not only giving away more than you should, you're also not improving the relationship itself, so you're not even getting what you think you are "paying" for. Furthermore, you're probably making matters worse: Appeasing your counterpart encourages his behavior, and you'll likely see it again and again. More important, you're not addressing the issues at stake or the circumstances that may have put the relationship on rocky footing.

To negotiate on two tracks, do the following:

- **Deal with the relationship head-on.** It may seem easier to bury relationship issues, but it isn't. If your preparation raised any concerns, or if you suspect that your counterpart has some, name them, jointly diagnose them, and explore possible solutions. A strained relationship will make it difficult for you to tackle specific terms, conditions, price, and so on.

- **Separate relationship issues from the substance of the negotiation.** If your counterpart says, "If you were a good partner, you'd agree with my plan," or uses your relationship as a basis for requesting a special discount or privileged information, don't get sucked in. Instead, actively establish two tracks for the conversation. Say something like, "If you feel that I'm not being a good partner, let's discuss that. I'd like to know what you look for in a good partner, and what I'm doing or not doing, and what we both can do differently to improve our partnership. If you want to discuss the plan," or the price, or the protocols for information sharing, "that feels like something else—we should explore that on its own merits by discussing interests, options, and standards. Which of these would you like to address first?"
- **Work unconditionally to grow the relationship.** Whether or not there are existing issues in the relationship, always work on making it stronger. Set the stage for a collaborative approach from the get-go by being respectful, well prepared, and ready to listen. Always be trustworthy in your interactions. Don't worry about whether your counterpart is trustworthy or reciprocating your

> respect, and don't wait for him to make the first move; just do this unconditionally. Similarly, if at first your counterpart does something that you feel harms your relationship, don't take an eye-for-an-eye approach: Keep working on your end to make the relationship stronger. My former colleagues Roger Fisher and Scott Brown first talked about this in their book *Getting Together: Building Relationships as We Negotiate*, explaining that rather than reacting in kind, you should always keep your goal of a successful negotiation in mind and adopt an "unconditionally constructive" strategy for building the relationship with your counterpart.

Negotiating on two separate tracks is particularly important if you're trying to repair an already-damaged relationship; see the box "Negotiating on Two Tracks: An Example."

If you have a good relationship, but you fear that your request—a raise, additional resources, or a discount—will strain it, you can use the same approach. Raise the issue respectfully and with an openness to think and work it through together. Be explicit about the relationship factor: "I have enormous respect for you and don't want to strain our relationship in any way, and yet I have what I think is an important request. I'd love to find a way to discuss my request on its merits and in a respectful and creative manner." If you enter into the conversation and sense from your counterpart's responses that he does feel that you are hurting the

NEGOTIATING ON TWO TRACKS: AN EXAMPLE

My colleagues and I worked with an IT outsourcing company that was reaching the end of a seven-year contract with a customer. The customer wanted to sign a new agreement, but managers there were still concerned about a service outage that occurred a few years earlier. They pointed out that it had taken our client four days to respond, and the outage ended up costing them several million dollars. Trust had been broken, and the customer demanded, for the sake of the relationship, a 20% discount on what would amount to a multi-hundred-million-dollar deal.

Our client was tempted to give the discount—perhaps not the full 20% but something close—but we knew that wasn't going to solve the real problem: The customer was still not going to trust our client to respond on time, since the issues that had caused the lack of trust had not been addressed at all. Instead our client needed to break the problem in two and deal with the relationship first and the pricing for the new contract separately.

Our client then acknowledged to the customer that they had not handled the outage effectively and they understood it had led to distrust and a strain on the relationship. They also noted that while they were very open to discussing pricing for the new contract, they thought these were unrelated issues and wanted to solve them one at a time.

NEGOTIATING ON TWO TRACKS: AN EXAMPLE

Based on the ensuing discussion, our client worked with the customer to develop a new set of procedures to ensure that kind of outage would not occur again and if any other problem occurred, it would be dealt with swiftly and would involve close ongoing contact with the customer team and the CIO. They also identified the actual cost of the outage to the customer and agreed to cover this cost as part of the new deal under negotiation. They were then able to use industry standards when pricing the new contract. Thus the client was much better off than they would have been if they had unnecessarily given up millions of dollars and ignored the issues that had caused the problem to begin with.

relationship, that's the time to move the conversation to the separate track and deal with any feelings of hurt or disrespect head-on.

In all cases, your goal is to negotiate on the merits of the deal rather than making concessions or offering discounts to build rapport or trust.

Opening the lines of communication and establishing a productive working relationship allow you to move into the circle of value and then work together to negotiate a solution. You'll keep applying these approaches to communication and the relationship that you learned in this chapter throughout the negotiation.

Chapter 7

Create and Refine Your Options

Make the most of your time together.

Once you've established lines of communication and begun to build (or rebuild) the relationship, start discussing the substance of your negotiation.

As you move further into the circle of value, you'll continue to test out your hypotheses and learn new information about what the other party's interests might be. Continuously update the Seven Elements Tool you filled out earlier. Whether you do this in your head in the midst of the negotiation or update the physical document between meetings, make sure you're recording what you learn along the way.

Draw Out Interests

When preparing, you created a list of what you believed the other party's interests to be. Now is the time to clarify, confirm, deny, and add to those, as well as choose which of your own interests to convey.

This step of the process requires careful thought and discipline. Don't forget to use the tactics you learned in the last chapter about how to handle communications throughout the negotiation: asking questions of your counterpart and actively listening, as well as making your own messages clear.

Uncover their interests

To begin understanding your counterpart's interests, ask what hers might be. "What are your key aims, objectives, and concerns around the issues we are discussing?" Or, prime the pump by testing your hypotheses about her interests and fill in the gaps. Reflect back to your counterpart what, when you prepared, you suspected those interests might be and ask what you got wrong, what you got right, and, most importantly, what interests you might have missed altogether.

It's possible, even likely, that your counterpart will initially respond to these questions by stating a position: "I want a guarantee that we're getting 5% less than what your other customers pay, and I'd like you to throw in two engineers to come train my people for three months." Don't react to this. Instead, keep probing for actual interests. Ask "Why?" or "For what purpose?" or "What are you trying to achieve?" Dig deeper to find out what's driving the other party's position.

Listen carefully, because it's not often that your counterpart will come out and just say what those interests are; you'll likely have to ask a number of questions, probe deeply and even read between the lines. When you hear something that sounds like an interest, check it. "I think I heard you just say that being able to defend the price to your executive committee is important to you. Did I understand that correctly?" Adding "What am I missing?" is also helpful, because it will keep the conversation going and you might learn more.

If you're having trouble drawing out the other party's interests, suggest possible options and solicit criticism. Asking "What would be wrong with that?" can help you solicit interests from a counterpart who isn't being forthcoming otherwise: "I know this is a crazy idea and I'm not really proposing it, but what if we raised prices 20% and cut our support in half? What would be wrong with that?" It's often easier for your counterpart to point out why a potential solution won't work than to state her interests directly. (Most people will jump at an opportunity to criticize an idea. Use this to your advantage.) Then infer the embedded interests from her explanation: "I could never do that! If I did, I wouldn't be able to fund a critical R&D project; I'd have to fire people; I'd look like a terrible negotiator and might lose my own job; I'd have to personally take time to provide support to our people when I should be out developing new partnerships; or there's no way that I could justify this to my new boss."

Don't get defensive if your counterpart reacts negatively; after all, you put this forward as a "crazy idea." Instead, listen carefully: You just uncovered a gold mine of interests. Your job here is not to show that you're "right"; rather, it's to get your counterpart to tell you where you're wrong so that you can understand her interests more fully and more accurately.

Keep pushing for answers. Press for criticism. Listen for the interests within it. Test to ensure that the interests you are hearing are, in fact, her interests. Don't go so far as to frustrate her, but constructively push, listen, and test. The more interests you uncover, the easier it will be to develop creative options later.

Share your interests—carefully

It's also important that your counterpart understands the driving force behind *your* interests. Sharing your own interests may also prompt him to respond in kind. But be smart about which interests you share at this point. Though your counterpart may already know or suspect some of them, there are others that he doesn't that he could use against you.

For example, a sales representative might say, "Let me share some of my goals for this negotiation. I need to find a way to cover the increasing cost of raw materials, achieve the kind of profit that will allow us to invest in new product development, and better manage inventory as storage costs are becoming less predictable." He didn't just say he needed a high price, but instead shared what he was trying to achieve with that price.

But the representative has other interests he has chosen not to share: He really needs a solid reference to use with other accounts and he wants to set a good price precedent here so that he can use it when selling this new product to another customer. He might share that later in the negotiation, but right now, at the beginning of the negotiation, he is worried (rightly so) that his counterpart could use those interests against him: "Oh, we'd be thrilled to serve as a reference for other customers . . . for a 15% discount."

There is also information here that he would never share: the fact that without this sale, he won't make his quarterly numbers, and that he's already tried to convince every other leading customer in this industry to adopt this new product. Both of these statements would show how weak his alternatives are.

Most often, you don't want to put all of your interests on the table, at least not at the outset. But you want to get enough out there so that your counterpart follows suit.

Capture both sets of interests

Push hard and generate as many interests as possible. During the negotiation, list your interests on a common piece of paper, computer screen, or flip chart so that you can refer to them when you move on to brainstorming options. Don't worry; the whole process is iterative, so you'll still have opportunities to add to or adjust the list of interests later.

Jointly Brainstorm Possible Options

With both parties' interests on the table, imagine solutions that might satisfy all or most of them. This discussion works best when accomplished in two steps: Generate ideas first, and then evaluate and refine them.

Generate options

Before you begin, tell your counterpart that you'd like to move into a joint problem-solving mode and brainstorm together to come up with possibilities, withholding judgment for the time being. Refer to the interests that you captured earlier and ask what you could do to address each one or, better yet, combinations of them. Bring in any options you came up with in your preparation that are still relevant based on the interests you discussed.

Engage your counterpart so that she's also creating possibilities. We've had experienced salespeople tell us that once they have everyone's interests on the table, they throw out a few options and the customer chooses one and they go from there. That's OK, but it would be better to have the customer build off the solutions she's offered and jointly come up with even better options. When you invent ideas together, it's easier to reach an agreement later on because you'll have more options to choose from and you'll feel joint ownership over them.

Focus on generating *possibilities*, not evaluating them, and certainly not eliminating them. The word *possibilities* is important for three reasons:

- First, whatever options you come up with together at this point are just that: possibilities, not offers or commitments. Be clear that you and your counterpart should feel free to come up with ideas even if you can't commit to them. Your options need not be fully formed either; if you want to suggest something without assigning a concrete number to it, it's fine to leave that blank for now.

- Second, the options should be within the realm of what's possible. You don't need to spend a lot of time at this point thinking about whether they're better than your best alternative or if they meet fair standards, however. The options should be possible, but they don't need to be good at this point.

- Third, the "s" is very important: Invent more than one option. If you toss out only one possibility, even if it is creative, it may be heard as an offer rather than one of many options. Throwing out multiple options at once encourages your counterpart to build on your ideas and avoids an unproductive back-and-forth. Offering three or four possibilities increases your chances of iterating together to find a solution that meets both your interests.

As you invent options, you might also discover new interests—yours and your counterpart's. If an option either of you comes up with sounds odd, think about why it might actually make sense and if it reflects an interest you haven't identified yet. Iterating between options and interests and back to options is a good sign that you're being open to the fluid nature of this process.

When you've generated as many options as you can, go back to your lists of interests and check that you have an option that addresses each one.

GENERATING OPTIONS: AN EXAMPLE

Imagine that you and your colleague are negotiating how to allocate a limited budget for next year. You say, "We could split it 50–50." Neither of you is satisfied, so you offer, "Or maybe I could take more of it and compensate you by lending you some needed resources. Or—wait—crazy idea: We could go try to negotiate with Pablo to drop one of his key projects this year and give us some of his budget."

Your colleague thinks for a minute and then adds to your ideas. "Well, maybe that idea isn't so crazy. You or I could also consider dropping a key project and giving the other one the budget for that. Or, since you said one key reason you needed more budget this year was to make investments in that new market you've been pursuing, maybe I could help since we've already started tapping into that market."

This makes sense to you, so you build further on the ideas: "If we went together to discuss with our boss

Be prepared for this process to take a while, sometimes multiple sessions. To see how this process of generating options might look in action, see the box "Generating Options: An Example."

Evaluate and refine your options

Once you feel as if you have truly exhausted the options you both can develop and have gone back to your and your

GENERATING OPTIONS: AN EXAMPLE

that either we need to get some more funding or one of us will need to drop a key project, we'd have more power than if one of us went alone. And, I forgot that you already have a small team in that market. Can we make use of some of your people to do some prospecting work for us?"

"I'm not ready to commit," she replies, "but we should be able to work with you part-time or introduce you to some people we're starting to work with in the market."

Because you and your counterpart understood each other's interests and weren't afraid to suggest "crazy" ideas, you were able to come up with a plan that not only works for both of you but may also save the company money. If you'd agreed to the first option—a 50-50 budget split—or spent time haggling over who got what percent, you wouldn't have realized that these opportunities were available.

counterpart's lists of interests to see if they spark any new ideas, narrow down your brainstormed list. If there are obvious options that don't meet your or your counterpart's interests well, now is a good time to weed them out.

For example, if you and your customer have developed various options for pricing and payment terms for a project, you might note that two of the options where he pays the bulk of the fee at the end is problematic for you, given that you are hoping to pay for highly specialized engineering resources that you need to subcontract out and pay for up front. He might share that the option in which you get a success bonus for delivering early is interesting, but since he is not funded for that event, he would not be able to pay you in that way.

As you each explain your thinking, you are, of course, not only winnowing down some options, but highlighting some interests that might spark new options. Don't rush to get your list of options down to just one or two yet, but do refine the list to ensure most options are ones that meet your and his interests well.

Use Standards to Narrow Options

Holding an objective yardstick up to your options will help you further improve some and eliminate others, leaving you with few solid options to take forward. Apply standards to make sure that each option would seem fair and reasonable to an unbiased outside party. Also use standards to fill in any gaps in the options, such as what percentage of time your counterpart's team might devote to your projects or what exact price increase you'll ask a customer for.

You already have some standards at your fingertips from your prep work. But now that you better understand the other party's interests and have some real options to work with, brainstorm useful and relevant criteria together. You might prompt your counterpart, "Considering the individuals we will need to explain our agreement to, what kinds of standards might we use to refine and evaluate the options we've come up with?"

Use sources and data that will be the most persuasive to you and the other party. For example, if you are negotiating with a customer, you might share the kinds of deals you have struck with other companies she respects and feels are similar to her company. In the alternative, avoid talking about terms and conditions, or pricing used with customers who purchase a lot less or buy a very different product or service from you. And don't pick standards that favor only your viewpoint. Choose ones that would seem fair whichever side you were on. The goal here is to make sure that any options still on the table are truly defensible to *both* parties.

For larger, more complex negotiations, think about how the deal would come across in a press release describing the final agreement. Draft one to share with the other party so that you both can assess how others would evaluate the option in front of you.

Use standards to support an appealing option

When discussing an option that you believe is a good solution, use a standard to support it. Though the goal here is to persuade the other party to believe that the solution is a valid one, also make it clear that you're bringing up this standard to make sure the final decision is fair and defensible. If you ask your supplier to consider decreasing his price by 10%, for example, you'll be more persuasive if you show that similar suppliers are also decreasing their prices by 8% to 12%. He may not like the decrease, but he'll see that your request isn't arbitrary, and you've given him evidence so that he can go back to the company's stakeholders to discuss the request.

Citing a standard doesn't necessarily mean that the other party will accept it. In the example earlier, the supplier might come back with a persuasive argument about why his company is different from the suppliers who are lowering their prices. Either way, you're now focused on what the right number or term or policy ought to be and the defensible reasons for it, not simply what one party wants it to be.

Use standards to eliminate an unfavorable option

When the other party advocates for an option that you don't feel is fair or defensible, use standards to support your argument against it. Ask your counterpart, "Why that number?" or "On what are you basing that amount?" or, often even more effectively, "How would I justify that figure to my boss?" Have her explain to you why the option is fair or defensible, especially if you have a standard that shows it might not be.

If she can't, suggest a standard that might make sense instead.

Identify and reconcile conflicting standards

Of course, it's very possible that you and your counterpart will bring conflicting standards to the table. Perhaps you found data that shows people in your position get paid an average of $20K more than you do, but your boss says that he has evidence that your salary is on the high end of average. Be sure that you're comparing apples with apples. Perhaps your data assumes that you have an advanced degree, and your boss is looking only at how much programming experience you have and doesn't think a master's in international relations is relevant to your role. Discuss which data is appropriate for your situation.

If this doesn't work, research additional standards on your own that you think might be applicable or helpful, jointly define what you think would make a good standard, or appeal to an unbiased third party who can provide insight on what an appropriate number would be.

If you're truly at an impasse, circle back to your interests and options, and try to get more solutions on the table that could hold up to both your standards.

Be persuasive—and open to persuasion

Applying standards can be tricky because you need to persuade the other party that some options are acceptable (or not). When brandishing a standard, it can be easy to act dismissive or antagonize the person across the table. Be both assertive and empathetic. Remember what you learned about communication and keep reflecting what you've heard back to your counterpart as you ask for more information: "I'm hearing that what you really are interested in is *x*. Help me understand why that might be fair."

One of the ironies of negotiation is that you're more persuasive if you seem open to persuasion yourself. Don't roll over; that won't help. But listen, consider the other person's point of view, and assume you might have something to learn. As your counterpart sees you do this, she will do the same.

Eventually, by applying standards and iterating and refining the options, you'll arrive at a few workable solutions. The options on the table should meet both of your interests and should be defensible by both parties. Now you move to using your alternatives and commitments to make a good choice among these options.

Chapter 8
Select the Right Outcome

Narrow in on a workable solution and commit with care.

With a few solutions left in front of you, it's time to move toward a final agreement. Do this by applying your alternative and making sure what's on the table is better. Then make commitments carefully so that the agreement is workable for all parties.

Compare Your Options to Alternatives

It's possible, maybe even inevitable, that you and your counterpart will have already stumbled on a discussion of alternatives by this point. As with all of the elements, consider addressing them as they come up in the conversation. But if that hasn't happened yet, now is the time.

Evaluate the remaining options

As we've already discussed, you want a solution that's better than your best alternative. Measure the remaining solutions against this alternative. If one of them passes, you're in good shape. In many negotiations, you never need to share your alternatives with the other party; you silently measure the solution against your best one.

Push for a better solution

If the options left after applying fair standards are not better than your best alternative, use that fact to push you—and your counterpart—to come up with better options.

For example, you could say, "Right now, the options on the table are good, but not nearly as good as what I can do on my own. Is the same true for you?" Or you might say, "For us to reach an agreement, we need to work harder to come up with something better than my team could do elsewhere. Right now I believe I could get 10% more value by going with another vendor, and perhaps as much if we simply used what's left in inventory of your old product."

Be sure to frame the discussion as an effort to do better than your alternative, not as a threat. You might have said, "If you can't do better than what's on the table, I'm going to go with a different vendor," but while threats like these sometimes get the other party to pay attention, most often they derail the negotiation. Your counterpart will likely make her own threat and you'll get stuck in a back-and-forth.

If your alternatives are weak to begin with, you likely will not want to reveal them, no matter the message. In this case, focus all the more on getting creative with your options.

Challenge the Other Party's Alternatives

Remember that even if your own alternatives are weak, the other party's may not be any better. Throughout the negotiation, look for signals of how good your counterpart believes his alternatives to be. You took an educated guess during your prep work, but listen to what he actually says in the negotiation. Watch for clues about what he would do if he had to walk away.

Keep in mind that your counterpart might exaggerate how good his alternatives are. If you suspect that's the case, do some research or even ask some questions to find out how realistic what he's told you is. Does his organization really have other vendors who provide a similar service? Might they truly be able to do it on their own? Can they really wait you out a few quarters until you do what they want?

Furthermore, just because some of these things are possible doesn't mean your counterpart actually wants to see them come to pass. Ask questions that challenge how attractive his alternative is. Can the other vendor his company is considering really meet its volume needs and deliver the same quality you can? What costs would the other party's organization incur doing it themselves? You're not just testing the strength of the other party's alternatives here; you're also making your counterpart see his weaknesses. Educate him: “It can take months to transfer to a new provider when you take into account all of the equipment that needs to be replaced.” “The operating life of our competitors’ products is two years with no guarantee. Ours, while slightly more expensive, have an operating life of twice that, and we are the only ones who provide a two-year guarantee.” This may not change your counterpart’s view right away, but it will give him food for thought.

When to walk away

If you still aren’t able to identify an option that’s better than your best alternative, then you may need to resort to that alternative. That’s OK: It’s not a failure to walk away if you can’t negotiate an agreement that’s better. Never negotiate just to agree. Instead of walking away, you may also be able to wait it out until you can develop a stronger alternative or until the other party’s weakens. Perhaps you can negotiate with others in your counterpart’s organization or find other companies that can meet your needs.

However, if you have successfully come up with solutions that surpass your best alternative, it’s time to think about commitments.

Make Commitments Carefully

Now that you have a few strong options left on the table, assess them against the following three criteria to narrow them down further and make sure you should commit.

1. **It’s operational and sufficient.** The timeline, terms, and conditions in the given option need

to be realistic and detailed enough to be implemented. Imagine putting the agreement into action, thinking about each step you'd need to take, and make sure you haven't left out anything that still needs to be agreed upon.

2. **You have the authority to commit to it.** Don't get carried away in the room and make agreements you're not allowed to (or let your counterpart do the same). Look at what's about to be agreed to, and think through whether you're allowed to sign on the dotted line or if you need approval from others.

3. **You'll be able to sell it internally to key stakeholders.** Test the solution with the right people before you make any commitment. This may be your boss, upper management, your team, or, in a negotiation that would affect your family, your spouse or children. They may have concerns or ideas you haven't considered.

You can apply these three criteria during the discussion silently, or you might need to step away from the table and talk to others before making a commitment. Either way, devote careful attention to this step. You want to see through what you've agreed to and be sure the other party can do the same.

Leave committing to any options until the very end. Even if you seem to have found options that meet all the criteria, force yourself to stay in the circle a bit longer, inventing and refining, to make sure you've come up with the *best* possible arrangement. Do this whether your negotiation is a five-minute hallway discussion or a months-long formal process. In the same way that you want to start preparing for a negotiation as early as possible, you also want to commit to its outcome as late as you can. As you do, make sure you've avoided the common mistakes in the box "Watch Out for Common Mistakes."

At this point, if all has gone well, you should have a final agreement that meets the seven elements of success.

Of course, not every negotiation goes this smoothly. Every negotiator faces obstacles and struggles, and even in the circle of value, there may be contention. In the next chapter, I'll talk about how to adjust to realities in the room; in the next section, I'll talk about problems people most often encounter and how to handle them.

WATCH OUT FOR COMMON MISTAKES

There are a few places where many negotiators get tripped up when using the circle of value approach. Here are the most common ones to watch out for and avoid:

- **Failing to listen.** When you've put hours or days into your preparation, it makes sense that you want to share your interests, lay out options, and so forth. But when you get into the room, focus on listening and asking questions as much as—if not more than—presenting.

WATCH OUT FOR COMMON MISTAKES

- **Sacrificing your interests in order to preserve the relationship.** Deal with the relationship separately. Resolve any trust issues before you move on to the substance of the negotiation.
- **Focusing on positions, not interests.** It's easy to get wrapped up in what you or the other party wants and move too quickly into the specifics of the potential agreements. But unless you both understand the drivers behind your positions, you won't be able to find an agreement that satisfies both parties' interests.
- **Evaluating options too soon.** When your counterpart throws out an option that's not appealing to you, don't start pointing out what's wrong with it. Spend time coming up with many options together before you start criticizing.
- **Using your best alternative as your only bar for success.** Your goal shouldn't be doing "well enough." Press for more options that meet your interests better and apply real standards so that you don't accept an offer that is too low. It might be tempting to agree to a 5% raise simply because it's better than your current salary, but if others with your talent are getting 8% and 10% increases, then you're leaving value on the

WATCH OUT FOR COMMON MISTAKES

table that you can capture with more work and discipline.

- **Committing too early in the process.** Your counterpart may suggest an option early on that sounds perfect to you and is based on a very reasonable standard. Don't jump on it, though. Agreeing to one suggestion prematurely will limit creativity. Be patient and take time to act thoughtfully and carefully. You may come up with an even better option.

Chapter 9
Continuously Adapt Your Approach

Be prepared to change course.

One of the things many negotiators find frustrating is the fact that you can't control what the other party does. All of the preparation you've done will help you shape and direct the process, and the circle of value approach will optimize your chances of working together toward a joint solution, but the reality is that you don't know what your counterpart will say, do, propose, or reject—or in what order. It's therefore important to be flexible when you're in the room.

Here are several ways to stay nimble and adjust your approach when necessary.

Role-Play

When you're between negotiation sessions and not sure in what direction to go, or you want to feel more confident implementing your planned approach, it's helpful to practice with someone else before going back into the room with your counterpart. Seeing and feeling the approach in action helps you decide whether or not you're on the right course.

Practicing your approach

Maybe you haven't been able to get your counterpart to discuss interests or your attempt to negotiate on two tracks doesn't seem to be working. Maybe you're not sure how to begin brainstorming options in your next session or you're uncomfortable presenting the standards you want to bring to the table. Ask a colleague to play the role of your counterpart as you test out what you might say and do. If possible, choose someone who doesn't have a stake in the outcome of the negotiation so that she can be objective. If you have to work with someone who is directly involved, pick someone who you know will be honest with you.

Explain the situation to her, perhaps even sharing your preparation tool so that she can orient herself, and then try out different approaches. Play it out multiple times. Ask for feedback after each try. "How did that sound? How did that feel? Was that persuasive?" Adjust your approach and repeat.

Your colleague might even make some suggestions. "What if you tried sharing a few more of your interests first or explained why you are asking about that there?" Keep practicing. When you feel comfortable—and have a range of moves you can use—you're ready to go back to the table.

Understanding your counterpart

If you're struggling to understand why your counterpart is behaving in a certain way, try a role reversal: You play your counterpart and ask a trusted colleague to play you. Before you begin, have your colleague interview you (being yourself) so that he can begin to understand how you think, what you feel, and what things you've been saying and doing in the negotiation. This will also allow him to accurately play your role when you're ready.

Next, have your colleague interview you again, this time with you playing your counterpart, so that you can begin to feel, think, speak, and act the way she does. Keep doing this until you really feel and speak like her.

Then, negotiate: your colleague as you, and you as your counterpart. After a few minutes, stop and review: What did you learn about your counterpart by getting inside her head? Do you better understand her perspective? Perhaps you have a better sense of why she has been acting the way she has.

Consider what you learned about the impact of your own words (spoken by your colleague). Are you being persuasive? Is your counterpart likely hearing what you're trying to say? Ask your colleague for observations as well.

Make adjustments to your approach. Perhaps you could be more persuasive on certain points or maybe you need to be more empathetic to build trust.

Become a Fly on the Wall

Any good athlete knows how to hop off the field or the court for a moment and assess what's going on. She becomes a "fly on the wall," stepping out of the action briefly to observe what she, her teammates, and her opponent are doing. Successful athletes adjust their approach (or consciously choose to stick to it) given what they see, and jump back into the game and execute.

A good negotiator has the same skill. Throughout the negotiation, pop out of the action and look at what's happening. Narrate to yourself what's taking place: "She has explained her interests. I shared mine. Now we're moving into options. Is this going smoothly? If not, I could stay with interests a bit longer, or I could move to standards next, or I could even ask for a time-out." Avoid getting stuck in your narrow view of the situation so that you can adjust as necessary.

Ideally you'll be able to do this yourself while at the table, but you can also assign people on your team to monitor certain slices of the negotiation. For example, you might ask Bob to watch how the other party reacts to certain options and Joan to monitor how your counterpart responds to messages you're sending.

Take an Occasional Break

If you have trouble becoming a fly on the wall in the heat of the negotiation, consider asking for a brief pause in the discussion. Don't hesitate to request a break if you're not sure what to do next, if you get annoyed and need time to calm down, or if you want to consult with colleagues who aren't at the table. Also consider asking for a time-out if you learn something unexpected or are truly surprised.

A break could be 10 minutes or it could be a few days. You can explain the reason for the time away from the table, or, if you're concerned about sending the wrong signal to your counterpart, you can always ask for a chance to use the restroom, check your e-mail, or grab a cup of coffee.

It's often less awkward if you establish up front that either of you can call a break at any time. That way it doesn't look odd if you ask for a time-out right after your counterpart has suggested an option you especially don't like, or if you head to the restroom when you're stumped about which standards to apply.

Conduct Frequent Reviews and Make Corrections

A smart negotiator also takes a more complete step back at certain points to review what's happening in the negotiation. Do this frequently—after each negotiation session to update prep documents, anytime you're stuck or things get heated, and prior to making any commitments.

At each of these junctures, ask yourself what's working and what you might do differently. Even if you only do this in your head for 10 minutes while driving home, you'll learn something and generate concrete ideas for adjusting your approach.

If you're stuck, do a more formal review, preferably with a colleague or two who can ask you tough questions:

"What did you say right before they threatened to walk away? What led you to say that? Why do you think they might have reacted that way?"

When you're preparing to commit, ask your colleagues to walk through the seven elements for a good outcome. "Does this truly meet your full range of critical interests very well? How many options did you consider? Why do you think this is the best one? Is it truly better than your best alternative?"

Then make any necessary adjustments. Perhaps you need to spend more time coming up with options or focus more on repairing the relationship before you talk about interests. If things aren't moving forward, consider a change of venue, timeline, or even players. Can you bring in someone from your or your counterpart's side who can help?

Don't think of midcourse corrections as failures; it's not uncommon that you'd have to make changes as the negotiation progresses (in fact, it likely means you are truly learning things along the way). Expect to make these kinds of shifts to move the discussion in the right direction and reach a more successful agreement.

Section 3
The Common Challenges

Tools and techniques you can use in specific situations.

All the advice we've given you so far optimizes your chances of reaching a successful agreement. But even with diligent preparation and a thoughtful approach, sometimes the most flexible negotiators can still find themselves stuck.

The four most common problems that negotiators may face are:

1. **There are multiple parties involved.** With numerous people at the table, the complexity of the negotiation has slowed it down or stopped it altogether.

2. **Your counterpart is a hard bargainer.** Your fellow negotiator resists your attempts to work collaboratively and instead states a position and demands concessions.

3. **Communication breaks down.** You and the other party keep talking past each other, unable to understand each other's perspectives, never mind reach an agreement.

4. **The conversation gets heated.** Emotions run high and either you or your counterpart is upset, angry, or offended.

In the chapters that follow, I'll explain how to overcome each of these issues in turn.

Chapter 10
Align Multiple Parties

Avoid inefficiency and chaos.

The Problem

Many negotiations involve more than two parties, all of whom need to subscribe to a final agreement. These are situations in which there aren't just multiple stakeholders behind the scenes, but also multiple parties sitting at the table: Perhaps you're negotiating the details of a go-to-market strategy with multiple channel partners; maybe you work for a research institution that is collaborating with several others on a government contract; or perhaps you're working on a complex services sale that involves a number of individuals from both the customer's and your organizations. When you have more than two parties that want to agree on a final solution, the circle of value approach becomes more complicated.

Why It Happens

There are two primary reasons that these negotiations are more complex:

- **People overload.** Getting the parties to commit to an option or agreement typically takes longer simply because there are more individuals involved. Start by discussing agenda items and ground rules at the beginning of the negotiation. You can also try to make things easier by identifying who the decision makers are and leaving everyone else out of the mix, but that can backfire if you find out later that there are others who need to have a voice as well.
- **Process complexity.** Negotiating with multiple parties means you have more interests to meet, more options to sort through, and more alternatives to consider.

Balancing the need to include and consult many different parties with the reality of how long it may take to consider all the options that satisfy their interests is not easy.

What to Do About It

There are ways to accelerate the process and still make sure that all points of view are considered.

Make it clear who decides

You can work through complex decisions more efficiently—and avoid confusion and frustration—by establishing expectations up front about who gets to decide what.

People have different interests in the negotiation, so they should play different roles in making a final decision. Those roles fall into three categories:

- **Inform.** Those who need to know about a decision and its rationale but don't need to (and likely, when pressed, don't really want to) be involved in the negotiation itself. This broad category of people includes those who have to implement the agreement or are otherwise affected by it, but don't have particular expertise or viewpoints needed in the discussion itself. For example, the vast majority of end users of a new product or service being purchased would fall into this category.
- **Consult.** Those whose input should inform the decision. These are the advisers to the decision makers. Consider their needs or advice before making a decision, though ultimately they don't need or get a vote. These participants typically have a unique perspective or expertise that you want to draw upon.
- **Negotiate.** Those who are ultimately responsible for all or key parts of the final agreement. These are people who need to make the decision because of their position, roles, responsibilities, or authority. It can be helpful to subdivide this group into those who have veto power (the agreement cannot go forward without their consent) and those who

can simply vote on an issue (the group can proceed without their approval if necessary).

It's best to formally establish these roles early in the negotiation, ideally in advance of sitting down together or when you first get in the room. At the very least, you want to have a discussion about roles before you begin refining options.

To decide who goes in which category:

1. **List each decision that will need to be made.** When you were preparing for the negotiation, you laid out the various issues that needed to be addressed in a negotiation. Using those, make a list of the specific decisions that need to be made.

2. **Assign each person a role for each decision.** Identify all the parties who have a stake in each decision and place them in one of the three buckets: Inform, Consult, or Negotiate (veto/vote). Keep in mind that the same person might be in different buckets for different decisions; your boss might have veto rights on the decision about pricing but needs to be consulted only about the length of the service contract. Use a chart like the one in table 10-1 to capture this work.

   You may be tempted to put most people in the "Negotiate" category, but that's not realistic, and many of them don't actually need or want to be that closely involved. Instead, aim to put each person in the bucket as far to the left side as

TABLE 10-1

Assigning negotiation roles

Decision	Inform	Consult	Negotiate—Has a Vote	Negotiate—Has a Veto
Product Pricing	**Seller:** Sales Representatives, Product Representatives **Buyer:** Business Unit Manager	**Seller:** Product Manager, Account Executive **Buyer:** Procurement Lead, Finance Lead	**Seller:** VP of Pricing, Finance Lead **Buyer:** VP of Procurement	**Seller:** SVP of Sales **Buyer:** Business Unit General Manager
Level of Product Support	**Both companies:** Finance	**Seller:** Service Line Leads **Buyer:** Procurement VP and Lead **Both companies:** Legal	**Seller:** Head of Sales **Buyer:** Business Unit General Manager	**Seller:** VP of Services **Buyer:** Business Unit VP of Quality

possible, limiting those in this crucial group to those who really must be there.

3. **Share and get feedback.** Be clear with everyone about the role you expect them to play and why. Ask for their input. Negotiate as necessary with people over their roles, and get their commitment to honor them during the negotiation.

   Sometimes people will easily fall into these roles, and other times it will take some discussion. If there is disagreement, discuss why the person feels she needs to be in the role she's requesting. Is she truly prepared to put in the effort and time necessary? Can a different role meet her interests? For example, you might say something like, "You had said you want to be in the Negotiate role because you want to share your opinion on the risks here. Could that be achieved in the Consult role, especially since your boss is already in the Negotiate role?"

This process can add work to your negotiation, but it will also help streamline the decision-making process, ultimately saving time.

Get people on the same page—literally

Even with agreed-upon responsibilities, it can be difficult to get everyone in a multiparty situation to agree to a solution.

Often each party will simply present their ideal solution and wait for the other parties to react or add more detail. This can jump-start a long, unproductive game of positional bargaining that leads to a lowest-common-denominator solution. Even if you don't fall into these traps and manage to draft a single proposal and circulate it to others for feedback, sorting through their reactions can descend into chaos.

Instead, use what we call the *one-text procedure*. As its name suggests, this process forces everyone to focus on one draft of an agreement. The parties work together on that single shared document, seeking to improve it along the way by offering criticism (not suggestions), allowing the drafter to creatively edit the draft from one round of feedback to the next.

Here's how it works:

1. **Choose a drafter.** Work together to select one individual who will be solely responsible for all writing and editing. Find someone who is known to be respected and trusted, a good listener, and creative. Look for a person who has built enough credibility with everyone at the table to be considered neutral. Ideally, he'll have no direct stake in the decision but understand the context and the issues. If everyone can't agree on who should play this role, create a small team composed of representatives from each party. You can also use an uninvolved outsider.

   If you're unable to find someone for this role, you may decide that you are the best person to draft the agreement. If this is the case, be very clear throughout the process which hat you're wearing when; at times, you will be the balanced facilitator soliciting and capturing feedback from others, while at other times, you will play the role of critiquing your own draft. No matter what, you'll need to take a fair, balanced approach to the discussion and to the drafting, understanding that you can't just focus on your own interests.

2. **Listen to each party's views.** The drafter then elicits interests from each party. He may do this in separate interviews or while everyone is together in the room. Each side is likely to make the case for what the solution should be, but it's the drafter's responsibility to ask questions that get at the interests underlying the preferred solutions and current positions. The drafter will want to probe deeply, asking, "Why?" "For what purpose?" and "What are you trying to achieve (or avoid)?"

3. **Create a rough draft.** The drafter then creates a rough solution that is impartial and responsive to what he's heard. It should be clear that this is a draft and not final in any way. Driving that point home can be as simple as writing "draft for discussion only" on each page.

4. **Ask for criticism.** The drafter shares the one text, asking each party in what ways the current draft does not meet their interests. Usually in this first round, he asks them as a group, as it is helpful for each participant to hear the others' answers. The drafter should not defend or explain the draft.

Instead, he asks questions like, "What would be wrong with something like this?" "Which interests of yours are not reasonably met with this proposal?" If he gets back a suggestion ("You should just change that term, and I will be set"), he should always ask about the interests behind it ("Why might that make more sense than what is there?"). His tone should not be defensive, but inquisitive.

Capitalizing on people's natural willingness to criticize, this approach further exposes their underlying interests. Ideally, the drafter will record all of those new interests heard in a place where everyone can see them. (See the box "Questions to Ask in the One-Text Procedure.")

5. **Make revisions.** The drafter then refines the text. He looks for new creative solutions, ideas that reconcile differences, and ways to create joint gains. If he believes certain interests are still not being shared, he might even put in a controversial idea or a few to spur criticism in the next round. The drafter should do this transparently, by noting what he has done and why. He again marks it as a "draft" and brings it back to the negotiators.

6. **Repeat.** The drafter once again asks all parties for their criticism, probing for interests, testing them, recording them, and digging more deeply for what is driving any proposed change. Most often this is done in live sessions, but if necessary,

he might send out a draft with numbered lines and ask the negotiating parties to write up their feedback in a separate document. Some individuals might beg to mark their changes directly on the draft, but the drafter should not give in. The result would be too many unreconciled versions, and all those productive steps toward one organized solution would be lost.

In this next round, the drafter gathers up the criticism, shares his appreciation with the negotiators, and goes back to improve the draft on his own. He then continues to alternate between soliciting criticism and revising. He continues iterating this way until he believes he cannot make the draft any better, the benefits of further improvement seem not worth the cost in time and effort, or he runs out of time.

7. **Present a choice.** At this point, the drafter presents all parties with a stark choice: Accept the draft as is or accept the consequences of not coming to an agreement. He might say something like:

   "I have done the very best I can. I can't promise everyone will be 100% happy, but I've listened to all of you and tried hard to meet many of your underlying interests. This is a final proposal. I don't think we can make it any better. If you all say yes, then we have ourselves an agreement. If you say no, we may all have to revert to our best alternative. I now need a simple yes or no from each of you."

QUESTIONS TO ASK IN THE ONE-TEXT PROCEDURE

- What is wrong with this draft as it is presented now?
- Do you have important interests that this draft does not adequately address? Which ones? Why are they important?
- What else seems wrong or is missing from the draft? Why are these things important?
- Do you have other ideas for improvement? What are your reasons for suggesting these items? What key unmet interests do they address?
- Do you have other ideas for how conflicting interests might be creatively and fairly resolved?
- Understanding why you would like this particular interest met, but given that it has become clear that it is in direct conflict with others' interests, why should meeting your interest here take priority over meeting theirs? What standards or fair process might we apply to deciding this?

My colleagues and I have used the one-text procedure in complex multiparty situations, such as peace negotiations, complex sales, mergers and acquisitions, and large-scale organizational change initiatives, and seemingly straightforward discussions, such as who gets which office, how a new policy should read, how to set budgets for the next fiscal year, and even where to go on vacation with the extended family.

The process leads to much better outcomes and builds relationships. Despite the number of people involved, people have a voice, they feel heard, and they begin to view crafting an agreement as a joint problem.

While the process as a whole may seem like it would take longer than putting everyone in a room and letting them fight it out, that approach usually just leads to deadlock or forced compromises that themselves often lead to unworkable agreements that can't be implemented properly. In the end, the one-text approach often saves time.

This process works very well for situations in which there are multiple parties at the table, but it can also be helpful for one-on-one negotiations in which you know your counterpart is going to have to vet the agreement with an array of internal constituents. You might develop a rough draft together, and then she can run the one-text procedure inside her organization. Of course, you have interests that need to be met, too, so remain involved to ensure your interests are taken into account in future drafts.

Negotiating with many individuals who have widely disparate interests can be daunting, but clarifying decision-making roles and using the one-text procedure is a disciplined way to bring all those voices together to reach one solution.

Chapter 11
Tame the Hard Bargainer

Shift the conversation.

The Problem

You've worked hard to prepare for the negotiation, and you're ready to enter the circle of value. But every time you try to better understand your counterpart's interests or jointly brainstorm options, he resists. Rather than following your approach, he's wedded to using typical negotiation tactics: laying out his position, making threats, and waiting for you to make concessions. He dismisses your questions about what's driving his demands, saying instead, "That's not relevant. I want what I want."

Take, for example, Ruben, a salesperson trying to sell a large piece of equipment to George, his potential customer. George makes an opening demand: "I'm going to need a 10% discount." He explains that none of his other suppliers would get away with charging more, not even his top suppliers. When Ruben asks George why, explaining that he wants to understand his underlying interests, George cuts him off. “Listen, I’m doing you a favor because I like working with you. If this were someone else, I’d ask for an even steeper discount.” He adds, “If you were a good partner, you’d give us this discount. Just remember, my boss is an old friend of your boss, and he can call him anytime.”

This kind of answer is frustrating, but panicking, reacting in kind, walking out—or even worse, just giving in—won’t get you anywhere. George, as a hard bargainer, is playing a kind of game. Don’t get lured into playing the game yourself; it often leads to a compromised solution and a strained relationship.

Why It Happens

You’re in this uncomfortable situation because no matter how good your intentions or how well prepared you are, you can’t demand that your counterpart negotiate the way you want. There are many reasons people choose to use the unproductive tactics George is using here:

- **This is the only approach they know.** They may assume that this is how negotiations are supposed to be done. If this is the case, you can sometimes show or teach them a better way.

- **This has worked for them in the past.** When they’ve played the hard bargainer before, they may have been rewarded by previous counterparts who have given concessions and let them “win.” Here, too, you may need to show them a more productive approach and make it clear that you're not going to continue to reward their bad behavior.

- **They've been told to negotiate this way by a boss or other superior.** It's possible that someone in their organization pays them to negotiate this way (for example, gives a bonus based on the discount they achieve) or gives them positional instructions, such as "Go get a 10% discount," with no explanation of why or for what purpose. Or perhaps the hard bargainer has seen someone she respects negotiate this way. You don't know what pressure they're under, but you can show them that they might get a better result using a different process.

- **They aren't prepared to negotiate any other way.** They haven't thought through what their interests are, what they might do if they can't reach an agreement, who needs to approve an agreement, and so forth. Give them time to regroup and guidance on how to prepare.

Considering why your counterpart is driving a hard bargain can help you determine how best to respond.

What to Do About It

Your job in this situation is to spot "the game," diagnose what's going on, and then change the tone and direction of the conversation so that you don't mimic your counterpart's style.

Don't react

The first step is to use the skills we talked about in chapter 9 and become a "fly on the wall." Instead of panicking or reacting to threats or demands, take a deep breath, mentally pop out of the negotiation, and objectively look at what's happening. Take a calm, disciplined approach so that you can systematically and strategically decide how to move forward.

Diagnose what's happening

Seek to understand what's going on by using the seven elements to spot the "game" and assess what "moves" your counterpart is making. Determine which of the elements he's using and how he's using them—and, importantly, which elements he's not.

Sometimes you'll see that he's using the elements, but in ways that aren't ideal; he's actually *mis*using them. Where you're trying to brainstorm options that meet both parties' interests, he's pressing for options that meet only his. Where you share very concrete standards based on research and analysis, he might toss out a fuzzy generalization such as, "Everyone agrees to those terms these days." Where you try to build the relationship, he might hold the relationship hostage by making threats if you don't give in.

Let's return to the large equipment sales example from earlier. George made the following four moves:

1. "I'm going to need a 10% discount."
2. "None of our suppliers would get away with charging more."

3. "I'm doing you a favor because I like working with you" and "If you were a good partner, you'd give us this discount."

4. "My boss is an old friend of your boss, and he can call him anytime."

Thinking of the elements, Ruben should note:

- With Move #1, George used commitment to demand that Ruben agree to his position.
- With Move #2, he tossed out just one, very general standard, without supporting it with evidence, and implied that Ruben should take his word for it.
- With Move #3, he tried to use the relationship to get Ruben to make a concession and perhaps even threaten the relationship if he doesn't.
- With Move #4, George is focused on alternatives, sharing that he has a pretty good one and that he can easily exercise it if Ruben doesn't cooperate.

Ruben should also note that George didn't address the other three elements: interests, options, or communication. Now he knows what elements are in play (and which aren't) and how they're being used.

Lastly, consider, too, how you may be contributing to the unhealthy dynamic. What is your body language saying? What's your tone of voice? How did you frame what you shared or asked? Are you acting defensive? Have you responded to his demand with a counter-demand? You can't expect him to exhibit collaborative behaviors if you aren't.

Change the game

Now that you know what's happening, you can work to change it. Here are three approaches you can use:

1. **Introduce an element your counterpart is not using.** Bringing in another element often helps move the conversation forward. If your counterpart is focused on her alternative and keeps pushing you to come to a final resolution, consider presenting some new options, asking about her interests, sharing standards that would allow you to both defend yourselves to relevant stakeholders, and so on.

   In the sales example earlier, Ruben could bring in one of the following elements George has not used:

   - **Interests.** George wasn't forthcoming about his interests, but Ruben needs to persevere. He should ask why George wants the 10% discount a number of times in a variety of different ways. Why 10%? Why not 8% or 12%? How will George use this extra money?

     If this tack does not work, Ruben should test his own hypotheses about what George's interests might be. Is he trying to improve the margins on his product into which these parts go? Is he trying to fund another project? Does he need to save money to invest in training and support? Alternatively, he could share some of his interests to prime the pump.

- **Options.** Ruben could also say, "Let's consider 10% as one possibility. What are three other ways we could structure this deal?" Or, even better, he could bring in George's interests as well: "I'm guessing the 10% is being driven by your increased production costs, and if so, I can imagine these three other ways we might structure this deal to address that problem."

2. **Take an element your counterpart *is* using and use it in a different way.** For example, Ruben might recognize George's invocation of his alternative and decide to stay focused on that element. Instead of threatening George with his own alternatives, Ruben can push George on how good his alternative really is. Ruben might ask George what it would look like if he had to go back and get his boss involved, or he could share with George that he's already discussed this deal with his own boss, and any call to his boss would just get directed back to him. He could possibly even remind him of the cost to George's company if the deal falls apart (for example, the costs of switching to a competitor's product).

   Ruben could also note that both of them have good alternatives and then steer the conversation in a different direction: "We both have alternatives, so let's see if we can come up with some better options, and then we can each go back and decide if what we created is better or worse than our alternatives."

Last, Ruben could continue with one of the other elements that George invoked:

- **Standards.** Ruben might inquire into George's suggestion that other potential partners would accept a lower price. He could ask which other suppliers provide a 10% discount or ask if George has *ever* purchased from a supplier who didn't provide such a discount. Any of these questions might be persuasive in and of themselves, or they might lead to a conversation about what standards George would need to persuade his constituents that he was getting a good deal.
- **Commitment.** Ruben could test George's authority to go below 10% and consider trading an immediate commitment to a 5% discount for an agreement to "sign" today. While not a move back into the circle, this exception could be a useful game-changing move. Ruben could ask who in George's organization could commit to something less than 10% and explore how to get that person to the table, or arm George with the arguments he needs to get approval.
- **Relationship.** Finally, Ruben could tell George that he likes doing business with him, too, and that the appropriate discount (if any) to apply here has nothing to do with their relationship and more to do with both sides being treated

fairly. Or he might ask if there's anything straining the relationship now (short of price) and address those issues head on, before moving back to how they both determine what a fair price should be.

3. **Call your counterpart out on the game she's playing.** Explicitly say what she's doing, explain the downsides of the tactic she's using, and suggest the circle of value approach instead. You might say something like, "I notice that you're making a unilateral demand, and it seems you'd like me to make a concession in return. That feels like a losing game for both of us. If we put our heads together, we could come up with a solution that would be a lot more valuable to both of us." Don't force a new process down her throat, though; ask: "What would be your concerns about that approach?" Stepping back and explicitly negotiating over the process itself can be a powerful move to refocus the discussion.

To change the game, you'll likely need to use a combination of these three approaches. Which you lead with depends on your unique situation, but often it is easiest to go to an element that isn't being used. Bringing in something new can breathe fresh air into a tense conversation.

Some negotiators have an element or two with which they feel particularly comfortable, so you might go with that element first. There isn't one right move. Rather, think of the seven elements as seven options to choose from whenever you get stuck.

Whichever move you decide to make, persevere. If your first attempt doesn't work, try again. Your first question, "Why do you need 10%?" may not be answered, so ask it again in different ways. If that move does not work, then try one of the other six elements. The good news is that you have seven different places to go, and if you stay focused and disciplined, you'll make progress.

When you can't change the game

On rare occasions, you may simply not be able to change the game. This happens most frequently when your counterpart has an actual interest in being a hard bargainer. For example, he takes some delight in seeing who will back down first or making concessions back and forth. If you have truly exhausted the strategies without success, you have a few choices.

1. Play the game, but play it better than he does. For example, if you are going to engage in the horse-trading game of positional bargaining, be well prepared on all seven elements, keep your measure of success in view, and use this to get the upper hand in his game. For example, use prepared standards to reinforce your positions, brainstormed options to select and use low-cost concessions as you extract high-cost ones from him, and so forth. Keep in mind, though, that you should do this only on very rare occasions. Even if you succeed, you risk setting a bad precedent.

2. Resort to your best alternative, but do so in a way that leaves the door open for the other party

> to come back to the table later. You might say, "I wish we could make this work, but as is, I'd simply do better losing this deal than agreeing to it. I have a number of other customers and think it would be better if I focus my attention there. If things change for you, I'd be thrilled if you gave me a call." Sometimes your counterpart won't call, but other times he'll realize his best alternative wasn't quite as good as he thought, is going nowhere, or worse yet, is leading to bad results, and your phone will ring.

Changing the game can save a negotiation that is going nowhere. It often sets a good precedent for future interactions, too. For example, if you bring in a standard that works against a tough negotiator, you've done two things: first, you've established a criterion you both can agree on and point to in the future, and second, you've made it clear that you want to negotiate fairly, rather than using one-sided power plays. Create the history you want to repeat.

This all may sound easier said than done, but armed with the advice here and some practice, you too will be able to do this. Start by watching tough negotiations and thinking about how you would steer your counterpart away from the hard bargainer's tactics. Then practice on some low-risk negotiations, gradually building your way up. As you get more experienced, make sure each time that you step back, diagnose, and make active choices about how you want to reshape the conversation.

Chapter 12
When Communication Breaks Down

Build understanding.

The Problem

Sometimes when you get in the room, you find that you and your counterpart can't get on the same page. Perhaps the conversation has turned contentious quickly, and your counterpart was offended by something you said, even though you didn't mean it that way. Maybe you don't understand why the options that you've suggested don't work for the other party. Or perhaps you find yourselves debating over how you each see the situation or issues in the negotiation. No matter what you do, there seems to be a disconnect.

Take this example from an R&D joint venture between an automobile manufacturer and a producer of electric car parts. Alfredo, one of the executives with the manufacturer, tried to persuade Deirdre, his counterpart with the electronics producer, to move the venture's main site to the Midwest, where the manufacturing of the vehicles took place. Deirdre was resistant, so Alfredo went out of his way to explain the benefits: They would have access to more-talented engineers, and the whole venture would be closer to "where the action was." Every time they spoke and he indicated another benefit, she'd shoot him down. Despite the fact that he had a counterargument ready for every issue she raised—like the fact that they'd save more in the cost of operations than what they'd have to spend on the relocation—still she said no, but would never explain why.

Their relationship was getting strained, since Alfredo simply couldn't understand where Deirdre was coming from, and he was beginning to assume that she was just being difficult. Further proof of this was her odd reaction to something he had said weeks earlier. In trying to be a helpful partner, he had told her proudly that the engineers at his company had finally come up with a method to integrate her company's very complex components into all their car models. He thought she'd be thrilled by this development. Instead, she glared at him and stomped off.

Despite Alfredo's best intentions, several common breakdowns in communication are evident here: Deirdre won't tell Alfredo why his proposals won't work for her; Alfredo has managed to offend Deirdre without knowing why; and Alfredo hasn't created an option that takes Deirdre's perspective and her interests into account.

Why It Happens

Breakdowns in communication aren't an infrequent occurrence in negotiations. To understand why, think about the classic black-and-white drawing that to some people looks like a young girl and, to others, like an old woman. It's the same picture, but people simply see it differently. These are called *partisan perceptions*, and they apply to negotiations the same way. You see the whole negotiation differently—the very act of the negotiation, one another, and the issues at hand.

These perceived differences are dangerous because we often amplify them in our minds. Research has shown that we have a tendency to enhance our own side of an issue—to think of it as more honest or real—while vilifying others into "the opposition." This often leads to negative perceptions of the other party and their reasoning, behavior, or position.

The gaps between your stories can be hard to fill. But if you don't explore the difference together, you're likely to be left debating conclusions instead of reducing conflict and solving problems.

What to Do About It

You can bridge this gap by building mutual understanding. This starts with you: Figure out what information you are lacking and how to get it. After all, you can't change someone's mind unless you know where his mind is. Once you do, you have a better chance of working together to form a solution that works for both of you.

Make understanding a collaborative effort

It helps to acknowledge that partisan perceptions exist and to assume that you will encounter them as a matter of course. When you do, you'll have to deliberately seek to understand your counterpart's perspective, and have that person understand yours:

1. **Ask her to share her reasoning.** Ask questions until you fully understand the other party's story and can see how she would've reached her conclusion (though you don't have to agree with it). Focus on the data she's using to reach conclusions and make clear how you're interpreting the data to reach *your* conclusions.

2. **Repeat it.** Tell your counterpart's story back to her. Test it, and demonstrate that you understand it. If she tells you that you missed something, play back what you learned.

3. **Share *your* story.** Don't present it as an airtight case, but explain how you got to your conclusion so that she understands your reasoning. Openly admit that it's possible that you might not have all the facts and that there may be other legitimate ways to view the situation.

4. **Invite your counterpart to ask questions.** She might ask about your story and how it leads to your conclusion, or she might critique it.

Stay away from the question of who's right. Use this method to get away from "agreeing to disagree" and move toward a mutual understanding of how and why you disagree and building trust.

If you expect partisan perceptions to be particularly divergent in your negotiation, consider discussing them early on in the negotiation process.

Manage impact, not intent

If your counterpart feels offended or hurt by something you said, but you didn't mean it that way, that may be another symptom of a communication breakdown. As someone who didn't mean to offend, it's natural to focus on correcting your counterpart's perception and demonstrating what you *did* intend to say. But your intentions shouldn't be the focus here. Instead, address the impact you might have had.

Begin by exploring the emotions your counterpart is feeling as a result of what you did or said. If he is not forthcoming about his feelings, test what you think your impact might have been: "While it was not my intent, I fear what I did yesterday ended up putting you in an embarrassing situation with your boss," or "I am truly worried that what I said sounded like I was criticizing your team, when I didn't mean to." Open up the conversation, explore unintended results, and let him talk. Show empathy or at least understanding, and never hesitate to apologize. You are not apologizing for good intent; you are apologizing for the impact.

Consider the example in which Alfredo's intent was to share how he had helped Deirdre and her company.

Unfortunately, from her reaction, Alfredo could tell that Deirdre hadn't understood it that way. What Alfredo didn't know was that Deirdre had heard many times how much better the engineering talent was at Alfredo's company than at hers. So based on her own experience, she heard one-upmanship and boasting—and, in effect, criticism. She was hurt by being reminded of what she failed to accomplish.

But Alfredo did not know that; to him, her reaction was baffling. Alfredo's next step was to follow up with Deirdre, explaining that he had expected a different reaction and asking her what was wrong. Still angry, Deirdre accused him of insulting her and showing off. But Alfredo kept asking questions about her reaction. When she calmed down, Deirdre explained how she had understood his remark and the background behind her reaction. She explained that she had always seen her failure to create an easier-to-use product as a pivotal moment in her career, and she hadn't been truly happy with her job since. Alfredo then had the opportunity to respond, "I can imagine how that makes you feel. I'm so sorry for bringing it all up and hurting you."

By managing the negative impact of what he had said, rather than insisting that Deirdre understand his intent, Alfredo learned more about Deirdre's interests, which then helped him in the course of his negotiation with her: She was competitive, she wished she could solve her company's problems, and she wanted to improve her job. He also gained Deirdre's trust; he put the relationship back on track by asking questions, listening carefully, and acknowledging the impact of his words and the validity of Deirdre's feelings.

Create a "yesable" proposition

If your counterpart keeps saying no to your proposals and options and you can't understand why, that's also a sign of miscommunication. While it's easy to assume that the person is being irrational or stubborn, neither conclusion is helpful nor, most often, true. People do what they think is in their best interests, whether we understand those interests or not.

Alfredo already shared with Deirdre all the reasons the move makes sense to him and explained away every concern she raised. It was unlikely he would get anywhere by continuing to try to persuade her.

Instead, after their conversation, Alfredo realized that his proposal must not meet Deirdre's interests well. Instead of continuing to press her, he stepped into her shoes to try to better understand *why* his idea wasn't winning her over. His goal was to uncover which of her interests weren't being met and to brainstorm new options that might work better for her.

My partner Roger Fisher always advised people to think about the decision from the other party's point of view and to use this to craft a *yesable proposition*. To create a yesable proposition in your negotiation, follow these five steps:

1. **Ask yourself whether you're trying to persuade the right person.** Sometimes the person with

whom you're negotiating may be saying no because the options don't satisfy other key parties. This could indicate that you should negotiate with someone else, or it might simply mean that you need to keep in mind that your counterpart will later need to get buy-in from someone else. In either case, you need to analyze the interests of these outside stakeholders and even get them directly involved in the discussion. For example, Alfredo might have talked to Deirdre's boss instead if he had realized that Deirdre didn't have the authority to make the decision whether to move the venture.

2. **Imagine what choice your counterpart believes you're asking her to make.** Think about how your counterpart might describe that choice to herself from her perspective, not yours. Alfredo, for example, might realize that he has been thinking about the question in Deirdre's mind as, "Shall I finally agree to Alfredo's excellent proposal to create closer collaboration, more efficiency, and lower operating costs for me?" when she's really thinking something more like, "Shall I today give in to another demand from superstar Alfredo, have to lay people off in one location only to have to hire people in the new location, and have people from his company more easily poke their noses into our business?"

   Imagining this tougher and not very appealing choice for Deirdre would help Alfredo realize more of her interests and come up with new options that meet them.

3. **Make a list of the negative consequences the other party might perceive in saying yes to the current proposal.** Carefully gauge what would happen for your counterpart if she said yes to your proposal. Make a list of the potential negative outcomes. (Put the positives aside for now; you've already tried to use those to convince her, and they haven't worked.) Then, make a separate list of reasons it would *benefit* her to say no to you. Put yourself in her shoes. If you think, "Wow, if I saw things this way, I would say no, too," you're headed in the right direction.

   When you do this analysis, don't just use your imagination to complete the lists. Talk to people who know your counterpart and her company. Do research on what's happening within the company.

   Alfredo started in on his lists. Considering what would happen if Deirdre said yes, he realized that she'd have to relocate people, fire others, take the time to hire new employees where perhaps the required specialized skills were in short supply, and explain her decision to the local union with which her company had strong relations. If she said no, Alfredo listed, she'd look strong to her colleagues and her team, keep her promise of no relocations, remain close to her company's headquarters where she could position herself for her next job, continue to have a team of engineers travel to Alfredo's company once a month, and use videoconference the other three weeks. And if things changed for some reason, she could always say yes tomorrow to what would likely be a sweeter deal from Alfredo.

It was no wonder that Deirdre was not saying yes, Alfredo realized; not only did the option on the table go against some of her key interests, but her best alternative was actually sounding pretty good.

Armed with a better understanding of Deirdre's unmet interests, Alfredo could now consider other options; research standards that could help Deirdre defend her choice to others if she did agree to his proposal; or demonstrate that her best alternative was weaker than she thought (perhaps the option to move her department wouldn't last forever!).

4. **Share and check your analysis.** Show your counterpart that you've thought through her perspective and make sure you're on the right track by sharing your conclusions. Say something like, "I was having trouble understanding your point of view, so I tried to list out the reasons you were saying no. What do I have wrong? What am I missing?" Your counterpart will appreciate that you took the time to think through her choice from her perspective, and even if you did a poor job, she'll pick up a pen and begin marking up

your list. This conversation clarifies unmet interests and helps you to move the negotiation back to inventing new options.

5. **Develop a new proposal.** Try to influence your counterpart by coming up with a different choice. This might involve developing a new solution altogether or simply refining or adding to the one already on the table. The goal is to find a way to meet more key interests of hers (as well as meeting your own) and make her alternatives look weaker, so she'll be more likely to say yes.

Using his analysis, Alfredo created new options that he felt would be more attractive to Deirdre:

1. Actively assist with recruiting in the new location.

2. Share criteria on the lower cost of living and help draft a press release that will address the concerns of Deirdre's strongest critic—the union. These standards could help her sell the idea to her stakeholders.

3. House Deirdre's people for the next six months, but don't ask them to move permanently.

Notice that the first two options are just slight adjustments to the option that had been on the table all along, while the third is a very different proposal.

Lastly, Alfredo let Deirdre know that this window of opportunity wouldn't last forever because the funding for the move wouldn't be available after the end of the fiscal year. He helped her see that her best alternative—saying no and waiting for him to make a better offer—wasn't as appealing as she thought.

The goal here is to create a new, more appealing option by better understanding the other party's interests. Remember, most people start with a position and hold on to it tightly. Once you understand the reasons behind their grip, you can address their needs and yours with a yesable proposition.

Making understanding a collaborative effort and creating a proposition to which your counterpart can say yes will both help address communication breakdowns and move you toward a more productive solution.

Chapter 13

When Emotions Get in the Way

Go from boiling to cool.

The Problem

Many people fear that no matter how they prepare, their negotiation will spiral into an unproductive debate or a shouting match. Even if you're approaching the negotiation with a collaborative, joint problem-solving mindset, it's possible that things will get heated. You know when it's happening: Perhaps you feel yourself getting emotional; you sense that your blood pressure is rising, that you're becoming angry or anxious. Maybe your counterpart is doing the same. The volume might be getting louder, or perhaps one or both of you have started to yell.

Let's look at an example inside a company doing its annual budget planning. Betty, the head of sales, is preparing her budget for next year, and she's meeting with

Amit, the director of finance. Betty has asked Amit several times for revised numbers that she can include in her budget. Instead of delivering, however, he keeps coming back to her with more questions.

Betty's draft budget is due to the CFO first thing tomorrow morning, so she sends Amit a meeting request to discuss what's going on. Amit accepts, but shows up 15 minutes late. After explaining why she needs the numbers today, Betty asks what's preventing Amit from just giving her the numbers she's asked for. He begins to explain that she hasn't shared enough information and that he's been working hard to make sense of what she *has* given him.

Betty raises her voice: "I've asked you four times to give me those numbers, you showed up late to this meeting, and this is somehow my fault. Why can't you just do what I asked?"

Amit can't believe she's not getting it. "I've been working on your numbers for weeks! But I can't get you the final figures until you give me all the information I need. Don't you understand that this is on you?"

This may not strike you as a negotiation at first glance, but it is: There are two parties, with different incentives and interests, who are trying to come to an agreement about how to proceed. In this case, a conflict has erupted, but it doesn't have to hurt Betty and Amit's relationship or Betty's draft budget.

Why It Happens

Emotions get heated during a negotiation because there are high stakes: people's jobs, their standing with their bosses, their confidence, the success of a venture, or the future of their business.

A negotiation can also get emotional when you and your counterpart haven't communicated well (as we saw in the previous chapter). Perhaps you misunderstood each other's intentions or offended each other by accident, and feelings were hurt.

What to Do About It

Whatever the reason the conversation has turned combative, help your counterpart—or yourself—go from boiling to cool. Remain calm, work to understand what's triggered both of you, see if you can use any of your emotions to help you make your case, and address any systemic problems.

Keep calm

If your counterpart is worked up, try to stay calm. This is easier said than done. Here are a few ways to help defuse the situation:

1. **Focus on your physical reaction.** Breathe deeply rather than tensing up and holding your breath. Ground yourself by putting your hands on the table or your feet on the floor. The physical motions you make will influence how your mind reacts. If you start wringing your hands, you're signaling to your mind that there is something to worry about. On the other hand, if you move slowly and deliberately, you send the message to your brain to remain calm.

2. **Listen to what your counterpart is saying.** Let him vent. Some people need to boil over as a kind of release. After yelling or banging the table, they might calm down by themselves. Don't always feel you need to respond to the outburst. If you can, let it go and move on to a more productive way of interacting.

3. **Show you've heard him.** Calmly paraphrase what you heard. Acknowledging the reason that your counterpart got upset can often help turn things around. Sometimes people just want to be heard.

4. **Show some empathy.** If he's mad because of something that doesn't have anything to do with you, acknowledge that it seems like a tough situation. Perhaps even frame the issue as a joint problem on which you two can work together.

5. **Find out more.** If you're the cause for his frustration, dig in and find out what's happening. Borrowing strategies from the previous chapter, try to understand what you did and how the two of you might be seeing things differently.

6. **Take a break.** If you're the one who's getting angry or emotional, consider taking a break. Go for a walk around the building. Ask someone on your team to help you talk it through. Some deep breathing, or even a little meditation, can help you reground yourself.

When Amit snapped back at her, Betty took a deep breath and sat back in her chair, putting both feet on the ground. With her body steady, she was able to begin calming down, but she couldn't help noticing that Amit still had a red face and crossed arms.

Betty's next step was to apologize for her outburst. She didn't stop there, though. She also asked Amit why he was upset. She moved forward to listen and let him go at it.

Amit said that he was under a lot of pressure given that it was budget time. He admitted that Betty wasn't the first person to get angry with him that week. He talked about how he was missing his targets because he did not get enough resources last year. He even shared a situation two months back when he had asked Betty for help and had gotten nothing. She had no idea what he was referring to, but she didn't stop him; instead, she asked what the consequences had been. With all that off his chest—and with Betty's evident openness to hearing from him—Amit calmed down, too. Betty watched, relieved, as Amit's shoulders began to relax and he uncrossed his arms.

Understand the triggers

As you try to move forward, it's helpful to know what's gotten you worked up in the first place. We all have pet peeves or behaviors that push our buttons. Develop an awareness of what typically makes you upset. Perhaps you don't like it when someone challenges your truthfulness or integrity. Maybe you get mad when someone exaggerates her point or keeps repeating it. Perhaps it's when someone calls you on something you know you need to work on or something you pride yourself on that the person is now framing as a negative. Sometimes simply understanding the underlying reason for your anger can help you regain control.

Pay attention to what makes your counterpart upset as well. Observe when she gets emotional. Are there certain words or behaviors that seem to provoke her? If you've negotiated with her in the past, try to think back to other occasions when she has gotten upset. Do you notice any patterns?

Once Betty and Amit began to calm down, Betty reminded herself that she always got angry when people showed up late to meetings because it made her feel disrespected. She worked many hours in the evening and on the weekends to ensure she was never late, and here not only was Amit late for the meeting, but he was on the verge of making her late submitting her budget. She recognized that this was *her* trigger and that was probably what made her particularly upset.

Betty also remembered that the sales team was known for being overly punctual, and finance just the opposite (perhaps, she now realized, due to the workload created by the demanding sales team). She had worked with Amit for several years and had seen him get upset before: It happened most often when people questioned his work ethic. Amit, too, worked long days, often staying into the evening, and he prided himself on the quality of his work, even if it didn't always get finished on time. To him, working hard and getting things right were more important than meeting a deadline.

Betty suggested that she stay late with Amit that evening so that they could work on the numbers together. Amit would get the information he needed to get the calculations right, and Betty would be able to submit her budget on time. Amit agreed, and both left the meeting feeling much better about the plan and each other.

Use your emotions

Some people think that they aren't supposed to be emotional in a negotiation, that they shouldn't reveal what they're feeling, whether it's good *or* bad. But there are times that showing passion can be helpful. While perhaps Betty derailed the conversation by losing her cool in the meeting, at least Amit now understood how much she cared about getting those numbers and delivering her draft budget on time.

If something upsets you, or if someone pushes your buttons, it's fine to show that you're angry, frustrated, or disappointed. (Reacting without forethought by banging the table, jumping up and down, storming out of the room, or verbally attacking your counterpart, however, is a different story; being out of control is never helpful.) If you're really excited about something positive, such as a feature of the agreement, or something of concern, such as the need to solve a key problem, it's OK to express your passion. Of course, do so as a conscious choice. You certainly don't want to accidentally signal that you're particularly needy (that you care about this interest over all else) or desperate (that your alternatives aren't very good). Instead of letting your emotion control you, harness that emotion and use it to make your point.

You can also harness your counterpart's emotion. Use it to uncover his interests (especially fears or concerns) or as a catalyst to invent options. "You're steaming mad, and I am, too, so what can we do about this?" or "You're clearly hurt. What are some ways we might fix this?" If the person is emotional, he is engaged, and this is often the best time to move into the circle of value. As the emotion dissipates, you might move to sit beside him, focus on a common piece of paper or flip chart, and begin recording interests, options, and standards together.

Address recurring conflicts

Sometimes emotions run high not because of something specific that's happening in the room but because there is a long-standing unhealthy relationship between the two parties. If you sense the underlying reason for your counterpart yelling at you has little to do with what you've just said, try talking about that.

If you're surprised by the negotiation turning emotional, or if negotiations with a particular counterpart turn sour on a consistent basis, it is likely a sign that something systemic is going on. Discover what the underlying cause is: missed deadlines, other broken commitments, lack of preparation, disrespectful comments or behaviors, past threats or escalations, or truth stretched. Use what you learned in chapter 6 about managing the relationship: Explicitly bring these issues up instead of letting them fester, and discuss how to solve the underlying problem rather than just temporarily smoothing things over.

Emotional outbursts can be scary, and it's often hard to imagine how to get past them in the moment. But balancing your and your counterpart's reactions—allowing emotions to be expressed but also thinking analytically about what's really going on and how to address it—helps the conversation stay productive and helps you find solutions that work for everyone.

Section 4
Postgame

Careful review drives learning and improvement.

How you conclude your negotiation is just as important as how you begin it. End on the right note so that what comes next—implementation of the agreement and any future negotiations—goes smoothly.

In the next chapter, I'll discuss how to wrap up the negotiation and communicate the results with the right people. In the final chapter, I'll explain how to learn from your negotiation to continuously improve your organization's approach to similar transactions, as well as to refine your own skills.

Chapter 14
Wrap Up the Negotiation

Know when you're done, and communicate the final decisions.

If you've successfully negotiated an agreement that meets the criteria you set out earlier for a good outcome, congratulations! It's tough work to get to this point.

You might assume that you've now reached the end of the negotiation and all that's left is the signing of the papers. However, you'll need to take three last steps before considering the negotiation final: documenting the terms, communicating with stakeholders, and prepping for implementation of the agreement.

Document the Terms

If you used the one-text procedure described in the "Get People on the Same Page—Literally" part of chapter 10, you've already written out the terms that you've agreed to. But if you haven't, now is a good time to record where you ended up so that you both have a shared understanding of the specifics.

Incorporate any notes you and your counterpart made along the way, any points you recorded on flip charts or in postsession memos. In a more formal setting, this is where you would create a formal contract that captures your agreement and requires signatures. Whether you use an e-mail, memo, or contract, have your counterpart review and agree to the text, and be sure you each have a copy. Even for quick negotiations in a hallway, you'll likely want to follow up with some sort of written confirmation of your discussion to share with your counterpart and any other stakeholders.

Documenting serves two purposes: One, it ensures that everyone is on the same page. You and your counterpart can share the e-mail or contract as a draft with others in your organizations. Two, the final approved version serves as a record of what you agreed to in case you, your counterpart, or anyone implementing the agreement later needs a reminder of the details.

Caution: Unless you are the sole stakeholder in your party, make clear to your counterpart that you are not yet making a final commitment at this stage. You still need to take your documentation back to your colleagues for review.

Communicate to Make Sure You Have Agreement

Throughout the negotiation, you've been keeping your stakeholders informed. Now is the time to confirm that everyone with decision rights is onboard. Your legal or finance teams may need to review the terms closely, your operations team may be interested in what's coming their way, or perhaps your boss just needs to give her blessing. Share your documentation and explain why you recommend it, focusing on the interests and standards it meets.

Sometimes this review will just be a formality; in other cases, you may need to work to persuade others or, on rare occasion, to revisit parts of the agreement if they have issues.

Whether it's your boss, key functional leaders, or your family, getting those who truly matter onboard will significantly increase your chances of successfully implementing your agreement.

Think Through the Implementation

Before you declare victory and move on, think about what steps will ensure a smooth transition from agreement to implementation.

Perhaps the agreement is something you'll be carrying out yourself, like a new role you just negotiated with your boss. If that's the case, talk about follow-up steps before leaving the room. Who will write up a new job description? Will you need certain resources, and if so, who will acquire them and how? What's the timeline? How will progress be tracked and success be measured? Explicitly discuss how to move from conceptual agreement to action.

If you're wrapping up a more complex negotiation, you'll probably already have addressed important milestones and deadlines and captured them in the contract. But before everything is finalized, think one last time about how the agreement will be carried out and by whom, and what could change or go wrong. Have you discussed what happens if you or your counterpart cannot hit these milestones? What process will you use to make adjustments? Will there be any penalties? What happens if you or your counterpart, or other prominent stakeholders, leave your organization before the project is complete? Perhaps you and the other party agreed that there were some risky terms in the agreement and you need to put something up for collateral; if so, what is the plan for doing this?

If your job is simply to negotiate, and you'll hand off the implementation responsibility to others, think about what *they* need to effectively carry out the agreement. These may feel like logistical issues that are extraneous to the negotiation, but in fact they are integral details that you need to consider, discuss with your counterpart, and perhaps also formally add into your documentation. All the work you did to negotiate your agreement will be for naught if it cannot be implemented.

Put the Agreement into Action

Once the agreement is (finally!) final, brief anyone involved in its implementation on what has been negotiated, the intent behind it, what you've learned about your counterpart and his interests, and any predictable future risks or stumbling blocks. Sharing sticking points from the negotiation process can be helpful as well, since this can indicate where future problems may occur. Certainly take time to explain any element of the agreement that is new to your organization, such as a particularly creative delivery or payment method.

Take, for example, a salesperson for a service provider who just closed a deal. Because of the deal's complexity, the contract required a lot of legal language, so the salesperson should convey the key terms to the delivery team in plain English. The customer emphasized throughout the negotiations concerns about certain deadlines or dependencies, so he should convey those to his delivery team as well. He also noticed during the process that representatives of the customer's organization approached conflict head-on: He'll tell her team that as well, in case disagreements come up over time.

Don't consider the negotiation "finished" until you've conveyed all relevant information about the agreement to anyone who will be working to put it into action; use the "Communicating to Implementers Checklist" box to make sure you've covered everything. Of course, some of these items will not be appropriate in every negotiation. In each case, consider how complex the contract is, how challenging you expect the implementation will be, the depth and dynamics of the past history with this counterpart, and how contentious the negotiation was, and share that with anyone who may be affected by the agreement.

COMMUNICATING TO IMPLEMENTERS CHECKLIST

(1) To help the implementers truly understand the agreement, I have:

- Shared the contract
- Highlighted key points
- Documented our and the other party's core interests behind important terms
- Shared the intent behind terms where it might not be clear

(2) To forewarn them about potential future conflicts, I have:

- Noted where, and why, there was significant contention during the negotiation around a particular issue or term
- Pointed out key areas where there was uncertainty in the negotiation about how to deal with a core issue or difference between the parties
- Highlighted areas where the issue or term creates, leaves open, or tries to manage some substantial risk for either or both parties
- Documented any areas where we are worried about the other party living up to their commitments and any areas where they seem worried about us living up to our commitments

COMMUNICATING TO IMPLEMENTERS CHECKLIST

(3) To assist implementers in managing the ongoing relationship with the other party, I have:

- Shared what I learned from the negotiation about how the other party's organization operates
- Highlighted key differences between our and their priorities, methods, ways of interacting, values, and so on
- Informed them about any relationship tensions, difficult people in the other organization, great people with whom to work, particularly strong and helpful relationships between certain people in our organization and certain people in the other organization, and so on
- Passed on any insights into who influences whom in the other organization, about what kinds of issues, and in what ways: in other words, the details of a fleshed-out Relationship Map for the other organization

(4) To help the implementers get started, I have:

- Made introductions between them and key people in the other party's organization
- Highlighted near-term goals, activities to launch, commitments to be fulfilled, deadlines, and so on

COMMUNICATING TO IMPLEMENTERS CHECKLIST

- Noted any key dependencies between what they need to do and what we need to do, and especially between what we and they committed to do
- Shared how both we and they will be measuring near-term success

Chapter 15

Review What Happened

Use "lessons learned" today for improvement tomorrow.

When the negotiation is truly finished, don't just pat yourself on the back. Every negotiation is an opportunity to learn and to improve your skills as a negotiator.

Set Up a Review

Unfortunately, most people don't formally look back over their negotiations unless things went horribly wrong. Of course, you'll learn a lot from your failures, but there are valuable takeaways from successes, too. Make sure to review, capture what you learned, and get feedback.

Set aside time as close to the end of the negotiation as possible so that the events of the negotiation are still fresh in your mind. For a simpler negotiation, take 15 minutes in your car to think through your lessons learned. For one that's more complex, set up reviews after each session. Consider doing another review after you've lived with the agreement for a few months to gauge if there are things that have come up in the implementation that might cause you to think differently about what to do or avoid the next time you negotiate.

If you negotiated on your own, get help from a trusted colleague and walk her through the process. For a more complex negotiation, set up a meeting with any colleagues who were involved. This includes anyone who was in the room, as well as those who played an important role behind the scenes.

Determine what worked well and where to improve

Identify areas to improve your and your organization's negotiation skills and strategies you may want to use again in other situations.

When you convene this review meeting (or when you sit down to think it through on your own), ask the following questions:

- What worked well? Why? What should I continue doing next time?
- What didn't work well? Why? What should I do differently next time?
- Where did I get stuck in the negotiation and why? If I was able to work my way out, how did I do it?
- Were there things the other party, or his organization, did from which I might learn?

- Are there new interests, creative options, persuasive standards, or effective game-changing moves that I might want to capture to use again or share with colleagues who have similar kinds of negotiations?

For more complex negotiations, consider asking these questions for each phase of the negotiation: preparing, conducting, making midcourse corrections, and closing it out.

Also go back and gauge your final agreement against each of the seven elements as a measure of success. If the agreement meets your interests well, but you can't quite say the same about standards, you now know where you need to prepare or practice more in the future.

Capture what you learned

Document everything discussed in your review session. Be prescriptive. Translate what you've learned into advice to use the next time you negotiate.

Consider keeping a journal that captures lessons from each of your negotiations, including inventive options, compelling standards, ways of improving relationships, or other strategies that worked well for you. That way, you can review these practical tips before your next negotiation and put them to use for a better result.

Share what you've learned with others

Capture your lessons in a way that others who were not part of the process can understand them. Lessons learned in the negotiation too often stay with the negotiator alone. Help others benefit from your experience by highlighting what you learned about the process and the other parties, creative ways you structured the agreement, and successful strategies. Some organizations create negotiation strategy playbooks in which they document this kind of information.

Aim for Continuous Improvement

The best way to get better at negotiation is to prepare, conduct, review, and repeat. While your next negotiation may be about a different set of issues, the process and skills you'll need to be successful are likely quite similar.

If you approach the whole process with discipline, over time you will not only become increasingly confident, you will also achieve better results, build productive relationships, and create valuable agreements with bosses, colleagues, customers, suppliers, and partners alike.

Learn More

If you're interested in learning more about negotiation, the books listed here are a great place to start. These publications are by my colleagues, and each one defined or helped shape the strategies and advice in this guide.

Ertel, Danny, and Mark Gordon. *The Point of the Deal: How to Negotiate When Yes Is Not Enough.* Boston: Harvard Business School Press, 2007.

Fisher, Roger, and Scott Brown. *Getting Together: Building Relationships as We Negotiate.* Boston: Houghton Mifflin, 1988. (Paperback edition: New York: Penguin Books, 1989.)

Fisher, Roger, and Daniel Shapiro. *Beyond Reason: Using Emotions as You Negotiate.* New York: Viking/Penguin, 2005.

Fisher, Roger, William L. Ury, and Bruce Patton. *Getting to YES: Negotiating Agreement Without Giving In*, 2nd edition. New York: Penguin Books, 1991. (1st edition: Boston: Houghton Mifflin, 1981.)

Stone, Douglas, Bruce Patton, and Sheila Heen. *Difficult Conversations: How to Discuss What Matters Most.* New York: Viking/Penguin, 1999.

Index

About the Author

Jeff Weiss is a partner at Vantage Partners, a global consultancy specializing in corporate negotiations, relationship management, partnering, and complex change management. At Vantage, Jeff has led both the Alliances and the Sales Advisory practices, and worked extensively both in the Strategic Sourcing and Supply Chain Management practice and in Vantage's training business. Jeff also serves on the faculties of the Tuck School of Business and the United States Military Academy at West Point, where he is also the codirector of the West Point Negotiation Project.

Notes

Notes

Notes

Notes

Notes

Notes

Notes

Notes

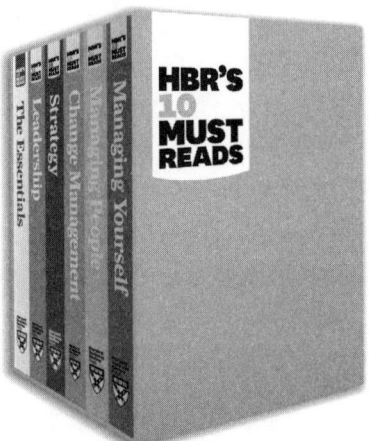

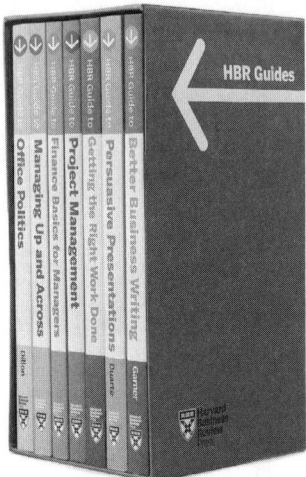

HBR Guide to **Making Every Meeting Matter**

Harvard Business Review Guides

Arm yourself with the advice you need to succeed on the job, from the most trusted brand in business. Packed with how-to essentials from leading experts, the HBR Guides provide smart answers to your most pressing work challenges.

The titles include:

HBR Guide to Better Business Writing

HBR Guide to Building Your Business Case

HBR Guide to Buying a Small Business

HBR Guide to Coaching Employees

HBR Guide to Dealing with Conflict

HBR Guide to Delivering Effective Feedback

HBR Guide to Finance Basics for Managers

HBR Guide to Getting the Mentoring You Need

HBR Guide to Getting the Right Job

HBR Guide to Getting the Right Work Done

HBR Guide to Leading Teams

HBR Guide to Making Every Meeting Matter

HBR Guide to Managing Stress at Work

HBR Guide to Managing Up and Across

HBR Guide to Negotiating

HBR Guide to Networking

HBR Guide to Office Politics

HBR Guide to Persuasive Presentations

HBR Guide to Project Management

HBR Guide to **Making Every Meeting Matter**

HARVARD BUSINESS REVIEW PRESS

Boston, Massachusetts

Printed in the United States of America

10 9 8 7 6 5

Library of Congress Cataloging-in-Publication Data

Title: HBR guide to making every meeting matter.
Other titles: Harvard business review guides.
Description: Boston, Massachusetts : Harvard Business Review Press, [2016] |
Series: Harvard Business Review guides
Identifiers: LCCN 2016025614 | ISBN 9781633692176 (pbk.)
Subjects: LCSH: Business meetings—Handbooks, manuals, etc. | Business meetings—Planning—Handbooks, manuals, etc.
Classification: LCC HF5734.5 .H397 2016 | DDC 658.4/56—dc23
LC record available at https://lccn.loc.gov/2016025614

ISBN: 9781633692176
eISBN: 9781633692183

The paper used in this publication meets the requirements of the American National Standard for Permanence of Paper for Publications and Documents in Libraries and Archives Z39.48-1992.

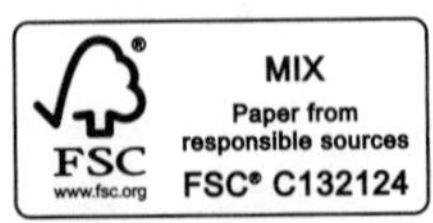

What You'll Learn

We all know what we're supposed to do to run meetings effectively, but we seldom do them well. Why? Perhaps we think it's just not worth the time to clarify what we hope to accomplish, craft an agenda, handpick participants, issue prework, and send out follow-up notes that detail key decisions and next steps. So we run meetings off the cuff or saddle participants with an overly ambitious agenda we have no hope of working through. Other meeting problems feel beyond our control. People nod their heads in our decision-making meeting but then show their true feelings with their lack of follow-through. Derailers. Latecomers. Blowhards. Nonparticipants. People who bring *their* agenda to *your* meeting.

The best way to prevent or overcome any of these obstacles is thoughtful and thorough preparation. This guide offers tips and scripts for curbing inappropriate behavior and making your meetings easier to prepare for, more efficient to conduct—and more productive.

You'll learn how to:

- Determine whether you even need to meet
- Prepare a realistic agenda

What You'll Learn

- Identify why you're meeting—and articulate your purpose to attendees
- Orchestrate group decision making
- Prevent implementation roadblocks by giving participants equal airtime
- Cope with chronic latecomers, windbags, and other people problems
- Turn around a bad meeting
- Run any type of meeting—from a status stand-up to a one-on-one walking check-in to a strategy off-site
- Get the most out of digital meeting tools
- Hold people accountable without hounding or micromanaging
- Keep the momentum going with prompt meeting follow-up

Contents

PREFACE

The Condensed Guide to Running Meetings

by Amy Gallo

> ***Editor's note:*** Here's where to start if you need to organize a meeting soon—and you don't have a ton of time to prepare, but you want to do it right. When you're not so pressed for time, take a look at the rest of the book, which expands on themes raised here.

We love to hate meetings. And with good reason—they clog up our days, making it hard to get work done in the gaps, and so many feel like a waste of time.

Adapted from content posted on hbr.org on July 6, 2015.

Paul Axtell, author of *Meetings Matter: 8 Powerful Strategies for Remarkable Conversations,* says that this is a major pain point for nearly every manager he works with. "People are absolutely resigned," he says. "They have given up on the hope that it could be different." Axtell and Francesca Gino, author of *Sidetracked: Why Our Decisions Get Derailed, and How We Can Stick to the Plan* and a professor at Harvard Business School, weigh in here on whether much of the conventional wisdom on meetings holds true.

"Keep the meeting as small as possible. No more than seven people."

Though research does not point to a precise number that's ideal, "there is evidence to suggest that keeping the meeting small is beneficial," says Gino. For one thing, you're better able to notice body language when there are fewer people. "In a group of 20 or more, you can't keep track of the subtle cues you need to pick up," says Axtell. And if you want people to have the opportunity to contribute, limit attendance. In Axtell's experience, limiting it to four or five people is the only way to make sure everyone has the chance to talk in a 60-minute meeting.

The challenge with large meetings isn't just that everyone won't have a chance to talk but that many of them won't feel the need to. "When many hands are available, people work less hard than they ought to," explains Gino. "Social psychology research has shown that when people perform group tasks (such as brainstorming or discussing information in a meeting), they show a sizable decrease in individual effort from when they perform alone." This is known as "social loafing" and tends to get worse as the size of the group increases.

That's not to say that your 20-person meeting is doomed for failure. You just need to plan more carefully. "The degree of facilitation has to go up," says Axtell. You have to be more thoughtful about getting input from the group and reading people in the room. "You need someone who is masterful at managing the conversation."

"Ban devices."

Both experts agree this is a good idea, for two reasons. First, we know devices distract us. Gino points out that many people think they can multitask—finish an e-mail or read through their Twitter feed while listening to someone in a meeting. But research shows they really can't. "Recent neuroscience research makes the point quite clear on this issue. Multitasking is simply a mythical activity. We can do simple tasks like walking and talking at the same time, but the brain can't handle multitasking," says Gino. "In fact, studies show that a person who is attempting to multitask takes 50% longer to accomplish a task and makes up to 50% more mistakes."

And those who pick up their devices during meetings may well be the worst multitaskers. "The research finds that the more time people spend using multiple forms of media simultaneously, the less likely they are to perform well on a standardized test of multitasking abilities," explains Gino.

The second reason to ban devices is that they distract others. Gino recently conducted a simple survey that assessed whether people thought reaching for a phone, posting a status on Facebook, or writing a tweet during a meeting was distracting or socially inappropriate. The subjects "found the same action to be much more problematic if their friend or colleague engaged in it but did not find it to be very problematic when they were the ones who were (arguably) being rude," she says. These results suggest that we feel annoyed when others are on their devices during a meeting. "Yet we fail to realize that our actions will have the same effect on others when we are the ones engaging in them," she says. This is what Axtell sees in practice: People feel insulted when someone reaches for their phone, especially if that person is a senior leader. "If you're presenting or talking about an idea, and you see a senior manager on their phone, it hurts," he says.

Still there are some good reasons to use technology in a meeting, says Axtell. You may want to take notes or retrieve reference material. "Perhaps they need to be available because something important is going on in their lives," he says. But if these circumstances don't apply to your participants, have everyone turn their devices off and pay attention.

"Keep it as short as possible— no longer than an hour."

Research shows that there are advantages to keeping meetings short. One reason is that people stay more focused during shorter time spans. "Classic studies have found that groups adjust both their rate of work and their style of interaction in response to deadlines and time constraints," says Gino. For example, one study showed that "groups solving problems communicated at a faster rate and used more autocratic decision-making processes under high time pressure than they did when time pressure was low."

"Once people realize you're tight on time, they stop asking questions or talking and focus on getting the work done," says Axtell.

This doesn't mean you should try to cram every meeting into a 30-minute slot. Axtell warns that there are conversations that necessitate more time, and you shouldn't rush over certain topics. "If the purpose of your meeting is to talk through something, you need to give people enough time to voice their opinions, build on one another's ideas, and reach a conclusion," he says. Time pressure will make this more efficient, but you don't want to make the time so short that you truncate important conversations (chapters 6 and 7 offer suggestions for ideal meeting length).

"Stand-up meetings are more productive."

While some might feel that stand-up meetings are a gimmick, Gino points out that there is empirical data that proves they work. In one study (done in 1999 before stand-up meetings were a staple in most offices), Allen Bluedorn from the University of Missouri and his colleagues concluded that stand-up meetings were about 34% shorter than sit-down meetings, yet they produced the same solutions. (For a different take on stand-up meetings, see chapter 29.)

Axtell finds these types of solutions encouraging. "I like that people are trying to do something bold to change up meetings—going for a walk, standing up," he says. But, he warns, don't let the format distract you from doing what really matters: running an effective meeting. "I'd prefer people have the guts to say 'I'm going to run this meeting well.'"

"Make sure everyone participates, and call on those who don't."

Some people may want to speak up in your meeting but feel like they can't unless they're asked, says Axtell. This may be due to "cultural reasons, or language barriers, or general disposition." Axtell believes that people who hold back often have the best perspective on the conversation, and you need to draw them out.

Having everyone contribute isn't just good for the end result of your meeting, it's good for the participants as well. People like to know that their opinions are being heard and considered, says Gino. And "just by asking people in the meeting for their opinion, you're going to raise their commitment to the issues being discussed."

For people you know may feel too put on the spot, talk to them ahead of time and tell them that you're hoping they'll contribute. That way they'll have time to plan what they'll say. Then in the meeting, you may still need to prompt them by asking for their perspective, but they'll be primed to do so.

"Never hold a meeting just to update people."

"If you're already meeting for worthwhile topics, it's okay to give a quick update," says Axtell. You might ask at the end if there's anything the group needs to be aware of or if there's something going on in the department that others need to know about. "But if you're only meeting to transfer information, rethink your approach," Axtell urges. "Why take up valuable time saying something you could just send in an email?"

Wasting time isn't the only problem with update meetings. Gino explains that research by Roy Baumeister, Kathleen Vohs, and their colleagues suggests that we have a limited amount of what they call "executive resources." "Once they get depleted, we make bad decisions or choices," says Gino. "Business meetings often require people to commit, focus, and make decisions with little or no attention paid to the depletion of the finite cognitive resources of the participants—particularly when the meetings are long or too frequent." She finds that in her own research, "depletion of our executive resources can even lead to poor judgment and unethical behavior." So if you can avoid scheduling yet another meeting, you should.

"Always set an agenda ahead of time, and be clear about the purpose of the meeting."

It's hard to imagine more sound advice about meetings. Axtell and Gino agree that designing the meeting and setting an agenda ahead of time is critical. "You should explain what's going to happen so participants come knowing what they're going to do," says Axtell. In her book, *Sidetracked,* Gino talks about how lacking a clear plan of action is often why groups get derailed in decision making. "Having a plan gives us the opportunity to clarify our intentions and think through the forces that could make it difficult for us to accomplish our goals," she says.

Following the advice given here will ensure that the next time you need to bring a group together, you'll make it a good use of everyone's time—including your own.

Amy Gallo is a contributing editor at *Harvard Business Review* and the author of the *HBR Guide to Dealing with Conflict*. She writes and speaks about workplace dynamics. Follow her on Twitter @amyegallo.

SECTION ONE

Prepare

CHAPTER 1

Do You Really Need to Hold That Meeting?

by Elizabeth Grace Saunders

"Let's schedule a meeting" has become the universal default response to most business issues. Not sure what to do on a project? Let's schedule a meeting. Have a few ideas to share? Let's schedule a meeting. Struggling to take action? Let's schedule a meeting.

Although scheduling a meeting can be the right solution in many instances, it's not always the best answer. Here's a decision tree to help you quickly determine if holding a meeting makes the most sense (see figure 1-1).

Adapted from content posted on hbr.org on March 20, 2015.

FIGURE 1-1

Should I hold a meeting?

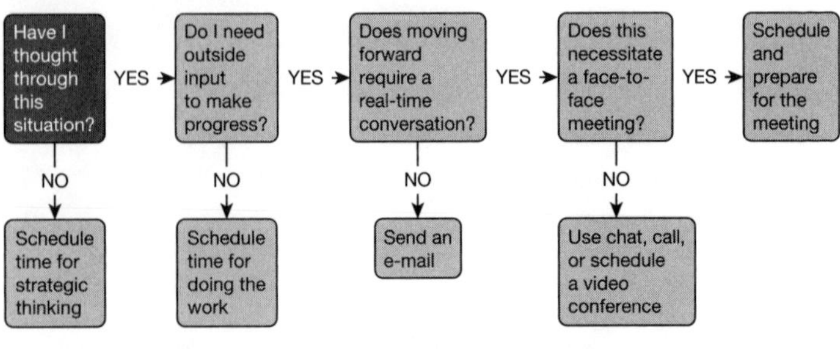

Copy this decision tree, and keep it handy. It makes it quick and easy to decide whether or not to hold a meeting. Here's what you should consider at each step.

Have I thought through this situation?

When you don't have clarity about what you're doing on a project, it's tempting to schedule a meeting to give you the feeling that you're making progress. But unless the meeting's intent is to structure the project, scheduling a meeting is probably an inefficient use of your time—and your colleagues'. Instead, do some strategic thinking. Evaluate the scope of the project, its current status, and the potential milestones, and lay out a plan of action for making meaningful progress. Once you've completed your own strategic thinking prep work you can consider if it makes sense to hold a meeting.

Do I need outside input to make progress?

You may be in a situation where you know what needs to be done, and you simply need to do the work. If so, don't schedule a meeting; update your to-do list, and take action instead. However, if after clarifying what needs to be done you require outside input to answer questions or give feedback before you feel comfortable jumping into action, continue on.

Does moving forward require a real-time conversation?

If you have questions that need to be answered but don't require a two-way conversation, e-mail can be an excellent alternative to a meeting. This is particularly true when you're looking for feedback on your written plans or documents. It's much more efficient for everyone involved if you send over items that they can look at on their own (while you're not awkwardly watching them read during an in-person meeting) and then shoot you back feedback. If you feel your situation does require a real-time conversation, examine different communication channels.

Does this necessitate a face-to-face meeting?

When you need two-way communication but don't necessarily need to see the person, you have a variety of options. An online chat can help you answer questions quickly, or for more in-depth conversations, scheduling a phone call or video conference can work well. This not only saves you the transition time of going to and from a meeting place, it also allows you to continue working if someone is late, rather than having to sit somewhere and wait for them to show up.

If in the end you decide that you need face-to-face, in-person communication, then schedule a meeting, and think through in advance how you can make it as efficient and effective as possible. That means considering your intent for the meeting, establishing your desired outcomes, and preparing any materials that should be sent out or reviewed in advance.

This decision-making process can help you radically reduce the number of meetings you attend and increase the amount of work that gets done.

Elizabeth Grace Saunders is the author of *How to Invest Your Time Like Money* (Harvard Business Review Press, 2015), a time coach, and the founder of Real Life E Time Coaching and Training. Find out more at the website www.RealLifeE.com.

CHAPTER 2

Stop Calling Every Conversation a "Meeting"

by Al Pittampalli

When both a 500-attendee event and a two-person discussion are referred to as "meetings," it's difficult to suss out a gathering's true purpose and to know how to prepare to make it successful. In order to have fewer, more purposeful meetings, we need a more robust vocabulary to describe them. So let's do some renaming, starting with three common "meetings" that you'll soon realize aren't really meetings at all.

Meetings with just two people are actually **conversations**. Whereas meetings with ample attendee lists

Adapted from content posted on hbr.org on November 3, 2015.

require an agenda, plenty of preparation, and an articulable purpose, one-on-one discussions need not be as rigorous. They aren't weapons of mass interruption, and humans are naturally good at them. So keep conversations casual, and hold them as often as you'd like.

Another kind of meeting that needs to be renamed is one in which work actually gets done. Management expert Peter Drucker famously noted that a "working meeting" was impossible: "One either meets or one works. One cannot do both at the same time." And, for the most part, he's right. Most meetings involve planning and coordinating the work, not executing it. But sometimes people—writers, programmers, mathematicians—do huddle around a laptop or whiteboard to do real work together. Let's call these **group work sessions** and make sure to disinvite the bureaucrats.

Then there are meetings where the primary goal is to generate ideas. If you want people to be truly imaginative and express themselves, don't dare call it a brainstorming meeting. Just call it a **brainstorm**. Since these sessions are designed to maximize creativity, it's a good idea to play a warm-up game, get people standing and active, and give people permission to have fun—free of judgment and criticism. If someone walks past the conference room and thinks you're having a "meeting," you're probably not doing it right.

Now let's consider a few types of meetings that are difficult to justify if you name them correctly. Take, for example, meetings that are called primarily because managers have information to disseminate. Rather than distributing a memo or having several one-on-one conversations, these bosses decide to save time by wasting the time of their colleagues, disrupting work, and corralling the team into a room together. These are **convenience meetings** and almost always a bad idea. They're typically convenient for the individual and inconvenient for everyone else.

Meetings called as a matter of tradition or habit—**formality meetings**—should also be banned. These gatherings may have served a purpose at one time but do so no longer. Rather than considering an issue and asking "Is a meeting the best way to address it?" we treat the event as a given and ask "What issues do we need to address at this meeting?" This ensures we always find things to discuss, no matter how trivial they are.

Some meetings are called under the guise of collaboration or alignment when it's really connection we're after. These are **social meetings**. Connection is a laudable goal, but meetings are a pretty lousy way to foster it. Instead, invite people to a team-building activity, a retreat, or a party. But make it optional. While the extroverts on the team might love the chance to socialize, the introverts may want to stay back and get some work done.

Finally, we come to the **decision-making meeting**, a total misnomer as it implies that the meeting itself is making the decision. But meetings don't make decisions; leaders do. Group discussions can help support that process, of course, so let's rename these types of gatherings **decision-supporting meetings** to remind the leader that it's her job, and hers alone, to make sure action follows. It's also helpful to distinguish between high-stakes, low-stakes, and no-stakes decision-supporting meetings.

In a high-stakes meeting, you want to facilitate a real honest debate. Research shows that moderate task conflict leads to more accurate decisions, so demand candor from attendees, and encourage them to disagree. Identifying these meetings as high-stakes will remind you to let the best decision prevail, even if it's not yours.

When the decisions to be made are less consequential, the goal isn't to slow down, it's to speed up. Propose a plan for moving forward, and focus on generating buy-in. Of course you should allow for disagreement and be prepared to revise your plan if participants offer good reasons. But aim for quick resolution so you can spend most of the time coordinating implementation. As for meetings called to support inconsequential, no-stakes decisions? They should obviously never see the light of day.

Imagine a culture where people regularly talk about meetings using this kind of precise language. Picture someone pushing back on a meeting invitation by calling it a formality meeting. Envision the leader of a decision-supporting meeting asking whether her gathering qualifies as high stakes or low stakes. Think about someone canceling an upcoming staff meeting and requesting a few conversations instead. Better language isn't the only step you must take to transform your meeting culture, but it's a powerful start.

Al Pittampalli is the author of *Persuadable: How Great Leaders Change Their Minds to Change the World* (HarperBusiness, 2016).

CHAPTER 3

If You Can't Say What Your Meeting Will Accomplish, You Shouldn't Have It

by Bob Frisch and Cary Greene

How many times have you walked out of a theoretically important meeting—a leadership off-site, a C-suite pow-wow, a sit-down with the board—thinking, "That was a great discussion, but I'm not sure we really accomplished anything?" More often than not, the problem lies not in

Adapted from content posted on hbr.org on April 18, 2016.

what did or didn't happen at the meeting itself but in the fact that you didn't get anything done because the goals for the meeting were never firmly established in the first place.

We see this happen all the time when clients hire us to help manage off-sites. Often, they start by handing us a pretty well-developed (and usually packed) agenda full of already-booked speakers and a finalized list of confirmed attendees. Beyond logistics, the actual substance of the off-site is nearly set. But then we always ask the meeting owner—the most senior executive hosting it—the same two questions:

- What do you want to have debated, decided, or discovered at the end of this session that you and the team haven't already debated, decided, or discovered?
- What do you want attendees to say when their team members ask, "What happened at the big meeting?"

In almost every case, the response is the same: "That's a good question—I hadn't actually thought about those things."

It doesn't matter if it's an 8-person board meeting, a 15-person executive team meeting, a 150-person leadership conference, or a regularly recurring status meeting: Your first step when planning an important meeting should be to draft an initial set of goals based on the answers to the two questions above. In the words of Stephen Covey, "Begin with the end in mind." These objectives are not the activities you will be engaged in or the time slots on the agenda. They are more high level: your desired outcomes for the meeting.

The list needn't be very long or complicated. As a starting point, three to five short bullet points or sentences that articulate what you want to accomplish is more than enough.

But this process may take some time. You could go through two to three iterations before you have a straw-model set of objectives that are ready to be tested with other key meeting stakeholders, who should then be asked to review the list and identify any missing or unnecessary goals. Once everyone is aligned, agree and communicate to all other attendees that these objectives are locked in. This will help keep the agenda focused and give you cover if someone asks to add an unrelated presentation or discussion at the last minute.

Here are some sample objectives from different types of meetings we've facilitated recently.

Regularly recurring weekly meeting

- Share updates and review progress-to-date, including major milestones or upcoming activities (ask and answer "What did I do? What will I do?").
- Identify questions and concerns related to progress (ask and answer "What are the potential roadblocks?").
- Prioritize and resolve issues and address additional questions.

- Agree on next steps (for example, escalation of issues, clear accountabilities, etc.).

Board meeting

- Provide board input as management formulates the new five-year strategy.
  - Agree on how much runway remains on the current core strategy.
  - Identify new strategies to potentially pursue.
- Finalize the operating model for strategic governance.
  - Launch annual strategic planning process.
  - Put in place long-term (five-plus-year) strategic oversight.
- Agree on the topics and timing for additional board input into the current planning cycle.

Executive team meeting

- Develop a list of growth opportunities for the team to assess further.
- Begin to define select growth opportunities, including the future-state description for each and potential measures of success.
- Confirm the accountable executive and team leader for each opportunity.
- Understand the time line and activities over the next three months.

Leadership conference

- Establish the purpose and positioning of the extended leadership team.
- Impart a meaningful understanding of the company's vision, mission, and strategy, including top priorities for the next three years.
- Understand priority issues raised by attendees, and develop potential solutions.
- Align around next steps.

Your list of objectives must also drive important decisions about aspects of the meeting.

Agenda. Draft an agenda, and map each activity to your stated goals. Do all of them help you achieve one or more of your objectives? Are there any objectives that can't be achieved through what you have planned?

Attendees. The number and identity of attendees should be based on the scope and objectives of the meeting. For example, if you need to make decisions, we recommend a smaller group. If your aim is to generate ideas or achieve broad organizational buy-in for an initiative, you should invite a larger group.

Pre-reads. Don't overload people with voluminous meeting pre-reads full of assorted plans, reports, and studies that aren't directly related to your objectives. Instead, use your list to organize, filter, and focus the content you send in advance.

Location. The location of your meeting should reflect its objectives, too. For example, if your goals focus on a specific region, go there. If an explicit objective is for participants to get to know each other better, pick a venue designed for socializing.

When you set out and share your objectives in this way, it ensures that everyone is "coming to the same meeting." Attendees will be energized and ready to accomplish those goals.

Bob Frisch is the managing partner of the Strategic Offsites Group, a Boston-based consultancy, and is the author of *Who's In The Room? How Great Leaders Structure and Manage the Teams Around Them* (Jossey-Bass, 2012). He is the author of four *Harvard Business Review* articles, including "Off-Sites That Work" (June 2006). **Cary Greene** is a partner of the Strategic Offsites Group. They are coauthors of *Simple Sabotage: A Modern Field Manual for Detecting & Rooting Out Everyday Behaviors That Undermine Your Workplace* (HarperOne, 2015) and are frequent contributors to hbr.org.

CHAPTER 4

How to Design an Agenda for an Effective Meeting

by Roger Schwarz

An effective agenda sets clear expectations for what needs to occur before and during a meeting. It helps team members prepare and allocate time wisely, quickly gets everyone focused on the same topic, and makes it clear when the discussion is complete. If problems occur during the meeting, a well-designed agenda promotes the team's ability to address them right away.

Here are some tips for designing an effective agenda for your next meeting. You'll find sample agendas and

---

Adapted from content posted on hbr.org on March 19, 2015.

a blank template in appendix B. These suggestions will be helpful whether your meeting lasts one hour or three days or whether you're meeting with a group of five people or forty.

Seek input from team members. If you want your team to be engaged in meetings, make sure the agenda includes topics that reflect their needs. Ask team members to suggest agenda items and an explanation of why each area needs to be addressed in a team setting. If you ultimately decide not to include an item, be accountable: Explain your reasoning to the team member who suggested it.

Select topics that are relevant to the entire team. Team meeting time is expensive and difficult to schedule. It should mainly be used to discuss and make decisions on issues that affect the whole team—and that need the whole team to solve them. These are likely to be areas in which individuals must coordinate their actions because their parts of the organization are interdependent. They are also likely to be issues for which people have different information and needs. Examples might include: How do we best allocate shared resources? How do we reduce response time? If the team isn't spending most of the meeting talking about interdependent issues, members will disengage and ultimately not attend.

List agenda topics as questions the team needs to answer. Most agenda items are simply several words strung together to form a phrase, such as: "office space reallocation." This leaves meeting participants wondering, "What about office space reallocation?" When you list a topic as a question (or questions) to be answered, it instead reads like this: "Under what conditions, if any, should we reallocate office space?"

A question enables team members to better prepare for the discussion and to monitor whether their own and others' comments are on track. During the meeting, anyone who thinks a comment is off track can say something like, "I'm not seeing how your comment relates to the question we're trying to answer. Can you help me understand the connection?" The team knows that when the question has been answered, the discussion is complete.

Note whether the purpose of the topic is to share information, seek input for a decision, or make a decision. It's difficult for team members to participate effectively if they don't know whether to simply listen, give their input, or be part of the decision-making process. If people think they are involved in making a decision, but you simply want their input, everyone is likely to feel frustrated by the end of the conversation. Updates are better distributed—and read—prior to the meeting, with a brief part of the meeting allocated to answering participants' questions. If the purpose of the topic is to make a decision, state the decision-making rule. If you're the formal leader, at the beginning of the agenda item you might say, "If possible, I want us to make this decision by consensus. That means that everyone can support and implement the decision given their roles on the team. If we're not able to reach consensus after an hour of discussion, I reserve the right to make the decision based on the conversation we've had. I'll tell you my decision and my reasoning for making it." (For more on group decision making, see chapter 12.)

Estimate a realistic amount of time for each topic. This serves two purposes. First, it requires you to do the math: to calculate how much time the team will need for introducing the topic, answering questions, resolving different points of view, generating potential solutions, and agreeing on the action items that follow from discussion and decisions. Leaders typically underestimate the amount of time needed. If there are 10 people in your meeting and you have allocated 10 minutes to decide under what conditions, if any, you will reallocate office space, you have probably underestimated the time. By doing some simple math, you would realize that the team would have to reach a decision immediately after each of the ten members had spoken for a minute.

Second, the estimated time enables team members to either adapt their comments to fit within the allotted time frame or to suggest that more time may be needed. The purpose of listing the time is not to stop discussion when the time has elapsed; that simply contributes to poor decision making and frustration. The purpose is to get better at allocating enough time for the team to effectively and efficiently answer relevant questions.

Propose a process for addressing each agenda item. A defined process makes it possible to identify the steps the team should take to complete a discussion or make a decision. Agreeing on a process significantly increases meeting effectiveness, yet leaders rarely do it. Unless a team has agreed on a process, members will, in good faith, participate based on their own process. You've probably seen this in action: Some team members are trying to define the problem, while other team members are wondering why the topic is on the agenda, and still other members are already identifying and evaluating solutions.

The process for addressing an item should appear on the written agenda. When you reach that item during the meeting, explain the process and seek agreement. For example: "I suggest we use the following process. First, let's take about 10 minutes to get all the relevant information on the table. Second, let's take 10 minutes to identify and agree on any assumptions we need to make. Third, let's take another 10 minutes to identify and agree on the interests that should be met for any solution. Finally, we'll use about 15 minutes to craft a solution that ideally takes into account all the interests and is consistent with our relevant information and assumptions. Any suggestions for improving this process?"

Specify how members should prepare for the meeting. Distribute the agenda with sufficient time before the meeting so the team can read background materials and prepare their initial thoughts for each agenda item ahead of time.

Identify who is responsible for leading each topic. Someone other than the formal meeting leader can be responsible for leading the discussion of a particular agenda item. This person may provide context for the topic, explain data, or have organizational responsibility for that area. Identifying this person next to the agenda item ensures that anyone who is responsible for leading part of the agenda knows it—and prepares for it—before the meeting.

Make the first topic "review and modify agenda as needed." Even if you and your team jointly developed the agenda before the meeting, take a minute to see if anything needs to be changed due to late-breaking events. I once had a meeting scheduled with a senior leadership team. As we reviewed the agenda, I asked if we needed to modify anything. The CEO stated that he had just told the board of directors that he planned to resign and that we probably needed to significantly change the agenda. Not all agenda modifications are that dramatic, but by checking in at the beginning of the meeting, you increase the chance that the team will use its meeting time most effectively.

End the meeting with a plus delta evaluation. If your team meets regularly, two questions should form a simple continuous improvement process: What did we do well? and What do we want to do differently for the next meeting? Investing 5 or 10 minutes will enable the team to improve performance, working relationships, and team member satisfaction. Here are some questions to consider when identifying what the team has done well and what it wants to do differently.

- Was the agenda distributed in time for everyone to prepare?
- How well did team members prepare for the meeting?
- How well did we estimate the time needed for each agenda item?
- How well did we allocate our time for decision making and discussion?
- How well did everyone stay on topic? Did team members speak up when they thought someone was off topic?
- How effective was the process for each agenda item?

To ensure that your team follows through, review the results of the plus delta evaluation at the beginning of the next meeting.

If you develop agendas using these tips, your team will have an easier time getting—and staying—focused in meetings.

Roger Schwarz is an organizational psychologist, speaker, leadership team consultant, and president and CEO of Roger Schwarz & Associates. He is the author of *Smart Leaders, Smarter Teams: How You and Your Team Get Unstuck to Get Results* (Jossey-Bass, 2013). For more, visit www.schwarzassociates.com or find him on Twitter @LeadSmarter.

CHAPTER 5

The Key to Shorter, Better Meetings

by Anthony Tjan

Your meetings may often cut across multiple objectives, but setting and articulating the purpose of your meeting will help participants prepare and contribute more effectively. Outside general relationship-building, consider that a business meeting has only three functional purposes:

1. To inform and bring people up to speed.
2. To seek input from people.
3. To ask for approval.

Adapted from content posted on hbr.org on June 23, 2009.

Use this as a filter to determine why you're having a meeting, to clarify your agenda viewing items through this lens, and to explain your purpose to your audience.

Consider a meeting that sets its agenda goals along the lines of "I want to bring you up to speed on these two things," or "I need input on this item," or "I would like to get your approval on these outstanding issues." That's it: a simple, three-purpose rule that frames the goals of the meeting from the perspective of each participant.

Anthony Tjan is CEO, managing partner, and founder of the venture capital firm Cue Ball. He is coauthor of *Heart, Smarts, Guts, and Luck: What It Takes to Be an Entrepreneur and Build a Great Business* (Harvard Business Review Press, 2012).

CHAPTER 6

The 50-Minute Meeting

by David Silverman

I have a life-changing proposal for businesspeople everywhere: 50-minute hours. Start a productivity revolution by scheduling business meetings that, by default, run 50 minutes long instead of 60.

How often do you find that by 11 a.m. you're running late, and by 3 p.m. you've either been forced to dump a meeting to reset your day or are 100 e-mails behind because you've gone straight from one appointment to another all day long? Either way, you're leaving someone (or many people) in the lurch. It's a stressful and unsatisfying existence.

Adapted from content posted on hbr.org on August 6, 2009.

There's another group of people who are scheduled in back-to-back sessions all day long, five days a week. I speak, of course, of students. All the way through school we're taught in 50-minute blocks, a schedule that lets us get to our next class on time. The buildings even have bells to remind the person running the meeting—er, class—to end on time.

Why is it, then, that when we graduate, they take away our bells, replace them with an irritating "doink" sound signaling "15 minutes until your next meeting," and assume we can now teleport to the next location? What could cause such madness? In two words: Microsoft Outlook. (Not without blame would also be IBM Notes, Google Calendar, Apple's Calendar, and others.)

By default, Outlook sets up meetings that are 30, 60, 90, or 120 minutes long. There's no room for travel time, to compose yourself, to answer a couple of e-mails, or for a coffee or bathroom break.

Next time you're faced with scheduling a meeting, consider booking a 20-minute or 50-minute session. See what you can accomplish in that time, and if you can still get to your next meeting. You may just start a new trend in your organization.

David Silverman has been an entrepreneur, an executive, and a business-writing teacher. He is the author of *Typo: The Last American Typesetter or How I Made and Lost 4 Million Dollars* (Soft Skull Press, 2009).

CHAPTER 7

The Magic of 30-Minute Meetings

by Peter Bregman

Often we schedule one-hour time slots. Why? How did an hour become our standard time allotment for so many meetings, phone calls, and appointments? Recently I tried a new experiment: I cut the time I allot for many activities in half.

I started with something easy. I used to work out for an hour a day. Now it's down to 30 minutes. My results—weight and conditioning—improved.

Adapted from content posted on hbr.org on February 22, 2016.

Here's why: My intensity is higher (I know I only have 30 minutes), I eat better (I don't rely on my workout to keep slim), I integrate movement more into my day (I don't rely on my workout to take care of all my fitness needs), and I never miss a workout (I can always find 30 minutes).

If you have half the time to accomplish something, you become hyperaware of how you're using that time. And hyperfocused during it. Most of my meetings are now 30 minutes or less. My podcast is 15 to 20 minutes. Even many of my conference calls, with multiple parties, are 30 minutes or less. People on the calls, aware of the time constraint, are more thoughtful about when they speak and more careful not to follow tangents that aren't useful.

People also listen better because when things are moving faster, we tend to be more alert. We know that a single distracted moment will leave us behind. And, since that keeps us more engaged, we end up having more fun in the process.

Nowhere has this impact been more transformational —and more evident—than in the leadership coaching we do at Bregman Partners. For the past several years, all of our coaching is accomplished in 30-minute sessions. The advantages are obvious: Everyone saves time and money. But here's what's less obvious: The coaching isn't simply as powerful as what we could do in a longer session, it's vastly more so. When the coach and the client both know they have only 30 minutes, they move into high gear.

- **People show up.** Just as with my workouts, clients are far less likely to skip a 30-minute session than they are an hour-long one.
- **Everyone is on time.** Every minute counts in a 30-minute conversation, and people know it. The session gets started more quickly, because everyone's aware that the relationship is built on doing good work, not on making small talk.
- **People are much more likely to come prepared.** There's no time wasted on off-topic items and going-nowhere conversations. Clients know what they want to cover and have put some thought into it beforehand.
- **The time pressure enhances focus and attention.** People don't focus on multiple issues; they tackle the single biggest opportunity or most persistent, intractable obstacle. And they move on it.
- **Coaches are more willing to be courageous, and clients are more willing to be prodded.** In a 30-minute session, coaches can't waste time beating around the bush. They get to the point faster and earlier, interrupt more bravely, and ask more provocative questions.

The compressed, focused coaching session hones the skill of getting to the point quickly, focusing on the most essential elements of a situation, and taking action. The downside? I haven't seen one yet. Try it yourself. Transition some of your hour-long meetings to

30 minutes. As you do, consider these three steps as a way to make the 30 minutes most powerful:

1. Read what you need to beforehand, and tell everyone else to do the same. Think about your questions and concerns. Decide what's important to you and what you can let go of. Ask yourself the most important question: What outcome do you want?

2. Decide on the one thing that will make the biggest difference, and spend the 30 minutes on that issue, topic, or opportunity. Get started right on time, no matter who isn't there, and be bold and disciplined at keeping the conversation on track. Let go of anything that is less critical. Make decisions quickly, even if they are imperfect. Getting traction on a single thing is far more useful than touching on many issues without forward momentum on any.

3. Save at least the last five minutes to summarize what you learned, articulate what was valuable, commit to what you're going to do as a result of the meeting, and clarify how you'll assess the success of your next steps. The sign of a great meeting isn't the meeting itself—it's what happens after that meeting.

Like our coaches, you'll need these "get to the most critical point fast" skills—and the courage to use them—if you're going to make the most of your time. You need to be bold and even provocative. You need to be willing to interrupt, thoughtfully and for the greater good of moving ambitiously toward what is most important. You need to let go of things that don't really matter.

And you need to be fully present. No multitasking. No texting under the table. No distractions. Which is also the upside: you get to be fully present in what you are doing.

There is a cost. While it's energizing, it also takes a lot of energy to be so focused, even for a short amount of time. It's a sprinter's tactic.

On the other hand, when you cut your meetings in half, you'll have a lot more time to relax at dinner, write, sleep, and spend unstructured time with people you love.

Peter Bregman is CEO of Bregman Partners, a company that strengthens leadership in people and in organizations through programs (including the Bregman Leadership Intensive), coaching, and by consulting with their CEOs and leadership teams. He is the best-selling author of *18 Minutes* (Business Plus, 2011), and his most recent book is *Four Seconds* (HarperOne, 2015).

CHAPTER 8

Meetings Need a Shot Clock

by Bob Frisch and Cary Greene

We've all been invited to meetings with agendas so long that it's impossible to cover every item. The early speakers run long. The early proposals get debated. But those at the end get short shrift or are tabled until the next gathering, even if they're equally important.

How can you avoid this problem? One option is to limit your ambitions, to be more realistic about what you can get done in the hour or hours you're meeting. Simply resign yourself to covering less. In our view, however, there's a better solution, one that allows you to accomplish more while still ensuring that each person or topic gets adequate time. As crazy as it sounds, the answer is

---

Adapted from content posted on hbr.org on March 16, 2016.

a shot clock. Yes, an actual shot clock, like the ones they use in high school, college, and professional basketball games. The NBA and the NCAA put the shot clock in place years ago to quicken the pace of play, because some teams (especially when leading near the end) passed the ball endlessly without penalty. Now there's a limit on the time a team has to shoot—24 seconds in the NBA, 30 seconds in the NCAA—and if that time runs out, the ball goes to the opponent.

We've experimented with the same system in business meetings—especially when fair process is important to uphold—and had great success. Although most attendees tend to be a bit skeptical at first, they quickly recognize the purpose and value of the shot clock: It ensures that all agenda items are covered and each is allocated appropriate time.

Here's how it works: Before a meeting begins, explain that you want to devote a certain amount of time to each topic. For example, if you're leading an annual budget review and have 40 investment proposals on the table, you might say, "We're going to spend exactly 10 minutes on each topic. Speakers will have three minutes to present, followed by seven minutes of discussion."

Of course, sometimes different topics require different amounts of discussion time. A relatively straightforward issue might warrant five minutes, while a more contentious one merits 20. If you can identify the more time-consuming items in advance, great. If not, consider using a few minutes at the start of a meeting to determine how much time each agenda item deserves. One organization we worked with listed topics on a wall chart and asked attendees to put a green, yellow, or red dot next to each one to signify whether it deserved 7, 10, or 15 minutes of discussion, respectively. To limit the number of 15-minute conversations, each person only had three red dots to dole out.

Once you've determined appropriate time allocations, set up the shot clock. A smartphone stopwatch works nicely. It should buzz—loudly—when time runs out and keep buzzing until the person stops talking.

When people are introduced to this tool, they usually both love it and hate it. They like the fact that it limits others from commandeering too much time, overanalyzing decisions, and beating dead horses in debates, but they don't enjoy getting cut off themselves. Still, we often find that by the end of that first meeting, everyone has grown more comfortable with it and even fond of it. The shot clock is impersonal—even obnoxious—but that's what makes it effective. It's fair. Everyone is guaranteed to get a turn, and each issue is given the attention it needs. No one gets to "buy" extra floor time because of their status. It grants no wiggle room.

The shot clock also keeps meetings lively, focused, and sharp. And it's a great training tool. At several meetings, we've observed that executives who are tasked with speaking on multiple agenda items progressively get better at managing the clock. The first time they might run a tad over. The second time they come in right at the buzzer. By the third or fourth time, they're expressing themselves much more succinctly and wrapping up well before their minutes run out. They are more careful with their time because—just like the best basketball players—they know it's fixed.

Bob Frisch is the managing partner of the Strategic Offsites Group, a Boston-based consultancy, and is the author of *Who's In The Room? How Great Leaders Structure and Manage the Teams Around Them* (Jossey-Bass, 2012). He is the author of four *Harvard Business Review* articles, including "Off-Sites That Work" (June 2006). **Cary Greene** is a partner of the Strategic Offsites Group. They are coauthors of *Simple Sabotage: A Modern Field Manual for Detecting & Rooting Out Everyday Behaviors That Undermine Your Workplace* (HarperOne, 2015) and are frequent contributors to hbr.org.

CHAPTER 9

Are There Too Many People in Your Meeting?

When you set up a meeting, the people you invite are just as important as what you need to get done.

It may be easy to default to inviting a crowd of people to a meeting—that way, you don't really have to identify the most critical participants, you can avoid any ruffled feathers, you'll have everyone involved on hand for a decision, and you won't have to repeat your communications separately afterward. Or maybe your tendency is to keep things small, to invite just a handful of people whose opinions you value most.

Adapted from content posted on hbr.org on March 18, 2015 and from *Running Meetings* (20-Minute Manager series; product#17003), Harvard Business Review Press, 2014.

But for a meeting to be most useful, you have to have the right people—and only the right people—in the room. With too many attendees, you might have trouble focusing everyone's time and attention and not accomplish anything; with too few, you might not have the right decision makers or information providers in the room.

As you plan your attendee list, consider who will help you accomplish your meeting's goal and who will be most affected by its outcome. You'll likely want to include a combination of people who will offer a variety of perspectives. Take the time to methodically list each individual and place them into the following categories to make sure you include the right people:

- The key decision makers for the issues involved
- Those with information and knowledge about the topics under discussion
- People who have a commitment to or a stake in the issues
- Those who need to know about the information in order to do their jobs
- Anyone who will be required to implement decisions made

Consult with other stakeholders to make sure you've made the right list. Often another key stakeholder can remind you of a perspective you forgot to bring into the room.

Just because someone's name is on your list, however, doesn't mean they must be at the meeting. How many people should you actually invite? There are no hard-and-fast rules, but in principle, a small meeting is best for deciding or accomplishing something, a medium-sized meeting is ideal for brainstorming, and a large meeting makes the most sense for communicating and rallying. Some people use what's known as the 8–18-1800 rule as a rough guideline:

- If you have to solve a problem or make a decision, invite no more than 8 people. If you have more participants, you may receive so much conflicting input that it's difficult to deal with the problem or make the decision at hand.
- If you want to brainstorm, then you can go as high as 18 people.
- If the purpose of the meeting is to provide updates, invite however many people need to receive the information. However, if everyone attending the meeting will be providing updates, limit the number of participants to no more than 18.
- If the purpose of the meeting is for you to rally the troops, go for 1,800—or more!

If you decide not to invite individuals you listed as likely to be affected by the meeting's outcome, have a plan to communicate the substance of the meeting to them afterward.

SECTION TWO

Conduct

CHAPTER 10

Before a Meeting, Tell Your Team That Silence Denotes Agreement

by Bob Frisch and Cary Greene

The meeting seemed to go smoothly. Bill, the executive vice president of sales at a global company, had gathered his extended leadership team—a group of more than 20 people—and outlined his latest plan to reconfigure the sales organization. When he asked if anyone had

---

Adapted from content posted on hbr.org on February 3, 2016.

concerns, there were a few questions, but no one raised any significant obstacles or issues, and some of the more senior team members spoke up in support of the plan. Bill felt that everyone was on board and ready to go.

But later that week, one of the meeting attendees came into Bill's office. "Do you remember when you were talking about reconfiguring the sales organization?" the attendee asked. "I'm not sure we've got Latin America quite right." Similar scenes played out with other direct reports and more-junior employees in the halls and cafeteria over the next few days. People had opinions they hadn't shared at the meeting. The plan, which had seemed unanimously popular, was now unraveling. What happened?

Most bosses assume that when they directly ask for feedback, people will offer their thoughts candidly. It's great when that happens. But it often doesn't, especially in public settings and high-stakes situations. If you get unanimous, but mostly unvoiced, support for a decision that you thought might be contentious, it should be a warning sign.

Why do people hold back from weighing in? In some cases, junior people may hesitate to disagree with bosses or senior colleagues. In others, the most powerful team members may be disinclined, for political or other reasons, to express candid opinions in front of the group because they know they can always get access to decision makers or launch a covert campaign to sway support their way after the fact.

How can you prevent this from happening? Set one key ground rule: Silence denotes agreement.

These three words do a great job of forcing people to open up, no matter how reluctant they may be feeling (or how passive-aggressive they are). Explain to people that if they don't say anything when given a proposal or plan, they're voting "yes" for it. Silence doesn't mean "I'm not voting" or "I reserve the right to weigh in later." It means "I'm completely on board with what's being discussed."

You must then commit to enforcing the rule. If someone—even a powerful team member or friend—comes up to you after a meeting to express reservations about what was said, the response should be "You should have spoken up at the meeting. Now everyone is on board and the ship has sailed. Next time, say something."

Sometimes the establishment and reinforcement of "silence denotes agreement" as a ground rule is enough to get the opinions flowing. But if you sense that some participants are still finding it difficult to express themselves freely, consider the following tactics, which allow perspectives to be aired in a way that focuses on the ideas rather than on the individuals voicing them.

- **Take anonymous polls.** Ask people to write down questions or concerns on index cards, put them into a bowl, and read them aloud without using names. Better yet, use a polling app or device to query meeting participants and see their answers in real time.

- **Heat map the topic.** Put poster-sized charts of the components of an idea or plan on the wall. Ask participants to place yellow dots on the charts where they have a question and red dots where they have a significant concern. Use the dots to guide the conversation.

- **Break up a big group.** People are more likely to participate in small group discussions, so divide people into teams with specific instructions to discuss any challenges to the proposal at hand. Appoint a representative from each group to summarize everyone's thoughts.
- **Ask them to empathize.** People are often more willing to speak on others' behalf than on their own. So when you solicit opinions with a question like "What objections or concerns might your direct reports have?" it can open the floodgates of reaction. That's because it allows those in the room to externalize criticism. It's not what they don't like. It's what they think their *people* won't like.

When you enforce the discipline of "silence denotes agreement" and use the tactics described here, everyone is motivated to say what they really think immediately and discuss it openly, rather than flagging problems after the fact.

Bob Frisch is the managing partner of the Strategic Offsites Group, a Boston-based consultancy, and is the author of *Who's In The Room? How Great Leaders Structure and Manage the Teams Around Them* (Jossey-Bass, 2012). He is the author of four *Harvard Business Review* articles, including "Off-Sites That Work" (June 2006).

Cary Greene is a partner of the Strategic Offsites Group. They are coauthors of *Simple Sabotage: A Modern Field Manual for Detecting & Rooting Out Everyday Behaviors That Undermine Your Workplace* (HarperOne, 2015) and are frequent contributors to hbr.org.

CHAPTER 11

Establish Ground Rules

Setting guidelines at the beginning of a meeting encourages everyone's participation and keeps the conversation on track. The guidelines don't have to be rigid or overly formal but should serve as a set of shared expectations for behavior that reflect your time constraints, the size of your group, and your meeting's intentions and goals. For example, your group may decide to let only one person speak at a time, not allow interruptions, set time limits on contributions, table issues that aren't easily resolved, limit conversations that stray from the topic at hand, and make sure that everyone is heard from.

Adapted from *Running Meetings* (20-Minute Manager series; product #17003), Harvard Business Review Press, 2014; and Martha Craumer, "How to Run an Effective Meeting: The Basics."

If you're meeting with the same group of people on a regular basis, the group can develop these guidelines together. Otherwise, suggest some ground rules at the beginning of your meeting, and get buy-in from the attendees.

Specifying ground rules signals to participants that you intend to keep things moving efficiently.

- Reassert that you're committed to beginning and ending on time (and then really do it).
- Ask for everyone's participation and openness to new ideas.
- Agree to listen to each other and limit interruptions—and as the leader, enforce that rule.
- Clarify how decisions will be made. Let the group know right up front if this will be a group-decision meeting, a meeting that calls for participants' input, or a meeting that shares a decision that has already been made.
- Explain your policy on multitasking and device use.

You may also need to establish ground rules for specific agenda items:

- Clarify constraints that exist for any issue that will be under discussion—for example, upper-management decisions or policy or budget restrictions that may limit the group's range of options.

- Identify the final decision maker for each item—especially if it's not someone in the meeting (such as the CEO or department manager).

Martha Craumer is a senior writer at The Boston Consulting Group.

CHAPTER 12

Reach Group Decisions During Meetings

Facilitating group decisions in meetings is rarely easy. The following suggestions for choosing the right decision-making method will help ensure that everyone leaves your meetings with clear decisions and next steps for implementing those decisions.

You can use three common decision-making methods with groups: group consensus, majority vote, or leader's choice. Each has its own benefits and challenges.

Adapted from *Running Meetings* (20-Minute Manager series; product #17003), Harvard Business Review Press, 2014.

Group Consensus

Group consensus does not mean arguing and lobbying until everyone agrees. It means reaching a decision that everyone understands, supports, and is willing to help implement.

Advantages:

- Allows all meeting participants to share their expertise in order to arrive at the best decision.
- Results in all participants understanding the decision and its implications.
- Greatly enhances the chance for buy-in from all parties.

Disadvantages:

- Participants may not be familiar with this decision-making process: They may think that they all have to agree to and believe in the final outcome, so it may feel like people are spinning their wheels or heading in the wrong direction.
- May take more time than other decision-making approaches.
- May require that you have an alternative decision-making process (for example, leader's choice) in case consensus cannot be reached within given time constraints.

How do you know when you have a genuine consensus? You'll hear comments such as "Option A isn't my first choice, but I believe it incorporates everyone's needs." Or "I don't think Option A satisfies all our criteria, but I'm prepared to implement it as fully as possible."

Majority Vote

The proposal or idea with the most votes wins.

Advantages:

- The group arrives at a decision relatively quickly.
- The group perceives the decision to be fair.
- You hear from everyone, even people who are usually quiet.

Disadvantages:

- Open voting requires taking public stands on issues and can result in perceived winners and losers.
- People may not feel comfortable voting according to their true feelings or voicing reservations they might have about decisions.
- Losers often feel their voices have not been heard.
- Not everyone buys into the decision.

Leader's Choice

In some ways, having the leader decide is similar to a majority rule because the leader needs to hear what the participants think and is most likely to agree with the majority view.

Advantages:

- It's the fastest approach to decision making and may be the best approach when time is short or when there is a crisis.
- If the meeting participants respect the leader and understand why they are making a certain decision, people are somewhat more likely to buy into the decision.

Disadvantages:

- Meeting participants may feel that the leader is ignoring their views, particularly if they haven't been given the chance to state their ideas.
- You may encounter resistance during implementation, as meeting participants may feel less ownership or may not have bought in completely.

CHAPTER 13

The Right Way to Cut People Off in Meetings

by Bob Frisch and Cary Greene

You've spent hours preparing for the meeting. The objectives are clear. The agenda is tight. Relevant material was distributed to attendees in advance. Smartphones are put away, and your team seems focused and ready to work.

The conversation begins, but after 10 minutes of good discussion on the first agenda item, someone goes off on a tangent that, while interesting, is only marginally related to the designated topic. Then another person jumps in to elaborate, and the two start talking in detail

---

Adapted from content posted on hbr.org on April 8, 2016.

about issues relevant only to them. Other attendees begin to tune out. Now 20 minutes have passed—and you haven't made any progress.

We've all seen scenes like this play out, whether in an hour-long meeting or at a multiday off-site. Participants veer off topic or take the conversation into the weeds, and because no one feels comfortable doing anything about it, critical agenda items are left untouched. In fact, research suggests that "getting off the subject" is the number one challenge to meeting productivity. When leaders or peers do try to intervene, it's often after too much time has passed (since they've waited for the perfect opportunity to interrupt), and the typical approach—"This is really interesting, but can I suggest we get back to the topic at hand?"—leaves everyone feeling awkward.

Thankfully, there is a simple solution to this predicament: the word "jellyfish." Jellyfish are, of course, those funny-looking creatures with no brain, no blood, and no heart that have drifted along on ocean currents for millions of years. We use the word to prevent meetings from drifting.

Here's how it works. At the start of your gathering, introduce the jellyfish ground rule: If any attendee feels the conversation is heading off course or delving into an inappropriate level of detail, they can and should employ the word to indicate that opinion. Simply say "jellyfish" or "I think we're having a jellyfish moment" or "Gee, did I just see a jellyfish swim by?" It's a catchall for "Why don't you take this offline—the rest of us would like our meeting back."

Of all things, why is "jellyfish" so effective?

It's safe. The word is both simple and funny, and if set up correctly at the start of a meeting, it carries the same effect as other, more traditional (and less comfortable) ways of interrupting and redirecting the conversation. Of course, you can pick another, similarly silly word, but we've been using this one for years and have found that people—indeed, entire organizations—quickly embrace it.

It's accessible. Anyone can invoke it. The meeting owner or facilitator may be the first to use it, but they don't have to be the only one. Any participant can ask, "This feels like jellyfish. Do you agree?" prompting the person or people on the tangent to ask themselves if they are using the group's time well.

It raises awareness. When meeting participants know that jellyfish will be used, they can't help but become more self-aware about staying on topic. In many cases we've even seen attendees call jellyfish on themselves.

In decades of helping clients conduct better meetings, we've found "jellyfish" to be one of the most effective ways of keeping the discussion on target.

Bob Frisch is the managing partner of the Strategic Offsites Group, a Boston-based consultancy, and is the author of *Who's In The Room? How Great Leaders Structure and Manage the Teams Around Them* (Jossey-Bass,

2012). He is the author of four *Harvard Business Review* articles, including "Off-Sites That Work" (June 2006). **Cary Greene** is a partner of the Strategic Offsites Group. They are coauthors of *Simple Sabotage: A Modern Field Manual for Detecting & Rooting Out Everyday Behaviors That Undermine Your Workplace* (HarperOne, 2015) and are frequent contributors to hbr.org.

CHAPTER 14

Dealing with People Who Derail Meetings

by Roger Schwarz

What does your team do when someone takes a meeting off track? If your team is like most, the leader says something like, "Lee, that's not what we're talking about now" or "Let's get back on track" or the team simply ignores Lee's comment and tries to bring the conversation back to the original topic.

But if your team responds in any of these ways, Lee may continue to press his off-topic point, the meeting may drag on with members getting more frustrated with

---

Adapted from content posted on hbr.org on September 20, 2013.

Lee, and the team may not accomplish its meeting goals. Or Lee may stop participating for the rest of the meeting and the team, without realizing it, will lose Lee's critical input and support for implementing a team decision.

If you assume that Lee or others who derail a meeting are the problem and the solution is to get them back on track or stop them from talking, you may be off track. These team members' behaviors are often a symptom of larger team problems. People often make off-track comments when there isn't clear agreement on the meeting's purpose or process, or when the team doesn't provide time to hear everyone's thoughts on a topic. Sometimes the problem is that you think others are off track when they aren't. So what should you do?

Agree on the track before going down it.

If your team doesn't explicitly agree on the purpose and topic for each part of the meeting, then people will use their own understanding to decide what is appropriate. Because team members will naturally have different interpretations, one person's comments can easily seem off track to others.

Start your meeting by saying something like, "My understanding of the purpose of this meeting is *X*; does anyone have a different understanding or think we need to add anything?" This ensures that if people think other issues need to be addressed, they can say so and have them considered for the agenda, rather than raising them as off-track items. If it's not your meeting and there is no agenda, simply ask "Can we take a minute to get clear on the purpose and topics for the meeting to make sure we accomplish what you need?"

Check that others are ready to move down the track.

Rather than saying "Okay, let's move on" or simply shifting to a new topic, say something like "I think we're ready to move to topic *Y*. Anyone have anything else we haven't fully addressed on *X*?" If some people aren't ready to move on, find out what needs to happen before they can move forward. This reduces the chance that people will raise issues later that you thought had been fully discussed. If your team is staying focused but regularly runs out of time before completing its agenda, then you're underestimating the amount of time necessary to make high-quality decisions that generate commitment. When you and the team agree on the goals and make sure everyone is ready to move on, you're jointly designing next steps, and that builds commitment to decisions.

Test your assumption that the meeting is getting derailed.

If the team has agreed on the topic to discuss and you still think that someone is off track, say something like, "Lee, I'm not seeing how your point about outsourcing is related to the topic of our planning process. Help me understand the connection." When Lee responds, you and other team members might discover a link between the two topics that you hadn't considered. For example, Lee might say that outsourcing will free up internal resources so that the team can complete the planning process in less time. If there is a connection, the team can decide whether it makes more sense to explore Lee's idea now or later. If it turns out that Lee's comment isn't related but is still relevant for the team, you can suggest placing it on a future agenda. One caveat: There are times when it is critical to address team members' issues immediately, even if they're off track. If team members raise highly emotional issues about how the group is working together, it's important to acknowledge the issue's importance and then decide whether it's more essential to address it than the current agenda topic. Sometimes focusing on how the team works together is more critical than sticking with the team's substantive topics.

This is more than a polite way of dealing with people who get off track: It's a way to suspend your assumption that you understand the situation and others don't, to be curious about others' views, and to ask people to be accountable for their own contributions so that the team can make an informed choice about how best to move forward. For this approach to work, you can't just say the words; you have to believe that Lee's topic might be connected and that you don't see it.

By getting explicit agreement about the meeting's purpose and topics and by being genuinely curious when people seem off track, you and your team can move faster and accomplish more in your meetings.

Roger Schwarz is an organizational psychologist, speaker, leadership team consultant, and president and CEO of

Roger Schwarz & Associates. He is the author of *Smart Leaders, Smarter Teams: How You and Your Team Get Unstuck to Get Results* (Jossey-Bass, 2013). For more, visit www.schwarzassociates.com or find him on Twitter @LeadSmarter.

CHAPTER 15

Refocus a Meeting After Someone Interrupts

by Rebecca Knight

You did everything you were supposed to do: invited all the right people, sent out an agenda in advance, and got everyone's agreement on the process. But despite your diligence, your meeting is being hijacked. How should you handle a persistent interrupter? Will it work to just ignore the person? And how can you regain control of the meeting?

Adapted from content posted on hbr.org on April 16, 2015.

What the Experts Say

Whether it's a team member who disagrees with your approach, an employee from another department who brings up irrelevant information, or a colleague who wants to use your meeting as a soapbox for their own personal agenda, dealing with interrupters during a meeting is challenging. "When someone interrupts you, blocks you, or otherwise thwarts your intended action, it's natural to feel upset," says Judith White, visiting associate professor at Dartmouth's Tuck School of Business. "This is a basic instinct, and you will always have a flash of annoyance." The key to successfully dealing with interrupters is to quash your frustration and instead "operate from a mind-set of curiosity," says Roger Schwarz, an organizational psychologist and the author of *Smart Leaders, Smarter Teams*. Here's how to handle disruptors and regain control.

Gather Input Ahead of Time

"A well-designed agenda both provides a structure for the meeting and serves as a point of reference," Schwarz explains. People are less likely to disrupt a meeting if they feel like they had a hand in shaping it. So send out a proposed agenda ahead of time, and ask your team for input. Give them a time frame for making recommendations, and ask that they include a reason why they think an item is worthy of discussion. Everyone should have a say, but "the team leader gets the final decision about what to include." While an agenda does not entirely prevent interruptions, "it becomes the basis of your intervention," says Schwarz. Once you're in the meeting, if someone interrupts with an off-topic remark, Schwarz suggests saying something like, "I don't see how your comment connects to the issue we're talking about now. Help me understand how the two relate." If the speaker can't draw a connection, "then you use the agenda to pick up where you left off," he says.

Stay Calm

When someone interrupts or challenges you in a meeting, manage your response. "Don't get emotional" says White. "If you look threatened or angry, you will lose the trust of everyone in the room." Rather, your goal should be to "react with humor, kindness, inclusion, and assertiveness." Modulate your tone of voice and inflection, too. When you respond to the person who is interrupting, Schwarz says, "Speak in a genuinely curious, not frustrated, way."

Listen, Validate, Redirect

Don't be tempted to ignore the interruption and move on. At the point of interruption, "you need to stop talking and listen to what the person has to say," White explains. Then summarize his points "to let him know he's been heard." Let's say, for instance, you're leading a meeting about new corporate initiatives, and your colleague, Bob, interjects with, "Why are we bothering to discuss this? We don't have money in the budget to execute these ideas." You should then say, "Bob, your point is that we don't have money in the budget for this. And that's a good point." After validating his comments, redirect the discussion. Start by restating the purpose of the meeting. In this instance, White suggests you could say something along the lines of, “We have great minds in this room, and the president of our company asked us to work together to come up with cost-efficient ideas. I am confident we can do it.”

Probe Further

Don’t always rush to redirect the conversation, however, warns Schwarz. It’s not necessarily your goal to move through the meeting agenda as quickly as possible. Rather, he says, your aim is to “address issues efficiently, but also in a way that leads to a sustainable solution. When a colleague interrupts you with a comment you think is off topic, that’s not a fact; it’s an inference.” Ask your colleague to elaborate on his point. if you’re still unsure how what he’s saying relates to the topic at hand, ask others at the meeting for help. Frame the interruption as “an opportunity for learning a new perspective,” he says. “Think: What does he know that I don’t know?” It may be that he has a perspective you haven’t thought of. Says Schwarz: “Take time to address legitimate issues, because they’re not going away.”

Be Resolute and Direct

When a colleague persists in interrupting, is off on a tangent, or keeps on making the same point over and over, be direct and firm, says White. She suggests saying something like “Rich, you’ve brought this issue up before, and we heard you. If you would like to stay after the meeting and talk with me, I’d be happy to discuss the matter further, but now we need to get back on track." Or you could directly address the colleague who keeps on interrupting. Schwarz recommends a script like this: "Bob, I'm seeing a pattern, and I'm trying to figure out what's happening here. Is there something going on that's leading you to bring up these items?" While some might contend that this strategy puts Bob on the spot, Schwarz says "you need to deal with the issue in the place where the data lies—within the team." Handling situations in the open also allows you to model to your team how to have challenging conversations and provides a forum for others to add relevant information.

Use Body Language to Take Back Control

When your meeting is in danger of derailment because of insistent or hostile interrupters, regain control using body language and nonverbal communication. "If you're already standing, take a step or two toward the person who's interrupting you," says White. "Face that person and hold his gaze for five seconds—it will feel like an eternity." Never cross your arms. "You should appear open," she says. Then, walk slowly around the table, "stand directly behind the person who's disrupting the meeting, and address the rest of the room." Proceed accordingly. This, of course, requires confidence and finesse. Even though it's not always easy, "it's a powerful way to exert influence," she says.

Consider Having a One-on-One Conversation

After a meeting filled with tense and numerous interruptions, you might spend a little time alone reflecting on

WHEN A SIT-DOWN IS CALLED FOR

Sometimes nothing you do in a meeting will help break someone of their problematic behavior. If this is the case, sit down with that person and speak directly with them. Here are tips for approaching the encounter.

1. ***Ask permission.*** "May I talk to you about today's meeting?"
2. ***Clarify goals.*** Ask the person what they hope to get out of the meeting. Discuss what you see as the meeting's core goals.
3. ***Describe the behavior.*** "I see you doing *X*." This way, you each have a common reference point.
4. ***Describe the consequences.*** Explain how the behavior is affecting the group's performance,

whether you're doing anything to contribute to the problem, says Schwarz. It might also be worth approaching the interrupter for a one-on-one conversation. "Don't argue with him after the meeting, and never scold," says White. "He wants to feel heard." Instead, pose questions and listen. Ask: What is your thinking on this issue? What would you like done differently? What's important to you? "It may turn out that you both want the same thing, in which case, propose that you become allies," she says. On the other hand, "you can agree to disagree." (See

and detail the consequences you see it having for the group.

5. ***Inquire about the root of the behavior.*** Ask, for example, if the person is upset about a particular issue.
6. ***Make a specific suggestion or request.*** "At the next meeting, please try not to dismiss an idea until others have had a chance to finish their thoughts." Being unambiguous increases the likelihood that they will change their behavior.
7. ***Agree on next steps.*** Getting the person to commit to changing their behavior will help them actually do so.

Adapted from *Harvard Management Communication Letter* (product #C0504B), Spring 2005.

the sidebar "When a Sit-Down Is Called For" for more ideas on conducting this conversation.)

Rebecca Knight is a freelance journalist based in Boston and a lecturer at Wesleyan University. Her work has been published in the *New York Times, USA Today,* and the *Financial Times.*

SECTION THREE

Participate

CHAPTER 16

Polite Ways to Decline a Meeting Invitation

by Liane Davey

There it is in your inbox: an invitation to a meeting you really don't want to attend. Maybe because it's shoehorned into one of the few open spaces in your calendar. Or perhaps it's at a time that's already booked, and now you're left to decide whom to turn down. Sometimes you just need to click "decline."

Your first challenge is deciding which meetings to say no to. Establish a set of criteria for participation, and stick with it. Ask yourself the following questions.

Adapted from content posted on hbr.org on May 17, 2016.

What is the value of the meeting?

Start by assessing whether the meeting is about something important, timely, and worthwhile. Is it set up for success by having a clear purpose and an agenda? Is there background information available to inform participants in advance? Are the appropriate people invited so that meaningful progress can be made? If the value of the meeting isn't clear from the invitation, reply back with a few open-ended questions before making your decision:

- "Could you please provide some additional information on the agenda?"
- "What stage of decision making are we at on this topic?"
- "How should I prepare for the discussion?"

Am I the right person to attend?

If it's clear that the meeting is worthwhile, your next question is whether or not you should be there. Are the issues within the purview of your role? Do you have the expertise to contribute to the conversation? Are you underqualified or overqualified for the level of decision making on the table? If you're questioning why you were invited, reach out to the meeting organizer before responding:

- "What are you looking for me to contribute at this meeting?"
- "Who else will be there from my department?"
- "Who will I be representing?"

Is the meeting a priority for me right now?

If you believe the meeting will be valuable and that you would make a contribution to the discussion, consider how it aligns with your goals and work. How central is the meeting topic to your role? Where does the issue fit relative to your other immediate demands? How unique is your contribution, and could your seat be better filled by someone else?

If you ask yourself these questions and find that your participation isn't essential, then it's appropriate to decline the meeting. Even if you choose not to attend, the following options can help you demonstrate that you're a good team player and a positive contributor, even if you can't be in the room.

Can I stop the meeting altogether?

If the meeting failed your first criteria because you don't believe it's set up for success, talk with the organizer about your concerns. It's possible the person will dismiss your comments, but you could also trigger one of two positive outcomes: Either the meeting gets better positioned for success or gets cancelled. Try one of the following approaches:

- "This is an interesting topic. Based on our current-year priorities, I'm not sure we're ready for a productive conversation yet. Would it be possible to push this meeting back and let the working group make a little more progress before we meet?"

- "I'm looking forward to making some decisions on this issue. From the meeting invite, it doesn't look like Production is involved. I would like to wait until someone from that team is willing to join. Otherwise, we won't be able to make any decisions."
- "Based on the information in the invitation, it looks like this meeting is for informational purposes. Would it be possible to get a summary sent out rather than hold a meeting?"

Can I recommend someone else?

If the meeting is important, but it failed your second criteria because you're not the right person for the job, try nominating someone else. Invest some effort in finding the right person so you don't appear to be shirking the responsibility. Try floating these options:

- "I'm glad that you're interested in my input, but I don't believe I'm the most qualified person on this topic. I did a little digging, and it looks like Pat would have the necessary context. Would you be comfortable inviting Pat rather than me?"
- "Given that this is a decision-making meeting, I think it's more appropriate to have my manager represent our team."
- "Thanks for the invite to this meeting. I don't think I'm required at this point. If it's okay with you, I'd like to send José as my delegate."

Can I contribute in advance?

If the meeting failed your third criteria (you determined that it was an important topic on which you could add unique value, but attending the meeting doesn't fit with your schedule or priorities), consider adding value in advance. Take a few minutes to pull together some notes and to brief the chair or a suitable participant. That will be much more efficient than attending the entire meeting. You can respond to the organizer by saying:

- "This is going to be an important discussion. I'm not able to attend, but I will find some time to share my thoughts so you can include them in the conversation."
- "I'm sorry that I can't attend the meeting. If I prepare you in advance, could I ask that you represent my ideas at the meeting?"

Can I attend only part of the meeting?

If one or more agenda items meets all three of your criteria but others don't, you might have the option of attending only part of the meeting. Respond with one of the following approaches:

- "Thanks for the invite. I think it's really important for me to be part of the discussion on rebranding. Given a few other priorities at the moment, I'm going to excuse myself once that item is complete."
- "Would it be possible to cover the rebranding discussion as the first agenda item? I can't stay for

> the entire meeting but I'd really like to contribute on that one."

Regardless of which option you choose, you're trying to do three things. First, model deliberateness about the use of time. Second, share your rationale so that the meeting organizer has some context for why you're not participating. Third, make an effort to meet the organizer's needs, even if it's not in the way they had originally envisioned.

It might be a bit of a culture shock at first, but all the overwhelmed people with 35 hours a week of meetings will quickly admire your discipline, and you may find folks declining your invites based on similar criteria.

Liane Davey is the cofounder of 3COze Inc. She is the author of *You First: Inspire Your Team to Grow Up, Get Along, and Get Stuff Done* (Wiley, 2013) and a coauthor of *Leadership Solutions: The Pathway to Bridge the Leadership Gap* (Jossey-Bass, 2007). Follow her on Twitter @LianeDavey.

CHAPTER 17

How to Interject in a Meeting

by Jodi Glickman

How many times have you sat through a meeting with something brilliant to say but without knowing quite when to say it? Or realized halfway through the meeting that your colleague said something completely erroneous? Or, worse yet, found yourself nodding and smiling in agreement while wondering what in the world the discussion was actually about?

Speaking up in meetings—to interject, correct someone else, or ask for clarification—can be extremely intimidating. Having a few useful phrases at hand can go a

---

Adapted from content posted on hbr.org on November 3, 2010.

long way toward giving you the confidence and tools you need to be able to introduce your thoughts and opinions effectively in meetings.

When You've Got an Idea

Often people don't speak up because they're afraid of going on the record as wrong, uninformed, or the proponent of a dumb idea. A great way to sidestep this inherent fear is to depersonalize your idea, putting a question to the group. When you think you might have a good idea but aren't overly confident about it, go ahead and lob in an offhanded caveat, such as:

- "*Have we thought about* . . . getting Steve involved in the PR campaign directly?"
- "*Did anyone mention* . . . the Brealy report? I seem to recall it covered some of the same topics Andrew has raised here."
- "*Another option we may want to consider* . . . is pushing back the timeline until early October."
- "*Is it worth revisiting* . . . last week's minutes from the meeting to review the agreed-upon product specifications?"

The subtext here is that you're contributing to the discussion and adding value to the group—but not taking ownership of an idea or commandeering the conversation. By using a more informal question or caveat, you'll make your voice and idea heard without overstating your commitment to that idea.

When You Disagree

It's hard to disagree without being disagreeable. When the conversation is heading in a direction that doesn't work for you, it may be difficult to keep your mouth shut. Of course, it's your right (and perhaps even your responsibility) to speak up when you've got something contrarian to say; the key, however, is knowing how to finesse your comments so you don't come off sounding like a jerk. Here are a few strategies and helpful phrases to use in those awkward or tense moments:

- **Be blunt.** "I respectfully disagree with that assessment, Jon." Or "My experience has actually been quite different. I found the team to be highly engaging."
- **Be cagey.** "I just want to play devil's advocate here for a moment. What if we were to go with the opposite approach and use direct-mail marketing instead of relying solely on social media efforts?"
- **Be provocative.** "I want to throw out a curveball here and challenge our assumption that we have to take the deal."

When You're Confused

What's worse than sitting in on a meeting and having no idea what's going on? You may have stumbled in late, tuned out at exactly the wrong moment, or simply never known much about the topic at hand—and found yourself falling further and further in the dark as the meeting progressed. No matter the cause, the longer you wait to ask for clarification, the harder it is to meaningfully reinsert yourself into the conversation.

Here are some good phrases to use the next time you find yourself lost in a meeting:

- "*I'm not entirely sure I'm following you. Could you please recap what you just mentioned regarding* . . . the August delivery?"
- "*I'm sure I'm supposed to know this already, but* . . . how many attendees are we expecting at the conference next week?"
- "*I apologize if this is totally obvious to everyone here, but* . . . what does CAFE stand for?"
- "*This may be a dumb question, but I'm still not up to speed on why* . . . we're not using rail instead of truck."

It's best if you speak up in meetings and make your case—whether to push a new idea, correct a misconception, or simply keep yourself up-to-date on what's really going on. You owe it to yourself and your team to contribute to your fullest potential. It's far less intimidating than you might think.

Jodi Glickman is a speaker, the founder of the communication training firm Great on the Job, and the author of *Great on the Job: What to Say, How to Say It. The Secrets of Getting Ahead* (St. Martin's Griffin, 2011). Follow Jodi on Twitter @greatonthejob.

CHAPTER 18

Stuck in a Meeting from Hell? Here's What to Do

by Melissa Raffoni

We've all been in meetings that seem to go on forever, whether they're being dominated by windbags or bounce aimlessly from one topic to the next. Don't just sit there and roll your eyes. Take control by trying one of the following options.

Be brave. Play dumb.

Even if you think you know what's going on, you may not really get it, or you may sense others don't get it. Consider the power of the statement, "I'm sorry, I'm lost.

Adapted from content posted on hbr.org on January 29, 2010.

Can somebody help me understand what problem we're trying to solve and what needs to happen to resolve it? Joe, can you help me out?" The key to the success of this tactic isn't your question. It's Joe. The person you appeal to should be one of the strongest communicators in the room. It forces the group to stop and hear clarification from the most articulate person. It often helps get a group back on track. Playing dumb is pretty smart.

Be a helper. Create shared visuals. Use some technology.

Another great question to ask: "Would it be helpful if I took some notes?" Flip open your laptop, and take notes on a projected screen or in a shared document (such as a Google Docs). This is much better than using a marker and flip chart, which don't allow for good group editing and require transcription. Taking and projecting notes serves two purposes. First, it refocuses participants on what they can see before them, which could be a list of questions, decisions to be made, individual commentary, or whatever makes sense.

Second, if you can sort it out, you can use the documentation to drive problem solving. Framing the discussion with a simple outline, such as "Problem, Objectives, Facts, Questions, Action Items, Next Steps," will help move the team from *A* to *B*. Better yet, it will keep the team from wandering off to *Y* and *Z*.

Also, don't neglect to wrap up the meeting without committing summaries and next steps to the document. Now, given your efforts, the group has a working document that serves as a reference for next time. It sounds simple, but it works. What's really happening is you're volunteering to do the facilitating that the facilitator has failed to do.

Find the root cause of the meeting's lack of focus, and suggest a solution.

Politely observe that "we seem to be spinning our wheels here," and ask what's causing the endless cycles. Sometimes identifying the reason for meetings from hell allows you to refocus them or call a new one to sort through the problem more productively.

Identifying root causes of bad meetings is not always easy. Here are some common examples of barriers that may be making that meeting interminable and unproductive:

- **Lack of preparation.** Often, meetings get stuck because not everyone (or no one) has prepared. Whether that meeting-prep document is sent out early or 20 minutes before the meeting starts, people may not stop to read it. Other times, someone conducts the meeting off the cuff or tosses out issues for brainstorming. These approaches waste everybody's time.

- **Who has the D?** Just ask the question, "Who's responsible for this decision?" Ask that person if they're comfortable making a decision, right now.

- **The right people aren't in the room.** Save a meeting from droning on by identifying the people who are needed but absent. "We really can't move forward on this without Jane." Then cancel the meeting, and reschedule it with Jane.

Taking some of these steps and saying some of these things when you're not in charge might seem professionally precocious, but they're good leadership and management skills. And if you think you're in the meeting from hell, it's likely many of your colleagues do, too. They'll appreciate your effort to get the meeting back on track.

Melissa Raffoni is founder and CEO of The Raffoni Group.

CHAPTER 19

7 Ways to Stop a Meeting from Dragging On

by Joseph Grenny

When I got a speeding ticket a few years ago, I was offered the option of attending traffic school in lieu of a black mark on my otherwise spotless driving record. I showed up at city hall promptly at 6 p.m., hoping my educational experience would end at 8:30 as advertised. The instructor was 25 minutes late and quite disorganized. By 8:15, he was on slide 18 of 123 and seemed to be just getting into the groove. My heart sunk and I was quickly getting resentful. At 8:26 he launched into what

Adapted from content posted on hbr.org on April 25, 2016.

promised to be a lengthy story about a multicar accident. I felt a toxic sense of dread and powerlessness.

In 1964, social psychologists John Darley and Bibb Latané conducted an experiment on group powerlessness. Subjects were led to believe they were part of a group discussion about personal problems, when one participant is struck with an epileptic seizure. Darley and Latané wondered what conditions would predict whether the subject witnessing the seizure would either sit passively or interrupt the gathering and take action to help. It turned out that the larger the group, the less likely the subject was to break ranks from powerless peers and leave the room in search of help. This has become known as bystander apathy.

If human beings can act so passively when health and safety are on the line, it should be no wonder that we turn ourselves into victims when the sole risk is an hour or two of wasted time. Meetings are notoriously ineffective, because most participants act like passive victims rather than responsible actors.

Interestingly, even meeting leaders often view themselves as constrained by unstated and untested group expectations that limit their ability to intervene effectively in the group process. They allow dysfunctional time-wasting behavior to go unchecked because they imagine it is the vox populi.

I've made myself a meeting victim more often than I'd like to admit, but over the years I've discovered that if I'm suffering, others are likely suffering too, and it's in my power to do something. There are tactful things I can do to not only take responsibility for my own investment of time, but also to become a healthy voice for the silent majority. In fact, most people silently cheer when someone takes action to refocus or cut off time-wasting activities.

Here are seven of my favorite interventions for stopping meandering in a meeting:

- **Come prepared.** You can organize a chaotic conversation and gain disproportionate influence by simply arriving with a clearly articulated straw position on the topic to be discussed. Don't push it on people, but do offer to share it if others believe that it will help accelerate discussion. More often than not they will.

- **Set boundaries.** Take responsibility for your time. If a meeting is notorious for starting late and running over, let people know when the meeting begins what your boundaries are. For example, you might say, "I understand we're starting late but I have a commitment to the Murphy team I want to keep, so I have a hard stop at 10:45."

- **Trust your gut. Go public. Check with the group.** Notice, honor, and trust your gut. If you're feeling lost, pay attention. If you're feeling bored, take notice. There's a good chance others are, too. Then, tactfully and tentatively share your concern. Don't express it as truth; instead, own the fact that it is simply your experience. Next, check to see if others are feeling similarly. Here's what that might sound like: "I'm not sure I'm tracking the discussion.

We seem to be moving between three different agenda items. Are others seeing that, too?"

- **Restate the less than obvious.** If the discussion is toggling between two or more problems, summarize the topics on the table, and suggest the group tackle one at a time. For example, "I'm hearing points about both whether this is a good investment and when we should make the purchase. I think we've already made the purchase decision and timing is the only question. Is that right?"

- **Ask the question no one's asking.** If a sacred cow is glaringly obvious, ask for confirmation of its existence. For example, "I'm getting from the comments that some of us question the wisdom of the original decision. Is that right?"

- **Spot the weeds.** Periodically point out digressions into unproductive detail or tangents. Everyone in the group is responsible for the group process, so if you say nothing, you're part of the problem (see chapter 10 for more on silence in meetings). Say something to the effect of, "It sounds like we're in agreement about the policy. Rather than wordsmith it now, it might be better to have someone do a draft."

- **Clarify responsibilities at the end.** It's rare that someone in the meeting takes the time to summarize decisions and clarify commitments at the end. This usually only takes 60 seconds but can save hours in misunderstanding and unneces-

> sary future meetings. Even if you aren't running the meeting, you can speak up and ask, "Can we take a second to summarize what we've agreed to and who will do what by when? Maybe I'm the only one who's fuzzy, but I want to be sure I follow through on my commitments."

As I sat festering in my misery in traffic school, I began to suspect I was not alone. I had 175 other classmates who might be playing victim right alongside me. So I checked my gut, went public, and addressed the person running the meeting.

"Officer, I'm anxious to hear the end of this story, but I'm wondering what time class ends."

He looked a bit uncertain. "I thought it ended at 9:30."

I heard an audible groan from my classmates.

"What time were you told it ended?" he inquired.

"8:30," I said.

He looked at his watch. Then announced, "Class dismissed." The cheers were audible. I felt like the valedictorian of the class.

Joseph Grenny is a four-time *New York Times* best-selling author, keynote speaker, and social scientist. His work has been translated into 28 languages, is available in 36 countries, and has generated results for 300 of the *Fortune* 500. He is the cofounder of VitalSmarts, an innovator in corporate training and leadership development.

CHAPTER 20

When Your Boss Is Terrible at Leading Meetings

by Paul Axtell

If you think your boss is ineffective at leading meetings, you're not alone. Few managers have mastered the art of meetings, and even fewer organizations have made it a priority. Add to that the fact that leaders are busy—and often don't have the time to adequately prepare—and you've got a recipe for ineffective meetings. The question is, what can you do about it?

Adapted from content posted on hbr.org on May 16, 2016.

Three broad perspectives are available to you in every meeting:

1. You can offer to do things to support your boss in preparing, leading, and following up after the meeting.
2. You have the right to ask for whatever you need to be effective in the meeting.
3. You can choose to be responsible for the experience of other people in the meeting.

Let's look at each of these options individually.

What might you offer to do?

I love this perspective because it allows you to be supportive without making your boss wrong. A key aspect of influence is the ability to state a problem without blaming anyone. Offering to supply elements that may be missing is a powerful way to do this. Here are some things you might offer to do:

- Collect agenda suggestions from the group, and then prepare an agenda for your boss to review and edit.
- Find team members to lead the different agenda items, or offer to lead the meeting so the boss can more fully focus on the conversation.
- Handle all of the room arrangements—and be there early to make sure it's all set.
- Help bring the conversation back when it wanders away from the intended path.

- Notice who isn't yet involved in the conversation, and invite them to speak.
- Take notes so that a written summary can be prepared quickly after the meeting.
- Chart complex conversations on a whiteboard as they unfold so the group can stay on track and see what has been said.
- Listen for commitments and actions that are voiced, and then review them during the closing for each topic.
- Write and distribute a summary shortly after the meeting ends.

Stepping up and offering to do something will usually be appreciated and respected. However, we all know that our ability to speak frankly with our boss is determined by the level of trust and respect that exists between us. If your boss values what you bring to the group, you can be straightforward: "Sam, I think we can improve the quality of our meetings by doing a couple of things differently. If you agree, I would be willing to do the following."

If your boss takes offense at your offer or says, "No thanks, I've got it under control," then respond with, "OK, and if you change your mind, let me know. I just want to do whatever I can to support you." None of us are as open-minded or coachable in the moment as we think we are. There is a good chance that your boss will continue to think about your suggestion during the next few meetings. Without your offer, nothing will change; with your offer, it just might.

What do you need to be effective?

What are your most common complaints about these meetings? What could you ask for that would resolve each complaint? If you need something in order to be both present and productive in a meeting, find a diplomatic way to ask for it. Other people will probably be having the same experience and will welcome your initiative. Here are some suggestions for asking for what you need.

- **An agenda:** "Most of the time, I think it's fine to find out what's on the agenda when we walk into the meeting. On a few topics, like the budget, however, I would appreciate knowing the agenda ahead of time so I can prepare in a way that lets me add value to the conversation."
- **Proper setup for each topic:** "Before we start this conversation, I'd like to know what input you're looking for from us and where you want to be at the end of this discussion."
- **Broader participation:** "I realize we're a bit pressed for time, but there are a couple of people I'd really like to hear from in this conversation. So I'd appreciate if we could stay with this topic a bit longer so Sarah, Ganesh, and Tori can give us their views."
- **Clarity:** "I might be the only person struggling with this conversation, but I need to get clear on where we are with this and what we've said so far."

- **To stay on track:** "It appears that we're now talking about something different than what's on the agenda. Do we want to stay with this new topic or go back to our intended discussion?"
- **Alignment:** "It seems the group has settled on a direction. I'd like to ensure the decision works for everyone."
- **Next steps:** "This was a great conversation, and I want to be clear about what, if anything, I need to do as a result. Could we nail down what actions will be taken next and when we should have them completed?"

How can you affect the experience of other participants?

Usually we go into a meeting thinking about one person: ourselves. Fair enough, but looking out for others is an easy way to add value and impact in an organization.

Consider these questions:

- Who is not yet participating in the conversation who might have something to say or ask?
- Who is affected by the decision and has not yet voiced their concerns or ideas?
- Who might not be able to attend and would like you to take notes or represent them in the meeting?
- Who would appreciate your collaboration on small-group work that is assigned during the meeting?

OK, now it's up to you. This is wonderful place to trust your instincts. Sincerity trumps all conversational skills. Take your boss to coffee, and offer to help. And, try the ideas that resonate with you in other meetings that you attend. You'll be pleased with the results.

Paul Axtell provides consulting and personal effectiveness training to a wide variety of clients, from *Fortune* 500 companies to universities. His latest book, *Meetings Matter: 8 Powerful Strategies for Remarkable Conversations* (Jackson Creek, 2015), received awards from the Nonfiction Book Awards and the Benjamin Franklin Book Awards, a Silver award in the Nautilus Book Awards, and was first runner-up for the Eric Hoffer Prize.

SECTION FOUR

Close and Follow Up

CHAPTER 21

The Right Way to End a Meeting

by Paul Axtell

A common complaint among managers is that the conversations they have with employees aren't producing results. "We keep talking about the same issue over and over, but nothing seems to ever happen!" they say. That's because most managers are missing a vital skill: the ability to deliberately close a conversation. If you end a conversation well, it will improve each and every interaction you have, ultimately creating impact.

Meetings are a series of conversations—an opportunity to clarify issues, set direction, sharpen focus, and move objectives forward. To maximize their effect, you need to actively design the conversation. While the

---

Adapted from content posted on hbr.org on March 11, 2015.

overall approach is straightforward—and may seem like basic stuff—not enough managers are actually doing this in practice.

- **Set up each conversation** so everyone knows the intended outcomes and how to participate.
- **Manage the conversation rigorously** so the discussion stays on track and everyone is engaged.
- **Close the conversation** to ensure alignment, clarity on next steps, and awareness of the value created.

In my 35 years of experience as a corporate trainer, I've found that closure is more often than not the missing link between meetings and impact. Without it, things can be left unsaid, unchallenged, unclear, and uncommitted. Each agenda item should be considered incomplete unless it is wrapped up in a thoughtful, deliberate way.

To deliberately close a conversation, do these five things:

Check for completion. If you move to the next topic on an agenda too quickly, people will either cycle back to that topic later or they'll leave the meeting with their thoughts unclear or misaligned. Ask, "Is there anything else someone needs to say or ask before we change topics or adjourn the meeting?" Giving people the space to address their lingering concerns and questions allows you to deal with those issues promptly and move forward.

Check for alignment. If someone can't live with the decisions being made in the meeting or the potential outcome of those decisions, ask that person what it would take to get them on board. People prefer to be united with the group, and if they aren't, there's a reason behind it that needs to be surfaced. Asking the question, "Is everyone OK with where we ended up?" will surface questions or concerns so they can be resolved as soon as possible.

Agree on next steps. Getting firm, clear commitments is the primary way to ensure progress between meetings. In order for a conversation to lead to action, you need to clearly state what you will do by when and ask others to do the same. To maintain the momentum of any project, nail down agreed-upon next steps, firm timelines, and individual responsibilities, and then follow up often. The question to ask here is "What, exactly, will we do by our next meeting to ensure progress?"

Reflect on the value of what you accomplished. This is one of the most powerful acknowledgment and appreciation tools. People rarely state the value created by a conversation, and therefore lose a wonderful opportunity to validate both the conversation and the individuals who are a part of it. After a presentation don't just say, "That was good." Instead, say "Let me tell you the five things I'm taking away from your presentation."

Check for acknowledgments. Did anyone contribute to the conversation in a way that needs to be highlighted? While you don't want to use acknowledgment and appreciation so frequently that it becomes a commodity with no value, at times someone's questions or remarks do help provide the tipping point that turns an ordinary conversation into an extraordinary one—and that's worth acknowledging. Doing so reinforces the conversations that occurred, supports the people in the meeting, and encourages everyone's desire to produce the expected results.

Try spending the next three weeks working on closing every conversation in this deliberate, thoughtful way. You'll see an immediate impact on how and when things get done.

Paul Axtell provides consulting and personal effectiveness training to a wide variety of clients, from *Fortune* 500 companies to universities. His latest book, *Meetings Matter: 8 Powerful Strategies for Remarkable Conversations* (Jackson Creek, 2015), received awards from the Nonfiction Book Awards and the Benjamin Franklin Book Awards, a Silver award in the Nautilus Book Awards, and was first runner-up for the Eric Hoffer Prize.

CHAPTER 22

Don't End a Meeting Without Doing These 3 Things

by Bob Frisch and Cary Greene

When a sports team finishes a game, they usually don't gather up their gear and immediately leave the court, rink, field, or locker room. The players and coaches take a few minutes for a post-game meeting—a ritual that's just as important as the pre-game warm-up.

Meeting participants can benefit from the same exercise. A quick wrap-up discussion before attendees leave the room goes a long way toward ensuring the gathering

Adapted from content posted on hbr.org on April 26, 2016.

achieved what it set out to do and that future get-togethers will also prove successful. Here are three steps to take at the end of each meeting (though you can, of course, dial up or down each component as the situation warrants). Once you've done this in person, follow up in writing.

Confirm key decisions and next steps.

Recap what was decided in the meeting, who is accountable for following through, when implementation will occur, and how it will be communicated. You want every attendee to leave the meeting with the same understanding of what was agreed on so there's little chance of anyone reopening the issues later. One client we've worked with preps for this end-of-meeting review by writing on a flip chart to capture decisions as they're made so nothing is forgotten or overlooked. He also notes action items, including who is responsible, when things should happen, and how status will be reported back to the group.

Develop communication points.

If a colleague who missed the meeting asks an attendee "What happened?" the person who went to the meeting should know what to say. So before you wrap up, put the question to the group. "What are the most important things we accomplished in our time together here?" As the group responds, capture the key points on a flip chart, whiteboard, or shared document, and briefly summarize them. Once you have alignment on what should be communicated to others, ask everyone if there are any parts of the discussion that they wouldn't want to be shared. Some information might be confidential; perhaps some ideas aren't quite ready for dissemination. Be as specific as possible here so everyone clearly understands what is off-limits. Then, as soon as possible after the meeting, send your agreed-upon talking points to everyone in an e-mail. The goal of this exercise is not to give people a script to read from. It's to provide guidance on the key messages they should convey and what they should keep to themselves, if asked, so the rest of the organization gets a consistent picture of what went on. After a recent strategy meeting of the top 30 executives at a major technology company, for example, the group decided on these communication points:

- This was not a one-time event but rather the beginning of this group coming together as a senior leadership team.
- We talked about our strategy, which is to build a collection of great businesses in strong categories.
- We agreed that each business should focus on driving its own growth, but where it makes sense, units and functions should leverage each other's best practices and capabilities. We captured some ideas for how to start doing this and talked about opportunities for leaders to grow and take on new boundary-spanning roles.

Gather session feedback.

Especially if your group will meet regularly, ask attendees for feedback on the session while it's fresh in their minds. This is an often-missed opportunity to learn what people liked and what they would change. Instead of asking a broad question like “What feedback do you have?” which often yields equally vague and unhelpful responses, break the discussion into what we call “roses” (positives) and “thorns” (negatives). Start with the latter. Tell attendees to think about everything they have received or done related to the meeting from the time they were invited right through the review, including any pre-reads or prework and aspects of the meeting itself (such as location and use of time). Then ask, “What could be improved?” Avoid debating the suggestions raised, but do ask questions to clarify what’s being said. Finally, turn to roses. Ask the group, “What went well? What should we be sure to do again in the future?” Combined with the recap of decisions, next steps, and talking points, this last discussion helps you end the session on a positive note.

When you embed a regular post-meeting debrief that incorporates these three elements into your meetings, you’ll help your team dramatically improve its play.

Bob Frisch is the managing partner of the Strategic Offsites Group, a Boston-based consultancy, and is the author of *Who’s In The Room? How Great Leaders Structure and Manage the Teams Around Them* (Jossey-Bass, 2012). He is the author of four *Harvard Business Review* articles, including “Off-Sites That Work” (June 2006).

Cary Greene is a partner of the Strategic Offsites Group. They are coauthors of *Simple Sabotage: A Modern Field Manual for Detecting & Rooting Out Everyday Behaviors That Undermine Your Workplace* (HarperOne, 2015) and are frequent contributors to hbr.org.

SECTION FIVE

Specific Types of Meetings

CHAPTER 23

What Everyone Should Know About Running Virtual Meetings

by Paul Axtell

To make sure that your virtual meetings are adding value and velocity to your projects, do three things:

Focus on relationships.

The quality of people's relationships in a meeting determines the quality of the conversations that will occur during the meeting. That's why it's important to set aside time to build relationships among team members.

Adapted from content posted on hbr.org on April 14, 2016.

Start with casual conversation.

Make it a practice for the conference lines to be open 10 minutes early, and designate that time for catching up. Ask someone to be there to greet and talk with people once the lines are open. If you're leading the meeting, prepare ahead of time so that you can spend time chatting rather than answering e-mails or reviewing your notes. Encourage others to make it a practice to show up early to converse.

Then, at the start of each meeting, ask three people to take a couple of minutes to share what's happening with them. Here are my favorite ways to start this brief conversation:

- Please catch us up on one of your other projects.
- What's happening in your country?
- How's your family?

Use people's names.

During the meeting, credit people when you refer to their earlier comments. Keep a chart next to you to help remember who's out there. People love to be recognized, and in virtual meetings, it builds a sense of community that can otherwise be diminished by not being in the same space. It also pulls meeting participants into a zone of being more attentive and thoughtful.

Meet face-to-face.

When team members visit from out of town or from another country, find time to see them. Schedule a working dinner. Invite them to coffee. If there's driving involved, ride together. Pick them up at the airport. This lays the foundation for authentic conversation—so you'll feel less distant on your next virtual encounter.

Prepare, so you can be present and productive.

Publish an agenda.

A clear agenda helps your participants understand how you'll conduct the virtual meeting and allows them to think about and prepare for each topic in advance. This is particularly important for those who speak English as a second language. When people have time to prepare, they can participate more fully and powerfully. Expecting people to develop their thinking and then express it clearly in the moment during a meeting is asking too much.

The agenda doesn't need to be elaborate. For each topic, answer these questions:

- Why is this topic on our agenda?
- How much time is allocated for this topic?
- Where do we want to be at the end of our discussion?
- What do we need from participants?

Give yourself more time.

Plan on 20% more time than you think you'll need for each topic. The process of getting broad participation and checking to see if everyone has had a chance to express their views and ask their questions takes time—lots of time. You don't want to feel any pressure to get through an agenda. You'll sacrifice clarity and alignment if you or your team members feel rushed. You can always end early if the extra time you've built in isn't needed.

Identify who you want to hear from.

Before the meeting, consider:

- Who would get the conversation off to a great start?
- Who will be most affected by the topic?
- Who is likely to have different views and ideas?
- Whose experience needs to be brought into the conversation?

Part of feeling included and adding value in a group is having the opportunity to share what you're thinking about the topic. This can be difficult when you're in the same room and even harder virtually. Once you've thought about who you want to hear from, tell people which topics you'd like their input on. Letting people know that you want broad participation is the first step; calling on people strategically and gently is the second step. Knowing ahead of time who you want to get into the conversation for each topic will make this easy.

Lead to accomplish the agenda and to get broad participation.

Review how you'll manage the conversation.

Virtual meetings require a stronger leadership approach because you don't have access to the nonverbal cues about whether people have questions or would like to get into the conversation. These meetings also require more empathy and thoughtfulness on your part because people have this sense of being less connected than when they're in the same room.

Ask for the permission you need to be able to relax and enjoy leading the meeting. This is what I usually request:

- Permission to be firm about keeping the conversation on track
- Freedom to call on different people when it seems appropriate
- Agreement from everyone about setting aside their technology, unless they have a good reason for keeping it available

I also let people know that while I have a plan for the meeting, I'm open to their coaching and ideas on making the meeting work for everyone.

Asking for what you want gives you the opportunity to guide the group without making anyone wrong. It also gives people in the group permission to step outside of their normal ways of interacting and participate authentically. It's easy to be ourselves in small groups of four or five people over coffee. In larger groups and virtual groups, the conversation needs to be set up to be safe and effective.

Consider covering these points in your opening:

- "With your permission, I'd like to manage our conversation today in a deliberate fashion so that we all stay on track and to make sure that everyone gets heard. This doesn't mean that I intend to be heavy-handed; I'd just like more freedom to keep the conversation focused and permission to call on people to ensure we have everyone's questions and views expressed before we end a topic."
- "For each item, I'd like to ask certain people to start the topic off. I've made notes on who I think might be affected and will check with each of you. Of course, if I haven't called on you and you want to add something, please do so. You always have permission to get into any conversation if your ideas, questions, and views have not yet been expressed."

Then, manage the conversation thoughtfully.

Go slowly. Without being able to see people as they speak, it's not only harder to hear, it's more difficult to process what's being said. Speaking succinctly will help, and a calmer pace will provide openings for people to ask their questions. Refer to your chart of who's in the meeting to keep track of who's already spoken and to remind you to invite others to add to the conversation.

Consider adding a process step to check for clarity on each topic. Without visual clues, you can't always tell when people aren't understanding or are disagreeing. If you have people with different language or cultural backgrounds, getting to clarity and alignment may require more time going back and forth.

Paul Axtell provides consulting and personal effectiveness training to a wide variety of clients, from *Fortune* 500 companies to universities. His latest book, *Meetings Matter: 8 Powerful Strategies for Remarkable Conversations* (Jackson Creek, 2015), received awards from the Nonfiction Book Awards and the Benjamin Franklin Book Awards, a Silver award in the Nautilus Book Awards, and was first runner-up for the Eric Hoffer Prize.

CHAPTER 24

How to Run a Great Virtual Meeting

by Keith Ferrazzi

Virtual meetings have the potential to be more valuable than traditional face-to-face meetings. Beyond the fact that they're an inexpensive way to get people together—no travel costs and readily available technology—they're also a great opportunity to build engagement, trust, and candor among teams.

Virtual meetings are just as effective as in-person gatherings if key rules and processes are maintained and respected. Here's my comprehensive list of simple steps you can take to get the most out of your next one.

Adapted from content posted on hbr.org on March 27, 2015.

Before the Meeting

Turn the video on.

Since everyone on the call is separated by distance, using video is the best thing you can do to make everyone feel like they're in the same room. Choose from several options, including WebEx and Skype. Video makes people feel more engaged because it lets team members see each other's emotions and reactions, which immediately humanizes things. No longer are they just voices on a phone line; they're the faces of your coworkers responding to what you and others are saying. Without video, you'll never know if the dead silence in a virtual meeting is happening because somebody isn't paying attention, someone's rolling their eyes in exasperation, or an individual is nodding their head in agreement. Facial expressions matter.

Cut out status updates.

Too many meetings, virtual and otherwise, are reminiscent of a bunch of fifth graders reading to each other around the table: a waste of the valuable time and opportunity of having people together. The solution is to send out a simple half-page document in advance of the meeting to report on key agenda items—and then only spend time on it in the meeting if people need to ask questions or want to comment.

This type of prework prepares participants to take full advantage of the meeting by thinking ahead about the content, formulating ideas, or getting to know others in the group. This can help keep team members engaged, says business consultant Nancy M. Settle-Murphy in her book *Leading Effective Virtual Teams.* But one thing is critical: It has to be assumed that everyone has read the pre-reading. Not doing so becomes an ethical violation against the team. I use the word "ethical" because it's stealing time from the team—and that's a disrespectful habit. The leader needs to aggressively set the tone that the pre-reading should be done in advance of the meeting.

Come prepared with the team's opinions.

Not only do you need to do your pre-reading, but after seeing the agenda, you should also discuss what's going to be covered with your team—that is, do your own due diligence. Often people get on a virtual call with a point of view, but because they haven't done any real homework beforehand, they end up reversing their opinions once the call has ended and they've learned new information that they could have easily obtained in advance. If there's a topic that seems to have interdependencies with people who work in another location, get their input ahead of time so you're best representing those constituents in the meeting.

During the Meeting

Encourage collaborative problem solving.

Replace the standard detailed status updates that can weigh meetings down with a group problem-solving session. How do they work? Raise a topic for discussion, and the team works together—viewing their fellow team members as sources of advice—to unearth information and viewpoints and to generate fresh ideas in response to business challenges.

Give each person time on the agenda.

Along with collaborative problem solving, giving each person time on the agenda fosters greater collaboration and helps all team members weigh in. Here's how it works: In advance of the session, have team members write up an issue they've been struggling with and bring it to the group, one at a time. Each team member then gets five minutes on the agenda to discuss their issue. The group then goes around the table so everyone gets a chance to either ask a question about it or pass. After the team member answers everyone's questions, people then get an opportunity to offer advice in the "I might suggest" format, or pass. Then you move on to the next issue until everyone has had the opportunity to present their challenge and receive ideas for addressing it.

Kill mute.

In an in-person meeting, there are social norms: You don't get up and walk around the room, not paying attention. Nor do you make a phone call and "check out" from the meeting. Virtual meetings should be no different. You can't press mute and leave the room to get something or strike up a conversation with your spouse. So establish a standard: Just because you're in a virtual meeting and it's possible to be disrespectful without others knowing, such behavior is unacceptable. If you wouldn't do something in person, don't do it virtually.

Turning the volume on for everyone's phones will keep people in line and raises the potential for lively discussion, shared laughter, and creativity.

Ban multitasking.

Once thought of as a way to get many things done at once, multitasking is now understood to be a way to do many things poorly. Science shows us that despite the brain's remarkable complexity and power, there's a bottleneck in information processing when it tries to perform two distinct tasks at once. Not only is this bad for your brain, it's bad for your team. Set a firm policy that multitasking during your meeting is unacceptable, as it's important for everyone to be mentally present.

Here are three ways to make sure the ban on multitasking is followed:

- **Use video.** It essentially eliminates multitasking, because your colleagues can see you.
- **Call on specific people.** Ask someone, by name, to share their thoughts. Since no one likes to be caught off-guard, they'll be more apt to pay attention.
- **Give people different tasks in the meeting.** To keep people engaged, have a different team member keep the minutes of the meeting each time; track action items, owners and deadlines; and try coming up with a fun question to ask everyone at the conclusion of the meeting. If you meet regularly, rotate assignments to keep things fresh.

Check in.

Nick Morgan, president of consulting company Public Words, recommends having constant touch points. "In a virtual meeting, you need to stop regularly to take everyone's temperature. And I do mean everyone. Go right around the list, asking each locale or person for input."

Assign a Yoda.

Candor is difficult even for co-located teams, but it's the number one gauge of team productivity. To keep people engaged during virtual meetings, appoint a "Yoda." Like the wise Jedi master in *Star Wars,* the Yoda keeps team members in line and makes sure everyone stays active and on topic. By being courageous and calling out any inappropriate behaviors, the Yoda keeps honesty from boiling over into disrespect. At critical points during the meeting, the leader should turn to the Yoda and ask, "So, what's going on here that nobody's talking about?" This allows the Yoda to express what they see happening and encourage risk-taking.

After the Meeting

Formalize the watercooler.

Have you ever been in a meeting, and after it's over everybody walks out and vents their frustrations next to the water cooler? Make the water cooler conversation the formal ending of your next virtual meeting. Roughly 10 minutes before the meeting ends, do what everybody would have done after the physical meeting—but do it *in* the meeting and make sure it's transparent and conscious, reflecting people's real feelings.

How? Have everyone go around and say what they would've done differently in the meeting. This is the final Yoda moment—the chance to "speak now or forever hold your peace." This is the time when you say what you disagreed with, what you're challenged with, what you're concerned about, what you didn't like, and so on. Make it clear that all the watercooler–type conversations need to happen right now or never happen again. And if they do happen later, you're violating the ethics of the team.

Most important, civility and respect must be the norm in virtual meetings. There must be inalienable ethical rules that you follow before, during, and after a virtual meeting if it is to be truly successful. And that means adhering to two fundamental principles: Be respectful of others' time, and be present.

Keith Ferrazzi is the CEO of Ferrazzi Greenlight, a research-based consulting and training company, and the author of *Who's Got Your Back* (Broadway Books, 2009).

CHAPTER 25

Conduct a Meeting of People from Different Cultures

by Rebecca Knight

When you're running a meeting with participants from different cultures, consider your colleagues' various needs and approaches. How do you brainstorm ideas, make decisions, and address conflict in a way that is comfortable for everyone? Which culture's preferences should be the default? And how can you be sure that people who aren't from the dominant culture participate and are heard?

Adapted from content posted on hbr.org on December 4, 2015.

What the Experts Say

Multicultural meetings can be challenging to lead. "People bring their cultural baggage with them wherever they go—and that includes the workplace," says Jeanne M. Brett, professor of dispute resolution and negotiations at Northwestern University's Kellogg School of Management. Communication styles vary from culture to culture, as do notions of authority and hierarchy, which only heightens the potential for misunderstanding and hard feelings. "If you don't prepare for cultural differences and anticipate them at the front end, they're a lot harder to deal with after the fact," she says. It's daunting, but you needn't feel overwhelmed, says Erin Meyer, a professor at INSEAD and the author of the book *The Culture Maps*. Approach your cross-cultural meeting with an open mind. And have faith in your abilities, because "you likely have more experience than you know," adds Andy Molinsky, professor of organizational behavior at Brandeis University International Business School and the author of the book *Global Dexterity*. "You've probably run meetings where there was quite a lot of diversity, be it gender diversity, functional diversity, seniority diversity, or just different personalities. Culture is one more element," he says. Here are some ideas to help your multicultural meetings go smoothly.

Be mindful of differences . . .

The key to showing cultural sensitivity in the workplace is being aware of the variations that exist among cultures and how they play out, says Molinsky. "There are differences in how and where people are supposed to sit in meetings, the extent to which they get down to business at the start of a meeting versus how much time they spend socializing, the extent to which they're willing to provide feedback or argue publicly—there are so many different elements." Meyer recommends "learning as much as you possibly can about the people and the regions of the world you are collaborating with so that you can adjust your management style in small ways." Study up on a country's customs and professional practices, and become an expert observer of others. It's a team effort. Provide your colleagues with reading material on cultural differences, and encourage colleagues to "think about how their behavior is viewed so they can make adjustments too," she adds.

. . . But don't obsess over them

And yet, says Molinsky, "sometimes culture matters, sometimes it doesn't, and you can't always anticipate" how cultural differences will play out. It's important to respect cultural norms, but don't be rigid about them—and especially don't pigeonhole individuals and groups of people. "Culture is only one potential influence on a person's style, his behavior, and how he perceives things," he says. "You should have a working hypothesis but test it against evidence." As the person in charge of the meeting, you'll probably need to make some adjustments and adaptations to your leadership style, but stay true to yourself, too. Don't be boorish or ignorant, but don't pretend to be someone you're not.

Set expectations

It's important to "create protocols and establish norms at the beginning" of your meetings, says Brett. "You want to be clear about what you expect and how meetings will run," she says. "This gives certain people the freedom to move outside their comfort zone, and it also gives you the freedom to rein in others." Say, for instance, some of your colleagues come from a culture where punctuality is not adhered to, but you want meetings to start and end in a timely manner. "You need to demonstrate that you understand different cultural behavior but also explain why you think it's critical for people to show up to meetings on time—and that people [who are late] will suffer the consequences," says Molinsky. "Be explicit. There are deal breakers." Structure and protocol "can override or supersede cultural norms" in other ways, too. If, for instance, you want to hold a group brainstorming session but some of your colleagues are from a culture that's typically reticent, ensure participation by asking "everyone to go around the room and spend two minutes describing their point of view on a particular problem," he says. "Institute rules" that are clear and that everyone follows.

Build relationships

Getting to know the personalities on your team is sound management practice in any culture, but it's especially important when your team is made up of people from different countries. "You need to know the people on your team and figure out the extent to which culture is an issue for each individual," says Molinsky. Say, for instance, one of your team members comes from a hierarchical culture and is loath to provide feedback to a senior colleague. "If you would like him to speak up in a meeting, you need to talk with him beforehand and strategize with him on how he can adapt his behavior," he says. Alternatively, "you need to forgive him for not doing it." Focus, too, on forging bonds and fostering trust among your team members, says Meyer. "Invest time up front on building emotional bonds so that people on your team have opportunities to get to know each other by sharing meals or talking over drinks," she says. "That way a lot of the cultural differences [that appear in the workplace] won't matter as much."

Be creative with conflict

When it comes to professional meetings, one of the biggest cultural differences is the degree to which open debate and disagreement are viewed as a positive, according to Meyer. "In countries like Korea, Indonesia, and Thailand, saying: 'I disagree,' is seen as very aggressive and could lead to a break in the relationship, whereas in France and Russia, it's seen as a great opportunity to build a relationship," she says. While "individual adjustments like softening your language" can be effective, it's also worth trying to make your team more comfortable with conflict. Meyers suggests that before the meeting, you ask your team members to e-mail their ideas and thoughts to a central organizing body that will be grouped by theme and shared when everyone is together. "That way you're disagreeing with an idea, not a colleague," she says. "It's not personal."

Be flexible

Meetings are only one element of the flow of workplace decision making. There are pre-meetings, post-meetings, informal, one-on-one conversations in the corridor, and impromptu group discussions. If cultural differences are making group meetings particularly challenging, try "soliciting coworkers' opinions in other venues and giving people an opportunity to provide feedback in different ways," says Molinsky. "Be flexible about the process," says Brett. "Consider breaking up your group into smaller subgroups." And remember, adds Meyer, "In many countries, the formal meeting is not the place to hash out ideas—it's for putting a stamp on what we've already decided in pre-meetings," she says. In other words, don't put too much stock in what takes place in the conference room. "Recognize that in many cultures the tough stuff is done off-line, one-on-one."

Consider rewards

"It's really hard for people to overcome their cultural behaviors because they're so ingrained," says Brett. But if you're concerned that cultural differences are having a negative impact on your team's capacity for growth and change, think about ways to push your colleagues outside their cultural comfort zones during meetings. "You need to institutionalize rewards around what you're trying to motivate people to do so that it's hardwired in," says Molinsky. Say, for instance, you want to encourage more-open conflict and feedback at meetings, but your workforce is conflict averse. In that case, you could "make providing feedback part of their performance evaluations" and a prerequisite for promotion. They get rewards when they do it well and perhaps even penalties if they fail. It's not easy, but "it's definitely possible to encourage and train people to behave in ways that might not feel natural," says Meyer.

Rebecca Knight is a freelance journalist based in Boston and a lecturer at Wesleyan University. Her work has been published in the *New York Times, USA Today,* and the *Financial Times.*

CHAPTER 26

Making Global Meetings Work

by June Delano

Running a virtual team is an interesting challenge, especially if people are spread across countries and time zones and have different levels of language proficiency. At one time I had a team of about 17 people spread across 10 countries, and we needed to have a meeting weekly or at least every other week. The challenge was that somebody was always in the meeting in the middle of the night, somebody was always the only person in a room while other people were in small groups.

This content originally appeared in the Virtual Teams module of *Harvard ManageMentor* (product #6789AR).

So we experimented and came up with a model we called “inconvenience everybody equally.” That meant that we rotated our meeting time so that at some point, everyone—whether they were in London, Berlin, New Delhi, or New York—was up in the middle of the night or in the middle of their normal workday. And it meant that everybody got a chance to be drowsy and falling asleep, as well as wide awake and full of energy at the peak of their day.

We also came up with a rule that, at first, was very hard to enforce: Even if there were several people in one location, each needed to be on the phone separately—not in a room together. It completely changes the dynamic of a meeting if some people are together in one place and can see and talk to one another off-line.

So although several of us were sitting in a row in cubicles in the same office, we made sure that we all got on the phone equally with everybody else. That meant no side conversations and that everybody needed to put their expression into their voice rather than rely on facial expressions.

We also learned that it was really important to have an agenda go out ahead of time, particularly when you have people who are speaking a second or a third language. Seeing the agenda in advance gave them a chance to read and get familiar with the content and what was going to be discussed.

Finally, we made sure that we kept the agenda to those things that really mattered to everyone who was on the phone. If there are 17 people on the line, you don’t want to have people getting bored and losing their sense of involvement and engagement in the meeting.

June Delano is a managing partner and cofounder of The ClearLake Group.

CHAPTER 27

Give Your Standing Meetings a Makeover

by Martha Craumer

Regularly scheduled meetings (staff meetings, progress report meetings, and sales meetings) sometimes seem to be called out of habit or a sense of duty rather than need. They're valuable not only for the information they allow people to share but also for the face time they offer. However, their importance doesn't necessarily make them interesting. Meeting with the same people in the same room every week to discuss the same topics can get boring, resulting in many empty chairs—and a lack of enthusiasm among the remaining attendees. Here are

---

Adapted from the "The Effective Meeting: A Checklist for Success," *Harvard Management Communication Letter* (reprint #C0103A), March 2001.

some ways to keep your regular meetings fresh—and attendance high.

Regularly review the meeting's purpose

From time to time remind participants of the reasons for meeting, and ask if the meeting still serves that purpose. For example, a project team may hold twice-weekly status reports at the beginning of a project, when there are a lot of new developments and many decisions to make. Once the initial frenzy subsides, though, there may only be enough new information to warrant a monthly meeting.

Solicit agenda items from the group in advance

This gives attendees a chance to bring up issues that are of interest to them.

Cancel when there is no reason to meet

Nothing on the agenda? Don't meet. There's no sense in gathering together just because it's what you do on Tuesdays at 11 a.m. People will come to appreciate that your meetings won't be a waste of time.

Rotate leadership of the meeting

Have each attendee take a turn running the meeting—setting the agenda, preparing materials, and introducing topics. It's a great way to inspire ownership of the meeting.

Martha Craumer is a senior writer at The Boston Consulting Group.

CHAPTER 28

How to Do Walking Meetings Right

by Russell Clayton, Christopher Thomas, and Jack Smothers

Fran Melmed is the founder of Context, a communication and change management consulting firm. She spends her days performing communication audits for organizations and meeting with clients. Sounds like a recipe for a sedentary workday, right? On the contrary. Fran is part of a growing trend known as walking meetings or "walk and talk."

A walking meeting is simply that: a meeting that takes place during a walk instead of in an office, board-

---

Adapted from content posted on hbr.org on August 5, 2015.

room, or coffee shop. Nilofer Merchant wrote in *Harvard Business Review* about her own transition to walking meetings after realizing that, like many Americans, she was sitting way too much while she worked. Merchant traded her coffee shop meetings for walking meetings and immediately saw the benefits. Likewise, Melmed finds that merely holding some of her meetings while walking has given her the necessary time to "unplug" that she needs in order to be an effective writer.

Recent research finds that the act of walking leads to increases in creative thinking. This certainly supports the idea that walking meetings are useful. Plenty of anecdotal evidence also suggests that walking meetings lead to more honest exchanges with employees and are more productive than traditional sit-down meetings.

Based on this, we undertook an exploratory study of the benefits associated with walking. We surveyed a population of approximately 150 working adults in the United States to gather input about their walking meeting and work habits. In short, we found that those who participate in walking meetings are 5.25% more likely to report being creative at their jobs than those who do not. Additionally, the responses suggest that walking meetings support cognitive engagement—or focus—on the job. Those who participate in walking meetings are 8.5% more likely to report high levels of engagement.

What we found adds support to the notion that walking meetings are beneficial for workers. Is an increase in creativity of 5.25% likely to make or break a business? Probably not. But look at these findings through the lens of a cost-benefit analysis. The costs associated with regularly participating in walking meetings are next to nil. Keep in mind that walking meetings are *not* breaks from work. They are meetings that would have taken place regardless of whether they were held in someone's office or while walking around your building complex. There may be no cheaper way to achieve moderate increases in creativity and engagement.

Just how do walking meetings produce these positive benefits in the workplace? Ted Eytan, a physician and medical director of the Kaiser Permanente Center for Total Health and a vocal advocate of walking meetings, has some ideas. First, from a neurochemical perspective, Eytan emphasizes that our brains are more relaxed during walks due to the release of certain chemicals. This aids executive function, which governs how we focus on tasks and deal with unforeseen events, among other things. Open-ended responses to our survey seemed to back this up in that people said they had moments of creativity sparked by walking meetings.

Furthermore, Eytan believes walking meetings lead to better employee engagement by breaking down barriers between supervisor and subordinate or between coworkers. He sees the bonding achieved through walking meetings as a micro version of the connection often made between coworkers who travel together on business trips. David Haimes, a senior director of product development at Oracle, has experienced this in his meetings with team members: "The fact that we are walking side by side means the conversation is more peer to peer than when I'm in my office and they're across a desk from me, which reinforces the organizational hierarchy."

To be sure, walking meetings aren't always the right choice (and not everyone is physically able to participate in them). Sometimes it is valuable to have materials or a whiteboard close at hand, and sometimes, as in an intense negotiation, it is important to be face-to-face. The best choices for walking meetings are situations in which colleagues are conferring on decisions or exploring possible solutions. Indeed, in our survey, participants who held managerial and professional positions experienced more of a creativity boost from walking meetings than those in technical or administrative jobs (though all categories realized some benefits).

If you are inspired to give walking meetings a try, here are a few tips that can help your walking meeting go well:

Consider including an "extracurricular" destination on your route.

Eytan, whose office is located in Washington, D.C., often mentions the nearby Washington Coliseum as a place to stroll by and notes it's where the Beatles played their first U.S. concert. Naming a point of interest, he says, provides more rationale and incentive for others to go for a walk.

Avoid making the destination a source of unneeded calories.

One of the arguments in favor of walking meetings is the health benefit. However, this is easily negated if the walking meeting leads to a 425-calorie white-chocolate mocha that wouldn't otherwise be consumed.

Don't surprise colleagues or clients with walking meetings.

It's fine to suggest a walk if it seems appropriate in the moment, as long as it's clear that you'll be fine with a "maybe next time." But if you're planning ahead to spend your time with someone in a walking meeting, have the courtesy to notify them in advance. Doing so allows them to arrive dressed for comfort, perhaps having changed shoes. You might also keep water bottles on hand to offer on warm days.

Stick to small groups.

Haimes recommends a maximum of three people for a walking meeting.

Have fun.

Enjoy the experience of combining work with a bit of exercise and fresh air. Our data shows that those who participate in walking meetings are more satisfied in their jobs than their colleagues who don't.

Based on our survey and the clear case to be made for walking in general as a key to good health, it's smart to make walking meetings a habit—or at least to give them a try.

Russell Clayton is an assistant professor of management at Saint Leo University's Donald R. Tapia School of Business. Follow him on Twitter @ProfessorRWC. **Christopher Thomas** is an assistant professor of management at Saint Louis University's John Cook School of Business. **Jack Smothers** is an assistant professor of management at the University of Southern Indiana's Romain College of Business.

CHAPTER 29

Stand-Up Meetings Don't Work for Everybody

by Bob Frisch

Stand-up meetings have become a routine part of the workday in many organizations, mostly due to the adoption of agile and other innovative management methods. These are usually brief daily progress sessions in which an initiative team updates and coordinates efforts. The phrase "stand up" is literal—participants remain standing for the duration of the meeting—and the reason is

---

Adapted from content posted on hbr.org on May 27, 2016.

speed. You want people to rapidly surface issues and solve disagreements. As the Wikipedia entry for stand-up meetings explains, "The discomfort of standing for long periods is intended to keep the meetings short."

While it's hard to argue with the success of agile tactics, it's worth taking a moment to question the wisdom of an organization adopting stand-up meetings on a widespread basis. They don't work for all interactions, and as with anything, treating them as a one-size-fits-all solution can have unintended consequences.

When I was a managing partner at Accenture, our organization and change strategy team helped design a new conference facility for one of our offices. We specifically varied the table shapes and sizes. Some rooms had a large round one in the center, others the classic boat-shaped, boardroom model. We had open-ended rectangles and squares, as well as U-shaped (with the boss typically seated at the center of the bottom of the U) and V-shaped (where the facilitator can move forward to stand in front of the individual participants) options. The reason for such variety is clear: The dynamics of a meeting are directly related to how people are seated relative to the boss, to one another, and to the presenter or facilitator.

Now think about a stand-up meeting, in which there is no rhyme or reason to how people are positioned. And overlay that with physical differences between teammates. Imagine someone who is 5′3″ trying to make a point when a 6′4″ colleague is standing in front of them, or picture the two debating the pros and cons of a critical problem while standing up. Don't think that's an issue? Then I'd bet you're not 5′3″. Remember too that, statistically speaking, the average male is taller than the average female, so height-ism often carries over into sexism.

Consider also a healthy 25-year-old negotiating a difficult compromise with a 63-year-old peer who suffers from a mild heart condition, with the "time clock" for resolution set by the fact that both have to stand for the length of the conversation. The higher stamina of the younger worker could certainly put an unappreciated thumb on the scale in their favor. Attempting to compensate for these differences by, for example, telling the short people to stand in front or offering the older worker a seat while everyone else stands only serves to reinforce these inequalities. Chairs may make meetings longer, but, depending on the layout of the table, they also put everyone on equal footing (so to speak).

I'm not advocating for eliminating stand-up meetings. They can be effective in certain circumstances, and research has shown that they can boost group productivity (see the preface of this book for more on the benefits of stand-up meetings). But any organization that uses them regularly should review how, when, and why they're being held. Is one stand-up per day or week appropriate for your team instead of several? Should stand-up meetings be limited to 5 or 10 minutes or allowed to go longer, occasionally substantially so? Will people really perform better at the desired activity—brainstorming, discussing, decision making, and so on—while on their feet?

Assume you were 5′3″ or in ill health or the most petite female in your organization having a raging disagreement with a tall, young, fit male. Would you want to be standing or seated?

Bob Frisch is the managing partner of the Strategic Offsites Group, a Boston-based consultancy; author of *Who's In The Room? How Great Leaders Structure and Manage the Teams Around Them* (Jossey-Bass, 2012); and coauthor, with Cary Greene, of *Simple Sabotage: A Modern Field Manual for Detecting and Rooting Out Everyday Behaviors That Undermine Your Workplace* (HarperOne, 2015). He is the author of four *Harvard Business Review* articles, including "Off-Sites That Work" (June 2006), and is a frequent contributor to hbr.org.

CHAPTER 30

Leadership Summits That Work

by Bob Frisch and Cary Greene

Every year, in virtually all large and midsize companies, high-level leaders come together for a leadership summit. These events usually last two to four days and can rack up millions of dollars in costs: airfare and accommodations for the 50 to 500 or so attendees, fees for outside speakers, production expenses, the many person days that go into planning, and the enormous opportunity cost incurred by taking so many top managers away from their normal duties for several days.

Reprinted from *Harvard Business Review*, March 2015 (product #R1503F).

When executed well, these meetings are certainly worth the time and expense. They can serve as a powerful catalyst to align leaders, develop solutions to problems, introduce new strategies, and fuel collaboration across the organization. But many companies squander this rare opportunity to harness the collective knowledge of their frontline leaders.

The typical summit begins with a numbing sequence of platform presentations from a parade of C-level executives. Later sessions address topics, such as a new ad campaign or a product rollout schedule, that concern only a portion of the people in the room. A motivational speaker adds a dollop of entertainment. Some breakout sessions and an open mic Q&A with the top team, emceed by the CEO, pass for an exchange of ideas.

Information, proposals, and solutions flow in only one direction—from the top down—and not all that coherently. Attendees leave only slightly better informed and better networked than when they arrived. It's usually not clear whether they've understood the messages they're supposed to take back to their people, much less what anyone would be expected to do as a result. A huge opportunity has been missed. Contrary to what leaders and planners assume, you *can* have genuine and productive conversations with hundreds of people at once. Over the past decade we have designed and conducted leadership summits for thousands of executives in scores of companies, ranging from *Fortune* 500 multinationals to German *Mittelstand* family businesses, and we've seen such conversations take place. Remarkably straightforward strategies and practices can ensure that information flows not only down from the top but also up from the group, and across it, in a way that allows leaders to direct the conversation without inhibiting creative responses. By applying the appropriate techniques before, during, and after the meeting, C-level leaders can get the full value of the knowledge of their frontline executives; see to it that participants leave with unambiguous messages that their employees can turn into action; and transform a meeting that often lulls people to sleep into an event that gets the organization's synapses firing.

Before the Summit

Why do CEOs and their top teams settle for less-than-optimal leadership conferences? A few executives may shy away from a real exchange of ideas for fear of losing control of the meeting. But most leaders and meeting planners simply assume that the events are too unwieldy to allow for much more than an annual update and marching orders from the top.

Here's how the planning process generally unfolds: Some 6 to 12 months in advance, a midlevel executive from HR, finance, strategy, marketing, or corporate communications is charged by the CEO or another top executive with planning the summit. He struggles to get on the executive team's calendar to discuss it. When he does, he uses his allotted 15 minutes to offer up some possible locations, three to five potential guest speakers, and a preliminary agenda seemingly related to a theme. Such themes are often so laughably vacuous—"One company, one vision," "Forward together," "Creating a common future"—that virtually any presentation or activity could be made to fit them. Executive team members spend a few minutes reacting to the locations. They may suggest a few more speakers. And then they promptly forget about the summit until a few weeks before the event, when the planner starts reminding them that they need to pull their presentations together.

That's when people start paying attention. C-level executives, division presidents, and function heads begin lobbying to add speaking slots or favored subjects to the agenda. The planner, lacking any real authority, attempts to allot them all time. Sometimes the CEO suddenly remakes the entire agenda. The result is a highly fragmented or superficial meeting conceived entirely from the perspective of top executives, with hardly a thought given to what the attendees are likely to take away from it, much less what they might contribute.

It doesn't have to be like this. Because these complicated conferences are scheduled so far in advance, there's plenty of time to take the steps needed to create a coherent, focused event. (Table 30-2 at the end of this chapter lays out the timeframe and important milestones for a summit from prep work to post-summit follow-up.)

Assign clear roles that have real authority.

Because the lines between directing, designing, planning, and coordinating a summit can blur, it often turns out that no one is clearly in charge of shaping the event. Roles and responsibilities should be clarified at the outset (see the sidebar "Who Should Do What?"). Rather than viewing meeting planning as a lower-level administrative function, the top executive convening the summit (the "meeting owner") should designate a summit director and grant that person the authority to control the agenda and to say no to people asking to add things that don't fit its focus. Working with a design team, the director should oversee the creation of all pre-meeting, in-meeting, and post-meeting materials and activities. A coordinator, reporting to the director, should be appointed to handle scheduling, travel, production, and logistics with the venue. An emcee should be selected to introduce the sessions and speakers, smooth transitions, clarify questions from the audience to the speakers, and present instant polls and other social media input during the event. Facilitators are also needed to help guide small-group discussions.

WHO SHOULD DO WHAT?

Meeting Owner

- ***Who***
  - The CEO or a member of the executive team
- ***What***
  - Initiates the meeting and designates a Summit Director
  - Makes final decisions on the meeting's objectives, structure, and design
  - Retains ultimate accountability for achievement of the objectives

(*continued*)

WHO SHOULD DO WHAT?

Executive Team

- ***What***
    - Provides input on the objectives and agenda
    - Develops content with the help of the Content Editor
    - Participates in presentations and panels
    - Tracks progress on commitments made at the summit

Summit Director

- ***Who***
    - An internal or external strategy, HR, or marketing executive; reports to the Meeting Owner
- ***What***
    - Works with the Meeting Owner and the Executive Team to confirm objectives
    - Owns the agenda
    - Works with the design team to create all meeting materials and activities
    - Manages the planning on a daily basis

Design Team

- ***Who***
    - Led by the Summit Director; includes two or three other senior executives

- ***What***
  - Creates the detailed agenda
  - Deploys and analyzes all meeting surveys
  - Confirms meeting design

Content Editor

- ***Who***
  - A midlevel strategy or communications executive or a third-party speechwriter
- ***What***
  - Tasked by the Meeting Owner with overseeing development of content, ensuring that all presentations are aligned with the objectives and coordinated with one another
  - Attends rehearsals and provides feedback to presenters

Coordinator

- ***Who***
  - A midlevel event planning or HR executive
- ***What***
  - Coordinates scheduling, travel, and lodging
  - Handles venue logistics
  - Coordinates with speakers and other outside vendors

(continued)

WHO SHOULD DO WHAT?

Emcee

- ***Who***
    - Could be the Meeting Owner, the Summit Director, or someone outside the company
- ***What***
    - Introduces sessions and speakers
    - Creates smooth transitions between sessions
    - Summarizes discussions, clarifies questions from audience members, and presents instant polling and social media input during the event

Facilitators

- ***What***
    - Guide small-group discussions in breakout or table sessions

Define a clear set of objectives for the conference by starting with the right questions.

The summit director's first contact with the CEO and the executive team may need to include a discussion of locations—an issue that requires a long lead time. But that's not the most important topic. The director should begin by asking two questions: "What do you want the outcome of the meeting to be from the perspective of the attendees?" and "What do you want them to say when their teams ask, 'What happened at the big meeting?'"

The answers aren't always readily apparent. But after some discussion, most executive teams develop a few concrete objectives. Depending on a company's circumstances, objectives might include aligning everyone around a common set of priorities, solving problems impeding company progress, driving a cultural transformation, or accelerating the integration of a major acquisition. Typically, executives will want to specify several outcomes, but the important point is to formulate them as outcomes, not as a grab bag of agenda items loosely connected by a vague theme.

Take, for example, a consumer products company we'll call Kallos, which has more than 35,000 employees and hundreds of thousands of sales reps. A new leader had succeeded a celebrity CEO, who in his wake left financial problems, low morale, and a culture that tolerated broken promises on the part of managers. The new CEO and his team, wishing to shake things up, developed five objectives for their summit of 200 executives: reach a realistic understanding of the current state of the company, including the need to drive growth; restore employees' faith in the brand; prepare to embark on a cost-reduction program in a way that would not adversely affect consumers; ensure that everyone understood what they needed to do in the near and long term to fulfill those goals; and lay the groundwork to make sure everyone followed through on his or her promises.

Start the conversation before anyone leaves home.

Eight to ten weeks before the meeting, attendees should be surveyed so that the summit director can determine how much time to spend on each objective and identify related issues that should be addressed. To gauge people's current view of the five objectives, Kallos administered an anonymous survey that asked respondents, among other things, how proud they were of the quality and performance of the company's products, how comfortable they would be describing the financial situation of the company to a newly hired employee, and to what extent they believed that managers they dealt with on a day-to-day basis behaved as if they were accountable for their actions. When 90% of the 200 respondents indicated that they were proud of the brand, the focus of the objective "restore faith in the brand" was shifted to "determine how to communicate our pride in the brand to sales reps." Open-ended survey questions included the standard "What's the one question you or your team would like addressed at the upcoming conference?" and "If you were riding in the elevator with the CEO and could tell him the one thing that would most improve the company's prospects, what would it be?"

Design the summit around the objectives and coordinate the content.

Podium presentations, breakouts, and interactive sessions should be not only relevant to the meeting objectives but also coordinated so that together they form a coherent whole. This is commonsensical, but rare. That's because the first time anyone other than a speaker or a few of his reports hears any of the podium presentations is often at the meeting itself.

Focusing C-level and other stage presentations on the objectives and making sure the presentations tie together requires appointing an individual as a single point of editorial contact. This role may be filled by someone from HR or corporate communications, or by a third-party speechwriter, but whoever it is should enjoy the protection of the meeting owner, who must deflect attempts to interfere. Four to six weeks before the meeting, the content editor should begin to assist all presenters, including outside speakers, in using one or more of the meeting's objectives as the starting point and backbone of their presentations and to coordinate the presentations with one another. The editor should attend rehearsals and provide feedback. He must hold the line against presenters who say they have a few extra slides but promise they can get through them in the allotted time and those who try to cram mountains of information onto each slide. With the guidance of a firm editorial hand, hours of formerly "must have" presentations by a succession of C-level executives will be transformed into short, pithy, coordinated talks.

Engage participants in the issues in the days leading up to the summit.

Seven to ten days before the meeting, attendees can be given reading material focused on the objectives. Include only the minimum amount necessary to set up discussions planned for the event. We've found that carefully focused and framed material usually takes no more than 60 minutes to read.

An orientation webcast, similarly lasting no more than an hour, can also prepare participants to make meaningful contributions at the summit. For one luxury goods company, a key objective of an upcoming leadership conference was to prepare the organization for a new global e-commerce division, which would supplant an outmoded regional structure. Before the meeting, participants were required to join in on one of three webcasts conducted by the new division head, who used a few simple diagrams to explain the new operating structure and then answered typed-in questions from participants. Instead of wasting valuable conference time explaining the structure, top leaders were able to have a problem-solving session about its implementation with knowledgeable, well-prepared attendees—the people who would ultimately have to make the new structure work.

During the Summit

Solid pre-meeting work clarifies the objectives, coordinates the content, and initiates engagement with attendees. The design and execution of the meeting itself should make that work come alive in what is in essence a series of structured conversations, carefully orchestrated to generate ideas, alignment, and, often, surprises along the way. Employing some simple principles and tools can make that happen.

Pay attention to the pace and rhythm of the meeting.

Kallos kicked off its conference with a brief (15-minute) keynote in which the CEO introduced the meeting objectives and framed what was going to unfold. Day one was devoted to the first two objectives: understanding the current state of the company and communicating pride in the brand. Two 20-minute podium presentations, each focused on one objective, were broken up by exercises performed by each table and breakout sessions, followed by reports to the entire assembly. During lunch, a guest speaker addressed the drivers of successful direct selling, offered a case study, and took questions from the audience. After lunch, presentations from the product and marketing group, along with several exercises, focused on communicating pride in the brand, particularly to sales reps. Day two—featuring a similar mix of presentations, exercises, and breakouts, and a Q&A with the executive team—was devoted to the remaining objectives: cost reduction, accountability, and commitment. An abbreviated day three included breakouts by region and concluded with a call to action from the CEO and promises from the executive team to track and support the commitments individuals and groups had made during the summit.

IT'S TIME TO BREAK UP WITH BREAKOUT GROUPS

by Andrew McAfee

Does anyone actually enjoy breakout groups? It's a serious question. I participate in more than a few full-day or longer meetings every year—management retreats, training sessions, meetings of centers and professional

(continued)

IT'S TIME TO BREAK UP WITH BREAKOUT GROUPS

societies, and so on—and there's nothing I dread seeing on the agenda more than a time slot devoted to "breakout groups."

This time slot usually follows a presentation on an important topic. The organizers then ask participants to split up into breakout groups for an hour. Groups could be organized in any number of other ways, and participants are typically assigned into these groups randomly. The groups report back for 30 minutes, then everyone goes to lunch.

I find this a complete waste of an hour and a half. For one thing, the random assignments mean that many (most?) people spend the time in a group where they know little about the topic and probably also care little about it. For another, the reporting back is rushed, superficial ("we talked about *X*, then we talked about *Y*"), and rarely questioned. And finally, I don't think I've ever seen the results of breakout groups actually used for anything.

I have also noticed that breakout groups are a great way to take energy out of the room. People usually head off to them with an air of resignation and report back from them in monotone.

Breakouts aren't the product of sadistic minds, though. They're put into agendas by well-meaning people who don't want participants to passively sit all day while one person after another drones on at them from onstage. Breakout groups are intended to break up the monotony of a long meeting and get people talking to each other about key topics. These are worthy goals; breakout groups are just lousy at realizing them.

What could work better? I think time slots devoted to mini "unconferences" would. I first came across the concept at FOO ("friends of O'Reilly") events organized by tech guru Tim O'Reilly. At an unconference, time slots and meeting rooms are predetermined, but nothing else is. Using whiteboards or sticky notes, people propose sessions that they want to lead or facilitate and also decide (by looking at the whiteboards or sticky notes) which ones they want to attend. The photo here shows a portion of the agenda for the recently completed FOO Camp.

This agenda was assembled on the fly and reflected the topics participants cared enough about to volunteer their time, energy, and knowledge. Attendance at each session reflected relative interest in the topic among all participants. Attendance varies widely, but

(*continued*)

IT'S TIME TO BREAK UP WITH BREAKOUT GROUPS

this is not perceived as a problem; some topics are just of narrower interest than others.

I think it would be straightforward to adopt the unconference approach to time slots at corporate meetings. If the organizers had a couple of topics that they wanted to be sure to cover, they could put them on the whiteboard before opening it up to others. And the organizers could wander around the rooms while sessions were taking place to see which ones had the most attendance and energy. Those should be the ones whose leaders report back to the group as a whole.

Andrew McAfee is the codirector of the Initiative on the Digital Economy in the MIT Sloan School of Management. He is the author of *Enterprise 2.0* and the coauthor, with Erik Brynjolfsson, of *The Second Machine Age*.

Adapted from content posted on hbr.org on July 18, 2012.

Allow for flexibility within sessions.

Given the many moving parts of large, multiday meetings—presentations, breaks, meals, breakouts, audiovisual setup, and the like—deviation from the schedule is impossible. Even so, flexibility can be maintained *within* sessions to address issues that arise or to pursue productive lines of discussion. For example, at the luxury goods company's leadership summit, the division president conducted an instant poll asking attendees if they would feel comfortable explaining to others a strategy she'd just outlined. When a large percentage of the 90 people there said no, she asked participants to anonymously submit written questions, which she addressed on the spot. Only after a second instant poll indicated that virtually all attendees were comfortable explaining the strategy to others did the session proceed as planned.

Improve the quality and effectiveness of top-down communication.

During conferences, top-down communication generally takes place in three ways: podium presentations, videos, and Q&As with the executive team. If the editor responsible for coordinating content has done a good job, the podium presentations will be succinct and integrated. We have found that an ideal podium session includes no more than four presenters who speak for 15 to 20 minutes each, using just five to seven slides.

Most leadership summits also include an open mic Q&A session in which attendees ask questions of the CEO or the executive team. The worthy intent is to provide unvarnished answers from the top in response to what's really on people's minds. But what actually happens is wearyingly predictable: impromptu speeches disguised as questions, multipart inquiries requiring time-consuming answers, softball questions intended to curry favor with the leaders, and questions relevant to only a handful of people in the room—to all of which the leaders must extemporize answers. Meanwhile, attendees who are hesitant to raise provocative (or any) issues in front of a large audience remain silent.

There is a better way. If you hold the Q&A on the second day, you can ask people to submit questions at the end of day one. That evening, the summit director, editor, and meeting owner can select the best questions and add ones they feel should have been asked; the executive team can formulate responses to the more provocative ones; and the rest can be parceled out to the appropriate executive team members. Many leaders resist this technique as somehow manipulative or undemocratic, feeling that an open mic is more honest. We argue that, in fact, this approach is ultimately *more* democratic, because it ensures that a cross section of questions are answered in a way that brings substance to what is often an empty exercise.

Use high- and low-tech approaches to capture the thinking of frontline executives and communicate it upward.

Numerous techniques can be employed to harvest the ideas of conference attendees. To determine which tool to use when, the director should ask four closely related questions:

- What kind of input is needed: Opinions? Questions? Brainstorming? Solutions to a specific problem? Complex judgments?
- What characteristics should the communication have: Anonymous or public? Guided or open-ended? In real time or delayed?

- What's the right unit from which to get that kind of input: Individuals? Small tables? Larger breakout groups?
- What are the most effective tools for gathering that kind of input from that unit: Polling? Discussion templates? Worksheets? Complex exercises? (See table 30-1.)

Polling technology as simple as a wireless keypad or an app accessed through a smartphone or web browser allows participants to respond to yes or no questions or to indicate how much they agree with statements such as "I am confident that we will achieve our revenue goals for the next two years." Polling results can be projected at the front of the room in real time for everyone to see (the luxury goods company did this). Text messages work well when more-substantive answers are desired, as when 140 attendees at a leadership conference for an information management company were asked to name the biggest obstacle to the company achieving its growth goals. Among the responses were: "We lack focus," "Too many initiatives distract our attention," "We lack new products," "The plan to grow is not clear," and "Our ability to attract and retain top-notch talent is questionable." The responses were compiled, and a subset was displayed on a screen at the front of the room for discussion.

Such audience response systems can also facilitate highly complex group deliberations during breakout sessions. Take, for example, an exercise we call "the poker chip game," first described in the 2006 *Harvard Business Review* article "Off-Sites That Work," which allows

TABLE 30-1

The right tool to gather input from a crowd

	Response		Participants		Questions	
	Anonymous	**Public**	**Individual**	**Group**	**Open-ended**	**Pre-defined options**
PRE-MEETING						
Survey	●	●	●		●	●
Webcast Q&A		●	●		●	
IN-MEETING						
Question cards	●		●	●	●	
Keypad polling	●		●	●		●
Poker chip game		●	●	●		●
Text-in answers	●		●	●	●	●
Table discussions		●		●	●	
Breakouts		●		●	●	
Pairs		●		●	●	
Commitment worksheets		●	●	●	●	
Give and Get		●	●		●	
POST-MEETING						
Survey	●	●	●		●	●
Intracorporate social network	●	●	●		●	

small groups using a game board and some poker chips to determine how a company should allocate its resources. Thanks to technology advances, the results of such exercises can be displayed instantly, providing comprehensive feedback to guide further deliberation.

Kallos conducted this game with its 200 attendees, who were divided among 20 tables. Each table was given 66 poker chips and a game board on which to allocate the discretionary portion of the annual $3.3 billion operating budget. The result was eye-opening for top management. Every table significantly reduced the amount of money budgeted for product development and packaging and increased the allocation for marketing. In the healthy discussion that ensued, a consensus emerged that growth was being constrained by an inability to tell consumers a compelling story.

Many old-school, low-tech tools are still remarkably effective in gathering input, including 3 × 5 cards on which participants write questions; color-coded cards, which participants can hold up in response to questions; templates to guide small-group discussions; and reports from breakout sessions.

Such tools can make brainstorming—often unwieldy and unfocused when conducted with hundreds of people—more productive. Using a technique called "self-facilitated dialogue," Kallos had pairs of participants spend 10 minutes in a conversation, guided by a paper template, about what the company should *start* doing, *stop* doing, and *continue* doing in the next 6 months to implement a strategy for increasing revenue. A member of each pair recorded the results of the conversation on the template. Another template was used to capture the suggestions from all five dialogues around the table and to communicate those results to the entire assembly.

A "round robin" variation of the breakout can be particularly effective in eliciting a full range of reactions to a series of issues. Instead of having 200 people sit through podium presentations on each of the 5 objectives, for instance, Kallos broke attendees into 5 groups of 40. Five executive team members, each responsible for explaining one of the objectives, rotated through the groups. Participants asked questions and provided input on every objective (captured on the lowly flowchart), an opportunity that top-down podium explanations cannot provide.

Make sure ideas flow across the meeting to lay the groundwork for genuine collaboration afterward.

The summit may be the only time in the year when many participants see one another. Yet all too often, connections are left to happen by chance—at meals, in breakout groups, or during coffee breaks and cocktail hours. To connect in a deliberate and more constructive way, we use an exercise we call "Give and Get."

Typically, this exercise is part of a breakout session with anywhere from 30 to 60 people. Two charts, one labeled "Give" and the other marked "Get," hang on opposite walls. On each chart, each participant is assigned a column with his or her photo, name, function, business unit, and location at the top.

In the Get column, each participant posts a card that completes this sentence: "If I could get help in one area that would make me and my team more successful in the coming year, it would be . . ." The card is like a classified ad, asking for a particular type of expertise or assistance. Perhaps someone needs help developing a product feature, reconfiguring a plant layout, or adjusting a customer contract to achieve a certain outcome. In the Give column, the participant posts a card that completes the sentence, "If I could name one area in which my team and I have developed expertise that may be useful to others in the company, it would be . . ."

After all the Give and Get cards have been posted, participants are given Post-it notes and asked to circulate around the room. If a participant sees a Get that she or someone she knows could address, she leaves a Post-it with a message about how she might be able to assist. If she sees a Give that could be helpful to her, she places a Post-it with a message under the card.

Once participants have posted all their offers to assist and requests for help, they switch rooms with another breakout group and survey the Gives and Gets on those walls. If each breakout room holds 50 people, each participant will see 100 requests for help and 100 offers. Those 200 Gives and Gets typically generate hundreds of Post-its, creating a network of connections across locations, functions, and business units. After the meeting, all the Gives and Gets are recorded and distributed to the appropriate individuals for follow-up.

These and other exercises, designed to ripple far beyond the walls of the meeting venue, can be explicitly tied to the objectives of the summit. Kallos, for instance, used a technique called the Wall of Commitments to further its goal of getting participants to follow through on their promises.

Here's how it worked: The packet each participant received on arrival contained worksheets printed on carbonless copy paper. At the end of day one, largely devoted to top-line growth, participants filled out a worksheet that asked them to list specific steps they and their teams would take to increase revenue immediately, in the coming 3 months, and in the coming 12 months. They handed in the original and kept the copy.

During the evening, unbeknownst to the attendees, 200 linear feet of eight-foot foam board walls were constructed in the auditorium. Participants' commitment sheets were posted on the walls under their names, affiliations, and photos. After dinner, the nine members of the executive committee went around the room with a stack of Post-it notes imprinted with their own names and posted comments on the commitment sheets. The comments ranged from "Great idea" and "Let me know if I can help with that" to "This is disappointing" and "I was hoping you were more ambitious than this."

The following morning, when the 200 participants walked into the auditorium, their reaction, as intended, was shock. As they wandered the perimeter of the room reading the comments about their own and their colleagues' commitments, some were visibly embarrassed. During the next two days, the commitment sheets that were generated to address the other objectives—which were added to the walls—became more thoughtful. Not only did the quality of the promised actions greatly improve, but attendees learned what colleagues throughout the organization would be focusing on in the coming months, creating opportunities for collaboration. In several instances, participants formed teams to work on initiatives, coordinate their efforts, or establish discussion groups about commitments that dovetailed.

The element of surprise in this exercise can have a galvanizing effect, and identifying individuals creates opportunities for networking. But both features can be adjusted. For example, to spur ambitious commitments from the outset, participants can be warned that the executive team members will comment on their posts. To avoid embarrassing participants, the comments can be provided to them individually rather than posted publicly. Because Kallos was looking to jump-start a culture change, it dialed up both features.

After the Summit

Because companies generally don't design leadership conferences around concrete objectives, they typically pay little attention to what happens afterward. Morale may have been lifted, but the absence of clear direction usually results in halfhearted follow-up and few tangible outcomes. If, however, you've begun with a purpose in mind, you can do some simple things to make sure it is achieved.

Create succinct materials for attendees to take home.

The real moment of truth for a summit occurs when leaders return to their divisions, regions, or functions, and people ask, "So, what happened at the meeting?" Those leaders should be able to answer clearly and explain the implications. But that's hard to do if all they've brought back is a notepad full of haphazard observations, doodles, and a few vague slogans, as so often happens. Far better to supply them with communication aids such as talking points, pithy presentations, or video links to drive home the objectives of the meeting and form the basis of discussions with their teams. Meeting participants are encouraged to add their own content to make the messaging relevant. In some cases we have conducted sessions before the close of the meeting in which leaders, working with tablemates, simulate communicating major points to their teams and get feedback on both content and style.

Ensure that all commitments made at the summit—up, down, and across the organization—are kept.

Answers to all questions that were not addressed at the meeting, whether from executive team leaders or from attendees, should be provided within one to two weeks. What's more, the executive team should track progress on any initiatives or commitments undertaken. Thirty days after the Kallos summit, each participant received an e-mail from an executive committee member listing the actions that person had committed to in the "next

30 days" section of his or her worksheet, followed by a single sentence: "Shoot me a quick e-mail letting me know how these went."

Continue the conversation.

Within 48 hours of the meeting's conclusion, conduct a survey to see if the goals were fulfilled and to ask participants about what worked, what could be improved, and what should be jettisoned for next year's summit. Repeating the pre-meeting survey questions will give you valuable insights into the impact of the event. For example, the percentage of people saying they fully understood the company's growth strategy rose from 37% in Kallos's pre-meeting survey to 82% after the summit, and the percentage describing themselves as "optimistic" or "very optimistic" about the company's prospects rose from 49% to 80%. To encourage collaboration within teams or discussion groups that emerged at the summit, either by design or by happenstance, enable attendees to continue the conversation among themselves through an intracorporate social network.

By adjusting how information flows—more up, more effectively down, and a lot more across—you can turn a leadership summit into a high point of the annual management calendar, one that makes a real difference. Leaders will know in advance that they'll be heard. People across the organization will understand what the results of the meeting mean for them. Executive committee members will know that they're going to get valuable

TABLE 30-2

Countdown to the leadership summit

Objectives	Content	Meeting design and structure	Speakers and presenters	Logistics
		4–6 Months		
Begin conversations on desired outcomes.		Appoint Summit Director and assemble design team.	Identify potential outside speakers.	Select venue and finalize dates.
		90 Days		
Discuss potential objectives.	Determine required materials for pre-meeting readings and summit presentations.	Determine topics and sequencing.	Secure outside speakers.	Send meeting invites. Finalize travel arrangements.
		60 Days		
Solicit input on potential objectives from key stakeholders.	Hold pre-meeting webcast. Deploy pre-meeting survey.	Design high-level agenda.	Determine internal presenters and discuss potential objectives. Select Emcee.	

30 Days				
Establish final set of objectives.	Compile survey results. Draft pre-meeting readings and session material.	Refine structure on the basis of survey results. Draft detailed agenda, including tools to gather input.	Review internal presentations.	Walk through the venue and confirm details, including agenda timing.
1–2 Weeks				
Include objectives in pre-meeting reading material.	Distribute reading material to attendees. Finalize session content.	Conduct final walk-through of detailed agenda.	Conduct rehearsals with presenters and Emcee. Confirm external speakers.	Secure supplies and make table and breakout assignments. Test audiovisual equipment.
During				
Regularly remind attendees of the objectives.	Compile input gathered through breakouts, keypad polls, etc.	Remind attendees of structure and agenda	Ensure that speakers and presenters understand their roles.	Coordinate ad hoc needs with venue.
After				
	Deploy post-meeting survey. Distribute summit output and other communication aids.	Follow up on commitments. Establish forums for continued collaboration.		

input and that the meeting will be well worth the considerable investment. And enthusiasm will build for each succeeding summit, as people look forward to a memorable event that's strategically significant for everyone.

Bob Frisch is the managing partner of the Strategic Offsites Group, a Boston-based consultancy, and is the author of *Who's In The Room? How Great Leaders Structure and Manage the Teams Around Them* (Jossey-Bass, 2012). He is the author of four *Harvard Business Review* articles, including "Off-Sites That Work" (June 2006). **Cary Greene** is a partner of the Strategic Offsites Group. They are coauthors of *Simple Sabotage: A Modern Field Manual for Detecting & Rooting Out Everyday Behaviors That Undermine Your Workplace* (HarperOne, 2015) and are frequent contributors to hbr.org.

APPENDIX A

Meeting Preparation Checklist

Use this tool to prepare for your next meeting.

Have you . . .

- ☐ Identified the specific purpose of the meeting?
- ☐ Made sure you need a meeting at all?
- ☐ Developed a preliminary agenda?
- ☐ Selected the right participants?
- ☐ Assigned roles to participants?

Adapted from *Running Meetings* (20-Minute Manager series; product #17003), Harvard Business Review Press, 2014.

- ☐ Decided where and when to hold the meeting and confirmed availability of the space?
- ☐ Sent the invitation, notifying participants when and where the meeting will be held?
- ☐ Sent the preliminary agenda to key participants and other stakeholders?
- ☐ Sent any reports or items needing advance preparation to participants?
- ☐ Followed up with invitees in person, if appropriate?
- ☐ Identified, if appropriate, the decision-making process that will be used in the meeting?
- ☐ Identified, arranged for, and tested any required equipment?
- ☐ Finalized the agenda and distributed it to all participants?
- ☐ Verified that all key participants will attend and know their roles?
- ☐ Prepared yourself?

APPENDIX B

Sample Agendas

A sample meeting agenda

Topic	Preparation	Proposed process
1 **What changes, if any, should we make to the agenda?** TIME: 2 minutes PURPOSE: Decision LEADER: Mike	None	• Mike polls team.
2 **What deltas from the previous meeting will we focus on in this meeting?** TIME: 3 minutes PURPOSE: Decision LEADER: Anne	Review applicable deltas from previous meeting notes.	• Anne reviews areas of improvement that we agreed to focus on during this meeting.

(*continued*)

Adapted from "How to Design an Agenda for an Effective Meeting," by Roger Schwarz, posted on hbr.org on March 19, 2015.

Topic	Preparation	Proposed process
3 **How do we best manage the fluctuating internal demand for our services?** TIME: 50 minutes PURPOSE: Decision LEADER: Peg	Identify relevant information, criteria, and assumptions that you believe should guide the decision.	• Statement of the problem. TIME: 5 minutes • Team identifies and agrees on relevant information to consider. TIME: 10 minutes • Identify and agree on criteria for acceptable solutions. TIME: 10 minutes • Identify and agree on assumptions. TIME: 10 minutes • Craft solutions that meet the above constraints. TIME: 15 minutes
4 **Which firm should we select for the adjacent markets acquisition study?** TIME: 15 minutes PURPOSE: Decision LEADER: Martin	Read the attached memo recommending three firms. Be prepared to ask questions and share your initial preference and your reasoning.	• Questions and additional information regarding the recommendations of the three firms. • Decision to select one firm.
5 **What developmental assignments are available during the next FY for high-potentials?** TIME: 15 minutes PURPOSE: Decision LEADER: Noah	Review the attached memo identifying the current high-potential managers and the areas in which we are seeking developmental assignments for them. If feasible, be prepared to offer an appropriate developmental assignment.	• Identify the available developmental assignments. • Match the assignments to the pool of high-potential managers. • Agree on next steps for any high-potential managers who have not been given a developmental assignment.
6 PLUS/DELTA: **What did we do well for this meeting? What should we do differently for the next meeting?** TIME: 5 minutes PURPOSE: Decision LEADER: Carrie	None	• Members identify pluses and deltas. • Team agrees on deltas to work on for next meeting.

A blank meeting agenda template

Meeting agenda

MEETING NAME ________________
DATE ________________
TIME ________________

Topic	Preparation	Proposed process
1 TIME ALLOTTED: PURPOSE: LEADER:		
2 TIME ALLOTTED: PURPOSE: LEADER:		
3 TIME ALLOTTED: PURPOSE: LEADER:		
4 TIME ALLOTTED: PURPOSE: LEADER:		
5 TIME ALLOTTED: PURPOSE: LEADER:		

Branded Books Meeting: sales, marketing, production, editorial team

9/17/16; 10:00–11:00; 307W

Jessica, Erin, Lisa, Mary, Jane, Audra, Sarah, Alex, Jen, Kate

Meeting objective:

To coordinate our marketing, sales, production, and editorial activities in order to execute our plan to generate $750,000 in sales of branded e-books across all channels: retail, e-tail, and our own website this fiscal year.

What	How	Who	Time
Introduction	• How did it go? What's the word on the new lines of books?	Mary	5 min

Book revision planning	• Overarching strategy: Need to revise/refresh before a potential customer picks up the book and says, "Outdated!"
	• Options:
	  ○ Since book display plans are done 4 months in advance, should the reprint schedule be on an 18–24 month cycle?
	  ○ Should we coordinate the revision schedule with the reprint schedule? Do we know the reprint schedule far enough in advance—or is that driven by sales?
	• Next steps
		Jane	15 min

(continued)

What	How	Who	Time
Paperback & e-book publication schedule	• We agreed that we'd offer the e-book and PDF versions of the paperbacks one month pre-bound book date, so the first group of five will be live and promoted on 2/14/17. • How do we develop an informed point of view about e-book/print book publication schedules? How do we gather best practices? • Next steps	Mary	15 min
Pre-sales meeting	• Scheduled for mid-October. • How can the team help prepare? • Should we pursue the possibility of pre-loading the first 10 Must Reads book on an e-reader? • Next steps	Mary	10 min
Merchan-dising idea	• How about grouping our books by topic rather than by series? For example, what if we grouped all of our Managing People books together? ○ *10 Must Reads on Managing People* ○ *HBR on Finding and Keeping the Best People* ○ *HBR Guide to Delivering Effective Feedback* • Next steps	Jane	10 min
Recap	• What we decided • Next steps—who's doing what	Jane	5 min

APPENDIX C

Meeting Follow-Up Checklist

Have you . . .

- ☐ Written a succinct follow-up note, including what, who, and when?
- ☐ Distributed the note to all participants?
- ☐ Recorded any task due dates in your calendar so you can follow up to make sure they're completed?
- ☐ Distributed the note to all other relevant stakeholders?

Adapted from *Running Meetings* (20-Minute Manager series; product #17003), Harvard Business Review Press, 2014.

- ☐ Followed up with key stakeholders in person to make sure they're aware of meeting highlights?
- ☐ Assessed yourself as leader?
- ☐ Assessed the outcome of the meeting?
- ☐ Met with critics?
- ☐ Thought through what you could do better next time?

APPENDIX D

Sample Follow-Up Memo

Branded Books Meeting: sales, marketing, production, editorial team

9/17/16 Follow-Up Notes

Attendees: Jessica, Erin, Lisa, Mary, Jane, Audra, Sarah, Alex, Jen, Kate

Meeting objective:

To coordinate our marketing, sales, production, and editorial activities in order to execute our plan to generate $750,000 in sales of branded e-books across all channels—retail, e-tail, and our own website this fiscal year.

What	How	Who	When
Pre-sales meeting	• Most important meeting in the buying cycle • 25 national account reps • Loved the jackets! • Sell sheets very helpful ○ Thanks to Sarah, Mary, and Alex for creating them!	Team	Done

Book revision planning	• Overarching principles
	  ○ When a content area (managing supply chains, doing business in China, marketing) undergoes a sea change, we should be ready to update ASAP.
	  ○ The new content in a refreshed book needs to be game changing.
	  ○ And we must be sure we're going to sell a lot more of the refreshed book; otherwise, we'll lose money on returns.
	  ○ Need to revise/refresh before a potential customer picks up the book and says, "Outdated!"
		Jane
		
		Jane w/ Mary and Jess
			Ongoing
			
			Ongoing

Paperback & e-book publication schedule	• We agreed that we'd offer the e-book and PDF versions of the paperbacks one month pre–bound book date, so the first group of five will be live and promoted on **2/14/17.** ○ We agreed that we'd use the branded lines as an experiment for figuring out nontraditional digital/print book release, marketing, and merchandising.	Jane Team	2/14/17

(*continued*)

What	How	Who	When
Merchan-dising idea	• What if we suggested grouping our books—all of our books, not just the branded lines—by topic rather than by series (for example, when all six 10 Must Reads are out, as well as the new paperbacks and authored books [such as Grote on performance appraisal]): ○ What if we grouped all the Managing People books together: ▪ *10 Must Reads on Managing People* ▪ *HBR on Finding and Keeping the Best People* ▪ Grote's new book on performance appraisal • In e-tail, we already do this type of grouping (Sarah and Alex); that is, thematic book lists with focus on core topics.		
	○ Need to look at Alex and Sarah's e-tail promotion of *10 Must Reads: The Essentials* with each author's related books.	Sarah	9/18/17
	○ Also need to take a field trip to some physical bookstores—before the winter weather!	Mary	10/18/17

APPENDIX E

Digital Tools to Make Your Next Meeting More Productive

by Alexandra Samuel

Meetings may seem like the ultimate holdout against the digitization of working life: After all, what's more analog than talking directly with another person? Even though the core work of a meeting—listening to and connecting with other people—hasn't changed, there are lots of ways technology can make that work easier and more effec-

---

Adapted from content posted on hbr.org on March 12, 2015 and July 3, 2015

tive. Given how much of our working lives we spend in meetings, building a digital meeting toolkit is one of the smartest investments you can make in tech-savvy productivity. Here are the tools you need.

Before Your Meeting

Find a group meeting time with Doodle, which lets you poll the various people who are part of your meeting and find a time that works for everyone. You'll get the best results if you hook it up to your own calendar (so you only offer people options that actually work for you) and if you set expectations by explaining you're using Doodle to find the time that works for as many people as possible—even if you can't find one that works for everyone.

Quickly schedule one-on-one meetings so the process of finding a time doesn't consume more time than the meeting itself. Use Google appointment slots or Calendly to set up times when you're available for calls or meetings, and when you want to take a meeting, share the link to your open slots.

If you're booking a call with someone in another time zone, make sure you're actually booking the same time into your calendars. Send an actual calendar invitation, rather than just agreeing on a time via e-mail, and as long as your calendaring app has built-in time zone support (nearly all of them do), you can avoid making a mistake. And use Every Time Zone to figure out what the time zone difference actually is, so you don't invite someone to a 4 a.m. meeting.

Find a place to meet. On-demand services like Liquidspace or Desks Near Me give you lots of options for identifying a meeting space, even when you're on the road. You can book weekly, daily, or even by the hour.

During Your Meeting

Take notes in Evernote or another dedicated digital notebook application. Capturing good, searchable notes makes meetings much more valuable, and the right note-taking tool will make it easy for you to file your meeting notes with the project or topics they relate to. Best of all, if you use the Evernote mobile app to snap pictures of your meeting whiteboard or flip charts, optical character recognition makes those handwritten notes searchable, too.

Share note taking with Google Docs. When you use a Google Docs document to capture meeting updates in more-or-less real time, you'll be able to see and contribute to each other's notes as long as you have an internet connection. (Be sure to copy the meeting notes in Evernote afterward, if that's where you like to keep all your project notes.) That means you and your team can take notes collaboratively, so that if one person's talking, another person records what's being said. This is a particularly nifty trick if you're working with one or more colleagues on a meeting with a client or another team, because you have a kind of psychic link—you can suggest ideas to one another alongside the notes you're taking. And if you don't have an internet connection but you and your colleagues all work on Macs, you can use the fab SubEthaEdit to collaborate with even less lag than you get on Google Docs, simply by creating a computer-to-computer network.

Bring an extra screen to view reference materials. The one downside of digital note taking is that if you need to refer to a document during your meeting, you have to flip back and forth between your note-taking application and your reference document. That's why I always carry my iPad. I use the application GoodReader to store any PDFs or documents I might need to look at during a meeting. And because GoodReader is hooked up to my DropBox account, I can always access a document I need to have open, even if I didn't think to preload it in GoodReader.

Collaborate with mind mapping. I'm a huge fan of mind mapping: diagramming ideas and information visually, using something that looks like a tree or flowchart. While some people actually take their meeting notes in mind map form (been there, done that, reverted to text), I find mind maps most useful when I'm part of a group discussion where we need to capture and organize ideas together. My two favorite mind-mapping apps for meetings are MindMeister (very flexible and powerful) and Popplet (less expensive, a little easier to use, less flexible). If you're using mind mapping in a face-to-face meeting, you can simply hook a projector up to one computer, but the real-time collaboration support in these apps mean they're great for using during virtual meetings, too.

Inspire new thinking. Your meeting outcomes will only be as good as the thinking that goes into them. But huddling around a PowerPoint presentation is hardly a recipe for inspiring bold new ideas. Instead, think about using a collaborative visual tool like Popplet to share ideas, so that you can reorganize them on the fly.

Convert action items to tasks. Once you leave a meeting, it's easy for follow-up steps to fall by the wayside. It really helps if everyone in a meeting actually puts their action items into their task manager—something that's a lot easier with TaskClone. A reader put me onto this service, which can scan Evernote to find any action items and then import them into your favorite task management tool.

Access your outcomes. Too often, we leave meetings with a tangible outcome, only to lose it in the digital morass. Even if you generally take your meeting notes in Evernote or another digital note-taking program, you may still have trouble tracking down that brilliant brainstorm that occurred on a pile of Post-its, the inspired idea you wrote in your paper notebook, or the meeting notes written on a flipchart. That's why it's handy to snap a photo of any written output and add it to Evernote, so that it becomes searchable.

For Virtual or Phone Meetings

While all the tools I've mentioned here are useful in both face-to-face and virtual meetings, there are a few extra tools I'd recommend for people conducting virtual or phone meetings.

Share screens faster with Join.me. I've tried GoToMeeting, WebEx, Google Hangouts, and Skype. They all work some (or even most) of the time. But the only bullet-proof screen-sharing tool I've used is Join.me. It works for me every time, and because it's so fast to set up a meeting and share a link, it works even if I'm already midcall when I realize I need to share my screen.

Choose a back channel. If you're doing a client or prospect call with colleagues who are in another office or location, keep yourselves in sync by choosing an instant messaging back channel before your meeting begins. There's nothing worse than needing to send your copresenter an urgent note but discovering you have to wait for him to read his e-mail so he can see it. A back channel chat provides a way of discreetly asking someone to let the conversation move forward or of checking in with other meeting attendees to see if they feel like your meeting has lost focus. Your back channel can be Skype, Lync, MSN, Apple Messages, or Gmail Chat—any messaging application works, as long as it has desktop support (so you're not trying to type urgent messages into your phone) and you have connected to your colleague before the meeting begins. (Send a test message just to be sure.) Even if you're using a virtual meeting application that supports private messaging, I recommend using a separate app as your back channel so you don't accidentally share your message with the client.

Record crucial phone meetings. If you're participating in a phone meeting and aren't in a position to take notes (or can't type fast enough), consider recording your call for future reference. TapeACall, which is available for both iPhone and Android, makes it really easy: Just install the app, and then conference the TapeACall number into your call. (Note that in many jurisdictions it's illegal to tape a call unless everyone consents.)

Set up these tools on your computer and mobile devices, and you'll be better equipped to make the most of your meetings. Far from distracting you from your work and colleagues, this is one place technology can help you reconnect with them—by making the time you spend together as valuable as possible.

Alexandra Samuel is a speaker, researcher, and writer who works with the world's leading companies to understand their online customers and craft data-driven reports such as "Sharing Is the New Buying." The author of *Work Smarter with Social Media* (Harvard Business Review Press, 2015), Alex holds a PhD in political science from Harvard University. Follow Alex on Twitter @awsamuel.

Index

Index

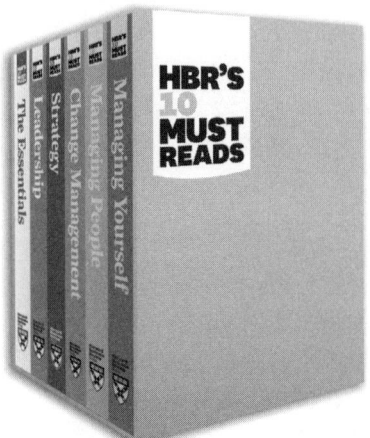

HBR Guide to **Data Analytics Basics for Managers**

Harvard Business Review Guides

Arm yourself with the advice you need to succeed on the job, from the most trusted brand in business. Packed with how-to essentials from leading experts, the HBR Guides provide smart answers to your most pressing work challenges.

The titles include:

HBR Guide to Being More Productive

HBR Guide to Better Business Writing

HBR Guide to Building Your Business Case

HBR Guide to Buying a Small Business

HBR Guide to Coaching Employees

HBR Guide to Data Analytics Basics for Managers

HBR Guide to Delivering Effective Feedback

HBR Guide to Emotional Intelligence

HBR Guide to Finance Basics for Managers

HBR Guide to Getting the Right Work Done

HBR Guide to Leading Teams

HBR Guide to Making Every Meeting Matter

HBR Guide to Managing Stress at Work

HBR Guide to Managing Up and Across

HBR Guide to Negotiating

HBR Guide to Office Politics

HBR Guide to Performance Management

HBR Guide to Persuasive Presentations

HBR Guide to Project Management

HBR Guide to **Data Analytics Basics for Managers**

HARVARD BUSINESS REVIEW PRESS

Boston, Massachusetts

Printed in the United States of America

10 9 8 7 6

Cataloging-in-Publication data is forthcoming

ISBN: 9781633694286

eISBN: 9781633694293

The paper used in this publication meets the requirements of the American National Standard for Permanence of Paper for Publications and Documents in Libraries and Archives Z39.48-1992.

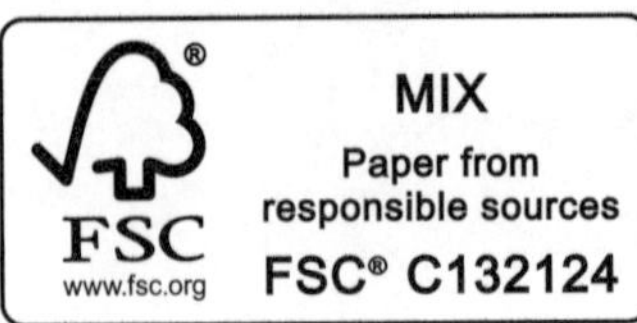

What You'll Learn

The vast amounts of data that companies accumulate today can help you understand the past, make predictions about the future, and guide your decision making. But how do you use all this data effectively? How do you assess whether your findings are accurate or significant? How do you distinguish between causation and correlation? And how do you present your results in a way that will persuade others?

Understanding data analytics is an essential skill for every manager. It's no longer enough to hand this responsibility off to data experts. To be able to rely on the evidence your analysts give you, you need to know where it comes from and how it was generated—and what it can and can't teach you.

Using quantitative analysis as part of your decision making helps you uncover new information and provides you with more confidence in your choices—and you don't need to be deeply proficient in statistics to do it. This guide gives you the basics so you can better understand how to use data and analytics as you make tough choices in your daily work. It walks you through three fundamental steps of data analysis: gathering the information you need, making sense of the numbers, and communicating those findings to get buy-in and spur others to action.

You'll learn to:

- Ask the right questions to get the information you need
- Work more effectively with data scientists
- Run business experiments and A/B tests
- Choose the right metrics to evaluate predictions and performance
- Assess whether you can trust your data
- Understand the basics of regression analysis and statistical significance
- Distinguish between correlation and causation
- Sidestep cognitive biases when making decisions
- Identify when to invest in machine learning—and how to proceed
- Communicate and defend your findings to stakeholders
- Visualize your data clearly and powerfully

Contents

Introduction

Data is coming into companies at remarkable speed and volume. From small, manageable data sets to big data that is recorded every time a consumer buys a product or likes a social media post, this information offers a range of opportunities to managers.

Data allows you to make better predictions about the future—whether a new retail location is likely to succeed, for example, or what a reasonable budget for the next fiscal year might look like. It helps you identify the causes of certain events—a failed advertising campaign, a bad quarter, or even poor employee performance—so you can adjust course if necessary. It allows you to isolate variables so that you can identify your customers' wants or needs or assess the chances an initiative will succeed. Data gives you insight on factors affecting your industry or marketplace and can inform your decisions about anything from new product development to hiring choices.

But with so much information coming in, how do you sort through it all and make sense of everything? It's tempting to hand that role off to your experts and analysts. But even if you have the brightest minds handling your data, it won't make a difference if you don't know what they're doing or what it means. Unless you know how to use that data to inform your decisions, all you have is a set of numbers.

It's quickly becoming a requirement that every decision maker have a basic understanding of data analytics. But if the thought of statistical analysis makes you sweat, have no fear. You don't need to become a data scientist or statistician to understand what the numbers mean (even if data scientists have the "sexiest job of the 21st century"—see the bonus article we've included in the appendix). Instead, you as a manager need a clear understanding of how these experts reach their results and how to best use that information to guide your own decisions. You must know where their findings come from, ask the right questions of data sets, and translate the results to your colleagues and other stakeholders in a way that convinces and persuades.

This book is not for analytics experts—the data scientists, analysts, and other specialists who do this work day in, day out. Instead, it's meant for managers who may not have a background in statistical analysis but still want to improve their decisions using data. This book will not give you a detailed course in statistics. Rather, it will help you better *use* data, so you can understand what the numbers are telling you, identify where the results of those calculations may be falling short, and make stronger choices about how to run your business.

What This Book Will Do

This guide walks you through three key areas of the data analytics process: gathering the information you need, analyzing it, and communicating your findings to others. These three steps form the core of managerial data analytics.

To fully understand these steps, you need to see the process of data analytics and your role within it at a high level. Section 1, "Getting Started," provides two pieces to help you digest the process from start to finish. First, Thomas Davenport outlines your role in data analysis and describes how you can work more effectively with your data scientist and become a better consumer of analytics. Then, you'll find an easy exercise you can do yourself to gather your own data, analyze it, and identify what to do next in light of what you've discovered.

Once you have this basic understanding of the process, you can move on to learn the specifics about each step, starting with the data search.

Gather the right information

For any analysis, you need data—that's obvious. But what data you need and how to get it can be less clear and can vary, depending on the problem to be solved. Section 2 begins by providing a list of questions to ask for a targeted data search.

There are two ways to get the information you need: by asking others for existing data and analysis or by running your own experiment to gather new data. We explore both of these approaches in turn, covering how to request information from your data experts (taking into account their needs and concerns) and using the scientific method and A/B testing for well-thought-out tests.

But any data search won't matter if you don't measure useful things. Defining the right metrics ensures that your results align with your needs. Jeff Bladt, chief data officer at DoSomething.org, and Bob Filbin, chief data scientist at Crisis Text Line, use the example of their own social media campaign to explain how to identify and work toward metrics that matter.

We end this section with a helpful process by data expert and company adviser Thomas C. Redman. Before you can move forward with any analysis, you must know if the information you have can be trusted. By following his advice, you can assess the quality of your data, make corrections as necessary, and move forward accordingly, even if the data isn't perfect.

Analyze the data

You have the numbers—now what? It's usually at this point in the process that managers flash back to their college statistics courses and nervously leave the analysis to an expert or a computer algorithm. Certainly, the data scientists on your team are there to help. But you can learn the basics of analysis without needing to understand every mathematical calculation. By focusing on how data experts and companies *use* these equations (instead of how they run them), we help you ask the right questions and inform your decisions in real-world managerial situations.

We begin section 3 by describing some basic terms and processes. We define predictive analytics and how to use them, and explain statistical concepts like regression analysis, correlation versus causation, and statistical significance. You'll also learn how to assess if machine learning can help solve your problem—and how to proceed if it does.

In this section, we also aim to help you avoid common traps as you study data and make decisions. You'll discover how to look at numbers in nonlinear ways, so your predictions are more accurate. And you will find practical ways to avoid injecting subconscious bias into your choices.

Finally, recognize when the story you're being told may be too good to be true. Even with the best data—and the best data analysts—the results may not be as clear as you think. As Michael Schrage, research fellow at MIT's Sloan School Center for Digital Business, points out in the last piece in this section, an unmentioned outlier can throw an entire conclusion off base, which is a risk you can't take with your decision making.

Communicate your findings

"Never make the mistake of assuming that the results will 'speak for themselves,'" warns Thomas Davenport in the final section of this book. You must know how to communicate the results of your analysis and use that information to persuade others and drive your decision forward—the third step in the data analytics process.

Section 4 explains how to share data with others so that the numbers support your message, rather than distract from it. The next few chapters outline when visualizations will be helpful to your data—and when they won't be—as well as the basics of making persuasive charts. You'll learn how to depict and explain the uncertainty and the probability of events, as well as what to do if someone questions your findings.

Data alone will not elicit change, though; you must use this evidence in the right way to inform and change the mindset of the person who sees it. Data is merely supporting material, says presentations expert Nick Morgan in the final chapter. To truly persuade, you need a story with emotional power.

Set your organization up for success

While we hope that you'll continue to learn and grow your own analytical skills, it's likely that you'll continue to work with data experts and quants throughout your data journey. Understanding the role of the data scientist will be crucial to ensuring your organization has the capabilities it needs to grow through data.

Data scientists bring with them intense curiosity and make new discoveries that managers and analysts may not see themselves. As an appendix at the end of this book, you'll find Thomas H. Davenport and D.J. Patil's popular article "Data Scientist: The Sexiest Job of the 21st Century." Davenport and Patil's piece aims to help you better understand this key player in an organization—someone they describe as a "hybrid of data hacker, analyst, communicator, and trusted adviser." These individuals have rare qualities that, as a manager, you may not fully understand. By reading through this piece, you'll have insight into how they think about and work with data. What's more, you'll learn how to find, attract, and develop data scientists to keep your company on the competing edge.

Moving Forward

Data-driven decisions won't come easily. But by understanding the basics of data analytics, you'll be able to ask the right questions of data to pull the most useful information out of the numbers. Before diving in to the chapters that follow, though, ask yourself how often you're incorporating data into your daily work. The assessment "Are You Data Driven?" is a brief test that will help you target your efforts. With that knowledge in mind, move through the next sections with an open mind, ready to weave data into each of your decisions.

ARE YOU DATA DRIVEN?

by Thomas C. Redman

Look at the list below and give yourself a point for every behavior you demonstrate consistently and half a point for those you follow most—but not all—of the time. Be hard on yourself. If you can only cite an instance or two, don't give yourself any credit.

- ☐ I push decisions down to the lowest possible level.
- ☐ I bring as much diverse data and as many diverse viewpoints to any situation as I possibly can.

(continued)

ARE YOU DATA DRIVEN?

(*continued*)

- ☐ I use data to develop a deeper understanding of the business context and the problem at hand.
- ☐ I develop an appreciation for variation.
- ☐ I deal reasonably well with uncertainty.
- ☐ I integrate my understanding of the data and its implications with my intuition.
- ☐ I recognize the importance of high-quality data and invest to make improvements.
- ☐ I conduct experiments and research to supplement existing data and address new questions.
- ☐ I recognize that decision criteria can vary with circumstances.
- ☐ I realize that making a decision is only the first step, and I revise decisions as new data comes to light.
- ☐ I work to learn new skills, and bring new data and data technologies into my organization.
- ☐ I learn from my mistakes and help others to do so as well.
- ☐ I strive to be a role model when it comes to data, and work with leaders, peers, and subordinates to help them become data driven.

Tally your points. If you score less than 7, it's imperative that you start changing the way you work as soon as possible. Target those behaviors where you gave yourself partial credit first and fully embed those skills into your daily work. Then build on your success by targeting those behaviors that you were unable to give yourself any credit for. It may help to enlist a colleague's aid—the two of you can improve together.

If you score a 7 or higher, you're showing signs of being data driven. Still, strive for ongoing improvement. Set a goal of learning a new behavior or two every year. Take this test every six months to make sure that you're on track.

Adapted from "Are You Data Driven? Take a Hard Look in the Mirror" on hbr.org, July 11, 2013 (product # H00AX2).

Thomas C. Redman, "the Data Doc," is President of Data Quality Solutions. He helps companies and people, including startups, multinationals, executives, and leaders at all levels, chart their courses to data-driven futures. He places special emphasis on quality, analytics, and organizational capabilities.

SECTION ONE

Getting Started

CHAPTER 1

Keep Up with Your Quants

by Thomas H. Davenport

"I don't know why we didn't get the mortgages off our books," a senior quantitative analyst at a large U.S. bank told me a few years ago. "I had a model strongly indicating that a lot of them wouldn't be repaid, and I sent it to the head of our mortgage business."

When I asked the leader of the mortgage business why he'd ignored the advice, he said, "If the analyst showed me a model, it wasn't in terms I could make sense of. I didn't even know his group was working on repayment probabilities." The bank ended up losing billions in bad loans.

We live in an era of big data. Whether you work in financial services, consumer goods, travel and transpor-

---

Reprinted from *Harvard Business Review*, July–August 2013 (product #R1307L).

tation, or industrial products, analytics are becoming a competitive necessity for your organization. But as the banking example shows, having big data—and even people who can manipulate it successfully—is not enough. Companies need general managers who can partner effectively with "quants" to ensure that their work yields better strategic and tactical decisions.

For people fluent in analytics—such as Gary Loveman of Caesars Entertainment (with a PhD from MIT), Jeff Bezos of Amazon (an electrical engineering and computer science major from Princeton), or Sergey Brin and Larry Page of Google (computer science PhD dropouts from Stanford)—there's no problem. But if you're a typical executive, your math and statistics background probably amounts to a college class or two. You might be adept at using spreadsheets and know your way around a bar graph or a pie chart, but when it comes to analytics, you often feel quantitatively challenged.

So what does the shift toward data-driven decision making mean for you? How do you avoid the fate of the loss-making mortgage bank head and instead lead your company into the analytical revolution, or at least become a good foot soldier in it? This article—a primer for non-quants—is based on extensive interviews with executives, including some with whom I've worked as a teacher or a consultant.

You, the Consumer

Start by thinking of yourself as a consumer of analytics. The producers are the quants whose analyses and models you'll integrate with your business experience and intuition as you make decisions. Producers are, of course, good at gathering the available data and making predictions about the future. But most lack sufficient knowledge to identify hypotheses and relevant variables and to know when the ground beneath an organization is shifting. Your job as a data consumer—to generate hypotheses and determine whether results and recommendations make sense in a changing business environment—is therefore critically important. That means accepting a few key responsibilities. Some require only changes in attitude and perspective; others demand a bit of study.

Learn a little about analytics

If you remember the content of your college-level statistics course, you may be fine. If not, bone up on the basics of regression analysis, statistical inference, and experimental design. You need to understand the process for making analytical decisions, including when you should step in as a consumer, and you must recognize that every analytical model is built on assumptions that producers ought to explain and defend. (See the sidebar "Analytics-Based Decision Making—in Six Steps.") As the famous statistician George Box noted, "All models are wrong, but some are useful." In other words, models intentionally simplify our complex world.

To become more data literate, enroll in an executive education program in statistics, take an online course, or learn from the quants in your organization by working closely with them on one or more projects.

Jennifer Joy, the vice president of clinical operations at Cigna, took the third approach. Joy has a nursing

ANALYTICS-BASED DECISION MAKING—IN SIX KEY STEPS

When using big data to make big decisions, non-quants should focus on the first and the last steps of the process. The numbers people typically handle the details in the middle, but wise non-quants ask lots of questions along the way.

1. ***Recognize the problem or question.*** Frame the decision or business problem, and identify possible alternatives to the framing.

2. ***Review previous findings.*** Identify people who have tried to solve this problem or similar ones—and the approaches they used.

3. ***Model the solution and select the variables.*** Formulate a detailed hypothesis about how particular variables affect the outcome.

4. ***Collect the data.*** Gather primary and secondary data on the hypothesized variables.

5. ***Analyze the data.*** Run a statistical model, assess its appropriateness for the data, and repeat the process until a good fit is found.

6. ***Present and act on the results.*** Use the data to tell a story to decision makers and stakeholders so that they will take action.

degree and an MBA, but she wasn't entirely comfortable with her analytical skills. She knew, however, that the voluminous reports she received about her call center operations weren't telling her whether the coaching calls made to patients were actually helping to manage their diseases and to keep them out of the hospital.

So Joy reached out to Cigna's analytics group, in particular to the experts on experimental design—the only analytical approach that can potentially demonstrate cause and effect. She learned, for example, that she could conduct pilot studies to discover which segments of her targeted population benefit the most (and which the least) from her call center's services. Specifically, she uses analytics to "prematch" pairs of patients and then to randomly assign one member of the pair to receive those services, while the other gets an alternative such as a mail-order or an online-support intervention. Each pilot lasts just a couple of months, and multiple studies are run simultaneously—so Joy now gets information about the effectiveness of her programs on a rolling basis.

In the end, Joy and her quant partners learned that the coaching worked for people with certain diseases but not for other patients, and some call center staff members were redeployed as a result. Now her group regularly conducts 20 to 30 such tests a year to find out what really makes a difference for patients. She may not understand all the methodological details, but as Michael Cousins, the vice president of U.S. research and analytics at Cigna, attests, she's learned to be "very analytically oriented."

Align yourself with the right kind of quant

Karl Kempf, a leader in Intel's decision-engineering group, is known at the company as the "überquant" or "chief mathematician." He often says that effective quantitative decisions "are not about the math; they're about the relationships." What he means is that quants and the consumers of their data get much better results if they form deep, trusting ties that allow them to exchange information and ideas freely.

Of course, highly analytical people are not always known for their social skills, so this can be hard work. As one wag jokingly advised, "Look for the quants who stare at your shoes, instead of their own, when you engage them in conversation." But it's possible to find people who communicate well and have a passion for solving business—rather than mathematical—problems and, after you've established a relationship, to encourage frank dialogue and data-driven dissent between the two of you.

Katy Knox, at Bank of America, has learned how to align with data producers. As the head of retail strategy and distribution for the bank's consumer division, she oversees 5,400-plus branches serving more than 50 million consumers and small businesses. For several years she's been pushing her direct reports to use analytics to make better decisions—for example, about which branches to open or close, how to reduce customer wait times, what incentives lead to multichannel interactions, and why some salespeople are more productive than others.

Bank of America has hundreds of quants, but most of them were pooled in a group that managers could not easily access. Knox insisted on having her own analytics team, and she established a strong working relationship with its members through frequent meetings and project-reporting sessions. She worked especially closely with two team leaders, Justin Addis and Michael Hyzy, who have backgrounds in retail banking and Six Sigma, so they're able to understand her unit's business problems and communicate them to the hard-core quants they manage. After Knox set the precedent, Bank of America created a matrix structure for its analysts in the consumer bank, and most now report to both a business line and a centralized analytical group.

Focus on the beginning and the end

Framing a problem—identifying it and understanding how others might have solved it in the past—is the most important stage of the analytical process for a consumer of big data. It's where your business experience and intuition matter most. After all, a hypothesis is simply a hunch about how the world works. The difference with analytical thinking, of course, is that you use rigorous methods to test the hypothesis.

For example, executives at the two corporate parent organizations of Transitions Optical believed that the photochromic lens company might not be investing in marketing at optimal levels, but no empirical data confirmed or refuted that idea. Grady Lenski, who headed the marketing division at the time, decided to hire analytics consultants to measure the effectiveness of different sales campaigns—a constructive framing that expanded on the simple binary question of whether or not costs were too high.

If you're a non-quant, you should also focus on the final step in the process—presenting and communicating results to other executives—because it's one that many quants discount or overlook and that you'll probably have to take on yourself at some point. If analytics is largely about "telling a story with data," what type of story would you favor? What kind of language and tone would you use? Should the story be told in narrative or visual terms? What types of graphics do you like? No matter how sophisticated their analyses, quants should be encouraged to explain their results in a straightforward way so that everyone can understand—or you should do it for them. A statistical methods story ("first we ran a chi-square test, and then we converted the categorical data to ordinal, next we ran a logistic regression, and then we lagged the economic data by a year") is rarely acceptable.

Many businesspeople settle on an ROI story: How will the new decision-making model increase conversions, revenue, or profitability? For example, a Merck executive with responsibility for a global business unit has worked closely with the pharmaceutical company's commercial analytics group for many years to answer a variety of questions, including what the ROIs of direct-to-consumer promotions are. Before an ROI analysis, he and the group discuss what actions they will take when they find out whether promotions are highly, marginally, or not successful—to make clear that the effort isn't merely an academic exercise. After the analysis, the executive sits the analysts down at a table with his management team to present and debate the results.

Ask lots of questions along the way

Former U.S. Treasury Secretary Larry Summers, who once served as an adviser to a quantitative hedge fund, told me that his primary responsibility in that job was to "look over shoulders"—that is, to ask the smart quants in the firm equally smart questions about their models and assumptions. Many of them hadn't been pressed like that before; they needed an intelligent consumer of data to help them think through and improve their work.

No matter how much you trust your quants, don't stop asking them tough questions. Here are a few that almost always lead to more-rigorous, defensible analyses. (If you don't understand a reply, ask for one that uses simpler language.)

1. What was the source of your data?
2. How well do the sample data represent the population?
3. Does your data distribution include outliers? How did they affect the results?
4. What assumptions are behind your analysis? Might certain conditions render your assumptions and your model invalid?
5. Why did you decide on that particular analytical approach? What alternatives did you consider?

6. How likely is it that the independent variables are actually causing the changes in the dependent variable? Might other analyses establish causality more clearly?

Frank Friedman, the chief financial officer and managing partner for finance and administration of Deloitte's U.S. business, is an inveterate questioner. He has assembled a group of data scientists and quantitative analysts to help him with several initiatives, including optimizing the pricing of services, developing models that predict employee performance, and identifying factors that drive receivables. "People who work with me know I question a lot—everything—always," Friedman says. "After the questioning, they know they will have to go back and redo some of their analyses." He also believes it's vital to admit when you don't understand something: "I know I am not the smartest person in the room in my meetings with these people. I'm always pushing for greater clarity [because] if I can't articulate it, I can't defend it to others."

Establish a culture of inquiry, not advocacy

We all know how easily "figures lie and liars figure." Analytics consumers should never pressure their producers with comments like "See if you can find some evidence in the data to support my idea." Instead, your explicit goal should be to find the truth. As the head of Merck's commercial analytics group says, "Our management team wants us to be like Switzerland. We work only for the shareholders."

In fact, some senior executives push their analysts to play devil's advocate. This sets the right cultural tone and helps to refine the models. "All organizations seek to please the leader," explains Gary Loveman, of Caesars, "so it's critical to cultivate an environment that views ideas as separate from people and insists on rigorous evidence to distinguish among those ideas."

Loveman encourages his subordinates to put forth data and analysis, rather than opinions, and reveals his own faulty hypotheses, conclusions, and decisions. That way managers and quants alike understand that his sometimes "lame and ill-considered views," as he describes them, need as much objective, unbiased testing as anyone else's. For example, he often says that his greatest mistake as a new CEO was choosing not to fire property managers who didn't share his analytical orientation. He thought their experience would be enough. Loveman uses the example to show both that he's fallible and that he insists on being a consumer of analytics.

When It All Adds Up

Warren Buffett once said, "Beware of geeks . . . bearing formulas." But in today's data-driven world, you can't afford to do that. Instead you need to combine the science of analytics with the art of intuition. Be a manager who knows the geeks, understands their formulas, helps improve their analytic processes, effectively interprets and communicates the findings to others, and makes better decisions as a result.

Contrast the bank mentioned at the beginning of this article with Toronto-Dominion Bank. TD's CEO, Ed Clark, is quantitatively literate (with a PhD in economics), and he also insists that his managers understand the math behind any financial product the company depends on. As a result, TD knew to avoid the riskiest-structured products and get out of others before incurring major losses during the 2008–2009 financial crisis.

TD's emphasis on data and analytics affects other areas of the business as well. Compensation is closely tied to performance-management measures, for example. And TD's branches stay open longer than most other banks' because Tim Hockey, the former head of retail banking, insisted on systematically testing the effect of extended retail hours (with control groups) and found that they brought in more deposits. If anyone at a management meeting suggests a new direction, he or she is pressed for data and analysis to support it. TD is not perfect, Clark acknowledges, but "nobody ever accuses us of not running the numbers."

Your organization may not be as analytical as TD, and your CEO may not be like Ed Clark. But that doesn't mean you can't become a great consumer of analytics on your own—and set an example for the rest of your company.

Thomas H. Davenport is the President's Distinguished Professor in Management and Information Technology at Babson College, a research fellow at the MIT Initiative on the Digital Economy, and a senior adviser at Deloitte Analytics. Author of over a dozen management books, his latest is *Only Humans Need Apply: Winners and Losers in the Age of Smart Machines*.

CHAPTER 2

A Simple Exercise to Help You Think Like a Data Scientist

by Thomas C. Redman

For 20 years, I've used a simple exercise to help those with an open mind (and a pencil, paper, and calculator) get started with data. One activity won't make you data savvy, but it will help you become data literate, open your eyes to the millions of small data opportunities, and enable you to work a bit more effectively with data scientists, analytics, and all things quantitative.

Adapted from "How to Start Thinking Like a Data Scientist" on hbr.org, November 29, 2013.

While the exercise is very much a how-to, each step also illustrates an important concept in analytics—from understanding variation to visualization.

First, start with something that interests, even bothers, you at work, like consistently late-starting meetings. Form it up as a question and write it down: "Meetings always seem to start late. Is that really true?"

Next, think through the data that can help answer your question and develop a plan for creating it. Write down all the relevant definitions and your protocol for collecting the data. For this particular example, you have to define when the meeting actually begins. Is it the time someone says, "OK, let's begin"? Or the time the real business of the meeting starts? Does kibitzing count?

Now collect the data. It is critical that you trust the data. And, as you go, you're almost certain to find gaps in data collection. You may find that even though a meeting has started, it starts anew when a more senior person joins in. Modify your definition and protocol as you go along.

Sooner than you think, you'll be ready to start drawing some pictures. Good pictures make it easier for you to both understand the data and communicate main points to others. There are plenty of good tools to help, but I like to draw my first picture by hand. My go-to plot is a time-series plot, where the horizontal axis has the date and time and the vertical axis has the variable of interest. Thus, a point on the graph in figure 2-1 is the date and time of a meeting versus the number of minutes late.

Now return to the question that you started with and develop summary statistics. Have you discovered an

FIGURE 2-1

How late are meetings?

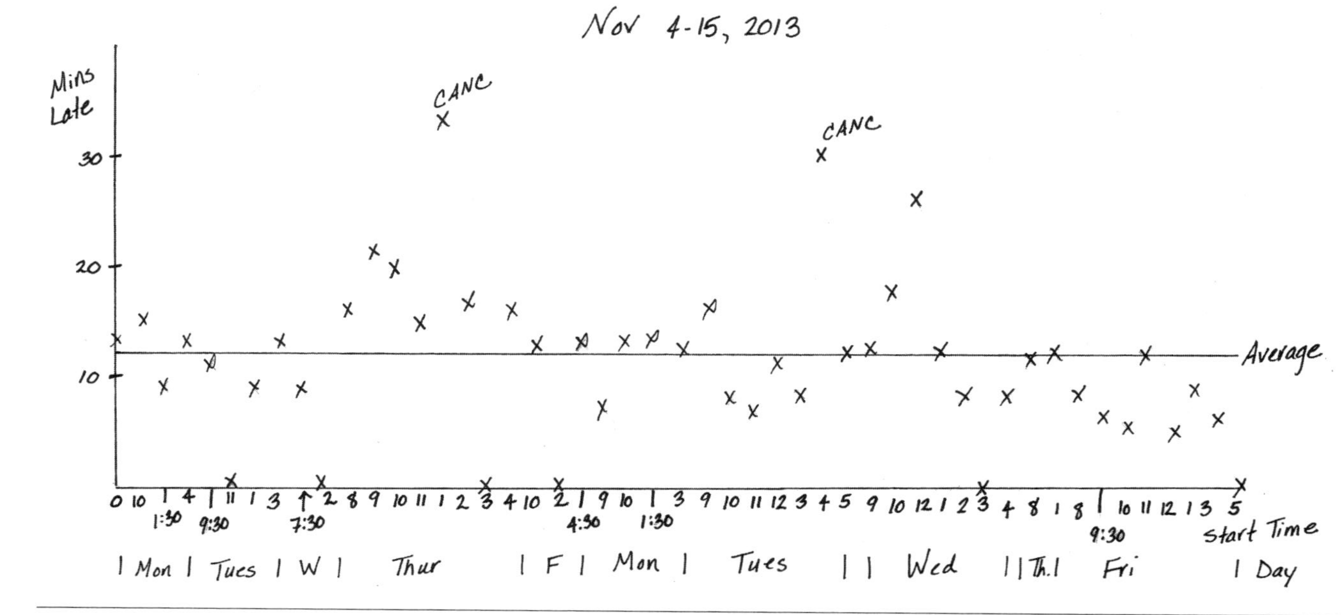

answer? In this case, "Over a two-week period, 10% of the meetings I attended started on time. And on average, they started 12 minutes late."

But don't stop there. Ask yourself, "So what?" In this case, "If those two weeks are typical, I waste an hour a day. And that costs the company x dollars a year."

Many analyses end because there is no "so what?" Certainly if 80% of meetings start within a few minutes of their scheduled start times, the answer to the original question is, "No, meetings start pretty much on time," and there is no need to go further.

But this case demands more, as some analyses do. Get a feel for variation. Understanding variation leads to a better feel for the overall problem, deeper insights, and novel ideas for improvement. Note on the graph that 8–20 minutes late is typical. A few meetings start right on time, others nearly a full 30 minutes late. It would be great if you could conclude, "I can get to meetings 10 minutes late, just in time for them to start," but the variation is too great.

Now ask, "What else does the data reveal?" It strikes me that six meetings began exactly on time, while every other meeting began at least seven minutes late. In this case, bringing meeting notes to bear reveals that all six on-time meetings were called by the vice president of finance. Evidently, she starts all her meetings on time.

So where do you go from here? Are there important next steps? This example illustrates a common dichotomy. On a personal level, results pass both the "interesting" and "important" test. Most of us would give almost anything to get back an hour a day. And you may not be able to make all meetings start on time, but if the VP can, you can certainly start the meetings you control promptly.

On the company level, results so far pass only the interesting test. You don't know whether your results are typical, nor whether others can be as hard-nosed as the VP when it comes to starting meetings. But a deeper look is surely in order: Are your results consistent with others' experiences in the company? Are some days worse than others? Which starts later: conference calls or face-to-face meetings? Is there a relationship between meeting start time and most senior attendee? Return to step one, pose the next group of questions, and repeat the process. Keep the focus narrow—two or three questions at most.

I hope you'll have fun with this exercise. Many find joy in teasing insights from data. But whether you experience that joy or not, don't take this exercise lightly. There are fewer and fewer places for the "data illiterate" and, in my humble opinion, no more excuses.

Thomas C. Redman, "the Data Doc," is President of Data Quality Solutions. He helps companies and people, including startups, multinationals, executives, and leaders at all levels, chart their courses to data-driven futures. He places special emphasis on quality, analytics, and organizational capabilities.

SECTION TWO

Gather the Right Information

CHAPTER 3

Do You Need All That Data?

by Ron Ashkenas

Organizations love data: numbers, reports, trend lines, graphs, spreadsheets—the more the better. And, as a result, many organizations have a substantial internal factory that churns out data on a regular basis, as well as external resources on call that produce data for onetime studies and questions. But what's the evidence (or dare I say "the data") that all this data leads to better business decisions? Is some amount of data collection unnecessary, and perhaps even damaging by creating complexity and confusion?

Let's look at a quick case study: For many years the CEO of a premier consumer products company insisted

---

Adapted from content posted on hbr.org, March 1, 2010 (product #H004FC).

on a monthly business review process that was highly data-intensive. At its core was a "book" that contained cost and sales data for every product sold by the company, broken down by business unit, channel, geography, and consumer segment. This book (available electronically but always printed by the executive team) was several inches thick. It was produced each month by many hundreds of finance, product management, and information technology people who spent thousands of hours collecting, assessing, analyzing, reconciling, and sorting the data.

Since this was the CEO's way of running the business, no one really questioned whether all of this activity was worth it, although many complained about the time required. When a new CEO came on the scene a couple of years ago, however, he decided that the business would do just fine with quarterly reviews and exception-only reporting. Suddenly the entire data-production industry of the company was reduced substantially—and the company didn't miss a beat.

Obviously, different CEOs have different needs for data. Some want their decisions to be based on as much hard data as possible; others want just enough to either reinforce or challenge their intuition; and still others may prefer a combination of hard, analytical data with anecdotal and qualitative input. In all cases, though, managers would do well to ask themselves four questions about their data process as a way of improving the return on what is often a substantial (but not always visible) investment:

1. **Are we asking the right questions?** Many companies collect the data that is available, rather than the information that is needed to help make decisions and run the business. So the starting point is to be clear about a limited number of key questions that you want the data to help you answer—and then focus the data collection around those rather than everything else that is possible.
2. **Does our data tell a story?** Most data comes in fragments. To be useful, these individual bits of information need to be put together into a coherent explanation of the business situation, which means integrating data into a "story." While enterprise data systems have been useful in driving consistent data definitions so that points can be added and compared, they don't automatically create the story. Instead, managers should consider in advance what data is needed to convey the story that they will be required to tell.
3. **Does our data help us look ahead rather than behind?** Most of the data that is collected in companies tells managers how they performed in a past period—but is less effective in predicting future performance. Therefore, it is important to ask what data, in what time frames, will help us get ahead of the curve instead of just reacting.
4. **Do we have a good mix of quantitative and qualitative data?** Neither quantitative nor qualitative data tells the whole story. For example, to make

> good product and pricing decisions, we need to know not only what is being sold to whom, but also why some products are selling more than others.

Clearly, business data and its analysis are critical for organizations to succeed, which is underscored by the fact that companies like IBM are investing billions of dollars in acquisitions in the business intelligence and analytics space. But even the best automated tools won't be effective unless managers are clear about these four questions.

Ron Ashkenas is an Emeritus Partner with Schaffer Consulting, a frequent contributor to *Harvard Business Review*, and the author or coauthor of four books on organizational transformation. He has worked with hundreds of managers over the years to help them translate strategy into results and simplify the way things get done. He also is the coauthor (with Brook Manville) of *The Harvard Business Review Leader's Handbook* (Harvard Business Review Press; forthcoming in 2018). He can be reached at rashkenas@gmail.com.

CHAPTER 4

How to Ask Your Data Scientists for Data and Analytics

by Michael Li, Madina Kassengaliyeva, and Raymond Perkins

The intersection of big data and business is growing daily. Although enterprises have been studying analytics for decades, data science is a relatively new capability. And interacting in a new data-driven culture can be difficult, particularly for those who aren't data experts.

One particular challenge that many of these individuals face is how to request new data or analytics from data scientists. They don't know the right questions to ask, the correct terms to use, or the range of factors to consider to get the information they need. In the end, analysts are left uncertain about how to proceed, and managers are frustrated when the information they get isn't what they intended.

At The Data Incubator, we work with hundreds of companies looking to hire data scientists and data engineers or enroll their employees in our corporate training programs. We often field questions from our hiring and training clients about how to interact with their data experts. While it's impossible to give an exhaustive account, here are some important factors to think about when communicating with data scientists, particularly as you begin a data search.

What Question Should We Ask?

As you begin working with your data analysts, be clear about what you hope to achieve. Think about the business impact you want the data to have and the company's ability to act on that information. By hearing what you hope to gain from their assistance, the data scientist can collaborate with you to define the right set of questions to answer and better understand exactly what information to seek.

Even the subtlest ambiguity can have major implications. For example, advertising managers may ask analysts, "What is the most efficient way to use ads to increase sales?" Though this seems reasonable, it may not be the right question since the ultimate objective of most firms isn't to increase sales, but to maximize profit. Research from the Institute of Practitioners in Advertising shows that using ads to reduce price sensitivity is typically twice as profitable as trying to increase sales.[1] The value of the insight obtained will depend heavily on the question asked. Be as specific and actionable as possible.

What Data Do We Need?

As you define the right question and objectives for analysis, you and your data scientist should assess the availability of the data. Ask if someone has already collected the relevant data and performed analysis. The ever-growing breadth of public data often provides easily accessible answers to common questions. Cerner, a supplier of health care IT solutions, uses data sets from the U.S. Department of Health and Human Services to supplement their own data. iMedicare uses information from the Centers for Medicare and Medicaid Services to select policies. Consider whether public data could be used toward your problem as well. You can also work with other analysts in the organization to determine if the data has previously been examined for similar reasons by others internally.

Then, assess whether the available data is sufficient. Data may not contain all the relevant information needed to answer your questions. It may also be influenced by latent factors that can be difficult to recognize. Consider the vintage effect in private lending data: Even seemingly identical loans typically perform very differently based on the time of issuance, despite the fact they may have had identical data at that time. The effect comes from fluctuations in the underlying underwriting standards at issuance, information that is not typically represented in loan data.

You should also inquire if the data is unbiased, since sample size alone is not sufficient to guarantee its validity. Finally, ask if the data scientist has enough data to answer the question. By identifying what information is needed, you can help data scientists plan better analyses going forward.

How Do We Obtain the Data?

If more information is needed, data scientists must decide between using data compiled by the company through the normal course of business, such as through observational studies, and collecting new data through experiments. As part of your conversation with analysts, ask about the costs and benefits of these options. Observational studies may be easier and less expensive to arrange since they do not require direct interaction with subjects, for example, but they are typically far less reliable than experiments because they are only able to establish correlation, not causation.

Experiments allow substantially more control and provide more reliable information about causality, but they are often expensive and difficult to perform. Even seemingly harmless experiments may carry ethical or social implications with real financial consequences. Facebook, for example, faced public fury over its manipulation of its own newsfeed to test how emotions spread on social media. Though the experiments were completely legal, many users resented being unwitting participants in Facebook's tests. Managers must think beyond the data and consider the greater brand repercussions of data collection and work with data scientists to understand these consequences. (See the sidebar, "Understanding the Cost of Data.")

Before investing resources in new analysis, validate that the company can use the insights derived from it in a productive and meaningful way. This may entail integration with existing technology projects, providing new data to automated systems, and establishing new processes.

UNDERSTANDING THE COST OF DATA

Though effective data analysis has been shown to generate substantial financial gains, there can be many different costs and complexities associated with it. Obtaining good data may not only be difficult, but very expensive. For example, in the health care and pharmaceutical industry, data collection is often associated with medical experimentation and patient observations. These randomized control trials can easily cost millions. Data storage can cost millions annually as well. When interacting with data scientists, managers should ask about the specific risks and costs associated with obtaining and analyzing the data before moving forward with a project.

But not all costs associated with data collection are financial. Violations of user privacy can have enormous legal and reputational repercussions. Privacy is one of the most significant concerns regarding consumer data. Managers must consider and weigh the legal and ethical implications of their data collection and analysis methods. Even seemingly anonymized data can be used to identify individuals. Safely anonymized

(*continued*)

UNDERSTANDING THE COST OF DATA

(*continued*)

data can be de-anonymized when combined with other data sets. In a famous case, Carnegie Mellon University researchers were able to identify anonymized health care records of a former Massachusetts governor using only his ZIP code, birthday, and gender.[2] The Gartner Data Center predicted that through 2016, over 25% of firms using consumer data would incur reputation damage due to privacy violation issues.[3] Managers must ask data scientists about these risks when working with the company's potentially sensitive consumer data.

Is the Data Clean and Easy to Analyze?

In general, data comes in two forms: structured and unstructured. Structured data is structured, as its name implies, and easy to add to a database. Most analysts find it easier and faster to manipulate. Unstructured data is often free form and cannot be as easily stored in the types of relational databases most commonly used in enterprises. While unstructured data is estimated to make up 95% of the world's data, according to a report by professors Amir Gandomi and Murtaza Haider of Ryerson University, for many large companies, storing and manipulating unstructured data may require a significant investment of resources to extract necessary information.[4] Working with your data scientists, evaluate the additional costs of using unstructured data when defining your initial objectives.

Even if the data is structured it still may need to be cleaned or checked for incompleteness and inaccuracies. When possible, encourage analysts to use clean data first. Otherwise, they will have to waste valuable time and resources identifying and correcting inaccurate records. A 2014 survey conducted by Ascend2, a marketing research company, found that nearly 54% of respondents complained that a "lack of data quality/completeness" was their most prominent impediment. By searching for clean data, you can avoid significant problems and loss of time.

Is the Model Too Complicated?

Statistical techniques and open-source tools to analyze data abound, but simplicity is often the best choice. More complex and flexible tools expose themselves to overfitting and can take more time to develop (read more about overfitting in chapter 15, "Pitfalls of Data-Driven Decisions"). Work with your data scientists to identify the simpler techniques and tools and move to more complex models only if the simpler ones prove insufficient. It is important to observe the *KISS* rule: "Keep It Simple, Stupid!"

It may not be possible to avoid all of the expenses and issues related to data collection and analysis. But you can take steps to mitigate these costs and risks. By asking the right questions of your analysts, you can ensure proper collaboration and get the information you need to move forward confidently.

Michael Li is the founder and executive director of The Data Incubator, a big data company that trains and places data scientists. A data scientist himself, he has worked at Google, Foursquare, and Andreessen Horowitz. He is a regular contributor to VentureBeat, *The Next Web*, and *Harvard Business Review*. **Madina Kassengaliyeva** is a client services director with Think Big, a Teradata company. She helps clients realize high-impact business opportunities through effective implementation of big data and analytics solutions. Madina has managed accounts in the financial services and insurance industries and led successful strategy, solution development, and analytics engagements. **Raymond Perkins** is a researcher at Princeton University working at the intersection of statistics, data, and finance and is the executive director of the Princeton Quant Trading Conference. He has also conducted research at Hong Kong University of Science and Technology, the Mathematical Sciences Research Institute (MSRI), and Michigan State University.

NOTES

1. P. F. Mouncey, "Marketing in the Era of Accountability," *Journal of Direct, Data and Digital Marketing Practice* 9, no. 2 (December 2007): 225–228.
2. N. Anderson, "'Anonymized' Data Really Isn't—and Here's Why Not," Ars Technica, September 8, 2009, https://arstechnica.com/tech-policy/2009/09/your-secrets-live-online-in-databases-of-ruin/.
3. D. Laney, "Information Innovation Key Initiative Overview," Gartner Research, April 22, 2014, https://www.gartner.com/doc/2715317/information-innovation-key-initiative-overview.
4. A. Gandomi and M. Haider, "Beyond the Hype: Big Data Concepts, Methods, and Analytics," *International Journal of Information Management* 35, no. 2 (April 2015): 137–144.

CHAPTER 5

How to Design a Business Experiment

by Oliver Hauser and Michael Luca

The rise of experimental evaluations within organizations—or what economists refer to as field experiments—has the potential to transform organizational decision making, providing fresh insight into areas ranging from product design to human resources to public policy. Companies that invest in randomized evaluations can gain a game-changing advantage.

Yet while there has been a rapid growth in experiments, especially within tech companies, we've seen too

Adapted from "How to Design (and Analyze) a Business Experiment" on hbr.org, October 29, 2015 (product #H02FSL).

many run incorrectly. Even when they're set up properly, avoidable mistakes often happen during implementation. As a result, many organizations fail to receive the real benefits of the scientific method.

This chapter lays out seven steps to ensure that your experiment delivers the data and insight you need. These principles draw on the academic research on field experiments as well as our work with a variety of organizations ranging from Yelp to the UK government.

1. Identify a Narrow Question

It is tempting to run an experiment around a question such as "Is advertising worth the cost?" or "Should we reduce (or increase) our annual bonuses?" Indeed, beginning with a question that is central to your broader goals is a good start. But it's misguided to think that a single experiment will do the trick. The reason is simple: Multiple factors go into answering these types of big questions.

Take the issue of whether advertising is worth the cost. What form of advertising are we talking about, and for which products, in which media, over which time periods? Your question should be testable, which means it must be narrow and clearly defined. A better question might be, "How much does advertising our brand name on Google AdWords increase monthly sales?" This is an empirical question that an experiment can answer—and that feeds into the question you ultimately hope to resolve. In fact, through just such an experiment, researchers at eBay discovered that a long-standing brand-advertising strategy on Google had no effect on the rate at which paying customers visited eBay.

2. Use a Big Hammer

Companies experiment when they don't know what will work best. Faced with this uncertainty, it may sound appealing to start small in order to avoid disrupting things. But your goal should be to see whether some version of your intervention—your new change—will make a difference to your customers. This requires a large-enough intervention.

For example, suppose a grocery store is considering adding labels to items to show consumers that it sources mainly from local farms. How big should the labels be and where should they be attached? We would suggest starting with large labels on the front of the packages, because if the labels were small or on the backs of the packages, and there were no effect (a common outcome for subtle interventions), the store managers would be left to wonder whether consumers simply didn't notice the tags (the treatment wasn't large enough) or truly didn't care (there was no treatment effect). By starting with a big hammer, the store would learn whether customers care about local sourcing. If there's no effect from large labels on the package fronts, then the store should give up on the idea. If there *is* an effect, the experimenters can later refine the labels to the desired characteristics.

3. Perform a Data Audit

Once you know what your intervention is, you need to choose what data to look at. Make a list of all the internal data related to the outcome you would like to influence and when you will need to do the measurements.

Include data both about things you hope will change and things you hope *won't* change as a result of the intervention, because you'll need to be alert for unintended consequences. Think, too, about sources of external data that might add perspective.

Say you're launching a new cosmetics product and you want to know which type of packaging leads to the highest customer loyalty and satisfaction. You decide to run a randomized controlled trial across geographical areas. In addition to measuring recurring orders and customer service feedback (internal data), you can track user reviews on Amazon and look for differences among customers in different states (external data).

4. Select a Study Population

Choose a subgroup among your customers that matches the customer profile you are hoping to understand. It might be tempting to look for the easiest avenue to get a subgroup, such as online users, but beware: If your subgroup is not a good representation of your target customers, the findings of your experiment may not be applicable. For example, younger online customers who shop exclusively on your e-commerce platform may behave very differently than older in-store customers. You could use the former to generalize to your online platform strategy, but you may be misguided if you try to draw inferences from that group for your physical stores.

5. Randomize

Randomly assign some people to a treatment group and others to a control group. The treatment group receives the change you want to test, while the control group receives what you previously had on offer—and make sure there are no differences other than what you are testing. The first rule of randomization is to not let participants decide which group they are in, or the results will be meaningless. The second is to make sure there really are no differences between treatment and control.

It's not always easy to follow the second rule. For example, we've seen companies experiment by offering a different coupon on Sunday than on Monday. The problem is that Sunday shoppers may be systematically different from Monday shoppers, even if you control for the volume of shoppers on each day.

6. Commit to a Plan, and Stick to It

Before you run an experiment, lay out your plans in detail. How many observations will you collect? How long will you let the experiment run? What variables will be collected and analyzed? Record these details. This can be as simple as creating a Google spreadsheet or as official as using a public trial registry. Not only will this level of transparency make sure that everyone is on the same page, it will also help you avoid well-known pitfalls in the implementation of experiments.

Once your experiment is running, leave it alone! If you get a result you expected, great; if not, that's fine too. The one thing that's not OK: running your experiment until your results look as though they fit your hypothesis, rather than until the study has run its planned course. This type of practice has led to a "replication crisis" in psychology research; it can seriously bias your results and reduce the insight you receive. Stick to the plan, to the extent possible.

7. Let the Data Speak

To give a complete picture of your results, report multiple outcomes. Sure, some might be unchanged, unimpressive, or downright inexplicable. But better to be transparent about them than to ignore them. Once you've surveyed the main results, ask yourself whether you've really discovered the underlying mechanism behind your results—the factor that is driving them. If you're not sure, refine your experiment and run another trial to learn more.

Experiments are already a central part of the social sciences; they are quickly becoming central to organizations as well. If your experiments are well designed, they will tell you something valuable. The most successful will puncture your assumptions, change your practices, and put you ahead of competitors. Experimentation is a long-term, richly informative process, with each trial forming the starting point for the next.

Oliver Hauser is a research fellow at Harvard Business School and Harvard Kennedy School. He conducts research and runs experiments with organizations and governments around the world. **Michael Luca** is the Lee J. Styslinger III Associate Professor of Business Administration at Harvard Business School and works with a variety of organizations to design experiments.

CHAPTER 6

Know the Difference Between Your Data and Your Metrics

by Jeff Bladt and Bob Filbin

How many views make a YouTube video a success? How about 1.5 million? That's how many views a video posted in 2011 by our organization, DoSomething.org, received. It featured some well-known YouTube celebrities, who asked young people to donate their used sports equipment to youth in need. It was twice as popular as any video DoSomething.org had posted to date. Success! Then came the data report: only eight viewers had signed up to donate equipment, and no one actually donated.

Adapted from content posted on hbr.org, March 4, 2013.

Zero donations from 1.5 million views. Suddenly, it was clear that for DoSomething.org, views did not equal success. In terms of donations, the video was a complete failure.

What happened? We were concerned with the wrong metric. A metric contains a single type of data—video views or equipment donations. A successful organization can only measure so many things well and what it measures ties to its definition of success. For DoSomething.org, that's social change. In the case above, success meant donations, not video views. As we learned, there is a difference between numbers and numbers that matter. This is what separates data from metrics.

You Can't Pick Your Data, but You Must Pick Your Metrics

Take baseball. Every team has the same definition of success—winning the World Series. This requires one main asset: good players. But what makes a player good? In baseball, teams used to answer this question with a handful of simple metrics like batting average and runs batted in (RBIs). Then came the statisticians (remember *Moneyball*?). New metrics provided teams with the ability to slice their data in new ways, find better ways of defining good players, and thus win more games.

Keep in mind that all metrics are proxies for what ultimately matters (in the case of baseball, a combination of championships and profitability), but some are better than others. The data of the game has never changed—there are still RBIs and batting averages. What has changed is how we look at the data. And those teams that slice the data in smarter ways are able to find good players who have been traditionally undervalued.

Organizations Become Their Metrics

Metrics are what you measure. And what you measure is what you manage to. In baseball, a critical question is, how effective is a player when he steps up to the plate? One measure is hits. A better measure turns out to be the sabermetric "OPS"—a combination of on-base percentage (which includes hits and walks) and total bases (slugging). Teams that look only at batting average suffer. Players on these teams walk less, with no offsetting gains in hits. In short, players play to the metrics their management values, even at the cost of the team.

The same happens in workplaces. Measure YouTube views? Your employees will strive for more and more views. Measure downloads of a product? You'll get more of that. But if your actual goal is to boost sales or acquire members, better measures might be return-on-investment (ROI), on-site conversion, or retention. Do people who download the product keep using it or share it with others? If not, all the downloads in the world won't help your business. (See the sidebar, "Picking Statistics," to learn how to choose metrics that that align with a specific performance objective.)

In the business world, we talk about the difference between vanity metrics and meaningful metrics. Vanity metrics are like dandelions—they might look pretty, but to most of us, they're weeds, using up resources and doing nothing for your property value. Vanity metrics for your organization might include website visitors per month, Twitter followers, Facebook fans, and media impressions. Here's the thing: If these numbers go up, they might drive up sales of your product. But can you prove it? If yes, great. Measure away. But if you can't, they aren't valuable.

PICKING STATISTICS

by Michael Mauboussin

The following is a process for choosing metrics that allow you to understand, track, and manage the cause-and-effect relationships that determine your company's performance. I will illustrate the process in a simplified way using a retail bank that is based on an analysis of 115 banks by Venky Nagar of the University of Michigan and Madhav Rajan of Stanford. Leave aside, for the moment, which metrics you currently use or which ones Wall Street analysts or bankers say you should. Start with a blank slate and work through these four steps in sequence.

1. Define Your Governing Objective

A clear objective is essential to business success because it guides the allocation of capital. Creating economic value is a logical governing objective for a company that operates in a free market system. Companies may choose a different objective, such as maximizing the firm's longevity. We will assume that the retail bank seeks to create economic value.

2. Develop a Theory of Cause and Effect to Assess Presumed Drivers of the Objective

The three commonly cited financial drivers of value creation are sales, costs, and investments. More-specific financial drivers vary among companies and can include earnings growth, cash flow growth, and return on invested capital.

Naturally, financial metrics can't capture all value-creating activities. You also need to assess nonfinancial measures such as customer loyalty, customer satisfaction, and product quality, and determine if they can be directly linked to the financial measures that ultimately deliver value. As we've discussed, the link between value creation and financial and nonfinancial measures like these is variable and must be evaluated on a case-by-case basis.

In our example, the bank starts with the theory that customer satisfaction drives the use of bank services and that usage is the main driver of value. This theory links a nonfinancial and a financial driver. The bank then measures the correlations statistically to see if the theory is correct and determines that satisfied customers indeed use more services, allowing the bank to

(*continued*)

PICKING STATISTICS

(*continued*)

generate cash earnings growth and attractive returns on assets, both indicators of value creation. Having determined that customer satisfaction is persistently and predictively linked to returns on assets, the bank must now figure out which employee activities drive satisfaction.

3. Identify the Specific Activities That Employees Can Do to Help Achieve the Governing Objective

The goal is to make the link between your objective and the measures that employees can control through the application of skill. The relationship between these activities and the objective must also be persistent and predictive.

In the previous step, the bank determined that customer satisfaction drives value (it is predictive). The bank now has to find reliable drivers of customer satisfaction. Statistical analysis shows that the rates consumers receive on their loans, the speed of loan processing, and low teller turnover all affect customer satisfaction. Because these are within the control of employees and management, they are persistent. The bank can use this information to, for example, make sure that its process for reviewing and approving loans is quick and efficient.

4. Evaluate Your Statistics

Finally, you must regularly reevaluate the measures you are using to link employee activities with the governing objective. The drivers of value change over time, and so must your statistics. For example, the demographics of the retail bank's customer base are changing, so the bank needs to review the drivers of customer satisfaction. As the customer base becomes younger and more digitally savvy, teller turnover becomes less relevant and the bank's online interface and customer service become more so. Companies have access to a growing torrent of statistics that could improve their performance, but executives still cling to old-fashioned and often flawed methods for choosing metrics. In the past, companies could get away with going on gut and ignoring the right statistics because that's what everyone else was doing. Today, using them is necessary to compete. More to the point, identifying and exploiting them before rivals do will be the key to seizing advantage.

Excerpted from "The True Measures of Success" in *Harvard Business Review,* October 2012 (product #R1210B).

Michael Mauboussin is an investment strategist and an adjunct professor at Columbia Business School. His latest book is *The Success Equation* (Harvard Business Review Press, 2012).

Metrics Are Only Valuable if You Can Manage to Them

Good metrics have three key attributes: Their data is consistent, cheap, and quick to collect. A simple rule of thumb: If you can't measure results within a week for free (and if you can't replicate the process), then you're prioritizing the wrong ones. There are exceptions, but they are rare. In baseball, the metrics an organization uses to measure a successful plate appearance will affect player strategy in the short term (do they draw more walks, prioritize home runs, etc.?) and personnel strategy in the mid- and long terms. The data to make these decisions is readily available and continuously updated.

Organizations can't control their data, but they do control what they care about. If our metric on the YouTube video had been views, we would have called it a huge success. In fact, we wrote it off as a massive failure. Does that mean no more videos? Not necessarily, but for now, we'll be spending our resources elsewhere, collecting data on metrics that matter.

Jeff Bladt is chief data officer at DoSomething.org, America's largest organization for young people and social change. **Bob Filbin** is chief data scientist at Crisis Text Line, the first large-scale 24/7 national crisis line for teens on the medium they use most: texting.

CHAPTER 7

The Fundamentals of A/B Testing

by Amy Gallo

As we learned in chapter 5, running an experiment is a straightforward way to collect new data about a specific question or problem. One of the most common methods of experimentation, particularly in online settings, is A/B testing.

To better understand what A/B testing is, where it originated, and how to use it, I spoke with Kaiser Fung, who founded the applied analytics program at Columbia University and is author of *Junk Charts*, a blog devoted to the critical examination of data and graphics in the mass media. His latest book is *Numbersense: How to Use Big Data to Your Advantage.*

Adapted from "A Refresher on A/B Testing" on hbr.org, June 28, 2017 (product #H03R3D).

What Is A/B Testing?

A/B testing is a way to compare two versions of something to figure out which performs better. While it's most often associated with websites and apps, Fung says the method is almost 100 years old.

In the 1920s, statistician and biologist Ronald Fisher discovered the most important principles behind A/B testing and randomized controlled experiments in general. "He wasn't the first to run an experiment like this, but he was the first to figure out the basic principles and mathematics and make them a science," Fung says.

Fisher ran agricultural experiments, asking questions such as, "What happens if I put more fertilizer on this land?" The principles persisted, and in the early 1950s scientists started running clinical trials in medicine. In the 1960s and 1970s, the concept was adapted by marketers to evaluate direct-response campaigns (for example, "Would a postcard or a letter sent to target customers result in more sales?").

A/B testing in its current form came into existence in the 1990s. Fung says that throughout the past century, the math behind the tests hasn't changed: "It's the same core concepts, but now you're doing it online, in a real-time environment, and on a different scale in terms of number of participants and number of experiments."

How Does A/B Testing Work?

You start an A/B test by deciding what it is you want to test. Fung gives a simple example: the size of the "Subscribe" button on your website. Then you need to know how you want to evaluate its performance. In this case, let's say your metric is the number of visitors who click on the button. To run the test, you show two sets of users (assigned at random when they visit the site) the different versions (where the only thing different is the size of the button) and determine which influenced your success metric the most—in this case, which button size caused more visitors to click.

There are a lot of things that influence whether someone clicks. For example, it may be that those using a mobile device are more likely to click a button of a certain size, while those on desktop are drawn to a different size. This is where randomization is critical. By randomizing which users are in which group, you minimize the chances that other factors, like mobile versus desktop, will drive your results on average.

"The A/B test can be considered the most basic kind of randomized controlled experiment," Fung says. "In its simplest form, there are two treatments and one acts as the control for the other." As with all randomized controlled experiments, you must estimate the sample size you need to achieve a statistical significance, which will help you make sure the result you're seeing "isn't just because of background noise," Fung says.

Sometimes you know that certain variables, usually those that are not easily manipulated, have a strong effect on the success metric. For example, maybe mobile users of your website tend to click less in general, compared with desktop users. Randomization may result in set A containing slightly more mobile users than set B, which may cause set A to have a lower click rate regardless of the button size they're seeing. To level the playing field, the test analyst should first divide the users by mobile and desktop and then randomly assign them to each version. This is called *blocking*.

The size of the "Subscribe" button is a very basic example, Fung says. In actuality, you might not be testing just size but also color, text, typeface, and font size. Lots of managers run sequential tests—testing size first (large versus small), then color (blue versus red), then typeface (Times versus Arial), and so on—because they believe they shouldn't vary two or more factors at the same time. But according to Fung, that view has been debunked by statisticians. Sequential tests are in fact suboptimal, because you're not measuring what happens when factors interact. For example, it may be that users prefer blue on average but prefer red when it's combined with an Arial font. This kind of result is regularly missed in sequential A/B testing because the typeface test is run on blue buttons that have "won" the previous test.

Instead, Fung says, you should run more-complex tests. This can be hard for some managers, since the appeal of A/B tests is how straightforward and simple they are to run (and many people designing these experiments, Fung points out, don't have a statistics background). "With A/B testing, we tend to want to run a large number of simultaneous, independent tests," he says, in large part because the mind reels at the number of possible combinations that can be tested. But using mathematics, you can "smartly pick and run only certain subsets of those treatments; then you can infer the rest from the data." This is called *multivariate* testing in the A/B testing world, and it means you often end up doing an A/B/C test or even an A/B/C/D test. In the colors and size example, it might include showing different groups a large red button, a small red button, a large blue button, and a small blue button. If you wanted to test fonts too, you would need even more test groups.

How Do You Interpret the Results of an A/B Test?

Chances are that your company will use software that handles the calculations, and it may even employ a statistician who can interpret those results for you. But it's helpful to have a basic understanding of how to make sense of the output and decide whether to move forward with the test variation (the new button, in the example Fung describes).

Fung says that most software programs report two conversion rates for A/B testing: one for users who saw the control version, and the other for users who saw the test version. "The conversion rate may measure clicks or other actions taken by users," he says. The report might look like this: "Control: 15% (+/- 2.1%); Variation 18% (+/- 2.3%)." This means that 18% of your users clicked through on the new variation (perhaps the larger blue button) with a margin of error of 2.3%. You might be tempted to interpret this as the actual conversion rate falling between 15.7% and 20.3%, but that wouldn't be technically correct. "The real interpretation is that if you ran your A/B test multiple times, 95% of the ranges will capture the true conversion rate—in other words, the conversion rate falls outside the margin of error 5% of the time (or whatever level of statistical significance you've set)," Fung explains.

This can be a difficult concept to wrap your head around. But what's important to know is that the 18% conversion rate isn't a guarantee. This is where your judgment comes in. An 18% conversation rate is certainly better than a 15% one, even allowing for the margin of error (12.9% to 17.1% versus 15.7% to 20.3%). You might hear people talk about this as a "3% lift" (*lift* is the percentage difference in conversion rate between your control version and a successful test treatment). In this case, it's most likely a good decision to switch to your new version, but that will depend on the costs of implementing it. If they're low, you might try out the switch and see what happens in actuality (versus in tests). One of the big advantages to testing in the online world is that you can usually revert back to your original pretty easily.

How Do Companies Use A/B Testing?

Fung says that the popularity of the methodology has risen as companies have realized that the online environment is well suited to help managers, especially marketers, answer questions like, "What is most likely to make people click? Or buy our product? Or register with our site?" A/B testing is now used to evaluate everything from website design to online offers to headlines to product descriptions. (See the sidebar "A/B Testing in

Action" to see an example from the creative marketplace Shutterstock.)

Most of these experiments run without the subjects even knowing. As users, Fung says, "we're part of these tests all the time and don't know it."

And it's not just websites. You can test marketing emails or ads as well. For example, you might send two versions of an email to your customer list (randomizing the list first, of course) and figure out which one generates more sales. Then you can just send out the winning version next time. Or you might test two versions of ad copy and see which one converts visitors more often. Then you know to spend more getting the most successful one out there.

A/B TESTING IN ACTION

by Wyatt Jenkins

At Shutterstock, we test everything: copy and link colors, relevance algorithms that rank our search results, language-detection functions, usability in downloading, pricing, video-playback design, and anything else you can see on our site (plus a lot you can't).

Shutterstock is the world's largest creative marketplace, serving photography, illustrations, and video to more than 750,000 customers. And those customers

(continued)

A/B TESTING IN ACTION

(*continued*)

have heavy image needs; we serve over three downloads per second. That's a ton of data.

This means that we know more about our customers, statistically, than anyone else in our market. It also means that we can run more experiments with statistical significance faster than businesses with less user data. It's one of our most important competitive advantages.

Search results are among the highest-trafficked pages on our site. A few years back, we started experimenting with a mosaic-display search-results page in our Labs area—an experimentation platform we use to try things quickly and get user feedback. In qualitative testing, customers really liked the design of the mosaic search grid, so we A/B tested it within the core Shutterstock experience.

Here are some of the details of the experiment, and what we learned:

- ***Image sizes:*** We tested different image sizes to get just the right number of pixels on the screen.
- ***New customers:*** We watched to see if new customers to our site would increase conversion. New customers act differently than existing ones, so you need to account for that. Sometimes existing customers suffer from change aversion.

- ***Viewport size:*** We tracked the viewport size (the size of the screen customers used) to understand how they were viewing the page.
- ***Watermarks:*** We tested including an image watermark versus no watermark. Was including the watermark distracting?
- ***Hover:*** We experimented with the behavior of a hover feature when a user paused on a particular image.

Before the test, we were convinced that removing the watermark on our images would increase conversion because there would be less visual clutter on the page. But in testing we learned that removing the watermark created the opposite effect, disproving our gut instinct.

We ran enough tests to find two different designs that increased conversion, so we iterated on those designs and re-tested them before deciding on one. And we continue to test this search grid and make improvements for our customers on a regular basis.

Adapted from "A/B Testing and the Benefits of an Experimentation Culture" posted on hbr.org, February 5, 2014 (product #H00NTO).

Wyatt Jenkins is a product executive with a focus on marketplaces, personalization, optimization, and international growth. He has acted as SVP of Product at Hired.com and Optimizely, and was VP of Product at Shutterstock for five years. Wyatt was an early partner in Beatport from 2003 to 2009, and he served on the board until 2013.

What Mistakes Do People Make When Doing A/B Tests?

Fung identified three common mistakes he sees companies make when performing A/B tests.

First, too many managers don't let the tests run their course. Because most of the software for running these tests lets you watch results in real time, managers want to make decisions too quickly. This mistake, Fung says, "evolves out of impatience," and many software vendors have played into this overeagerness by offering a type of A/B testing called *real-time optimization*, in which you can use algorithms to make adjustments as results come in. The problem is that, because of randomization, it's possible that if you let the test run to its natural end, you might get a different result.

The second mistake is looking at too many metrics. "I cringe every time I see software that tries to please everyone by giving you a panel of hundreds of metrics," he says. The problem is that if you're looking at such a large number of metrics at the same time, you're at risk of making what statisticians call *spurious correlations* (a topic discussed in more detail in chapter 10). In proper test design, "you should decide on the metrics you're going to look at before you execute an experiment and select a few. The more you're measuring, the more likely that you're going to see random fluctuations." With too many metrics, instead of asking yourself, "What's happening with this variable?" you're asking, "What interesting (and potentially insignificant) changes am I seeing?"

Lastly, Fung says, few companies do enough retesting. "We tend to test it once and then we believe it. But even with a statistically significant result, there's a quite large probability of false positive error. Unless you retest once in a while, you don't rule out the possibility of being wrong." False positives can occur for several reasons. For example, even though there may be little chance that any given A/B result is driven by random chance, if you do lots of A/B tests, the chances that at least one of your results is wrong grows rapidly.

This can be particularly difficult to do because it is likely that managers would end up with contradictory results, and no one wants to discover that they've undermined previous findings, especially in the online world, where managers want to make changes—and capture value—quickly. But this focus on value can be misguided. Fung says, "People are not very vigilant about the practical value of the findings. They want to believe that every little amount of improvement is valuable even when the test results are not fully reliable. In fact, the smaller the improvement, the less reliable the results."

It's clear that A/B testing is not a panacea for all your data-testing needs. There are more complex kinds of experiments that are more efficient and will give you more reliable data, Fung says. But A/B testing is a great way to gain quick information about a specific question you have, particularly in an online setting. And, as Fung says, "the good news about the A/B testing world is that everything happens so quickly, so if you run it and it doesn't work, you can try something else. You can always flip back to the old tactic."

Amy Gallo is a contributing editor at *Harvard Business Review* and the author of the *HBR Guide to Dealing with Conflict*. Follow her on Twitter @amyegallo.

CHAPTER 8

Can Your Data Be Trusted?

by Thomas C. Redman

You've just learned of some new data that, when combined with existing data, could offer potentially game-changing insights. But there isn't a clear indication whether this new information can be trusted. How should you proceed?

There is, of course, no simple answer. While many managers are skeptical of new data and others embrace it wholeheartedly, the more thoughtful managers take a nuanced approach. They know that some data (maybe even most of it) is bad and can't be used, and some is good and should be trusted implicitly. But they also realize that some data is flawed but usable with caution.

Adapted from content posted on hbr.org, October 29, 2015 (product #H02G61).

They find this data intriguing and are eager to push the data to its limits, as they know game-changing insights may reside there.

Fortunately, you can work with your data scientists to assess whether the data you're considering is safe to use and just how far you can go with flawed data. Indeed, following some basic steps can help you proceed with greater confidence—or caution—as the quality of the data dictates.

Evaluate Where It Came From

You can trust data when it is created in accordance with a first-rate data quality program. They feature clear accountabilities for managers to create data correctly, input controls, and find and eliminate the root causes of error. You won't have to opine whether the data is good—data quality statistics will tell you. You'll find an expert who will be happy to explain what you may expect and answer your questions. If the data quality stats look good and the conversation goes well, trust the data. This is the "gold standard" against which the other steps should be calibrated.

Assess Data Quality Independently

Much, perhaps most, data will not meet the gold standard, so adopt a cautious attitude by doing your own assessment of data quality. Make sure you know where the data was created and how it is defined, not just how your data scientist accessed it. It is easy to be misled by a casual, "We took it from our cloud-based data warehouse, which employs the latest technology," and completely miss the fact that the data was created in a dubious public forum. Figure out which organization created the data. Then dig deeper: What do colleagues advise about this organization and data? Does it have a good or poor reputation for quality? What do others say on social media? Do some research both inside and outside your company.

At the same time, develop your own data quality statistics, using what I call the "Friday afternoon measurement," tailor-made for this situation. Briefly, you, the data scientist providing the analysis, or both of you, should lay out 10 or 15 important data elements for 100 data records on a spreadsheet. If the new data involves customer purchases, such data elements may include "customer name," "purchased item," and "price." Then work record by record, taking a hard look at each data element. The obvious errors will jump out at you—customer names will be misspelled, the purchased item will be a product you don't sell, or the price may be missing. Mark these obvious errors with a red pen or highlight them in a bright color. Then count the number of records with no errors. (See figure 8-1 for an example.) In many cases you'll see a lot of red—don't trust this data! If you see only a little red, say, less than 5% of records with an obvious error, you can use this data with caution.

Look, too, at patterns of the errors. If, for instance, there are 25 total errors, 24 of which occur in the price, eliminate that data element going forward. But if the rest of the data looks pretty good, use it with caution.

FIGURE 8-1

Example: Friday afternoon measurement spreadsheet

Record	Attribute 1 **Name**	Attribute 2 **Size**	Attribute 3 **Amount**	Attribute 15	**Perfect record?**
1	Jane Doe	Null	$472.13		No
2	John Smith	Medium	$126.93		Yes
3	Stuart Madnick	XXXL	Null		No
4	Thoams Jones				No
100	James Olsen	24 Lockwood Road	$76.24		No
					Number of perfect records = 67

Source: Thomas C. Redman, "Assess Whether You Have a Data Quality Problem" on hbr.org, July 28, 2016 (product #H030SQ).

Clean the Data

I think of data cleaning in three levels: rinse, wash, and scrub. "Rinse" replaces obvious errors with "missing value" or corrects them if doing so is very easy; "scrub" involves deep study, even making corrections one at a time, by hand, if necessary; and "wash" occupies a middle ground.

Even if time is short, scrub a small random sample (say, 1,000 records), making them as pristine as you possibly can. Your goal is to arrive at a sample of data you know you can trust. Employ all possible means of scrubbing and be ruthless! Eliminate erroneous data records and data elements that you cannot correct, and mark data as "uncertain" when applicable.

When you are done, take a hard look. When the scrubbing has gone really well (and you'll know if it has), you've created a data set that rates high on the trustworthy scale. It's OK to move forward using this data.

Sometimes the scrubbing is less satisfying. If you've done the best you can, but still feel uncertain, put this data in the "use with caution" category. If the scrubbing goes poorly—for example, too many prices just look wrong and you can't make corrections—you must rate this data, and all like it, as untrustworthy. The sample strongly suggests none of the data should be used to inform your decision.

After the initial scrub, move on to the second cleaning exercise: washing the remaining data that was not in the scrubbing sample. This step should be performed by a truly competent data scientist. Since scrubbing can be a time-consuming, manual process, the wash allows you to make corrections using more automatic processes. For example, one wash technique involves "imputing" missing values using statistical means. Or your data scientist may have discovered algorithms during scrubbing. If the washing goes well, put this data into the "use with caution" category.

The flow chart in figure 8-2 will help you see this process in action. Once you've identified a set of data that you can trust or use with caution, move on to the next step of integration.

Ensure High-Quality Data Integration

Align the data you can trust—or the data that you're moving forward with cautiously—with your existing data. There is a lot of technical work here, so probe your data scientist to ensure three things are done well:

- **Identification:** Verify that the Courtney Smith in one data set is the same Courtney Smith in others.
- **Alignment of units of measure and data definitions:** Make sure Courtney's purchases and prices paid, expressed in "pallets" and "dollars" in one set, are aligned with "units" and "euros" in another.
- **De-duplication:** Check that the Courtney Smith record does not appear multiple times in different ways (say as C. Smith or Courtney E. Smith).

At this point in the process, you're ready to perform whatever analytics (from simple summaries to more complex analyses) you need to guide your decision. Pay

FIGURE 8-2

Should you trust your data?

A simple process to help you decide

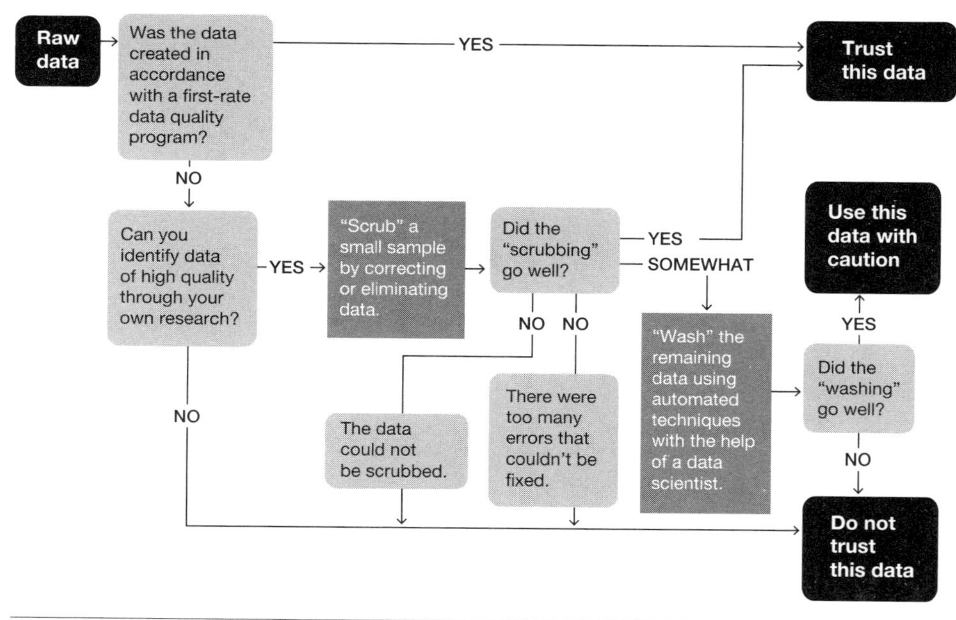

particular attention when you get different results based on "use with caution" and "trusted" data. Both great insights and great traps lie here. When a result looks intriguing, isolate the data and repeat the steps above, making more detailed measurements, scrubbing the data, and improving wash routines. As you do so, develop a feel for how deeply you should trust this data.

Data doesn't have to be perfect to yield new insights, but you must exercise caution by understanding where the flaws lie, working around errors, cleaning them up, and backing off when the data simply isn't good enough.

Thomas C. Redman, "the Data Doc," is President of Data Quality Solutions. He helps companies and people, including startups, multinationals, executives, and leaders at all levels, chart their courses to data-driven futures. He places special emphasis on quality, analytics, and organizational capabilities.

SECTION THREE

Analyze the Data

CHAPTER 9

A Predictive Analytics Primer

by Thomas H. Davenport

No one has the ability to capture and analyze data from the future. However, there is a way to predict the future using data from the past. It's called predictive analytics, and organizations do it every day.

Has your company, for example, developed a customer lifetime value (CLTV) measure? That's using predictive analytics to determine how much a customer will buy from the company over time. Do you have a "next best offer" or product recommendation capability? That's an analytical prediction of the product or service that your customer is most likely to buy next. Have you made a

---

Adapted from content posted on hbr.org, September 2, 2014 (product #H00YO1).

forecast of next quarter's sales? Used digital marketing models to determine what ad to place on what publisher's site? All of these are forms of predictive analytics.

Predictive analytics are gaining in popularity, but what do you really need to know in order to interpret results and make better decisions? By understanding a few basics, you will feel more comfortable working with and communicating with others in your organization about the results and recommendations from predictive analytics. The quantitative analysis isn't magic—but it is normally done with a lot of past data, a little statistical wizardry, and some important assumptions.

The Data

Lack of good data is the most common barrier to organizations seeking to employ predictive analytics. To make predictions about what customers will buy in the future, for example, you need to have good data on what they are buying (which may require a loyalty program, or at least a lot of analysis of their credit cards), what they have bought in the past, the attributes of those products (attribute-based predictions are often more accurate than the "people who buy this also buy this" type of model), and perhaps some demographic attributes of the customer (age, gender, residential location, socioeconomic status, etc.). If you have multiple channels or customer touchpoints, you need to make sure that they capture data on customer purchases in the same way your previous channels did.

All in all, it's a fairly tough job to create a single customer data warehouse with unique customer IDs on everyone, and all past purchases customers have made through all channels. If you've already done that, you've got an incredible asset for predictive customer analytics.

The Statistics

Regression analysis in its various forms is the primary tool that organizations use for predictive analytics. It works like this, in general: An analyst hypothesizes that a set of independent variables (say, gender, income, visits to a website) are statistically correlated with the purchase of a product for a sample of customers. The analyst performs a regression analysis to see just how correlated each variable is; this usually requires some iteration to find the right combination of variables and the best model. Let's say that the analyst succeeds and finds that each variable in the model is important in explaining the product purchase, and together the variables explain a lot of variation in the product's sales. Using that regression equation, the analyst can then use the regression coefficients—the degree to which each variable affects the purchase behavior—to create a score predicting the likelihood of the purchase.

Voilà! You have created a predictive model for other customers who weren't in the sample. All you have to do is compute their score and offer them the product if their score exceeds a certain level. It's quite likely that the high-scoring customers will want to buy the product—assuming the analyst did the statistical work well and that the data was of good quality. (For more on regression analysis, read on to the next chapter.)

The Assumptions

Another key factor in any predictive model is the assumptions that underlie it. Every model has them, and it's important to know what they are and monitor whether they are still true. The big assumption in predictive analytics is that the future will continue to be like the past. As Charles Duhigg describes in his book *The Power of Habit*, people establish strong patterns of behavior that they usually keep up over time. Sometimes, however, they change those behaviors, and the models that were used to predict them may no longer be valid.

What makes assumptions invalid? The most common reason is time. If your model was created several years ago, it may no longer accurately predict current behavior. The greater the elapsed time, the more likely it is that customer behavior has changed. Some Netflix predictive models, for example, that were created on early internet users had to be retired because later internet users were substantially different. The pioneers were more technically focused and relatively young; later users were essentially everyone.

Another reason a predictive model's assumptions may no longer be valid is if the analyst didn't include a key variable in the model, and that variable has changed substantially over time. The great—and scary—example here is the financial crisis of 2008–2009, caused largely by invalid models predicting how likely mortgage customers were to repay their loans. The models didn't include the possibility that housing prices might stop rising, and that they even might fall. When they did start falling, it turned out that the models were poor predictors of mortgage repayment. In essence, the belief that housing prices would always rise was a hidden assumption in the models.

Since faulty or obsolete assumptions can clearly bring down whole banks and even (nearly!) whole economies, it's pretty important that they be carefully examined. Managers should always ask analysts what the key assumptions are, and what would have to happen for them to no longer be valid. And both managers and analysts should continually monitor the world to see if key factors involved in assumptions have changed over time.

With these fundamentals in mind, here are a few good questions to ask your analysts:

- Can you tell me something about the source of the data you used in your analysis?
- Are you sure the sample data is representative of the population?
- Are there any outliers in your data distribution? How did they affect the results?
- What assumptions are behind your analysis?
- Are there any conditions that would make your assumptions invalid?

Even with those cautions, it's still pretty amazing that we can use analytics to predict the future. All we have to do is gather the right data, do the right type of statistical model, and be careful of our assumptions. Analytical predictions may be harder to generate than those by the late-night television soothsayer Carnac the Magnificent, but they are usually considerably more accurate.

Thomas H. Davenport is the President's Distinguished Professor in Management and Information Technology at Babson College, a research fellow at the MIT Initiative on the Digital Economy, and a senior adviser at Deloitte Analytics. Author of over a dozen management books, his latest is *Only Humans Need Apply: Winners and Losers in the Age of Smart Machines*.

CHAPTER 10

Understanding Regression Analysis

by Amy Gallo

One of the most important types of data analysis is **regression**. It is a common approach used to draw conclusions from and make predictions based on data, but for those without a statistical or analytical background, it can also be complex and confusing.

To better understand this method and how companies use it, I talked with Thomas Redman, author of *Data Driven: Profiting from Your Most Important Business Asset*. He also advises organizations on their data and data quality programs.

Adapted from "A Refresher on Regression Analysis" on hbr.org, November 4, 2015 (product #H02GBP).

What Is Regression Analysis?

Redman offers this example scenario: Suppose you're a sales manager trying to predict next month's numbers. You know that dozens, perhaps even hundreds, of factors from the weather to a competitor's promotion to the rumor of a new and improved model can impact the number. Perhaps people in your organization even have a theory about what will have the biggest effect on sales. "Trust me. The more rain we have, the more we sell." "Six weeks after the competitor's promotion, sales jump."

Regression analysis is a way of mathematically sorting out which of those variables do indeed have an impact. It answers the questions: Which factors matter most? Which can we ignore? How do those factors interact with one another? And, perhaps most importantly, how certain are we about all of these factors?

In regression analysis, those factors are called variables. You have your **dependent variable**—the main factor that you're trying to understand or predict. In Redman's example above, the dependent variable is monthly sales. And then you have your **independent variables**—the factors you suspect have an impact on your dependent variable.

How Does It Work?

In order to conduct a regression analysis, you gather data on the variables in question. You take all of your monthly sales numbers for, say, the past three years and any data on the independent variables you're interested in. So, in this case, let's say you find out the average monthly rainfall for the past three years as well. Then you plot all of that information on a chart that looks like figure 10-1.

The y-axis is the amount of sales (the dependent variable, the thing you're interested in, is always on the y-axis) and the x-axis is the total rainfall. Each dot represents one month's data—how much it rained that month and how many sales you made that same month.

Glancing at this data, you probably notice that sales are higher on days when it rains a lot. That's interesting to know, but by how much? If it rains three inches, do you know how much you'll sell? What about if it rains four inches?

FIGURE 10-1

Is there a relationship between these two variables?

Plotting your data is the first step to figuring that out.

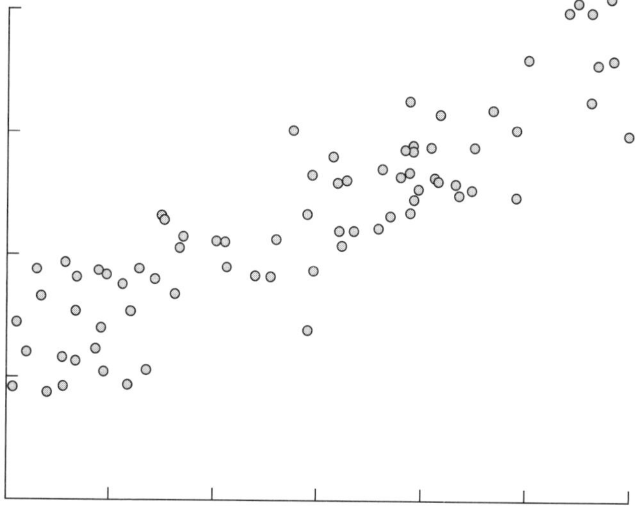

FIGURE 10-2

Building a regression model

The line summarizes the relationship between x and y.

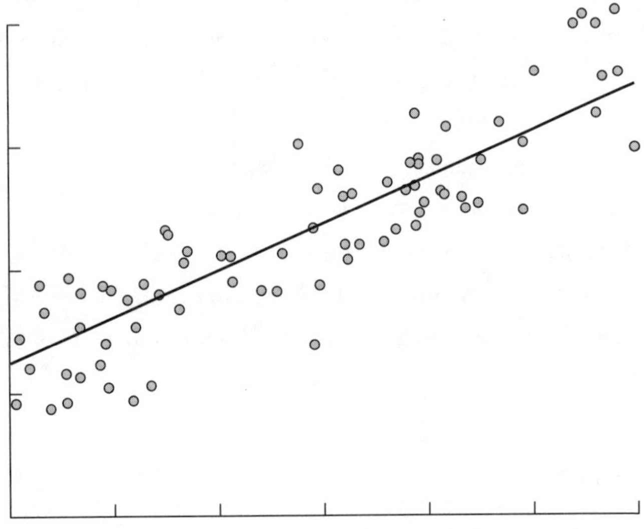

Now imagine drawing a line through the chart, one that runs roughly through the middle of all the data points, as shown in figure 10-2. This line will help you answer, with some degree of certainty, how much you typically sell when it rains a certain amount.

This is called the regression line and it's drawn (using a statistics program like SPSS or STATA or even Excel) to show the line that best fits the data. In other words, explains Redman, "The line is the best explanation of the relationship between the independent variable and dependent variable."

In addition to drawing the line, your statistics program also outputs a formula that explains the slope of the line and looks something like this:

$$y = 200 + 5x + \text{error term}$$

Ignore the error term for now. It refers to the fact that regression isn't perfectly precise. Just focus on the model:

$$y = 200 + 5x$$

What this formula is telling you is that if there is no x then $y = 200$. So, historically, when it didn't rain at all, you made an average of 200 sales and you can expect to do the same going forward assuming other variables stay the same. And in the past, for every additional inch of rain, you made an average of five more sales. "For every increment that x goes up one, y goes up by five," says Redman.

Now let's return to the **error term**. You might be tempted to say that rain has a big impact on sales if for every inch you get five more sales, but whether this variable is worth your attention will depend on the error term. A regression line always has an error term because, in real life, independent variables are never perfect predictors of the dependent variables. Rather, the line is an estimate based on the available data. So the error term tells you how certain you can be about the formula. The larger it is, the less certain the regression line.

This example uses only one variable to predict the factor of interest—in this case, rain to predict sales. Typically, you start a regression analysis wanting to understand the impact of several independent variables. So you might include not just rain but also data about a competitor's promotion. "You keep doing this until the error term is very small," says Redman. "You're trying to get the line that fits best with your data." While there can be dangers in trying to include too many variables in a regression analysis, skilled analysts can minimize those risks. And considering the impact of multiple variables at once is one of the biggest advantages of regression.

How Do Companies Use It?

Regression analysis is the "go-to method in analytics," says Redman. And smart companies use it to make decisions about all sorts of business issues. "As managers, we want to figure out how we can impact sales or employee retention or recruiting the best people. It helps us figure out what we can do."

Most companies use regression analysis to explain a phenomenon they want to understand (why did customer service calls drop last month?); to predict things about the future (what will sales look like over the next six months?); or to decide what to do (should we go with this promotion or a different one?).

Does Correlation Imply Causation?

Whenever you work with regression analysis or any other analysis that tries to explain the impact of one factor on another, you need to remember the important adage: Correlation is not causation. This is critical and here's why: It's easy to say that there is a correlation between rain and monthly sales. The regression shows that they are indeed related. But it's an entirely different thing to say that rain *caused* the sales. Unless you're selling umbrellas, it might be difficult to prove that there is cause and effect.

Sometimes factors are correlated that are obviously not connected by cause and effect, but more often in business it's not so obvious (see the sidebar, "Beware Spurious Correlations," at the end of this chapter). When you see a correlation from a regression analysis, you can't make assumptions, says Redman. Instead, "You have to go out and see what's happening in the real world. What's the physical mechanism that's causing the relationship?" Go out and observe consumers buying your product in the rain, talk to them, and find out what is actually causing them to make the purchase. "A lot of people skip this step and I think it's because they're lazy. The goal is not to figure out what is going on in the data but to figure out what is going on in the world. You have to go out and pound the pavement," he says.

Redman once ran his own experiment and analysis in order to better understand the connection between his travel and weight gain. He noticed that when he traveled, he ate more and exercised less. Was his weight gain caused by travel? Not necessarily. "It was nice to quantify what was happening but travel isn't the cause. It may be related," he says, but it's not like his being on the road put those extra pounds on. He had to understand more about what was happening during his trips. "I'm often in new environments so maybe I'm eating more because I'm nervous." He needed to look more closely at the correlation. And this is his advice to managers. Use the data to guide more experiments, not to make conclusions about cause and effect.

What Mistakes Do People Make When Working with Regression Analysis?

As a consumer of regression analysis, there are several things you need to keep in mind.

First, don't tell your data analyst to go figure out what is affecting sales. "The way most analyses go haywire is the manager hasn't narrowed the focus on what he or she is looking for," says Redman. It's your job to identify the factors that you suspect are having an impact and ask your analyst to look at those. "If you tell a data scientist to go on a fishing expedition, or to tell you something you don't know, then you deserve what you get, which is bad analysis," he says. In other words, don't ask your analysts to look at every variable they can possibly get their hands on all at once. If you do, you're likely to find relationships that don't really exist. It's the same principle as flipping a coin: Do it enough times, you'll eventually *think* you see something interesting, like a bunch of heads all in a row. (For more on how to communicate your data needs to experts, see chapter 4.)

Also keep in mind whether or not you can do anything about the independent variable you're considering. You can't change how much it rains, so how important is it to understand that? "We can't do anything about weather or our competitor's promotion but we can affect our own promotions or add features, for example," says Redman. Always ask yourself what you will do with the data. What actions will you take? What decisions will you make?

Second, "analyses are very sensitive to bad data" so be careful about the data you collect and how you collect it, and know whether you can trust it (as we learned in chapter 8). "All the data doesn't have to be correct or perfect," explains Redman, but consider what you will be doing with the analysis. If the decisions you'll make as a result don't have a huge impact on your business, then it's OK if the data is "kind of leaky." But, "if you're trying to decide whether to build 8 or 10 of something and each one costs $1 million to build, then it's a bigger deal," he says.

Redman also says that some managers who are new to understanding regression analysis make the mistake of ignoring the error term. This is dangerous because they're making the relationship between two variables more certain than it is. "Oftentimes the results spit out of a computer and managers think, 'That's great, let's use this going forward.'" But remember that the results are always uncertain. As Redman points out, "If the regression explains 90% of the relationship, that's great. But if it explains 10%, and you act like it's 90%, that's not good." The point of the analysis is to quantify the certainty that something will happen. "It's not telling you how rain will influence your sales, but it's telling you the probability that rain may influence your sales."

The last mistake that Redman warns against is letting data replace your intuition. "You always have to lay your intuition on top of the data," he explains. Ask yourself whether the results fit with your understanding of the situation. And if you see something that doesn't make sense, ask whether the data was right or whether there is indeed a large error term. Redman suggests you look to more experienced managers or other analyses if you're getting something that doesn't make sense. And, he says, never forget to look beyond the numbers to what's happening outside your office: "You need to pair any analysis with study of the real world. The best scientists—and managers—look at both."

Amy Gallo is a contributing editor at *Harvard Business Review* and the author of the *HBR Guide to Dealing with Conflict*. Follow her on Twitter @amyegallo.

BEWARE SPURIOUS CORRELATIONS

We all know the truism "Correlation doesn't imply causation," but when we see lines sloping together, bars rising together, or points on a scatterplot clustering, the data practically begs us to assign a reason. We want to believe one exists.

Statistically we can't make that leap, however. Charts that show a close correlation are often relying on a visual parlor trick to imply a relationship. Tyler Vigen, a JD student at Harvard Law School and the author of *Spurious Correlations*, has made sport of this on his website, which charts farcical correlations—for example, between U.S. per capita margarine consumption and the divorce rate in Maine.

Vigen has programmed his site so that anyone can find and chart absurd correlations in large data sets. We tried a few of our own and came up with these gems:

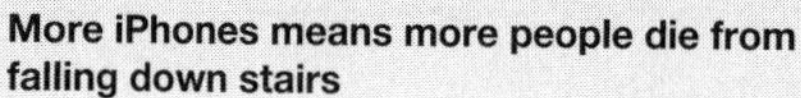

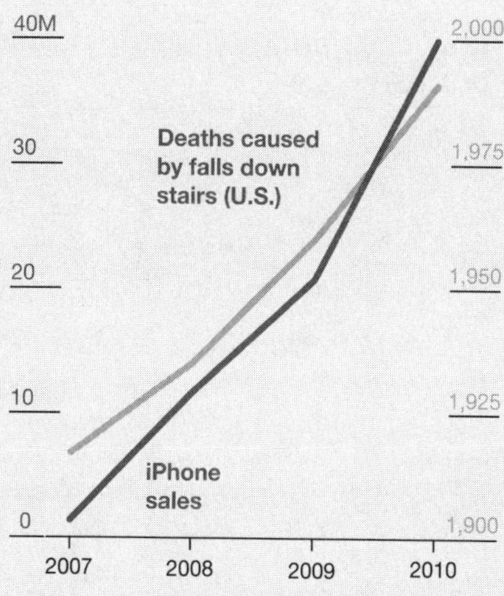

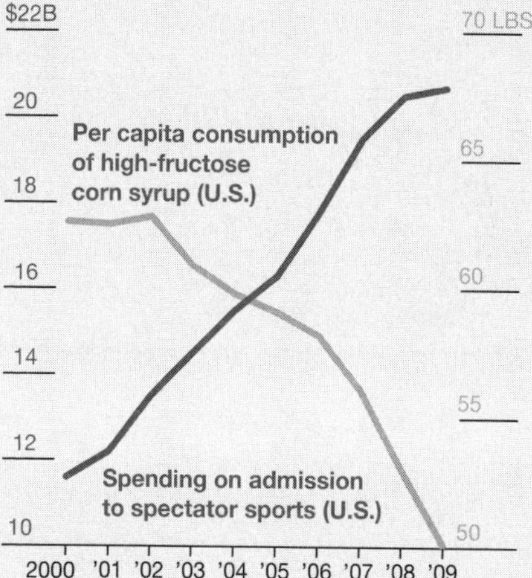

Source: Tylervigen.com

(continued)

BEWARE SPURIOUS CORRELATIONS

(continued)

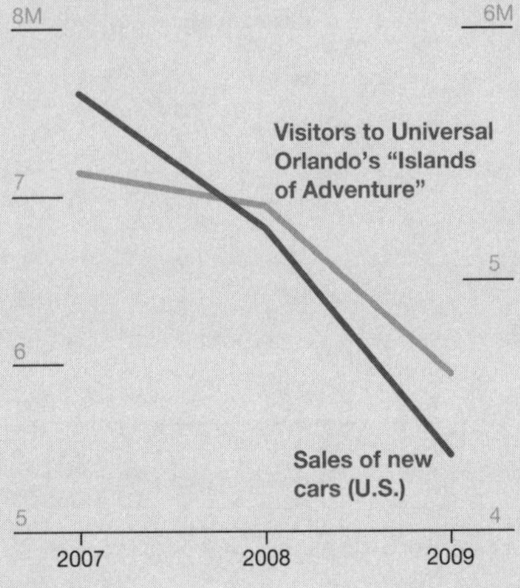

Source: Tylervigen.com

Although it's easy to spot and explain away absurd examples, like these, you're likely to encounter rigged but plausible charts in your daily work. Here are three types to watch out for:

Apples and Oranges: Comparing Dissimilar Variables

Y axis scales that measure different values may show similar curves that shouldn't be paired. This becomes pernicious when the values appear to be related but aren't.

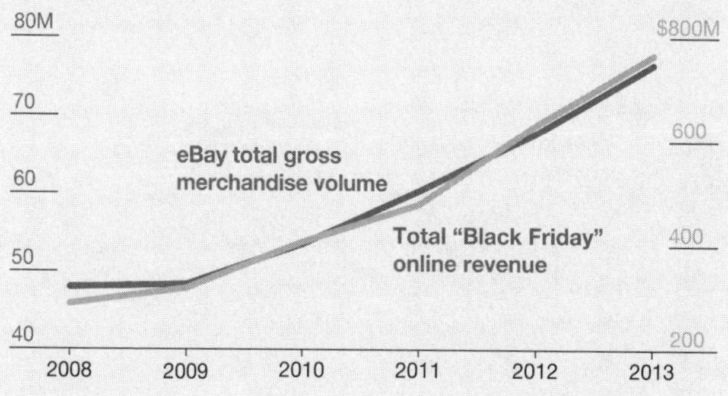

It's best to chart them separately.

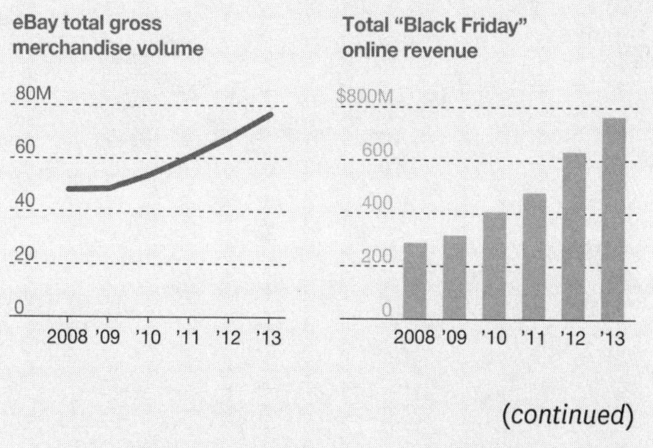

(continued)

BEWARE SPURIOUS CORRELATIONS

(continued)

Skewed Scales: Manipulating Ranges to Align Data

Even when *y* axes measure the same category, changing the scales can alter the lines to suggest a correlation. These *y* axes for RetailCo's monthly revenue difference in range and proportional increase.

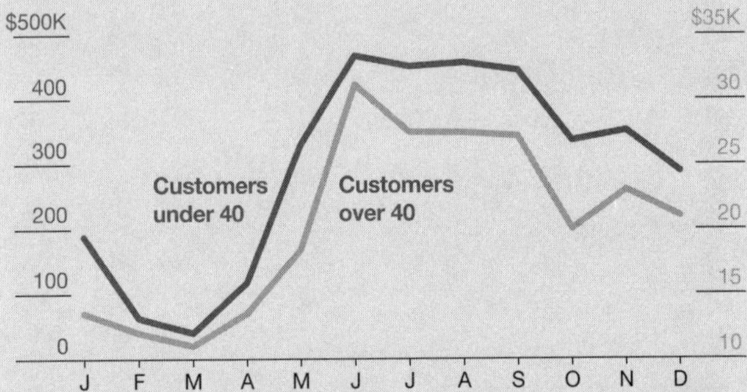

Eliminating the second axis shows how skewed this chart is.

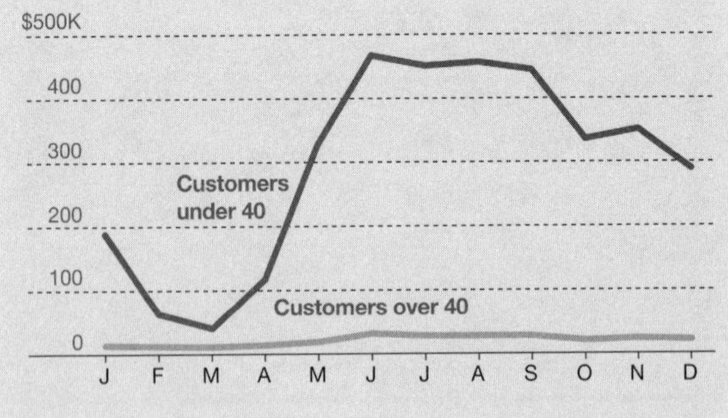

Ifs and *Thens*: Implying Cause and Effect

Plotting unrelated data sets together can make it seem that changes in one variable are causing changes in the other.

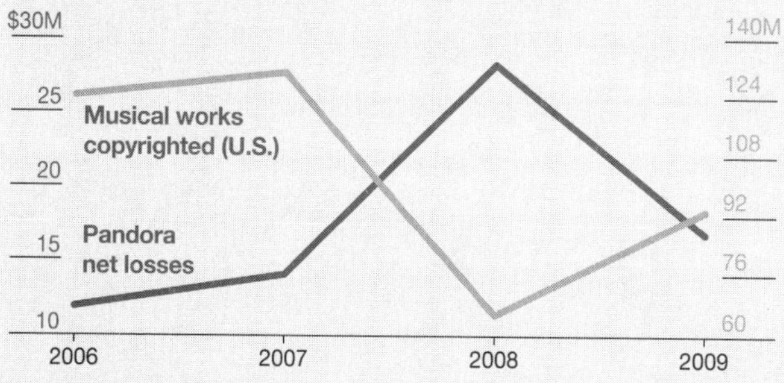

We try to create a narrative—*if* Pandora loses less money, *then* more music is copyrighted—from what is probably a coincidence.

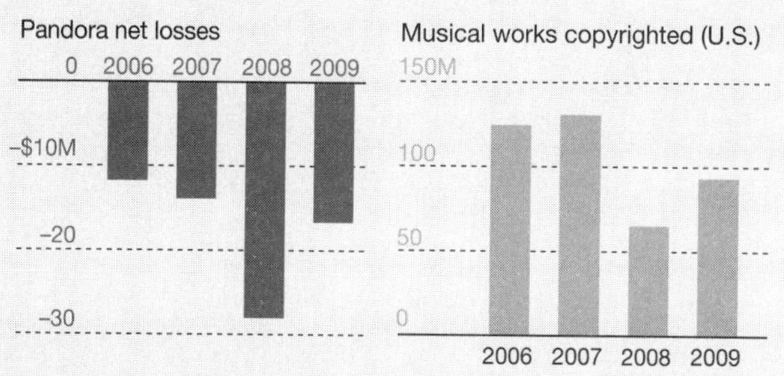

Adapted from "Beware Spurious Correlations," *Harvard Business Review*, June 2015 (product #F1506Z).

CHAPTER 11

When to Act On a Correlation, and When Not To

by David Ritter

> "Petabytes allow us to say: 'Correlation is enough.'"
>
> —**Chris Anderson,**
> ***Wired*, June 23, 2008**

The sentiment expressed by Chris Anderson in 2008 is a popular meme in the big data community. "Causality is dead," say the priests of analytics and machine learning. They argue that given enough statistical evidence, it's no longer necessary to understand why things happen—we need only know what things happen together.

Adapted from content posted on hbr.org, March 19, 2014 (product #H00Q1X).

But inquiring whether correlation is enough is asking the wrong question. For consumers of big data, the key question is, "Can I take action on the basis of a correlation finding?" The answer to that question is, "It depends"—primarily on two factors:

- **Confidence that the correlation will reliably recur in the future.** The higher that confidence level, the more reasonable it is to take action in response.
- **The trade-off between the risk and reward of acting.** If the risk of acting and being wrong is extremely high, for example, acting on even a strong correlation may be a mistake.

The first factor—the confidence that the correlation will recur—is in turn a function of two things: the frequency with which the correlation has historically occurred (the more often events occur together in real life, the more likely it is that they are connected) and an understanding of what is causing that statistical finding. This second element—what we call "clarity of causality"—stems from the fact that the fewer possible explanations there are for a correlation, the higher the likelihood that the two events are linked. Considering frequency and clarity together yields a more reliable gauge of the overall confidence in the finding than evaluating only one or the other in isolation.

Understanding the interplay between the confidence level and the risk/reward trade-off enables sound decisions on what action—if any—makes sense in light of a particular statistical finding. The bottom line: Causality can matter tremendously. And efforts to gain better insight into the cause of a correlation can drive up the confidence level of taking action.

These concepts allowed The Boston Consulting Group (BCG) to develop a prism through which any potential action can be evaluated. If the value of acting is high, and the cost of acting when wrong is low, it can make sense to act based on even a weak correlation. We choose to look both ways before crossing the street because the cost of looking is low and the potential loss from not looking is high (in statistical jargon what is known as "asymmetric loss function"). Alternatively, if the confidence in the finding is low due to the fact you don't have a handle on why two events are linked, you should be less willing to take actions that have significant potential downside, illustrated in figure 11-1.

FIGURE 11-1

When to act on a correlation in your data

How confident are you in the relationship? And do the benefits of action outweigh the risk?

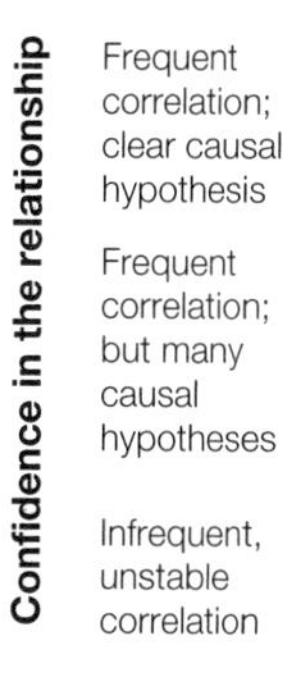

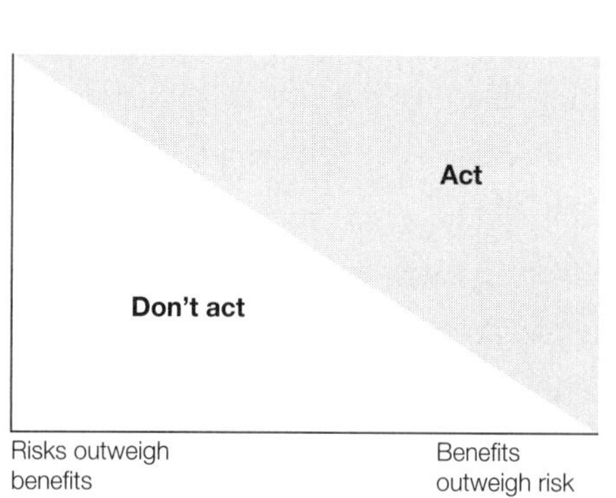

Source: David Ritter, BCG

Consider the case of New York City's sewer sensors. These sensors detect the amount of grease flowing into the sewer system at various locations throughout the city. If the data collected shows a concentration of grease at an unexpected location—perhaps due to an unlicensed restaurant—officials will send a car out to determine the source. The confidence in the meaning of the data from the sensors is on the low side—there may be many other explanations for the excessive influx of grease. But there's little cost if the inspection finds nothing amiss.

Recent decisions around routine PSA screening tests for prostate cancer involved a very different risk/reward trade-off. Confidence that PSA blood tests are a good predictor of cancer is low because the correlation itself is weak—elevated PSA levels are found often in men without prostate cancer. There is also no clear causal explanation for how PSA is related to the development of cancer. In addition, preventative surgery prompted by the test did not increase long-term survival rates. And the risk associated with screening was high, with false positives leading to unnecessary, debilitating treatment. The result: The American Medical Association reversed its previous recommendation that men over 50 have routine PSA blood tests.

Of course, there is usually not just one, but a range of possible actions in response to a statistical finding. This came into play recently in a partnership between an Australian supermarket and an auto insurance company. Combining data from the supermarket's loyalty card program with auto claims information revealed interesting correlations. The data showed that people who buy red meat and milk are good car insurance risks while people who buy pasta and spirits and who fuel their cars at night are poor risks. Though this statistical relationship could be an indicator of risky behaviors (driving under the influence of spirits, for example), there are a number of other possible reasons for the finding.

Potential responses to the finding included:

- Targeting insurance marketing to loyalty card holders in the low-risk group
- Pricing car insurance based on these buying patterns

The latter approach, however, could lead to brand-damaging backlash should the practice be exposed. Looking at the two options via our framework in figure 11-2 makes clear that without additional confidence in the finding, the former approach is preferable.

FIGURE 11-2

If supermarket purchases correlate with auto insurance claims, what should an insurer do?

With the case of relationship unclear, low risk actions are advisible.

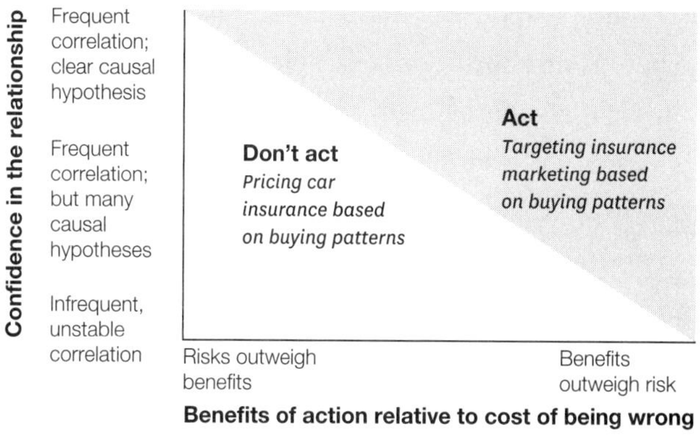

Confidence in the relationship

Frequent correlation; clear causal hypothesis

Frequent correlation; but many causal hypotheses

Infrequent, unstable correlation

Don't act
Pricing car insurance based on buying patterns

Act
Targeting insurance marketing based on buying patterns

Risks outweigh benefits

Benefits outweigh risk

Benefits of action relative to cost of being wrong

Source: David Ritter, BCG

However, if we are able to find a clear causal explanation for this correlation, we may be able to increase confidence sufficiently to take the riskier, higher-value action of increasing rates. For example, the buying patterns associated with higher risks could be leading indicators of an impending life transition such as loss of employment or a divorce. This possible explanation could be tested by adding additional data to the analysis.

In this case causality is critical. New factors can potentially be identified that create a better understanding of the dynamics at work. The goal is to rule out some possible causes and shed light on what is really driving that correlation. That understanding will increase the overall level of confidence that the correlation will continue in the future—essentially shifting possible actions into the upper portion of the framework. The result may be that previously ruled-out responses are now appropriate. In addition, insight on the cause of a correlation can allow you to look for changes that cause the linkage to weaken or disappear. And that knowledge makes it possible to monitor and respond to events that might make a previously sound response outdated.

There is no shortage of examples where the selection of the right response hinges on this "clarity of cause." The U.S. Army, for example, has developed image processing software that uses flashes of light to locate the possible position of a sniper. But similar flashes also come from a camera. With two potential reasons for the imaging pattern, the confidence in the finding is lower than it would be if there were just one. And that, of course, will determine how to respond—and what level of risk is acceptable.

When working with big data, sometimes correlation is enough. But other times understanding the cause is vital. The key is to know when correlation is enough—and what to do when it is not.

David Ritter is a director in the Technology Advantage practice of The Boston Consulting Group (BCG), where he advises clients on the use of technology for competitive advantage, open innovation, and other topics.

CHAPTER 12

Can Machine Learning Solve Your Business Problem?

by Anastassia Fedyk

As you consider ways to analyze large swaths of data, you may ask yourself how the latest technological tools and automation can help. *AI*, *big data*, and *machine learning* are all trending buzzwords, but how can you know which problems in your business are amenable to machine learning?

Adapted from "How to Tell If Machine Learning Can Solve Your Business Problem" on hbr.org, November 25, 2016 (product #H03A8R).

To decide, you need to think about the problem to be solved and the available data, and ask questions about feasibility, intuition, and expectations.

Assess Whether Your Problem Requires Learning

Machine learning can help automate your processes, but not all automation problems require learning.

Automation without learning is appropriate when the problem is relatively straightforward—the kinds of tasks where you have a clear, predefined sequence of steps that is currently being executed by a human, but could conceivably be transitioned to a machine. This sort of automation has been happening in businesses for decades. Screening incoming data from an outside data provider for well-defined potential errors is an example of a problem ready for automation. (For example, hedge funds automatically filter out bad data in the form of a negative value for trading volume, which can't be negative.) On the other hand, encoding human language into a structured data set is something that is just a tad too ambitious for a straightforward set of rules.

For the second type of problem, standard automation is not enough. Such complex problems require learning from data—and now we venture into the arena of machine learning. *Machine learning*, at its core, is a set of statistical methods meant to find patterns of predictability in data sets. These methods are great at determining how certain features of the data are related to the outcomes you are interested in. What these methods cannot do is access any knowledge outside of the data you provide. For example, researchers at the University of Pittsburg in the late 1990s evaluated machine-learning algorithms for predicting mortality rates from pneumonia.[1] The algorithms recommended that hospitals send home pneumonia patients who were also asthma sufferers, estimating their risk of death from pneumonia to be lower. It turned out that the data set fed into the algorithms did not account for the fact that asthma sufferers had been immediately sent to intensive care, and had fared better only because of the additional attention.[2]

So what are good business problems for machine learning methods? Essentially, any problems that meet the following two criteria:

1. They require prediction rather than causal inference.
2. They are sufficiently self-contained or relatively insulated from outside influences.

The first means that you are interested in understanding how, on average, certain aspects of the data relate to each other, and not in the causal channels of their relationship. (Keep in mind that the statistical methods do not bring to the table the intuition, theory, or domain knowledge of human analysts.) The second means that you are relatively certain that the data you feed to your learning algorithm includes more or less all there is to the problem. If, in the future, the thing you're trying to predict changes unexpectedly and no longer matches prior patterns in the data, the algorithm will not know what to make of it.

Examples of good machine learning problems include predicting the likelihood that a certain type of user will click on a certain kind of ad, or evaluating the extent to which a piece of text is similar to previous texts you have seen. (To see an example of how an artificial intelligence algorithm learned from existing customer data and test marketing campaigns to find new sales leads, see the sidebar "Artificial Intelligence at Harley-Davidson.")

Bad examples include predicting profits from the introduction of a completely new and revolutionary product line, or extrapolating next year's sales from past data when an important new competitor just entered the market.

ARTIFICIAL INTELLIGENCE AT HARLEY-DAVIDSON

by Brad Power

It was winter in New York City, and Asaf Jacobi's Harley-Davidson dealership was selling one or two motorcycles a week. It wasn't enough.

Jacobi went for a long walk in Riverside Park and happened to bump into Or Shani, CEO of an AI firm, Adgorithms. After discussing Jacobi's sales woes, Shani suggested he try out Albert, Adgorithm's AI-driven marketing platform. It works across digital channels, like Facebook and Google, to measure and then autonomously optimize the outcomes of marketing campaigns. Jacobi decided he'd give Albert a one-weekend audition.

That weekend, Jacobi sold 15 motorcycles—almost twice his all-time summer weekend sales record of eight.

Naturally, Jacobi kept using Albert. His dealership went from getting one qualified lead per day to 40. In the first month, 15% of those new leads were lookalikes, meaning that the people calling the dealership to set up a visit resembled previous high-value customers and therefore were more likely to make a purchase. By the third month, the dealership's leads had increased 2,930%, 50% of them lookalikes, leaving Jacobi scrambling to set up a new call center with six new employees to handle all the new business.

While Jacobi had estimated that only 2% of New York City's population were potential buyers, Albert revealed that his target market was larger—much larger—and began finding customers Jacobi didn't even know existed.

How did it do that?

Albert drove in-store traffic by generating leads, defined as customers who express interest in speaking to a salesperson by filling out a form on the dealership's website. Armed with creative content (headlines and visuals) provided by Harley-Davidson and key performance targets, Albert began by analyzing existing customer data from Jacobi's customer relationship management system to isolate defining characteristics and

(*continued*)

ARTIFICIAL INTELLIGENCE AT HARLEY-DAVIDSON

(*continued*)

behaviors of high-value past customers: those who either had completed a purchase, added an item to an online cart, viewed website content, or were among the top 25% in terms of time spent on the website.

Using this information, Albert identified lookalikes who resembled these past customers and created micro segments—small sample groups with whom it could run test campaigns before extending its efforts more widely. Albert used the data gathered through these tests to predict which possible headlines and visual combinations, and thousands of other campaign variables, would most likely convert different audience segments through various digital channels (social media, search, display, and email or SMS).

Once it determined what was working and what wasn't, Albert scaled the campaigns, autonomously allocating resources from channel to channel, making content recommendations, and so on.

For example, when it discovered that ads with the word *call*—such as, "Don't miss out on a pre-owned Harley with a great price! Call now!"—performed 447% better than ads containing the word *buy*, such as, "Buy a pre-owned Harley from our store now!" Albert immediately changed *buy* to *call* in all ads across all relevant channels. The results spoke for themselves.

For Harley-Davidson, AI evaluated what was working across digital channels and what wasn't, and used what it learned to create more opportunities for conversion. In other words, the system allocated resources only to what had been proven to work, thereby increasing digital marketing ROI. Using AI, Harley-Davidson was able to eliminate guesswork, gather and analyze enormous volumes of data, and optimally leverage the resulting insights.

Adapted from "How Harley-Davidson Used Artificial Intelligence to Increase New York Sales Leads by 2,930%" on hbr.org, May 30, 2017 (product #H03NFD).

Brad Power is a consultant who helps organizations that must make faster changes to their products, services, and systems to compete with startups and leading software companies.

Find the Appropriate Data

Once you verify that your problem is suitable for machine learning, the next step is to evaluate whether you have the right data to solve it. The data might come from you or from an external provider. In the latter case, ask enough questions to get a good feel for the data's scope and whether it is likely to be a good fit for your problem.

Ask Questions and Look for Mistakes

Once you've determined that your problem is a classic machine learning problem and you have the data to fit it, check your intuition. Machine learning methods, however proprietary and seemingly magical, are statistics. And statistics *can* be explained in intuitive terms.

Instead of trusting that the brilliant proposed method will seamlessly work, ask lots of questions.

Get yourself comfortable with how the method works. Does the intuition of the method roughly make sense? Does it fit conceptually into the framework of the particular setting or problem you are dealing with? What makes this method especially well-suited to your problem? If you are encoding a set of steps, perhaps sequential models or decision trees are a good choice. If you need to separate two classes of outcome, perhaps a binary support vector machine would be best aligned with your needs.

With understanding come more realistic expectations. Once you ask enough questions and receive enough answers to have an intuitive understanding of how the methodology works, you will see that it is far from magical. Every human makes mistakes, and every algorithm is error prone too. For all but the simplest of problems, there *will* be times when things go wrong. The machine learning prediction engine will get things right on average but will reliably make mistakes. And these errors will happen most often in ways that you cannot anticipate.

Decide How to Move Forward

The last step is to evaluate the extent to which you can allow for exceptions or statistical errors in your process. Is your problem the kind where getting things right 80% of the time is enough? Can you deal with a 10% error rate? 5%? 1%? Are there certain kinds of errors that should never be allowed? Be clear and upfront about your needs and expectations, both with yourself and with your solution provider. And once both of you are comfortably on the same page, go ahead. Armed with knowledge, understanding, and reasonable expectations, you are set to reap the benefits of machine learning. Just please be patient.

Anastassia Fedyk is a PhD candidate in business economics at Harvard Business School. Her research focuses on finance and behavioral economics.

NOTES

1. G. F. Cooper et al., "An Evaluation of Machine-Learning Methods for Predicting Pneumonia Mortality," *Artificial Intelligence in Medicine* 9 (1997): 107–138.
2. A. M. Bornstein, "Is Artificial Intelligence Permanently Inscrutable?" *Nautilus*, September 1, 2016, http://nautil.us/issue/40/learning/is-artificial-intelligence-permanently-inscrutable.

CHAPTER 13

A Refresher on Statistical Significance

by Amy Gallo

When you run an experiment or analyze data, you want to know if your findings are significant. But business relevance (that is, practical significance) isn't always the same thing as confidence that a result isn't due purely to chance (that is, statistical significance). This is an important distinction; unfortunately, **statistical significance** is often misunderstood and misused in organizations today. And because more and more companies are relying on data to make critical business decisions, it's an essential concept for managers to understand.

Adapted from content posted on hbr.org, February 16, 2016 (product #H02NMS).

To better understand what statistical significance really means, I talked with Thomas Redman, author of *Data Driven: Profiting from Your Most Important Business Asset*, and adviser to organizations on their data and data quality programs.

What Is Statistical Significance?

"Statistical significance helps quantify whether a result is likely due to chance or to some factor of interest," says Redman. When a finding is significant, it simply means you can feel confident that it's real, not that you just got lucky (or unlucky) in choosing the sample.

When you run an experiment, conduct a survey, take a poll, or analyze a data set, you're taking a sample of some population of interest, not looking at every single data point that you possibly can. Consider the example of a marketing campaign. You've come up with a new concept and you want to see if it works better than your current one. You can't show it to every single target customer, of course, so you choose a sample group.

When you run the results, you find that those who saw the new campaign spent $10.17 on average, more than the $8.41 spent by those who saw the old campaign. This $1.76 might seem like a big—and perhaps important—difference. But in reality you may have been unlucky, drawing a sample of people who do not represent the larger population; in fact, maybe there was no difference between the two campaigns and their influence on consumers' purchasing behaviors. This is called a sampling error, something you must contend with in any test that does not include the entire population of interest.

Redman notes that there are two main contributors to sampling error: the size of the sample and the variation in the underlying population. Sample size may be intuitive enough. Think about flipping a coin 5 times versus flipping it 500 times. The more times you flip, the less likely you'll end up with a great majority of heads. The same is true of statistical significance: With bigger sample sizes, you're less likely to get results that reflect randomness. All else being equal, you'll feel more comfortable in the accuracy of the campaigns' $1.76 difference if you showed the new one to 1,000 people rather than just 25. Of course, showing the campaign to more people costs more money, so you have to balance the need for a larger sample size with your budget.

Variation is a little trickier to understand, but Redman insists that developing a sense for it is critical for all managers who use data. Consider the images in figure 13-1. Each expresses a different possible distribution of customer purchases under campaign A. Looking at the chart on the left (with less variation), most people spend roughly the same amount. Some people spend a few dollars more or less, but if you pick a customer at random, chances are pretty good that they'll be close to the average. So it's less likely that you'll select a sample that looks vastly different from the total population, which means you can be relatively confident in your results.

Compare that with the chart on the right (with more variation). Here, people vary more widely in how much they spend. The average is still the same, but quite a few people spend more or less. If you pick a customer at random, chances are higher that they are pretty far from

FIGURE 13-1

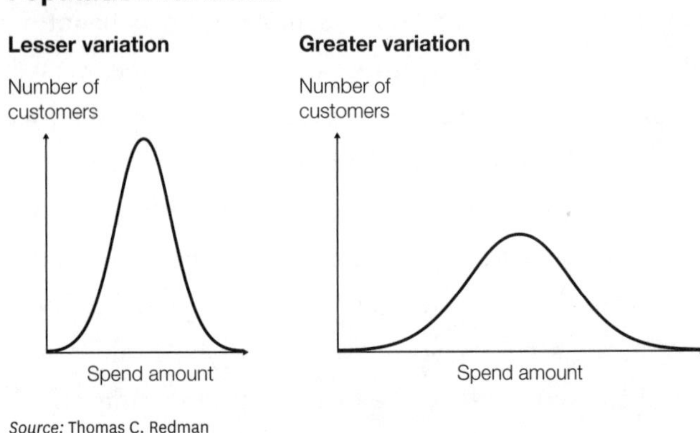

Source: Thomas C. Redman

the average. So if you select a sample from a more varied population, you can't be as confident in your results.

To summarize, the important thing to understand is that the greater the variation in the underlying population, the larger the sampling error.

Redman advises that you should plot your data and make pictures like these when you analyze the numbers. The graphs will help you get a feel for variation, the sampling error, and in turn, the statistical significance.

No matter what you're studying, the process for evaluating significance is the same. You start by stating a null hypothesis. In the experiment about the marketing campaign, the null hypothesis might be, "On average, customers don't prefer our new campaign to the old one." Before you begin, you should also state an alternative hypothesis, such as, "On average, customers prefer the new one," and a target significance level. The significance level is an expression of how rare your results are, under the assumption that the null hypothesis is true. It is usually expressed as a *p*-value, and the lower the *p*-value, the less likely the results are due purely to chance.

Setting a target and interpreting *p*-values can be dauntingly complex. Redman says it depends a lot on what you are analyzing. "If you're searching for the Higgs boson, you probably want an extremely low *p*-value, maybe 0.00001," he says. "But if you're testing for whether your new marketing concept is better or the new drill bits your engineer designed work faster than your existing bits, then you're probably willing to take a higher value, maybe even as high as 0.25."

Note that in many business experiments, managers skip these two initial steps and don't worry about significance until after the results are in. However, it's good scientific practice to do these two things ahead of time.

Then you collect your data, plot the results, and calculate statistics, including the *p*-value, which incorporates variation and the sample size. If you get a *p*-value lower than your target, then you reject the null hypothesis in favor of the alternative. Again, this means the probability is small that your results were due solely to chance.

How Is It Calculated?

As a manager, chances are you won't ever calculate statistical significance yourself. "Most good statistical packages will report the significance along with the results," says Redman. There is also a formula in Microsoft Excel and a number of other online tools that will calculate it for you.

Still, it's helpful to know the process in order to understand and interpret the results. As Redman advises, "Managers should not trust a model they don't understand."

How Do Companies Use It?

Companies use statistical significance to understand how strongly the results of an experiment, survey, or poll they've conducted should influence the decisions they make. For example, if a manager runs a pricing study to understand how best to price a new product, they will calculate the statistical significance (with the help of an analyst, most likely) so that they know whether the findings should affect the final price.

Remember the new marketing campaign that produced a $1.76 boost (more than 20%) in the average sale? It's surely of practical significance. If the *p*-value comes in at 0.03 the result is also statistically significant, and you should adopt the new campaign. If the *p*-value comes in at 0.2 the result is not statistically significant, but since the boost is so large you'll probably still proceed, though perhaps with a bit more caution.

But what if the difference were only a few cents? If the *p*-value comes in at 0.2, you'll stick with your current campaign or explore other options. But even if it had a significance level of 0.03, the result is probably real, though quite small. In this case, your decision probably will be based on other factors, such as the cost of implementing the new campaign.

Closely related to the idea of a significance level is the notion of a confidence interval. Let's take the example of a political poll. Say there are two candidates: A and B. The pollsters conduct an experiment with 1,000 "likely voters." From the sample, 49% say they'll vote for A and 51% say they'll vote for B. The pollsters also report a margin of error of +/- 3%.

"Technically, 49% plus or minus 3% is a 95% confidence interval for the true proportion of A voters in the population," says Redman. Unfortunately, he adds, most people interpret this as "there's a 95% chance that A's true percentage lies between 46% and 52%," but that isn't correct. Instead, it says that if the pollsters were to do the result many times, 95% of intervals constructed this way would contain the true proportion.

If your head is spinning at that last sentence, you're not alone. As Redman says, this interpretation is "maddeningly subtle, too subtle for most managers and even many researchers with advanced degrees." He says the more practical interpretation of this would be "Don't get too excited that B has a lock on the election" or "B appears to have a lead, but it's not a statistically significant one." Of course, the practical interpretation would be very different if 70% of the likely voters said they'd vote for B and the margin of error was 3%.

The reason managers bother with statistical significance is they want to know what findings say about what they should do in the real world. But "confidence intervals and hypothesis tests were designed to support 'science,' where the idea is to learn something that will stand the test of time," says Redman. Even if a finding isn't statistically significant, it may have utility to you and your company. On the other hand, when you're working with large data sets, it's possible to obtain results that are statistically significant but practically meaningless, for example, that a group of customers is 0.000001% more likely to click on campaign A over campaign B. So rather than obsessing about whether your findings are precisely right, think about the implication of each finding for the decision you're hoping to make. What would you do differently if the finding were different?

What Mistakes Do People Make When Working with Statistical Significance?

"Statistical significance is a slippery concept and is often misunderstood," warns Redman. "I don't run into very many situations where managers need to understand it deeply, but they need to know how to not misuse it."

Of course, data scientists don't have a monopoly on the word "significant," and often in businesses it's used to mean whether a finding is strategically important. It's good practice to use language that's as clear as possible when talking about data findings. If you want to discuss whether the finding has implications for your strategy or decisions, it's fine to use the word "significant," but if you want to know whether something is *statistically* significant, be precise in your language. Next time you look at results of a survey or experiment, ask about the statistical significance if the analyst hasn't reported it.

Remember that statistical significance tests help you account for potential sampling errors, but Redman says what is often more worrisome is the non-sampling error: "Non-sampling error involves things where the experimental and/or measurement protocols didn't happen according to plan, such as people lying on the survey, data getting lost, or mistakes being made in the analysis." This is where Redman sees more troubling results. "There is so much that can happen from the time you plan the survey or experiment to the time you get the results. I'm more worried about whether the raw data is trustworthy than how many people they talked to," he says. Clean data and careful analysis are more important than statistical significance.

Always keep in mind the practical application of the finding. And don't get too hung up on setting a strict confidence interval. Redman says there's a bias in scientific literature that "a result wasn't publishable unless it hit a $p = 0.05$ (or less)." But for many decisions—like which marketing approach to use—you'll need a much lower confidence interval. In business, says Redman, there's often more important criteria than statistical significance. The important question is, "Does the result stand up in the market, if only for a brief period of time?"

As Redman says, the results only give you so much information: "I'm all for using statistics, but always wed it with good judgment."

Amy Gallo is a contributing editor at *Harvard Business Review* and the author of the *HBR Guide to Dealing with Conflict*. Follow her on Twitter @amyegallo.

CHAPTER 14

Linear Thinking in a Nonlinear World

by Bart de Langhe, Stefano Puntoni, and Richard Larrick

Test yourself with this word problem: Imagine you're responsible for your company's car fleet. You manage two models, an SUV that gets 10 miles to the gallon and a sedan that gets 20. The fleet has equal numbers of each, and all the cars travel 10,000 miles a year. You have enough capital to replace one model with more-fuel-efficient vehicles to lower operational costs and help meet sustainability goals.

Which upgrade is better?

A. Replacing the 10 MPG vehicles with 20 MPG vehicles

Reprinted from *Harvard Business Review*, May-June 2017 (product #R1703K).

B. Replacing the 20 MPG vehicles with 50 MPG vehicles

Intuitively, option B seems more impressive—an increase of 30 MPG is a lot larger than a 10 MPG one. And the percentage increase is greater, too. But B is not the better deal. In fact, it's not even close. Let's compare.

Gallons used per 10,000 miles

	Current	After upgrade	Savings
A.	1,000 (@10 MPG)	500 (@20 MPG)	500
B.	500 (@20 MPG)	200 (@50 MPG)	300

Is this surprising? For many of us, it is. That's because in our minds the relationship between MPG and fuel consumption is simpler than it really is. We tend to think it's linear and looks like this:

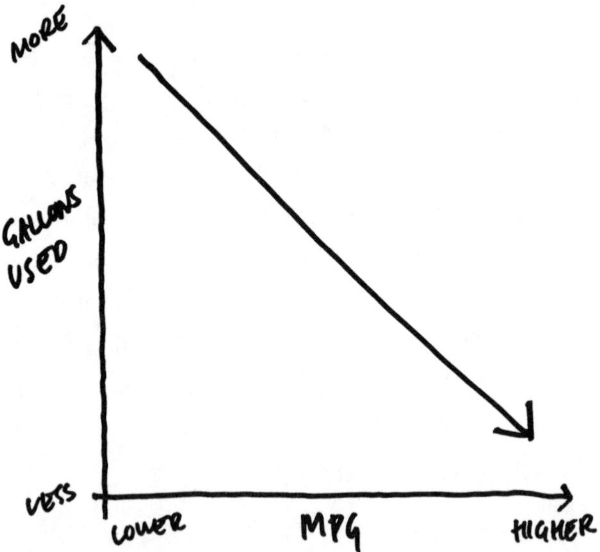

But that graph is incorrect. Gas consumption is not a linear function of MPG. When you do the math, the relationship actually looks like this:

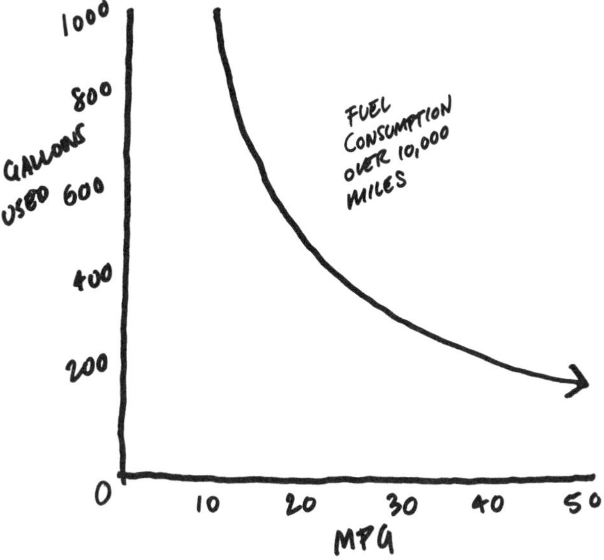

And when you dissect the curve to show each upgrade scenario, it becomes clear how much more effective it is to replace the 10 MPG cars.

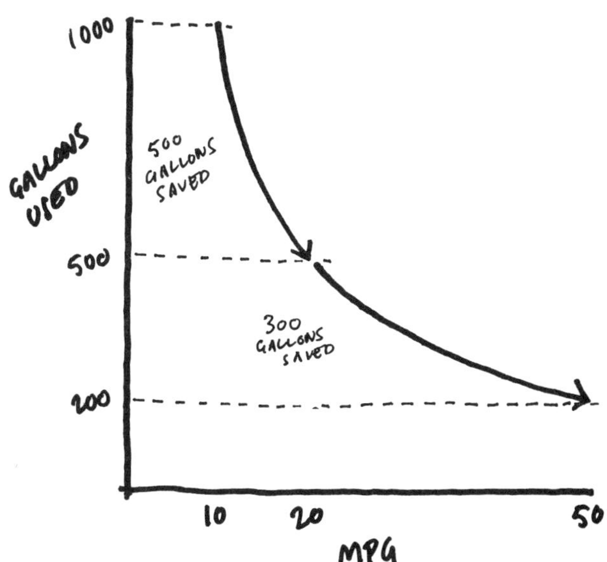

Shockingly, upgrading fuel efficiency from 20 to 100 MPG *still* wouldn't save as much gas as upgrading from 10 to 20 MPG.

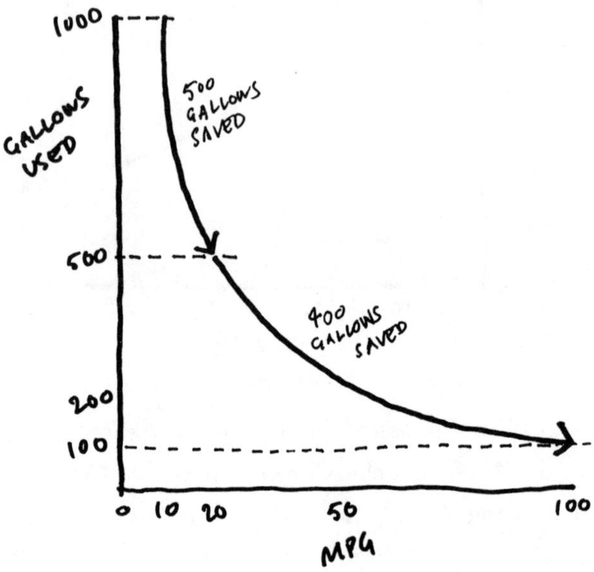

But choosing the lower-mileage upgrade remains counterintuitive, even in the face of the visual evidence. It just doesn't feel right.

If you're still having trouble grasping this, it's not your fault. Decades of research in cognitive psychology show that the human mind struggles to understand nonlinear relationships. Our brain wants to make simple straight lines. In many situations, that kind of thinking serves us well: If you can store 50 books on a shelf, you can store 100 books if you add another shelf, and 150 books if you add yet another. Similarly, if the price of coffee is $2, you can buy five coffees with $10, 10 coffees with $20, and 15 coffees with $30.

But in business there are many highly nonlinear relationships, and we need to recognize when they're in play. This is true for generalists and specialists alike, because even experts who are aware of nonlinearity in their fields can fail to take it into account and default instead to relying on their gut. But when people do that, they often end up making poor decisions.

Linear Bias in Practice

We've seen consumers and companies fall victim to linear bias in numerous real-world scenarios. A common one concerns an important business objective: profits.

Three main factors affect profits: costs, volume, and price. A change in one often requires action on the others to maintain profits. For example, rising costs must be offset by an increase in either price or volume. And if you cut price, lower costs or higher volumes are needed to prevent profits from dipping.

Unfortunately, managers' intuitions about the relationships between these profit levers aren't always good. For years experts have advised companies that changes in price affect profits more than changes in volume or costs. Nevertheless, executives often focus too much on volume and costs instead of getting the price right.

Why? Because the large volume increases they see after reducing prices are very exciting. What people don't realize is just how large those increases need to be to maintain profits, especially when margins are low.

Imagine you manage a brand of paper towels. They sell for 50 cents a roll, and the marginal cost of producing a roll is 15 cents. You recently did two price promotions. Here's how they compare:

	Normal	Promo A: 20% off	Promo B: 40% off
Price/Roll	50¢	40¢	30¢
Sales	1,000	1,200 (+20%)	1,800 (+80%)

Intuitively, B looks more impressive—an 80% increase in volume for a 40% decrease in price seems a lot more profitable than a 20% increase in volume for a 20% cut in price. But you may have guessed by now that B is not the most profitable strategy.

In fact, both promotions decrease profits, but B's negative impact is much bigger than A's. Here are the profits in each scenario:

	Normal	Promo A: 20% off	Promo B: 40% off
Price/Roll	50¢	40¢	30¢
Sales	1,000	1,200 (+20%)	1,800 (+80%)
Profit/Roll	35¢	25¢	15¢
Profit	$350	$300	$270

Although promotion B nearly doubled sales, profits sank almost 25%. To maintain the usual $350 profit during the 40%-off sale, you would have to sell more than 2,300 units, an increase of 133%. The curve looks like this:

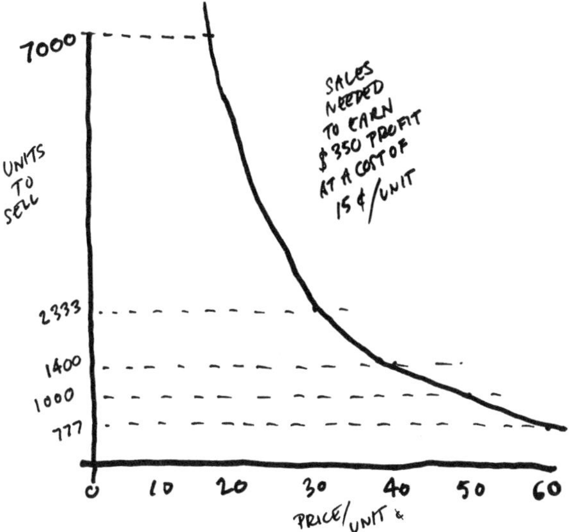

The nonlinear phenomenon also extends to intangibles, like consumer attitudes. Take consumers and sustainability. We frequently hear executives complain that while people say they care about the environment, they are not willing to pay extra for ecofriendly products. Quantitative analyses bear this out. A survey by the National Geographic Society and GlobeScan finds that, across 18 countries, concerns about environmental problems have increased markedly over time, but consumer behavior has changed much more slowly. While nearly all consumers surveyed agree that food production and consumption should be more sustainable, few of them alter their habits to support that goal.

What's going on? It turns out that the relationship between what consumers say they care about and their actions is often highly nonlinear. But managers often believe that classic quantitative tools, like surveys using 1-to-5 scales of importance, will predict behavior in a linear fashion. In reality, research shows little or no behavioral difference between consumers who, on a five-point scale, give their environmental concern the lowest rating, 1, and consumers who rate it a 4. But the difference between 4s and 5s is huge. Behavior maps to attitudes on a curve, not a straight line.

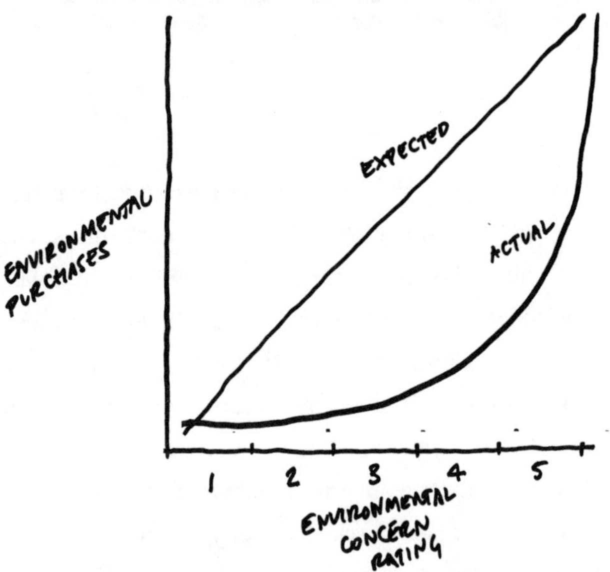

Companies typically fail to account for this pattern—in part because they focus on averages. Averages mask nonlinearity and lead to prediction errors. For example, suppose a firm did a sustainability survey among two of its target segments. All consumers in one segment rate their concern about the environment a 4, while 50% of consumers in the other segment rate it a 3 and 50% rate it a 5. The average level of concern is the same for the two segments, but people in the second segment are overall much more likely to buy green products. That's because a customer scoring 5 is much more likely to make environmental choices than a customer scoring 4, whereas a customer scoring 4 is not more likely to than a customer scoring 3.

The nonlinear relationship between attitudes and behavior shows up repeatedly in important domains, including consumers' privacy concerns. A large-scale survey in the Netherlands, for example, revealed little difference in the number of loyalty-program cards carried by consumers who said they were quite concerned versus only weakly concerned about privacy. How is it possible that people said they were worried about privacy but then agreed to sign up for loyalty programs that require the disclosure of sensitive personal information? Again, because only people who say they are extremely concerned about privacy take significant steps to protect it, while most others, regardless of their concern rating, don't adjust their behavior.

Awareness of nonlinear relationships is also important when choosing performance metrics. For instance, to assess the effectiveness of their inventory management, some firms track days of supply, or the number of days that products are held in inventory, while other firms track the number of times their inventory turns over annually. Most managers don't know why their firm uses one metric and not the other. But the choice may have unintended consequences—for instance, on employee motivation. Assume a firm was able to reduce days of supply from 12 to six and that with additional research, it could further reduce days of supply to four. This is the same as saying that the inventory turn rate could increase from 30 times a year to 60 times a year and that it could be raised again to 90 times a year. But employees are much more motivated to achieve improvements if the firm tracks turnover instead of days of supply, research by the University of Cologne's Tobias Stangl and Ulrich Thonemann shows. That's because they appear to get decreasing returns on their efforts when they improve the days-of-supply metric—but constant returns when they improve the turnover metric.

Other areas where companies can choose different metrics include warehousing (picking time versus picking rate), production (production time versus production rate), and quality control (time between failures versus failure rate).

Nonlinearity is all around us. Let's now explore the forms it takes.

The Four Types of Nonlinear Relationships

The best way to understand nonlinear patterns is to see them. There are four types.

Increasing gradually, then rising more steeply

Say a company has two customer segments that both have annual contribution margins of $100. Segment A has a retention rate of 20% while segment B has one of 60%. Most managers believe that it makes little difference to the bottom line which segment's retention they increase. If anything, most people find doubling the weaker retention rate more appealing than increasing the stronger one by, say, a third.

But customer lifetime value is a nonlinear function of retention rate, as you'll see when you apply the formula for calculating CLV:

$$\frac{\text{Margin} \times \text{Retention Rate}}{1 + \text{Discount Rate} - \text{Retention Rate}}$$

When the retention rate rises from 20% to 40%, CLV goes up about $35 (assuming a discount rate of 10% to adjust future profits to their current worth), but when retention rates rise from 60% to 80%, CLV goes up about $147. As retention rates rise, customer lifetime value increases gradually at first and then suddenly shoots up.

Most companies focus on identifying customers who are most likely to defect and then target them with marketing programs. However, it's usually more profitable to focus on customers who are more likely to stay. Linear thinking leads managers to underestimate the benefits of small increases to high retention rates.

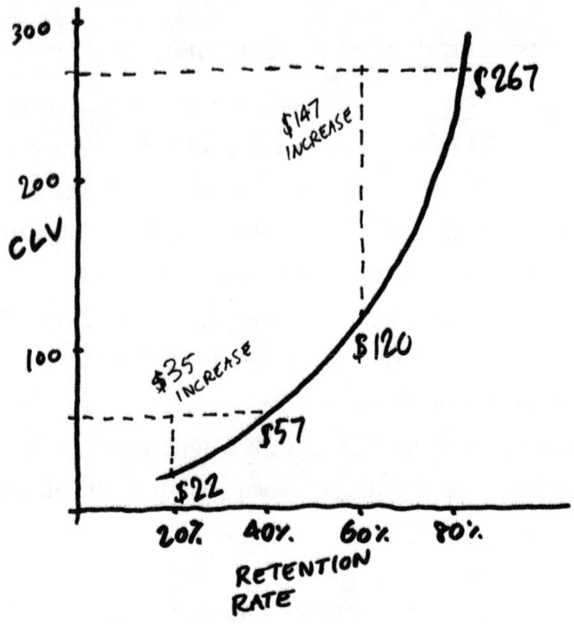

Decreasing gradually, then dropping quickly

The classic example of this can be seen in mortgages. Property owners are often surprised by how slowly they chip away at their debt during the early years of their loan terms. But in a mortgage with a fixed interest rate and fixed term, less of each payment goes toward the principal at the beginning. The principal doesn't decrease linearly. On a 30-year $165,000 loan at a 4.5% interest rate, the balance decreases by only about $15,000 over the first five years. By year 25 the balance will have dropped below $45,000. So the owner will pay off less than 10% of the principal in the first 16% of the loan's term but more than a quarter of it in the last 16%.

Because they're misled by their linear thinking in this context, mortgage payers are often surprised when they

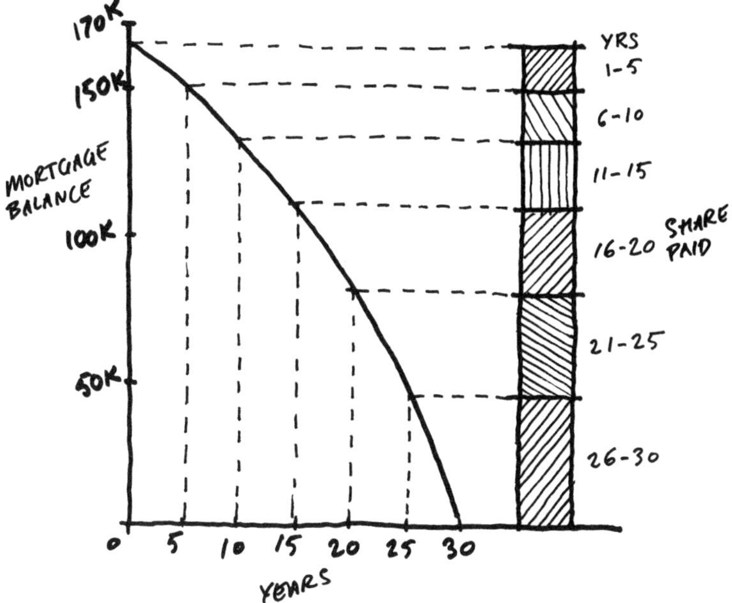

sell a property after a few years (and pay brokerage costs) and have only small net gains to show for it.

Climbing quickly, then tapering off

Selling more of a product allows companies to achieve economies of scale and boost per unit profit, a metric often used to gauge a firm's efficiency. Executives use this formula to calculate per unit profit:

$$\frac{(\text{Volume} \times \text{unit price}) - \text{Fixed Costs} - (\text{Volume} \times \text{Unit Variable Costs})}{\text{Volume}}$$

Say a firm sells 100,000 widgets each year at $2 a widget, and producing those widgets costs $100,000—$50,000 in fixed costs and 50 cents in unit variable costs. The per unit profit is $1. The firm can increase per unit profit by producing and selling more widgets, because it will spread fixed costs over more units. If it doubles the number of widgets sold to 200,000, profit per unit will rise to $1.25 (assuming that unit variable costs remain the same). That attractive increase might tempt you into thinking per unit profit will skyrocket if you increase sales from 100,000 to 800,000 units. Not so.

If the firm doubles widget sales from 400,000 to 800,000 (which is much harder to do than going from 100,000 to 200,000), the per unit profit increases only by about 6 cents.

Managers focus a great deal on the benefits of economies of scale and growth. However, linear thinking may lead them to overestimate volume as a driver of profit and thus underestimate other more impactful drivers, like price.

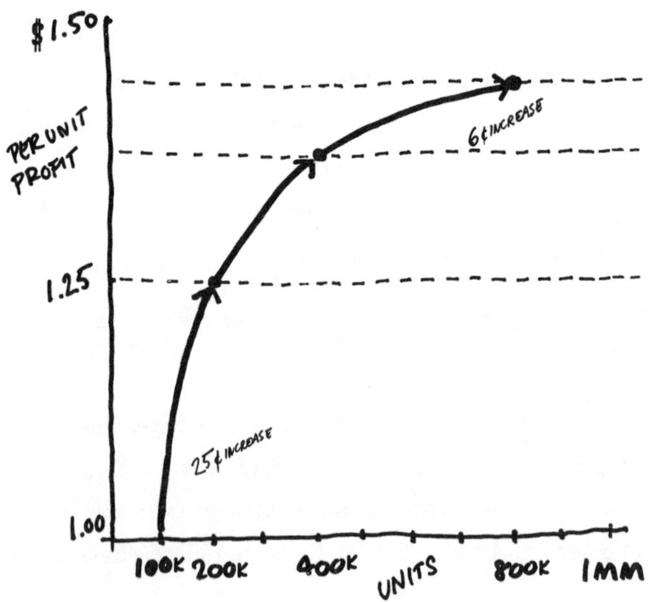

Falling sharply, then gradually

Firms often base evaluations of investments on the payback period, the amount of time required to recover the costs. Obviously, shorter paybacks are more favorable. Say you have two projects slated for funding. Project A has a payback period of two years, and project B has one of four years. Both teams believe they can cut their payback period in half. Many managers may find B more attractive because they'll save two years, double the time they'll save with A.

Company leadership, however, may ultimately care more about return on investment than time to break-even. A one-year payback has an annual rate of return (ARR) of 100%. A two-year payback yields one of 50%—a 50-point difference. A four-year payback yields one of 25%—a 25-point difference. So as the payback period increases, ARR drops steeply at first and then more slowly. If your focus is achieving a higher ARR, halving the payback period of project A is a better choice.

Managers comparing portfolios of similar-sized projects may also be surprised to learn that the return on investment is higher on one containing a project with a one-year payback and another with a four-year payback than on a portfolio containing two projects expected to pay back in two years. They should be careful not to underestimate the effect that decreases in relatively short payback periods will have on ARR.

How to Limit the Pitfalls of Linear Bias

As long as people are employed as managers, biases that are hardwired into the human brain will affect the quality of business decisions. Nevertheless, it is possible to minimize the pitfalls of linear thinking.

Step 1: Increase awareness of linear bias

MBA programs should explicitly warn future managers about this phenomenon and teach them ways to deal with it. Companies can also undertake initiatives to educate employees by, for instance, presenting them with puzzles that involve nonlinear relationships. In our experience, people find such exercises engaging and eye-opening.

Broader educational efforts are already under way in several fields. One is Ocean Tipping Points, an initiative that aims to make people more sensitive to nonlinear relationships in marine ecosystems. Scientists and managers often assume that the relationship between a stressor (such as fishing) and an ecological response (a decline in fish population) is linear. However, a small change in a stressor sometimes does disproportionately large damage: A fish stock can collapse following a small increase in fishing. The project's goal is to identify relevant tipping points in ocean ecology to help improve the management of natural resources.

Step 2: Focus on outcomes, not indicators

One of senior management's most important tasks is to set the organization's direction and incentives. But frequently, desired outcomes are far removed from everyday business decisions, so firms identify relevant intermediate metrics and create incentives to maximize them. To lift sales, for instance, many companies try to improve their websites' positioning in organic search results.

The problem is, these intermediate metrics can become the end rather than the means, a phenomenon academics call "medium maximization." That bodes trouble if a metric and the outcome don't have a linear relationship—as is the case with organic search position and sales. When a search rank drops, sales decrease quickly at first and then more gradually: The impact on sales is much greater when a site drops from the first to the second position in search results than when it drops from the 20th to the 25th position.

Other times, a single indicator can be used to predict multiple outcomes, and that may confuse people and lead them astray. Take annual rates of return, which a manager who wants to maximize the future value of an investment may consider. If you map the relationship between investment products' ARR and their total accumulated returns, you'll see that as ARR rises, total returns increase gradually and then suddenly shoot up.

Another manager may wish to minimize the time it takes to achieve a particular investment goal. The relationship here is the reverse: As ARR rises, the time it takes to reach a goal drops steeply at first and then declines gradually.

Because ARR is related to multiple outcomes in different nonlinear ways, people often under- or overestimate its effect. A manager who wants to maximize overall returns may care a great deal about a change in the rate from 0.30% to 0.70% but be insensitive to a change from 6.4% to 6.6%. In fact, increasing a low return rate has a much smaller effect on accumulated future returns than increasing a high rate does. In contrast, a manager focused on minimizing the time it takes to reach an investment goal may decide to take on additional risk to increase returns from 6.3% to 6.7% but be insensitive to a change from 0.40% to 0.60%. In this case the effect of increasing a high interest rate on time to completing a savings goal is much smaller than the effect of increasing a low interest rate.

Step 3: Discover the type of nonlinearity you're dealing with

As Thomas Jones and W. Earl Sasser Jr. pointed out in HBR back in 1995 (see "Why Satisfied Customers Defect"), the relationship between customer satisfaction ratings and customer retention is often nonlinear—but in ways that vary according to the industry. In highly competitive industries, such as automobiles, retention rises gradually and then climbs up steeply as satisfaction ratings increase. For noncompetitive industries retention shoots up quickly and then levels off.

In both situations linear thinking will lead to errors. If the industry is competitive, managers will overestimate the benefit of increasing the satisfaction of completely dissatisfied customers. If the industry is not competitive, managers will overestimate the benefit of increasing the satisfaction of already satisfied customers.

The point is that managers should avoid making generalizations about nonlinear relationships across contexts and work to understand the cause and effect in their specific situation.

Field experiments are an increasingly popular way to do this. When designing them, managers should be sure to account for nonlinearity. For instance, many people

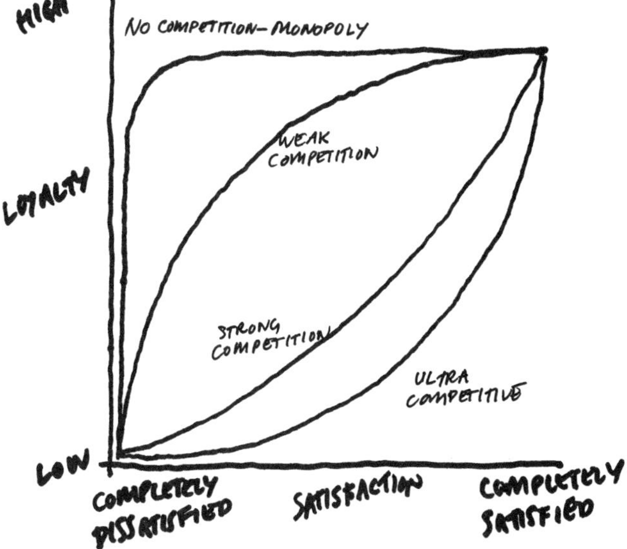

try to measure the impact of price on sales by offering a product at a low price (condition A in the chart on the next page) and a high price (condition B) and then measuring differences in sales. But testing two prices won't reveal nonlinear relationships. You need to use at least three price levels—low, medium (condition C), and high—to get a sense of them.

Step 4: Map nonlinearity whenever you can

In addition to providing the right training, companies can build support systems that warn managers when they might be making bad decisions because of the inclination to think linearly.

Ideally, algorithms and artificial intelligence could identify situations in which that bias is likely to strike and then offer information to counteract it. Of course,

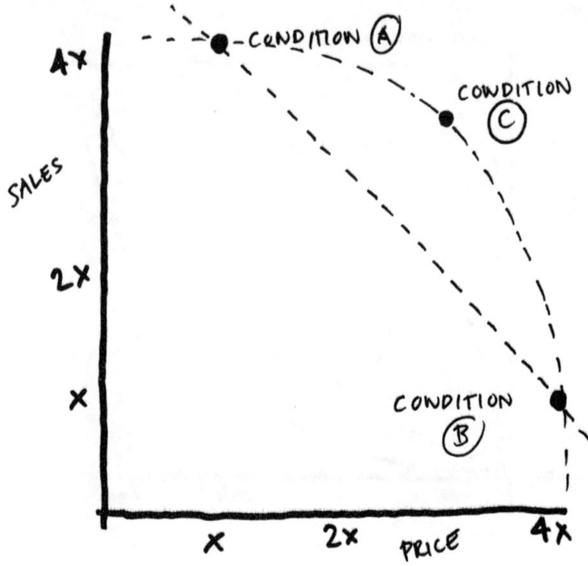

while advances in AI make this possible in formal settings, it can't account for decisions that take place offline and in conversations. And building such systems could eat up a lot of time and money.

A low-tech but highly effective technique for fighting linear bias is data visualization. As you've noticed in this article, whenever we wanted you to understand some linear bias, we showed you the nonlinear relationships. They're much easier to grasp when plotted out in a chart than when described in a list of statistics. A visual representation also helps you see threshold points where outcomes change dramatically and gives you a good sense of the degree of nonlinearity in play.

Putting charts of nonlinear relationships in dashboards and even mapping them out in "what if" scenarios will make managers more familiar with nonlinearity and thus more likely to check for it before making decisions.

Visualization is also a good tool for companies interested in helping customers make good decisions. For example, to make drivers aware of how little time they save by accelerating when they're already traveling at high speed, you could add a visual cue for time savings to car dashboards. One way to do this is with what Eyal Pe'er and Eyal Gamliel call a "paceometer," which shows how many minutes it takes to drive 10 miles. It will surprise most drivers that going from 40 to 65 will save you about six minutes per 10 miles, but going from 65 to 90 saves only about two and a half minutes—even though you're increasing your speed 25 miles per hour in both instances.

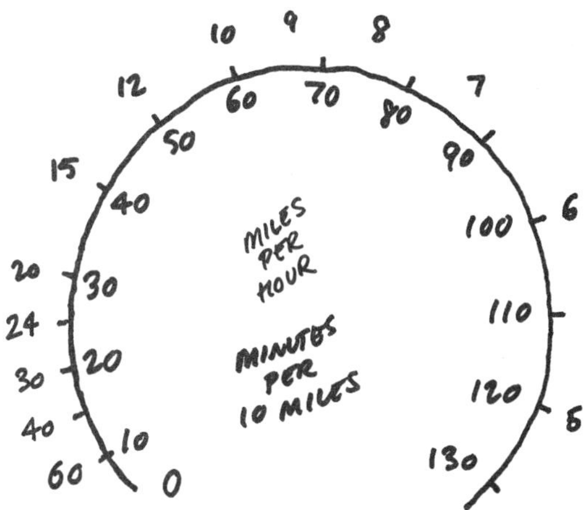

The Implications for Marketers

A cornerstone of modern marketing is the idea that by focusing more on consumer benefits than on product attributes, you can sell more. Apple, for instance, realized that people would perceive an MP3 player that provided "1,000 songs in your pocket" to be more attractive than one with an "internal storage capacity of 5GB."

Our framework, however, highlights the fact that in many situations companies actually profit from promoting attributes rather than benefits. They're taking advantage of consumers' tendency to assume that the relationship between attributes and benefits is linear. And that is not always the case.

We can list any number of instances where showing customers the actual benefits would reveal where they may be overspending and probably change their buying behavior: printer pages per minute, points in loyalty programs, and sun protection factor, to name just a few. Bandwidth upgrades are another good example. Our research shows that internet connections are priced linearly: Consumers pay the same for increases in speed from a low base and from a high base. But the relationship between download speed and download time is nonlinear. As download speed increases, download time drops rapidly at first and then gradually. Upgrading from five to 25 megabits per second will lead to time savings of 21 minutes per gigabyte, while the increase from 25 to 100 Mbps buys only four minutes. When consumers see the actual gains from raising their speed to 100 Mbps, they may prefer a cheaper, slower internet connection.

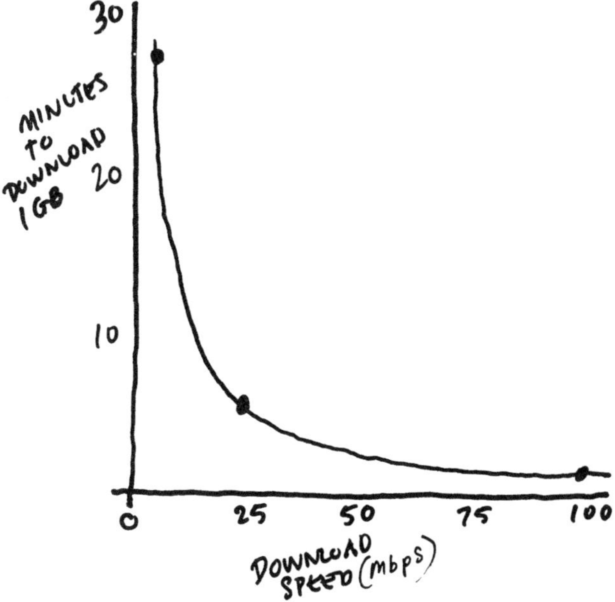

Of course, willfully exploiting consumers' flawed perceptions of attribute-benefit relationships is a questionable marketing strategy. It's widely regarded as unethical for companies to take advantage of customers' ignorance.

In recent years a number of professions, including ecologists, physiologists, and physicians, have begun to routinely factor nonlinear relationships into their decision making. But nonlinearity is just as prevalent in the business world as anywhere else. It's time that management professionals joined these other disciplines in developing greater awareness of the pitfalls of linear thinking in a nonlinear world. This will increase their ability to choose wisely—and to help the people around them make good decisions too.

Bart de Langhe is an associate professor of marketing at Esade Business School, Ramon Llull University, and an assistant professor of marketing at the Leeds School of Business, University of Colorado–Boulder. **Stefano Puntoni** is a professor of marketing at the Rotterdam School of Management, Erasmus University. **Richard Larrick** is the Hanes Corporation Foundation Professor at Duke University's Fuqua School of Business.

CHAPTER 15

Pitfalls of Data-Driven Decisions

by Megan MacGarvie and Kristina McElheran

Even with impressively large data sets, the best analytics tools, and careful statistical methods, managers can still be vulnerable to a range of pitfalls when using data to back up their toughest choices—especially when information overload leads us to take shortcuts in reasoning. In some instances, data and analytics actually make matters worse.

Psychologists, behavioral economists, and other scholars of human behavior have identified several common decision-making traps. Many of these traps stem from the fact that people don't carefully process every piece of information in every decision. Instead, we often rely on *heuristics*—simplified procedures that allow us to make decisions in the face of uncertainty or when extensive analysis is too costly or time-consuming. These heuristics lead us to believe we are making sound decisions when we are actually making systematic mistakes. What's more, human brains are wired for certain biases that creep in and distort our thinking, typically without our awareness.

There are three main cognitive traps that regularly skew decision making, even when informed by the best data. Here are each of these three pitfalls in detail, as well as a number of suggestions for how to escape them.

The Confirmation Trap

When we pay more attention to findings that align with our prior beliefs, and ignore other facts and patterns in the data, we fall into the confirmation trap. With a huge data set and numerous correlations between variables, analyzing all possible correlations is often both costly and counterproductive. Even with smaller data sets, it can be easy to inadvertently focus on correlations that confirm our expectations of how the world should work, and dismiss counterintuitive or inconclusive patterns in the data when they don't align.

Consider the following example: In the late 1960s and early 1970s, researchers conducted one of the most well-designed studies on how different types of fats affect heart health and mortality. But the results of this study, known as the Minnesota Coronary Experiment, were not published at the time. A recent *New York Times* article suggests that these results stayed unpublished for so long because they contradicted the beliefs of both the researchers and the medical establishment.[1] In fact, it wasn't until 2016 that the medical journal *BMJ* published a piece referencing this data, when growing skepticism about the relationship between saturated fat consumption and heart disease led researchers to analyze data from the original experiment—more than 40 years later.[2] These and similar findings cast doubt on decades of unchallenged medical advice to avoid saturated fats. While it's unclear whether one experiment would have changed standard dietary and health recommendations, this example demonstrates that even with the best possible data, when we look at numbers we may ignore important facts when they contradict the dominant paradigm or don't confirm our beliefs, with potentially troublesome results.

This is a sobering prospect for decision makers in companies. And confirmation bias becomes that much harder to avoid when individuals face pressure from bosses and peers. Organizations frequently reward employees who can provide empirical support for existing managerial preferences. Those who decide what parts of the data to examine and present to senior managers may feel compelled to choose only the evidence that reinforces what their supervisors want to see or that confirms a prevalent attitude within the firm.

To get a fair assessment of what the data has to say, don't avoid information that counters your (or your boss's) beliefs. Instead, embrace it by doing the following:

- Specify in advance the data and analytical approaches on which you'll base your decision, to reduce the temptation to cherry-pick findings that agree with your prejudices.
- Actively look for findings that disprove your beliefs. Ask yourself, "If my expectations are wrong, what pattern would I likely see in the data?" Enlist a skeptic to help you. Seek people who like to play devil's advocate or assign contrary positions for active debate.
- Don't automatically dismiss findings that fall below your threshold for statistical or practical significance. Both noisy relationships (those with large standard errors) and small, precisely measured relationships can point to flaws in your beliefs and presumptions. Ask yourself, what would it take for this to appear important? Make sure your key takeaway is not sensitive to reasonable changes in your model or sample size.
- Assign multiple independent teams to analyze the data separately. Do they come to similar conclusions? If not, isolate and study the points of divergence to determine whether the differences are due to error, inconsistent methods, or bias.
- Treat your findings like predictions, and test them. If you uncover a correlation from which you think your organization can profit, use an experiment to validate that correlation.

The Overconfidence Trap

In their book *Judgment in Managerial Decision Making*, behavioral researchers Max Bazerman and Don Moore refer to overconfidence as "The Mother of All Biases." Time and time again, psychologists have found that decision makers are too sure of themselves. We tend to assume that the accuracy of our judgments or the probability of success in our endeavors is more favorable than the data would suggest. When there are risks, we alter our read of the odds to assume we'll come out on the winning side. Senior decision makers who have been promoted based on past successes are especially susceptible to this bias, since they have received positive signals about their decision-making abilities throughout their careers.

Overconfidence also reinforces many other pitfalls of data interpretation, be it psychological or procedural. It prevents us from questioning our methods, motivation, and the way we communicate our findings to others. It makes it easy to underinvest in data and analysis; when we feel too confident in our understanding, we don't spend enough time or money acquiring more information or running further analyses. To make matters worse, more information can increase overconfidence without improving accuracy. More data in and of itself is not a guaranteed solution.

Going from data to insight requires quality inputs, skill, and sound processes. Because it can be so difficult to recognize our own biases, good processes are essential for avoiding overconfidence when analyzing data. Here are a few procedural tips to avoid the overconfidence trap:

- Describe your perfect experiment—the type of information you would use to answer your question if you had limitless resources for data collection and the ability to measure any variable. Compare this ideal with your actual data to understand where it might fall short. Identify places where you might be able to close the gap with more data collection or analytical techniques.
- Make it a formal part of your process to be your own devil's advocate. In *Thinking, Fast and Slow*, Nobel laureate Daniel Kahneman suggests asking yourself why your analysis might be wrong, and recommends that you do this for every analysis you perform. Taking this contrarian view can help you see the flaws in your own arguments and reduce mistakes across the board.
- Before making a decision or launching a project, perform a "pre-mortem," an approach suggested by psychologist Gary Klein. Ask others with knowledge about the project to imagine its failure a year into the future and to write stories of that failure. In doing so, you'll benefit from the wisdom of multiple perspectives, while also providing an opportunity to bring to the surface potential flaws in the analysis that you may otherwise overlook.

- Keep track of your predictions and systematically compare them with what actually happens. Which of your predictions turned out to be true and which ones fell short? Persistent biases can creep back into our decision making; revisit these reports on a regular basis so you can prevent mistakes in the future.

The Overfitting Trap

When your model yields surprising or counterintuitive predictions, you may have made an exciting new discovery—or it may be the result of overfitting. In *The Signal and the Noise*, Nate Silver famously dubbed this "the most important scientific problem you've never heard of." This trap occurs when a statistical model describes random noise, rather than the underlying relationship we need to capture. Overfit models generally do a suspiciously good job of explaining many nuances of what happened in the past, but they have great difficulty predicting the future.

For instance, when Google's Flu Trends application was introduced in 2008, it was heralded as an innovative way to predict flu outbreaks by tracking search terms associated with early flu symptoms. But early versions of the algorithm looked for correlations between flu outbreaks and millions of search terms. With such a large number of terms, some correlations appeared significant when they were really due to chance (searches for "high school basketball," for example, were highly correlated with the flu). The application was ultimately scrapped only a few years later due to failures of prediction.

In order to overcome this bias, you need to discern between the data that matters and the noise around it. Here's how you can guard against the overfitting trap:

- Randomly divide the data into two sets: a training set, with which you'll estimate the model, and a "validation set," with which you'll test the accuracy of the model's predictions. An overfit model might be great at making predictions within the training set, but raise warning flags by performing poorly in the validation set.

- Much like you would for the confirmation trap, specify the relationships you want to test and how you plan to test them *before* analyzing the data, to avoid cherry-picking.

- Keep your analysis simple. Look for relationships that measure important effects related to clear and logical hypotheses before digging into nuances. Be on guard against spurious correlations—the ones that occur only by chance—that you can rule out based on experience or common sense (see the sidebar, "Beware Spurious Correlations," in chapter 10). Remember that data can never truly "speak for itself" and must rely on human interpreters to make sense of it.

- Construct alternative narratives. Is there another story you could tell with the same data? If so, you cannot be confident that the relationship you have uncovered is the right—or only—one.

- Beware of the all-too-human tendency to see patterns in random data. For example, consider a baseball player with a .325 batting average who has no hits in a championship series game. His coach may see a cold streak and want to replace him, but he's only looking at handful of games. Statistically, it would be better to keep him in the lineup than substitute the .200 hitter who had four hits in the previous game.

From Bias to Better Decisions

Data analytics can be an effective tool to promote consistent decisions and shared understanding. It can highlight blind spots in our individual or collective awareness and can offer evidence of risks and benefits for particular paths of action. But it can also make us complacent.

Managers need to be aware of these common decision-making pitfalls and employ sound processes and cognitive strategies to prevent them. It can be difficult to recognize the flaws in your own reasoning—but proactively tackling these biases with the right mindset and procedures can lead to better analysis of data and better decisions overall.

Megan MacGarvie is an associate professor in the markets, public policy, and law group at Boston University's Questrom School of Business, where she teaches data-driven decision making and business analytics.

She is also a research associate of the National Bureau of Economic Research. **Kristina McElheran** is an assistant professor of strategic management at the University of Toronto and a digital fellow at the MIT Initiative on the Digital Economy. Her ongoing work on data-driven decision making with Erik Brynjolfsson has been featured on HBR online and in the *American Economic Review*.

NOTES

1. A. E. Carroll, "A Study on Fats That Doesn't Fit the Story Line," *New York Times*, April 15, 2016.
2. C. E. Ramsden et al., "Re-evaluation of the Traditional Diet-Heart Hypothesis: Analysis of Recovered Data from Minnesota Coronary Experiment (1968-73)," *BMJ* (April 2016), 353:i1246, doi: 10.1136.

CHAPTER 16

Don't Let Your Analytics Cheat the Truth

by Michael Schrage

Everyone's heard the truism that there are lies, damned lies, and statistics. But sitting through a welter of analytics-driven, top-management presentations provokes me into proposing a cynical revision: There are liars, damned liars, and statisticians.

The rise of analytics-informed insight and decision making is welcome. The disingenuous and deceptive manner in which many of these statistics are presented is not. I'm simultaneously stunned and disappointed

Adapted from "Do Your Analytics Cheat the Truth?" on hbr.org, October 10, 2011.

by how egregiously manipulative these analytics have become at the very highest levels of enterprise oversight. The only thing more surprising—and more disappointing—is how unwilling or unable so many senior executives are about asking simple questions about the analytics they see.

At one financial services firm, for example, call center analytics showed spike after spike of negative customer satisfaction numbers. Hold times and problem resolution times had noticeably increased. The presenting executive clearly sought greater funding and training for her group. The implied threat was that the firm's reputation for swift and responsive service was at risk.

Three simple but pointed questions later, her analytic gamesmanship became clear. What had been presented as a disturbing customer service trend was in large part due to a policy change affecting about 20% of the firm's newly retired customers. Between their age, possible tax implications, and an approval process requiring coordination with another department, these calls frequently stretched beyond 35 to 45 minutes.

What made the situation worse (and what might explain why the presenter chose not to break out the data) was a management decision not to route those calls to a specially trained team but instead to allow any customer representative to process the query. The additional delays undermined the entire function's performance.

Every single one of the presenter's numbers was technically accurate. But they were aggregated in a manner that made it look as if the function was underresourced. The analytics deliberately concealed the outlier statistically responsible for making the numbers dramatically worse.

More damning was a simple queuing theory simulation demonstrating that if the call center had made even marginal changes in how it chose to manage that exceptional 20%, the aggregate call center performance numbers would have been virtually unaffected. Poor management, not systems underinvestment, was the real root cause problem.

Increasingly, I observe statistical sophisticates indulging in analytic advocacy—that is, the numbers are deployed to influence and win arguments rather than identify underlying dynamics and generate insight. This is particularly disturbing because while the analytics—in the strictest technical sense—accurately portray a situation, they do so in a way that discourages useful inquiry.

I always insist that analytics presentations and presenters explicitly identify the outliers, how they were defined and dealt with, and—most importantly—what the analytics would look like if they didn't exist. It's astonishing what you find when you make the outliers as important as the aggregates and averages in understanding the analytics. (To guide your discussion, consider the questions in the sidebar "Investigating Outliers.")

My favorite example of this comes, naturally enough, from Harvard. Few people realize that, in fact, the average net worth of Harvard dropouts vastly exceeds the average net worth of Harvard graduates.

The reason for that is simple. There are many, many more Harvard graduates than there are Harvard dropouts. But the ranks of Harvard dropouts include Bill

INVESTIGATING OUTLIERS

by Janice H. Hammond

When you notice an outlier in data, you must investigate why the anomaly exists. Consider asking some of the following questions:

- Is it just an unusual, but valid, value?
- Could it be a data entry error?
- Was it collected in a different way than the rest of the data? At a different time?

After making an effort to understand where an outlier comes from, you should have a deeper understanding of the situation the data represent. Then think about how to handle the outlier in your analysis. Typically, you can do one of three things: leave it alone, or—very rarely—remove it or change it to a corrected value.

Excluding or changing data is not something we do often—and it should be done only after examining the underlying situation in great detail. We should never do it to help the data "fit" a conclusion we want to draw. Changes to a data set should be made on a case-by-case basis only after careful investigation of the situation.

Adapted from "Quantitative Methods Online Course," Harvard Business Publishing, October 24, 2004, revised January 24, 2017 (product #504702).

Janice H. Hammond is the Jesse Philips Professor of Manufacturing at Harvard Business School. She serves as program chair for the HBS Executive Education International Women's Foundation and Women's Leadership Programs, and created the online Business Analytics course for HBX CORe.

Gates, Mark Zuckerberg, and Polaroid's Edwin Land, whose combined, inflation-adjusted net worth probably tops $100 billion. That megarich numerator divided by the smaller "dropout" denominator creates the statistically accurate illusion that the average Harvard dropout is much, much wealthier than the Harvard student who actually got their degree.

This is, of course, ridiculous. Unfortunately, it is no more ridiculous than what one finds, on average, in a statistically significant number of analytics-driven boardroom presentations. The misdirection—and mismanagement—associated with outliers is the most disturbingly common pathology I experience, even in stats-savvy organizations.

Always ask for the outliers. Always make the analysts display what their data looks like with the outliers removed. There are other equally important ways to wring greater utility from aggregated analytics, but start from the outliers in. Because analytics that mishandle outliers are "outliars."

Michael Schrage, a research fellow at MIT Sloan School's Center for Digital Business, is the author of the books *Serious Play, Who Do You Want Your Customers to Become?* and *The Innovator's Hypothesis.*

SECTION FOUR

Communicate Your Findings

CHAPTER 17

Data Is Worthless If You Don't Communicate It

by Thomas H. Davenport

Too many managers are, with the help of their analyst colleagues, simply compiling vast databases of information that never see the light of day, or that only get disseminated in autogenerated business intelligence reports. As a manager, it's not your job to crunch the numbers, but it is your job to communicate them. Never make the mistake of assuming that the results will speak for themselves.

Consider the cautionary tale of Gregor Mendel. Although he discovered the concept of genetic inheritance,

---

Adapted from content posted on hbr.org, June 18, 2013 (product #H00ASW).

his ideas were not adopted during his lifetime because he only published his findings in an obscure Moravian scientific journal, a few reprints of which he mailed to leading scientists. It's said that Darwin, to whom Mendel sent a reprint of his findings, never even cut the pages to read the geneticist's work. Although Mendel carried out his groundbreaking experiments between 1856 and 1863—eight years of painstaking research—their significance was not recognized until the turn of the 20th century, long after his death. The lesson: If you're going to spend the better part of a decade on a research project, also put some time and effort into disseminating your results.

One person who has done this very well is Dr. John Gottman, the well-known marriage scientist at the University of Washington. Gottman, working with a statistical colleague, developed a marriage equation predicting how likely a marriage is to last over the long term. The equation is based on a couple's ratio of positive to negative interactions during a 15-minute conversation on a difficult topic such as money or in-laws. Pairs who showed affection, humor, or happiness while talking about contentious topics were given a maximum number of points, while those who displayed belligerence or contempt received the minimum. Observing several hundred couples, Gottman and his team were able to score couples' interactions and identify the patterns that predict divorce or a happy marriage.

This was great work in itself, but Gottman didn't stop there. He and his wife, Julie, founded a nonprofit research institute and a for-profit organization to apply the results through books, DVDs, workshops, and therapist training. They've influenced exponentially more marriages through these outlets than they could possibly ever have done in their own clinic—or if they'd just issued a press release with their findings.

Similarly, during his tenure at Intuit, George Roumeliotis was head of a data science group that analyzed and created product features based on the vast amount of online data that Intuit collected. For his projects, he recommended a simple framework for communicating about each analysis:

1. My understanding of the business problem
2. How I will measure the business impact
3. What data is available
4. The initial solution hypothesis
5. The solution
6. The business impact of the solution

Note what's not here: details on statistical methods used, regression coefficients, or logarithmic transformations. Most audiences neither understand nor appreciate those details; they care about results and implications. It may be useful to make such information available in an appendix to a report or presentation, but don't let it get in the way of telling a good story with your data—starting with what your audience really needs to know.

Thomas H. Davenport is the President's Distinguished Professor in Management and Information Technology at Babson College, a research fellow at the MIT Initiative on the Digital Economy, and a senior adviser at Deloitte Analytics. Author of over a dozen management books, his latest is *Only Humans Need Apply: Winners and Losers in the Age of Smart Machines.*

CHAPTER 18

When Data Visualization Works—and When It Doesn't

by Jim Stikeleather

I am uncomfortable with the growing emphasis on big data and its stylist, visualization. Don't get me wrong—I love infographic representations of large data sets. The value of representing information concisely and effectively dates back to Florence Nightingale, when she developed a new type of pie chart to clearly show that more soldiers were dying from preventable illnesses than

Adapted from content posted on hbr.org, March 27, 2013 (product #H00ADJ).

from their wounds. On the other hand, I see beautiful exercises in special effects that show off statistical and technical skills, but do not clearly serve an informing purpose. That's what makes me squirm.

Ultimately, data visualization is about communicating an idea that will drive action. Understanding the criteria for information to provide valuable insights and the reasoning behind constructing data visualizations will help you do that with efficiency and impact.

For information to provide valuable insights, it must be interpretable, relevant, and novel. With so much unstructured data today, it is critical that the data being analyzed generates interpretable information. Collecting lots of data without the associated metadata—such as what is it, where was it collected, when, how, and by whom—reduces the opportunity to play with, interpret, and draw conclusions from the data. It must also be relevant to the people who are looking to gain insights, and to the purpose for which the information is being examined (see the sidebar "Understand Your Audience"). Finally, it must be original, or shed new light on an area. If the information fails any one of these criteria, then no visualization can make it valuable. That means that only a tiny slice of the data we can bring to life visually will actually be worth the effort.

Once we've narrowed the universe of data down to that which satisfies these three requirements, we must also understand the legitimate reasons to construct data visualizations, and recognize what factors affect the quality of data visualizations. There are three broad reasons for visualizing data:

- **Confirmation:** If we already have a set of assumptions about how the system we are interested in operates—for example, a market, customers, or competitors—visualizations can help us check those assumptions. They can also enable us to observe whether the underlying system has deviated from the model we had and assess the risk of the actions we are about to undertake based on those assumptions. You see this approach in some enterprise dashboards.
- **Education:** There are two forms of education that visualization offers. One is simply reporting: here is how we measure the underlying system of interest, and here are the values of those measures in some comparative form—for instance, over time, or against other systems or models. The other is to develop intuition and new insights on the behavior of a known system as it evolves and changes over time, so that humans can get an experiential feel of the system in an extremely compressed time frame. You often see this model in the "gamification" of training and development.
- **Exploration:** When we have large sets of data about a system we are interested in and the goal is to provide optimal human-machine interactions (HMI) to that data to tease out relationships, processes, models, etc., we can use visualization to help build a model to allow us to predict and better manage the system. The practice of using visual

UNDERSTAND YOUR AUDIENCE

Before you throw up (pun intended) data in a visualization, start with the goal, which is to convey great quantities of information in a format that is easily assimilated by the consumers of this information—decision makers. A successful visualization is based on the designer understanding whom the visualization is targeting, and executing on three key points:

- Who is the audience, and how will it read and interpret the information? Can you assume these individuals have knowledge of the terminology and concepts you'll use, or do you need to guide them with clues in the visualization (for example, good is indicated with a green arrow going up)? An audience of experts will have different expectations than a general audience.
- What are viewers' expectations, and what type of information is most useful to them?
- What is the visualization's functional role, and how can viewers take action from it? An exploratory visualization should leave viewers with questions to pursue; educational or confirmational graphics should not.

Adapted from "The Three Elements of Successful Data Visualizations" on hbr.org by Jim Stikeleather, April 19, 2013.

discovery in lieu of statistics is called exploratory data analysis (EDA), and too few businesses make use of it.

Assuming the visualization creator has gotten it all right—a well-defined purpose, the necessary and sufficient amount of data and metadata to make the visualization interpretable, enabling relevant and original insights for the business—what gives us confidence that these findings are now worthy of action? Our ability to understand and to a degree control three areas of risk can define the visualization's resulting value to the business:

- **Data quality:** The quality of the underlying data is crucial to the value of visualization. How complete and reliable is it? As with all analytical processes, putting garbage in means getting garbage out.
- **Context:** The point of visualization is to make large amounts of data approachable so we can apply our evolutionarily honed pattern detection computer—our brain—to draw insights from it. To do so, we need to access all of the potential relationships of the data elements. This context is the source of insight. To leave out any contextual information or metadata (or more appropriately, "metacontent") is to risk hampering our understanding.
- **Biases:** The creator of the visualization may influence the visualization's semantics and the syntax of the elements through color choices, positioning,

> and visual tricks (such as unnecessary 3D, or 2D when 3D is more informative)—any of which can challenge the interpretation of the data. This also creates the risk of pre-specifying discoverable features and results via the embedded algorithms used by the creator (something EDA is intended to overcome). These in turn can significantly influence how viewers understand the visualization, and what insight they will gather from it.

Ignoring these requirements and risks can undermine the visualization's purpose and confuse rather than enlighten.

Jim Stikeleather, DBA, is a serial entrepreneur and was formerly Chief Innovation Officer at Dell. He teaches innovation, business models, strategy, governance, and change management at the graduate level at the University of South Florida and The Innovation Academy at Trinity College Dublin. He is also a senior executive coach.

CHAPTER 19

How to Make Charts That Pop and Persuade

by Nancy Duarte

Displaying data can be a tricky proposition, because different rules apply in different contexts. A sales director presenting financial projections to a group of field representatives wouldn't visualize her data the same way that a design consultant would in a written proposal to a potential client.

So how do you make the right choices for your situation? Before displaying your data, ask yourself these five questions:

Adapted from "The Quick and Dirty on Data Visualization" on hbr.org, April 16, 2014 (product #H00RKA).

1. Am I Presenting or Circulating My Data?

Context plays a huge role in how best to render data. When delivering a presentation, show the conclusions you've drawn, not all the details that led you to those conclusions. Because your slides will be up for only a few seconds, your audience will need to process them quickly. People won't have time to chew on a lot of complex information, and they're not likely to run up to the wall for a closer look at the numbers. Think in broad strokes when you're putting your charts together: What's the overall trend you're highlighting? What's the most striking comparison you're making? These are the sorts of questions to answer with projected data.

Scales, grid lines, tick marks, and such should provide context, but without competing with the data. Use a light neutral color, such as gray, for these elements so they'll recede to the background, and plot your data in a slightly stronger neutral color, such as blue or green. Then use a bright color to emphasize the point you're making.

It's fine to display more detail in documents or in decks that you email rather than present. Readers can study them at their own pace—examine the axes, the legends, the layers—and draw their own conclusions from your body of work. Still, you don't want to overwhelm them, especially since they won't have you there in person to explain what your main points are. Use white space, section heads, and a clear hierarchy of visual elements to help your readers navigate dense content and guide them to key pieces of data.

2. Am I Using the Right Kind of Chart or Table?

When you choose how to visualize your data, you're deciding what type of relationship you want to emphasize. Take a look at figure 19-1, which shows the breakdown of an investment portfolio.

In the pie, it's clear that this person holds a number of investments in different areas—but that's about all you see.

Figure 19-2 shows the same data in a bar chart. In this form it's much easier to discern how much is invested in each category. If your focus is on comparing categories, the bar chart is the better choice. A pie chart would be more useful if you were trying to make the point that a single investment made up a significant portion of the portfolio.

FIGURE 19-1

Investment portfolio breakdown

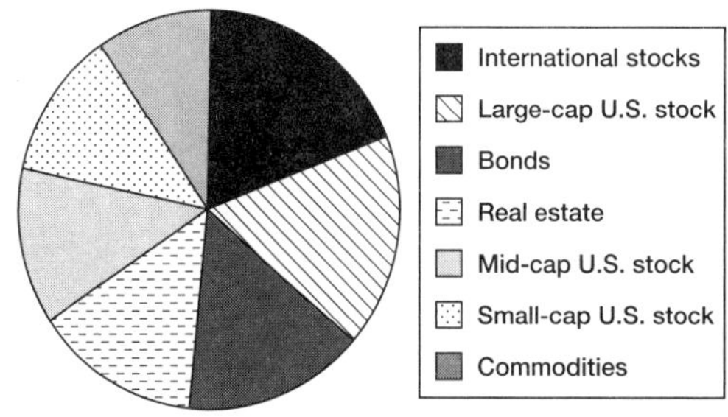

FIGURE 19-2

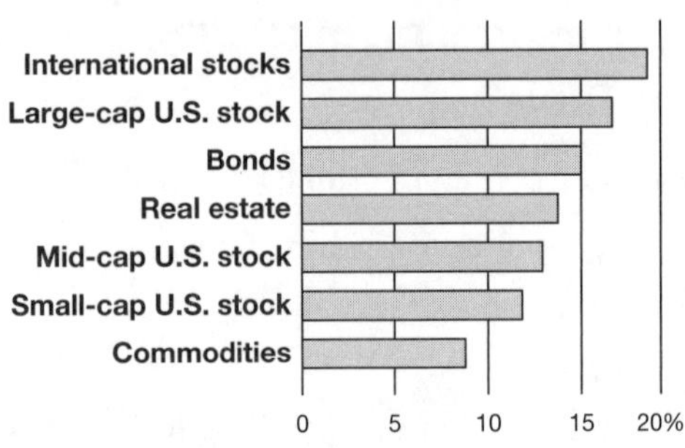

3. What Message Am I Trying to Convey?

Whether you're presenting or circulating your charts, you need to highlight the most important items to ensure that your audience can follow your train of thought and focus on the right elements. For example, figure 19-3 is difficult to interpret because all the information is displayed with equal visual value.

Are we comparing regions? Quarters? Positive versus negative numbers? It's difficult to determine what matters most. By adding color or shading, you can draw the eye to specific areas, as shown in figure 19-4.

We now know that we should be focusing on when and in which regions revenue dropped.

4. Do My Visuals Accurately Reflect the Numbers?

Using a lot of crazy colors, extra labels, and fancy effects won't captivate an audience. That kind of visual clutter

FIGURE 19-3

Revenue trends

	Q1	Q2	Q3	Q4	Total
Americas	–18%	7%	25%	2%	2%
Australia	47%	–7%	26%	15%	17%
China	15%	–5%	1%	7%	19%
Europe	57%	10%	–3%	7%	13%
India	57%	6%	–3%	8%	13%

FIGURE 19-4

Revenue trends

	Q1	Q2	Q3	Q4	Total
Americas	–18%	7%	25%	2%	2%
Australia	47%	–7%	26%	15%	17%
China	15%	–5%	1%	7%	19%
Europe	57%	10%	–3%	7%	13%
India	57%	6%	–3%	8%	13%

dilutes the information and can even misrepresent it. Consider the chart in figure 19-5.

Can you figure out the northern territory's revenue for year one? Is it 17? Or maybe 19? The way some programs create 3D charts would lead any rational person to think that the bar in question is well below 20. However, the data behind the chart actually says that bar represents 20.4 units. You can see that if you look at the chart in a very specific way, but it's difficult to tell which way that should be—even with plenty of time to scrutinize it.

It's much clearer if you simply flatten the chart, as in figure 19-6.

5. Is My Data Memorable?

Even if you've rendered your data clearly and accurately, it's another challenge altogether to make the information stick. Consider using a meaningful visual metaphor to il-

FIGURE 19-5

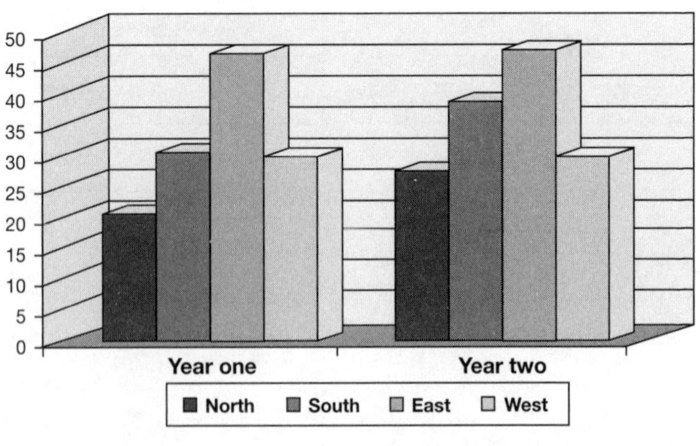

FIGURE 19-6

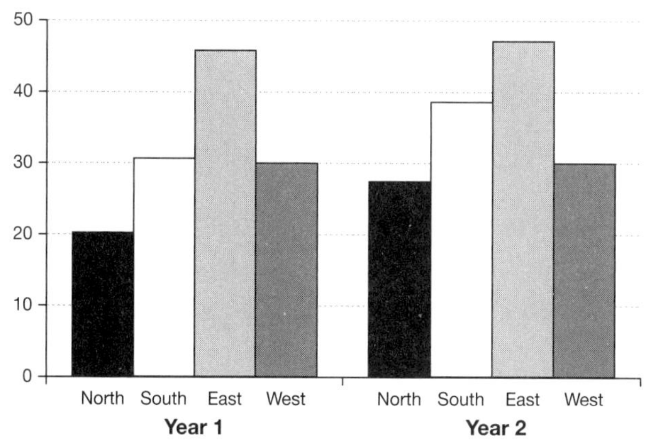

lustrate the scale of your numbers and cement the data in the minds of your audience members. A metaphor can also tie your insights to something that your audience already knows and cares about.

Author and activist Michael Pollan showed how much crude oil goes into making a McDonald's Double Quarter Pounder with Cheese through a striking visual demonstration: He placed glasses on a table and filled them with oil to represent the amount of oil consumed during each stage of the production process. At the end, he took a taste of the oil to drive home his point. (To add an element of humor, he later revealed that his prop "oil" was actually chocolate syrup.)

Pollan could have shown a chart, but this was more effective because he gave the audience a tangible visual—one that triggered a visceral response.

By answering these five questions as you're laying out your data, you'll visualize it in a way that helps people understand and engage with each point in your presentation, document, or deck. As a result, your audience will be more likely to adopt your overall message.

Nancy Duarte has published her latest book, *Illuminate*, with coauthor Patti Sanchez. Duarte is also the author of the *HBR Guide to Persuasive Presentations*, as well as two award-winning books on the art of presenting, *Slide:ology* and *Resonate*. Her team at Duarte Inc. has created more than a quarter million presentations for its clients and teaches public and corporate workshops on presenting. Find Duarte on LinkedIn or follow her on Twitter @nancyduarte.

CHAPTER 20

Why It's So Hard for Us to Communicate Uncertainty

An interview with Scott Berinato by Nicole Torres

We use data to make predictions. But predictions are just educated guesses—they're uncertain. And when they're being communicated, they're incredibly difficult to explain or clearly illustrate.

A case in point: The 2016 U.S. presidential election did not unfold the way so many predicted it would. We now know some of the reasons why—polling failed—but

---

Adapted from "Why It's So Hard for Us to Visualize Uncertainty" on hbr.org, November 11, 2016 (product #H039NV).

watching the real-time results on the night of Tuesday, November 8, wasn't just surprising, it was confusing. Predictions swung back and forth, and it was hard to process the information that was coming in. Not only did the data seem wrong, the way we were presenting that data seemed wrong too.

I asked my colleague Scott Berinato, *Harvard Business Review* editor and author of *Good Charts: The HBR Guide to Making Smarter, More Persuasive Data Visualizations*, if he would help explain this uncertainty—how we dealt with it, why it was so hard to grasp, and what's so challenging about communicating and visualizing it.

Torres: What did you notice about how election predictions were being shown election night?

Berinato: A lot of people were looking at the *New York Times'* live presidential forecast, where you'd see a series of gauges (half-circle gauges, like a gas gauge on your car) that updated frequently.[1] The needle moved left if data showed that Hillary Clinton had a higher chance of winning, and right if Donald Trump did. But the needle also jittered back and forth, making it look like the statistical likelihood of winning was changing rapidly. This caused a lot of anxiety. People were confused. They were trying to interpret what was going on in the election and why the data was changing so drastically in real time, and it was really hard to understand what was going on.

The thing was, the needle wasn't swinging to represent statistical likelihood; it was a hard-coded effect meant to represent uncertainty in the statistical forecast. So trying to show real-time changes in the race, while accounting for uncertainty, was a good engagement effort, but the execution fell short because it confused and unnerved people. The jitter wasn't the best visual approach.

What do we mean by "uncertainty"?

When thinking about showing uncertainty, we think mostly about two types. One is *statistical uncertainty*, which applies if I said something like, "Here are my values, and statistically my confidence in them is 95%." Think about margin of error built into polls. Statisticians use things like box-and-whisker plots to represent this, where a box shows the upper and lower ranges of the first and third quartiles in a data set, a line in the box marks the median, and thin bar "whiskers" reaching above and below the box to indicate the range of the data. Dots can also be used beyond the whiskers to show outliers. There are lots of variations of these, and they work reasonably well, though academics try other approaches sometimes and the lay audience isn't used to these visualizations, for the most part.

The other kind of uncertainty is *data uncertainty*. This applies when we're not sure where within a range our data falls. Instead of having a value and a confidence in that value, we have a range of possible values. A friend recently gave me a data set with two values. One was "the estimate ranges from 1 in 2,000 to 1 in 4,500" and the other was "an estimate ranging from 1 in 5,500 to 1 in 8,000." There's not an accepted or right way to visualize something like this.

Finding ways to accurately and effectively represent uncertainty is one of the most important challenges in data visualization today. And it's important to know that visualizing uncertainty in general is extremely difficult to do.

Why?

When you think about it, visualizations make something abstract—numbers, statistics—concrete. You are representing an idea like 20% with a thing like a bar or dot. A dot on a line that represents 20% looks pretty certain. How do you then express the idea that "five times out of a hundred this isn't the right answer, and it could be all these other answers"?

So are there good ways of visualizing uncertainty like this?

A lot of the time people just don't represent their uncertainty, because it's hard. We don't want to do that. Uncertainty is an important thing to be able to communicate. For example, consider health care, where outcomes of care may be uncertain but you want people to understand their decisions. How do you show them the possible range of outcomes, instead of only what is the most likely or least likely to happen? Or say there's an outbreak of a disease like Ebola and we want to model the worst case, the most likely, and the best-case scenarios. How do we represent those different outcomes? Weather forecasts, hurricane models are the same thing. Risk analysts and probability experts think about how to solve these problems all the time. It's not easy.

There are a number of other approaches, though. Some people use bars to represent the range of uncertainty. Some use solid lines to show an average value and dotted lines above and below to show the upper and lower boundaries. Using color saturation or gradients to show that values are becoming less and less likely—but still in the realm of possibility—is another way.

On top of uncertainty, we're also dealing with probability.

Yes, it's really hard for our brains to perceive probability. When we say something has an 80% chance of happening, it's not the simplest thing to understand. You can't really feel what 80% likelihood really means. I mean, it seems like it will probably happen. But the important thing to remember is that if it doesn't happen, that doesn't mean you were wrong. It just means the 20% likelihood happened instead.

Statistics are weird. Even if we felt like we understood what a "20% chance" was, we don't think of it as the same as "1 in 5." We tend to think that "1 in 5" is more likely to happen than "20%." It's less abstract. If you say 1 in 5 people commits a crime, you actually picture that one person. We "image the numerator." But "20%" doesn't commit a crime. It's not a thing that acts. It's a statistic.

What do we do when the 20% or 10% chance thing happens?

How do you tell someone who has had the very rare thing happen to them that, based on the probability we gave you, it was the right advice, even though it didn't work out for you? That's really difficult, and security executives and risk experts think about this all the time. When you think about it, businesses need to learn this because it's easy in hindsight to say "Our models were wrong—the unlikely bad thing happened." Not true! We all along were communicating there was some small chance that the bad thing could happen. Still, as humans, that's hard for us to grasp.

Is it because we try to hang on to the hope of a more favorable outcome?

It's because likely things happen more of the time. When unlikely things happen, we want to make sense of it. We weren't expecting it. We shouldn't have been expecting it because it was unlikely. But it's still possible, however unlikely. Already just hearing myself say this, you see how elliptical it sounds. When a natural disaster strikes, you often hear people afterward say "It was a 100-year storm, no one could have seen this coming." Not true! Risk experts always see it coming. It was always a statistical possibility. It's just not likely.

I get probability, but I still can't help but feel misled by the presidential election predictions. What am I missing?

Three things are going on with the election models. (1) Even if a candidate had a 10% chance of winning 10 days ago and they end up winning, it doesn't mean the model was wrong. It means the unlikely happened. (2) This whole notion of using probability to determine who will win an election (based on whether they have an 80% chance, etc.) is hard for the audience to grasp, because we tend to think about elections in more binary terms—this person will win versus that person will win. (3) We revisit the probabilities every day and update them. And when one candidate says something stupid, their probability of winning goes down and the others go up. This makes us feel like these winning probabilities are reactive, not speculative. So we, the lay audience, end up thinking we're looking at data that tells us something about how the candidates are behaving, not how likely it is they'll win. It starts to feel more like an approval rating than a forecast.

That first point must come up in business all the time.

The election brings the subject of visualizing uncertainty into focus but it's an increasingly common challenge in businesses building out their data science operations. As data science becomes more and more important for companies, managers are starting to deal with types of data that show multiple possible outcomes, where there is statistical uncertainty and data uncertainty that they have to communicate to their bosses. If they don't help their bosses understand the uncertainty, they will look at their charts and say that's the answer when it's only the likelihood. It's okay to focus on what is most likely, but you don't want to forgo showing the range of possible outcomes.

For example, if you're looking at a way to model customer adoption and you're using statistical models, you want to make sure you demonstrate what you think is most likely to happen, but also how this outcome is one of a range of potential outcomes based on your models. You need to be able to communicate that visually, or your boss or client will misinterpret what you're saying. If the data scientists say we have a 90% chance of succeeding if we adopt this model, but then it doesn't happen, the boss should know that you weren't wrong—you really just fell into the 10%. You rolled snake eyes. It happens. This is a really hard thing for our brains to deal with and communicate, and it's an important challenge for companies investing in a data-driven approach to their businesses.

Scott Berinato is a senior editor at *Harvard Business Review* and the author of *Good Charts: The HBR Guide to Making Smarter, More Persuasive Data Visualizations* (Harvard Business Review Press, 2016). **Nicole Torres** is an associate editor at *Harvard Business Review*.

NOTE

"Live Presidential Forecast," *New York Times*, November 9, 2016, https://www.nytimes.com/elections/forecast/president.

CHAPTER 21

Responding to Someone Who Challenges Your Data

by Jon M. Jachimowicz

I recently conducted a study with a large, multinational company to figure out how to increase employee engagement. After the data collection was complete, I ran the data analysis and found some intriguing findings that I was excited to share with the firm. But a troubling result became apparent in my analysis: The organization had rampant discrimination against women, especially

---

Adapted from "What to Do When Someone Angrily Challenges Your Data" on hbr.org, April 5, 2017 (product #H03L2M).

ambitious, passionate, talented women. Although this result was based on initial data and was not particularly rigorous, I was convinced that managers at the collaborating organization would like to hear it so that they could address the issue.

I couldn't have been more wrong. In a meeting with the company's head of HR and a few members of his team, I first presented my overall findings about employee engagement. In my last few slides, I turned the presentation toward the results of the gender discrimination analysis that I had conducted. I was expecting an animated conversation, and perhaps even some internal questioning into why the discrimination was occurring and how they could rectify it.

Instead, the head of HR got very angry. He accused me of misrepresenting the facts, and countered by citing data from his own records that showed men and women were equally likely to be promoted. In addition, he had never heard from anyone within the organization that gender discrimination was a problem. He strongly believed that the diversity practices his team had championed were industry leading, and that they were sufficient to ward off gender discrimination. Clearly, this topic was important to him, and my findings had touched a nerve.

After his fury (and my shock) had cooled, I reminded him that the data I presented was just initial pilot data and should be treated as such. Perhaps if we were to do a more thorough assessment, I argued, we would find that the initial data was inaccurate. In addition, I proposed that a follow-on study that focused on gender discrimination could pinpoint which aspects of the diversity policies were working particularly well, and that he could use these insights to further advocate for his agenda. We landed on a compromise: I would design and run an additional study with a focus on gender discrimination, connecting survey responses to important outcomes such as promotions and turnover.

A few months later, the data came in. My data analysis showed that my initial findings were correct: Gender discrimination *was* happening in the company. But the head of HR's major claim wasn't wrong: Men and women were *equally* likely to be promoted.

The improved data set allowed us to see how both facts could be true at the same time. We now had detailed insights into which employees were—and, more important, were *not*—being promoted. Although ambitious, passionate, and talented men were advancing in the company, their female counterparts were being passed over for promotion, time and again—effectively being pushed out of the organization. That is, the best men were moving up, but not the best women. Those women who were being promoted were given these opportunities out of tokenism: They weren't particularly high performing, and often reached a "natural" ceiling early on in their careers due to their limited abilities.

We also now had data on the specific kind of advancement opportunities male and female employees received to learn new skills, make new connections, and increase their visibility in the organization. Compared with their male counterparts, passionate women were less likely to get these kinds of chances.

Armed with this new data, I was invited to present to the head of HR again. Remembering our last meeting, I expected him to be upset. But we had a very different conversation this time. Instead of being met with anger, the data I presented prompted concern. I could place the fact of men and women being equally likely to be promoted in a fuller context, complete with rigorous data from the organization. We had a lively debate about why this asymmetry between men and women existed. Most important, we concluded that the data he measured to track gender discrimination was unable to provide him with the necessary insight to understand whether gender discrimination was a problem.

He has since appointed a task force to tackle the problem of gender discrimination head-on, something he wouldn't have done if we hadn't collected the data that we did. This is the power of collecting thorough data in your own organization: Instead of making assumptions on what may or may not be occurring, a thoughtful design of data-collection practices allows you to gather the right information to come to better conclusions.

So it's not just about the data you have. Existing data blinds us, and it is important to shift the focus away from readily available information. Crucially, not having the right data is no excuse. In the case of the head of HR, not hearing about gender discrimination from anyone in the organization allowed him to conclude that women did not face this issue. Think about what data is *not* being collected that may help embed existing data in a richer context.

Next time someone angrily challenges your data, there are a few steps you can take:

First, take their perspective. Understand why your counterpart is responding so forcefully. In many cases, it may simply be that they really care about the outcome. Your goals may even be aligned, and framing your data in a way where their goals are achieved may help you circumvent their anger.

Second, collect more data that specifically takes their criticism to heart. Every comment is a useful comment. Just as a fiction author can't be upset when readers don't get the point of what they are trying to say, a researcher must understand how their findings are being understood. What is the upset recipient of your analysis responding to, and how can further data collection help you address their concerns?

Last, view your challenger not as an opponent, but as an ally. Find a way to collaborate, because once you have their buy-in, they are invested in the joint investigation. As a result, they will be more likely to view you as being part of the team. And then you can channel the energy that prompted their fury for good.

Defending your data analysis can be stressful—especially if your findings cause conflict. But by following these steps, you can diffuse any tension and attack the problem in a productive way.

Jon M. Jachimowicz is a PhD candidate at Columbia Business School. In his research, he investigates the antecedents, perceptions, and consequences of passion for work. His website can be found at jonmjachimowicz.com.

CHAPTER 22

Decisions Don't Start with Data

by Nick Morgan

I recently worked with an executive keen to persuade his colleagues that their company should drop a longtime vendor in favor of a new one. He knew that members of the executive team opposed the idea (in part because of their well-established relationships with the vendor) but he didn't want to confront them directly, so he put together a PowerPoint presentation full of stats and charts showing the cost savings that might be achieved by the change.

He hoped the data would speak for itself.

But it didn't.

Adapted from content posted on hbr.org, May 14, 2014 (product #H00T3S).

The team stopped listening about a third of the way through the presentation. Why? It was good data. The executive was right. But, even in business meetings, numbers don't ever speak for themselves, no matter how visually appealing the presentation may be.

To influence human decision making, you have to get to the place where decisions are really made—in the unconscious mind, where emotions rule, and data is mostly absent. Yes, even the most savvy executives begin to make choices this way. They get an intent, a desire, or a want in their unconscious minds, and then decide to pursue it and act on that decision. Only after that do they become consciously aware of the choice they've made and start to justify it with rational argument. In fact, research from Carnegie Mellon University indicates that our unconscious minds actually make *better* decisions when left alone to deal with complex issues.

Data is helpful as supporting material, of course. But, because it spurs thinking in the conscious mind, it must be used with care. Effective persuasion starts not with numbers, but with stories that have emotional power because that's the best way to tap into unconscious decision making. We decide to invest in a new company or business line not because the financial model shows it will succeed but because we're drawn to the story told by the people pitching it. We buy goods and services because we believe the stories marketers build around them: "A diamond is forever" (De Beers), "Real beauty" (Dove), "Think different" (Apple), "Just do it" (Nike). We take jobs not only for the pay and benefits but also for the self-advancement story we're told, and tell ourselves, about working at the new place.

Sometimes we describe this as having a good "gut feeling." What that really means is that we've already unconsciously decided to go forward, based on desire, and our conscious mind is seeking some rationale for that otherwise invisible decision.

I advised the executive to scrap his PowerPoint and tell a story about the opportunities for future growth with the new vendor, reframing and trumping the loyalty story the opposition camp was going to tell. And so, in his next attempt, rather than just presenting data, he told his colleagues that they should all be striving toward a new vision for the company, no longer held back by a tether to the past. He began with an alluring description of the future state—improved margins, a cooler, higher-tech product line, and excited customers—then asked his audience to move forward with him to reach that goal. It was a quest story, and it worked.

Data can provide new insight and evidence to inform your toughest decisions. But numbers alone won't convince others. Good stories—with a few key facts woven in—are what attach emotions to your argument, prompt people into unconscious decision making, and ultimately move them to action.

Nick Morgan is a speaker, coach, and the president and founder of Public Words, a communications consulting firm. He is the author of *Power Cues: The Subtle Science of Leading Groups, Persuading Others, and Maximizing Your Personal Impact* (Harvard Business Review Press, 2014).

APPENDIX

Data Scientist: The Sexiest Job of the 21st Century

by Thomas H. Davenport and D.J. Patil

When Jonathan Goldman arrived for work in June 2006 at LinkedIn, the business networking site, the place still felt like a startup. The company had just under 8 million accounts, and the number was growing quickly as existing members invited their friends and colleagues to join. But users weren't seeking out connections with the people who were already on the site at the rate executives had expected. Something was apparently missing in the social experience. As one LinkedIn manager put it, "It

---

Reprinted from *Harvard Business Review*, October 2012 (product #R1210D).

was like arriving at a conference reception and realizing you don't know anyone. So you just stand in the corner sipping your drink—and you probably leave early."

Goldman, a PhD in physics from Stanford, was intrigued by the linking he did see going on and by the richness of the user profiles. It all made for messy data and unwieldy analysis, but as he began exploring people's connections, he started to see possibilities. He began forming theories, testing hunches, and finding patterns that allowed him to predict whose networks a given profile would land in. He could imagine that new features capitalizing on the heuristics he was developing might provide value to users. But LinkedIn's engineering team, caught up in the challenges of scaling up the site, seemed uninterested. Some colleagues were openly dismissive of Goldman's ideas. Why would users need LinkedIn to figure out their networks for them? The site already had an address book importer that could pull in all a member's connections.

Luckily, Reid Hoffman, LinkedIn's cofounder and CEO at the time (now its executive chairman), had faith in the power of analytics because of his experiences at PayPal, and he had granted Goldman a high degree of autonomy. For one thing, he had given Goldman a way to circumvent the traditional product release cycle by publishing small modules in the form of ads on the site's most popular pages.

Through one such module, Goldman started to test what would happen if you presented users with names of people they hadn't yet connected with but seemed likely to know—for example, people who had shared their tenures at schools and workplaces. He did this by ginning up a custom ad that displayed the three best new matches for each user based on the background entered in his or her LinkedIn profile. Within days it was obvious that something remarkable was taking place. The click-through rate on those ads was the highest ever seen. Goldman continued to refine how the suggestions were generated, incorporating networking ideas such as "triangle closing"—the notion that if you know Larry and Sue, there's a good chance that Larry and Sue know each other. Goldman and his team also got the action required to respond to a suggestion down to one click.

It didn't take long for LinkedIn's top managers to recognize a good idea and make it a standard feature. That's when things really took off. "People You May Know" ads achieved a click-through rate 30% higher than the rate obtained by other prompts to visit more pages on the site. They generated millions of new page views. Thanks to this one feature, LinkedIn's growth trajectory shifted significantly upward.

A New Breed

Goldman is a good example of a new key player in organizations: the "data scientist." It's a high-ranking professional with the training and curiosity to make discoveries in the world of big data. The title has been around for only a few years. (It was coined in 2008 by one of us, D.J. Patil, and Jeff Hammerbacher, then the respective leads of data and analytics efforts at LinkedIn and Facebook.) But thousands of data scientists are already working at both startups and well-established companies.

Their sudden appearance on the business scene reflects the fact that companies are now wrestling with information that comes in varieties and volumes never encountered before. If your organization stores multiple petabytes of data, if the information most critical to your business resides in forms other than rows and columns of numbers, or if answering your biggest question would involve a "mashup" of several analytical efforts, you've got a big data opportunity.

Much of the current enthusiasm for big data focuses on technologies that make taming it possible, including Hadoop (the most widely used framework for distributed file system processing) and related open-source tools, cloud computing, and data visualization. While those are important breakthroughs, at least as important are the people with the skill set (and the mindset) to put them to good use. On this front, demand has raced ahead of supply. Indeed, the shortage of data scientists is becoming a serious constraint in some sectors. Greylock Partners, an early-stage venture firm that has backed companies such as Facebook, LinkedIn, Palo Alto Networks, and Workday, is worried enough about the tight labor pool that it has built its own specialized recruiting team to channel talent to businesses in its portfolio. "Once they have data," says Dan Portillo, who leads that team, "they really need people who can manage it and find insights in it."

Who Are These People?

If capitalizing on big data depends on hiring scarce data scientists, then the challenge for managers is to learn how to identify that talent, attract it to an enterprise, and make it productive. None of those tasks is as straightforward as it is with other, established organizational roles. Start with the fact that there are no university programs offering degrees in data science. There is also little consensus on where the role fits in an organization, how data scientists can add the most value, and how their performance should be measured.

The first step in filling the need for data scientists, therefore, is to understand what they do in businesses. Then ask, What skills do they need? And what fields are those skills most readily found in?

More than anything, what data scientists do is make discoveries while swimming in data. It's their preferred method of navigating the world around them. At ease in the digital realm, they are able to bring structure to large quantities of formless data and make analysis possible. They identify rich data sources, join them with other, potentially incomplete data sources, and clean the resulting set. In a competitive landscape where challenges keep changing and data never stop flowing, data scientists help decision makers shift from ad hoc analysis to an ongoing conversation with data.

Data scientists realize that they face technical limitations, but they don't allow that to bog down their search for novel solutions. As they make discoveries, they communicate what they've learned and suggest its implications for new business directions. Often they are creative in displaying information visually and making the patterns they find clear and compelling. They advise executives and product managers on the implications of the data for products, processes, and decisions.

Given the nascent state of their trade, it often falls to data scientists to fashion their own tools and even conduct academic-style research. Yahoo, one of the firms that employed a group of data scientists early on, was instrumental in developing Hadoop. Facebook's data team created the language Hive for programming Hadoop projects. Many other data scientists, especially at data-driven companies such as Google, Amazon, Microsoft, Walmart, eBay, LinkedIn, and Twitter, have added to and refined the tool kit.

What kind of person does all this? What abilities make a data scientist successful? Think of him or her as a hybrid of data hacker, analyst, communicator, and trusted adviser. The combination is extremely powerful—and rare.

Data scientists' most basic, universal skill is the ability to write code. This may be less true in five years' time, when many more people will have the title "data scientist" on their business cards. More enduring will be the need for data scientists to communicate in language that all their stakeholders understand—and to demonstrate the special skills involved in storytelling with data, whether verbally, visually, or—ideally—both.

But we would say the dominant trait among data scientists is an intense curiosity—a desire to go beneath the surface of a problem, find the questions at its heart, and distill them into a very clear set of hypotheses that can be tested. This often entails the associative thinking that characterizes the most creative scientists in any field. For example, we know of a data scientist studying a fraud problem who realized that it was analogous to a type of DNA sequencing problem. By bringing together those disparate worlds, he and his team were able to craft a solution that dramatically reduced fraud losses.

Perhaps it's becoming clear why the word "scientist" fits this emerging role. Experimental physicists, for example, also have to design equipment, gather data, conduct multiple experiments, and communicate their results. Thus, companies looking for people who can work with complex data have had good luck recruiting among those with educational and work backgrounds in the physical or social sciences. Some of the best and brightest data scientists are PhDs in esoteric fields like ecology and systems biology. George Roumeliotis, the head of a data science team at Intuit in Silicon Valley, holds a doctorate in astrophysics. A little less surprisingly, many of the data scientists working in business today were formally trained in computer science, math, or economics. They can emerge from any field that has a strong data and computational focus.

It's important to keep that image of the scientist in mind—because the word "data" might easily send a search for talent down the wrong path. As Portillo told us, "The traditional backgrounds of people you saw 10 to 15 years ago just don't cut it these days." A quantitative analyst can be great at analyzing data but not at subduing a mass of unstructured data and getting it into a form in which it can be analyzed. A data management expert might be great at generating and organizing data in structured form but not at turning unstructured data into structured data—and also not at actually analyzing the data. And while people without strong social skills might thrive in traditional data professions, data scientists must have such skills to be effective.

Roumeliotis was clear with us that he doesn't hire on the basis of statistical or analytical capabilities. He begins his search for data scientists by asking candidates if they can develop prototypes in a mainstream programming language such as Java. Roumeliotis seeks both a skill set—a solid foundation in math, statistics, probability, and computer science—and certain habits of mind. He wants people with a feel for business issues and empathy for customers. Then, he says, he builds on all that with on-the-job training and an occasional course in a particular technology.

Several universities are planning to launch data science programs, and existing programs in analytics, such as the Master of Science in Analytics program at North Carolina State, are busy adding big data exercises and coursework. Some companies are also trying to develop their own data scientists. After acquiring the big data firm Greenplum, EMC decided that the availability of data scientists would be a gating factor in its own—and customers'—exploitation of big data. So its Education Services division launched a data science and big data analytics training and certification program. EMC makes the program available to both employees and customers, and some of its graduates are already working on internal big data initiatives.

As educational offerings proliferate, the pipeline of talent should expand. Vendors of big data technologies are also working to make them easier to use. In the meantime one data scientist has come up with a creative approach to closing the gap. The Insight Data Science Fellows Program, a postdoctoral fellowship designed by

HOW TO FIND THE DATA SCIENTISTS YOU NEED

1. Focus recruiting at the "usual suspect" universities (Stanford, MIT, Berkeley, Harvard, Carnegie Mellon) and also at a few others with proven strengths: North Carolina State, UC Santa Cruz, the University of Maryland, the University of Washington, and UT Austin.

2. Scan the membership rolls of user groups devoted to data science tools. The R User Groups (for an open-source statistical tool favored by data scientists) and Python Interest Groups (for PIGgies) are good places to start.

3. Search for data scientists on LinkedIn—they're almost all on there, and you can see if they have the skills you want.

4. Hang out with data scientists at the Strata, Structure:Data, and Hadoop World conferences and similar gatherings (there is almost one a week now) or at informal data scientist "meet-ups" in the Bay Area; Boston; New York; Washington, DC; London; Singapore; and Sydney.

5. Make friends with a local venture capitalist, who is likely to have gotten a variety of big data proposals over the past year.

(*continued*)

HOW TO FIND THE DATA SCIENTISTS YOU NEED

(*continued*)

6. Host a competition on Kaggle or TopCoder, the analytics and coding competition sites. Follow up with the most-creative entrants.

7. Don't bother with any candidate who can't code. Coding skills don't have to be at a world-class level but should be good enough to get by. Look for evidence, too, that candidates learn rapidly about new technologies and methods.

8. Make sure a candidate can find a story in a data set and provide a coherent narrative about a key data insight. Test whether he or she can communicate with numbers, visually and verbally.

9. Be wary of candidates who are too detached from the business world. When you ask how their work might apply to your management challenges, are they stuck for answers?

10. Ask candidates about their favorite analysis or insight and how they are keeping their skills sharp. Have they gotten a certificate in the advanced track of Stanford's online Machine Learning course, contributed to open-source projects, or built an online repository of code to share (for example, on GitHub)?

Jake Klamka (a high-energy physicist by training), takes scientists from academia and in six weeks prepares them to succeed as data scientists. The program combines mentoring by data experts from local companies (such as Facebook, Twitter, Google, and LinkedIn) with exposure to actual big data challenges. Originally aiming for 10 fellows, Klamka wound up accepting 30, from an applicant pool numbering more than 200. More organizations are now lining up to participate. "The demand from companies has been phenomenal," Klamka told us. "They just can't get this kind of high-quality talent."

Why Would a Data Scientist Want to Work Here?

Even as the ranks of data scientists swell, competition for top talent will remain fierce. Expect candidates to size up employment opportunities on the basis of how interesting the big data challenges are. As one of them commented, "If we wanted to work with structured data, we'd be on Wall Street." Given that today's most qualified prospects come from nonbusiness backgrounds, hiring managers may need to figure out how to paint an exciting picture of the potential for breakthroughs that their problems offer.

Pay will of course be a factor. A good data scientist will have many doors open to him or her, and salaries will be bid upward. Several data scientists working at startups commented that they'd demanded and got large stock option packages. Even for someone accepting a position for other reasons, compensation signals a level of respect and the value the role is expected to add to the business. But our informal survey of the priorities of data scientists revealed something more fundamentally important. They want to be “on the bridge.” The reference is to the 1960s television show *Star Trek,* in which the starship captain James Kirk relies heavily on data supplied by Mr. Spock. Data scientists want to be in the thick of a developing situation, with real-time awareness of the evolving set of choices it presents.

Considering the difficulty of finding and keeping data scientists, one would think that a good strategy would involve hiring them as consultants. Most consulting firms have yet to assemble many of them. Even the largest firms, such as Accenture, Deloitte, and IBM Global Services, are in the early stages of leading big data projects for their clients. The skills of the data scientists they do have on staff are mainly being applied to more-conventional quantitative analysis problems. Offshore analytics services firms, such as Mu Sigma, might be the ones to make the first major inroads with data scientists.

But the data scientists we’ve spoken with say they want to build things, not just give advice to a decision maker. One described being a consultant as “the dead zone—all you get to do is tell someone else what the analyses say they should do.” By creating solutions that work, they can have more impact and leave their marks as pioneers of their profession.

Care and Feeding

Data scientists don’t do well on a short leash. They should have the freedom to experiment and explore possibilities. That said, they need close relationships with the rest of the business. The most important ties for them to forge are with executives in charge of products and services rather than with people overseeing business functions. As the story of Jonathan Goldman illustrates, their greatest opportunity to add value is not in creating reports or presentations for senior executives but in innovating with customer-facing products and processes.

LinkedIn isn't the only company to use data scientists to generate ideas for products, features, and value-adding services. At Intuit data scientists are asked to develop insights for small-business customers and consumers and report to a new senior vice president of big data, social design, and marketing. GE is already using data science to optimize the service contracts and maintenance intervals for industrial products. Google, of course, uses data scientists to refine its core search and ad-serving algorithms. Zynga uses data scientists to optimize the game experience for both long-term engagement and revenue. Netflix created the well-known Netflix Prize, given to the data science team that developed the best way to improve the company's movie recommendation system. The test-preparation firm Kaplan uses its data scientists to uncover effective learning strategies.

There is, however, a potential downside to having people with sophisticated skills in a fast-evolving field spend their time among general management colleagues. They'll have less interaction with similar specialists, which they need to keep their skills sharp and their tool kit state-of-the-art. Data scientists have to connect with communities of practice, either within large firms or externally. New conferences and informal associations are springing up to support collaboration and technology sharing, and companies should encourage scientists to become involved in them with the understanding that "more water in the harbor floats all boats."

Data scientists tend to be more motivated, too, when more is expected of them. The challenges of accessing and structuring big data sometimes leave little time or energy for sophisticated analytics involving prediction or optimization. Yet if executives make it clear that simple reports are not enough, data scientists will devote more effort to advanced analytics. Big data shouldn't equal "small math."

The Hot Job of the Decade

Hal Varian, the chief economist at Google, is known to have said, "The sexy job in the next 10 years will be statisticians. People think I'm joking, but who would've guessed that computer engineers would've been the sexy job of the 1990s?"

If "sexy" means having rare qualities that are much in demand, data scientists are already there. They are difficult and expensive to hire and, given the very competitive market for their services, difficult to retain. There simply aren't a lot of people with their combination of scientific background and computational and analytical skills.

Data scientists today are akin to Wall Street "quants" of the 1980s and 1990s. In those days people with backgrounds in physics and math streamed to investment banks and hedge funds, where they could devise entirely new algorithms and data strategies. Then a variety of universities developed master's programs in financial engineering, which churned out a second generation of talent that was more accessible to mainstream firms. The pattern was repeated later in the 1990s with search engineers, whose rarefied skills soon came to be taught in computer science programs.

One question raised by this is whether some firms would be wise to wait until that second generation of data scientists emerges, and the candidates are more numerous, less expensive, and easier to vet and assimilate in a business setting. Why not leave the trouble of hunting down and domesticating exotic talent to the big data startups and to firms like GE and Walmart, whose aggressive strategies require them to be at the forefront?

The problem with that reasoning is that the advance of big data shows no signs of slowing. If companies sit out this trend's early days for lack of talent, they risk falling behind as competitors and channel partners gain nearly unassailable advantages. Think of big data as an epic wave gathering now, starting to crest. If you want to catch it, you need people who can surf.

Thomas H. Davenport is the President's Distinguished Professor in Management and Information Technology at Babson College, a research fellow at the MIT Initiative on the Digital Economy, and a senior adviser at Deloitte Analytics. Author of over a dozen management books, his latest is *Only Humans Need Apply: Winners and Losers in the Age of Smart Machines.* **D.J. Patil** was appointed as the first U.S. chief data scientist and has led product development at LinkedIn, eBay, and PayPal. He is the author of *Data Jujitsu: The Art of Turning Data into Product.*

Index

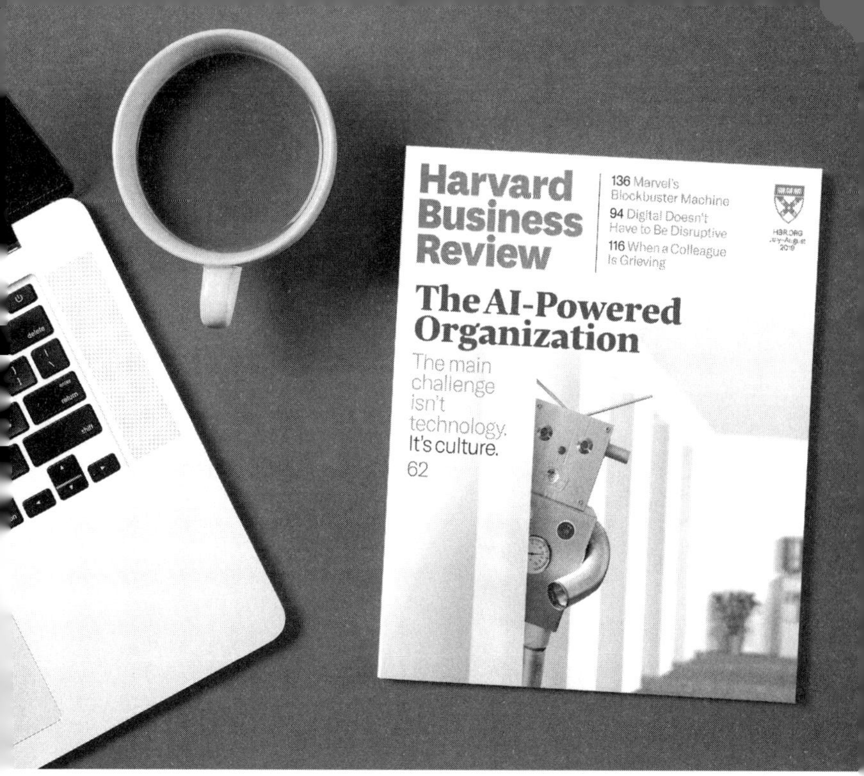
Harvard Business Review
136 Marvel's Blockbuster Machine
94 Digital Doesn't Have to Be Disruptive
116 When a Colleague Is Grieving
The AI-Powered Organization
The main challenge isn't technology. It's culture. 62

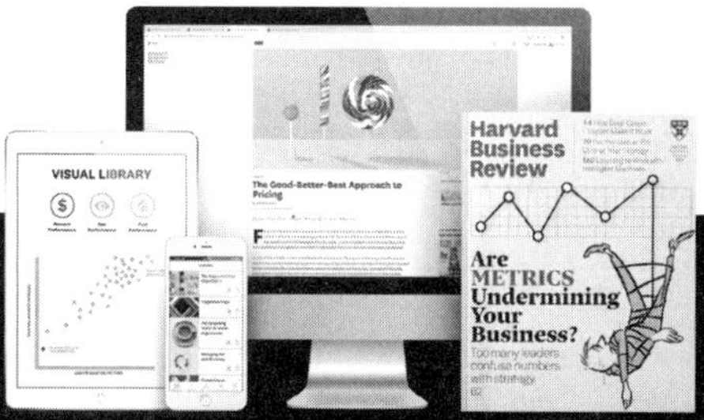
VISUAL LIBRARY
Harvard Business Review
Are METRICS Undermining Your Business?

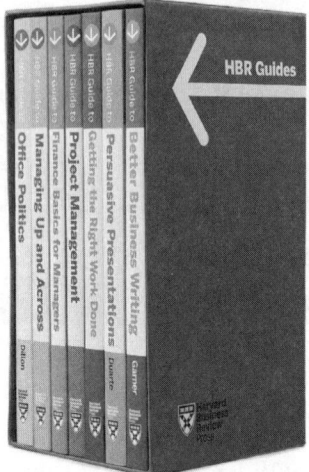

Notes

Notes

Notes

Notes

Notes

Notes

Notes

Notes

Notes

Notes

Notes

Notes

HBR Guide to
Persuasive Presentations

Harvard Business Review Guides

Arm yourself with the advice you need to succeed on the job, from the most trusted brand in business. Packed with how-to essentials from leading experts, the HBR Guides provide smart answers to your most pressing work challenges.

The titles include:

HBR Guide to Better Business Writing

HBR Guide to Finance Basics for Managers

HBR Guide to Getting the Mentoring You Need

HBR Guide to Getting the Right Job

HBR Guide to Getting the Right Work Done

HBR Guide to Giving Effective Feedback

HBR Guide to Making Every Meeting Matter

HBR Guide to Managing Stress at Work

HBR Guide to Managing Up and Across

HBR Guide to Persuasive Presentations

HBR Guide to Project Management

HBR Guide to **Persuasive Presentations**

Nancy Duarte

HARVARD BUSINESS REVIEW PRESS

Boston, Massachusetts

Printed in the United States of America

21

Library of Congress Cataloging-in-Publication Data

Duarte, Nancy.

HBR guide to persuasive presentations / Nancy Duarte.

p. cm.

ISBN 978-1-4221-8710-4 (alk. paper)

1. Business presentations. 2. Persuasion (Psychology) I. Title.

HF5718.22.D817 2012

658.4′52—dc23

2012019634

The paper used in this publication meets the requirements of the American National Standard for Permanence of Paper for Publications and Documents in Libraries and Archives Z39.48–1992.

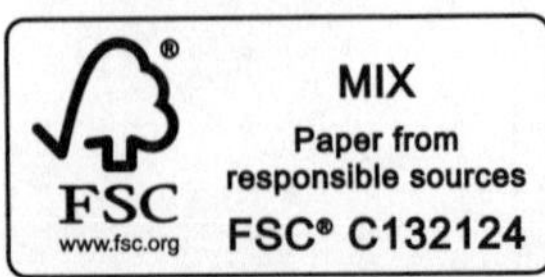

What You'll Learn

Do you dread giving presentations? Maybe your mind goes blank when you sit down to generate ideas, or you struggle to organize your fragmented thoughts and data into a coherent, persuasive message. Is it tough to connect with customers you're wooing, senior executives you're hitting up for funding, or employees you're training? Do you fumble for the right words, get lost in your slide deck, run out of time before you've hit your main points—and leave the room uncertain you've gotten through to *anyone*?

This guide will give you the confidence and tools you need to engage your audience, sell your ideas, and inspire people to act. You'll get better at:

- Showing people why your ideas matter to *them*
- Winning over tough crowds
- Balancing analytical and emotional appeal
- Crafting memorable messages
- Creating powerful visuals

- Striking the right tone
- Holding your audience's attention
- Measuring your impact

Contents

Section 4: MEDIA

Identify the best modes for communicating your message.

Section 5: SLIDES

Conceptualize and simplify the display of information.

Introduction

> If I am to speak for ten minutes, I need a week for preparation; if fifteen minutes, three days; if half an hour, two days; if an hour, I am ready now.
>
> **—Woodrow T. Wilson**

We work in a first-draft culture. Type an e-mail. Send. Write a blog entry. Post. Whip up some slides. Speak.

But it's in crafting and recrafting—in iteration and rehearsal—that excellence emerges.

Why worry about being an excellent communicator when you have so many other pressing things to do? Because it will help you *get those things done.*

So as you conceive, visualize, and present your message, don't skimp on preparation, even if you're giving a short talk. It actually takes more careful planning to distill your ideas into a few key takeaways than it does to create an hour-long presentation (see figure I-1). And gather lots of feedback so you'll be all the more effective when you start the process again.

FIGURE I-1

Planning a presentation

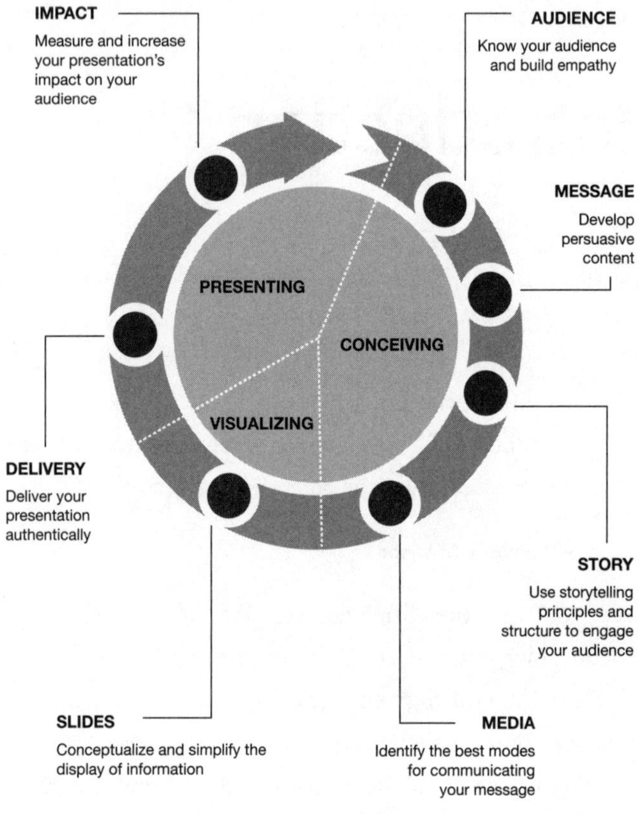

Since 1990, I've run a firm that specializes in writing and producing presentations—and then I became a presenter myself. This book is loaded with insights learned from supporting other presenters and giving my own talks. But, trust me, I've had my share of embarrassing moments, many of which could have been avoided with a little planning. Loading the wrong presentation onto my laptop. Walking onstage with my skirt tucked into my underwear. Botching my delivery to executives at an $8 billion company because I hadn't rehearsed enough—and getting cut from their continuing series of meetings. Experience is a powerful teacher.

I've also learned a lot from success. When audiences can see that you've prepared—that you care about their needs and value their time—they'll want to connect with you and support you. You'll get people to adopt your ideas, and you'll win the resources to carry them out. You'll close more deals. You'll earn the backing of decision makers. You'll gain influence. In short, you'll go farther in your organization—and your career.

Special thanks to:

- The wonderful Lisa Burrell, who edited my mess into coherence
- The entire team at Duarte, who supported me with case studies
- Members of the Twitterverse who answered my questions: @annzerega, @caddguru, @carolmquig, @catiehargrove, @charlesgreene3, @ckallaos, @conniewinch, @iamanshul, @karlparry, @managebetternow, @matthewmccull, @moniquemaley, @mpacc, @speakingtall, and @zupermik

Section 1
Audience

Designing a presentation without an audience in mind is like writing a love letter and addressing it "to whom it may concern."

—**Ken Haemer,**
Presentation Research Manager, AT&T

Understand the Audience's Power

When you walk into a room as a presenter, it's easy to feel as if you're in a position of power: You're up front, perhaps even elevated on a stage, and people came to hear you speak. In reality, though, you're not the star of the show. The audience is.

Why? The people you're addressing will determine whether your idea spreads or dies, simply by embracing or rejecting it. You need them more than they need you. Since they have that control, it's crucial to be humble in your approach. Use their desires and goals as a filter for everything you present.

Presenters tend to be self-focused. They have a lot to say, they want to say it well, and they have little time to prepare. These pressures make them forget what's important to the audience. A self-focused presenter might just describe a new initiative and explain what needs to get done—outlining how to do it, when to do it, and the budget required. Then maybe, if the audience is lucky, he'll have a slide at the very end about "why it matters."

This format screams, "I pay you to do this, so just do it!" The presenter is so consumed by the mission that he forgets to say why people would want or need to be involved.

Spend a moment in your audience's shoes. Walk people through why the initiative matters to them and to the organization, what internal and external factors are driving it, and why their support will make it successful. Yes, get through the nitty-gritty details, but set up the valuable role they'll play in the scenario rather than dictate a laundry list of to-do's.

Though presentations and audiences vary, one important fact remains constant: The people in your audience came to see what you can do for them, not what they must do for you. So look at the audience as the "hero" of your idea—and yourself as the mentor who helps people see themselves in that role so they'll want to get behind your idea and propel it forward.

Think of Yoda—a classic example of a wise, humble mentor. In the *Star Wars* movies, he gives the hero, Luke Skywalker, a special gift (a deeper understanding of the "Force"), trains him to use a magical tool (the lightsaber), and helps him in his fight against the Empire.

Like Yoda and other mentors in mythology, presenters should:

- **Give the hero a special gift:** Give people insights that will improve their lives. Perhaps you introduce senior managers at your company to an exciting new way to compete in the marketplace. Or maybe you show a roomful of potential clients that you can save them money and time.

- **Teach the hero to use a "magical" tool:** This is where the people in your audience pick up a new skill or mind-set from you—something that enables them to reach their objectives *and* yours.
- **Help the hero get "unstuck":** Ideally, you'll come with an idea or a solution that gets the audience out of a difficult or painful situation.

So if you're gearing up to launch a new service offering, for example, give your team a clear roadmap (tool) and a promise to bring in consultants for training and support (gift)—and describe how these will help everyone rise to the challenge ahead.

Segment the Audience

If you see your audience as a homogenous, faceless clump of people, you'll have a hard time making a connection and moving them to action. Instead, think of them as a line of individuals waiting to have a conversation with you.

Your audience will usually include a mix of people—individuals in diverse roles, with various levels of decision-making authority, from different parts of the organization—each needing to hear your message for different reasons. Decide which subgroup is the most important to you, and zero in on that subgroup's needs when you develop your presentation.

When you're segmenting your audience, take a look at:

- **Politics:** Power, influence, decision process
- **Demographics:** Age, education, ethnicity, gender, and geography
- **Psychographics:** Personality, values, attitudes, interests, communities, and lifestyle

- **Firmographics:** Number of employees, revenue size, industry, number of locations, location of headquarters
- **Ethnographics:** Social and cultural needs

After you've segmented the group, figure out which members will have the greatest impact on the adoption of your idea. Is there a layer of management you need to appeal to? Is there a type of customer in the room with a lot of sway over the industry?

Then view yourself as a curator of content for your most valuable and powerful stakeholders. Pick the one type of person in the room with the most influence, and write your presentation as if just to that subgroup. The presentation can't be so specialized that it will alienate everyone else—you'll need some content that appeals to the greater group. But tailor most of your specifics to the subgroup you've targeted.

Say you're presenting a new product concept to the executive team, and you know you won't get their buy-in unless Trent, the president of the enterprise division, gets excited about the idea, because they always defer to his instincts on new initiatives. Appeal first to Trent's entrepreneurial nature by describing how exciting the new market is—while keeping in mind what the other executives will care about. Here's where your segmentation work will come in handy (table 1-1).

Draw on your understanding of the team members as you prepare your talk. In addition to fanning the flames of Trent's entrepreneurism, for example, have data in your pocket to respond to Marco, the analytical and

TABLE 1-1

Segmenting your audience

Executive team member	Qualities
Bert, CEO	Hierarchical, micromanager, dominant, fear-driven, needs to be liked
Carol, president of Consumer division	Visionary, creative, disruptive, scattered, wants to stand on own feet
Trent, president of Enterprise division	Entrepreneurial, design thinker, systematic, found self after near-death experience
Martin, CMO	CEO's favorite, empirically minded, arrogant, sabotages projects
Marco, CTO	Political, risk-averse, analytical, introverted, has self-doubt

risk-averse CTO, when he inevitably balks. And try to work with, not against, your CMO's arrogance: Ask for his counsel on a key marketing point or two before the group meets, and he'll be less likely to lash out during the presentation or sit there quietly plotting a coup, as is his wont.

What if some audience members are already familiar with your idea and others need to be brought up to speed? (This is most likely to happen when you're presenting within your organization.) Consider evening things out by giving the newbies a crash course before you conduct the larger presentation. Or you may decide just to do two separate presentations.

Present Clearly and Concisely to Senior Executives

Senior executives are a tough segment to reach. They usually have very little time in their schedules to give you. Though that's true of many audiences, what sets this crowd apart is that they need to make huge decisions based on accurate information delivered quickly. Long presentations with a big reveal at the end do not work for them. They'll want you to get to the bottom line right away—and they often won't let you finish your shtick without interrupting. (Never mind that you would have answered their questions if they'd just let you get through the next three slides.)

When presenting to an audience of senior executives, do everything you can to make their decision making easier and more efficient:

- **Get to the point:** Take less time than you were allocated. If you were given 30 minutes, create your talk within that timeframe but then pretend that your slot got cut to 5 minutes. That'll force you to be succinct and lead with the things they care about—high-level findings, conclusions, recommendations, your call to action. Hit those points clearly and simply before you venture into supporting data or tangential areas of importance to you.

- **Give them what they asked for:** Stay on topic. If you were invited to give an update about the flooding of the manufacturing plant in Indonesia, do that before covering anything else. They've invited you because they felt you could supply a missing piece of information, so answer that specific request quickly.

- **Set expectations:** At the beginning, let the audience know you will spend the first 5 of your 30 minutes presenting your summary and the remaining time on discussion. Most executives will be patient for 5 minutes and let you present your main points well if they know they'll be able to ask questions fairly soon.

- **Create executive summary slides:** Develop a clear, short overview of your key points, and place it in a set of executive summary slides at the front of the deck; have the rest of your slides serve as an appendix. Follow a 10% rule of thumb: If your appendix is 50 slides, devote about 5 slides to your summary at the beginning. After you present the summary, let the group drive the conversation.

Often, executives will want to go deeper on the points that will aid their decision making. You can quickly pull up any slides in the appendix that speak to those points.

- **Rehearse:** Before presenting, run your slides by someone who has success getting ideas adopted at the executive level and who will serve as an honest coach. Is your message coming through clearly and quickly? Do your summary slides boil everything down into skimmable key insights? Are you missing anything your audience is likely to expect?

Sounds like a lot of work, right? It is, but presenting to an executive team is a great honor and can open tremendous doors. If you nail this, people with a lot of influence will become strong advocates for your ideas.

Get to Know Your Audience

Segmenting your audience members politically, demographically, psychographically, and so on is a great start, but connecting with people means understanding them on a more personal level. To develop resonant content for them, dig for deeper insights about them. Ask yourself:

- **What are they like?** Think through a day in their lives. Describe what that looks like so they'll know you "get" them.

- **Why are they here?** What do they think they're going to get out of this presentation? Are they willing participants or mandatory attendees? Highlight what's in it for them.

- **What keeps them up at night?** Everyone has a fear, a pain point, a thorn in the side. Let your audience know that you empathize—and that you're here to help.

- **How can you solve their problems?** How are you going to make their lives better? Point to benefits you know they'll care about.
- **What do you want them to do?** What's their part in your plan? Make sure there's a clear action for your audience to take. (See "Build an Effective Call to Action" in the Message section of this guide.)
- **How might they resist?** What will keep them from adopting your message and carrying out your call to action? Remove any obstacles you can.
- **How can you best reach them?** How do they prefer to receive information? Do they like the room to be set up a certain way? Do they want materials to review before the presentation? Afterward? What atmosphere or type of media will best help them see your point of view? Give them what they want, how they want it.

When getting ready to present to an audience you've never met, do some research online. If you know the names of stakeholders in your audience, look up their bios. If you know only generalities about the audience, find the event on social media feeds and read what's on the minds of those who'll be attending. If you'll be presenting to a company, find recent press mentions, look at how the company positions itself against competitors, read its annual report, and have Google Alerts send new articles about the company to your e-mail.

One time, I was preparing to present to beer executives, and I don't like beer or know anything about the industry. So I hosted a beer-tasting event at my shop, read their annual report, read recent press, studied key influencers, and looked up each attendee online. During the Q&A, a question came from one of the top executives (I knew he was at the top because I'd looked him up)—and I answered his question with timely examples.

When your audience is familiar—say, a group of your direct reports or colleagues—think through the pressures they are under and find ways to create an empathic connection.

Knowing people—*really* knowing them—makes it easier to influence them. You engage in a conversation, exchange insights, tell stories. Usually, both you and they change a bit in the process.

People don't fall asleep during conversations, but they often do during presentations—and that's because many presentations don't *feel conversational.* Knowing your audience well helps you feel warmly toward the people in the room and take on a more conversational tone. Speak sincerely to your audience, and people will want to listen to your message and root for and contribute to the success of your idea.

Define How You'll Change the Audience

When you present, you're asking the people in the room to change their behavior or beliefs in some way, big or small. Before you begin writing your presentation, map out that transformation—where your audience is starting, and where you want people to end up. This is the most critical step in planning your presentation, because that desired endpoint is the whole reason you're presenting in the first place, and people won't get there on their own.

Ask yourself, "What new beliefs do I want them to adopt? How do I want them to behave differently? How must their attitudes or emotions change before their behavior can change?"

By thinking through who they are before they enter the room and who you want them to be when they leave, you'll define their transformation arc, much as a screenwriter plans the protagonist's transformation in a film.

Let's say you work in the development office at a university and you're delivering a presentation to potential donors. The audience transformation might look like the one shown in table 1-2.

TABLE 1-2

Transforming your audience

Move audience from:	Move audience to:
Skepticism that the school will make good use of the money	Excitement about innovative research by faculty, students, and alumni—and an impulse to give

Change typically doesn't happen without a struggle. It's hard to convince people to move away from a view that is comfortable or widely held as true, or change a behavioral pattern that has become their norm. You are persuading members of your audience to let go of old beliefs or habits and adopt new ones. Once you understand their transformation, you can demonstrate empathy for the sacrifices they may need to make to move your idea forward.

Find Common Ground

Whether you evoke frenzied enthusiasm or puzzled stares or glassy-eyed boredom depends largely on how well your message resonates with the audience.

Resonance is a physics phenomenon. If you tap into an object's natural rate of vibration, or *resonant frequency*, it will move: It may vibrate, shudder, or even play a sympathetic musical note—think tuning forks. The same is true, metaphorically, when you present to an audience. If you tap into the group's resonant frequency, you can *move* the people listening to you.

But how do you resonate deeply enough to move them toward your objective? Figure out where you have common ground, and communicate on that frequency. Think about what's inside them that's also inside you. That way, you're not pushing or pulling them; they're moving because you tapped into something they already believe.

All this may sound highly unscientific and touchy-feely, but you can find your audience's resonant frequency by doing a little research. You'll want to examine:

- **Shared experiences:** What from your past do you have in common. Do you share memories, historical events, interests?
- **Common goals:** Where are you all headed in the future? What types of outcomes are mutually desired?
- **Qualifications:** Why are you uniquely qualified to be the audience's guiding expert? What did you learn when you faced similar challenges of your own, and how will your audience benefit from that insight?

The amount of common ground you discover will depend on the depth of your relationship with the group.

Lots of common ground

If you are presenting to family, friends, club members, or a religous group, it's easy to find common ground because you know the people well and tend to share many experiences, interests, and values.

Moderate common ground

With your colleagues, the challenge is a bit tougher. You know them a bit, but not as much as close friends or relatives. You share some interests but possibly only around one or two things. Examine those points of intersection for a way in.

Let's say you're a scientist working for a biotech company and you've been asked to speak at an all-hands meeting. Most of the audience members will be scientists, but you'll also be addressing executives and administrative employees. To find common ground with them, think about why you decided to work for this company and what motivates you to do your job day to day. Maybe you wanted to use your research and problem-solving skills to help people stay healthy—a mission the others in the room will share or at least support. Finding such commonalities will help you connect with them.

Minimal common ground

With a broad audience—for instance, a group of seminar participants from a variety of organizations and industries—you'll have many types of people to think about. The overlap won't be immediately evident, because there are so many perspectives and backgrounds to consider. You'll need to work hard to find or create it, but that work will pay off.

Before I went to China on a book tour, for example, I researched communication and storytelling in modern and ancient Chinese culture. I identified three great communicators in Chinese history and analyzed their speeches. When I shared my analysis with audiences, it was clear to them that I understood the historical context surrounding the speeches—I could even provide detailed answers to their questions about it. I got feedback multiple times on that trip that people could see I cared enough to really study and understand their perspective.

Section 2
Message

Are ideas born interesting or made interesting?

—**Chip and Dan Heath,**
authors of *Switch: How to Change Things When Change Is Hard*

Define Your Big Idea

Your big idea is that one key message you *must* communicate. It's what compels the audience to change course. (Screenwriters call this the "controlling idea.") It has two components:

- **Your point of view:** The big idea needs to express *your* perspective on a subject, not a generalization like "Q4 financials." Otherwise, why present? You may as well e-mail your stakeholders a spreadsheet and be done with it.

- **What's at stake:** You'll also want to convey why the audience should care about your perspective. This helps people recognize their need to participate rather than continue with the status quo.

Express your big idea in a complete sentence. It needs a subject (often some version of "you," to highlight the audience's role) and a verb (to convey action and elicit emotion).

When asked, "What's your presentation about?" most people answer with a phrase like "Software updates." That's not a big idea; it's a topic—no point of view, no stakes. Change it to "Your department needs to update its workflow management software," and you're getting closer. You've added your point of view, but the stakes still aren't clear. So try this instead: "Your department will struggle to meet key production deadlines until we update the workflow management software."

Another example: If you say your presentation is about "the Florida wetlands," that's also just a topic. Add your point of view and what's at stake. For instance: "We need to restrict commercial and residential development in Florida's wetlands, because we're destroying the fragile ecosystem there and killing off endangered species."

People will move away from pain and toward pleasure. Prod them (with words like "struggle" from the first example; "destroying" and "killing" from the second) so they feel uncomfortable staying in their current position. Lure them toward your idea with encouragement and rewards (the promise of meeting deadlines; protection of endangered species).

Generate Content to Support the Big Idea

Now that you've articulated your big idea, it's time to create your content, but don't fire up your presentation software quite yet. Software forces linear thinking—one slide after another—so it's not the best tool for early brainstorming.

Instead, change up your usual environment. Move to a new room, turn off your e-mail and cell phone, maybe play some music. Use tactile tools like paper, whiteboards, and sticky notes.

Generate as many ideas as possible by:

- **Gathering existing content:** You don't have to start from scratch. Dig up other presentations, industry studies, news articles, reports, surveys—anything that's relevant to your big idea.
- **Building on existing content:** Push on the ideas in the content you've gathered. Challenge them,

or consider them from a new angle. Draw new connections.

- **Creating new content:** Be curious, take risks, and let your intuition guide you. Experiment and dream.

For brainstorming to be successful, you have to suspend judgment and stay receptive to seemingly unrelated ideas—they may lead to something great. Increase your creative yield by moving back and forth between brainstorming alone and brainstorming in a group.

Brainstorm alone

It's intimidating to approach a blank piece of paper or whiteboard, but you have to start somewhere. Write down a key word and riff off that. Let your mind move in random directions. Then draw connections with lines. Keep brainstorming until you have a messy web of concepts and relationships to explore. This is called *mind mapping* (see figure 2-1). You can get special software to do it, but paper or sticky notes will work just as well.

Brainstorm in a group

When you work with others, you get more gems to choose from—and someone else's idea may spark even more creative ones in you. Be extra kind to the folks with enough guts to put half-baked or embarrassing ideas out there. Treat every idea as valuable. Have someone facilitate and capture the ideas so the discussion can move at a fast clip (if it slows down, people will start to question and censor themselves). Or ask brainstormers to scribble ideas on

FIGURE 2-1

Mind map

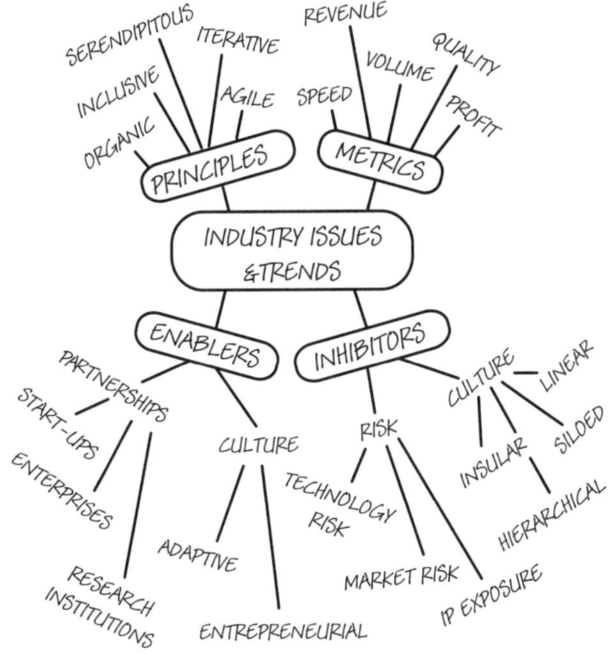

sticky notes and post them on a wall. Sticky notes are the perfect brainstorming tool. They're small, convenient, and moveable—great for collecting and organizing material. Limit yourselves to one idea per sticky note so it's easier to sort and cluster thoughts.

Brainstorm alone again

Take the seeds of ideas that came from the rapid-fire group session and do another round of quiet brainstorming on your own. This will give those latent ideas a chance to develop.

Go for quantity, not quality. You may work your way through five, ten, twenty ideas until you find ones that are distinctive and memorable. This is not the time to edit yourself. Even if an idea has been expressed or used before, add it to the mix. You may later find a unique way of incorporating it.

Anticipate Resistance

As a presenter, you're asking people to change their beliefs or behavior. That's not something they'll enjoy or find easy, so every audience will resist in some way. People will adamantly defend their own perspectives to avoid adopting yours. While listening to you, they'll catalog what they hear. Having come into the room with their own knowledge and biases, they'll constantly evaluate whether what you say fits within or falls outside their views.

So think through why and how they might resist, and plan accordingly. Here are the most common types of resistance, and how to get ready for them:

Logical resistance: Can you find logical arguments against your perspective? Dig up articles, blog posts, and reports that challenge your stance to familiarize yourself with alternate lines of reasoning. This kind of research prepares you for skeptical questions and comments you may have to field—and it helps you develop a deeper understanding of the topic and a more nuanced point of view.

Emotional resistance: Do the people you're addressing hold fast to a bias, dogma, or moral code—and does your idea violate that in some way? Hitting raw nerves will set off an audience, so proceed carefully. For example, if you're at a medical conference launching a new HPV vaccination for kids, also emphasize the importance of abstinence in youth.

Practical resistance: Is it physically or geographically difficult for the audience to do what you're asking? Will it take more financial means than people have? Be sensitive if you're asking employees to hang in there as you temporarily freeze salaries to weather a recession, for instance, or giving your team a deadline that will take nights and weekends to meet. Acknowledge the sacrifices people are making—and show that you're shouldering some of the burden yourself. Say that your salary will be frozen, too. Or explain that you'll be in 24/7 mode right along with your team until the big project is wrapped up—and that everyone will get comp time afterward.

Prepare for these types of resistance, and you'll stand a much better chance of winning over an entrenched audience. You can raise and address concerns before they become mental roadblocks—for example, by sharing at the beginning of your talk that you too were skeptical until you'd looked more closely at the data, or by meeting with particularly tough critics in advance to "pre-sell" your ideas. By showing that you've considered opposing points of view, you demonstrate an open mind—and invite your audience to respond in kind.

If you're struggling to come up with opposing viewpoints, share your big idea with others and ask them to pressure-test it. You may be so deeply connected to your perspective that you're having a hard time anticipating the most simple and obvious forms of resistance. Use your boss as a sounding board as you prepare to speak to the executive committee, for example. Or ask a key stakeholder for a reality check before you present to other managers in her group.

Amplify Your Message Through Contrast

People are naturally drawn to contrast because life is filled with it: Day and night. Male and female. Love and hate.

A skilled communicator captures an audience's interest by creating tension between contrasting elements—and then provides relief by resolving that tension. It's how you build a bridge between others' views and yours.

Try brainstorming ideas around polar opposites such as the ones in table 2-1.

TABLE 2-1

Dynamic opposites

Past/present	Future
Need	Fulfillment
Speed	Endurance
Ambition	Humility
Stagnation	Growth
Roadblocks	Clear passage
Sacrifice	Reward
Budget	Quality

Suppose you manage an airline's maintenance division, and you're asking for money to invest in analytics. Table 2-2 shows pairs of opposites you might explore as you figure out how to make your case.

TABLE 2-2

Using the tension of extremes

Customer complaints	Customer satisfaction
We're getting low ratings on customer surveys because of flight delays and missed connections caused by simple maintenance issues.	What if we could better schedule our planes' maintenance by digging into our repair data?
We currently follow the manufacturer's recommended maintenance schedule—and it's not sufficient. Planes get held up at the gate while mechanics do routine repairs.	By tracking and studying how often we actually perform certain kinds of repairs, we can create a schedule that's more realistic. We'll be able to prevent problems instead of fixing them when they pop up.

By embracing the tension between the extremes, you can propel your message—and the movement will feel natural.

The familiar will comfort people; the new will stimulate them and keep them interested. Generate plenty of content on both sides of the contrast or you'll lose momentum—and your audience.

Build an Effective Call to Action

Presentations move people to act—but only if you explicitly state what actions you want them to take, and when. Are you asking them to be doers, suppliers, influencers, or innovators (see table 2-3)?

To get to this list of four things an audience can do for you, I read hundreds of speeches and classified their calls to action. Whether your audience is corporate, political, scientific, or academic, the people you're addressing should fall into one of these categories.

Make it clear what you need to accomplish together and break that down into discrete tasks and deadlines that feel manageable to the audience. Let's consider an example where the call to action is to "innovate"—since that can be tough to pull off. Suppose you have an aging product that needs reinvention. Not all great ideas have to come from engineering. So after you say that the organization is open to ideas from all departments, you might break down the tasks like this:

- Identify enthusiastic brainstormers from all departments.
- Have engineers facilitate a cross-departmental brainstorming session that week.
- Assign a team member to take notes.
- Filter ideas at the engineering summit the following week.

You might ask everyone to take just one action, or you might provide a few actions people can choose from. Either way, be explicit in your request—and about how it will benefit the audience.

TABLE 2-3

What your audience can do for you

	Doers	Suppliers	Influencers	Innovators
What they do for you	Instigate activities	Get resources	Change perceptions	Generate ideas
How they do it	Doers are the worker bees. Once they know what needs to get done, they'll take on the tasks. They also recruit and motivate others to complete important activities.	Suppliers are the people with resources—financial, human, or material. They have the means to get you what you need to move forward.	Influencers can sway individuals or groups, large or small, mobilizing them to adopt and evangelize your idea.	Innovators think outside the box for new ways to add value to and spread your idea. They create strategies, perspectives, and products.

Choose Your Best Ideas

Up to this point, we've been focusing on how to generate presentation ideas and content. That's actually the easy part. It's much harder to trim everything down so only the most effective messages remain. But the quality of your presentation depends as much on what you choose to remove as on what you choose to include.

Many of your ideas may be fascinating and clever, but you can't fit them all in—and no one wants to hear them all, anyway. Connect, analyze, sort, and filter the ideas so you use only the ones that will yield the best outcomes. Designers call this part of the process *convergent thinking*, and they refer to its opposite, idea generation, as *divergent thinking* (see figure 2-2). As Tim Brown, the CEO of IDEO, explains: "In the divergent phase, new options emerge. In the convergent phase, it is just the reverse. Now it's time to eliminate options and make choices."

Your primary filter should be your big idea (see "Define Your Big Idea" at the beginning of the Message section). Everything you keep in your talk must support it.

FIGURE 2-2

Filter your best ideas

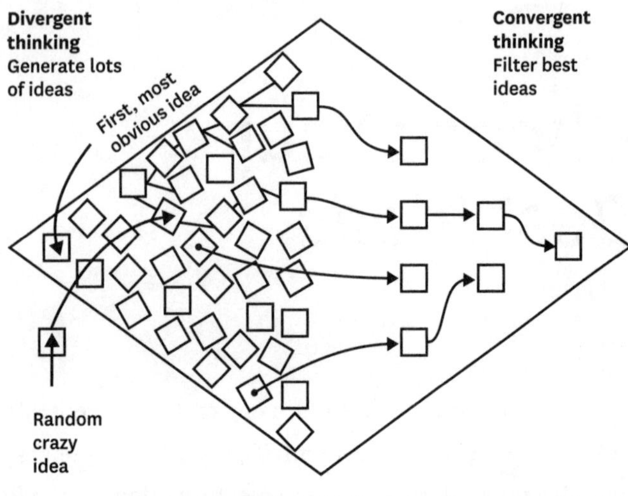

If you don't filter your presentation, the audience will have to—and people will resent you for making them work too hard to identify the most important points. Cut mercilessly on their behalf. Say you're presenting a business case for acquiring a company. You might brainstorm things to cover, like:

- The competencies your company would gain
- Estimated return on investment
- Lessons learned from the last acquisition
- Threat R&D might perceive
- Bringing in culture consultants

- Receivables are at net 45 days
- Need to retool the factory floor

All these ideas fit into the big idea except the fact that receivables are at net 45 days. Though that may be important, it would be a distraction during this meeting. Save it for another meeting.

Even if all you do is sort and filter the ideas you've generated, you're technically ready to present. You can place your sticky notes on the inside of a file folder and use those as your speaking notes, as I did at a launch party for my book *Resonate*. I had only to glance down once in a while.

Or you can begin to put your ideas into the presentation software of your choice.

Organize Your Thoughts

Because presentation programs such as PowerPoint are visual tools, we often jump too quickly into visually expressing our ideas when we use them—before we've spent enough time arranging our thoughts and crafting our words. When moving ideas from sticky notes to software, enter each point you plan to cover as a clearly worded title in outline or slide-sorter mode rather than going straight to slide-creation mode (figure 2-3). That allows you to read the titles in sequence, without the distractions of supporting details or graphics, to make sure your presentation flows from point to point.

Ask yourself, "If people read just the titles, will they get what I'm saying?" That's not just an academic exercise. You really want to know the answer, because your audience members often won't read past your slide titles when you present. They'll scan them the way they do headlines of news articles—and make snap decisions

FIGURE 2-3

Convey a clear message with each title

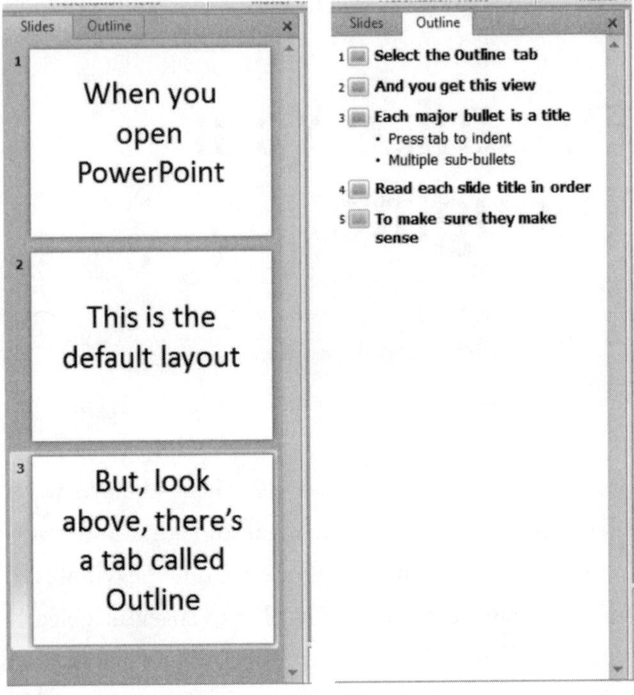

about whether they'd like to learn more. So convey a clear message with each title, arrange them in an order that will make sense to your audience, and infuse them with personality where you can. You'll want to come across as a real person, not an automaton. Include verbs to show action.

Compare the examples shown in table 2-4.

TABLE 2-4

Convey clear meaning with titles

Vague, passive	Clear, active
Market overview	We're neck-and-neck with an aggressive rival.
Productivity gains	Production time shrank from 21 days to 8.

Agonize over your titles as marketing copywriters do in their campaigns to get more click-throughs and sales. You, too, are selling something—your big idea—and the more quickly you grab people's attention, the higher your "conversion rate" will be.

Balance Analytical and Emotional Appeal

Now that you've outlined your message, consider how you'll appeal to people's minds and hearts.

Strike the wrong balance of analytical and emotional content in your presentation, and you risk alienating the audience and diminishing your credibility. But how do you get it right? Take your cues from the topic and the audience.

Certain topics—like layoffs and product launches—are inherently charged and naturally lend themselves to emotional appeal. Others—like science, engineering, and finance—invite more analytic treatment.

Weigh the subject against the group you're addressing. Suppose you're making a case for personnel cuts to a group of managers who'll soon have to decide which direct reports to let go. They may see you as cold and inhumane if you focus primarily on cost savings, with nary a word about people losing jobs. A numbers-based approach will probably go over better with a group of executives charged with improving the bottom line—though even they will expect you to at least acknowledge that layoffs are difficult.

No presentation should be devoid of emotional content, no matter how cerebral the topic or the audience. In a business setting, it may feel more comfortable to just "state the facts," but look through your deck and see if you can add emotional texture to any content that's purely analytical (see figure 2-4).

FIGURE 2-4

Strike a balance

Analytical	Emotional
Features	Benefits illustrated through stories (personal, true, fictional)
Data/evidence	Metaphors and analogies that make data meaningful
Exhibits	Thought-provoking questions
Logical arguments	Slow reveal (builds suspense)
Proofs	
Examples	
Case studies	

There are two basic classes of emotion: pain and pleasure. Determine how you'd like people to feel at various points in your presentation. Where would you like them to feel happy? To cringe? To be inspired?

Ask "why" questions to unearth your big idea's emotional appeal. For example, if you're requesting funding to pay for cloud storage, start by asking, "Why do we need to buy cloud storage?" Your answer may be "to facilitate data sharing with colleagues in remote locations." So then ask, "Why do we need to facilitate data sharing with colleagues in remote locations?" Eventually you'll get to the human beings whose lives will be affected by your idea, and that's where you'll discover your emotional appeal: Maybe you need cloud storage "to help those remote colleagues coordinate disaster relief efforts and save lives."

Once you know what that hook is, use words or phrases that have emotional weight to them—like "save lives" in the cloud example above. Tell personal stories with conviction and describe not just what people did, but how they felt. (See "Add Emotional Texture" in the Story section of this guide.)

Lose the Jargon

Have you ever listened to a presenter who sounded supersmart—without having any idea what she *really* said?

Each field has its own lexicon, filled with words that are familiar to experts but foreign to everyone else. Even different departments within the same organization use niche language and acronyms that mean nothing to other groups. And the more companies and individuals innovate within their areas of expertise, the bigger and gnarlier their vocabularies get.

Unless you're presenting to a roomful of specialists cut from the same cloth, don't assume that everyone will understand your jargon. Modify your language so it resonates with the people whose support and influence you need. If they can't follow your ideas, they won't adopt them.

What's more, delivering abstruse presentations can hurt your career. As communications coach Carmine Gallo puts it, "Speaking over people's heads may cost you a job or prevent you from advancing as far as your capabilities might take you otherwise."

So lose the jargon. If a specialized term is central to your message, translate it. Would your grandmother understand what you're talking about? Rework your message until it's *that clear.*

The presenter in the following example (figure 2-5) spoke to an audience of 800 people who could fund his

FIGURE 2-5

Drop the jargon

Before: Developed from a scientific perspective	After: Reworked for a lay audience
I am currently the lead researcher developing a microbially induced brine-mining technology, where bacteria are employed to accumulate selected minerals from desalination brine, producing a minable sediment, which may indirectly reduce the cost of desalinated water and the environmental impact of the desalination process. Initial experiments have shown how certain bacterial cultures are able to mine selected metals from desalination brine. I am now hoping to prove the economic viability of the process through qualitative and quantitative studies of the metals produced. Conventional mechanical and chemical mining technologies are restrictive due to technological and economic constraints. Biological processes, however, present an efficient and environmentally benign alternative, which must be seen in the context of a future where urban ecological systems are in harmony with the ecological cycles of our planet.	Desalination is a process that removes salt from water so it can be used for drinking and irrigation. Removing salt from water—in particular sea water—via reverse osmosis requires energy to produce clean water. This process also creates a toxic saltwater solution, or brine, that is generally dumped back out at sea and is harmful for the ecology of the receiving water body. This is where my collaboration with bacteria comes in. Introducing bacteria into the brine draws out metals such as calcium, potassium, and magnesium from desalination brine. The value of magnesium alone in the volume of brine potentially needed for Singapore represents 4.5 billon U.S. dollars—indirectly lowering the cost of the desalinated water produced, while reducing the environmental impact of the process. Imagine a mining industry in a way it hasn't existed before. Imagine a mining industry that doesn't mean defiling the earth. Imagine bacteria helping us achieve this industry, as they accumulate and sediment minerals out of desalination brine. In other words, imagine a mining industry in harmony with nature.

idea but didn't have deep knowledge of the science behind it. The first column shows what he said during rehearsal; the second shows what he said at the presentation, after he got feedback and reworked his talk for an intelligent lay audience.

Craft Sound Bites

Your words are now clear—but are they memorable? Will people share them with others?

Great quotes get picked up and repeated—whether at the water cooler, in blog posts, or on social networking sites. Brilliant ones end up on the front pages of newspapers. So embed well-crafted sound bites into every talk.

Steve Jobs made this an art form. He relied on rhetorical devices to drive his messages home and get pickup from audiences and press alike. Here are a few that he used to great effect:

Rhythmic repetition: Repeated phrase at beginning, middle, or end of a sentence.

In 2010, Jobs had to deliver an emergency press conference about the performance of the antenna in the iPhone 4. If users held the phone a certain way, it dropped calls. As social media scientist Dan Zarrella, at HubSpot, points out, Jobs repeated the phrase "We want to make all our users happy" several times during his talk. Midway through, Jobs flashed a slide showing that the antenna issue affected only a fraction of users. Soon, a message appeared at the bottom: "We care about *every* user." A few slides later: "We love our users." Then "We love our users" appeared again on the next slide. And the next. And the next. "We love our users, we love them," Jobs concluded. "We do this [provide a free phone case that will solve the problem] because we love our users." That "love" was the message the press took away from his piece of "crisis communication."

Concrete comparison: Simile or metaphor.

In his iPhone keynote speech at MacWorld 2007, Jobs likened Apple's switch to Intel processors to a "huge *heart transplant.*"

Slogan: A concise statement that's easy to remember.

At the iPhone launch, Jobs said "reinvent the phone" several times—and the slogan was all over the press release Apple sent out before his keynote. "Reinvent the phone" ended up in *PCWorld*'s headlines the next day.

As Jobs did, take time to create repeatable sound bites. But don't deliver them with a lot of fanfare. Make them appear spontaneous, so people will *want* to repeat them.

Section 3
Story

[Stories] are the currency of human contact.

—**Robert McKee,**
author of *Story: Substance, Structure, Style, and the Principles of Screenwriting*

Apply Storytelling Principles

Stories have the power to win customers, align colleagues, and motivate employees. They're the most compelling platform we have for managing imaginations. Those who master this art form can gain great influence and an enduring legacy.

If you use stories in your presentation, the audience can recall what they've learned from you and even spread the word. Just as the plot of a compelling play, movie, or novel makes a writer's themes more vivid and memorable, well-crafted stories can give your message real staying power, for two key reasons:

- **Stories feature transformation:** When people hear a story, they root for the protagonist as she overcomes obstacles and emerges changed in some important way (perhaps a new outlook helps her complete a difficult physical journey). It's doubly powerful to incorporate stories that demonstrate how others have adopted the same beliefs and behaviors you're proposing—that is, show others going through a similar transformation that your audience will go through. This will help you get people to cross over from their everyday world into the world of your ideas—and come back to their world transformed, with new insights and tools from your presentation.

- **Stories have a clear structure:** All effective stories adhere to the same basic three-part structure that Aristotle pointed out ages ago: They have a beginning, a middle, and an end. It makes them easy to digest and retell—and it's how audiences have been conditioned for centuries to receive information. Make sure your presentation—and any story you tell within it—has all three parts, with clear transitions between them.

In this section of the guide, you'll learn how to use storytelling principles to structure your presentation and incorporate anecdotes that add emotional appeal.

Create a Solid Structure

All good presentations—like all good stories—convey and resolve some kind of conflict or imbalance. The sense of discord is what makes audiences care enough to get on board.

After gleaning story insights from films and books, studying hundreds of speeches, and spending 22 years creating customized presentations for companies and thought leaders, I've found that the most persuasive communicators create conflict by juxtaposing *what is* with *what could be.* That is, they alternately build tension and provide release by toggling back and forth between the status quo and a better way—finally arriving at the "new bliss" people will discover by adopting the proposed beliefs and behaviors. That conflict resolution plays out within the basic beginning-middle-end storytelling structure we all know and love (figure 3-1).

The tips in this section will help you weave conflict and resolution throughout the beginning, middle, and end of your presentation.

FIGURE 3-1

Persuasive story pattern

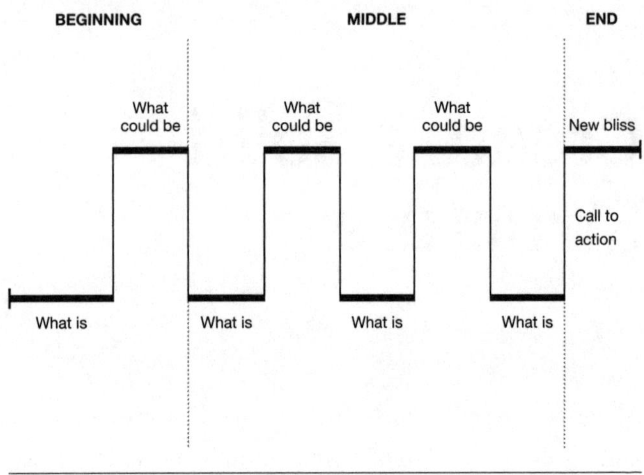

Craft the Beginning

Begin by describing life as the audience knows it. People should be nodding their heads in recognition because you're articulating what they already understand. This creates a bond between you and them and opens them up to hear your ideas for change.

After you set that baseline of *what is*, introduce your ideas of *what could be*. The gap between the two will throw the audience a bit off balance, and that's a good thing—because it creates tension that needs to be resolved (figure 3-2).

FIGURE 3-2

Create dramatic tension

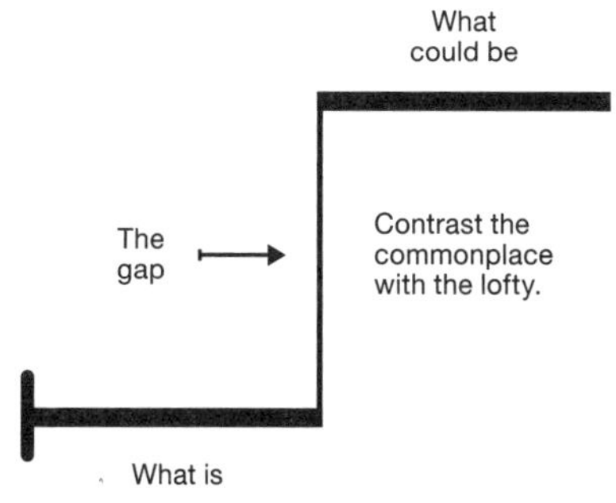

If you proposed what could be without first establishing what is, you'd fail to connect with the audience before swooping in with your ideas, and your message would lose momentum.

The gap shouldn't feel contrived—you wouldn't say "Okay, I've described what is. Now let's move to what could be." Present it naturally so people will feel moved, not manipulated. For instance:

> *What is:* We fell short of our Q3 financial goals partly because we're understaffed and everyone's spread too thin.
>
> *What could be:* But what if we could solve the worst of our problems by bringing in a couple of powerhouse clients? Well, we can.

Here's another example:

> *What is:* Analysts have been placing our products at the top of three out of five categories. One competitor just shook up the industry with the launch of its T3xR—heralded as the most innovative product in our space. Analysts predict that firms like ours will have no future unless we license this technology from our rival.
>
> *What could be:* But we will not concede! In fact, we will retain our lead. I'm pleased to tell you that five years ago we had the same product idea, but after rapid prototyping we discovered a way to leapfrog that generation of technology. So today, we're launch-

> ing a product so revolutionary that we'll gain a ten-year lead in our industry.

Once you establish the gap between what is and what could be, use the remainder of the presentation to bridge it.

Develop the Middle

The middle is, in many ways, the most compelling part of your presentation, because that's where most of the "action" takes place.

People in your audience now realize their world is off-kilter—you've brought that to their attention and at least hinted at a solution at the beginning of your presentation. Now continue to emphasize the contrast between what is and what could be, moving back and forth between them, and the audience will start to find the former unappealing and the latter alluring.

Let's go back to that Q3 financial update example from "Craft the Beginning." Revenues are down, but you want to motivate employees to make up for it. Table 3-1 shows one way you could approach the middle of your presentation.

Earlier, you brainstormed around pairs of contrasting themes (see "Amplify Your Message Through Contrast" in the Message section). Try using one of those pairs—for instance, sacrifice versus reward—to drum up material to flesh out this structure.

TABLE 3-1

Creating "action" in the middle of your story

What is	What could be
We missed our Q3 forecast by 15%.	Q4 numbers must be strong for us to pay out bonuses.
We have six new clients on our roster.	Two of them have the potential to bring in more revenue than our best clients do now.
The new clients will require extensive retooling in manufacturing.	We'll be bringing in experts from Germany to help.

Make the Ending Powerful

Your ending should leave people with a heightened sense of what could be—and willingness to believe or do something new. Here's where you describe how blissful their world will be when they adopt your ideas.

Let's return to our Q3 example from "Craft the Beginning" and "Develop the Middle" in this section. You might wrap up your presentation along the lines of figure 3-3.

FIGURE 3-3

Making the ending powerful

Call to action	New bliss
It will take extra work from all departments to make Q4 numbers, but we can deliver products to our important new clients on time and with no errors.	I know everyone's running on fumes—but hang in there. This is our chance to pull together like a championship team, and things will get easier if we make this work. The reward if we meet our Q4 targets? Bonuses, plus days off at the end of the year.

Many presentations simply end with a list of action items, but that isn't exactly inspiring. You want the last thing you say to move your audience to tackle those items. You want people to feel ready to right the wrong, to conquer the problem.

By skillfully defining future rewards, you compel people to get on board with your ideas. Show them that taking action will be worth their effort. Highlight:

- **Benefits to them:** What needs of theirs will your ideas meet? What freedoms will the audience gain? How will your ideas give the audience greater influence or status?

- **Benefits to their "sphere":** How will your ideas help the audience's peers, direct reports, customers, students, or friends?

- **Benefits to the world:** How will your ideas help the masses? How will they improve public health, for instance, or help the environment?

In the example above, we've called out a key benefit to the organization (making up for Q3 revenue shortfall), plus three benefits to employees (bonuses, time off, and—probably most important—the promise of a saner workload).

Add Emotional Texture

Now step back and review all your content so far. Do you have the right mix of analysis and emotion? (See "Balance Analytical and Emotional Appeal" in the Message section.) If you need more emotional impact, you can add it with storytelling.

A message matters to people when it hits them in the gut. Visceral response, not pure analysis, is what will push your audience away from the status quo and toward your perspective. Stories elicit that kind of response. When we hear stories, our eyes dilate, our hearts race, we feel chills. We laugh, clap, lean forward or back. These reactions are mostly involuntary, because they're grounded in emotion.

While you're describing what is, tell a story that makes people shudder, or guffaw at the ridiculousness of their situation, or feel disappointment. While you're describing what could be, tell a story that strikes a little awe or fear into their hearts—something that inspires them to change.

Table 3-2 shows a template (with an example plugged in) that can help you transform supporting information into a story with emotional impact.

You may be thinking that people don't go to work to feel; they go to get stuff done. But by making them feel, you move them to action—and help them get stuff done. It's not about issuing a gushing, weepy plea. It's about

TABLE 3-2

Making an emotional impact with data

Point you want to make	Every cross-divisional function could benefit from a steering committee.	
STORY ABOUT ORGANIZATIONAL CHANGE		
Beginning	When, who, where	A few years ago, the sales team tackled a cross-divisional problem with the help of a steering committee.
Middle	Context	At the time, all sales groups were independent.
	Conflict	This means we were confusing customers with many different rules, processes, and formats.
	Proposed resolution	So we decided to create a sales steering committee.
	Complication	You can imagine how hard it was to reach agreement on anything.
End	Actual resolution	But we agreed to meet every two weeks to find common ground. Over the next year, we standardized all our processes and learned a lot from each other. The customers became much happier with our service.

Source: Glenn Hughes, SMART as Hell.

adding emotional texture to the logical case you've built with data, case studies, and other supporting evidence.

Personal stories told with conviction are the most effective ones in your arsenal. You can repeat stories you've heard, but audiences feel more affection for presenters who reveal their own challenges and vulnerability.

Use relevant stories that are appropriately dramatic, or you may come across as manipulative or out of touch with reality. When giving an update at a small staff meeting on a project you're leading, you wouldn't tell a melodramatic story about the "just-in-time delivery" of multiple vendors you managed at your daughter's wedding. It would waste everyone's time.

But one U.S. government official *did* effectively tell a story about his daughter's wedding—to get new remote-communication technology adopted in his organization. Many of his relatives couldn't travel to the wedding, so he used a commercial version of the technology to push the wedding pictures quickly to the remote family members, helping all feel more included in the event. He argued that adopting the enterprise version of this technology would similarly include distant employees in the development of important agency initiatives. The senior executives not only understood this with their minds but felt it in their hearts. They could relate this story about a father doing his best to serve his family to their agency doing its best to serve the citizenry.

Take out a notepad and start cataloging personal stories and the emotions they summon. This exercise takes time, but it will yield material you can draw on again and again. Do your first pass when you have an uninterrupted hour or so to reflect. You can use the checklist that follows to trigger your memory. As you recall past events, jot down how you felt when you experienced them.

Inventory of Personal Stories

- ☐ ***Important times in your life:*** Childhood, adolescence, young adulthood, later years
- ☐ ***Relatives:*** Parents, grandparents, siblings, children, in-laws
- ☐ ***Authority figures:*** Teachers, bosses, coaches, mentors, leaders, political figures, other influencers
- ☐ ***Peers:*** Colleagues, social networks, club members, friends, neighbors, teammates
- ☐ ***Subordinates:*** Employees, mentees, trainees, interns, volunteers, students
- ☐ ***Enemies:*** Competitors, bullies, people with challenging personalities, people you've been hurt by, people you've hurt
- ☐ ***Important places:*** Offices, homes, schools, places of worship, local hangouts, camps, vacation spots, foreign lands
- ☐ ***Things you cherish:*** Gifts, photos, certificates/awards, keepsakes
- ☐ ***Things that have injured you:*** Sharp objects, animal bites, spoiled food, allergens

Spending time with each item on this list, you'll unearth many stories you've forgotten. Even after you've selected stories for whatever presentation you're currently working on, save your notes and continue adding to them here and there, as you find time. They'll come in handy when you're creating future presentations.

Use Metaphors as Your Glue

Metaphors are a powerful literary device. In Dr. Martin Luther King Jr.'s "I Have a Dream" speech, about 20% of what he said was metaphorical. For example, he likened his lack of freedom to a bad check that "America has given the Negro people . . . a check which has come back marked 'insufficient funds.'" King introduced this metaphor three minutes into his 16-minute talk, and it was the first time the audience roared and clapped.

Presenters tend to overrely on tired visual metaphors instead of using powerful words to stir hearts. King's speech would not have been nearly as beautiful if he'd used slides with pictures of bad checks and piles of gold symbolizing "freedom and the security of justice."

For each point you make in your presentation, try to come up with a metaphor to connect people's minds to the concept. You might even weave it like a thread throughout the presentation.

When developing metaphors, reject overused themes like racecars and sporting events—and avoid stock photos along those lines. If you want to tell a story of triumph, dig into one of your own stories for the right metaphor: Describe, for instance, how it felt to struggle to the top of Yosemite's Half Dome, run your first marathon, or win the citywide Boy Scout trophy. Identify metaphors that will be meaningful to the audience.

Create Something They'll Always Remember

Place *Something They'll Always Remember*—a climactic S.T.A.R. moment—in your presentation to drive your big idea home. That moment is what the audience will chat (or tweet) about after your talk. It can also help your message go viral through social media and news coverage. Use it to make people uncomfortable with what is or to draw them toward what could be. Here are four ways to create a S.T.A.R. moment that captivates your audience and generates buzz.

Shocking statistics

If statistics are shocking, don't glide over them—amplify them. For example, in his 2010 Consumer Electronics Show presentation, Intel CEO Paul Otellini used startling numbers to convey the speed and impact of the company's newest technology. "Today we have the industry's first-shipping 32-nanometer process technology. A

32-nanometer microprocessor is 5,000 times faster; its transistors are 100,000 times cheaper than the 4004 processor that we began with. With all respect to our friends in the auto industry, if their products had produced the same kind of innovation, cars today would go 470,000 miles per hour. They'd get 100,000 miles per gallon, and they'd cost three cents."

Evocative visuals

Audiences connect with emotionally potent visuals. When asking donors to help raise $1.7 million, Conservation International contrasted dreamy, glistening, surreal under-ocean images (captioned with phrases like "90% of our oxygen" describing how dependent we are on the ocean) with photos of grimy rubbish that washes up on the beach (where "14 billion pounds of trash" roll in on the waves). That approach tapped the power of evocative visuals and shocking stats—and people responded by getting out their wallets.

Memorable dramatization

Bring your message to life by dramatizing it. As Bill Gates spoke about the importance of malaria eradication at a TED conference in 2009, he released a jar of mosquitoes into the auditorium and said, "There is no reason only poor people should be infected." It got the audience's attention—and effectively made the point that we don't spend nearly enough money on fighting the disease. The mosquitoes were malaria-free, but he let people squirm a minute or two before he let them know that.

Consider another example. When Mirran Raphaely, CEO of Dr. Hauschka Skin Care, presented to the cosmetics industry, she wanted to draw a sharp contrast between industrial agriculture and biodynamic farming practices. She showed two photos side by side—a container of chemicals and an herb called horsetail—and compared the toxicity of the two substances. In industrial agriculture, farmers rely on glyphosate, a synthetic chemical linked to cancer in animals and humans. In biodynamic agriculture, farmers treat crops with an extract made from horsetail. Holding up two glasses—one filled with the chemical weed killer, the other with the horsetail extract—she asked the audience, "Which one of these would you want on the crops you consume?" After the audience finished laughing, she took a sip of the biodynamic solution.

Emotive anecdote

Sometimes S.T.A.R. moments are gripping personal stories (see "Add Emotional Texture" earlier in this section).

Here's one such story, told by Symantec.cloud group president Rowan Trollope in May 2012, to encourage his organization to innovate:

> *I went mountain climbing at Mount Laurel, in the eastern Sierras, with two of my friends. I'm not very experienced, but both of them were even less experienced. We'd been climbing for about 19 hours. We were up at 11,000 feet, and it was getting dark. Fast.*
>
> *We needed to get down the side of this mountain . . . and we needed to do it fast. Descending first, I got to a ledge and started to get our line ready.*
>
> *Climbers carry two emergency pitons with them for just this purpose. I'd never used them before, but I knew*

how they worked. I took out my hammer and started hammering one into the rock. The books tell you that you'll hear the tone of the hammer strike change when it's "in." I heard a loud ping with each strike of the hammer and decided it was in "good enough."

The books also tell you, though, to always use two, so I used two. As I hammered in the second one, I heard a sharp, high-pitched ping at the end, so I tied the knots and got our line ready. By this time, my buddies had reached the ledge, and I started to hook us in.

Something was bugging me. I looked at the knot between the two pitons and it looked like this [prop: climbing rope with two pitons]. The problem with a knot like that is that if one piton fails, you'll fall. You need to tie it instead like this [prop: retie knot].

My buddies were all clipped in and wanted to get going. It was getting darker. The way I tied the knot seemed good enough, but something in the back of my head told me to stop. So I did.

We all unclipped, and I retied the knot, and then we clipped in again and started the climb down.

The moment I put weight on my line, the first piton popped out and hit me smack in the middle of the helmet. Had I not unclipped and retied the knot, I would have died on that ledge. My life rushed through my mind. And I suddenly and irrevocably got *the danger of "good enough."*

When I pounded in that first piton, I decided it was good enough.

When I tied the knot that first time, I decided that it wasn't, so I did it again.

I still have that piton that popped out. I brought it with me today because I thought you might like to see it [prop: piton]. The other one? The one that saved my life? It's still in a crack on the Laurel Cliffs. Still doing its job.

I came back to work, and everything had new meaning for me. Retying my knots became a sort of metaphor. I realized that in every job I did, every project I touched, I was making piton decisions every time. I was deciding, with every one of those moves, whether good enough was good enough for me.

I picked that story for today because I think we're facing a similar climb as a company. And we're making piton decisions every day. For my buddies and me, there was nothing but sky beneath us. When you and I look down, we see the PC business changing dramatically. We can see physical things being driven into the cloud, and we can agree that the Internet is not yet a secure place.

Unfortunately, it will take more than one piton to address these dangers. But I think it starts by reawakening in our company some of the qualities that made us great in the first place. And to do that, I think we need to change how we approach our work.

Section 4
Media

People who know what they're talking about don't need PowerPoint.

—Steve Jobs

Choose the Right Vehicle for Your Message

Now that you've carefully considered your audience's needs and tailored your message and content accordingly, it's time to determine how the people you're addressing prefer to process information so you can select the best vehicle for reaching them. Just because you have something to communicate and a time slot to fill doesn't mean a formal presentation with slides is the right choice. Some audiences—a group of analysts, for example—may find a thoughtfully written memo more persuasive. Others, such as young professionals, might prefer a video.

It's your job to determine the best way to connect with your audience. Presentations aren't limited to a single time or place anymore. They can be broadcasted, streamed, downloaded, and distributed. Slides aren't a must-have, either. You can use props, handouts, sketches, tablets, videos, flipcharts—pretty much anything that will help people receive your message.

Before opening your presentation software, think about your audience and venue. Will you be speaking to a few team members in an intimate setting? A big crowd in an auditorium? A small group who will be connecting remotely? The size of your audience and the level of interaction that your setting allows should determine which media you choose.

See figure 4-1 for a sampling of ideas on how to deliver your message to one person or many, in a staged or more spontaneous setting.

There's also an element of common sense. Delivering a stand-up formal presentation in a small conference room just doesn't make sense if you're speaking to two of your direct reports—but it does if you're speaking to a couple of venture capitalists who may invest in your business.

Although technology has opened up new ways of communicating, a low-tech approach is sometimes your best bet. If you show up with a slick slide deck, everything seems final. But sketching out ideas while people watch and listen signals that your thinking is in the formative stages and that the audience can still weigh in.

Maybe the "presentation" you're developing should really be a carefully mapped-out conversation with a planned whiteboard drawing. When my firm was buying a new digital storage system, we met with two potential vendors: One brought a deck of slides and didn't deviate from its spiel. The other, which won our business, whiteboarded out a full storage and network plan. That rep came across as having listened to our needs and understood what we wanted. Her presentation felt collaborative, not canned.

FIGURE 4-1

Choosing your delivery style

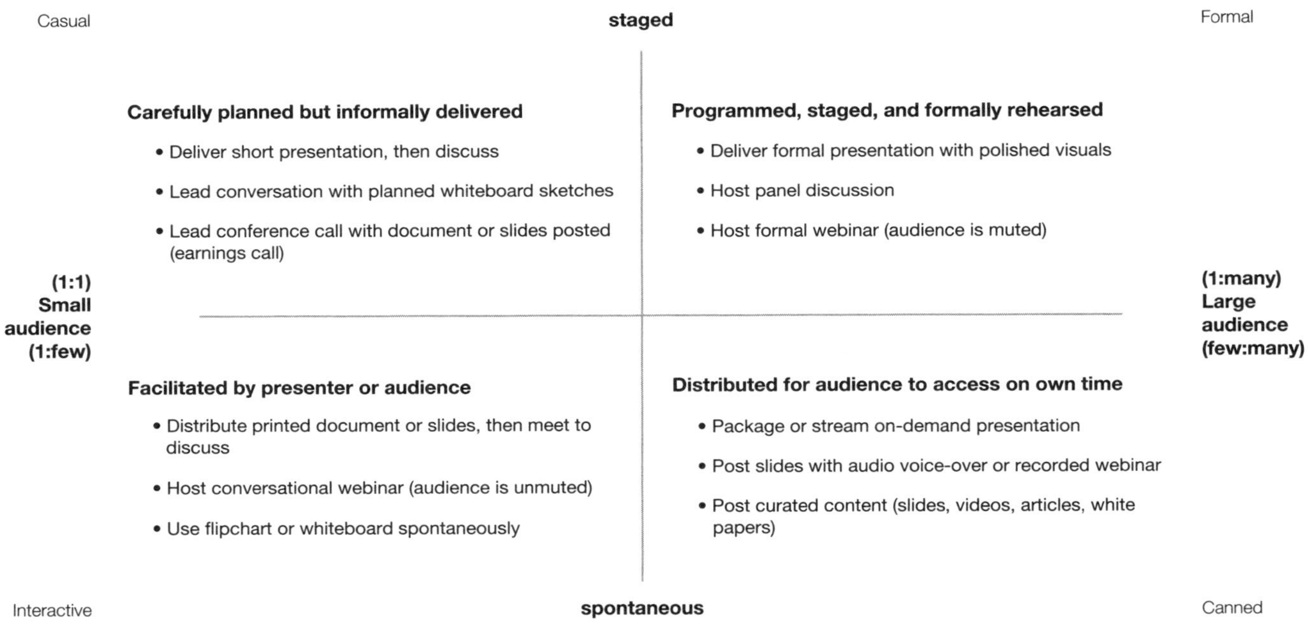

Casual | **staged** | Formal

(1:1) Small audience (1:few)

(1:many) Large audience (few:many)

Carefully planned but informally delivered

- Deliver short presentation, then discuss
- Lead conversation with planned whiteboard sketches
- Lead conference call with document or slides posted (earnings call)

Programmed, staged, and formally rehearsed

- Deliver formal presentation with polished visuals
- Host panel discussion
- Host formal webinar (audience is muted)

Facilitated by presenter or audience

- Distribute printed document or slides, then meet to discuss
- Host conversational webinar (audience is unmuted)
- Use flipchart or whiteboard spontaneously

Distributed for audience to access on own time

- Package or stream on-demand presentation
- Post slides with audio voice-over or recorded webinar
- Post curated content (slides, videos, articles, white papers)

Interactive | **spontaneous** | Canned

Make the Most of Slide Software

Presentation software is widely reviled. The press has called PowerPoint evil, and corporations have cried for its banishment. The software isn't at fault. It's an empty shell, a container for our ideas. It's not a bad communication tool unless it's in the hands of a bad communicator.

So how do you use it without abusing it—and your audience? Know exactly what you're trying to accomplish and rely on the software to achieve that—and nothing more.

You can use presentation software to create documents, compose teleprompter notes, and visualize ideas. But keep those tasks *separate* to avoid the most common PowerPoint pitfalls. The trick is to show audience members only what they want to see, when they want to see it.

Create documents

Presentation software is great for laying out dense material in easy-to-read documents. In fact, that functionality is built right in—the default setting is a document template, not a slide template. You can swiftly compose and format your text and move sections around—and best of all, when it's time to derive a presentation from that document, you don't have to copy and paste from Word.

That said, don't *project* your entire document when you speak. No one wants to attend a plodding read-along. It's boring, and people can read more efficiently on their own, anyway. Circulate your document before or after the presentation so you won't need to project text-heavy slides—which Garr Reynolds, author of *Presentation Zen*, aptly calls *slideuments*. If your content can be distributed and clearly understood without a presenter, you've created a document, not a presentation—and that's fine as long as you treat it as such. That might be all you need if you're giving a status update, for instance.

If you step back and realize you've created a slideument, it may be a sign that you need to distribute a document. Make some adjustments so it looks and feels more like a document before you circulate it. Try dividing the content into clear sections, creating a table of contents that links to each one, adding page numbers, converting fragments and phrases into complete sentences, and distributing the file as a PDF rather than a slide deck. Nolan Haims, the presentation director at the global PR firm Edelman, sets up slideuments in portrait layout instead of landscape so it's very clear to staff members that they're documents in the making, not visual aids to be projected.

Compose teleprompter notes

What if you have to deliver several presentations per month, each customized for a different audience? (Think of sales pitches tailored to corporate clients, for example.) In situations like that, it's impossible to memorize what you'll say every time—and you shouldn't have to.

For decades, great orators have relied on note cards, notepaper, even full scripts. You can use bulleted slides as teleprompter material—but again, *don't project them.* You'll run into the same read-along problems (boredom and inefficiency) you encounter when you project slideuments. Sheryl Sandberg, the COO of Facebook, didn't show any slides at her eloquent TEDWomen presentation "Why We Have Too Few Women Leaders." But when the camera panned to her view of the audience, you could see her bulleted slides on the comfort monitor. Those slides were her teleprompter notes, and she was the only person in the room viewing them.

If you're using PowerPoint to compose teleprompter notes, write them in "Notes" view, and then go to "Set Up Show." After you attach your projector, select "Presenter View." Everything in your notes will appear on your laptop screen or comfort monitor, and only your slides will project behind you. Bring printouts of your teleprompter notes in case anything technical goes wrong.

Visualize ideas

The only things you should actually project are images, graphics, and phrases that move your ideas along—and cement them in the audience's memory long after your presentation is over. Strip everything off your slides that's there to remind you what to say; keep only elements that will help the audience understand and retain what you're saying. Developing clear visuals that add emotion, emphasis, or nuance to your delivery is no easy task—but when you do this well, your ideas will resonate with your audience. (See the Slides section in this guide for detailed tips on creating powerful visual aids.)

Determine the Right Length for Your Presentation

If you ask around, "What do great presentations have in common?" you'll get one consistent answer: "They're short." It's no secret that people value their time.

But many presenters don't realize that it costs *them* time to save the audience time. It's easier to blather on for an hour than to craft a tight, succinct presentation. Some of the magic of TED is in the 18-minute limit. A great talk goes by quickly. A bad one—well, people can endure it if it's only 18 minutes.

People in your audience won't scold you for ending early, but they will for ending late. Out of consideration for them and the day's agenda, treat the time slot assigned to you as sacred. And keep in mind that people have a 30- to 40-minute presentation tolerance (they're conditioned by TV shows with creatively produced commercial breaks). Go longer than that, and they'll begin to squirm.

Here are five ways to tighten your talk and keep your audience engaged:

1. **Plan content for 60% of your time slot:** If you're given a full hour, take no more than 40 minutes. That will leave time for Q&A, a panel, or some other form of discussion. It's hard to keep people's attention for much longer than 40 minutes unless you've built in interesting guest speakers, video clips, interactive exercises, and such. As Thomas Jefferson put it, "Speeches that are measured by the hour will die with the hour."

2. **Trim your slide deck:** If you created an hour-long presentation and want to deliver it in 40 minutes, cut your slides by a third. You can work in slide-sorter mode in PowerPoint, dragging slides to a "slide cemetery" at the very end of the file. Don't delete them, because you might have to resurrect one or more at the last minute, when you're answering questions.

3. **Practice with the clock counting up:** As you're cutting material, rehearse with a clock counting up, not with a timer counting down. If you go over, you need to know how much you're over. Give critical content the most stage time; cut sections that are more important to you than to the audience. Keep trimming and practicing until you're consistently within your desired time frame.

4. **Practice with a timer counting down:** Once you're within the time frame, begin practicing with a timer counting down. Divide your content into quarters and calculate a time stamp for the end of each quarter. For example, if you're giving a 40-minute talk, know the exact slide you should be on at the 10-, 20-, and 30-minute marks so you can gauge throughout the talk if you're on time or running over. That way you can trim more easily on the fly.

5. **Have two natural ending points:** Create a false ending (a summary of the ideas covered, for example) and a real ending—perhaps a rousing, inspirational story that drives the message home. If you're running long, you can drop the second ending and still get your message across. Once at a TED event in India, I was given a 15-minute time slot and had rehearsed it to a T. Two days before the talk, I caught a severe chest cold, so I was heavily medicated when I walked on stage. Before I knew it, the "time's up" light was blinking, and I wasn't done. Fortunately, I'd planned two natural places to end my talk, so I wrapped things up with my first ending, citing a beautiful salutation to the land of India from a famous Indian speech. As far as the people in the audience knew, that was the real ending—and they responded warmly.

Persuade Beyond the Stage

Your presentation doesn't start the moment you enter the room; it starts the moment you've committed to speak—and it continues after the actual talk, as you follow up with the audience. If you take advantage of opportunities to reinforce your message at all three stages, you're much more likely to change people's thinking and behavior.

Before

How you position the talk before you even deliver it will have a big impact on the audience's level of interest. Consider the most effective forms of communication to send out in advance. If you're presenting to colleagues, you might e-mail them a summary of your message and a rough list of points you plan to cover, for example, or send a meeting request with a detailed agenda. If you're going to speak to people from outside your organization—conference attendees, for instance—you may post your biography and talking points online and provide links to prereading material (published articles, abstracts of white papers, and so on).

Preparing strong supporting material may take as long as developing the presentation itself. However you choose to orient your audience members, make it clear how they will benefit from this talk.

During

If you need to distribute handouts during your talk, bring more than enough copies and recruit volunteers to pass them out at the right time. You can also tape secret messages under people's chairs for retrieval at a key moment during your talk, have audience members hold up color-coded cards to give you feedback in real time, or give them all a prop to interact with, such as a product prototype.

And if you're trying to create external buzz—about a launch, for example—post your slides online along with any videos or photos that support your presentation. Downloadable assets like these will make it easier for journalists, bloggers, and fans in social media circles to write about your talk. If appropriate, use webinar or streaming technology to further increase your audience reach.

After

Follow up with a thank-you note, a survey, or supplementary reading or viewing material to keep your message fresh in people's minds. But don't overtly solicit your audience. People should feel they're getting additional insights and value—not doing extra work that benefits you more than it does them. For example, if you send a survey to find out what they think about a new service you're offering, make it worth their time: Explain how their feedback will lead to benefits they'll care about, and offer a relevant, attractive free product in exchange for their participation. When I wrap up a webinar on presentations, I set up a URL where the audience can access free digital content from my books on the topic. Attendees love getting free, useful tools like this. More than a quarter of them download the files.

By adding points of contact before, during, and after your presentation, you'll make a lasting impression and increase the likelihood that your ideas will gain traction.

Share the Stage

Audiences find monologues boring. Thanks to advances in entertainment, they've become accustomed to quick action, rapid scene changes, intense visual stimulation, and soundtracks that make the heart race. They're no longer willing to sit attentively for an hour while a single speaker drones on.

The key to getting and holding their attention is having new things continually happen. You can do that by:

- **Bringing in other presenters:** Invite others to join you on the stage or by video. Consider which experts or analysts in your organization or industry would add meat and credibility to your presentation. And look for ways your team members can play to their strengths. If your colleague Sam is quick on his feet, for example, have him lead the Q&A.

- **Mixing up your media:** Try alternating between slides and other media. Hang posters and exhibits on the wall, place tchotchkes on the table that tie into the theme of your talk, or have a helper unveil

> a prop or new product while you speak. Add video to inject humor, boost credibility through testimonials, or clarify concepts with animated infographics. If you're talking about a product, demo it—hold it, display it, allow people to interact with it. If you're explaining a concept, try drawing on a flipchart or a whiteboard—it varies the pace and audiences often find it endearing because it makes all but the most artistic presenters vulnerable and thus accessible. Or you can hire a graphic recorder to capture your message visually on a large strip of butcher paper while you talk. She can synthesize what's being said in real time, creating a mural that memorializes the talk. Display it somewhere prominent in your department as a reminder of the goals everyone agreed on at the last vision meeting.

You can reengage your audience several times during your talk by alternating presenters and changing up your media. Of course, all those moving parts require planning and rehearsal—but they'll also keep people tuned in.

Section 5
Slides

At our studio we don't write our stories, we draw them.

—**Walt Disney**

Think Like a Designer

To make the point that design thinking goes "hand-in-hand with financial success" in business, *Fast Company* cited an intriguing Design Council study in its October 2007 letter from the editor: "A portfolio of 63 design-driven British companies . . . trounced the FTSE 100 index over 13 years."

A chart like the one in figure 5-1 accompanied the letter.

What does this have to do with presentations? A lot.

Presentations are one of the most popular business communication tools, second only to e-mail. They attract clients and keep employees on track. And the most effective presenters think like designers. Good presenters display data clearly, simply, and compellingly, as in the chart in figure 5-1. They select visuals that convey meaning and brand value. They create and arrange slides that persuade audiences and help them solve problems.

After reading the tips in the Slides section of this guide, you won't be a master designer—but you'll make better choices when confronted by the empty expanse of a virgin slide.

FIGURE 5-1

Design contributes to the bottom line

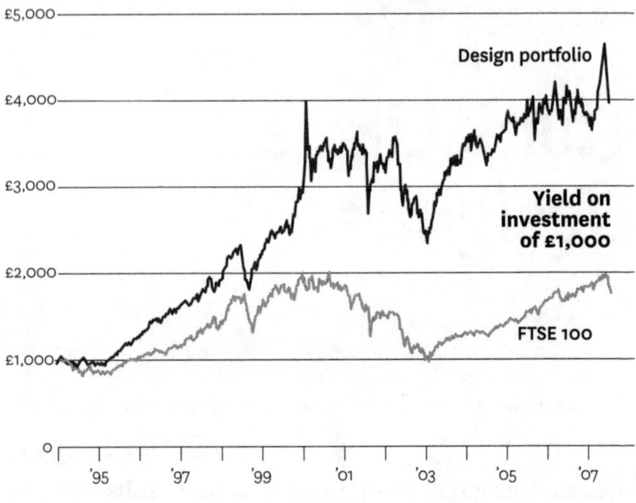

Source: Fast Company, Design Council, and FTSE.

Create Slides People Can "Get" in Three Seconds

Audiences can process only one stream of information at a time. They'll either listen to you speak or read your slides—they won't do both simultaneously (not without missing key parts of your message, anyway). So make sure they can quickly comprehend your visuals and then turn their attention back to what you're saying.

Let's say you're using the default template in PowerPoint, and you completely fill in the field that says "Click to Add Text" each time you create a slide. That field holds about 80 words, and the average reading speed is 250 words per minute. So, if you develop 40 text-heavy slides for a 40-minute presentation, people will miss about 13 minutes (one-third!) of your talk just because they're too busy reading your slides to listen.

Another important reason to keep your slides simple: Research shows that people learn more effectively from multimedia messages when they're stripped of extraneous words, graphics, animation, and sounds. The extras actually *take away* meaning because they become a distraction. They overtax the audience's cognitive resources.

Each slide should pass what I call the *glance test*: People should be able to comprehend it in three seconds. Think of your slides as billboards. When people drive, they only briefly take their eyes off their main focus—the road—to process billboard information. Similarly, your audience should focus intently on what you're saying, looking only briefly at your slides when you display them.

To create slides that pass the glance test:

- **Start with a clean surface:** Instead of using the default "Click to Add Title" and "Click to Add Text" slide master, turn off all the master prompts and start with a blank slide. And when you add elements, make sure you have a good reason. Does the audience need to see your logo on each slide to remember who you work for? Does that blue swoosh add meaning? If not, leave it off.

- **Limit your text:** Keep the text short and easy to skim. Scale the type as large as possible so the people in the back of the room can see it.

- **Coordinate visual elements:** Select one typeface—two at most—for the entire slide deck. Use a consistent color palette throughout (limit yourself to three complementary colors, plus a couple of neutral shades, like gray or pale blue). Photos should be taken by the same photographer or look as if they are. Illustrations should be done in the same style.

- **Arrange elements with care:** When you project your slides, they'll be many times larger than they are on your laptop screen—so they need to be tidy. (Blown up, unkempt slides look downright chaotic.) Align your graphics and text blocks. Size objects appropriately. If one element is larger than another, the audience will interpret that to mean the larger object is more important.

Take a look at the "before" slide (figure 5-2). It fails the glance test because it's packed with text.

But when you streamline the text and incorporate simple visual elements—as in figure 5-3—you help the audience process the information much more quickly.

Presentation software gives us many shiny, seductive elements to work with. But there's beauty and clarity in

FIGURE 5-2

Before

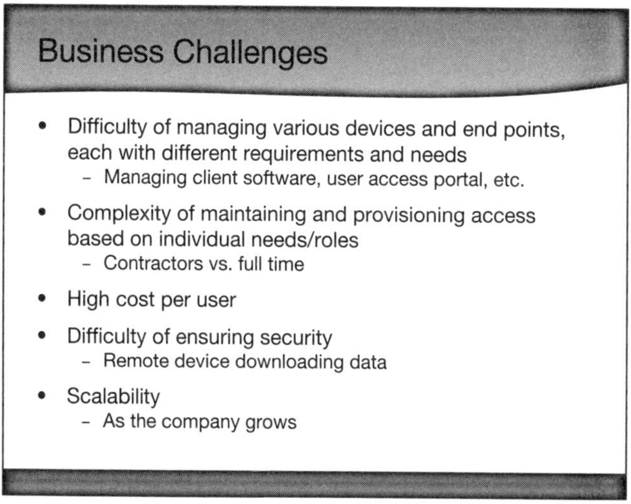

Business Challenges

- Difficulty of managing various devices and end points, each with different requirements and needs
  - Managing client software, user access portal, etc.
- Complexity of maintaining and provisioning access based on individual needs/roles
  - Contractors vs. full time
- High cost per user
- Difficulty of ensuring security
  - Remote device downloading data
- Scalability
  - As the company grows

FIGURE 5-3

After

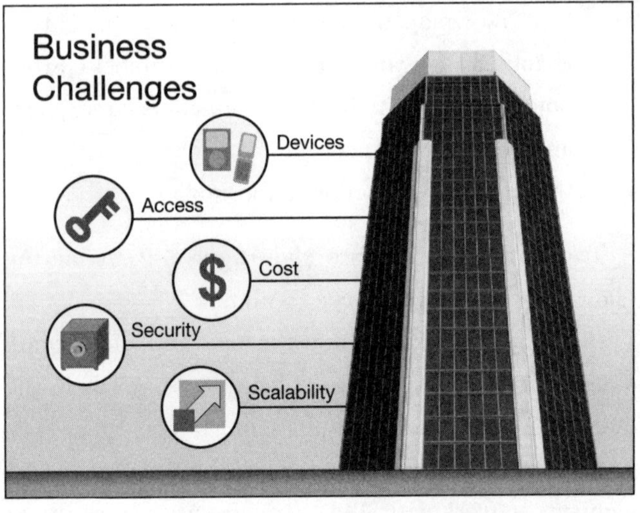

restraint. Though you can develop your visual sensibility by studying well-designed publications, you may also want to ask a professional designer to customize a template for you so you'll have a solid foundation to build from.

Choose the Right Type of Slide

If you're feeling overwhelmed by endless possibilities as you're creating slides, rest assured—all slides can be boiled down to the following types. Here's how they work, and when you'll use them.

Walk-in slide

This slide is already up when people enter the room. It creates the first impression. You may want it to display your company's branding, for example, or an image that sets the tone for your presentation.

Title slide

Here's where you show the title of your talk and (if you're addressing an external crowd) your name, title, and company. Include a title slide even if you don't state the title when you speak; it helps orient and focus the audience.

Navigation slide

This type of slide helps the audience see where you are in the presentation. You can, for example, show section

FIGURE 5-4

Navigation slide

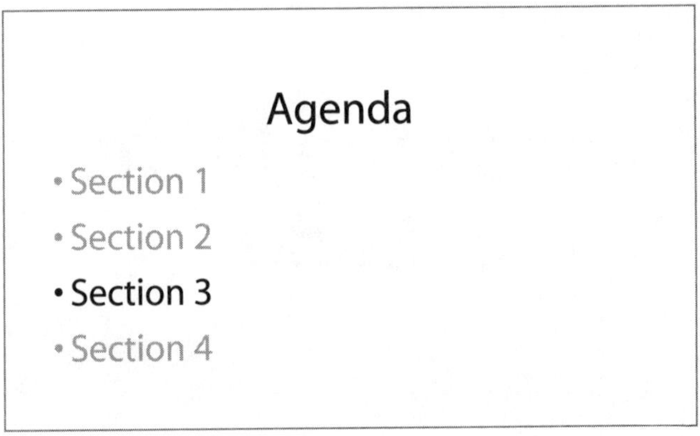

titles as you move from point to point or periodically show an agenda slide that highlights where you are in your talk (see figure 5-4).

Bullet slide

Use bullets to cluster related ideas into a list, but don't display them all at once. If you do, your audience will get ahead of you—and get bored. Instead, control your pacing with a "build" (have each bullet appear as you cover it by animating each one). If the bullets on your slide don't have to be associated together, give each point its own slide.

Big-word slide

This type of slide shows a single word or short phrase in large type—the one message or idea you want to convey at that moment. Sometimes I use a single word to set up a visual surprise on the next slide. When I was speaking at a high-tech company's annual sales meeting, for instance, I told a story about my first sales job: selling candy for the Camp Fire Girls as a kid. I had clipped a newspaper photo of my troop with a trophy for selling the most candy—but I wanted that part to be a surprise. So first, I slipped in a slide that said, "Victory is sweet." This text not only explained an important reason *why* people sell but also teed up the photo showing our goofy fifth-grade smiles and our skinny arms holding up a trophy that was bigger than we were.

Quote slide

Project quotes by experts or from important documents to add credibility or factual support to your message, but clearly show where the material came from. Use quotation marks and include a source line. Project only one quote at a time—more than one will muddy the focus. And try not to exceed 30 words. That allows you to fit in attribution without sacrificing readability. You can also borrow a technique that I've seen several TED presenters use effectively: Supplement the visual with a recording of the person you're quoting or (if that's not available) add voice-over so the audience feels as if it's reading along with the author of the quote.

Data slide

You may need to display data when explaining your research, for example, or reporting on your business unit's performance, or making a controversial argument that requires proof. Be judicious, though, so you don't overwhelm people with numbers they don't really need to know. Visually emphasize what part of the data you want people to look at by rendering everything else in the chart in gray (see "Clarify the Data" later in this section of the guide).

Diagram slide

Diagrams translate abstract, invisible concepts into something people can see. Use them to show connections between ideas or to illustrate processes. You may want to transform some of your bullet slides into diagrams to clarify the type of relationship your points and subpoints have with each other (see "Turn Words into Diagrams" later in this section).

Conceptual image slide

Sometimes showing is more powerful than telling. Project photos or illustrations to convey concepts or even

FIGURE 5-5

Conceptual image slide

combine them. Slaveryfootprint.org used the familiar image of a clothing tag with provocative wording to open consumers' eyes to the realities of slave labor in supply chains (figure 5-5).

Video slide

A video slide provides a nice break from a series of static slides. Use videos of talking heads to endorse your concept, for example, or animated infographics to explain it. Many images from stock photography houses also come in video versions.

Walk-out slide

Leave people with something useful as they exit the room. You may want to re-project a rousing call to action, show your contact information, or display a nicely branded slide and play music that reinforces the mood you've created.

Storyboard One Idea per Slide

Filmmakers sketch out their shots *before* production begins to make sure they'll hang together structurally, conceptually, and visually. Good presenters use a similar planning process before they sweat over their slides.

Sure, you're not Steven Spielberg, but don't be intimidated. Basic storyboarding isn't hard, and it saves you more time than it takes.

When you're storyboarding a presentation:

- **Keep it simple:** Draw small visual representations of your ideas on 1.5″ × 2″ sticky notes (see figure 5-6). Constraining your ideas to a small sketch space forces you to use simple, clear words and pictures as proof of concept before creating slides in presentation software. Don't be embarrassed by rudimentary sketches. This is an ideation phase; doodles work fine as long as you understand them (and if you don't, the concept is probably too complex anyway).

FIGURE 5-6

Use stickies to keep it simple

- **Limit yourself to one idea per slide:** There's no reason to crowd several ideas onto one slide. Slides are free. Make as many as you need to give each idea its own moment onstage (as in figure 5-7).

The sketching process helps you clarify what you want to say and how you want to say it. As Dan Roam, author of *The Back of the Napkin*, points out, "All the real problems of today are multidimensional. . . . There is no way to fully understand them—thus no way to effectively begin solving them—without at some point literally drawing them out."

FIGURE 5-7

One idea per slide

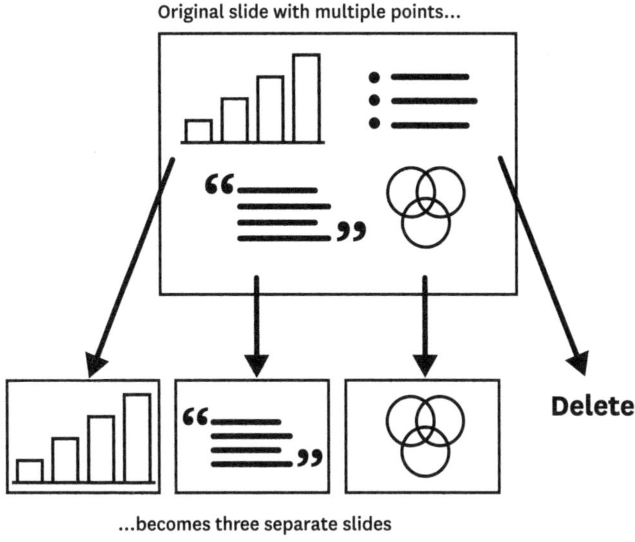

As you storyboard, you'll be able to tell immediately which concepts are clunky or overly complex (you'll run out of space on your sticky notes). Eliminate them, and brainstorm new ways to communicate those messages.

Chances are good you can develop at least a couple of your storyboarding doodles into graphics or diagrams you'll actually use in the presentation. If they'll help the audience understand or remember your verbal message, they're worth including. But even if you don't display any images when you present, nice big type on the screen is better than dense prose.

Avoid Visual Clichés

When your CFO announces at an all-staff meeting that the company's financials are "right on target," does he treat you and your colleagues to the all-too-familiar image of a bull's-eye?

Nothing gets eyes a-glazing like a visual cliché. If you want your presentation to stand out (in a good way) from the others your audience has seen, throw out the first visual concepts that come to mind. They're the ones that occur to everyone else, too. Brainstorm several ideas for

TABLE 5-1

Find new visual metaphors

Concept	Cliché	Unique
Goal	Bull's-eye	Maze; threshold
Partnership	Handshake in front of globe	Reef ecosystem; Fred Astaire and Ginger Rogers
Security	Lock and key	Doberman pinscher; pepper spray

each concept you want to illustrate—and you'll work your way toward fresh, surprising images.

Table 5-1 gives some examples of visual clichés and more-creative ways to illustrate the same concepts.

Arrange Slide Elements with Care

By carefully arranging your slide elements, you can help your audience process the information more easily—and that, as we've discussed, frees up people to hear what you're saying.

Follow these five design principles when arranging elements to simplify your slides.

Flow

Placement governs flow—that is, how the eye travels across a space. You can direct people's eyes to certain areas of a slide and help your audience get to the important points quickly. People should be able to move their eyes across your slide in one back-and-forth motion and be done processing the information.

In figure 5-8, your eye takes in the cluster of grapes, then moves to the text, then focuses on one individual grape.

FIGURE 5-8

Flow—Part 1

The next example (figure 5-9) shows one of a series of five points made. Your eye moves from left to right: You see the number 5 and the title, then your eye follows the path to the ridgeline.

Contrast

Our eyes are drawn to things that stand out, so designers use contrast to focus attention. Create contrast through your elements' size, shape, color, and proximity.

Look at figure 5-10, where the presenter compared cross-sections of skin and soil to show that tending to both requires an understanding of the microbiological activity beneath the surface. Notice how the blurred

FIGURE 5-9

Flow—Part 2

FIGURE 5-10

Contrast

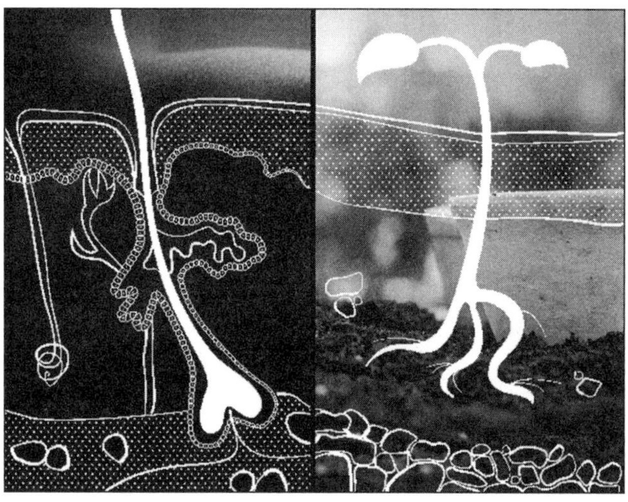

background images set off the stark white illustrations in high relief so they can be processed quickly.

White space

White space is the open space surrounding items of interest. Presenters are often tempted to fill it up with additional content that competes for attention. But including a healthy amount of white space imparts a feeling of luxury (advertisers have discovered that it creates higher perceived value) and sharpens viewers' focus by isolating elements.

That doesn't necessarily mean that everything is literally "white"—just that the design feels spacious. See the example in figure 5-11:

FIGURE 5-11

White space

PABCO
"Products are made in the factory, but brands are created in the mind."
Walter Landor
Founder of Landor Associates

If we'd paired the quote with a larger or more detailed image, your eye wouldn't know where to begin. Buried, the quote's message would have lost its power.

Hierarchy

A clear visual hierarchy allows viewers to quickly ascertain a slide's most important elements.

The sample slide in figure 5-12, citing a statistic from a recent McKinsey study, has a top-down hierarchy: You process the picture, and then the large percentage, and then the supporting copy.

Unity

Slides with visual unity look as though the same person created them and make your message feel cohesive. You

FIGURE 5-12

Hierarchy

FIGURE 5-13

Unity—Part 1

FIGURE 5-14

Unity—Part 2

can achieve this through consistent type styles, color, image treatment, and element placement throughout the slide deck.

The slides in figures 5-13 and 5-14 feel united for a couple of reasons: Both of their backgrounds are dark around the edges and lighter in the middle. Also, all the type and the images are black.

Clarify the Data

When displaying data in a presentation, pursue clarity above all else. The people in your audience can't spend extra time with your projected charts or pull them closer to examine them, as they do with charts in print. They have to get meaning from your numbers at a distance, before you click away.

People will interpret your data slides first by reading the titles, then by looking at the shapes the data make, and then by reading the axes. It's a multistep process, complex to begin with. So if the information you're displaying is *visually complex,* the audience won't have time to comprehend it.

These rules of thumb will help you clarify—and simplify—your data.

Highlight what's important

Start by asking, "What would I like people to remember about the data?"—and give that point visual emphasis. If you're projecting a chart about sales trends over five years but talking specifically about how sales are consistently low in the first quarter, show the first-quarter bar of each year in a rich color and other bars in a neutral color, like gray. Deemphasize grid lines, borders, axes, and labels—you'll provide that kind of context when you speak, so your visuals don't have to—and use contrast (color, size, or position) to draw the viewer's eye to where the meaning is.

Notice in figure 5-15 (top) how the grid lines and borders all have the same weight as the data, so the eye doesn't know where to go first. But the bottom image—borderless, with muted axes and gridlines—takes viewers right to the point: They see immediately that revenue leveled off after a spike early in the year.

Tell the truth

This may seem obvious, but many presenters play fast and loose with their charts. If you don't have a *z*-axis in

FIGURE 5-15

Highlight what's important

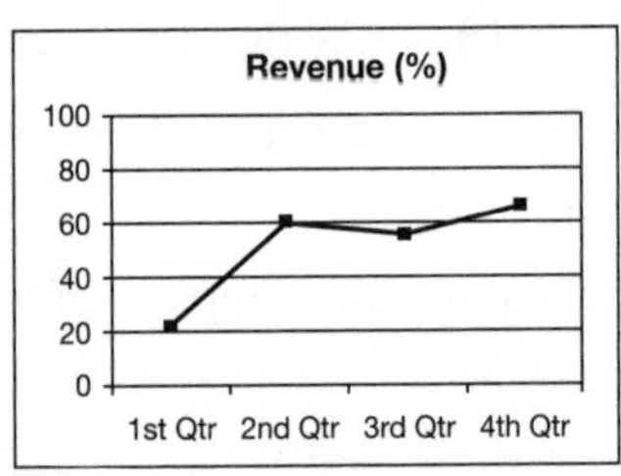

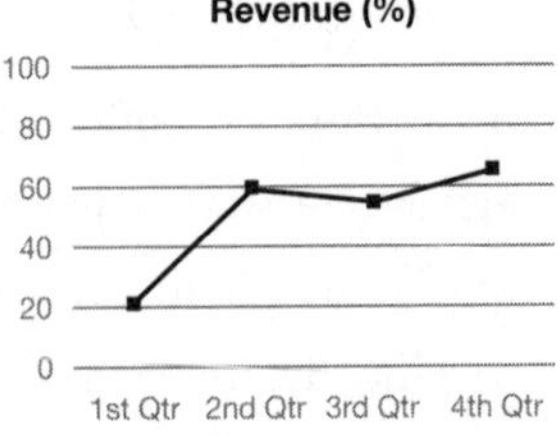

your data, omit 3-D effects—the depth can make your numbers look larger than they are. In a 3-D pie chart, for example, the pie piece in the foreground appears deceptively larger than the rest. Also, don't alter the proportions of your axes. Doing so can make a change in the numbers look more significant (figure 5-16a) or less so (figure 5-16b). Square grid lines (figure 5-16c) will keep your data true.

Pick the right chart for the job

The most common charts in business are pies, bars, matrixes, and line graphs. They serve different purposes, though. Use a line graph instead of a bar chart if the shape of the line will draw attention to your most impor-

FIGURE 5-16

Tell the truth

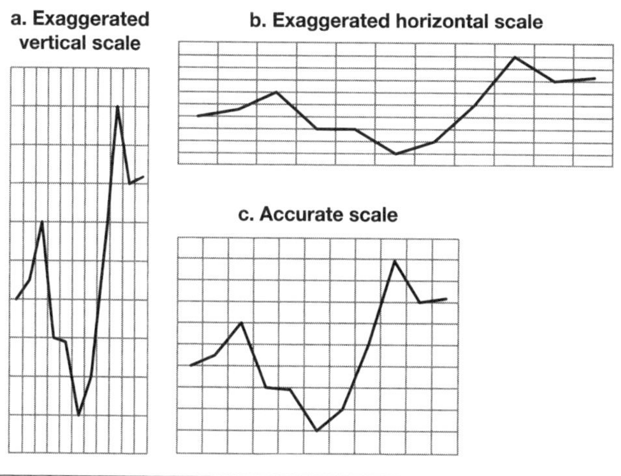

tant point. Use a matrix instead of multiple pie charts if you want to show relationships between the data points.

For example, the slide in figure 5-17 uses pie charts to show how airline ticket sales break down between three different sales channels: online, agents, and direct sales. But there's not much you can deduce from these charts, because they're visually similar.

Lay out the data in a matrix, however, and suddenly it's clear that total sales for Airline 3 are almost double the others (figure 5-18).

Sometimes the best chart is no chart at all. If a number conveys your key message most clearly on its own, show just that number—huge—on the slide.

FIGURE 5-17

The wrong chart for the job

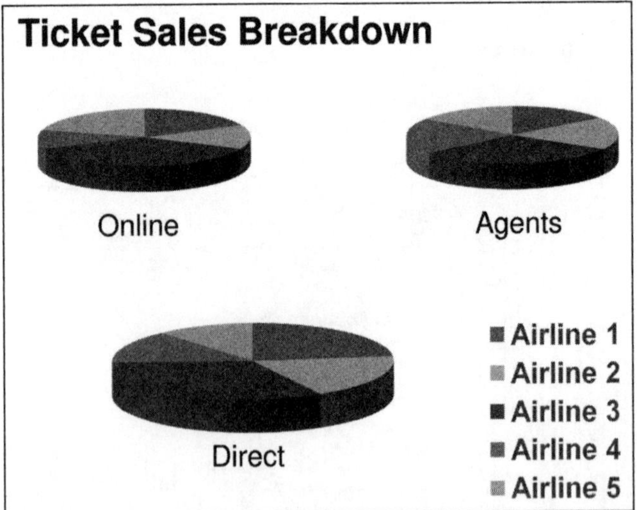

FIGURE 5-18

The right chart for the job

Ticket Sales Breakdown

	Airline 1	Airline 2	Airline 3	Airline 4	Airline 5
Online	20	15	40	12	22
Agents	15	18	30	20	15
Direct	25	20	35	15	12
Total	**60**	**53**	**105**	**47**	**49**

Find the narrative in the data

Explain not just the "what," but the "why" and the "how" of your data. Maybe the numbers went up, but what *made* them go up? What impact did people have on them? How will people be affected *by* them?

Use concrete comparisons to express magnitude

The bigger a number is, the tougher it is to grasp. Millions, billions, and trillions sound a lot alike, but they're nowhere near each other in magnitude. Help your audience understand scale by communicating large numbers in concrete terms. For example, if you're trying to get an audience to visualize a billion square feet, hold up a carpet square that's 12″ × 12″ and tell them it would take a billion of those squares to cover Manhattan.

Turn Words into Diagrams

Diagrams are great tools for illustrating relationships. They clarify concepts so an audience can see at a glance how parts of a whole work together. For example, if your organization is merging with two others, you can use a diagram of three overlapping circles to signify redundancies between departments. Or if you want to encourage your team members to innovate iteratively, try using a flow diagram that loops back on itself in several places to illustrate the process of working out kinks in a prototype.

When you're creating your presentation visuals, try turning some of your words into diagrams that *reinforce* your speech. It's easy to translate words into diagrams when you have a visual taxonomy at your disposal—and I'm providing one here.

Because my firm has visualized concepts for companies and brands for more than 20 years, my designers' notebooks are filled with great business diagrams. Looking for patterns, I clipped thousands of sketches from those notebooks and sorted them into the following commonly used (and universally understood) types of diagrams.

FIGURE 5-19

Types of diagrams

A Network

HUB AND SPOKES

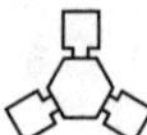

SPOKES

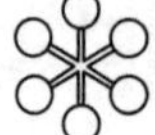

FLARE

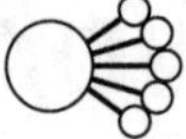

RING

B Segment

DONUT

PIE

C Join

HOOK

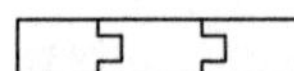

OVERLAP

D Flow

LOOP

PARALLEL

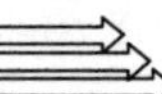

LINEAR

MERGE AND DIVIDE

E Stack

VERTICAL

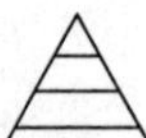

HORIZONTAL

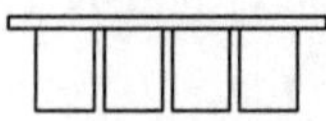

CONCENTRIC

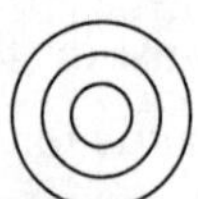

The diagrams in figure 5-19 illustrate these kinds of relationships:

- **Network**

  Example: A hub-and-spokes diagram can illustrate the stakeholders from various departments who come together to make an initiative successful.

- **Segment**

  Example: A donut can show how separate products fit into a suite of offerings.

- **Join**

  Example: A hook diagram can depict a relationship between supply chain partners.

- **Flow**

  Example: Parallel arrows can show two teams working in concert toward a goal.

- **Stack**

  Example: Vertical layers can illustrate discrete fiscal-year goals as building blocks that will lead to profitability.

So, how can you use these diagrams in your presentation? Look through your slides and find a list of bullets. Those bullets should "feel" related—that's why you grouped them together in the first place. Circle the verbs or nouns on the slide and consider *how* they're related.

That relationship will most likely fall into one of the categories in figure 5-19. Now see if you can use one of the diagrams in that category to replace your bullet slide. Repeat the process with other text slides.

Consider two sets of slides (figures 5-20a and 5-20b; figures 5-21a and 5-21b) showing how a list of bullet points ("Before") can be turned into a diagram ("After").

The taxonomy in figure 5-19 isn't exhaustive, and there's room for creativity within each category. You can use different shapes and styles for the nodes and connectors, and so on (go to diagrammer.com for thousands of choices). But it covers most of the bases, so it takes some of the pressure off as you're working to meet your deadline.

FIGURE 5-20a

Before

We follow the same basic process every time

- We start with the invention. We take early stage ideas and turn them into demos—not technical demos but conceptual ones, like the rough version of Flare you saw.
- Then our team takes this seed of an idea to customers, in conferences and forums, to get feedback that helps us shape it into something even more useful.
- We improve it and build a prototype that we give to a set of early adopters, who use it and give us more feedback.
- Eventually, after a few quick cycles of this process, we standardize the product features.
- Only then is it ready to go out to our larger group of customers, like the finished version of Flare you saw.

FIGURE 5-20b

After

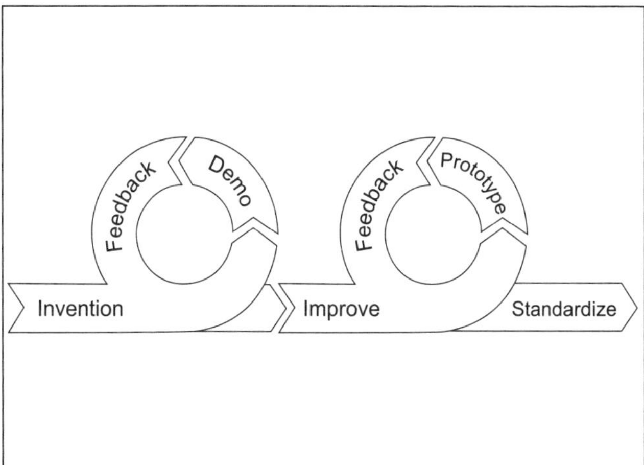

FIGURE 5-21a

Before

Research Programs

Concentrate on four research programs

- Domestic Energy Development
- Environmental Technologies
- Carbon Management
- Energy Efficiency

The potential impact of all of our programs will extend beyond policy makers to corporations and citizens around the world.

FIGURE 5-21b

After

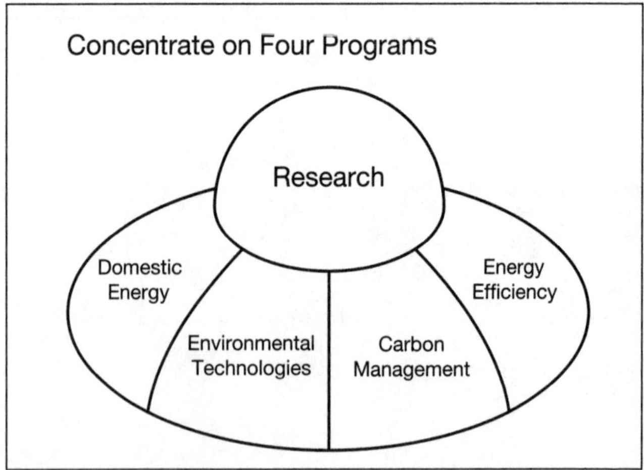

Use the Right Number of Slides

How many slides should you have? That depends on your audience, the technology you're using, the setting you're in, your own sense of pacing, and how comfortable you are with a clicker. Some presenters could spend an hour on three slides; others could go through 200 or more and you'd never know it.

Consider these slide-count variables as you're creating your presentation.

No slides

If you need to make a very personal connection with your audience or you're delivering a short talk in a casual environment, go without slides. They don't work in every situation. As Andrew Dlugan says in his "Six Minutes" blog about public speaking, presenters shouldn't use slides in a commencement speech, a eulogy, a wedding toast, or a layoff announcement. If you're unsure whether they're appropriate, bring them with you but also carry a printout of your slide notes in case you decide when you arrive that it's best to leave your laptop off.

Moderate slide count

Some experts recommend 1 to 2 slides per minute, or 30 to 60 slides for an hour-long talk. That's about the average count in corporate presentations—but most of them cram too much information on each slide. If you've broken your content down to one idea per slide (see "Storyboard One Idea per Slide" earlier in the Slides section), you may end up with more than 60.

High slide count

Some presenters use 5 slides per minute. This rapid-fire style keeps the audience extra alert because people will visually reengage with each click—but it requires a lot of rehearsal and careful pacing. In a 40-minute talk, I typically use 145 slides. (If you count "builds" within each slide—where I reveal bullets one at a time, and so forth—I click up to 300 times.) But when I ask audiences how many slides they think I used, they usually say between 30 and 50.

Social media slide count

The most popular presentations on social media sites like slideshare.com have more than 75 slides that you can read in 2 to 3 minutes. They also tend to be built like children's books—sentence, visual, sentence, visual—to facilitate quick clicking.

Don't worry about slide count. Just make your *slides* count.

Know When to Animate

When things move, eyes are drawn to them. So animation is a powerful communication tool—but only when applied judiciously and in a way that enhances your message.

It's tempting to include every feature and flashy effect that's available—but that would be like adding rhinestones to every outfit in your closet. You'd be blinded by all the bling when you opened the door, and you wouldn't know what to pick.

Effective animation:

- **Shows how things work:** Use animation and motion to control eye movement as you reveal how things are put together, explain changes, show direction, or illustrate sequence. If, for example, you've got a stack of boxes showing how parts of your software application fit together, you can provide information on one part at a time, without crowding the visual: When you click on a box, have a "drawer" slide out from behind it to reveal details.

- **Creates contrast:** Show many slides with no animation so that when you do use it, it stands out.
- **Looks natural:** Just like actors on a stage, elements can enter your slide, interact, and then leave the scene. But the movement should seem natural and controlled, not busy and frenetic.
- **Does not annoy:** Most content isn't any clearer if you make it spin, twitch, or twirl. Gratuitous features like these just get on people's nerves, so don't waste time on them.

Section 6
Delivery

Golden Rule: Never deliver a presentation you wouldn't want to sit through.

—Motto at Duarte, Inc.

Rehearse Your Material Well

There's no such thing as overrehearsing your delivery. Not that you should memorize your talk—if you do, you'll come across as stiff and struggle to connect with the audience. But know your material inside and out. That way, you can adapt more easily if the environment, audience, or technology suddenly changes on you (something often does). Also, audiences can tell if you try to wing it—and they feel slighted. It sends the message that you don't value them or their time. Perhaps most important, rehearsing frees you up to be more *present* in your talk and fully engage with the people in front of you.

When you rehearse, leave plenty of time to:

- **Get honest feedback from a skilled presenter:** As the presenter, you're so familiar with (and probably attached to) your ideas that you may think you're making each point more clearly and persuasively than you are. So ask a skilled presenter to give you honest feedback. Give her a printout of your slides and have her jot down what you say well, what you don't, what's essential to keep, and what's distracting. She might say things like: "When you put it that way, people won't follow you," and "That term sounds derogatory to me," and "I thought you expressed it better last time, when you said . . ." The extra set of eyes and ears helps you see and hear yourself as the audience will.

- **Prepare a short version:** Many variables in a presentation can go wrong, leaving you with less time than you expected. The technology doesn't always work. Other speakers might cut into your time slot by running long. An impatient executive may interrupt you with lots of questions. Prepare a presentation that fits your scheduled time, but also craft and rehearse a version that's much shorter, just in case.

- **Fiddle with your slides:** Continue to tweak your slides until the day you present. Refining a bit of text here and adding an image there is a form of rehearsal. You become more deeply familiar with the content as you engage with your slides—so when you present, they feel seamlessly integrated with your message, not tacked-on or disruptive.

- **Rehearse a few times in slide-show mode:** Because slide-show mode doesn't allow you to peek at the notes view, it forces you into an even greater familiarity with the material and allows you to focus on pacing and visualize the flow. Look for choppy transitions from slide to slide, inconsistent graphics, and awkward builds as you reveal new bullets, so you can smooth things out.

- **Practice on camera:** Record some of your final rehearsals on video. You don't need a professional setup. Use a webcam or the camera on your cell phone or tablet. Pretend you are in front of an audience, and address the camera as if it's a person. When you're done, review the video to assess not just your content but also your stage presence, eye contact, facial expressions, gestures, and ease of movement. Identify where you don't appear natural, relaxed, or in command of your material—and work on those areas.

Know the Venue and Schedule

Scoping out the room in advance will help you navigate it. If you can't check it out in person, look for details online or ask the host to describe it. Sometimes, if you get this information early enough, you can change the setup to meet your preferences. If you're leading an off-site meeting for a team of six, for example, and you've been assigned a large conference space, see if you can get a cozier room—or at least a smaller table to encourage discussion.

Don't make any assumptions about the space. When I was invited to speak to 70 people at Google, in my head I pictured rows of chairs. But when I got there, I was taken to a tiny conference room with 20 people crammed in—and 50 small faces of webcam participants projected on the wall. If I'd known what the room would be like, I would have prepared to facilitate a conversation instead of delivering a formal presentation. Instead, I found myself making lots of last-minute mental adjustments, like figuring out where to stand and where to focus my eye contact, and that threw me off my stride.

Avoid such surprises by getting information about:

- **Floor and seating plan:** How is the room arranged? Does it have classroom seating? Round tables? Is the size of the room appropriate for the number of attendees you expect? It's better for people to sit close together, feeding off one another's energy, than to feel lost and disconnected in a cavernous space. Will you be elevated on a stage? Will the audience be able to see you if you stand on the same level as everyone else to make your talk feel less like a lecture? Do you have room to walk around and connect with people? If you'll be on stage, where will the lights hit the floor? Mark any pockets of darkness with tape so you can avoid them (important for talks recorded on video). Does the room have any poles that will obstruct the audience's view? Do what you can to work around them. Is there a podium? Remove it—it's a visual barrier that puts distance between you and the audience—unless you need a place to put your notes.

- **Food plan:** Are you presenting near a mealtime? Find out whether food will be provided. If not, build in time for people—including yourself—to grab a bite. Or if you're presenting within your organization, bring some snacks. A hungry audience won't focus on your message. Will you be speaking during a sit-down meal? You'll need adequate amplification so people can hear you above the sounds of forks and knives. Or see if you can wait until the food service crew clears the dishes before you speak.

- **Show flow:** What will the order of events be? Check with the organizer. Will you be introduced, or do you need to prepare your own introduction? Who will speak before you and after you? What messages will others present? It's nice to reference things others are saying. If you're toward the end of a long list of speakers, keep your message short and simple—the audience will already be tired and overloaded with information. And if you're following a presenter with a contrary view, you can prepare to address any seeds of resistance he might plant in the audience. Speaking at a conference? Look at sessions in the same time slot as yours to find out if you'll be competing with a popular workshop, for example, or a famous author doing a book signing. That'll help you gauge whether the room will fill up.
- **Recording:** Will your talk be recorded? If so, locate the cameras and look at them often to connect with remote viewers or listeners. Do you want to restrict distribution of your recorded presentation? Make that clear to the organizers. Once, when I spoke to a group of 250 professional women about overcoming obstacles, I knew I was being

recorded but thought only attendees could access the recording, via a password-protected website. A local TV channel ended up broadcasting my entire presentation. My talk was very raw. I wouldn't have gotten so personal if I'd known it would go beyond the room.

Anticipate Technology Glitches

Equipment often malfunctions—even for people who aren't as technologically challenged as I am. So arrange a tech walkthrough or, if that's not possible, give yourself *at least* 30 minutes to set up.

Here's a checklist I've developed after years of trial by fire to avoid last-minute frenzy from tech glitches:

- **Get to know the AV person:** Learn his name and treat him well. He'll work extra hard and extra fast for you if he likes you.

- **Test all the equipment:** Do a dry run using the projector, the clicker, and any audio equipment beforehand. Make sure it all works.

- **Bring backups:** If a piece of technology is critical to the success of your talk, request that it be provided—but also bring your own. That goes for the projector, the cables needed to connect it, the clicker, and any audio equipment you'll need. I travel with my own speakers because at-venue audio often doesn't work. Venture capitalist and former Apple marketer Guy Kawasaki even brings his own in-ear microphone when he presents. Also, back up the content of your presentation on drives and in the cloud—and make printouts of your slides and notes.

- **Prerecord your demos:** If you're planning to demonstrate software, an app, or a website, have a recorded version of your demo on your machine in case the Internet connection is slow or down at the time of your talk.

- **Test your slide deck:** Click through every single slide. This is your last time to see what the slides look like projected in the room. You want to confirm that you've grabbed the right version, that everything is legible from the back of the room, and that each time you click, the slides advance to the right content. Sometimes the distance between the clicker and the computer backstage is too far for the signal to reach, and the AV team has to make adjustments.

- **Try out the comfort monitors:** Confirm that your comfort monitors (teleprompters) work and you can read from them. At a technical walkthrough the day before a presentation, I discovered that my comfort monitors were so small I couldn't read anything from the stage. I wanted to use monitors rather than rely solely on printouts because I'd be quoting lengthy excerpts from famous speeches. So that night, I doubled the font size and saved myself a lot of embarrassment.

- **Play all media:** When transferring files to a venue's machines, it's easy to forget to grab video and audio files. Double-check that you have all your media in one folder and that the file types will play on the machines you'll be using.

- **Confirm type of projection:** Check the screen's aspect ratio (usually 16:9 or 4:3), and make sure your slides are the right dimensions. Also consider whether they'll be front- or rear-projected—and mark the floor with tape so you won't walk through the light beam and have slides projected across your face when you're speaking.

- **Find out if people will attend remotely:** The odds of technical mishaps go way up in remote presentations—especially ones that involve last-minute equipment changes. Once I tested all my videos before walking onstage, only to discover moments before I began speaking that the AV crew switched machines to accommodate a large remote group. The crew forgot to copy over my video files—so I did my best to describe what people *would have seen* if we had those files.

Manage Your Stage Fright

Before you present, does your heart speed up? Do you sweat? Does your mouth go dry and your breathing become erratic? That's your fight-or-flight instinct kicking in. Your body is telling you to flee because your brain perceives the audience as a possible threat: People might judge, challenge, or resist you.

You may also fear the fact that presentation delivery can't be undone. It's live, and it's final.

A little bit of fear can be a good thing. I actually do a better job of presenting when I'm mildly nervous—it's like a shot of adrenaline. But don't let it overwhelm you.

Here are a few ways to manage your stage fright before you present:

- **Quiet your mind:** Stop the self-critical internal chatter and think instead about something that calms you. Take a short walk outside. Listen to soothing music.

- **Breathe:** Sit on a chair or the floor, breathe deeply, and hold it in. Then take in one more gasp of air to fill your lungs even more—and let it all out very slowly. By doing this four times in a row, I can calm my body down in less than a minute.

- **Laugh:** Read your favorite humor website or watch a funny video. Laughing doesn't just distract you from your fear—it releases tension.

- **Visualize:** Communication coach Nick Morgan, the author of *Trust Me,* suggests my favorite fear-busting technique: "Role-play in your mind a communication between you and your favorite person. . . . Form a memory of what that feels like physically, not about what you say. Notice everything you can about your behavior. . . .What are you doing with your hands? . . . How close are you? . . . Catalogue and remember the behavior, and then use that behavior."

- **Remember your audience's flaws:** You've spent time thinking about how the people in your audience might resist your message—and rightly so. They do have that power. But, having studied them, you should also have insights into what makes *them* human and frail. Remembering that they're just as flawed as you are will help calm your nerves.

Set the Right Tone for Your Talk

Your audience will size you up before you utter a word—so it's critical to make a positive, message-appropriate first impression.

What's the first thing you want people to think or experience? What mood do you want to create? Set the right tone for your talk by attending to the following details.

Precommunication

When you invite others to your presentation, send a thoughtfully written agenda with a concise but telling subject line—and be explicit about what the audience will get out of it. All communication leading up to your talk will affect your credibility and impact—so put as much thought and care into it as into the presentation itself. (See "Persuade Beyond the Stage" in the Media section.)

Atmosphere

Special touches in the room let people know what to expect and prime them for the type of experience you want them to have. If you're giving a calculated, chilling speech, a cold, sparsely appointed room works. Use bright lighting for a casual talk; go a bit darker for a formal one. Provide refreshments (even for small, familiar groups) to make people feel welcome. Music, props, and projected images can also help set the tone.

Appearance

As much as you want the audience to like you for your mind, people will make quick judgments based on your appearance. Suit up to address potential clients, for example, or investors. Dress more casually when introducing yourself to a new group of direct reports, to signal that you're accessible. In *Enchantment: The Art of Changing Hearts, Minds, and Actions,* Guy Kawasaki suggests matching your audience (or dressing for a "tie"). If you underdress, you're saying, "I don't respect you"; and if you overdress, you're saying, "I'm better than you."

Disposition

The moment people see you, your disposition should prepare them for your message. For your content to ring true, do you need to come across as passionate? Humbled by the challenges ahead? If you're announcing a layoff, be somber, not smiley. If your talk is upbeat, chat with individuals as the group gathers; shake hands if you're meeting for the first time. No matter what tone you're trying to establish, be available and sincere.

Be Yourself

Transparency wins people over. Though you'll want to come across as smart and articulate, it's even more important to be open and sincere so people will trust you and your ideas.

It's OK if you're nervous. Audiences are gracious. As business communication expert Victoria Labalme points out, they'll "forgive a stumble, an 'um,' or a section where you backtrack as long as they know that your heart is in the right place."

She adds: "Your audience wants you to be real. So avoid sounding like a corporate spokesperson—but don't portray false humility, either. Playing small and meek when inside you know (and the audience knows) you're a giant will not win you any fans. Authenticity means claiming who you are."

If you love what you do, for instance, let your enthusiasm show.

Microsoft CEO Steve Ballmer explodes with so much passion when he presents that his sweaty, breathless dancing became a YouTube phenomenon (figure 6-1).

FIGURE 6-1

Steve Ballmer's famous "monkey boy" dance

In a January 2012 article about Ballmer, *Business-Week* mused, "He plays the cheerleader in public appearances in an apparent effort to prove that no one can top his love of Microsoft—and he succeeds cringingly well." It's over-the-top, but it's all him. No one questions his authenticity, and the man can rally his troops.

And then there's Susan Cain, who took the opposite tack when she gave one of the most buzzed-about talks at TED 2012. Cain spoke quietly and convincingly about being an introvert in a world that rewards extroverts. Her style suited her—and her subject matter—perfectly. She seemed comfortable onstage, but she certainly wasn't dramatic or even passionate. That wouldn't have been natural, given her personality and her topic. Instead, she delivered her message in a way that would resonate with fellow introverts: "The world needs you, and it needs the things you carry. So I wish you the best of all possible journeys and the courage to speak softly."

Communicate with Your Body

People will read your body language to decide if they can trust you and your expertise. Constricted and contrived gestures will make you seem insecure. Larger movement conveys confidence and openness.

Use your physical expression to its fullest with the following techniques:

- **Project emotion with your face:** Connect with the audience by using your face to convey your feelings. Smile, laugh, open your mouth in disbelief. Before you begin your talk, try moving every facial muscle you can—it'll help you warm up.

- **Peel yourself away from your slides:** If you turn your back to the audience to look at your slides, you put up a barrier. As much as you can, keep your eyes on the people who have come to hear you.

- **Open up your posture:** Avoid a "closed" stance, such as folding your arms, standing with legs crossed, putting your hands in your pockets, or clasping your hands behind or in front of you. It signals discomfort.

- **Exaggerate your movements:** Fill the space around you, especially if you're speaking in a large room. Use the same types of gestures you would if you were having a personal conversation—but make them bigger and more deliberate. Before your presentation, stretch your arms as wide as you can and as tall as you can (even stand on your toes). This helps you open up your chest cavity and practice exaggerating your gestures.

- **Match gestures with content:** Gestures should complement or amplify what you're saying. If you're presenting a record year in sales, go "big" with your arms and your smile. If your team barely missed its targets, bring everything in, perhaps showing a tiny little gap between your thumb and forefinger.

Brain scientist Jill Bolte Taylor coordinated her gestures and content beautifully when she described in her 2008 TED talk what it was like to have a massive stroke. She threw her arms upward to convey the unexpected rush of euphoria she'd felt as the left side of her brain shut down (figure 6-2a); she brought them back down when she described how she'd surrendered her spirit, ready to transition out of this world (figure 6-2b).

When you tape yourself in rehearsal, you may identify gestures, movements, or facial expressions that look

FIGURE 6-2a

Jill Bolte Taylor, arms up

FIGURE 6-2b

Jill Bolte Taylor, arms down

lackluster or unnatural. Re-create those gestures so you can physically feel them, and then practice new ones that would be appropriate replacements. As with golf, focus on how it feels as you do it so you can create "muscle memory" of what works.

Communicate with Your Voice

Your voice is multitalented. It can sound:

- **Assertive:** Firm, unyielding, significant, focused
- **Cautious:** Measured, enunciated, understated
- **Critical:** Harsh, angry, upset, pointed, caustic
- **Humorous:** Comedic, light, novel, irreverent
- **Motivational:** Uplifting, encouraging, friendly
- **Sympathetic:** Emotional, moving, personal, delicate
- **Neutral:** Casual, technical, dispassionate, informative

And it does all this through pitch, tone, volume, pacing, and enunciation.

Many business presenters have a dispassionate vocal style, assuming that it makes them sound objective or authoritative. But a flat delivery will bore your audience.

Instead, create contrast—and emphasis—through vocal variation. You can do this on your own or by tag-teaming with someone else. When my husband and I copresent our company's vision each year, our contrasting styles come through: He's soft-spoken and charmingly funny, whereas I'm dramatic and passionate. That mix works well for our content. He gets everyone to reflect on the firm's success, and I talk about the future with bold enthusiasm.

To ensure that your content comes through clearly, identify and remove verbal tics. Because silence makes most speakers uncomfortable, they tend to use words such as "um," "uh," "you know," "like," and "anyway" to fill up space between points. They'd almost always be better served by a pause, which gives the audience a chance to reflect.

I didn't think I had any verbal tics until I watched myself on video. After each key point, I said, "Right?" with an annoying lilt in my tone. It didn't take me long to remove that from my repertoire. I watched the video several times to cement it in my mind. At my very next speaking gig, I said it. Once. This word I didn't even know I used suddenly sounded like fingernails on a chalkboard. I caught myself two more times about to say it—and stopped. Becoming self-aware and really hearing how bad it sounded helped me correct myself in the moment.

Make Your Stories Come to Life

The beauty of an honest story—whether comedic or dramatic—is that it touches people. (See the Story section for details on how to apply storytelling principles when crafting and structuring your content.) But even the most compelling stories lose their power if they're not told well. How do you make yours come to life? Try the following two tips from business communication expert Victoria Labalme.

Reexperience your stories

Broadway actors relive stories each time they perform. It's how they keep their material fresh and engage audiences show after show. You can do the same. If you're talking about the time you got lost in a strange city at night to make a point about finding your way when there's no one around to guide you, re-create that scene. Don't be melodramatic or ridiculous. But narrate the story as if you're still in the moment, and you'll increase its impact on your audience. Use evocative, descriptive words. Enhance them with your stance and gestures.

One CEO reenacts the moment when his CFO came into his office and recommended that they not invest in subprime mortgages. The story is riveting partly because audiences know, in hindsight, how high the stakes were—but also because the CEO brings people *into* the scene. He describes the wood-paneled room, the view out the window on a clear day, and the moment of his razor's-edge decision—a decision that ultimately saved the company hundreds of millions of dollars. He then acknowledges his CFO for his sage advice at this critical juncture.

Rarely does someone approach a speaker weeks after a presentation to say, "I loved your third point on leadership." What people do say, however, is "I still think of the story you told . . ."

Use sensory details to set the scene

The more you can invoke the senses when telling a story, the better. Paint a visual picture, or the audience is left with a blank canvas. Also describe sounds, tastes, smells, and how things feel to the touch. "I waited in a chilly, mildewed alcove the size of an elevator" says a lot more than "I waited in a small room." By grounding yourself in such details, you'll avoid flowery, empty language reminiscent of greeting cards and embroidery pillows. You'll give your stories credibility and staying power.

Work Effectively with Your Interpreter

As companies do business farther and farther from home, presenters increasingly need translation. And working with an interpreter always complicates things. You can make it easier, though, with preparation.

Start by picking the right type of interpreter for your situation. Three types are available:

- **Simultaneous:** The interpreter sits in a soundproof booth while you present without disruption. Audience members who need translation wear earphones. When I spoke to a large group of business leaders in Taiwan, more than half the audience used earphones. As a result, I got through a lot of material with little time lost. Simultaneous interpretation requires more overhead than the other types do, since it involves technology.

- **Consecutive:** The interpreter shares the stage with you. After you make a point, you pause for her to relay what you've said. You can use this approach in less-formal settings or if you don't have the budget for simultaneous interpretation.

- **Whispering:** Here, the interpreter whispers translation to you when audience members make comments or raise questions. This approach works best if you are familiar enough with the language to understand most of what's said but need help here and there with specific words and phrases.

Once you've sorted out which kind you need, here's how to choose the right person and work effectively with her. If you can, allow up to a month to do the following:

- **Test your chemistry:** Some interpreters bring energy to the presentation; others can drain you. Spend time speaking with yours before you hire her. If you have time to interview a few candidates, all the better. You'll know someone's a good fit if she makes you laugh, for example, or calms you down. The interpreter shouldn't agitate you in any way—public speaking in a different culture is hard enough as it is. You should trust that she values your material and will represent it well.

- **Call in reinforcements:** If you can't find an excellent interpreter who's also a subject matter expert (a rare breed), use the professional interpreter as your primary source of translation—but also enlist an expert who speaks both languages to help out. That way you'll have someone who can correct the interpreter if she makes content mistakes here and there, in real time, or who can simply step in at a point where the material gets highly specialized or technical.

- **Prepare half as much material:** If you are given an hour, prepare 30 minutes' worth of material. It takes twice as long to convey your message with a consecutive interpreter—and even with the other types, you'll need extra time to translate any Q&A discussion.
- **Send your notes:** A week ahead of time, send over your notes or a transcript of a similar talk so the interpreter can practice. Even if you don't deliver your presentation exactly the same way, she'll get a feel for your material and style.
- **Work through idioms and metaphors:** Many phrases and sayings have no direct corollaries in other languages. If you've sent your notes or a transcript in advance, your interpreter will have time to flag anything that doesn't translate clearly. She can then suggest regional stories and metaphors that would work in her culture.
- **Practice pacing:** Rehearse with your interpreter when you arrive to get a sense of how much material she can translate at a time. Have her coach you

on your speed of delivery, so she can keep up *and* audience members can process what you're saying.

- **Complete each thought:** Each burst of content should be a concise but complete thought. Otherwise, you'll leave people hanging midphrase while the interpreter translates the first half of your point. Keeping your statements short and sweet makes it easy for the audience to follow you and engage with you.

Get the Most out of Your Q&A

A Q&A is a powerful, interactive way to address your audience's concerns *and* drive your point home. Always allow time for Q&A in a business presentation—trim your talk if necessary. When people leave the room with burning, unanswered questions, they won't adopt your ideas.

Get the most out of your Q&A by:

- **Planning when you'll take questions:** Establish early on if you want to field questions throughout your talk or save them until the end. If you need to build a thorough case, ask people at the very beginning to hold questions until the end. But if you're making a series of points, you can take questions after each one, while they're fresh in people's minds.

- **Anticipating questions:** You can spend hours preparing a presentation and deliver it beautifully—and then undo all your hard work and undermine your credibility by fumbling a response to an unexpected question. Think through *any* questions the audience might raise, from the mundane to the hostile. (See "Anticipate Resistance" in the Message section.) Prepare answers ahead of time so you won't be thrown off your game when all eyes are on you. Rehearse those answers, but still be mentally prepared for curveballs. Some questioners may feel a need to publicly challenge your idea. When that happens, it's important to keep your composure. Knowing your material inside-out will help immensely.

- **Listening empathetically for subtext:** Answer questions directly, but also try to identify and address any deeper ones behind them. (You'll often find a larger issue or unspoken motive lurking in the shadows.) Say you're in HR and you're hosting an orientation for employees from a recently acquired company. If people ask why they don't get to have monthly employee birthday parties anymore, you may be tempted to brush that off as silly—but the parties are probably a symbol of a bigger underlying problem. The question *behind* the question might be: "The culture we used to have isn't valued here. How can we hang on to some of the traditions that made our organization feel like a family?"

- **Admitting when you don't know something:** Don't fake an answer. Ever. Your audience will see right through it. If you don't know the answer to a question, say that—and offer to do some research after the presentation and get back to the group.

- **Keeping a tight rein on large or tough crowds:** If you're presenting to a large group, ask a Q&A moderator to graciously take the microphone back after each question is asked. That way, one aggressive question won't turn into a barrage. Or, if you don't have a moderator, let the audience know up front that you're answering one question per person so more folks will have a chance to participate.

  When I took delivery training classes, I learned to acknowledge questions from angry inquisitors—but to look at *other* audience members when answering them so it's easier to move on to the next person and keep the discussion constructive. If your topic is emotionally charged or you're addressing a crisis—a safety recall, for example—have a facilitator filter the questions. He can compile a mix of tough questions and lighter ones that might get a laugh, and omit those that stray off topic or seem to have a personal agenda behind them. He can also plant questions the audience might be too intimidated to ask—for instance, "Will people lose their jobs if we don't make our numbers this year?"

- **Leaving a strong final impression:** Don't end abruptly after the Q&A—it feels incomplete and unsatisfying to the audience, and you'll miss an opportunity to reinforce your message. Wrap up the discussion with a brief summary that recaps the "new bliss" you're helping the audience achieve. (See "Make the Ending Powerful" in the Story section.)

Build Trust with a Remote Audience

Thanks to easily accessible webinar and teleconference technology, about 80% of corporate presentations are delivered remotely, according to several live surveys I've conducted with audiences at large companies in a range of industries. That's a stunning percentage. Any time technology revolutionizes how we communicate, there's a trade-off: Communication theorist Marshall McLuhan pointed it out when he proposed his system for examining the impact of new media on society. Use his system to examine remote presenting (figure 6-3), and you'll see both positive and negative outcomes.

Even though it's designed to connect people remotely and even globally, the technology isolates participants from human contact. So how do you solve that problem? How do you build trust with your remote audience? That depends on whether you incorporate video streaming.

With video streaming

When you're visible to the audience, your body language—particularly eye contact and gestures—can help

FIGURE 6-3

Pros and cons of remote presenting

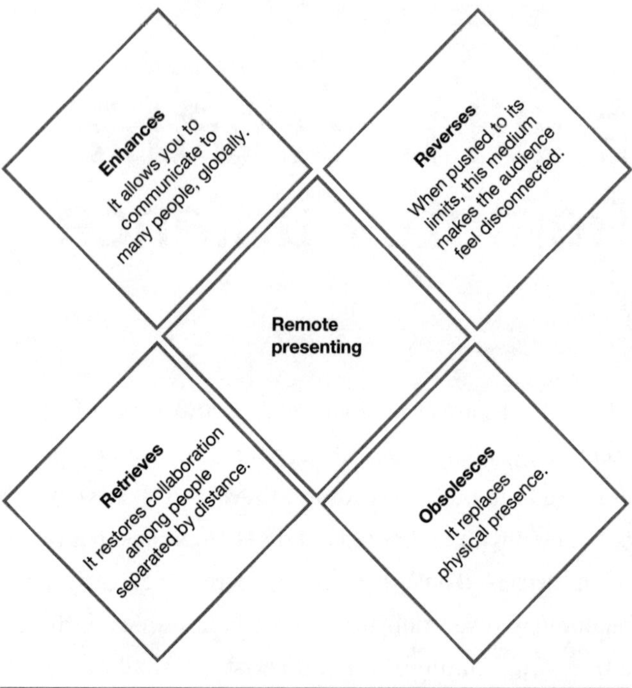

you connect with people (see “Communicate with Your Body” earlier in this section). If you glance at your notes or slides too often, your eyes will look shifty, so keep them trained on the camera as much as possible. Place the camera at eye level so you and the audience are on even ground. Looking down at it forces viewers to look up at you. Cinematographers use that trick to show a character's superiority—but the last thing you want to do is appear condescending.

If you can, deliver your presentation standing rather than seated. This allows you to move naturally—use your hands freely, lean forward, step back—which puts viewers at ease. Overall, make your movements expansive to connect with the people in the room. But when you want remote viewers to see certain gestures, keep those hand motions closer to your chest so they'll stay in the video frame. Use a high-quality video recorder and light yourself well: A professional-looking setup makes the audience feel valued.

Without video streaming

Your voice is your most valuable tool for building trust when the audience can't see you. But again, stand up—you'll sound more open and relaxed than if you're hunched over your computer. Hold people's attention by varying your volume, pitch, and tone (see "Keep Remote Listeners Interested" in this section). But don't overdo it—melodrama doesn't earn anyone's trust.

You can also build trust through the visuals you post. Create slides that convey an "open" feel by using type that's easy to read and keeping the graphics simple and clean. Also, in the spirit of transparency, let your audience download your deck.

Keep Remote Listeners Interested

When people tune in to a webinar or dial in to a teleconference, you can't see them, so their temptation to multitask is great.

My firm recently surveyed almost 400 people who've attended a webinar within the last year, and it turns out that more of them checked e-mail than doing any other activity—including *watching the webinar* (figure 6-4). That makes people's in-boxes your biggest competitor.

So what can you do to lure people away from their other tasks?

- **Break the content down into small bites:** Feed participants small, tasty morsels one by one so they stay tuned in. Move through your points quickly—don't spend a long time explaining concepts. And if you have slides, change them up about every 20 seconds.

FIGURE 6-4

E-mail is your biggest competitor

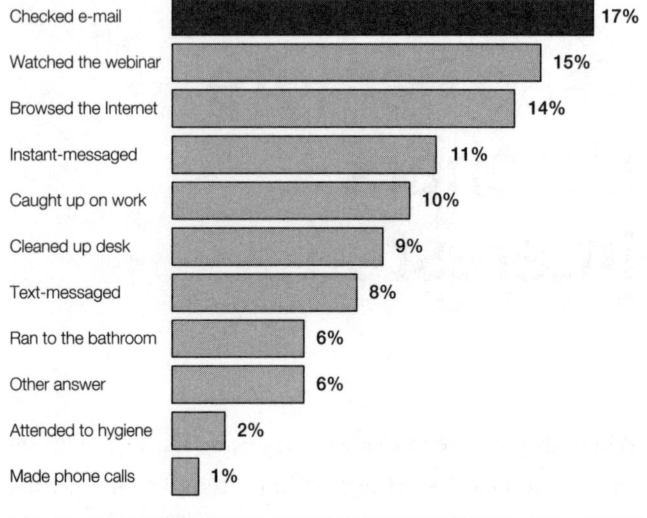

- **Make your presentation interactive:** Create useful activities for audience members to do, like spending a few minutes researching something and posting their findings in the chat window for everyone to see. If you ask people to take a survey, make sure the results will be of interest to them. And reward participants for paying close attention. When I was a guest on marketing consultant Chris Brogan's video blog, I placed a sign behind me that said, "First one who posts on Twitter that they saw this sign wins a free book."
- **Enjoy your own material:** Your enthusiasm needs to come through in your voice, especially if the

audience can't see you on video. Smile as you share your material—and your voice will automatically take on a more cheerful tone. And if you say something funny, laugh a bit even if no one's in the room with you—it invites listeners to laugh, too.

- **Vary the voices:** Bring in other voices for interest. Try cohosting your presentation with another subject matter expert and bantering like morning show hosts. The audience will reengage each time a new speaker talks.
- **Pause strategically:** When audiences tune out remote presenters, the presentations sound like white noise to them. Sprinkle in pauses before points you really want people to hear. That'll cut through the white noise. When you begin speaking again, people will notice. Sometimes pausing also makes the audience think there's a problem with the technology—and people reengage to fiddle with their computers.
- **Picture your listeners:** Remember that you're talking to people, not machines. Picture their faces in your mind and imagine that you're having a live conversation with them. When I first started to present remotely, I struggled with talking naturally to the camera. So I took photos of my smiley staff members, cut out their faces, and taped them above my monitor (figure 6-5). This served as a visual reminder that I was speaking to real people.

FIGURE 6-5

Visualizing real people

Keep Your Remote Presentation Running Smoothly

Since remote audiences are so susceptible to distraction, even minor annoyances can derail your presentation. Keep things running smoothly with the following checklist:

- **Provide clear instructions:** When you send out an invitation explaining what the presentation is about, spell out how to register and log in, and explain any technical requirements up front so people don't sign up only to discover later that they don't have the equipment to participate.
- **Plan for technology snafus:** Give the audience contact information for technical questions. E-mail handouts ahead of time, and have slides in a handy location online just in case the webinar technology fails.

- **Test your slides:** Some webinar software "breaks" your slides by not properly displaying animations, builds, and transitions. Many path-based animations don't work or are so choppy they are ineffective. Color contrast can fade, and photos become pixilated. Test your slides on the exact same machine you're presenting from, because different operating systems and software behave differently. Click through each slide in the software and fix any problems.

- **Start on time:** Set up at least 30 minutes in advance to make sure your audio and video are working properly. You don't want attendees to think you're ill prepared as they listen to you fuss with technology issues.

- **Reduce personal noise:** Remove loud jewelry like bangle bracelets or earrings that can bang loudly against a headset. Minimize fidgeting. Don't drum your fingers, click pens, shuffle paper, or take sips of water near the microphone.

- **Reduce environmental noise:** Close your door and turn off fans and music. Close out of computer applications that have alert noises. Mute your microphone in the remote app when someone else is speaking so people won't hear your breathing or throat clearing. Turn off your cell phone, and put your office phone on the "Do Not Disturb" setting. If people are dialing in for a teleconference, don't put your phone on hold—they'll hear your hold music. Mute it.

- **Reduce visual noise:** Hide unnecessary software application windows and icons on your computer desktop to help focus the audience's attention. Use your mouse as a pointing device; don't frantically zing the arrow around your slides.
- **Reduce communal noise:** Remote listeners can hear just one person at a time, so don't have multiple conversations going at once during a teleconference. If someone in your room asks a question, repeat it so the remote audience can hear it.
- **Use a facilitator:** Relieve some of your pre-presentation stress by asking a facilitator to manage many of the details, like wrangling the technology, setting up the room, sending out the agenda and slides ahead of time, monitoring chat rooms, conducting surveys, and making sure people in all locations get a chance to be heard.

Section 7
Impact

We are competing for relevance.

—**Brian Solis,**
principal analyst at Altimeter Group

Build Relationships Through Social Media

Social media channels give your audience a lot of control over your PR. People can broadcast bits of your content to their followers—quoting you, synthesizing your ideas, adding their own comments. Even if you have only 30 people in front of you when you speak, hundreds more—perhaps thousands, if your audience is highly networked—might catch a glimpse of what you're saying and what others think of it.

When the comments are positive, your ideas gain traction. At one event, a group of new attendees came to my talk about 15 minutes after I started. I found out afterward that an audience member had tweeted about my session, so some of his followers came to check it out.

But sometimes the comments aren't positive. Look at these sample tweets that went out during a higher-education conference presentation in Milwaukee:

@jrodgers
Starting to see the OMG I AM TRAPPED looks on faces. #heweb09

@jShelK
We need a drinking game for every time he says "actually" and "actionable." #heweb09

@stomer
We need a tshirt, "I survived the keynote disaster of 09." #heweb09

Within hours, someone created a shirt on CafePress and shared it with conference attendees (figure 7-1).

FIGURE 7-1

CafePress T-shirt

In *The Backchannel,* communication consultant Cliff Atkinson writes about social media's impact on presentations. He points out that the "backchannel"—the stream of chatter before, during, and after your talk—is constructive when it:

- Enriches your message as people take notes, add commentary, and suggest additional resources on the topic
- Provides a valuable archive of information to review after the presentation
- Connects people in the room, building a community around the ideas
- Allows people who can't attend your live talk to follow dispatches and engage in conversations about it
- Increases your reach to more people

It's destructive when it:

- Distracts audience members so they pay more attention to the backchannel than to you
- Steers the conversation to unrelated topics
- Excludes audience members who are unaware of the backchannel or unable to join
- Limits people's ability to convey nuance or context, because of the brevity of the posts
- Injects a rude or snarky tone, since people feel comfortable tweeting thoughts they wouldn't say out loud

Your goal is to avoid a backchannel revolt, where people rally one another to reject your message. How? By making the folks online feel *heard.*

With or without your involvement, they'll have conversations about you. So participate. Engage with people like a skilled conversationalist, and they'll engage more fully and fairly with your ideas.

Build relationships with them by:

- **Observing their behavior:** Pay attention to what else they're commenting on. Active social media users can point you to hot spots online—a LinkedIn discussion group, for instance, or a brand's fan page—where you can begin or join conversations with potential customers or advocates.

- **Providing a channel:** Create a Twitter hashtag for your presentation and invite audience members to use it to chat with you and one another about your message. (Of course, this is appropriate only for external presentations with broad audiences. You wouldn't broadcast content from confidential company meetings, for example, or client sales calls.) Encourage attendees to use the backchannel before, during, and after your presentation; display your hashtag on an introductory slide.

- **Asking for their input:** Try presenting a partially developed idea and asking people to help you refine it through social media. I do this all the time and get useful replies. When I don't know much about an audience I'm preparing to address, I'll do some digging on my own—but I'll also ask my Twitter channel what might be on the minds of people attending a certain event, for instance, or working for a particular company or industry.

Spread Your Ideas with Social Media

Use social media content the way you use stories, visuals, and sound bites: to reinforce and spread your message.

You can write blog entries, post photos, commission infographics, and produce videos that enhance your ideas so your audience feels compelled to share them with others. If you want to get started but don't generate a lot of content yet, tweet links to other experts' articles and blog posts that support your talk.

Social media activity usually spikes during a presentation, with moderate chatter beforehand and afterward. Facilitate the conversation at its peak by:

- **Streaming your presentation:** Post a live video stream of your talk so people can attend remotely. This is the most direct way of extending your reach online, because the full message comes through, not just the chatter around it.
- **Time-releasing messages and slides:** Craft messages and slides expressly for social me-

dia channels, and use technology to automatically push them out at key moments during the presentation. You can download social media tools to program the time-release. Or you can add 140-character phrases to your notes field in PowerPoint and set them to auto-tweet when you advance the slides.

- **Selecting a moderator:** Assign someone—a colleague, a guest blogger, an audience member—to keep the social media thread constructive. Pick a person who's quick-witted, with a strong command of your material. Ask her to tweet key phrases as you say them, raise thought-provoking questions online, and bring the chatter back on topic when it starts to stray. Also have your moderator send out links to your slides (post them on slideshare.com or as pdfs on your website).

- **Repeating audience sentiment:** In addition to broadcasting your message, the moderator should repeat (and validate) what live audience members are saying. The currency of social media is reciprocity: If you don't spread the ideas of others, yours probably won't get anywhere.

- **Posting photos of your talk:** Enlist someone to photograph your presentation. To give social media users a sense of immediacy, he can work with your moderator to post the images while you're speaking.

- **Encouraging blogging:** Invite bloggers, journalists, and social media specialists to attend and cover your presentation. You'll increase your reach exponentially through their outlets and followers.

Social media guru Dan Zarrella studied what types of social media content people like to share during presentations. Here are a couple of tips from his research:

- **Don't be too overt:** People want to identify what's worth spreading on their own. So resist the temptation to use a little Twitter bird to flag sound bites you want the audience to spread. They'll actually get shared *less*.

- **Be novel:** Close to 30% of respondents in Zarrella's study said they were more likely to tweet or blog about a presentation if it was novel or newsworthy. For an idea to spread, it needs to be distinct and stand out.

After you present, post a video of your talk on your website and on LinkedIn, Facebook, and other social media sites. Though most backchannel activity typically happens during the talk, presentations sometimes go viral after the fact. (Great ones can get hundreds of thousands of views week after week.) Posting a video will also help you capture new audience members who didn't know about your presentation when you gave it or weren't able to tune in to the streamed version or the backchannel.

Gauge Whether You've Connected with People

Gathering feedback on your talk in real time and after you're done gives you different kinds of insights—all of them valuable.

Watch the backchannel

Have a moderator keep an eye on social media and send text messages to your cell phone if she thinks you should address any criticisms in a Q&A at the end of your talk. (She should pass along tough but fair comments—and filter out any chatter that would completely throw you off-kilter.) Or, if you're comfortable tweaking your message as you go, try putting your phone in silent mode, setting it on the podium or table in front of you, and glancing at it throughout the presentation. If the audience begins to revolt on the backchannel, you can change direction. Let people know you've monitored their sentiment because you want to address their concerns.

Watch the live audience

People in the room will show how they're feeling through their posture and facial expressions. Keep a keen eye out for physical cues that they're engaged in your material. One reason Steve Jobs could maintain a heightened sense of anticipation during a 90-minute keynote is because he had a gift for eliciting frequent physical reactions. In his 2007 iPhone launch presentation, the audience laughed 79 times and clapped 98 times—that's about one reaction every 30 seconds.

It's important to pick up on negative cues, too, so you can change course. Are audience members leaning back with their arms crossed? That could be a sign of resistance. Do they look tired? Are they fidgeting? Looking around? Checking e-mail? They may be bored or apathetic toward your ideas. If they're not demonstrating engagement by leaning forward, nodding, smiling, and taking notes, find a way of drawing them in.

One conference presenter could easily tell from body language that he was missing the mark with his audience—people clearly weren't into his message. Instead of dragging on, he stopped, admitted that he'd miscalculated when he'd prepared, and asked if he'd be given a chance to speak at the next conference if he promised to do a better job of understanding the group's needs. He got a standing ovation and an invitation to come back the next year.

Survey your audience

A survey isn't quite as immediate as backchannel chatter and other real-time feedback, but it gives you more control over the kinds of insights you'll get from the audience—and the comments may be more thoughtful. Make it short and direct, and have people fill it out on paper, online, or by e-mail. Explicitly ask them to be candid. Project a slide at the end of your talk encouraging people to rate you either right away, with their phones or tablets, or at their leisure.

Organizers of large events often survey audiences at all the sessions. If you're speaking at such an event, ask for the results. Even if you're doing a much smaller, less-formal presentation, you can ask one or two audience members whose opinion you value to give you an honest read on how it went. Tell them you're trying to refine your skills, and they'll probably be glad to help.

Analyze sentiment

If you're giving a high-stakes talk to a large group—a keynote address, for example—it's probably worth analyzing social media data, such as how many people blogged about your talk, how much traffic was driven to the press announcement through social media, and whether the coverage and comments were negative or positive. This will give you an even finer-grained picture of how well you've connected with your audience.

But the data can be daunting if you don't know what you're doing. Hire an analytics specialist to really dig in and help you see where you did well and where you can improve. In the analysis, you may discover a rival you didn't know about, for instance, or a new key influencer who drives buying behavior.

Analyze your reach

You can also use analytics tools to measure how many people spread your message through social media, how many clicked on the shared links, and whether your message was picked up by the people you'd want to hear it. Again, work with a data specialist.

It takes an iron gut to digest critical feedback. But it will make you a better presenter. Look closely at what the audience is saying about you, and modify your message, visuals, and delivery so you'll resonate more deeply with people in the future.

I launched my speaking career at a small annual conference. The first survey I got back said that I delivered a fire hose of valuable information, but the audience felt no connection. The event organizer told me I should incorporate more personal stories. It was painful to hear, but true. I took the feedback very seriously. In fact, it sent me on a several-year journey studying story principles and structure, which I now apply to presentations.

I'm not suggesting that every piece of feedback you get will be useful or even true. Usually, though, if you put the audience's needs first when you create your content and you're sincere in your approach when you deliver it, people will want to help you succeed.

Follow Up After Your Talk

Your presentation is done, and the adrenaline has stopped pumping. Now what?

Once you've won people over to your point of view, help them implement your ideas. Encourage them. Bring them new insights. Remove roadblocks. Keep your message alive by:

- **Sending personal notes:** It's rare to get a nice handwritten note these days, and people appreciate it when they do. Send a note whenever you feel grateful—to a colleague who helped you set up your presentation, for example, or to a busy executive who made time to attend and voice her support. (I've sent a few "I'm sorry" notes, too—it works both ways.) It can be a formal branded thank-you note or a clever card that touches on a personal conversation you had with an audience member. In a world of digital communications, a human touch stands out.

- **E-mailing the audience:** Follow up with an e-mail thanking people for their time. If appropriate, summarize your big idea, key points, call to action, and "new bliss." Many times, event organizers will share their attendees' e-mail addresses with you in lieu of paying speaking fees.

- **Being accessible:** If you presented within your organization, being accessible can mean hosting a lunch immediately after your talk, for instance, or blocking off your calendar so you can have an open door to answer questions in more detail. If you spoke to a broader audience and don't have people's contact information, send out thank-yous and other follow-up messages through blog and social media posts. Respond to anyone who starts a thoughtful conversation with you.

- **Sending materials:** If you promised the audience any materials in your talk, get them out right away. You might want to offer thank-you gifts such as free books or access to secure content, but check with the audience first. Many people have contracts with their employers that don't allow them to accept gifts from vendors or industry influencers.

- **Calling or meeting with individuals:** Suppose you presented a new initiative that's going to be demanding on your team. Spend time listening to each member's concerns. Pick up the phone if it's not possible to talk to everyone in person. Insights from these conversations can help shape your next piece of communication with the group. If you discover, for instance, that people are most worried about limited resources, describe your plans for shoring them up.

- **Booking "next steps" meetings:** Gather folks afterward to answer questions that require some research or analysis, and work together on a roadmap for achieving your goals. Facilitate collaboration in any way you can—for instance, order in lunch and ask your project leaders to brainstorm ways of marketing your initiative internally.
- **Presenting again:** Though your presentation is done, you may need to do a few more like it to share your message with other groups and move your ideas along. If you're selling a product or service, the purpose of the first presentation is usually to get a second presentation—that is, face-to-face time with a decision maker.

Think of each interaction as one moment in a larger relationship with your audience. That's the mind-set it takes to persuade people to change their thinking and behavior—and their world of work.

Index

About the Author

Communication expert **Nancy Duarte** has more than 20 years of experience working with global organizations and thought leaders from a wide range of industries and fields. Her company, Duarte, Inc., has created more than a quarter of a million presentations for its clients. Her team also teaches corporate and public workshops on writing and storyboarding effective presentations.

Duarte is the author of two award-winning books: *Resonate: Present Visual Stories That Transform Audiences,* which spent nearly a year on Amazon's top 100 business book bestsellers list; and *Slide:ology: The Art and Science of Creating Great Presentations.*

Duarte has been featured in *Fortune, Forbes, Fast Company, Wired,* the *Wall Street Journal,* the *New York Times,* and the *LA Times,* and on CNN.

Notes

Notes

Notes

Notes

Notes

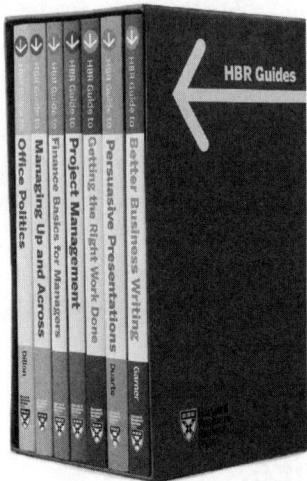

HBR Guide to **Better Business Writing**

Harvard Business Review Guides

Arm yourself with the advice you need to succeed on the job, from the most trusted brand in business. Packed with how-to essentials from leading experts, the HBR Guides provide smart answers to your most pressing work challenges.

The titles include:

HBR Guide to Better Business Writing

HBR Guide to Finance Basics for Managers

HBR Guide to Getting the Mentoring You Need

HBR Guide to Getting the Right Job

HBR Guide to Getting the Right Work Done

HBR Guide to Giving Effective Feedback

HBR Guide to Making Every Meeting Matter

HBR Guide to Managing Stress at Work

HBR Guide to Managing Up and Across

HBR Guide to Persuasive Presentations

HBR Guide to Project Management

Other Books Written or Edited by Bryan A. Garner

Garner's Modern American Usage

Garner's Dictionary of Legal Usage

Black's Law Dictionary (all editions since 1996)

Reading Law: The Interpretation of Legal Texts, with Justice Antonin Scalia

Making Your Case: The Art of Persuading Judges, with Justice Antonin Scalia

Garner on Language and Writing

The Redbook: A Manual on Legal Style

The Elements of Legal Style

The Chicago Manual of Style, Ch. 5, "Grammar and Usage" (15th & 16th eds.)

The Winning Brief

Legal Writing in Plain English

Ethical Communications for Lawyers

Securities Disclosure in Plain English

Guidelines for Drafting and Editing Court Rules

The Oxford Dictionary of American Usage and Style

A Handbook of Basic Legal Terms

A Handbook of Business Law Terms

A Handbook of Criminal Law Terms

A Handbook of Family Law Terms

HBR Guide to **Better Business Writing**

Bryan A. Garner

HARVARD BUSINESS REVIEW PRESS

Boston, Massachusetts

Printed in the United States of America

20 19 18 17

Library of Congress Cataloging-in-Publication Data

Garner, Bryan A.
HBR guide to better business writing / Bryan A. Garner.
p. cm. — (Harvard business review guides)
Includes bibliographical references and index.
ISBN 978-1-4221-8403-5 (alk. paper)
1. Commercial correspondence. 2. Business writing. I. Harvard business review. II. Title. III. Title: Guide to better business writing.
HF5718.3.G37 2013
808.06′665—dc23

2012032809

The paper used in this publication meets the requirements of the American National Standard for Permanence of Paper for Publications and Documents in Libraries and Archives Z39.48-1992.

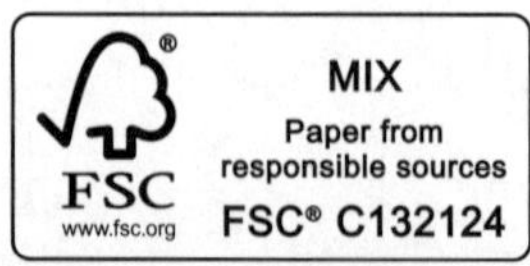

To J.P. Allen,
my lifelong friend

What You'll Learn

Do you freeze up when writing memos to senior executives? Do your reports meander and raise more questions than they answer for key stakeholders? Do your e-mails to colleagues disappear into a void, never to be answered or acted on? Do your proposals fail to win clients?

You'll lose a lot of time, money, and influence if you struggle with business writing. And it's a common problem. Many of us fumble for the right words and tone in our documents, even if we're articulate when we speak. But it doesn't have to be that way. Writing clearly and persuasively requires neither magic nor luck. It's a skill—and this guide will give you the confidence and the tools you need to cultivate it.

You'll get better at:

- Pushing past writer's block.
- Motivating readers to act.
- Organizing your ideas.
- Expressing your main points clearly.

- Cutting to the chase.
- Holding readers' attention.
- Writing concise, useful summaries.
- Trimming the fat from your documents.
- Striking the right tone.
- Avoiding grammar gaffes.

Contents

Introduction: Why you need to write well

You may think you shouldn't fuss about your writing—that good enough is good enough. But that mind-set is costly. Supervisors, colleagues, employees, clients, partners, and anyone else you communicate with will form an opinion of you from your writing. If it's artless and sloppy, they may assume your thinking is the same. And if you fail to convince them that they should care about your message, they *won't* care. They may even decide you're not worth doing business with. The stakes are that high.

Some people say it's not a big deal. They may feel complacent. Or they may think it's ideas that matter—not writing. But good writing gets ideas noticed. It gets them realized. So don't be misled: Writing well *is* a big deal.

Those who write poorly create barriers between themselves and their readers; those who write well connect with readers, open their minds, and achieve goals.

All it takes is a few words to make a strong impression, good or bad. Let's look at four brief passages—two effective and two not. See whether you can tell which ones are which:

1. In the business climate as it exists at this point in time, one might be justified in having the expectation that the recruitment and retention of new employees would be facilitated by the economic woes of the current job market. However, a number of entrepreneurial business people have discovered that it is no small accomplishment to add to their staff people who will contribute to their bottom line in a positive, beneficial way.

2. In this job market, you might think that hiring productive new employees would be easy. But many entrepreneurs still struggle to find good people.

3. The idea of compensating a celebrity who routinely uses social media to the tune of thousands of dollars to promote one's company by tweeting about it may strike one as unorthodox, to say the least. But the number of businesses appropriating and expending funds for such activities year on year as a means of promotion is very much on the rise.

4. Paying a celebrity thousands of dollars to promote your company in 140-character tweets

> may seem crazy. But more and more businesses are doing just that.

Can you tell the difference? Of course you can. The first and third examples are verbose and redundant. The syntax is convoluted and occasionally derails. The second and fourth examples are easy to understand, economical, and straightforward. They don't waste the reader's time.

You already recognize business writing that gets the job done—and trust me, you can learn to produce it. Maybe you think writing is a bother. Many people do. But there are time-tested methods for reducing the worry and labor. That's what you'll find in this book, along with lots of "before" and "after" examples that show these methods in action. (They're adapted from real documents, but disguised.)

Good writing isn't an inborn gift. It's a skill you cultivate, like so many others. Anyone of normal athletic ability can learn to shoot a basketball or hit a golf ball reasonably well. Anyone of normal intelligence and coordination can learn to play a musical instrument competently. And if you've read this far, you can learn to write well—probably very well—with the help of a few guiding principles.

Think of yourself as a professional writer

If you're in business, and you're writing anything to get results—e-mails, proposals, reports, you name it—then you're a professional writer. Broadly speaking, you belong to the same club as journalists, ad agencies, and book authors: Your success may well depend on the writing you produce and its effect on readers. That's why what you produce should be as polished as you can make it.

Here's an example you may be familiar with. Various versions of this story exist—it's sometimes placed in different cities and told with different twists:

> *A blind man sits in a park with a scrawled sign hanging from his neck saying, "I AM BLIND," and a tin cup in front of him. A passing ad writer pauses, seeing only three quarters in the cup. He asks, "Sir, may I change your sign?" "But this is my sign. My sister wrote it just as I said." "I understand. But I think I can help. Let me write on the back, and you can try it out." The blind man hesitantly agrees. Within two hours the cup is full of coins and bills. As another passerby donates, the blind man says: "Stop for a moment, please. What does my sign say?" "Just seven words," says the newest contributor: "It is spring, and I am blind."*

It matters how you say something.

Read carefully to pick up good style

To express yourself clearly and persuasively, you'll need to develop several qualities:

- An intense focus on your reason for writing—and on your readers' needs.
- A decided preference for the simplest words possible to express an idea accurately.

- A feel for natural idioms.
- An aversion to jargon and business-speak.
- An appreciation for the right words in the right places.
- An ear for tone.

How can you acquire these traits? Start by noticing their presence or absence in everything you read. Slow down just a little to study the work of pros. This shouldn't be a chore, and it shouldn't be squeezed in at the end of a long day. Grab a few spare minutes, over your morning coffee or between tasks, and read closely. Find good material that you enjoy. It could be the *Economist* or the *Wall Street Journal*, or even *Sports Illustrated*, which contains tremendous writing.

If you can, read at least one piece aloud each day as if you were a news announcer. (Yes, literally aloud.) Read with *feeling*. Heed the punctuation, the phrasing, the pacing of ideas, and the paragraphing. This habit will help cultivate an appreciation of the skills you're trying to acquire. And once you've honed your awareness, all you need is practice.

Recognize the payoff

An ambiguous letter or e-mail message will require a "corrective communication" to clear up a misunderstanding—which saps resources and goodwill. A poorly phrased and poorly reasoned memo may lead to bad decision-making. An ill-organized report can obscure important information and cause readers to overlook vital facts. A heavy, uninviting proposal will get put aside and forgotten. A badly drafted pitch to a key client will only consume the time of higher-ups who must rewrite it at the eleventh hour to make it passable—lowering its chances of success because of the hectic circumstances surrounding its preparation.

That's a lot of wasted time—and a drag on profits. But you can prevent these problems with clear, concise writing. It's not some mysterious art, secret and remote. It's an indispensable business tool. Learn how to use it, and achieve the results you're after.

One prefatory note: Asterisks are used in the text throughout this book to mark examples of incorrect English grammar, spelling, or usage.

Section 1
Delivering the Goods Quickly and Clearly

Chapter 1
Know why you're writing

Many people begin writing before they know what they're trying to accomplish. As a result, their readers don't know where to focus their attention or what they're supposed to do with the message. So much depends on your *purpose* in writing that you must fix it firmly in your mind. What do you want the outcome to be? Do you want to persuade someone to sign a franchise contract, for instance? Or to stop using your trademark without permission? Or to come to a company reception?

Say clearly and convincingly what the issue is and what you want to accomplish. With every sentence, ask yourself whether you're advancing the cause. That will help you find the best words to get your message across.

Form follows function

Say your firm rents space in an office building that has thoroughly renovated the entrance and the entire first floor. Your general counsel has alerted you that the landlord has violated the Americans with Disabilities Act (ADA). For example, there are no wheelchair-access ramps or automatic doors. You've decided to write to the landlord. But *why* are you writing? The answer to that question determines much of what you'll say and *all* of the tone that you'll use. Consider three versions of the letter you might write:

Version #1

You're good friends with the landlord, but you think that the law should be followed for the good of your employees and your customers. Purpose: to gather more information. Tone: friendly.

Dear Ann:

The new foyer looks fantastic. What a great way for us and others in the building to greet customers and other visitors. Thank you for undertaking the renovations.

Could it be that the work isn't finished? No accommodations have yet been made for wheelchair accessibility—as required by law. Perhaps I'm jumping the gun, and that part of the work just hasn't begun? Please let me know.

Let's get together for lunch soon.

All the best,

Version #2

You're on good terms with the landlord, but on principle, you don't like being in a building that isn't ADA-compliant. You have a disabled employee on staff, and you want the situation righted. Purpose: to correct the oversight. Tone: more urgent.

Dear Ann:

Here at Bergson Company, we were delighted when you renovated the first floor and made it so much more inviting to both tenants and visitors. We are troubled, however, by the lack of wheelchair-access ramps and automatic doors for handicapped employees and customers, both of which are required by state and federal law. Perhaps you're still planning that part of the renovations. If so, please advise.

If this was a mere oversight, can you assure us that construction on ramps and automatic doors will begin within 60 days? Otherwise, as we understand it, we may be obliged to report the violation to the Vermont Buildings Commission. Without the fixes, you may be subject to some hefty fines—but we feel certain that you have every intention of complying with the law.

Sincerely,

Version #3

You've had repeated problems with the landlord, and you have found a better rental property elsewhere for your company. Purpose: to terminate your lease. Tone: firm, but without burning bridges.

Dear Ms. Reynolds:

Four weeks ago you finished renovating the first floor of our building. Did you not seek legal counsel? You have violated the Americans with Disabilities Act—as well as state law—by failing to provide a wheelchair-access ramp and automatic doors for handicapped visitors and employees. Because four weeks have elapsed since you completed the work, we are entitled under state law to terminate our lease. This letter will serve as our 30 days' notice.

Although we have no doubt that your oversight was a good-faith error, we hope that you understand why we can't stay in the building and have made plans to go elsewhere.

We hope to remain on friendly terms during and after the move.

Sincerely,

These three letters are quite different because you are writing them to accomplish different things. Focus on the reaction you're trying to elicit from the reader. You want results. Yet notice how even the sternest letter—Version 3—maintains a civil tone to foster goodwill. No hostility is necessary.

Recap

- Consider your purpose and your audience *before* you begin writing, and let these guide both what you say and how you say it.
- Plainly state the issue you're addressing and what you hope to achieve.
- Keep your goal in mind: Don't undermine your efforts with a hostile or inappropriate tone.

Chapter 2
Understand your readers

Communication is a two-way exercise. Without knowing something about your readers—and about psychology in general, for that matter—you'll rarely get your ideas across. What are their goals and priorities? What pressures do they face? What motivates them?

Respect readers' time constraints

The most important things to realize about all business audiences are these:

- Your readers are busy—*very* busy.
- They have little if any sense of duty to read what you put before them.
- If you don't get to your point pretty quickly, they'll ignore you—just as you tend to ignore long, rambling messages when you receive them.

- At the slightest need to struggle to understand you, they'll stop trying—and think less of you.
- If they don't buy your message, you may as well have stayed in bed that day.

Each of these universal tendencies becomes magnified as you ascend the ranks of an organization. Your job as a writer, then, is to:

- Prove quickly that you have something valuable to say—valuable to *your readers,* not just to you.
- Waste no time in saying it.
- Write with such clarity and efficiency that reading your material is easy—even enjoyable.
- Use a tone that makes you likable, so that your readers will want to spend time with you and your message.

Do these things and you'll develop a larger reservoir of goodwill. You'll not only have a genuinely competitive edge, but you'll also save time and money.

Tailor your message

If you're writing a memo to colleagues, for example, consider where they sit in the organization and what they're expected to contribute to its success. Or if you're responding to a client's request for proposal, address every need outlined in the RFP—but also think about the client's industry, company size, and culture. Your tone will change depending on your recipients, and so will your content. You'll highlight the things they care about most—the ever-important "what's in it for them."

Connect with particular readers to connect with large audiences

It's challenging to write for a large, diverse group of readers, especially if you don't know them. But you can make it easier by focusing on some specific person you know. In his preface to the U.S. Securities and Exchange Commission's *Plain English Handbook*, Warren Buffett suggests grounding your prose by having a particular reader in mind:

> When writing Berkshire Hathaway's annual report, I pretend that I'm talking to my sisters. I have no trouble picturing them: Though highly intelligent, they are not experts in accounting or finance. They will understand plain English, but jargon may puzzle them. My goal is simply to give them the information I would wish them to supply me if our positions were reversed. To succeed, I don't need to be Shakespeare; I must, though, have a sincere desire to inform.

If you focus on a smart nonspecialist who's actually in your audience—or, like Buffett, imagine that you're writing for a relative or a friend—you'll strike a balance between sophistication and accessibility. Your writing will be more appealing and more persuasive.

Your readers may have little or no prior knowledge about the facts or analysis you're disclosing. But assume that they're intelligent people. They'll be able to follow you if you give them the information they need, and they won't be bamboozled by empty, airy talk.

NOT THIS:	BUT THIS:
We aspire to be a partner primarily concerned with providing our clients the maximal acquisition of future profits and assets and focus mainly on clients with complex and multi-product needs, large and midsized corporate entities, individual or multiple entrepreneurial agents, and profit-maximizing institutional clients. By listening attentively to their needs and offering them paramount solutions, we empower those who wish to gain access to our services with the optimal set of decisions in their possible action portfolio given the economic climate at the time of the advice as well as the fiscal constraints that you are subject to. Against the backdrop of significant changes within our industry, we strive to ensure that we consistently help our clients realize their goals and thrive, and we continue to strengthen the coverage of our key clients by process-dedicated teams of senior executives who can deliver and utilize our integrated business model. On the back of a strong capital position and high levels of client satisfaction and brand recognition, we have achieved significant gains in market share. We hope that you have a favorable impression of our company's quantitative and qualitative attributes and will be inclined to utilize our services as you embark on your financial endeavors.	We're a client-focused firm dedicated to making sure you get the most out of our services. Our client base includes individual entrepreneurs, midsized companies, and large corporations. If you decide to do business with us, we'll give you financial advice that is in tune with the current economy and with what you can afford to invest. For years, we've consistently received the highest possible industry ratings, and we have won the coveted Claiborne Award for exceptional client satisfaction 17 of our 37 years in business. We hope to have the opportunity to work with you in your financial endeavors.

Recap

- Understand that your readers have no time to waste: Get to the point quickly and clearly to ensure that your message gets read.
- Use a tone appropriate for your audience.
- Emphasize the items most important to your readers. If they can easily see how your message is relevant to them, they will be more likely to read it and respond.
- Choose an intelligent, nonspecialist member of your audience to write for—or invent one—and focus on writing for that person. Your message will be more accessible and persuasive to all your readers as a result.

Chapter 3

Divide the writing process into four separate tasks

Do you feel anxious every time you sit down to write? Your main difficulty is probably figuring out how to begin. Don't try to picture the completed piece before you've gathered and organized your material. It's much too soon to think about the final, polished product—and you will just make the challenge ahead of you seem overwhelming. The worry can take more out of you than the actual writing.

Instead, break up your work. Think of writing not as one huge task but as a series of smaller tasks. The poet, writer, and teacher Betty Sue Flowers has envisioned them as belonging to different characters in your brain: MACJ.[1] That stands for Madman–Architect–Carpenter–

1. Betty S. Flowers, "Madman, Architect, Carpenter, Judge: Roles and the Writing Process," *Proceedings of the Conference of College Teachers of English* 44 (1979): 7–10.

Judge, representing the phases that a writer must go through:

- **The Madman** gathers material and generates ideas.
- **The Architect** organizes information by drawing up an outline, however simple.
- **The Carpenter** puts your thoughts into words, laying out sentences and paragraphs by following the Architect's plan.
- **The Judge** is your quality-control character, polishing the expression throughout—everything from tightening language to correcting grammar and punctuation.

You'll be most efficient if you carry out these tasks pretty much in this order. Sure, you'll do some looping back. For example, you may need to draft more material after you've identified holes to fill. But do your best to compartmentalize the discrete tasks and address them in order.

Get the Madman started

Accept your good ideas gratefully whenever they come. But if you're methodical about brainstorming at the beginning of the process, you'll find that more and more of your good ideas will come to you early—and you'll largely prevent the problem of finally thinking of your best point after you've finished and distributed your document.

Get your material from memory, from research, from observation, from conversations with colleagues and others, and from reasoning, speculation, and imagination. The problem you're trying to solve may seem intractable, and you may struggle to find a good approach. (How on earth will you persuade the folks in finance to approve your budget request when they're turning down requests left and right? How will you get the executive board to adopt a new mind-set about a proposed merger?) Don't get hung up on the size of the challenge. Gathering ideas and facts up front will help you push through and defuse anxiety about the writing.

How do you keep track of all this preliminary material? In the old days, people used index cards. (I wrote my first several books that way.) But today the easiest way is to create a rough spreadsheet that contains the following:

- Labels indicating the points you're trying to support.
- The data, facts, and opinions you're recording under each point—taking care to put direct quotes within quotation marks.
- Your sources. Include the title and page number if citing a book or an article, the URL if citing an online source. (When writing a formal document, such as a report, see *The Chicago Manual of Style* for information on proper sourcing.)

As you're taking notes, distinguish facts from opinions. Be sure to give credit where it's due. You'll run aground if you claim others' assertions as your own, because you'll probably be unable to back them up convincingly. Worse, you'll be guilty of plagiarism.

This groundwork will save you loads of time when you're drafting and will help you create a well-supported, persuasive document.

Let the Architect take the lead

You may feel frustrated at first as you're groping for a way to organize your document. If a sensible approach doesn't come to mind after you've done your research and scouted for ideas, you may need to do more hunting and gathering. You want to arrive at the point of writing down three sentences—complete propositions—that convey your ideas. Then arrange them in the most logical order from the reader's point of view (see chapter 4). That's your bare-bones outline, which is all you typically need before you start drafting.

Give the Carpenter a tight schedule

The key to writing a sound first draft is to write as swiftly as you can (you'll read more about this in chapter 5). Later, you'll make corrections. But for now, don't slow yourself down to perfect your wording. If you do, you'll invite writer's block. Lock the Judge away at this stage, and try to write in a headlong rush.

Call in the Judge

Once you've got it all down, it's time for deliberation—weighing your words, filling in gaps, amplifying here and curtailing there. Make several sweeps, checking for one thing at a time: the accuracy of your citations, the tone, the quality of your transitions, and so on. (For an editorial checklist, see chapter 6.) If you try to do many things at once, you won't be doing any of them superbly. So leave plenty of time for multiple rounds of editing—at least as much time as you spent researching and writing. You'll ferret out more problems, and you'll find better fixes for them.

Recap

- Approach a writing project as a series of manageable tasks using the MACJ method.
- Use the Madman to gather research and other material for the project, diligently keeping track of quotations and sources. And allow more of your best ideas to come early by methodically brainstorming at the beginning of the process.
- As the Architect, organize the Madman's raw material into a sensible outline. Distill your ideas into three main propositions.
- In the Carpenter phase, write as quickly as possible—without worrying about perfecting your prose.
- Finally, assume the role of the Judge to edit, polish, and improve the piece. Do this in several distinct passes, each time focusing on only one element of your writing.

Chapter 4

Before writing in earnest, jot down your three main points—in complete sentences

A mathematician once told me that there are really only four numbers in the world: one, two, three, and many. There's something to that: Four items just seem to be one too many for most people to hold in their memory. But a proposal, a report, or any other piece of business writing feels underdeveloped when it's supported by only one or two points.

So write down your three main points as full sentences, and spell out your logic as clearly as you can. That way, you'll force yourself to think through your reasons for recommending a vendor, for example, or pitching an offer to a client—and you'll make a stronger case.

If you try to simply think things out as you write, you'll run into trouble because you won't really know yet what you're hoping your reader will think or do. You'll flail about, gradually clarifying your point as you make several runs at it. In the end, after multiple attempts, you may finally figure out what you have to say, but you probably won't say it in a way that your reader can follow.

An example of finding your focus

Let's say your name is Carol Sommers, and you work at a small management-consulting firm. Your boss, Steve, owns the business and is considering acquiring a 17,000-square-foot building as his new office. Because you're the office manager, Steve has asked you to think through the logistics and to write up your recommendations before the company makes an offer to purchase the building. At first, you're at a loss—there are so many issues to sort through. But you've got to start somewhere.

So before you write your memo, you put on your Madman hat and brainstorm a list of considerations:

- Ownership
- Maintenance
- Buildout
- Security
- Offices vs. cubicles
- Real-estate values—comparables?

- The move—bids on movers?
- Timing
- Tax consequences
- Employee and visitor parking
- Environmental inspection and related issues
- Smooth transitioning: phone and Internet service, mail forwarding, new stationery, updating business contacts, subscriptions, etc.
- Insurance
- Leaving current landlord on good terms
- Taking signage to new location?

These are just *topics,* not fully formed thoughts. But now that you have a rough list, you can start the Architect phase of writing and categorize in threes.

Steve's responsibilities (before acquisition):

- Consider an environmental inspection to make sure that the building has no hidden issues. Our commercial realtor can help.
- Check with our accountant to find out what tax consequences we might have depending on how we time the closing.
- Ask the accountant and perhaps a tax lawyer whether Steve should own the property personally, whether the company should own it, or whether a

newly formed entity (an LLC, for example) should own it. There may be liability issues.

My responsibilities (before acquisition):

- Cost out insurance coverage.
- Interview contractors for building out the space to our satisfaction. (Note to self: Confirm that we can roll the buildout into the mortgage.)
- Cost out the annual bill for providing the kind of security we currently have.

My responsibilities (postacquisition):

- Contract for maintenance (cleaning and trash services, lawn and parking-lot care).
- Plan the move, with a smooth transition in operations (the physical move, mail forwarding, phone and Internet, new stationery, address updates, announcement to customers, moving signage, etc.).
- Help Steve plan the architectural buildout to foster collaboration and use space efficiently.

To come up with all this, put yourself in Steve's place, imagining what you'd want *your* office manager to think of to help you do your job better. But it also takes a little legwork—for example, talking to people at firms that have recently changed locations or acquired buildings. Can't find anyone like that through your network? Ask the commercial realtor to put you in touch with one or two of its clients.

For each stage, we've listed the three big issues—at least what we *think* they are. Look how easy it is now to begin your Carpenter work (writing a useful memo to Steve):

Memo

To: Steve Haskell
From: Carol Sommers

Re: The Prospective Purchase of 1242 Maple Avenue
Date: April 12, 2012

As you requested, I've thought through the logistics of purchasing and moving into the Maple Avenue property. Here are my suggestions for each stage of the process.

Now

I'd like your approval to tackle the following tasks immediately because they'll give us a more complete picture of how expensive the acquisition and move would be:

- Cost out insurance coverage.
- Interview contractors for building out the space to our satisfaction. (I've checked with the bank to see if we can roll the buildout into the mortgage, and we can.)
- Cost out the annual bill for providing the kind of security we currently have.

Preclosing

If you decide to go forward with the purchase and your offer is accepted, I'll take care of these items before we close on the loan:

- Arrange for at least one thorough inspection of the building.
- Work with our accountant, to the extent you'd like, to get papers in order for obtaining the bank financing you mentioned.
- Ensure that all due-diligence deadlines are met.

After Closing

After closing, I'll get into the nuts and bolts of the move:

- Help you plan the architectural buildout to foster collaboration and use space efficiently.
- Plan the move, with a smooth transition in operations (the physical move, mail forwarding, phone and Internet, new stationery, address updates, announcement to customers, moving signage, etc.).
- Contract for maintenance (cleaning and trash services, lawn and parking-lot care).

Issues for You to Think About

While I'm attending to the details above, you might want to:

- Consider environmental and structural inspections to make sure the building has no hidden issues. Our commercial realtor says he can provide guidance—I'd be happy to set up a meeting if you like.
- Check with our accountant to find out what tax consequences we might have depending on how we time the closing.
- Ask the accountant and perhaps a tax lawyer whether you should own the property person-

> ally (highly unlikely), whether Haskell Company should own it, or whether a newly formed entity (such as an LLC) should own it. You or the company may face liability issues with outright ownership.

> Of course, I'm always on hand to take on whatever tasks you need. Just let me know.

Prewriting in threes resulted in a clear, useful memo. It helped us forestall writer's block, organize the material, and make concise, well-reasoned recommendations.

But did you notice that the finished memo breaks things down into four categories, not three? As hard as I tried to think of everything before writing the memo, I couldn't. Looking at my preliminary list, I identified a gap in time—a period in which there would be other necessary tasks. So I added the preclosing category and wrote those items on the fly. But I probably wouldn't have come up with them if I hadn't started with a plan. Organizing my main points in sets of three helped me see the preclosing gap; after that, filling it in wasn't difficult.

The order of categories changed, too. Why move Steve's tasks from the beginning to the end? The memo was about what you, Carol Sommers, the office manager, could do for Steve. To think of your responsibilities, you needed to think of Steve's. That was your starting point for brainstorming—but not for your memo.

You couldn't very well lead by telling your boss what he needs to do. That's not your place, and that's not what he asked for. So Steve's to-dos can go at the end, as helpful reminders. That way, you can focus his attention mainly on items you'll take care of to make his decisions easier.

Recap

- Find your focus by first generating a list of topics to cover.
- Develop these raw ideas into full sentences and categorize your main points in sets of three.
- Arrange these sets in a logical order, keeping your reader's needs in mind.

Chapter 5
Write in full—rapidly

Once you've written your three main points so that you know where you're going, you're in Carpenter mode—ready to put together the ideas you've generated and organized. Write as quickly as possible. Your sentences will be shorter than they otherwise would be, your idioms will be more natural, and your draft should start taking shape before you know it. If there's a painful part of writing, it's doing the first draft. When you shorten the duration, it's not as painful.

Time yourself

To prevent premature fussing, write against the clock. (Creative writers call this speed writing. They often use it as an exercise to get juices flowing.) Allow yourself 5 or 10 minutes to draft each section—the opener, the body, and the closer—and set the timer on your computer or phone to keep yourself honest.

Don't edit as you go

It's counterproductive to allow the Judge and the Carpenter to work side by side. That's essentially multitasking—you're just doing two things inefficiently rather than simultaneously. And besides, the editorial part of the brain is simply incompatible with the production part. Who needs a fault-finding critic's kibitzing when you're trying to create something new and fresh? You're best off keeping the Judge away as you produce your first draft. You'll spend plenty of time editing later.

Don't wait for inspiration

Inspiration rarely comes when you want it to. After the careful planning you've done, you won't need it anyway. As the management expert Peter Drucker famously said about innovation, good writing takes careful, conscious work, not a "flash of genius."

If you follow the MACJ process, you'll inspire *yourself*—and minimize your procrastinating. Once the Madman and the Architect have worked, you should be primed to write. Schedule the time when the Carpenter is to begin, and when the appointed time comes, get started.

Begin by writing in support of what you're most comfortable addressing. When you get stuck, skip to something else. You need to get into a flow. If you're still struggling when you come back to that problem passage, say out loud (to yourself or to a colleague) what you're trying to convey. Sometimes speaking will help you find the right words. The point is to get your ideas on paper—knowing that you'll still have time to elaborate and perfect them at the next stage.

Recap

- Write your first draft as quickly as you can.
- Don't get stuck waiting for inspiration. Try giving yourself 5 to 10 minutes for each section when drafting.
- Resist the urge to perfect as you write. Saving the editing until the draft is finished will keep the Judge from getting in your way.
- Schedule a time for the Carpenter to work—and when that time comes, begin.
- If you find yourself stumped, move on to a different section you're more comfortable with and come back to the problem once you've found your flow.

Chapter 6

Improve what you've written

Once you've written a complete draft, you'll revise first and then edit. Revising is a reconsideration of what you're saying as a whole, and where you're saying it. It's rethinking the floor plan. Editing is more a matter of fine-tuning sentences and paragraphs. You need to allow time for both. On the one hand, don't let some neurotic obsession with perfectionism delay important projects. On the other hand, don't rashly send things out without proper vetting and improvement.

Revising

As a reviser, you're asking several questions:

- Have I been utterly truthful?
- Have I said all that I need to say?
- Have I been appropriately diplomatic and fair?

- Do I have three parts to the piece—an opener, a middle, and a closer?
- In my opener, have I made my points quickly and clearly? And concretely?
- Have I avoided a slow wind-up that unnecessarily postpones the message?
- In the middle, have I proved my points with specifics?
- Is the structure immediately apparent to my readers? Have I used informative headings?
- Is my closer consistent with the rest—yet expressed freshly? Have I avoided lame repetition?

Editing

When it comes to editing, you're asking different questions as you read through your sentences and paragraphs:

- Can I save some words here?
- Is there a better way of phrasing this idea?
- Is my meaning unmistakable?
- Can I make it more interesting?
- Is the expression relaxed but refined?
- Does one sentence glide into the next, without discontinuities?

An example of revising and editing

To understand the process more concretely, let's take a look at how an internal memo takes shape through three drafts. The first draft is not very clear and omits important information, but the germ of an idea is there:

First Draft

> To: All Sales Personnel
> From: Chris Hedron
> Subject: Changes in Order-Processing Procedure
>
> In order to facilitate the customers' placement of orders, a new order-processing procedure has been designed. The process will require a customer to enter the product and/or service code into our order-entry system, which will then generate a quote for the job and return it to the customer for approval. This will make time for the customer to review the quote and transmit any changes before work begins. Upon receipt of the customer's written approval, the quote will be transformed into a work order. This procedure will make it easier and faster for us to process customers' orders.

This memo needs some amplification, especially in the realms of who, what, why, and when. The second draft, a full-fledged revision, fleshes out much that was unclear about the first draft.

Second Draft

> To: All Sales Personnel
> From: Chris Hedron
> Subject: New Work-Order-Processing Procedure
>
> Because our current work-order-processing procedure requires a lot of paperwork and phone calls, it's difficult for customers to make changes prior to the

> commencement of work. The procedure is inefficient and subject to numerous errors. And it takes up to four weeks from quote to approval to work order. So we have designed a new four-step order-processing procedure that will allow customers to place orders through our website and allow us to begin jobs faster.
>
> Beginning in January 2013, we will inform our customers about the new procedure, and on April 20, 2013, we will implement the new procedure, which will work as follows. First, to initiate or change a work order, customers can visit our website to request a quote by filling out a detailed form and providing a purchase-order number. Second, we will transmit a quote to the customer for approval. Third, if the customer approves, they can return the quote with an electronic signature and purchase-order number. Fourth, we will transform the quote to a work order immediately. Work-order changes can be made using the same procedure except that instead of a quote, customers will request a work-order change.

The focus there was on saying all that needed to be said—not on refining the expression. Now, though, it's possible to engage in fine-tuning and to produce a much-improved draft.

Third Draft

> To: All Sales Personnel
> From: Chris Hedron
> Subject: New Work-Order-Processing Procedure
>
> Our current work-order processing takes a lot of paperwork and phone calls, so it's hard for our customers to

make changes to the work before it begins. The procedure is inefficient and subject to error. And it takes up to four weeks from quote to approval to work order. We have therefore designed a new four-step procedure that has two key benefits: (1) Customers can place orders through our website, and (2) we can start jobs faster.

Beginning January 2013, we'll tell our customers about the new procedure. On April 20, 2013, we'll implement it. The new procedure will work in four steps:

- Customers can visit our website to request a quote for a job by filling out a form and providing a purchase-order number.
- We'll then send a quote for the customer's approval.
- The customer can return the approved quote with a digital signature.
- We'll instantly convert the quote to a work order.

Work-order changes can be made using the same procedure except that instead of a quote, customers will request a work-order change.

Recap

- Allow yourself ample time to revise and edit your work.

- Consider your draft in its entirety. Take a fresh look at your content and structure: Have you said everything you need to—and in the most effective way?

- Then edit your work, fine-tuning to tighten, sharpen, and refine your prose.

Chapter 7

Use graphics to illustrate and clarify

When you're writing about complex ideas, for example, or looking for useful ways to break up a long stretch of text, you can use a simple, elegant chart to convey critical information at a glance. Such graphics especially serve people who want to skim what you've written.

A few crucial principles:

- Make sure your graphics illustrate something discussed in the text.
- Place them near the text they illustrate, preferably on the same page or on a facing page.
- Use legends and keys that readers can easily grasp.

To learn how to produce effective graphics, consult the books of Edward Tufte, especially *Envisioning*

Information and *Beautiful Evidence.* You'll marvel at the amount of learning and the sophisticated thought that lie behind superb visuals.

It would be gross negligence to leave off without a graphic, so here's one to round out the section. Note that when you flip through this book, your eye stops here. That's because any departure from the norm achieves a special emphasis. If every third or fourth page had such a

FIGURE 7-1

The Who-Why-What-When-How Chart

Who are you writing for?	Key point: Consider your audience's concerns, motivations, and background.
Why are you writing?	Key point: Keep your purpose firmly in mind. Every sentence should advance it.
What needs saying?	Key point: Include only the main points and details that will get your message across.
When are you expecting actions to be taken?	Key point: State your time frame.
How will your communication benefit your readers?	Key point: Make it clear to readers how you're meeting their needs.

chart, the effect would be nullified. So make your graphics distinctive—and don't overuse them.

Recap

- Distill your report (or part of it) into a chart, diagram, or other visual aid that helps your audience understand the content and its import.
- Take your design cues from visuals you have found effective.
- Read the books of Edward Tufte to develop this skill.

Section 2
Developing Your Skills

Chapter 8
Be relentlessly clear

Clarity can be a double-edged sword. When you're forthright enough to take a position or recommend a course of action, you're sticking your neck out. People who don't want to commit make their writing muddy. Perhaps they're trying to leave room for their views to evolve as events unfold. Or perhaps they're hoping they can later claim credit for good results and deny responsibility for bad ones.

The fact is, though, that many readers will perceive them not as savvy wait-and-see participants but as spineless herd-followers who are slow to see (much less seize) opportunities within their reach. So clean up the mud.

Adopt the reader's perspective

Always judge clarity from the reader's standpoint—not your own. Try showing a draft to colleagues with fresh eyes and asking them what they think your main points are. If they can't do that accurately, then you're not being clear enough.

Your ideal should be to write so unmistakably that your readers can't possibly misunderstand or misinterpret. Anything that requires undue effort from them won't be read with full attention—and is bound to be misunderstood.

Keep your language simple

Simplicity breeds clarity. Strive to use short words and sentences. Over the years, research has confirmed again and again that the optimal average for readable sentences is no more than 20 words. You'll need variety to hold interest—some very short sentences and some longer ones—but aim for an average of 20 words. With every sentence, ask yourself whether you can say it more briefly.

NOT THIS:	BUT THIS:
Efficiency measures that have been implemented by the company with strong involvement of senior management have generated cost savings while at the very same time assisting in the building of a culture that is centered around the value of efficiency. We anticipate that, given this excising of unnecessary expenditures and enhanced control of other expenditures, the overall profitability of the company will be increased in the near term of up to four quarters.	Our senior management team has cut costs and made the company more efficient. We expect to be more profitable for the next four quarters.

If you're writing about technical matters for an audience of nonspecialists—for example, explaining the benefits of a software upgrade to end users or putting together an investment primer for your company's 401(k) participants—don't try to define each term in the sentence where it first appears. That will bulk up your sentences and make the material even harder for people to grasp. Sometimes you'll need a new sentence or even a new paragraph to explain a term or concept in simple, straightforward English.

Show, don't tell

You probably heard writing teachers in school say, "Show, don't tell." It's excellent advice no matter what you're writing—even business documents. The point is to be specific enough that you lead your readers to draw their own conclusions (conclusions that match yours, of course), as opposed to simply expressing your opinions without support and hoping people will buy them.

Consider these examples:

NOT THIS:	BUT THIS:
He was a bad boss.	He got a promotion based on his assistant's detailed reports, but then—despite the company's record profits—denied that assistant even routine cost-of-living raises.
The company lost its focus and floundered.	The CEO acquired five unrelated subsidiaries—as far afield as a paper company and a retailer of children's toys—and then couldn't service the $26 million in debt.
The shares of OJM stock issued to Pantheon stockholders in the merger will constitute a significant proportion of the outstanding stock of OJM after the merger. Based on this significant proportion, it is expected that OJM will issue millions of OJM shares to Pantheon stockholders in the merger.	We expect that OJM will issue about 320 million shares of its stock to Pantheon shareholders in the merger. That figure will account for about 42% of OJM's outstanding stock after the merger.

WRITE LETTERS TO SHARPEN YOUR SKILLS

Your letter writing is the best barometer of your writing skills generally. And it's a safe way to practice—to prepare yourself for your more difficult writing tasks. Write thank-you letters, congratulatory letters, letters of recommendation (when asked), complaint letters, letters to the editor, personal notes (handwritten), and all sorts of others. If you can write good letters, you can write just about anything. (See chapter 19, "Business Letters," for pointers on how.) That's because they help you to focus on *others*. When you write a letter, you're connecting with one particular recipient. And letters help you build goodwill with people. An e-mail message may create an impression, but it's far less likely to be remembered than a personal letter is.

To develop the habit, try writing a few letters a week. Make many of them handwritten notes. (When you receive one in a stack of mail, isn't that the first thing that grabs your attention?) They're personal and, if well done, memorable and even savable. They'll help you build and maintain relationships. Write them to tell those you supervise how much you appreciate their hard work, congratulate colleagues on promotions, motivate team members to meet goals, let new partners know you're eager to start collaborating, and so on. To write a good one, keep it neat, try limiting it to one page, make it warm and friendly, use *you* more than *I*, and use tasteful, mature stationery.

A short, vague sentence (like "He was a bad boss") may register in the readers' minds—but only as a personal impression that's potentially biased. It's credible only if its source is highly credible. As for the long, vague sentence about OJM stock, there's nothing for readers to hold on to, and they'll get tired trying.

Concrete business writing is persuasive because it's evidence-based, clear, and memorable. When you supply meaningful, objective details (explaining, for example, that the floundering company "couldn't service the $26 million in debt"), you're sharing information, not just your opinion that the company "lost its focus." You earn credibility by demonstrating a command of the facts. You also give your message staying power. People don't care about—or even remember—abstractions the way they do specifics.

So if you're marketing your firm's consulting services to potential clients, don't just tell them you'll save them money. Say how much money you've saved others. Don't just promise that you'll make their lives easier. List the time-consuming tasks you'll take off their hands. Don't just claim to have deep experience in the health care industry. *Name names:* Mention several hospitals and medical centers you've done work for, and include testimonials saying how happy clients are with the time and money you've saved them.

Recap

- Put yourself in the reader's shoes to assess your clarity. Better yet, see whether a colleague can accurately summarize the main points of your draft from a quick read-through.

- Phrase your ideas as plainly and briefly as possible, aiming for an average sentence length of 20 or fewer words.
- Pave your readers' way with concrete details. Don't try to push them there with abstract assertions.
- Cultivate your letter writing to improve your writing skills more generally.

Chapter 9
Learn to summarize—accurately

A good summary is focused and specific—and it's at the beginning of your document so readers don't have to dig. It gets to the point. It lays the foundation for what's to follow. There's no holding back on the crucial information.

Consider the difference between these two openers to a recommendation that a proposal be rejected:

NOT THIS:

Summary

The cell phone changeover that has been proposed should be rejected. For the reasons stated below, the company would not be well served by accepting the proposal.

BUT THIS:

Summary

Last year, we adopted an officewide policy of issuing cell phones to all executives and sales reps at an annual cost of $58,000 (including voice and data plans). The Persephone company has proposed that we switch to its phones and service at an annual cost of $37,000. The committee charged with evaluating this proposal recommends that we reject it for four reasons:

1. The new plans would have significantly less coverage in Europe and Asia, so our international sales reps might suffer lost opportunities.
2. Our current provider has been highly responsive and has tailored its service to our needs.
3. The $21,000 savings is dwarfed by potential costs (even one dropped sales call could result in a loss of much more money than that).
4. Persephone's customer service appears from credible online reviews to be inferior.

What makes the second version better? It can be fully understood by anyone who reads it—at any time. The first version, by contrast, assumes familiarity: It's clear to only a few "insiders"—and for only a limited period. And because it's vague, it lacks the credibility that the second version earns through specifics.

Struggling to incorporate the right amount of detail to make your summary clear and useful? Write a descriptive outline of your document—summarize each paragraph or section with a sentence that captures the who, what, when, where, why, and how—and try creating your overall summary out of that. Also, keep your readers' needs foremost in your mind. What questions will people have when they open your document? Provide brief but concrete answers to those questions. These will assure readers that what follows will matter to them.

Be brief—but not too brief

People often assume that shorter is better when it comes to summaries. But brevity without substance is worthless. Never say more than the occasion demands—but never say less, either. Adopt the reader's perspective: Fill in as much information as it takes to get people up to speed. Think of your summary as the CliffsNotes version of your document. Although the second example is longer, it conveys the whole gist of the message. And there's not one wasted word, which brings us to our next chapter.

Recap

- Summarize the vital information at the beginning of the document.
- Summarize each section with a sentence that addresses "the five Ws" (who, what, when, where, why) and how—and use these sentences to build your general summary.
- Provide only the information the reader needs to understand the issue—no more and no less.

Chapter 10
Waste no words

Make every word count. When you mean *before,* don't say or write *prior to,* much less *prior to the time when.*

Though *prior to* is a linguistic choice that the dictionary offers us, it's a bad choice. Never use two words for one, three words for two, and so on. Syllables add up fast and slow people down. Of course, stick to idiomatic English. Don't start dropping articles (*a, an, the*) where we'd all normally expect them. And don't cut the important word *that* left and right—more often than not, you really need it to be clear. But remove all the words that aren't performing a real function. Doing so saves readers time and effort and makes your ideas easier to grasp and apply.

Wordiness can exist on many levels, from rambling statements to unnecessary repetition to verbose expressions that could be replaced by shorter, sharper alternatives. Whatever the manifestation, it's bad. Consider the following examples:

NOT THIS:	BUT THIS:
The trend in the industry is toward self-generation by some companies of their own websites, and Internet technology is changing the nature of training necessary to acquire the skill of website development at an acceptable level of sophistication, so that this activity can more and more be handled in-house. [49 words]	Since Internet technology makes it easier than ever to develop sophisticated websites, some companies now develop their own in-house. [19 words]
We are unable to fill your order at this point in time because there is an ongoing dock strike that affects our operations. [23 words]	We cannot fill your order right now because of the dock strike. [12 words]
I am writing in response to a number of issues that have arisen with regard to the recent announcement that there will be an increase in the charge for the use of our lobby computers. [35 words]	You may have heard that we're raising the fees for using our lobby computers. [14 words]
The greater number of these problems can readily be dealt with in such a way as to bring about satisfactory solutions. [21 words]	Most of these problems can be readily solved. [8 words]

To trim extra words from your documents, try:

- Deleting every preposition that you can, especially *of*: change *April of 2013* to *April 2013* and *point of view* to *viewpoint.*

- Replacing every *–ion* word with a verb if you can. Change *was in violation of* to *violated* and *provided protection to* to *protected.*

- Replacing *is, are, was,* and *were* with stronger verbs where you can. Change *was hanging* to *hung* and *is indicative of* to *indicates.*

You'll see all three tricks at work here:

NOT THIS:	**BUT THIS:**
The manufacturers of tools for gardening have been the victims of a compression factor that has resulted in an increase in units on the market accompanied by a negative disproportionate rise of prices. [36 words]	The garden-tool industry has suffered from an oversupply of units coupled with rising prices. [14 words]
For the near and intermediate future in terms of growth goals, Bromodrotics, Inc., is evaluating its corporate design needs. The purpose of this short-term and intermediate-term evaluation is to make a determination as to how the image of the company might best be positioned to be of assistance to the sales force in meeting its growth goals. [57 words]	To increase sales, Bromodrotics needs to improve its image. [9 words]

Ruthlessly cut words from your first draft, so long as you remain faithful to the sounds and rhythms of normal, down-to-earth English. Don't compress words to the point of sounding curt or unnatural.

One other trick in that last example: eliminating padding such as *in terms of* and *the purpose of.* Sometimes you'll find even worse phrases:

in this connection it might be observed that

it is important to bear in mind that

it is interesting that

it is notable that

it is worthwhile to note that

it should be pointed out that

it will be remembered that

Leave all these things unsaid—without saying *it goes without saying that . . . .*

Recap

- Never use more words than necessary: If you can say it in two words instead of three, do so—as long as the result still sounds natural.
- Tighten your prose by removing inessential prepositions, replacing abstract *-ion* nouns with action verbs where possible, and replacing wordy *be*-verb phrases with more direct simple verbs.
- Eliminate padding that doesn't contribute to your meaning.

Chapter 11

Be plain-spoken: Avoid bizspeak

It's mission-critical to be plain-spoken, whether you're trying to be best-of-breed at outside-the-box thinking or simply incentivizing colleagues to achieve a paradigm shift in core-performance value-adds. Leading-edge leveraging of your plain-English skill set will ensure that your actionable items synergize future-proof assets with your global-knowledge repository.

Just kidding. Seriously, though, it's important to write plainly. You want to sound like a person, not an institution. But it's hard to do, especially if you work with people who are addicted to buzzwords. It takes a lot of practice.

Back when journalists were somewhat more fastidious with the language than they are today, newspaper editors often kept an "index expurgatorius": a roster of words and phrases that under no circumstances (except perhaps in a damning quote) would find their way into print. Here's such a list for the business writer. Of course, it's just a starting point—add to it as you come across other examples of bizspeak that hinder communication by substituting clichés for actual thought.

Bizspeak Blacklist

actionable (apart from legal action)

agreeance

as per

at the end of the day

back of the envelope

bandwidth (outside electronics)

bring our A game

client-centered

come-to-Jesus

core competency

CYA

drill down

ducks in a row

forward initiative

going forward

go rogue

guesstimate

harvesting efficiencies

hit the ground running

impact (as verb)

incent

incentivize

impactful

kick the can down the road

Let's do lunch.

Let's take this offline.

level the playing field

leverage (as verb)

liaise

mission-critical

monetize

net-net

on the same page

operationalize

optimize

out of pocket (except in reference to expenses)

paradigm shift

parameters

per

planful

pursuant to

push the envelope

putting lipstick on a pig

recontextualize

repurpose

rightsized

sacred cow

scalable

seamless integration

seismic shift (outside earthquake references)

smartsized

strategic alliance

strategic dynamism

synergize; synergy

think outside the box

throw it against the wall and see if it sticks

throw under the bus

turnkey

under the radar

utilization; utilize

value-added

verbage (the correct term is *verbiage*—in reference only to verbose phrasings)

where the rubber meets the road

win-win

These phrases have become voguish in business—abstain if you can. Sometimes people use them to enhance their own sense of belonging or to sound "in the know." Or they've been taught that good writing is hyperformal, so they stiffen up when they use a keyboard or pick up a pen, and they pile on the clichés.

It takes experience to bring your written voice into line with your spoken voice and to polish it so well that no one notices the polish.

NOT THIS:	BUT THIS:
The reduction in monthly assessments which will occur beginning next month has been made financially feasible *as a result of leveraging* our substantial reductions in expenditures.	We'll be cutting your assessments beginning next month because we've saved on expenses.
It is to be noted that a considerable amount of savings has been made possible *by reason of our planful initiation of* more efficient and effective purchasing procedures.	We've saved considerable sums by streamlining our purchases.

Hunt for offending phrases

Start looking for bizspeak in all kinds of documents, from memos to marketing plans, and you'll find it everywhere. You'll eventually learn to spot it—and avoid it—in your own writing. You'll omit canned language such as *Attached please find* and other phrases that only clutter your message.

Bizspeak may seem like a convenient shorthand, but it suggests to readers that you're on autopilot, thoughtlessly using boilerplate phrases that people have heard over and over. Brief, readable documents, by contrast, show care and thought. *Attached please find* is just one example among many:

NOT THIS:	**BUT THIS:**
at your earliest convenience	as soon as you can
in light of the fact that	because
we are in receipt of	we've received
as per our telephone conversation on today's date	as we discussed this morning
Pursuant to your instructions, I met with Roger Smith today regarding the above-mentioned.	As you asked, I met with Roger Smith today.
Please be advised that the deadline for the above-mentioned competition is Monday, April 2, 2012.	The deadline is April 2, 2012.
Thank you for your courtesy and cooperation regarding this matter.	Thank you.
Thank you in advance for your courtesy and cooperation in this regard. Please do not hesitate to contact me if you have any questions regarding this request.	Thank you. If you have any questions, please call.

Writing plainly means expressing ideas as straightforwardly as you can—without sacrificing meaning or tone.

Take Warren Buffett again, one of the smartest business leaders on the planet—and someone, by the way, who cares a lot about good business writing. Consider how he rewrote a short passage that he found in a financial-services firm's business prospectus. Read through the first excerpt before you read Buffett's translation below it, and note the bizspeak phrases that landed on the cutting-room floor as Buffett tightened and translated:

NOT THIS:

Maturity and duration management decisions are made *in the context of* an intermediate maturity orientation. The maturity structure of the portfolio is adjusted *in the anticipation of* cyclical interest-rate changes. Such adjustments are not made *in an effort to* capture short-term, day-to-day movements in the market, but instead *are implemented in anticipation of* longer-term, secular shifts in the interest rates (*i.e.*, shifts transcending *and/or* not inherent to the business cycle). Adjustments made to shorten portfolio maturity and duration are made to limit capital losses during periods when interest rates are expected to rise. Conversely, adjustments made to lengthen maturation for the portfolio's maturity and duration strategy lies *in the analysis of* the U.S. and global economies, focusing on levels of real interest rates, monetary and fiscal policy actions, and cyclical indicators.

Words: 136
Sentences: 5 (All passive voice)
Average sentence length: 27.2
Flesch Reading Ease: 8.2

BUT THIS:

We will try to profit by correctly predicting future interest rates. When we have no strong opinion, we will generally hold intermediate-term bonds. But when we expect a major and sustained increase in rates, we will concentrate on short-term issues. And conversely, if we expect a major shift to lower rates, we will buy long bonds. We will focus on the big picture and won't make moves based on short-term considerations.

Words: 74
Sentences: 5 (None passive voice)
Average sentence length: 14.8
Flesch Reading Ease: 60.1

If you analyze the before-and-after prospectuses under the Flesch Reading Ease (FRE) scale—a test developed by readability expert Rudolf Flesch to measure the comprehensibility of written passages using word and sentence length—you can quantify the difference. The higher the score, the easier the passage is to read and comprehend. On a scale of 0–100, the original 136-word prospectus on top scores an 8.2. In contrast, Warren Buffett's revision below it scores a 60.1. To give some perspective, *Reader's Digest* scores 65 on the FRE scale, *Time* magazine around 52, and the *Harvard Law Review* in the low 30s. Increasing a passage's readability is not the same as "dumbing it down." The revised passage above gives the reader the same information—but more clearly.

Here's a shorter example, this time from a community college's mission statement:

NOT THIS:

The object of this enterprise is *to facilitate the development of greater capacities* for community colleges and not-for-profit neighborhood organizations to *engage in heightened collaboration in regard to the provision of* community services that would *maximize the available resources* from a number of community stakeholders and to *provide a greater level of* communication about local prioritization of educational needs with the particular community.

[63 words]

BUT THIS:

This project seeks to help community colleges and nonprofit neighborhood groups work more efficiently together.

[15 words]

In both the Buffett example and the community-college example, the original versions seem to be aiming at something other than getting the point across. Perhaps the writers wanted to sound impressive, or wanted to obscure what they were actually up to, or wanted to cover up the fact that they weren't entirely sure what they were up to. Whatever the answer, the original styles won't work on any target audience.

Recap

- Aim to write as naturally as you speak: Sound like a human being, not a corporation.
- Avoid boilerplate phrases that weigh down your language and suggest lazy thinking.
- Increase readability by expressing your ideas as directly as possible.

Chapter 12

Use chronology when giving a factual account

Stories are inherently chronological. One thing happens, then another, then another. That structure works well not only in books and films but also in business writing. It's more likely to be clear and efficient, and to keep readers interested. So include "just the facts, ma'am," as Joe Friday on the old TV series *Dragnet* used to say. Just the facts that *matter*, and in the right order.

In theory this point seems obvious, but in practice writers find storytelling difficult. They often dive straight into the middle without orienting their readers, and the inevitable result is confusion on the receiving end. You're familiar with this phenomenon. It happens all the time in conversations with friends or family members: "Wait a minute. Back up. When was this? Where were you? And why were you talking to this guy? And where'd he come from?"

Suppose you're sending an e-mail message to give the status of an ongoing project, and it's been some time since the last update. The recipient isn't as immersed in the project as you are and probably has many other things going on. So remind your reader where things stood when you last communicated about the subject, and describe what's happened since then:

NOT THIS:	**BUT THIS:**
Sarah— It was hard making headway with Jim Martinez, but finally we're looking (in the best-case scenario) at a demonstration of what our software can do by mid-May, as I established in my first telephone conference with Jim last Monday at 9:00 a.m. He was out Wednesday and Thursday (I didn't see any reason to try calling on Tuesday), but on Friday he told me that we'd need a sample app. But prior to that, Magnabilify requires an NDA. Tuesday's meeting should clarify things. Let me know what you think. Frank	Sarah— Last week you asked me to approach Magnabilify Corporation, the software developers, to see whether they might have any interest in our customizing some security applications for their computer systems. I finally got through to Jim Martinez, corporate vice president in charge of software, and we have planned a face-to-face meeting at his office next Tuesday. The next steps, as I understand them under Magnabilify's protocol, will be to enter into a nondisclosure agreement, to develop a sample application (in less than two weeks), and to schedule a demonstration shortly after. Can you and I chat before Tuesday's meeting? Frank

The version on the left reads like stream-of-consciousness. The writer didn't take the time to step back, think of the message from the reader's perspective, and then lay out the important points chronologically. A story, even a short one like the narrative on the right, holds the reader's interest more effectively than jumbled facts interspersed with opinions.

Plot out what happened, and when

When a serious dispute arises within a company, the lawyers will typically ask their clients to produce a "chronology of relevant events," detailing the most important incidents leading up to the dispute. This document helps everyone involved think more clearly about how things unfolded. Try taking a similar approach when writing a document that walks the reader through a series of events—whether you're sending someone a project update or preparing an employee's performance evaluation. Create a chronology of relevant events to organize the narrative. Say you did that before drafting your e-mail message to Sarah in the right-hand example. Here's how it might look:

Chronology of relevant events

Last week	Sarah asked me to gauge Magnabilify's interest in having us build customized security applications.
Today	I spoke with Jim Martinez.
Next Tuesday	Jim and I will meet at his office to discuss.
In two weeks	If Magnabilify is interested, we'll do an NDA, develop a sample app, and schedule a demo.

Once you've laid out the chronology like this, drafting the e-mail message becomes a lot easier—just a matter of stringing the events together and asking to meet with Sarah before next Tuesday's meeting.

Recap

- Include only the relevant facts.
- Provide them in chronological order to make it easy for your readers to follow you.
- Organize your narrative by creating a chronology of relevant events before you write; then string the events together in your draft. But avoid the rote recitation of unnecessary dates.

Chapter 13

Be a stickler for continuity

Smooth writing consists of a sequence of well-joined sentences and paragraphs, not a mere collection of them. This smooth sequencing requires good planning and skill in handling transitions, or links that help readers follow your train of thought.

Watch how a good writer on business ethics, Manuel G. Velasquez, does it with a series of paragraph openers (the links are indicated here by italics):

A Series of Paragraph Openers from Manuel G. Velasquez's* Business Ethics *(2011)

1. *How well* does a free monopoly market succeed in achieving the moral values that characterize perfectly competitive free markets? Not well.

2. The *most obvious failure* of monopoly markets lies in the high prices they enable the

monopolist to charge and the high profits they enable him to reap, a failure that violates capitalist justice.

3. A monopoly market *also* results in a decline in the efficiency with which it allocates and distributes goods.

4. *First,* the monopoly market allows resources to be used in ways that will produce shortages of those things buyers want and cause them to be sold at higher prices than necessary.

5. *Second,* monopoly markets do not encourage suppliers to use resources in ways that will minimize the resources consumed to produce a certain amount of a commodity.

6. *Third,* a monopoly market allows the seller to introduce price differentials that block consumers from putting together the most satisfying bundle of commodities they can purchase given the commodities available and the money they can spend.

7. Monopoly markets *also* embody restrictions on the negative rights that perfectly free markets respect.

8. A monopoly market, *then,* is one that deviates from the ideals of capitalist justice, economic utility, and negative rights.

The italicized transitional phrases steer us from one idea to the next. Normally, we wouldn't even notice them. The transitions in really good writing are almost subliminal—but they're carefully placed where readers will need them. These connections take readers forward in different ways. They can:

- **Establish a time sequence:** *then, at that point, afterward, as soon as, at last, before, after, first, initially, meanwhile, later, next, now, once, originally, since, then, until, finally*
- **Establish place:** *there, in that place, at the front, in back, farther back, in the rear, at the center, to the left (right), up front, way back*
- **Add a point:** *and, or, further, also, in fact, moreover, not only . . . but also*
- **Underscore a point:** *above all, after all, and so, chiefly, equally important, more so, indeed, more important*
- **Concede a point:** *although, and yet, admittedly, at the same time, certainly, even though, doubtless, granted, no doubt, of course, still, though, to be sure, whereas, yet, while*
- **Return to a point:** *even so, nevertheless, nonetheless, still*
- **Give an example:** *for example, for instance, in particular*
- **Provide a reason:** *because, hence, thus, for, it follows, since, so, then, therefore*

- **Set up a contrast:** *but, yet, and yet, conversely, despite, by contrast, instead, on the other hand, still, then, while*

- **Set up a conclusion:** *so, as a result, finally, in conclusion, in short, in sum, on the whole, therefore, thus, to sum up*

Use subheads as transitions

No matter how smooth your transitions are between sentences and paragraphs, time-pressed readers will zone out if you place a solid wall of text in front of them. Break up your documents (even e-mails that are longer than a paragraph) with some signposts to lead people from section to section and help them quickly locate the parts they're particularly interested in. A "summary" subhead, for example, tells readers where to find just the highlights. And subheads that concisely yet clearly lay out your key points allow people to skim and still get the gist of your message.

Make your subheads as consistent as you can. For instance, if you're leading a task force that's recommending ways to forge direct customer relationships through social media, you might write each subhead in your body text as a directive, along these lines:

Use LinkedIn to Get Feedback on Current Products

Use Facebook to Test New Concepts

Use Twitter to Facilitate Chats About Live Events

The parallelism will help your document hang together both rhetorically and logically.

Recap

- Use well-placed transitional phrases to guide the reader to your next idea and indicate its relationship to what came before.
- Break up documents with concise, descriptive subheads to increase readability and help readers quickly locate the information most important to them.
- Use a "summary" subhead to point your readers to the document's highlights.
- Use consistent style and parallel syntax in your subheads to reinforce the document's logical and rhetorical cohesion.

Chapter 14

Learn the basics of correct grammar

Why nitpick about grammar? Because readers may see your language—especially your use of your native language—as a reflection of your competence. Make lots of mistakes and you'll come across as uneducated and uninformed. People will hesitate to trust your recommendation to launch a resource-intensive project, for example, or to buy goods or services. They may think you don't know what you're talking about.

Telltale indicators

Consider pronouns. If you don't know how to handle *I* and *me,* many of your colleagues, partners, and customers won't take you seriously. Some errors will predictably get you in trouble:

- "She placed an order *with Megan and I." (Correct: She placed an order with Megan and me.)
- (On the phone:) "*This is him." (Correct: This is he.)

- "Just keep this matter *between you and I." (CORRECT: Just keep this matter between you and me.)
- "*Whom may I say is calling?" (CORRECT: Who may I say is calling?)

The rule, very simply, is that *I, we, he,* and *she* are subjects of clauses <Leslie and I were delighted to work with you>; *me, us, him,* and *her* are objects of either verbs or prepositions <Please call either Leslie or me> <You might want to consult with Leslie and me>. In the compound phrasings, try leaving out *Leslie and*—and you'll know the correct form immediately.

Besides pronoun problems, here are the main types of grammatical errors to watch out for. As for dozens of other wording issues that can torpedo your credibility, see Appendixes D and F.

Subject-verb disagreement

A verb must agree in person and number with its subject <I am aware of that> <You are aware of that> <Pat is aware of that> <We are all aware of that>. But syntax can make things tricky.

There is poses a problem because *There* appears to be the subject. It's not. It's what grammarians call an expletive—not a bad-word expletive (as in "expletive deleted"), but a word that stands in for the subject in an inverted sentence. In these sentences, *there is* just means "exists." Take, for example, *There is a vacancy on the hiring committee.* The uninverted sentence would be *A vacancy (exists) on the hiring committee.* Because *there* seems to some people to resemble a singular subject, they tend to use a singular verb. But *there* inverts the word order, and the true subject follows the verb <There are several reasons for approving the plan>. And, of course, when the subject is plural, a plural verb is needed.

NOT THIS:	BUT THIS:
There *is* always risk and liability *considerations* to take into account.	There *are* always risk and liability *considerations* to take into account.
There *is* many *options* to avoid a takeover.	There *are* many *options* to avoid a takeover.

Another troublesome area for subject–verb disagreement involves prepositional phrases that follow the subject. By "false attraction," they often mislead writers to choose the wrong verb (singular for plural or vice versa). The object of a prepositional phrase is never the subject of a sentence. It may be nearer the verb, but the number of the subject controls the number of the verb:

NOT THIS:	BUT THIS:
The *details* of the customized work *is delaying* the project.	The *details* of the customized work *are delaying* the project.
The *source* of our replacement parts and maintenance *have not been selected* yet.	The *source* for our replacement parts and maintenance supplies *has not been selected* yet.

In the first example, *work* is the object of the preposition *of,* so the plural subject *details* controls the verb. In the second, *source* takes the singular *has not been selected.*

Disagreements can also arise with compound subjects connected by *or, either . . . or,* or *neither . . . nor.* If the subjects are all singular then the verb is singular as well. But when one or more are plural, the number of the verb must match the number of the noun that follows the *or* or *nor*:

NOT THIS:	BUT THIS:
Special services *or* a new product *target* a niche market.	Special services *or* a new product *targets* a niche market.
Neither the education fund *nor* the training costs *is* without budget constraints.	Neither the education fund *nor* the training costs *are* without budget constraints.

In the first example, the singular subject *a new product* after the *or* mandates a singular verb. In the second example, the plural subject after *nor* makes the verb plural as well. Notice that it's more idiomatic to use the *singular subject or plural subject + plural verb* form.

Noun–pronoun disagreement

Strictly speaking, a pronoun must have the same gender and number as the subject.

NOT THIS:	BUT THIS:
A shareholder may cast *their* vote for only one member of the board.	*A shareholder* may cast *his or her* vote for only one member of the board.

Although *their* is colloquially used as a genderless singular pronoun, this usage is not yet widely accepted in formal writing. And unless you know the sex of the subject, try to avoid using a masculine or feminine pronoun. If you wish to make a political statement with pronoun gender (by always choosing the generic feminine, for example), do so: Just know that some of your readers may be distracted by it or may discount your credibility. The safest course is to use some ingenuity to write in an invisibly gender-neutral way.

NOT THIS:	BUT THIS:
Either the receptionist or the sales assistant will have to change *their* lunch hour so that at least one will be in the office at all times.	*Either* the receptionist or the sales assistant will have to start taking lunch earlier or later so that at least one will be in the office at all times.
Three candidates responded to the advertisement for the financial-officer position. *Each* submitted *their* résumé.	*Three candidates* responded to the advertisement for the financial-officer position. *Each* submitted *a* résumé.

But back to grammar. When the subject of a sentence is a singular pronoun such as *either, neither, each,* or *every,* other nouns that accompany it have no effect on the number of the verb:

NOT THIS:	BUT THIS:
Have either of our clients arrived yet?	*Has either* of our clients arrived yet?
Neither of the new products have sold spectacularly this year.	*Neither* of the new products *has* sold spectacularly this year.
Each of us *are* responsible for the tasks assigned.	*Each* of us *is* responsible for the tasks assigned.

Double negatives

A double negative occurs when back-to-back negatives are meant to intensify, not cancel, each other. It's easy to recognize in dialect (for example, *we didn't have no choice* or *it didn't hardly matter*), but the problems can be more subtle in formal writing. Watch for the word *not* plus another word with a negative sense.

NOT THIS:	BUT THIS:
We *couldn't scarcely* manage to keep up with the demand.	We *could scarcely* manage to keep up with the demand.

Another subtle double-negative combination is *not . . . but.*

NOT THIS:	BUT THIS:
The clerk *couldn't* help *but* call the manager for advice.	The clerk *couldn't* help calling the manager for advice.

But indicates a negative or contradiction, so *not . . . but* may be ambiguous. The first sentence could mean the clerk had some other option. The second sentence clearly states there was no alternative.

Nonstandard vocabulary

In business writing, always use standard English—unless you're writing specifically for a niche audience of non-standard speakers. Broadly speaking, standard English is characterized by attention to accepted conventions for grammar, vocabulary, spelling, and punctuation.

You needn't always be strictly formal—in appropriate situations, use less formal English. But your prose and speech must always be professional and respectful.

Dialect is always nonstandard. Avoid using it in business:

NOT THIS:	BUT THIS:
Where's the meeting *at?*	*Where's* the meeting?
Me and Kim will handle the Brewster account.	*Kim and I* will handle the Brewster account.

Nonstandard language may also creep in when writers rely on the spoken sounds of words:

NOT THIS:	BUT THIS:
They *shouldn't of* submitted those incomplete reports.	They *shouldn't have* submitted those incomplete reports.

Irregular verbs are also fertile ground for nonstandard language.

NOT THIS:	BUT THIS:
We *drug* our heels getting into the mid-Atlantic market.	We *dragged* our heels getting into the mid-Atlantic market.
Our late entry almost *sunk* our chances against established competitors.	Our late entry almost *sank* our chances against established competitors.

How to correct yourself

Here are three good ways to brush up: (1) Read first-rate nonfiction; (2) have knowledgeable colleagues proof your material and explain their corrections; and (3) browse through guides on grammar and usage, consulting them whenever questions arise.

This last method will help you distinguish between the real rules and the artificial ones that plague so much writing. For example, were you told in school never to begin a sentence with a conjunction? So was I. But look at all the *and*s and *but*s that begin sentences in first-rate prose. They're everywhere. These words, as sentence-starters, keep readers going smoothly with the train of thought. They don't break any real rules—and they never have.

Grammatically, there's nothing wrong with using *additionally* and *however* as sentence-starters. But stylistically, they're inferior. The multisyllable connectors don't join as cleanly and as tightly as monosyllables do.

Do you worry that your readers will *think* a sentence-starting conjunction is wrong? They won't even notice it, just as you never do. Good style gets readers focused on your clear, concise message. Bad style, by contrast, draws attention to itself.

For a handy collection of grammar guidelines, see Appendix B, "A Dozen Grammatical Rules You Absolutely Need to Know." And be sure to spend some quality time with Appendix F, "A Primer of Good Usage." Fall in love with the language, and it will love you back.

Recap

- When considering verb number, watch for compound subjects, inverted syntax, and prepositional phrases that follow the subject.

- Never mistake the object of a preposition for the subject of a sentence.

- Avoid using *they/them/their* as genderless singular pronouns in formal writing.

- Avoid double negatives.

- Follow the conventions of standard English.

- Improve your grasp of standard English by reading quality nonfiction, having colleagues review your writing, and referring to grammar and usage guides when you have questions.

Chapter 15
Get feedback on your drafts from colleagues

Say you've drafted a budget request. Ask people on your team to read it and make sure you've explained clearly, concisely, and persuasively why you should receive the funding, for example, to hire two more staff members. And if possible, get constructive feedback from an objective peer in a different department—preferably someone who is good at lobbying for resources.

Pay attention to what your colleagues say: Their reactions will probably be quite close to those of your intended readers.

Accept suggestions graciously

A good writer welcomes good edits—yearns for them, in fact. A bad writer resents them, seeing them only as personal attacks. A good writer has many ideas and tends to value them cheaply. A bad writer has few ideas and values them too dearly. So share your material while it's still rough—the feedback will help you make it shipshape much faster than if you were toiling in isolation.

Try to avoid having your colleagues explain their edits in person. You may get defensive and have a hard time recognizing good advice. Invite them to mark up your document, and thank them for their help.

If you have the people you supervise tightening and brightening your prose regularly, you'll benefit in two ways: Your documents will be more polished, and the people you manage will, with practice, become better editors and writers. Give them direction, though: Ask them to look not just for outright errors but also for passages that are verbose, unclear, or awkwardly expressed. Ideally, you'll get to the point where you're accepting 80 percent of their suggestions.

Create a culture where editing flourishes

At my company, everyone who edits or proofreads must suggest at least two changes per page. No one is allowed to hand something back—even a short letter—and say, "It looks good to me!" People can always make improvements by asking, "What did the writer not say that should have been said? How could the tone be improved? Isn't there a better, shorter way of phrasing one of the ideas?" And so on.

If each reader suggests at least two edits per page, your typos will get caught—believe me. Typos are generally the easiest things to catch, so readers will usually mark those before trying the more difficult task of suggesting stylistic improvements. In the end, awkwardness will disappear. You and your team will look better because you'll *perform* better. You'll make stronger, clearer arguments. You'll put together more persuasive pitches.

Does this seem like overkill? Consider that every communication you send is a commentary on your team or company and its level of professionalism. If it's a printed brochure or a commercial e-mail with wide distribution, the more feedback the better. You simply cannot have too many sets of knowledgeable eyes review the copy.

A dumb mistake can be disastrous—as a major university discovered after printing thousands of commencement brochures with "School of Pubic Affairs" in large type on the front cover. A photo of this embarrassing gaffe almost instantly popped up on the Internet, of course, and the university became the target of many jokes.

When it comes to writing, you want a culture of unneurotic helpfulness. There's no shame in needing edits from others. People should freely seek them and freely give them—without any unpleasant overtones of one-upmanship. Everyone in an organization, regardless of rank, can benefit from good editing.

Recap

- Routinely ask your colleagues and those you supervise to read your drafts and suggest edits.
- Have them mark up the document and submit their edits in writing, rather than explaining them in person, to avoid reacting defensively. Always thank them for their help.
- Foster an environment where edits are freely sought and offered—without overtones of petty one-upmanship.

Section 3
Avoiding the Quirks That Turn Readers Off

Chapter 16

Don't anesthetize your readers

It seems obvious that you shouldn't put your audience to sleep, doesn't it? It should also be obvious to people who talk in circles at dinner parties or deliver dull lectures, but consider how many boring speakers you've had to listen to. It doesn't have to be that way—whether in conversation or in writing.

Ponder the best conversationalists and the best lecturers you've ever heard. No matter how obscure the topic, they make it fascinating through their technique. They avoid trite expressions. They use strong, simple words. Think of Winston Churchill's famous phrase "blood, toil, tears, and sweat." And remember what George Washington reputedly said when questioned about the fallen cherry tree: not "It was accomplished by utilizing a small sharp-edged implement," but "I used my little hatchet."

Effective writers use the same techniques. Why do you read some books all the way through but set others aside?

It's their style: the way they explain things, the way they tell the story.

Here are several tips for writing business documents that hold readers' attention.

Use personal pronouns skillfully

Don't overuse *I* (try not to begin paragraphs or successive sentences with it), but do lean heavily on *we, our, you,* and *your.* Those are personal, friendly words that add human interest and pull readers into a document. Rudolf Flesch, a leading figure in plain-English circles and the author of *How to Be Brief,* was one of the first to explain the need for *you:*

> Keep a running conversation with your reader. Use the second-person pronoun whenever you can. Translate everything into *you* language. *This applies to citizens over 65* = *if you're over 65, this applies to you. It must be remembered that* = *you must remember. Many people don't realize* = *perhaps you don't realize.* Always write directly to *you*, the person you're trying to reach with your message.

Likewise, the words *we* and *our*—in reference to your firm or company—make corporations and other legal entities sound as if they have collective personalities (as they should and typically do). People usually appreciate this down-to-earth approach over the sterile, distancing effect of third-person prose. Compare the following examples:

NOT THIS:	**BUT THIS:**
Whether or not *a stockholder* plans to attend a meeting, *he or she* should take the time to vote by completing and mailing the enclosed proxy card to *the Company*. If a *stockholder* signs, dates, and mails a proxy card without indicating how *he or she* wants to vote, *that stockholder's* proxy will be counted as a vote in favor of the merger. If *a stockholder* fails to return a proxy card, the effect in most cases will be a vote against the merger.	Whether or not *you* plan to attend a meeting, please take the time to vote by completing and mailing the enclosed proxy card to *us*. If *you* sign, date, and mail *your* proxy card without indicating how *you* want to vote, *your* proxy will count as a vote in favor of the merger. If *you* don't return *your* card, in most cases *you'll* be counted as voting against the merger.

Use contractions

Many writers have a morbid fear of contractions, having been taught in school to avoid them. But you won't be breaking any real rules if you use them—and they counteract stuffiness, a major cause of poor writing.

This doesn't mean that you should become breezy or use much slang—just that it's good to be relaxed. If you would say something as a contraction, then write it that way. If you wouldn't, then don't.

NOT THIS:	**BUT THIS:**
For those customers who do not participate in West Bank's online banking program, and do not wish to consider doing so, West Bank will continue sending them statements by U.S. Mail.	If you prefer not to use our online banking program, we'll continue mailing your statements to you.
We would like to remind you that it is not necessary to be present to win. We will inform all winners by telephone subsequent to the drawing.	Remember: You needn't be present to win the drawing. We'll call you if you win.

Stick to simple language

I know I repeat this again and again—but it bears repeating. Readers who can't follow you will stop trying.

Avoid passive voice

Don't say "The closing documents were prepared by Sue," but instead "Sue prepared the closing documents"; not "The message was sent by George," but either "George sent the message" or "The message came from George." This guideline is hardly absolute—sometimes passive voice is the most natural way to say what you're saying. Sometimes it can't be avoided. (See?) But if you develop a strong habit of using active voice, you'll largely prevent convoluted, backward-sounding sentences in your writing.

How do you identify passive voice? Remember that it's invariably a *be*-verb (typically *is, are, was, were*) or *get,* plus a past-tense verb. There are eight *be*-verbs and countless past participles.

Examples of Passive Voice

is + delivered

are + finished

was + awarded

were + praised

been + adjusted

being + flown

be + served

am + relieved

got + promoted

You will improve your writing if you minimize passive voice. (Not: Your writing will be improved if passive voice is minimized by you.)

Vary the length and structure of your sentences

Monotony, as Cicero once said, is in all things the mother of boredom. It's true of syntax no less than it's true of eating or anything else. Sameness cloys. So you want short sentences and long; main clauses and subordinate ones. You want variety.

NOT THIS:	BUT THIS:
Over a significant period of time, we have gained experience helping our clients improve operational performance and maximize both the efficiency of their human resources and the economical utilization of their capital. Ours is an integrated approach that both diagnoses and streamlines operating practices and procedures using lean maintenance and optimization tools, while at the same time implementing change-management techniques involving mind-sets and behaviors of those involved in managerial positions within a given organization.	For many years, we have helped clients better use their resources and improve performance. How? By streamlining operations and changing managers' mind-sets and behaviors.

NOT THIS:	BUT THIS:
In order to provide you, the user of our products, the option of obtaining free replacements for defective products from the nearest office, we offer a simplified processing without acknowledgment of the statutory duty ("goodwill") regardless of whether the product has been purchased there or has reached the user by another route.	What should you do if you need a free replacement for a defective product? Go to the nearest office. Any of our offices can help even if you did not purchase the item there.

Avoid alphabet soup

Readers find acronyms tiresome, especially ones they're not familiar with. So use them judiciously. It might be convenient to refer to COGS instead of spelling out "cost of goods sold." If you also throw in acronyms such as ABC ("activity-based costing"), EBITDA ("earnings before interest, tax, depreciation, and amortization"), and VBM ("value-based management"), the accountants in your audience will follow you—but you'll lose everyone else. Small wonder, too. People don't want to master your arcane vocabulary to get what you're saying.

Surely you've had this experience as a reader: You encounter an acronym (a long one if you're particularly unlucky) and can't connect it with anything you've read in the article or document so far. You find yourself scanning backward through the text, hoping to find the first appearance of that acronym or words that might fit it. By the time you find it (or give up trying), you've completely lost the writer's train of thought. Never put your own readers through that.

Stick to words when you can. Acronyms make writing easier but reading harder. Your shortcut is the reader's hindrance.

Recap

- Don't overuse *I*. Use *we, our, you,* and *your* instead to add a personal touch and appeal to your reader.
- Avoid stuffiness by overcoming any fear you might have of contractions.
- For clearer, more straightforward writing, prefer active voice—unless the passive in a particular context sounds more natural.
- Vary the length and structure of your sentences.
- Make the reader's job easier by avoiding acronyms when you can.

Chapter 17

Watch your tone

Striking the right tone takes work—but it's critical to the success of your business documents. If you sound likable and professional, people will want to work with you and respond to you. So adopt a relaxed tone, as if speaking directly to the recipient of your document.

Avoid hyperformality

What do you think of colleagues who say or write "How may I be of assistance?" instead of "How may I help you?" Or "subsequent to our conversation" instead of "after we spoke"? When they choose overblown words over everyday equivalents, don't they strike you as pompous?

Too much formality will spoil your style. Keep your writing down to earth and achieve a personal touch by:

- Writing your message more or less as you'd say it, but without all the casualisms (*like*s and *you know*s).
- Including courtesies such as *thank you, we're happy to,* and *we appreciate.*

- Using the names of the people you're writing about (*David Green*, not *the above-mentioned patient*).
- Using personal pronouns (*you, he, she*—not *the reader, the decedent, the applicant; we understand*—not *it is understood; we recommend*—not *it is recommended by the undersigned*).

Be collegial

You'll have better luck delivering most kinds of messages, even tough ones, if you approach people collegially. Imagine that everything you write will be paraded before a jury in a contentious lawsuit. You'll want that jury to think you've behaved admirably. Of course, sometimes you'll need to take an aggressive stance—for example, when you're at the last stage before litigation. But do this *only* as a last resort, and preferably on advice of counsel.

Be yourself. Just be your most careful, circumspect self. People have gotten their companies into terrible trouble—and have lost their jobs—by writing ill-considered letters, memos, and e-mails. So always summon your best judgment.

Even if you're collegial and fairly relaxed, your language will vary somewhat depending on your relationship with the recipient. You'll be okay if you ask yourself, "How would I say this to so-and-so if he were right here with me?" You don't want a distant tone with your closest colleagues, and you don't want a chummy tone with someone you don't know all that well.

Never try to make your readers admit that they're in the wrong. It's unwise to say that they *labor under a delusion*, or *claim to understand*, or *fail to understand*, or *complain*, or *erroneously assert*, or *distort*. These expressions, and others like them, breed ill will. Instead, treat your readers with integrity and fairness—and show your willingness to meet them halfway.

Drop the sarcasm

Sarcasm expresses contempt and superiority. It doesn't shame people into compliance. Rather, it's a surefire way of irritating and alienating them. Compare:

NOT THIS:	BUT THIS:
Given that Monday was a bank holiday, as declared by federal statute no less, your e-mail of the 17th of the present month did not come to my attention until yesterday. It is with no small degree of regret that we note that you deemed it necessary to send a follow-up e-mail to us regarding this matter, since we are desirous of establishing a relationship of mutual trust and respect.	Because Monday was a bank holiday, I didn't receive your e-mail message of the 17th until yesterday. Naturally I was chagrined that you had to write a second time. But of course I want you to call on me whenever I might help.

In the left-hand column, note the deadly combination of hyperformality and sarcasm, and the annoying subtext: "You wrote on a holiday, you DOPE. Of course you had to wait for a response." The chance of "establishing a relationship of mutual trust and respect" is very likely diminished.

Recap

- Arrive at a relaxed but professional tone by writing your message as if you were speaking to the recipient in person.
- Refer to people by name, use personal pronouns as you naturally would, and shun fancy substitutes for everyday words.
- Always use your best judgment and a collegial tone in composing your messages, even if the content isn't positive. You'll get better responses from your recipients and keep yourself—and your company—out of trouble.
- Adopt a tone appropriate to your relationship with the recipient.
- Never use sarcasm in professional messages. It will result in a step away from—not toward—your desired outcome.

Section 4
Common Forms of Business Writing

Chapter 18
E-mails

When you send e-mails, do you usually receive a useful, friendly, timely response? Or one that falls short of that ideal? Or no response at all? If you're struggling to get your recipients to focus on your messages, it's because you're competing with a lot of senders—in some cases, hundreds per day.

Here's how to write e-mails that people will actually read, answer, and act on:

- **Get straight to the point—politely, of course—in your first few sentences.** Be direct when making a request. Don't fulsomely butter up the recipient first—although a brief compliment may help ("Great interview. Thanks for sending it. May I ask a favor?"). Spell out deadlines and other details the recipient will need to get the job done right and on time.

- **Copy people judiciously.** Include only those who will immediately grasp why they're on the thread.

And avoid "Reply All." Your correspondent may have been overinclusive with the "Copy" list, and if you repeat that mistake, you'll continue to annoy the recipients who shouldn't be there.

- **Keep your message brief.** People find long e-mails irksome and energy-sapping. The more they have to scroll or swipe, the less receptive they'll be to your message. They'll probably just skim it and miss important details. Many people immediately close long e-mails to read the shorter ones. So rarely compose more than a single screen of reading. Focus your content and tighten your language.

- **Write a short but informative subject line.** With a generic—or blank—subject line, your message will get buried in your recipient's overstuffed inbox. (Not "Program," but "The Nov. 15 Leadership Program.") If you're asking someone to take action, highlight that in the subject line. By making your request easy to find, you'll improve your chances of getting it fulfilled.

- **Stick to standard capitalization and punctuation.** Good writing conventions may seem like a waste of time for e-mail, especially when you're tapping out messages on a handheld device. But it's a matter of getting things right—the little things. Even if people in your group don't capitalize or punctuate in their messages, stand out as someone who does. Rushed e-mails that violate the basic norms of written language bespeak carelessness. And their abbreviated style can be confusing. It takes less time to write a clear message the first time around than it does to follow up to explain what you meant to say.

- **Use a signature that displays your title and contact information.** It should look professional (not too long or ornate) and make it convenient for others to choose how to reach you.

These tips are pretty commonsensical—but they're not common practice. To show you how well they work, let's compare some sample e-mails.

Say you're trying to help a young friend of yours, a budding journalist, land an internship. You happen to know the editor of a metropolitan newspaper, and you send him a message. Consider these two approaches:

NOT THIS:

Subject: Hello there!

Hal—

It's been ages, I know, but I've been meaning to tell you just how effective I think you've been as the editor of the *Daily Metropolitan* these past seven years. Although I canceled my subscription a few years back (LOL)—the papers kept cluttering the driveway—I buy a copy at the coffee shop almost every day, and I always tell people there just how good the paper is. Who knows, I may have won you some subscribers with all my gushing praise! Believe me, I'm *always* touting the good old *DM*.

Anyhoo, I have a mentee I'd like you to meet. You'll soon be thanking me for introducing you to her. She would like an internship, and I know she'll be the best intern you've ever had. Her name is Glenda Jones, and she is A-1 in every way. May I tell her you will contact her? (With good news, I hope!) It can be unpaid. I know your paper has fallen on tough times—but she wants to get into the business anyway! Silly girl. Ah, well, what can you do when journalism seems like it's just in the blood?

Expectantly yours,
Myra

P.S. You'll thank me for this!

BUT THIS:

Subject: Request for an Interview

Hal—

May I ask a favor of you? Glenda Jones, a really sharp mentee in the township's Young Leaders program, wants to pursue a career in journalism, and she's eager to learn how commercial news organizations work. Would you spend 15 minutes chatting with her at your office sometime this month, before school lets out? I know it would be a meaningful introduction for her. You'll find that she is a poised, mature, smart, and incredibly self-possessed young woman.

She tells me that she's looking for an unpaid internship. After a brief interview, perhaps you'd consider giving her a one-week tryout as your assistant. I know you've been a mentor to many aspiring journalists over the years, but here you have a real standout: editor of her college newspaper, Phi Beta Kappa member, state debate champion.

No pressure here. If it's a bad summer for you to take on an intern, I'll completely understand. But please meet with her if you can. I've asked her to write to you independently, enclosing her résumé, to give you a sense of her writing skills.

Thanks very much. Hope you and your family are doing well.

Myra

The first version is colossally ineffective—and if Glenda gets an internship it will be very much *despite* the message from her mentor. The writer is inconsiderate (suggesting that journalism is a thankless career), insensitive (confessing to having canceled her subscription), and horribly presumptuous (acting as if the recipient owes her for "always touting" the newspaper and for suggesting this "A-1" intern—as well as assuming that Glenda must get the job).

The second version is effective because it's humble, *you*-centered, considerate ("No pressure here"), and mildly flattering ("I know you've been a mentor to many"). Though it's a little longer than the first one, it gets to the point sooner, and it provides only helpful information. If

Glenda has any real potential, she stands a decent chance of getting that interview and possibly landing an internship with this version.

You may occasionally need to reprimand someone in an e-mail—to clearly explain a misstep, to make a record of it, or both. Compare these two examples, which show the right and wrong way to deal with an employee who sent an offensive e-mail to the whole team:

NOT THIS:

Subject: You Are in Trouble

Ted—

What on earth were you thinking when you sent that "joke"? Your coworkers sure didn't appreciate it one bit, and neither did I. Don't tell me it was "just a joke." Haven't you cracked your employee handbook and read our company's policies? You've never done this before, that I am aware of. Don't ever send an e-mail like this one again.

Bill Morton
Office Manager

BUT THIS:

Subject: Disruption Caused by Your E-mail

Ted—

What one person considers funny, another may find offensive and insulting. Several people have complained to me about the e-mail headed "Have You Heard This One" that you sent everyone yesterday. I was as upset as they were by the foul language, which is inappropriate for an e-mail sent at work. Our company's policy does not make an exception for offensive language, even when used in jest. Please think about how future e-mails will affect your coworkers. If I receive complaints again, HR will have to get involved. But I trust that won't be necessary.

Bill

In the first version, the writer's anger is clear—and that's about all that's clear. Ted will certainly feel stupid ("What on earth were you thinking" and "Haven't you cracked your employee handbook") and scared ("Don't ever"). But the writer doesn't detail what Ted did wrong and why. And Ted isn't likely to ask ("Don't tell me it was 'just a joke'").

The tone of the second version won't immediately put the recipient on the defensive. This time, the writer explicitly identifies the source of the problem ("the e-mail headed 'Have You Heard This One' that you sent everyone yesterday") and explains the effects, the policy violated, and the consequences. Ted is much more likely to understand his mistake.

Recap

- Be as direct as possible while maintaining a polite tone. Come to the point of your e-mail within the first two or three sentences.
- Never click "Reply All" without first checking the recipient list. Send your e-mail only to people who need to know its contents.
- Keep e-mails brief. Restrict yourself to one screen's worth of text and keep the message tight and focused so your readers get the point fast.
- Write a concise subject line that tells your recipients why you're writing and what it means to them. If they need to act on your message, make that clear in the subject line.
- Diligently adhere to standard writing conventions—even when typing with your thumbs on a handheld device.

Chapter 19
Business Letters

Business letters aren't a quaint thing of the past. They're necessary in all sorts of situations—from correcting a vendor's error to recommending a job candidate to announcing a new service. Effective ones can increase your profitability—by getting key customers to renew large orders, for example, or persuading service providers to charge you less for repeat business. They can also create goodwill, which may eventually yield financial returns.

The pointers in this chapter will help you get those kinds of results.

Use direct, personal language

You see canned phrases like *enclosed please find* and *as per* all the time in letters. They're high-sounding but low-performing. Your letters will be much clearer and more engaging without them.

TIPS FOR WRITING CLEAR, PERSUASIVE LETTERS

- ***Focus on the reader.*** Try not to begin with the word *I;* make it *you,* if possible ("You were so kind to . . . ," "You might be interested . . . ," etc.). Keep your recipient in the forefront because—let's face it—that's what will hold the reader's interest. Not: "I just thought I'd drop you a note to say that I really enjoyed my time as your guest last week." But instead: "What a wonderful host you were last week."
- ***Say something that matters.*** Make your message pointed but substantive—not just airy filler. Not: "I trust this finds you prospering in business, thriving in your personal life, and continuing to seek the wisdom that will bring lasting satisfaction in all your dealings." But instead: "I hope you and your family and friends all dodged the fires last week in Maniton Springs—which sounded devastating."
- ***Avoid hedging and equivocating.*** Not: "It is with regret that we acknowledge that we do not appear at this time to be in a position to extend an offer of employment." But instead: "We're sorry to say that we aren't now hiring."

NOT THIS:	BUT THIS:
Enclosed please find . . .	Here are . . .; Enclosed are . . .
As per your request . . .	As you requested . . .
We are in receipt of . . .	We've received . . .
We shall advise you . . .	We'll let you know . . .
As per your letter . . .	As your letter notes . . .
We have your order and will transmit same . . .	We'll forward your order promptly . . .
We take pleasure . . .	We're glad . . .
Due to the fact that . . .	Because . . .
At an early date . . .	Soon . . .
In respect of the matter of . . .	Regarding . . .

People often overwrite their letters—studding their language with stiff, wordy expressions—when they're uncomfortable with the message. Consider the difference between the two examples that follow. The first letter is a greeting to customers from a hotel manager; the second is my revision.

NOT THIS:

Dear Valued Guest:

Welcome to the Milford Hotel Santa Clara. We are delighted that you have selected our hotel during the time when you will be here in the Silicon Valley area. Our staff is ready to assist you in any way and ensure that your stay here is an enjoyable and excellent one in every way.

During your time here at the Milford Hotel Santa Clara, we would like to inform you that the hotel is installing new toilet facilities in all guest rooms. This project will begin on Tuesday, May 8 until Tuesday, May 29. The project engineers will begin at 9:00 a.m. and conclude for the day at 5:30 p.m. The team of associates will begin work on the 14th floor and will work in descending order until completion. During these hours, you may see the new or old toilets in the guest room corridors during the exchange process, and we will ensure that a high level of cleanliness standards will be upheld. We think you'll soon appreciate fresh toilet seats. Should you be in your guest room during the toilet exchange and/or wish not to be disturbed, we recommend that you please utilize your Do Not Disturb sign by placing it on the handle of your guest room door.

The vending area should remain sanitary, so feel free to have a candy bar or beverage of your preference. For your convenience, there are safes located in the bottom nightstand drawer in your guest room to safely store your valuables. There may also be available to you utilization of our safe deposit boxes located at the Front Desk.

We appreciate your cooperation and understanding while we continue to improve the delivery system and appearance of our guest room product. Our goal is to minimize any inconvenience related to the toilet-exchange project. Please contact our Manager on Duty should you have any questions or concerns. Once again, please be assured of our utmost devotion to the total quality of your stay within the confines of the Milford Hotel Santa Clara. On behalf of myself and all the other management personnel and staff of employees here, we wish to reiterate our thanks for your selection and confidence that each and every factor of your stay here will be more than satisfactory.

Sincerely,

[386 words]

BUT THIS:

Dear Valued Guest:

Welcome to the Milford Hotel Santa Clara. We're delighted you're staying here, and we're ready to help make your stay both enjoyable and productive.

This month, we're renovating the bathrooms, starting with the 14th floor and working our way down. Although you may have occasion to see or hear workers (during the day), we're striving to minimize disruptions.

Always feel free to use your "Do Not Disturb" sign while you're in your room to ensure that our staff will respect your privacy. And if the renovations ever become a nuisance, please call me (extension 4505): I'll see what I can do. The renovations are but one example of our commitment to providing first-rate lodging.

Thank you again for joining us.

Sincerely,

[125 words]

The original is verbose (*guest room product*), perversely repetitious (the word *toilet* appears five times), hyperbolic (*excellent . . . in every way*), bureaucratic-sounding (*there may also be available to you utilization*), unpleasantly vivid (*you may see the new or old toilets*), and even gross (*have a candy bar* right after *you may see the new or old toilets*). It seems destined to arouse ill-feeling and to drive away customers who bother to read it. The revised version, by contrast, conveys warmth and consideration with its "you" focus.

Start fast, and say what you need to say in the simplest way you can. Think of Olympic diving: neatly in, no splash, soon out. And if you're writing on behalf of your firm, use *we.* It's much warmer and friendlier than the passive voice (*It has been decided* vs. *We have decided*) or the impersonal third person (*this organization* vs. *we*). Consider the difference:

NOT THIS:	BUT THIS:
The Mercantile Association of Greater Gotham is delighted to count you among its newest members. The Mercantile Association will provide not only networking opportunities but also advantageous insurance rates, concierge services, and Internet advertising to its members. If you ever confront business issues with which the Mercantile Association might be able to devote its resources, it stands ready to be of assistance.	Here at the Mercantile Association of Greater Gotham, we're delighted to count you among our newest members. We provide not only networking opportunities but also advantageous insurance rates, concierge services, and Internet advertising. If you ever confront business issues we can help with, we'll do whatever we can. Just let us know.

In the left-hand example, passive voice (*is delighted*) and repetition of the organization's name (it appears in every sentence) put distance between the writer and the reader. They make the communication sound like a commercial or promotion. But the *you*s and *we*s in the version on the right create a sense of belonging, a personal connection.

Motivate readers to act

Business letters get results when they meet readers' needs. To get people to do something, give them reasons they'll care about.

Consider one of the most challenging kinds of letters to write: a fund-raising appeal for a nonprofit group. The key is to understand why people give money to charitable organizations. Although marketers often cite seven "fundamental motivators" to explain responses—fear, guilt, exclusivity, greed, anger, salvation, and flattery—the reality is a bit more nuanced. Some combination of eight major reasons might motivate donors to send money in response to your appeal:

- They believe their gifts will make a difference.
- They believe in the value of organizations like yours.
- They will receive favorable recognition for the gift.
- They will be associated with a famous or respected person.
- They will enhance their sense of belonging to a worthy group.
- They will be able to relieve emotional burdens such as fear and guilt.

- They feel a sense of duty.
- They will receive tax benefits.

Certain principles follow from these reasons for giving. A successful fund-raising letter must (1) appeal directly from one person to another; (2) depict an opportunity for the recipient to satisfy personal needs by supporting a worthwhile aim; and (3) prompt the recipient to take a specific, decisive action. (These principles apply to other types of business letters as well.)

Note how all this theory plays out in an actual fund-raising letter:

Dear Marion:

May I count you in as a table sponsor at the Annual Dinner of the Tascosa Children's Home of North Texas? Your sponsorship will pay a month's room and board for one of the 50 orphaned teenagers that we care for.

The event will be held at 6:00 p.m. on July 1 at Snowdon Country Club, and the emcee will be the nationally syndicated television host Spooner Hudson—our longtime national spokesperson. Celebrity chef Margrit Lafleur promises to serve up one of his memorable dinners, and the wines will be personally selected by master sommelier Peter Brunswick. Most excitingly, two mystery guests from Beverly Hills will be there that evening—among the best-known philanthropists in the world.

As a table sponsor, you'll be credited as one of our Patron Angels—and, believe me, the tangible gratitude of our kids will bring you the lasting satisfaction that you have vastly improved their lives and well-being. Our kids are reachable and teachable, but only through the generosity of our community's philanthropic leaders.

Many people, of course, can't help us in our mission. We count on our Patron Angels. I hope you'll spend a few minutes browsing through the Home's brochure (enclosed) and that you'll fill out the card committing to fill ten seats at your table (a $1,500 tax-deductible gift).

I look forward to hearing from you soon.

Sincerely,

Now look again at the bulleted list that precedes the letter to Marion (our fictitious recipient): The writer deals with every item on the list. With a letter like that, you can hope to elicit prompt action from an acceptable percentage of recipients.

Ease into bad news

If you have a rejection to deliver in your letter, sandwich it between happier elements. Don't start with a direct "no." Your readers can bear disappointment more easily if you begin on a genuine positive note and then explain the reason for the negative decision. They'll also be more likely to grant your wishes—make a purchase, sign up for your webinar, renew a membership—despite your denying theirs.

NOT THIS:	**BUT THIS:**
We regret to inform you that we cannot supply the 500 copies of *Negotiate It Now!* at the 60% discount that you have requested. No one—not even one of our authors, and not even the biggest bookselling chains—receives such a hefty discount. If you would care to resubmit your order at the more modest figure of 30%, we will gladly consider the order at that time. But I can offer no guarantees.	How rewarding to hear that you intend to use *Negotiate It Now!* as part of your business summit. You've chosen the best book on the subject, and we'd be delighted to supply it. Although you've requested a 60% discount off list price, the most we can offer is 30%. That's the largest discount available to anyone, and we're happy to extend it to you with a purchase of 500 copies.

Recipients of bad news will probably be unhappy no matter what. But to some extent you can control just how unhappy they'll be. Some tips:

- Adopt the reader's perspective—and be your best self. If your correspondent is rude, be polite; if anxious, be sympathetic; if confused, be lucid; if stubborn, be patient; if helpful, show gratitude; if accusatory, be reasonable and just in admitting any faults.
- Answer questions directly.
- Don't overexplain. Say only as much as necessary to get your point across.
- Put things in the simplest possible terms—never use "insider talk" or bizspeak.
- Use the voice of a thoughtful human being, not a robot.

Even if your letter grants a benefit or request, it may irk the recipient if it does so in a way that puzzles, sounds grudging, or seems indifferent to the reader's predicament.

NOT THIS:	BUT THIS:
Joan— In response to your request for a travel subsidy to the conference where your award will be given, Jonathan has reminded me of our current discretionary-spending freeze. He has decided, however, to make an exception in this instance so long as your flight is no more than $400 and you stick to a $50 per diem. Please submit your fully documented expenses upon your return. Sincerely, Rebekah	Joan— Congratulations on your Spivey Award! We're delighted for you. Jonathan hastened to tell me that despite our current discretionary-spending freeze, he wants to support your travel to accept your award. We can manage a $400 flight reimbursement and a $50 per diem for on-the-ground expenses. You'll be a great company representative, I know, and I only wish I could be there myself to see you honored. Sincerely, Rebekah
Brandy— At this time you have now used up all your available sick-leave days and vacation days for the year. A sister-in-law does not qualify for the closeness of relation required for an employee to be eligible for compensated bereavement leave, so you will be docked for any days you choose to be absent next week around the time of the funeral. I'm afraid that policy is simply inflexible, and I checked with Jane to confirm this. Sincerely, Pamela	Brandy— Once again I want to extend my condolences for your family's loss. Take the time you need next week to be with your family. I'm sorry to report that the days will be uncompensated, according to our policies for bereavement leave, but I hope you'll call on me if I can do anything else for you in this time of need. Jane joins me in sending our heartfelt sympathies. Sincerely, Pamela

ENCLOSED PLEASE FIND

See what business-writing authors have long said about this wooden phrase and others like it:

Richard Grant White (1880): "[*Please find enclosed:*] A more ridiculous use of words, it seems to me, there could not be."

Sherwin Cody (1908): "All stereotyped words [that] are not used in talking should be avoided in letter writing. There is an idea that a certain peculiar commercial jargon is appropriate in business letters. The fact is, nothing injures business more than this system of words found only in business letters. The test of a word or phrase or method of expression should be, 'Is it what I would say to my customer if I were talking to him instead of writing to him?'"

Wallace E. Bartholomew & Floyd Hurlbut (1924): "*Inclosed herewith please find. Inclosed* and *herewith* mean the same thing. How foolish to tell your reader twice exactly where the check is, and then to suggest that he look around to see if he can find it anywhere. Say, 'We are inclosing our check for $25.50.'"

A. Charles Babenroth (1942): "*Enclosed please find.* Needless and faulty phraseology. The word *please* has little meaning in this instance, and the word *find* is improperly used. POOR: Enclosed please find sample of our #1939 black elastic ribbon. BETTER: We are enclosing (or We enclose) a sample of our #1939 black elastic ribbon."

***L. E. Frailey (1965)*:** "So much for the worn-out, hackneyed expressions [*enclosed herewith, enclosed please find, herewith please find*] so often seen in business letters—whiskers, rubber-stamps, chestnuts, call them what you please. They are sleeping pills [that] defeat the aim of making every letter a warm, personal contact with the reader."

***Gerald J. Alred, Charles T. Brusaw, & Walter E. Oliu (1993)*:** "Using unnecessarily formal words (such as *herewith*) and outdated phrases (such as *please find enclosed*) is another cause of affectation."

***Kelly Cannon (2004)*:** "[I]n any business letter, certain principles are universal. 'Inure to the benefit of' is four words too long, 'enclosed please find' sounds pompous and silly, and 'I am writing this letter to inform you that . . .' is a thoughtless statement of the obvious."

Don't write in anger

Be kind and diplomatic, and say *please* and *thank you.* Courtesy is necessary to all business transactions—even letters of complaint. Omit it, and you'll be dismissed as a crank. You can be courteous while still being direct.

NOT THIS:	BUT THIS:
We are astonished at your complaint. The brochures that we printed were exactly as you specified. You okayed the sample paper, the typesetting, and the proofreading (we gave you an extra three hours). You chose the hot-pink borders with the fine-screen halftones in the body type against our advice. You insisted on drop-shipping by the 18th, and as you know, a rushed job does not allow for first-rate press work. Moreover, we quoted you a bargain-basement price. Under the circumstances we believe that any unbiased observer would say that we performed remarkably well under the impossible conditions you imposed.	We agree with you that the brochures did not match the high standards you have a right to expect from us. But we believed, in this instance, that you considered the color quality less crucial than a low price and a quick turnaround. So we pushed the work through production in three days' less time than we usually require. We advised against your using hot-pink borders and fine-screen halftones on the grade of paper you chose. Still, we exercised some ingenuity to achieve better results than are ordinarily possible. I mention this not to avoid responsibility but merely to suggest that we did the best that could be done under difficult circumstances. If you'll allow us a few more days next time, as you ordinarily do, the results will be better.

As you can see, a combative, superior tone irritates and alienates the reader—and probably loses a customer. A more diplomatic approach still gets the point across (rush jobs always take a hit on quality), but without souring the relationship.

When you receive unreasonable letters, don't ever respond in kind. That just starts a negative chain reaction. Approach complaints with a dedication to first-rate service. Write with the same warmth and friendliness you'd use in face-to-face conversations. If you or your company made a mistake, avoid the temptation to ignore it, cover it up, or shift the blame. Instead of deceiving readers, you'll provoke more ire. When you blunder, admit error and say what you've done (or will be doing) to correct it. Stress the desire to improve service.

Recap

- Keep your language simple, personal, and direct. Avoid canned phrases that add little but pomposity and verbiage to your letter.
- Motivate your readers to act on your letter by giving them reasons that matter to them.
- When conveying bad news, soften the blow by opening on a positive note. Follow up by explaining the reason for the unfavorable outcome—without overexplaining.
- Consider the reader: Be polite, sympathetic, and professional.
- Remain courteous and diplomatic. Accept responsibility for any mistakes you may have made.

Chapter 20

Memos and Reports

Memos and reports are often used to get people up to speed on an issue, to induce action, or both. So make it immediately clear in each element—your title, summary, body, and conclusion—what you want readers to learn about or do.

Pick a short, clear title

Whether you're writing a memo's subject line or a report title, choose concise, sure-footed language that says exactly what the document is about.

NOT THIS:	BUT THIS:
Subject: Siegelson	Subject: Approval of Siegelson Acquisition
Subject: Settlement	Subject: Why We Should Reject Frost's Settlement Offer
Subject: Print Run	Subject: Ginsburg Autobiography Print Run

The titles on the left hint at the topics covered but don't let readers know what they're supposed to do with the information. Those on the right are more pointed (without being wordy): The first and third titles promise status updates; the second asks readers to follow a recommendation.

Summarize key specifics up front

Figure out how many main issues you're addressing—preferably no more than three (see chapter 4)—and then for each one state: (1) the issue in a way that *anyone* can understand, (2) your solution, and (3) the reason for your solution. Here's an example:

> **Summary**
>
> **Issue:** Arnold Paper Supply has consistently failed to meet our deadlines for delivery of multicolor, printed cardstock.
>
> **Proposed Solution:** Switch to National Paper and Plastics Company, which has a higher fixed fee.
>
> **Reason:** Though National Paper and Plastics Company has a higher rate per delivery, its turnaround is quicker. This will increase efficiency in the warehouse, allow us to fill more orders, and help us to establish goodwill with retailers who have been angry with us for not meeting their deadlines.

By sharing everything important at the beginning of the document, you'll end up repeating yourself—but in a way that's reinforcing, not redundant. Readers will get a quick orientation with your very short version up front;

the fully elaborated version in the body will unpack each point, providing details and data for support. I recommend going back and forth between the summary and the body when writing your first draft: Start by stating the problem and offering your best shot at the answer in your summary. As you do more work on the body of the memo or report, you'll go back and refine the problem and the answer.

Write your summary for three types of readers:

- A primary audience of one or more executives interested only in a quick status update, your findings and conclusions about a problem, or your recommendations.
- A line of readers who may be called in (with or without your knowledge) to assess the soundness of your document, judging its merits according to their own fact-checking and critical analysis.
- Future readers (including those in the first category two years from now) who will be required to quarry information from your document some time after you've written it. (After all, memos and reports are rarely acted on quickly: They may be laid aside for weeks or months or even years before anyone has the resources—or a mandate—to act.)

All three types of readers have a legitimate claim to your attention. More important, you need to win them all over if you want your recommendations to go anywhere.

Even if someone else has assigned you the question you're exploring, you must define it in your summary.

WHEN WRITING A REPORT . . .

- Make sure you understand why you're writing and what you're reporting on.
- Do your best, in light of your background knowledge and initial research, to write a summary that concisely states the problem, your solution, and why your solution will work or why it's preferable to alternatives.
- Discern sources of relevant information.
- From those sources, gather all the data and explanations that you can.
- Synthesize relevant observations and inferences and throw out the rest.
- Put your findings into report form.
- Revise your summary to match your body text.

You, the writer, are in the best position to limit its scope: The person who did the assigning may not know enough about the problem to raise the right question—or to understand that it actually contains three subquestions.

In fact, you won't know these things until you do your research, which may involve digging up data that reveal where the problem lurks, reading about how other organizations have tried to solve it, talking with people who have discovered some helpful workarounds, and so on.

You should do enough research to understand the problem. *Then* you state the problem so clearly that anyone could understand why it's worth solving.

If you're making a recommendation, say (1) what needs to be done, (2) who should do it, (3) when and where it should be done, (4) why it should be done, and (5) how it should be done.

A brief marketing report might look like this:

Marketing Strategy for Skinny Mini Line of Chocolates

Summary

Issue: Within the last fiscal year, Pantheon Chocolate's sales have dropped from $13,320,000 to $10,730,000, but its market share remains unchanged at 37%.

Proposed Solution: Increase promotion of the Skinny Mini line of chocolates. These chocolates contain less sugar and fat than the regular line.

Reason: Health-conscious consumers want low-calorie options but don't want to sacrifice full flavor. The Skinny Mini chocolates have fewer calories than Pantheon's regular chocolates but the same flavor.

Consumers are buying more "healthy alternative" chocolates

Because consumers increasingly regard sugar and fat as unhealthy, they are not buying as much high-end gourmet chocolate as they were a year ago. This has led to a decline in sales for all high-end chocolate makers, including Pantheon. But for candies marketed as "healthy alternatives" with less sugar and fat and fewer calories, sales have increased 42% in the same period. Marketing studies show that consumers of "healthy alternative" candies are most attracted to low-calorie chocolates that are packaged in specific-calorie portions rather than by weight.

These consumers also complain that low-calorie candies lack the rich flavor that they are used to, and they are willing to pay more for quality. Pantheon already produces a line of low-calorie gourmet chocolates, Skinny Minis, that have fewer calories than Pantheon's regular candies but the same flavor. They're currently sold by the pound or in gift boxes in high-end chocolate boutiques and as elegantly wrapped bars in coffee shops.

Recommendations

- To reach more health-conscious consumers, Pantheon should package Skinny Mini chocolates in a variety of portion-controlled sizes and make them available in health-food stores and supermarkets as well as the chocolate and coffee shops.
- The marketing campaign should stress the controlled portion and limited calories of each Skinny Mini bar or gift box, and the packaging should boldly display the low calorie count.

Recap

- Choose a concise title or subject line that tells readers what topics the memo or report covers and what they should do about it (or why they should care).

- Begin your document by addressing your main points and outlining the issue, your solution, and the reason for it.
- Work from this summary when elaborating the body of your first draft.
- Modify the summary as you go to ensure that it accurately reflects what's in the body.

Chapter 21
Performance Appraisals

Writing performance appraisals, sometimes called employee reviews, needn't be a dreaded responsibility. As long as you have gathered your facts in advance—reviewed the notes you've taken throughout the year, asked others for feedback on the people you supervise, and carefully read people's self-assessments—the drafting isn't onerous if you have an ample evaluative vocabulary. I've written this chapter so you'll have some helpful phrases at the ready.

The sample phrases that follow address seven aspects of work: attitude, efficiency, human relations, judgment, knowledge, reliability, and communication skills. But you can adapt the wording to suit whatever qualities you'd like to focus on. Then it's a matter of pairing the phrases with specifics that support them. For example: "When we had several layoffs last June, Lauren *remained utterly calm and collected* while *demonstrating keen sensitivity* to those who lost their jobs. She [fill in whatever particular action was noteworthy]."

Attitude

Superb	• shows unwavering commitment • always gives maximal effort • is always friendly and happy to help • always brings out the best in others
Good	• shows strong commitment • usually makes a strong effort • is usually friendly and happy to help • usually brings out the best in others
Acceptable	• shows adequate commitment • makes an effort • is often friendly and happy to help • is often a positive influence on the group
Needs Improvement	• could show more commitment • doesn't always make an effort • is sometimes quarrelsome • sometimes creates tension within the group
Poor	• lacks commitment • rarely makes a real effort • is quarrelsome and sometimes even hostile • often creates tension within the group

Efficiency

Superb	• never wastes time or effort • delegates effectively • always completes tasks on time • can manage many projects at a time
Good	• rarely wastes time or effort • usually delegates appropriately • almost always completes tasks on time • can manage several projects at a time
Acceptable	• usually doesn't waste time or effort • delegates pretty well • usually completes tasks on time • can manage more than one project at a time
Needs Improvement	• sometimes wastes time and effort • tries to do too much without delegating • fails to complete tasks on time • cannot manage more than one project at a time
Poor	• often wastes time and effort • usually fails to delegate when appropriate • can't be counted on to complete tasks on time • struggles to manage even one project at a time

Human relations

Superb	• demonstrates keen sensitivity to others and an uncanny ability to understand their needs • participates actively and collegially in meetings • works exceptionally well on teams • relates to customers extremely well

Good	• usually demonstrates sensitivity to others • participates effectively in meetings • works effectively on teams • relates to customers well
Acceptable	• often demonstrates sensitivity to others • participates adequately in meetings • gets along with fellow team members • relates to customers competently
Needs Improvement	• does not always pick up on interpersonal cues • sometimes wastes others' time in meetings • is sometimes motivated more by personal goals than by team goals • sometimes alienates customers through inattention
Poor	• rarely pays attention to others' reactions • often wastes others' time in meetings • does not work well on teams • often alienates customers with impoliteness and sarcasm

Judgment

Superb	• makes excellent choices and informed decisions • remains utterly calm and collected even in times of crisis • knows precisely which problems need immediate attention and which ones can wait • behaves professionally and appropriately in every situation
Good	• makes sound choices and reasonable decisions • remains relatively calm and collected even in times of crisis • generally knows which problems need immediate attention and which ones can wait • behaves professionally and appropriately
Acceptable	• generally makes sound choices and informed decisions • remains mostly calm and collected except in times of crisis • does a pretty good job distinguishing between problems that need immediate attention and those that can wait • generally behaves professionally and appropriately
Needs Improvement	• sometimes makes poor choices and ill-informed decisions • sometimes lacks the calm and collected demeanor required in high-pressure circumstances • often doesn't distinguish between problems that need immediate attention and those that can wait • sometimes behaves unprofessionally and inappropriately

Judgment (*continued*)

Poor	• often makes poor choices and ill-informed decisions • often lacks the calm and collected demeanor required in high-pressure circumstances • typically fails to distinguish between problems that need immediate attention and those that can wait • often behaves unprofessionally and inappropriately

Knowledge

Superb	• is exceptionally well informed about all aspects of the job • demonstrates extraordinarily comprehensive knowledge • skillfully handles complex assignments without supervision • has a comprehensive knowledge of the industry
Good	• is well informed about key aspects of the job • demonstrates thorough knowledge • can handle complex assignments with some supervision • has strong knowledge of the industry
Acceptable	• understands the job • demonstrates adequate knowledge • can handle moderately complex assignments with supervision • has an acceptable degree of knowledge of the industry
Needs Improvement	• doesn't fully understand the job • demonstrates less than satisfactory knowledge • sometimes mishandles assignments of moderate complexity, even with supervision • has insufficient knowledge of the industry
Poor	• is ill-informed about many aspects of the job • demonstrates inadequate knowledge • mishandles basic assignments • has little knowledge of the industry

Reliability

Superb	• always meets deadlines • is unfailingly dependable • achieves excellent results in urgent situations • always delivers on promises
Good	• meets deadlines • is highly dependable • achieves good results in urgent situations • almost always delivers on promises
Acceptable	• meets most deadlines • is dependable • achieves acceptable results in urgent situations • delivers pretty consistently on promises

Needs Improvement	• sometimes fails to meet important deadlines • is sometimes undependable • sometimes fails to achieve acceptable results in urgent situations • sometimes fails to deliver on promises
Poor	• often fails to meet important deadlines • is rarely dependable • often fails to achieve acceptable results in urgent situations • can't be counted on to deliver on promises

Communication skills

Superb	• writes and speaks with remarkable clarity • never gets bogged down in unnecessary details • has superior communication skills in person and over the phone • develops and delivers imaginative, clear, and concise presentations
Good	• writes and speaks clearly • rarely gets bogged down in unnecessary details • has sound communication skills in person and over the phone • develops and delivers clear, concise presentations
Acceptable	• generally writes and speaks clearly • usually avoids getting bogged down in unnecessary details • has adequate communication skills in person and over the phone • develops and delivers acceptable presentations
Needs Improvement	• sometimes writes and speaks unclearly and with undue complexity • sometimes gets bogged down in unnecessary details • sometimes struggles to communicate in person and over the phone • develops and delivers presentations in need of further work and polish
Poor	• writes and speaks unclearly and with undue complexity • gets bogged down in unnecessary details • fails to communicate effectively in person and over the phone • develops and delivers presentations that ramble and lack clarity

Recap

- Prepare by gathering your facts in advance: Keep performance notes throughout the year and review them before writing. Ask other colleagues for feedback on those you're evaluating. Carefully review the employees' self-assessments.
- Use the sample phrases provided here to help articulate your impressions.
- Always pair your general statements with specific examples that support them.

Appendix A

A Checklist for the Four Stages of Writing

Madman

- ☐ Consider why you're writing: What's moved you to write? What's the assignment? What do you hope to achieve?
- ☐ Think about who your readers are and what they need to know.
- ☐ Figure out how much time you have, and work out a rough schedule for gathering ideas and material, outlining, preparing a draft, and revising.
- ☐ Research with imagination and gusto. Take notes on relevant information.
- ☐ Push yourself to be creative. Don't be content with obvious ideas that just anyone would think of.

Architect

- ☐ Jot down your three main points in complete sentences—with as much specificity as you can.
- ☐ Consider the best order of the three points and reorganize them if necessary.
- ☐ Decide how to open and conclude the document.
- ☐ Think about what visual aids might be helpful in conveying your ideas.

Carpenter

- ☐ If possible, turn away from all distractions. Silence your phone and your computer alerts, and find an hour or so of solitude. You'll be writing.
- ☐ Use your three-point outline as a guide.
- ☐ Start writing paragraphs that support the point you find easiest to start with—then move to the other points.
- ☐ Write swiftly without stopping to edit or polish.
- ☐ Try to write a full section in one sitting. If you must get up in the middle of a section, start the next sentence with a few words and then leave. (When you come back, you'll find it easier to resume a half-completed sentence than to start a new one.)

Judge

- ☐ Immediately after completing your draft, read it through with the idea of amplifying ideas here and there.
- ☐ Then let it cool off—overnight, if you can, or for a few minutes if you're working under an urgent deadline.
- ☐ When you return to your draft, consider it from the audience's perspective. Will it be clear to everyone who looks at it, or does it require inside knowledge? Is it concise, or does it waste words and time?
- ☐ Identify the draft's two biggest flaws and try to fix them.
- ☐ Ask yourself:
    - Is anything essential missing?
    - Are important points stressed?
    - Is the meaning of each sentence clear and accurate?
    - Are my transitions smooth?
    - What can I trim without sacrificing important content?
    - Are there any vague passages I can sharpen with specific facts?
    - Are there boring passages I can word more vividly?
    - Can I improve the phrasing?
    - Can I improve the punctuation?
    - Are there any typos?

Appendix B
A Dozen Grammatical Rules You Absolutely Need to Know

1. **It is perfectly acceptable to start a sentence with *And* or *But*.**
   The single most important element in fluid writing is the use of effective transitions between sentences and paragraphs. And no transition is more effective than the plain single-syllable words *and* and *but*.

   The notion that it's ungrammatical to start a sentence with a conjunction has long been ignored by the best writers and debunked by reputable grammarians. Look at the op-ed page of any major newspaper or scan through some pages of any well-edited magazine and you'll see plenty of examples. Why? Because conjunctions are excellent transition tools, signaling how the sentence to follow fits in with what came before—and because they're short, sharp, and fleet. *And* and *but* are usually more effective than clunky conjunctive adverbs such as *additionally* and *however*, which add syllables and demand a comma after them.

2. **It is perfectly acceptable to end a sentence with a preposition.**

The "rule" that you should not end a sentence with a preposition is a misbegotten notion based on Latin syntax and expounded by a few (a very few) 19th-century writers. Grammarians have long since dismissed it as ill-founded and unnecessary.

Often a sentence that ends with a preposition sounds far more natural than the same sentence forced into avoiding the terminal preposition. Consider: *What will the new product be used for*? versus *For what purpose will the new product be used*?

That said, a strong sentence should end forcefully because the end of a sentence is the most emphatic position. A preposition is rarely a powerful sentence-ender, but it is not an ungrammatical one.

3. **The adverb corresponding to the adjective *good* is *well*.**

When describing performance, manner, action, and the like, use the adverb *well* <The intern

works well under pressure> <The research and development stage is going well> <We wish them well in the future>. Though becoming more widespread, the adverbial use of *good* is nonstandard English <The vice presidents *worked good as a team> <The new water pump *is running good>. The question whether to use *good* or *well* frequently arises when someone asks "How are you doing?" The best answer—assuming a positive response—is "I'm doing well" (or "I'm fine, thank you"). Saying "I'm good" is common but unrefined. The response "I'm *doing good" is substandard because *good* is there being used as an adverb. An exception to the rule against using *good* as an adverb applies with certain set phrases <a good many more> <did it but good>.

4. **The subject of the sentence determines the number of the verb.**
A subject and its verb must both be either singular or plural. Grammar Girl says so. (*Grammar Girl* and *says* are both singular.) All grammarians say so. (*Grammarians* and *say* are both plural.) The rule seems so elementary as to be trivial. But a lot can go wrong. A prepositional phrase modifying the subject is a common source of trouble: Should *an oversupply of foreign imports* take a singular or plural verb? The answer is singular, to match the subject *oversupply*. Although compound

subjects generally take plural verbs, sometimes a subject really expresses a single (and singular) idea <The company's bread and butter is still shipping>. The subject, *bread and butter,* is plural in form but singular in sense, so it takes the singular verb *is.*

There (in its use as a subject stand-in, as in *There is another way*) presents a special problem, one that some authorities call the most common grammatical error today. In inverted sentences, the true subject follows the verb <There go our fourth-quarter profits>. The subject *profits* is after the verb *go.* Yet people seem to want singular verbs with *there* regardless of what follows, and errors result <*There is still market capacity and established competition to be considered>. The compound subject *capacity and competition* should take the plural verb *are,* not the singular verb *is.*

Illusory compounds can also cause trouble. These occur with constructions such as *together with, as well as,* and the like, none of which forms a plural. <The board, along with the president and CFO, endorses the stock split>. The subject is the singular *board,* which takes the singular verb *endorses.*

5. **Both *either* and *neither,* as subjects, take singular verbs.**

Beware of distractions caused by prepositional phrases containing plural objects: The subject—*either* or *neither*—is still singular <Either of the marketing plans *involves* [not *involve*] capital investment> <Neither of our expansion options *provides* [not *provide*] a total solution>.

6. **With *neither/nor* and *either/or* in the subject position, the second element controls the number of the verb.**
When the correlative conjunctions *either/or* or *neither/nor* frame alternatives in the singular, the verb is singular <Either phone or fax *is* acceptable for your response>. When the alternatives are plural, the verb is plural <Neither our accountants nor our lawyers *are* concerned about the merger>. But when one element is singular and the other is plural, match the verb to the second element <Neither the regional managers nor the vice-president for sales *likes* [not *like*] the proposed campaign's theme> <Either the home office or the branch managers *are* [not *is*] largely responsible for employee morale>.

7. **A flat adverb like *thus* or *doubtless* takes no *-ly* ending.**
Most adverbs are formed by adding the *-ly* suffix to adjectives (*large* makes *largely, quick* makes *quickly*) or changing the *-able* suffix to *-ably* (*amicable* makes *amicably, capable* makes *capably*). But the English language also contains a fair number of adverbs that do not

end in -*ly* (such as *fast, ill,* and *seldom*). With these, it is unnecessary—and unidiomatic—to add the suffix -*ly*. The two most common examples are **doubtlessly* and **thusly*.

8. **The words *however, therefore,* and *otherwise* cannot join independent clauses without additional punctuation.**
An independent clause (1) contains a subject and a verb and (2) expresses a complete thought. It can stand alone as a sentence, or it can be connected with another clause by a comma and a conjunction (such as *and, but, or*) <The new advertising campaign is ready, but the CEO has yet to approve it>. When two independent clauses are joined with a conjunctive adverb like *however,* a semicolon must go in front of the connector and a comma after <Mr. Bingham can't attend the meeting; however, he hopes to call before we adjourn>. Omitting the semicolon or replacing it with a comma creates what is known as a "comma splice" <*We were supposed to arrive at 4:00 p.m., however, we didn't arrive until 5:00>.

9. **With a verb phrase, the adverb usually goes after the first auxiliary verb.**
Writing authorities have long agreed that midphrase is the strongest and most natural place for an adverb <Industry experts *have long agreed* on the product's effectiveness>. The alternatives are awkward <Industry experts

long have agreed on the product's effectiveness> or nonsensical <Industry experts *have agreed long* on the product's effectiveness>. Resistance to this guidance may be due to the old superstition that it's ungrammatical to split an infinitive (it isn't), since that is one type of split verb <We expect the new product line and expanded territory *to almost double* our sales in the next two years>.

When the phrase has more than one auxiliary verb, the most natural placement is usually after the first one (as in *has long been assumed*).

10. **Relative pronouns (*that, which,* and *who*) must appear alongside their antecedents.**

A relative pronoun (*that, which, who, whom,* and various forms with the *-ever* suffix) serves one of two purposes. First, it can link a dependent clause to an independent one <Whoever wants to participate is welcome>. The dependent clause (*whoever wants to participate*) serves as the subject of the main clause. Second, it can join a clause with its antecedent <Those who want to participate are welcome>. Here, the dependent clause (*who want to participate*) adds crucial information about its antecedent, *those.*

The second type of relative pronoun should be close to its antecedent—preferably immediately after it. The link must be clear because trouble can occur when the reference becomes uncertain <*Please discuss the customer-service position in the accounting department that is being eliminated>. Which is being eliminated, the position or the department? Restating the sentence clarifies it <Please discuss the customer-service position that is being eliminated in the accounting department>. The relative pronoun *that* immediately follows its antecedent, *customer-service position.*

11. **An appositive is set off by commas when it is not essential to the sentence (when it is nonrestrictive), but is not set off by commas when it is essential (restrictive).**

An appositive is a noun or noun phrase that follows another noun (or pronoun) and identifies or depicts it more fully <My colleague Pat agrees> <The customer, a tall man in an oversized suit, left his keys on the counter>.

In the first example, the appositive *Pat* is not set off by commas from the rest of the sentence. In the second, *a tall man in an oversized suit* is set off. The reason is that appositives, like relative clauses (those introduced by *which, who,* and *whom*), may or may not be essential to the meaning of the sentence. *Pat,* in the first sentence, is essential—it specifies which colleague (presumably out of several) is being referred to. In the second sentence, the appositive merely adds description. We could also say that *Pat,* in the first sentence, defines or restricts its referent, *colleague,* while the appositive in the second sense is indefinite or nonrestrictive. Current stylebooks use the terms *restrictive* and *nonrestrictive* to label these qualities.

Appositives may also be set off by em-dashes (typically for emphasis) or parentheses (typically for deemphasis) instead of commas.

12. **Correlative conjunctions (those used in pairs) require parallel phrasing.**
Correlative conjunctions (such as *both . . . and, neither . . . nor,* and *not only . . . but also*) work in pairs, joining related constructions that match in syntax. Each conjunction should immediately precede the part of speech it describes. Parallelism is rarely a problem with simple nouns <neither time nor money>, but it becomes tricky with phrases and clauses, as in the erroneous phrasing **We not only raised our regional market share but also our profit margin,* which should read: *We raised not only our regional market share but also our profit margin.* The verb *raised* must be outside the first correlative conjunction (*not only*) to apply to both possessive phrases (*our regional market share* and *our profit margin*).

Appendix C

A Dozen Punctuation Rules You Absolutely Need to Know

1. **Hyphenate your phrasal adjectives.**

   A *small-business incentive* is different from a *small business incentive.* A *limited-liability clause* is different from a *limited liability clause.* When two or more words as a unit modify a noun, they must be hyphenated (unless certain exceptions apply). So a hotel's door sign advising the staff not to disturb the guests would be a *do-not-disturb sign.* A company that is 25 years old is a *25-year-old company.*

   There are some exceptions: (1) Don't hyphenate simple phrases formed by an *-ly* adverb and a past-participial adjective <a greatly

exaggerated claim>. (2) Don't hyphenate phrases formed with proper nouns <New Zealand exports> or foreign words <a post facto rationalization>. (3) Generally, don't hyphenate phrasal adjectives used after the noun they modify <a job well done>, but there are exceptions based solely on conventions of usage <our HR manager is risk-averse by nature> <the information is time-sensitive>.

2. **Use a comma before *and* or *or* when listing three or more items.**
   Although simple series <*red, white, and blue*> might not require the so-called serial comma before the conjunction to be perfectly clear, clarity fades fast as series become longer and more complex <We hope to boost sales in the target area, to build the company's name-recognition statewide and beyond, and to attract investors for possible franchise opportunities>. So what is the rule?

   The Chicago Manual of Style and other authorities on professional, technical, and scholarly writing almost universally endorse using the serial comma in *all* series for one good reason: It is sometimes wrong (ambiguous or worse) to omit it, but never wrong to include it.

3. **Don't use a comma to separate two compound predicates. Do use punctuation—usually a comma but a semicolon if needed for clarity—to separate a series of three or more compound predicates.**

When two predicates share the same subject, it's common not to repeat the subject. If the second clause repeats the subject, then the comma is proper before the conjunction <I stopped by yesterday, and I will call today>. But if the subject isn't repeated (is shared by both predicates), there should be no comma before the conjunction <I stopped by yesterday and will call today>. When three or more such clauses are combined (sharing the same subject), the predicates become a series and do require at least a comma to separate them <I wrote him yesterday, stopped by yesterday, and will call today>.

When one or more of the parts in the series contain commas, use semicolons instead to separate the predicates <I wrote him last week; I stopped by yesterday with the paperwork, the deposit check, and the keys; and I will call him today>. The same principle holds for a compound predicate <I wrote him last week; stopped by yesterday with the paperwork, the deposit check, and the keys; and will call him today>.

4. **Don't use an apostrophe to form plural nouns.** The use of apostrophes to form plurals (rather than possessives or contractions) is almost always incorrect. Most proper nouns take a simple *-s,* while those ending in *-s, -x, -z,* and sibilant *-ch* or *-sh* take *-es.* The exceptions to the no-apostrophe rule are for lowercase

letters <Mind your p's and q's> and capital letters when an apostrophe might prevent a miscue <all A's on the audit report>. Don't use apostrophes to pluralize numbers or capitalized abbreviations without periods <ATMs became ubiquitous in the 1990s>. The usual way to pluralize words and letters is to italicize the word or letter and append *-s* in roman type <Please delete the first two *or*s in the sentence>.

The incorrect use of apostrophes is especially common when pluralizing names. Mr. and Mrs. Smith are *the Smiths,* not **the Smith's* (or **the Smiths'*). Mr. and Mrs. Stevens are *the Stevenses* (not **the Steven's* or **the Stevens'*).

5. **Don't separate the grammatical subject from the verb, unless there's a set-off intervening phrase.** As a rule, words and phrases that *go* together should *be* together, not unduly separated. So an appositive, for example, is next to the noun or pronoun it elaborates <Maeve Peterson, the new CEO, is . . .> and a pronoun should not be so far from its antecedent as to make the connection unclear. On the same principle, the subject and verb in a sentence are best kept close together so that the sentence does not wander off on tangents.

   That's not to say that an intervening phrase or clause between the subject and verb is always wrong. It can be an effective way to modify the sense or add information <Ms. Peterson, whose leadership at McLaughlin Enterprises has been credited with that firm's turnaround, will take the reins here on June 1>. Although this technique adds emphasis to the modifying matter, it's often clearer to make the phrase or clause introductory so that the subject and verb remain close <Credited with turning around McLaughlin Enterprises during her four years as CEO, Ms. Peterson starts work here on June 1>.

6. **Use bullets as attention-getting devices, but don't overuse them.**
   Bullets draw the reader's eye to a list of points without signaling that they're presented in a certain order. The best lists follow these rules:
   - Set up the list with an explanatory sentence in the form of an introduction that ends with a colon.
   - Keep all the items parallel in grammatical form (all noun phrases, say, or all predicates starting with verbs) and somewhat similar in length.
   - Present the items with a hanging indent so the bullets stand out to the left and all the lines of type align.
   - Typeset the items single-spaced, perhaps with a bit of extra spacing between items.

- Keep the bullets simple in appearance, eschewing whimsical artwork in favor of solid bullet dots about the size of a lowercase *o*.

As with any other design device aimed at signaling emphasis or attracting the reader's attention, the overuse of bulleted lists dilutes their impact.

7. **Avoid quotation marks as a way of emphasizing words.**

Quotation marks can send mixed signals. Most often they signal their traditional function: to set off a quotation. Sometimes they suggest a snide attitude <an “expert” in negotiation>, or perhaps imply that what they contain is not what it purports to be at all <Here's the “final” schedule>. They can be the equivalent of introducing the words with “so-called.” Given all these different possible meanings, quotation marks are a poor choice for emphasizing words and phrases. That is traditionally the role of italic type, an unambiguous signal.

Also avoid (1) underlining, the italic font's uglier equivalent from the typewriter era; (2) overuse of boldface type, which is best reserved for titles and headings; and (3) all caps, which is irritating and hard to read if longer than a word or two.

8. **Don't hyphenate most prefixed terms.**

American English is generally averse to hyphenating its prefixes (*anteroom, biennial, deselect, proactive, quarterfinal, semisweet*). Avoid the practice of inserting a hyphen, even when it results in a doubled letter (*cooperate, reelect, misspeak*). But there are a few exceptions: (1) when it's needed to avoid a miscue or an ambiguity (*re-create, re-lease, re-sign*); (2) when the root word is a proper noun (*pre-Halloween sales*); and (3) when using certain prefixes such as *all-* (*all-inclusive*), *ex-* (*ex-partner*), and *self-* (*self-correcting*).

9. **Use a colon or a comma—never a semicolon—after a salutation.**
   Colons are standard in business correspondence <Dear Ms. Wilson:>, commas in personal letters <Dear Barbara,>. Commas may also be permissible for business letters, depending on the personal relationship between the sender and the recipient. But to use a semicolon (**Dear Mr. Jones;*) is always incorrect.

10. **Long dashes have two defensible—and valuable—uses: to frame and to emphasize.**
    First, long dashes—called *em-dashes*—frame what is basically parenthetical matter and make it stand out. Notice in the first sentence how "called *em-dashes*" stands out. It could just as easily have been set off from the rest of the sentence by commas or placed inside parentheses. But the dashes give an interruptive phrase special emphasis (while parentheses

almost beg to be skipped over). It's a strong technique that should be used but, like all effective writing devices, not overused.

Second, em-dashes are handy for short tags that sit apart from the main sentence. The em-dash replaces the colon but adds emphasis. The setoff can come at the beginning of the sentence <Customer service—it's our top priority> or at the end <No matter what the field, an able workforce starts with and continues with one thing—professional training>.

11. **Don't use a comma when writing a month and year.**

Stylebooks have long agreed that no comma should appear between the month and year <February 2012>. With the standard American format of month–day–year, do use a comma after the day <February 23, 2012>. No comma is necessary with the day–month–year format <23 February 2012>. Use a comma after the year <Groundbreaking was held February 23, 2012, in Menomonee Falls> unless the date is used adjectivally <the February 23, 2012 groundbreaking ceremonies>.

12. **For singular possessives, add *'s* even if the word ends with an *-s, -z, -x,* or *-ss*.**

This is the first rule in Strunk & White's famous book *The Elements of Style:* A singular possessive takes *'s* <Kansas's business climate> <Holtz's contract> <Xerox's patents> <the

actress's endorsement>. But note that personal pronouns and *who* have their own form without the *'s* (*mine, our, ours, your, yours, his, her, hers, its, their, theirs, whose*). Also, if the name of a corporation or other entity is formed from a plural word, add only the apostrophe <United Airlines' quarterly report> <The United Arab Emirates' capital is Abu Dhabi>.

When forming a plural possessive, use the word's standard plural form and add an apostrophe to the final *-s* <caterers' fees> <the bosses' offices>. An exception applies to plural words that don't end in *-s:* they follow the same rule as singular possessives <a line of children's clothing> <the alumnae's reunion>.

Appendix D
Common Usage Gaffes

In this top-20 list of usage points that distinguish sloppy from refined language, an asterisk precedes erroneous words and phrases.

NOT THIS:	BUT THIS:
I *feel badly about the oversight.	I feel bad about the oversight.
I'm *feeling very well about the sales figures.	I feel good (contented). I feel well (healthy).
They're *doing good.	They're doing well.
Just *between you and I.	Just between you and me.
He expected *Helen and I to help him.	He expected Helen and me to help him.
She *could care less.	She couldn't care less.
He's *laying down on the couch.	He's lying down on the couch.
*Where are you at?	Where are you?
*If I would have been there	If I had been there . . . .

NOT THIS:	BUT THIS:
She serves on the board; *as such, she has fiduciary duties.	She's a board member; as such, she has fiduciary duties.
The letter was sent *on accident.	The letter was sent by accident.
I *wish he was faster.	I wish he were faster.
I *could of done it.	I could have done it.
*in regards to	in regard to, or regarding
*less items	fewer items
He was *undoubtably guilty.	He was undoubtedly guilty.
*preventative	preventive
*There's lots of reasons.	There are lots of reasons.
*as best as she can	as best she can
*irregardless	regardless, or irrespective

For more on usage, see Appendix F.

Appendix E

Some Dos and Don'ts of Business-Writing Etiquette

Dos:

1. Proofread all documents before sending them out to make sure the spelling and grammar are correct.

2. Double-check that the recipient's name is spelled correctly and that the form of address is proper (Ms., Mrs., Miss, Mr., Dr., Judge, Justice, Honorable, etc.). Double-check the envelope, too, if there is one.

3. Sign business letters with your full name unless you're friends with the recipient. If the salutation is "Dear Mr. Smith," sign your full name; if it's "Dear George," sign your first name only.

4. Sign your letters with an ink pen and not with a stamp of your signature.

5. Always include your contact information so that the recipient will know how to respond to you.

6. If you're sending a handwritten note to a business contact or friend, use a stamp to mail the letter rather than meter-stamping the envelope.

7. Before sending an e-mail, make sure that you have (a) included everyone you need in the address block and (b) incorporated any attachments you refer to in the e-mail.

8. Use white space effectively so that the document reads well and is not a strain on people's eyes. Create generous margins, leave spaces between paragraphs, break up text with subheads if appropriate, and indent appropriately.

9. Date your communications (except e-mails, which will date themselves) so that they give the reader a reference time.

10. Write distinctive thank-you notes if you're writing them to several people in the same office. It's counterproductive if recipients compare their notes and realize you mass-produced them.

Don'ts:

1. Don't use all caps. It amounts to shouting at the reader.

2. Don't return a letter to its sender by writing on it to save time or paper. A reply should be on a separate piece of paper, even if it's a short note. Contracts and other agreements are a separate issue.

3. Don't write "Thank you in advance." If you want to thank people in a request, simply make the request and then write "Thank you." Also, be sure to say thanks (perhaps in person) again when the task has been completed.

4. Don't use BCC on an e-mail unless you are quite sure that it is necessary. It could get you a bad reputation as being indiscreet.

5. Don't use tiny or unusual fonts that make your writing hard to read or that make you seem flippant.

6. Don't write a very long topic in the subject line of an e-mail.

7. Don't write a thank-you note on a card with a preprinted "Thank you!" or "Merci" (it's not considered good manners).

8. Don't let the passage of time stop you from writing to express congratulations, gratitude,

condolences, or whatever other sentiment your instincts say you *ought* to express.

9. Don't write a letter in anger or frustration. Step back, take some time, and detach yourself from the situation. Come back to writing when you have had time to reflect on the matter and can express yourself calmly.

10. Don't put anything in writing that you would be ashamed to see reported on the front page of the *Wall Street Journal.*

Appendix F
A Primer of Good Usage

abstruse. See **obtuse.**

accede; exceed. *Accede* = to agree or yield <We acceded to your request>. *Exceed* = to surpass, to be greater than <Your needs exceeded our capacity for production>.

access; excess. Both are traditionally nouns. *Access* = the act or opportunity of approaching or entering. *Excess* = an amount beyond what is required. Of course, *access* is also common today as a verb meaning "to gain entry to; to penetrate" <I couldn't access those files> <I accessed the storage unit>.

accord; accordance. *Accord* = agreement <The partners are in accord about expanding plant capacity>. *Accordance* = conformance <The materials weren't in accordance with our specs>.

administer; administrate. The first is standard. Avoid **administrate,* a back-formation from *administration.*

admission; admittance. *Admission* = permission or authority to enter <The price of admission is steep>. *Admittance* = physical entry <No admittance after 6 p.m.>.

adopt; adapt. *Adopt* = take up as one's own <Adopt this cause>. *Adapt* = modify <Adapt your leadership style>. Note that the nouns are *adoption* and *adaptation.*

adverse; averse. *Adverse* = unfavorable or contrary to <The expansion plan was postponed in face of adverse market conditions>. *Averse* = reluctant or unwilling; having distaste of, fear of, or hostility toward <The company is risk-averse>.

advise; advice. *Advise* is the verb <Our CFO advised against the merger>. *Advice* is the noun <We took the consultant's advice>.

affect; effect. *Affect* is usually a verb meaning "to have an influence" <The ordinance may affect our sales>. *Effect* is usually a noun denoting a result or outcome <It may be a positive effect>. *Effect* may also be a verb meaning "to bring about" <The new manager effected several changes>.

aggravate; irritate. *Aggravate* = to make worse <This news aggravates an already-bad situation>. *Irritate* = to annoy. Using *aggravate* to mean "irritate" is a common colloquialism, but it will still annoy some readers.

aide; aid. *Aide* is an assistant. *Aid* is assistance.

allusion; illusion. *Allusion* = an indirect reference, as to a cultural work, historical event, or other form of shared knowledge <"Sage of Omaha" is an allusion to Warren Buffett>. *Illusion* = a misperception or a mistaken belief <Their profitability turned out to be an illusion>.

a lot. Always two words.

already; all ready. *Already* = previously, by this time <She was already taking notes>. *All ready* = completely prepared <The corporate minutes were all ready for the secretary's sign-off>.

alternative; alternate. As a noun, *alternative* = one option (among one or more others) <We came up with an alternative design>; *alternate* = a substitute <The delegate's alternate attended>.

altogether; all together. *Altogether* = entirely or completely <This trip was altogether useless>. *All together* = collectively or in a group <That day we reported to him all together>.

ambiguous; ambivalent. *Ambiguous* = inviting more than one reasonable interpretation <Please clarify the

ambiguous policy>. *Ambivalent* = having mixed emotions about something <The CFO has ambivalent feelings about the trade-off>.

amend; emend. *Amend* = to add to a document, esp. a law or other legal document <Amend the contract>. *Emend* = to make corrections or edits to a piece of writing <Emend the proposal before you circulate it>.

among. See **between.**

amuse; bemuse. *Amuse* = to entertain or delight. *Bemuse* = to befuddle.

antidote; anecdote. *Antidote* = anything that counteracts a bad situation <Preparation is the antidote for nervousness>. *Anecdote* = an amusing, illustrative story <She told an anecdote about her first day on the job>.

anxious; eager. *Anxious* = anticipating with unease or worry <We grew anxious about the IPO>. *Eager* = anticipating with enthusiasm <Customers were eager for the retail stores to open>.

appraise; apprise. *Appraise* = to assess in value <Appraise the property at $1 million>. *Apprise* = to keep someone informed <Apprise me of any changes>.

arbiter; arbitrator. *Arbiter* = a person with final say over a matter <You're the arbiter of company policy>. *Arbitrator* = a person who conducts an arbitration to settle a dispute <The arbitrator decided the dispute in our favor>.

as. See **like.**

assure; ensure; insure. *Assure* = to try to satisfy someone of something <He assured me he'd attend>. *Ensure* = to make certain that something will happen or that things will be as expected <We made a schedule to ensure that we'd meet our deadline>. *Insure* = to indemnify against loss or damage <The warehouse was insured for less than market value>.

attain; obtain. *Attain* = to achieve or accomplish something <The regional division attained its quarterly sales target>. *Obtain* = to get something <We had no trouble obtaining raw materials>.

averse. See **adverse.**

avocation. See **vocation.**

awhile; a while. *Awhile* is an adverb meaning "for a short time" <Let's talk awhile before deciding>. *A while* is a noun phrase meaning "a period of time" <Let's talk for a while before deciding>.

bear; born; borne. *Bear* = (1) to carry or support <Corporate suitors come bearing gifts> or (2) to give birth <bear a child>. *Borne* refers to sense 1 <Airborne particulates make the product unsafe>, and *born* to sense 2 <You're a born leader>.

bemuse. See **amuse.**

beside; besides. *Beside* = (1) next to or at the side of <The seat beside the window is taken> or (2) outside of <That's beside the point> <she was beside herself with joy>. *Besides* = in addition to <Besides coffee, we sell tea and baked goods>.

between; among. *Between* shows one-to-one connections <Between payroll and health care, our costs are up>, even when more than two things are involved <Talks began between the firm and its various suitors>. *Among* connotes a looser relationship with three or more <There was one standout among applicants>.

blatant; flagrant. *Blatant* = obvious, overt <That's a blatant lie>. *Flagrant* = conspicuously rude or abusive <Refusing to shake hands was a flagrant break of protocol>.

bombastic = pompous, pretentious <Bombastic speeches stretched out the meeting>. The word has nothing to do with violence.

born; borne. See **bear.**

breach; broach. *Breach* = to break <That's a breach of contract> or break though <Expansion plans will breach the market's boundaries>. *Broach* = to bring up <I hate to broach the subject>.

can; may. Most properly, *can* expresses power or ability <We can ship your order next week>. *May* expresses permission or possibility <May we ship your order by UPS?>.

canvas; canvass. *Canvas* = coarse cloth <We ordered a canvas awning>. *Canvass* = a noun meaning "a poll or survey" or a verb meaning "to conduct a poll or survey" <Canvass your customers before you brainstorm new products>.

capital; Capitol. *Capitol* = the building where the U.S. Congress or a state legislature meets. In all other senses, the spelling is *capital* <capital expenses> <capital letter> <a capital crime> <the capital city>.

censor; censure. *Censor* = to inspect and possibly restrict the release of matter judged to be objectionable. *Censure* = to reprimand someone.

clench; clinch. *Clench* = to tighten, esp. in anger or determination <clenched fist>. *Clinch* = to secure or fasten <clinch the sale>.

climatic; climactic. *Climatic* = of the weather, esp. climate <climatic change>. *Climactic* = dramatic, riveting, moving toward a climax <climactic tension>.

clinch. See **clench.**

closure; cloture. *Closure* = the act or fact of concluding or resolving. *Cloture* = the parliamentary procedure for ending debate and calling for a vote.

collaborate; corroborate. *Collaborate* = to cooperate in an enterprise <We once collaborated in a joint venture>. *Corroborate* = to lend support, esp. by confirming information <Two studies corroborate the claims>.

common. See **mutual.**

compare to; compare with. To compare something *to* something else is to liken the two things; to compare it *with* something else is to note both similarities and differences.

compel; impel. *Compel* = to force, esp. by dint of authority or necessity <I felt compelled to report the error>. *Impel* = to drive forward, as by circumstances or weight of argument <Better opportunities impelled her to relocate>.

compendious; voluminous. *Compendious* = concise, condensed. *Voluminous* = large, roomy.

complementary; complimentary. *Complementary* = (1) making complete or perfect or (2) matching or harmonious <a bundle of complementary products>. *Complimentary* = (1) free <complimentary tickets> or (2) flattering <complimentary reviews>.

comprise; compose. *Comprise* = to include <The company comprises three business units>. *Compose* = to make up <The company is composed of three business units>. The phrase **is comprised of* is always faulty.

compulsive; compulsory. *Compulsive* = prone to or caused by uncontrollable urges <compulsive behavior>. *Compulsory* = mandatory <compulsory training>.

connote. See **denote.**

consequent; subsequent. *Consequent* = following as a result (consequence) <Our supplier took responsibility for consequent costs>. *Subsequent* = following in time <Subsequent ads included a disclaimer>.

continual; continuous. *Continual* = recurring, intermittent <continual calls for tech support>. *Continuous* = ceaseless, uninterrupted <continuous efforts to meet our goals>.

convince; persuade. *Convince . . . of* = to win over, to prove a point <convince the board of the need to expand>. *Persuade . . . to* = convince and cause to take action <persuade the board to fund the building program>.

corroborate. See **collaborate.**

council; counsel. *Council* = a board <the city council>. *Counsel* = (1) adviser <corporate counsel>, (2) advice <She heeded the counsel of her CFO>, or (3) to advise <My mentor counseled patience>.

credible; credulous; incredulous; creditable. *Credible* = believable, trustworthy <a credible argument>. *Credulous* = gullible <credulous acceptance>. *Incredulous* =

unbelieving <an incredulous audience>. *Creditable* = respectable but not outstanding <a creditable performance>.

damage; damages. *Damage* = harm <damage caused by the false rumor>. *Damages* = judicial compensation for harm <judgment for $2 million in damages>.

declaim. See **disclaim.**

definite; definitive. *Definite* = clear, explicit, unmistakable <a definite asset to the department>. *Definitive* = authoritative <the definitive source of information>.

delegate. See **relegate.**

deliberate; deliberative. *Deliberate* = purposeful <a deliberate affront>. *Deliberative* = of or relating to debate or discussion <a deliberative decision-making process>.

denote; connote. *Denote* = to signify; to be the name of <*Mortgagee* denotes the lender, not the borrower>. *Connote* = to imply; to suggest something beyond the literal sense of a term <An open workspace connotes collaboration>.

depreciate; deprecate. *Depreciate* = to fall in value <The car will depreciate by 40% when you drive it away>. *Deprecate* = to disapprove of, to plead against <The manager deprecated the use of company meal allowances for those working solo>.

detract; distract. *Detract* = take away (some quality) <His abrupt manner detracted from his effectiveness>. *Distract* = divert <An accomplice distracted the cashier>.

device; devise. *Device* = a tool or apparatus <a handy device>. *Devise* = to create or invent <devise a better system>.

different. Prefer *different from* over *different than.*

differ from; differ with. To *differ from* is simply to be different <Gross profits differ from net profits>; to *differ with* is to disagree <I differ with you on that point>.

disburse. See **disperse.**

disclaim; declaim. *Disclaim* = deny or disavow <disclaim any knowledge of the report>. *Declaim* = to orate <declaim against corruption>.

discrete; discreet. *Discrete* = distinct <three discrete sources of funding>. *Discreet* = circumspect, tactful <a discreet phone call>.

disinterested; uninterested. *Disinterested* = unbiased; lacking any financial or emotional stake in a dispute <The arbitrator must be a disinterested third party>. *Uninterested* = uncaring <The audience was uninterested>.

disperse; disburse. *Disperse* = to scatter <disperse an unruly crowd>. *Disburse* = to distribute funds <disburse grants>.

distinct; distinctive. *Distinct* = clear, well-defined <We set three distinct goals this quarter>. *Distinctive* = marking a difference, characteristic <her distinctive management style is unlike any we've ever seen>.

distract. See **detract.**

dominant; dominate. *Dominant* = supreme <the dominant player>. *Dominate* = to control <dominate the market>.

eager. See **anxious.**

effect. See **affect.**

e.g.; i.e. *E.g.* = for example <big-ticket items (e.g., cars, refrigerators, and furnaces)>. *I.e.* = that is <numismatics (i.e., coin-collecting)>.

elicit; illicit. *Elicit* = to draw a response <The verbal gaffe elicited laughter>. *Illicit* = forbidden, illegal <illicit behavior>.

eligible; illegible. *Eligible* = fit to be chosen; suitable. *Illegible* = incapable of being read because of bad handwriting, poor printing, etc.

embarrass. So spelled.

emend. See **amend.**

eminent. See **imminent.**

empathy; sympathy. *Empathy* = understanding <empathy for a kindred spirit>. *Sympathy* = compassion <sympathy for the displaced survivors>.

ensure. See **assure.**

equally. Avoid **equally as*. Good usage dictates *equally profitable,* not **equally as profitable.*

evoke; invoke. *Evoke* = to draw out <evoke memories>. *Invoke* = to call on, esp. for authority or assistance <invoke the right to counsel>.

explicit; implicit. *Explicit* = (1) unambiguous <an explicit disclaimer> or (2) graphic, lurid <explicit photos>. *Implicit* = (1) implied <an implicit warranty> or (2) absolute <implicit trust>.

farther; further. *Farther* = physically more distant <Drive three miles farther>. *Further* = more advanced <Further study is needed>.

faze; phase. *Faze* = to agitate <not fazed by the rude caller>. *Phase* = a stage of development <a growing phase>.

fewer. See **less.**

first, second, third. So written—preferably not **firstly,* **secondly,* **thirdly.*

flagrant. See **blatant.**

flair; flare. *Flair* = (1) an innate talent <a flair for pitching ideas> or (2) stylishness <write with flair>. *Flare* = a burst, as of light, activity, etc. <an emotional flare-up>.

flaunt; flout. *Flaunt* = to show off something <flaunting new jewelry>. Flout = to openly disobey or disregard <flouting the rules>.

flounder; founder. *Flounder* = to struggle or thrash about <The campaign was floundering>. *Founder* = (1) to sink <The stock foundered when profits fell> or (2) to fail <The company foundered after the scandal>.

forbear; forebear. *Forbear* = to refrain from an impulse <We must forbear any thoughts of retaliating>. *Forebear* = an ancestor <My grandmother and other forebears were mostly Irish>.

forgo; forego. *Forgo* = to do without <forgo help>. *Forego* = to precede <the foregoing events>.

formally; formerly. *Formally* = properly <We haven't been formally introduced>. *Formerly* = previously <He was formerly with Hastings>.

founder. See **flounder.**

further. See **farther.**

gibe; jibe. *Gibe* = a taunt or tease <The manager's talk was interrupted by good-natured gibes>. *Jibe* = agree <That jibes with what I expected>.

harass. So spelled.

horde; hoard. *Horde* = large group of people <hordes of customers>. *Hoard* = a cache, esp. of valuable things <a hoard of cash>. As a verb, to *hoard* is to accumulate to an excessive degree.

i.e. See **e.g.**

if; whether. A fine but useful distinction: *If* = on the condition that. So, e.g., *Let me know if you need a catalog* means most rigorously not to call if you don't want a catalog. *Whether* = which way you decide about. So *Let me know whether you need a catalog* means, again most rigorously, to please call either way.

illegible. See **eligible.**

illicit. See **elicit.**

illusion. See **allusion.**

imminent; eminent. *Imminent* = looming and inevitable <an imminent announcement>. *Eminent* = prominent and respected <an eminent authority on the subject>.

impel. See **compel.**

implicit. See **explicit.**

imply; infer. *Imply* = to suggest something without saying it expressly <There's an implied threat>. *Infer* = to read into <Can we infer from the announcement that they will build stores close to ours?>.

in behalf of. See **on behalf of.**

incredulous. See **credible.**

infer. See **imply.**

ingenious; ingenuous. *Ingenious* = clever, skillful <That is an ingenious solution>. *Ingenuous* = frank, innocent, free of ulterior motive <Security released the child, who they said was open and ingenuous under questioning>.

in order to. Usually you can shorten this expression to *to.* Do so whenever you can with no loss in clarity.

insure. See **assure.**

invoke. See **evoke.**

irritate. See **aggravate.**

it's; its. *It's* = it is <it's no mistake>. *Its* = the possessive form of *it* <each branch has its responsibilities>.

jibe. See **gibe.**

just deserts (what one deserves) is so spelled—not **just desserts*. *Deserve* and *desert* [pronounced /di-ZURT/] are related words.

lay > laid > laid. To *lay* is to put down or arrange <I'll lay it on his desk> <I laid it on his desk yesterday> <if only I'd laid it there>.

lend; loan. *Lend* = to provide, to grant the temporary use of <Could you lend me that calculator?>. *Loan* = a sum of money that has been lent <We're paying back the loan>. Though traditionally a noun, *loan* is also acceptable as a verb when the object is money <We asked the bank to loan us $50,000>.

less; fewer. *Less* = a smaller amount <less waste>. *Fewer* = a smaller number <fewer losses>.

lie > lay > lain. To *lie* is to recline <I should lie down> <I lay down earlier this afternoon> <if I'd lain down this afternoon, I'd have more energy now>.

like; as. *Like* precedes a noun or pronoun <like a rock>. *As* precedes a subject and verb <as you said>.

loan. See **lend.**

loathe; loath. *Loathe* is the verb meaning "to abhor" <He loathes broccoli>. *Loath* is the adjective meaning "reluctant" <He's loath to admit that he loves spinach>.

loose; lose. *Loose* is an adjective meaning “not tight” or “not constrained” <loose lips> or a verb meaning “to free” <loose the dogs of war>. *Lose,* the verb <lose customers>, is often misspelled *loose.*

make do = to get by with <We’ll have to make do with what’s available>. The phrase is often mistakenly rendered **make due.*

marshal. Both the noun <the fire marshal> and the verb <marshal our arguments> are so spelled.

may. See **can.**

mete out = to allocate. So rendered, not **meet out.*

militate. See **mitigate.**

minuscule = tiny <a minuscule amount>. So spelled, not **miniscule.*

mitigate; militate. *Mitigate* = to make less harsh <I normally would have filed a complaint, but there were mitigating circumstances>. *Militate* = to weight heavily in one direction <A long history of conflict militated against the agreement>.

mutual; common. *Mutual* = reciprocal <mutual admiration>. *Common* = shared <common interests>.

nonplussed = frozen by surprise, perplexed <nonplussed by the shocking news>.

number. See **quantity.**

obtain. See **attain.**

obtuse; abstruse. *Obtuse* = dull, dim-witted <I was too obtuse to catch the allusion>. *Abstruse* = obscure, arcane <But it turns out that no one caught the abstruse allusion>.

on behalf of; in behalf of. *On behalf of* = representing <accepting the award on behalf of>. *In behalf of* = in support of <speaking in behalf of the motion>.

orient; *orientate. *Orient* = to get one's bearings <spend the first day getting oriented>. **Orientate* is an ostentatious variant to be avoided.

past; passed. *Past* is the noun <in the past>, adjective <past efforts>, adverb <walk on past>, and preposition <past the park>. *Passed* is the past tense and past participle of the verb *pass* <time passed slowly>.

peak; peek; pique. *Peak* = a high point, esp. a pointed one such as a mountaintop or a spike on a chart <reach the peak>. *Peek* = a quick, furtive look <take a peek at this file>. *Pique* = (1) indignation <a fit of pique> or (2) to arouse <piqued her interest>.

peddle; pedal. *Peddle* = to sell <peddle hot dogs>. *Pedal* = to operate a foot lever <pedal a bike>.

peek. See **peak.**

pejorative = having negative implications; tending to belittle. So spelled, not **perjorative.*

pendant; pendent. *Pendant* = a piece of dangling jewelry <a silver pendant>. *Pendent* = pending, unsettled <a pendent lawsuit>.

people. See **persons.**

percent. This word (meaning "by the hundred") was formerly spelled as two words. Today it is one.

perquisite; prerequisite. *Perquisite* = a privilege or benefit, esp. one attached to a position; usually shortened to *perk* <Perks included a company car>. *Prerequisite* = a necessary condition <This position has job-training prerequisites>.

persecute; prosecute. *Persecute* = treat harshly, esp. as a group <a persecuted minority>. *Prosecute* = pursue legal action <prosecuted for embezzlement >.

personal; personnel. *Personal* = an adjective meaning "private, individual." *Personnel* = a noun meaning "the whole group of persons employed in a business."

persuade. See **convince.**

persons; people. In most contexts, the plural *persons* sounds stilted. Except for set phrases <missing-persons report>, reserve *person* for singular use <Only one person showed up> and use *people* for the plural.

perspicuous; perspicacious. *Perspicuous* = lucid <a perspicuous argument>. *Perspicacious* = insightful, shrewd <a perspicacious observer of the market>.

phase. See **faze.**

pique. See **peak.**

populace; populous. *Populace* = the inhabitants of a place, collectively <the Swiss populace>. *Populous* = heavily populated <populous northeastern cities>.

pore; pour. To *pore* is to read intently <poring over the financial statements>. To *pour* is to make (a liquid) flow downward.

practical; practicable. *Practical* = pertaining to experience or actual use; adapted to useful action instead of to contemplation <There must be a practical way of shipping these goods>. *Practicable* = capable of being done or used <Scientists have long known that a perpetual-motion machine is impracticable>.

precede; proceed. *Precede* = to occur before something else <An extensive campaign preceded the launch>. **Preceed* is a common misspelling. *Proceed* = (1) to start <Proceed with your report> or (2) to continue <From St. Louis, proceed to Chicago>.

precipitate; precipitous. *Precipitate* is most commonly a verb meaning "to cause suddenly or recklessly" <precipitate a riot>. As an adjective, it means "sudden, rash, or violent" <a precipitate run on the banks>. *Precipitous* = steep <a precipitous decline in demand>.

prerequisite. See **perquisite.**

prescribe; proscribe. *Prescribe* = to direct a course of action <The consultants prescribed a plan>. *Proscribe* = to forbid or outlaw <Insider trading is proscribed>.

presumptive; presumptuous. *Presumptive* = assumed to be <the presumptive nominee>. *Presumptuous* = arrogant, impudent <making presumptuous demands>.

preventive; *preventative. *Preventive* = intended to ward off harm <preventive measures>. **Preventative* is a corrupt form.

principal; principle. *Principal* = main, first <the principal reason>. As a noun, it refers to the main person <a principal at a consulting firm> or, in finance, the original sum of money lent or invested <the principal continues to earn interest>. *Principle* = a belief, tenet, or law <stand on principle> <the principles of economics>.

proceed. See **precede.**

prophesy; prophecy. *Prophesy* = to predict <prophesy great success>. *Prophecy* = the prediction <another doomsday prophecy>.

proposition; proposal. *Proposition* = something that is offered for consideration <We reject the proposition that

plants should be located only on rivers>. *Proposal* = a formal offer <His proposal was silent on the personnel required to make it work>.

proscribe. See **prescribe.**

prosecute. See **persecute.**

prostrate; prostate. *Prostrate* = lying face down. *Prostate* = a gland in male mammals.

proved; proven. *Proved* = the long-preferred past participle of *prove* <last year's financial projections have proved accurate>. An exception is the set phrase *innocent until proven guilty. Proven* is an adjective <Our new software line is already a proven seller in the market>.

quandary = state of confusion <in a quandary about how to proceed>, not the cause of that confusion.

quantity; number. *Quantity* = an unspecified mass <The farm produces large quantities of grain>. *Number* = a collection of individually countable objects <The number of units we sold last year exceeded that of any previous year>.

rack. See **wrack.**

rebut; refute. *Rebut* = to answer a charge or argument. *Refute* = to disprove a charge or argument.

reek; wreak. *Reek* = (1) to stink <The stagnant water reeks> or (2) the bad odor <We could smell the reek of an open sewer>. *Wreak* = to cause a specified type of harm <wreak havoc>.

refute. See **rebut.**

regrettable; regretful. *Regrettable* = unfortunate <a regrettable decision>. *Regretful* = sorry about <regretful about not calling>.

rein; reign. *Rein* = a bridle strap. Figuratively, the means of control <give free rein> <to rein in>. The homophone *reign* (= to rule over) is sometimes mistakenly used in those and similar idioms.

relegate; delegate. *Relegate* = to reassign to a lower position or task <relegated to traffic control>. *Delegate* = to entrust (a person) to act on one's behalf <delegated the research to Terry>.

reluctant. See **reticent.**

respectfully; respectively. *Respectfully* = in a polite manner <May I respectfully ask you to wait another five minutes>. *Respectively* = in regular order <So $500,000 and $600,000 are the benchmarks, respectively, for Ted and Carol>.

reticent; reluctant. *Reticent* = taciturn, not open about one's thought; reluctant to talk <Veterans can be reticent

about their experiences>. Avoid using it as a substitute for being *reluctant* to act.

role; roll. *Role* (in the sense "a part in an organization, a movie, etc.") and *roll* (in the sense "a list of participants, actors, etc.") are often confounded.

sanction = (1) a penalty <The commission imposed sanctions for the incident> or (2) an endorsement <The board gave its sanction for continued talks>.

species; specie. *Species* = a type of plant or animal. The word is both singular and plural. *Specie* = coined money.

stanch. See **staunch.**

stationary; stationery. *Stationary* = unmoving <The gym has five stationary bikes>. *Stationery* = writing paper <We received 12 boxes of stationery>.

staunch; stanch. *Staunch* = loyal and devoted <He's a staunch supporter>. *Stanch* = to stop or control the actual or figurative loss of liquid <stanch the red ink>.

strait; straight. *Strait* = a tight spot <Strait of Magellan> <in dire straits>. *Straight* often displaces *strait* in *straitjacket* and *straitlaced.*

strategy; tactics. *Strategy* = big-picture planning <competitive strategy>. *Tactics* = actions and techniques that support your strategy <flash mobs and other guerrilla-marketing tactics>.

subsequent. See **consequent.**

supersede = to take the place of <It supersedes last year's employee handbook>. The word is often misspelled **supercede.*

sympathy. See **empathy.**

tactics. See **strategy.**

than. See **then.**

that; which. Use *that* to introduce a clause that's essential to meaning (a restrictive clause), and don't set it off with commas. If you write, "The departments that made their numbers last quarter received budget increases," readers will infer that some departments didn't receive increases. Use *which* with a clause that isn't essential (a nonrestrictive clause). If you write, "The departments, which made their numbers last quarter, received budget increases," you're saying that all departments received increases. You can leave out a *which* clause set off by commas and still convey the gist of the sentence.

their. See **there.**

then; than. *Then* = at that time; in that case; therefore. *Than* expresses comparison <more successful than any other start-up>.

there; their; they're. *There* refers to direction <over there> or place <where there is life>; *their* is the possessive of *they* <all their worldly belongings>; and *they're* is the contraction of *they are* <they're on the way>.

torpid. See **turgid.**

toward; towards. *Toward* dominates in American English, *towards* in British English.

try and. Make it **try to.**

turgid; torpid. *Turgid* = (1) swollen <the turgid river after Friday's rain>, or (2) bombastic <a turgid harangue>. *Torpid* = dormant or sluggish <Demand is usually torpid after the holidays>.

uninterested. See **disinterested.**

unique; unusual. *Unique* = one of a kind, unmatched <a unique handmade quilt>. As an absolute term, *unique* should not take modifiers such as *very.* It is not a synonym of *unusual.*

use; utilize. Prefer the simple term.

venal; venial. *Venal* = corrupt, susceptible to bribery <a venal border guard>. *Venial* = pardonable <a venial mistake>.

veracity; voracity. *Veracity* = truthfulness <Veracity earns trust>. *Voracity* = gluttony <His voracity was his downfall>.

verbiage = wordiness, not the words in a message. *Excess verbiage* is redundant. Avoid the misspelling **verbage.*

vocation; avocation. *Vocation* = career <His vocation is nursing>. *Avocation* = (1) hobby or (2) second occupation <On weekends he works on his avocation, flint-knapping>.

voluminous. See **compendious.**

voracity. See **veracity.**

wangle. See **wrangle.**

whether. See **if.**

whether; whether or not. In most instances *whether* can stand alone: *or not* adds nothing. But when the sense is "regardless of whether," the additional words are needed <We're going whether or not you can make it>.

which. See **that.**

who's; whose. *Who's* = who is. *Whose* = the possessive form of *who* or *whom.*

whosever; whoever's. *Whosever* is the standard possessive form of *whoever. Whoever's* is a contraction for *whoever is.*

workers' compensation. This gender-neutral phrase has replaced *workmen's compensation* as standard.

wrack; rack. *Wrack* = (1) to destroy <wracked by fraud> or (2) wreckage <go to wrack and ruin>. *Rack* = to torture as on a rack <rack my brains>.

wrangle; wangle. *Wrangle* = to argue noisily <wrangling over licensing rights>. *Wangle* = to obtain by manipulation <wangle an invitation>.

wreak. See **reek.**

your; you're. *Your* = possessive form of *you. You're* = contraction of *you are.*

Desk References

Writing well is not just one skill but a combination of many—and it's something you must constantly work at. In addition to this guide you might want to keep the following desk references handy.

The Basic Writer's Bookshelf

- *The American Heritage Dictionary of the English Language.* 5th ed. Boston: Houghton Mifflin Harcourt, 2011.
- Garner, Bryan A. *Garner's Dictionary of Modern American Usage.* 3d ed. New York: Oxford, 2009.
- *Merriam-Webster's Collegiate Dictionary.* 11th ed. Springfield, MA: Merriam-Webster, 2008.
- *Roget's Thesaurus of English Words and Phrases.* George Davidson, ed. Avon, MA: Adams Media, 2011.
- Trimble, John R. *Writing with Style.* 3d ed. Upper Saddle River, NJ: Pearson, 2010.

The Connoisseur's Bookshelf

- Flesch, Rudolf. *The Art of Plain Talk*. New York: Harper & Brothers, 1946.
- Flesch, Rudolf. *How to Write Plain English: A Book for Lawyers and Consumers*. New York: Harper & Row, 1979.
- Fowler, H. W. *A Dictionary of Modern English Usage*. 2d ed. Edited by Ernest Gowers. New York: Oxford University Press, 1965.
- Garner, Bryan A. *Legal Writing in Plain English*. 2d ed. Chicago: University of Chicago Press, 2013.
- Gowers, Ernest. *The Complete Plain Words*. 3d ed. Edited by Sidney Greenbaum and Janet Whitcut. Boston: David R. Godine, 1986.
- Graves, Robert, and Alan Hodge. *The Reader over Your Shoulder*. 2d ed. London: Cape, 1947.
- Partridge, Eric. *Usage and Abusage: A Guide to Good English*. New York: Harper & Brothers, 1942.
- Strunk, William, and E. B. White. *The Elements of Style*. 4th ed. Boston: Allyn & Bacon, 1999.
- Tufte, Edward R. *Beautiful Evidence*. Cheshire, Conn.: Graphics Press, 2006.
- Tufte, Edward R. *Envisioning Information*. Cheshire, Conn.: Graphics Press, 1990.

- Wallace, David Foster. *Consider the Lobster.* New York: Little, Brown & Co., 2005.
- Zinsser, William. *On Writing Well.* New York: HarperCollins, 30th Ann. ed., 2006.

Index

Acknowledgments

My profound gratitude goes to Lisa Burrell of HBR, who suggested and edited the book through several revisions; to the LawProse employees Heather C. Haines, Becky R. McDaniel, Tiger Jackson, Jeff Newman, David Zheng, and Ryden McComas Anderson—all of whom helped in developing and refining the text; my Twitter followers (I'm @bryanagarner) who suggested examples of bizspeak to be avoided; my mother-in-law Sandra W. Cheng, her brother Daniel Wu, and my sister-in-law Linda Garner, all of whom suggested lines of inquiry from their many years in business; and most of all my wife, Karolyne H.C. Garner, who cheered and goaded and inspired me in the months when this book was being written—as she has before and since.

The book is dedicated to J.P. Allen, the filmmaker, who has been my close friend from childhood (I was 5, he was 3): We developed our interest in language and writing as teenagers, while also reading intensively about entrepreneurship and business management—never worrying that we might be considered nerds or eggheads. We always thought learning was cool, and ignorance uncool. Nothing has changed.

B.A.G.

August 2012

About the Author

Bryan A. Garner is a noted lexicographer, grammarian, lawyer, and business owner. Since founding LawProse Inc. in 1991, he has trained more than 150,000 lawyers in the techniques of written persuasion and effective contract drafting. His clients include the legal departments of dozens of *Fortune* 500 companies.

Garner is the author of *Garner's Modern American Usage*, *The Elements of Legal Style*, and *The Winning Brief*, and the editor in chief of all in-print editions of *Black's Law Dictionary*. He has coauthored two best-selling books about judicial decision-making with Justice Antonin Scalia.

Notes

Notes

Notes

Notes

Notes

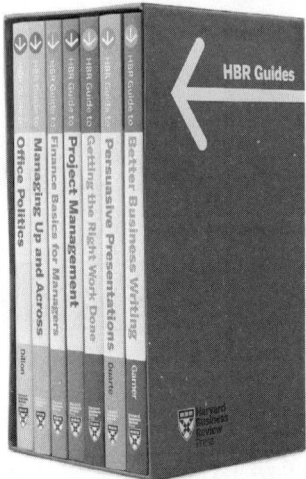

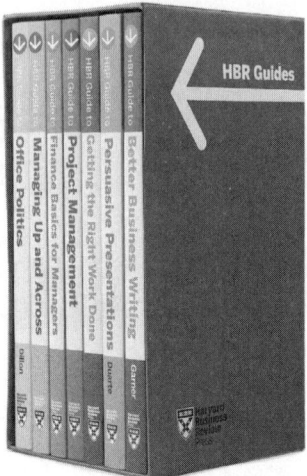

HBR Guide to **Building Your Business Case**

Harvard Business Review Guides

Arm yourself with the advice you need to succeed on the job, from the most trusted brand in business. Packed with how-to essentials from leading experts, the HBR Guides provide smart answers to your most pressing work challenges.

The titles include:

HBR Guide to Better Business Writing

HBR Guide to Building Your Business Case

HBR Guide to Coaching Employees

HBR Guide to Finance Basics for Managers

HBR Guide to Getting the Mentoring You Need

HBR Guide to Getting the Right Job

HBR Guide to Getting the Right Work Done

HBR Guide to Giving Effective Feedback

HBR Guide to Leading Teams

HBR Guide to Making Every Meeting Matter

HBR Guide to Managing Stress at Work

HBR Guide to Managing Up and Across

HBR Guide to Negotiating

HBR Guide to Office Politics

HBR Guide to Persuasive Presentations

HBR Guide to Project Management

HBR Guide to **Building Your Business Case**

Raymond Sheen

with **Amy Gallo**

HARVARD BUSINESS REVIEW PRESS

Boston, Massachusetts

HBR Press Quantity Sales Discounts

Harvard Business Review Press titles are available at significant quantity discounts when purchased in bulk for client gifts, sales promotions, and premiums. Special editions, including books with corporate logos, customized covers, and letters from the company or CEO printed in the front matter, as well as excerpts of existing books, can also be created in large quantities for special needs.

For details and discount information for both print and ebook formats, contact booksales@harvardbusiness.org, tel. 800-988-0886, or www.hbr.org/bulksales.

Printed in the United States of America
10 9 8 7 6

Library of Congress Cataloging-in-Publication Data

Sheen, Raymond.
HBR guide to building your business case / Raymond Sheen with Amy Gallo.
pages cm. — (Hbr guide)
ISBN 978-1-63369-002-8 (paperback)
1. Business planning. 2. Strategic planning. 3. New business enterprises—Planning. I. Gallo, Amy. II. Title.
HD30.28.S428 2015
658.4′012—dc23

2015002965

The paper used in this publication meets the requirements of the American National Standard for Permanence of Paper for Publications and Documents in Libraries and Archives Z39.48–1992.

What You'll Learn

You've got a great idea that will increase revenue or productivity—but how do you get approval to make it happen? By building a business case that clearly shows its value.

Maybe you struggle to win support for your projects because you're not sure what kind of data your stakeholders will trust, or naysayers tend to shoot down your ideas at the last minute. Perhaps you're intimidated by analysis and number crunching, so you just take a stab at estimating costs and benefits, with little confidence in your accuracy.

To get any idea off the ground in your company, you'll have to make a strong case for it. This guide gives you the tools to do that.

You'll get better at:

- Spelling out the business need for your idea
- Aligning your case with strategic goals
- Building the right team to shape and test your idea
- Calculating the return on investment

- Analyzing risks and opportunities
- Gaining support from colleagues
- Presenting your case to stakeholders
- Securing the resources your project needs

Contents

Section 3: BUILD THE CASE

Section 4: CRUNCH THE NUMBERS

Section 5: PRESENT YOUR CASE AND MOVE FORWARD

Introduction

Whether you're pitching a new project at your company or seeking funds for a start-up, you'll need to develop a persuasive business case if you want your idea to go anywhere.

Your primary goal is to help people decide whether to invest resources in your idea. If you're making a case for a project or initiative within an organization, you're not starting in a vacuum. You have insight into your company's strategic priorities, and you probably know the people you're pitching to. But you've still got plenty of work to do. Your audience—the leaders of your unit or company—will expect you to put yourself in their shoes. (What are their chief concerns? How does your project address them?) They'll also expect a thoughtful analysis of the financials and the risks. They'll want to understand what impact your project will have on the P&L so they can intelligently weigh the costs and benefits.

How does that differ from pitching a start-up? As an entrepreneur, you're selling potential partners and funders on *you* as well as on your idea. Though that's an important distinction—it affects what you're trying to achieve and what you'll emphasize in your presentation—you'll take the same general approach you would inside an organization. In both situations, you must identify a clear business need, get to know your stakeholders, and tell them a compelling story about how to profitably meet that need.

That's what you'll learn to do in this guide. We'll focus on building internal business cases because that's the challenge most managers face—but the principles and tools will benefit entrepreneurs, too.

Internal business cases can serve many purposes, but here are three common reasons for developing one:

1. **You want to create a new product or service.** Here, your goal is to demonstrate the profits your offering would add to the bottom line. You'll help decision makers weigh sales estimates against the costs of development, manufacturing, and delivery.

2. **You want to invest in a large IT system.** When you're making a case for a new enterprise resource planning (ERP) system or a customer relationship management (CRM) database, for instance, you'll take into account the impact on the entire business—which departments will benefit and which will incur the costs.

3. **You want to improve your company's facilities.** This type of business case is becoming more common as organizations try to save money through energy efficiency. You may propose buying a

new building, for example, or remodeling an existing one.

You might also create a business case to prioritize projects and propose cutting a few; obtain additional resources for an ongoing initiative; invest in building a new capability; or decide whether to outsource a function.

Anytime you want your company to dedicate resources beyond what's already budgeted, you need to make a case. But you're not just doing legwork to persuade others to support your efforts. You're trying to figure out the best way to capture an opportunity or solve a problem. Developing a case will force you to generate and evaluate ideas in a disciplined way.

For that reason, success doesn't necessarily mean getting a "yes." It means enabling your leadership team to make a wise investment decision. A business case addresses the question "What happens if we take this course of action?" (*not* "Why is this a good idea?"). If the answer doesn't demonstrate that the benefits outweigh the costs or that the results align with the company's strategy, you haven't failed. On the contrary, you've saved your company from making a poor investment.

Let's look at a couple of fictional examples that make this point:

Jim, a brand manager, had an idea for a product that would help his midsize media company compete against larger rivals. His boss asked him to develop a business case, so Jim talked to customers, researched competitors, and looked at several alternatives. He worked with colleagues in finance, marketing, and sales to project revenues 10 years out and calculate ROI. His initial calculations showed promise for the new product. But his risk analysis revealed that if just one competitor got to market first, his company's market share would take a huge hit. During a quarterly review meeting with senior managers, Jim presented a well-researched, clearly articulated business case that incorporated both his original estimates and a worst-case scenario. They said the product looked like a good opportunity, but they agreed with Jim that it felt too risky, so they didn't fund it.

Now consider Catherine, a VP of IT at a manufacturing firm. Her boss asked her to put together a business case for a new inventory-management system. The managers of the company's six plants had been clamoring for this for more than a year, saying that they didn't have enough visibility into one another's inventory levels. Catherine traveled to the plants to learn more about what each one needed the new system to do. She then met with several vendors to review off-the-shelf options and discuss what customization might be required. After getting rough cost estimates, she worked with each plant manager to project how much the new system would speed up fulfillment times and then calculated the savings over the next five years. She presented a well-researched, clearly articulated business case to the CFO, the CEO, and her boss, the CIO. They gave her approval to select a vendor, develop an implementation plan, and cost out the system in detail.

So, who did a better job—Jim or Catherine? You might be tempted to say Catherine, because her project won approval and moved to the next stage. But ultimately, *both* succeeded. They both helped senior managers make an informed decision. Not gaining support for a project after you've devoted time and energy to it is never fun. But as long as you've presented a well-constructed business case, it's OK—and sometimes desirable—to get a "no" from the powers that be. Even if you've persuaded senior managers *not* to approve your project, you'll have earned their trust by showing how carefully you've thought it through. The first step in helping your company decide whether or not to invest in your idea is understanding what goes into a business case.

Section 1
Prepare

Chapter 1
Know the Basics of Making a Case

No matter where you work or what type of idea you're pitching, you should follow the same basic process for any business case you develop. I'll briefly outline it here to give you a sense of the whole before delving into the individual steps in later chapters.

Here, in section 1, "Prepare," you learn how to put yourself in the right frame of mind. Don't even think about constructing a logical argument yet or wrestling with the numbers—it's much too soon for that level of detail. Instead, imagine you're telling a story.

The story starts, as all good ones do, with a problem. This is the *business need* you're trying to solve. For example: Are customers complaining about a particular product feature? Is finance struggling to produce accurate reports because of an outdated IT system? Has your company lost market share to a competitor that's offering adjacent services?

You may spot the need yourself. Or your manager may ask you to address a concern that came up during a strategic-planning discussion or a product-line review. Once you've pinpointed the problem or opportunity, it's time to identify your story's characters:

- Your *stakeholders* have the authority to approve or reject your business case. They might include your boss, your boss's boss, or your company's senior leadership team (section 2, "Get to Know Your Audience").

- *Beneficiaries* are those who stand to gain from what you're proposing. You'll usually have more than one group to consider, either inside or outside the organization. If you're recommending a new IT system for the finance department, you'll have two sets of beneficiaries: the people who run the financial reports and those who receive them.

- You'll draw on *subject-matter experts* to create the case. They're the people with insight into what it will take to solve the problem. If you're proposing a new product, you'll probably pull in colleagues from R&D, sales, and marketing. For any type of project, you'll work closely with finance to come up with cost estimates.

Then you'll consider alternatives for meeting the business need—different ways your story might play out (section 3, "Build the Case"). With the experts you've brought in, you'll explore several options: Which is the most efficient? The most cost-effective? The most appropriate for the organization's culture and capabilities?

After making the best choice in light of what you know at that point, you'll create a very high-level project plan to roughly gauge the amount of time and resources you'll need and the value your solution will bring. Estimating costs and benefits can be daunting for managers who are new to developing business cases. But as you'll see in section 4, "Crunch the Numbers," it's pretty straightforward if you've got the rest of your story clearly laid out: your business need, the alternatives you've considered, and your recommended approach to meeting the need.

You'll enter those numbers into a spreadsheet to determine the return on investment (ROI). A classic ROI calculation (benefits divided by cost) is static—it provides a snapshot of one point in time—so very few companies still rely on it alone. It's better to use a more nuanced version of ROI and look at a stream of costs and benefits over months or years by examining the break-even point, payback period, net present value, or internal rate of return—or some combination of those measures (which we'll cover in chapter 10).

Finally, it's time to tell your story. Package it in whatever format your company uses for business cases and present it to your stakeholders. If no templates exist, create your own logical format (you'll find suggestions and samples in section 5, "Present Your Case and Move Forward"). Above all else, your story needs to be clear—it should *not* be a mystery. Your stakeholders won't be receptive if they have to puzzle out which solution you're recommending, what divisions it will affect, or what it will cost.

Whether you get a yea or nay on your business case, you're not done, so chapter 17, "What Next?" will walk you through the first few steps. If your case is approved, you'll kick off your project and get started. If it's not approved, you still have work to do, such as wrapping things up so you can easily dust off your business case in the future if need be.

Knowing the basic components of a business case will help you get into the right frame of mind to gather, polish, and present your compelling story. But before you dive into the work, you need to know what the decision makers look for in a business case.

Chapter 2
Learn How Your Company Evaluates Cases

How you tell the story of your business case depends on how your organization reviews and approves projects and initiatives.

To figure that out, you need to answer questions such as:

- Does your company have a formal process for evaluating cases? If so, what's involved—and is it connected to other processes, such as the budget review cycle?
- Does your company review cases as they come up, or at specific times tied to your fiscal year or budgeting season?
- Do stakeholders look at projects individually or as a portfolio?

- What level of detail will your audience want? For instance, are they looking for sales projections by region, product line, year, or a combination of the three?
- Does the organization approve entire projects at once or in discrete phases?

Find out as much as you can from a colleague who knows the ins and outs of the process. Reach out to your boss and members of your internal network to connect you with someone who's made a successful pitch. What forms should you use? Which decision makers should you talk to in advance? What types of projects typically get approved?

Large companies like GE, where I spent several years on the corporate staff, usually have a formal process with preset templates. And they typically review business cases at specific times during the year. Some other companies I've worked with do it as part of their annual budgeting process: Senior leaders look at a portfolio of 20 to 30 cases at a time and decide which to fund with the budget that's available. Say they've got $10 million to work with. After reviewing the company's strategic priorities, they may decide to spend roughly $5 million on product development; for instance, $3 million on compliance projects and $2 million on cost-reduction projects. They'll evaluate the portfolio against those numbers and do the necessary juggling to hit them. Companies that review business cases annually often set aside a small portion of the budget for off-cycle opportunities that pop up throughout the year.

Many large companies also have a *tollgate process.* That means a project lead prepares a business case for an initial discovery phase—not for the entire project. If stakeholders give that a green light, they'll ask the team to break the rest of the project into phases (such as design, development, testing, and commercialization, if you're proposing a new product) and to return for approvals along the way. This allows senior managers to hedge their bets, committing more resources only as it becomes clearer that the benefits will outweigh the costs.

Though they sometimes have less structure, smaller organizations work similarly. They may have set times to review cases, for example, and approve initial phases before committing to an entire project.

One small internet service provider I worked with reviewed its business cases at a monthly leadership meeting. After going over the previous month's sales and costs, senior managers would discuss which new projects to fund. Another company—an automotive supplier—developed business cases before responding to requests for proposals (RFPs). That exercise helped stakeholders decide whether to bid on new-vehicle projects and how aggressive their bids should be.

Regardless of company size, you'll need to know who has the authority to approve or reject your case. In some organizations, even small projects require approval by senior leaders. The decisions may be made at the functional, unit, or regional level.

If your organization doesn't dictate a process for business cases or you're requesting resources during an off-cycle time, find out what others have done to get approval. Ask around to see which colleagues have a track record of success and request meetings with them to learn what materials they used, whose help they enlisted, what twists and turns they encountered, and what mistakes they're now careful not to repeat.

Knowing what's worked—and what hasn't—is the best way to develop a case that stands a chance of being approved. We'll dig into learning more about strategic priorities and figuring out who has the authority to approve your case in the next section.

Section 2

Get to Know Your Audience

Chapter 3
Figure Out Who's Calling the Shots

The fate of your project or initiative will usually lie with a small group or even one individual.

Early on, ask your boss who will be evaluating your idea so you can build a case that speaks to their priorities (see chapter 4, "Understand Your Audience's Objectives"). Maybe it's your boss's boss or the division head. Or perhaps the review committee consists of eight leaders representing different parts of the organization—and they take a vote on every idea presented.

Knowing which people will review your business case isn't the same as understanding who makes the final decision. At one company I worked with, a committee of six executives looked at cases during the annual budget meeting. But everyone knew that the CFO had the last word.

It's not always clear who's calling the shots, but you can get important clues by looking at business cases that have been approved. If projects that benefit marketing often get a green light, some decision-making power may lie with the CMO. If cases from HR and finance tend to sail through, the heads of those departments may have a large say in what gets approved.

Once you've figured out who has decision rights, how do you appeal to that person or group? By finding sources of influence and support.

Who Has Influence?

In most organizations, there's a dominant department—and its leader wields informal authority, regardless of his title. At P&G, marketing is king. At GE, it's finance. And at General Motors, it's manufacturing. You can assume that the dominant department's objectives will trump others when decision makers review business cases.

Which area of your company has that kind of power? Projects under its purview stand the best chance of approval, especially in a close race for resources. At P&G, leaders reviewing cases will ask "Which projects promise the most market growth?" At GE, "Which ones will give us the best financial returns?" At General Motors, "Which ones will make our plants most efficient?" Identify your company's dominant department—and cast your idea in light of its goals.

Who Will Have Your Back?

Finding a champion on the review committee—or one who's close to it—will help you get a fair review, because she will lobby on behalf of your case. But how do you find a project champion?

Look at each member of the review committee: Whose goals and concerns will your project address most directly? That person is a potential champion. Reach out and ask what her department is trying to achieve in the coming year. Get a sense of what big projects are under way and which need more support. Explain how your initiative can help fill in gaps or address trouble spots. This is a time when your personal network will pay dividends. Work with people you know in that department or division to clarify the problem or business need that your project will address. Ask them specifically what the champion will care most about and how to address those concerns. Then, ask your contacts to introduce you to the potential champion or to set up a meeting so you can clarify the need and explain your ideas. Even if you've never met the potential champion, you're more likely to get her ear since you're working on a problem that affects her division. If she is interested, ask her to review your business case when it's ready and champion it within the review committee. You'll also want to keep her informed and use her as a sounding board along the way.

Of course, having someone influential on your side does little good if you don't have a strong case that meets a business need and well-thought-out financials. If those elements are missing, even a powerful champion can't help you. So now that you've won over one person, it's time to tailor your pitch to meet the objectives of the organization and the broader committee.

Chapter 4
Understand Your Audience's Objectives

Once you know who the decision makers are, the next step is to discover what they care about most. Senior leaders are looking for projects and initiatives that fit the company's strategy, and they're likely to reject those that don't.

But many managers don't understand that, so they have trouble getting even solid business cases approved. They believe that the benefits are obvious—and neglect to align their cases with broader objectives.

Very few organizations have money or people sitting around waiting to be deployed. So when you're making a business case, you're inevitably competing with others for limited resources. The best way to come out on top is to explicitly demonstrate how your idea supports the company's priorities.

GETTING TO KNOW POTENTIAL INVESTORS OR PARTNERS

If you're an entrepreneur developing a business case, it can be tough to unearth your audience's objectives. After all, you may not know the people you're pitching to. But with a little creativity, you can get the information.

Find other entrepreneurs who have worked with your audience. Sometimes investors will offer this information if asked; otherwise, you may need to tap your network to see if anyone knows whom else they've funded.

Reach out to these fellow entrepreneurs through LinkedIn, Twitter, or mutual acquaintances to get the inside scoop. And don't just ask about your audience's business priorities. You also want to understand what they're passionate about and tailor your business case to that. They're more likely to invest in or partner with you if they have an emotional connection to your project, in addition to confidence in the financials.

If you're not entirely sure what those are, look at the annual report, the CEO's letter to shareholders, and all-staff memos. Consider: What are we trying to do this year overall? Are we in growth mode or cutting costs? Are we attempting to go global quickly or focusing on one or two regions? As you comb through those external and internal communications, you'll probably find a few main themes. Typically, the people evaluating your business case are also charged with meeting those larger objectives—and they'll want to understand how your idea helps them do that. If your executive team has set a goal of 5% top-line growth, demonstrate how your project will add directly to revenue. If you can't do that, highlight metrics that show an indirect connection: Will your idea reduce the time to market by 3%? Will it save cycle time? Whatever the benefits, clearly explain how they relate to overarching goals.

That strategy paid off for one utility company I worked with. Several years ago, market research firm J.D. Power evaluated customer satisfaction at 300 utility companies. The company I worked with came in dead last. Worst in the nation. For the next two years, the executive committee set its sights on reversing that dismal rating, approving any solid business case that dealt with the problem. If you couldn't make a case for improving customer satisfaction in some way, it didn't matter how much money your project would save the company or how much growth it would generate—you'd get turned down. Five years later, when J.D. Power did a follow-up study, the company scored in the top 50% on customer satisfaction—a huge improvement.

Even if your company's goals are that narrowly defined, your stakeholders may not agree on how to achieve them, so you have to understand each decision maker's perspective on execution. Say your organization is keen to reduce costs. The CFO may feel the best way to do that is to streamline manufacturing processes, but the COO may advocate outsourcing.

That's one reason it's critical to pull in experts from various functions to help you build your business case (see chapter 6, "Build a Cross-Functional Team," for more on this). They'll shed light on what their department's leaders care about. For example, someone from finance can probably give you insight into what the CFO thinks about the company's strategic goals and how to achieve them.

How else can you get the information you need about your audience?

1. **Gather intelligence from above.** In addition to tapping cross-functional experts, ask your boss about your stakeholders' priorities, values, goals, and decision-making styles. What might they gain or lose from the opportunity you're presenting? How are they influenced? Do they like to be presented with strong opinions supported by facts, or do they prefer to go through the thinking process with you and then reach their own conclusions? How do they like to receive information? Are they numbers oriented? Customer focused?

   Your champion can be a good source of intelligence, too. Ask her the same questions. In addition, inquire about anything you *shouldn't* include in the proposal because it might push the buttons of one of the decision makers.

   If you have direct access to stakeholders, approach them with three simple questions: What are your group's chief objectives this year? How do you measure success? What are your barriers? Then use their answers to inform your case. If they're struggling to respond to increasingly stringent environmental protection regulations, for example, highlight how your idea will help them do that.

2. **Examine your stakeholders' track records.** Look at the projects they've approved over the past two years. What do they have in common? Do they all focus on improving customer satisfaction? Lowering costs? Growing your product line? Finding new sources of revenue? Adding capabilities? Now look at projects your stakeholders have killed—they, too, may have telling similarities. Of course, it's important to put those approvals and rejections in context. If your company just acquired a business or went through a restructuring, the goals may have changed.

As you're digging for insights into your stakeholders, also consider what *their* stakeholders care about. Even if the people reviewing your business case have decision-making authority, they'll have to justify their choices when actual revenues and costs start rolling in. So think carefully about your audience's audience: If you pitch to the CEO, he'll probably try to anticipate the board of directors' reactions and concerns. A marketing VP will channel the CMO. Put yourself in your stakeholders' shoes and give them what they'll need to convey the value of your idea to those above them.

Now that you know what your audience cares about most, you can turn to gathering the specific information you need, starting with the pain point or opportunity you've identified.

Section 3
Build the Case

Chapter 5
Clarify the Need

You can't build your team, brainstorm solutions, or crunch the numbers until the business need is crystal clear.

Try thinking of it as a pain point: Plant managers don't have an effective way to share performance information. The sales force in Europe is losing bids because of a new competitor. Whatever the pain, that's the source of the need, and your task is to figure out how to alleviate the suffering.

Of course, some projects are driven by opportunities, not by urgent problems. Your company might save 40% in operating costs by switching to a new CRM system, for example, or become eligible for $2 million in tax incentives by updating its wastewater treatment facility by year-end.

You may identify the pain point or opportunity yourself—maybe you have an idea about how to remedy a product defect or make a process more efficient. But more often, stakeholders will hand you a problem and say, "Fix this," or point to an opportunity and say, "Check this out." In either situation, research the business need so you'll have a thorough understanding of it.

Let's look at an example that shows how you might do this.

Imagine that a manufacturing VP comes to a strategic-planning meeting and says, "We can't meet our goals this year if we don't fix or replace our inventory system. Our counts are all wrong. In some places, we have excess; in others, we keep running out." The CEO asks you, an IT manager, to look into it. Now it's your responsibility to build a case for investing in a new system, or not, depending on what you find.

Your primary challenge at this point? Learn *why* the inventory levels are off and which parts of the business suffer as a result. Here are the steps you'll take.

Talk to Beneficiaries

First, ask the manufacturing people who use the current system what they think is going on: When did the problem start? How does it manifest itself? How often? How does the problem prevent their teams from doing their work effectively? Who else in the company does it affect? Talk to those individuals as well, and gather relevant data, reports, surveys—whatever evidence your beneficiaries can provide. If possible, observe the issue firsthand. You might visit plants and watch how inventory is captured and entered into the system. You could shadow the people who use the system and observe how they complete their tasks.

Your job is to listen *and* probe further. The beneficiaries may not know the underlying reason for the problem: "We're not sure why the inventories keep showing up wrong. But when we go to the warehouse floor, the count is always off." It's up to you to discover the cause and identify a reasonable solution.

The beneficiaries may have a solution in mind. (Perhaps the manufacturing VP learned about an inventory management system that he believes will provide a more accurate count.) But sometimes what they want isn't the best fix. Of course you need to look into this option, but it might not be your final recommendation, especially if it's costly or difficult to adopt.

Analyze Processes

Next, examine the problem yourself. Don't just take people's word for it. Use a process-flow analysis—a visual representation of the various stages. Through conversations with beneficiaries and your own observations, develop a full picture of how inventory moves and where amounts are captured. Lay out all the steps of the inventory flow, illustrating how they conncct and noting decision points (for example, who decides when to enter amounts into the system?). This is critical because you may find out that it isn't an IT problem at all. Maybe there's a training issue or a communication breakdown in the supply chain. You could discover places where the process falls apart.

Look at the sample flowchart in figure 5-1. Note how many parts of the process depend on manual updates

FIGURE 5-1

Process-flow analysis

By creating a visual process map like this sample flowchart, you'll develop a more complete picture of the business need you're trying to address.

Inventory management process

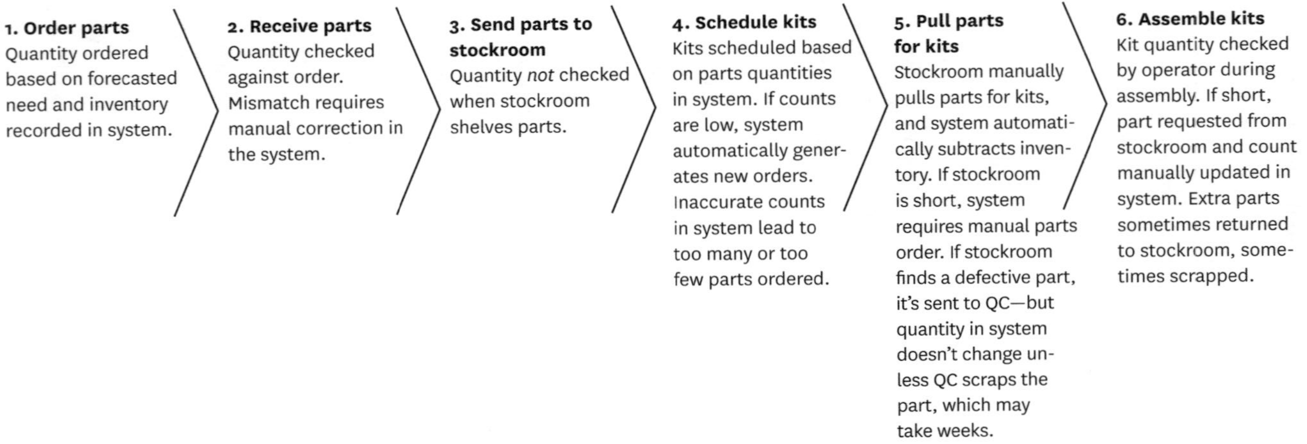

1. Order parts
Quantity ordered based on forecasted need and inventory recorded in system.

2. Receive parts
Quantity checked against order. Mismatch requires manual correction in the system.

3. Send parts to stockroom
Quantity *not* checked when stockroom shelves parts.

4. Schedule kits
Kits scheduled based on parts quantities in system. If counts are low, system automatically generates new orders. Inaccurate counts in system lead to too many or too few parts ordered.

5. Pull parts for kits
Stockroom manually pulls parts for kits, and system automatically subtracts inventory. If stockroom is short, system requires manual parts order. If stockroom finds a defective part, it's sent to QC—but quantity in system doesn't change unless QC scraps the part, which may take weeks.

6. Assemble kits
Kit quantity checked by operator during assembly. If short, part requested from stockroom and count manually updated in system. Extra parts sometimes returned to stockroom, sometimes scrapped.

—we've got lots of room for human error. And the lag time after quality control identifies a defective part makes it even harder for the inventory system to reflect accurate counts. You'll want to examine all these pain points to fully expose the need.

Agree on What the Solution Should Accomplish

Once you've gathered all this information and formed a clearer picture of the business need, go back to your stakeholders (the CEO and the manufacturing VP) and make sure your assumptions match theirs about what the solution should do and what the constraints are. For example, a new inventory system may need to work in Europe as well as in the United States—that's an assumption you'll want to confirm with your stakeholders, even if it seems obvious to you. Constraints might include compatibility with other IT systems or short windows of time when the rollout can take place. Use the following questions to guide the discussion with your stakeholders:

- Where will the solution be used? In what offices or facilities? In how many countries?
- Who will be affected by the solution? A single department or the entire organization?
- How quickly does the solution need to be in place? Will we roll it out over time or all at once?
- How should we measure the solution's effectiveness? Do we have a baseline that we can compare against?

TESTING THE NEED WITH A STEALTH PROJECT

What if you *suspect* a market need but lack data to back it up? Or senior managers don't want to alter a product, despite customer complaints? Or they tend to reject out-of-the-mainstream ideas like yours?

Try demonstrating the importance of your business case—to yourself and others—by doing a stealth project as proof of concept. A small pilot project can help you test your hypothesis about the need before you develop and present a solution.

Take this example: At GE, we had some problems with a product that my engineering team was responsible for. We thought fixing them would require a time-consuming, expensive redesign, but then one of my engineers suggested a minor change in the manufacturing process. Not everyone agreed it would work, so he and the manufacturing manager pulled operators aside and asked them to collect product and process data over

- Should we combine the solution with another related initiative?

Stakeholders may not have the answers to all these questions, or they may ask you to make recommendations. When that happens, it usually means there's no constraint with respect to that question, which is helpful to know.

a two-week period. The data demonstrated the validity of his idea, and he got approval for it.

The stealth approach has its risks, of course. You might annoy people or even get into trouble, particularly if you're spending funds meant for other projects. Doing a proof of concept without getting approval can also signal to senior managers that you don't trust them to make smart decisions.

To reduce these risks, keep your project lean and focused—and frame it as a fact-finding experiment.

Know what you want to learn, and spend only as much money as it takes to do that. Get your answer and move on. Don't let the project carry on for months. And document everything you learn so you can include your findings in your business case.

You may discover that the business need isn't so great, after all—so be prepared to abandon your idea.

Document, Document, Document

Record everything you learn: where the pain comes from, who's experiencing it, and what the solution needs to accomplish. This documentation will save you time later as you prepare your presentation to stakeholders—they'll want to see what you're basing your recommendations on (see Section 5, "Present Your Case and Move Forward").

The process can be as straightforward as jotting down notes or entering them in an Excel or PowerPoint file—or you might use your company's project management software to log evidence of the need. Keep track of who told you what. That way, you can go back for clarification in the likely event that you receive conflicting or partial information from beneficiaries. This will also help you refer stakeholders' questions to the right people.

After doing all this work, what if you find out the business need isn't strong? That's OK. You're still helping your stakeholders make an informed decision about whether to invest, and how much. This is a good time to meet with your champion and ask for guidance. Should you continue to develop a business case even though there isn't much benefit? Is there an additional benefit that you haven't considered that should be added to the business case? For instance, you may find that a new inventory system will speed up delivery time by just 5%—and that the project won't generate any return for several years, given software and innovation costs. But stakeholders may still want to go ahead if the new system brings manufacturing up-to-date with competitors. When I sat on the review committee at a medical device company, we saw many projects that didn't immediately deliver huge revenues or cost savings. Still, they had to get done—sometimes to comply with new FDA guidelines, sometimes to address concerns of key hospitals or doctors and gain their support for new products.

Figuring out the specifics of how to address the business need and with what resources can be a daunting task. Fortunately, you don't typically have to go it alone. Your next step is to gather a team of internal experts who can help you get the information you need.

Chapter 6

Build a Cross-Functional Team

Unless you're an entrepreneur, you probably won't build the business case on your own. Inside established companies, it's a team effort. Both beneficiaries and subject-matter experts will help you determine which solution to the underlying problem will work best, how much it will cost, how much revenue it will bring in, and so on.

You probably won't have a full-time, dedicated team at your disposal. Instead, you'll bring people together from various departments at different points in the process—when it's time to brainstorm alternatives, for instance, or estimate the costs and benefits.

Building a cross-functional team allows you to examine solutions from multiple angles. Otherwise, you'll develop the case from a particular point of view—most likely your department's—and run the risk of overlooking an option or important costs and benefits.

Include the following types of team members:

- **A finance representative.** Too many people assume that finance is the enemy. This couldn't be further from the truth, especially when you're developing a business case. Someone from finance can establish current costs and benefits, and make accurate projections. And the earlier you bring in this person, the better. Don't attempt to do the forecasting and ROI calculations on your own, even if you're good with numbers. You might make incorrect assumptions about industry dynamics, depreciation, personnel costs, and so on without guidance from someone with a big-picture view of the company's revenues and expenses.
- **Beneficiaries.** If you're proposing a product fix, engineering may be your primary internal beneficiary, but salespeople could also gain an advantage. So include someone from each group. Don't overemphasize the role of your beneficiaries—since they're the ones feeling the pain, they're not going to be your most objective problem solvers. But ask them to voice their chief concerns as the team identifies and weighs solutions, just as they did when they helped you gain a deeper understanding of the business need.
- **Someone who regularly talks with customers.** If customers feel the pain most acutely, or the proposed solution will affect them in any way (most new ideas do), consult with someone who knows

what they care about—or who can ask them. This may be an account manager, a customer service rep, or a marketing associate who conducts customer surveys.

- **External experts.** You might not get all the information and insight you need in-house. If your company has never solved this kind of problem before, ask outside experts for their recommendations. Considering a new ERP system? Reach out to your network of IT professionals, online communities, vendors, and partners. Find out what they use and how well it's working for them.

What might a team that includes all those members look like? Let's return to the inventory problem we looked at in chapter 5, "Clarify the Need." You'd want to bring in people most affected by the incorrect counts: several manufacturing representatives (from different plants), colleagues from finance and sales, and someone who can speak to the concerns of suppliers. You could also consult with vendors who sell inventory systems to find out what additional features the latest software provides.

By involving these people in building the business case, you don't just gain access to information (though that's important); you also gain their *support*. They're engaged, right along with you, in finding the right solution. And it's much easier to get approval if your stakeholders know that people from their departments helped create the proposal.

Once you know what types of team members you need, handpick individuals you work well with—those who will be generous with their time and information. You can add occasional "guest stars" to the lineup. For instance, if you're bringing the team together to brainstorm solutions, include people who thrive in meetings like that—creative colleagues who are quick on their feet, not black-and-white thinkers wedded to their own ideas.

But keep the core group small—no more than six people, if possible. You'd lose momentum and focus if you spent weeks or months consulting everyone who knows something about the problem. You want a tight team of experts who can efficiently help you work out the best solution.

Even with a dream team, it's rare you'll come up with the best solution out of the gate. That's because there's rarely one solution to any given problem. You'll need to generate and weigh several alternatives.

Chapter 7
Consider Alternatives

Now that you've selected your team, it's time to start brainstorming. Bring your experts and beneficiaries together to think about potential solutions. Briefly describe the pain, who's feeling it, and its underlying cause—just to orient the group—and ask for suggestions on how to alleviate it. Lay out the ideas that stakeholders or beneficiaries proposed early on, and ask your team to generate several more. Encourage people to look beyond their own unit or function: How have other departments met this need? What have other companies done? What's worked, and what hasn't?

At the beginning of a meeting like this, don't put constraints on people. Let them think out loud. Then, after the team generates options, you can mention limitations to focus their thinking and spur additional ideas: Remind people that the solution can't involve relocating staff, for instance, or that it must take into account the products the company will launch in the coming year.

Open the floor to any and all ideas for solving the problem with the following guidelines in mind.

Forgo Precision—and Push Beyond the Obvious

Generate alternatives quickly. You aren't drafting project plans or identifying specific vendors or product names. Instead, you're coming up with a generic system, initiative, or product to recommend. Don't get hung up on particulars. If your team starts laying out specifications for a solution, pull them back to the big picture. You'll gather basic specs later, after you've narrowed down your options and begun assessing them. And once you get approval, you'll have time to sort out the nitty-gritty details. The goal right now is to sketch out several directions you might take, not to pave the actual path.

Often there's a front-runner idea from the very beginning—perhaps a solution suggested by your champion or adopted by leaders in your industry. Don't fixate on this option, even if it's the CEO's idea. Stakeholders will expect you to seriously consider multiple options. After all, they want to see that you've conducted a thorough analysis, not just gone with the obvious solution.

If you struggle to come up with other options, try these techniques to broaden your perspective:

- **Start with the desired end state.** Look at how other organizations have achieved the business performance you're aiming for, whether it's faster time to market or improved quality. Would those approaches work for your company?

- **Think about how other departments would address the issue.** What would the project look like if IT took the lead? How about sales? HR? Engineering? Supply chain?
- **Consider how you'd do the project with different constraints.** What if you had twice the time to complete the project? Or half the time? What would change if you outsourced (or insourced) the work? What if you had to scale the solution to do the same thing 100 times?

Consider a Do-Nothing Option

A business case addresses the question "What happens if we take this course of action?" But you also need to consider the consequences of doing nothing. That will help you articulate the business need when you present your case. For example: "If we stick with our current line, sales will continue to drop 10% a year. This new product will reverse that trend—in fact, we project a 20% increase in sales over the next five years."

Sometimes doing nothing is a viable option. That's often true of internal improvement projects. Suppose the supply chain organization wants to modify its parts-traceability program to meet the industry standard. The manager developing the business case will include a do-nothing option to show stakeholders what costs they'll avoid by approving the project. She'll answer questions along these lines: "If we don't get in line with the industry standard, what work-arounds will we need in order to keep selling our products? Will we lose any customers?" If the do-nothing costs aren't prohibitive, stakeholders may decide to absorb them rather than invest in changing the program.

Narrow Down Your Possibilities

When I reviewed business cases at GE, I didn't like being given one option and told that was the way we had to do it. Nor did I want someone to walk me through 25 alternatives. Chances are your review committee members are looking for the same thoughtful balance. Present stakeholders with two or three reasonable choices. This means you need to whittle down the list from your brainstorming session. Questions like these will help:

- Which option costs the least?
- Which is the fastest to implement?
- Which has the fewest risks?
- Which brings in the most revenue?

Often, one option will meet several of those conditions—but each idea you present should have at least one big thing going for it. Don't offer an obviously unacceptable solution in contrast to your preferred choice. It will appear that you're trying to manipulate the review board.

Once you've selected a few options, talk with the champion you identified early on—ask her what she thinks of your alternatives and which ones stand the best chance of approval. Also, review the options with your subject-matter experts. If there is something in an option that is impossible or unacceptable, modify the option or drop it. For instance, if one option violates existing codes or standards, revise it to make it compliant.

When you prepare the financials, one of your options may stand out as a clear winner. So you'll present it to the review committee—but also share other options you considered. If you looked at three alternatives but immediately saw that two would generate no revenue growth (or would cost too much, or present a compliance problem), explain that in your presentation. Stakeholders expect to see which viable choices you rejected and on what grounds.

You have several good ideas for solving the problem, but that's only half the work. Now it's time to dig a bit deeper and consider what it would mean to implement them.

Chapter 8
Think Through the "How" at a High Level

To build a strong case, you'll need to paint a picture—in very broad strokes—of how the organization would implement the solution you're proposing. You're not doing a detailed project plan at this point. Far from it. You're just sketching a basic outline of what the project requires so your estimates of costs and benefits will be realistic.

This helps you see more clearly whose support you'll need. If you start to think through the "how" and suddenly realize that marketing and sales will have to contribute resources, you'll need to tap them for information when you're working on the financials and get their buy-in before you present the case.

This process also reveals transition costs, which many managers overlook (see chapter 9, "Estimate Costs and Benefits"). They're often so gung ho about their pet solution that they forget to consider how they're going to migrate the company's data into that fancy new system, how they'll train everyone to use it, or how they'll shut down and archive the old system. To get the fullest picture of what implementation will mean to your project, you'll need to work with your team to get their feedback and to set a rough plan.

Consult Your Team

Here again, you'll bring in your subject-matter experts to get their input on various practical questions. For example:

- What work must be done before the company can switch to the new system?
- Who needs to do it?
- What—and whom—will the actual switch involve?
- Where will major costs be incurred before, during, and after the switch?
- Will we roll out the system once companywide or multiple times for different customers, departments, or locations?
- What training will employees need?
- What systems, products, or processes will be eliminated when this new system is implemented?

Beneficiaries will have strong opinions on how to implement the solution since they're often the ones who will do the work. They may believe the system needs to be rolled out across the organization all at once. Or they may think that their department should be responsible for managing the project. Make sure your case reflects their input so you'll have their buy-in when it's time for them to contribute. Let's say you're proposing to develop a new product for the Asian market. The marketing and sales force in Asia may think that they should manage the project. If your recommendation is that the project will be managed by the R&D department in Germany, you might add that a person from the Asian marketing team will relocate to Germany or that the prototype reviews and design reviews will be done in Hong Kong. That way, the team in Asia won't stand in your way when it's time to roll out the project.

Make the Plan Directionally Correct

You're still not at the point where you need a detailed project plan, so don't go too far into the weeds. But you'll want to figure out, for instance, whether you'll use the new system in three countries or five. You can think later about which country you'll do first, and so on, depending on what's happening in those markets. For now, just knowing the "where" at a high level will help you consider what kind of work will go into getting the system ready (translating it into three or five languages, testing it with user groups in each country, and so on). You're not sorting out every task—just the types of tasks and the people involved.

As you do this, you may realize that one or more of your alternatives aren't feasible, after all. Perhaps you discover a large hidden cost or see that one of the solutions, when implemented, would violate a stated constraint. In that case, go back to your team of experts to reconsider other options or generate new ones.

With the key issues identified and your rough plan mapped out, you're ready to turn to the financials.

Section 4
Crunch the Numbers

Chapter 9
Estimate Costs and Benefits

Before you calculate the ROI, you'll need a more accurate projection of costs and benefits. For many people (especially nontechnical folks), working with these numbers can be intimidating. But now that you've identified and clarified the business need, gathered the right team, and tested your assumptions, this part won't be hard.

Start by estimating costs and benefits for the option that you and your team consider to be the most viable. Once you've done that, explore the alternatives by adjusting the numbers. Will they cost more to implement? Will they return revenue sooner? Usually you'll change just a few figures. For example, one option may be to do a phased rollout instead of a universal launch. Your project costs are likely to be similar, but some of your benefits won't show up until later—so you'll decrease those numbers for the first year or two.

Stick to two or three alternatives. You'll drive yourself—and your team—crazy if you explore all the possibilities available to you. On rare occasions, you may need to develop a full-blown case for more than one alternative. For example, in a financial services company I worked with, some executives wanted to outsource the call center; others pushed to keep it in-house and update the antiquated system. We knew the review team had advocates on both sides, so we had to create two separate cases—one to outsource, one to upgrade—for equal consideration. In this case, the outsourcing option had a faster payback, but ultimately did not deliver as much value to the company. The organization decided to upgrade the existing system. This option cost more and took longer, but it also created a long-term capability that grew in value over time.

Exceptions like this aside, once you have your alternatives identified, you'll want to assemble the figures that will be most useful in helping your stakeholders make a solid decision.

The Numbers You Need

Base your estimates on the categories in your company's income statement (P&L)—those are the numbers your reviewers will care about. Together, your costs and benefits make up the cash flow for your project. Consider when they'll begin and how they'll change over time. Don't look at the total pot of money your company will "net" at the end of five or ten years. Instead, show a stream of expenses and income: Generate estimates for each year until the benefits run out.

How many years out do you go? It depends on the project. Your company may have guidelines—or your stakeholders may have a preference. But if not, follow these rules of thumb: For IT projects, estimate three to five years of cash flows. (After that, most IT systems become obsolete.) For product development cases, look at the product life cycle. In some industries, such as consumer electronics, that's three years. In others, like the aircraft industry, it's 15. Facilities projects usually need a minimum of 15 years.

With those rough guidelines in mind, gather the cost and benefit information.

Costs

You'll look at two main types of costs. The first type, *project costs,* consists of project expenditures and capital expenditures. Project expenditures usually occur at the beginning—they tend to include development, testing and qualification, training and deployment, and travel costs. They're pretty straightforward to estimate: You consider the type of work to be done on the project and approximately how long it will take, and then put together your estimate for completing that work. I generally start by assessing how many people I need on the team and, using an average salary rate, I can project the personnel costs. Then I do a rough estimate of travel and supplies to be purchased on the project.

Capital expenditures aren't as simple. A project cost becomes a capital expenditure when you've spent the money to acquire or develop an asset. Anything that is capitalized must be depreciated—which means finance must show the decrease in value over the asset's life. On your project ROI calculation, you can record the cost of an asset as a single number, under the year the company acquired the asset, or you can spread the cost over the years it's depreciated. (Either way, you capture the total cost.) Check with your finance person to find out how you must represent the costs in your analysis. The financial rules for capital expenditures are complex, and they often change, so you'll want expert guidance.

The second type of costs, *operating costs,* can be tricky because you're estimating how much money it will take to maintain whatever you're proposing. These include overhead—costs, such as personnel, office space, maintenance and licensing fees, and any other ongoing expenses. Consider: Will you need a part-time staff member to monitor your new centralized procurement system? Or will your new product require a dedicated sales team that understands its technical features? What about changes to the help desk? Some projects will reduce operating costs, so look at expenses you'll eliminate as well as those you'll add.

The department doing the project work incurs the project costs (IT, if it's creating a new customer management system). By contrast, operating costs can crop up anywhere in the business (for instance, in the departments that will use the system).

As discussed in chapter 8, "Think Through the 'How' at a High Level," many managers overlook *transition costs,* the type of operating expense that kicks in when the organization switches from something old to something new. These costs might include a temporary spike in manufacturing defects, say, or an increase in calls to the help desk. Most major projects will cause some disruption, and you need to account for it in your estimates. The subject-matter experts on your team should be able to identify transition costs for their departments; these should be included as a separate line on our ROI worksheet.

Benefits

Benefits consist mainly of *revenue* (money you'll bring in through sales) and *productivity savings* (costs you'll avoid through greater efficiency). Let's look at each.

Revenue

Ask your sales and marketing subject-matter experts to work with you to estimate revenue. They'll help you set realistic targets—both how much to expect and when to expect it.

They'll also help you anticipate the response from competitors—a critical long-term factor. For example, the revenue stream for a new product may plateau or decrease when a rival comes to market with a similar or better offering. Look with your team at what's happened with previous products—and base your assumptions on that. Did sales grow steadily for the first three years and then decay once competitors entered the market?

When considering revenue, factor in the *cost of goods sold* (listed as COGS on the income statement). This puts a price tag on the materials and labor required to produce what you're selling. Of course, to do that, you'll first have to estimate how many units you'll sell each year—once again, your team members from sales and marketing can help with those numbers. People often neglect to take COGS into account and so accidentally inflate their revenue estimates. But your stakeholders will want to see that you've deducted them from your revenues—that's how you calculate your gross profit margin.

Productivity savings

Some productivity savings relate to product costs, others to overhead costs. You can achieve the former by changing materials or automating assembly. These savings change the product cost baseline and, therefore, the gross profit margin. You'll base these estimates on how many units you'll produce each year. By contrast, overhead productivity savings come from cutting current, ongoing expenses that stem from how you run the business. Maybe a security system you're proposing would enable your company to hire fewer guards without compromising safety. Such savings are usually flat—in other words, they are the same every year.

If you say your project will save personnel overhead costs, your stakeholders will probably ask, "Who are we going to lay off?"—and for good reason. Unless you get rid of people, you still have to pay them. Even if you make the argument that they'll do other things instead, you're not really saving money. You're just moving expenses around to other parts of the organization. But you might be able to cut other types of operating expenses: Maybe your initiative will eliminate the need for overtime or reduce costly errors by giving people more time to focus on their tasks. Or perhaps the company will spend less on maintenance contracts.

Intangible costs and benefits

Some costs and benefits are tough to measure. For example, a new employee time-tracking system may hurt morale—but how do you quantify the cost to the company? If a new product feature will increase overall customer satisfaction, how do you translate that benefit into dollars?

Whenever possible, assign numbers to your costs and benefits. Derive those figures from expected changes in behavior—those are the business consequences you can measure. If morale will be hurt, will you see an increase in absenteeism? By how much? What about error rates and training costs? How much will they go up? If customers will be happier, how many repeat customers will you gain? How much will you save in advertising as a result? If you think your new performance management system will improve employee satisfaction, how much will the turnover rate drop? And how much will that save the company in new-hire training?

If you truly can't quantify certain costs or benefits, you can't use them in your calculations—though you should still mention them when you present your case.

Where to Get the Numbers

As you've probably gathered by now, you're not making up these estimates alone in your office. You're reaching out to beneficiaries and experts in various departments to get accurate information. If you're proposing an initiative to improve the contracting process with vendors, get input from procurement. If your case is for a new product in a new market, ask sales and marketing colleagues how much revenue growth they expect and whether the product will cannibalize other offerings. The experts on your team have already helped you identify types of costs and benefits—now they can suggest actual numbers from their functions' perspectives.

Since it's nobody's job to give you the numbers you need, you have to rely on relationships—often going beyond your core team—to get them. If you're an IT manager proposing a new system to track sales leads, ask one of your contacts in sales to vet your costs and benefits. Don't have anyone to call? See if your manager or a member of your team can put you in touch with somebody.

When you're making a case for an entirely new type of project for your company, tap your broader professional network for figures, as you did when you were weighing various options and narrowing them down. Ask people in other companies what they've spent on similar projects. They're not going to hand over their detailed plans—those would be considered proprietary. But they may be willing to give you a ballpark number, saying that it cost them about $20 million to put in SAP software. You can also get general estimates from vendors, based on their experience doing similar work for other clients. If you work for a large corporation, ask other operating divisions for their input.

Whatever the source, don't take the numbers at face value. Your sales contact may give you five-year forecasts that seem low. Find out what he's basing them on, how they compare with other product sales, and whether he's willing to back up the numbers when you share them with the review committee. And keep in mind that certain departments are inclined to either pad or lowball numbers. Salespeople rewarded with commissions may underestimate so they can exceed their targets. Marketing colleagues, wanting to see a new product get approved, may give you a higher number. Understanding biases like these will help you ask the right questions to get the most accurate, balanced numbers possible. Of course, people won't tell you that their numbers are biased. They'll say that they're realistic. To assess how accurate their estimates are, ask them what the impact would be if the number were 20% higher or 20% lower. If you get an emotional response to such questions, there's a good chance that, whether they realize it or not, they've given you a biased number. In that case, check with another subject-matter expert to confirm the initial figures you received. If you've got a large range for one of your estimates, that signals a project risk. Select the value that you believe is most realistic and test the best-case and worst-case numbers (see chapter 11, "Account for Risks").

Only use—and present—numbers that have buy-in from the departments affected. When the CFO questions your forecasts, you want to be able to tell him that his team has endorsed them. If you can't back up numbers when stakeholders scrutinize them, your entire case loses credibility.

Again, this is where friends in the finance department can be enormously helpful in putting together estimates. They have insight into where money is spent across functions and quick access to those numbers. They're familiar with each line of the P&L, and they know what past projects have cost the company. If you don't have a helpful contact in finance already, it's worth your time to find one and cultivate that relationship. Ask your boss who supports your department in the finance group. Then reach out to the person and say you're interested in understanding your department's numbers and how your work can affect them. It's smart to do this right after the quarterly report comes out. Showing that interest will win you a friend, and you'll probably learn something along the way.

Track Where Each Number Comes From

As you gather figures, collect them in a spreadsheet like the one in chapter 10, "Calculate ROI" (see figure 10-1). You can tailor this spreadsheet to fit your circumstances. For instance, if you are doing an IT project, you'll forecast only three to five years out, not 10. List your costs and benefits—and capture the assumptions and sources along with them. This is critical information to have when it's time to do your risk analysis and present to stakeholders. For example, if one of your expenses is new software, list the amount, how many licenses it includes, and any other assumptions you've made about the price. Then document who gave you the estimate. Later, when you're asked where the number came from, you'll have the information right there in the spreadsheet.

Your completed spreadsheet may have 50 rows, or more than 100—whatever it takes to accurately cost out the project and account for its benefits. Tracking the source of your figures may sound tedious, but will save you time later. And being able to answer questions from the review committee during your presentation will definitely enhance your credibility.

Manage Uncertainty

You're dealing with estimates and forecasts, so work with round numbers. If you're forecasting sales, it's OK to say that you'll see $5 million the first year, $8 million the next year, and $12 million the year after that. No one expects you to have a detailed, 100% accurate list of costs and benefits at this point in the process.

In fact, many of your numbers will be educated guesses. I worked with a company a couple of years ago that wanted to install an ERP system. The IT manager building the case reached out to three of his contacts at other companies to ask what they had spent on similar systems. He got three wildly different numbers. Which did he use? The one in the middle. But he also ran the calculation using the high figure (considering it the worst case) and the low one (the best case). That's what you should do if there's a high level of uncertainty with some of your numbers. Identify a range, and use the middle number.

You can also reduce uncertainty by benchmarking your project against others your company has undertaken. These comparisons will often give you the most-accurate numbers because you're dealing with known systems, processes, and people.

Even so, some uncertainty will remain, and senior managers understand that. If you're off—say you initially estimate $7 million in costs but discover later that the project will run closer to $8 million—people probably won't blame you, demanding to know why you were wrong. More likely (assuming you've developed and presented a solid case), they'll ask, "OK, so what will $7 million get us?"

Ignore Sunk Costs

On occasion, you may do a business case for a project that's already in progress so stakeholders can decide whether to continue it or alter its direction. In a situation like that, you need to keep track of *sunk costs*—the money already spent—but don't include them in your estimates or ROI calculation. Know the total amount in case stakeholders have questions, but don't allow it to factor too heavily in their decision. If you do, they may choose to keep funding the project since they've already spent so much on it—and that's how companies dig themselves into gigantic financial holes.

Take an equipment rental company I worked with that wanted to go completely paperless. The project lead estimated that it would take three years and $25 million. Three years later, the company had spent $35 million, with only one quarter of the work done. The team redid the business case, wisely ignoring the $35 million already spent, and the stakeholders decided not to move forward—it wasn't worthwhile in light of all the hassles they now knew to expect.

Using the costs and benefits you've outlined, you can now calculate the return on your investment.

Chapter 10
Calculate ROI

Return on investment (ROI) is a more pointed look at the financial value of your proposal. Think of it as a measure of relative "goodness" because it helps organizations compare projects and decide which ones to pursue.

Good news for mathphobes: It takes nanoseconds to calculate ROI in a spreadsheet (Excel saves you from doing fifth-order partial differential equations by hand). Many companies have templates, like the one in figure 10-1, where you just plug in your numbers and the software does the rest.

Here's the classic formula for ROI:

ROI = Net Benefit/Total Cost

(Net benefit is the total benefit minus the total cost.)

A positive ROI is good. A negative one means the project's not worth doing. The larger the ROI value, the better the project. But this is a static measure that doesn't take into consideration changes to benefits and costs over time. Therefore, most companies use one of the more advanced, dynamic techniques described in figure 10-2.

FIGURE 10-1

Your basic ROI spreadsheet

Before selecting a method for calculating ROI, enter your costs and benefits into a spreadsheet like the one shown here. This serves as your starting point for any ROI technique.

Project estimating & approval

Worksheet

Project investment	Amount	Year 1	Year 2	Year 3	Year 4	Year 5	Year 6	Year 7	Year 8	Year 9	Year 10	Estimate rationale
Capital												
Category 1 *(ex: HW procurement)*												
Category 2 *(ex: Facility upgrade)*												
Total capital costs	$ -											
Project expense (one-time expense)												
Category 1 *(ex: Project personnel costs)*												
Category 2 *(ex: Project travel)*												
Total project expense	$ -											
Total project investment	$ -	$ -	$ -	$ -	$ -	$ -	$ -	$ -	$ -	$ -	$ -	

Operating costs (OpEx)	Amount	Year 1	Year 2	Year 3	Year 4	Year 5	Year 6	Year 7	Year 8	Year 9	Year 10	
Category 1 *(ex: SW license)*												
Category 2 *(ex: Maintenance)*												
Total operating costs		$ -	$ -	$ -	$ -	$ -	$ -	$ -	$ -	$ -	$ -	

Project benefits (amount & timing)	Amount	Year 1	Year 2	Year 3	Year 4	Year 5	Year 6	Year 7	Year 8	Year 9	Year 10	
Sales benefits												
Incremental sales												
Infrastructure changes (savings +, costs -)												
Support personnel, etc. (list all)												
Operations impacts (savings +, costs -)												
Product support cost reduction												
Other benefits												
Total benefits		$ -	$ -	$ -	$ -	$ -	$ -	$ -	$ -	$ -	$ -	
	Annual total	$ -	$ -	$ -	$ -	$ -	$ -	$ -	$ -	$ -	$ -	
	Cumulative total	$ -	$ -	$ -	$ -	$ -	$ -	$ -	$ -	$ -	$ -	

FIGURE 10-2

Four ways to calculate ROI

Method	Answers the question...	Expressed in...	Typically used for...
Break-even analysis	How many sales do we need to recoup the investment?	Units sold	Market-focused projects, such as product development; entrepreneurial endeavors
Payback period	How long will it take to recoup the investment?	Months or years	Projects with a heavy up-front investment, such as facilities projects; productivity projects that accumulate benefits over time
Net present value	How much is this project worth to the business?	Dollars	Projects with large expenditures
Internal rate of return	What rate of return will this project deliver over its life cycle?	Percentage	Projects that the company reports on externally, especially those that require you to borrow money

The best method for you—break-even analysis, payback period, net present value (NPV), or internal rate of return (IRR)—will depend on the nature of your project and what's most important to the business. If your company has a standard approach, go with that so your stakeholders can easily compare your project with others. Or you may need to apply several methods to accommodate a variety of preferences.

Fortunately, you can start with the same basic spreadsheet shown in figure 10-1, no matter which techniques you use. Once you've loaded your estimates into that, you create other worksheets from it, with slight variations to perform the different types of calculations.

Break-Even Analysis

Break-even analysis tells you how many units you need to sell in order to pay for the project (see figure 10-3). Companies typically use it for new products and other projects that have a marketing focus—they weigh their analysis against the size of the market opportunity. This technique doesn't reveal how *long* it takes to break even, so it's most useful when you're unsure about timing—when the project will start, how long it will last, and so on. Entrepreneurs often use break-even analysis to show investors how many units must be sold before they'll turn a profit.

It's not the best method when you have high, time-dependent operating costs or infrastructure benefits that aren't related to product volume, since it's impossible to quantify the impact of those factors on unit sales. In those cases, you'll probably want to determine NPV instead.

FIGURE 10-3

Break-even example

When you tailor your basic ROI worksheet to determine your break-even point, it should look like this.

Project estimating & approval — Break-even

Project investment	Amount	Estimate rationale
Capital		
Category 1 *(ex: HW procurement)*	$ -	none
Total capital costs	$ -	
Project expense (one-time expense)		
Concept analysis	$ (50,000)	similar to project XYZ
Development	$ (300,000)	similar to project XYZ
Test and validation	$ (100,000)	based on current compliance matrix
Industrialization and commercialization	$ (50,000)	similar to project XYZ
Total project expense	$ (500,000)	
Total project investment	**$ (500,000)**	

Operating costs (OpEx)	Amount	Estimate rationale
Category 1 *(ex: SW license)*	$ -	none
Total operating costs		

Project benefits (amount & timing)	Amount	Estimate rationale
Sales benefits		
Incremental sales	$300,000/Year	sales increase by $1M with $1K price and 30% gross margin rate per Bob in mktg
Infrastructure changes (savings +, costs -)		none
Operations impacts (savings +, costs -)		
Product support cost reduction	$100,000/Year	reduction in warranty and help desk costs per Sue in service
Other benefits	$ -	none
Total benefits		

To calculate your break-even point, you'll first determine the gross profit margin from selling one unit of your product:

Revenue − COGS = Gross Margin

Then you can figure out how many units you need to sell for your sales benefit to equal your total costs:

Break-Even Number of Units = Net Project Cost/Gross Margin

Here's what those calculations look like when you plug in numbers from the spreadsheet in figure 10-3.

Our gross margin from selling one unit is $300. (See "Estimate Rationale" for sales benefits in the spreadsheet: 30% of $1,000 is $300. If you don't already know the gross margin, calculate it by subtracting COGS from revenue, as described above.) And in this case, we'll get our net project cost ($400,000) by adding one year of the productivity benefit ($100,000) to the total project investment (−$500,000).

Now we can enter these numbers into our break-even formula:

Break-Even Number of Units = $400,000/$300

We'll break even when we sell 1,334 units (rounding up from 1,333.33 because we can't sell one-third of a unit).

Payback Period

Payback period, one of the simplest ways of calculating ROI that accounts for time, tells you how long it will take to earn back the money invested.

You can create a basic payback spreadsheet that lists the total costs and benefits and spreads them over time, either by month or year (usually the latter—see figures 10-4 and 10-5 for examples). You'll determine period totals by summing each month's or year's numbers—these reflect the monthly or annual cash flow. And then you'll figure out the cumulative cash flow by adding period totals.

Typically, you'll start off with a negative cash flow because you're spending on the project but you haven't yet reaped the benefits. Eventually, benefits should offset costs. The payback point occurs when the cumulative cash flow changes from negative to positive—that's when the cumulative benefits exceed the cumulative costs.

You can start your timing for payback either after you complete the project, when benefits kick in (as in figure 10-4, which shows what's known as Type 0), or when the project work begins, to capture the time and money invested throughout (as in figure 10-5, which shows Type 1). Neither approach is better or worse. Just make sure you're following your company's standard or you agree with stakeholders ahead of time on which method to use.

In our Type 0 example (figure 10-4), when the project is done, we start off $500,000 in the hole. Then, in Year 1, we gain $400,000 in benefit—so we're still $100,000 in the negative, but we're making our way out. The project goes positive in Year 2, so we know the payback period will be one full year plus some fraction of the second year. To figure that out, take the last year of negative cumulative cash flow (Year 1) and using the absolute value of that

FIGURE 10-4

Type 0 payback example

To calculate payback starting from project completion, use a Type 0 spreadsheet. The first column (labeled "Project") captures costs incurred throughout the project, whether it takes a few months or a few years to complete. Benefits appear in the second column (Year 1) and subsequent columns.

Project estimating & approval **Type 0 payback**

	Amount	Project	Year 1	Year 2	Year 3	Estimate rationale
Project investment						
Capital						
Category 1 *(ex: HW procurement)*	$ -					none
Total capital costs	$ -					
Project expense (one-time expense)						
Concept analysis	$ (50,000)	$ (50,000)				similar to project XYZ
Development	$ (300,000)	$ (300,000)				similar to project XYZ
Test and validation	$ (100,000)	$ (100,000)				based on current compliance matrix
Industrialization and commercialization	$ (50,000)	$ (50,000)				similar to project XYZ
Total project expense	$ (500,000)					
Total project investment	**$ (500,000)**	**$ (500,000)**	**$ -**	**$ -**	**$ -**	

	Amount	Project	Year 1	Year 2	Year 3	Estimate rationale
Operating costs (OpEx)						
Category 1 *(ex: SW license)*	$ -					none
Total operating costs		**$ -**	**$ -**	**$ -**	**$ -**	

	Amount	Project	Year 1	Year 2	Year 3	Estimate rationale
Project benefits (amount & timing)						
Sales benefits						sales increase by $1M with $1K price and 30%
Incremental sales	$300,000/Year		$ 300,000	$ 300,000	$ 300,000	gross margin rate per Bob in mktg
Infrastructure changes (savings +, costs -)						none
Operations impacts (savings +, costs -)						reduction in warranty and help desk costs per
Product cost savings	$100,000/Year		$ 100,000	$ 100,000	$ 100,000	Sue in service
Other benefits	$ -					none
Total benefits		**$ -**	**$ 400,000**	**$ 400,000**	**$ 400,000**	
Annual total		**$ (500,000)**	**$ 400,000**	**$ 400,000**	**$ 400,000**	
Cumulative total		**$ (500,000)**	**$ (100,000)**	**$ 300,000**	**$ 700,000**	

FIGURE 10-5

Type 1 Payback Example

In a Type 1 spreadsheet, you begin calculating the payback period from the day you launch the project. Each column typically represents one year. If the project takes less than a year to complete, the first column will contain both project costs and benefits. If it takes more than a year, the first column will have only project costs; benefits will appear in a later column.

Project estimating & approval **Type 1 payback**

	Amount	Year 1	Year 2	Year 3	Year 4	Estimate rationale
Project investment						
Capital						
Category 1 *(ex: HW procurement)*	$ -					none
Total capital costs	$ -					
Project expense (one-time expense)						
Concept analysis	$ (50,000)	$ (50,000)				similar to project XYZ
Development	$ (300,000)	$ (300,000)				similar to project XYZ
Test and validation	$ (100,000)	$ (50,000)	$ (50,000)			based on current compliance matrix
Industrialization and commercialization	$ (50,000)		$ (50,000)			similar to project XYZ
Total project expense	$ (500,000)					
Total project investment	**$ (500,000)**	**$ (400,000)**	**$ (100,000)**	**$ -**	**$ -**	
Operating costs (OpEx)	**Amount**	**Year 1**	**Year 2**	**Year 3**	**Year 4**	
Category 1 *(ex: SW license)*	$ -					none
Total operating costs		$ -	$ -	$ -	$ -	
Project benefits (amount & timing)	**Amount**	**Year 1**	**Year 2**	**Year 3**	**Year 4**	
Sales benefits						
Incremental sales	$300,000/Year		$ 225,000	$ 300,000	$ 300,000	sales increase by $1M with $1K price and 30% gross margin rate per Bob in mktg
Infrastructure changes (savings +, costs -)						none
Operations impacts (savings +, costs -)						
Product cost savings	$100,000/Year		$ 75,000	$ 100,000	$ 100,000	reduction in warranty and help desk costs per Sue in service
Other benefits	$ -					none
Total benefits		**$ -**	**$ 300,000**	**$ 400,000**	**$ 400,000**	
Annual total		**$ (400,000)**	**$ 200,000**	**$ 400,000**	**$ 400,000**	
Cumulative total		**$ (400,000)**	**$ (200,000)**	**$ 200,000**	**$ 600,000**	

year's cumulative total, divide by the following year's annual cash flow.

In this case, it's $100,000 divided by $400,000, or .25 (note that we drop the negative of the first figure—we're using the absolute value). It will take us 1.25 years to recoup our investment.

Now take a look at our Type 1 example (figure 10–5). By the end of Year 1, we'll have racked up most of our project costs ($400,000), with no benefits to show for them yet. In Year 2, we'll spend another $100,000 in the first three months to finish the project, but that's offset by productivity savings and new sales in the final nine months, so we'll be $200,000 in the hole at year-end. In Year 3, we'll get the full $400,000 of benefit.

To figure out our payback period in Type 1, we take the last year that our cumulative cash flow was still negative (Year 2) and again using the absolute value of that year's cumulative cash flow, divide by the following year's annual cash flow (in this case, $200,000 divided by $400,000). So it will be 2.5 years before we recoup our investment.

With each type of calculation, you get completely different numbers. Companies often use Type 0 to analyze smaller projects with uncertain time frames. For larger projects that tie up a lot of money, companies prefer Type 1 because they want to know when they're going to get the investment back. But to use Type 1, you need to have a good sense of how long the project will take—otherwise, your calculations will be way off.

One downside of the payback period method: It doesn't show what happens after you earn the money back. Let's say you'll recoup the investment in a new product in two years, and after that you expect exponential sales growth. With this technique, your stakeholders wouldn't know the difference between your product and a similar one for which sales start to decay after two years. If your company uses the payback calculation as its standard but you expect benefits to increase or decrease significantly after the payback point, you should calculate net present value as well.

Net Present Value (NPV)

Net present value (NPV) shows today's value of a long-term investment by discounting future cash flows, so you can see what the impact of your 10-year project would be in today's dollars. This is my preferred method for calculating ROI—I believe it gives the most complete view of a project's value. Both NPV and the next technique, IRR, rely on the principle of the time value of money, which states that the buying power of money today is greater than the buying power of the same amount of money in the future.

If the NPV is negative, the project is not a good one. It will ultimately drain cash from the business, and you shouldn't even bring it to the table. If it's positive, you can make a solid case for the project. The larger the positive number, the greater the benefit.

NPV is particularly useful in comparing the intrinsic value of two mutually exclusive projects. Your stakeholders can look at the NPV of your project and a completely different one and make a fair comparison.

Here's the calculation:

$$\text{Net Present Value} = \sum \frac{\text{Year n Total Cash Flow}}{(1 + \text{Discount Rate})^{n}}$$

Where "n" is the year whose cash flow is being discounted.

This is the sum of the present value of cash flows (positive and negative) for each year associated with the investment, discounted so that it's expressed in today's dollars.

Luckily, you don't have to do this by hand. Excel does it for you when you enter the stream of costs and benefits over a set time period.

As you can see, the example in figure 10-6 has a high NPV compared with the level of investment (even $1 in the positive is considered good). We'd have a strong chance of getting that project approved, as long as it's aligned with business objectives and not up against projects with a higher value.

Assuming your project costs will only be accurate to plus or minus 25%, don't recommend an option with an NPV that's less than 25% of the project cost. Otherwise, stakeholders might worry that once the project gets started, the true NPV will be closer to $0.

One note about the formula: The "NPV" function in Excel starts discounting the first year inside the formula. However, any costs or benefits in the current year shouldn't be discounted—they're already in today's dollars. So you'll need to remove the value for the current year from the Excel NPV formula and manually add that to your total NPV for the remaining years.

FIGURE 10-6

NPV example

Calculate NPV when you want to show the value of a long-term investment in today's dollars.

Project estimating & approval — NPV

Project investment	Amount	Year 1	Year 2	Year 3	Year 4	Year 5	Year 6	Estimate rationale
Capital								
Category 1 *(ex: HW procurement)*	$ -							none
Total capital costs	$ -							
Project expense (one-time expense)								
Concept analysis	$ (50,000)	$ (50,000)						similar to project XYZ
Development	$ (300,000)	$ (300,000)						similar to project XYZ
Test and validation	$ (100,000)	$ (50,000)	$ (50,000)					based on current compliance matrix
Industrialization and commercialization	$ (50,000)		$ (50,000)					similar to project XYZ
Total project expense	$ (500,000)							
Total project investment	**$ (500,000)**	**$ (400,000)**	**$ (100,000)**	**$ -**	**$ -**	**$ -**	**$ -**	

Operating costs (OpEx)	Amount	Year 1	Year 2	Year 3	Year 4	Year 5	Year 6	Estimate rationale
Category 1 *(ex: SW license)*	$ -							none
Total operating costs		**$ -**	**$ -**	**$ -**	**$ -**	**$ -**	**$ -**	

Project benefits (amount & timing)	Amount	Year 1	Year 2	Year 3	Year 4	Year 5	Year 6	Estimate rationale
Sales benefits								
Incremental sales	$300,000/Year		$ 225,000	$ 300,000	$ 300,000	$ 300,000	$ 300,000	sales increase by $1M with $1K price and 30% gross margin rate per Bob in mktg
Infrastructure changes (savings +, costs -)								none
Operations impacts (savings +, costs -)								
Product support cost reduction	$100,000/Year		$ 75,000	$ 100,000	$ 100,000	$ 100,000	$ 100,000	reduction in warranty and help desk costs per Sue in service
Other benefits	$ -							none
Total benefits		**$ -**	**$ 300,000**	**$ 400,000**	**$ 400,000**	**$ 400,000**	**$ 400,000**	
Annual total		**$ (400,000)**	**$ 200,000**	**$ 400,000**	**$ 400,000**	**$ 400,000**	**$ 400,000**	

Discount rate: 8.0%

NPV: $1,011,899

CHOOSING A DISCOUNT RATE FOR NPV

To calculate NPV, you need to include a discount rate in your formula. This is tied to the current cost of money. It will change from year to year, depending on the health of the company, the health of the economy, and your stakeholders' risk tolerance. In today's economy, most companies are using 5% to 10%. In a good economy, they'll use 10% to 15%. Someone in finance can probably tell you what rate to use, or it will already be filled in on your company's template. If this isn't the case, or if you're an entrepreneur, you can use your company's interest rate or the prime rate (whichever is higher) plus 5%.

Internal Rate of Return (IRR)

Internal rate of return (IRR) shows a project's investment value. It essentially tells you what rate of return you would get if you invested the same amount of money in a CD that performed as well as your project.

If the IRR is small, you shouldn't do the project—there are better ways to spend your money. If it's large, you have a good shot at approval (as with NPV, the greater the rate, the greater the benefit). Finance experts often use this technique to determine whether it's worth borrowing money for a project. Bankers will want to know the return rate on the money they lend, to make sure your company can pay back the interest and principal.

Entrepreneurs, take note: Investors often want to understand the IRR in the same way that bankers do. The rate of return indicates what they can expect to receive from their investment when they cash out.

Here's the calculation:

$$0 = \sum \frac{\text{Year n Total Cash Flow}}{(1 + \text{Rate of Return})^n}$$

Where "n" is the year whose cash flow is being discounted.

Again, thank goodness for software.

Many people run IRR when they run NPV since both use the same numbers, and it's just another formula in the spreadsheet. The example in figure 10-7 shows an IRR of 72.4%—a great result. You're not likely to get that much of a return on other types of investments.

What to Do with Negative or Low Numbers

When your calculations show a negative NPV or a very low IRR, for example, you need to reevaluate the case you're trying to make. If the project was your idea, go back and check your assumptions and numbers carefully. Unless you find errors, it may be time to pull the plug on your case. Stakeholders usually won't approve a project that doesn't return value to the company (occasional exceptions apply—more on this later).

By contrast, if you were assigned the business case, your beneficiaries may insist that the project is necessary even if the numbers don't support it. In a situation like that, go ahead and present the case with the bad ROI—but provide stakeholders with other viable options. Suppose your sales team decides that the company needs a certain new product to compete in the low-price market, and you're tapped to develop the case. After running the

FIGURE 10-7

IRR example

You calculate IRR to determine your project's investment value. It's a useful metric if you want to borrow funds from a bank, for example, or attract investors for a start-up venture.

Project estimating & approval — IRR

Project investment	Amount	Year 1	Year 2	Year 3	Year 4	Year 5	Year 6	Estimate rationale
Capital								
Category 1 *(ex: HW procurement)*	$ -							none
Total capital costs	$ -							
Project expense (one-time expense)								
Concept analysis	$ (50,000)	$ (50,000)						similar to project XYZ
Development	$ (300,000)	$ (300,000)						similar to project XYZ
Test and validation	$ (100,000)	$ (50,000)	$ (50,000)					based on current compliance matrix
Industrialization and commercialization	$ (50,000)		$ (50,000)					similar to project XYZ
Total project expense	$ (500,000)							
Total project investment	**$ (500,000)**	**$ (400,000)**	**$ (100,000)**	**$ -**	**$ -**	**$ -**	**$ -**	

Operating costs (OpEx)	Amount	Year 1	Year 2	Year 3	Year 4	Year 5	Year 6	Estimate rationale
Category 1 *(ex: SW license)*	$ -							none
Total operating costs		$ -	$ -	$ -	$ -	$ -	$ -	

Project benefits (amount & timing)	Amount	Year 1	Year 2	Year 3	Year 4	Year 5	Year 6	Estimate rationale
Sales benefits								sales increase by $1M with $1K price and 30%
Incremental sales	$300,000/Year		$ 225,000	$ 300,000	$ 300,000	$ 300,000	$ 300,000	gross margin rate per Bob in mktg
Infrastructure changes (savings +, costs -)								none
Operations impacts (savings +, costs -)								reduction in warranty and help desk costs per
Product support cost reduction	$100,000/Year		$ 75,000	$ 100,000	$ 100,000	$ 100,000	$ 100,000	Sue in service
Other benefits	$ -							none
Total benefits		$ -	**$ 300,000**	**$ 400,000**	**$ 400,000**	**$ 400,000**	**$ 400,000**	
Annual total		**$ (400,000)**	**$ 200,000**	**$ 400,000**	**$ 400,000**	**$ 400,000**	**$ 400,000**	
IRR:		**72.4%**						

numbers, you get a negative NPV. Perhaps the competitor has patent protection or a strong hold on the market that you don't think you can crack. Present the case, but also suggest another way to address the sales team's concerns. Maybe your company should take out features to bring down the product's price, for instance, or go to that market with a different type of offering.

In some cases, such as compliance projects, you can expect a negative return because you'll get no new revenue or productivity (although staying in business is obviously a benefit). Say you have to meet new air-emissions standards or upgrade your financial reporting system to comply with a new regulation. The numbers won't be good, but you may have to do the project anyway. The medical device folks I worked with needed to get rid of certain product materials that the FDA had deemed potentially hazardous. They'd been making products with some of these materials for 20 years, so they had to go through major redesigns. They're now in the process of removing more than 20 materials that are no longer compliant—a major investment that doesn't show any increase in sales or productivity. But they have to do it to sell compliant products.

When evaluating projects, stakeholders look for the best numbers: the lowest break-even point, the quickest payback period, or the highest NPV or IRR. But that's not all they base their decision on. Remember that you are telling a story to convince them your project is worthwhile—the ROI number is just one data point.

Chapter 11
Account for Risks

After you've run the ROI, you still have some number crunching left to do. None of the ROI techniques will account for risks, so it's a separate step to identify them and consider what impact they'll have on your final figures.

Gut-Check the Numbers

If you're looking at a low ROI and thinking, "Wait—I thought this was going to be a great project," question your numbers. Could you have underestimated revenue? Or overestimated transition costs? Or entered a wrong figure? (As you'd imagine, leaving off a zero makes a big difference.) Scrutinize each line item and ask whether the number—or the timing—could be off.

You may need to go back to your subject-matter experts and ask them to double-check their estimates. For example: "Can we get 20% more in sales? What would you need to deliver that?" Or: "Can we train call center employees on the new system sooner?"

You've based every line of your spreadsheet on assumptions—which you've carefully documented. But what if they're wrong and things don't go as you planned? What if the worst (or best) case occurs?

Analyzing risk helps you see what will happen to the project's value if your assumptions are off. Most people focus on threats. (What if the vendor doesn't deliver on time? What if the cost of raw materials goes through the roof?) But you need to consider opportunities as well. (How can you get a higher NPV or a faster payback? Can you complete the project sooner? Can you put your best team on it?) Go through your estimates line by line and consider what factors might alter them. For instance:

- **Personnel:** What if the person running this project leaves the company? What if you don't get all the resources you requested? Or conversely: What if you're able to pull together an all-star team or hire an outside expert?

- **Technology:** What if you encounter bugs when testing? What if employees struggle to adapt to the new system? What if you run into intellectual-property issues with the technology?

- **Quality/Performance:** What if the product doesn't perform as you expect it to—for better or worse? What if quality suffers because of a tight schedule?

- **Scope:** What if the project needs to include more (or fewer) geographic regions, employees, or customers? What if the stakeholders change requirements? What if a regulatory change creates a new opportunity?

- **Schedule:** What if you aren't able to hit the launch date? What would allow you to get ahead of schedule? Does anything outside the project need to happen before you can complete it?

Think about what concerns your stakeholders will have. Where will they see risks? Does your CTO always assume projects take twice as long as planned? Does your CMO distrust any project that relies on vendors? Identify the questions they might ask so you can account for them in your calculations and, ultimately, in your presentation. Once you've listed the risks, identify your biggest threats and opportunities (see figure 11-1): Which are most likely to happen, and which would have the greatest impact on

FIGURE 11-1

Assessing threats and opportunities

When reviewing project risks with decision makers, draw their attention to the threats and opportunities with the highest probability and impact—those that would fall in the upper-right corner of this matrix.

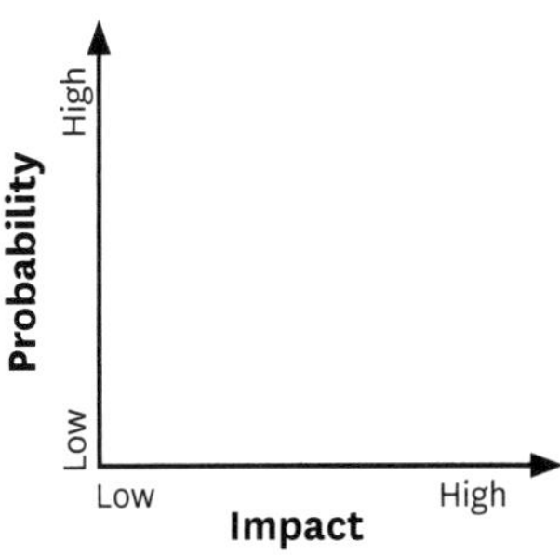

your project? Those are the ones to highlight when you present to your stakeholders.

Test the Numbers

In light of the risks you've identified, rerun your calculations. What happens if your project costs run over by 20%? How does that change the NPV? What if the product launches six months later than you expected (see figure 11-2)?

Play with the numbers. Plug in your best guess for each line, then the best- and worst-case figures, and see what happens to your spreadsheets. You're likely to choose a middle number for most lines, but you may have reason to be conservative or aggressive on certain items. If one of your critical stakeholders is risk-averse, for example, you may go with lower numbers on your benefit stream. If you face severe penalties for completing the project late, you may want to build some buffer into your timing assumptions. Conservative assumptions lower your risk; aggressive assumptions increase it. Often you can mention contingencies and say that the team will develop plans for them when it's time to put together a detailed project plan—but sometimes stakeholders want to know up front what types of contingencies you're considering.

Ultimately, each number you settle on is a judgment call. Check with your subject-matter experts, your manager, and your project champion for feedback on major costs and benefits. Do your final figures seem reasonable to them?

As you tinker, you'll start to see what it would take to get the best ROI figure. But you need to present realistic

FIGURE 11-2

Factoring risks into your spreadsheets

When calculating ROI, you'll consider many "what ifs" and adjust your numbers to reflect likely scenarios. In this example, which uses estimates from Figure 10-6, a six-month project delay stretches the project costs, delays the benefit start, and causes a 26% drop in NPV (see shaded cells).

Project estimating & approval — NPV with six-month project delay

Project investment	Amount	Year 1	Year 2	Year 3	Year 4	Year 5	Year 6	Estimate rationale
Capital								
Category 1 *(ex: HW procurement)*	$ -							none
Total capital costs	$ -							
Project expense (one-time expense)								
Concept analysis	$ (50,000)	$ (50,000)						similar to project RST
Development	$ (300,000)	$ (200,000)	$ (100,000)					similar to project RST
Test and validation	$ (100,000)		$ (100,000)					based on current compliance matrix
Industrialization and commercialization	$ (50,000)		$ (50,000)					similar to project RST
Total project expense	$ (500,000)							
Total project investment	**$ (500,000)**	**$ (250,000)**	**$ (250,000)**	**$ -**	**$ -**	**$ -**	**$ -**	

Operating costs (OpEx)	Amount	Year 1	Year 2	Year 3	Year 4	Year 5	Year 6	Estimate rationale
Category 1 *(ex: SW License)*	$ -							none
Total operating costs		$ -	$ -	$ -	$ -	$ -	$ -	

Project benefits (amount & timing)	Amount	Year 1	Year 2	Year 3	Year 4	Year 5	Year 6	Estimate rationale
Sales benefits								sales increase by $1M with $1K price and 30% gross margin rate per Bob in mktg
Incremental sales	$300,000/Year			$ 300,000	$ 300,000	$ 300,000	$ 300,000	
Infrastructure changes (savings +, costs -)								none
Operations impacts (savings +, costs -)								reduction in warranty and help desk costs per Sue in service
Product support cost reduction	$100,000/Year			$ 100,000	$ 100,000	$ 100,000	$ 100,000	
Other benefits	$ -							none
Total benefits		$ -	$ -	**$ 400,000**	**$ 400,000**	**$ 400,000**	**$ 400,000**	
	Annual total	**$ (250,000)**	**$ (250,000)**	**$ 400,000**	**$ 400,000**	**$ 400,000**	**$ 400,000**	

Discount rate: 8.0%

NPV: **$745,232**

risks, not just ones that make the case look good. Change an assumption if you have reason to believe it is wrong. Use wisdom and experience to make these decisions—don't pick arbitrary numbers to pad or manipulate your ROI. And make your risk assessment consistent with the numbers you have selected.

All of your information gathering, pressure-testing, and documenting sources will pay off as you assemble your winning presentation.

Section 5

Present Your Case and Move Forward

Chapter 12
Prepare Your Document

To get buy-in from your stakeholders, you must tell your "story" in a compelling way so they'll easily grasp the need, the solution (or solutions) you're proposing, and the benefits to the company. Typically, your audience will care most about ROI and how your project relates to strategic objectives—so keep those issues front and center. (See appendix B: How to Give a Killer Presentation by TED curator Chris Anderson for further advice on crafting your story, finding the right mix of data and narrative, and sharpening your delivery.) Here are some things to keep in mind as you prepare your presentation.

Your Document Should Speak for Itself

In some companies, especially large ones, you may not get to present your case. You might simply submit a Word document, Excel file, or slide deck and wait for the committee's decision. Or you might have just a few minutes in front of stakeholders who are considering 40 projects in a half-day meeting. Increasingly, companies decide on projects over conference calls or videoconferences to include stakeholders in different locations—so you can't even assume that your audience will pay undivided attention to your pitch. People may multitask, catching up on e-mail or getting other work done during the call.

For all those reasons, your document needs to stand on its own. Stakeholders must be able to comprehend the case without your voice-over. So don't distribute a deck as thick as a dictionary. Keep your slides crisp, clear, and to the point. But share enough data to show that you've done your homework.

Follow your company's process for presenting cases. Some firms want you to fill out forms or templates. That helps them review a large number of projects in one batch and make fair comparisons. Sure, the process may feel bureaucratic, but if you want your case approved, you have to go through the system.

Look at Past Presentations

Whether or not there's a standard format, find out what other presenters in your company have done. This will give you ideas for your own presentation—and a sense of what stakeholders might expect from you. Reach out to several coworkers who have recently gotten approval for business cases and ask to see their documents. Look for similarities. Did your colleagues use PowerPoint or Word? How did they describe the business need? What kind of data did they include in backup slides? How did they render the data? Also get your hands on a few rejected cases, if you can, to see what their project leads did differently. Did they fail to address risk? Were their documents too long or not substantial enough?

Make a Structured Argument

If your company doesn't provide templates and you can't track down helpful examples, you may need to start from scratch. In that case, I recommend the following structure:

1. **Opening slide:** Begin with an executive summary that briefly states the problem or opportunity, describes how you plan to address it, and explains why your solution is sensible and its expected ROI.

2. **Business need:** Describe why you're proposing the project. Explicitly connect the need to the company's strategic goals, and share data points that convey its urgency.

3. **Project overview:** Give a high-level description of the solution. If it's a new product, lay out the general concept and explain how it fits with existing offerings. For a productivity initiative (such as an IT project), specify which business processes it will affect and which costs it will eliminate or reduce. For a facility project, describe its magnitude, and name the facility systems it will touch (power, HVAC, water, sewage, and so on).

TELLING YOUR STORY IN THE EXECUTIVE SUMMARY

Your stakeholders are extremely busy, with competing demands on their time and attention. So think of your executive summary as a hook: It's a concise, compelling story about the business need, your solution, and the impact your solution will have.

Here's an example:

Executive Summary

We're facing tough new competitors in our Southeast Asian market—and losing a lot of sales as a result [the need]. *So I'm proposing a new product that will help us regain market share* [the solution]. *When we get it out through our distribution channels, we expect to see sales double within the first six weeks—and we'll recoup our investment in just under three years* [the impact].

Of course, if you're presenting with slides, you'll want to break up the text, perhaps like this:

Executive Summary

Problem:

- *Tough new competitors in Southeast Asia*
- *Loss of market share*

Solution:

- *New product*

Benefits:

- *Double sales in first six weeks*
- *Recoup investment in fewer than three years*

Clearly state the result of your ROI calculation: Above, it's the payback period of *fewer than three years*. But use whatever figure your stakeholders care most about: *The NPV is $20,000*. Or: *We'll get $30 million in new sales*. Or: *We'll cut $1.5 million in costs*.

Display the ROI prominently—it's the satisfying ending to your story. Then, in the rest of your document or presentation, demonstrate with data and other supporting material why your audience should have confidence in that story.

4. **Schedule and team:** Provide a high-level project plan. Include basic milestones, major deliverables, and core team members (by name or function).

5. **Impact:** Describe the benefits. Say which departments the project will affect, and how. Quantify the impact as precisely as you can.

6. **Risk:** Explain what might not go as planned—whether positive or negative. Include major risks associated both with doing the project and with not doing it.

7. **Financials:** Summarize the costs and benefits, and restate the ROI.

8. **Closing slide:** Restate the need, why your solution is a good one, and, once again, the ROI.

How long you make each section and how much supporting material you include will depend on how much time you have to present and your stakeholders' appetite for data. Again, use other successful cases as guides.

Your opening slide is crucial. It grabs reviewers' attention and sets the stage for everything to come (see sidebar "Telling Your Story in the Executive Summary"). And remember, you may not get beyond the opening slide if your review committee is busy or distracted. In fact, one time when I presented a business case at GE, previous presenters had gone long, and members of the review committee needed to wrap things up—they had to catch a plane. So I got five minutes to make my case (I was scheduled for 30 minutes). I did the presentation using only my executive summary slide and told reviewers they could find details in the rest of the deck. My project was one of the few they approved that day.

Document in hand, it's time to gather more feedback before you go in front of the official review committee.

Chapter 13
Shop Your Case Around

You've drafted your case, but you're not ready to present it just yet. First, you need to get buy-in from your stakeholders—because you'll want allies in the room when tough questions come up.

Two people in particular are critical: the head of the department that will lead the work and the head of the department that will benefit most from it. With these individuals on board, you'll defuse many concerns and greatly increase your chances of getting that green light.

Work with Your Champion

Go back to the champion you identified early in the case-development process. Ideally, you've asked for her input and kept her updated all along. But if not, definitely connect before the presentation.

If your champion believes in the value of your project, she'll defend it against naysayers or play a critical role in a tie-breaker situation.

Meet with Other Stakeholders in Advance

It's also helpful to give individuals on the review committee a preview and ask about their concerns. Get feedback from as many stakeholders as you can—you want to know where they stand, especially on new projects that are out of the ordinary for your company.

If you can't schedule meetings with them, you might be able to reach out through your subject-matter experts. Enlist a team member who is close to someone on the review board to go over the highlights with her. He might mention that he helped develop the business case and thinks it's a good project. He can then share her reaction with you and relay any questions or concerns she had.

Most questions you'll get at this point shouldn't come as a surprise if you've thoroughly prepared your case. (You know the CMO will ask about brand implications of the new product feature. Or that the CFO doesn't want to approve any projects over $5 million this year.) But on occasion, you'll discover concerns that haven't come up yet. It's always better to bring them to the surface before review time. Big surprises during the review meeting may sink your case and will almost certainly delay a decision. Of course, you'll need to adjust your content in response to what you hear. You may drop some features, for example, or tweak a few numbers. Let your stakeholders know you've made changes to allay their concerns so they can give the project their support at the review meeting.

Anticipate New Concerns

Other issues may arise when the committee is in the room, comparing your case with others.

Anticipate those concerns by getting inside the heads of your stakeholders: What do they care most about? What are their hot buttons? Ask around to find out what happened in similar review meetings. What unexpected questions came up? What issues became sticking points?

And think carefully about what's been going on in the business over the past week or month. Recent events can play a big role in review meetings. At a pharmaceutical company I worked with, the focus one year was growth, so people knew to explain how their proposed projects would grow sales, increase market share, or expand the customer base. But two days before the review committee met, one of the company's products got recalled. Quality hadn't been a major concern a few days earlier—and now, suddenly, it was the top priority. Stakeholders grilled project leads on quality assurance, testing, validation, and clinical trial strategy. They rejected cases that weren't airtight on quality, no matter how much growth those projects promised.

Size Up the Competition

Find out what other business cases are being considered. Talk with your boss to see if he knows of any initiatives up for approval. Ask your subject-matter experts (particularly those in finance) if they've been consulted about other projects. You probably won't change your numbers or general approach to beat out another project, but you might change what you emphasize in your presentation. If six other projects focus on market differentiation, as yours does, you may want to play up other benefits as well to distinguish your case.

Now that you've had a chance to socialize your case and gather and incorporate feedback, you're almost ready to go before the board. Time to quickly double-check that you have everything you need to deliver a great presentation.

Chapter 14
Are You Ready to Present?

Congratulations—you've developed your business case, and now you're ready to present it. Or are you?

Use this checklist to confirm that you've covered all your bases. If you answer "no" to any of these questions, go back and rework your case.

Did You . . .

- ☐ Lay out a clear business need and frame it as a compelling story that will grab stakeholders' attention?
- ☐ Align your objectives with strategic priorities, directly connecting your case to one of the company's stated goals?
- ☐ Identify each stakeholder's objectives and address as many as possible?

- ☐ Meet with your beneficiaries and accurately capture their needs?
- ☐ Identify a champion on the review committee who will support your project in front of the group?
- ☐ Consult subject-matter experts in different departments or functions to estimate costs and benefits, assess risks, calculate ROI, and get buy-in?
- ☐ Factor in transition costs?
- ☐ Document the assumptions behind each estimate—and note the source of each number?
- ☐ Double-check the numbers?
- ☐ Consider best- and worst-case scenarios?
- ☐ Consider several viable solutions along with the one you're proposing?
- ☐ Meet with stakeholders to preview your case and ask for input?
- ☐ Gain support from the department that will do the work?
- ☐ Gain support from the department that will benefit most from the project?
- ☐ Create a clear, concise document or slide deck?
- ☐ Gather enough information to move immediately into project planning if you get the green light?

Chapter 15
Make Your Pitch

On decision day, some stakeholders focus entirely on ROI. Others want to know who you worked with to gather information. Still others scrutinize the risk plan. If one person will decide your project's fate, play to her preferences. But when presenting to multiple stakeholders, include something for everyone.

Start with the Need

If stakeholders don't believe you've identified a real business need that's connected to the company's strategic priorities, they'll stop listening—or even ask you to stop talking. So describe that need at the outset, and remember to tell it like a story to engage your audience.

Be Brief

Review each slide, providing only pertinent information on major points. Your busy stakeholders will appreciate a concise, direct presentation. And don't just read your slides to them—you'll bore them to tears. As communication expert Nancy Duarte suggests in the *HBR Guide to Persuasive Presentations,* you can use the "notes" field in PowerPoint to spell out everything you want to say without projecting teleprompter text on the wall for everyone to see.

While reviewing the proposed solution, you might explain other alternatives you considered and then ruled out. Or when talking about risks, you might share the perspective of an important team member. But touch on these things quickly, then move on. Stay away from tangents. Many managers make the mistake of going deep into the risks, trying to head off doubts. It's better to mention them at a high level. For instance: *We thought about product introduction, technology transfer, and supplier issues and have included ways to mitigate these issues.* Stakeholders will request more detail if they want it—and then you can speak directly to their concerns.

Personalize the Presentation

Involve your beneficiaries and stakeholders in the discussion. If you're talking about the need, turn to the stakeholder who's feeling the most pain and invite her to comment on it. You might say something like, "Because this product line hasn't lived up to expectations, sales won't make its numbers"—and then ask the sales VP for quick observations on what's happening in the field. You might also have finance chime in with how much gross profit the company is short. This will enroll people in building and supporting your case in front of their peers.

Shine a Light on Your Experts

In some instances, stakeholders will be more (or less) inclined to approve your project depending on which subject-matter experts you worked with. You've chosen your team members carefully for their smarts and their perspective—now it's time to showcase their contributions. For example: *Bob gave me these forecasts and feels confident we'll hit the numbers.* If Bob is a superstar in his department, his endorsement will mean something. People who trust him will trust you.

Handle the Naysayers

Even the strongest business cases will get some push-back. Here are the most common types of resistance and tips on how to address them:

1. **"This is too good to be true."** Stakeholders may not believe that the benefits, sales, or savings you've identified are realistic. This happens in organizations where people frequently overpromise. If you think you'll face this roadblock, take extra care in backing up your numbers. For each benefit stream, identify a subject-matter expert who can credibly speak to the figure you've listed. If you're promising 25% sales growth, have your sales expert say how the team arrived at that estimate.

2. **"But you haven't thought of . . ."** Many stake-holders like to point out gaps: *You haven't even talked about how this will play out in Europe,*

and that's a critical region for us. They may also bring up risks that you didn't address in your presentation. Give honest, direct responses. If you haven't considered the issue, say so. Offer to look into it and get back to the committee. If you don't believe Europe is critical, you can ask the group whether they'd like you to do more research. If others agree with you, they may step in to say so.

3. **"We'll never get this done."** Another common concern is timing. Stakeholders may think you're being overly optimistic about when the project will be completed. Here, again, it's essential to have the support of those who will do the work. You can reply, "I've shared these timelines with IT and manufacturing, and they agree the work will take no longer than six months."

If people try to shoot down your case with objections like these, don't get defensive. Instead, "invite the lions in," as leadership and change expert John Kotter advises in his book *Buy-In.* When someone voices skepticism, thank him for his comment and engage him directly. Say something like, "Yes, I hear your concern. Let's go back to that issue and discuss how we're planning to address it." If you give a thorough, straightforward answer, chances are that your skeptic will back off—or people in the room will come to your defense. Invite your champion to comment if she can credibly address the concern.

End on a Positive Note

It's always a good sign when stakeholders say, "Tell me more." You know you're on the right track if they ask who would be assigned to the project or when you could get started. Whenever possible, close your presentation on a high note. Reiterate a positive NPV or highlight the significant need your project fills. No matter what questions arose during the discussion, you want stakeholders to remember the good your initiative will bring the company.

Chapter 16
Get to a Decision

After you've submitted or presented your case, you probably won't have to sit around biting your nails for long. Usually, decision makers respond either in the meeting itself or within a few days. You'll get one of four answers.

"No, the Project Isn't a Priority."

When cases get rejected, it's typically because they're not in sync with strategic goals, the ROI isn't high enough, or the organization simply doesn't have the funds or people to get it done. While this can be disappointing, keep in mind that "no" is sometimes the best answer for the business (as discussed in the introduction). Depending on the reason for the rejection, you may be able to build a stronger case later. If the project wasn't aligned closely enough with the company's objectives, you could propose it again when the goals evolve. Or you might collect information over the next year or so showing that the benefits are even stronger than you initially thought. Whether you plan to let your proposal go or revisit it in the next approval cycle, thank your champion, your subject-matter experts, and everyone else who helped you build the case. You might need their help later on.

"We Can't Make a Decision Yet."

Stakeholders who agree about the business need but don't think you've found the right solution may send you back to the drawing board. (This can also happen if you haven't told the story clearly or provided enough data.) Find out from your stakeholders what the sticking points are. Does the project take too long? Does it cost too much? Is a strategic element missing? In light of these concerns, revisit other alternatives that you and your team considered. Sometimes stakeholders already have another project in mind and your proposal just doesn't align with it. Have someone who's close to your stakeholders—whether it's your champion or a trusted subject-matter expert—work with them to understand more about the project they do want. Evaluate that idea and include it as one of the alternatives you come back with.

"We Can Approve Only Part of the Project."

Typically, there are two reasons why a review board will give you the go-ahead on just a portion of your case: process or issues.

On long projects or those with many risks, decision makers may hedge their bets and give you an OK to go up to some key milestone. Leaders at companies with this type of tollgate process intentionally fund only early stages so they can see if the assumptions are valid. The "yes" has a caveat—you'll need to reapply for funding for the next year or possibly even the next phase. This partial approval can be a blessing, since it gives you the opportunity to refine the solution as you move forward.

Sometimes review boards grant partial approval due to funding issues. It's not uncommon for a review committee to say that it can't greenlight your $2 million project, but it can give you part of that money. When that happens, you're expected to come back and explain what you can do with fewer resources.

The complexities surrounding partial approvals are discussed in chapter 17, "What Next?"

"Yes, Let's Move Ahead."

If you get a "yes," stakeholders will immediately start asking questions about resources: Who will lead the project (if not you)? How soon can you have a project plan in place? When can you pull together a team and get started on the work? Be ready with answers—you don't want to lose momentum after securing your hard-won approval.

A note of caution, though: "Yes" doesn't always mean yes. Conflict-averse leaders sometimes approve a project but then never allocate resources for it. If they withhold the dollars, people, and time it will take to do the work, they might as well have said no. You may be able to prevent this from happening by following up immediately with a detailed request for resources. Ask for the names of individuals assigned to the project. If managers won't give you names, they probably aren't assigning resources. In that case, ask your champion to talk with them and find out the reasons for the holdup—then address whatever concerns you can in the detailed project plan.

You can make a quick decision more likely by putting a time frame on your project. Explain that a window of opportunity will close if you don't move forward soon—perhaps it's an opening in the market because a competitor's product just flopped or the chance to upgrade an IT system during a facility upgrade. Don't be the boy who cried wolf, though. The urgency needs to be legitimate. Assuming it is, bringing this up in your presentation can help you get closure sooner rather than later.

No matter what the outcome of the decision, don't rest on your laurels. You can take steps forward whether your project was rejected or approved.

Chapter 17
What Next?

Whether you're popping a bottle of bubbly, walking despondently back to your desk, or pulling your hair out because you have to create and present a case all over again, remember that you've done your job—you've helped the company make a wise decision.

But the work is not over. If you got a yes, it's time to begin implementing your project. And even if the decision makers said no, there are steps you can and should take.

If You Heard "No, the Project Isn't a Priority."

First off, don't despair if your project isn't approved. Although it may feel like failure to hear "no," keep in mind that you've contributed to the success of the company by helping it identify that the project wasn't a worthwhile investment. The real purpose of a business case is not to necessarily win approval for your proposal, but to provide enough information so the committee can make an informed decision.

But don't just accept the "no" by saying thank you and walking away. Instead, always ask "Why?" If you know precisely why the decision makers rejected the case, then you'll be able to follow up appropriately. Ask this question in the meeting or in a subsequent email. Don't pick a fight or try to use the response to change the outcome, but seek to understand their reasoning. You might say, "Thanks for letting me know about your decision. I'd love any feedback you have on why the project wasn't approved."

The reviewers may have passed on your project for any of several reasons. For example, they might tell you that the project doesn't align with the company strategy. In this case, let it die. Any project that doesn't fit with the company's imperatives should be rejected.

If they thought the project wasn't viable—that the approach you described wouldn't yield the results you promised—you can go back and address their concerns. Do you need more data to show why the approach works? Can you create a prototype that will assuage their worries? You might ask for a small amount of funding to run a quick pilot to prove the project can succeed.

If the higher-ups say no because there aren't enough resources, hold on to your case in the event that resources become available. That actually happened to me at GE. Partway through the year, corporate decided to give our business unit some additional funding to invest in strategic product development projects. Some market dynamics had changed, making our market segments more attractive than others. The product manager and I quickly dusted off several business cases that had not been funded due to lack of resources during the previous year's strategic planning process. In less than a month, projects were approved and teams were getting down to work. Staying in close touch with your project champion so that she can keep you apprised of any changes will help you prepare for such opportunities.

When you ask for the reasons behind the rejection, you have to hope you'll get an honest answer. In most cases, you will. It may not be direct—the CEO may not say to you, "We didn't think you could pull off the project"—but you'll likely be able to infer the reasons. Try to read between the lines. If you're still not sure, ask the project champion for her insight. Whatever response you get, don't argue with the logic or take it personally. That's not a way to win allies—or support—for this or future projects.

If You Heard "We Can't Make a Decision Yet."

Having your proposal tabled is better than an outright "no," but it's still disappointing. In most cases, you'll just have to trust that you built and presented a solid case and then wait and see what happens. Any additional measures you take will depend on the decision makers' rationale. Typically, it's for one of three reasons.

The case hasn't made the first cut.

It could be that your case didn't make it into the "definite yes" pile. If the decision committee is reviewing multiple cases at once, it may divide proposals into yes, no, and maybe piles. At least you know your project is in the mix. There's no need to lobby for your case at this point, especially if your project champion is representing you to the decision makers.

The decision makers just haven't decided yet.

Sometimes you've got a management team full of ditherers who are unable or unwilling to make decisions on the spot. They might want to hold off until they're behind closed doors to make the final call. Of course, your project is more likely to be approved if your proposal clarifies what's in it for each of the decision makers. While you wait, though, you may want to periodically work through your champion to be sure your idea is still in front of people and to check if there's anyone else's ear you should get.

Sometimes, the committee hasn't decided because they're waiting for the outcome of another decision that has farther-reaching impact. This happened to me once, when a project I'd proposed was hanging in the balance while we waited to find out if an acquisition that was in the works would be successful. If the acquisition went through, our project wouldn't be needed. If the deal didn't go through, our project would help fill a larger product development void.

The strategy is on hold.

The third reason for tabling projects is that the strategy it supports is on hold or being reconceived. Use your internal network to stay abreast of where the strategy is going. Once you have that information, you'll have to tweak your case to reflect new goals, assumptions, or constraints. If your proposal focuses on U.S. customers, and your company has decided to focus more on European customers, for example, explore whether your idea could be carried out in the United Kingdom. Since you've done a good job preparing your business case, you'll easily be able to tweak it. This can be a great opportunity. Typically, senior leaders will want to do a project right away that aligns with the new imperatives to demonstrate support for the new strategy. With your carefully prepared plan, you could be first in line with a project that fits. Don't shoehorn your project into the new strategy, of course. If your case doesn't support it, don't make it.

Sometimes waiting for a final decision takes time—days, weeks, and even months. And the reason for the project—the pain point it's designed to address—likely isn't going away. There may not be a whole lot you can do, but look for opportunities to alleviate the pain a bit. If your case proposed a new system that would allow customer service representatives to respond more quickly to complaints, look for workarounds. Collaborate with the person heading up that department to see if he has any short-term ideas that will make things better.

While you're waiting, it's not a bad idea to find a simple, easy way to collect more information about the problem and its magnitude. Document what's happening so that when you have the opportunity to go back to the decision makers or to your project champion you can say, "This problem hasn't gone away; in fact, it's gotten worse." This will make your case stronger. If the problem is getting severe, you'll provide people with new information and change the story of your case: The boat's not just taking on water—it's sinking.

If You Heard "We Can Approve Only Part of the Project."

What if your case has three parts but the decision makers only approve one? Or they sign off on the first phase of your project but ask you to come back in six months or more to request the additional funding? This happens more often than people think. It's frustrating, but it doesn't have to demotivate you and your team. Instead, focus on the fact that the committee liked your idea and want to move it forward.

Chapter 16, "Get to a Decision," discussed how approval of just one part of your project is particularly common at companies that use a tollgate process. If this is the situation you're in, ask the review committee what risks or questions need to be resolved by the time you reach the first milestone. Then proceed as though your project will be fully funded. That will give you the best sense of whether the project will be a success. At the end of the funding period, be prepared to go back and explain which of your assumptions held true and which didn't. For instance, you might have determined that the product cost can be 10% less than planned or that the launch date will need to change by three months. Since you documented the source of all your original numbers and assumptions, it will be easy to check with those individuals for updates. Prepare to come back and present the business case again with updated information on the benefits or costs based on what you learned so far.

The most common scenario, however—and the most challenging—is when the decision makers come back and say, "OK, we know you wanted $2 million, but what can you do for $1 million?" When asked if you can do the project or reach the same goals with less time or money, never say yes right away. Instead, tell the reviewers that you'll get back to them—very quickly—so you have time to redo the business case with those new constraints.

When you commit to doing just part of the project, resist the temptation to overpromise. First, don't do an across-the-board cut. If the committee wants you to submit a proposal for a project that costs 30% less, don't try to do everything the original case did with 30% less resources. It's better to restructure the project completely. Ask yourself and your team: What is a viable business opportunity that we can fund with this much money to achieve a portion of the goal? Can we drop the European sales arm? Can we cut down the rollout time? Second, don't agree to a cut in resources without a cut in the benefits. This creates an almost impossible situation. If your original case promised $800,000 in revenue from the new product but now you're asked to cut the budget by 20%, chances are you won't be able to realize the full $800,000. You'll need to bring that number down as well. After all, if you don't have a full tank of gas, you can't go as far.

You'll be prepared for this conversation if you ran several scenarios in your spreadsheet (as described in chapter 7, "Consider Alternatives"). It's great if you have those numbers in your back pocket, but if not, go back and rerun your numbers. Fortunately, this is pretty easy because you've structured your spreadsheet well. Simply create another tab and change the relevant figures.

It's rare that a company can afford to fund every good idea. Instead of harping on the cuts you needed to make, focus your team on creating and implementing a new plan that will help pave the way for the rest of your project to be approved later on.

If You Heard "Yes, Let's Move Ahead."

First, celebrate. Open a bottle of champagne or take your team out for dinner. Then get to work. After all, the decision makers just opened a door and you've got to walk through it. You'll need to figure out how you transition from getting your project approved to implementing it.

Don't wait for the check. In most companies, a formal funding mechanism doesn't exist—nobody actually writes you a check. More likely you're told: OK, you've got the resources and people you need, get started.

After your celebration, the first step is to set up your project management process. Some companies have a methodology for this. If that's the case at your organization, reach out to your contact in the project planning or management group. This person can set you up with the appropriate tools, templates, checklists, or software to start the project.

If there isn't a formal process at your company, get the project moving yourself. Start by gathering your team and working on a project charter. Review the high-level implementation plan you outlined in the case and make sure it's still actionable. And keep the business case handy. It was the initial road map for the project and it will be helpful to refer to as you structure the work. See the *HBR Guide to Project Management* for more information on tools and templates to help you manage a project effectively.

You've succeeded in getting the organization behind your solution to an important business need, but this is just the beginning. Think of it as building a house: You've chosen the architect and the builders, you've agreed on a blueprint, the bank has approved the funding, and you have a rough schedule and budget—but you haven't broken ground yet. Now comes the real work.

Appendix A
Avoid Common Mistakes

When creating and pitching business cases, even experienced managers fall into these traps—but you can avoid them.

Mistake #1: Failing to Address the Company's Goals

Too many managers assume that the benefits of their proposed projects speak for themselves or are implicit in a strong ROI.

This often happens with IT initiatives. Take, for example, a project lead who wants to put in a new system because it's the industry standard and he fears the firm will fall behind the competition without it. He'll probably build a case demonstrating how the system will pay off in a few years. But how will it support the company's strategy? That's what senior leaders really want to know, because that's what they're on the hook to deliver. They won't approve anything that doesn't help them on that front. So when you're creating your case, show that you're meeting a clear business need that aligns with their goals.

Mistake #2: Ignoring Other Perspectives

Ideas rarely touch just one department—yet the people pitching them often fail to consider how they'll affect others in the organization.

Proposing a new product? It will be produced, marketed, and sold by colleagues in other functions, so you'll need their buy-in. Suppose the product makes three other lines obsolete: It's important to anticipate the impact on manufacturing processes, marketing, and sales projections. You can't just say, "Oh, and these three lines will go away."

Involve a cross-functional team when developing your case. Bring in experts whose departments will be affected by your idea. Share drafts of estimated costs and benefits with them, and ask if you've accurately gauged the impact on their teams. And think about your idea from their perspective: How will it benefit them? What will they need to contribute? What new work will they have to do? Include this information in your case—the review committee will expect it.

Mistake #3: Neglecting Transition Costs and Timing

Most managers realize they need to identify all the costs and benefits of a new system, facility, product, and so on—but they often don't factor in what it takes to make the switch.

Senior leaders need a handle on transition costs and how long it will take to fully realize benefits before they can decide whether to invest. Even if you can't give them exact figures, include rough estimates based on similar projects. This shows stakeholders that you're looking at the big picture and helps you gain support across the organization (see Mistake #2). If your colleagues in the quality department know you're asking for money to upgrade their systems and provide training for your product launch, for example, they're more likely to endorse your case. Amounts can be adjusted later on, when you have a better sense of the project's scope.

Mistake #4: Glossing Over Risks

The easiest way to poke holes in a business case is to ask, "What if?" I see executive teams do this all the time: "What if our competitors beat us to market? What happens to your projections then?" Or: "What if our key partner bails? What will it take to get a backup plan in place?" Unless you've adequately addressed things that could go wrong, your reviewers will surely ask about them.

It's not enough to throw in a brief nod to risks at the end of the presentation—or to say you'll examine them in the project's next phase. Executives want to see that you've thought through contingencies from the beginning. Of course, you can't account for every imaginable scenario, and stakeholders shouldn't expect you to. But look at the most likely possibilities, especially in light of recent business experience. For example, if the project will require you to outsource work, consider what happens if you can't find a qualified vendor or if your chosen vendor doesn't deliver on time.

It can be difficult to spot risks on your own, so appoint someone on your team to help you. As you're building your case, ask that person to challenge assumptions, to think like your stakeholders and raise the concerns they'll have. Or ask each member of your team to come up with five "What if?" questions. Encourage them to channel the approval committee when identifying risks. Does your CFO worry that the housing market will crash again? Is your division head preoccupied with a particular competitor? Those are the sorts of issues that will come up during review.

Mistake #5: Cluttering the Presentation with Jargon

Use plain language in your presentation so you won't bore and alienate your audience. The technical folks in the room will know what you mean by "backward compatibility" and "dual-layer technology," but others may not. People from several different functions will probably weigh in on your case, and if they can't understand it, you're in trouble. To avoid this problem, ask colleagues in other functions to review drafts, noting any opaque terms you should define or cut altogether.

In many firms, leaders review business cases on paper or on conference calls, so you may not get the chance to present face-to-face. Even if you do, you probably won't have time to give lengthy explanations—and your audience won't have the patience to listen to them. A clear, concise document always wins the day.

Appendix B
How to Give a Killer Presentation

by Chris Anderson

Editor's note: Though giving a TED Talk to a large, diverse audience is different from presenting a business case to the handful of stakeholders who will assess your project's value, this article provides helpful tips on crafting and delivering your message.

A little more than a year ago, on a trip to Nairobi, Kenya, some colleagues and I met a 12-year-old Masai boy named Richard Turere, who told us a fascinating story. His family raises livestock on the edge of a vast national park, and one of the biggest challenges is protecting the animals from lions—especially at night. Richard had noticed

---

Reprinted from *Harvard Business Review*, June 2013 (product #R1306K)

FIGURE B-1

Find the perfect mix of data and narrative *by Nancy Duarte*

Report
Literal, Informational, Factual, Exhaustive

Most presentations lie somewhere on the continuum between a report and a story. A report is data-rich, exhaustive, and informative—but not very engaging. Stories help a speaker connect with an audience, but listeners often want facts and information, too. Great presenters layer story and information like a cake, and understand that different types of talks require differing ingredients.

Story
Dramatic, Experiential, Evocative, Persuasive

Research Findings
If your goal is to communicate information from a written report, send the full document to the audience in advance, and limit the presentation to key takeaways. Don't do a long slide show that repeats all your findings. Anyone who's really interested can read the report; everyone else will appreciate brevity.

Financial Presentation
Financial audiences love data, and they'll want the details. Satisfy their analytical appetite with facts, but add a thread of narrative to appeal to their emotional side. Then present the key takeaways visually, to help them find meaning in the numbers.

Product Launch
Instead of covering only specs and features, focus on the value your product brings to the world. Tell stories that show how real people will use it and why it will change their lives.

VC Pitch
For 30 minutes with a VC, prepare a crisp, well-structured story arc that conveys your idea compellingly in 10 minutes or less; then let Q&A drive the rest of the meeting. Anticipate questions and rehearse clear and concise answers.

Keynote Address
Formal talks at big events are high-stakes, high-impact opportunities to take your listeners on a transformative journey. Use a clear story framework and aim to engage them emotionally.

Nancy Duarte is the author of *HBR Guide to Persuasive Presentations*, *Slide:ology,* and *Resonate*. She is the CEO of Duarte, Inc., which designs presentations and teaches presentation development.

that placing lamps in a field didn't deter lion attacks, but when he walked the field with a torch, the lions stayed away. From a young age, he'd been interested in electronics, teaching himself by, for example, taking apart his parents' radio. He used that experience to devise a system of lights that would turn on and off in sequence—using solar panels, a car battery, and a motorcycle indicator box—and thereby create a sense of movement that he hoped would scare off the lions. He installed the lights, and the lions stopped attacking. Soon villages elsewhere in Kenya began installing Richard's "lion lights."

The story was inspiring and worthy of the broader audience that our TED conference could offer, but on the surface, Richard seemed an unlikely candidate to give a TED Talk. He was painfully shy. His English was halting. When he tried to describe his invention, the sentences tumbled out incoherently. And frankly, it was hard to imagine a preteenager standing on a stage in front of 1,400 people accustomed to hearing from polished speakers such as Bill Gates, Sir Ken Robinson, and Jill Bolte Taylor.

But Richard's story was so compelling that we invited him to speak. In the months before the 2013 conference, we worked with him to frame his story—to find the right place to begin, and to develop a succinct and logical arc of events. On the back of his invention, Richard had won a scholarship to one of Kenya's best schools, and there he had the chance to practice the talk several times in front of a live audience. It was critical that he build his confidence to the point where his personality could shine through. When he finally gave his talk at TED, in Long

Beach, you could tell he was nervous, but that only made him more engaging—people were hanging on his every word. The confidence was there, and every time Richard smiled, the audience melted. When he finished, the response was instantaneous: a sustained standing ovation. Since the first TED conference, 30 years ago, speakers have run the gamut from political figures, musicians, and TV personalities who are completely at ease before a crowd to lesser-known academics, scientists, and writers—some of whom feel deeply uncomfortable giving presentations. Over the years, we've sought to develop a process for helping inexperienced presenters to frame, practice, and deliver talks that people enjoy watching. It typically begins six to nine months before the event, and involves cycles of devising (and revising) a script, repeated rehearsals, and plenty of fine-tuning. We're continually tweaking our approach—because the art of public speaking is evolving in real time—but judging by public response, our basic regimen works well: Since we began putting TED Talks online, in 2006, they've been viewed more than one billion times.

On the basis of this experience, I'm convinced that giving a good talk is highly coachable. In a matter of hours, a speaker's content and delivery can be transformed from muddled to mesmerizing. And while my team's experience has focused on TED's 18-minutes-or-shorter format, the lessons we've learned are surely useful to other presenters—whether it's a CEO doing an IPO road show, a brand manager unveiling a new product, or a start-up pitching to VCs.

Frame Your Story

There's no way you can give a good talk unless you have something worth talking about. Conceptualizing and framing what you want to say is the most vital part of preparation.

We all know that humans are wired to listen to stories, and metaphors abound for the narrative structures that work best to engage people. When I think about compelling presentations, I think about taking an audience on a journey. A successful talk is a little miracle—people see the world differently afterward.

If you frame the talk as a journey, the biggest decisions are figuring out where to start and where to end. To find the right place to start, consider what people in the audience already know about your subject—and how much they care about it. If you assume they have more knowledge or interest than they do, or if you start using jargon or get too technical, you'll lose them. The most engaging speakers do a superb job of very quickly introducing the topic, explaining why they care so deeply about it, and convincing the audience members that they should, too.

The biggest problem I see in first drafts of presentations is that they try to cover too much ground. You can't summarize an entire career in a single talk. If you try to cram in everything you know, you won't have time to include key details, and your talk will disappear into abstract language that may make sense if your listeners are familiar with the subject matter but will be completely opaque if they're new to it. You need specific examples to flesh out your ideas. So limit the scope of your talk to that which can be explained, and brought to life with examples, in the available time. Much of the early feedback we give aims to correct the impulse to sweep too broadly. Instead, go deeper. Give more detail. Don't tell us about your entire field of study—tell us about your unique contribution.

Of course, it can be just as damaging to overexplain or painstakingly draw out the implications of a talk. And there the remedy is different: Remember that the people in the audience are intelligent. Let them figure some things out for themselves. Let them draw their own conclusions.

Many of the best talks have a narrative structure that loosely follows a detective story. The speaker starts out by presenting a problem and then describes the search for a solution. There's an "aha" moment, and the audience's perspective shifts in a meaningful way.

If a talk fails, it's almost always because the speaker didn't frame it correctly, misjudged the audience's level of interest, or neglected to tell a story. Even if the topic is important, random pontification without narrative is always deeply unsatisfying. There's no progression, and you don't feel that you're learning.

I was at an energy conference recently where two people—a city mayor and a former governor—gave back-to-back talks. The mayor's talk was essentially a list of impressive projects his city had undertaken. It came off as boasting, like a report card or an advertisement for his reelection. It quickly got boring. When the governor spoke, she didn't list achievements; instead, she shared an idea. Yes, she recounted anecdotes from her time in office, but the idea was central—and the stories explanatory or illustrative (and also funny). It was so much more interesting. The mayor's underlying point seemed to be how great he was, while the governor's message was "Here's a compelling idea that would benefit us all."

As a general rule, people are not very interested in talks about organizations or institutions (unless they're members of them). Ideas and stories fascinate us; organizations bore us—they're much harder to relate to. (Businesspeople especially take note: Don't boast about your company; rather, tell us about the problem you're solving.)

Plan Your Delivery

Once you've got the framing down, it's time to focus on your delivery. There are three main ways to deliver a talk. You can read it directly off a script or a teleprompter. You can develop a set of bullet points that map out what you're going to say in each section rather than scripting the whole thing word for word. Or you can memorize your talk, which entails rehearsing it to the point where you internalize every word—verbatim.

My advice: Don't read it, and don't use a teleprompter. It's usually just too distancing—people will know you're reading. And as soon as they sense it, the way they receive your talk will shift. Suddenly your intimate connection evaporates, and everything feels a lot more formal. We generally outlaw reading approaches of any kind at TED, though we made an exception a few years ago for a man who insisted on using a monitor. We set up a screen at the back of the auditorium, in the hope that the audience wouldn't notice it. At first he spoke naturally. But soon he stiffened up, and you could see this horrible sinking feeling pass through the audience as people realized, "Oh, no, he's reading to us!" The words were great, but the talk got poor ratings.

Obviously, not every presentation is worth that kind of investment of time. But if you do decide to memorize your talk, be aware that there's a predictable arc to the learning curve. Most people go through what I call the "valley of awkwardness," where they haven't quite memorized the talk. If they give the talk while stuck in that valley, the audience will sense it. Their words will sound recited, or there will be painful moments where they stare into the middle distance, or cast their eyes upward, as they struggle to remember their lines. This creates distance between the speaker and the audience.

Getting past this point is simple, fortunately. It's just a matter of rehearsing enough times that the flow of words becomes second nature. Then you can focus on delivering the talk with meaning and authenticity. Don't worry—you'll get there.

But if you don't have time to learn a speech thoroughly and get past that awkward valley, don't try. Go with bullet points on note cards. As long as you know what you want to say for each one, you'll be fine. Focus on remembering the transitions from one bullet point to the next.

Also pay attention to your tone. Some speakers may want to come across as authoritative or wise or powerful or passionate, but it's usually much better to just sound conversational. Don't force it. Don't orate. Just be you.

If a successful talk is a journey, make sure you don't start to annoy your travel companions along the way. Some speakers project too much ego. They sound condescending or full of themselves, and the audience shuts down. Don't let that happen.

Develop Stage Presence

For inexperienced speakers, the physical act of being on stage can be the most difficult part of giving a presentation—but people tend to overestimate its importance. Getting the words, story, and substance right is a much bigger determinant of success or failure than how you stand or whether you're visibly nervous. And when it comes to stage presence, a little coaching can go a long way.

The biggest mistake we see in early rehearsals is that people move their bodies too much. They sway from side to side, or shift their weight from one leg to the other. People do this naturally when they're nervous, but it's distracting and makes the speaker seem weak. Simply getting a person to keep his or her lower body motionless can dramatically improve stage presence. There are some people who are able to walk around a stage during a presentation, and that's fine if it comes naturally. But the vast majority are better off standing still and relying on hand gestures for emphasis.

Perhaps the most important physical act onstage is making eye contact. Find five or six friendly-looking people in different parts of the audience and look them in the eye as you speak. Think of them as friends you haven't seen in a year, whom you're bringing up to date on your work. That eye contact is incredibly powerful, and it will do more than anything else to help your talk land. Even if you don't have time to prepare fully and have to read from a script, looking up and making eye contact will make a huge difference.

Another big hurdle for inexperienced speakers is nervousness—both in advance of the talk and while they're onstage. People deal with this in different ways. Many speakers stay out in the audience until the moment they go on; this can work well, because keeping your mind engaged in the earlier speakers can distract you and limit nervousness. Amy Cuddy, a Harvard Business School professor who studies how certain body poses can affect power, utilized one of the more unusual preparation techniques I've seen. She recommends that people spend time before a talk striding around, standing tall, and extending their bodies; these poses make you feel more powerful. It's what she did before going onstage, and she delivered a phenomenal talk. But I think the single best advice is simply to breathe deeply before you go onstage. It works.

In general, people worry too much about nervousness. Nerves are not a disaster. The audience expects you to be nervous. It's a natural body response that can actually improve your performance: It gives you energy to perform and keeps your mind sharp. Just keep breathing, and you'll be fine.

Acknowledging nervousness can also create engagement. Showing your vulnerability, whether through nerves or tone of voice, is one of the most powerful ways to win over an audience, provided it is authentic. Susan

Cain, who wrote a book about introverts and spoke at our 2012 conference, was terrified about giving her talk. You could feel her fragility onstage, and it created this dynamic where the audience was rooting for her—everybody wanted to hug her afterward. The fact that we knew she was fighting to keep herself up there made it beautiful, and it was the most popular talk that year.

Many of our best and most popular TED Talks have been memorized word for word. If you're giving an important talk and you have the time to do this, it's the best way to go. But don't underestimate the work involved. One of our most memorable speakers was Jill Bolte Taylor, a brain researcher who had suffered a stroke. She talked about what she learned during the eight years it took her to recover. After crafting her story and undertaking many hours of solo practice, she rehearsed her talk dozens of times in front of an audience to be sure she had it down.

Plan the Multimedia

With so much technology at our disposal, it may feel almost mandatory to use, at a minimum, presentation slides. By now most people have heard the advice about PowerPoint: Keep it simple; don't use a slide deck as a substitute for notes (by, say, listing the bullet points you'll discuss—those are best put on note cards); and don't repeat out loud words that are on the slide. Not only is reciting slides a variation of the teleprompter problem—"Oh, no, she's reading to us, too!"—but information is interesting only once, and hearing and seeing the same words feels repetitive. That advice may seem universal by now, but go into any company and you'll see presenters violating it every day.

Many of the best TED speakers don't use slides at all, and many talks don't require them. If you have photographs or illustrations that make the topic come alive, then yes, show them. If not, consider doing without, at least for some parts of the presentation. And if you're going to use slides, it's worth exploring alternatives to PowerPoint. For instance, TED has invested in the company Prezi, which makes presentation software that offers a camera's-eye view of a two-dimensional landscape. Instead of a flat sequence of images, you can move around the landscape and zoom in to it if need be. Used properly, such techniques can dramatically boost the visual punch of a talk and enhance its meaning.

Artists, architects, photographers, and designers have the best opportunity to use visuals. Slides can help frame and pace a talk and help speakers avoid getting lost in jargon or overly intellectual language. (Art can be hard to talk about—better to experience it visually.) I've seen great presentations in which the artist or designer put slides on an automatic timer so that the image changed every 15 seconds. I've also seen presenters give a talk accompanied by video, speaking along to it. That can help sustain momentum. The industrial designer Ross Lovegrove's highly visual TED Talk, for instance, used this technique to bring the audience along on a remarkable creative journey.

Another approach creative types might consider is to build silence into their talks, and just let the work speak for itself. The kinetic sculptor Reuben Margolin used that approach to powerful effect. The idea is not to think

"I'm giving a talk." Instead, think "I want to give this audience a powerful experience of my work." The single worst thing artists and architects can do is to retreat into abstract or conceptual language.

Video has obvious uses for many speakers. In a TED Talk about the intelligence of crows, for instance, the scientist showed a clip of a crow bending a hook to fish a piece of food out of a tube—essentially creating a tool. It illustrated his point far better than anything he could have said.

Used well, video can be very effective, but there are common mistakes that should be avoided. A clip needs to be short—if it's more than 60 seconds, you risk losing people. Don't use videos—particularly corporate ones—that sound self-promotional or like infomercials; people are conditioned to tune those out. Anything with a soundtrack can be dangerously off-putting. And whatever you do, don't show a clip of yourself being interviewed on, say, CNN. I've seen speakers do this, and it's a really bad idea—no one wants to go along with you on your ego trip. The people in your audience are already listening to you live; why would they want to simultaneously watch your talking-head clip on a screen?

Putting It Together

We start helping speakers prepare their talks six months (or more) in advance so that they'll have plenty of time to practice. We want people's talks to be in final form at least a month before the event. The more practice they can do in the final weeks, the better off they'll be. Ideally, they'll practice the talk on their own and in front of an audience.

The tricky part about rehearsing a presentation in front of other people is that they will feel obligated to offer feedback and constructive criticism. Often the feedback from different people will vary or directly conflict. This can be confusing or even paralyzing, which is why it's important to be choosy about the people you use as a test audience and whom you invite to offer feedback. In general, the more experience a person has as a presenter, the better the criticism he or she can offer.

I learned many of these lessons myself in 2011. My colleague Bruno Giussani, who curates our TEDGlobal event, pointed out that although I'd worked at TED for nine years, served as the emcee at our conferences, and introduced many of the speakers, I'd never actually given a TED Talk myself. So he invited me to give one, and I accepted.

It was more stressful than I'd expected. Even though I spend time helping others frame their stories, framing my own in a way that felt compelling was difficult. I decided to memorize my presentation, which was about how web video powers global innovation, and that was really hard: Even though I was putting in a lot of hours and getting sound advice from my colleagues, I definitely hit a point where I didn't quite have it down and began to doubt I ever would. I really thought I might bomb. I was nervous right up until the moment I took the stage. But it ended up going fine. It's definitely not one of the all-time great TED Talks, but it got a positive reaction—and I survived the stress of going through it.

Ultimately, I learned firsthand what our speakers have been discovering for three decades: Presentations rise or fall on the quality of the idea, the narrative, and the passion of the speaker. It's about substance, not speaking style or multimedia pyrotechnics. It's fairly easy to "coach out" the problems in a talk, but there's no way to "coach in" the basic story—the presenter has to have the raw material. If you have something to say, you can build a great talk. But if the central theme isn't there, you're better off not speaking. Decline the invitation. Go back to work and wait until you have a compelling idea that's really worth sharing.

The single most important thing to remember is that there is no one good way to do a talk. The most memorable talks offer something fresh, something no one has seen before. The worst ones are those that feel formulaic. So do not on any account try to emulate every piece of advice I've offered here. Take the bulk of it on board, sure. But make the talk your own. You know what's distinctive about you and your idea. Play to your strengths and give a talk that is truly authentic to you.

Chris Anderson is the curator of TED.

Glossary

Beneficiaries. Those inside or outside the organization who stand to gain from the project or initiative you are proposing.

Break-Even Point. Method of calculating ROI that determines how many units you need to sell in order to pay for the project.

Capital Expenditures. Money spent to acquire or develop an asset—which then depreciates, or decreases in value, over its life.

Internal Rate of Return (IRR). Method of calculating ROI that shows a project's investment value—essentially, the percentage of return you would get by investing the same amount of money in a CD that performed equally well.

Net Present Value (NPV). Method of calculating ROI that expresses the value of a long-term investment in today's dollars.

Operating Costs. Amount of money it will take to maintain the result of the project you are proposing. Includes ongoing expenses and overhead such as personnel, office space, and maintenance and licensing fees.

Payback Period. Method of calculating ROI that shows how many months or years it will take to earn back the money invested.

Productivity Savings. Costs you avoid through greater efficiency. Achieved either by changing the product cost baseline (with less-expensive materials, for example) or by cutting overhead costs (ongoing expenses that stem from how you run the business).

Project Expenditures. Onetime costs of doing the upfront project work, such as development, testing, training and deployment, and travel.

Proof of Concept. A small pilot project that tests your hypothesis about the business need for a project before you develop and present a solution.

Return on Investment (ROI). An estimate of the project's value. Four ROI measures calculated by using a stream of costs and benefits over time: break-even point, payback period, net present value, and internal rate of return.

Revenue. Money brought into the organization through sales.

Stakeholders. People with the authority to approve or reject your business case.

Sunk Costs. Money your organization has already spent on a project and will never get back.

Tollgate Process. Multiphased project approval, allowing stakeholders to decide one phase at a time whether to commit resources.

Index

Index

About the Authors

Raymond Sheen, PMP, is the president of Product & Process Innovation, a consulting firm specializing in project management, product development, and process improvement. He teaches seminars on developing and reviewing business cases at Worcester Polytechnic Institute, Clemson University, and the China Institute for Innovation. Sheen has managed projects for both government and private organizations. He prepared and reviewed hundreds of business cases when he worked at General Electric—both as a member of corporate staff and as an engineering executive within GE's Industrial Systems business. He holds engineering degrees from the U.S. Air Force Academy and the Massachusetts Institute of Technology. He and his family reside in South Carolina.

Amy Gallo is a contributing editor at *Harvard Business Review* and is the author of the forthcoming *HBR Guide to Managing Conflict at Work*. Her writing appears regularly on HBR.org. Before working as a writer and editor, she was a consultant at Katzenbach Partners, a strategy and organization consulting firm based in New York.

Notes

Notes

Notes

Notes

Notes

Notes

Notes

Notes

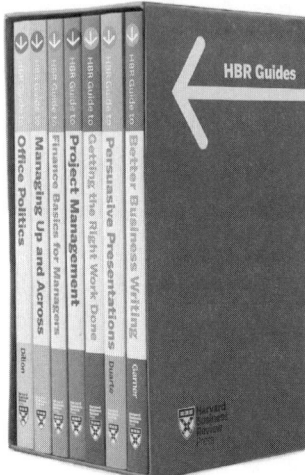

HBR Guide to
Leading Teams

Harvard Business Review Guides

Arm yourself with the advice you need to succeed on the job, from the most trusted brand in business. Packed with how-to essentials from leading experts, the HBR Guides provide smart answers to your most pressing work challenges.

The titles include:

HBR Guide to Better Business Writing

HBR Guide to Building Your Business Case

HBR Guide to Coaching Employees

HBR Guide to Finance Basics for Managers

HBR Guide to Getting the Mentoring You Need

HBR Guide to Getting the Right Job

HBR Guide to Getting the Right Work Done

HBR Guide to Giving Effective Feedback

HBR Guide to Leading Teams

HBR Guide to Making Every Meeting Matter

HBR Guide to Managing Stress at Work

HBR Guide to Managing Up and Across

HBR Guide to Negotiating

HBR Guide to Networking

HBR Guide to Office Politics

HBR Guide to Persuasive Presentations

HBR Guide to Project Management

HBR Guide to
Leading Teams

Mary Shapiro

HARVARD BUSINESS REVIEW PRESS

Boston, Massachusetts

Printed in the United States of America

10 9 8 7 6

Library of Congress Cataloging-in-Publication Data

Shapiro, Mary.
HBR guide to leading teams / Mary Shapiro.
pages cm
ISBN 978-1-63369-041-7 (alk. paper)
1. Teams in the workplace—Management. 2. Leadership. I. Title.
HD66.S4844 2015
659.4'022—dc23

2015007184

ISBN: 9781633690417

eISBN: 9781633690424

The paper used in this publication meets the requirements of the American National Standard for Permanence of Paper for Publications and Documents in Libraries and Archives Z39.48-1992.

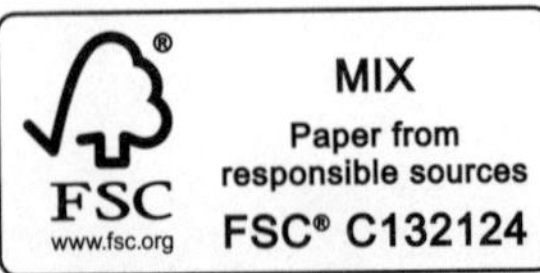

What You'll Learn

How often have you sat in team meetings, grousing to yourself, "What a colossal waste of time. Why does it take forever for us to make a simple decision? What are we even trying to *achieve* here?"

Dysfunctional teams are maddening—and sadly, they seem to be endemic to organizational life. But as the team leader, you have the power to change things for the better. It's up to you to get people to work well together and produce results.

How do you avoid the pitfalls you've experienced so painfully in the past? This guide offers step-by-step advice, drawing on time-tested principles, practical exercises, guidelines for structured team conversations, and examples from a range of industries and organizational settings.

You'll get better at:

- Picking the right team members
- Cultivating their skills
- Setting clear, smart goals

- Rallying support both within and outside the team
- Fostering camaraderie and cooperation
- Addressing bad behavior before it gets out of hand
- Promoting healthy dissent
- Resolving conflict when it rears its head
- Holding members accountable to one another, not just to you
- Keeping them focused and motivated to the end
- Identifying best practices for your next team

Contents

Section 3: CLOSE OUT YOUR TEAM

Introduction

Whether you're taking over an existing team, launching a new one, or have been leading a group for a while, getting people to work together to produce excellent outcomes is not easy. Each team is different, and each poses a distinct set of challenges. Maybe you've just been assigned to chair a task force of people from different units to launch a companywide initiative. Perhaps you manage five people who have to work together daily as a part of ongoing operations. Or maybe you've been struggling at the helm of a team so mired in conflict that the members couldn't reach agreement on anything if their lives depended on it. No matter what type of team you're leading, you probably face tight deadlines and high expectations and feel the pressure to churn out project plans, assign tasks, and, above all, execute.

It's only natural. We create teams to accomplish work, after all, so we tend to focus mainly on tasks. But that's just one side of the equation; we also need to focus on the *people* who will be carrying out those tasks.

If your team members don't have good relationships with one another, your team won't do good work. People will squabble. They won't trust each other. They'll feel underappreciated, grumbling that others aren't carrying their share of the load. They'll stop collaborating. Tempers will flare—and productivity will grind to a halt.

It takes time and energy to prevent complications like these and to get team members working well together. You have to explain tasks clearly, coordinate efforts, motivate people, resolve conflicts, give feedback, and develop skills. In short, you have to manage the people with as much discipline as you manage the work.

Before investing all that effort, consider whether you even need a team to do the job at hand. We've all been on teams assembled for the wrong reasons—to rubber-stamp an already-made decision, for example, or to spread out the risk and blame in case a project goes badly. To ensure that your team has a solid reason for being, conduct a straightforward cost/benefit analysis: Will it help you meet your goals and improve your outcomes? Or can you do the work just as well yourself, with greater efficiency and fewer headaches?

If you decide the investment is worthwhile, you'll want to create a *winning* team, of course—not one that crashes and burns or limps along indefinitely. This book will help you do just that. Effective team leadership unfolds in three stages: build-up, managing, and closing out.

Stage 1: Build Your Team's Infrastructure

Just like a house, a solid team needs a strong foundation. But instead of stones or cement, your materials will be early discussions about goals, roles, rules of conduct, and the metrics you'll use to gauge progress. Once you've enlisted people with the required skills and perspectives, the group must explicitly agree on what it's trying to achieve, how it will get there, and what success will look like. This is how team building really works. It's not about ropes courses or whitewater-rafting trips, it's about reconciling individual temperaments and work styles to get the most out of each contributor and the team as a whole.

You may be thinking, "Who has time for all these conversations? We have a job to do, and we're already in a pinch to get it done." But agreeing on *how* you'll do that work beforehand will make it go more quickly and smoothly. You'll have fewer conflicts to navigate, decisions to revisit, and tasks to redo.

Because each group has its own quirks, you'll need to build this infrastructure every time you create a new team—and every time you lose or add members.

Stage 2: Manage Your Team

If you've ever led a project, you know what it takes to manage tasks: You acknowledge when they're done well and on time. And when something misses the mark, you stipulate changes to get it back on track. Throughout the project, you strive for continuous improvement.

The same principles apply to leading a team. When people exhibit useful behavior—such as warning others before a deadline slips—point it out. This motivates them to keep it up and reminds others of what they should do to support team goals. It's just as important to nip negative behavior in the bud—a team member stops participating in meetings, for example, or verbally attacks those who disagree with her. Just as you monitor and tweak tasks to follow a project plan, keep a close eye on how people are doing relative to the goals, roles, and rules you've all agreed on—and talk openly about problems as soon as they crop up.

It sounds simple, but most team leaders don't do this. Instead, they let issues go unaddressed until someone explodes in frustration, or until everyone mentally checks out, bringing work to a standstill.

Stage 3: Close Out Your Team

Say you're almost ready to turn your prototype over to engineering, for example, or to present recommendations to the board of directors. You should be elated, right? The team is so *close* to achieving its goals. But you've noticed that people are skipping meetings or spending time on other work. What's happening?

When the finish line is in sight, team members often lose their focus, drive, and patience. They start thinking about the *next* project or obsessing about all their other work that has piled up. You may feel the same impatience to move on. Now more than ever, it's critical to motivate team members—and yourself—to wrap things up properly and capture best practices to apply next time around.

That's what this third stage is about. If you solicit your team's input on what went well and what didn't, you'll manage those problems better in the future. You'll grow as a team leader—and your team members will improve their own skills.

We'll cover each of these stages in this guide. Throughout, I provide sample structured conversations and activities developed from my experience of more than 20 years of consulting with teams. I draw on many real examples (some of them disguised) to show how team leaders have applied the advice in a range of situations.

You may feel uncomfortable with some of the activities, at least initially, since they deal with the "people" side of teams (an area where many leaders struggle, especially those who were promoted because of their technical expertise). But give them a try. I've seen them work for new and existing teams, large and small, colocated and virtual, and in just about every organizational setting—including financial services, manufacturing, customer service, technology, nonprofits, and government agencies. They'll help your team to grow, prevent and fix hard problems, and produce the results you're after.

Section 1
Build Your Team's Infrastructure

Chapter 1
Pull Together a Winning Team

If you've ever led a team, you've dealt with maddening members: Those who dominate meetings. Slowpokes who analyze every problem from every angle when the schedule is tight. Those who harp on reasons *not* to support decisions the group made months ago. Quiet folks who say nothing in meetings, but then complain endlessly at the coffee station about decisions that were made in their presence. Those who compete for "resident expert" status without actually contributing much at all.

You may have wondered: Do they stay up all night thinking of ways to torment me? What's wrong with them? Why can't they be more like *me?*

That's a common—though a bit melodramatic—response to the challenge of leading a team of diverse individuals. Socially we all gravitate toward people who are like us—those who understand our humor, enjoy doing the same things we do, and don't get offended when we cancel at the last minute (after all, they do it, too). Sameness minimizes conflict and misunderstanding. Yet, to paraphrase U.S. gum maker William Wrigley Jr. when two people think alike on a team, one of them is redundant. Assemble a team of people who are just like you, and you'll undoubtedly experience less frustration. The group will reach decisions more quickly, and members will approach the work in the same way.

But lack of diversity has a serious downside. If everyone on the team prefers big-picture thinking, who comes up with the practical steps necessary to realize the group's vision? If everyone likes taking risks, who plans a soft landing before you leap? Who handles the tasks you don't like to do or can't do well?

Research repeatedly shows that greater diversity on a team yields more innovation and higher-quality work. That's why each individual on your team should bring some unique combination of expertise and skills that will help you produce great work (see figure 1-1).

To achieve the diversity "sweet spot" you're aiming for, you must first envision the results you want, and then determine what strengths and capabilities you'll need to achieve them. If you're building a business case, for instance, you'll need expertise in data mining and proposal writing. Tap your network for people who are good at those things or ask your colleagues whom they'd recommend. Once you've got someone on board who possesses a critical skill, don't add another team mem-

FIGURE 1-1

Making the most of diversity

Use this list of task- and people-related strengths to determine what mix of knowledge and skills your team requires.

To complete the tasks at hand, you may need members who bring:	To get everyone working well together, enlist members who excel at:
• Relevant functional expertise (for example, in engineering, accounting, marketing, finance, or customer service) • Relevant industry knowledge (for example, in manufacturing, technology, health care, or financial services) • Technological skill • An appetite for research • The ability to mine and analyze data • A knack for writing and presenting	• Facilitating meetings • Building consensus • Giving feedback • Communicating in groups • Resolving conflicts • Negotiating • Motivating others • Exercising emotional intelligence • Influencing others • Networking with people outside the team who can provide resources

ber who excels at the same thing. Remember to address both task-related strengths and people skills when assembling your team.

Consider this hypothetical example illustrating the value of diversity on a team.

Imagine that your company has experienced a dramatic increase in products returned from customers. If you pull together a team of six engineers to analyze the problem, chances are they'll quickly come to one conclusion and make a recommendation consistent with their common backgrounds: It's an engineering issue, and the solution is to rework the design.

I know this is a cliché, but it applies here: When everyone on your team is a "hammer," then every problem will look like a nail, and every solution will be to pound it. Outcomes will be quick, consistent, and harmonious—but not innovative.

Now suppose you add people from customer service and marketing to your team. Team members will look at the problem from different viewpoints. Maybe it's an engineering problem, maybe customers don't understand how to use the product correctly, or maybe they're buying the wrong model for their purposes.

That's the good news—a variety of perspectives expands the number of possible solutions. But the team still must work together to come up with a single creative solution. The decision making takes much longer, and relationships may get strained as members hash out conflicting ideas.

So what's the right amount of diversity? Jon Katzenbach and Douglas Smith define the optimal makeup of a team in their classic *Harvard Business Review* article "The Discipline of Teams" this way: "A small number of people with complementary skills who are committed to a common purpose, set of performance goals, and approach for which they hold themselves mutually accountable."

Building on this definition and drawing on my years of experience consulting with teams and leading my own, I've developed the following principles for assembling an effective team:

Make It Small

The larger the team, the more difficult it is to find meeting times, the longer it takes to make decisions, and the tougher it is to manage information and work flow. So bring together the smallest number of people necessary to provide the skills and perspectives you need. That's usually somewhere between three and seven members. Other contributors who will be needed only occasionally—organizational allies, content experts, and advisers—should not be included as full-fledged members: That just wastes everyone's time. Instead, consult them at specific points and assign one member to serve as a conduit of information back and forth. For example, a finance representative should weigh in as you put together a budget request for a project, but that person obviously shouldn't participate in all the team building and ongoing work that doesn't require financial expertise.

If you are assuming leadership of an existing team, you'll need to start by deciding whom to keep and whom to cut loose. If the numbers feel bloated, consider defining a core team of a few essential people and moving others onto a "support" team that you enlist on an ad hoc basis. This strategy is particularly useful if you have inherited some noncontributors, complainers, or obstructionists. If you can't eliminate them, you can at least marginalize their impact.

Incorporate Skills and Knowledge

List the skills and types of expertise you'll need to tackle the team's responsibilities—not just what's needed to accomplish the work but also what will facilitate collaboration. (Again, use figure 1-1 to get started.) Then identify the fewest number of people who can cover most of those requirements.

You can also conduct this inventory to reevaluate your current team. If certain members aren't contributing much, ideally you'll remove them. But if you don't have that authority, try giving them "support team" status as suggested above. Does your team lack key competencies? Add people to fill those gaps—or at least identify advisers you can call on periodically.

Include Diverse Approaches to Work

The best teams offer a mix of work styles: people who carefully address one task at a time and those who can multitask, folks who excel at contingency planning and those who nimbly adjust when problems strike, and so on. Here, we're talking about people's natural inclinations, not the skills they've acquired through training or experience. When assembling your team, consider how people differ in their outlooks, priorities, and attitudes about decision making, change, and risk.

Don't drive yourself crazy trying to include every conceivable work style on your team. It's just not possible. But identify people whose wiring differs from your own and who possess characteristics essential for your team's success. If you're leading a team that will drive deep change in the organization, you may want members on both sides of the "change" spectrum: early adopters to generate creative ideas and late adopters to anticipate sources of resistance (see figure 1-2).

FIGURE 1-2

How are they wired?

When you're selecting team members, think about how they're naturally inclined to act. On each dimension below, most people will gravitate toward one end of the continuum or the other when they're on "autopilot," though they can adjust their behaviors with effort—when under deadline pressure, for instance.

←		→
Is detail oriented	OUTLOOK	Focuses on the big picture
Focuses on the next project deadline	OUTLOOK	Looks one to three years down the road
Decides on the basis of data	DECISION MAKING	Relies on intuition
Decides deliberately with analyses and contemplation	DECISION MAKING	Decides spontaneously
Is a late adopter of trends; prefers certainty and clarity	CHANGE	Is an early adopter; is comfortable with uncertainty
Prefers incremental change; builds on what works	CHANGE	Prefers large, sweeping change; likes a "clean slate"
Places task completion ahead of relationships	PRIORITIES	Places relationships and harmony ahead of tasks
Focuses on the tasks themselves	PRIORITIES	Focuses on how the work gets done (the process)
Prefers a slow and methodical environment	WORK	Prefers a fast and fluid environment
Works on one task at a time	WORK	Multitasks
Spends time analyzing and preparing for risk	RISK	Faces risk with minimal planning
Identifies all possible outcomes and generates contingencies ahead of time	RISK	Prefers to make real-time adjustments as needed

Though work quality will benefit from a mix of personalities and approaches, relationships may suffer. For example, the big-picture thinkers might regard the detail-oriented people as data geeks crippled by "analysis paralysis." And the detail people may dismiss the big-picture folks as unrealistic or people who "shoot from the hip."

Why would you want both types on your team? Imagine how much work would get done with only big-picture thinkers to execute ideas. Probably very little. They'd generate lots of excitement and creative thought, but the goals would keep changing and expanding, and no one would focus on how exactly to accomplish them. And you wouldn't be any better off with an entire team of detail-oriented colleagues. They'd provide clarity, structure, and solid documentation of progress—but their outcomes would probably resemble what's been done in the past. They wouldn't break new ground.

So the differences are worth the potential headaches. We'll talk more about how to handle the conflict—both destructive and beneficial—that is a natural by-product of diversity in chapter 11, "Resolve Conflicts Constructively." But let's now look at ways to minimize the headaches by anticipating some of the problems members will have.

Chapter 2

Get to Know One Another

Now that you've identified the skills and expertise your project needs and pulled together your team, it's time for your launch meeting. You've made a PowerPoint deck outlining the project. You've provided coffee and donuts, and everyone's sitting around the table expectantly. How do you begin? If you're like most of us, you welcome everyone, introduce yourself, and then ask each person to share his or her name, title, and maybe "a little about yourself."

But hang on. Don't zip past those introductions. Before you dig into that deck and start explaining and organizing tasks, it's essential to gather some personal data to help the group establish effective goals, roles, and rules of conduct. I'm not suggesting that your team members should share their favorite reality TV shows or "fun facts" about themselves. Rather, I'm encouraging you to connect with them in a meaningful way so that you—and the rest of the group—will know what each person needs to do his or her best work.

Begin by addressing the fundamental questions they're privately contemplating while munching on their donuts:

- Why am I on this team, and what are your expectations of me?
- Why are others on this team?
- How do you see us working together?

If your team members understand why you chose them, they'll have a clearer sense of how they can contribute. And just as important, they'll learn what other team members bring to the table. You're also helping people recognize from the outset the purpose for the team's diversity, so they'll be less likely later to snipe about how some members "leap before they look" and others can't "analyze their way out of a paper bag." By naming differences from the beginning, you're acknowledging the need to work across them and highlighting the value each person brings.

Having everyone say "Hi, my name is Ellen, and I'm from St. Louis" doesn't accomplish any of that.

As the team leader, you've intentionally chosen people with complementary skills and perspectives. Now you need to shed light, in a series of group conversations, on members' personal strengths, work styles, and priorities.

Personal Strengths

Each member's skills, knowledge, and work style will add to the pool of valuable team resources. A simple way of getting the group up to speed on those resources is to go around the room and ask individuals to share what strengths they bring to the team and what others say they do well. Because many people are reluctant to talk about themselves, you may need to prompt them with a structured conversation (see, for example, the sidebar "Artifact Exercise").

You can also invite them to talk about one another. For existing teams or for members who have collaborated before, ask people to complete this sentence about each colleague: "In the past, I've relied on this person to . . . ."

Then it's your turn to speak up: Say why you placed each individual on the team and what contributions you expect each member to make.

One project leader at a large pharmaceutical company did this in a quirky way: He cut a poster of his business unit's logo into jigsaw-puzzle pieces. At his team's first meeting, he explained why he'd asked each person to participate, handing him or her a puzzle piece as he did so. Then he had the seven members assemble the puzzle.

You may be thinking, "There's no way I can do that—it's too hokey." And that might be true for your team. Members have to be receptive for this to work, but when they are, it packs a punch. The team leader in the example above had enough seniority that people were willing to suspend disbelief and give the exercise a fair

ARTIFACT EXERCISE

Before meeting as a group for the first time, ask each team member to come prepared with a five-minute story about a past accomplishment. This can be a personal or business achievement—anything the storyteller is proud of. Have everyone bring an artifact (some physical object, whether it's a photo, a diploma, or a rock from Mount McKinley) that symbolizes the achievement.

When people share their stories in the meeting, prompt them to describe the opportunities or challenges they faced, the actions they took, and the outcomes they produced. Then debrief by asking the team:

- What was your reaction to hearing everyone's stories?
- What do these stories tell us about the skills that each person brings to the team?

It's never too late to do this exercise, even with existing teams or those you inherit. People are often amazed by their colleagues' accomplishments. The stories may uncover hidden resources the team can put to use. They also give members a chance to communicate their own strengths and help them appreciate one another.

One manager at a government agency found this exercise particularly helpful when she was tapped to lead a team of account managers and engineers. She knew she had to neutralize a lot of pent-up mistrust—not a small feat—because the two groups had a long history of organizational conflict. They didn't like or work well with each other.

So she used the artifact exercise. By listening to team members' stories of achievement, each group gained a new appreciation for the other's challenges. It took time to break down the long-standing barriers between them, but this exercise gave them a good start. It opened their minds so they could find new, better ways of working together.

shake. He also articulated a clear goal for doing it: He wanted to convey that everyone's voice had equal weight, even though the scientists in the group outranked the administrators and junior members in the corporate hierarchy. It was an important point to make, because the team's ability to produce meaningful recommendations for the company depended on the full commitment and engagement of all its members. The scientists got the message that, at least on this team, they had to collaborate with their junior colleagues. And the junior folks felt empowered.

Work Styles

Some of your team members may prefer a "divide and conquer" approach, where you break projects into small tasks and have people work independently on their sections, with limited interaction until it's time to assemble the final report. Others may prefer to work together in all aspects of the project, believing that collaboration generates a better outcome. Not surprisingly, the first group will probably feel micromanaged if forced to work with others constantly, and people in the second group will feel isolated if left on their own for too long.

By finding out how individuals prefer to operate, you and the team can develop rules that enable all members to contribute meaningfully (see chapter 5, "Agree on Rules of Conduct"). Yes, the "divide and conquer" members will have to collaborate occasionally, and the "let's stay joined at the hip" members will have to work independently at times. But understanding those conflicting preferences helps you and the team anticipate members' needs and determine how to work together productively.

So how do you figure out individuals' preferences? In a meeting, have each member talk about prior team experiences. This allows people to learn how their teammates naturally behave when deadlines loom and stress increases. Ask everyone:

- What was your best team experience and why? What made it so good? What did team members or the leader do that made it such a good experience? What was the atmosphere like?

- What was your worst team experience and why? What made it so bad? What behaviors drove you crazy?

Another approach is to have each team member complete a diagnostic like the Myers-Briggs Type Indicator. People's traits—how decisive, detailed, intuitive, or adaptable they are—have an impact on their behavior and on how they'd prefer to operate on your team.

You have many diagnostics to choose from (see the sidebar "Personality and Work Style Assessments" for a few examples). The goal in using any of them is to help people on your team understand their own traits and styles and recognize how other members differ. This sets the stage for the team to craft a "team style" of working.

Such diagnostics are powerful partly because they reinforce the notion that people's intentions are generally good and that the way they behave isn't random, arbitrary, or malicious. Rather, their behavior reflects what makes sense to them. It may not make sense to others until people can more clearly see the motives behind it.

That's what happened with Nancy, a nurse at a community-based health care center where each patient is assigned a team: a physician, a nurse practitioner, several nurses, and a patient care manager. Whenever Nancy met with a team to determine a patient's care, she asked lots of questions because she preferred to make decisions on the basis of abundant data. However, team members with different styles misinterpreted her

PERSONALITY AND WORK STYLE ASSESSMENTS

Myers-Briggs Type Indicator

Indicates how people get their energy (working alone or working with others), how they make decisions (using intuition or data), what they base their decisions on (emotions or objective information), and how they manage their lives (with or without structure).

Howard Gardner's Multiple Intelligences

Recognizes different types of intelligences beyond standard IQ, which measures only logical and mathematical intelligences. Teams benefit when they bring additional intelligences (linguistic, musical, kinesthetic, intrapersonal, interpersonal, and spatial-visual) to bear on their work.

DISC

Identifies the level of dominance (control of environment), influence, steadiness (cooperation), and conscientiousness (accuracy and completeness) each member brings to the team.

Big Five Personality Test

Assesses individuals' extraversion (how outgoing or solitary they are), agreeableness (how cooperative or not), conscientiousness (how organized or casual), openness (how curious or cautious about diverse people and experiences), and emotional stability (how steady or impulsive).

motives. The physician thought Nancy saw herself as smarter than her teammates; others assumed she didn't trust them to make good decisions.

It wasn't until the team did a personality diagnostic that they discovered what really drove Nancy's behavior. She scored much higher on conscientiousness and the need for detail and control than the other team members. And most of them scored higher than she did on valuing relationships. With their focus on maintaining harmony in the group, they were reluctant to bring up dissenting ideas when making decisions together. They usually agreed to the first idea offered and didn't ask people to explain their opinions, fearing that disagreement would be seen as a challenge. Nancy, whose assessment revealed a focus on tasks rather than relationships, didn't view questions and disagreement as personal attacks. She saw them as tools for making the best decision.

Unnamed, these differences between Nancy and her teammates had created a big problem. But now when Nancy asks a lot of questions, the rest of the team understands that it's just how she operates—and that her questions may actually prevent errors.

Priorities

It's also critical to identify up front where the team ranks on each member's personal priority list. This is particularly true for ad hoc teams, where you're given a limited amount of time, and you're adding work to people's already-full plates. It's also important when you've borrowed team members from their "real" jobs, because they're now accountable to you *and* their managers. As

ALLAYING FEARS ABOUT ASSESSMENTS

As helpful as diagnostics can be, they make some people feel exposed or vulnerable. To put them at ease, you can:

Make It Optional

Allow members to opt out. The team needs to be OK with that and to understand that people differ in their need for privacy.

Explain the Purpose

If people understand that the results will help the team define its goals and ways of working together, they'll be more receptive to the exercise. Remind them that these assessments are *not* evaluative or judgmental—it's neither good nor bad to be identified as decisive, for instance, or collaborative. Rather, effective assessments simply describe individuals' traits, increasing self-awareness and others' understanding.

Emphasize Confidentiality

Assure team members that you won't share results with anyone outside the group, and set the expectation that no one else will, either. The insights are for the team's use only.

Let Members Choose What to Share

If people don't feel comfortable discussing individual results, that's all right—you can still get value from reviewing results in the aggregate. But if they're willing to disclose what they've learned about themselves, ask how they think their colleagues scored and have them explain what behaviors they're basing their conclusions on. People usually guess others' styles correctly, as you can imagine. That member who loves to create PERT charts for projects? Of *course* she scored high on conscientiousness. And the person who loves to deliver presentations? He probably scored high on extroversion.

Discuss Impact on the Work

Ease people into sharing their experiences. If you're leading a small team, give them time to think before they speak. If it's a larger team, you might group them according to their styles. That way, they can trade stories with similarly wired members before opening up to the whole team. Someone might say, for example, "I scored high on introversion. That explains why I usually gravitate toward task management. I love making sure the hundreds of moving parts are in alignment. However, because I'm an introvert, I have a hard time asking others for input. I prefer making decisions alone and sometimes miss important points as a result."

When you break into small groups, you can also ask people to discuss what they need from a team to do their best work, what they like about teams, what

(*continued*)

(*continued*)

they struggle with, and how they define a good team member, leader, and meeting. Gathering this kind of data now will help the team figure out its rules and processes later.

Collect Results in a Chart

Create a visual to show members where they overlap and where they differ. You can match traits with names or just indicate how many team members have each tendency. Even if you do the latter, names often come up as people discuss the diagnostic, guess one another's styles, or talk about themselves. Either way, it's useful to discuss which traits the team has in abundance and which it lacks. For new teams, consider how the distribution of styles might shape what the group is likely to do well and what it might overlook. For existing teams, ask what impact the various styles have had on group dynamics (both positive and negative). The health care team, for instance, found it enlightening that Nancy was the only one who scored high on conscientiousness. No wonder her behavior frustrated the others—she was an outlier.

Emphasize Value Added

Have people with similar traits brainstorm in small groups—that way, they'll come up with a long list of all the good things they bring. Then ask the groups to share their lists with the rest of the team. This helps people appreciate the value of having different styles in the mix. For example, those who love big, sweeping change are more likely than others to challenge the status quo and prompt innovation. Conversely, those who prefer small, incremental adjustments will prevent the team from making changes too hastily or without due cause.

you assembled the team, you probably negotiated for the amount of time each ad hoc member would give. But even your full-time members have personal (and often invisible) limits to their availability.

For that reason, a group conversation about individuals' priorities yields useful information for all types of teams. Members come with their own goals, ambitions, and outside commitments. So ask how many hours they can realistically devote to your team every week. Also get them to specify competing demands on their time. Sometimes I have each member draw up and share a rough pie chart showing how they'll allocate their time across their multiple commitments.

By finding all this out early, you can make smart assignments that align with individuals' priorities and availability. While this may not seem like a fair way to distribute the work, it's the right way. The team's outcomes will be only as ambitious as its members' availability allows.

And the team can boost its performance and avoid missing deadlines by funneling more tasks to members with more time and a greater level of investment.

Beware the usual expectation that everyone will participate equally. This is unrealistic and sets everyone up for disappointment. Expecting equity also hurts performance, since members who give the work a lower priority may do just what's minimally required. And it hurts members for whom the work is a *high* priority: They aren't given as much responsibility as they'd like, and they may feel they have to scale back their contributions to the lowest common denominator. Instead of looking for equal participation, expect members to contribute to the best of their abilities.

Once everyone has a clear sense of what each member brings to the team and how individuals' styles and priorities differ, you're well positioned to establish the team's goals, roles, and rules of conduct, which we'll cover in the chapters that follow.

Chapter 3
Establish Your Team's Goals

No matter what kind of team you're leading, the group must set two types of goals: *Task goals* specify what your outcomes should look like. They direct *what* gets done, defining the work of the team. *Process goals* describe the team's approach to working together. They direct *how* individuals do the work and interact with one another. (You'll work out the "how" in more detail when you create rules of conduct, addressed in chapter 5.)

Although it's tempting to skimp on the goal setting and immediately start planning tasks, taking the time up front to develop both task and process goals yields several benefits:

- Group decision making becomes clearer and more efficient—and conflicts are easier to resolve. The team can cull its options by asking, "Which ideas move us closer to our goals?"

- Individual members approach autonomous decisions consistently. This allows for a smoother discussion when people report back to the group, and it expedites the team's progress.
- Goals provide a framework for holding team members accountable. When giving feedback (positive or negative) or evaluating a team member's performance, you can answer the question: "Did this outcome or behavior support our goals?"

Let's take a closer look at both types of goals.

Task Goals

Suppose you've been asked to lead a team to plan how your company will store and ship products during warehouse renovations.

First, you need to agree on outcomes—your task goals. To develop them, ask members to describe what an optimal future would look like. Have them envision the warehouse layout, for instance, and the staffing. Also consider as a group what failure would look like. Often, people can easily articulate what they *don't* want; recasting their language reveals what they would like to see happen. Finally, discuss the desired customer experience from beginning to end.

During this conversation, your team may decide, for example, that the final plan should include the fewest possible moves (of people, equipment, and inventory), a way of updating all affected departments on progress to facilitate their planning, a continual feedback loop to permit real-time adjustments, and sufficient procedures and staffing to keep the renovation process invisible to customers. Once you've got those overarching goals in place, the team needs to define three components:

Actions

What steps will the team take to achieve its task goals? Teams often rely on one or two members with project management skills to create and present a plan, which others then add to or revise. However you develop it, any plan should include key activities, contingencies, checkpoints for monitoring the work, guidelines for keeping stakeholders informed, and details about who needs to sign off on which steps.

Deadlines

When will the team take each step? Without deadlines to drive you forward, the actions you've planned will remain a wish list. Work backward from the final due date, and estimate (realistically) how long each step should take. Allow buffer for actions outside the team's control, such as waiting for go-aheads from senior management.

Metrics

How will the team measure progress on its tasks? What are the criteria for completion? Clear measures of team success will help individuals understand what's expected of them and how they'll be evaluated. You may want to gauge financial performance (reduced costs, for example, or increased margins), productivity (reduced time), or quality (reduced errors). Metrics should spur team members to work hard and "stretch"—but they'll discourage people if they aren't within reach. And they need to be specific so that team members won't interpret tasks differently ("What do we mean by 'accurate' reports?").

Process Goals

Clear process goals allow you to blend individual team members into one cohesive unit, so these goals are every bit as critical to your success as planning the work. Most teams don't even bother with process goals—they assume they already know how to work together. But remember all the diversity you purposely embedded in your team? Each member probably has a different understanding of how to collaborate, not to mention different styles and preferences.

Identifying process goals requires that you define the team's culture. You'll explicitly address the following questions:

- **What will it feel like to work with the team?** Will it be inclusive with shared responsibility or dictatorial with autocratic decrees? Will there be mutual respect or backstabbing and political alliances? Will the tone be optimistic or pessimistic? Supportive or competitive?

- **What will the relationships look like?** Will they be equal or hierarchical? Open or closed? Trusting or suspicious? Social and personal or all-business?

- **What do we want from those relationships?** Do we want to simply get the tasks done or develop longer-term connections? Divide and conquer tasks with minimal interaction or learn from and mentor one another?

- **What do we value?** Do we care more about speed or accuracy? Risk taking or compliance? Innovation or building on core strengths?

Of course, no team in the universe *tries* to establish a culture of suspicion, backstabbing, and passivity. But we've all been on a team like that. A team's culture evolves whether you talk about it or not—so it's better to spell out what you're aiming for, giving people the opportunity to explicitly reject undesirable behaviors. Otherwise, you're likely to wind up with a culture that evolves by itself in the wrong direction—one, for example, where people stop contributing because they see only a few individuals getting all the credit, or one where the mantra is "CYA."

It's important to incorporate members' personal goals into your team's process goals. Otherwise, people may act against the group's interests to satisfy their own. Say, for instance, that one member is eager to gain visibility with senior leaders. It's best to know that *before* he decides to leak messy work-in-progress details to a stakeholder over lunch. (You can prevent that sort of problem by creating a "team of equals," where all members get visibility and credit, not just the team leader.) But how do you uncover his personal agenda? You'll need to read between the lines. If you asked, "What do you want to get out of this team project?" he would never say, "More visibility to advance my career." But he might reveal that objective through his questions ("Who will get to present the final proposal to senior management?") or through his comments on what success or failure would look like ("We need to be seen as innovators in the company").

There's no set formula for creating process goals beyond focusing on behaviors and the feelings they elicit, but here's an example of what process goals can look like.

At a large Midwestern college, the Student Life Department faced deep resource cuts and needed to figure out how the team could do more with less (including fewer people). Group members developed these process goals to guide them:

As a team, we aspire to:

Support each other fully. *We will understand and appreciate one another's lives, both at work and outside of work. We will create a climate where team members feel free to ask for help, offer help, and listen.*

Communicate fully. *We will share information and best practices; we will share what we do at work and in our lives, to better support one another; and we will share our successes to motivate ourselves and position our team to build upon those accomplishments.*

Be innovative. *We will develop a climate where it feels safe to take risks (including expressing ourselves) and experiment, and where downsides are identified but upsides are protected from naysaying.*

Those process goals enabled the new team of 10, down 30% from its original size, to do the hard work of deciding which programs to keep and which to cut, and to put in the longer hours needed to maintain most of its regular programming. One academic year later, the director was pleased to see that all 10 staffers were still on the team; she had not lost a single member to burnout.

So how can you get the conversation about process goals started? Ask members to recall the best and worst team experiences they shared when getting to know one another. Call out common themes, and build your goals around them. Usually the "worst" stories are the most vividly told. They also powerfully convey what problems people don't want to encounter on the new team.

If you used a diagnostic tool to highlight diversity when building your team, revisit the results. Not surprisingly, people's personality traits will influence the types of relationships they want with team members and what qualities they value in a team setting. Once again, group individuals according to their traits, and ask each subgroup to propose a set of process goals. Then, as a full team, negotiate goals that work across diverse traits.

Usually, you'll want process goals to accommodate most people's preferences, on the theory that individuals contribute most effectively when they feel comfortable. In the example mentioned earlier, the goals of the Student Life Department reflected its members' high interpersonal intelligence (from Howard Gardner's Multiple Intelligences diagnostic). But sometimes it's good to go against the grain and set process goals that stretch people and build future capacity. For instance, if most members shy away from conflict, your team may set a goal of engaging in rigorous discussions, encouraging constructive dissent, and seeking honest feedback.

Process goals should tap into team members' aspirations as well as their styles. Here are two exercises for doing that:

Capture ideals

Ask each person to prepare a one-paragraph e-mail that he or she would like to send to a friend, at the close of the project or initiative, about the team's fantastic experience working together. When you meet, have members share their hypothetical e-mails and identify themes. These idealized visions of the future can inform both task *and* process goals: What do people want to accomplish? How do they want to accomplish it?

Channel hopes and concerns

Have each member write down two hopes for the team and two concerns. Discuss these as a group, again looking for areas of overlap. Often one person will articulate something as a hope and another will frame the same thought as a concern. For example, "I hope we'll work efficiently together" is equivalent to saying, "I'm concerned that the project will take much longer with us working as a team than it would if we tackled the tasks individually." For both statements, the theme is making the best use of everyone's time. Translate common themes into three to five process goals for the team. To continue with the example above, one process goal might be, "We will work efficiently and respect everyone's time."

This exercise can be effective even for large groups. Consider how well it worked for a regional nonprofit that brought together about 60 people to build a new program strategy. The team included representatives from the staff, the nonprofit's board of directors, and other organizations with overlapping missions, as well as current and potential funders. To decide how they would work together over a series of several weekends, each person was asked to submit by e-mail two hopes and two concerns for the sessions. The hopes of all 60 people were compiled into one list, the concerns into another—with no indication of who said what.

On their first weekend together, the team members divided into 10 working groups. Half of the groups received the list of hopes; the other half, the list of concerns. Each group chose up to five themes from its respective list and posted them on a flip chart. The full group of 60 then looked at all 10 charts and went through the same process of identifying three to five recurring themes. After doing so, the team broke into groups again and crafted the themes into goals.

In about two hours, then, 60 people agreed on five process goals defining how they would work together.

Once you've established process goals, keep reinforcing them. State them at the beginning of each team meeting or reflect on them at the meeting's close (answering

"What did we do today that advanced our process goals?"). Consider including them as a footer in every team e-mail or posting them in office common areas. These reminders prevent members from reverting to old behaviors and drifting from the team's agreed-upon way of operating.

At the same time, though, consider the process goals a set of living principles that will evolve as team membership changes and people develop their team skills. To keep these goals salient in a changing environment, periodically review them by asking, "Which ones have we accomplished? Which ones are still priorities? Which should be more ambitious, or less so?" Conduct this review at least quarterly and at your project or initiative's end, as you're gathering lessons learned to apply to the next team experience.

Chapter 4
Agree on Individuals' Roles

Once you've set task and process goals, establish the roles that each member will play. That includes your role, too: You may have the title "leader," but what does that mean—to you and to the rest of the team? Even though everyone has worked on teams before, each individual will bring different ideas about leadership to *this* team. Some people may expect you to make all decisions unilaterally and tell them what to do. Others may expect you to lead the team in making decisions together and build consensus on who will handle which activities.

To prevent confusion, you must have an explicit conversation about who will do what on the team. (Here, we're talking about "internal" roles, essential to producing solid work together. In chapter 13, "Manage Outside the Team," we'll look at "external" roles for managing relationships outside the team.) Each member needs to know what his or her role is and what it means to succeed in that role. Without that discussion, some members may jump in and take on tasks that don't have clear owners—and some may see that "initiative" as grabbing power, or at least overstepping boundaries. By agreeing explicitly on who has what responsibilities, teams avoid misinterpreting motives, duplicating effort, and fighting turf battles.

You've already considered roles in terms of expertise. When assembling your team, you chose people because of what they can do, whether it's computer programming, for instance, or managing vendors. And you've already shared, during introductions, what kind of expertise each individual brings to the team (see chapter 2, "Get to Know One Another"). But here are two other ways to define roles in teams:

- **By structure:** Most teams have a basic structure of one leader and multiple team members. The leader has one role to play; each of the members, another.

- **By activity:** The team must complete many activities to reach its goals. For example, someone will plan the project; someone else will keep senior management informed. Each of those activities constitutes a role.

You can take either approach to frame the group's discussion about roles. One way is not any better than the other. The same is true for how roles are distributed. You can match roles to strengths or, conversely, give people opportunities to stretch. Growth assignments will mean more work for you because of the monitoring and coaching they require, but they can help you develop new competencies in your people.

Defining Roles by Structure

To clarify which behaviors people can expect from the leader and which they can expect from team members, try completing the form in table 4-1 as a group.

As you capture and discuss everyone's input, you'll expose differences in thinking. Work together to reconcile them. You might, for example, ask each team member to write down five behaviors of a good team member, and

TABLE 4-1

Clarifying behaviors

Leader	Team members
Here's what I propose to do as the leader:	Here's what we propose to do as members:
Here's what I need from you as members:	Here's what we need from our leader:

five of a good team leader, and then have people share what they wrote. Identify points of agreement, and use those to establish basic roles for you as the leader and for your team's members.

Another useful exercise is to lead the team through developing a "job description" for the ideal team member, as if you were going to post an ad to attract strong candidates.

When teams do this, they often list obligations such as those in table 4-2.

Your team will need to define each obligation to ensure consistent understanding: For instance, what does it mean for members to "pull their weight"? One way of clarifying expectations is to ask each person, "What would you need to *see* to know that someone is pulling his or her weight?" Team members may suggest specific behaviors, such as volunteering for new assignments or offering to assist others who are not meeting deadlines.

At a large pharmaceutical company, a "client express" team (assembled to improve communication between customers and account managers) wrote a job description for its members. After the group spent hours crafting it, one person observed, "There is no human being alive capable of meeting all those requirements!" Rather than feeling that they'd just wasted a lot of time creating something that wasn't doable, team members realized that they needed to prioritize their job requirements, which helped them set more reasonable expectations for themselves.

It's critical to explicitly define leader and member roles if you're on a team of peers. When no one has for-

TABLE 4-2

Defining expectations

Regarding:	Team members are expected to:
Task work	• meet deadlines • keep everyone informed on progress • meet targets
Relationships	• manage their own emotional responses • maintain good working relationships • resolve conflicts
Collaboration	• pull their weight • accept and support team decisions
Meetings	• attend all required meetings • come prepared • actively participate
Time management	• give advance notice before pushing back a due date • return all team-related e-mails, texts, and calls by close of business each day

mal authority, teams are often tempted to decide, "We don't need a leader. We can all share that role." Although that can work, most leaderless teams find that tasks take longer, the quality of the work is lower, and more conflicts arise among members.

Instead, consider rotating leadership throughout the project. For example, during data collection, the team's analytics expert might act as the leader. When it's time to create the final report for stakeholders, the person with the best writing skills might assume the role.

However, it's usually a good idea to designate an overall leader, as well. You'll want someone to maintain a big-picture view of the team's work (both task progress and relationship dynamics) and to serve as a tie breaker when the group has a hard time making a decision.

Defining Roles by Activity

Teams that define roles by activity often divide them into two essential categories: those that manage tasks (focusing on getting the work done) and those that manage processes (making sure members work well together). See table 4-3 for an example.

When looking at all these roles, you'll quickly see that you, the team leader, can't do them all. Think about what happens at just one meeting: Perhaps you take up the facilitator role to guide the team through all the agenda points you want to cover. While you're doing that, you can't also play gatekeeper, devil's advocate, and consensus taker.

To distribute roles, make assignments based on what you've learned about members' strengths and natural tendencies, or allow people to volunteer for what they would feel competent doing. Either way, people's dominant traits often indicate what roles they'd do well and enjoy. For example, Myers-Briggs "judgers," who need structure and order, can make great project managers or note takers. Extroverts, who get their energy from working with people, may prefer the liaison role.

Team members can fill multiple roles simultaneously or over time. For example, if Janice is detail oriented and good at organizing, she may play project manager in the beginning, shift to note taker and goal/rule keeper as

TABLE 4-3

Defining roles

Task roles	Process roles
Meeting facilitator: puts the agenda together, leads the discussion, and makes sure the meeting starts and ends on time **Project manager:** sets up the project sequence and timeline; holds members accountable to that plan **Task specialist:** organizes and leads a portion of the larger project, such as conducting the research or doing the analysis **Note taker:** records all key decisions; documents the progress of the team **Liaison:** informs stakeholders (clients, boss, customers) about team activities; brings their ideas and concerns back to the group	**Gatekeeper:** pays attention to who is and isn't talking; invites quiet members into the conversation **Mediator:** names conflicts (often the "elephant in the room") and then guides conflict resolution **Devil's advocate:** challenges the team's thinking to increase rigor in decision making **Morale manager:** keeps members energized by remembering birthdays, organizing social events, and so on **Consensus taker:** monitors the commitment level during team discussions to see if people really agree with decisions **Goal/rule keeper:** monitors adherence to team goals and rules; facilitates ongoing "continuous improvement" discussions

specialists step in to manage different aspects of the project, and then come back as project manager at the end to tie everything together and capture lessons learned.

The roles your team needs may evolve. When one team's leader announced his retirement, the group created a new role: succession planner. That person became responsible for working with the retiring leader to capture his institutional knowledge before the team lost it.

Periodically ask, "Are our roles still working for us?" If they aren't, the team may need to redefine them or change who does what.

Reconciling Individual and Team Interests

No matter how you clarify roles, it's important to recognize a dilemma that's central to teamwork: balancing each person's need for control and autonomy (including your own) with the team's shared goals and accountability. Why is that difficult? Because members will be evaluated on what the *team* produces, not what they do on their own. Their reputations (and future opportunities for assignments and promotions) may suffer if the team doesn't produce good work. No wonder team members often want to do it *all* themselves and micromanage one another.

To work together productively, they need to trust that their teammates will do a good job, and they must accept that the team's outcomes will differ from what they would have done individually. They need to feel ownership and pride in those joint outcomes—yet they also need the autonomy to perform their individual tasks as they see fit. Otherwise, they'll throw up their hands and say, "Why bother working hard? You're just going to redo it anyway."

You can avoid frustration and prevent duplicated or discarded work by creating clear boundaries. Within those boundaries, give members control over their own tasks. Spell out what can be done autonomously within each role and what needs approval by others inside or outside the team. Decide when progress reports for each role are required, and in what format, so the team feels assured that tasks will be accomplished on time and according to specifications. Also specify opportunities for team members to weigh in on someone else's decisions or actions. For example, before any subgroup goes off to plan a task, the whole team might brainstorm about it and suggest performance metrics. And then the subgroup can use this input—or not.

You may occasionally have to "invade" the boundaries you have so carefully defined. That becomes easier if you've clearly articulated the criteria for success within each role: When individuals fail to meet certain standards, you can simply redistribute their delegated responsibilities. Suppose one member of your team is responsible for synthesizing customer data collected by the group. Say you've specified how the report should be structured and how much secondary research to include, and you've set expectations for accurate numbers, solid grammar, and correct spelling. If the first, and certainly the second, draft doesn't meet those criteria, give the role to someone else.

With the team's goals and roles established, you've agreed on what the team seeks to accomplish and who will be responsible for which activities. You're now ready to craft the team's operating rules, which map out how the team will work together.

Chapter 5
Agree on Rules of Conduct

If you ask six team members what they think "completing work on time" entails, you'll probably get six different answers. The same holds true for your team's other aspirations.

Now that you've talked openly about roles, the group shares a broad understanding of what a good team member is. But you must also sort out what a good member *does*—that is, the rules that will guide everyone's behavior.

We each have our own rules of conduct, of course. Yours may tell you that getting to a 9:00 a.m. meeting at 9:03 is just fine. Or that it's OK to chime in mid-presentation when you're enthusiastic about an idea. Or that you should remain silent to avoid rocking the boat when you disagree with a decision the majority of people seem to support.

So what happens when you work with someone who thinks that a 9:00 start time really means 8:55? And that interrupting is rude? And that silence signals agreement? One or both of you end up frustrated, angry, or feeling disrespected, and tensions will mount.

Generally speaking, people want to do a good job and work well together. But when individuals' rules of conduct are unspoken, motives are often misinterpreted ("He's just doing that because he always has to be right" or "She's trying to hog the spotlight").

Rules of conduct build on the team's process goals (see chapter 3, "Establish Your Team's Goals") to clarify how you'll make decisions, keep everyone informed, run meetings, play nicely, hold one another accountable, assess progress, and continually improve.

Here's an example: An executive committee at a large pharmaceutical company had a reputation for behaving territorially and bad-mouthing each other. When a new chair took over, the group established an important new goal: "We will project a unified sense of mission and strategy across silos." The committee then identified a few rules of conduct to guide members' behavior:

1. Support the team's final decisions, even when you would have made a different call.

2. Express your support when communicating decisions to constituents.

3. Share decisions with stakeholders, but keep the discussions that led to them confidential.

The chair relentlessly held members accountable to these rules. As a result, when the company announced a reorganization of its regional offices, there was no finger-pointing or back-channel griping, and executives in lower ranks said they noticed a more collegial tone at the top.

Teams often skip discussing rules of conduct for the same reason they tend to gloss over process goals: They assume their members all know how to work on teams. Yes, they all do, but they do it *differently*. For example, some may be accustomed to having an agenda for every meeting, while others find agendas restrictive for short meetings, say, or brainstorming sessions. The purpose of discussing your team's rules isn't to determine the *one right way* of running a team. It's to agree on the *one consistent way* you'll run this particular team.

Rules of conduct:

- Clarify what others expect of you, the leader.
- Make members' behavior more predictable.
- Rein in members' behavior so you won't have to play "cop" as often.
- Reduce the amount of time you spend rehashing processes, such as how team decisions are made.
- Provide criteria for objective feedback and conflict resolution.

Like process goals, rules of conduct will form and evolve whether you talk about them or not. Without deliberate conversations, you'll find that unproductive rules crop up as people mimic what you and other influential team members do in practice. If you, the leader, routinely show up five minutes late for meetings, lateness becomes the norm, overriding any notion that punctuality is important. Rules also evolve according to what you reward. By listening to a team member complain about another member, you reward that behavior—you're giving the complainer your attention. And that kind of exchange becomes an accepted way of operating, even if the team originally agreed that members should try to resolve conflicts without your intervention.

Get your team members thinking about rules by asking them, "How do you want to handle X?" (fill in the blank with meetings, conflict, delegation, feedback, and so on). If they've completed a personality diagnostic, have them work with people with similar styles, and reframe the question: "According to your style, what is the best way to handle X?" This allows them to ask for what they want in an objective, nonpersonal way. It also brings different ideas to the surface, none of them "wrong." The team can discuss their respective merits and then agree on one way.

Reconciling personality and style differences isn't the only reason to create rules of conduct (though it's a big one). If you're leading a cross-unit team, you'll need to blend the different approaches. If you've added new people to a team, you'll have to take their perspectives into account. If you're managing two teams that must collaborate to achieve larger goals, you'll have to establish a third, overarching set of rules. You get the picture:

Any time you bring people together, you have to create explicit rules of conduct—or the work will suffer.

Here are a couple of exercises to help your team establish its rules.

Begin with a Boilerplate List

Rather than having open-ended discussions about desired conduct—which can take a lot of time and exhaust everyone—use an existing framework. For example, the Rules Inventory in appendix A lists basic rules for respect and trust; meeting discussions and decision making; dissent and innovation; feedback and reporting; and conflict resolution.

A framework like this serves as a starting point for establishing your team's top 10 rules (a manageable number to generate and remember). You can then reach agreement on them through what's called the *nominal method of decision making:*

- Ask individuals to do their own assessments: Which rules has the team followed from the get-go? Which would they like to add? Which would they rate as their top 10?
- At a meeting, post everyone's lists on the wall.
- Have team members walk around, view everyone's lists, and put checks next to the 10 rules they value the most (with fresh ideas in the room, their picks are likely to differ from their original 10).
- The rules with the most votes become the team's top 10.

This exercise works well for new and existing teams. At a large technology retailer, a team of eight Service Center staffers had worked together for several years, but they had never held team-building conversations. As a result, some counterproductive rules of conduct had emerged: For instance, team members weren't following up on customer requests. As more and more of those requests went unaddressed, people started pointing fingers. The team decided it was time to create explicit rules of conduct; members consulted the Rules Inventory and worked together to come up with the following list:

1. Bring up problems (regarding tasks or relationships) when they arise. Don't expect them to go away; instead, name the "elephant in the room."

2. Take ownership and follow through on problems.

3. Don't let things fall through the cracks. Even if the next step is someone else's responsibility, stay in touch until it's done.

4. Tell people what you need. Don't expect them to guess.

5. When responding to someone's request, always explain why you are doing what you are doing, especially when you have to say no.

6. When asking for something, always explain why you are making the request. This allows the person to come up with an alternative solution if what you are asking for isn't possible.

7. If you need training or tools in order to be successful, ask for them.

8. Take risks, but inform key people so that they don't get blindsided. Analyze the risks, identify the unexpected consequences, and plan for them.

9. Think Center-wide. When your actions diverge from usual practice, always ask, "What impact will this have on the team?"

10. Start each meeting with individuals sharing "what I did this week that constituted excellent customer service."

To make these rules stick, the team regularly reviewed them, especially when they experienced backsliding. And when the Service Center added three employees, veteran staffers used orientation as an opportunity to reexamine the rules. They invited the new hires to propose different rules or suggest changes to existing ones.

Even if the makeup of your team doesn't change, members should periodically reassess its rules. As with goals and roles, you can do this quarterly or each time you close out a project. That keeps the rules relevant as tasks and timelines change. It also helps quash undesirable behaviors that emerge, as the Service Center staffers discovered.

Conduct a Cultural Audit

A cultural audit helps newly blended or ongoing teams with new members identify rules of conduct that already exist—whether explicitly established or unofficially evolved. The team can then decide what to keep, modify, discontinue, or add.

A few days before you meet, ask people to think about how they would describe to a new member "the way things are done around here." Use the following questions as prompts:

- What rules were you told explicitly when you joined the team? Did someone take you aside and give you the "inside story"? If so, what did that person say?
- What rules do you *wish* you'd been told about early on?
- Has a teammate ever told you, "That's not how it's done around here"? (Violating an unknown rule is often the quickest way to learn!)
- What criticisms have you heard about others' behavior? Name the criticisms but *not* the people involved.

As the leader, conduct your own audit of the culture. Don't spend too long on it: Your spontaneous responses are probably the most accurate. (To prompt thinking, see appendix B, "Cultural Audit," for a list of behaviors.) When the team meets, ask members to share their perceptions. Take time to highlight differences—they're often a source of conflict (or at least confusion). As in the Rules Inventory exercise, ask members to vote for the top 10 rules they'd like to see the team adopt.

A team I consulted with at a large health care company used the Cultural Audit to identify and resolve a culture clash. The leader, a VP of marketing, had brought together some internal folks and a group of contractors to create a social media campaign. But the two camps had problems gelling. The internal folks complained that the consultants were too lax about details and deadlines, and too informal. Not surprisingly, the contractors saw the company insiders as bureaucratic and stodgy. When each group fell back on its own home rules, conflicts arose. The Cultural Audit gave the team a nonjudgmental way of recognizing the two sets of rules, which took the heat out of the conversation. Members then negotiated one common set of rules to guide interactions within the blended team.

Rules of conduct should help your team work together smoothly and productively, so keep things simple and practical. Focus on behaviors that will improve collaboration and the quality of the work. Early on, though, it's usually best to err on the side of more structure (and a few more rules), which you can adjust or relax as the team hits its stride. For instance, you might start out with a rule about answering e-mails by the end of the day. As that behavior becomes ingrained, you may no longer need that rule to ensure responsiveness. When teams don't have clear, specific rules at the outset, they often have to impose structure later as confusion and conflict arise, which takes more time and energy than spelling out desired behaviors in the first place.

You'll find more suggestions for rules when we cover decision making (chapter 8, "Make Optimal Team Decisions") and accountability (chapter 9, "Hold People Accountable").

Chapter 6
Set the Stage for Accountability

"Step into my office . . . I have a little feedback for you."

If you're like most people, that sentence strikes fear into your heart. You expect the worst: bad news. A pink slip. The end of life as you know it.

Understanding how it feels to be on the receiving end is part of what makes giving feedback to *others* so hard. But providing it is an essential part of your job as team leader. It's how you ensure that the work gets done on time, on budget, and according to quality standards. It's how you sharpen people's skills and keep them motivated. It's how you demonstrate commitment to their development and recognize their efforts to grow.

To all those ends, you must monitor tasks against project plans and track people's behavior against the team's process goals, roles, and rules of conduct. You may find the task-monitoring side easier, but you'll achieve good outcomes on tasks only if team members work together productively.

Say you've got one team member who holds forth during meetings. That violates a team rule—"Share air-time"—yet no one calls her on her behavior. Instead, people roll their eyes when she starts talking, cross their arms, and hunker down for a long, irritating meeting. If this dynamic continues, you'll end up with lots of frustrated and silenced members—and poor decisions.

Better to correct the behavior before it gets out of hand. Hold people accountable by reminding them of the rules for working together that everyone agreed on. When that troublesome team member starts pontificating, you can say, "Let's follow our rule of sharing airtime and give someone else a chance to comment."

The good news is, you shouldn't be the only one paying attention to the goals, roles, and rules. *Everyone* should. Members' behavior affects the whole team, not just you. By involving the whole team in monitoring behavior, you foster team ownership of the rules, making it more likely that each person will internalize and follow them.

Yet you may still need to persuade team members to hold one another accountable and give candid feedback, for a few reasons:

- **They avoid the negative.** When people think of accountability, they usually envision calling people out for poor behavior. They don't enjoy bearing bad news, so they try to avoid it. But remind them that giving positive feedback is an equally important part of the equation. Rather than just focusing on what needs fixing, you and other team members will want to acknowledge and reinforce productive behaviors.

- **They're not used to giving feedback.** Growing up, many of us were taught to bounce complaints, injustices, or rule violations up to our parents or teachers or bosses. So we don't have much experience sitting down with a peer and explaining, for example, how that person's late contribution had a negative impact on our own work. We just aren't skilled at it—and we need practice to improve.
- **They don't want to hurt anyone's feelings.** Any feedback conversation has two components: the message you need to deliver and the relationship you want to preserve with the recipient. We often worry that the feedback (particularly if it's peer-to-peer) will harm the relationship. We fear that the recipient will take it personally—that he'll be hurt by the message, angry, suspicious of our intentions, and so on. So it seems easier to keep mum. Instead, you may avoid him, complain about him to others, or become resentful—all of which damages the relationship further. As a result, there's less collaboration and less shared effort, and the work goes downhill.

So how do you get other team members to participate willingly in the monitoring? It can be helpful to lead a frank discussion about feedback itself. Ask how people feel about giving it—and what makes it so hard for them.

Also ask why they think it's worth pushing past that initial difficulty and holding one another accountable. By raising these questions, you'll make everyone's discomfort normal and understandable while signaling that it's something you'll all have to work through together.

You can also frame accountability as a continuous improvement process. That's what we do to refine tasks. It's also what we should do to strengthen relationships. When you see disruptive behaviors and do nothing, you're setting yourself up for frustration: People won't change on their own—they may not even realize they *need* to. Like subpar work, problem behavior will improve only if it's identified and corrected. Enlist your entire team in applauding the good conduct of others (a great motivator and energizer) and in speaking up when unproductive behavior emerges. With that sense of mutual—and ongoing—accountability, the team *will* improve over time, resulting in better outcomes and relationships.

Agreeing on a Process for Accountability

The next step is to sort out how the team will enforce the agreed-upon goals, roles, and rules. (Then in chapter 9, "Hold People Accountable," you'll find exercises to help structure your feedback conversations.) At this point, you'll want to:

Decide how to celebrate successes

Never let a well-done task or accomplishment go by without celebrating it with the team. Plan how you'll recognize achievements and link those rewards to performance metrics and due dates. For example, when the team hits an important milestone, a celebratory dinner out can be a satisfying reward—and an effective motivator.

Schedule periodic continuous improvement meetings

Just as the team monitors its progress toward its goals through regular check-ins, it must also occasionally assess how people are working together (as noted in chapters 3–5). Set aside time for continuous improvement meetings up front, while you're planning the work: When people know that the conversations are coming, they're more inclined to hold *themselves* accountable along the way. Scheduling these meetings also prevents the need for convening a postmortem after things go wrong, which tends to amp up the anxiety.

In the meetings, the team should identify the behaviors and processes that support its goals and those that are getting in the way. Focus on:

- How the *team* is doing as a whole ("Do we need to drop, change, or add any processes or rules in order to work together more effectively?")
- How *individual members* are doing ("What should we continue to do and what should we change?")

Schedule a final debrief

A wrap-up conversation about overall team performance and individual contributions is essential to learning from the experience. (We'll cover this in more detail in chapter 15, "Learn from Your Team's Experiences.")

Again, get this meeting on the calendar up front to make sure that it happens. If you wait until you're nearing the end, you'll find that team members have scattered and you've lost the opportunity to glean lessons and apply them to the next team. This final debrief isn't a remedial intervention; it's just the conclusion of the continuous improvement process you've implemented throughout the team's work together.

Assign the role of goal/rule keeper

As noted in chapter 4, "Agree on Individuals' Roles," it's useful to charge a team member with monitoring compliance and facilitating continuous improvement discussions. This can be one person, or the role can rotate project to project, or even meeting to meeting.

Agree on rules for evaluating work

Determine as a group how you will conduct feedback sessions: Establish, for example, when feedback should be given one-on-one and when it should be offered in a team setting. For example, your team may decide to spend the final five to ten minutes of each meeting discussing "what we did well today" and "what we could have done better." Also set guidelines for how to give and receive feedback.

Building Feedback Skills

Many people have no idea when to give feedback or how to deliver and receive it effectively. As noted earlier, they particularly struggle with negative messages, euphemistically called "constructive feedback" (which we all know means "I don't like what you are doing, and I want you to change"). As a team leader, it's your job to set a good example and provide some training. At the very least, the team should talk about the following principles.

When to give feedback

It's *always* appropriate to give positive feedback, as long as it's specific and genuine—so encourage team members to do it often, both publicly and privately. Negative feedback requires more deliberate timing. Here are some guidelines:

- Provide feedback when someone's behavior prevents you from meeting team goals. *Don't* give it when it's a matter of personal taste and you'd just like to see the other person do things your way.

- Speak up as soon as you can. The longer you wait, the more likely you are either to drop the issue altogether (resolving nothing) or to explode. Those on the receiving end of your pent-up frustration will probably be embarrassed or angry that you've been harboring negative thoughts about them for so long.

- Give negative feedback in a one-on-one conversation whenever possible. Not *all* disruptive behavior merits a group discussion, and you don't want to gang up on individuals—that puts them on the defensive and prevents them from hearing your message. For example, if you had to recheck every number in a teammate's spreadsheet to correct multiple errors, take her aside and ask her to do more checking herself next time before sending the spreadsheet to you.

- Establish rules for when it is appropriate to give negative feedback in a team setting: for instance, when someone's behavior has a negative impact on the entire team or on many members, when the person has already received private feedback but has not demonstrated a willingness to change, or when the feedback is likely to lead to changes in goals, roles, or rules. If you have warring factions inside the team, avoid frustrating "he said, she said" conversations by bringing them together to hear each other's concerns and work out a solution. (More on this in chapter 11, "Resolve Conflicts Constructively.")

How to give feedback

Although the team should follow standard best practices for giving feedback, lead the group in defining its own preferences. They may include principles like these:

- Describe the behavior ("You interrupted me several times"), not the personality ("You were rude").
- Avoid casting behaviors and people as good or bad, right or wrong.
- Don't try to interpret motives behind the behavior; stick with your observations. Say, "You've been late

three times," not "It's obvious you aren't committed to this project."

- Point out the behavior's impact on your work. For example: "You waited until after my presentation to say what you didn't like, so I couldn't take your points into consideration before our client meeting."
- Be specific. This is important even for positive feedback. A simple "good job" without details won't show that you've paid attention and really appreciate the work. Give examples, such as "I particularly liked how you answered the customer's questions about our data collection methodology. You avoided jargon and limited your response to exactly what was asked."
- Invite discussion about the problem and alternative solutions.
- Suggest behavior that would be more helpful. In the presentation example above, you might say: "It would be helpful to get your input in advance next time."
- Ask colleagues for permission to give feedback, especially in peer-to-peer situations, where no one has clear authority. For example: "I have some feedback on how you organized your proposal that might make your main idea come through more clearly. Would you like to hear it?" Highlight a

benefit (in this case, clarifying the idea) to get your audience to listen.

How to receive feedback

The natural human response to receiving negative stimulus is "fight or flight": We either lash out or withdraw from the situation. It's much more difficult to respond openly and objectively, but that's how people grow and improve. Consider with your team the following ground rules for receiving feedback:

- Control your emotional response. Breathe. If you find it tough to remain calm in the moment, ask for a "time out" to think about the feedback, and resume the conversation later.
- Remember that while all feedback is subjective, it also represents someone else's "reality"—so don't dismiss it if it doesn't align with your perceptions.
- Assume that people giving you feedback have good intentions (that is, that they want to improve how the team works together—they're not out to get you). Resist interpreting their motives. Take their stated reasons at face value.
- Demonstrate that you care about what they're saying. Listen. Request clarification and examples if you're not sure you understand the message.
- Ask people to rephrase their feedback if their delivery doesn't follow agreed-upon team guidelines.

- Ask if they'd like to hear your point of view if you disagree with their feedback. (You might have a different recollection of events, for example.) Someone with good intentions will say yes. Someone who just doesn't like you will say no—or simply not listen.

As with setting rules of conduct, start with a more structured approach to accountability and then ease up. You might, for instance, schedule monthly continuous improvement meetings up front if the team will be working together for a year. Early on you'll want to regularly remind people what the team's goals, roles, and rules are; signal the importance of compliance; and provide some basic training on giving and receiving feedback. You can reduce the frequency or duration of the meetings as team members develop trust and internalize rules. It's easier to cancel unneeded meetings than to add meetings when conflict reaches a crisis level. There's a lot of groundwork to be laid, but once that's done, you switch to maintenance mode.

Finally, you need to consistently hold yourself accountable to meeting the team's goals, respecting its roles, and following its rules. If you don't, you can't credibly hold others accountable for doing the same.

Chapter 7
Commit to a Team Contract

If you've made it this far, you've done a lot of work to build your team's infrastructure. Now it's time to seal the deal.

Nothing secures commitment more than writing up a contract—summarizing what you've agreed to in team-building conversations—and having all members sign it. This solidifies their understanding of what's expected of them, helps in resolving future disagreements, and reminds them of what they've agreed to as you track progress, hold one another accountable, and strive for improvement.

Signing the contract also serves as a symbolic bridge from building the team to working as a team. Consider recognizing the achievement with a dinner out or a toast—a lot of time, energy, and human capital has gone into building a solid foundation for the team.

There's no set format for a team contract, but it's useful to include the following:

- The team's task and process goals
- The team members' roles—how they'll be designated and who will hold them
- Rules of conduct
- How you'll hold one another accountable for producing good work and nurturing strong relationships

See appendix C for a basic template, which you can adapt to suit your team. The contract shouldn't be a lengthy document filled with legalese. Rather, it should be a living document that will evolve and change along with the team.

Once you've got a written and signed agreement, keep it visible to all members as a continual reminder of guiding team principles. You might, for example, display it in a wiki where team members regularly post updates on their tasks. A team of sales reps in a medical devices group made a poster out of its contract, titled the "Declaration of Interdependence," and tacked it up in their conference room. A team at a military manufacturing company summed up its process goals in a slogan ("On time, on place, on target") that members included in their e-mail signatures. If you're leading a long-term or ongoing team, you may even want to put your slogan on coffee mugs so members will have it in front of them all the time.

Rest assured that all this foundational work will pay off: Although teams that jump right into assigning and executing tasks may get a head start on reaching performance goals, research consistently shows that they're soon overtaken by teams that have invested time in establishing their task and process goals, roles, and rules of conduct. Why? Because in all those team-building conversations, members develop trust, the ability to learn from one another, an understanding of how to collaborate fruitfully, and a clear sense of how everyone can best contribute. They then feel more empowered to take on work and solve problems. All of that leads to stronger performance, greater efficiency, and continuous improvement.

Now it's time to focus on the work itself and reap the rewards of your investment.

Section 2
Manage Your Team

Chapter 8

Make Optimal Team Decisions

Much of your team's time together will be devoted to making decisions about the work: planning tasks, monitoring progress, evaluating outcomes, changing strategies, or responding to crises. Teams often struggle with decision making, though. We all have our stories about leaving a meeting confident that everyone knows who's doing what—only to later discover that isn't true. Or getting bogged down in long, tedious discussions about minutiae, losing sight of what's important. Or realizing that hours were spent essentially endorsing a decision the boss had already made.

But you're now well equipped to avoid pitfalls like these. While you were building the team's infrastructure (its goals, roles, and rules), you were also developing the skills a team needs to make good decisions together:

airing dissent, tolerating others' points of view, and making trade-offs, to name a few.

In this chapter, we'll examine best practices for group decision making in the moment.

Think "Good," Not "Right"

We tend to believe deep in our hearts that there's one "right" answer out there, and that it will become evident if we collect enough data and apply enough analytic rigor. Sadly, for most decisions, that's not the case.

Having a discussion about what constitutes an *optimal* decision for the group, versus one that's right, saves everyone the frustration of pursuing unachievable perfection. When your team discussed rules of conduct, members may have agreed on decision-making criteria such as these:

- Take all key factors into account.
- Use the best (often limited) information available.
- Balance data and intuition.
- Rigorously generate multiple options.
- Weigh the pros and cons of each option.
- Get input from everyone who will feel the impact of the decision.
- Support the team's goals.
- Improve the team's ability to solve future problems.

These criteria are not about discovering an end-all, be-all solution. You're just trying to find the best possible answer given whatever constraints the team faces.

Here's an example to show how clear decision-making criteria will expedite that process. A faculty team at a small college found itself at a stalemate after more than a year of debating which core courses all undergraduates must take. Even though all the professors could link their own departments' courses to the school's mission (a critical selection factor), they couldn't agree across departmental lines. But then, after discussing what would constitute a good decision, the team decided that "made in a reasonable period of time" should be a guiding principle. That put everyone in a better frame of mind to meet the fast-approaching deadline for the next year's catalog. The team made compromises on all sides and finalized the curriculum.

Look at the Context

We often associate teams with building consensus. Didn't you pull your team together precisely because you wanted its members' collective brainpower? Yet reaching consensus takes a lot of time and energy—sometimes more than it's worth. Instead of using that as your default approach, consider which type of decision is best for the current situation. Ask yourself:

- **How much time do I have?** If it's in short supply, you may need to make the decision yourself or appoint someone on the team to do it.

- **Who has the expertise?** When one or a few people within the team have greater insight about an issue because of their knowledge or experience, let them make the call—or at least a strong recommendation to the group.

- **Is growth a goal?** If you want members to learn from a decision, spend time discussing it as a group rather than delegating it or making it on your own. Less-experienced members will benefit from hearing subject-matter experts debate which solution is optimal. Members can also develop key skills—such as advocating for a position or challenging someone's point of view—through the decision-making process.

- **How much buy-in do I need?** The greater the commitment you need from team members to implement a decision, the more you'll want to build consensus or at least solicit their input. You'd probably want everyone's buy-in when deciding on the team's strategy for pitching to prospective clients, for example. However, you don't need it to select the PowerPoint template you'll use. Many of those supportive, operational decisions are best delegated to individuals or subgroups.

- **How much creativity does the decision require?** If you're trying to generate really fresh ideas—say you're looking for a new fund-raising concept—don't just sit down at your computer and type up what comes to mind. Ask others to contribute ideas or, better yet, conduct a brainstorming session. Once the team has come up with a long list of possibilities, you'll shift to a different mode of decision making: evaluating and selecting (possibly through the nominal group technique described in chapter 5, "Agree on Rules of Conduct").

Bottom line: Use consensus only when a decision will affect every team member. For big-picture, direction-setting decisions—sorting out or changing rules of conduct, for example—it makes sense. But remember, reaching consensus is not about agreeing on a decision that every member *likes*. You'll drive yourself—and others—mad attempting to arrive at this elusive, usually impossible, destination. Consensus really just means that all members feel they've had a fair hearing so that they'll publicly defend the decision even if it's not in line with their personal preferences.

Majority vote is another option, but use it sparingly. It creates winners and losers—and that division in the group can impede progress, especially if you need people in the minority to implement the decision. People may also interpret your call for a vote as a power play. If it's pretty clear beforehand which side will win, a vote will simply shut down further debate. They know that, and they know you do, too. So save voting for when a deadline looms, when additional delays will damage the team's work, or when the team has already spent too much time trying to reach an agreement. When stalemates occur, it's often because the options are equally good or bad. In that case, vote just to end the gridlock.

Whatever decision-making method you choose, remember to factor in members' need for control and autonomy. Empower people to make decisions connected to their individual roles. If you're delegating a decision to a small group within the team, specify when others can offer input (and when they can't) and have the team agree on what criteria the subgroup should use in making the final decision.

Make It Easy to Contribute

Create an environment where every team member comes to meetings prepared to participate in decision making by advocating, challenging, and proposing alternatives—and by getting behind the group's final choice. You've already set the stage for this by establishing rules for decision making, but people will sometimes need reminders about those rules.

One board chair had several trustees who dominated every decision-making discussion and several who, as a result, rarely bothered to say much. To address that problem, she handed each member five poker chips at a meeting and explained that every time someone spoke, that person had to turn in one chip. Once members used up their chips, they could no longer chime in. The group thought she was joking until she began telling people they'd lost the floor because they'd used up their chips. She made her point, and the team took it to heart. Board members continued to hold one another accountable even without the chips, occasionally saying, "Hey, you've used up your chips. Let's hear from someone else."

Other ways to encourage equal participation include:

- **Acting as a gatekeeper:** Explicitly invite quiet members to speak up. Don't assume that they agree with their teammates or have nothing to add. They may just feel uncomfortable about interrupting to get into the conversation.
- **Resisting the impulse to speed up a decision:** The team may try to quickly narrow down its options or accept the first one on the table just to move things along. But there's value in broadening the field of possibilities before evaluating any of them. Instead of that first or second idea, it may be the ninth or tenth that best meets your needs. You won't get that far if you cut your discussion short.

As team leader, you may feel forced to make a final call, since the team looks to you for guidance. If you want the others to own the decision, push it back on them. Boomerang their "What should we do?" back to them by asking, "What do *you* think we should do?" Or say, "That's up to the group."

That's often a good way to go, because offering your input too soon can quickly shut down a discussion. Once you say, "Wow, that's a great idea—that's what we should do," team members may be reluctant to offer any competing (and possibly better) alternatives. Try waiting until the end of the discussion to offer your ideas or endorse suggestions. When a team member shares an idea that conflicts with your own, watch your body language. You can "kill the messenger" with just one disapproving look.

Of course, when you have expertise that would benefit the discussion, you won't do the team any favors by remaining silent. In a case like that, consider relinquishing your team leader role momentarily so that you're free to participate as a regular member. You might ask an outsider to come in and facilitate. One team leader communicated this role shift by moving out of his usual seat at the head of the table. Another did it by saying, "I'm taking my 'team lead' hat off . . . " before adding her perspectives.

Use Your Experts Wisely

You've included subject-matter experts on your team to provide knowledge, but what if they don't express their insights effectively? Perhaps they give too little input or withhold ideas altogether because they don't want to be held responsible for decisions. You may need to prompt them to share their thoughts so that quality doesn't suffer.

By contrast, when experts give *too much* input, others may see them as condescending and dominating. Or their teammates may abdicate their own responsibility for decisions, thinking, "It's up to the expert." So continually remind all team members of the value they bring: different ideas, new perspectives, ideas not limited to those that worked in the past. Ask them to keep voicing their opinions and to avoid acquiescing too quickly.

Periodically remind the team that each expert's role is to share expertise, not to make decisions unilaterally because of it. You may decide it's best for experts to weigh in later in the discussion if their comments appear to be silencing others early on.

Invite Dissent

Dissent is at the heart of why you've created a team in the first place. Consulting a variety of data sources and examining conflicting ideas will lead to better decisions. If everyone prefers to work with Vendor A, then you won't explore other options, which could include a cheaper supplier with a better track record. If you all agree right away on what the data indicates then you won't conduct further analysis, which might have revealed serious breaches in collection integrity.

Dissent infuses problem solving with energy and creativity. It also promotes closer relationships (as members grow to appreciate one another's contributions), greater social competence (as people learn how to persuade, advocate, and challenge constructively), and psychological well-being (as individuals recognize the value they add in the exchange of ideas).

So why don't teams foster dissent more often? When they're in decision-making mode, the conversation has a task component (evaluating the information) and a people component (maintaining the relationships). Destructive conflict can ensue if dissent starts to feel personal. When someone questions your thinking in a meeting, you might wonder, "Is he trying to make me look bad?" That kind of dissent hurts relationships.

Not surprisingly, many teams attempt to ward off interpersonal conflict by suppressing dissent. We see a team's lack of disagreement as a good thing—but really, it may signal apathy, disengagement, or alienation.

The best teams explore opposing ideas while preserving relationships. But how do you make that happen?

First, agree on what you're trying to accomplish with the decision—perhaps you're looking to woo back a lost client, for example—and then collect as many ideas and views as you reasonably can. Don't finalize big decisions until the group has rigorously examined several options and weighed the pros and cons: This can take the form of a cost/benefit analysis or a discussion of risks and rewards. If the group agrees on one idea quickly, solicit dissent by saying, "Let's see if we can come up with reasons *not* to move forward with this" or "I'd like to hear at least one other proposal before we continue down this path."

You may also provide some time to reflect before making the decision. Ask everyone to think about it until the next meeting. In the interim, talk to people one-on-one. Some members may feel comfortable expressing opposing views in a team setting, but others may not. You may find in these conversations that people start to change their minds—or they may remain aligned. Sometimes early agreement is just that—it's not always a symptom of "groupthink."

Keep the tone constructive. When members state opposing views, have them first paraphrase the other perspective to show that they listened to it and understand it. And protect the dissenters on your team. As they raise concerns, encourage them to say more. As they propose new ideas, ask the team to point out the positives as well as the negatives so people don't simply shoot them down.

Here are several activities for fostering constructive dissent:

Post before you discuss

After you define the problem to solve or the decision to make, have team members post their ideas on a wall (sticky notes work well), and then proceed with a discussion. This brings out views that might otherwise be suppressed once a majority opinion becomes obvious or once the team leader or a major influencer states a position.

Build on written ideas

Have everyone come up with as many ideas as possible, writing each one on a separate piece of paper and placing it in the center of the table. Once members have finished doing this, they can pull out others' papers, read them, jot down why they disagree or how they'd expand the ideas, and put the papers back into the middle. When people stop writing comments, the team reads the ideas out loud and discusses the points others have added to them. You can also do this with flip charts or large sheets of paper tacked on the wall: Members write their ideas on their flip chart and then move around the room to the other charts, reading teammates' ideas and adding comments.

Use advocacy groups

After identifying a few main options, assign each alternative to an advocacy group within the team. Task those groups with developing "best cases" for their assigned options and presenting their positions to the whole team. Once all the groups have presented their cases, they can challenge one another's information, rationales, and conclusions. The outcome is a clearer understanding of the strengths and weaknesses of each position.

Here's an example: In an IT company, an eight-person team was formed to streamline the process of filling customer requests. The team consisted of representatives from two very siloed, embattled functions: customer reps, who took the orders, and technical developers, who completed the orders. The reps proposed a process that made sense to them, but the developers hated it. The developers responded with their own proposal, and the reps hated that. To break the stalemate, the team leader told the reps to strongly advocate for the developers' proposal, and vice versa. This required each side to look at the problem from the other's perspective. As a result, both camps recognized the limitations of their own proposals and the merits of the other side's. They then worked together to create a third proposal that addressed the needs and concerns of both functions.

Play devil's advocate

Early in a discussion, team members may hesitate to actively disagree with one another. Make it safe to do so by assigning the role of devil's advocate to an individual or a subgroup of members. Whenever an idea or position is presented, it's their responsibility to challenge it and identify its weaknesses. This allows people to ask the hard questions or dispute positions without fear of hurting their relationships with their colleagues. It's their *role* to disagree—so others are less likely to take it personally.

To use key decision meetings as learning opportunities, consider ending them with a debrief about the process. You won't do this every time, but it can be useful after a particularly rigorous or contentious debate. Take a few minutes to capture best practices for future decisions, nip bad behaviors in the bud, and review team rules. Try to evaluate the process while it's still fresh. But if people need a little cooling off or reflection time, it's fine to do the debrief at the next meeting or before the next decision. Continuous improvement is your goal.

Chapter 9
Hold People Accountable

When do you start holding the team accountable for its work? Right away.

Don't wait for deadlines to slip—or even for someone to show up 15 minutes late more than once. An accountable team strives for continuous improvement from the outset. There's no time like the present to become more efficient and effective as a group.

Initially, focus your accountability discussions on the team as a whole. Use them to build trust and develop skills in giving and receiving useful feedback. Then you can start having more difficult conversations about individual performance.

Team Accountability

Start small and simple. Do a brief "plus/delta" at the end of every meeting, asking "What did we do well today?

What do we need to change for the next meeting?" Team members might say, for example, that they generated lots of promising ideas but that next time they shouldn't begin analyzing and eliminating options so quickly. You'll want to end the team's conversations about continuous improvement with a plus/delta, too. It may sound circular, but it's the only way your team will get better at giving feedback and holding one another accountable.

These exercises are also useful in assessing team performance.

Discuss what to stop, start, or continue

These three questions are fundamental to any continuous improvement process: "What should we stop? What should we start? What should we continue?" Asking them regularly will build members' feedback skills and trust within the group. A different way of framing this sort of conversation is to ask, "What are some of our greatest achievements so far, and what factors have contributed to those successes? What have been our greatest challenges, and how might we overcome them in the future?"

Rate your team in one area

Ask each member to privately rate the group on some activity or event. It might be as general as "How do you feel about the team's performance on the last project?" or as specific as "How do you feel about the level of support you received from your teammates in the final stretch?" Use a scale of 1 (highly unsatisfied) to 10 (greatly satisfied). When you meet, ask each person to share his or her rating, explain the reason for it, and say what would have to change to increase it.

Even though some team members are inevitably harder "graders" than others, the ratings help people see more clearly what's working for the team and what's not. Saying why they gave the ratings they did will shed light on their own preferences, and saying what needs to change will help the team figure out which rules to fix.

One team leader used this exercise when he noticed tension brewing in his group. No one had complained to him, but people had been uncharacteristically quiet at the past few meetings. He had everyone rate the level of trust among team members. Though several members gave high ratings, two people gave 3s. After they explained their ratings, the problem became clear: In writing a client report together, the two members had divided it into sections that each would prepare. But then one member completely rewrote the other's material when combining the drafted sections into one document. It was a breakdown in roles: One had assumed the editor role, unbeknownst to the other. They agreed that in future joint efforts, they would decide on roles up front.

Rate your team's processes

Want to conduct a more comprehensive review of your team's performance? Try the Process Ratings Exercise (see sidebar). For ongoing teams and long projects, schedule time for this activity quarterly or semiannually; for ad hoc teams or shorter projects, do it at their conclusion.

This exercise measures performance on several key dimensions of teamwork, such as infrastructure, accountability, workload, and trust. However, you can adjust it to meet your needs: Rate only a few elements, for instance. Modify the descriptions at the ends of the scales to include specific behaviors. Or add new scales. If the team consists of people from different parts of the business, you might assess collaboration across functional lines.

Don't buckle under time pressure and skip these conversations because you have 100 tasks that need to be

PROCESS RATINGS EXERCISE

Ask members to score the team on the following elements of teamwork, and then meet to discuss. Have them share their ratings, explain their reasoning, and suggest changes that would improve the ratings.

1. Team infrastructure (goals, roles, and rules)

1	2	3	4	5	6	7	8	9	10
Never clearly established; members don't know what's expected of them.									Clearly established; members know what's expected of them.

2. Accountability

1	2	3	4	5	6	7	8	9	10
Members don't comply with team goals and rules; they aren't held accountable.									Members comply with goals and rules; they're held accountable.

3. Workload

1	2	3	4	5	6	7	8	9	10
Team has "free riders" who don't contribute or volunteer; their work gets ignored or is done by a dominant few.									Team has no "free riders"; work is fairly distributed.

4. Problem solving and decision making

1 2 3 4 5 6 7 8 9 10

A few members make all the decisions, with little or no rigor; the team doesn't appreciate opposing ideas.

Team discusses decisions rigorously, seeks diverse ideas, invites dissent, and includes affected stakeholders.

5. Managing conflict

1 2 3 4 5 6 7 8 9 10

Members avoid conflict or pretend it doesn't exist; people complain about others behind their backs.

Members explicitly discuss conflicts with all those involved.

6. Task/project progression

1 2 3 4 5 6 7 8 9 10

Members do poor-quality work and miss deadlines.

Members produce high-quality work on time.

7. Communication

1 2 3 4 5 6 7 8 9 10

Members don't communicate; they fail to disclose decisions, rationales, goals, and other information critical to performance.

Members communicate frequently and fluidly; they fully disclose decisions, rationales, goals, and other information critical to performance.

8. Trust

1 2 3 4 5 6 7 8 9 10

Members don't trust one another, which stifles innovation, risk taking, and rigorous decision making; they expect their input to be misinterpreted or leaked to people outside the team.

Members have a high degree of trust, which fosters innovation, risk taking, and rigorous decision making; they expect their input to be received openly and kept confidential.

done. It's tempting to do so, even when things are going well on a team. But resist that urge. It's as important to acknowledge what's going well, so people continue that behavior, as it is to identify and fix what's broken.

As with any continuous improvement discussion, have someone record the group's observations and resulting decisions. This record will help you update the team's roles and rules as they evolve.

Individual Accountability

As members gain experience in holding the team accountable, it's time to add in discussions that focus on individuals. To help people with that transition, allow them time to carefully prepare their remarks in advance. You'll also want to review the team's rules about how to give and receive feedback (see chapter 6, "Set the Stage for Accountability") and remind people that the overarching goal of the discussion is to continuously improve individual performance for the benefit of the team. Members should always use that lens when deciding what to share in a feedback session.

To keep discussions focused and constructive, you can modify the team exercises described earlier in this chapter. Familiarity with those structured conversations may help members overcome their natural reluctance to give their peers feedback.

The stop-start-continue exercise works particularly well for individuals. Approach it the same way you would a team-focused discussion: Ask everyone to consider each member: "What do you want this person to stop doing? What do you want him to start doing? What do you want him to continue doing?" Have people write down their comments in advance and then meet to share their thoughts. Remind them to describe specific behaviors, not personalities, so their observations don't come across as personal attacks.

Remember the community health care team that Nancy, the nurse, drove crazy with all her questions (chapter 2, "Get to Know One Another")? To avoid future misunderstandings about one another's intentions, members began conducting stop-start-continue discussions on a quarterly basis. Over time, they dubbed these "Kudos and Concerns" meetings, where members could give each person an unlimited number of kudos (for behaviors to continue) and point out two areas of concern (behaviors to manage).

It's essential to limit the number of behaviors to manage. Realistically, most people can work on one or two areas at a time. They may feel overwhelmed by more than that.

After each member receives feedback, call out themes and ask individuals what behaviors they'll commit to stopping, starting, or continuing. You may need to give them time to think about this first, as it involves digesting and accepting what they've heard. Allowing them to decide what they'll do empowers them. Feedback is subjective, after all, and members may have conflicting responses to behaviors (for instance, one may appreciate someone's close attention to detail, and another may find it frustrating).

Group feedback is powerful because we all feel a basic need for affiliation. Team discussions harness the power of the group and compel individuals to get with the program—it's like high-school peer pressure channeled for the good. This approach (versus a one-on-one conversation) is most useful when:

- **The behavior affects the whole team's ability to perform.** Talking with the group enables people to see the broader impact of their actions. Completing tasks late doesn't just hurt the person waiting for them—it hurts the full team. That realization usually prompts members to comply with the team's expectations.

- **The behavior is best handled by adjusting the team's expectations.** Take Isaac, a financial analyst on a client support team who was continually late for the group's daily 9:00 a.m. check-in meeting. Through the stop-start-continue exercise, team members told Isaac he needed to change this behavior. He then revealed that he was responsible for dropping off his son at day care, and even when he arrived there at the earliest possible drop-off time, the public transportation schedule didn't permit him to get to work by 9:00. With that information, the team changed the meeting time to 9:30.

Despite the power of accountability, some individuals may choose to not do the work or comply with agreed-upon rules. It's your job as team leader to manage individual performance. After you've let problem members know that they aren't doing what's expected of them, here are some other steps you can take:

- **Confirm that they have the skills to do what your team needs.** Can they demonstrate those skills? Have they used those skills in other situations? If not, you will need to train and coach them or work more closely with them to build the required competencies. Although you may enlist team members to assist in their skill development—for example, by partnering up on tasks—the coaching responsibility primarily falls to you. As people are getting up to speed, give them smaller tasks, shorter timelines, more observation, and more feedback.
- **Make sure they have the resources to do the work and follow team rules.** Isaac, in the earlier example, couldn't get to team meetings on time because of child care and transportation constraints, so his team changed the meeting time. Consider how you can provide missing resources for your team members or help them overcome obstacles to performance.
- **Zero in on what motivates them.** If your team members know that they're not meeting expectations, they possess the skills and resources to do the work, and you don't see any other barriers impeding their performance, then they are probably lacking motivation. Again, as the team leader, it's up to you to identify whether they respond best to

> recognition, control, achievement, or affiliation—all big motivators. The first three can be tricky to satisfy in a team setting: Recognition for group accomplishments must be shared. So must control. And depending on others to produce results can dampen an individual's sense of achievement. You may have more luck appealing to each member's need to belong to the group. But keep in mind that lack of motivation is often a reason to cut someone loose.

Ideally, you'll have the authority to remove nonproductive or disruptive members from your team. If that is not automatically granted, negotiate for it. Without this authority, you may get stuck with people who don't carry their weight, which can have a demoralizing effect on the rest of the team.

The IT team leader who used advocacy groups (from chapter 8, "Make Optimal Team Decisions") faced that problem. After multiple accountability conversations, one technical developer kept reverting to the old siloed way of filling customer requests instead of following the new protocols the team had agreed on. His recalcitrance led to unhappy customers and frustrated colleagues. Unfortunately, the team leader didn't have the authority to remove anyone from the group. So he isolated the offending member, protecting the rest of the team from the disruptive behavior. The engineer followed his own protocol: Instead of collaborating with the team to fill requests, he worked alone. The team leader held him accountable only for his own outcomes, and he did not participate in any team meetings. The developer pulled his weight but was essentially an individual contributor.

Although this may seem like an inequitable or easy-way-out solution, it's sometimes the best one for the team, the individual, and even you (fewer headaches!). You need to decide how much time and energy you want to invest in fixing the behaviors or outcomes of a problem member. If you've chosen that person for his content expertise, you might treat him like a consultant, pulling him in as needed without involving him in ongoing team building and maintenance.

Accountability conversations are important throughout the life of the team. Here, we've discussed how to continuously improve by aligning behavior with the team's aspirations (embedded in its rules). In the next chapter, we'll turn to another aspect: giving team members recognition for their good work. And chapter 15 covers the final step of accountability: reviewing each individual's contributions to identify which behaviors and processes to bring to future teams and which to change. This enables you to learn from each team experience and build your own competence as a team leader over time.

Chapter 10
Give People Recognition

Even in team environments, recognition remains one of the top four human motivators (along with the need for achievement, control, and a sense of belonging).

It's relatively easy to recognize the full team for good task work, such as meeting goals and hitting deadlines, or for exemplary behavior, such as conducting a difficult feedback session constructively. It can be harder, in a team setting, to recognize *individuals* for their good work or behaviors. Teams are based on collaboration, equity, and fairness. How can you give individuals their due while fostering the cohesiveness that comes when everyone works toward the same goals and follows the same rules?

The Japanese proverb, "The nail that sticks up gets hammered down," comes to mind. Sadly, that's what often happens to individuals who get a lot of praise from their team leader: Other team members may begin competing for your attention or, worse, sabotaging the work of your "pets."

You need to give recognition to motivate individuals—and certain team members do regularly go the extra mile. Here are some tips.

Connect One-to-One

You can do lots of things to discreetly show your appreciation for individuals' contributions. For starters, get to know each member personally. Find out about people's backgrounds, lives outside work, and interests. For example, does a team member bike for a cancer charity? If so, ask about her latest race and consider donating to the cause.

Learn about people's career aspirations, too, and pass along relevant articles, blog posts, or other information you come across. Introduce team members to people in your network who can help advance their careers. You might even sponsor them in professional development training or write letters of recommendation for school or fellowship applications.

You can also privately provide extra feedback, going beyond the performance appraisals the team conducts. One of the most powerful forms of recognition is to help people grow. Assign them challenging tasks, and coach them. Pass on positive comments you've heard about them from others. And give them as much time and attention as you reasonably can.

Written acknowledgments go a long way, too. Send a note of thanks, for example, and copy senior management and HR.

Include Positive Feedback

Make sure the team gives positive feedback in its accountability discussions (chapter 9, "Hold People Accountable"). Don't just focus on behaviors that should be added, dropped, or changed. Give recognition during discussions about behaviors that people should continue, and occasionally conduct a session devoted just to sharing positive feedback. Go around the room, and ask everyone to say what they appreciate about each team member. Try prompting people to comment on specific contributions (to a particular task or project) as well as general strengths (skills, attitude, and so on).

A design team at an engineering company conducted a positive feedback session immediately following a big team failure: The prototype it had produced came back from the engineering group with a long list of attributes deemed infeasible. While the team pondered everything that had contributed to this failure, its leader wanted to boost morale by reminding people of the talents and strengths they brought to the new challenge. The appreciation exercise helped the team members see that they had the skills and smarts to come up with a successful new design.

Share Credit Publicly

Visibility outside the group is another effective form of recognition. Consider having every member sign the proposals and project reports submitted by the team. Or ask every member to participate in final presentations to clients or senior management.

A senior scientist in a pharmaceutical laboratory saw a dramatic increase in individuals' motivation (and, consequently, their contributions) when she changed how the lab gave credit to employees. She didn't like the fact that only her name would appear on research reports and academic articles in medical journals. This made the rest of the team's work invisible to the outside world. Over time, it became increasingly difficult to get junior scientists and research analysts to put in the extra time and energy needed to meet project deadlines. So she changed the lab's practice, giving recognition to junior scientists and research analysts. When team members could claim authorship on reports and articles, their motivation soared. The lab began meeting its deadlines and found itself deluged with applications for junior positions.

Think about your interactions with team members as bank transactions: Every time you give constructive feedback or hold someone accountable, you're withdrawing on your account. Every time you give positive feedback or recognition, you're making a deposit. Clearly, you always want to be "in the black." This means making timely, consistent deposits. You'll get a great return on your investment.

Chapter 11
Resolve Conflicts Constructively

Most of us go to great lengths to avoid conflicts. We smile and nod instead of proposing alternatives. We give in and do things "their way." We'll deny outright that conflicts even exist when asked (the "Nothing's wrong—everything's great" scenario). But on teams, conflicts are inevitable.

Why Conflicts Arise

Typically, team members don't try to cause trouble or seek negative attention. More often, they become embroiled in conflicts for several reasons:

- **Different work styles.** To arrive at a team contract, members had to compromise. Most likely, at least a few rules of conduct don't jibe with their own personal preferences. That's why team-building conversations can be so difficult: It's not easy for people to change their ways. It's even harder when the stakes are high. After all, a team's output can affect individuals' salaries, careers, and reputations. Before signing the contract, people may have resisted certain rules—not out of petulance but from a desire to do what's worked for them in the past.

You've done a lot of work to preempt style-based conflicts, yet they'll still flare up now and then, particularly when deadlines loom, people get overworked, or the team experiences a setback. When we're tired or stressed, we all tend to revert to the way we act most naturally, with no mental pause, no behavioral adjustment. For example, under time pressure, a team member might make a decision unilaterally, despite what the team had agreed.

- **Opposing ideas, perspectives, and opinions.** As we discussed earlier, the diversity you carefully built into your team often leads to disagreements. If your team is operating as it should, people will voice dissenting opinions—and that's a healthy kind of conflict. Your team's rules of conduct will help keep tempers in check, warding off feelings of being dismissed or "spoken down to." When people give in to those feelings, however, teams experience the third source of conflict.

- **Anger or hurt feelings.** This is what most people think of when they hear the word *conflict:* One member mad at another. One person offended by someone's comments. Subgroups vying to "win" a decision. Individuals taking outcomes personally. We've all been on teams that feel like a war zone.

How do *you* react in situations like these? Do you lash out, raising your voice and slinging a few choice words? Or do you try to bargain your way out of the conflict, suggesting that you and your opponent "split the difference" or "agree to disagree"? If you're like many people, you won't directly confront the colleague who offended you (although you might talk to *others* about the problem). You delay answering her calls and avoid eye contact at meetings.

We often avoid dealing with interpersonal conflict because we don't know how to handle it or because we had disastrous experiences in the past. We withdraw and hope it goes away on its own.

The individuals seated around your table may respond in any of those ways. But that's exactly why you spent time creating rules for dealing with conflict back in your team-building conversations (see chapter 5, "Agree on Rules of Conduct").

Before you even start talking about the problem, first review those rules with the team. For instance, you all may have agreed to acknowledge the ways in which you've each contributed to the problem. You also may have decided to discuss conflicts openly with the people involved, to resist the impulse to counterattack, and to control emotional responses (no profanity, threats, or stalking out of the room).

Taking the time to review the rules you established when you were not actually *in* conflict will allow you to have a more productive conversation, and perhaps even to act in accordance with the ideal behaviors you laid out when it was all hypothetical.

How to Handle Conflicts

Yelling or giving in won't fix anything. Nor will splitting the difference, which often compromises quality or results in an outcome no one likes. How, then, can you pave the way to resolution?

Identify the cause

Instead of viewing conflict as something to avoid, look at it as a red flag: Something is breaking down, but what is it? Just as you'd investigate why a product line didn't perform up to expectations or why a marketing launch didn't yield the targeted response rate, you need to understand *why* the conflict has arisen. Ask those involved what they are hoping to achieve. Their answers may reveal opposing intentions—for instance, one person wants to finish a project quickly, while the other wants to do it perfectly.

Opposing intentions may mean that individuals are operating with different goals in mind—often the most fundamental reason for conflict. Even though you worked together up front to formulate *team* goals, over time people's interpretations may have splintered into different directions. Certain goals may no longer be salient, or new ones may need to be added. Reconfirming *why* you're working together and what you're all trying to accomplish helps get everyone back on the same page.

If you've reviewed your goals together and yet there's still a problem, you'll need to dig deeper. Try asking the same questions you'd use to uncover a task breakdown:

- What's working?
- What's not working?
- When did it stop working? What in the environment changed at the time of the shift—team membership? The task? Other events?
- Who is part of the conflict? Who isn't? Why?
- Who has the upper hand, and in what way? Who is "losing," and in what way? (Answers to both these questions can uncover resistance to resolving the conflict.)

You can also explore what's going on *around* the conflict:

- What driving forces are exacerbating the problem? (A client's increasing dissatisfaction? A competitive threat in the marketplace? Factors like these can ratchet up the urgency.)
- What's preventing the situation from getting better? (Competing demands on time? Understaffing? You'll need to address these to resolve the conflict.)

Revisit the team's rules

Most people operate with good intentions, believing that they're contributing to the team's goals and behaving in accordance with team norms. Conflict can still creep in, however, because it's impossible to outline expectations for every scenario you'll encounter. What's more, people often assign different meanings to the same words. Conflict is a good opportunity to investigate and repair whether you need to create new rules, clarify existing ones, or pull individuals back into alignment.

For example, your team may be ready to strangle one member who keeps repeating his idea over and over again as the team tries to reach agreement. His behavior, which other team members find rigid and overbearing, means it takes forever to make a decision. Increasingly, they just "give up" and let his ideas prevail. Revisiting the team's rules as a group will allow members to take such behavior into account, focusing on:

- **Gaps we may not have noticed when articulating our rules.** Did we anticipate all the challenges we might encounter? Now that we've lived as a team for a while, do we need to create new rules?

- **Whether our existing rules are explicit and effective.** Is the language clear enough? For example, when the team created the rule "Advocate your position well in team decisions" our goal was to encourage rigorous exploration of lots of good options. But in practice, "advocate" means different things to different people (relentless hounding, in this case). Conflict can arise from even well-intentioned behavior (for example, we thought having a devil's advocate during decision making would be useful, but perhaps we need to scale it back to having someone play that role only for certain types of decisions).

- **Whether individuals have "drifted" from the rules.** Even if everyone was in lock-step with the rules in the beginning, over time, people's recollections and interpretations may have shifted. Our memories often fail us when we're under stress or we may revert to our own preferred behavior in a crisis.

One way to expose the differences in people's expectations or interpretations is to ask team members to write down what they believe the team's goals and rules are. Then, review the responses as a group, and note how consistent their answers are. Go over the team contract together and ask the group, "Are these goals and rules still valid? Should we change them? What's missing?" If most people aren't following what's documented, make tweaks to reflect actual practice.

Point out strengths

In times of conflict, it's easy to demonize others. *They're* the ones who yelled. *They're* the ones who caused a bottleneck. And so on. During all the finger-pointing, people forget about the value everyone brings to the team. So bring the strengths and skills of others to their attention before talking about the conflict. These next two structured conversations can help cut through the tension, remind people that they're complementary teammates (not adversaries), and preempt defensiveness.

Even if you've already used the Artifact Exercise to highlight individuals' strengths back when you introduced your team members (see chapter 2, "Get to Know One Another"), try it again. Ask each person to share an accomplishment external to the team. This allows members to see everyone in a positive light and get a fuller picture of one another, beyond the work they do together.

The power of this next exercise comes from having others sing each member's praises. Have the team sit in a circle around a table. Ask one person at a time to turn her back to the group while the rest of you talk about her strengths, what she brings to the team, and how she contributes. She's not allowed to say a word in response. Speak loudly enough for her to hear all the good things you're saying. Spend about two minutes per person.

Foster empathy

Empathy is a critical ingredient in conflict resolution. Do what you can to promote it. For instance, you might ask individuals or small subgroups with different perspectives to prepare three-minute skits acting out, on fast-forward, a day in their hectic lives. This gives them all a chance to highlight—in an entertaining way—some of the daily challenges they face. Encourage them to exaggerate, both to punch up the humor and to drive their points home. This exercise helps everyone recognize that seemingly combative behaviors, such as curt language or omitting colleagues from an e-mail thread, are often attempts to deal with time pressure, reconcile competing demands, and so on. With that empathic view, people are less likely to assume malicious intent and may lower their defenses.

The sales and fulfillment groups at a consumer products distribution company used this exercise to address a classic conflict: Fulfillment folks felt that sales reps made ridiculous promises to customers, and they resented having to "move heaven and earth" to deliver on those contracts. They complained about frequent rush orders and exceptions to shipping protocols. Sales reps viewed the people in fulfillment as inflexible and totally out of touch with the realities of the marketplace.

After a little prodding, each group created a "day in the life" skit. These skits featured every imaginable disruption, setback, screw-up, and bad-news event. Both groups came away with a clearer sense of their colleagues' challenges and pressures. They then worked together to redesign their fulfillment processes. Sales reps had previously tagged most customer requests as "special" or "rush"; after seeing what fulfillment had to deal with as a result, sales put a cap on those, making them exceptions rather than the norm. And fulfillment redistributed routine tasks to free up staff time and capacity to satisfy special requests when they came through.

Reframe the conflict

By phrasing the conflict in constructive language and focusing on solutions, you'll depersonalize the problem. If one member consistently fails to finish tasks on time, the group does need to hold her accountable, but avoid defining it this way: "Maura always turns her work in late." Instead, ask each member to state the problem in a solution-oriented way: "how to create processes that enable Maura to complete her work on time." That gets people thinking about the future instead of wallowing in

TRUTHS ABOUT CONFLICT

Consulting with teams and leading my own, I've experienced the following truths about conflict again and again. Once you absorb them, have a discussion with your team early on, preferably *before* any problems crop up.

Unnamed conflicts remain unresolved. Conflicts do not go away on their own. Rather, they intensify as work pressures mount. So discuss them as soon as possible. Task-oriented team members tend to believe they can "just push through this," hoping to complete their work and meet their deadlines. They often feel they don't have time to talk about conflicts. People-oriented members worry that discussion will lead to hurt feelings and severed relationships. And members of ad hoc teams may think, "I have to work with this group for only three more weeks, so why bother talking about this? I can put up with anything for that long." However, avoidance leads to the next problem.

Ignored conflicts hurt the team's work. People focus less on their tasks if they're wasting time and energy avoiding one another, and quality suffers as a result. Withdrawal from the group amounts to lost

the past. If Maura doesn't have to sit through rehashing of her continual lateness, she's less likely to be defensive—and more likely to engage in the conversation and change her behavior. Plus, having every team member state the problem brings out different perspectives. For

resources (brainpower, sets of hands). As members stop talking to one another, they may duplicate work or find at the end of a project, when writing up the final report, that their work isn't cohesive. For all these reasons, members must get problems out in the open.

You can't resolve every conflict. This is hard for team leaders to accept: Unless all affected parties want to resolve a conflict, they won't. So what should you do if someone deliberately perpetuates the conflict—drawing it out as a way of holding a decision hostage, for example? What if he passive-aggressively signals his unhappiness by sabotaging tasks—skipping important steps or not verifying data? Refusal to resolve conflict is a violation of basic team rules. If someone refuses to discuss an issue, or nothing changes after you've talked, you might need to isolate that member from the others (as discussed in chapter 9, "Hold People Accountable") so that their behaviors don't bring the work to a halt or threaten its quality. Or, if you have the authority, remove that person from the team.

example, one member may see the problem as "how to get the project done on time"; another may see it as "how to develop people's skills so they can get their portions done on time"; still another may see it as "how to prioritize all the challenges each member faces." To craft a viable solution, everyone needs to be solving the same problem.

As discussed earlier, it's equally important to look at what *is* working. In Maura's case, the team could talk about times when she did get her work in on deadline. This acknowledges the good work Maura does, and it may somewhat reduce her need to defend herself. (Rarely is a member *always* late or *always* creating problems.) It also provides the team with data for coming up with a solution: What variables allowed her to meet her deadlines? Did a different person do the delegating? How did the tasks differ? Were they less complex? More squarely in her comfort zone? Did she have more time? Did the work require fewer interactions with others? Identifying contextual differences often reveals a solution.

Envision the future

The more you gear your conversations toward the future, the more productive they will be. Rigorously deconstructing the events that led up to a conflict, even with the best intentions of understanding the causes, can still put people in a blaming frame of mind.

Once again, think continuous improvement. Ask the team, "What do we need to do differently going forward?" For instance, what reporting relationships need to change? What timelines? What team processes? How can you or others change the context to prevent unhelpful behavior in the future?

Teams in conflict often feel consumed by how terrible and overwhelming their current situation is. Try to get people to lift their heads up from the present and look toward where they want to go. Ask them to describe how they'd *like* the team to operate, what kinds of relationships they *want* with their teammates, what caliber of work they'd *like* to produce. You've had this conversation before (see chapter 3, "Establish Your Team's Goals"); but you'll want to revisit these issues now and then, and a conflict is a good opportunity to do so. The next exercise is one way of doing this.

Ask each member to prepare a "farewell letter" to the team. Have people reflect on what they'd be most proud of about the team's work and, more important, the way members worked together. At the meeting, invite individuals to share their letters, and then discuss what was important to each person. Often themes will emerge across letters, revealing the source of the conflict and what needs to change.

That's what happened when an alumni board at a small college did this exercise. Over the years, the group had served largely as a mouthpiece for its president and the college deans. As new people joined, they became increasingly frustrated with the board's passive, complacent culture. To root out the conflict between new and legacy members, each person wrote a farewell letter answering the question "In what position do you want the school to be in when you leave?" They used that as a starting point for crafting a unified vision and, from there, agreed on which actions the team would take to push for that vision.

The goals and rules you've already established will guide your team in resolving conflicts. But as you can see, those conflicts will serve to refine the goals and rules to prevent problems down the road (see the sidebar "Truths About Conflict"). Once again, it's a process of continuous learning and improvement.

Chapter 12
Welcome New Members

When your team gains or loses even one member, its composition changes. It becomes a new team, with a different mix of skills and temperaments, so you'll need to review (and possibly redefine) goals, roles, and rules. If you don't, here's the kind of problem you might encounter:

As VP of market development at a fairly young health care start-up, Steve had built a tight team of eight account reps, each in charge of a different region of the New England area. After three years, the team lost one of its reps and brought in Carol as a replacement. Carol quickly learned the business, but she had trouble integrating with her new team. Other members complained about her to Steve: They said she was taking over client relationships without permission, writing "sharp" e-mails, and challenging them in embarrassing ways. They thought she was aggressive, disrespectful, and inconsiderate. How, they wondered, had they misjudged her so badly when interviewing her for the job?

Maybe Carol had pulled the wool over their eyes during the hiring process and was really a ruthless, competitive colleague who didn't care about people. But more likely, she hadn't been brought up to speed on the team's expectations. Had anyone told her that before taking on a client relationship she needed to speak to the rep in charge of that region? Or that the team valued its collaborative culture? Or that if she disagreed with someone, she needed to discuss it privately? Probably not, Steve realized.

Ideally, a team's veteran members will orient the new ones, filling them in on the rules. Even better, the whole (new) team will discuss whether the old ways of working still apply and what may need to change. Unfortunately, that's not what usually happens. When adding someone new, teams tend to explain what the tasks are but gloss over how the group prefers to interact. They expect their new teammate to pick up that information along the way, or they point out rules after she violates them ("Yeah, not a good idea to just pop into his office with a question—you really need an appointment").

Given the time you've already spent on team building, you might not relish the thought of revisiting the process. You may be thinking, "We've done all that! We've got work to do!" But think of the rewards you'll reap: a fully invested, integrated new member and a more cohesive, productive team.

As you're taking a fresh look at your team's infrastructure, you'll want to:

- **Recognize the impact of any departures.** Before new people come on board, acknowledge how the team has changed as a result of losing a member. At this point, you're not just wondering who's going to become the resident software expert. That's only the "task" side of the loss. You'll certainly need to deal with it—missing competencies should guide who you hire or how you redistribute responsibilities among remaining team members. But there's also a "people" side: Legacy members may feel sad, abandoned, envious, or even relieved when a teammate leaves. It's critical to give them a chance to air their emotional responses, whether it's through a good-bye lunch or a conversation about how they're feeling. It allows the team to clear the air of past issues, identify important changes to make, and refocus members on their work.

- **Celebrate the addition of new members.** If you're hiring new employees, of course you'll do all the regular onboarding: setting up their new work spaces, training them, explaining their responsibilities, familiarizing them with company policies, and so on. But again, those are task-related activities. What can you do on the "people" side to help new members? As the team leader, how can you address their anxiety, excitement, or feelings of separateness?

  Throughout the centuries, groups have performed ceremonies to receive new members into adulthood, religious sects, the military, fraternities, and gangs. Though you probably won't give your new members tattoos or have them fast for a week, the basic idea is the same: Accept them into the group with some sort of celebration or initiation rite. You might host a dinner at your house, for example. One team leader situated newcomers in the office next to his. The close proximity allowed for frequent informal check-ins and ensured that lots of foot traffic passed by the new person's desk.

- **Make meaningful introductions.** Legacy members already know about everyone's skills, interests, and idiosyncrasies. But you need to share all that information with your new members—it will help them bond and interact with the group. This can be fun. Try having veterans introduce one another to their new teammates by going around the room and completing the following sentence: "What you should know about Ava is . . . ." Or you might ask people to describe the funniest (or worst or most embarrassing) thing that's happened to them since they've joined the team. It doesn't really matter how you frame the exercise, as long as it gives new members a sense of what individuals are like.

- **Highlight personalities and work styles.** The goal here is to reveal how each person works in a team setting, as you did in chapter 2, "Get to Know One Another." If continuing members completed a personality diagnostic such as Myers-Briggs, have new ones do it, too. Then invite all members to share their results. You may even want legacy folks to comment on one another's traits, describing how they've seen those tendencies play out ("I could see that Debbie was an ESFP type when she . . . "). Or have people talk about their own work styles, completing sentences such as "When I make decisions, my biggest concern is . . . " and "When I'm under pressure, I tend to . . . ."

- **Adjust your team's process.** Although you want new people to learn about the team's established ways of working together, you also want veterans to learn about the new members' preferences. That way, the team can renegotiate an infrastructure that reflects everybody. Revisit the exercises you've done to define goals, roles, and rules (see chapters 3–5), and by all means, share the team contract with the new person. But make sure that legacy members comment on how things work in practice—and then update the goals, roles, and rules accordingly. And ask new members to talk about their experiences on past teams: what worked well, what didn't, and what lessons might apply in this new context.

Integrating new members in a deliberate way enables them to contribute more quickly and the team to adjust to its new future together. You've already invested lots of time in recruiting the right members, old and new. It's worth investing a little more in keeping the group humming.

Chapter 13
Manage Outside the Team

You've already done a lot of work to organize, motivate, and manage your team. But to meet your goals, it's equally important to motivate and manage people *outside* your team, up and down the hierarchy.

MIT management professor Deborah Ancona calls this *boundary management:* You cultivate mutually beneficial relationships with colleagues elsewhere in the organization—particularly the people your team relies on for information and resources. If you don't manage boundaries, team performance suffers.

Consider this cautionary tale: A branch manager at a regional bank had high aspirations (task goals) for innovative customer service, so he worked with his team of 10 employees to define them and put them into practice. Though customers liked the changes they saw, internal relationships across the organization became strained.

The corporate compliance department grew frustrated as branch employees continually asked for exceptions to existing rules. Corporate marketing resisted the branch's requests for variations to branding protocols. And other branch managers resented this branch for getting "special treatment." Within a year, it had a reputation as a problem child, not as an innovator. Eventually the executive team replaced the branch manager.

If the manager had thought about the impact his team's innovations would have on others in the organization, he could have partnered with them instead of alienating them. For example, he might have included them in brainstorming sessions or solicited their input before changes came their way.

So consider your team's work from the perspective of your stakeholders—the individuals and groups who will have the greatest impact on your team's success. They may include:

- senior managers who control your resources
- leaders of other teams competing for company resources
- managers of groups whose collaboration or input your team needs
- managers who have "loaned" people to your team on an ad hoc basis
- functional groups (marketing, engineering, accounting) who provide support

To identify your stakeholders and map out your relationships with them, draw an X on a whiteboard and say, "This is us." Next draw incoming arrows labeled with all the resources you need (and who owns them) and outgoing arrows labeled with all the people and groups who will use what you're producing. Your project plans also reveal the interconnected relationships your work entails.

Once you've identified which parties will require care and feeding, manage your team's boundaries by establishing a reputation, providing external value, and assigning boundary roles. Let's look at each of those steps in more detail.

Establish a Reputation

To obtain the people, funding, commitment to timing, and cross-functional collaboration your team requires, you must earn a favorable reputation early on with decision makers in the senior ranks. As Deborah Ancona's research shows, their first impression of your team will stick—and it will significantly influence your team's success or failure. If your stakeholders like what they see, they'll spread the word, and others in the organization will eagerly help you out. Everyone likes backing a winner.

For a brief period after you've assembled your team, you've got a clean slate: Senior managers haven't formed an opinion about you either way. That's your chance to forge a positive impression.

Suppose you're submitting your team's first progress report, for instance, or releasing a beta version of your software program. From this early glimpse of your team's work, top management will form its opinion, which will then spread rapidly through the organization.

Initial communication matters a lot. If it reveals any kind of struggle within your team—difficulty meeting a deadline or a goal, for example—you'll have to fight the uphill battle from then on of overcoming a bad reputation. Senior managers may question your team's competence, reconsider whether the work you're doing is even necessary, or signal in some way their withdrawal of confidence or support. Others inside the organization will follow suit, thinking why get behind a losing team? Additionally, people will view your subsequent efforts through that lens of negativity, emphasizing missteps and even attributing any success to luck instead of competence. Expectations of failure will become a self-fulfilling prophecy.

How do you manage your reputation to prevent that from happening? By controlling information flow. Discuss up front with your team who should communicate with whom, and what information to share. At one small nonprofit, the executive committee actually used the last part of every team meeting to craft external talking points so that they'd all be on the same page once they'd left the conference room.

Carefully consider who will be the "face" of your team. Send only the most positive, articulate, and politically savvy team members to meet with senior managers, deliver status updates, and so on.

Also, embed small, early wins in your project plan—important outcomes the team can quickly and easily accomplish. Delivering right away on these promises shows that the team is competent, well organized, and primed for success. Even if you then miss a deadline later on, the senior team will probably see it as a temporary setback. Identifying early wins often involves breaking a larger task into smaller pieces. One team at a nonprofit, which focused on giving children access to science education, was charged with getting six new corporations to fund community outreach programs. Instead of waiting to achieve all six goals, the team widely publicized its first success—and then its second. Word quickly spread that the team was on a roll.

Provide External Value

As a team leader, you can't require that people in other groups support you. You have to make them *want* to. You can win them over by invoking what Allan Cohen and David Bradford call "the law of reciprocity" in their book *Influence Without Authority*. It's the "almost universal belief that people should be paid back for what they do." When colleagues do something for you, they expect you to help them at some point—and when you do something for them, they feel obliged to reciprocate.

Once you've identified the people and groups you need to rely on to meet your goals, figure out what you can do for them. Consider how you might support them in achieving their own goals. They may respond well, as Cohen and Bradford suggest, to an exchange "of tangible goods, such as a budget increase, new equipment, or more personnel; of tangible services, such as a faster response time, more information, or public support; or of sentiments, such as gratitude, admiration, or praise."

Determine which "currencies" they value, and start paying. You can earn reciprocity points with your finance colleagues simply by submitting your budget proposal on time and in good shape. Timeliness, accuracy, and attention to detail are all valuable to them. And they'll be more inclined to reciprocate when you ask for help on a task that calls for number crunching, such as building a business case.

You'll gain influence with people only when you're "in the black"—when you've done more for them than they've done for you. That's not to say you should keep a running tally of favors exchanged. But make an ongoing effort to be helpful. Don't wait until you need something to do something for them.

Assign Boundary Roles

To manage your team's boundaries properly, it's helpful to understand the roles Deborah Ancona outlines for controlling the flow of information. Their overall purpose is to make sure outgoing messages enhance the team's reputation and incoming messages enable the group to do its best work.

Managing two-way flow

The "task coordinator" occupies the role we most typically associate with boundary management. This is the person who gathers external approvals to proceed with tasks, negotiates for resources, coordinates the team's activities with other people's schedules, and solicits external feedback. The task coordinator both shares and receives information across the team's boundaries.

Managing outward flow

The “ambassador” focuses on team PR. This person establishes relationships with key stakeholders, updates them on progress, and strategically shares information to influence perceptions and generate support. The “guard,” conversely, ensures that confidential information remains inside the team, often creating and enforcing protocols for data storage and dissemination.

Managing inward flow

The “scout” actively seeks external information so that the team avoids surprises and can capitalize on opportunities. This person scans the environment for trends in markets, technology, competitive products, and ideas, and identifies potential allies and opponents. The “sentry,” on the other hand, monitors the data that comes into the team, protecting members from information overload and distractions.

You can assign these roles in a number of ways (see chapter 4, “Agree on Individuals’ Roles”). You might play to individuals’ strengths, asking someone with good interpersonal skills to serve as ambassador, for example. Or you could use the roles to complement the work that members do inside the team. Your team’s project manager might act as the task coordinator, since she’d be doing many of those activities anyway.

One team I worked with managed its stakeholders like clients: Individuals “owned” entire relationships and maintained them by taking on multiple roles rather than divvying them among members. For a given stakeholder, the same team member would manage perception of the team (ambassador), make sure the work went smoothly (task coordinator), and inform the team of important challenges its clients faced (scout).

Whatever approach your team chooses, the critical takeaway is this: To succeed internally, it must also succeed externally. By managing the people and groups that will have an impact on your team, you avoid getting blindsided by surprises, gain input into significant decisions, and build a reputation that precedes you in a *good* way.

Section 3
Close Out Your Team

Chapter 14
Deliver the Goods

As your team's work begins to wrap up, you may find yourself starting to mentally and emotionally move on. It's hard *not* to. You're thinking about everything you've put on hold during this project—all the other work that's once again screaming for your attention. Maybe your mind is starting to wander a little in meetings or you're quicker to lose patience with a team member who grates on your nerves. You might be tempted to cut a corner or two just to finish things up.

Chances are, your team members feel the same way. How do you keep everyone, including yourself, focused and working productively so that your team delivers the goods on time and up to quality standards? By devoting as much care to maintaining the relationships as you do to completing the tasks—up until the very end.

Manage Emotions

As your project draws to a close, members may feel fulfilled by a job well done, relieved that the pressure is finally letting up, sad to stop working together, or regretful about conflicts that erupted along the way. They may be anxious about what they'll be doing next or whom they'll report to. Or, after putting in so much hard work, they may worry about passing the baton to others in the organization: What if they ignore the team's recommendations or make ill-considered changes?

Help members deal with the ups and downs by reminding them that closure is imminent. Talk openly, as a group, about how everyone's feeling to signal that those emotions are normal but still need to be managed. Agree on how the team will safeguard against letting emotions compromise the work that remains.

One team leader became very adept at anticipating, recognizing, and dealing with members' feelings. He ran the training program for new hires at a boutique financial firm. Two times a year, he would get a class of about 15 to 20 new hires. In addition to educating them about the company's products, he tried to "mold them into a tight unit." During the six months of training, he encouraged individuals to study together and quiz one another as they prepared for the exam they would take at the end. He knew that their anxiety would dramatically increase as the exam drew near—and that they'd need one another's support as they transitioned from the safe haven of the program to the demanding real world. In the last few weeks, he did weekly assessments with the group, asking questions like these: "On a scale of 1 (terrible) to 10 (great), how are you feeling about exam prep? How are you feeling about starting your 'real' job? How are you feeling about this unit?" As members shared their ratings, he acknowledged their feelings, focusing on what individuals, the team, or he could do to manage them. One outcome from the discussions was a new wiki where people could post questions to the entire group. This not only helped with exam prep but also reminded individuals that they were part of a larger group that would face the exam together.

Orchestrate Your Delivery

A strong handoff is essential to your team's overall success. Otherwise, all the accumulated time and effort is wasted.

Suppose senior executives asked your team to analyze a problem and make a recommendation. Unless members make a solid case for their proposed solution—documenting and presenting their findings in a clear, engaging way—their research and analysis won't amount to anything. Or say the team explored a new product idea and created a prototype. That developed idea won't become a reality unless you get people in manufacturing to buy in to the specifications.

So keep in close contact, as you did in the team's early days, by increasing the number of check-ins and amount of face time. That will keep the energy up and prevent people from taking shortcuts or dropping tasks altogether. One team leader posted a calendar in the office 15 days before the final deadline and, with great flourish, crossed off each passing day. Another held brief "countdown" meetings toward the end. First thing every morning, she assembled her team in the hallway (standing, to signal urgency) and asked members to quickly report on their plans for that day.

Another way to keep people alert is to include them in delivering the end result. It's easy to disengage if you've completed all of your delegated tasks. But if your name is on the final report or you'll participate in the presentation to senior management, you'll stay focused.

And make sure to give your team something to look forward to. Whether you celebrate completion with a dinner out or bring pizza to the last meeting, let people know what you're planning to do. That will give productivity a nice boost as you head to the finish line. It's a way of saying, "Just a *little* more, and we'll be done."

Provide Closure

We have diplomas and graduation ceremonies to mark the end of school, retirement parties to commemorate a career, trophies to recognize our sports achievements. So why don't we close out our teams and projects with some gesture, act, or event? Often, it's because we're busy or we've already leapt to the next team or project. Sometimes we don't want to acknowledge that our work or relationships will end and that change is imminent.

So teams tend to drift apart rather than come to a clear, definitive close. They keep canceling or postponing their increasingly unnecessary meetings. Attendance dwindles, and those who do come get frustrated. And the opportunity to show the team how much you appreciate and respect everyone's effort and time slips away.

Providing closure and wrapping up on a positive note makes members more inclined to join future teams if you invite them. Here are some ways of doing that:

- Hand out awards (humorous or real) that show appreciation for individual contributions.
- Send letters to their managers outlining their contributions, and give copies to your team members so that they can see the accolades.
- Invite senior executives to the final meeting. Have them express their thanks and discuss how the team's work supports the company's strategic priorities.
- Ask team members to talk about which tasks gave them the greatest sense of accomplishment.
- Discuss the team's successes and what could be done better in the future.

That last point is crucial. Don't forget to acknowledge the failures. It's even more important than celebrating the successes. What if senior management rejects the team's recommendations? What if the prototype can't be reproduced on the factory floor? Help members recover, and put them in a constructive frame of mind for the next project. You might, for example, have a champagne toast to the prospect "that got away" or hold a funeral for a proposal that got killed. One engineering team actually filled a box with copies of project-related materials and buried it in a hole behind the company parking lot. Then each member took a moment to reminisce about the project. It added some levity to the situation and put the loss into perspective.

Learning from the past, in preparation for future teams and projects, is your next and final step as a team leader.

Chapter 15

Learn from Your Team's Experiences

Before rushing off to the next big project, reflect on what worked and what didn't for your team. That way, you carry forward processes that served you well and change those that didn't on work with future teams. You don't want to experience déjà vu as the same people create bottlenecks, for example, or the same decision-making processes create "winners" who dominate and "losers" who drag their feet.

As veteran project manager Ray Sheen points out in the *HBR Guide to Project Management,* many organizations provide templates to evaluate the work and the outcomes. You fill out those reports and send them up to senior managers for review, both to inform them about your initiative and to contribute institutional knowledge that will help managers of future projects in their own planning and execution.

For each project you complete, you'll need to evaluate how well the team met its targets (task outcomes, timelines, budgets, resource usage) and analyze the lessons learned at each stage.

You'll also want to conduct an evaluation of people and processes. Do a review at both the team level (rules and processes) and the individual level (behaviors).

Evaluate the Team

When examining the group's performance, pose questions such as:

1. Did we adhere to our rules and processes?
2. Did we achieve our process goals?
3. What factors (planned and unplanned, inside and outside the team) contributed to our success? What got in our way?
4. What did we do well? What should we continue doing on future teams?
5. What did we not do well? What changes should we make going forward?

You can use accountability exercises (see chapter 9, "Hold People Accountable") to facilitate the discussion. Just shift the focus from the here and now ("What can we do better on *this* team?") to future ("What can we do better on our *next* teams?").

Or try this exercise, which highlights personal reactions to the group dynamic: Ask members to reflect on their entire experience working together and share their thoughts with the full team. Here are some questions to consider:

1. What gave you the greatest satisfaction working on this team?
2. What was the most difficult or frustrating aspect?
3. What did you learn about working with others?
4. What did you learn about accomplishing tasks?
5. What would you suggest doing again on future teams? What would you change?

Evaluate Individuals

Next take a look at individual contributions and behaviors. Team members need to know which behaviors they personally should continue and which they should stop or adjust as they move to future teams. Ask members to answer the following two questions about each of their colleagues.

1. How did this person contribute?
2. What could he or she do differently to become an even more valuable team member?

During the team's final feedback session, have members share their comments about one another. And ask someone to take notes so that people can reflect later on what was said.

If your team members have grown skilled at giving and receiving honest feedback, you may want them to conduct a more rigorous review. Have them rate one another on dimensions such as sharing the workload and solving problems, perhaps with the same assessments they used for continuous improvement discussions (see the Process Ratings Exercise in chapter 9) or an abbreviated one, such as the Final Ratings Exercise (see sidebar).

In a growing number of organizations, individuals' compensation depends partly on peer ratings like these. That practice stems from the assumption that peers are in the best position to know how much work employees do and the level of quality they achieve. Though the boss—which may be you, the team leader—will still conduct annual performance appraisals, peer assessments add useful data to the mix. But in my experience, it's best to use them only if you've made that explicit in the original team contract; peer ratings should not be used as a response to uneven work or disruptive behavior. Otherwise, you'll sacrifice the trust you've worked so hard to develop in the group. Ideally, peer ratings are a natural extension of team feedback. If you feel the need to collect them privately to ensure honesty, consider that a red flag, and don't use them. Your team isn't ready.

After members hear their feedback, encourage them to digest it and align their self-perceptions with those of the group. Suggest that they write down what they've learned, what they disagree with, how they feel they've contributed to the team's outcomes and processes, how they may have hindered progress, what they'll do

FINAL RATINGS EXERCISE

Before meeting to discuss individuals' performance, ask people to score each team member on these dimensions (or others the team deems relevant). As individuals share their ratings, they should explain their thinking and offer suggestions for ways their colleagues can improve.

1. Adhered to team rules

1 2 3 4 5 6 7 8 9 10

2. Fully contributed to our process goals and team culture

1 2 3 4 5 6 7 8 9 10

3. Completed tasks on time and with care

1 2 3 4 5 6 7 8 9 10

4. Engaged in and supported team decisions

1 2 3 4 5 6 7 8 9 10

5. Gave and received feedback appropriately

1 2 3 4 5 6 7 8 9 10

6. Resolved conflicts and promoted harmony

1 2 3 4 5 6 7 8 9 10

OVERALL SCORE

1 2 3 4 5 6 7 8 9 10

differently on future teams, and what they'll do to keep developing their team membership skills. They'll be more likely to act on the feedback if you have them process it on their own.

You might also work with individuals to craft a development plan together, if appropriate. Ask members to keep their written reflections as a reminder of what they're committing to do (stop, start, continue) on future teams.

Agree on Principles

These end-of-team discussions and exercises help provide closure. They also wipe the slate clean for the next team experience. Often the conversations are cathartic, helping people move beyond grudges or perceived injuries and prime them for a fresh start.

Make your final review as productive as possible by:

- **Agreeing up front how you'll handle it.** This is your last conversation about accountability. It will go much more smoothly—and people will get more out of it—if the team has decided earlier, in discussions about rules and processes, what will happen at this stage. Members need to know in advance how they'll be held accountable along the way *and* at the end so that they can monitor their behavior accordingly. Nothing is more demoralizing than being critiqued for something without receiving fair warning.

- **Giving people time to consider what they will say.** People should avoid speaking off the cuff, especially when delivering feedback to individual members.

- **Providing guidance on what to say and how to say it.** Regarding the "what," remind everyone that this conversation is about the future. The final review is *not* the time to rehash past mistakes or bring up new pain points. Instead, it's a chance to acknowledge what people (as a team and as individuals) did well and should continue on future teams, and what they could do differently to improve the next team experience. Regarding the "how," remind members of the team's feedback and accountability rules (see chapters 5 and 6), and ask them to frame their comments constructively.

Since the beginning, you've led your team through continuous improvement: You established goals, roles, and rules; helped members build essential team skills; and held them accountable to the contract they agreed on. Now, at the end, you're identifying best practices for the future.

The final review promotes learning and improvement *across* teams: Individuals hone their team behaviors into even more productive ones; you sharpen your leadership skills; and future teams benefit from the growth all around.

Appendix A
Rules Inventory

This exercise provides structure for a team conversation about desired behaviors, or rules of conduct. Under each category, you'll find open questions to help identify rules the team may already be following, followed by prompts for considering new ones. If you're leading a new team, you might revise the open questions and ask people what has worked well (or not) for them on previous teams.

NORMS

	Do Now	Add
RESPECT AND TRUST		
What do we do well? What might we do differently?		
Keep conversations confidential.		
Be punctual.		
Return phone calls and e-mails by close of business each day.		
Avoid sarcasm, snide remarks, or melodramatic body language (such as eye rolling) when conveying disagreement.		
Don't sulk or give the silent treatment when your position has not prevailed.		
Respect other people's ways of accomplishing tasks; don't redo work or impose your way on others.		
Be flexible.		
Listen without interpreting people's motives. Ask why they said, did, or asked for something.		
Volunteer to take on work when you can without doing the "who's doing more/less" calculation.		
Other:		

	Do Now	Add
MEETING DISCUSSIONS/ DECISION MAKING		
What do we do well? What might we do differently?		
Share "airtime," listen, and don't interrupt others.		
Invite quiet people to speak.		
Resist regarding an opposing view as a personal affront.		
Be willing to change your position or compromise.		
Support the team's final decision, even when it's different from the one you proposed.		
Stop advocating your position after a decision has been made.		
Make sure people have been given the floor to present their views before a decision is made.		
Other:		

(continued)

(*continued*)

	Do Now	Add
DISSENT AND INNOVATION		
What do we do well? What might we do differently?		
Rigorously examine multiple options, and their respective strengths and weaknesses, before evaluating alternatives and making decisions.		
Protect dissenting views by encouraging the speaker to explain and preventing others from immediately dismissing the ideas.		
Encourage innovation by delaying evaluation.		
Reframe “This will never work” as “How could we make it work?”		
Other:		

	Do Now	Add
FEEDBACK AND REPORTING		
What do we do well? What might we do differently?		
Give the team status updates according to the prescribed process (which the team determines).		
Give a "heads-up" and be responsible for the consequences if you have to miss a deadline.		
Give positive feedback frequently; speak up when someone's behavior helps the team.		
Give negative feedback constructively. State the observed behavior and its impact on the team, ask for the other person's perceptions, and suggest a preferred behavior.		
Admit your own mistakes.		
Listen and avoid defensiveness when receiving constructive feedback.		
When giving or receiving feedback, put it in the context of helping the team move toward its goals.		
Other:		

(continued)

(*continued*)

	Do Now	Add
CONFLICT RESOLUTION		
What do we do well? What might we do differently?		
Assume that every team member is working in good faith toward the team's goals.		
Put conflict "on the table" for discussion.		
Discuss conflict with the goal of identifying what is best for the team's future.		
Discuss the conflict first with the person involved; avoid talking behind anyone's back.		
Don't yell, use profanity, make threats, or walk out of discussions.		
Other:		

Appendix B
Cultural Audit

Ask team members to describe the group's way of operating, as if you were bringing someone new onboard. Have them quickly answer the following questions, without overthinking their responses.

What would you tell new team members about how we:

Communicate

- How do we share information? (Through what channels? What's the tone and level of formality?)
- Who can—or can't—we communicate with? What chain of command do we need to honor?
- What's the expected response time? Is it ever OK to be "offline"? If so, when, and how do we inform others of our availability?

- What are the standards for presentations?
- What are the standards for written documents?

Conduct meetings

- How do we run meetings? How long are they? How frequent? What's the tone and level of formality?
- Why do we hold meetings?
- Who should attend? When is it OK to meet in subgroups, and when is the full team required? How and when do we invite outsiders?
- How do we handle sensitive or confidential issues?

Make decisions

- What is our process for making decisions?
- Who makes them? Who is included and who isn't?
- How do we communicate decisions? Who gets told about them? Through what medium? What's the tone and level of formality?

Handle differing viewpoints

- How do we solicit dissent (if at all)? At meetings? In e-mail? One-on-one?

- How do people offer dissenting ideas or opinions? How direct should the language be?
- Is dissent allowed from everyone?
- Are some people never to be challenged?

Delegate work

- How do we negotiate timelines and resources (if at all)?
- How do we communicate assignments? (Through what medium? At what level of detail? What's the tone and level of formality?)
- How do we make sure that all team members understand their roles?
- How do we reach agreement on outcomes and schedules?
- How do people get feedback on their tasks?

Manage projects

- How do we keep teammates and stakeholders up to date on progress? (Through scheduled status reports? When things go wrong? At project milestones?)
- Who gets told? How frequently?

- What's included?
- What happens with problems, missed deadlines, changes, adjustments, and so on? How do we communicate them? How do we get back on track?

Appendix C
Team Contract

Here's a template for capturing the goals, roles, rules, and metrics your team has agreed to. Update your contract periodically, as members, tasks, and timelines change.

Brief team description:

Date:

Team members:

Name	Contact information	Signature

Goals that will serve as a unifying force in the work ahead:

Task goals (what we'll accomplish)
Process goals (how we'll work together)

Roles we've identified to ensure performance:

Roles	Names

Rules of conduct:

Meetings	
Communication	
Decision making	
Managing tasks	
Managing relationships	

Evaluation plan (how we'll determine that we've achieved our goals):

Index

About the Author

Mary Shapiro has worked with *Fortune* 500 companies, nonprofit organizations, and government agencies as a consultant and executive trainer for more than 20 years. She has developed and delivered executive education programs at Simmons College since 1988 and joined the Simmons MBA faculty in 1993. She holds the Trust Professorship of Leadership Development at Simmons College School of Management. Shapiro specializes in four areas: team building and intervention, communicating in a diverse and virtual environment, personal effectiveness in influence and motivation, and strategic career management.

Notes

Notes

Notes

Notes

Notes

Notes

Notes

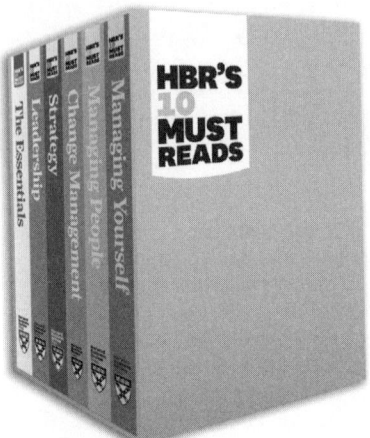

HBR Guide to **Dealing with Conflict**

Harvard Business Review Guides

Arm yourself with the advice you need to succeed on the job, from the most trusted brand in business. Packed with how-to essentials from leading experts, the HBR Guides provide smart answers to your most pressing work challenges.

The titles include:

HBR Guide to Being More Productive

HBR Guide to Better Business Writing

HBR Guide to Building Your Business Case

HBR Guide to Buying a Small Business

HBR Guide to Coaching Employees

HBR Guide to Data Analytics Basics for Managers

HBR Guide to Delivering Effective Feedback

HBR Guide to Emotional Intelligence

HBR Guide to Finance Basics for Managers

HBR Guide to Getting the Right Work Done

HBR Guide to Leading Teams

HBR Guide to Making Every Meeting Matter

HBR Guide to Managing Stress at Work

HBR Guide to Managing Up and Across

HBR Guide to Negotiating

HBR Guide to Office Politics

HBR Guide to Performance Management

HBR Guide to Persuasive Presentations

HBR Guide to Project Management

HBR Guide to **Dealing with Conflict**

Amy Gallo

HARVARD BUSINESS REVIEW PRESS

Boston, Massachusetts

Printed in the United States of America
10 9 8 7 6 5

Library of Congress Cataloging-in-Publication Data

Names: Gallo, Amy, author.
Title: HBR guide to dealing with conflict / by Amy Gallo.
Other titles: Harvard Business Review guide to dealing with conflict | Harvard business review guides.
Description: Boston, Massachusetts : Harvard Business Review Press, [2017] | Series: Harvard Business Review guides
Identifiers: LCCN 2016044710 | ISBN 9781633692152 (pbk. : alk. paper)
Subjects: LCSH: Conflict management. | Work environment.
Classification: LCC HD42 .G33 2017 | DDC 658.4/053--dc23 LC record available at https://lccn.loc.gov/2016044710

ISBN: 9781633692152
eISBN: 9781633692169

The paper used in this publication meets the requirements of the American National Standard for Permanence of Paper for Publications and Documents in Libraries and Archives Z39.48-1992.

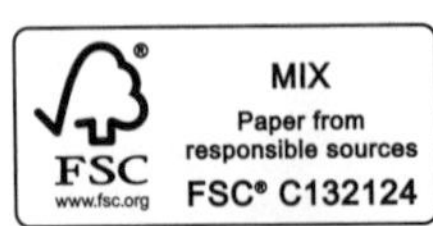

What You'll Learn

While some of us enjoy a lively debate with colleagues and others prefer to suppress our feelings over disagreements, we all struggle with conflict at work. Every day we navigate an office full of competing interests, clashing personalities, limited time and resources, and fragile egos. Sure, we share the same goals as our colleagues, but we don't always agree on how to achieve them. We work differently. We rub each other the wrong way. We jockey for position. But disagreements don't have to be a source of unhealthy tension. So how can you deal with conflict in a way that is both professional and productive—where it improves both your work and your relationships? This guide lays out a straightforward process for addressing nebulous situations. You start by understanding whether you generally seek or avoid conflict, identifying the most frequent reasons for disagreement, and knowing what approaches work for what scenarios. Then, if you decide to address your situation, you use that information to plan and conduct a productive conversation. Knowing there is a process to follow can make conflict more manageable. This guide will give you the advice you need to:

- Understand the most common sources of conflict
- Explore your options for addressing a disagreement
- Recognize whether you—and your counterpart—typically seek or avoid conflict
- Assess the situation that's making you feel uncomfortable
- Prepare for and engage in a difficult conversation
- Manage your and your counterpart's emotions
- Develop a resolution together
- Know when to walk away
- Repair relationships

Contents

SECTION TWO

Managing a Conflict

SECTION THREE

Resolving a Conflict

Preface

by Linda Hill

Years ago, a colleague and I got into a fight. I had been selected to lead a cross-functional task force to review a portion of our MBA curricula. This was a diverse group of people—a few fellow junior faculty, people from other departments, and professors who had been at the school for decades, including my senior colleague and friend, whom I'll call Elizabeth. I was a brand-new tenured professor, and although I was surprised that I'd been picked to lead the team, I was also honored. And I was glad that I would be able to rely on Elizabeth for her expertise. After all, she had much more experience than I did.

Yet each time the group met, Elizabeth wasn't participating. She sat silently and rarely, if ever, had anything positive to contribute. We'd be talking about a topic that I knew she had an opinion on, and still she didn't say anything.

When she did open her mouth, it was to disparage me. In front of the group, she picked on what I felt were trivial things, like the fact that I didn't have all the supplemental materials in the same order as they were listed in the agenda. I could tell that something was wrong.

So could the rest of the team. People exchanged glances when Elizabeth openly criticized me for not being prepared. Some people tried to jump in and move things along when things got tense between us. But it was clear that the situation was making the whole team uncomfortable—me, Elizabeth, and everybody else.

I was confounded. Elizabeth and I had always gotten along, and whenever we'd collaborated in the past, it went well. After a few weeks of enduring her alternating silent treatment and carping, I decided to talk to her. I closed her office door behind me, sat down, and asked, "We aren't really working well together, are we?"

I wasn't prepared for what came next. She started yelling at me. She thought that I was doing a horrible job of running the group, that we weren't making progress on the evaluation, and that I was wasting her and everyone else's time. I felt backed into a corner, and as a result, I raised my voice, too, defending myself against her accusations.

This was not a smart way to handle the situation. It quickly became clear that neither of us wanted to be fighting. I didn't know what to do. I was concerned that without Elizabeth on board, the group would never be able to finish our work. And more importantly, I worried that Elizabeth's and my relationship, a relationship that I valued, was going to be irreparably damaged. And she didn't seem to be doing any better.

I'm not proud of what I did—you should never raise your voice at people at work. It felt horrible at the time; I was exasperated, angry, upset, questioning myself and Elizabeth. But our disagreement over who should be in charge of the group, how it should be run, and whose expertise needed to be tapped and in what way was not necessarily negative in and of itself. These questions needed to be addressed for the group to do its best work and for me to be effective as a leader.

During our heated exchange we got those issues out into the open. But how we handled that initial discussion was problematic—we weren't going to solve the issues we'd raised if we were both defensive. We needed to work together.

And that's just the thing—conflict at work is going to happen, no matter what you do. And it should. It can be good for you, your team, and your organization. But how you deal with it can make the difference between a negative interaction and a productive one.

That's why you've turned to this guide. We don't want to have screaming matches with colleagues. We don't want to feel as if our projects will fail unless we give in to what someone else wants. We don't want to lose sleep over an intense interaction. We *want* to better understand why conflict happens, our options for addressing it, and how to navigate these disagreements so that we end up with our dignity and relationships intact.

Imagine how things with Elizabeth would've gone if I hadn't just waltzed into her office and confronted her. What if I had thought through the discussion in advance, considering what Elizabeth and I were actually disagreeing about, and thinking about our different personalities? What if I had chosen the right time and place for us to talk, framed my message carefully, heard her out, and explained my position? Or what if Elizabeth had come to me earlier and explained why she wasn't participating, made clear that her issues weren't personal but had to do with how I was running the group or what the team was trying to achieve? Instead of sitting there staring at each other, fuming, we might've been engaged in a thoughtful, productive discussion.

Learning to navigate conflicts such as the one I had with Elizabeth is not really a choice in today's organizations. There's always going to be diversity, interdependence, and competition over scarce resources. And that's not a bad thing. When passionate people with different perspectives collaborate to address a problem or an opportunity, there can be give-and-take and productive disagreement. That healthy competition helps create better products, features, and solutions. The research on innovation is clear: Without "creative abrasion" you won't have a robust marketplace of new ideas. The most effective people are those who can disagree constructively, not destructively, and keep difficult conversations substantive, not personal.

Thankfully, mercifully really, in the middle of our fight, Elizabeth paused and asked if I wanted to get coffee with her across campus. Not sure what else to do, I agreed.

The change of scenery was exactly what we needed. As we walked across campus, we both calmed down and Elizabeth opened up about the source of her frustrations. It turns out that I was driving her crazy. I'm not a linear thinker and she is. The process I was using was infuriating to her. She wanted to know how each step led to the next, and I was willing to let things evolve more organically. Plus she felt as if I wasn't using her expertise. I assumed people would speak up if they had ideas—that those with the most experience, such as Elizabeth, would chime in when they wanted to, so I didn't call on anyone in particular and never met with individual team members outside the group to get their perspective. By not calling on her, or openly acknowledging her expertise and asking for her opinion, I had upset her. She felt that I hadn't shown her enough respect. It's not that I didn't feel it (in fact, I assumed that she assumed that I respected her), but I didn't demonstrate it.

Perhaps what really got me in trouble was that I hadn't tried to see the situation from her perspective. I didn't think about how she might feel having someone with far less experience be in charge of something she cared about so much.

We didn't see eye to eye on how the committee should be managed—and she felt mistreated. We both were unafraid of conflict and typically approached it head-on, which is why we ended up in such a heated exchange in her office.

Her complaints made me realize that perhaps others in the group were having similar reactions. I wasn't adapting my style for what worked best for the team—I was doing what was most comfortable to me. Also, I had assumed that by virtue of holding the leadership position, I had credibility. I didn't think I needed to earn everyone's trust, but I absolutely did.

Once we understood what exactly we were fighting about, and we had heard each other out, we were able to move toward a resolution. I asked for Elizabeth's advice. How would she run the group? I was a new leader, and I wanted to learn from her. We both wanted the same thing—to produce the best curricula for our students—and to get there, I vowed to be more respectful of the wisdom and experience she brought to the group and to be more explicit about the process I was using to run the meetings. I started to ask her opinion before the team met. If I thought there was something she wouldn't agree with, I gave her a heads-up. And I started regularly asking everyone to suggest options before we started evaluating them so that we could objectively look at the pros and cons.

Elizabeth made changes after our discussion, too. She stopped nitpicking. She backed off and gave me more space. Because everyone deeply respected her, the change in her attitude influenced the group positively. People were more at ease and offered ideas freely. Suggestions were no longer "Elizabeth's idea" or "Linda's idea"; they were all viable options we could evaluate based on their merits.

I was fortunate. I was able to preserve my relationship with Elizabeth, and the task force's work was better as a consequence of our fight.

Looking back, I wish I had had the advice in this book before I spoke to Elizabeth. I could've saved us both a lot of grief if I had better understood the common sources of conflict, how people approach it differently, and the various options and strategies for solving it.

That's what you'll get in the pages ahead. You'll learn how to effectively navigate conflicts with your boss, your peers, your direct reports, and partners outside your company. You'll do the foundational work of better understanding the different types of conflict, your own tendency toward approaching it, and your options for resolving it. Then you'll learn the process to follow when a specific conflict arises—from assessing what kind of conflict it is, to preparing for the conversation, to hearing your counterpart out, and to ultimately reaching a satisfying resolution and repairing your relationship, if necessary.

Mastering all of this will not absolve you from having fights at work. I still have them, for sure. We all do, and maybe on occasion you will lose your temper, say something ugly, and behave in a way that you regret. But by following the advice in this book, those occasions will be fewer and less painful—for you and your colleagues.

Introduction: A Practical Plan for Dealing with Conflict

Let's face it: There's no such thing as a conflict-free office. We fight at work. We disagree about how to implement a new IT system. We battle over which strategy to pursue. We engage in turf wars about who gets to lead the website redesign project. And sometimes, we just act like passive-aggressive jerks toward one another.

And as uncomfortable and draining as conflict can be, conflict in and of itself isn't really the problem. It's how we handle it that matters.

Consider these two fictional stories:

Celia and her colleague, Sara, disagreed about how to word an important provision in a client contract. As the legal expert, Celia felt Sara's suggestion was too vague and perhaps even intentionally deceptive to the customer—implying better payment terms than their company was willing to allow. When Celia pointed out how the language might be misinterpreted, Sara stood her ground. Celia knew that this was an important customer for the company, and the CEO was eagerly awaiting news that the deal was closed, so she let it go. But she worried for several weeks whether she should've pushed harder. She lost sleep over it, avoided Sara at the office, and dreaded the date when the customer would receive its first invoice. And rightly so—when that time came, the customer was extremely unhappy and Celia ended up with Sara in the CEO's office having an all-out fight over whose fault it was. The two colleagues didn't speak for weeks afterward, and it took months for Celia's manager to regain trust that she could handle important contracts.

Now, let's take a look at what happened with a manager named Antonio.

Antonio had always had a positive relationship with his boss, Rebecca, but lately he noticed that she was frequently talking over him. As soon as Antonio started to say something, Rebecca would interrupt, often dismissing his view and presenting an opposing one. Antonio was annoyed. He wanted to pull Rebecca aside and tell her to quit it. But before doing that, he spent some time trying to understand what was going on and seeing things from Rebecca's perspective. He knew that she wasn't afraid of conflict and that she might not see her behavior as rudely as he did. He also remembered a conversation in which Rebecca revealed that she was under pressure from the company's senior team to demonstrate that she had fresh ideas. With these things in mind, he asked Rebecca out for coffee, explained that he wanted to maintain their relationship but that he was hurt by her behavior. At first, Rebecca was defen-

sive, claiming that it was all in Antonio's head, but when he gave a few examples, she conceded that she'd been stressed and was perhaps taking it out on him. He offered to support her in meetings, even brainstorming ideas with her beforehand, and she vowed to watch the interruptions. They continued to work together for five more years and relied on each other for candid feedback and advice.

You might be tempted to think that Celia was in a tougher situation than Antonio—she was dealing with a stubborn peer and an important client situation. She had the CEO breathing down her neck, too. But Celia's conflict wasn't any worse or more intense than Antonio's. He was dealing with his boss—the most influential person in his work life—and stood to lose a lot if things went south. Antonio simply handled the situation better. He took time to think through what was really happening, to see the conflict from Rebecca's perspective, and to prepare for his discussion with her.

Celia, of course, is not alone. When we perceive the risks of engaging in conflict to be greater than the potential upsides, many of us prefer to stifle our feelings and move on rather than speak up. And understandably so, as there are negative consequences to mishandling disagreements.

The Downsides of Conflict

Linda Hill's story in the preface and Celia's story here illustrate that when handled poorly—or avoided altogether—conflict can derail projects, damage client relationships, or lose company business. Initiatives slow to a standstill, while warring factions sort out their differences or teams risk not meeting their goals at all. "Energy and creativity get siphoned off," explains Annie McKee, an expert in emotional intelligence, and rather than focusing on accomplishing their objectives, team members are absorbed by their differences. And people in organizations, says McKee, "often have a very long memory when it comes to fighting at work. It doesn't matter what the underlying cause was or who was right or wrong. All people remember is that it was a mess, and that you were involved."

Avoiding conflict (as Celia chose to do) can just make things worse. In fact, unspoken disagreements can have consequences that are as significant as a conference room shouting match. Jeanne Brett, a negotiations professor, warns, "Conflict that's not expressed can be worse than conflict that is." Sometimes we're upset with people and they have no idea we're struggling with them. This negativity can bleed into your interactions. Or worse, your feelings simmer underneath the surface until your coworker does something that makes you explode, blindsiding your unsuspecting colleague.

Conflict also takes an emotional toll. "When you're consumed with a fight, it's hard to draw the boundary and it often spills over into your life," says McKee. We shred our nails worrying about what to say to a colleague with whom we're fighting, or we waste hours agonizing over whether we could have better articulated our perspective on a contentious issue. Over time, persistent conflict causes health problems. A Duke University Medical Center study showed that an intensely angry episode can lead to an eightfold increase in risk of heart attack, and anger has been linked to strokes, irregular heartbeat, sleep problems, excess eating, and insulin resistance, which can help cause diabetes.

The Benefits of Conflict

Luckily, however, when handled well, conflict can have positive outcomes: It can help you be more creative, spark new ideas, and even strengthen bonds with your coworkers, as it did between Antonio and Rebecca. You might dream of living in a peaceful utopia, but it wouldn't be good for your company, your work, or you. "Conflict allows the team to come to terms with difficult situations, to synthesize diverse perspectives, and to make sure solutions are well thought out. Conflict is uncomfortable, but it is the source of true innovation and also a critical process in identifying and mitigating risks," says Liane Davey, an expert in team dynamics.

Here are some of the specific benefits:

- **Better work outcomes:** When you and your coworkers push one another to continuously ask if there's a better approach, that creative friction is likely to lead to new solutions. And there's rarely a fixed amount of value to be gained in a disagreement. If you and your colleague are arguing about the best way to roll out a new initiative—he wants to launch in a single market first and you want to enter several at one time—you'll be forced to explore the pros and cons of each approach and ideally find the best solutions. It may be that you decide to run the pilot he wants but on a shorter time frame so that you get the revenue from reaching the other markets sooner.

- **Opportunity to learn and grow:** As uncomfortable as it may feel when someone challenges your ideas, it's an opportunity to learn. You gain experience from incorporating feedback, try new things, and evolve as a manager. When a peer chews you out after an important presentation because you didn't give her team credit for their work, the words may sting, but you're more likely to think through everyone's perspectives before preparing your next talk.
- **Improved relationships:** By working through conflict together, you'll feel closer to the people around you and gain a better understanding of what matters to them and how they prefer to work. You'll also set an important precedent: that it's possible to have "good" fights and then move on. Two regional managers who engage in a lengthy debate about who should be responsible for maintaining quality in their region have, at the end of the day, learned information about each other that will help them work better together in the future. And they've shown their teams that it's possible to move beyond conflict, to not get entrenched in a viewpoint but to make progress toward a resolution.
- **Job satisfaction:** When you're not afraid to constructively disagree, or even fight, about issues at work, you're likely to be happier to go to the office, be satisfied with what you accomplish, and enjoy interactions with your colleagues. Instead of

> feeling as if you have to walk on eggshells, you can focus on getting your work done. A study in China showed a correlation between the use of certain approaches to conflict management—ones in which employees pursue a win-win situation, care for others, and focus on common interests—and an employee's happiness at work.

For conflict to have any of these benefits, you have to learn the skills to proactively address problems and engage in healthy discussions. Fortunately, you have ample opportunity to try. The average person spends nearly three hours each week dealing with conflict at work, according to a study by CPP Global. Another study by CPP showed that managers report spending 18% to 26% of their time dealing with conflicts. Since we spend so much time engaged in disagreements, it's worth our effort to get them right—to temper our reactions and manage the conflict so that it's more productive.

How do you do that? This book will help you break through the scary, emotional stuff and take a practical, ordered approach to dealing with conflict.

A Plan for Handling Conflict

I'll briefly outline here a better approach for handling conflict so that you get a sense of the whole process before delving into the individual steps and specific scenarios in later chapters.

You start by understanding conflict better. Before we engage in an unhealthy way, it helps to know what's at the root of the disagreement. First, you need to know the various sources of conflict (see chapter 1, "Types of Conflict"). There are four main types: **relationship** (a personal disagreement), **task** (disagreement over what the goal is), **process** (disagreement over the means or process for achieving a goal), and **status** (disagreement over your standing in a group). These categories will help you figure out what's actually happening when you get into a conflict—even when your fight doesn't neatly fit into one bucket.

The second piece of information you need is to understand your options (see chapter 2, "Your Options for Handling Conflict"). In general, there are four from which to choose when confronting a conflict. The first, which is more common than you might think, is to **do nothing**. You don't say anything to your colleague, you let the comment go, or you simply walk away and go on as if the conflict hasn't happened. The second option is to address the conflict, but **indirectly**. Instead of talking through what's going on with your coworker, you might involve your boss or a third party, or hint at the conflict without ever candidly naming it. This option is more common in cultures such as East Asia, where saving face is important. The third option is to address the conflict **directly.** This is where the rest of the book focuses—on preparing for and having a direct conversation with your counterpart. The final option—and typically your last resort—is to **exit** the relationship.

The third and final aspect to having a more productive conflict is to know what people's natural tendencies are when it comes to conflict. There are generally two types of people: those who gravitate toward conflict and those who want to take cover under their desks whenever tensions rise. **Avoiders** tend to shy away or even hide from disagreements. **Seekers** are more eager to engage in conflict when it arises (or even find ways to create it). In chapter 3 ("Recognize Your Natural Tendency"), you'll get to know which style you gravitate toward (and tips for sussing out your counterpart's tendency) so that you can make a conscious choice about how to address a disagreement.

Table I-1 gives you an overview of this foundational work.

Once you've completed this groundwork, it's time to put your knowledge into practice. When faced with a specific situation—your colleague raises his voice, you're battling with your finance counterpart over next year's budget, your boss is acting like a jerk—start by quickly taking stock of what you know about your counterpart

TABLE I-1

Conflict at a glance

Types of conflict (conflict is over . . .)	Options for handling	Natural tendencies
1. Relationship (personal issues, such as how you're being treated)	**1. Do nothing.**	**1. Conflict avoider** • Shies away from disagreements • Cares most about harmony
2. Task (the goal, *what* you're trying to achieve)	**2. Address indirectly.**	
3. Process (the process, *how* work gets done)	**3. Address directly.**	**2. Conflict seeker** • Eager to engage in disagreements • Cares most about directness and honesty
4. Status (your standing in a group or who's in charge)	**4. Exit the relationship.**	

(is she a seeker like you, or are you both avoiders?) and the type of conflict you're having (see chapter 4, "Assess the Situation"). This will give you a better picture of what you're up against.

You'll also need to sort out what your goal is: Do you want to move your stalled project forward? Preserve the relationship? Just move on? That will help you make a smart choice about which of your four options to exercise. If you choose to do nothing or exit the relationship, this is where your journey ends. You can skip to chapter 8 ("Repair the Relationship") and focus on how to rebuild trust and move on. If you prefer to address the conflict indirectly, you'll choose one of the tactics laid out in chapter 4. If you decide to address the conflict directly, then you'll start to prepare for the conversation (see chapter 5, "Get Ready for the Conversation"). This involves the following eight steps:

1. Check your mindset.
2. See the situation from your counterpart's perspective.
3. Consider the larger organizational context.
4. Plan your message.
5. Prepare for multiple scenarios.
6. Pick the right time.
7. Choose the right place.
8. Vent.

Then you're ready to sit down with your colleague and talk through what's happening (see chapter 6, "Have a Productive Conversation"). You'll start by framing the conversation so that you get off on the right foot. You want to form a bond with your counterpart by focusing on where you agree. Then you'll do three things simultaneously: Manage your and your counterpart's emotions, listen to your colleague's perspective, and make your viewpoint heard. These are all toward the goal of trying to find a solution to the underlying conflict.

Ideally in that conversation, or in subsequent ones, you'll find a resolution that meets both of your needs (see chapter 7, "Get to a Resolution and Make a Plan"). And if you aren't able to reach a conclusion, you'll at least agree on how to move forward.

No matter what sort of end your conflict comes to, you'll need to figure out how to repair the relationship and move on (see chapter 8). Conflict can bring up lots of negative emotions—anger, frustration, annoyance, resentment—and it's important to clear the air and lay the groundwork for a strong relationship going forward.

Conflict can feel less scary and more manageable when you approach it methodically. You'll need to be flexible and adapt as the situation takes unexpected turns, but this book will help you develop the basic skills and strategies you need. There are many examples throughout (real stories disguised and combined) to show you how others have tackled similar challenges. Of course, nothing ever goes exactly as planned, so the final chapter addresses specific scenarios, such as what to do when you're dealing with a bully or how to navigate a disagreement with a vendor (see chapter 9, "Navigate Common Situations"). When you learn to manage conflict, it has fewer downsides and more benefits, and it boosts your overall productivity. "If you're going to be a truly effective manager, you're going to have to deal with conflict. Otherwise you're going to end up fighting with everyone or simply giving them what they want," says John Ratey, a professor of psychiatry at Harvard Medical School. By following the process in this guide, you can reap the benefits of conflict while mitigating its risks. You will also become more confident in proactively addressing disagreements and engaging in difficult discussions.

SECTION ONE

Preparing for Conflict Before It Happens

CHAPTER 1

Types of Conflict

In the middle of a dispute, when your brain kicks into overdrive, you might be stuck wondering, Where did this conversation go wrong? or Why is my coworker so mad? It might feel as if your colleague is being unreasonable, that the situation is intractable, or that your relationship will never recover.

Uncovering what's truly going on—what's at the root of the disagreement—will help you set aside your emotional reaction and begin to solve the problem.

There are generally four types of conflict: relationship, task, process, and status (see table 1-1).

The common sources of conflict are neatly delineated here, but in reality, disagreements rarely fall into just one of these categories. More often, there are multiple things going on and a conflict may start as one type and expand into another. We'll follow the story of a cross-functional team at TechCorp, a fictional tech company, to illustrate what these categories look like in the real world.

TABLE 1-1

Types of conflict

Type of conflict	What it is	For example . . .	Outcomes if you get it right
Relationship	A clash of personalities	Your counterpart interrupts and talks over you in a meeting.	• Better understanding of your counterpart • Improved relationship
Task	A disagreement over the intended goal of a task or project	You and your colleague in the legal department don't agree on how much risk the company should assume in a partnership agreement.	• Clearer understanding of the trade-offs to be made • Better results • Innovation
Process	A disagreement over how to carry out a project or task	You think it's important to roll out a new initiative quickly, even if it means sacrificing some quality, while your counterpart believes it needs to be perfect before it hits the market.	• Process innovation • More potential solutions to the problem
Status	A disagreement over who's in charge or gets credit for the work	You and your peer are competing to run a high-profile project.	• Clear hierarchy • Easier coordination of the work

Relationship

This is what we most often assume is happening when we get into a conflict—a clash of personalities.

What it is

A personal disagreement. Sometimes called an interpersonal or emotional conflict, it's when one or both of you feel disrespected or hurt. It includes:

- Snapping at each other in meetings
- Exchanging snarky emails
- Avoiding eye contact in the hallway
- Interrupting, or talking over, a colleague in a meeting
- Using a condescending tone to indicate your disagreement
- Arguing over who's right and who's wrong

Quite often a relationship conflict starts as something else. A disagreement over a project schedule escalates to bickering that disrupts a team meeting. Or a difference of opinion on the company's strategy devolves into a heated debate about who's right and who's wrong. You may both have valid points, and good intentions, but some disagreements turn ugly. Annie McKee describes it this way: "In a perfect world, we follow the textbook advice, treat conflict logically, behave like adults, and get on with it. The problem is, we're not working in a perfect world, and none of us is perfect. We each bring our own baggage to work every day. And some of our issues—insecurity, the desire for power and control, habitual victimhood—rear their heads again and again."

Example

A team of functional leaders at TechCorp all agree that one of their best-performing products needs a new feature, but the SVP of product development and the SVP of engineering can't agree on the ultimate goal. Their differing views gradually escalated from lively debate to a public blowout. Now they trade passive-aggressive barbs over group emails and interrupt each other in meetings. Some teammates have become so uncomfortable witnessing the interactions that they've started declining meetings in which they know both will be present. Not only do the SVPs disagree, they can't believe that the other person doesn't see it the same way. It's no longer about what's best for TechCorp and the customer. For both of them, it's about being right.

The benefits of managing it well

There are typically few benefits to relationship conflict, says Jeanne Brett. When our egos and sense of pride get involved, it's painful, and challenging to manage effectively.

But even uncomfortable interpersonal conflict can have positive outcomes. Jonathan Hughes, an expert on corporate negotiations and relationship management, points out that these types of disputes give us the opportunity to learn more about ourselves and our colleagues. We better understand each other's values, working styles, and personalities and therefore build better relationships, "which creates a virtuous cycle," he says. If you've established that you can successfully navigate conflict, you're more likely to give honest feedback and challenge each other when necessary.

Task

The most common source of disagreement at work is task conflict.

What it is

A dispute over the goal of a task or project or what you're trying to achieve. This includes disagreements about:

- The agenda for a staff meeting
- How the success of a new initiative should be defined or measured
- Whether the customers or the employees should come first
- How much risk a company should assume when partnering with other organizations
- Whether to prioritize revenue or customer satisfaction

"The most common form of task conflict in organizations is functional," explains Brett. Marketing, legal, and finance may look at the same problem and see it completely differently. For example, marketing may lobby to put the customer first, while legal's aim is to protect the company from risk, and finance is trying to cut costs. Each may argue that their perspective on how to solve the problem is more important. "In reality, all those viewpoints and each functional way of addressing the problem are relevant and should be integrated into the solution," says Brett.

Example

The functional leaders at TechCorp all agree that they want the new feature, but they can't agree on the objective. Marketing sees it as an opportunity to expand the company's market share. Finance is focused on improving the business's margins. And the engineers on the team care about developing something cool that integrates the latest technology. If they can't agree on what success means for the new feature, they won't be able to move the project forward—or even worse, they'll each take it in a separate direction, wasting time and the company's resources. The engineers spent all weekend developing a prototype of the new feature, but the finance managers are worried that it will be too expensive to produce and the marketing lead isn't sure users will appreciate the added functionality.

The benefits of managing it well

When we have productive discussions about our different views of project goals or how we should define success, we gain valuable insights, says Hughes. "We live in a world of finite resources, and this type of conversation is helpful in terms of coming to smart decisions about which trade-offs to make." Should the new feature have less functionality and be more affordable to make? Or is it important to delight customers so that they stay with the company longer? At TechCorp, the new feature is likely to be more robust and useful to the customer precisely because each of the functions is pushing its own agenda. The new feature won't satisfy everyone, but airing each group's goals is likely to serve up new ideas and generate productive conversations about what will make the feature successful—more so than if the team had just driven toward one person's objective.

Process

Another common type of conflict is not about *what* you're doing but *how* you're doing it.

What it is

A disagreement over how to carry out a project or task, the means or process you use to reach your goal. This includes differences on:

- The best tactic for reaching a quarterly target
- How to implement a new HR policy
- How decisions should be made in a meeting
- How quickly a project should be completed
- Who should be consulted and included as the project is carried out

Process disagreements are easily confused with task conflicts. You think you're arguing over the outcome when really you can't agree on how to make a decision.

For example, you might get locked into a battle with a coworker over the right strategy for a new project when what you need to settle is not the specific tactic but who gets to make the final call. Or you think the company should do customer research first and a coworker thinks it should get a good-enough product out in the market and see what happens.

Example

At TechCorp, finance thinks that the group should come up with a proposal for the new feature that everyone can agree on, but marketing is lobbying to take a vote and let the majority rule. Marketing is also at odds with the engineers because they think they should conduct customer focus groups throughout the course of development, starting as soon as possible, while the engineers think they should wait until they have an internally approved prototype. None of the three functions agrees on the timeline for completing the project—in time for an important trade show or within the fiscal year.

The benefits of managing it well

Disagreements over how to get something done can help bring about process improvements or unearth hidden benefits. A good way to come up with several viable options, Hughes suggests, is to ask, "What other ways can we imagine meeting our goals?" and then allow your team to offer answers. "People tend to frame things in an unnecessary binary fashion: should we do this or that, but there's almost always a third or fourth way as well," he says. It's natural for finance to lobby for production schedules that align with fiscal year milestones. But discussing the timing with the entire group reveals a critical trade show date, reminds the group of key fiscal-year dates, and allows everyone to share their own team's schedule and resource constraints. As with task conflict, process conflict can improve results by drawing on the expertise of the whole group.

Status

A less common—but still problematic—source of conflict is when people disagree over their standing within a group.

What it is

A disagreement over who's in charge or who deserves credit for the work. For example, you think you should be leading an initiative, while your worker thinks he should. It can also include:

- Jockeying for leadership, especially in a team without a formal or designated leader
- Competing to run a high-profile project
- Arguing over or dominating shared resources
- Competing for status symbols, such as the corner office, the latest technology, or having an administrative assistant

Example

The SVP of engineering at TechCorp and the SVP of new product development are going head to head over which one of them should lead the group that's designing the new feature. In an effort to gain an advantage in this horse race, when the senior leaders congratulate the team on the work so far, the SVP of engineering credits the long hours his group put in, while the SVP of new product development claims it was her team's brainstorming sessions and market research that led to the concept for the snazzy new feature.

The benefits of managing it well

When a status conflict is resolved, there's clarity for the team and anyone working with them. "A clear status hierarchy is efficient in that everyone knows his or her role and responsibility," says Brett. This makes it easier to coordinate work and get things done smoothly. "In stable social hierarchies, lower-status individuals defer to those with higher status, and higher-status individuals look out for the welfare of lower-status ones. At least that is how it is supposed to work," she says.

It bears repeating that it's rare to have a conflict that fits neatly into just one of these categories. Often, as the TechCorp example shows, disagreements have elements of all four, and many that start as another type end up as relationship conflicts. Separating out each type cuts through the noise of the conflict to what's really at hand. Instead of a morass of disagreements, you have an organized list of issues to resolve. "Finding the root causes helps you get into problem-solving mode," says Hughes. "It doesn't automatically solve everything. It's not like the heavens open and the angels sing and the conflict is over. But it does make it easier to resolve."

No matter what kind of conflict you're having—or if your conflict is a mess of all four types—you aren't stuck. You have options for moving forward.

CHAPTER 2

Your Options for Handling Conflict

Some people might tell you that the only way to manage work disagreements is to dive right in and straighten things out. This isn't true. While dealing with the conflict directly can be the most effective route, it isn't the only one.

In this chapter I explain your four options: Do nothing, address it indirectly, address it directly, and exit the relationship (see table 4-2 in chapter 4, "Assess the Situation," for an overview of these options).

Do Nothing

When you choose to do nothing, you don't say anything to your colleague, you let the comment go, or you simply walk away and carry on as if the conflict didn't happen. Instead of acting on any feelings or impulses you have about a disagreement, you swallow them and move on. This isn't a cop-out—it's a seemingly easy and low-effort option for managing conflict. "Most people tend toward loyalty," says Brian Uzzi, a leadership professor. "That's because it's easier to lower your expectations than deal with the real issues at hand." To be clear, this isn't taking your bat and ball and going home or storming off. This is simply keeping an issue to yourself rather than raising it.

We do this all the time, often without realizing it. "We put up with an awful lot on a day-to-day basis. We lump conflict all the time without consciously making a decision to do so," says Jeanne Brett. For many conflicts, it's a perfectly good approach. It can be a smart move, especially if the risks of addressing the issue feel greater than the potential rewards. "There are certain discussions you're just better off not having at all, and knowing when to let it go is just as critical as knowing when to engage," she says. (For more on making that call, see chapter 4, "Assess the Situation.")

It may not be worth having the conversation if you don't think it's going to go anywhere. "If your colleague is stuck in her ways and has never demonstrated a willingness to concede, what do you gain by pushing her yet again? If the damage is already done—say the project was defunded last week and you're just finding out about it—it's probably better to forget about it and move on," says Brett.

The risk in selecting this option is that your resolve may not stick. The issue may not go away, so your feelings about it may come out sideways as you blow up at your colleague about an unrelated matter. Or your colleague's behavior may continue or worsen because he is unaware of the problem.

Note that this option and the "address it indirectly" option are different than avoiding conflict altogether. Conflict avoidance is a natural tendency to steer away from conflict whenever possible (see chapter 3, "Recognize Your Natural Tendency"). These are active, conscious decisions you make to handle a situation. If you tend to avoid conflict, check yourself if you find that you gravitate toward these two options.

Use when . . .

- You don't have the energy or time to invest in preparing for and having a conversation
- You suspect the other person is unwilling to have a constructive conversation
- You have little or no power, particularly in conflicts with people above you
- You won't beat yourself up or stew about it

Keep in mind that this option . . .

- Requires little work on your part, but it can be frustrating to dismiss your feelings
- Keeps the relationship stable, assuming you can both truly move on
- Won't work if you're unable to put it behind you and you risk having an outburst later or acting passive-aggressively toward your counterpart
- May cause your work to suffer if you continue to feel bad

- Can reinforce bad behavior—if your counterpart got away with it once, she might try again

What it looks like in practice

Clara, a project manager, was helping Lisa, a product manager, develop a launch schedule for testing a new product line, and she thought that Lisa was being overly optimistic. She tried to point out that Lisa's dates weren't realistic, but Lisa wouldn't listen. "I was new, and while her time frame seemed aggressive to me, I couldn't be sure," Clara says. "Plus she isn't the warmest person, and she made it clear she wasn't really open to my feedback." When the plan went to the wider team, things blew up. The production manager couldn't believe that Clara thought her team would drop everything to meet her dates. But Lisa had already shared the schedule with the head of marketing, who had announced the launch date in the market. When the team discussed the schedule, Lisa never once explained that Clara had a difference of opinion and, in fact, implied that the dates were Clara's work.

"I was livid," explains Clara, "but I didn't want to get into a fight in front of our bosses." She later explained the situation to her manager but decided not to talk with Lisa about it. "She didn't strike me as the kind of person who would be interested in hashing it out, and this wasn't the last time we'd have to work together," she says. "I didn't see what good would come of it, other than creating more tension." Instead, she put it behind her and continued to work with Lisa. Though they never directly discussed the issue, Clara says that Lisa was more open to her input on schedules in the future.

Address It Indirectly: Skirt the Issue

If you decide to try to change the situation by addressing it, there are two ways to do that. The first is to confront someone indirectly.

Indirect confrontation is when you choose to circle around an issue rather than naming it and addressing it together. Maybe you appeal to someone else who can talk to your counterpart (say, your boss or a coworker who knows the person better), or you talk about the situation without ever naming the issue. To those in certain cultures that tend to address conflict directly, this may sound backhanded and completely ineffective. But in some places, particularly those where saving face is important, this is the approach of choice. "In many Asian cultures, group harmony is incredibly important. It's not appropriate to say, 'We have a disagreement,'" says Erin Meyer, author of *The Culture Map: Breaking Through the Invisible Boundaries of Global Business*. "If you have a conflict with someone on a Japanese team, for example, you would not sit down and talk it through."

Brett explains that one tactic is to use a story or a metaphor. For example, if you're upset about a colleague who is constantly interrupting you, you might tell a story about an employee you previously managed who struggled to listen. The moral of the story—that listening is a valuable but tough-to-learn skill—may prompt your counterpart to reflect on her own behavior. "You see this all the time in China and other Asian countries. They are respecting the other party to understand the problem and do something about it rather than telling them what to do," says Brett.

Another way to indirectly address a conflict is to get a third party involved. "In some African cultures, when you have a conflict, you work through a friend. That person works it out for you so that you never have a direct confrontation," says Meyer. You might go to your boss and explain that your interrupting colleague is preventing you from conducting a successful meeting. In some cultures it may be clear that you expect that she will talk to your coworker. In others, you may need to ask. Similarly, if you and another team member don't agree on how to spend money in your shared budget, you might ask your boss to make the decision so that neither of you is seen as losing. Instead, you're just carrying out your manager's orders. Again, in Western cultures, this might be frowned upon because you may be seen as giving away your power or failing to step up to the plate, but in other places, this is an effective way to handle the disagreement.

This option has several risks. If your indirect approach is too indirect, your counterpart may completely miss the message you're trying to send and may not change, or he may just think that "someone else" really messed up. Another risk is that your counterpart hears that you were reaching out to other people about his behavior and may resent that you went around him rather than speaking with him about it first. Lastly, if your counterpart is from a more direct culture, he may not respect what he perceives to be a passive approach.

Remember that this option and the "do nothing" option are different than avoiding conflict altogether. Steering away from conflict is not the same as making a conscious choice to address it indirectly. Watch out if you tend to avoid conflict and find yourself exercising this option regularly.

Use when . . .

- It's important in your culture to save face and not embarrass people
- You work in a place (office or country) where direct confrontation is inappropriate
- You think the other person will be more willing to take feedback from someone else—either someone more powerful than you, such as a boss, or someone he trusts, such as a close confidant

Keep in mind that this option . . .

- May not work in Western cultures, where the expectation is generally to speak directly with someone when you have a problem
- Can backfire if your counterpart finds out about your behind-the-scenes work and is unhappy about it
- May fail if your counterpart doesn't understand your story or metaphor

What it looks like in practice

Carlos worked as an estimator for a large contractor company, and his new boss, Peter, was a classic micromanager.

"He was very operations focused and wanted to know what I was doing all the time," says Carlos. "I was constantly getting emails from him asking about details on my projects that he didn't need to know." Carlos was afraid that if he told Peter he was micromanaging him, Peter would get worse, not trusting that Carlos would do the work the way Peter wanted. "I was good at my job. I just needed him to back off some," explains Carlos.

He decided to approach the conversation by talking to Peter about one of his own direct reports, Vince. "I told him that since Vince was new, he probably needed some closer managing, but that I really saw our job as helping these younger people to learn the job on their own and empower them as much as possible," he says. Peter was a bit hesitant and tried to argue that some people needed to be micromanaged. The two then got into a discussion about who needed closer supervision and who didn't. Without addressing the issue directly, Carlos was able to make the case that he didn't need Peter always looking over his shoulder. And it worked. Peter still managed Carlos more closely than Carlos preferred, but the conversation seemed to encourage Peter to give Carlos a longer leash.

Address It Directly: Confront the Issue

You can also try to change the situation by explicitly addressing it. A direct confrontation is when you talk to the other person—either in the moment the conflict arises or at a later time. Generally this involves explaining your side of the conflict, listening to the other person's perspective, and then, ideally, agreeing on a resolution.

For those in more assertive cultures such as the United States, this can be an effective option, and it's the one I focus on for most of this book. Meyer also points to other countries, such as France, Russia, and Spain, where it's acceptable to have "open, vigorous, strong" disagreements. Some organizational cultures are also more prone to addressing conflict directly, says Brett. The financial industry, for example, has a reputation for people openly disagreeing, sometimes in seemingly harsh ways.

This can be a risky option if it's not handled well because it might heighten the conflict rather than defuse it. That's why the majority of this book is dedicated to showing you how to prepare for the conversation, engage productively, and reach a resolution.

Use when . . .

- You worry that there will be lingering resentment if you don't clear the air
- You've tried to do nothing or indirectly address it and the problem persists
- You previously had a positive relationship with the person and you want to get it back on track

Keep in mind that this option . . .

- Can be good for a relationship—going through difficult experiences together can make your connection stronger and your relationship more resilient

- Allows you to voice your opinion or feelings, if that's important to you
- Helps you develop a better understanding of yourself and your counterpart
- Can improve your work if you can incorporate others' views and opinions
- Could earn you a reputation as aggressive or combative if you do it too often (or not well)

What it looks like in practice

A close work friend of Aparna's pulled her aside to tell her that another coworker of theirs, Zia, had been spreading rumors that Aparna was looking for a new job. Aparna knew that Zia was competitive with her—their jobs were closely related—and that in Zia's ideal world, she would take over several of Aparna's projects. But Aparna was not on the job market. "It was absurd. I hadn't had one networking conversation, and I'd barely updated my résumé in years," she says. She and Zia had small disagreements in the past over what direction to take particular projects, but they'd always been able to move past them. "I always thought we were healthy competitors. We made each other work harder."

Worried that Zia's rumors would put her position at risk, especially if her boss heard them, she decided to talk with Zia directly. She asked Zia out for coffee and explained what she heard and asked for her perspective on it. At first Zia denied that she had said anything to anyone, but she eventually conceded that she'd heard something about Aparna talking with a competitor and she may have mentioned it to a few people. Aparna explained that that was not the case and asked Zia to stop. She agreed, and while they continued to compete on occasion, Aparna didn't hear news of Zia talking behind her back again.

Exit: Get Out of the Situation Entirely

Your final option is to extricate yourself from the situation by either getting reassigned to another project, finding a new boss, or leaving the company. This is usually a last resort. "You can't always leave a relationship, especially at work," Uzzi says. When you're disagreeing with a boss or someone on your team, you may just be stuck with that person, unless you're willing to find another job. But if the conflict is with someone in another department or a person outside your company, such as a vendor, you may be able to reduce your contact.

Exiting doesn't mean that you end the relationship by making a dramatic scene. Instead, look for a way to stop interacting with that person. If it's a client with whom you have an ongoing conflict, you may explain the situation to your supervisor and propose that one of your equally qualified colleagues replaces you on the account. If it's someone you work with in the finance department, you can begin to build a relationship with someone else on that team so that you have an alternative contact. If your boss is the problem, you might apply to jobs in other departments; you can start by building a broader network in the organization or connecting with people on teams you may want to join.

This sounds easier said than done, and often it is. Exiting is a risky option because it's not something you can typically do overnight or even in a week's time. More likely it's something you'll build toward slowly, while you dust off your résumé, expand your network, and have conversations with people who may be able to support you in making the move.

Brett says that it's usually worth trying the other three options before ending things completely. But there are situations in which the conflict is so bad and seemingly intractable that severing the relationship is the best option.

Use when . . .

- You're dealing with someone from another department or outside your company where your jobs aren't interdependent
- You can easily find another job somewhere else
- You've tried other options and nothing has worked

Keep in mind that this option . . .

- May give you a sense of relief because it gives you a clean break
- Can protect you from further time wasted, stress, and discomfort
- Is likely to take a lot of work from you (including potentially difficult conversations) to change departments, get reassigned, or leave your job

- May hurt other relationships as you sever ties with this person
- Can have negative repercussions if you leave a project and then you're later blamed for its failure because you abandoned the team or client
- May make *you* seem as though you're difficult to work with

What it looks like in practice

When the 50-person department that Monique worked in was restructured, she wasn't happy with her new direct supervisor, Samir. "He didn't know how to manage. He was patronizing. He didn't seem interested in my contributions. And it wasn't clear what he wanted me to be doing," she explains. To make matters worse, she didn't believe in the direction Samir was taking the department, a unit that she had spent years helping to build. She repeatedly tried to get clearer directions from him, but the conversations quickly disintegrated, leaving Monique frustrated and Samir confused. "It felt near impossible to have a constructive conversation with him," she says.

After six months of pulling her hair out, Monique went to the head of HR, with whom she had a positive relationship. She didn't want to complain openly for fear that it would get back to her boss. "That would've felt like tattle telling. Instead, I explained to her that as Samir's responsibilities were expanding, he probably had more than enough to do," she says. She suggested that maybe she could report to a different manager. "She thought it was an interesting idea," she says. A couple of weeks went by, and during one of her one-on-one meetings with Samir, he proposed the new reporting structure and asked how she felt about it. Her response, "Whatever's best for the team, I'm willing to do." Monique was very happy with her new manager and felt she had done the best she could do under the circumstances. "If things hadn't changed, I would've left the company," she says.

When Your Counterpart Takes the Lead

Sometimes you're not the one who gets to decide which option to pursue. Your counterpart may ask to be taken off your project. Or a colleague may start yelling at you in the hallway after a meeting. "If it's the other party who's having the problem, you may not be able to completely avoid having the conversation," says Brett. If you're put on the spot, try to delay the conversation for when you're in a better frame of mind so that you can make a smart choice about the option that will work best. (See chapter 4 for more on walking away from a conflict.)

Here are a few examples of language you could use to put off a fight with someone who's upset:

- "I understand you want to discuss this, but now isn't the best time. Can we schedule something at a later date so that we can talk it through?"

- "I can see you're really upset about this. Can we talk about this when we're both calmer?"

- "I'm not ready to have this conversation right now. I'm going to step outside to clear my head, and then perhaps we can meet tomorrow to talk about this."

If your counterpart makes the first move, then you must choose how to react. Your options are the same, but it would be hard for you to do nothing, for example, if he's requested that you sit down and talk about an issue. And you certainly won't need to exercise your right to exit if he's already done so.

Whether you're choosing an approach or whether your counterpart initiates a difficult conversation, there's work for you to do. You'll have to deal with your anger or hurt if you elect to do nothing, finagle a new position or job if you decide to exit the relationship, make a careful plan if you decide to address it indirectly, or prepare for a difficult conversation if you decide to address it directly. That work will be easier if you understand the two general approaches to conflict and which one you tend to favor.

CHAPTER 3

Recognize Your Natural Tendency

There are generally two types of people: those who avoid conflict and those who seek it. Neither style is better or worse, so instead of beating yourself up for being resistant to conflict or being drawn to it, accept that you have a default approach, says Amy Jen Su, an executive coach. Knowing which style is your (and eventually your counterpart's) natural tendency allows you to make smart choices about how to address the conflict and, if you decide to confront it, have a constructive conversation.

Of course, it's rare for a person to avoid conflict or seek it out all of the time. It's more likely that you adjust your style based on the context (are you at home or at work?); whom you're having the conflict with (your boss or your direct report?); and other things going on (is the organization under extensive scrutiny from investors; are you feeling particularly stressed-out, or did you just return

TABLE 3-1

Conflict styles at a glance

Avoiders	Seekers
• Shy away from disagreements. • Value harmony and positive relationships. • Often try to placate people or change the topic. • Don't want to hurt others' feelings. • Don't want to disrupt team dynamics.	• Are eager to engage in disagreements. • Care most about directness and honesty. • Strongly advocate for their own perspective. • Lose patience when people aren't being direct or honest. • Don't mind ruffling feathers.

from a rejuvenating vacation?). You might be willing to tell your sister that she's out of line, but you'd probably tone down a similar comment when you're directing it at a colleague. "This may be because we're more mindful with some audiences than others. With a customer you're trying to sell to, you might be more avoidant [of conflict]. With a peer you've worked with for years, you might be a seeker," says Jen Su.

Still, knowing which style you gravitate toward will help you make a conscious choice about how to address a disagreement. If you're an avoider, for example, your instinct may be to do nothing. But knowing that's your natural tendency can help you overcome your resistance to addressing issues. See table 3-1 for an overview of the characteristics of each. The following sections offer more detail to help you identify your most common approach.

Conflict Avoiders

Conflict avoiders are generally people who value harmony in the workplace. When they sense a disagreement brewing, they will often try to placate the other person or change the topic. These aren't passive behaviors, but active things they do to prevent conflict from becoming an issue. They believe having positive relationships with their colleagues is extremely important and are often seen as easy to get along with. Liane Davey describes these people this way: "They worry that disagreeing might hurt someone's feelings or disrupt harmonious team dynamics. They fret that their perspective isn't as valid as someone else's, so they hold back."

This strategy is meant to make things easier, but it can take a toll. Conflict avoiders try to be nice and often avoid contentious topics. But "[these people] end up spending an inordinate amount of time talking to themselves or others—complaining, feeling frustrated, ruminating on something that already happened, or anticipating something that might happen," says Jen Su. This avoidance can have physical manifestations as well. Some of Jen Su's more conflict-avoidant clients have experienced headaches, back pain, and weight gain.

If you're a conflict avoider, here are some examples of how you might think:

> "My colleague interrupted me again. We're supposed to be leading this effort together, and this is his way of showing he's the boss. He just makes me look bad in front of the team. I've been replaying it in my mind over and over again."

> "Someone has to tell my direct report that her bad attitude is affecting the rest of the team, but I'm

dreading it. I've been thinking about it all day and haven't been able to get anything done."

"I know what they're going to say—that we can't have more resources due to budget constraints. This gives me such a knot in my stomach. I'll probably just give up on asking for this investment."

"If I can just keep a smile on my face at the meeting, people will understand that I don't want to talk about the bugs that came up last week."

Conflict Seekers

Conversely, conflict seekers will seize on brewing disputes and amplify them, often strongly advocating for their perspective. They don't have patience when they think people aren't being direct or honest, and they're willing to ruffle a few feathers. The tendency to dive into conflict may feed upon itself because of a neurochemical process, as Judith E. Glaser, a communications expert, explains: "When you argue and win, your brain floods with different hormones—adrenaline and dopamine—which make you feel good, dominant, even invincible. It's a feeling any of us would want to replicate. So the next time we're in a tense situation, we fight again."

This attraction to conflict also takes a toll, but often on others. "Seekers are extremely good at fighting for their point of view (which may or may not be right), yet they are completely unaware of the dampening effect their behavior has on the people around them. If one person is getting high off his dominance, others are being drummed into submission," says Glaser.

Although it may not negatively affect them in the moment, their effectiveness as leaders and colleagues suffers. Though they "win" the argument, conflict seekers may earn the reputation of being difficult to work with, quick to snap, or even mean. People may avoid working with them or even describe them as bullies.

If you're a conflict seeker, here are some examples of how you might think:

> "I can tell that many of them don't agree that we need to go with this vendor. But I know this is the right choice, even if they don't realize it yet."

> "Why can't we get into this right now? Everyone should just lay out what they think the new strategy should be, and then we'll choose the best option. Why are we being so nice?"

> "I couldn't believe my direct report had the nerve to question the deadline I laid out for the team. I was sure to shut her down and copied the others so that they all know in the future not to cross that line."

> "Sal's recommendation on this hiring issue is just plain stupid. I owed it to him to tell him when he tried to get me on board with the new policy."

Identify Yourself

After reading the descriptions above, you may immediately recognize yourself as an avoider or a seeker. If it's not clear to you, taking the time to get to know yourself better is worthwhile. If a conflict erupts with your boss, you're not going to run home to take a personality test or soul search about your personal relationship to conflict. You won't have time for that. Knowing your preferred approach before you get into a heated debate can help you be better prepared for a discussion when the time comes.

To better understand what your natural tendency is, look at the many factors that contribute to your default approach:

- **Past experience:** "Our relationship to conflict is anchored in a history of habit," says Jen Su. If you were shamed or criticized during a conflict early in your career, you might choose safety and harmony over speaking up, she says. Or perhaps your first mentor enjoyed sparring with coworkers, demonstrating that there was nothing to fear. Maybe you're from a large family, who thrived on lively dinner table debates, so you frequently adopt the role of devil's advocate to spark heated team discussions.
- **Cultural norms:** Brett makes it clear: "You confront based on the norm in your culture." As discussed in the previous chapter, in East Asian cultures, for example, it's common to use an indirect approach. Others are typically more direct, such as Latin American cultures. This doesn't mean that every Chinese manager is a conflict avoider or that every Mexican manager is a conflict seeker; it's just another factor.

- **Office context:** Every workplace has its own set of norms, and some teams have their own separate set of rules as well. In some offices, it's frowned upon to disagree openly; you're expected to resolve disagreements in private meetings or through email. In other offices, it's common to have a more open airing of conflict.

- **Gender norms:** There's a stereotype that most women are conflict avoiders and most men are conflict seekers, which stems from the view that women are more nurturing and care more about what others think, say Amy Jen Su and her coauthor Muriel Maignan Wilkins in their book, *Own the Room: Discover Your Signature Voice to Master Your Leadership Presence.* But in practice this isn't necessarily true. Some women may opt to take less direct approaches to conflict because they know they will be penalized for being assertive. In fact, researchers at Harvard Business School and Babson College have shown that when women negotiate, people (both men and women) are less likely to want to work with them. So some women may lean toward being avoiders not because it's their natural tendency but because they know the social costs of being a conflict seeker are higher for them.

If you're still not sure which camp you fall into, here are several tips for unearthing your preference.

Develop healthy self-awareness

Ask yourself some of the following questions about your current and previous relationship with conflict.

- Were you always more of a fighter? Or did you tend to accommodate others?
- Look back over particular moments of conflict early in your life or career—were you rewarded or punished for your approach?
- When you think about conflict now, do you get a pit in your stomach and feel like fleeing?
- Or does your heart race and you feel the urge to jump in?
- The last time tensions got high with someone at work or at home, how did you react?
- When you were growing up, how was conflict handled in your family?
- Do you come from a culture where conflict is handled more directly or one where it's frowned upon?
- What is the norm in your organization? In your unit? On your team? Do you adopt the typical approach or play against type?

Look for patterns in your answers. Perhaps you had always been a seeker until you were criticized as being "too aggressive" in an early performance review. Or maybe you notice that you tend to avoid conflict unless the issue is something you really care about, such as your team. You may be able to understand your tendency just by answering these questions. But it's also helpful to get more input.

Ask for feedback

It's tough to see ourselves for who we really are, so ask others to reality check your observations. Get feedback from trusted colleagues, a caring mentor, or even your spouse. Inquire specifically about conflict situations: "Do you see me as someone who backs away from disagreement? Or do I enjoy digging into an argument?" Jen Su warns that conflict seekers need to say explicitly that they want genuine and honest input. "More-aggressive people tend not to get the tough feedback they need because their colleagues are often afraid of them and don't want to trigger them." It's important, therefore, to ask someone who you know will be candid with you, perhaps someone who has little to lose in telling you the truth.

Take an assessment

Many of the psychometric tests that people use in the workplace, such as Myers-Briggs Type Indicator (MBTI), help you better understand how you handle conflict. However, there's one tool that's focused specifically on understanding your conflict style: the Thomas-Kilmann Conflict Mode Instrument (TKI). The tool categorizes you as having one of five conflict-handling styles—avoiding, accommodating, compromising, collaborating, or competing—based on your answers to several questions. It's not time intensive (it usually takes about 15 minutes to complete), but there is a fee.

Reflecting on your approach is only half the battle; you also need to get a sense of how your counterpart prefers to approach disagreements before you can have a productive conflict.

SECTION TWO

Managing a Conflict

CHAPTER 4

Assess the Situation

When you're faced with a specific situation, there are five things to do to assess the scenario at hand before taking action—understand your counterpart; identify the type of conflict you're facing; consider the organizational context; determine your goal; and, finally, pick one of the four options you'll take to deal with this particular situation.

The first time you analyze a conflict using these five steps it will take some time, but eventually the analysis will get easier. The goal is to be able to quickly do these steps in your head whenever a disagreement arises.

Understand Your Counterpart

First, consider whom you're dealing with. Is he a conflict seeker or avoider? How does he typically communicate and how does he prefer to be communicated with? Is he more of a straight shooter who says things like they are or does he tend to beat around the bush? If you frequently work with the person you're in conflict with, you may already be familiar with his style. If you rarely interact with the person, you'll have to do some digging. "More and more we're working with people whom we don't have the luxury of getting that kind of intelligence on," says Amy Jen Su. It may be that you're fighting with an overseas colleague whom you see in person only at annual meetings, or your conflict is with a manager in a different department who sits in another building. "It's better to know something about the person rather than fighting in a vacuum," Jen Su says. She suggests that you get whatever information is available. Here's how.

Look for patterns

Whether or not you know your counterpart well, play the role of observer. How does she handle a tense discussion in a meeting? What's the look on her face when other people are disagreeing? Does she like people to cut to the chase and lay out just the facts or does she want the complete picture with every gory detail? What have you observed about her communication style? Look for patterns in how she communicates and clues in her behavior. "People who are volatile and confrontational, for example, tend to be that way in a lot of different situations," says Brett. Ideally you'll observe the person over time in multiple scenarios. That may not be possible, so take what you can get. Just keep in mind that the fewer instances you see, the less likely you'll be able to deduce an accurate pattern.

Get input from others

In addition to examining your counterpart's behavior, you might ask a colleague or two for input. Don't go around grilling others about him, but ask people to confirm or deny your observations. Say something like, "I noticed Jim flew off the handle in that meeting. Is that typical?" or "I saw Katerina avoid engaging with Tomas when he questioned whether her figures were right. Did you see the same thing?" You can also ask more direct questions: "Can you tell me how this person typically navigates conflict?" Obviously, you have to trust the person you're asking—you don't want your colleague to find out you're snooping on him.

Use this same approach to figure out cultural and office norms. If you're dealing with a vendor based in a different country, for example, or a colleague who's located halfway around the world, ask someone who knows that person or is familiar with the culture or office environment how conflict is typically handled. Erin Meyer suggests saying something along these lines: "Here's how I would deal with this in my culture. How would you typically approach it?" She also recommends that you seek out "cultural bridges," people who work in your culture and in your counterpart's. These are often ex-pats who've relocated to another office or people based out of headquarters who have to work across multiple locations.

Ask directly

It's not always advisable to come out and ask: "How do you like to address conflict?" That can be awkward—few people will be prepared to answer this question. Instead, share your own preferences as a way to start the conversation: "You might have noticed that I am more of a conflict seeker. I don't shy away from arguments, and I tend to get worked up quickly." You could also share tactful observations about what you've noticed about your counterpart. "Based on how you responded to Corinne's questioning in this morning's meeting, it seems as if you prefer to steer away from conflict. Is that right?"

You're trying to learn what someone's style is, not judge it. Instead of saying "We've got a problem here because it seems as if you don't know how to discuss conflict," you might ask, "What do you do in your culture when people disagree?" It's better to ask questions than make statements, and use phrases that ask for confirmation, such as "Correct me if I'm wrong . . ." or "Do I have this right?" Meyer points out that there's nothing wrong with showing curiosity. "People always like to be asked about themselves," she says.

Once you learn more about the culture, use that knowledge to help you understand your situation better. Why did he speak to me like that? What did he mean? "If you're dealing with someone from the Netherlands and he speaks to you in a really direct way," says Meyer, "you can interpret that behavior differently than if someone from China was short with you." Was the person really being rude? Was he intentionally being vague and trying to hide something? Or is there a cultural reason for him to speak or behave like that?

If you come up empty-handed

If your digging doesn't turn up adequate information, all is not lost. Although it helps, having this information is not a prerequisite to a productive conversation. Instead, prepare by playing out a few scenarios. What if she's a conflict seeker and gets mad at me? What if he yells? What if she's an avoider and gets upset? Or tries to leave the room?

You may even want to role-play with another coworker. If you do, Jen Su suggests you play your counterpart and your coworker acts as you. That will help you take your counterpart's perspective and ask yourself, How would I want that person to interact with me? This will also allow you to better understand how your counterpart sees you.

How Your Styles Work Together

Now that you have a sense of your approach to conflict and have gleaned some insights into your counterpart's preferences, how will your styles interact? If you're both seekers, can you expect an all-out brawl? If you're both avoiders, should you forget the idea of directly addressing the conflict? See table 4-1 to get a sense of what typically happens between each of the types and how you might manage it.

Identify the Type of Conflict

Next, think about what's causing the conflict. Review the four types of conflict I identified in chapter 1, "Types

TABLE 4-1

How conflict approaches work together

	You are an *avoider*	You are a *seeker*
Your counterpart is an *avoider*	**What happens:** • Both of you lean toward doing nothing. • You may tamp down feelings that could explode later on. **How to manage:** • One of you needs to take the lead. • Say directly, "I know we both don't like conflict, but instead of doing nothing, should we consider other options?" • Do your best to draw the person out in a sensitive, thoughtful way. • If things get tough, don't shy away. Fight your natural instinct.	**What happens:** • You tend to bulldoze your counterpart into agreeing with you. • Your counterpart may act passive-aggressively to get his point across. **How to manage:** • Ask the person to participate actively in the conversation—not hide her opinions. • Don't be a bully. • Be patient with the pacing of the conversation.
Your counterpart is a *seeker*	**What happens:** • You are tempted to play the role of "good guy" and go along with what your counterpart wants. • You might get trampled by your counterpart's requests. **How to manage:** • Explicitly ask for what you need: "To have a productive conversation, I need you to be patient with me and watch the tone and volume of your voice." • Earn the seeker's respect by being direct and to the point. • Don't signal disrespect, which is likely to set the seeker off.	**What happens:** • Neither of you is afraid to say what's on your mind. • The discussion turns contentious. • You might end up saying things you don't believe. • You both feel disrespected. **How to manage:** • Since you'll both be eager to address the situation, take extra time to prepare for the conversation. • Know that you're likely to feel impatient and schedule your discussion in a way that allows you both to take breaks. • Be ready—things may get heated. Suggest a coffee break or a walk or a change of scenery to help even out emotions.

Source: Adapted from an interview with Amy Jen Su, coauthor with Muriel Maignan Wilkins of *Own the Room: Discover Your Signature Voice to Master Your Leadership Presence* (Boston: Harvard Business Review Press, 2013).

of Conflict," and suss out whether your disagreement is over issues related to relationship, task, process, or status (see table 1-1).

Go over what's happened so far with your counterpart—what she's said and done, who else has been involved, where the disagreement started, and what it's related to. With all that information, ask yourself: Are we disagreeing about the goal of a project, or how to achieve it? Does my counterpart think she should be leading the initiative? Have we exchanged barbs? Or all of the above?

Rarely do conflicts fall into just one of these categories, so try to identify each type of conflict that's occurring. Doing this helps you to:

- **Organize your own thoughts.** In the midst of a conflict, rational thinking often goes out the window. Considering what type of conflict you're having will help you set aside your emotional reactions and structure your thinking. If you decide to directly address the situation, parsing the conflict into categories will set you up for a successful conversation (see chapter 5, "Get Ready for the Conversation").

- **Identify common ground.** By labeling your differences of opinion, you'll also see where you and your counterpart concur. If you disagree on how exactly to compensate a customer who received bad service (process), you may note that you agree on the need to make the customer happy (task).

This shared goal becomes a foundation for reaching a resolution (see chapter 6, "Have a Productive Conversation").

- **Structure the conversation.** Before you begin your discussion with your counterpart, create a list of the types of conflict you're experiencing and the specific issues you disagree on. This will help guide your conversation and keep you focused on the issue at hand.

Be particularly careful when labeling a disagreement a "relationship conflict." Many disagreements do end up here, but personalities are not always to blame, says Ben Dattner, author of *The Blame Game: How the Hidden Rules of Credit and Blame Determine Our Success or Failure*. "More often than not, the real underlying cause of workplace strife is the situation itself rather than the people involved." What people *think* they're fighting about isn't actually what they *are* fighting about. For example, they might perceive the root cause of the struggle to be a personality clash when in fact it's a process conflict.

Dattner explains: "Perhaps the conflict is due to someone on the team simply not doing her job, in which case talking about personality as being the cause of conflict is a dangerous distraction from the real issue . . . Focusing too much on either hypothetical or irrelevant causes of conflict may work in the short term, but it creates the risk over the long term that the underlying causes will never be addressed or fixed."

Determine Your Goal

Before you decide which approach to take, determine what you hope to accomplish. Keeping in mind the personalities of the people involved, their communication styles, and the type of conflict you're having, reflect on your ultimate goal: Do you want to complete the project quickly? To deliver the best results you can? Does your relationship with this person matter more than the outcome of the work? Figure out what you need to get done. If you're under pressure to complete a presentation by a certain date and your counterpart in sales is complaining about how much data you need from him, you might consider doing nothing so that you can get the numbers you need and hit your deadline. Later you could explain to the sales guy how his griping impacted you and ask what would work better for him for future requests.

If you're having more than one type of conflict, you might set more than one goal. For example, if you're fighting with your conflict-seeking boss about which metrics to report to the senior leadership team (task conflict) and you and your boss have exchanged heated emails that challenge each other's understanding of web analytics (relationship conflict), your goal may be to come up with a set of stats that you can both live with *and* to make sure that your boss understands that you respect her and her expertise.

Make sure your goal is reasonable, suggests IMD's Jean-François Manzoni, who has conducted extensive research on conflict management. Ask yourself: Does what I want make sense? Is it realistic? If not, set your sights a little lower. Come up with a small, manageable goal, such as "agreeing on which of us will own the redesign project" or "creating a six-week plan for how our team will collaborate." If you're disagreeing over how to proceed on an important project, your goal might be to end the conversation by simply agreeing on the next step rather than cementing a full implementation plan.

It's not uncommon, particularly with relationship conflict, to want to set a goal that's about changing the other person. Perhaps you'd like to show your colleague that her passive-aggressive behavior doesn't work or make sure your boss knows what a jerk he's been for the past week. But these kinds of agendas are better dropped before they lead to full-on fights.

"It's easy to become aggravated by other people's actions and forget what you were trying to achieve in the first place," says Jeffrey Pfeffer, of Stanford's Graduate School of Business. But it's not likely you're going to change the other person, so focus on your goal. If the conflict were over and you found that you had won, what would that look like?

Pick Your Option

Now it's time to decide what to do. Taking into account your goal, and the other person's natural tendency and communication style, which of the four options discussed in chapter 2 is best for handling the specific situation you're in (see table 4-2)?

There is no magic formula that tells you which approach to take. It's not like two conflict seekers having a

TABLE 4-2

The four options for addressing conflict

The option	What it is	Use it when . . .
Do nothing	Ignoring and swallowing the conflict	• You don't have the energy or time. • You suspect the other person is unwilling to have a constructive conversation. • You have little or no power. • You won't beat yourself up or stew about it.
Address indirectly	Skirting the issue instead of naming it	• It's important in your culture to save face. • You work in a place where direct confrontation is inappropriate. • You think the other person will be more willing to take feedback from someone else.
Address directly	Actively trying to change the situation by talking to the other person	• You worry that there will be lingering resentment if you don't clear the air. • You've tried other options and the problem persists. • You want to get your relationship with your counterpart back on track.
Exit	Getting out of the situation entirely by being reassigned to another project, finding a new boss, or leaving the company	• You're dealing with someone from another department or outside your company where your jobs aren't interdependent. • You can easily find a job somewhere else. • You've tried other options and nothing has worked.

relationship conflict who want to restore a friendly rapport should always use the "address directly" approach. The reality is that the option you choose depends on all of the above factors as well as other circumstances, such as your office norms or the amount of time pressure you're under. Play out each option in your head and assess the pros and cons for your specific situation. If you do nothing, will you be able to let go of the conflict? If you directly confront, will your counterpart be able to engage constructively? There is no one right answer; there's just the one that's right for you and the circumstances you're in. (See also the sidebar "Know When to Walk Away.")

Be mindful of your natural tendency

Because the conflict may have triggered a fight-or-flight response in your brain, your immediate response—"We need to address this right away" or "I'm going to find a new job"—may not be the best one. Conflict avoiders often gravitate toward the first two options (doing nothing or addressing the conflict indirectly), while seekers prefer the latter two (addressing directly or exiting). Keep this in mind when you're choosing your option. Ask yourself whether you're doing what's best for the situation—and will most likely help you achieve your goal—or if you're opting for an approach that's most comfortable for you.

Cool down before deciding

Brett says that it's wise to take a breather before choosing an approach. "Weighing whether to bring up and try to resolve a conflict should be a rational decision. The first question to ask yourself: Am I too emotional right now?" she says. If so, take a step back from the conflict. Return to your desk and take a few deep breaths. Go for a walk outside. Or sleep on it. You want to be sure whatever route you choose is based on a lucid decision, not a rash one.

KNOW WHEN TO WALK AWAY

It's not an easy decision to walk away from a conflict—temporarily or permanently. But it's important to recognize when the situation calls for it. "If you're angry or upset—or your colleague is—it's not a good time to engage. It won't help if either of you is yelling or pounding the table," says Jeanne Brett. She explains that there's a lot of research that shows people are unable to be rational when their emotions are high (see more on managing your emotions in chapter 6).

Judith White, a leadership professor at the Tuck School of Business at Dartmouth, says there are several signs that you need to walk away—at least temporarily:

- Your counterpart is yelling or is otherwise out of control.
- You feel as if you're going to lose control in any way that might be dangerous to you, your counterpart, or your relationship.
- The fight is happening in a public setting where others can see or hear you.
- It becomes obvious that the discussion can't be resolved through the current conversation. You or your counterpart repeating the same argument over and over is the telltale sign here.
- Your colleague has never demonstrated a willingness to concede.

(*continued*)

KNOW WHEN TO WALK AWAY

(*continued*)

- The damage is already done. For example, maybe the project you're fighting over ended last week and the decision can't be reversed.

Once you've made the tough decision to walk away, how do you actually do it? Here are some tips:

- If the situation feels overly heated or dangerous, simply walk away. Leave the room, go to the bathroom, or take a walk outside the building.
- If you can, explain that you need some time to think through the conflict before coming back to it. "Don't ever tell someone he or she needs to calm down, because the person will lose face or only become more upset," advises White. (For more sample language examples, see chapter 2, "Your Options for Handling Conflict.")
- Take the time you need to cool down (or let your counterpart cool down). When you feel ready to make a smart and thoughtful choice about how to address the conflict, you can return to it.

Here's an example. Jonathan was meeting with his project manager, Rebecca, about why they were falling behind in their deadlines. As a conflict seeker, he was asking pointed questions to get at the root of what was behind the delays. Rebecca was getting more and more agitated as Jonathan went line by line through the plan. Soon Rebecca snapped. She stood up and pointed her finger at Jonathan, accusing him of badgering her. "This is your fault, not mine," she said. Jonathan quickly apologized for pushing so hard, but Rebecca wouldn't hear it. She yelled, "I don't need your apologies. I need you to stop %^@# harassing me." Jonathan realized he was stuck. Rebecca had lost control, and he didn't feel like anything he said would help. He stood up and said, "I'm sorry that this conversation has taken this turn. I'm going to go back to my desk to think through how we might resolve this. It'd be great if we could regroup tomorrow." Rebecca sent him an apology later that night, and when they had both calmed down the next day, they were able to have a more rational conversation about how to get the project back on track.

Sometimes delaying a tense conversation by a day helps, as it did with Rebecca and Jonathan. But sometimes, a day is not enough. You may be faced with a situation in which you decide to permanently walk away—by either doing nothing or exiting the relationship entirely. Whether or not you do this, says White, depends on two questions: How important is this relationship? How potentially valuable is this deal? As

(*continued*)

KNOW WHEN TO WALK AWAY

(*continued*)

Deepak Malhotra and Max H. Bazerman point out in *Negotiation Genius: How to Overcome Obstacles and Achieve Brilliant Results at the Bargaining Table and Beyond*, you shouldn't negotiate when the costs of negotiation exceed the potential gains.

Exiting the relationship is particularly advisable when the situation is causing you extreme discomfort—your health is suffering, for example. If you can't concentrate on anything else or are having panic attacks, there's no sense enduring more torture. Also, if your counterpart is singling you out and trying to prevent you from doing your job, it's time to take extreme measures. Speak to someone else, such as your boss or an HR representative, to see what support is available to you.

In a highly emotional conflict—in which one or both parties are extremely angry or upset—it can be tempting to exercise the exit option. But even situations in which feelings are running high can benefit from you opting to address it, or even doing nothing. Judith White says: "It's natural for people to feel strong emotion in a conflict situation. Once the conflict is identified and addressed, and parties are allowed to vent, emotion usually dissipates . . . Recognize the emotion, but don't let it stop you from negotiating."

Adapt Your Approach

Managing conflict is a fluid process. You may start with one approach and then find you need to switch to another if your selected approach is no longer working or the conflict grows or changes. For example, you may decide to directly address the situation by talking with your colleague about why you're disagreeing over the targets each of your teams should be hitting, but then find that you're getting nowhere: Your coworker is unresponsive or, worse, frustrated that you don't agree with her and just gets angrier. Then you may decide to do nothing and move on. You could also start with the do-nothing option and realize that the problem is getting worse, so you need to address it directly, by talking with your colleague, or indirectly, by going to your boss. As you weigh the options for your specific situation, you don't have to make a choice and stick to it no matter what. You can always change tactics as your conflict plays out.

Consider this example. Amara and Vivek work closely in a small design group. Amara has to complete her initial designs before Vivek can take over the presentations and do the formatting that is his responsibility. In a team meeting, Vivek made an offhand comment about Amara "taking her time" with the latest batch of presentations. Amara thought about the statement, and even talked about it with another colleague, and she concluded that it could be interpreted in several ways, but the implication was that Amara's speed was impacting Vivek's work. Amara tends to avoid conflict, so she didn't like the idea of bringing it up with Vivek. Plus they had worked well together for so long. She didn't see the point.

She thought she could let it go. And for a few weeks, she did. But soon she realized that it was still bothering her. Every time she handed something off to Vivek, she mentally replayed his saying "She's taking her time," so she decided to address the situation directly. She scheduled an appointment with Vivek to ask what he had meant and to find a way to move forward.

The fluidity of the process can work the other way, too. Take Marie's story. She called one of her long-time vendors to directly address and explain that her company's payment terms had changed. In the middle of the conversation, Claude, the finance manager at the vendor, hung up on her. She emailed him and said that she'd like to set up a time to talk. But when they got on the phone again, Claude wouldn't say anything other than "This doesn't work for us." Marie was offended and frustrated. Recognizing that the direct approach wasn't working, she decided to go to Claude's boss and appeal to him. She didn't want to get Claude in trouble, but they clearly weren't able to resolve the conflict on their own. Soon after she spoke with Claude's manager and explained the situation, Claude called her and offered to negotiate the terms.

The next two chapters talk about preparing for and conducting a conversation if you've decided to address the conflict directly. Even if you've chosen one of the other options, your approach may change, so it's best to be prepared.

CHAPTER 5

Get Ready for the Conversation

Once you've resolved to directly address the conflict, it's tempting to have the conversation immediately. But taking time to prepare will help you remain calm and increase the chances that you and your counterpart will come away with a better solution than either of you could have predicted.

Below are several guidelines to help you prepare for a productive discussion.

Check Your Mindset

If you're getting yourself ready for a conversation that you've labeled "difficult," you're more likely to feel nervous, stressed, angry, or upset. To minimize those negative emotions, try to think about it as a non-charged conversation, suggests Jean-François Manzoni. For example, instead of giving negative feedback, you're having a constructive conversation about development. Or you're not saying "no" to your boss; you're offering up an alternative solution.

"A difficult conversation tends to go best when you think about it as just a normal conversation," says Holly Weeks, a communications expert. This isn't sugarcoating. Be honest with yourself about how hard the conversation might be, but also put as constructive a frame on it as possible. You might tell yourself: We may have to talk about difficult things, but we'll work through them together because Carol and I have always respected each other.

And focus on what you stand to gain from the conversation. "Assume you have something to learn; assume there is a more creative solution than you've thought of," says Jeff Weiss, author of the *HBR Guide to Negotiating*. By entering the discussion with an open mind, regardless of your coworker's stance, you're more likely to find common ground.

Take Your Counterpart's Perspective

Try to get a sense of what your colleague might be thinking. Ideally you already did some thinking about this when you analyzed the conflict, but go a little deeper. She had a rationale for the way she's behaved so far (even if you don't agree with it). What might that reason be? "Try to imagine your way into their shoes as best you can. You can learn a lot by doing that simple mental exercise," says Jonathan Hughes. Think about what's going on for them. Ask yourself: What would I do if I were her, or if I were in R&D instead of marketing? What if I were someone reporting to me? What if I were my boss? Also ask yourself: What is she trying to achieve in the conflict? You'll need a sense of what her goal is if you want to resolve it. Identify places where you see eye to eye on the issues. This common ground will give you a foundation to joint problem-solve.

Ask a colleague what he thinks is going on in your counterpart's mind. Make sure it's someone you trust, says Hughes. You might say something like, "I'd love some advice and coaching. I haven't worked much with Akiko before, but I know you have. Can you help me understand how she might be seeing this situation?" Don't use the conversation to vent and seek validation. "Paint the situation for him as neutrally as you can," says Karen Dillon, author of the *HBR Guide to Office Politics*. "Cataloging every fault and misstep will probably get you sympathy but not constructive feedback, so focus on the problem."

It's unlikely that you'll be able to gather all the information you want about your colleague and her interests before you sit down together. Weiss says, "Craft a set of questions to ask in the room to uncover critical information and test any hypotheses you made." This will help you, once you're face-to-face, to show that you care enough about her perspective to think it through beforehand and to discover more about how she views the situation.

In addition to thinking about your counterpart's take on the situation, remember the work you did in the previous chapter to consider his natural tendency for handling conflict and his communication style.

Consider the Larger Organizational Context

While the conflict may revolve around you and your counterpart, the reality is that you're both part of a broader context—that of your organization or your industry. Consider how the larger playing field you're operating in might be affecting the conflict.

First, determine the culture of your organization or team. Do people in your unit generally try to avoid conflict? Or is it acceptable to have heated debates? Are you at odds with an external vendor and feeling less invested in working things out because you have several other partners who are courting your business? How might the larger culture be shaping the current conflict you're having? Is it making it worse than it needs to be?

Hughes points out that quite a few years ago Microsoft had a reputation for having an aggressive culture. "During your first few presentations their people would just tear into you. The culture was one that valued conflict. 'We're going to use rigorous, fiery debate to separate good from bad ideas,'" he says. In a company like this, which places a premium on being direct, you'd need to be prepared for a lively debate and know not to take criticism personally. On the other hand, there are companies where consensus is the norm. "In these places, you're going to take a slower, more iterative approach to conflict," says Hughes.

Second, reflect on the current circumstances surrounding your organization. Are there potential layoffs looming? Have budgets been cut? Is your industry on a downward trend? Your conflict may be intensified when tensions are high in the company, or it might take on a more severe or vicious tone. The answers to these questions may not change the approach you choose, but you should consider them as you get ready for the discussion. Also find out who else in the organization can help you both reach a resolution. Are there colleagues who need to be involved in the discussions? Should you consult your boss or HR?

Plan Your Message

Think about what you'll say when you get in the room *before* you get in the room, incorporating your goal and your colleague's perspective, interests, and style. What do you want your counterpart to take away from the conversation? "You'll have a better chance of being heard if you define your message and decide how you'll convey it," says Dillon. Plan how you'll approach the conversation—literally what you will and won't say. "View it as a presentation," suggests Dillon. "What information does your counterpart need to hear? Identify the key points you'd like to make, highlighting mutual benefits when possible." When you frame the conversation as trying to achieve a shared goal—such as meeting a deadline, coming in under budget, or having a positive work relationship—the conversation will go better.

But don't script the entire conversation. That's a waste of time. "It's very unlikely that it will go according to your plan," says Weeks. Your counterpart doesn't know "his lines," so when he "goes off script, you have no forward motion" and the exchange "becomes weirdly artificial." Your strategy for the conversation should be "flexible" and contain "a repertoire of possible responses," says Weeks. Jot down notes and key points before your conversation. Even with thoughtful planning, it's not uncommon for there to be misalignment between what you mean when you say something (your intention) and what the other person hears (your impact). "It doesn't matter if your intent is honorable if your impact is not," says Linda Hill, a leadership professor at Harvard Business School. Most people are very aware of what they meant to say but are less tuned in to what the other person heard or how they interpreted it. So choose your words wisely, and try to anticipate and address anything that might be misinterpreted (see chapter 6, "Have a Productive Conversation," for more discussion tips).

Prepare for Multiple Scenarios

Since you can't know how the conversation is going to go, you may want to play out a few scenarios, suggests Amy Jen Su. Find a trusted colleague with whom you can do a few role-plays. What if your counterpart gets upset and cries? What if she gets angry? Try responding using different approaches and test out phrases you might use for various possibilities. And ask your role-play partner to give you feedback.

Pick the Right Time

Knowing exactly when to have the conversation can be challenging. On the one hand, it might be easiest to get it over with quickly, when all the details are fresh in your mind. On the other hand, as discussed in the previous chapter, it's often a good idea for everyone to cool down before trying to get into problem-solving mode. Here are some tips on picking the right time:

- **Consider your tendency.** Check yourself before you decide to delay or get into the conversation. If you're a seeker, you're likely to want to get going and have the conversation. But if your counterpart is an avoider, he may need more time. And if you're an avoider, you may want to put the conversation off, but watch that you're not using that tactic as an "out" so that you don't have to face the issue at all.

- **Take into account any outside deadlines.** Sometimes you don't have the luxury of several days or weeks to work out your disagreement. If the budget you're fighting over is due to the executive committee by the end of the month and it's the 28th, you need to have the conversation sooner rather than later.

- **Check the emotions.** As discussed in the previous chapter, it's better to have the conversation when you and your counterpart can be levelheaded. Ask yourself: Am I too emotional right now? If so, you may say the wrong thing, embarrass yourself or your colleague, or create awkward scenes for others. In those instances, take a walk around the building, or change your surroundings by working in a small conference room or heading home to work in peace.

"Occasionally, you need to let it go and come back to it another time when you can both have the conversation," says Hill. It's OK to walk away and return to the discussion later. But if you decide to put off the conversation, make a plan for when you will have it so that you don't keep delaying it.

When you're ready, set up a meeting. Look for a time when you'll both be in a good frame of mind. "Not first thing on Monday when you're both coming in to a full inbox. Not last thing on Friday when you're eager for the weekend to begin," says Dillon. Be sure to schedule enough time so that you'll be able to reach a conclusion, or at least end in a constructive place where you can agree to meet again. In fact, you may want to have an initial meeting to hear each other out and then schedule a follow-up time when you can dig in to how to solve the disagreement after you've both had time to reflect on what the other person said.

Choose the Right Place

The venue will have an effect on whether you both feel able to speak freely, express any emotions, and ultimately reach a resolution, so select a location where you'll both be comfortable. "Right after lunch in a neutral conference room? Over coffee at the local greasy spoon?" suggests Dillon. You might take a walk outside together for a change of scenery. Avoid choosing a place that gives you or your counterpart an advantage. Inviting someone into your office puts you in a power position, for example, because it's your space and you're the one sitting behind a desk. And when choosing a conference room, think about who's in adjacent rooms. Sometimes walls are thinner than you think.

Ideally you want the conversation to happen face-to-face in private. "Don't try to solve differences using email, which does not do a good job of conveying tone or nuance," says Dillon. If the issue starts on email, send a gentle request such as "Could we continue this discussion in person?" or just call the person.

If you have a conflict with one person during a meeting, don't attempt to work it out in front of the group, even if others in the room have a stake in the outcome. It's better to take the conversation off-line and then report back to the group. For example, if you and a colleague start to debate the specific marketing language that will accompany the rollout of a new product and the conversation gets heated, you might say, "Tom and I seem to have the strongest viewpoints on this. Would it be OK with you, Tom, if we paused here and continued the discussion after the meeting? Then we can come back to the group with our recommendation." This will give you and Tom time to cool down, make sure you don't embarrass yourselves in front of everyone, and allow you to have a more candid and fruitful discussion later.

Vent

Before you get into the room, find a trusted colleague or a spouse or friend who can listen to you complain. Say everything you feel about the situation—the good, the bad, and the ugly. Don't hold back. Susan David, a psychologist and coauthor of the *Harvard Business Review* article "Emotional Agility," says that "suppressing your emotions—deciding not to say something when you're upset—can lead to bad results." She explains that if you don't express your emotions, they're likely to show up elsewhere.

Psychologists call this *emotional leakage*. "Have you ever yelled at your spouse or child after a frustrating day at work—a frustration that had nothing to do with him or her? When you bottle up your feelings, you're likely to express your emotions in unintended ways instead, either sarcastically or in a completely different context. Suppressing your emotions is associated with poor memory, difficulties in relationships, and physiological costs (such as cardiovascular health problems)," David explains. Prevent your emotions from seeping out—in the conversation or at home—by getting your feelings out ahead of time. You'll be more centered and calm when you're having the discussion.

Table 5-1 summarizes the guidelines. Use this checklist to prepare mentally, strategically, and logistically for your discussion.

When You Have No Time to Prepare

Sometimes there's no time to do this advance work. A decision needs to be made immediately, or your colleague catches you off guard, or your boss storms into

TABLE 5-1

Your pre-conversation checklist

MENTALLY		
	Do	**Don't**
☐ CHECK YOUR MINDSET Be positive, but also honest with yourself about how difficult the conversation may be. ☐ CONSIDER THE OTHER POSITIONS Look at the situation from your counterpart's perspective: What does she want? ☐ VENT Get your emotions out beforehand so you can be calm during the conversation.	• Focus on what you stand to gain from the discussion and assume you have something to learn. • Ask a trusted coworker for input if you're at a loss about what your counterpart is thinking. • Identify places where you see eye to eye. • Get your feelings out ahead of time so you'll be more centered and calm. • Come up with a list of questions you want to ask when you sit down together.	• Label the conversation as "difficult." • Sugarcoat what's going to happen. • Assume you can know everything your counterpart is thinking ahead of time. • Vent to a friend who typically riles you up.

STRATEGICALLY		
	Do	**Don't**
☐ PLAN YOUR MESSAGE Think about what you'll say ahead of time. ☐ PREPARE FOR MULTIPLE SCENARIOS Play out various ways the conversation might go.	• Plan how you'll approach the conversation—literally what you will and won't say. • Focus on a shared goal. • Find a trusted colleague with whom you can do a few role-plays. • Test out phrases you might say.	• Script the entire conversation—just jot down notes and key points. • Assume you know how the conversation is going to go.

(*continued*)

TABLE 5-1 (continued)

LOGISTICALLY	Do	Don't
☐ PICK THE RIGHT TIME Choose a time when you and your counterpart can be unrushed and calm. ☐ SELECT THE RIGHT PLACE Look for somewhere you can meet in private.	• Pick a time when you and your counterpart won't be rushed. • Consider an initial meeting to hear each other out, and then schedule a follow-up time when you can focus on problem-solving. • Talk in person, or at least on the phone. • Try a change of scenery—going to a coffee shop or taking a walk.	• Have the conversation over email • Try to talk to your colleague when emotions are high. • Have a fight in a group setting (such as in a team meeting). • Choose a "turf" setting where you or your counterpart has a power advantage.

your office. Jeanne Brett suggests you try to put off the conversation if at all feasible. You might say, "I see that this is a problem, and I'd like to take some time to think about ways to resolve it. I promise I'll come by your office tomorrow to discuss it." It's important to not be dismissive and to acknowledge your colleague's feelings—"I can see you're really upset about this"—and then ask whether you can set a time to talk when you're both calmer. If your counterpart insists that you have the discussion right then, you might have to go ahead. "The best you can do in these situations is to remain calm and stop yourself from getting into a negative emotional spiral," says Brett. (See chapter 6 for more on how to maintain your composure and manage your emotions.)

You may be wondering, Do I really need to do all of this for one 10-minute conversation? The answer is yes. While it takes time (though it will get easier the more you do it), there is a huge payoff. You'll go into the conversation with the right mindset, feeling confident, knowing what you want to achieve. This foundation is the key to a productive discussion.

CHAPTER 6

Have a Productive Conversation

You're now ready to have a constructive discussion. Your goal is to work with your counterpart to better understand "the underlying causes of the problem and what you can do to solve it together," says Jeanne Brett.

First, frame the discussion so that you and your counterpart start off on the right foot. Then there are three things you'll do simultaneously as the conversation flows: Manage your emotions, listen well, and be heard.

When you sit down with your counterpart, don't be overly wedded to the information you've gathered in advance. Be flexible. "You don't want to be so prepared that you anticipate a particular reaction and you're not able to take in what's actually happening," says Amy Jen Su. If you see the behavior you expected, then label it (in your head) and continue to observe. But allow yourself to be surprised, too. The same goes for cultural norms.

"Knowing something about your colleague's culture gives you hypotheses to test. But just because you have an East Asian at the table doesn't mean he will be indirect," says Brett.

Frame the Conversation

Your first few sentences can make or break the rest of the discussion. Set the conversation up for success by establishing common ground between you and your counterpart, labeling the type of conflict you're having, asking your counterpart for advice, laying out ground rules, and focusing on the future. Here's more on how to do that.

Focus on common ground

"Too often we end up framing a conflict as who's right or who's wrong," Linda Hill says. Instead of trying to understand what's really happening in a disagreement, we advocate for our position. Hill admits that it's normal to be defensive and even to blame the other person, but implying "You're wrong" will make matters worse. Instead, state what you agree on. In chapter 4, when you identified the type of conflict you're having, you noted where there was common ground, and in chapter 5, you identified where your goals might overlap. Put those commonalities out there as a way to connect. "We both want to make sure our patients get the best care possible" or "We agree that the new email system should integrate with our existing IT systems" or "We both want our department to get adequate funding."

If you weren't able to pinpoint something that you both agreed on beforehand or you're not sure you know what your counterpart's goal is, the easiest way to find out is to ask, says Jonathan Hughes, "although sometimes people need help crystallizing their goals." Explain what's important to you and then ask, "Is there any overlap with what you care about? Or do you have another goal?" Asking questions like these sets a collaborative tone.

Label the type of conflict

Acknowledge the type of conflict you're having—relationship, task, process, or status—and check with your counterpart that he sees it the same way. "It seems as if the crux of our disagreement is about where to launch the product first. Do you agree?" You may also want to reassure him that you value your relationship. This will convey to him that your point of contention is not a personal one. Say something like, "I really respect you and how you run your department. This is not about our relationship, but about how our two teams will work together on this project."

If your conflict covers several different types, as many do, name each one in turn so that they're all out on the table. Hughes suggests you say something along these lines: *It feels like we agree on the same goal here—to bring in revenue from this new product as soon as possible.* [Establishing common ground on task] *Our conflict seems to be more about how we do it—the timing of how quickly we roll out this product and whether we roll it out in target markets first.* [Labeling the process conflict] *In addition to that disagreement over the means, it seems—and I could be wrong about this—you feel some frustration with me about how I've approached this.* [Naming the relationship conflict] *I want to put that all on the table because success is going to depend on us working together.*

Ask for advice

Research by Katie Liljenquist at Brigham Young University's Department of Organizational Leadership and Strategy and Adam Galinsky, the chair of the Management Department at the Columbia Business School, has shown that asking for advice makes you appear more warm, humble, and cooperative—all of which can go a long way in resolving a conflict. "Being asked for advice is inherently flattering because it's an implicit endorsement of our opinions, values, and expertise. Furthermore, it works equally well up and down the hierarchy—subordinates are delighted and empowered by requests for their insights, and superiors appreciate the deference to their authority and experience," say Liljenquist and Galinsky. Of course, any goodwill garnered by this tactic will swiftly be undone if you ignore your counterpart's suggestions. Incorporate at least some small part of what she advises into your approach.

There are two other benefits to framing a conflict as a request for advice, according to Liljenquist and Galinsky. First, you nudge your counterpart to see things from your perspective. "The last time someone came to you for advice, most likely, you engaged in an instinctive mental exercise: You tried to put yourself in the other person's shoes and imagine the world through his eyes," they explain. The second benefit is that an adversary-turned-advisor may well become a champion for your cause. "When someone offers you advice, it represents an investment of his time and energy. Your request empowers your advisor to make good on his recommendations and become an advocate," they say.

Set up ground rules

The conversation will go more smoothly if you agree on a code of conduct. At a minimum, suggest no interrupting, no yelling, and no personal attacks. This is especially important for conflict seekers, who may see no problem in raising their voices. Acknowledge that you both may need to take a break at some point. Then ask what other rules are important to your counterpart. If you're concerned your colleague won't abide by the rules, write them down on a piece of paper to keep in front of you or on a whiteboard if you're in a conference room. If your counterpart begins to raise his voice, for example, you can nod toward the written rules and offer a gentle reminder. "We said we weren't going to yell. Can you lower your voice?" These rules may also be helpful if you need to change the tone of the conversation later on (see "Change the tenor of the conversation" later in the chapter).

Focus on the future

It's tempting to rehash everything that's happened up to this point. But it's generally not helpful to go over every detail or to focus too heavily on the past. "You can't resolve a battle over a problem that has already happened, but you can set a course going forward," says Judith White. Focus the discussion on solving the problem and moving on. You can start by saying "I know a lot has gone on between us. If it's OK with you, I'd like to talk about what we both might do to make sure this project gets completed on budget and how we can better work together in the future." If your counterpart starts to harp on the past, don't chastise her for it. Instead, refocus the conversation by saying something like "I hear you. How can we make sure that doesn't happen again?"

Each of these steps will establish the right tone for your conversation: that you and your counterpart are in it together and you need to reach a resolution that works for both of you.

Manage Your Emotions—and Theirs

Conflict can bring up all sorts of negative emotions for seekers and avoiders alike. Recognize the emotion, but don't let it stop you from having the conversation. To watch your own reaction while also recognizing your counterpart's feelings, understand why conflict can feel so bad. Remain calm, acknowledge and label your feelings, and allow for venting. Let's take a closer look at how to manage emotions and clear the way for a productive discussion.

Understand why you're so uncomfortable

In the middle of a tough conversation, it can be difficult to take a deep breath and think rationally about what to do next. This is because you're fighting your body's natural reaction, says psychiatry professor John Ratey. Your brain experiences conflict, particularly relationship conflict, as a threat: *I disagree with you. You haven't done your job. I don't like what you just said. You're wrong. I hate you.*

Leadership expert Annie McKee suggests that conflict makes us feel bad because it means we're going to have to give something up—our point of view, the way we're used to doing something, or maybe even power. That threat triggers your sympathetic nervous system. As a result, your heart rate and breathing rate spike, your muscles tighten, the blood in your body moves away from your organs. "Some people feel their stomach tense as acid moves into it," says Ratey.

Depending on the perceived size and intensity of the threat, you may then move into fight-or-flight mode. "When you're panicking, feeling crushed or overwhelmed, the body's response is to be aggressive—punch or push back—or to run away and hide," says Ratey. "This is when you're in it full-time and the discomfort goes all over your body. It's like seeing a bunch of snakes or spiders in front of you." When your brain perceives danger like this, it can be difficult to make rational decisions, which is precisely what you need to do in a difficult conversation. Luckily, it's possible to interrupt this physical response and restore calm in your body.

Remain calm

There are several things you can do to keep your cool during a conversation or to calm yourself down if you've gotten worked up. For conflict seekers, it's especially important to keep your temper in check. For avoiders, these tactics will help keep you from retreating from the conversation.

- **Take a deep breath.** Notice the sensation of air coming in and out of your lungs. Feel it pass through your nostrils or down the back of your throat. This will take your attention off the physical signs of panic and keep you centered.

- **Focus on your body.** "Standing up and walking around may activate the thinking part of your brain," says Ratey, and keep you from exploding. If you and your counterpart are seated at a table, instead of leaping to your feet, you can say, "I feel like I need to stretch some. Mind if I walk around a bit?" If that doesn't feel comfortable, do small things like crossing two fingers or placing your feet firmly on the ground and noticing what the floor feels like on the bottom of your shoes.

- **Look around the room.** Become more aware of the space between you and your counterpart, suggests Jen Su. Notice the color of the walls or any artwork hanging there. Watch the hands of the clock move. "Pay attention to the whole room," she says. "This will help you realize that there's more space in the room than you're currently allowing."

- **Say a mantra.** Jen Su also recommends repeating a phrase to yourself to remind you to stay calm. Some of her clients have found "Go to neutral" to be a helpful prompt. You can also try "This isn't about me," "This will pass," or "This is about the business."

- **Take a break.** You may need to excuse yourself for a moment—get a cup of coffee or a glass of water, go to the bathroom, or take a brief stroll around the office. If you agreed up front that this might happen, you can say, "I think I need that break now. OK if we come back in five minutes?" If pushing pause wasn't on your list of ground rules, you can still make the request: "I'm sorry to interrupt you, but I'd love to get a cup of coffee before we continue. Can I get you something while I'm up?"

Acknowledge and label your feelings

When you're feeling emotional, "the attention you give your thoughts and feelings crowds your mind; there's no room to examine them," says Susan David. To get distance from the feeling, label it. "Just as you call a spade a spade, call a thought a thought and an emotion an emotion," says David. *He is so wrong about that and it's making me mad* becomes *I'm having the thought that my coworker is wrong, and I'm feeling anger.* Labeling like this allows you to see your thoughts and feelings for what they are: "transient sources of data that may or may not prove helpful." When you put that space between these emotions and you, it's easier to let them go—and not bury them or let them explode.

Allow for venting

You're probably not the only one who's upset. When your counterpart expresses anger or frustration, don't stop him. Let him vent as much as possible and remain calm while this is happening. Seekers may naturally do this, while you may have to draw an avoider out. If you took the time to air your own feelings with someone else (as discussed at the end of the previous chapter), you'll understand the importance of giving your counterpart this space. That's not to say it's easy. Brett explains:

> *It's hard not to yell back when you're being attacked, but that's not going to help. To remain calm while your colleague is venting and perhaps even hurling a few insults, visualize your coworker's words going over your shoulder, not hitting you in the chest. Don't act aloof; it's important to indicate that you're listening. But if you don't feed your counterpart's negative emotion with your own, it's likely he or she will wind down. Without the fuel of your equally strong reaction, he or she will run out of steam.*

Don't interrupt the venting or interject your own commentary. "Hold back and let your counterpart say his or her piece. You don't have to agree with it, but listen," Hill says. While you're doing this, you might be completely quiet or you might indicate you're listening by using phrases such as "I get that" or "I understand." Avoid saying anything that assigns feeling or blame, such as "Calm down" or "What you need to understand is . . ." This can be an explosive trigger for a conflict seeker. If you can tolerate the venting, without judging, you'll soon be able to guide the conversation to a more productive place. Refocus the conversation on the substance of the conflict by saying "I'm glad I got to hear how this has affected you. What do you think we should do next?" This will begin to draw out potential solutions so that you can move toward a resolution.

Listen Well

"If you listen to what the other person is saying, you're more likely to address the right issues and the conversation always ends up being better," says Jean-François Manzoni. Hear your counterpart out and ask questions. Here are tips for doing that.

Hear your coworker out

Even if you think you already understand your coworker's point of view—and you've put yourself in her shoes ahead of time—hear what she has to say. This is especially important if you aren't sure of what the other person sees as the root of the conflict. Acknowledge that you don't know, and ask. This shows your counterpart "that you care," Manzoni says. "Express your interest in understanding how the other person feels" and "take time to process the other person's words and tone," he adds. Be considerate and show compassion by validating what she's saying with phrases such as "I get it" or "I hear you." According to Jeff Weiss, this requires that you "stop figuring out your next line" and actively listen. Your coworker's explanation of his side may uncover an important piece of information that leads to a resolution. For example, if he says he's just trying to keep his boss happy, you can help him craft a resolution that addresses his boss's concerns.

Ask thoughtful questions

It's better to ask questions than to make statements; questions demonstrate your receptiveness to a genuine dialogue. This is when you bring in the questions you crafted in the previous chapter to unearth your counterpart's viewpoint and test your hypotheses (see the sidebar "Questions to Draw Out Your Counterpart's Perspective"). Once you've had a chance to hear her thoughts, Hill suggests you paraphrase and ask, "I think you said X. Did I get that right?"

Don't just take what she says at face value. This is especially important for a conflict avoider, who may not tell you all that she's thinking. Ask what her viewpoint looks like in action. For example, says team expert Liane Davey, "If you are concerned about a proposed course of action, ask your teammates to think through the impact of implementing their plan. 'OK, we're contemplating launching this product only to our U.S. customers. How is that going to land with our two big customers in Latin America?' This is less aggressive than saying 'Our Latin American customers will be angry.'" She adds: "Anytime you can demonstrate that you're open to ideas and curious about the right approach, it will open up the discussion."

Hill suggests you also get to the underlying reason for the initiative, policy, or approach that you're disagreeing with. You've already labeled the conflict as relationship, task, process, and/or status, but return to those categories in your questions to give your counterpart the opportunity to share her view. How do you see the goal

QUESTIONS TO DRAW OUT YOUR COUNTERPART'S PERSPECTIVE

- What about this situation is most troubling to you?
- What's most important to you?
- Can you tell me about the assumptions you've made here?
- Can you help me understand your thinking here?
- What makes you say that?
- Can you tell me more about that?
- What leads you to believe that?
- How does this relate to your other concerns?
- What would it take for us to be able to move forward? How do we get there?
- What would you like to see happen?
- What does a resolution look like for you?
- What ideas do you have that would meet both our needs?
- If this was completely in your control, how would you handle it?

differently? Why do you think you're the best person to lead the team?

Figure out why your counterpart thinks his idea is a reasonable proposal. Say something like, "Sam, I want to understand what we're trying to accomplish with this initiative. Can you go back and explain the reasoning behind it?" Get Sam to talk more about what he wants to achieve and why. It's not enough to know that he wants the project to be done in six months. You need to know why that's important to him. Is it because he made a promise to his boss? Is it because the team that's dedicated to the project needs to be freed up to take on an important client initiative? These are his underlying interests, and they'll help you later when you're trying to craft a resolution that incorporates his viewpoint (see chapter 7, "Get to a Resolution and Make a Plan").

You can return to the notion of asking for advice here. Perhaps you genuinely don't understand something, or you're shocked by something your counterpart has said. Davey suggests that you be mildly self-deprecating and own the misunderstanding. "If something is really surprising to you (you can't believe anyone would propose anything so crazy), say so. 'I think I'm missing something here. Tell me how this will address our sales gap for Q1.' This will encourage the person to restate his perspective and give you time to understand it."

Respectfully listening to and acknowledging your counterpart's viewpoint sets the stage for you to share your side of the conflict. If he feels heard, he's more likely to hear you out as well.

Be Heard

When it's time to share your story, allow your counterpart to understand your perspective in a genuine way. "Letting down your guard and letting the other person in may help her understand your point of view," says Mark Gerzon, author of *Leading Through Conflict: How Successful Leaders Transform Differences into Opportunities*. Help your coworker see where you're coming from by speaking from your own perspective, thinking before you talk, and watching body language (yours and hers) for clues that the conversation may be going off the rails.

Own your perspective

If you feel mistreated, you may be tempted to launch into your account of the events: "I want to talk about how horribly you treated me in that meeting." But that's unlikely to go over well.

Instead, treat your opinion like what it is: your opinion. Start sentences with "I," not "you." Say "I'm annoyed that this project is six months behind schedule," rather than "You've missed every deadline we've set." This will help the other person see your perspective and understand that you're not trying to blame him.

With a relationship conflict, explain exactly what is bothering you and follow up by identifying what you hope will happen. You might say, "I appreciate your ideas, but I'm finding it hard to hear them because throughout this process, I've felt as if you didn't respect my ideas. That's my perception. I'm not saying that it's your intention. I'd like to clear the air so that we can continue to work together to make the project a success."

Dorie Clark, author of *Reinventing You: Define Your Brand, Imagine Your Future,* says that you should admit blame when appropriate. "It's easy to demonize your colleague. But you're almost certainly contributing to the dynamic in some way, as well," Clark says. To get anywhere, you have to understand—and acknowledge—your role in the situation. Admitting your faults will help set a tone of accountability for both of you, and your counterpart is more likely to own up to her missteps as well. If she doesn't, and instead seizes on your confession and harps on it—"That's exactly why we're in this mess"—let it go. See it as part of the venting process described earlier.

Pay attention to your words

Sometimes, regardless of your good intentions, what you say can further upset your counterpart and make the issue worse. Other times you might say the exact thing that helps the person go from boiling mad to cool as a cucumber. See the sidebar "Phrases to Make Sure You've Heard." There are some basic rules you can follow to keep from pushing your counterpart's buttons. Of course you should avoid name-calling and finger-pointing. Focus on your perspective, as discussed above, avoiding sentences that start with "you" and could be misinterpreted as accusations. Your language should be "simple, clear, direct, and neutral," says Holly Weeks. Don't apologize for your feelings, either. The worst thing you can do "is to ask your counterpart to have sympathy for you,"

PHRASES TO MAKE SURE YOU'RE HEARD

- "Here's what I'm thinking."
- "My perspective is based on the following assumptions . . ."
- "I came to this conclusion because . . ."
- "I'd love to hear your reaction to what I just said."
- "Do you see any flaws in my reasoning?"
- "Do you see the situation differently?"

she says. Don't say things like "I feel so bad about saying this" or "This is really hard for me to do," because it takes the focus away from the problem and toward your own neediness. While this can be hard, especially for conflict avoiders, this language can make your counterpart feel obligated to focus on making you feel better before moving on.

Davey provides two additional rules when it comes to what you say:

- **Say "and," not "but."** "When you need to disagree with someone, express your contrary opinion as an 'and.' It's not necessary for someone else to be wrong for you to be right," she says. When you're surprised to hear something your counterpart has said, don't interject with a "But that's not right!" Just add your perspective. Davey suggests something like this: "You think we need to leave room in the budget for a customer event, and I'm concerned that we need that money for employee training. What are our options?" This will engage your colleague in problem solving, which is inherently collaborative instead of combative.

- **Use hypotheticals.** Being contradicted doesn't feel very good, so don't try to tit-for-tat your counterpart, countering each of his arguments. Instead, says Davey, use hypothetical situations to get him imagining. "Imagining is the opposite of defending, so it gets the brain out of a rut," she says. She offers this example: "I hear your concern about getting the right salespeople to pull off this campaign. If we could get the right people . . . what could the campaign look like?"

Watch your body language—and your counterpart's

The words coming out of your mouth should match what you're saying with your body. Watch your facial expression and what you do with your arms, legs, and entire body. A lot of people unconsciously convey nonverbal messages. Are you slumping your shoulders? Rolling your eyes? Fidgeting with your pen?

Increase your awareness of the energy you give off. In Amy Jen Su and Muriel Maignan Wilkins's book, *Own the Room,* they offer six places where nonverbal messages are communicated through body language: your posture; eye contact; the natural gestures you make typically with your hands; the tone, tempo, and timing of your voice; your facial expressions; and how you occupy the space around you (see table 6-1).

Through each of those points, you signal to others what you're thinking and feeling. Jen Su and Maignan Wilkins use the acronym CENTER to help people remember these six cue points. Table 6-1 shows different signals you might be sending depending on whether you're in an aggressive, conflict-seeking mode or a more passive, conflict-avoidant mode. Reviewing the table and considering the questions will help you maintain body language that's as open as the language you're using.

During your conversation, pay attention to each of these areas and take stock of the overall impression you're giving. Do the same for your counterpart. Watch what she's conveying through her body language. Again, her nonverbal cues may be sending a different message than what she's articulating. If that's the case, or if you're noticing any body language, ask about it. For example, you might say, "I hear you saying that you're fine with this approach, but it looks as if maybe you still have some concerns. Is that right? Should we talk those through?"

Change the tenor of the conversation

Sometimes, despite your best intentions and all of the time you put into preparing for the conversation, things veer off course. You can't demand that your counterpart hold the discussion exactly the way you want.

If things get heated, don't panic. Take a deep breath, mentally pop out of the conversation as if you're a fly on the wall, and objectively look at what's happening.

TABLE 6-1

Manage your body language during a conflict

	What others see when you're avoiding conflict	What others see when you're being aggressive	Questions to ask yourself to keep your body language open
Core posture	• Slouched, loose posture	• Propped, tense, wound-up posture	• What happens to your core posture? Are you standing tall? Slouching?
Eye contact	• Not holding eye contact	• Intense eye contact	• Do you hold eye contact or lose it?
Natural gestures	• Nervous gestures, fidgeting	• Using aggressive gestures like finger-pointing	• What gestures do you start to make? What do you do with your shoulders, hands, and feet?
Tone, tempo, timing	• High pitch or soft volume • Use of filler words such as um, ahs, or stutters	• Fast pace or loud volume • Judgmental or condescending tone	• How does the tone, tempo, and timing of your speech change?
Expressions of the face	• Wide, deer-in-headlights eyes	• Furrowed brows	• What expressions do you make with your face?
Regions and territory	• Shrinks down, doesn't take up space or fill the room	• Takes up too much space at the table or in the room	• How do you take up space in the room?

Source: Adapted from Amy Jen Su and Muriel Maignan Wilkins, *Own the Room: Discover Your Signature Voice to Master Your Leadership Presence* (Boston: Harvard Business Review Press, 2013).

You might even describe to yourself (in your head) what's happening: "He keeps returning to the fact that I yelled at his team yesterday." "When I try to move the conversation away from what's gone wrong to what we can do going forward, he keeps shifting it back." "Every time I bring up the sales numbers, he raises his voice."

Then state what you're observing in a calm tone. "It looks as if whenever the sale numbers come up, you raise your voice." Suggest a different approach: "If we put our heads together, we could probably come up with a way to move past this. Do you have any ideas?"

"Stepping back and explicitly negotiating over the process itself can be a powerful game-changing move," says Weiss. If it seems as if you've entered into a power struggle in which you're no longer discussing the substance of your conflict but battling over who is right, step back and either return to your questions above or talk about what's not working. Say, "We seem to be getting locked into our positions. Could we return to our goals and see if we can brainstorm together some new ideas that might meet both our objectives?" See the sidebar "Phrases That Productively Move the Conversation Along." Returning your counterpart to his original goal may be enough to get the conversation back on track.

When to Bring in a Third Party

There are times, however, when you're getting nowhere with your counterpart and, even when you follow the principles above, you're still not able to have a productive discussion. Some problems are too entrenched, complicated, or emotional to sort out between two people. Or

PHRASES THAT PRODUCTIVELY MOVE THE CONVERSATION ALONG

- "You may be right, but I'd like to understand more."
- "I have a completely different perspective, but clearly you think this is unfair, so how can we fix this?"
- "Can you help me make the connection between this and the other issues we're talking about?"
- "I'd like to give my reaction to what you've said so far and see what you think."
- "I'm sensing there are some intense emotions about this. When you said 'X,' I had the impression you were feeling 'Y.' If so, I'd like to understand what upset you. Is there something I've said or done?"
- "This may be more my perception than yours, but when you said 'X,' I felt . . ."
- "Is there anything I can say or do that might convince you to consider other options here?"

your counterpart is too inflexible or unable to hear your side, insisting that it's her way or the highway.

The main indicator you may need outside help, says White, is when it seems as if your counterpart is perpetuating the conflict rather than trying to solve it. "She may be alternatively conciliatory and antagonistic. Every time you seem to be making progress, she walks back from the tentative agreement and accuses you of not negotiating in good faith," she explains.

This is not a failure. "Someone who is not involved in the conflict may be able to provide vital perspective for both parties," says Gerzon. Ideally, you'll both agree that a third party is necessary before going with this option. But if you can't reach agreement on anything else, this might be difficult. In these cases, you may have to ask someone else to get involved without your counterpart's permission.

Who you bring in will depend on the nature of the conflict. Choose someone whom you both trust and can rely on to understand the issues but also brings an outside perspective. It might be one or both of your bosses. "For example," says Ben Dattner, "if roles are poorly defined, a boss might help clarify who is responsible for what." If the conflict is over how people are rewarded, you might turn to HR or a union representative. Dattner shares another example: "If incentives reward individual rather than team performance, HR can be called in to help better align incentives with organizational goals."

When you've exhausted all your internal options, or if there is no one to appeal to, you might need a trained mediator to help.

In the process of having a productive discussion with your counterpart—expressing your point of view and listening to hers—a resolution may naturally arise. It may be that there was a misunderstanding and now it's cleared up. Or perhaps after hearing your colleague out, you realize you do agree with how she's approaching the project. Or as you talk through what her goals are, you stumble upon a solution that would work well for both of you.

If this doesn't happen organically, you'll have to more consciously work toward a resolution that meets both your and your counterpart's goals.

SECTION THREE

Resolving a Conflict

CHAPTER 7

Get to a Resolution and Make a Plan

When addressing the conflict directly, the final step is to broker a resolution between you and your counterpart. Start by understanding what a resolution looks like. Then with that goal in mind, take steps to narrow down the options and make the final call.

What a Resolution Looks Like

The details of each specific resolution will vary depending on the type of conflict you were having. With task conflict, the resolution is likely to be an agreement about what it is you want to accomplish—the stated objective for the project you're coleading or an agenda for the next managers' meeting. It will be something concrete that you can write down. The same goes for a process conflict.

Ideally you'll be able to document the process you'll use going forward—how to reach consensus before approving new projects or the sequencing for rolling out the IT initiative. With status conflict, the resolution may be reaching an understanding about who will lead a project or whose team is ultimately responsible for the success of the product launch.

Resolutions in a relationship conflict can be the most difficult to broker and recognize, especially because there are usually bruised feelings that take a while to heal. Often you might agree to each do something differently in the future—he will not raise his voice when he disagrees with you, and you will not run to your boss until you've talked with your counterpart first.

But no matter what type of conflict you were engaged in—relationship, task, process, or status—a resolution needs to meet the same three criteria.

It satisfies as many interests as possible

During your conversation, you spent a lot of time and energy explaining your perspective and goals. You also learned about your counterpart's underlying interests. Perhaps she wanted to be sure that her team was well represented at an important presentation so that they had an opportunity to show off their work, while you wanted the presentation to go quickly and smoothly so that there was plenty of time at the end for questions. It's possible—and preferable—that an agreement meets each of those interests reasonably well. "The essence of a resolution is that you get to what the underlying interests are and try to satisfy as many of them as possible," says Jonathan Hughes.

It's fair and reasonable

"We all want a resolution that feels fair and reasonable to everyone involved—and is defensible to others on the outside looking in," says Hughes. You should be able to answer yes to the following questions: "Do I think this is a reasonable solution?" "Does my counterpart?" "Can I defend it to my boss or anyone else who cares about the outcome?" We also want to feel as though we came to the agreement by ourselves and weren't pressured into conceding or giving in. So both the final arrangement and the process you used to reach it need to be fair.

The relationship is intact

If you reach a resolution that meets the business needs and is fair and reasonable, but you end up hating each other, then it's hard to call that a success. You want to be able to say that you maintained your relationship, or that you even improved it. "The icing on the cake is if you can honestly say to each other that you learned something about each other in the process," says Hughes, "and thus that the next disagreement or conflict will be that much easier to resolve together."

How You Reach a Resolution

Arriving at a resolution that meets those three criteria requires additional conversation, and it's up to you and your counterpart to come up with options. Be creative and collaborative as you do that. Then evaluate the options you generated and make the final call together.

Be creative

Keep in mind your goal, and that of your counterpart, and when all the data is on the table, offer different options that ideally meet both of your needs. Are there ways to satisfy both of your interests and build on that to discover new benefits neither one of you envisioned on your own? Consider a salary increase. You may be fighting for a 10% raise, while your boss thinks you deserve 7%. Instead of just duking it out over the exact percentage, find a way to include something in the raise that's valuable to both of you. Perhaps you can take on a new project for your region that allows you to travel and get exposure to more senior leaders. Taking a creative approach to the conflict, instead of focusing on and nitpicking over a number, increases what you can both get out of it.

Don't get locked into your answer and his answer. Proposing several alternatives helps the other person see a way out, and it also signals humility, that you don't believe there's just one way to resolve this dispute: your way. Don't offer what you originally came to the table with, but use the information you gathered during your conversation to come up with a better solution. There are always additional ways of solving a problem. "When you're creative about how to meet your interests, you can begin to imagine a third way that might meet your needs well and work for both of you," says Hughes.

Be collaborative

Brainstorm possibilities together. If you propose a potential solution, ask for your counterpart's input. Ask, "What other ideas might you have?" and let him build on your ideas or offer others. When you suggest a potential resolution, don't just say, "Do you like it?" but invite criticism. Weiss suggests you ask "What would be wrong with this solution?" That better helps you understand his viewpoint and encourages him to also be creative.

Consider what you can offer

If you've proposed a solution that potentially puts the other person in a difficult spot or takes something away from her, ask yourself: Is there something I can give back? says Holly Weeks. If, for instance, you're telling your boss that you can't take on a particular assignment, propose a viable alternative, such as someone else who can fill the role equally well. "Be constructive," says Jean-François Manzoni. Or if you're laying off someone you've worked with for a long time, "you could say, 'I have written what I think is a strong recommendation for you; would you like to see it?'"

Decide how to evaluate the possibilities

With several options on the table, begin evaluating them. Agree on the criteria you'll use to select the best option. Perhaps you'll ask a disinterested third party to weigh in on your resolution and see if it looks fair. Or maybe you'll agree on certain requirements that the resolution must meet, such as mitigating the risk of a lawsuit or being cost-effective. "It's often easier to agree on the criteria than the solution," says Hughes. These can be hard to establish in a relationship conflict, however. In those situations, fairness is usually the standard against which to evaluate possibilities.

This may all sound rational and reasonable, and maybe collaborating on a resolution will be exactly that. But just as emotions were a key element of the conflict up to this point, they're likely to be present in this part of the conversation as well. Continue to remain calm, acknowledge and label your feelings, and allow for venting when necessary. All the tips you learned for having a productive conversation in the previous chapter will continue to be useful here.

Make the final call

Often with task, process, and status conflict, there is a tangible decision to make. Are we going to finish this project in six months or one year? Can we fund this project and at the same time put a small amount of money toward another one that we'll plan to fully fund next year? Using the criteria you've laid out and the options you've developed, you and your counterpart must agree on which path to pursue and under which arrangements. Other times there is no decision to make, especially with relationship conflict. In those cases, "sometimes just talking it through will resolve it," says Hughes. Once you understand your counterpart's perspective, you may not feel so bad about the way he spoke to you in that meeting. And once he sees that you misinterpreted his reaction, he may be more forgiving of the fact that you left the room before the meeting was over. "No one's at fault," says Hughes. "No one's the bad guy. And accepting that can take the sting out of the fight."

Document the agreement

This doesn't have to be formal, such as a contract. Capture your discussion in an email and send it with a quick note that asks, "Did I get this right?" Confirming what you've agreed to ensures you're on the same page and gives you both something to refer to should any similar issues arise again. You want to do this as soon after your conversation as possible—definitely within a day or two. Leaving it any longer risks that you'll misremember what you both agreed to.

When to Accept That There Won't Be a Resolution

There are some situations in which, try as you might, you won't reach a resolution. You've engaged in a constructive discussion and come up with alternatives for resolving the particular conflict you're having, but you can't make the final call on which option to go with. It may be that your counterpart insists on one solution and you're unwilling to go with that one. Perhaps you have your heart set on a particular option, but it doesn't meet your counterpart's interests. Be realistic with yourself about what's possible so that you don't bang your head against the wall trying to force a solution when there isn't one.

If you can't reach a resolution, there are three things you can do:

- **Take a break.** Sometimes, if you step away from the conversation, let the emotions cool down a little, and return to it later, you might see a different option neither of you thought of before or an existing possibility may look more appealing to one or both of you. This is an especially good tactic if you feel bullied into accepting an outcome. "When someone threatens us, we tend to make irrational decisions, so we need time to figure out whether this is, in fact, something we are willing to accept, or whether it's worse than no agreement," says Judith White. "This will give you the time to consider the offer and save you from one of three mistakes: accepting something you should have rejected; rejecting something you should have accepted, or blowing up at the other person and thereby blowing up any hope of a mutually agreeable solution."

- **Appeal to someone more senior.** You can escalate the situation to a person in a higher position. You might say to your boss or your counterpart's boss, "We're in this fix and we need your help to make the decision." You might ask that person to "decide for the two of you, to intervene and offer another solution, or to change one of the constraints, such as giving you more resources or extending a deadline," explains Hughes.

- **Get your needs met another way.** In lieu of settling your conflict, what can you do instead? If you and a supplier disagree on the terms of your contract renewal, can you find another supplier? Or stay with this supplier, but escalate the conflict to his boss? Or you could hold out for a few months and see if the deal gets better with time. If you're in a dispute about how much of a raise you'll get, and it doesn't look as if HR is going to give you what you asked for, can you look for a different job or go freelance?

Learn from Your Experience

Once you've reached a successful conclusion, it's worthwhile to reflect and consider what went well and what didn't, says Manzoni. "Why did you have certain reactions, and what might you have said differently?" Weeks also recommends observing how others successfully cope with these situations and emulating their tactics. The goal is to constantly improve your approach to conflict by integrating new tactics and strategies. Talk with your boss, a mentor, or a trusted colleague about what you've learned and ask them to remind you and hold you accountable so that you don't repeat the same mistakes.

It's also a good time to talk with your counterpart about what you'll do if you enter into a conflict again. What do each of you want to do differently? How can you make sure that future disagreements don't turn ugly? Document these ideas (again an email is fine) so that you can both refer back to them if you need to.

Once the content of the disagreement has been solved, think about what other reparations you might need to make. Even if your dispute was purely task related or process related, be mindful that your relationship may have suffered. Restoring trust and accepting the situation are critical parts of moving on.

CHAPTER 8

Repair the Relationship

Whether you're shaking hands after a productive conversation, carrying on business as usual, returning to your desk knowing someone intervened on your behalf, trying to accept that there will be no resolution, or plotting how to find an entirely new job, it's important to put the conflict behind you and move on. And even if you've come to an agreeable resolution, sometimes the relationship needs to be mended. There may be some lingering resentment or you or your counterpart may be anxious that the situation will happen again.

If you opted to do nothing, you still need to think about the relationship. You don't want to harbor negative feelings toward the person, especially if you were the one who decided against other options for addressing the disagreement. "You need to tell yourself: 'I chose to let this go. I'm not going to ruminate or retaliate because it was my decision to let go,'" says Jeanne Brett. Even if you didn't make the decision about how to handle the situation, it's still in your best interest to move past it.

Putting your relationship back on track requires addressing your needs, those of your counterpart, and those of the people who may have been party to the conflict.

Pause and Reflect

You might feel amped from the tension even after it's been resolved, or plain exhausted from the mental gymnastics of trying to remain calm, listen, and balance your goals with your counterpart's all at the same time. Or perhaps you're worn out from working hard to let the conflict go. No matter what you're feeling, take a moment to consider what you've accomplished: Not only did you make it through the conflict in one piece, but you made smart choices about how to handle it, remained flexible, and pushed yourself to stay present. Well done. Now consider taking a break from work. After a heated discussion, you may want to take a walk outside, go to the gym, or meet up with a friend. Or you may just want to go home and get a good night's sleep. Chances are that with a little time and space, any lingering negative energy will dissipate and you'll return to work feeling clearer and more focused.

Look Forward

Although you'll want to reflect and learn from what happened, resist the tendency to analyze every detail of the conflict. Who said what? Why did they say it? That isn't productive. "Lots of people think that it's only by understanding the past that we get beyond it. But what you focus on is what grows," Susan David says. So contemplate what's worked well previously, what you like about the person, and what you want from the relationship. "Take a solution-focused approach, not a diagnostic one," she says. (See the sidebar "A Success Story" for one example of how a common purpose helped two people move beyond their conflict.)

Rebuild Rapport

If the relationship has suffered some damage, don't expect it to change overnight. "The real shifts in relationships happen less in those watershed moments and more in your everyday actions," David explains. Sitting down and talking is helpful, "but that's not where the work really happens. It's more subtle than that." Make an effort to change the tone of your everyday interactions. Say hello before you sit down at your desk in the morning. Offer to buy him a coffee. Small gestures of civility go a long way.

Reconnect Through Questions

One way to rebuild rapport is to ask questions, says Caroline Webb, author of *How to Have a Good Day: Harness the Power of Behavioral Science to Transform Your Working Life*. "It's inherently rewarding to people to get to talk about themselves or share their opinions." The trick is to move beyond more typical, factual questions like "When's the presentation due?" to what Webb calls "quality questions" that go beyond exchanging basic information. Instead of asking "How was your weekend?"

A SUCCESS STORY

Rachel had an ongoing conflict with her coworker, Pia. At the consultancy where they worked, it was Rachel's job to sell projects to clients, but it was Pia's role as the business director to vet the sales proposals and pricing. Whenever Rachel sent Pia a draft for review, Pia would increase the prices that Rachel was pitching. She'd send back a curt email that explained the prices were too low and told Rachel to fix them, which Rachel did. As a result, Rachel lost potential sales.

Because she didn't know Pia personally (she had met her only once at a team retreat), Rachel went to her boss, the regional manager, to explain that Pia was being unreasonable about the prices and rude to her. "I had targets I was supposed to meet, and every time Pia caused me to lose a sale, I was getting angrier and angrier," Rachel says. But Rachel's boss was not receptive to her appeals. "She told me that she trusted Pia's judgment implicitly and that I just had to find clients who were willing to pay the premium price," she says.

The circumstances were starting to affect Rachel's morale, not to mention her sales performance. She didn't enjoy going to work anymore because she wasn't making progress toward her goals. She cringed every time she got an email from Pia. One day, after learning that she'd lost yet another potential sale, she called Pia.

Rather than criticize her, though, Rachel explained how upset she was and the impact the situation was having on her: "I wanted to let her know that I really couldn't keep working like this, having strained relationships with my colleagues, bringing in clients and losing them again and again."

Pia was receptive to what she had to say. "She heard me out and said she wasn't aware of how she was coming across." It turned out that Pia was also frustrated by the lack of sales and her performance was also being affected. "This gave us a common purpose to address," Rachel says. So the two of them switched into problem-solving mode. How could they both do their jobs and close the deals together? "She taught me how she did the pricing, and we reached a compromise on what could be quoted," Rachel says.

Pia and Rachel ended up closing several big deals together. "We weren't best buds, but we didn't have any further disagreements either," she says. Both women eventually left the company, but they still keep in touch.

ask what your counterpart did specifically and follow up with something like, "That's interesting. What led you to do that?" If you don't have a personal relationship, ask questions that signal you value his opinion: "How did you think that meeting went?" "What are you working on at the moment?" The goal with these questions is to create what Susan David calls "a shared psychological space." Make it less about you and more about "creating a connection," she advises.

Reestablish Reciprocity

You'll also want to restore trust if it was broken. One smart way to do that, Brian Uzzi says, is to "offer things to the other person without asking for anything in return." Propose taking on a small project she hasn't been able to get to. Or bring her lunch one day. This will activate the law of reciprocity and restore the give-and-take of your previous relationship. But don't verbalize what's taking place. "That will get you into the tight accounting system of who's doing what for whom," warns Uzzi. Keep your word, too. "Being true to the things you've offered will continue to deepen the relationship and make sure it doesn't slip back into mistrust," says Uzzi.

Apologize

"You don't have to be completely at fault to say you're sorry or show some penance," says Adam Galinsky. It's rare that a conflict is completely one-sided, so chances are that you contributed to the situation in some way. Apologize for your part and express genuine regret that the situation occurred (only if you feel it). Doing this will often elicit a similar expression from your counterpart. But don't expect that. You don't want to resent the person if she doesn't apologize, too.

Focus on Commonalities

During the course of your conflict, you likely had disagreements that emphasized how different you were from one another. This can push you apart. Webb says that "if we see someone as part of our in-group, we're more likely to feel empathy for them and not see them as a threat." And fortunately, "it takes very, very little to perceive someone is like you." Find something you agree on. Perhaps it's the common ground you identified before your discussion or something as simple as a shared dislike of the new printer. If this is someone you've had a long-standing relationship with, talk about projects you've worked on together that went well. Reminisce about things you've done in the past. Consider paying the person a compliment or asking about his pet. "Flattery—no matter how ludicrous it is—always works," says Webb.

Spend More Time Together

"One of the best ways to repair a relationship is to work on a project that requires coordination," says Bob Sutton, a Stanford University management professor. This seems counterintuitive, since you may be sick of each other at this point. "Over time, if you work together closely, you may come to appreciate your colleague more and perhaps even develop some empathy," he says. You may discover there are reasons for your counterpart's actions: stress at home, pressure from his boss, or maybe he's tried to do what you're asking for and failed. Spending more time with him will also grant you the opportunity to have more-positive experiences.

Involve Other People

It's likely that throughout the conflict, you turned to other people for advice and commiseration. Your attempts to repair the relationship won't be successful if those people aren't included. "You need to get any involved third parties on board to fix it and keep it healthy," says Uzzi. Explain to your confidants that you're working on the relationship and that you'd appreciate their support in making it work. You might say: "I know Howard and I have been at odds over the past few weeks, and you've heard an earful from me. I want to let you know that we've sorted through our problems, and I'm determined to make our relationship work. It'd be great if you could help by calling me out if I start to complain again." This helps not only you but those around you as well. You're contributing to an office or team culture that allows for conflict to happen. "You're showing that it's safe to disagree," says Annie McKee. "It's not enough to deal with conflict well; you have to make sure everyone knows it was dealt with well."

Consider Providing Feedback

This isn't always possible, but if you've directly addressed the conflict and you've reached a resolution, you might want to give your colleague some feedback about the process. You can share observations with the intention of improving how you interact in the future. It may be that how your counterpart behaved with you is something that regularly gets in her way as a professional. "Don't assume the person knows how she is coming across," says Sutton. This isn't a diatribe about everything she did to annoy you—that will just pull you back into the fray. Focus on behaviors that she can control. Describe how they affected you and your work together with the aim of supporting change. Your carefully framed feedback can help her develop greater self-awareness and increase her effectiveness. And of course, you also need to be open to hearing feedback yourself. If you're seeing some things that your counterpart might change, she's liable to have her own observations to share with you.

However, weigh this option carefully. Daniel Goleman, author of *Emotional Intelligence: Why It Can Matter More Than IQ*, says whether you give feedback "depends on how artful you are as a communicator and how receptive they are as a person." If you feel your counterpart might be open and you can have a civilized conversation, then go ahead. But if this is a person you suspect will be vindictive or mad, or will turn it into a personal conflict, don't risk it. You'll be back to where you started.

For most of us, the word *conflict* conjures up a difficult struggle: We want people to like us, but we also want to get our way. It would be ideal if our colleagues always saw the brilliance in our ideas, gave us the resources we asked for, completely agreed with us on the best way to run the business, *and* still adored us at the end of the day. But work is not a perfect place. Fortunately, it doesn't have to be. And when we fight with people at work, it doesn't have to be scary or threatening. "Going through difficult experiences can be the makings of the strongest, most resilient relationships," says David. We make it through, and in the process, we learn about each other, and ourselves, as we make the next conflict less likely to occur or at least easier to manage.

CHAPTER 9

Navigate Common Situations

For every conflict you encounter, you'll tweak your approach depending on the circumstances. But there are some specific situations that commonly occur.

This chapter will walk you through the following challenges:

- You're fighting from afar
- Your counterpart is passive-aggressive
- Your colleague goes over your head
- You're caught in the middle of two warring colleagues
- You're mad at your boss
- You're dealing with a bully

- Your counterpart is suffering from a mental illness
- You manage two people who hate each other
- Your team turns on you
- You're fighting with someone outside the office

Knowing a bit more about why these situations happen can help you to better tackle them.

You're Fighting from Afar

The situation

You're coleading an important project with your London-based colleague, and his emails have turned snarky. You were initially debating when the project should launch, but now he's sending you emails with just a "?" in them if you don't respond within the hour. Since you're based in Hong Kong, that means you'd have to be up at midnight to receive his "urgent" 5 p.m. emails. He seems really mad, but who can tell, since you're just reading his words on a screen.

Why it happens

"Task-related disputes can more quickly devolve into relationship conflicts when there's no face-to-face contact, which helps to accelerate empathy," says Keith Ferrazzi, who studies virtual teams. A study by Syracuse's Kristin Byron showed that using email generally increases the likelihood of conflict and miscommunication. Cultural differences may also be contributing to the problem if you and your colleague are from different countries.

What to do about it

"The good news is that bad relationship conflicts don't occur as often because virtual team members are typically focused more on their work and less on interpersonal issues and office politics. Hence, bad blood is less likely to develop between coworkers," explains Ferrazzi. Still, it can be harder to solve these conflicts when they do arise because you don't know how the other person is reacting. Is he opting to do nothing and set aside his feelings, or is he actually stewing?

Assess your options

The approaches you might use for navigating conflict take on a different flavor when you work far apart. The do-nothing option can work well when you don't have to see your colleague every day; you may be able to get over the conflict more easily by not addressing it. Or you can indirectly address it by asking someone at your colleague's location to talk with her. Also, exiting the relationship can be easier in these situations because you can ask to work with someone else on the team, or you may be able to go around the person and work with her boss.

Move the conversation to a better medium

As discussed in chapter 5, "Get Ready for the Conversation," arguing through email can be tough, but sometimes that's your only form of communication. "People often behave with far less restraint in a virtual environment than in the physical world—a phenomenon that psychologists call the 'online disinhibition effect,'" says Ferrazzi. And it's just too difficult to interpret what's really going on. If you're arguing via email, stop. Pick up the phone and call your colleague, or schedule a time to do a video call.

Get to know how your counterpart works

Understanding your counterpart—his approach to conflict, his goal in the conversation, and so forth—is central to successfully navigating a conflict. But when you work in different offices, you need to take this task a step further. Do you know how the other person works? Are the tools and processes you use compatible? Pamela Hinds, who studies dispersed teams, says that when people share these kinds of details, or at least an understanding of their contextual differences, there is less conflict. "The challenge on global teams is that the contexts *are* different—that's unavoidable. But we found that as long as team members understand what is different, they're less likely to blame one another for incompatibilities," she says. If possible, visit your colleague's office, and vice versa, to get a sense of how he works. If you can't do that, spend extra time explaining your systems and processes, noting similarities and differences.

Increase informal communication

Research by Mark Mortensen of INSEAD and Hinds also showed that casual, unplanned communication dramatically reduces conflict when you're not in the same location. Take advantage of opportunities for informal interactions. Keep your messaging app open to share personal snippets or jokes throughout the day. Take virtual breaks together, chatting on the phone while you both sip tea. Or you might leave your computer cameras on so that you can see each other throughout the day. "These video links between offices create a shared space and provide more opportunities for these spontaneous—but often very productive—workplace conversations," says Mortensen.

Diane's story

Diane started a new job in the US office of an international NGO. After several weeks of building a rapport over email with Brigitte, a German colleague—and believing that they had started a friendship—Diane got an email from Brigitte that said, "People here in Europe are saying that you're not right for your job." Diane was hurt and assumed that her colleague didn't like her. Why else would she say something so mean and in such an abrupt way? But she didn't want to jump to conclusions, especially since she'd never met Brigitte in person. Diane didn't know anyone in Brigitte's office to turn to for advice or insights into Brigitte's style or personality. She opted to do nothing, ignore the email, and move on, but after a few days, it was still bothering her. She set up a Skype video call with Brigitte.

When the two connected, Diane was surprised to see Brigitte smiling at her. Diane carefully broached the subject of the email. "I told her I was taken aback by it because I thought we had been getting along well," she says. Brigitte explained that it was precisely because they were establishing a relationship that she'd told Diane about what others were thinking. "She thought she was helping me, giving me information that would be useful as I tried to prove myself in the new role. She did it so directly because that was an appropriate way to communicate in her culture, but I just misinterpreted her intentions," Diane says. The two women started turning on Skype when they got to the office and would chat throughout the day. It also gave others in the European office a way to get to know Diane better as they'd stop by Brigitte's desk to wave or say hello to Diane.

Your Counterpart Is Passive-Aggressive

The situation

Your colleague says one thing in a meeting but then does another. She passes you in the hallway without saying hello and talks over you in meetings, but when you ask to speak with her about it, she insists that everything's fine and the problem is all in your head.

Why it happens

It's not uncommon for colleagues to make a passive-aggressive remark once in a while over a particularly sensitive issue or when they're not sure how to directly address an issue. But persistent passive-aggressive behavior that manifests itself in a variety of situations is a different ball game. These individuals can be self-centered at best and narcissistic at worst, says Annie McKee. "These are people who will often do anything to get what they need, including lie." But it may not be all her fault, either. In many organizations, direct, overt disagreement is not allowed, so "some people have been trained to be passive-aggressive by their cultures," she explains.

What to do about it

Passive-aggressive people are not necessarily more engaged in conflict than most, but they're doing it in a way that's tough to deal with. It's not as clean as the indirect approach described in chapter 2, "Your Options for Handling Conflict," because they're not being honest about their intentions. "Fighting with these people is like shadowboxing," says McKee. It's best to do nothing and work around them or to distance yourself (exit), if possible. Also, try the following suggestions.

Accept that your counterpart's behavior likely has nothing to do with you

It's not in your head; it's in hers. Recognize the behavior for what it is, says McKee, but don't spend too much time psychoanalyzing her. Amy Jen Su and Muriel Maignan Wilkins say, "You need all the energy you can muster as a leader, so don't waste an ounce of it trying to figure out why she acts this way with you."

See through the behavior to the source of the conflict

Instead of harping on how much she bothers you, focus on what's causing the disagreement. Does she think that the way you're running the project isn't working (process conflict), but she hasn't directly said that? Or do you disagree about whether your team's ultimate goal is to increase revenue or boost brand recognition (task conflict)? As discussed in chapter 1, "Types of Conflict," knowing what's underneath the disagreement can help to depersonalize it, and when passive-aggressive behavior makes everything feel like a relationship conflict, understanding and labeling the real source can help you move forward.

Focus on a common goal

You've thought about what your goal is and what you suspect hers to be, but her behavior may prevent you from establishing common ground. Instead, focus on the objective you share with others, suggests McKee. If your project is at risk of not getting completed on time, that's the problem you need to deal with, not her infuriating conduct. Sure, you may be tempted to vent with others who also work with her, but limit those conversations. They aren't professional or productive. After a few minutes of complaining, redirect the discussion to your work. You might say: "Enough about her. Let's talk about how we can get this project done."

Enlist help from others

Amy Jen Su and Muriel Maignan Wilkins suggest you enroll your team in keeping your passive-aggressive colleague accountable. Have others confirm expectations that you agreed on. "For example," they explain, "if you're in a meeting discussing next steps, make sure everyone articulates what they heard and verbally communicates what they commit to in specific terms (not just head nodding)." Or you can send a follow-up email documenting who's going to do what. "Form an esprit de corps with your other colleagues," suggests McKee. And since your colleague is passive-aggressive with everyone, politely ask others what coping mechanisms or tactics work for them.

Darrell's story

Darrell's new coworker, Raquel, was turning out to be a nightmare. Their boss had asked Darrell to show Raquel how to complete several reports that she'd eventually be responsible for, and when he sat down with her, she acted like she already knew how to do them. "It was impossible since the reports were specific to our organization, but when I tried to point that out, she told me to not get so worked up," he says. "That was the first sign that something was wrong."

One day, Darrell overheard her telling their boss that she was still waiting for him to train her on the reports. He didn't want to get defensive in front of his manager, so instead he went to Raquel and tried to appeal to their shared goal. "I told her that we both wanted her to be able to take over the reports," he says. He again offered to show her, but she told him that she had it under control. Since the direct approach wasn't working, he decided to go to their boss. "It wasn't what I wanted. I really hoped I could work it out with her, but she acted like nothing was wrong every time I tried to address it," he says. Darrell explained his side to the boss. "I didn't ask him to talk to her because I thought that would make matters worse, but I wanted him to know that what she was saying wasn't true."

Darrell was extremely frustrated, but he didn't see a way out of the situation. He had to work with Raquel, and she wasn't changing her behavior. So he took the do-nothing option and didn't address it further, except to calmly explain his side of the story whenever Raquel told their boss a lie about him. "Luckily for me, I wasn't the only one whom she treated poorly. Two other people in our department noticed the same kind of thing, so we were able to commiserate," he says. None of them figured out a way to get Raquel to stop lying, but they all learned to laugh at the absurdity of her behavior. "I had a choice to be angry at work every day or to shrug her off." Happily for Darrell, Raquel stayed at the company for only a year.

Your Colleague Goes over Your Head

The situation

Your coworker comes to you with a new initiative and asks for your help. You agree that his idea is worthwhile but explain that you just don't have the time or resources to tackle it this quarter. After your conversation, he goes behind your back to share his brilliant idea with your boss. When your manager comes to you to ask why you're not helping your coworker, you're embarrassed and infuriated. Not only has your coworker undermined your authority, now your boss is questioning your decisions.

Why it happens

There are both practical and psychological reasons why a colleague might try to sidestep you. Practically speaking, he may want a different answer or outcome than you've given him. Psychologically, it's possible that he wants to show that he has more clout or authority than you do.

What to do about it

You may be tempted to stomp over to the person's desk and read him the riot act. "You have to be a saint to not be annoyed or stressed or nervous about something like this happening," says Caroline Webb. But, as with any conflict, even one where you feel you've been slighted, it's better to take a more measured approach. Keep in mind that some people don't know that going over your head may be frowned upon. In some cultures, it's not. So don't make assumptions about the person's intentions. Instead, try the following approaches.

Question your assumptions

To help you keep your cool, Webb suggests you start by sorting through what you actually know. You may think your coworker went over your head but that's not necessarily true. Ask yourself what the facts of the situation are and try to strip your explanation of emotional language. Rather than thinking, "He completely disregarded my authority to get a different answer from my boss," tell yourself, "He had a conversation with my boss about his initiative." Focus on what you know. And then ask yourself: What would be different ways to explain this situation? One might be that your coworker is just out for himself, but another could be that your boss asked him what exciting projects he was working on next quarter. "Work out three or four different scenarios," suggests Webb, "that broaden your aperture and help you question the assumption that they've been dastardly or ill-intended."

Find out more

As you think about what you know, also consider what you don't know. If you just heard about the conversation through the rumor mill, find out what really happened. You might go to your boss and ask in a neutral way about what transpired: "Hey, I heard you and Carlos were talking about his new idea." Take care to maintain a casual, nonaccusatory tone so that your boss doesn't think you're trying to start a feud.

Approach your colleague

If after gathering additional facts, you decide to directly address the issue, start with your coworker. You'll likely need to have a conversation with your boss, too (more on that later), but that discussion will go better if you can report on how you handled things with your colleague. Ask your coworker if you can talk—preferably in a private room. Keep an open mind as you enter the conversation, says Adam Galinsky. This is true anytime you directly address a conflict, but especially in a situation like this when you likely feel put upon or upset. Remember your goal, whether it's to have a strong working relationship, to restore trust, or to protect your time. Don't go into the conversation with the intention of sticking it to your coworker. That's just going to set you up for a battle. Instead, be open to hearing what he has to say about the situation and why he did what he did.

State what you know and how you feel

Begin by saying what you know and how it made you feel. "Make it a straightforward discussion," says Galinsky. Let the person know that you're disappointed by what he did but stay away from words like "angry" or "betrayed." That may be how you feel, but it's going to put your coworker on the defensive, advises Webb. Instead say: "I heard you talked to Roger about your initiative after we discussed it and that made me feel a bit concerned that we're not communicating well."

Problem-solve, together

Once you've shared what you know and heard his perspective, decide together how to remedy the situation. "Try asking them for their thoughts first, before building on their suggestions. Research shows that people feel far more attachment to any idea that they've had a hand in shaping," explains Webb. So instead of saying, "Here's how we should handle this situation," ask, "What do you think would be the best way to address this, given where we are now?" Once you've agreed on how to rectify the current issue, discuss how you'll handle similar situations in the future.

Clarify the lines of communication

Ideally, you'll both agree that your coworker should come directly to you next time and then actually follow through on that. But if he's not on board with that plan, prevent this situation from recurring by showing him that going over your head won't be effective. Make clear that you and your boss are in regular contact and if he goes to your manager, you're going to find out. You might say something along the lines of, "I meet with Roger regularly to discuss our group's priorities and he usually lets me know if he gets requests from other teams." You don't need to say this in a threatening way; think about it as educating him on the lines of communication.

Repair your relationship with your boss

You may be ticked off that your boss didn't redirect your colleague to you and wonder if he has faith in your judgment. And this breach in the chain of command may have also annoyed your boss or caused him to question your ability to do your job. So once you've settled things with your colleague, talk with your boss about what happened, why it happened, and how to avoid similar situations in the future. Start by considering what you want to get out of the conversation. Webb suggests you may "want to come off as wise, thoughtful, and in control." Your goal here may be to restore your reputation or to reestablish ground rules for communication. Then lay out what you know (for a fact) and how it made you feel: "I heard that Carlos talked to you about his initiative and that made me concerned that I might be out of the loop. Can I ask what happened or how you saw it from your perspective?" Then it's your job to listen. Once you've heard his side of things, you might ask, "What can we do differently when this happens in the future?" You can gently suggest that next time your colleague goes to him, he redirect him to you: "If Carlos comes to you again, would you mind sending him to me so we can address the issue without having to take up your time?"

Gina's story

Gina was responsible for helping new employees get up to speed on current processes and best practices for initiating sales with customers. She was training Dante, who had been hired to work with their biggest customer. Dante was more senior than Gina. "I could tell that he wasn't necessarily pleased to be taking direction from me and had a general air about him that told me that he didn't think I could really teach him anything," she says. Dante wasn't happy with the process and timeline that Gina explained the company typically used with customers. He thought it was too strict and wanted to bypass particular parts of the process, such as getting customer signoff before sending initial samples, in order to speed up the sale. So he went to Gina's manager to get approval to ship the samples.

Luckily, Gina's manager reiterated the company's standard process and the reasons behind it. "If he had said yes, it could have completely thrown off our timeline and been a disaster," Gina says. Then the manager had a conversation with Gina about what had happened with Dante.

Gina decided to talk with Dante directly, but she wanted to be careful. "I knew that if I approached him in a certain way, he could easily become defensive and maybe even combative. I didn't want to make any snap judgments about why he did what he did." While she appreciated his desire to move things along more quickly, she also knew that she had insight on why things were done the way they were.

She asked Dante to sit down with her to review the account once more. "I explained the processes thoroughly and stressed how important it was to follow the guidelines—and included the reasoning behind each step," she says. She casually mentioned that their manager had explained what he had tried to do and thanked him for "trying to think outside of the box and see how we could potentially get samples to the customer even faster." She was careful not to make it a huge deal and to focus on the process conflict they were having. "I didn't make it personal," she says. She ended the conversation on a positive note too, offering to help Dante in any way she could. Gina says this approach worked: The two had a great working relationship after that point, and Dante came to her—not their manager—with questions or concerns.

You're Caught in the Middle of Two Warring Colleagues

The situation

Two of your coworkers just don't get along. They exchange mean looks in meetings, and they both come to you to complain about each other. You want to be supportive, but you also don't want to be seen as taking sides.

Why it happens

We all want to have alliances at work—so when two people are having a conflict, it's not uncommon for them to drag other people in. They may want validation of their viewpoint or to demonstrate to the other person that they have more allies. Conflict avoiders often tend to get put in the middle because they generally don't push back when one coworker gossips about another.

What to do about it

When stuck between two adversaries, "people often find themselves in over their head," says Roderick Kramer, of Stanford Graduate School of Business. "They think they can intervene, make suggestions, feel good about themselves, and move the conflict forward in a constructive way. But that's not always possible."

Stay out of it

Whether or not you engage will depend on how enmeshed you already are in the situation. If you feel as if you're being used as a pawn in their war, draw the line and choose to do nothing. This is particularly tough for conflict avoiders to do, but try saying something such as "I'm sorry that you two aren't getting along, but I'd really prefer to stay out of it." If that feels too difficult to do, try to find ways to spend less time with each of them. After you've turned down a coffee break several times, they may get the hint. "Remember that you aren't a psychologist or a mediator," says Kramer. If the situation is outside your comfort zone or you think the disagreement is juvenile, there's nothing wrong with staying out of it. But always give one or both of your coworkers a next step to take. Say, "I'm not sure I'm the right person to help you with this, but you might want to sit down together or with HR."

On the other hand, if you want to lend a sympathetic ear and think you can help them work through it, take the next few steps.

Allow them to vent

It can be hard to listen to people complain about each other, but sometimes that's exactly what they need. By allowing each of them to process the situation with you, they may figure out on their own what the source of their conflict is and how they can sort it out between them. If you're worried that by hearing one person out, you'll upset the other, make an effort to get both sides of the story. Go to the other person and ask, "What's your take on what's going on between you and Harry?" This will give you a fuller picture of the conflict without earning you a reputation as a meddler. It will also equip you to help them solve it.

Empathize

While listening to each colleague, show that you understand how hard the situation is. You can say, "I'm sorry this is happening" or "It's tough when two people can't agree." Stay neutral and speak from your own experience. Offer observations such as, "It seemed as if Jane was stressed out and didn't mean what she said" or "I know that Joe is a direct person and can sometimes come off as harsh." If you're being pushed to choose a perspective, make it clear that you won't: "You seem hurt, but I can't take sides because I have to work with both of you."

Offer advice—cautiously

Before you give your two cents, ask your coworkers if they want your help. "We tend to offer unsolicited advice because we think we know better," says Anna Ranieri, a career counselor and executive coach. But people might not want your opinion, so start by saying something like, "I've observed what's happening between you two. Would it be helpful to hear my take?"

Explain the impact of their fighting

After you've demonstrated your concern, describe how the conflict is affecting the team. Say something like, "You two not getting along is distracting. We've got a lot on our plates right now with the quarter closing soon, so it'd be better if we were focused on getting the reports done." Or "I'm concerned that you're setting a bad example for the younger people on our team. They look up to both of you, and when they see you treating each other this way, they may think it's OK to do the same to others."

Problem-solve together

Just as you would focus on the future if this were your own conflict, help them do the same. Instead of offering concrete suggestions, help them find their own solutions. Ask open-ended questions as discussed in chapter 6, "Have a Productive Conversation." In this situation, those questions might sound more like "How do you hope this will be resolved?" or "What do you want out of your relationship with Greg?" Kramer says, "You should be more in problem-solving mode than gossip mode."

Gary's story

Gary was planning a partner meeting to make decisions about compensation. As the senior partner, it was his job to set the ground rules for the sensitive discussion. Each partner presented his or her accomplishments and progress against goals, then the other partners asked questions, typically polite requests for clarification, before deciding on that partner's bonus for the year. If there was a more serious issue, the partners usually brought it up before the meeting so that it could be addressed outside of this formal setting.

Everyone knew that two partners, Susan and Robert, had been at odds for some time, and each of them came to Gary ahead of time to complain about the other. Susan felt as if Robert wasn't pulling his weight at the firm and his compensation should reflect that. Robert said that Susan was mistreating her team members, especially junior analysts whom she often had stay late at the office for no reason. He wanted her compensation to be affected as well.

Gary heard them both out. He asked that they sort it out between them in advance of the meeting. When they came back a week later even more upset, he suggested that the three of them sit down together and talk about what could be done. He explained that if the two of them couldn't figure out how to stop fighting, they would have to postpone the compensation discussion, which would affect when the bonuses would get paid out. "But I didn't want—and I know they didn't want—to air all of this in front of the larger group," Gary says. He then asked if they wanted to know his opinion. They both said yes. He suggested they should recuse themselves in the discussion of each other's compensation. "That way it was basically a wash for them," he says.

At first, Susan was game and Robert pushed back. "He wanted to say his piece in front of the group," Gary says. But Gary explained to him that the goal of getting the discussion done was more important than his beef with Susan. So when the group met, Susan and Robert sat out for the discussion of each other's performance and compensation. "It was obvious to everyone in the room what was happening and why, but we accepted that because it let us get through the discussion with everyone saving face," he says. Susan and Robert never got along much better, but because they saw that Gary was unwilling to take sides, they stopped appealing to him.

You're Mad at Your Boss

The situation

You did all the work on the unit's big project, but your boss took all the credit. The executive team patted him on the back, and he didn't say a word about the late nights you pulled. You're angry, but you want to broach this sensitive issue with your boss productively.

Why it happens

"Your relationship with your boss is a significant predictor of your experience at work," says Liane Davey. A positive relationship is likely to lead to interesting assignments, meaningful feedback, and recognition for your contributions, so you want things to go well. But because of that desire, you may also hold your boss to a higher, unobtainable standard.

What to do about it

Fighting with your manager, says McKee, "sparks a deep, primal response: fear." And for good reason. "Bosses hold our lives in their hands—the keys to our futures, not to mention our daily bread." Given that, you could do nothing and move on—as discussed in chapter 2, this is a good option if you don't think your boss will change his ways or is unwilling to hear you. But if you're worried that your anger will only grow, you may want to take the following steps.

Cool down

Remember the advice in chapter 6 about walking away? You don't want to say anything you don't mean. First, give yourself some time—wait a day or two. Your anger may fade to the point where you're willing to let the irksome behavior go. If not, you may decide to address the conflict directly.

Show respect

This may be the last thing you want to do, especially when you feel slighted, but your boss expects—and hopefully deserves—your respect. You can still label your disagreement as a relationship conflict, but before explaining what's made you so mad, "assure your boss that you respect him and his position," says Joseph Grenny, author of *Crucial Conversations: Tools for Talking When Stakes Are High.* "When that sense of respect is secure, you can venture into expressing your views openly and honestly." You might say, "I enjoy working for you, and I know I have a lot to learn from you."

Focus on the business needs, not yours

When you talk to your boss, you can point out how surprised you were by what he did, but you'll get further with the conversation if you frame it in terms of your goals. What's best for the business? Where do your goals align? Your boss may be more willing to change his behavior if you explain that not sharing the credit could create a bottleneck because those above him think he's the only one who can get things done.

Explain your intent

As you would do any time you address conflict directly, tell your boss what your objective is in giving him this feedback. Do you want to show off the work of the team? Are you concerned that you'll become disengaged if your work isn't recognized? Grenny says that you can clarify your intent by contrasting what you mean with what you don't mean. "I'd like to share a concern, but I'm worried that it will sound as if I doubt your character. I don't. And yet I don't think I'd be fully loyal if I didn't share my perspective. May I do so?"

Alina's story

Alina's company had an informal policy that it wouldn't start work with clients (especially new ones) before there was a signed contract in place. Rodrigo, one of the firm's partners, asked Alina to start working with a new client before he'd gotten the contract finalized. "It was a busy time, and I was stretched incredibly thin, but the project started moving forward pretty quickly," she says. She worked nights and weekends to keep up only to find out that the client pulled out before the contract was signed. Rodrigo sent an email letting Alina and the rest of the team know. It ended with "Sorry about this!" which irked Alina. "It seemed flippant to me, and it was inadequately matched to the suckiness of the situation," she explains.

Rodrigo called her to talk through the logistics of how to wrap up the work, but she didn't feel ready to have the conversation. "I wanted to be prepared, and I was afraid I would talk about how personally annoyed I was when really what bothered me was how much of the firm's money was wasted," she explains. She asked Rodrigo if they could talk the following morning instead. She thought about it that night and decided she wouldn't be able to let it go. Rodrigo might not change, but she really needed to get it off her chest.

She knew that both she and Rodrigo were conflict seekers, so she set up a full hour for them to talk. Then she set the tone for the conversation. "I told him that my pushing back on him was not because I didn't respect him. I did. He was amazing at client service. But I felt as if it would be a disservice to him if I didn't point out why ignoring the policy was so bad." At first, Rodrigo was defensive, arguing about whether or not the contract would've made a difference. After she let him vent, he calmed down and vowed to be better about the contracts in the future. He even asked her to keep him accountable, refusing to do work for him if there wasn't a contract in place.

You're Dealing with a Bully

The situation

Your colleague consistently undermines you in meetings, withholds information you need to do your work, and speaks badly about you. This isn't just one jab on a bad day; it's persistent negative behavior over time. You feel sick to your stomach whenever you see her name in your inbox or hear her voice down the hall.

Why it happens

Research from Nathanael Fast, a professor at the University of Southern California's Marshall School of Business, proves a commonly held idea: People act out when their ego is threatened. "We often see powerful people behave aggressively toward less powerful people when their competence is questioned," he says. It's not just people in positions of authority who act this way. Whoever it is, chances are, she's singled you out for this bullying because she's jealous that others like you or that you have skills she doesn't, says Gary Namie, the founder of the Workplace Bullying Institute. You may also seem like an easy target, particularly if she sees that you shy away from conflict.

What to do about it

Just because you're a victim doesn't mean you can't take action. Try the following.

Understand the situation better

Being bullied can be downright painful. Stepping back and looking at the situation can help give you some insight into the dynamic between the two of you. Are you a conflict avoider while she's a seeker? Are your disagreements mostly relationship conflicts? Or are there elements of task conflict as well? Using the advice in this book can give you some distance from the pain of the situation and the emotional room to start to address it.

Stand up for yourself

Call out bad behavior when it happens. "I believe very strongly in making immediate corrections," says Michele Woodward, an executive coach. "If someone calls you honey in a meeting, say right then: 'I don't like being called that. Please use my name,'" she says. If you're uncomfortable with a direct, public response, Woodward advises saying something as soon as you're able. After the meeting, you could say, "I didn't like being called honey. It demeans me." Show that there is no reward for treating you that way. "The message should be: Don't mess with me; it won't be worth your effort," Namie says.

Enlist help

Talk to colleagues you trust and see what they can do, even if it's simply confirming your perspective. They might stand up for you in a meeting, defending your ideas or asking the bully not to call you honey. Or they might go speak to the bully one-on-one and explain how disruptive her behavior is to the larger group. This can be especially helpful if your supporters have power over the bully or the bully trusts them.

Know the limitations

If your colleagues' interventions don't help, escalate the situation to someone more senior or to HR. Your objective is to get the bullying behavior to stop. But that's not always possible. "The only time I've seen bullies change is when they are publicly fired. The sanctions don't work," says Woodward. Instead, protect yourself. Perhaps take time off from work. Or move on—when you're in an abusive situation at work, the most tenable solution may be to leave, if that's a possibility. The Workplace Bullying Institute has done online surveys that show more people stay in a bullying situation because of pride (40% of respondents) than because of economics (38%). If you're worried about letting the bully win, Namie says, you're better off worrying about your own well-being.

Cedric's story

Cedric took a new position at a veterinary clinic with the intention of buying into the practice, which he did after several months, becoming the business partner of the owner, Ruth. A year later, after what seemed like a minor disagreement, Ruth stopped speaking to Cedric for six weeks. When he confronted her, she told him she was contemplating dropping him as a partner. Cedric was shocked. He had taken out a loan to buy into the firm and felt financially stuck.

Cedric soon recognized a pattern in Ruth's behavior. She was a clear conflict seeker. Any time the two had a conflict, no matter what the original source of the disagreement (task, process), it immediately turned personal. "If I disagreed, she would ice me out. If I confronted her, she iced me out longer," he says. He eventually figured out that stroking her ego was more effective. "You could flatter her, tell her how great she was, how well she did in a case, and she'd be back on your side. I learned to do this sort of dance in order to survive."

But Ruth's harsh behavior wore Cedric down. Things got so bad at one point that she didn't speak to him for three months. He enlisted a professional coach, who helped him see that Ruth was a narcissist and a bully who was threatened by his skills. This gave him the confidence to set his limits: He told her he was looking for someone to buy out his part of the business, and she offered to do it. "It was the best thing I could've done," he says. "I wish I had left when she first showed me who she truly was."

Your Counterpart Is Suffering from a Mental Illness

The situation

You never know what frame of mind you'll catch your fellow team member in. Sometimes when you ask him why he didn't respond to an email you sent, he snaps at you and storms off. Other times, when coworkers challenge his ideas, he laughs inappropriately. When he doesn't show up to meetings or get his share of the team's work done, you're afraid to confront him because you have no idea how he'll react. You wonder whether there's more going on here than just a quirky personality—perhaps he has a mental illness.

Why it happens

In 2014, the National Institute of Mental Health estimated that 18.1% of adults in the United States had a mental illness, most of whom didn't have an official diagnosis. With percentages that high, you're likely to have coworkers with some sort of mental illness—depression, personality disorders, schizophrenia—"especially since many of these issues don't prevent people from working," McKee says.

What to do about it

We can't account for our colleagues' moods, nor should we. "There are clues, however, that let us know that there may be something more going on than a disagreement," says McKee. Your interactions or homework to better understand your counterpart may reveal things such as sudden changes in mood or communication style, personality, or personal habits, or social withdrawal—all of which are indications that your coworker may have an underlying mental health issue. Addressing the conflict could be dangerous—to your and your coworker's well-being. Instead, do the following.

Look for patterns

Is his behavior often erratic? Do his regular actions seem outside the norm? Don't jump to conclusions. "Occasionally people do things that others deem inappropriate, but if it happens on a consistent basis or every time the person feels threatened, it's an indication that there's a larger issue," says McKee.

Don't diagnose

Although it's helpful to recognize when something bigger might be affecting your colleague, don't try to come up with a specific diagnosis. Chances are that you aren't trained to evaluate emotional or psychological problems. "And we really don't know if there's truly something going on," says Judith White. What you can do instead, suggests White, is educate yourself about the symptoms you may be able to observe in family, friends, and colleagues. "The National Alliance on Mental Illness [https://www.nami.org/] is a good resource for friends and family members who either know or suspect mental illness," she says. This information can help you distinguish between an isolated incident that may be safe to address and a deeper problem that is better handled by a professional.

Don't let the problem lie

You might be tempted to steer clear and exercise your do-nothing option because you're afraid or unsure about what to do. Doing nothing may be the right approach to the conflict but not necessarily to the person. It's most certainly a sensitive situation, but that doesn't mean you have to completely ignore it. After all, it may be hard for this person to do his job if he can't get along with people. "Most job descriptions have requirements for 'interaction' or 'collaboration' of some kind baked in, and if the person can't fulfill this aspect of the job, then it's time to step in," says White. Indirectly addressing the conflict is often the right approach here. White recommends asking your boss or HR for help with the problem, or reaching out to your company's employee assistance program, if you have one.

Be compassionate

"Remember that everyone has a story," says McKee. Don't judge what's going on with your colleague. He might be suffering from his behavior as much as or more than you. If you have a close personal relationship and you suspect there is an underlying health issue, gently ask about what might be going on outside of work. But don't push. If he doesn't want to talk, don't force it.

Go by the book

Because of the sensitivity of the situation, this is not a place to wing it. White says to follow any formal rules your company has for resolving the conflict because informal persuasion or negotiation is unlikely to work. "Look up the legal or regulatory rules, and if they don't exist, then find out past precedent in your organization and write it down," says White. Then keep records of your interactions. If the conflict escalates, you'll be able to justify your actions to this person, and to any third parties.

Heather's story

Heather was concerned about her fellow professor, Jacques. "He had always been jovial, but his behavior changed midway through the year," Heather explained. "We were coleading an independent study for five students, and he basically stopped showing up," she says. Every time Heather tried to ask Jacques whether he had read the students' papers or was planning to come to the next meeting, Jacques would snap and insist he was fine. "I felt bad for him, but I was also annoyed because I was picking up his slack and I was already having a busy semester, and here he is yelling at me," says Heather. When she realized that the direct approach wasn't working, Heather thought about doing nothing. She knew that she could cover the class, and she hoped that after the summer break, Jacques might return feeling better. "But that didn't feel right. I didn't want to get him in trouble, but there was clearly something wrong. He had become a different person."

Heather decided to ask for help. She went to their department chair and explained the situation, telling him that some of the students had started to complain. The chair worked with HR to talk with Jacques and convince him to take a leave of absence. Heather found out a year later that Jacques had been suffering from severe depression. "I wasn't surprised, but it explained a lot. I'm glad I handled it the way I did. I tried to be as compassionate as I could."

You Manage Two People Who Hate Each Other

The situation

As a manager you probably didn't expect to play referee, but two of your team members just aren't getting along. They won't look at each other, they openly deride each other, and they refuse to cooperate. How you can right such a dysfunctional relationship?

Why it happens

Conflict, as discussed in chapter 5, is often based on the fear of losing something—ego, respect, status. Your team members may be insecure, anxious about their status in the team, or worried about their jobs. Instead of handling their emotions appropriately, they're taking them out on each other.

What to do about it

You have an obligation to help your team members. You don't have to hold their hands, but you do need to examine your role in the problem and offer suggestions for moving forward.

Hear them out

Give each person a chance to explain his point of view. First, sit down with each person one-on-one. "Redirect comments that include assumptions about what the other person is thinking or feeling," Davey suggests. For example, if he says, "She's trying to destroy my credibility," respond by reframing the idea: "We don't know her motive; I'm interested in how her behavior is being interpreted by you. How do you feel when she disagrees with you in front of the team?"

Determine if you've contributed to the problem

Make sure you haven't set these two up for failure, suggests Davey, by either being unclear about roles or sparking unhealthy competition. Ask: Do they have a clear understanding of what's expected of them? Are their metrics and rewards designed to promote collaboration rather than rivalry? If either answer is no, sit them down to make expectations clear and rejigger their goals so that they can work better together.

Manage your reaction

You may be fed up with these two. If you can't be empathetic, you won't be able to help because your annoyance is likely to further heighten the conflict. "Start with the positive assumption that your direct reports are good people experiencing something stressful," says Davey. This shift in mindset will help in the same way it does when you're addressing your own conflict (as discussed in chapter 5). It will also make you calmer: a key component of managing your emotions—and theirs.

Help them see the other side

Ask questions so that they can understand the other person's perspective. "How do you think she felt when she joined a team of people who are older and more experienced than she is?" "How might you help her get her point across so that she doesn't need to be so assertive?" If there's someone on the team they both get along with, ask that person to serve as a bridge and raise each other's awareness about what the other is thinking.

Bring them together

After they've had a chance to vent and see the situation from the other's perspective, bring them together. Davey suggests you start by saying, "I've been speaking with each of you about my concerns over your strained relationship, and I was hoping you felt ready to talk directly to each other." Interject as little as possible in the conversation, but when you know there is something that's not being said, provide a gentle nudge: "Heather, we talked about your reaction to Tony's tone of voice. Do you want to share that with him?"

Work toward a shared agreement

Ask them each to make commitments about what they'll change. "Heather, what are you planning to do differently going forward? And Tony, how about you?" Then tell them that you'd like to keep them accountable to those promises. Document what they said they would do differently and send it to both of them to confirm agreement.

Focus them on work

Leadership professor Richard Boyatzis says the best way to heal war wounds is to start working again. Give them a relatively easy task to rebuild their confidence as a team. As they restore their relationship, help them follow Bob Sutton's advice from chapter 8, "Repair the Relationship," about working together. Put them on projects that require deeper collaboration and give them the opportunity to work through task or process conflicts.

Prevent additional problems

Encourage your team members to handle issues themselves. Research by Grenny shows that top-performing teams immediately and respectfully confront one another when problems arise. “Not only does this drive greater innovation, trust, and productivity, but it also frees the boss from being the playground monitor,” says Grenny. Let new team members know up front that you expect them to hold *you* and others responsible. Call out positive examples and be a good model yourself. If people still come running to you whenever there’s a fight, refuse to get involved. If you’re not solving it for them, they’ll figure out how to do it on their own.

Marshall’s story

Marshall, the owner of an eco-lodge, employed four managers including Helga, a German expat who ran the front office and oversaw the staff when Marshall was offsite, and Carlos, a Belizean who was in charge of client services. Helga was incredibly organized and meticulous about her work. Carlos’s expertise was client service. “He had an ability to make every guest feel as if he or she is the first one to ever see a snake,” says Marshall.

But Helga and Carlos weren’t getting along. In fact, Helga asked Marshall to fire Carlos because she felt he wasn’t doing his job; he regularly forgot to do tasks and was sloppy with his paperwork. She was frustrated and felt as if she was working twice as hard as he was. Carlos had also previously complained about Helga. He resented her criticism and felt she was too cold to the clients.

As Marshall saw it, they were both failing to understand or appreciate each other’s talents. Marshall encouraged Helga to step back and look at the situation.

Carlos was failing to do part of his job description, but he was invaluable to the lodge. Helga conceded that Carlos's job description should be changed so that he could live up to expectations.

He spoke to both employees, explained why each one was extremely valuable to the team, and asked them to appreciate what the other brought. He asked them to focus on the larger purpose and to put their disputes behind them. With expectations reset, Carlos and Helga found a way to work together by accepting that they had completely different styles but both cared ultimately about the same thing—making the lodge successful.

Your Team Turns on You

The situation

Your team members disengage or stop coming to meetings. They simply don't do, or even refuse outright, what you ask of them. They begin meeting without you. You start to worry that you have a mutiny on your hands.

Why it happens

Your team may be upset about a decision you made (or didn't make) or fed up with you continually interrupting them, taking credit for their ideas, or not going to bat for them.

What to do about it

For a leader, this can be a disheartening and terrifying experience, but it's not irreparable. By being open to what's happening, listening to your team, and being direct, you can regain the group's confidence and your effectiveness as a leader.

Find out what's going on

Is one person driving the negativity, or are the feelings shared across the team? Are people taking issue with your leadership, or is fighting among team members causing them to rebel against you? Ask direct and open questions that get at the source of the conflict. It's easiest to do this in one-on-one meetings with team members you trust most. But if they tell you that others have an issue with you, ask them to send the others to talk to you directly.

Name what's happening

Once you've identified the source of the conflict, acknowledge it with your team. "It seems as if you all are upset with the way I've been gathering and incorporating your input into the new strategy. Is that right? Am I missing anything?" Trying to gloss over a problem can turn it into the elephant in the room. "If you're pretending that nothing's wrong and the rest of your team knows there is, it can be really problematic," says Deborah Ancona, an MIT professor. And while you may want to follow the team's lead in not directly addressing the situation, when they're letting the conflict seep out in other ways, doing nothing isn't a smart option.

Own the issue

No matter the cause of the problem, recognize the things that became destructive under your watch. Publicly acknowledge what you have done to contribute to the problem, and explain what you're going to do to address it. "Great leaders are able to get up and say, 'Thanks for the feedback. I realize I haven't been doing X. These are the steps I'm taking to correct this, and I'd appreciate feedback on how it's going,'" says Ancona.

Get outside help if necessary

When a team is particularly defiant or upset, you may not be able to resolve the conflict alone. Find a mediator—either an outside coach or an uninvolved person from another part of the organization—to get the issues out in the open and negotiate a resolution. Typically you do this when you've exhausted all options, as discussed in chapter 7, "Get to a Resolution and Make a Plan," but you may need to go this route sooner because there are so many people involved and you may not get the whole story as the boss. Working with a coach can help you understand why your style or approach is not effective with your team.

Katja's story

Katja was ready to close her marketing company. The business was doing OK, but there were some severe personnel problems: Morale was low, and her employees were angry and resentful. "The soul of my business was black," she recalls.

When she looked honestly at the situation, she saw that there wasn't disagreement over task or process or even status. It was pure relationship conflict. Her boyfriend at the time convinced her to work with an executive coach before she truly called it quits. The coach helped her to develop a plan to address the conflict. She started by talking with members of her staff to find out what was going on. But every time she spoke to anyone, they would claim they didn't have an issue, but someone else did. "Eventually, I started to realize that no one was going to own up to the conflict, so I had to get it out in the open."

Katja requested that they start communicating directly. There couldn't be any gossip if they were going to turn things around and improve their relationships. She also acknowledged her role in creating the destructive atmosphere. She herself had gossiped on occasion, and she knew she'd set a bad example. Once her employees started having the difficult conversations needed to resolve their conflicts with her and with one another, they began to feel more united and committed. Soon they realized there was pent-up client demand they hadn't been able to serve because they were so wrapped up in what was going on inside the business. In the next six years, the company's revenue tripled.

You're Fighting with Someone Outside the Office

The situation

Your vendor has missed several deadlines, and you're getting nervous the IT project isn't going to get done on time. But your contact there isn't answering your calls or emails. You're wondering if it's time to switch vendors.

Why it happens

When you're interacting with people in other organizations—a customer, supplier, a partner—you typically know little about them. Without the shared context of an office, colleagues, and other commonalities, it's easy for you and an external partner to misunderstand each other or misinterpret intentions.

What to do about it

Whether the person is a vendor who has missed several deadlines, a customer who complains about a rise in your product's price, or a colleague from a partner organization who is accusing you of not holding up your end of an agreement, approach the issue in the same way.

Don't overcompensate

It's tempting to treat the situation differently than fighting with someone inside your organization. You might think, "This is a key supplier. I should do whatever it takes to smooth over this disagreement" or "They're just a vendor. We can find a new one next week." You may feel less invested in the relationship because there are 10 vendors who want your business. But although you may have lots of alternatives, know what it would mean to pursue them. Sometimes the cost of switching vendors or suppliers is higher than you think. "With external parties, you don't want to fall on your sword, but you also don't want to treat them as if they don't matter," says Jeff Weiss.

Show respect

With people you don't see regularly, and perhaps with whom you communicate mostly via email, it's important to demonstrate that you value the relationship. This isn't always implicit. It's a good way to signal that you're invested in working through the issue. Plus, it establishes a foundation of trust from which you can solve the problem: "I know we don't see each other often, but I wanted you to know that I value this relationship and appreciate what your company does for ours."

Jointly diagnose the problem

As with any conflict, you want to understand what the root cause is, but because you work in different organizations, you may know less about your counterpart, his perspective, and his goals. Sit down to jointly diagnose what led to the conflict. Is there a communication problem? Are you perceiving an issue differently? What about your contribution to the issues? Have you not given the supplier clear instructions? Have you been too hands-off? Have you made it difficult for him to do his job?

Know your counterpart's stakeholders

You likely have a contact at your supplier, but this isn't the person who makes all of the decisions that affect you. You're frustrated that he's not getting back to you about pricing or delivery terms, but it may be that he's trying to get his boss or finance on board with the new terms. "You are at the interface of the conflict," says Jonathan Hughes. When you do the work to better understand your counterpart and your goals, don't just focus on your point of contact. Also consider anyone who may have a stake in the decision. And when you propose a resolution, figure out how you can help your contact sell it internally at his organization so that it fits into their goals. You can ask, "How can I help you get approval for this arrangement?"

Consider the precedent

Because you may have fewer interactions with this person than you do with coworkers, it's important to examine the tone you're setting as it's likely to influence any discussions that come next. "Think about the history you want to have behind you," advises Weiss. If you mistreat your counterpart, you're sending the message that he can do the same the next time an issue comes up between your two organizations—whereas if you are thoughtful and respectful, and take his (and his company's) perspective into consideration, you're paving the way for smoother interactions in the future.

Zach's story

As the project manager at a building company, Zach works with dozens of subcontractors at a time—plumbers, painters, carpenters, electricians. "I approach these relationships with one question in mind: 'How can we partner to get this project done for a client?'" he says. But he acknowledges that it's difficult to settle disputes because the subcontractors can walk away from the job. "They don't have the relationship with the client; I do," he says.

A plumber with whom he was working on a big redesign project was getting upset about the payment terms. "It's standard in the industry to pay subcontractors within 30 days, but we're not always able to do that," Zach says. The plumber had put a lot of time and material into the project, and he hadn't received any payment. "The trouble was that the client wasn't paying us, so we couldn't pay out our subs." The plumber threatened to walk off the job.

Although Zach knew he could find another subcontractor if necessary, he valued his relationship with this plumber and said so. He told him, "Look, you've always been a great partner, and as you know, we typically pay net 30, but we're stuck in a bind this time. Can you see it from my perspective? I'd love to pay you, but I just don't have the money." Zach then offered to let him know as soon as the client check came in. "I promised I'd send him his check the very same day," he says. "I don't think he was happy with the outcome because he still had to wait for his money, but he understood the position I was in."

Knowing how to manage conflict at work won't make it go away, but it will make dealing with any disagreements easier and less stressful. Whether you're experiencing conflict with your direct report or your boss—or someone outside your business—you now have the tools to assess the situation and choose an approach that works for you. As these scenarios show, directly addressing the conflict is just one alternative. You also need to know when to walk away or get out of the relationship altogether. But if you do choose to sit down with your counterpart, you're now better equipped to prepare for and engage in a difficult conversation, manage your and your counterpart's emotions, and develop a resolution together.

Sources

Introduction

- Karen Dillon, *HBR Guide to Office Politics*, Harvard Business Review Press, 2015.
- Jennifer Lawler, "The Real Cost of Workplace Conflict," Entrepreneur.com, June 10, 2010, http://www.entrepreneur.com/article/207196.
- Kenneth W. Thomas, "Making Conflict Management a Strategic Advantage," CPP, https://www.cpp.com/pdfs/conflict_whitepaper.pdf.
- Jeanne Whalen, "Angry Outbursts Really Do Hurt Your Health, Doctors Find," *Wall Street Journal*, March 23, 2015, http://www.wsj.com/articles/angry-outbursts-really-do-hurt-your-health-doctors-find-1427150596.

Chapter 1

- Annie McKee, "How Power Affects Your Productivity," HBR.org, February 9, 2015, https://hbr.org/2015/02/how-power-affects-your-productivity.

Chapter 2

- Jeanne Brett, "When and How to Let a Conflict Go," HBR.org, June 10, 2014, https://hbr.org/2014/06/when-and-how-to-let-a-conflict-go/.

Chapter 3

- Hannah Riley Bowles, "Why Women Don't Negotiate Their Job Offers," HBR.org, June 19, 2014, https://hbr.org/2014/06/why-women-dont-negotiate-their-job-offers.
- Liane Davey, "Conflict Strategies for Nice People," HBR.org, December 25, 2013, https://hbr.org/2013/12/conflict-strategies-for-nice-people/.
- Judith E. Glaser, "Your Brain Is Hooked on Being Right," HBR.org, February 28, 2013, https://hbr.org/2013/02/break-your-addiction-to-being/.
- Amy Jen Su, "Get Over Your Fear of Conflict," HBR.org, June 6, 2014, https://hbr.org/2014/06/get-over-your-fear-of-conflict.

Chapter 4

- Jeanne Brett, "When and How to Let a Conflict Go," HBR.org, June 10, 2104, https://hbr.org/2014/06/when-and-how-to-let-a-conflict-go/.
- Ben Dattner, "Most Work Conflicts Aren't Due to Personality," HBR.org, May 20, 2014, https://hbr

.org/2014/05/most-work-conflicts-arent-due-to-personality/.

- Karen Dillon, *HBR Guide to Office Politics,* Harvard Business Review Press, 2015.
- Jeffrey Pfeffer, "Win at Workplace Conflict," HBR.org, May 29, 2014, https://hbr.org/2014/05/win-at-workplace-conflict/.
- Judith White, "Two Kinds of People You Should Never Negotiate With," HBR.org, June 18, 2014, https://hbr.org/2014/06/two-kinds-of-people-you-should-never-negotiate-with/.

Chapter 5

- Jeanne Brett, "When and How to Let a Conflict Go," HBR.org, June 10, 2014, https://hbr.org/2014/06/when-and-how-to-let-a-conflict-go/.
- Susan David, "Manage a Difficult Conversation with Emotional Intelligence," HBR.org, June 19, 2014, https://hbr.org/2014/manage-a-difficult-conversation-with-emotional-intelligence/.
- Susan David and Christina Congleton, "Emotional Agility," *Harvard Business Review,* November 2013 (product R1311L).
- Amy Gallo, "Choose the Right Words in an Argument," HBR.org, June 16, 2014, https://hbr.org/2014/06/choose-the-right-words-in-an-argument/.

- Amy Gallo, "How to Work with Someone You Hate," HBR.org, January 30, 2012, https://hbr.org/2012/01/how-to-work-with-someone-you-h/.
- Amy Gallo, "The Right Way to Fight," HBR.org, May 12, 2010, https://hbr.org/2010/05/the-right-way-to-fight/.
- Rebecca Knight, "How to Handle Difficult Conversations at Work," HBR.org, January 9, 2015, https://hbr.org/2015/01/how-to-handle-difficult-conversations-at-work.

Chapter 6

- Dorie Clark, "How to Repair a Damaged Professional Relationship," HBR.org, June 5, 2014, https://hbr.org/2014/06/how-to-repair-a-damaged-professional-relationship.
- Liane Davey, "Conflict Strategies for Nice People," HBR.org, December 25, 2013, https://hbr.org/2013/12/conflict-strategies-for-nice-people/.
- Susan David and Christina Congleton, "Emotional Agility," *Harvard Business Review*, November 2013 (product R1311L).
- Amy Gallo, "Choose the Right Words in an Argument," HBR.org, June 16, 2014, https://hbr.org/2014/06/hoose-the-right-words-in-an-argument/.

- Amy Gallo, “The Right Way to Fight,” HBR.org, May 12, 2010, https://hbr.org/2010/05/the-right-way-to-fight/.
- Mark Gerzon, “To Resolve a Conflict, First Decide: Is It Hot or Cold?” HBR.org, June 26, 2014, https://hbr.org/2014/06/to-resolve-a-conflict-first-decide-is-it-hot-or-cold/.
- Rebecca Knight, “How to Handle Difficult Conversations at Work,” HBR.org, January 9, 2015, https://hbr.org/2015/01/how-to-handle-difficult-conversations-at-work.
- Katie Liljenquist and Adam Galinsky, “Win Over an Opponent by Asking for Advice,” HBR.org, June 27, 2014, https://hbr.org/2014/06/win-over-an-opponent-by-asking-for-advice.

Chapter 7

- Rebecca Knight, “How to Handle Difficult Conversations at Work,” HBR.org, January 9, 2015, https://hbr.org/2015/01/how-to-handle-difficult-conversations-at-work.
- Jeff Weiss, *HBR Guide to Negotiating,* Harvard Business Review Press, 2016.

Chapter 8

- Jeanne Brett, “When and How to Let a Conflict Go,” HBR.org, June 10, 2014, https://hbr.org/2014/06/when-and-how-to-let-a-conflict-go/.

- Dorie Clark, "How to Repair a Damaged Professional Relationship," HBR.org, June 5, 2014, https://hbr.org/2014/06/how-to-repair-a-damaged-professional-relationship.
- Amy Gallo, "Fixing a Work Relationship Gone Sour," HBR.org, August 20, 2014, https://hbr.org/2014/08/fixing-a-work-relationship-gone-sour/.
- Amy Gallo, "How to Build the Social Ties You Need at Work," HBR.org, September 23, 2015, https://hbr.org/2015/09/how-to-build-the-social-ties-you-need-at-work.
- Amy Gallo, "How to Deal with a Mean Colleague," HBR.org, October 16, 2014, https://hbr.org/2014/10/how-to-deal-with-a-mean-colleague/.
- Amy Gallo, "How to Manage Someone You Don't Like," HBR.org, August 29, 2013, https://hbr.org/2013/08/how-to-manage-someone-you-dont/.
- Amy Gallo, "How to Work with Someone You Hate," HBR.org, January 30, 2012, https://hbr.org/2012/01/how-to-work-with-someone-you-h/.
- Caroline Webb, "How to Tell a Coworker They're Annoying You," HBR.org, March 10, 2016, https://hbr.org/2016/03/how-to-tell-a-coworker-theyre-annoying-you.

Chapter 9

- Jeanne Brett, "When and How to Let a Conflict Go," HBR.org, June 10, 2014, https://hbr.org/2014/06/when-and-how-to-let-a-conflict-go/.
- Liane Davey, "Conflict Strategies for Nice People," HBR.org, December 25, 2013, https://hbr.org/2013/12/conflict-strategies-for-nice-people/.
- Liane Davey, "Managing Two People Who Hate Each Other," HBR.org, June 9, 2014, https://hbr.org/2014/06/managing-two-people-who-hate-each-other/.
- Liane Davey, "What to Do When Your Boss Doesn't Like You," HBR.org, December 8, 2014, https://hbr.org/2014/12/what-to-do-when-your-boss-doesnt-like-you.
- Karen Dillon, "Don't Hide When Your Boss Is Mad at You," HBR.org, June 11, 2014, https://hbr.org/2014/06/dont-hide-when-your-boss-is-mad-at-you/.
- Nathanael J. Fast, Ethan R. Burris, and Caroline A. Bartel, "Research: Insecure Managers Don't Want Your Suggestions," HBR.org, November 24, 2014, https://hbr.org/2014/11/research-insecure-managers-dont-want-your-suggestions/.
- Keith Ferrazzi, "How to Manage Conflict in Virtual Teams," HBR.org, November 19, 2012,

https://hbr.org/2012/11/how-to-manage-conflict-in-virt/.

- Amy Gallo, "Choose the Right Words in an Argument," HBR.org, June 16, 2014, https://hbr.org/2014/06/choose-the-right-words-in-an-argument/.
- Amy Gallo, "Get Your Team to Stop Fighting and Start Working," HBR.org, June 9, 2010, https://hbr.org/2010/06/get-your-team-to-stop-fighting/.
- Amy Gallo, "How to Deal with a Mean Colleague," HBR.org, October 16, 2014, https://hbr.org/2014/10/how-to-deal-with-a-mean-colleague.
- Amy Gallo, "The Right Way to Fight," HBR.org, May 12, 2010, https://hbr.org/2010/05/the-right-way-to-fight/.
- Amy Gallo, "When Two of Your Coworkers Are Fighting," HBR.org, July 3, 2014, https://hbr.org/2014/07/when-two-of-your-coworkers-are-fighting/.
- Amy Gallo, "When You Think the Strategy Is Wrong," HBR.org, February 4, 2010, https://hbr.org/2010/02/when-you-think-the-strategy-is.html.
- Daniel Goleman, "E-Mail Is Easy to Write (and to Misread)," *New York Times*, October 7, 2007, http://www.nytimes.com/2007/10/07/jobs/07pre.html?_r=0.

- Joseph Grenny, "How to Disagree with Your Boss," HBR.org, November 25, 2014, https://hbr.org/2014/11/how-to-disagree-with-your-boss.
- Joseph Grenny, "The Best Teams Hold Themselves Accountable," HBR.org, May 30, 2014, https://hbr.org/2014/05/the-best-teams-hold-themselves-accountable.
- Pamela Hinds, "4 Ways to Decrease Conflict Within Global Teams," HBR.org, June 27, 2014, https://hbr.org/2014/06/4-ways-to-decrease-conflict-within-global-teams.
- Amy Jen Su and Muriel Maignan Wilkins, "How to Deal with a Passive-Aggressive Peer," HBR.org, December 14, 2010, https://hbr.org/2010/12/how-to-deal-with-a-passive-agg.
- Rebecca Knight, "How to Manage Remote Direct Reports," HBR.org, February 10, 2015, https://hbr.org/2015/02/how-to-manage-remote-direct-reports.
- Annie McKee, "When Fighting with Your Boss, Protect Yourself First," HBR.org, July 22, 2014, https://hbr.org/2014/07/when-fighting-with-your-boss-protect-yourself-first/.
- Holly Weeks, "Say No Without Burning Bridges," HBR.org, June 24, 2014, https://hbr.org/2014/06/say-no-without-burning-bridges/.

Featured Experts

Deborah Ancona is the Seley Distinguished Professor of Management at the MIT Sloan School of Management and the faculty director of the MIT Leadership Center. She is also a coauthor of *X-Teams: How to Build Teams That Lead, Innovate, and Succeed* (with Henrik Bresman).

Richard Boyatzis is a Distinguished University Professor, and a professor in the departments of Organizational Behavior and Psychology Cognitive Science at Case Western Reserve University, where his MOOC "Inspiring Leadership Through Emotional Intelligence," has over 400,000 participants from over 200 countries. He is a coauthor of *Primal Leadership: Unleashing the Power of Emotional Intelligence* (with Daniel Goleman and Annie McKee), as well as *Resonant Leadership: Renewing Yourself and Connecting with Others Through Mindfulness, Hope, and Compassion* (with Annie Mckee) and *Becoming a Resonant Leader: Develop Your Emotional Intelligence, Renew Your Relationships, Sustain Your Effectiveness* (with Annie McKee and Fran Johnston).

Jeanne Brett is the DeWitt W. Buchanan, Jr. Distinguished Professor of Dispute Resolution and Organizations at the Kellogg School of Management, Northwestern University, and the director of the Kellogg School's Dispute Resolution Research Center. She is the author of *Negotiating Globally: How to Negotiate Deals, Resolve Disputes, and Make Decisions Across Cultural Boundaries* and a coauthor (with William Ury and Stephen B. Goldberg) of *Getting Disputes Resolved: Designing Systems to Cut the Costs of Conflict.*

Dorie Clark is a marketing strategist and professional speaker who teaches at Duke University's Fuqua School of Business. She is the author of *Reinventing You: Define Your Brand, Imagine Your Future* and *Stand Out: How to Find Your Breakthrough Idea and Build a Following Around It.* She is currently writing a book on being an entrepreneur for Harvard Business Review Press. You can access her free articles at dorieclark.com

Ben Dattner is an executive coach and the founder of Dattner Consulting in New York City. He is also the author of *The Blame Game: How the Hidden Rules of Credit and Blame Determine Our Success or Failure.*

Liane Davey is the cofounder of 3COze Inc. She is the author of *You First: Inspire Your Team to Grow Up, Get Along, and Get Stuff Done* and a coauthor (with David S. Weiss and Vince Molinaro) of *Leadership Solutions: The Pathway to Bridge the Leadership Gap.* Follow her on Twitter: @LianeDavey.

Susan David, PhD, a founder of the Harvard affiliated Institute of Coaching and CEO of Evidence Based Psychology, is an internationally recognized leader operating at the nexus of business and psychology. She routinely consults, speaks, and coaches at the most senior levels of *Fortune* 500 organizations and influential not-for-profits. She is the author of *Emotional Agility: Get Unstuck, Embrace Change, and Thrive in Work and Life* and coauthor of the definitive *Oxford Handbook of Happiness* (with Ilona Boniwell and Amanda Conley Ayers) and *Beyond Goals: Effective Strategies for Coaching and Mentoring* (with David Clutterbuck and David Megginson).

Karen Dillon is the author of the *HBR Guide to Office Politics* and a coauthor of *Competing Against Luck: The Story of Innovation and Customer Choice* (with Clayton M. Christensen, Taddy Hall, and David S. Duncan) and *How Will You Measure Your Life?* (with Clayton M. Christensen and James Allworth). She is the former editor of *Harvard Business Review*. Follow her on Twitter: @DillonHBR.

Nathanael Fast is an associate professor of management at the Marshall School of Business at the University of Southern California. He studies power and status in groups and organizations.

Keith Ferrazzi is the CEO of Ferrazzi Greenlight, a research-based consulting and coaching company, and the author of *Never Eat Alone* and the #1 best seller

Who's Got Your Back: The Breakthrough Program to Build Deep, Trusting Relationships That Create Success—and Won't Let You Fail.

Adam Galinsky is the Vikram S. Pandit Professor of Business and the chair of the Management Department at the Columbia Business School. He is the coauthor (with Maurice Schweitzer) of *Friend and Foe: When to Cooperate, When to Compete, and How to Succeed at Both.* His research focuses on leadership, power, negotiations, decision making, and ethics.

Mark Gerzon is the author of *Leading Through Conflict: How Successful Leaders Transform Differences into Opportunities* and the president of the Mediators Foundation.

Judith E. Glaser is the CEO of Benchmark Communications and the chairman of the Creating WE Institute. She is the author of six books, including *Creating WE: Change I-Thinking to We-Thinking and Build a Healthy, Thriving Organization* and *Conversational Intelligence: How Great Leaders Build Trust and Get Extraordinary Results.*

Daniel Goleman is a codirector of the Consortium for Research on Emotional Intelligence in Organizations at Rutgers University, a coauthor (with Richard Boyatzis and Annie McKee) of *Primal Leadership: Unleashing the Power of Emotional Intelligence,* and the author of *Focus: The Hidden Driver of Success, Emotional*

Intelligence: Why It Can Matter More Than IQ, The Brain and Emotional Intelligence: New Insights, and *Leadership: The Power of Emotional Intelligence, Selected Writings.*

Joseph Grenny is a cofounder of VitalSmarts, an innovator in corporate training and leadership development, and a coauthor of *Crucial Conversations: Tools for Talking When Stakes Are High* and *Crucial Accountability: Tools for Resolving Violated Expectations, Broken Commitments, and Bad Behavior* (with Kerry Patterson, Ron McMillan, and Al Switzler), as well as *Influencer: The New Science of Leading Change* and *Change Anything: The New Science of Personal Success* (with Kerry Patterson, David Maxfield, Ron McMillan, and Al Switzler).

Linda Hill is the Wallace Brett Donham Professor of Business Administration at Harvard Business School. She is a coauthor of *Being the Boss: The 3 Imperatives for Becoming a Great Leader* (with Kent Lineback) and *Collective Genius: The Art and Practice of Leading Innovation* (with Greg Brandeau, Emily Truelove, and Kent Lineback).

Pamela Hinds is a professor in management science and engineering at Stanford University. She studies the dynamics of globally distributed work teams and writes about issues of culture, language, and the transfer of work practices in global collaborations.

Jonathan Hughes is a partner at Vantage Partners, a global consultancy that advises companies on complex

B2B negotiations, strategic alliances, customer and supplier partnerships, and organizational transformation.

Amy Jen Su is a cofounder and managing partner of Paravis Partners, a boutique executive coaching and leadership development firm. She is a coauthor (with Muriel Maignan Wilkins) of *Own the Room: Discover Your Signature Voice to Master Your Leadership Presence.*

Roderick Kramer is the William R. Kimball Professor of Organizational Behavior, Stanford Graduate School of Business, a coeditor (with Todd Pittinsky) of *Restoring Trust in Organizations and Leaders*, and a coeditor (with George Goethals, Scott Allison, and David Messick) of *Conceptions of Leadership.*

Katie Liljenquist is on the faculty of Brigham Young University's Department of Organizational Leadership and Strategy. She studies decision making and interpersonal influence.

Muriel Maignan Wilkins is a cofounder and managing partner of Paravis Partners, a boutique executive coaching and leadership development firm. She is a coauthor (with Amy Jen Su) of *Own the Room: Discover Your Signature Voice to Master Your Leadership Presence.*

Jean-François Manzoni is the president and Nestlé Professor at IMD. He is a coauthor (with Jean-Louis Barsoux) of *The Set-Up-to-Fail Syndrome: How Good Managers Cause Great People to Fail.*

Annie McKee is a senior fellow at the University of Pennsylvania, the director of the PennCLO Executive Doctoral Program, and the founder of the Teleos Leadership Institute. She is a coauthor of *Primal Leadership: Unleashing the Power of Emotional Intelligence* (with Daniel Goleman and Richard Boyatzis), as well as *Resonant Leadership: Renewing Yourself and Connecting with Others Through Mindfulness, Hope, and Compassion* (with Richard Boyatzis), and *Becoming a Resonant Leader: Develop Your Emotional Intelligence, Renew Your Relationships, Sustain Your Effectiveness* (with Richard Boyatzis and Fran Johnston). She is also the author of the forthcoming *How to Be Happy at Work: The Power of Purpose, Hope, and Friendship.*

Erin Meyer is a professor specializing in cross-cultural management at INSEAD. She is the author of *The Culture Map: Breaking Through the Invisible Boundaries of Global Business.* Follow her @ErinMeyerINSEAD.

Mark Mortensen is an associate professor of organizational behavior at INSEAD. His work focuses on the changing nature of collaboration, particularly fluid, interdependent, and global teams.

Gary Namie is the founder of the Workplace Bullying Institute. He is a coauthor (with Ruth F. Namie) of *The Bully-Free Workplace: Stop Jerks, Weasels, and Snakes from Killing Your Organization* and *The Bully at Work: What You Can Do to Stop the Hurt and Reclaim Your Dignity on the Job.*

Jeffrey Pfeffer is Thomas D. Dee II Professor of Organizational Behavior at the Graduate School of Business, Stanford University. He is the author of *Leadership BS: Fixing Workplaces and Careers One Truth at a Time*, and *Power: Why Some People Have It and Others Don't.*

Anna Ranieri is a career counselor, an executive coach, and a coauthor (with Joe Gurkoff) of *How Can I Help? What You Can (and Can't) Do to Counsel a Friend, Colleague, or Family Member with a Problem.*

Dr. John Ratey is an associate clinical professor of psychiatry at Harvard Medical School. He is the author of *A User's Guide to the Brain.* He is also a coauthor of *Spark: The Revolutionary New Science of Exercise and the Brain* (with Eric Hagerman) and *Driven to Distraction: Recognizing and Coping with Attention Deficit Disorder from Childhood Through Adulthood, Answers to Distraction,* and *Delivered from Distraction: Getting the Most Out of Life with Attention Deficit Disorder* (with Edward M. Hallowell, MD).

Robert Sutton is a professor of management science and engineering in the Stanford Engineering School, where he is a cofounder and active member of the Stanford Technology Ventures Program, and the Hasso Plattner Institute of Design (the "d.school"). He is author or coauthor of six books, including *Good Boss, Bad Boss: How to Be the Best . . . and Learn from the Worst* and *The No Asshole Rule: Building a Civilized Workplace and Sur-*

viving One That Isn't, and *Scaling Up Excellence: Getting to More Without Settling for Less* (with Huggy Rao).

Brian Uzzi is the Richard L. Thomas Professor of Leadership and Organizational Change at Northwestern's Kellogg School of Management and the codirector of the Northwestern Institute on Complex Systems (NICO). He is a coauthor (with Shannon Dunlap) of the *Harvard Business Review* article "Make Your Enemies Your Allies."

Caroline Webb is the author of *How to Have a Good Day: Harness the Power of Behavioral Science to Transform Your Working Life.* She is also CEO of the coaching firm Sevenshift and a senior adviser to McKinsey & Company.

Holly Weeks is a communications consultant, an adjunct lecturer in public policy at the Harvard Kennedy School, and the author of *Failure to Communicate: How Conversations Go Wrong and What You Can Do to Right Them.*

Jeff Weiss is a partner at Vantage Partners, a global consultancy specializing in corporate negotiations, relationship management, partnering, and complex change management. He serves on the faculties of the Tuck School of Business at Dartmouth and the United States Military Academy at West Point, where he is also the codirector of the West Point Negotiation Project. He is author of the *HBR Guide to Negotiating.*

Judith White is a visiting associate professor of management at the Tuck School of Business at Dartmouth. Her research focuses on gender and diversity in groups, multidisciplinary teams, narcissism and negotiation, and conflict management.

Michele Woodward is a Master Certified Coach who coaches executives and trains other coaches.

Index

About the Author

Amy Gallo is a contributing editor at *Harvard Business Review,* where she covers a range of topics including managing yourself, leading people, and building your career. As a speaker and workshop facilitator, Amy has helped dozens of organizations deal with conflict more effectively and navigate complicated workplace dynamics. Previously, she was a management consultant at Katzenbach Partners, a strategy and organization consulting firm. She is a graduate of Yale University and has a master's in public policy from Brown University. Follow her on Twitter @amyegallo.

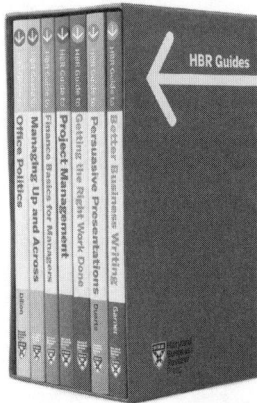

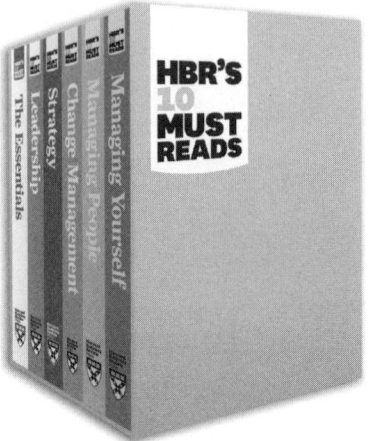

HBR Guide to **Project Management**

Harvard Business Review Guides

Arm yourself with the advice you need to succeed on the job, from the most trusted brand in business. Packed with how-to essentials from leading experts, the HBR Guides provide smart answers to your most pressing work challenges.

The titles include:

HBR Guide to Better Business Writing

HBR Guide to Finance Basics for Managers

HBR Guide to Getting the Mentoring You Need

HBR Guide to Getting the Right Job

HBR Guide to Getting the Right Work Done

HBR Guide to Giving Effective Feedback

HBR Guide to Making Every Meeting Matter

HBR Guide to Managing Stress at Work

HBR Guide to Managing Up and Across

HBR Guide to Persuasive Presentations

HBR Guide to Project Management

HBR Guide to
Project Management

HARVARD BUSINESS REVIEW PRESS

Boston, Massachusetts

Printed in the United States of America

20 19 18 17 16 15

Library of Congress Cataloging-in-Publication Data

HBR's guide to project management.
p. cm.
ISBN 978-1-4221-8729-6 (alk. paper)
1. Project management. I. Harvard business review. II. Title: Guide to project management.
HD69.P75H394 2013
658.4'04—dc23

2012026957

The paper used in this publication meets the requirements of the American National Standard for Permanence of Paper for Publications and Documents in Libraries and Archives Z39.48-1992.

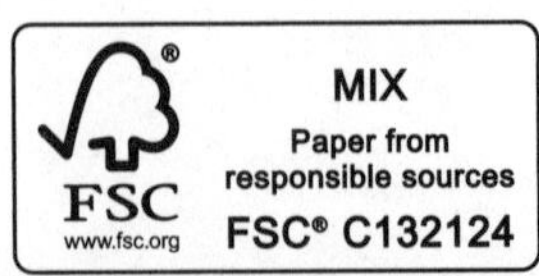

What You'll Learn

You've been asked to lead a project. You appreciate the vote of confidence, but are you panicking because you haven't a clue where to begin? Do you worry that stakeholders will tug you in a million directions, making it impossible to set clear goals, let alone deliver the goods on time and on budget? How will you know when to stick to your original plan and when to be flexible? And how will you keep all your team members excited about this project—when they have so many other pressures on them?

This guide will give you the confidence and tools you need to manage projects effectively. You'll get better at:

- Choosing the right team and keeping it humming
- Avoiding "scope creep"
- Zeroing in on critical tasks and mapping out a logical sequence
- Making heads or tails of Gantt and PERT charts
- Getting disruptive team members on board

- Keeping stakeholders in the loop
- Gauging your project's success
- Deciding when to cut bait
- Capturing—and using—lessons learned

Contents

Phase 3: IMPLEMENTATION

Phase 4: CLOSEOUT

Overview

Chapter 1
The Four Phases of Project Management

Whether you're in charge of developing a website, designing a car, moving a department to a new facility, updating an information system, or just about any other project (large or small), you'll go through the same four phases: planning, build-up, implementation, and closeout. Even though the phases have distinct qualities, they overlap. For example, you'll typically begin planning with a ballpark budget figure and an estimated completion date. Once you're in the build-up and implementation phases, you'll define and begin to execute the details of the project plan. That will give you new information, so you'll revise your budget and end date—in other words, do more planning—according to your clearer understanding of the big picture.

Adapted from *Pocket Mentor: Managing Projects* (product #1878), Harvard Business Review Press, 2006

Here's a chart that outlines the activities of each phase, plus the skills and tools you may need for doing the work:

PROJECT PHASES

Planning	Build-up	Implementation	Closeout
ACTIVITIES			
Determine the real problem to solve	Assemble your team	Monitor and control process and budget	Evaluate project performance
Identify stakeholders	Plan assignments	Report progress	Close the project
Define project objectives	Create the schedule	Hold weekly team meetings	Debrief with the team
Determine scope, resources, and major tasks	Hold a kickoff meeting	Manage problems	Develop a post-evaluation report
Prepare for tradeoffs	Develop a budget		
KEY SKILLS			
Task analysis	Process analysis	Supervising	Follow-through
Planning	Team building	Leading and motivating	Planning
Cost-benefit analysis of options	Delegating	Communication	Communication
	Negotiating	Conflict management	
	Recruiting and hiring	Problem solving	
	Communication		
TOOLS			
Work Breakdown Structure	Scheduling tools (CPM, PERT, Gantt)		Post-evaluation report: analysis and lessons learned

Planning: How to Map Out a Project

When people think of project planning, their minds tend to jump immediately to scheduling—but you won't even get to that part until the build-up phase. Planning is really about defining fundamentals: what problem needs solving, who will be involved, and what will be done.

Determine the real problem to solve

Before you begin, take time to pinpoint what issue the project is actually supposed to fix. It's not always obvious.

Say the CIO at your company has asked you, an IT manager, to develop a new database and data entry system. You may be eager to jump right into the project to tackle problems you have struggled with firsthand. But will that solve the *company's* problem? To increase the project's chances of success, you must look beyond the symptoms you have observed—"*We can't get the data out fast enough*" and "*I have to sift through four different reports just to compile an update on my clients' recent activity*"—to find the underlying issues the organization is trying to address. Before designing the database, you should ask what type of data is required, what will be done with it, how soon a fix is needed, and so on. If you don't, you'll run the risk of wasting time and money by creating a solution that is too simplistic, too complicated, or too late—or one that doesn't do what users need it to do.

Identify the stakeholders

The real problem will become even clearer once you figure out who all your **stakeholders** are—that is, which functions or people might be affected by the project's activities or outcomes, who will contribute resources (people, space, time, tools, and money), and who will use and benefit from the project's output. They will work with you to spell out exactly what success on the project means. Have them sign off on what they expect at the end of the project and what they are willing to contribute to it. And if the stakeholders change midstream, be prepared not only to respond to the new players but also to include all the others in any decision to redirect the project.

Whether you're managing a project in a corporation or working as an independent consultant, it's critical to have the support of the people you're working for. They may take a blue-sky view and demand an enormous amount of work within an unrealistic time period or expect you to perform miracles with inadequate resources or staffing. As the project manager, you'll need to make sure the requirements and resources line up fairly evenly, or you will set yourself up for failure.

Define project objectives

One of your most challenging planning tasks is to meld stakeholders' various expectations into a coherent and manageable set of goals. The project's success will be measured by how well you meet those goals. The more explicitly you state them at the outset, the less disagreement you will face later about whether you have met expectations. In the planning phase, however, much is still in flux, so you'll revise your objectives later on, as you gather information about what you need to achieve.

When defining objectives, think SMART. They should be:

- **S**pecific
- **M**easurable

- Action-oriented
- Realistic
- Time-limited

Suppose your HR department has been tasked with identifying potential new providers for your company's health benefits plan because the current ones aren't delivering the level of service they should given how much money employees have to pay for them. The project's SMART objectives may be to:

1. **Survey** <*action-oriented*> at least **six** <*measurable*> providers that meet the department's minimum threshold criteria for service quality.
2. **Recommend** <*action-oriented*>, at the **June** <*time-limited*> board of directors' meeting, the **three** <*specific*> that offer the best and broadest coverage at a cost that is at least **10%** <*realistic*> less than the company's current per-employee contribution.

Keep the following factors in mind as you define your project's objectives:

- **Quality.** Identify quality standards, and determine how to measure and satisfy them.
- **Organization.** Calibrate goals depending on the people and other resources you have available.
- **Communication.** Determine what information each stakeholder needs and how to deliver it.

Determine scope, resources, and major tasks

Many projects fail either because they bite off more than they can chew and thus grossly underestimate time and money or because a significant part of the work has been overlooked. One tool that can help you avoid these problems is the **Work Breakdown Structure (WBS)**, which aids in the process of determining scope and tasks and developing estimates. (See the sample later in this chapter.) The underlying concept is to subdivide complex activities into their most manageable units.

To create a WBS:

- Ask, "What will have to be done in order to accomplish X?"
- Continue to ask this question until your answer is broken down into tasks that cannot be subdivided further.
- Estimate how long it will take to complete these tasks and how much they will cost in terms of dollars and person-hours.

A WBS typically consists of three to six levels of subdivided activities. The more complex the project, the more levels it will have. As a general rule, you shouldn't have more than 20—and only an enormous project would require that many.

Here in the planning phase, don't worry about the sequence of activities. You will take care of scheduling in the build-up phase. Rather, use the WBS to create the framework that you'll fill in once you have a better sense of your staff, budget, and time constraints. Padding estimates is an acceptable way to reduce risk, but do it openly and communicate your reasons to the stakeholders.

As a result of your thoughtful planning, you'll be able to rough out an estimate of how many people—with what skills—you'll need for the project. You'll also have a good idea of how long the project will take.

Prepare for trade-offs

Time, cost, and quality are the three related variables that typically dictate what you can achieve.

Quality = Time + Cost

Change any of these variables, and you change your outcome. Of course, such alterations often occur in the middle of a project. If your time frame for developing a new database management system is suddenly cut in half, for instance, you will need to either employ twice the number of people or be satisfied with a system that isn't as robust as originally planned. Don't let bells and whistles get in the way of mission-critical activities. The key is to establish a level of quality that meets your stakeholders' needs.

Knowing from the start which variable is most important to each stakeholder will help you make the right changes along the way. It's your responsibility to keep everyone informed of any tweaks and tell them what the consequences will be in terms of time, cost, and quality.

WORK BREAKDOWN STRUCTURE

Sample Planning Document

Develop a Work Breakdown Structure (WBS) to ensure that you do not overlook a significant part of a complex activity or underestimate the time and money needed to complete the work. Use multiple pages as needed.

DESCRIBE THE OVERALL PROJECT:

The overall project will migrate 3 Web servers and databases to a new physical data center. The project requires that 5 new servers be provisioned in the new data center: these servers will mirror the production servers existing in the old data center. The new servers will be built to the same specifications as the old ones; they will run the same application and have the same content. Once implemented, the new equipment will be tested to confirm functionality. The sites will have a cutover and "go live" date. Finally, the old equipment will be decommissioned and reabsorbed into inventory.

MAJOR TASK

Obtain equipment.

Level 1 Sub Tasks

Purchase 3 Web servers and 2 databases.

Ship equipment to new data center.

Level 2 Sub Tasks

Cut P.O. and order servers.

Alert data center that equipment is slated for arrival.

Sub Task Duration

7 days

MAJOR TASK

Provision and implement equipment.

Level 1 Sub Tasks

Physically install hardware.

Load operating systems.

Load applications.

Mirror content to new servers.

Level 2 Sub Tasks

Rack and cable new equipment in data center and ensure physical and network connectivity.

Load base-level operating systems for Web and database servers.

Load application level software, including Web server software, database applications, and any required dependencies.

Copy configurations from production sites, transfer to new servers, and load appropriately.

Sub Task Duration

8 days

MAJOR TASK

Test equipment.

Level 1 Sub Tasks

Test machines.

Level 2 Sub Tasks

Ensure network connectivity, as well as Web and database access functionality and integrity.

Sub Task Duration

2 days

MAJOR TASK

Go live with new equipment.

Level 1 Sub Tasks

Cutover to new production site.

Data and content integrity check.

(continued)

MAJOR TASK (CONTINUED)

Level 2 Sub Tasks

Switch Web and database access to new sites.

Run a series of predetermined tests to ensure that data is accurate and that any updates since mirroring have been captured and applied as necessary.

Sub Task Duration

2 days

MAJOR TASK

Test again.

Level 1 Sub Tasks

Let sites burn in for 24 hours and check integrity once again.

Level 2 Sub Tasks

Run series of tests once more to ensure that updates and logging are functioning correctly.

Sub Task Duration

1 day

MAJOR TASK

Decommission old equipment.

Level 1 Sub Tasks

Remove equipment from data center.

Reabsorb equipment for future use.

Level 2 Sub Tasks

De-install equipment; erase software and content.

Ship equipment back to inventory.

Sub Task Duration

2 days

Build-Up: How to Get the Project Going

In the build-up phase, you bring your team together. Time estimates become schedules. Cost estimates become budgets. You gather your resources. You get commitments, and you make them.

Assemble your team

Your first task in this phase is to assess the skills needed for the project so you can get the right people on board. This assessment flows directly from the Work Breakdown Structure you did during the planning phase, in which you developed your best estimate of the necessary tasks and activities. You may need to bring in people—either temporary workers or employees from other parts of the organization—who have certain skills. Don't forget to budget time and money for training to cover any gaps you can't fill with people who are already up to speed.

Plan assignments

If you've built your own team, you've probably already decided who will do what. Or, if you've inherited a team but worked with the members before, you can still make the assignments yourself. But if a new, unfamiliar group is assigned to you, list the people on the team, list the skills required, and talk to each team member about her own skill set before you match people to tasks. This approach starts the process of team communication and cohesion. For example, if the project calls for a skill no one on the team possesses, members may know someone else who has it—or they may express interest in being trained themselves.

Clearly, you can't do everything yourself, even if you want to. After you've decided how you will assign tasks to team members, give each person the information and resources needed to succeed—and then back off and let your team members do their jobs. You may, as the project proceeds, have to delegate more tasks than originally anticipated. Be flexible enough to do so—without forgetting that you, as project manager, are the one who's accountable for results. (See the sidebar "Tips for Delegating Effectively.)

Create the schedule

It would be nice if you could tally up the to-dos and say, "With the resources we have, we will need this much time"—and then get exactly what you've asked for. But the reality is, most projects come with fixed beginning and end dates, regardless of available resources.

To create a realistic schedule within those constraints, work backward from any drop-dead deadlines you know about—that is, dates that cannot be changed—to see when your deliverables must be ready. For instance, if an annual report is due for a shareholder's meeting and you know it takes the printer two weeks, then all the final art and copy for the report must be ready to go to the printer two weeks before the meeting.

Depending on the complexity of your project, you may also rely on tools such as the **Critical Path Method** and a **Performance Evaluation and Review Technique (PERT) chart** to help with the sequencing of tasks and a **Gantt chart** to map out their chronological order and duration. You'll learn how to use these tools elsewhere in this guide. For now, though, keep in mind the "working backward" rule of thumb and these basic steps for scheduling:

1. Use the Work Breakdown Structure or a similar outline to develop a list of activities or tasks, and

TIPS FOR DELEGATING EFFECTIVELY

- Recognize the capabilities of your team members.
- Trust your team's ability to get the job done.
- Focus on results, and let go of your need to get involved in how tasks are accomplished.
- Consider delegation as a way to develop the skills of your team.
- Always delegate to the lowest possible level to make the best use of staff resources.
- Explain assignments clearly and provide resources needed for successful completion.
- Deflect reverse delegation. Do not automatically solve problems or make decisions for your staff members. Focus on generating alternatives together.

plot out their sequence by determining which ones are critical to achieving the desired final outcome.

2. Assign each task a deliverable—for instance, "compose rough draft of survey questions."
3. Use deliverables to create a schedule with realistic due dates.
4. Identify bottlenecks that could upset the schedule.
5. Determine ways to remove bottlenecks, or build in extra time to get around them.
6. Establish control and communication systems for updating and revising the schedule.
7. Keep all stakeholders involved in and informed of the project's progress and any schedule modifications.

Hold a kickoff meeting

As soon as you've chosen your players and set the schedule, bring everyone together for a kickoff meeting. Go over the project's plan and objectives with the group in as much detail as possible, and review the proposed time frame. Be sure to clarify roles and responsibilities.

Encourage people to point out spots where problems may occur and where improvements could be made. Take all suggestions seriously—especially in areas where the team members have more experience than you do—and adjust your estimates and activities accordingly.

Develop a budget

The first question to ask when developing a budget is, "What will it take to actually do the work?" To determine your costs, break down the project into the following categories:

- **Personnel.** Have you included all costs, both ongoing and extra, for employees and contract workers? (This is typically the largest part of a budget.)
- **Travel.** Is everyone onsite, or will employees be brought in from other locations?
- **Training.** Does everyone know how to use all the necessary equipment and software? Do the members of your team possess all the required skills? Will training involve travel? Will you need to teach users how to implement your project when it's completed?
- **Supplies.** Will your team need anything in addition to the usual computers, software, and so on?
- **Space.** Do people have to be relocated? How much room will be required in the new space, and at what cost? Will there be ongoing maintenance expenses?
- **Research.** Will you have to buy studies or data to support this project? How much research will your team have to perform itself? At what cost?
- **Capital expenditures.** What expensive equipment or technical upgrades will be necessary to do the

job? Will any capital expenditures pay for themselves? If so, how?

- **Overhead.** What is your projected overhead expense? Is it in line with your company's standard overhead percentage?

After you've entered the figures from these standard categories into the budget, ask a trusted adviser what you forgot. Did you overlook insurance? Licensing fees? Costs for legal or accounting support?

A budget, no matter how carefully planned, is just your best guess. Expect actual numbers to deviate from original estimates, and stay as flexible as possible within your limitations of time, quality demands, and total money available.

Implementation: How to Execute the Project

It's time to put the plan into action. The implementation phase is often the most gratifying, because work actually gets done, but it can also be the most frustrating. The details can be tedious and, at times, overwhelming.

Monitor and control process and budget

Whether you have a formal project control system in place or you do your own regular check-ups, try to maintain a big-picture perspective so that you don't become engulfed by details and petty problems. Project-monitoring software systems can help you measure your progress. No single approach works for all projects. A system that's right for a large project can easily swamp a small one with paperwork, whereas a system that works for small projects won't have enough muscle for a big one.

Respond quickly to changes in data or information as they come in, and look for early signs of problems so you can initiate corrective action. Otherwise, all you are doing is monitoring, not exercising control. Make it clear to your team that your responses to problems that arise won't do any good if you don't receive timely information. (In most cases, the weekly updates are fine.) But don't jump in to fix things too quickly—allow your team members to work out small problems on their own.

Watch the real numbers as they roll in to ensure that they are matching the budgeted amounts. Be ready to explain why extra costs are unavoidable. Common ones that sneak up on projects include increased overtime to keep things on schedule, consultant fees to resolve unforeseen problems, and fluctuations in currency exchange rates.

Report progress

Stakeholders will generally want regular updates and status reports. Consult with them to see how much information they'd like and in what format. Don't hide or downplay problems as they come up, or you can easily transform them into crises. If you keep your stakeholders informed, they may turn out to be good resources when issues do arise.

Hold weekly team meetings

When you're immersed in project details, it's easy to be diverted from critical activities to side paths that waste time. You and your team can stay focused by meeting

TIPS ON CONTROLLING PROJECT SLOWDOWNS

Try these approaches before accepting the inevitability of a delay in project completion:

- ***Renegotiate with stakeholders.*** Discuss the possibility of increasing the budget or extending the deadline.
- ***Use later steps to recover.*** Reexamine budgets and schedules to see if you can make up the time elsewhere.
- ***Narrow the project's scope.*** Can nonessential elements of the project be dropped to reduce costs and save time?
- ***Deploy more resources.*** Can you put more people or machines to work? Weigh the costs against the importance of the deadline.

once a week and periodically asking yourselves what's essential to the project's success.

Set clear agendas for your meetings. Try structuring them around production numbers, revenue goals, or whatever other metrics you've chosen to gauge performance. Many of your agenda items will naturally stem from targets the project has missed, met, or exceeded: For instance, you may need to discuss as a group whether to incorporate more travel into the project because you've

- ***Accept substitution.*** Can you go with a less expensive or more readily available item?
- ***Seek alternative sources.*** Can you get the missing item elsewhere?
- ***Accept partial delivery.*** Can you keep work going if you take the items that are ready now and receive the rest of the delivery later?
- ***Offer incentives.*** Can you provide bonuses or other enticements to facilitate on-time delivery?
- ***Demand compliance.*** Will insisting that people do what they said they would get the desired result? This may require support from upper management. Use this tactic selectively; be careful not to damage important relationships in pursuit of your goal.

noticed a decline in productivity at a satellite office. Or you might ask the product designers on your team to continue gathering among themselves on a biweekly basis because they've doubled their creative output since they've begun doing so. Keep the momentum going by following up each week on any to-dos and connecting them with the metrics for overall performance. Also, celebrate small successes along the way—that will rekindle the team's enthusiasm as you make progress toward your larger objectives.

Manage problems

Some problems have such far-reaching consequences that they can threaten the success of the entire project. Here are four of the biggest you'll face:

1. **Time slippage.** The most common problem in project management is falling behind schedule. Delays may be unavoidable, but you can usually at least improve the situation. The first step is to recognize that you're behind. If you've been monitoring the project's progress carefully, you'll quickly notice when schedules are being readjusted to accommodate delays or unexpected bottlenecks.
2. **Scope creep.** Time slippage can result from internal pressure to alter the scope of the project. When stakeholders ask for changes, it's your job to communicate clearly to them how those changes will affect cost, time, or quality.

   On some projects, scope creep is an ongoing battle for the project manager. After specific milestones and budgets have been agreed upon, people may begin to see more that could be achieved. Don't get caught up in trying to solve problems that lie beyond the established scope of your project—even ones that your company urgently needs to address.
3. **Quality issues.** Quality assurance plays a major role in any project's success. Unfortunately, it sometimes gives way to deadline pressure. Don't rush essential quality checks for the sake of the

schedule. And when you examine deliverables, use the most appropriate tools—such as detailed inspections, checklists, or statistical sampling—to accept or reject them. Return or rework rejected deliverables, depending on costs.

4. **People problems.** These are often the most difficult challenges a project manager must confront. They can generally be avoided or handled early on if you communicate frequently with each team member. Weekly staff meetings may not be enough; daily interaction—with individual team members or with the team as a whole—may be necessary.

Pay attention to small signs of emerging problems, such as a team member's increased tension and irritability, loss of enthusiasm, or inability to make decisions. When you see signs like these, get to the heart of the problem quickly and deal with it. Don't let it grow from a small irritant into a disaster.

Closeout: How to Handle End Matters

Though some projects *feel* endless, they all, eventually, come to a close. How do you, as project manager, know when to make that happen? And how do you go about it?

Evaluate project performance

Before closing out your project, your team needs to meet its goals (or determine, along with key stakeholders, that those goals no longer apply). Compare your progress with the scope everyone agreed on at the beginning. That

POST-EVALUATION REPORT

Sample Analysis and Lessons Learned

Project name: Project Phoenix **Date:** 5/29/200X

Present at this session: Rafael, Phil, and Carmen

PROJECT PHASE/TASK

Equipment acquisition

What Worked

Obtained the Web servers on time and on budget.

What Didn't Work

Logistical problems with availability of database servers—caused a delay. Expedited order that introduced additional expense.

Ways to Improve

Need to order equipment earlier.

PROJECT PHASE/TASK

Provision and implement equipment

What Worked

Two days were recovered through the efforts of Rafael and Carmen during provisioning phase.

PROJECT PHASE/TASK

Test equipment

What Worked

Testing phase was successful; during testing, a bug in the database content was discovered and corrected prior to cutover.

PROJECT PHASE/TASK

Go live with new equipment

What Worked

Smooth cutover with minimal downtime.

What Didn't Work

Some users were unaware that there would be a brief outage.

Ways to Improve

Publicize work window to user base more aggressively.

PROJECT PHASE/TASK

Test again

What Worked

Tested fine.

PROJECT PHASE/TASK

Decommission old equipment

What Worked

Decommissioned sites and erased content successfully; reabsorbed stock into inventory.

What Didn't Work

Some confusion over serial numbers and inventory, but straightened out in the end.

Ways to Improve

Check serial numbers at an earlier phase to minimize problems at the end of project.

TARGET ANALYSIS

How well did the project/team do...

In achieving goals and meeting project objectives?

Success: all goals were achieved.

At meeting deadlines and the final completion date?

Success: met our target date.

At monitoring and staying within budget?

Success: slight overrun was unavoidable.

(continued)

TARGET ANALYSIS (CONTINUED)

How well did the project/team do...

At communicating with stakeholders?

Partial success: we could have done better at communicating requirements earlier to individuals involved in the phases of the project.

RESOURCES ASSESSMENT

Were the allocated resources appropriate, sufficient, and efficiently used? (i.e., time, people, money)

Generally, the resource allocations were appropriate. The project went slightly over budget, but was not inappropriate. The people involved had the expertise necessary to carry out the highly technical phases of the project. The time resources were appropriate as the project was completed on time with no room to spare.

LESSONS LEARNED

What are the key lessons learned that can be applied to future projects?

At each phase of the project, it is crucial to anticipate the next steps and to alert groups or individuals of resource requirements as early as possible in the process. By so doing, we probably could have acquired the equipment in a more timely manner and would not have had to scramble so much in the later phases to meet our target dates.

---

will tell you how well the project has performed—and if there's still work to do. When you discuss your findings with your stakeholders, make sure you reach consensus with them on how "finished" the project is. Keep your scope front and center so everyone uses the same yardstick to measure success.

Close the project

The steps you take to wrap things up will depend on whether your team assumes ownership of its own deliverables, hands them off to others in the organization, or must terminate the project altogether. Later in this guide, you'll learn about these three types of closeouts and some techniques you can use to make them go smoothly. If all has gone as planned with your project, then it's time for celebration. Even if, as is more likely, there are some rough spots along the way—the project takes longer than expected, the result is less than hoped for, or the costs overtake your estimates—it's still important to recognize the team's efforts and accomplishments.

Debrief with the team

No matter what the outcome, make sure you have scheduled a **post-evaluation**—time to debrief and document the process so that the full benefits of lessons learned can be shared. The post-evaluation is an opportunity for discovery, not for criticism and blame. Team members who fear they'll be punished for past problems may try to hide them rather than help find better ways of handling them in the future.

Develop a post-evaluation report

The post-evaluation report documents all information that will be useful not only for the current team and stakeholders but also for future project managers who may use it to plan their own projects. (See the sample report in this chapter.) It should include:

- **Insights from the team.** Which lessons identified during the debrief should be applied going forward?

A NOTE ABOUT PROJECT MANAGEMENT OFFICES

Large companies often have what's called a **Project Management Office** (PMO), which does some combination of the following:

- Establishes processes and templates to guide project managers in planning and execution.
- Provides coaching and assistance to business leaders, project managers, and team members trying to apply the processes and templates.
- Directly manages projects to achieve desired objectives. (PMOs in heavily matrixed organizations don't usually take on this responsibility.)

A PMO that's well run helps each project team develop an appropriate plan, conduct a reasonable risk estimate, and track progress—and it allows teams room to deviate from standard procedure when it makes sense to do so.

- **Future status.** What will happen to the project now that it has been completed? Was it part of a larger project, or was it a self-contained entity that completed its goals?
- **Status of ongoing critical tasks.** What is the current state of ongoing tasks that contain a high level of technical risk or are being performed by outside vendors or subcontractors?

- **Risk assessment.** Could or did any risks cause financial loss, project failure, or other liabilities?
- **Limitations of the audit.** Do you have any reason to question the validity of the post-evaluation? Is any information missing or suspect? Did anyone in the group seem to resist providing details?

Even after you've completed your project, you can draw on the knowledge you've gained, the skills you've learned, and the relationships you've formed. You've accumulated valuable assets. The trick is to keep using them as you begin new projects.

Chapter 2
The Cast of Characters

To meet your project objectives, you need the right people on board—and they must have a clear understanding of their roles. Here's a breakdown of who does what.

Sponsor

The **sponsor** champions the project at the highest level in the company and gets rid of organizational obstructions. She should have the clout to communicate effectively with the CEO and key stakeholders, provide necessary resources, and approve or reject outcomes. It's also important that she have "skin in the game"—in other words, accountability for the project's performance.

Project Manager

The **project manager** identifies the central problem to solve and determines, with input from the sponsor and

---

Adapted from *Harvard Business Essentials: Managing Projects Large and Small* (product #6198BC), Harvard Business Review Press, 2004

stakeholders, how to tackle it: what the project's objectives and scope will be and which activities will deliver the desired results. He then plans and schedules tasks, oversees day-to-day execution, and monitors progress until he evaluates performance, brings the project to a close, and captures the lessons learned. The project manager receives authority from the sponsor. In many respects, he's like a traditional manager because he must:

- Provide a framework for the project's activities
- Identify needed resources
- Negotiate with higher authorities
- Recruit effective participants
- Set milestones
- Coordinate activities
- Keep the vision clear and the work on track
- Make sure everyone on the team contributes and benefits
- Mediate conflicts
- Make sure project goals are delivered on time and on budget

Team Leader

Large projects may include a **team leader,** who reports directly to the project manager. In small projects, the project manager wears both hats. The team leader cannot act like the boss and still obtain the benefits of team-based work. Instead, he must adopt the following important roles:

- **Initiator.** Rather than tell people what to do, the leader draws attention to actions that must be taken for team goals to be met.
- **Model.** He uses his own behavior to shape others' performance—by starting meetings on time, for example, and following through on between-meeting assignments. Leaders often rely heavily on this tactic, since they typically cannot use promotions, compensation, or threats of dismissal to influence team members.
- **Negotiator.** He gets what he needs from resource providers by framing the project as mutually beneficial.
- **Listener.** He gathers from the environment signals of impending trouble, employee discontent, and opportunities for gain.
- **Coach.** He finds ways to help team members maximize their potential and achieve agreed-upon goals. Coaching opportunities are abundant within teams because the skills members eventually need are often ones they don't already have.
- **Working member.** In addition to providing direction, the leader must do a share of the work,

particularly in areas where he has special competence. Ideally, he should also take on one or two of the unpleasant or unexciting jobs that no one else wants to do.

Team Members

The heart of any project, and the true engine of its work, is its membership. That's why bringing together the right people is extremely important.

Criteria for membership

Although the skills needed to accomplish the work should govern team selection, keep in mind that you're unlikely to get all the know-how you need without providing some training. Consider the following areas of proficiency:

- **Technical skills** in a specific discipline, such as market research, finance, or software programming
- **Problem-solving skills** enabling individuals to analyze difficult situations or impasses and to craft solutions
- **Interpersonal skills,** particularly the ability to collaborate effectively with others—a critical aspect of team-based work
- **Organizational skills,** including networking, communicating well with other parts of the company, and navigating the political landscape, all of which help the team get things done and avoid conflicts with operating units and their personnel

When forming project teams, people tend to focus too narrowly on technical skills and overlook interpersonal and organizational skills, which are just as important. For instance, a brilliant programmer may thwart team progress if she is unwilling to collaborate. By contrast, an organizationally savvy person with average technical skills may be the team's most valuable member, thanks to his ability to gather resources and enlist help from operating units.

Individuals who are strong on all four skill measures are few and far between. Make the most of the talent available, and take steps to neutralize weaknesses in your group. Look for people not just with valued skills but with the potential to learn new ones. Once you identify a candidate for membership, discuss her potential contribution with the sponsor. Consult her supervisor as well, since team membership absorbs time that would otherwise go toward regular assignments.

You may have to add new members and possibly bid thanks and good-bye to others over time, as tasks and needs change. One note of caution: Team members gradually develop effective patterns for working together, making decisions, and communicating. Cohesion is undermined when too many people join or exit the team.

Contributions and benefits

Free riders—team members who obtain the benefits of membership without doing their share—cannot be tolerated. However, not every member has to put in the same amount of time. For example, a senior manager who must direct much of his attention to other duties may still add value to the project by securing resources or by building support within the organization.

Just as each member must contribute to the team's work, each should receive clear benefits: a learning experience that will pay career dividends, for instance, or a fatter paycheck or bonus. Otherwise, individuals will not participate at a high level—at least not for long. The benefits they derive from their regular jobs will absorb their attention and make your project a secondary priority.

THE PROJECT STEERING COMMITTEE

Some projects have a **steering committee,** which consists of the sponsor and all key stakeholders. The committee's role is to approve the charter, secure resources, and adjudicate all requests to change key project elements, such as deliverables, the schedule, and the budget.

A steering committee is a good idea when different partnering companies, units, or individuals have a strong stake in the project. Because it represents these various interests, it is well positioned to sort out complicated interfirm or interdepartmental project problems. Likewise, it can be helpful if you anticipate many change requests. The downside to having a steering committee? It involves another level of oversight, and its meetings take up the time of some of the company's most expensive employees. So don't have a committee if you don't need one.

Alignment

The goals of the project team and those of its individual members must align with organizational objectives. For that reason, everyone's efforts should be coordinated through the company's rewards system. This kind of reinforcement begins at the top, with the sponsor. Since she is accountable for the team's success, some part of her compensation should be linked to the team's performance. Moving down the line, the project manager and team members should likewise see their compensation affected by team outcomes. Such alignment gets everyone moving in the same direction.

Phase 1
Planning

Chapter 3
A Written Charter

Every project should have a **charter** that spells out the nature and scope of the work and management's expectations for results. A charter is a concise written document containing some or all of the following:

- Name of the project's sponsor
- Project's benefits to the organization
- Brief description of the objectives
- Expected time frame
- Budget and resources available
- Project manager's authority
- Sponsor's signature

Creating a charter forces senior managers to clearly articulate what the project should do. Consider this example:

Adapted from *Harvard Business Essentials: Managing Projects Large and Small* (product #6211BC), Harvard Business Review Press, 2004

Phil was the sponsor of his company's effort to reengineer its order fulfillment and customer service operations. As an outspoken critic of these functions, he was the right person for the job. He had long been dissatisfied with the time it took to fill orders and with the company's mediocre customer service, and he thought the costs of these operations were too high. So he put Lila in charge of a project to improve them.

What sorts of cost cutting was Phil anticipating? What exactly were his complaints about the current system? What would success look like? Lila attempted to pin down Phil on those questions, but without success. He was too busy to think it all through and too eager to delegate responsibility for the project's outcome. Other company executives were also anxious to see improvements but, like Phil, had no clear ideas about the outcomes they wanted. So when Lila quizzed senior managers about the subject, they cited no specific goals. Lacking guidance, Lila and her team members developed their own goals and criteria for success.

The team pushed forward, and Lila reported progress to Phil over the course of the 10-month effort. Resources were always a problem, particularly since Lila was never sure how much money she could spend and how many people she could add to the team at key stages. Every request for resources had to be negotiated on a case-by-case basis with Phil.

The team eventually completed its tasks, meeting all of its self-declared goals. It had cut order-fulfillment time by one-third and the overall costs of fulfillment and customer service by 12%. And 90%

of customers could now get all their issues resolved with a single phone call. The team celebrated with a splendid dinner, and members went back to their regular duties.

Senior management, however, was not entirely pleased with the outcome. "You did a pretty good job," Phil told Lila. "The improvements you've made are significant, but we were looking for a more sweeping reorganization and larger cost savings." Lila was stunned and more than slightly angry. "If he wanted these things," she thought, "why didn't he say so?"

Situations like this are common but can be avoided with a charter that clarifies the project's objectives, time frame, and scope.

Objectives

As Lila's case demonstrates, project managers need more than a broad-brush description of the objectives for which they will be responsible. Ambiguous goals can lead to misunderstandings, disappointment, and expensive rework.

Take, for instance, the following statement: "Develop a website that's capable of providing fast, accurate product information and fulfillment to our customers in a cost-effective way." What exactly does that mean? What is "fast"? How should accuracy be defined? Is one error in 1,000 transactions acceptable? One in 10,000? To what degree must the site be cost-effective? Each of those questions should be answered in consultation with the project's sponsor and key stakeholders.

A thoughtful charter specifies the ends, but the means should be left to the project manager and team members. Telling the team what it should do *and* how to do it would undermine the benefits of having recruited a competent group. As J. Richard Hackman writes in *Leading Teams*: "When ends are specified but means are not, team members are able to—indeed, are implicitly encouraged to—draw on their full complement of knowledge, skill, and experience in devising and executing a way of operating that is well tuned to the team's purpose and circumstances."

Time Frame

In addition to setting specific, measurable objectives, you'll need to establish a time frame for achieving them. The project cannot be open-ended. In some cases, the deadline must be firm, and the scope becomes variable. Suppose a software company promises to deliver a new release every three months. The project team must make adjustments to the scope of its new releases—adding or dropping product features—to meet each deadline.

By contrast, if the project's scope is fixed, then a logical deadline can be established only after the project manager and team break down the objectives into sets of tasks and estimate the duration of each task. Nevertheless, the charter should contain a reasonable deadline—one that can be amended as the project team learns more about what it must do.

Scope

Of course, options are always more plentiful than time and resources. One useful technique for making the right choices is to have key stakeholders and project participants join in a brainstorming exercise to define what should be within scope and what should not.

Think of the sponsor's expectations (the ends to be sought) as part one of the charter and the project plan (the means) as part two. The project manager typically creates the plan, but it's important to get the sponsor's approval on it so you don't run into the same problems Lila faced with Phil. Ideally, it represents the best ideas from many or all team members. It's especially valuable for large, complex endeavors because it provides details about tasks, deliverables, risks, and timetables. It serves as a road map for the team.

Chapter 4
Dealing with a Project's "Fuzzy Front End"

by Loren Gary

Project management used to be about driving out uncertainty. You nailed down all the deliverables at the outset and fine-tuned your specs so implementation could be as routine as possible. Sure, there were always a few surprises, but overall you had a pretty good idea of what to expect. In many of today's complex projects, however—whether they involve new-product development, IT installation, or internal process improvement—uncertainty simply can't be eliminated.

If you were retooling a shoe company's manufacturing plant, says David Schmaltz, a Washington-based project management consultant, "perhaps only 10% of the

---

Adapted from *Harvard Management Update* (product #U0306C), June 2003

work would be devoted to building the new production line, but 50% would have to do with the uncertainty surrounding which shoe style will sell best in the next quarter. . . . Thus, instead of trying to cut its time to market by building production lines faster, the company focuses on building production lines that can more easily accommodate changing shoe styles."

Studies of exceptional project managers in fast time-to-market industries show that the initial phase of a complex project, often referred to as the **fuzzy front end,** has a disproportionately large impact on end results. So it's important to tread carefully. Resist the urge to dive right into implementation. "Defining the problem first gives you greater degrees of freedom in solving it," says Bob Gill, president of the Product Development and Management Association, a New Jersey–based nonprofit. "Instead of assuming that your riveting equipment is operating too slowly, if you step back and say, 'The real issue is that my cost of manufacturing the product is too high,' you enable other possible alternatives to solving the problem—for example, redesigning the process so that the product requires fewer rivets."

Build Your Community Early

You'll need input from key stakeholders before you can reach a robust understanding of the nature and scope of what needs to be done. Ask people in various groups likely to be affected by your project to help explore the opportunities, advises Peter Koen, a professor at the Stevens Institute of Technology, also in New Jersey. "Asking up front the questions about the unmet needs and the value of what you're doing can help prevent unsatisfactory results down the road—for example, bringing out products to a mature and declining market."

As you invite others into the work of defining the problem, you'll soon realize that your project's community is much larger than you originally imagined. And it will shift over time, points out Chuck Kolstad, CEO of Antara, a high-tech firm in California. "Stakeholders who have only informational input into the early phases of the project may wield decision-making power later on." If you make it clear in those early days that you value their insights and will incorporate them, your stakeholders will be much more inclined to give you the buy-in you need. Here's where your recruitment skills come into play: As you share your developing vision for the project with a colleague whose assistance you'll need, ask her what's in it for her. Help her find her project within yours.

Assuming a typical complex project, which lasts less than a year, "the week or two you spend at the outset just having conversations with people is far from useless, despite its appearance," says Schmaltz. When plans slip or new requirements are added, he continues, the relationships you've built during this initial phase will "constitute a benevolent conspiracy of people committed to figuring out how to make the project work."

Work Backward

Research about cognitive bias has shown that decision makers are unduly influenced by how they initially frame their thoughts about a topic. Once you've defined the problem, don't focus yet on the current process or product you want to improve. Instead, says Jim Goughenhour, vice president of information technology at Sealy, "imagine what the ideal end state would look like, then work back to put in as much of it as you can given the time, budget, and political realities."

The traditional approach to one of the projects Goughenhour oversees—creating a consistent sales reporting system—would have been to revisit the purpose of all the existing reports used by sales and marketing people throughout the company and explore ways of combining them. "If we'd done that," he says, "we'd have spent most of our money making minor improvements that didn't come close to the ideal."

Be the Voice of Reason

By the end of the project's initial phase, you'll produce a general plan that sets expectations within the project community and the company at large. That's certainly no small task, but it can be an even bigger challenge to manage the expectations of your sponsor—the project champion three or four levels above you who insists that the work be completed in four weeks.

Remember your "sacred responsibility to disappoint," says Schmaltz. You know that unsettling hunch you've got, now that the fuzzy-front-end conversations are winding down, that the project will take much longer than expected and will cost a lot more, too? "Only by disappointing the project champion with this news in the beginning can you delight him in the end," Schmaltz says.

"Otherwise you end up being a slave to his unrealistic expectations, and instead of guaranteeing success, you're almost certain to produce failure."

Loren Gary was the editor of *Harvard Management Update.*

Chapter 5

Performing a Project *Pre*mortem

by Gary Klein

Projects fail at a spectacular rate. One reason is that too many people are reluctant to speak up about their reservations during the all-important planning phase. By making it safe for dissenters who are knowledgeable about the undertaking and worried about its weaknesses to speak up, you can improve a project's chances of success.

Research conducted in 1989 by Deborah J. Mitchell, of the Wharton School; Jay Russo, of Cornell; and Nancy Pennington, of the University of Colorado, found that prospective hindsight—imagining that an event has already occurred—increases the ability to correctly identify reasons for future outcomes by 30%. We have used prospective hindsight to devise a method called a *premortem*, which helps project teams identify risks at the outset.

Reprint #F0709A. To order, visit hbr.org.

A premortem is the hypothetical opposite of a postmortem. A postmortem in a medical setting allows health professionals and the family to learn what caused a patient's death. Everyone benefits except, of course, the patient. A premortem in a business setting comes at the beginning of a project rather than the end, so that the project can be improved rather than autopsied. Unlike a typical critiquing session, in which project team members are asked what *might* go wrong, the premortem operates on the assumption that the "patient" has died, and so asks what *did* go wrong. The team members' task is to generate plausible reasons for the project's failure.

A typical premortem begins after the team has been briefed on the plan. The leader starts the exercise by informing everyone that the project has failed spectacularly. Over the next few minutes those in the room independently write down every reason they can think of for the failure—especially the kinds of things they ordinarily wouldn't mention as potential problems, for fear of being impolitic. For example, in a session held at one *Fortune* 50–size company, an executive suggested that a billion-dollar environmental sustainability project had "failed" because interest waned when the CEO retired. Another pinned the failure on a dilution of the business case after a government agency revised its policies.

Next the leader asks each team member, starting with the project manager, to read one reason from his or her list; everyone states a different reason until all have been recorded. After the session is over, the project manager reviews the list, looking for ways to strengthen the plan.

In a session regarding a project to make state-of-the-art computer algorithms available to military air-campaign planners, a team member who had been silent during the previous lengthy kickoff meeting volunteered that one of the algorithms wouldn't easily fit on certain laptop computers being used in the field. Accordingly, the software would take hours to run when users needed quick results. Unless the team could find a workaround, he argued, the project was impractical. It turned out that the algorithm developers had already created a powerful shortcut, which they had been reluctant to mention. Their shortcut was substituted, and the project went on to be highly successful.

In a session assessing a research project in a different organization, a senior executive suggested that the project's "failure" occurred because there had been insufficient time to prepare a business case prior to an upcoming corporate review of product initiatives. During the entire 90-minute kickoff meeting, no one had even mentioned any time constraints. The project manager quickly revised the plan to take the corporate decision cycle into account.

Although many project teams engage in prelaunch risk analysis, the premortem's prospective hindsight approach offers benefits that other methods don't. Indeed, the premortem doesn't just help teams to identify potential problems early on. It also reduces the kind of damn-the-torpedoes attitude often assumed by people who are overinvested in a project. Moreover, in describing weaknesses that no one else has mentioned, team members feel valued for their intelligence and experience, and others learn from them. The exercise also sensitizes the team to pick up early signs of trouble once the project gets under way. In the end, a premortem may be the best way to circumvent any need for a painful postmortem.

Gary Klein is a senior scientist at MacroCognition, in Yellow Springs, Ohio.

Chapter 6
Will Project Creep Cost You—or Create Value?

by Loren Gary

Allow the wrong changes to your project, and you can veer off course, run over budget, and miss key deadlines. Reject the right change, and you may fail to capitalize on a major opportunity. Hence the dilemma: How do you stay open to improvements without succumbing to "creep," in which small tweaks add up to budget- or schedule-busting modifications? By making sure the project's boundaries are sharply delineated and the impact of potential alterations or slippage can be quickly calculated.

The Planning Phase

A surprising number of projects get under way without a thorough attempt to define parameters. Haste is the chief

---

Adapted from *Harvard Management Update* (product #U0501C), January 2005

culprit here, says Dave Moffatt, who brings 40 years of industry project-management experience to his role as senior operations adviser at Harvard Business School (HBS). As you plan your project, clarify it in the following important ways:

Differentiate scope from purpose

"A project's purpose is the general benefit it will provide to the organization," explains Alex Walton, a Florida-based project consultant. "Its scope comprises the particular elements (or product attributes) that the project team can control and has agreed to deliver."

For example, a project's purpose may be to create a new electronic game that will increase a toy company's holiday sales by 40%. But the team developing the product needs to know what features it must have and what the budget for producing it will be. The **scope statement** provides this kind of information; it spells out, in a few sentences, how the team intends to achieve success and, thus, the criteria on which it will be evaluated. Get input on scope from your key stakeholders to align their expectations with the project's actual trajectory.

Plan in the aggregate

Defining scope isn't enough to ensure clear boundaries, however. "Organizations also need to do aggregate project planning," says HBS professor Steven Wheelwright, "in which they develop a strategy that lays out a pattern and rhythm for when subsequent projects will occur." This is especially important for product development.

Lacking a schedule for future projects, a product engineer with a new idea may grow concerned that it will never be implemented and thus try to slip it into the product that's now in development—regardless of the impact on the cost and schedule.

Analysis of prior projects serves as a valuable adjunct to aggregate planning. Study the past several internal IT projects your company has undertaken. What patterns emerge? Your findings can help you identify and better prepare for potential trouble spots in IT projects on the docket for the coming years.

Set the rules

Another way to minimize creep is to require conscious discussion and approval before significant changes can occur. For instance:

- **Set up a change control board.** In highly structured project environments, such a group is responsible for "gathering information about the impact that a proposed change will have on the schedule, budget, or scope; voting on the proposed change; and then sending a request-for-change document on for the project sponsors' signature," says Bob Tarne, a senior consultant who specializes in IT and telecommunications projects for PM Solutions in Pennsylvania.

  For an IT project affecting the sales, marketing, and logistics departments, your change control board would contain senior managers from those units. Smaller projects—costing less than $1 million and lasting less than 12 months—can effectively function without a formal board, says Tarne. The project manager can simply solicit the advice of key stakeholders as needed.

- **Establish thresholds for additional work.** Michele Reed, an independent project management consultant in Washington, says, "Any change entailing more than 5% of the original cost or hours budgeted for that particular line item in the project should trigger a formal request for a scope change."
- **Limit the number of new features.** Set guidelines for how many new major and minor features can be included in a project of a certain size. This helps the project team control the inherent fuzziness of front-end planning by forcing it to choose only the ones that are most important to customers right now.

The Execution Phase

When it's time to implement the project, break it into small components with short time frames and focus first on the tasks with the least uncertainty and variability.

For example, a software development team working on a product with four new features—the fourth of which it is not yet sure the market really wants—might choose to create the other three first because it is confident that the market wants them. The launch date for the fourth feature would be set to occur later, after the team has gathered enough additional customer input to confirm that it is critical.

But don't wait until all subprojects are complete before checking on whether the whole project (or product) is going to be a success, says Wheelwright. He recommends an approach known as **periodic system prototyping:** "At regular intervals during the execution phase, link up all the subprojects for a system test. This helps ensure that the subprojects you've created are coming together as planned."

Should *This* Add-On Be Approved?

During construction of McArthur Hall, HBS's residence for students in executive education programs (some of which last as long as eight weeks), a scope-change decision was made to create 10 rooms so guests of attendees could visit for a few days at a time.

Reducing the number of rooms for students by 10 would have cut into the program's long-term revenue potential by reducing the available space for registrants. Better to build 10 additional rooms to accommodate guests, the project's executive sponsor argued, and to pay for the additional cost over several years out of the larger income stream that would result from keeping the number of exec-ed suites as originally planned. Careful ROI analysis, in other words, helped the project's overseers find the optimal way of dealing with the proposed add-on.

By following the recommendations outlined here for your project's planning and execution phases, you can eliminate scope changes that don't merit such analysis. If you define clear boundaries up front, the change requests that come through are much more likely to be worth serious consideration.

When considering a scope change, make sure your stakeholders fully understand the purpose of the change. For example, have market conditions made it important to accelerate the schedule so that the product can ship earlier than originally planned? Do new industry standards, adopted since the planning phase, need to be accommodated? Or is a new technological solution required, because the one initially chosen hasn't panned out?

Next, explain how the proposed change affects everything: the scope statement and project plan, the available resources, the total cost, and the schedule. Finally, encourage stakeholders to consider what will happen if the change is not made. In these deliberations, says HBS's Moffatt, the opinions of people who represent the end users should be given the greatest weight.

As the project manager, if you're lobbying for a change, you've got to have a plan for funding it. If the future revenue generated by the add-on won't cover the cost, find other places in the project where you can save money, and focus on things you can directly control within the next 30 to 90 days in the schedule, advises Reed.

Loren Gary was the editor of *Harvard Management Update*.

Phase 2
Build-Up

Chapter 7
Setting Priorities Before Starting Your Project

by Ron Ashkenas

In a rush to demonstrate initiative and take action, new project managers often launch activities without first getting a sense of which ones are the most critical and what the sequence should be. As a result, they unwittingly slow things down.

Take this example: Plant managers at a global manufacturing company kept getting peppered with unnecessary, often redundant, data requests from corporate headquarters. To reduce this burden, the head of manufacturing asked a senior engineer to lead a project team to streamline data sharing. Upon receiving the assignment, the engineer enthusiastically (1) fired off an e-mail requesting that all heads of corporate functions nominate team members and send lists of the data they wanted from the plants; and (2) sent a note to a dozen plant managers asking for their views about which reports to eliminate. Within hours, the new project manager was overwhelmed and confused: Some of the corporate executives balked at her requests because this was the first they'd even heard of the project; others said they needed more details about the problem before they could respond; and still others sent long lists of required reports. The plant managers, too, came back with an odd mix of questions and requests. So instead of getting off to a fast start, the project manager stirred up resistance, created extra work for herself and others, and ended up with a pile of information that wasn't very useful.

It's not as difficult as you might think to avoid a situation like this. Here are three simple steps you can take to get your priorities right before you set your project in motion:

1. Clarify the assignment

Do not start any activities until your stakeholders have blessed your charter. You can easily spin your wheels on all sorts of misguided tasks if you're not clear on the overall objectives of the project and how success will be measured (what); the business context for it (why); the resources available (who); the timing (when); and any key constraints or interdependencies (how). Though it would be nice if your boss or project sponsor had sorted out these issues *before* giving you the assignment, the reality is that most projects are not commissioned with this level of specificity and clarity—so it will be up to you to get it. In the example above, if the project manager had done this before sending e-mails, she would have discovered that the head of manufacturing had talked only in general terms to the other corporate functional leaders about the data-overload problem—and had not told them he was starting a specific project with a defined goal and timetable.

2. *Organize your troops*

Once you've figured out what needs to be accomplished and recruited team members, get people engaged quickly so they feel ownership of the project. Ask for their reactions to the charter and their experiences regarding the issues, and treat them as partners rather than temporary subordinates. Work with them to develop a "modus operandi" for your team—how often you will meet, how you will communicate with one another, when you will review progress with the sponsor, and so on. If you don't get organized from the beginning, you'll waste time later chasing down people, coordinating calendars, and repeating key messages.

The same goes for identifying and reaching out to stakeholders. Have your team help you create a "map" of the people who will be affected in some way by the project. Sketch out how they relate to one another and to the project—and then do a political analysis of the key players. Which individuals or groups will be supportive and enthusiastic about your project? Which ones might be anxious or even resistant? Who will need to be won over or given special attention? Such analysis would have revealed to the project manager in our manufacturing example that some (or all) of the corporate functional leaders—who would have to

SAMPLE CHARTER FOR DATA-STREAMLINING PROJECT

What: Reduce corporate's requests for data from plants by 50%—and free up at least four hours per week for the plant managers and staff.

Why: The plants need to focus on increasing equipment utilization while managing a greater mix of products. This means spending more time planning and leading and less time reporting. Currently, every corporate function is asking for information from the plants—often the same information in different forms at different times.

Who: The project manager will recruit team members from plant operations, corporate finance, quality assurance, and human resources. Others may be called upon as necessary. All members will

change their way of collecting data to comply with her requests—would not be supportive of her project and may in fact be hostile. And with that insight, she might have approached them differently.

3. Pull your project plan together

You're now ready to develop a project plan, or at least a good working draft, given what you know about your objectives and your stakeholders. Conduct a brainstorming session with your team to identify all the activities that

be part-time but may have to dedicate 25% of their time to this effort.

When: The project should commence immediately. Develop an inventory of current reporting requirements within 30 days and recommendations for consolidation and streamlining within 60 days. Start eliminating redundant reports within 90 days. Complete implementation within 120 days.

How: The corporate functions must reach consensus about which common data requests can be met with existing systems and standardized reports. Data requests that are unique for particular plants should be exceptions, not the rule, and should involve minimal customization.

might be required to complete the project—including data collection, completion of "quick wins," stakeholder meetings, and presentations. Encourage your team to be creative and not to worry at this point about timing. Write each item on a sticky note, and post the notes on the wall.

Once all the activities are up there, organize them into categories and put the groupings in sequence. Some of the categories will "run" in parallel and represent separate (but probably related) work streams.

The notes on the wall, taken together, represent your project plan.

Now take a hard look at that total picture. Give each team member 100 "units" to allocate to the various activities (without discussion); ask them to pay close attention to which ones *must* be done successfully to achieve the project's objectives. Then compare the allocations and see which activities are considered critical as opposed to "nice to do." This should lead you to the tough discussion of which ones to drop or delay so the highest priorities will get the focus and the resources they require. After you've completed this exercise, go back to the overall project plan and make the necessary adjustments: Remove the low-value steps, and load the high-value ones for success.

Clearly, it's counterproductive to get things moving without prioritizing tasks. But controlling the all-too-natural impulse to jump the gun only at the beginning of your project is not sufficient. New opportunities, issues, ideas, and threats will continue to materialize, as will new steps and work streams—often without anyone understanding how these items even made their way onto the table. You'll need to keep setting and resetting priorities to make sure you and your people are always on target. To do this, bring your team together at least once a month to step back and reassess the project plan. At each of these meetings, ask your team two questions: First, "Has anything changed that should make us rethink our priorities?" And second, "If we were just given this assignment now, would we approach it differently?" This will help you keep your priorities clear—and your project on track.

Ron Ashkenas is a senior partner at Schaffer Consulting in Stamford, Connecticut, and the author of *Simply Effective: How to Cut Through Complexity in Your Organization and Get Things Done* (Harvard Business Review Press, 2009). He is a regular blogger for hbr.org.

Chapter 8
Boost Productivity with Time-Boxing

by Melissa Raffoni

Editor's note: To keep your project on schedule, you'll need team members who are focused and productive. Here are some tips for getting their calendars—and your own—under control.

Everybody needs more time—but since no one gets more than 24 hours a day, the only choice is to use those hours more effectively. One proven technique, time-boxing, involves just three steps.

First, list everything you and your team members want to accomplish in a given week, month, or quarter. Include project goals and the tasks necessary to achieve them. It may help to group activities by job function, such as strategy, business development, daily operations,

---

Adapted from *Harvard Management Update* (product #U99120), December 1999

and people management. With that kind of framework, you can see whether the team is spending its time in the right places.

Second, estimate how much time each item will require. Think carefully about the steps for completing the tasks. This is the part that "keeps me honest," says Beran Peter, CEO of Instruction Set, an educational consulting company in Massachusetts. "If I realize I'm not going to hit my estimate, I'm able to assess why and evaluate how I might make a change to get back on track."

Third, block off the appropriate amount of time for each item. If you think writing a business plan will take 32 hours, try setting aside four hours for every Tuesday and Thursday over the next four weeks. The challenge, of course, is prioritizing and fitting the time in where it makes sense. Don't forget to allow some leeway. Change is inevitable, and you may need to add tasks midstream.

Once you get started on time-boxing, you'll find it has several benefits:

- It forces you to think through project goals and figure out how much time you really need to make them happen.
- It provides a framework for setting expectations and boundaries. If a team member's calendar is full, she'll have to say no to extra requests—or you'll have to work with her to consciously reassess priorities.
- It improves your ability to estimate time demands.

- It enables you to assess—and pull the plug on—unproductive initiatives that suck up too much time.

Your team will feel better about the work it's doing. Everyone will be more focused. You'll all accomplish more. And—no small matter—people will avoid burnout from taking on more than they can handle.

Chapter 9

Scheduling the Work

Now that you've used the Work Breakdown Structure to identify and define your project's tasks and estimate how long each will take, you're ready to put them in sequence. That involves three steps:

- Examining relationships between tasks
- Creating a draft schedule
- Optimizing the schedule

Examining Relationships Between Tasks

Task relationships dictate the order of activities in a project. Suppose ABC Auto Company plans to introduce a new passenger car and has asked a team to design and test it. The team needs to build and test both external

---

Adapted from *Harvard Business Essentials: Managing Projects Large and Small* (product #6242BC), Harvard Business Review Press, 2004, and *Pocket Mentor: Managing Projects* (product #1878), Harvard Business Review Press, 2006

and internal components before it can test the whole car. Because of those dependencies, the project's tasks must be scheduled in this sequence: (1) design the vehicle, (2) build and test both external and internal components, and (3) test the vehicle built from those components. (See figure 1.)

Component building and testing, however, can simultaneously follow parallel tracks—one for external components, another for internal ones. Why? Because those two sets of build-and-test activities depend on vehicle design but not on each other. By recognizing opportunities to perform different activities in parallel, as in this example, you can reduce the amount of time your overall project takes.

Once you've evaluated the relationships between tasks, brainstorm with your team to come up with a rough sequence that makes sense in light of the dependencies you've identified.

FIGURE 1

Project network diagram: task relationships

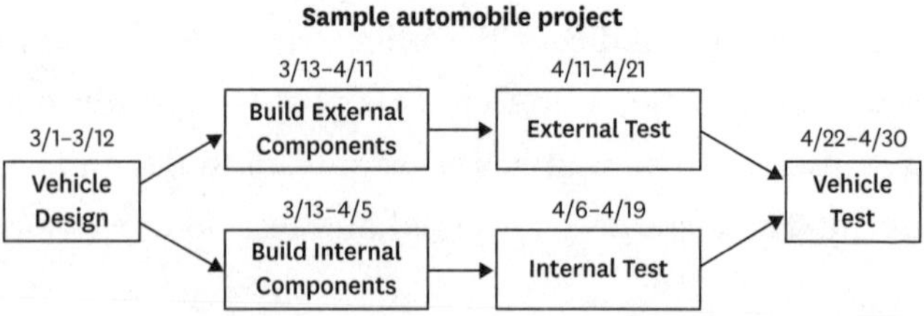

Source: Harvard ManageMentor® on Project Management (Boston: Harvard Business Publishing, 2002). Used with permission.

Creating a Draft Schedule

At this point, you're ready to create a draft schedule, which involves assigning a deliverable to each task (for instance, "build prototype for market testing"); setting realistic due dates; identifying bottlenecks so you can eliminate them, develop workarounds, or add time to accommodate them; and establishing a protocol for updating or revising the schedule. In your draft schedule, indicate start and end dates for all activities and recognize task relationships. Remember, this is just your first stab at scheduling—you'll make adjustments later, after the team has had a chance to review it.

Project managers rely on several tools for scheduling their teams' work. Here are a few useful ones to have at your disposal.

The Critical Path Method

As its name suggests, the **Critical Path Method (CPM)** helps you identify which tasks are critical—those that must be completed on time for the project to meet its deadlines—so you can allocate resources efficiently. Project managers often use CPM to plot the sequence of activities.

Consider a project involving six tasks with the following requirements and time expectations:

Activity	Requirement	Time to Complete
A		5 days
B		3 days

(continued)

Activity	Requirement	Time to Complete
C	A and B completed	4 days
D	B completed	7 days
E	A completed	7 days
F	C completed	1 day

You can diagram the critical path as shown in figure 2.

This chart tells you that at the earliest, you can complete the project in 12 days. It also shows that activities A and E are critical to your overall deadline. Given this information, you may want to readjust your resources and put more toward these tasks.

Let's revisit the ABC Auto Company project and the accompanying **network diagram,** discussed earlier. The diagram not only illustrates dependencies between tasks but also reveals the critical path: (1) vehicle design, (2) build external components, (3) external test, and (4) vehicle test. Why does this progression of tasks define the critical path? Because it's the longest path in the diagram. The other path—which passes through (1) build

FIGURE 2

Critical Path Method

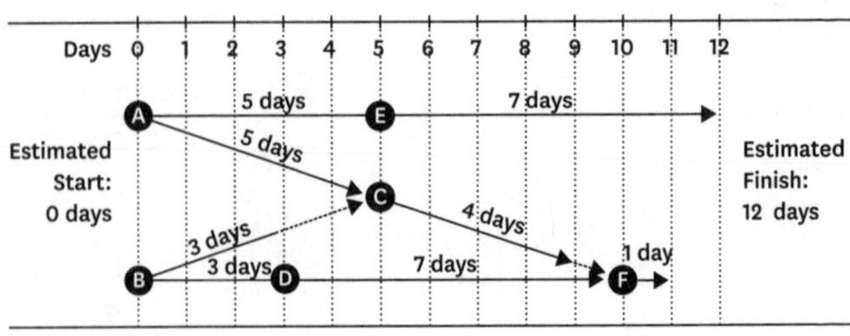

internal components and (2) internal test—is shorter by two days. Team members working on those activities could spend two extra days on them and still not throw the vehicle test off schedule. And they wouldn't shorten the overall schedule if they completed their work on non-critical-path activities ahead of time. The reason? **Tasks on the critical path determine total project duration.**

Gantt chart

If all you need is a way to show when activities should begin and when they should end, try making a **Gantt chart.** You can easily create one with spreadsheet or project-management software. (See figure 3.)

This is a popular scheduling tool because it's simple and it allows people to see the project at a glance. But it does not spell out relationships between tasks, as CPM does, so you may want to make note of dependencies inside the time blocks.

PERT charts

Some project managers use **Performance Evaluation and Review Technique** (**PERT**) as an alternative to the Gantt method for scheduling. Because it illustrates the critical path (it's essentially a network diagram) and lays out the project milestones, it's a handy tool for communicating the big picture to your team members. (See figure 4.) A PERT chart may have many parallel or interconnecting networks of tasks, so periodic reviews are essential for complex projects. As you're tracking your project's progress later on, you may need to come back and revise the chart. For example, if the time between dependent tasks exceeds your estimates, and those

FIGURE 3

Gantt chart

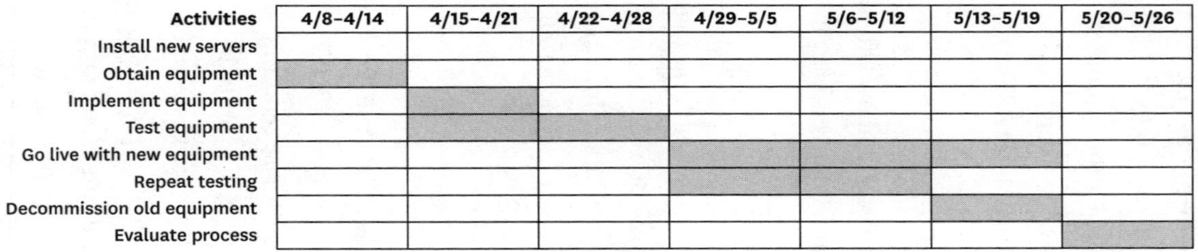

Activities	4/8–4/14	4/15–4/21	4/22–4/28	4/29–5/5	5/6–5/12	5/13–5/19	5/20–5/26
Install new servers							
Obtain equipment							
Implement equipment							
Test equipment							
Go live with new equipment							
Repeat testing							
Decommission old equipment							
Evaluate process							

Source: Harvard ManageMentor® on Project Management (Boston: Harvard Business Publishing, 2002), 26. Used with permission.

FIGURE 4

PERT chart

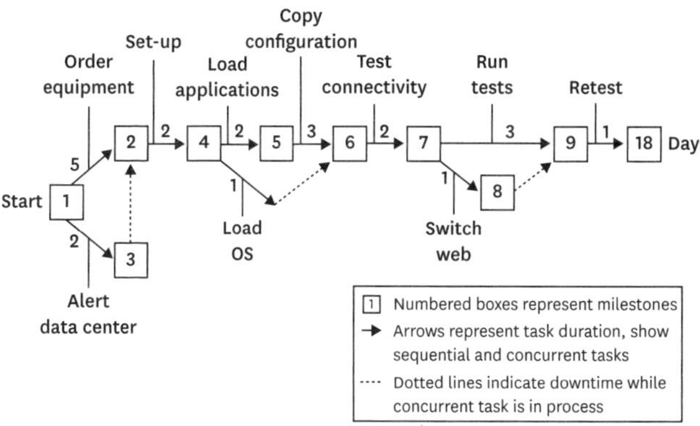

Source: Harvard ManageMentor® on Project Management (Boston: Harvard Business Publishing, 2002), 25. Used with permission.

tasks are on the critical path, you'll have to make up for lost time elsewhere in the schedule to avoid missing the project's overall deadline.

Which scheduling tools are best for your purposes? Whichever ones fit how you like to work, allow you to keep all team members informed, and remind people that they are part of a larger effort.

Optimizing the Schedule

After you've created the draft schedule, work with your team to improve it. Have the group help you look for:

- **Errors.** Are all time estimates realistic? Pay particular attention to tasks on the critical path because if any of these cannot be completed on time, the entire schedule will be off. Also, review the relationships between tasks. Does your schedule reflect the fact that some tasks can't start until others are completed?

- **Oversights.** Have any tasks been left out? Have you allowed time for training?
- **Overcommitments.** In reviewing the schedule, you may discover that some employees would have to work 10 to 12 hours per day for months on end to complete the tasks assigned to them, for instance, or that a piece of equipment is booked to deliver above and beyond its capacity. If you find such problems, redistribute the load.
- **Bottlenecks.** Any task that causes the work feeding it to pile up must be identified and dealt with. Think of an auto assembly line that stops periodically because the people who install the seats cannot keep up with the pace of the line. The usual way to handle this problem is to speed up the work process used in that task or add resources to it (for example, more people or better machinery).
- **Imbalances in the workload.** Are some team members being asked to do more than their share while others do very little? Rebalancing the load could reduce the overall schedule.
- **Slack time that can be filled.** You may be able to shorten the whole schedule by shifting resources

away from noncritical-path activities. For example, if you have four people working on a noncritical task that has four to five days of slack time, shift some or all of those people to a critical task for several days.

Even if you're using project-planning software to keep track of tasks and times, do this kind of thorough reality check with your team members. Any software you consider buying should make it easy to develop and change charts, calculate critical paths, produce schedules and budgets, factor in weekends and holidays, create different scenarios for contingency planning, and check for overscheduling of individuals and groups.

Chapter 10
HBR Case Study: A Rush to Failure?

by Tom Cross

Editor's note: HBR's case studies present fictionalized accounts of actual dilemmas faced by leaders, and offer solutions from experts.

"There is absolutely no reason why the contractors shouldn't be able to give us rapid product development and flawless products—speed and quality both," David MacDonagle said as he tried to light a cigarette. The warm wind, portending rain, kept blowing out his matches. Finally he gave up and slipped the cigarette back in his pocket.

MacDonagle, the head of the Canadian Aeronautics Administration, was nervous. Everyone at CAA headquarters was nervous. Very shortly, the project that many of them had devoted the past four years to would have its first real-world test, 350 kilometers above the earth.

Reprint #R1104N. Reprint Case only #R1104X. Reprint Commentary only #R1104Z

Feeling cooped up in the executive offices and oppressed by the presence of the media, MacDonagle had gone outside to breathe some air—actually, some tobacco smoke—and had invited the sharp young program manager Samantha Van Sant to join him.

Van Sant, a former Canadian army major, had a lot of skin in the project too. Since 2006 she'd been managing the two contractors the CAA had commissioned to build the $1.2 billion set of giant robotic arms known as Retractable Extended-Arms Compatible Holder, or REACH, for the International Space Station.

"So how do you deal with nerves?" MacDonagle asked.

"I usually go out for a run," Van Sant said, looking down the road that led from CAA headquarters through the cornfields, on which she'd logged many miles.

They turned to look back at the agency's buildings, which despite their grandeur looked small in the empty Quebec landscape. The sight reminded Van Sant of one of MacDonagle's catchphrases: "We are a small spacefaring nation. . . ."

Canada was indeed a small player in space compared with the U.S., Russia, Europe, and Japan. Always at risk of being marginalized, the CAA had done everything possible to get the REACH contractors, Hollenbeck Aircraft and Eskina Software Systems, to complete the first phase of the project in time to get it to the space station this year, when the orbiting lab would officially be complete. And, amazingly, they had made the deadline—and come in on budget. REACH was now attached to the station, though there was still much more to come, including an even more sophisticated set of "hands" that would fit on the ends of the robotic arms for extremely delicate work. The additions were to continue for two more years.

The contractors had been great about speed; the problem was quality. Glitches with the software, motors, and circuits had kept turning up. The fact was, not a single test in four years had gone flawlessly. "Yeah, yeah, we can fix that," the contractors' reps always said, dismissing the CAA's concerns. "Hey, this is life in the fast lane," a rep told Van Sant after one of REACH's arms had failed to retract on command. "Remember, we told you that the compressed schedule would increase the risk."

The contract that she managed called for parallel development, meaning that the project's phases—R&D, prototyping, testing, production, and quality control—overlapped, with each one beginning while the previous one was as much as 50% incomplete. That was sacrilege in some aerospace circles. But owing to the space station's construction deadline and the everpresent threat of cuts to the CAA's budget, the agency was aiming to do a decade's worth of work in six years. Computer simulations had to take the place of some real-world testing. Component quality control was less thorough. Because of all the unknowns in the project, the CAA had agreed to a cost-plus-fixed-fee contract, under which the contractors were paid a specified amount over their costs for labor, materials, and overhead.

MacDonagle's insistence on a rapid approach to development had been one of the main reasons Van Sant had been hired as a program manager. During her years in the army, she had established a bulletproof reputation for being aggressive and goal oriented. She and MacDonagle saw eye-to-eye. She knew speed was critical.

"We'd better go, I guess," MacDonagle said. "The media hounds are waiting. I told them I'd do quickie interviews once I got back. I know what they'll ask me: Is REACH going to work this time?" As they headed toward the building, the rain started. He looked at Van Sant. "So is it?"

Trouble in the Air

Red marker in hand, MacDonagle held forth before a group of reporters, asking whether they were aware that 50 years ago, the U.S. had blasted half a billion inch-long copper needles into orbit to reflect radio waves and thereby facilitate communications. Those needles were still floating around, and some had torn through one of the space station's solar collectors. "The solar arrays are the big bird's big red wings," he said, turning to the whiteboard and drawing the collectors.

He drew a gash in one of them. "A hole here means less electricity," he said, tapping the board. "Ever since the solar array got that hole from those flying needles, the space station has been operating on less power. Fixing it is tricky, because it's very far from the modules where the astronauts work and because of the risk of electrocution. Once an array is in place, you can't turn it off. It keeps generating power from sunlight. So if a spacewalker were to try to go out there and fix it, he'd be liable to get 100 volts of direct current through his body. That's where REACH comes in."

He took a moment to draw the Canadian creation, then stepped back to admire his sketch. The machine's two long arms stretched out toward the solar array in a nurturing embrace.

"Fixing solar arrays isn't what REACH was designed for," MacDonagle said. "It's meant to do the mundane work of replacing battery units on the exterior of the space station. But since REACH is up there, it's being pressed into service for the repair. It will stitch together the solar array while the astronauts control it from the safety of their module." He put the cap back on the marker and began fielding questions.

As Van Sant watched, someone tapped her on the arm. It was Alfred Siroy, the head of a CAA panel that had been trying to find out why there were so many quality issues with equipment from the Hollenbeck-Eskina venture.

"How long before they deploy it?" he asked.

"Soon—later—I'm not sure," she said.

Siroy always made Van Sant defensive. He'd made no secret of his disapproval of the way the REACH program was being managed, and of the parallel approach in particular. She knew that this viewpoint would figure in his forthcoming report. Fortunately, he was an overly meticulous writer, so the draft was taking forever. She asked him how the writing was going.

"Slow," he said, shaking his head. "But we do have a title: 'The Rush to Failure.'"

This gave her a start. "What failure?" she asked. "REACH is about to perform a critical repair task."

He shot her a skeptical look. "Rapid ramp-up was a laudable goal," he said. "But you have to give a contractor adequate time for QA. And you have to have a contract that gets the incentives right."

He continued: "We did an analysis. Your compressed schedule forces Hollenbeck-Eskina to cut corners, resulting in prototypes that fail. Substituting computer simulations for rigorous ground testing is a recipe for disaster. There isn't an electronic data management system that would allow the contractors and the CAA to access current test data for analysis. The prototypes aren't equipped with the instruments that would provide adequate test data. And the contractors have no incentive to push back: The cost-plus contract puts all the risk on the CAA. The agency and the contractors have different goals and objectives."

Van Sant couldn't disagree about the contract; its weaknesses had become increasingly evident to her. But if speed was the priority, they were unavoidable. "The contract language is ancient history," she said dismissively.

"You can rewrite history," Siroy said. "Any contract can be altered as long as both sides agree—you know that."

Suddenly, Van Sant saw, one of the staff members who'd been monitoring the goings-on at the space station began ushering MacDonagle away from the reporters, who, smelling blood, tried to follow. MacDonagle caught her eye, and Van Sant didn't like the look she saw on his face. Something bad had happened.

She slipped inside the communications room, where journalists weren't allowed, just before the door was shut. Over the speakers she could hear the astronauts at the space station talking about the power switching unit and using the word "failure." She heard someone say, "We have to go to Plan B."

REACH was probably experiencing the same problem that had come up during its last on-ground test. A system failure notification had gone off, but the contractors had dismissed it as a "reporting error," meaning it hadn't reflected a true mechanical breakdown. Still, no one wanted to deploy REACH while red lights were flashing. There was too great a risk that the robotic arms would fail at a critical moment.

"What's Plan B?" Van Sant asked MacDonagle.

"I don't know," he said quietly, "but whatever it is, it won't involve anything that came from us. REACH is Canada's only contribution to the space station."

Support from on High

"We've got video!" someone shouted, and there on the screens were multiple images of a man in a space suit dangling at the end of a loading crane.

It was well past midnight, but the reporters were still at CAA headquarters. They gathered around the screens. MacDonagle and Van Sant had long since given up trying to avoid them and were mingling with them as the repair attempt unfolded high above West Africa.

Everyone watched in silence as the crane, jury-rigged for the purpose, carried a spacewalker toward the space station's torn solar array. REACH couldn't even be seen—it was docked somewhere else.

"Harris Webb," MacDonagle said ruefully as he watched the figure in the shiny suit. "It's so fitting." Years ago, MacDonagle and Webb had been pilots on the same shuttle mission, and Webb, though much younger, had been chosen to lead it. A U.S. physician, mountaineer, author, pilot, and gourmet cook, as well as an astronaut, he was the ultimate go-to guy, brilliant and fearless—almost to the point of being foolhardy.

The reporters were excitedly discussing his stunt. Because REACH had failed, Webb was going out on the end of the crane to repair the array by hand. In one gloved hand he held what looked like an oversized hockey stick wrapped in insulation, so that he could stop himself from bumping into the arrays. In the other he carried several two-meter lengths of plastic cable that would be used to "stitch" the pliable solar array back together.

"Wow," a reporter gasped as Webb, reaching awkwardly, began threading one of the cables through the openings in the array.

"Cowboy," MacDonagle hissed under his breath. He put his hands on his head and looked at the ceiling.

Van Sant spotted Charlie Truss, one of the reps from Hollenbeck, sitting in a corner, his tie loose. He looked miserable. But she didn't feel pity for him—just annoyance. She went over to him.

"Whatever happens up there tonight," she said, "things are going to change down here. Our only way forward from this fiasco is to show that we've taken concrete steps to improve QA and finally get some positive results."

"I'm all for that," Truss said. "But anything you do to increase QA is going to slow things down. Once that happens, the costs start increasing and you become vulnerable to budget cuts. If we turn our existing contract into a traditional aerospace contract with all those sequential steps and inevitable delays, we might as well say good-bye to the improvements to REACH that are in the pipeline."

"If speed has to be sacrificed for a more reliable REACH, then so be it," Van Sant said. "The contract has major flaws. You're accountable for speed but not performance. We have to share the risk. We need a contract with performance-based incentives and penalties so that we can balance speed, quality, and results. Our goal is reliable components and systems that perform—and that should be your goal, too. We need to work as a unified team willing to push back on each other to get results."

Behind her the reporters gasped. She rushed to a screen and was relieved to see only that Webb, as he had finished his repair, had accidentally let go of a set of pliers, which was now drifting off into space.

But then Webb did something incredible. He turned to his Earth audience and began making a statement defending the failed REACH. "Everyone's going to blame REACH, but they shouldn't," he said. "It's a great piece of technology. I want to commend David MacDonagle and the CAA for overcoming a lot of technical obstacles in a big hurry and getting REACH up here on time. It's going to be a vital part of our operations. One little power-unit problem doesn't mean anything. Complex machines fail—that's just the way it is. We'll fix it, just like we fixed the solar array. I understand that the CAA has a great upgrade coming in the next couple of months—a new set of robot hands that are so nimble they can peel a hard-boiled egg. I say, Get it ready and shoot it up here. We'll start using it right away. I've got a few eggs that need peeling."

Van Sant was stunned, and she could see that Truss was, too. Then, giving her a small smile, he asked: "What were you saying about the contract?"

Tom Cross is a senior director in executive education at the University of Virginia's Darden School of Business, where he develops executive-learning programs for Department of Defense leaders. Previously he was a senior executive at such firms as KFC and Office Depot.

Should Van Sant push for a renegotiated contract for REACH?

See commentaries that follow.

Commentary #1

by Gary L. Moe

Whenever you hear about large, complex, costly government-sponsored tech initiatives that fail to meet expectations, the blame almost always falls on the "hurry up" schedule. If only the public agency hadn't pushed the contractors so hard, if only the developers had been given more time to refine the design, if only a few more months or years had been built into the production schedule, the technology would have worked perfectly. But it's not true.

Government sponsors can give contractors all the time and money in the world to complete a detailed requirements analysis and perfect a project design, and the finished product still probably won't work flawlessly. So-called big-bang design, in which developers labor mightily to get every last detail correct, is incapable of yielding a fully functioning, error-free product, because human beings, no matter how brilliant they are, cannot foresee all the issues that might arise in a complex technology.

What's needed instead is an iterative development process, whereby you build a prototype or even a fully fledged product and then put it out there, test it, and learn from its weaknesses, most of which you couldn't have seen on the drawing board or in a 3-D simulation. In the next iteration, you enhance the product. Then you run another round and another and another until finally you have something that works. The more complex a technology is, the more iterative the development needs to be.

This is how products are developed in the nongovernment sector. Take the auto industry. Cars are so complex that a manufacturer will put a model through a number of builds and a lot of testing before starting full production. In software, this process is called *agile development.* Developers write code for a week, test it to find out how to improve it, and then write some more code.

An interactive approach also works best when it comes to organizational change. No matter how hard you work on designing a reorganization, you will get it only 60% right, so you have to keep working at it, and finally you'll get to 90% right. (It never gets any better than that.)

Iterative development can work both for big long-term projects and for big one-offs, which is what many components of the International Space Station are. You break the development into pieces and apply the build-test, build-test method to the parts.

So why do government organizations, especially those that are defense- or space-related, favor the big-bang approach? There are a number of reasons, some involving the way procurement is handled. But the root of the problem is that iterative development entails experimentation, and experimentation entails failure. Government agencies don't like failure because it ruins political careers. So they try to avoid experimentation. But usually what they end up with is an even bigger failure—and no clue about why it happened.

My advice for Samantha Van Sant, then, is to restructure the contract to break further development of REACH into small chunks and require the contractors to practice iterative improvement, instead of striving for full initial functionality. Cutting down on the functionality delivered in each phase might help too, since 80% of cost and schedule overruns are usually due to the last 10% to 20% of requested functionality.

Gary L. Moe is a director in McKinsey's Business Technology Office and is based in Silicon Valley.

Commentary #2

by Tom Quinly

In the world of cutting-edge product development, the struggle between speed and quality is over. Speed has won—decisively. In today's highly competitive global markets, getting innovations out quickly can mean the difference between success and failure. But it's also a given that the quality must be high. Quality has become table stakes.

A lot of research has been published on the holy grail of lightning-speed development. Concurrent engineering programs, agile teams, risk mitigation programs, spiral development, outsourcing, harmonizing tools, and advanced simulation and modeling tools all can help you attain it, but your own people, processes, and market demands will determine the right recipe. What works best for us is forming small, seasoned, highly talented teams; being clear about time-to-market expectations; making sure developers have the right set of tools; and keeping our technical teams engaged, customer focused, and happy.

Bureaucracy, however, is an innovation killer. It's inevitable that as a business grows, things that don't add value creep into processes. With each slipup there's a tendency to add another process check. In isolation, each makes perfect sense, but in the aggregate, innovation is choked, and the team can't move nimbly.

I recall an experience early in my career, when a major development project had gone poorly. At an executive review, I was prepared to explain what had happened, what we'd learned, and what we'd done to stop the bleeding. Our CEO looked around at the others in attendance and said that he was disappointed—not in the group that had failed (mine), but in the other groups, because they *hadn't* failed. They weren't being as aggressive as he expected. That story lives on in the lore of the company, and it says a lot about our culture.

It's not that we encourage failure—we use it as a tool. Complex development programs rarely (if ever) come out of the gate perfectly; something unanticipated often happens. A lot can be learned from reviewing failures and looking at processes, expectations, people, and tools. Were our requirements too ambitious or ill defined? Did we not map the highest-risk areas and have well-designed mitigation plans? This relentless focus on learning improves predictability, reduces cycle time, and helps us get a high-quality offering to market ahead of the competition.

That's why I would advise Van Sant to give up the dinosaur perspective that speed means having to sacrifice quality. She should engage the entire team in examining the failures and exploring ways to achieve quality without upsetting the schedule. If REACH has few qualified alternative partners, then disrupting a long-standing contract with a highly experienced and specialized partner would be counterproductive. If Hollenbeck-Eskina is the best option, I would avoid having to reopen the contract and potentially lose the partner's deep project knowledge. However, if Hollenbeck-Eskina was not totally engaged and forthcoming in helping understand and correct the failures, it may be time to involve other potential partners or to stand firm on a contract renegotiation.

Tom Quinly is president of the motion control segment at Curtiss-Wright Controls, based in Charlotte, North Carolina, which develops products for aerospace, defense, and industrial markets.

Chapter 11
Getting Your Project Off on the Right Foot

With your project team formed, your charter delivered, and the team's tasks scheduled, you've still got a few critical matters to take care of before work commences. First, your project needs a **launch**—a special event that marks its official beginning. Second, you must set up activities and provide tools that foster team building. And third, you must institute behavioral norms that make collaborative work possible and communicate them to all participants.

Why Launch Meetings Matter

The launch represents the very first project milestone. If conducted properly, it has substantial symbolic value.

The best way to kick off a project is through an all-team meeting, one with appropriate levels of gravity and

---

Adapted from *Harvard Business Essentials: Managing Projects Large and Small* (product #6280BC), Harvard Business Review Press, 2004

fanfare. You'll have already held many planning sessions with key individuals—but those informal get-togethers are no substitute for a face-to-face meeting attended by all team members, the sponsor, your stakeholders, and, if appropriate, the organization's highest-ranking official.

Physical presence at this meeting has great psychological significance, particularly for geographically dispersed teams, whose members may have few future opportunities to convene as a group. Being together at the beginning of their long journey and getting to know one another on a personal level will build commitment and bolster participants' sense that this team and project are important. If certain people cannot attend the launch meeting because of their geographic location, they should participate virtually, through videoconferencing or, at the very least, speakerphone.

The sponsor's presence and demeanor at the launch speak volumes about the importance—or unimportance—ascribed to the project's mission. As Jon Katzenbach and Douglas Smith write in "The Discipline of Teams" (HBR March–April 1993):

> *When potential teams first gather, everyone monitors the signals given by others to confirm, suspend, or dispel assumptions and concerns. They pay particular attention to those in authority: the team leader and any executives who set up, oversee, or otherwise influence the team. And, as always, what such leaders do is more important than what they say. If a senior executive leaves the team kickoff to take a phone call ten minutes*

after the session has begun and he never returns, people get the message.

Here are your main tasks for the launch:

- **Welcome everyone aboard.** Acknowledge and thank all those who will contribute to the project. Mention each person by name. Many attendees will be core team members, and others will be peripheral members who participate for a limited time or in a limited way. But all are members.
- **Ask your sponsor to say a few words.** Have him articulate *why* the project's work is important and *how* its goals are aligned with larger organizational objectives. Otherwise, people won't see consequences for themselves and the company, and they won't make their best effort.
- **Make introductions.** Unless people are already familiar with one another, they probably won't know who has which skills. If the group isn't too large, ask participants to introduce themselves, to say something about their background and expertise, and to explain what they hope to contribute to and get from the project.
- **Share the charter.** Explain the goals, deliverables, and timetables you've documented.
- **Seek consensus.** Get everyone to agree on what the charter means.

- **Describe the resources available.** Although you'll certainly want to stoke the team's enthusiasm at the launch, it's equally important to set realistic expectations about the amount of support (both workers and budget) you'll have.
- **Describe incentives.** What will members receive, beyond their normal compensation, if the team meets or exceeds its goals?

Though participants will develop a sense of belonging and common goals only with time and through shared experiences, you'll have planted the seeds at the launch meeting. People should now begin to think of themselves as members of a real team.

Provide Activities and Tools for Working Together

Giving people collective goals and handing out free T-shirts with a team logo creates a team in name only. Project teams gel through joint work, idea sharing, and give-and-take in decision making and information exchange.

A project manager can facilitate that kind of collaboration through regularly scheduled meetings, communication tools such as project newsletters and websites, and the physical colocation of team members. Off-site social events may also be valuable, since they can help groups cohere. You'll want to encourage people to forge the bonds of trust and friendship that make team-based work stimulating and productive.

Establish Norms of Behavior

It takes time to build an effective project team. Individuals come to the effort with personal agendas. Some may view their new teammates as competitors for promotions, recognition, and rewards. Others may harbor grudges against one or more of those with whom they have been thrown together. And there's always a member or two lacking in social skills.

Such problems can undermine your project if they're not contained or neutralized. One of the best ways to manage them is to set up unambiguous norms of behavior that apply equally to all. As Jon Katzenbach and Douglas Smith point out in *The Wisdom of Teams*, the most critical rules pertain to:

- **Attendance.** The team cannot make decisions and accomplish its work if members fail to show up for meetings or joint work sessions. If you, the leader, are chronically late or absent, people will follow your example.

- **Interruptions.** Turn cell phones off during meetings and work sessions. Also, make it clear that people are not to interrupt others. Everyone has a right to speak.

- **Sacred cows.** Agree that no issues will be off-limits. For example, if a process-reengineering team knows that a change will upset a particular executive, its members should not be reluctant to discuss it.

- **Disagreements.** Team players are bound to come up with competing solutions as they tackle problems. Encourage them to vent disagreements in constructive ways.
- **Confidentiality.** Some team issues may be sensitive. Members will discuss them freely only if what is said within the team stays within the team.
- **Action orientation.** The purpose of teams is not to meet and discuss. It's to act and produce results. Make that clear from the beginning.

What behavioral norms should your group observe? That depends on the purpose of the group and the personalities of its members. But the basics include mutual respect, a commitment to active listening, and an understanding of how to voice concerns and handle conflict.

To guarantee the free flow of ideas, some groups may want to adopt specific guidelines that support calculated risk taking, for instance, or spell out procedures for acknowledging and handling failure. Whatever norms your group follows, make sure all members have a hand in establishing them—and that everyone agrees to abide by them. Members' participation and acceptance will head off many future problems.

Chapter 12
The Discipline of Teams

A summary of the full-length HBR article by **Jon R. Katzenbach** *and* **Douglas K. Smith,** *highlighting key ideas.*

THE IDEA IN BRIEF

The word *team* gets bandied about so loosely that many managers are oblivious to its real meaning—or its true potential. With a run-of-the-mill working group, performance is a function of what the members do as individuals. A team's performance, by contrast, calls for both individual and mutual accountability.

Though it may not seem like anything special, mutual accountability can lead to astonishing results. It enables a team to achieve performance levels that are far greater than the individual bests of the team's members.

Excerpted from Harvard Business Review, July–August 2005 (republished from 1993), Reprint #R0507P. To buy the full-length article, visit www.hbr.org.

To achieve these benefits, team members must do more than listen, respond constructively, and provide support to one another. In addition to sharing these team-building values, they must share an essential *discipline.*

THE IDEA IN PRACTICE

A team's essential discipline comprises five characteristics:

1. **A meaningful common purpose that the team has helped shape.** Most teams are responding to an initial mandate from outside the team. But to be successful, the team must "own" this purpose, develop its own spin on it.

2. **Specific performance goals that flow from the common purpose.** For example, getting a new product to market in less than half the normal time. Compelling goals inspire and challenge a team, give it a sense of urgency. They also have a leveling effect, requiring members to focus on the collective effort necessary rather than any differences in title or status.

3. **A mix of complementary skills.** These include technical or functional expertise, problem-solving and decision-making skills, and interpersonal skills. Successful teams rarely have all the needed skills at the outset—they develop them as they learn what the challenge requires.

4. **A strong commitment to how the work gets done.** Teams must agree on who will do what jobs, how schedules will be established and honored, and how decisions will be made and modified. On a genuine team, each member does equivalent amounts of real work; all members, the leader included, contribute in concrete ways to the team's collective work-products.

5. **Mutual accountability.** Trust and commitment cannot be coerced. The process of agreeing upon appropriate goals serves as the crucible in which members forge their accountability to each other—not just to the leader.

Once the essential discipline has been established, a team is free to concentrate on the critical challenges it faces:

- For a team whose purpose is to make recommendations, that means making a fast and constructive start and providing a clean handoff to those who will implement the recommendations.

- For a team that makes or does things, it's keeping the specific performance goals in sharp focus.

- For a team that runs things, the primary task is distinguishing the challenges that require a real team approach from those that don't.

If a task doesn't demand joint work-products, a working group can be the more effective option. Team opportunities are usually those in which hierarchy or organizational boundaries inhibit the skills and perspectives needed for optimal results. Little wonder, then, that teams have become the primary units of productivity in high-performance organizations.

Jon R. Katzenbach is a senior partner at Booz & Company and a former director of McKinsey & Company. **Douglas K. Smith** is an organizational consultant and a former partner at McKinsey & Company.

Phase 3
Implementation

Chapter 13
Effective Project Meetings

Run your meetings well, and you'll infuse your project with energy, momentum, and direction. How do you make them productive? Follow these simple guidelines.

Setting the Stage for the Meeting

- Make sure a meeting is even necessary. If you can accomplish your goal efficiently without calling one (via e-mail, for example), do so—and avoid eating up everyone's time.
- Clarify the meeting's objective. If it is to make a decision, explain that and give participants the time and materials needed to prepare.
- Sound out key participants on important agenda items ahead of time. What you discover may suggest that alterations are in order.

Adapted from *Harvard Business Essentials: Managing Projects Large and Small* (product #6198BC), Harvard Business Review Press, 2004, and Harvard ManageMentor, an online product of Harvard Business Publishing

- Invite only people who have something to contribute or who can learn from the discussion.
- Provide an agenda in advance that clearly supports the objective.
- Insist that people get up to speed on the issues before they arrive, bring relevant materials with them, and show up ready to contribute to the discussion.

Running the Meeting

- Restate the meeting's purpose. This will sharpen the group's focus.
- Let everyone have a say. If one or two individuals are dominating the conversation or if certain attendees are shy about leaping in, say, "Thanks for those ideas, Phil. What are your thoughts about this problem, Charlotte?"
- Keep the discussion centered on the key issues.
- End with confirmation and an action plan that includes a clear time frame: "OK, we've decided to hire DataWhack to install the new servers. And, as agreed, I will obtain the purchase order today, Bill will phone the salesperson later this week and set up the schedule, and Janet will begin looking for someone to take the old equipment off our hands. We'll regroup at the usual time next week to see where things stand."

Following Up

- Send out a note summarizing the meeting's outcomes. People will be encouraged by it because it's evidence that the team is one step closer to its goal.
- Remind individuals of their tasks and deadlines.
- Offer support to anyone who may be overwhelmed with other work or may struggle with a task. People are often reluctant to ask for assistance, even when they recognize that they need it.

Chapter 14

The Adaptive Approach to Project Management

Does your project involve an unfamiliar technology or material? Is it substantially larger than others you've overseen? Are the tasks different from those your team has handled in the past?

If you answered yes to one or more of those questions, the traditional approach to project management may not work. That's because it takes for granted that you can pinpoint what needs to be done, what it will cost, and how much time you'll need. In situations with higher levels of uncertainty—if you face unanticipated risks,

---

Adapted from "Project Adaptation: Dealing with What You Cannot Anticipate," *Harvard Business Essentials: Managing Projects Large and Small* (product #6273BC), Harvard Business Review Press, 2004

A NEW MODEL FOR SPONSORS

The adaptive model of project management creates a new role for project sponsors, one that Robert Austin likened to venture capitalism in the 2002 *Science* article "Project Management and Discovery." Rather than give teams a big pile of resources at the beginning, they support projects in stages, as results roll in. Like VCs, sponsors advance resources to purchase information and reduce uncertainty—and each investment gives them the option of remaining in the game.

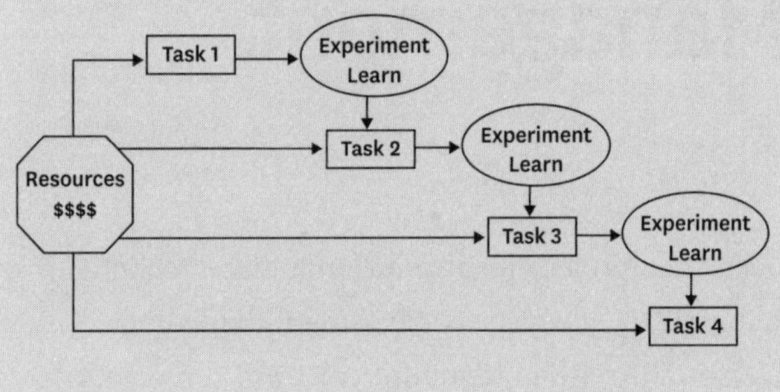

for instance, or if the range of potential outcomes is very wide—decision tools such as return on investment, net present value, and internal rate of return (which assume predictability of future cash flows) cease to be useful. You may have to consider a more adaptive approach.

In their research on large IT implementation projects, Lynda Applegate, Robert Austin, and Warren McFarlan (the authors of *Corporate Information Strategy and Management*) found that companies such as Cisco Systems have enjoyed success with adaptive project-management models that:

- **Approach tasks iteratively.** Teams engage in small incremental tasks, evaluate the outcomes of those tasks, and make adjustments as they move forward.
- **Have fast cycles.** Short lead times allow an iterative approach.
- **Emphasize early value delivery.** Small, early deliverables encourage feedback and the incorporation of learning into subsequent activities.
- **Staff the project with people who can adapt.** Some people are faster learners than others and are more amenable to change.

Cisco refers to its approach as "rapid iterative prototyping." Many tasks serve as probes—that is, as learning experiences for later steps. This tactic is analogous to the notion of the "cheap kills" that research and development organizations use to sort through many possibilities quickly and at low cost. When the right solution is not apparent, they try a number of simple experiments to separate promising and unpromising options. Even failed experiments provide insights into what will work.

WHAT-IF PLANNING AND CHUNKING

To enhance their ability to adapt to shifting conditions, some firms rely on the techniques that Cathleen Benko and F. Warren McFarlan call "what-if planning and chunking" in their book *Connecting the Dots: Aligning Projects with Objectives in Unpredictable Times.* Sweden-based software firm Ellipsus Systems used **what-if planning** to decide which programming standard—wireless application protocol (WAP) or Java—it would choose for its software. Since it was unclear which standard would dominate, cofounder Rikard Kjellberg designed projects based on both and then took early prototypes to a trade show to test participants' preferences. His contingency planning led to a successful partnership with Java-maker Sun Microsystems.

Minnesota hotel-management company Carlson Hospitality Worldwide uses **chunking** to break big, expensive projects into smaller, more manageable ones, thereby boosting their chances of receiving approval and funding. After the board of directors rejected a $15 million request to overhaul the company's central reservation system, managers broke the project into work units that each had stand-alone benefits and minimal mutual dependencies. That is, if one chunk was canceled, others could still move ahead. The board soon approved the first chunk. Ultimately, Carlson's new reservation system was voted best in the industry; its voice-reservation chunk alone generated $40 million in annual revenue by 2003. "Chunking helps us learn constantly and perpetually reassess our priorities," says CIO Scott Heintzeman. "It also reduces risk and focuses people's efforts on each work unit. And because the work on each chunk extends for no more than three to six months, people maintain their energy and enthusiasm."

Adapted from "Close the Gap Between Projects and Strategy," *Harvard Management Update* (product #U0406A), June 2004

Chapter 15
Why Good Projects Fail Anyway

A summary of the full-length HBR article by **Nadim F. Matta** *and* **Ronald N. Ashkenas,** *highlighting key ideas.*

THE IDEA IN BRIEF

Big projects fail at an astonishing rate—well over half, by some estimates. Why are efforts involving many people working over extended periods of time so problematic? Traditional project planning carries three serious risks:

- **White space:** Planners leave gaps in the project plan by failing to anticipate all the project's required activities and work streams.

- **Execution:** Project team members fail to carry out designated activities properly.

Excerpted from Harvard Business Review, September 2003, reprint #R0309H. To buy the full-length article, visit www.hbr.org.

- **Integration:** Team members execute all tasks flawlessly—on time and within budget—but don't knit all the project pieces together at the end. The project doesn't deliver the intended results.

Manage these risks with **rapid-results initiatives**: small projects designed to quickly deliver mini-versions of the big project's end results. Through rapid-results initiatives, project team members iron out kinks early and on a small scale. Rapid-results teams serve as models for subsequent teams who can roll out the initiative on a larger scale with greater confidence. The teams feel the satisfaction of delivering real value, and their company gets early payback on its investments.

THE IDEA IN PRACTICE

Rapid-results initiatives have several defining characteristics:

- **Results oriented:** The initiatives produce measurable payoffs on a small scale.

  Example: The World Bank wanted to improve the productivity of 120,000 small-scale farmers in Nicaragua by 30% in 16 years. Its rapid-results initiatives included "increase pig weight on 30 farms by 30% in 100 days using enhanced corn seed."

- **Vertical:** The initiatives include people from different parts of the organization—or even different organizations—who work in tandem within a very short time frame to implement slices of several horizontal—or parallel-track—activities. The traditional emphasis on disintegrated, horizontal, long-term activities gives way to the integrated, vertical, and short-term. The teams uncover activities falling in the white space between horizontal project streams, and properly integrate *all* the activities.

> *Example:* Take a companywide CRM project. Traditionally, one team might analyze customers, another select the software, a third develop training programs. When the project's finally complete, though, it may turn out that the salespeople won't enter the requisite data because they don't understand why they need to. Using rapid-results initiatives, a single team might be charged with increasing the revenues of one sales group in one region within four months. To reach that goal, team members would have to draw on the work of all the parallel teams. And they would quickly discover the salespeople's resistance and other unforeseen issues.

- **Fast:** The initiatives strive for results and lessons in less than 100 days. Designed to deliver quick wins, they more importantly change the way teams work. How? The short time frame establishes a sense of urgency from the start, poses personal challenges, and leaves no time to waste on inter-organizational bickering. It also stimulates creativity and encourages team members to experiment with new ideas that deliver concrete results.

Balancing Vertical and Horizontal Activities

Vertical, rapid-results initiatives offer many benefits. But that doesn't mean you should eliminate all horizontal activities. Such activities offer cost-effective economies of scale. The key is to *balance* vertical and horizontal, spread insights among teams, and blend all activities into an overall implementation strategy.

> *Example:* Dissatisfied with its 8% revenue increase in two years, office-products company Avery Dennison launched 15 rapid-results teams in three North American divisions. After only three months, the teams were meeting their goals—e.g., securing one new order for an enhanced product with one large customer within 100 days. Top management extended the rapid-results process throughout the company, reinforcing it with an extensive employee communication program. As horizontal activities continued, dozens more teams started rapid-results initiatives. Results? $8 million+ in new sales, and $50 million in sales forecast by year-end.

Nadim F. Matta is a managing partner, and **Ronald N. Ashkenas** is a senior partner, of Schaffer Consulting in Stamford, Connecticut.

Chapter 16
Monitoring and Controlling Your Project

by Ray Sheen

Unlike processes—where the same people repeatedly perform the same activities—projects often involve unique activities (such as using new technologies, building new buildings, or writing new software) carried out by individuals who may be working together for the first time. So as a project leader, you'll need to actively monitor progress to figure out whether your plan is really bringing the team closer to its objectives.

When monitoring and controlling a project, you'll follow five basic steps:

1. Track project activities

It's important to check in with team members regularly to make sure they're completing their tasks and meeting quality standards. You can do this most effectively through team meetings if everyone works at the same location. However, given how common distributed teams are in today's business environment, it can be difficult to get the entire group together. When that's the case, I conduct separate working sessions with individuals or small groups needed for particular activities. For example, I recently participated in a "live meeting" conference call where engineers from three locations helped prepare a product-development proposal for a customer. If I had created a draft, sent it around for comments, and then tried to integrate all the feedback, it could easily have taken weeks to complete the document. Instead, I had the right engineers reviewing it over the phone for about three hours, until everybody agreed on the wording. After a working session like this, I loop the rest of the team in at a larger group meeting or through e-mail.

I also use "buddy checks" to verify that tasks are done properly. When someone completes an activity, another team member looks at the results. This is not an in-depth technical analysis; it's a quick check to confirm that the person who did the work hasn't accidentally overlooked something or misunderstood the requirements. A team member checking a training plan for a new system, for example, would make certain that all departments in need of training have been included. If possible, have someone who will *use* the results of the activity do the buddy check. When I worked with a medical device company on developing a new product, I had its regulatory department review the design documentation and test data to flag any missing information that would be required later for regulatory submittal. If a team member with a stake in the activity's result is not available, you can do the buddy check yourself—but make it clear that it's not a performance appraisal. It's just one team member looking out for another.

2. *Collect performance data*

A few companies have project management information systems that automatically generate reports. If you have access to one, by all means use it—but also seek out performance data through short **pulse meetings,** where team members share status updates on activities and assess risks, either face-to-face or virtually. I limit these to 10 minutes and discuss only the tasks started or finished since the last meeting. The purpose is to get a quick sense of where things are, not to roll up sleeves. If the team identifies any problems or risks, I resolve them in a separate working session with the appropriate individuals.

I normally pulse projects on a weekly basis, which allows me to track progress adequately and identify problems in time to respond to them. However, when a project is in crisis mode, the "pulse rate" quickens. I once managed a project in which the power system for a new facility failed three days before the building needed to be up and running. An important business objective hinged on that deadline. The team worked around the clock to identify the cause of the failure, replace the destroyed component, and bring the facility back on line. All that would normally have taken two to three months, but we had three days, so I pulsed the project every three hours.

3. *Analyze performance to determine whether the plan still holds*

Activities seldom go precisely as anticipated. They may take more or less time; they may overrun or underrun the budget. A departure from your plan isn't a problem unless it's likely to compromise the team's objectives. On one project, I had an engineer report at a pulse meeting that a new mold would be two weeks late. But since the mold wasn't on our critical path and we had nearly six weeks of slack time in that portion of the schedule, the team didn't need to take special action. If the late deliverable had put us in danger of missing an important goal, I would have called a meeting with the appropriate team members to figure out a solution.

This is the time when careful project planning pays dividends. Knowing the critical path will help you decide which issues warrant a schedule change. If you've identified risks up front that could undermine your objectives, you can more easily recognize which snags are threats to the project's success. Having estimated each activity's duration and costs and carefully noted any uncertainties, you'll be able to distinguish between variances that aren't a big deal and those that suggest larger underlying problems.

When a plan does need revising, you may have to extend the end date, apply budget reserves, remove deliverables from the project's scope, or even cancel the project. On one software development project I oversaw, we had an excessively "buggy" first release. Before trying to fix the software, I quickly checked the requirements document and realized that the developers were using an out-of-date version. We had to reschedule the software development task for that module, causing us to delay project completion by about a month, but the change clearly needed to be made.

4. Report progress to your stakeholders

Some project managers and team members perceive **stakeholder reviews**—which involve preparing reports and conducting progress meetings—as wasted effort because they take time away from other activities. However, if managed properly, these reviews propel a project toward success. There are three types: management reviews, tollgate reviews, and technical reviews. For all three, record and circulate action items, and keep meeting minutes in the project file for future reference.

The purpose of the **management review** is to manage risk. Stakeholders may examine several projects at a time to see if the portfolio as a whole will generate the desired business performance and to identify systemic weaknesses. They'll look at individual projects on their own merits as well. Such reviews are normally held at regular intervals—monthly, for instance. When conducting them, keep in mind that your stakeholders care about reaching business goals, not about following the team's day-to-day activities. I recently attended a review where the project leader spent nearly 30 minutes describing technical designs the team was considering and testing, which only bored and frustrated the stakeholders. Instead, he should have spent five minutes telling them the project was on schedule (it was), that the team had made progress on its technical analysis (it had), and that no new risks had been identified.

Creating a **project dashboard** is a great way to summarize your objectives and show stakeholders whether the project, as currently planned and managed, will achieve them. (You can break it down into components such as schedule, cost, and performance.) This is often called a **stoplight chart,** since it usually indicates activity statuses in red, yellow, and green. Most companies have a standard format to help senior managers quickly and efficiently assess progress and risks on many projects. When using color coding, make sure everyone understands exactly what each color means. For example, do you list all incomplete tasks in red? Or are some of them green, because the plan for completion is approved and under way?

When you need to report bad news in a management review, always couch it in terms of risks to project objectives. Explain how certain task delays will prevent the team from realizing project goals on time, for instance, or how a resource shortage will reduce the rigor of an activity and thus the quality of its deliverable. When you present problems, also give options for responding to them and discuss the risks associated with each solution. The stakeholders will decide which risks they want the business to take.

The **tollgate review** (also called the **stage-gate review,** or **phase-gate review**) is a decision meeting, not a status check. It's used when a business plans and executes projects in discrete phases. In it, the project team summarizes the results of the preceding phase and presents a plan for the next phase. The stakeholders assess the plan, options, and risks, and then decide whether to approve, redirect, or cancel the project. If they say to proceed to the next phase, they also provide the team with the necessary resources, including funding.

At a **technical review** (sometimes referred to as a **peer review**), an independent team of experts—internal or external consultants, say, or representatives from a regulatory agency—provides an in-depth analysis of project results. The purpose is to ensure that team members did the work accurately, completely, and to the right quality standard. Stakeholders may give a stamp of approval at this time: If the team has successfully completed one phase of the project, it can now proceed to a tollgate review for approval to begin the next phase.

5. Manage changes to the plan

When revising a plan, you may make major changes or just minor tweaks that will allow the team to meet its objectives.

If you propose major changes to your stakeholders, spell out the costs and risks of adopting them and those of sticking with the original plan. A defense contractor that I work with was asked by the Air Force to improve performance of a weapon-system component. After the Air Force reviewed the proposed options (which included costs, risks, and schedules) and selected one, the contractor synchronized updates to design documentation, manufacturing processes, supplier contracts, the project schedule, and the budget so the transition would be as seamless as possible. When making such large-scale revisions, record them (along with the rationale) on some type of change log in the project records. You can use your normal project-planning processes and techniques to revise your plan. Send the new plan to your team members, and explain any changes that affect them.

Minor changes may come up as you're implementing a contingency plan or working out details of a portion of the project that was planned only at a high level. The project team can usually manage these on its own, without seeking stakeholder approval, unless the changes will directly affect stakeholders or their departments.

As you're monitoring your project, remember that meeting your objectives trumps everything else. Don't get hung up on compliance with the original plan. In my experience, almost every project plan must be revised at some point—especially when you're developing new products or systems, because what you learn in the early stages sheds light on how later-stage tasks should take shape. Don't be afraid to change course if it will bring you within reach of your goals.

Ray Sheen teaches and consults on project and process management. He has more than 25 years of experience leading projects in defense, product development, manufacturing, IT, and other areas, and has run a project management office in GE's Electrical Distribution business.

Chapter 17

Managing People Problems on Your Team

Your most important resource is your people. After you've done the hard work of selecting the right team members and getting them revved up for the project, you need to make sure they stay on task, pull their weight, work collaboratively, and reach the quality standards you've established with your stakeholders. If you don't, you're highly unlikely to meet your goals, let alone your deadlines and budget targets. Here's how to recognize and deal with various people problems you may encounter as a project manager.

Adapted from *Pocket Mentor: Managing Projects* (product #1878), Harvard Business Review Press, 2006

Team structure problems

Problem	Possible causes	Potential impact	Recommended action
• Your team lacks necessary skills.	• You overlooked certain skill requirements during planning. • You discovered a need for new skills in the midst of the project.	• The project doesn't move forward as fast as it should, or it stalls.	• Arrange for a team member to be trained in the skills needed. • Hire outside consultants or contractors who have the skills.

Problem	Possible causes	Potential impact	Recommended action
• A team member leaves.	• This could happen for many reasons, ranging from sudden illness to departure from the organization.	• Severity depends on the skills and knowledge lost: • If you can easily redistribute the work or hire someone with the same expertise, the impact may be slight. • If not, the loss could create a crisis.	• Have backup team members at the ready. • Cross-train people so they can fill in for one another. • Make one person's departure an opportunity to bring an even more skilled team member on board.

Interpersonal problems

Problem	Possible causes	Potential impact	Recommended action
• Team members are *too* friendly.	• They spend excessive amounts of time chatting or discussing personal problems.	• Overall productivity decreases. • Time is wasted, and the project slows down. • Hard-working team members resent those who work less efficiently.	• Emphasize that social gatherings need to be planned for after work. • Reorganize team subgroups to disrupt cliques.
• Conflicts exist within the team.	• People have a hard time reconciling different personalities, working styles, or areas of expertise.	• The schedule, quality of work, overall productivity, and team cohesiveness could all suffer.	• Focus team members on the project's goals, not on personal feelings. • Separate the underlying causes from the surface disturbances, so you can solve problems at the root. • Propose solutions, not blame.

(continued)

Productivity problems (continued)

Problem	Possible causes	Potential impact	Recommended action
• Time is spent on the wrong tasks.	• People manage their time poorly. • A team member prefers some tasks over others, regardless of relative importance. • You've sent the wrong message about priorities.	• Work on critical tasks is delayed. • The overall project is delayed.	• Clarify which tasks are most important. • Assign tasks to pairs of team members to work on together so they can keep each other in check. • Provide resources to help members improve time management skills.

Problem	Possible causes	Potential impact	Recommended action
• The quality of the work is poor.	• A team member misunderstands the requirements of the job. • Different people measure the work by different standards. • Someone doesn't have adequate skills to complete a task.	• Work must be redone, costing money and time. • The project fails.	• Be clear from the start about quality expectations and standards of measure. • Develop an action plan for improving the quality of the team member's work. • Provide training and support to develop skills.

Chapter 18
The Tools of Cooperation and Change

A summary of the full-length HBR article by **Clayton M. Christensen, Matt Marx,** *and* **Howard H. Stevenson,** *highlighting key ideas.*

> **Editor's note:** Sometimes you need to manage change within projects. Other times the projects themselves are agents of change in a company, and you have to overcome organizational resistance. Arm yourself with the right tools, and you can elicit cooperation rather than entrenchment.

THE IDEA IN BRIEF

Why do managers struggle so hard to get employees' cooperation on change initiatives? Even charismatic leaders

Excerpted from *Harvard Business Review,* October 2006, reprint #R0610D. To buy the full-length article, visit www.hbr.org.

have spotty records—winning commitment to change in some cases but failing dismally in others.

According to Christensen, Marx, and Stevenson, too many leaders use the wrong change tools at the wrong time—wasting energy and risking their credibility. For example, a vision statement helps get people on board if they already agree on where their organization should go. Without that consensus, vision statements won't change behavior—aside from provoking a collective rolling of eyes.

How to wield the *right* change tools, at the right time? Gauge how strongly your people agree on 1) where they want to go and 2) how to get there. Then select tools based on the nature of employees' agreement. For instance, if people disagree about goals and ways to achieve them (common during mergers), use power tools—such as threatening to make key decisions yourself. If employees have goals that differ from your company's but agree on how work should be done (think independent contractors), use management tools—including training and performance measurement systems.

Choose the correct tools, and you spur the changes your firm needs to stay ahead of rivals.

THE IDEA IN PRACTICE

Selecting the Right Change Tools

Scenario #1: If employees agree on goals but disagree on how to achieve them, use **leadership tools**: vision, charisma, salesmanship, and role modeling.

Example: In December 1995, Microsoft's Bill Gates published his visionary "Internet Tidal Wave" memo. The memo persuaded employees that the World Wide Web would become integral to computing (which countered most employees' beliefs). Employees responded with products that crippled Internet rival Netscape and maintained Microsoft's dominance in the software industry (which employees and the company wanted).

Scenario #2: If employees disagree on both goals and how to get there, use **power tools**: threats, hiring and promotion, control systems, and coercion.

Example: To merge JP Morgan with BankOne, CEO Jamie Dimon slashed hundreds of executives' salaries 20% to 50%. He threatened to select a single IT platform to replace the firm's myriad systems if the IT staff didn't pick one themselves in six weeks. And he told branch managers they'd lose their jobs if they failed to meet sales quotas.

Scenario #3: If employees agree on both goals and how to get there, use **culture tools** to counter complacence. In particular, use "disaggregation" (separating the organization into entities that each have their own agreed-upon goals and plans for achieving them) to disrupt high-level agreement about goals and methods that could otherwise preserve the status quo.

> *Example:* Hewlett-Packard recognized that its new inkjet printer business—with its unique technology and economics—could thrive only if it was protected from the cultural expectations of its traditional laser printing business. Disaggregating the two businesses eliminated the need for cooperation between them and enabled the groups to operate on very different profit models.

Scenario #4: If employees disagree on goals but agree on how work should be done, use **management tools**: measurement systems, standard operating procedures, and training.

> *Example:* In many companies, the reasons unionized manufacturing workers come to work differ markedly from those of senior managers. But as long as workers accept management's assertion that following certain manufacturing procedures will help them make products with desired quality and cost, they will follow those procedures.

Clayton M. Christensen is the Kim B. Clark Professor of Business Administration at Harvard Business School in Boston. **Matt Marx** was a doctoral student at HBS. **Howard H. Stevenson** is HBS's Sarofim-Rock Baker Foundation Professor of Business Administration, Emeritus, and the chairman of the board at Harvard Business Publishing.

Chapter 19
Don't Throw Good Money (or Time) After Bad

by Jimmy Guterman

You approved the development of a high-profile new product for your company a year ago—but now things aren't going well. Despite previous forecasts that customers needed your product, the market has changed, and the response is uncertain at best. But you're not going to give up and throw away $10 million, are you?

Actually, spending another dime on a doomed product is the wrong decision. Yet chasing after **sunk costs** (investments that are no longer recoverable) is a common error. *Just another couple hundred thousand dollars,* you say to yourself, *and we'll be able to recoup our investment.*

Adapted from *Harvard Management Update* (product #U0205D), May 2002

Don't fall for that line of reasoning. True managerial wisdom lies in a kind of forgetfulness—the ability to ignore prior investments, costs, and benefits, and to focus instead on the situation at hand. When faced with insufficient information and tight time constraints, managers regularly use simplifying strategies, known as **judgment heuristics,** as decision-making shortcuts. Problem is, human psychology always enters into the process, leading to cognitive biases—conclusions based on misperceptions or faulty inferences. The sunk-cost trap is a type of cognitive bias. Harvard Business School professor Max H. Bazerman, author of *Judgment in Managerial Decision Making,* likens this "nonrational escalation of commitment" to standing at a bus stop for hour after hour. At some point, you have to admit that the bus is not coming.

You can avoid escalating your company's commitment to a product, person, or strategy beyond a reasonable point. These guidelines will help.

Don't make choices merely to justify past decisions

Should you retain an underperforming, abusive contractor simply because you hired him and don't want to be accused of flip-flopping? Should you continue to extend credit to a company that has consistently failed to meet its obligations, since it promises that just one more loan will turn everything around? In the abstract, the answer to both questions is clearly no. But it's easy to let context obscure your better judgment.

Avoid this problem by gathering external evidence to support your choices. When deciding whether to move forward on a project, consult as many outside sources and devil's advocates as you can, so you're sure to consider how people other than your supervisor might view your quandary. Failure to see the big picture often results in overly cautious decision making, which in turn can lead to the sunk-cost trap.

Focus on the quality of the decision, not the quality of the outcome

Many people fall into the sunk-cost trap because they fear being judged for the unfortunate consequences of their good-at-the-time decisions. When things go sour, HBS professor emeritus Howard Raiffa explains, decision makers become "more worried about acts of commission, like changing course, than acts of omission, like continuing to take the company down the wrong road. *If I just go along as things are now,* the thinking goes, *things might change. If I commit an act of commission and admit that the current course is wrongheaded, that may trigger a review.* . . . There are huge internal and external pressures to keep going even if all parties realize it's wrong and it's going to stay wrong."

If you're managing a decision maker, you can prevent unnecessary escalations of commitment by making it clear that no one will be punished for not owning a crystal ball.

The more you equate time with money, the more susceptible you are to the sunk-cost trap

That's the conclusion Hong Kong University of Science and Technology marketing professor Dilip Soman reached after conducting a series of sunk-cost experiments. As he noted in a 2001 article in the *Journal of Behavioral Decision Making,* sunk costs don't usually trip us up when our main investment is time. But they do present a problem when we become more adept at converting that investment into a monetary equivalent.

Use decision rules to prevent cloudy thinking

In *Judgment in Managerial Decision Making*, Bazerman lays out a common scenario: "You personally decided to hire a new middle-level manager to work for you. Although you had expected excellent performance, early reports suggest that she is not performing as you had hoped. Should you fire her? Perhaps you really can't afford her current level of performance. On the other hand, you have invested a fair amount in her training. Furthermore, she may just be in the process of learning the ropes. So you decide to invest in her a bit longer and provide additional resources so that she can succeed. But still she does not perform as expected. Although you have more reason to 'cut your losses,' you now have even more invested in this employee."

Precise targets can help you avoid such rounds of rationalizing. Establish in advance how much time and money you're willing to pour into a project or person before you need to see specific results. As the investment sage Warren Buffett once said, "When you find yourself in a hole, the best thing you can do is stop digging." Targets tell you when to put down the shovel. They enable you to discriminate, says Bazerman, "between situations in which persistence will pay off and situations in which it will not."

Jimmy Guterman was a senior editor at hbr.org.

Phase 4
Closeout

Chapter 20

Handing Off Authority and Control

by Ray Sheen

Now that you've executed your project, it's time to gauge your success and then finalize activities, ranging from transferring control of new systems or facilities to presenting deliverables to stakeholders. Why not finalize activities first? Because you can't know when to close up shop until you've determined whether you've met your objectives.

In other words, success means achieving the goals in your charter and scope statement—not necessarily finishing all the tasks on your Gantt chart. Whether your team is releasing a product, adopting a new system, opening a facility, or improving a process, you'll need to validate that those goals, if still relevant, have been reached. Since stakeholders care far more about realizing business benefits than they do about adhering to the plan's "critical path," the team needs to get out of the weeds and sharpen its focus on those benefits as it completes the project.

Awhile back, I bumped into someone I had worked with years ago on a product-development initiative, and he mentioned that it was one of the best projects our organization had done. After we parted ways, I tried to reconstruct what was so good about it, because it was not well planned or executed. I realized it was the closeout phase that saved us. In our plan, we had overlooked some business systems that had to be changed to accommodate the new product; we were late getting staff assigned, so we soon fell behind schedule; and we had to replan the project on several occasions as a result of estimating errors and technical problems. Scrambling to recover from the delays, we went over budget by about 10%. In the endgame, however, we made up for those earlier problems by meeting market needs. We made sure that when the product launched, it worked well, it was easy for customers to order and for us to build, and our business systems could support it without difficulty. All that paid off—sales exceeded expectations. That's why stakeholders viewed the project as a success, despite the stumbles in planning and execution.

Once you've achieved your objectives—or determined that they're no longer relevant—you'll take one of three approaches to winding down your project:

The team hands off the project to itself

In such cases, team members become the primary users and maintainers of their own deliverables. When I was at GE, for example, we had a project team that designed and oversaw the installation of a new high-voltage power test facility. Once that was up and running, the head of the team and several other members went on to manage the facility. If your team inherits its own deliverables, it will need to close any administrative accounts or files (such as supplier contracts and purchase orders) associated with development and open new ones for operational deployment.

The team terminates the project

Here, all activities come to a halt, and the organization either releases or redeploys the resources. This can happen when a project has problems, such as a massive overrun, but sometimes it's due to forces outside the team's control. For instance, I once worked with several project teams on coordinating financial processes for two companies planning to merge. The teams had been in place for months and had made great progress when an unexpected government ruling barred the merger at the last minute. The teams disbanded within 24 hours. This type of closeout is administratively straightforward (the end is indisputable, after all), but it can be emotionally difficult because people often lose their assignments—or their jobs—without warning.

The team integrates the project

When using this approach—by far the most common and the most challenging—your team must ensure that others embrace its deliverables and apply them appropriately. In the dozens of new-product initiatives I've helped manage, it has taken as much or more time and work to hand off the product design to the manufacturing and quality organizations and to ensure the training of sales, marketing, and service staff as it has to design, develop, and validate the products themselves. As you integrate your project, you may face organizational resistance to change. If you think that will happen, you can add a transition phase to the project that includes pilot runs, beta tests, and any other activities that will make adoption easier.

Clearly, your closeout method will depend largely on business conditions—and so will the tools and techniques you'll apply within it. Here are a few I've found especially helpful in managing expectations as projects near completion:

The punchlist

This is used mainly in construction projects, but it works well for any type of project where people may try to slide in extra requests—for example, additional features—at the end. The team meets with the stakeholders and reviews the results of project activities. During that review, everyone helps identify remaining tasks, which you put on a "punchlist" of final action items. The team then tackles each item, and when everything on the punchlist is finished, so is the project. Because stakeholders have already agreed on your final to-dos, they'll be much less likely to ask for "just one more thing" at this stage. The punchlist is a good fit when you need to terminate a project, because the team may have a hard time letting go, and this focuses the group on closure. While working with a contract manufacturer of plastic parts several years ago, I helped a team use this tool to ensure that all the tests, inspections, and pilot runs needed to certify a new mold were done and that the mold was brought on line in a timely manner.

The "stakeholder handshake"

Projects that have a fuzzy scope statement—as many research initiatives and small, informal projects do—benefit from this technique because it keeps the work from going too far beyond the plan's boundaries. Meet with your key stakeholders to compare the project's accomplishments with the contract or scope statement, and ask them to agree on whether the project is indeed finished. Have them set an end point or elect to close the project now and, if necessary, open a new one. Such meetings tend to include wide-ranging discussions of options, so it's good to come prepared with several proposals. Following the meeting, document the stakeholders' decision and circulate it so there's no confusion. When I conduct a project-management assessment for an organization, I often close it in this fashion. Many times, I've been asked to "see what we need to improve." After I complete my review, I meet with the executive who hired me. Usually we agree that the assessment is over, discuss the findings, and then determine if I'm needed to help implement them.

The "scope creep parking lot"

During project execution, eager stakeholders may have proposed additional ideas, or team members may have been tempted to add bells and whistles. Ideally, you've captured those items in a list that some project managers call the "scope creep parking lot," so they're not lost—

but they also haven't derailed the plan by introducing new activities or changing boundaries. Now that you're closing the project, it's time to review this list so you can create follow-on proposals for your stakeholders. This technique can be effective when a team prepares to hand off a project to itself because stakeholders may be more likely to accept the deliverables if they know they'll have the opportunity to tweak them later. I've used the scope creep parking lot on several software-development projects. In each case, although minor issues were found during user-acceptance testing, the projects could close because we worked them into the scope for the next release.

Whichever closeout approach and tools you use, don't forget to celebrate your team's achievements. Success breeds success. Even on projects that weren't perfectly planned or executed, team members have worked hard to meet the business objectives and should be rewarded if they've done so. This will encourage them to do good work for you in the future—and the positive example will prompt other teams to achieve their project goals as well. Hold off on discussing opportunities for improvement. It's best to do that in a separate lessons-learned session that's focused on improving the way you manage the next project. For now, take a moment to "bask in the glow" of your current project.

Ray Sheen teaches and consults on project and process management. He has more than 25 years of experience leading projects in defense, product development, manufacturing, IT, and other areas, and has run a project management office in GE's Electrical Distribution business.

Chapter 21
Capturing Lessons Learned

by Ray Sheen

Though every project is different, you can and should always learn from what you've just done. Companies with a project management office (PMO) conduct a **lessons-learned session**—sometimes called a **postmortem** or an **after-action review**—as a formal part of each project's closeout. Those without a PMO typically share insights informally, as team members reminisce. Either way, it's important to capture learning while the experience is still fresh.

For example, I recently led a small project that lasted only a few months, and the team gathered for a dinner immediately after we wrapped things up to talk about what went right and what went wrong. It was a great conversation, and the next project we do will be better because of it. Since the project had a short time frame and the team was intact for the whole thing, it was relatively easy to discuss all aspects, from early planning through completion. When we returned from the dinner, one of the other team members and I updated the project folder with notes about our lessons learned.

By contrast, when I managed an engineering department at a *Fortune* 500 company, some of our projects lasted three years, and the core teams inevitably changed over time. I remember conducting a lessons-learned session with a product development team right after it had launched a new offering. Unfortunately, only one person in the room had been on board back when the project began—and she had moved into a different role by the time it was winding down. With the benefit of hindsight, we could spot errors that the original team had made in the project plan. But we could not identify the events or explain the thinking that led to those errors, since most of us had not been there. From then on, I took a different approach to long-term projects: I started gathering lessons after each phase rather than waiting until the project's end, so the team could clearly recall and accurately analyze what happened. This had the added bonus of allowing us to incorporate the lessons sooner.

When I conduct lessons-learned sessions, I follow a four-step process:

1. Evaluate the business case

The first question I ask is, "Has the project delivered on its promised result?" This isn't meant to help you judge how well the team did the work; it's to gauge whether the project has met senior management's expectations as clarified in the project selection and approval process—and whether those goals were really within reach. Projects are approved on the basis of forecasted business benefits, such as sales growth, cost reduction, cycle-time improvement, defect reduction, or increased capacity. Whatever the forecasted benefit, has it been realized? If not, were the original assumptions and project justifications inaccurate? By carefully examining these issues and sharing the findings with the project's sponsor, a team can improve its organization's ability to select projects and to establish realistic objectives in project charters. If you have a PMO, it will normally take responsibility for incorporating such lessons into project-initiation processes.

2. *Evaluate the project plan*

Next I ask, "Was the project plan reasonable and appropriate for the project goal and business conditions?" I consider whether it excluded any necessary activities or included any unnecessary ones. I also look at the cost and schedule estimates for each activity. These should reflect the business and technology conditions at the time the project began and provide sensible buffers. Then I review the initial risk assessment to determine which risks were not anticipated, which ones were improperly rated, and which response approaches were inadequate. Finally, I consider the practices established for both team and stakeholder communication. Did the plan allow enough opportunities for updates and information exchange? Did conversations take place at the right times, with the right people? Were decisions made in a timely fashion?

3. Evaluate the project-management methodology

The third question I ask is, "Were the organization's project-management procedures and systems beneficial?" To answer it, I focus on whether the company even *has* procedures, templates, or checklists; how current and relevant they are (if they do exist); how appropriate the mandated reviews and control points were for the project; and how useful the project-management information system was in communicating the project's plans and status to all the players.

Lessons learned are often embodied in companies' project-management procedures and systems. When I served as a consultant to a midsize contract manufacturer, I was surprised to find that it had no centralized project-management procedures, even though all of its work was project based. The firm simply hired experienced project managers and allowed them free rein. This led to a "rock star" mentality among project managers and no consistency in approach. Anyone assigned to a new project team had to learn new scheduling, budgeting, and reporting techniques. The duplication of systems and resulting inefficiency in project execution took a high toll on the organization. Individuals participating on multiple projects had to support multiple, often conflicting, meetings and report formats, leading to numerous "re-dos." The company established a PMO, and over the next three to four months we created the procedures and systems that allowed for coordinated, simplified project planning and execution.

4. Evaluate individuals' performance

Last, I ask, "What feedback do I need to give team members on their performance (good or bad), and what should I tell their supervisors?" I recommend following this step, even if it's not officially required, for all core team members. I typically ask the full team to help identify the "superheroes" among them. This both publicly reinforces the importance of contributing your best and minimizes the impression that the project leader is playing favorites. The members with poor performance I address individually. Of course, specific methods for conducting any performance appraisals must be in accordance with local human resource practices.

An effective lessons-learned process encourages continuous improvement. However, in my experience, the reports from these sessions are seldom read by anyone—so don't pin all your hopes on the documentation you've tucked away in the project file. Instead, turn the lessons into a list of action items for the PMO or for your team members to ensure that they are incorporated into the next project. Apply the insights right away by updating checklists, tweaking review processes, and making any other necessary adjustments before the next project launches.

Ray Sheen teaches and consults on project and process management. He has more than 25 years of experience leading projects in defense, product development, manufacturing, IT, and other areas, and has run a project management office in GE's Electrical Distribution business.

Glossary

Charter. A concise written description of the project's intended work. The charter may contain the name of the sponsor, the project's benefits to the organization, a description of the objectives, the expected time frame, and a budget.

Critical Path Method. A planning technique used for complex projects that consist of several activities. Any activities that need to be completed before others can move forward are considered "critical"—in other words, necessary for the on-time success of the project. The total duration of the project is defined by the critical path.

Gantt chart. A bar chart showing when project tasks should begin and when they should end.

Launch. A special meeting or event that marks a project's official beginning.

Adapted from *Harvard Business Essentials: Managing Projects Large and Small* (product #3213), Harvard Business Review Press, 2004.

Management review. A meeting where stakeholders may examine several projects together, as well as individually, to see if the portfolio as a whole will generate the desired business results and to identify weaknesses.

Network diagram. A scheduling chart that indicates all the relationships between tasks and reveals the critical path. Generally synonymous with a **PERT chart** (below).

Performance Evaluation and Review Technique (PERT). A scheduling method that, when charted, represents every task as a node that connects with other nodes required to complete the project. A **PERT chart** may have many parallel or interconnecting networks of tasks, so periodic reviews are encouraged for complex projects. Unlike the Gantt chart, it indicates all the important task relationships and project milestones.

Post-evaluation. A meeting where the project team debriefs and documents its process for the purpose of learning and sharing lessons and making improvements. Also called a **lessons-learned session,** a **postmortem,** or an **after-action review.**

Project management office. A corporate office (typically in a large company) that establishes processes and templates to guide an organization's project managers in planning and execution, provides assistance to individuals trying to apply those processes, and sometimes manages individual projects.

Project Steering Committee. A group that approves the project charter, secures resources, and adjudicates all requests to change key project elements, including deliverables, the schedule, and the budget.

Punchlist. The project team's final list of action items, approved by key stakeholders.

Scope creep. The tendency (often as a result of pressure from stakeholders) to permit changes that exceed a project's scope and may wreak havoc on the schedule, the quality of the work, or the budget.

Scope creep parking lot. A list of additional ideas or bells and whistles proposed during a project. The idea is to "park" them so they can be revisited later, without danger of derailing the current project.

Stoplight chart. A project-monitoring tool that uses red, yellow, and green color coding to indicate the status of each project activity.

Sunk costs. Project investments that are no longer recoverable.

Technical review. A meeting where an independent team of experts provides an in-depth analysis of project results to ensure that team members did the work accurately, completely, and to the right quality standard. Sometimes called a **peer review.**

Tollgate review. A meeting where the project team summarizes the results of the preceding phase and presents a plan for the next phase so stakeholders can decide whether to approve, redirect, or cancel the project. Also called a **stage-gate review,** or a **phase-gate review.**

Variance. The difference (positive or negative) between actual and expected results in the budget. Managers use variance to spot sources of trouble and areas of exceptional performance.

Work Breakdown Structure (WBS). A planning routine that breaks down a project's goal into the many tasks required to achieve it. The time and money needed to complete those tasks are then estimated.

Index

Notes

Notes

Notes

Notes

Notes

Notes

Notes

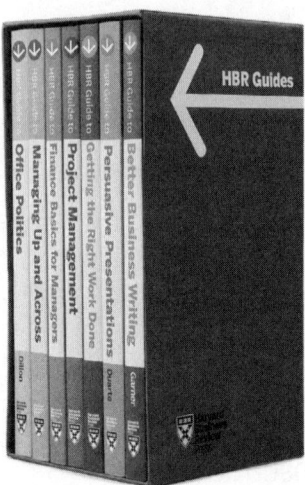

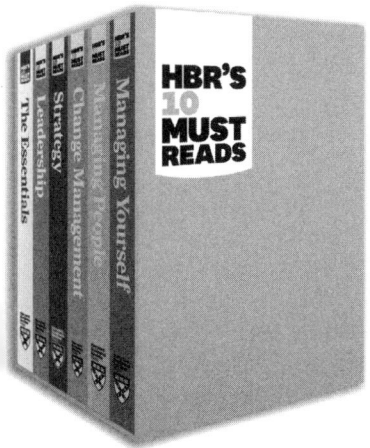

HBR Guide to **Performance Management**

Harvard Business Review Guides

Arm yourself with the advice you need to succeed on the job, from the most trusted brand in business. Packed with how-to essentials from leading experts, the HBR Guides provide smart answers to your most pressing work challenges.

The titles include:

HBR Guide to Being More Productive

HBR Guide to Better Business Writing

HBR Guide to Building Your Business Case

HBR Guide to Buying a Small Business

HBR Guide to Coaching Employees

HBR Guide to Data Analytics Basics for Managers

HBR Guide to Dealing with Conflict

HBR Guide to Delivering Effective Feedback

HBR Guide to Emotional Intelligence

HBR Guide to Finance Basics for Managers

HBR Guide to Getting the Right Work Done

HBR Guide to Giving Effective Feedback

HBR Guide to Leading Teams

HBR Guide to Making Every Meeting Matter

HBR Guide to Managing Up and Across

HBR Guide to Negotiating

HBR Guide to Office Politics

HBR Guide to Performance Management

HBR Guide to Persuasive Presentations

HBR Guide to Project Management

HBR Guide to **Performance Management**

HARVARD BUSINESS REVIEW PRESS

Boston, Massachusetts

Printed in the United States of America
10 9 8 7 6

Cataloging-in-Publication data is forthcoming.

ISBN: 978-1-63369-278-7
eISBN: 978-1-63369-279-4

The paper used in this publication meets the requirements of the American National Standard for Permanence of Paper for Publications and Documents in Libraries and Archives Z39.48–1992.

What You'll Learn

As a manager, you're accountable for ensuring your employees produce results that align with your organization's needs. But traditional approaches to tracking employee performance—while providing a dedicated opportunity for employee feedback and evaluation—are increasingly coming under fire. Holding a performance discussion once a year takes a lot of time and can cause stress for you and your employees—and it doesn't guarantee improvement. Organizations that use traditional performance management to engage, motivate, and develop their people are finding that those approaches don't achieve what they're after. And annual cycles that start with goal setting and culminate with a formal review aren't providing the agility you need from your employees in today's fast-paced business environment.

What you need is an ongoing, more flexible approach—one that keeps the best of the traditional performance management process but also incorporates new thinking and ideas. By following the advice in this guide, you'll discover new ways to fold managing performance into your day-to-day work, so you're monitoring employee progress, providing feedback, and offering opportunities for growth on a regular basis while still meeting any annual requirements your organization may have.

You'll learn how to:

- Help your employees set flexible goals that can adapt with the organization
- Define clear performance metrics and behavioral expectations
- Provide ongoing feedback to stop performance problems in their tracks
- Coach your people toward improvement
- Motivate your employees through recognition and rewards
- Identify growth opportunities that align with individual learning styles and preferences
- Consider development options outside the traditional promotional track
- Understand where formal appraisals are useful—and where they fall short
- Go beyond a simple number when using performance ratings
- Sidestep burnout on your team
- Manage the performance of employees who work remotely

Contents

SECTION TWO

Ongoing Performance Management

SECTION THREE

Developing Employees

SECTION FOUR

Formal Performance Reviews

SECTION FIVE

Tough Topics

Introduction

Performance Management for a New Age of Work

As a manager, you're responsible for the output and productivity of your team. But what steps should you take to track performance, communicate effectively with your direct reports, and encourage individual growth?

Performance management is an interconnected set of tools used to measure and improve the effectiveness of people in the workplace. High-performing organizations use performance management to achieve three goals: to develop individuals' skills and capabilities, to reward all employees equitably, and to drive overall organizational performance. As a manager, you can customize your performance management process to help your team and employees deliver strong results for the organization while helping them develop their professional aspirations.

Specific approaches to performance management differ based on organizations' strategies, values, and culture, but they typically include setting employee goals and tracking progress against these objectives, providing ongoing feedback and coaching, developing employees' skills and strengths, and, often, formal evaluations. Many elements of the process—assessing performance, giving feedback, and development, for example—are ongoing. Other activities, like goal setting and formal reviews, have historically been calendar driven and cyclical.

But traditional performance management approaches have come under fire in recent years. Many business leaders have begun to question the value of standard processes and whether they are effective in achieving the results they seek. With the growth of knowledge work, the traditional annual performance review cycle can seem like a rusty artifact ill-suited for today's nimble organizations. But stepping away from performance management entirely—leaving employees without a process for meeting their goals and managers without a method for developing their employees—risks many errors, missteps, and missed opportunities for growth. Some organizations have begun to adjust and revise their performance management processes, but even then, many managers are left wondering how to ensure the results and growth of their direct reports as more and more pieces of the process are debated.

As formal approaches to performance management evolve, managers must understand which elements of traditional best practices they should keep in place and which are fraught, which components of new processes are working and which should be avoided. This guide will introduce the essential elements of performance management so you can adjust your own process to best suit the needs of your company and your team, while also providing you with the information you need to understand the conversations surrounding performance management as it shifts to meet the needs of a changing, more agile organization.

The Evolution of Performance Management

The traditional process of managing performance began as a system for assessing and maximizing the productivity of industrial workers in manufacturing firms. The cycle generally began with the development of annual goals for each employee; at the end of the year, people were formally appraised based on how successfully they achieved those objectives. Performance assessment was based on straightforward, production-based metrics, so evaluating employees against goals was usually clear-cut: Did they produce the targeted number of units, with few errors? Appraisals were usually linked to employee ratings, which were used to calculate changes in compensation for high-performing workers. Those rated as low performing were often let go.

But processes originally developed to evaluate the performance of individual contributors in industrial firms and jobs in production don't necessarily align with the needs of today's businesses that prize creativity and innovation and those that are increasingly staffed by knowledge workers and teams whose results aren't so easy to measure. While the industrial model aimed to reduce variation (in manufacturing errors, for example), many organizations today aspire to innovate by *increasing* variation. An individual's appraisal, rating, and compensation once rested on the completion of annual goals—but today, those targets often become outdated before the year is out. In response, some organizations are embracing flexibility and shorter-term goals that can be modified over the course of the year.

Metrics to gauge performance, too, have become more complex: When an employee is dealing with ideas and knowledge rather than easily countable units, assessing performance against goals requires some ingenuity. What's more, with talent in shorter supply (and skills, particularly technical ones, becoming obsolete quickly), companies have used these metrics solely as a tool to identify individuals to advance or reward—but their actions didn't always result in better performance.

Many organizations now recognize that they need performance management processes that are better suited for their people and their needs. They want nimble, flexible instruments that can truly increase and accurately measure performance. Some organizations are shifting away from cyclical, calendar-based approaches toward those based on more communication throughout the year. Netflix, for example, eliminated formal evaluations in favor of regular performance discussions and informal 360-degree reviews, where people identify what their colleagues should stop, start, or continue doing either by supplying signed feedback or even taking part in face-to-face team meetings. Others are holding more-frequent reviews (often semiannually or quarterly) and complementing them with increased dialogue between bosses and employees that involve ongoing check-ins and opportunities for real-time feedback.

Some influential companies and business leaders are reappraising the established performance management approach—in some cases overhauling familiar processes in innovative, even unprecedented, ways. Deloitte, for example, conducted a public survey and found that 58% of executives questioned felt that their current method of managing performance neither drove employee engagement nor promoted high performance.[1] By focusing too much on looking at past results, the process provided no practical look to the future. With that in mind, Deloitte created a new approach that removed traditional elements such as 360-degree feedback, cascading objectives, and once-a-year reviews and instead focused on "performance snapshots," in which an employee's immediate manager answers four future-focused questions about an employee—essentially asking what they'd *do* with the employee rather than what they think of the individual.[2]

Companies are also discovering that a more individualized plan may work better for their employees. A different approach may be needed for, say, salaried professional staff eligible for incentive pay than for hourly employees. Some organizations are also taking steps to broaden traditional processes to weigh how teammates' contributions, in addition to system or organizational challenges, can significantly influence individual performance.

These organizations are signaling that while traditional approaches may be less effective than they once were, managers are still responsible for assessing their teams' work and output in one form or another. Few can realistically afford to dismiss the process altogether—nor should they.

Why Performance Management (Still) Matters

Despite the arguments against it, routinizing the management of employee performance can help every organization and every manager make the most of its most important resources—its people—so everyone benefits. That's because:

- Shareholders and investors observe better results when people are working in unison toward key goals.
- Supervisors are more successful when their reports focus on the right tasks and projects—and do them well.
- Employees appreciate focused goals, opportunities for career development, and recognition for outstanding performance.

An effective performance management process—one that takes into account how organizations are changing—can still keep employees focused on meaningful goals and offers managers a clear framework for appraising the quality of their people's work. At the very least, a calendar-based system—whether annual or more frequent—guarantees that direct reports will have a chance to discuss their work and get feedback from their managers at predictable intervals during the course of the year. (Managers can and should offer feedback more frequently than that, but this is a start.) The performance management cycle provides a logical time frame and process for assessing the quality of employees' work and making compensation-related decisions, whether or not companies stick with formal rating processes. And a thoughtful performance management approach will offer people opportunities to plan out learning and development efforts to boost their motivation and career satisfaction for the long term.

It's rare that an organization (or individual, for that matter) can make real progress without setting and working toward goals. And few companies can remain competitive or retain their best people without offering opportunities to grow. So as performance management evolves, it's important for managers to learn how to work within those changing processes to ensure the growth of their people and their contribution to their organization.

What's Ahead

This guide will offer tools and best practices you can tailor to manage your team's performance while meeting your organization's needs and supporting your people in today's agile business world. Whether you're looking to improve on a traditional process, seeking a more flexible option, or creating an approach where none exists, you'll learn the basics of performance management, so you can customize an approach that works for you.

In section 1, we'll explore employee goal setting: the characteristics of effective goals, how individual and organizational goals align, and how to develop metrics to measure people's progress toward their objectives. We'll also discuss creating specific plans for enabling direct reports to meet those targets to ensure that you'll be satisfied with progress. But because established goals may no longer remain static over the course of a year, we'll also explain how to assess whether set goals are still valid—and how to make changes as necessary.

In section 2, we'll discuss the process of observing, documenting, and improving performance throughout the year. You'll learn how to identify performance gaps and assess why they occur, effectively coach and deliver feedback, recognize good work, and motivate people to do their best.

In section 3, we'll address employee career development: how to ensure that your people are growing professionally. Regardless of how your organization's formal performance management process is run, employee development efforts are becoming a focus of every manager who wants to lead an engaged, high-performing team and drive business. You'll learn how to discover your employees' unique needs and ambitions, identify the tactics available to your direct reports to build their skills, determine a direction for growth, and create individualized development plans to propel people forward—even those who are struggling.

In section 4, we'll delve into the details of formal performance reviews. This section first presents current arguments for and against formal appraisals—and for those who do conduct them, offers a detailed process for success. We'll help you navigate the practice of assessing a direct report's progress toward previously established goals and show you how to put your appraisal in writing, including how to use ratings most effectively. We'll cover how to conduct the review session, from detailing performance to preparing for the review period ahead.

In section 5, we'll explore topics that managers struggle with in performance management. We'll begin by explaining how to support and nurture your B players: those who are neither ambitious standouts nor strugglers. We'll also discuss how to avoid burnout on your team—a problem that tends to affect the most valuable, hardest-working employees. Finally, you'll learn how to manage the performance of remote employees you rarely (or never) see in person.

While the rules of performance management are constantly changing, the need to work effectively with your employees and to encourage their success remains constant. This book will help you better understand how the landscape is changing, so you can adjust your own behavior while managing your people's performance and meet the needs of your organization. By following the advice in this guide, you'll be able to master each part of the process and make it an ongoing, flexible, and effective part of your daily work.

NOTES

1. Deloitte Consulting LLP and Bersin by Deloitte, "Global Human Capital Trends 2014: Engaging the 21st-Century Workforce," Deloitte University Press, 2014.
2. Marcus Buckingham and Ashley Goodall, "Reinventing Performance Management," *Harvard Business Review*, April 2015 (product #R1504B).

SECTION ONE

Goal Setting

CHAPTER 1

The Characteristics of Effective Goals

Setting clear goals is the starting point of managing performance. Goals define the results that your people should aim to achieve in a given period of time. When you work with your employees to establish targets, you help ensure that their time and energy will be spent on the things that matter most to them—and to your organization. Doing so enhances motivation, provides accountability, and boosts performance.

Agreeing on specific targets is only part of the goal-setting process, however. You must also define how your employee's progress toward these objectives will be evaluated and how to measure results and gauge behavioral expectations. Defining this information at the outset will make assessing performance easier for you later, and your employees will have a clear understanding of how to proceed throughout the year.

You will work with your people directly to craft a set of goals that are suitable for them. Before jumping into a goal-setting discussion, though, you need to know what characteristics goals should have and where to draw potential targets from. Finally, you must understand how challenging to make these objectives.

Attributes of Well-Defined Goals

Most managers are familiar with the SMART acronym, a set of five criteria that goals should meet: They should be specific, measurable, attainable, realistic, and time-bound. These five traits can be used to assess whether a goal statement has been constructed properly—like a spell-checker that can flag any misspelled words. But simply passing a SMART test isn't enough to make an objective valuable to your company or employees. A goal can be SMART without being important, challenging, or congruent with unit or organizational strategy.

Instead, consider different criteria. Effective goals must be:

- **Aligned with organizational strategy and beneficial to the company.** They focus your people's time, energy, and resources on the work that matters most.

- **Specific and measurable.** Spelling out the details of what your employee plans to achieve ensures that both of you will know when they have reached their goal.

- **Framed in time, with clear deadlines.** Including a target date for reaching a goal increases the likelihood that your employee will meet it.

- **Achievable but challenging.** Stretch goals that require individuals to reach can be energizing.

- **Future focused.** They should be geared toward improving current performance and spurring future growth.

- **Tailored to the individual.** When people are involved in setting objectives, they feel a valuable sense of ownership—and they'll naturally be more committed to things they own.

- **Documented but not forgotten.** Most organizations require that each employee's targets be written down, but too often, once they're filed away, they can fall off the radar till the next goal-setting meeting. Keeping these objectives front of mind and regularly assessing progress will prevent them from getting buried in day-to-day work.

These characteristics will help ensure that your direct reports focus their time and resources on the results that will most benefit the organization while still providing room for individual growth. Some of the attributes in this list align with SMART criteria, but you'll also see additional traits that point to a larger purpose. As you think about your employees' goals, strive to meet all of these criteria.

Sources of Goals

Each of your direct reports should have a set of goals that is based on their role, skill level, and development aims. Do this by drawing from a variety of sources directly related to your employee's needs, such as:

- **Organization, division, or department plans and strategies.** How could the employee contribute to bigger priorities? Consider your company's broader objectives, team aims, or your own targets as a manager in the process of developing an individual's goals.

- **Goals from previous review periods or those that are linked to critical job responsibilities.** Some objectives will be evergreen, and others will evolve: A salesperson will always have the goal of increasing sales, but specific numerical targets will change from year to year.

- **Comments from previous performance reviews and feedback discussions.** Perhaps there are performance gaps to close, strong skills to develop further, or greater responsibilities to take on once skills have been mastered. Performance management is a continuous process, so it can be helpful to link one period's goals with those of the next, especially when they are tied to an employee's ongoing growth or improvement.

You can also consider the "cheaper, faster, better" rubric, described by performance management expert Dick Grote in his book *How to Be Good at Performance Appraisals*. Start by thinking about the areas of an individual's job where they spend most of their time or that make the biggest impact. How can expenses be reduced (cheaper) or less time spent (faster) while still improving quality (better)? How can an employee's time and energy best be redirected to contribute to departmental or organizational success? These questions may be more apt for those with entry-level or support roles than for those in leadership positions; seeking ways to perform cheaper, faster, and better may already be a routine part of these higher-level jobs and unnecessary to identify as an additional goal.

You may be tempted to draw goals from a person's job description. After all, a well-written job description can be a clear way to define a position and its essential functions. But job descriptions tend to be more about the content of the role than about the aims that managers and their employees agree to pursue.

For example, consider this job description for an executive assistant:

> *The executive assistant to the director will plan, schedule, and coordinate meetings; record and circulate meeting minutes; manage and track communications by providing timely responses and distributing messages; assist in drafting, editing, copying, and distributing project reports and other materials; handle*

travel arrangements; assist with expense documentation and reimbursements; manage complicated schedules and day-to-day office systems; and perform other job-related duties as required.

There are many activities listed here, but not a single identifiable goal. The description doesn't provide any clarity on the objectives of the director or the organization—or about the professional ambitions of the employee. Using this write-up alone to establish effective targets for this role would be ill-advised.

As you think about potential goals for your employee (and they do the same), dig deeper than a simple job description. Think about the difference between "handle customer complaints" and "reduce customer attrition by 10%." Or "participate in a quality-control training program" versus "Cut production waste by 20%." The first is an activity, while the second is an end result to work toward. Aim toward descriptive, measurable targets in your goal setting.

The Tricky Balance of Challenge

Possibly the toughest factor in goal setting is how to make desired outcomes achievable but challenging. Stretch goals are objectives that require extra effort to reach. They're an important element of a high-performing culture and of employee development. People respond positively to challenge, and when motivated to reach a tough target, employees can push themselves to achieve more than they previously thought they could. Ambitious goals can create energy and momentum, spurring the greatest effort and highest performance. Conversely, aiming too low can lead to mediocrity. When people choose goals that are too easily attained, they don't see a need to push themselves, and they may disengage from their work.

Because they require significant effort, there's no guarantee these objectives will be achieved. And when they're too unrealistic, stretch goals can backfire. Employees may discount outcomes that are unreasonably ambitious. Faced with an impossible task or an overly aggressive objective, your direct report may end up frustrated, unmotivated, or demoralized. Worse, when faced with unrealistic targets, employees may act immorally. Michael E. Raynor and Derek Pankratz of Deloitte Consulting and Deloitte Services, respectively, have written that when trying to reach unrealistic goals, "people may feel increasingly tempted to cut corners or to resort to unethical or illegal behaviors that they would otherwise be loath even to contemplate."[1] That's not to say that all people faced with tough targets will cheat or misrepresent their performance. But driving to meet unachievable goals can pressure your employees in dangerous ways. You want your people to stretch, not to break.

Keep in mind, though, that what's an impossible ordeal for one person may be an exciting test for another. Ask an aspiring executive to lead a new team, and they may light up with excitement; ask a stellar solo contributor who had no interest in management to do the same, and you'll likely be disappointed with the results.

When developing a plan for your direct reports, collaborate with your employees to craft goals that are challenging, strategic, and in line with individual skill sets and aspirations. The next two chapters will give you the skills you need to do this.

NOTE

1. Michael E. Raynor and Derek Pankratz, "A Way to Know If Your Corporate Goals Are Too Aggressive," HBR.org, July 13, 2015 (product #H0278K).

CHAPTER 2

Define Employee Goals—and Decide How They're Measured

As a manager, you'll take the lead on setting objectives for your team as a whole. Each team member will be working toward these overarching targets, but each individual should also have unique, personalized expectations of their own.

From a purely logical perspective, goal setting should be a top-down process that begins in company strategy and cascades down from the top ranks of the organization—from the president to the VPs to the directors, all the way down the line. This system helps ensure that the goals of any employee in an organization would support their manager's team goals as well as the organization's broader objectives.

But the traditional "cascading goal" model has its downsides. When no one is able to set their own goals until their supervisor's goals have been established—which can't happen until *their* manager's goals are set—employees can feel like mere cogs in a wheel. The cascading model can directly or indirectly signal to your reports that they are truly subordinate, leaving them feeling less motivated than those who have had more ownership and control in setting their own goals. Imposed objectives dictated from on high are unlikely to motivate people as much as goals they had some say in developing. Inflexible, top-down goals can also fail to account for or take advantage of the unique interests, skills, and potential contributions of individuals throughout the organization.

Given this, consider a different approach: Let your direct reports take the lead in setting their goals. Targets that are defined by employees themselves (with managerial guidance and review) engender an important sense of ownership. A person who isn't invested in the creation of their goals may not have the same level of commitment to achieve them—and a person who isn't held accountable for results has no reason to take goals seriously. In his HBR.org article, "The Right Way to Hold People Accountable," leadership advisor Peter Bregman explains, "Accountability is not simply taking the blame when something goes wrong. . . . Accountability is about delivering on a commitment. It's responsibility to an outcome, not just a set of tasks. It's taking initiative with thoughtful, strategic follow-through."

Giving your employees the autonomy to define the details of their goals will help them take responsibility and accountability for the results they aim to achieve. It also helps ensure that they understand both the specifics and the greater importance of their objectives.

You can support your people by helping them understand what the organization's larger goals and strategy are and what your team needs to achieve. By reviewing and providing input on each objective your direct report suggests, you can help create opportunities that also support each person's growth and enable their engagement.

Set Up a Performance-Planning Session

In many organizations, new goals are set after a formal performance review, which serves as the natural end of a traditional performance management cycle and the beginning of a new one. Many experts suggest separating the review meeting from the goal-setting process for a more-focused discussion. Since appraisal sessions can cover a wide range of topics from criticism to compensation—and because many review conversations are at least somewhat emotionally loaded—separating out the goal-setting process allows you and your employee to give the conversation due consideration and focused attention. If possible, schedule a separate performance-planning session to discuss the employee's goals and your expectations.

While your employee may be setting goals for the year in this meeting, it's possible that those targets will need to be adjusted before the review period ends. In fast-changing industries, the goals you set may not be relevant for an entire year—or even for a quarter. Between constantly evolving technology and a rapidly changing economy, many organizations are becoming more agile; in that context, planning employee goals and tasks a year in advance may not be realistic or accurate. Some companies have replaced annual objectives with short-term ones. At the retailer Gap, for example, employees have quarterly targets; at GE, shorter-term "priorities" have taken the place of annual goals. Recognize that a person's goals may need to be adjusted or adapted during the year. It doesn't make sense for anyone to keep working toward an outdated target, so while you should aim to establish long-term objectives, recognize that you may need to meet again to revise or adapt them.

Before you and your employee get together at the performance-planning meeting, ask them to draft a list of goals for the two of you to review together. Give them some pointers about what makes for an effective goal, and review some promising sources for coming up with possibilities. Employees at every level should be able to articulate how their work feeds into the big-picture organizational strategy in addition to fitting with their individual strengths, skills, and ambitions.

Define Goals

When your employee has a list in place, assess their suggested goals. How do they fit into the larger picture? Can you see clear links between their expected contributions and the results they need to achieve as members of your team? Are the objectives realistic and challenging? Do they cover all the elements of the SMART rubric and meet the characteristics of well-defined goals? When reviewing the list, make sure both organizational needs and the employee's professional aspirations are accounted for.

Aligning goals with those of the organization

Each unit, team, and individual should have goals that directly support the organization's larger strategic objectives. Such alignment focuses each person's energy on the work that matters most to the company. Your employee may already understand your team and organization's strategic efforts, but don't assume that they do. Take the time now to discuss those efforts in detail. Understanding *why* a goal is important, on both an individual and an organizational level, will make it more meaningful to your employee.

With these aims in mind, review the employee's suggested list. Do each of their proposed goals line up with these big-picture efforts? Do they fit within a larger organizational or team strategy? By defining together how their goals can contribute to a larger organizational purpose, their sense of ownership and engagement can grow, and you can begin identifying which of their suggested goals should take priority.

If a target doesn't match a team or organizational aim, assess whether it's the right fit. You may be able to revise it to better serve the team or company, or you may choose to remove it from the list altogether. Also, discuss whether there are any goals that are missing from their list that would be important to add from an organizational perspective.

Aligning personal interests with professional goals

Understanding your direct reports at a personal level will help you not only in the goal-setting process but with every facet of performance management. How can the unit goals be crafted to inspire the highest level of enthusiasm and engagement from each person? What are your employees' career ambitions? Are their professional goals compatible with those the unit or organization must pursue?

By understanding your employees as individuals and learning about their personal strengths and interests, you may be able to help incorporate those elements into their professional goals. Activities that contribute to organizational success can also spur individual employee development—and people can find the intersection of professional goals and personal interests highly motivating.

Ask your team members if they would be comfortable telling you about their personal interests during your performance-planning meeting if their drafted list of goals doesn't seem to include them. Consider what adjustments can be made to workplace objectives to include those interests. A software developer with a stand-up comedy hobby may not have much opportunity to entertain at work, but if you know they thrive in the spotlight you can suggest them for any speaking opportunities that arise. A goal of delivering departmental presentations or pitching new clients may well suit their interests and skills.

WHEN PERSONAL AND UNIT GOALS CONFLICT

Every so often you'll encounter an employee who doesn't think that a unit goal is very important—at least not to them. For example, sales manager Natasha learns that Cory, her team's newest field sales representative, has a professional goal of landing a job in market research. He's in his current job only to help him gain essential skills to put on his résumé. Natasha needs to have a conversation with Cory in which she explains that, while he may want to be in a new role in the future, he has a job to do and goals to achieve in his current position. She should tell him that by achieving or exceeding his present goals, he may get the opportunity to develop skills that are applicable to market research or gain exposure to the work done by colleagues in that field.

If Cory devotes himself to meeting his sales goals and achieves strong results, Natasha will be more likely to help him get experience in his field of interest. But if he's just not willing to get on board with his team's goals, he may not be a good fit for the team or the organization.

Even employees who share identical titles and roles can adjust certain goals or take on specific tasks that best suit their interests, tap into their strengths, and reflect their personal traits. Your team of three marketers, for example, may share similar goals regarding the new marketing initiative your department is rolling out in the next few months, but each person can also have individually tailored goals that suit their unique interests. If one person likes social media, for example, they might set a goal of increasing the organization's followers and growing brand awareness on a specific platform. Their colleague with an interest in customer research and focus groups may set out to spearhead new research efforts to better target your department's marketing dollars, while another team member with a passion for data analytics could aim to analyze your current marketing effort's reach. By identifying your employee's interests, you can help them define objectives that let them explore and develop skills that are meaningful to them while producing valuable work results.

Once you've taken the time to understand your employee's strengths and aspirations, look again at their suggested list of goals to see if any align with those traits and objectives. In some cases, you may need to prioritize an organizational mission over a personal aim, but strive for balance to keep your employee engaged, motivated, and growing. (See the sidebar "When Personal and Unit Goals Conflict" for suggestions on what to do when your employees' aspirations don't match with unit goals.)

Set a Reasonable Number of Goals

Once you and your report have discussed the list of goals in detail, narrow down the list to a succinct set of objectives to pursue. Even stellar employees can only do so much. A person faced with two goals will probably make progress toward achieving both. But when faced with five, an individual may only make progress toward two or three. Any more than five, and your employee is unlikely to accomplish any, since their attention will be so divided. Instead of burying someone in a flurry of goals, prioritize: Focus on two to four challenging, specific, significant goals.

People can also be overwhelmed by complex and large goals—which is not to say they can't aim to meet them. It can be helpful, though, to break a goal into smaller pieces, or to set shorter-term aims. Setting monthly or quarterly goals, rather than annual ones, can narrow the focus enough to make the target achievable while still having a big impact.

Establish Ways to Measure Success

Once you and your employee agree on a set of meaningful goals, determine how you plan to assess progress toward each one. List anticipated outcomes and measures for each item.

Metrics provide objective evidence of goal achievement or progress toward it. Sales revenues, errors per thousand units of product, and time to market for new products are all clear examples of metrics that can be linked to goals, since they can be easily quantified.

It's worth noting, however, that not every goal can be easily measured, and you can fall into traps while establishing metrics. Keep the following pitfalls in mind as you define how objectives will be evaluated.

- **Missing metrics.** Some goals may not be obviously connected to clear performance metrics. "Increase unique visitors to the website by 5%" is simple to measure if you know the starting point, but a goal of "increase engagement on social platforms" is trickier to quantify.

- **Choosing the wrong metrics.** Not all that can be measured is equally important or worth targeting. While it's great to increase the number of customer complaints resolved in a given time period, it may be better to focus on reducing the number of complaints overall.

- **Overemphasizing metrics.** Performance is a combination of two factors: behaviors and results. If results are the "what" of performance, behaviors are the "how." Noting the behavior and work behind a specific goal is just as important as the metric itself, even if it's not easily quantifiable. Helping a colleague who's facing a tight deadline or coaching a new member of the team is unlikely to fit into anyone's formal goals, but such actions deserve recognition and acknowledgment.

When goals aren't easily quantified

Some goals are more qualitative and therefore harder to measure. In such cases, you should still be able to pinpoint tangible, measurable targets within them. If you're struggling to find a suitable unit of measure, set a more specific, metric-friendly goal targeting something that *can* be measured. Someone whose goal is to improve their public speaking skills may set a target of making six public presentations in the upcoming year, with the understanding that there will be a follow-up meeting to discuss that performance and ways to improve after each. Or, if your employee is tasked with increasing innovation, a suitable target might be to propose three new ideas to the department in the next six months or to meet certain deadlines for specific stages in a project's development.

Determine in advance how you plan to measure progress for each goal, whether it's a numerical or time-based target. Be specific: If you were evaluating an individual who wanted to improve their public speaking, you might want to agree on how you define "public presentations." Are they presentations to the department, to the organization as a whole, or outside the company? Additionally, define ways to measure engagement and people's reactions to determine if the speech was considered a success.

While goals and metrics are hugely important, they are not the be-all and end-all of performance management. Don't make the mistake of dismissing what you can't quantify. When it comes time to assess an employee's performance, you'll want to look beyond simply measured aspects.

Establish Expectations, Not Just Goals

When you discuss objectives with your employees, you should also talk about what you expect of them in terms of behavior. Your direct report may understand what they must achieve, but if they do so in a way that's detrimental to your team or the organization, their contributions won't matter.

Talk through your expectations for citizenship behaviors—like stepping in to help colleagues in need, serving as a resource for others, cooperating and demonstrating flexibility, and training new hires—as well as basic competencies like behaving professionally in the office and arriving to work on time. How individuals contribute to organizational culture may not fit into a goals framework but is still essential to achieving strong performance. Understanding behavioral expectations is important to creating a collaborative and productive work environment—and you should make it clear to your employees that you value their contributions and cooperation on this front as much as you do their work results.

When you make your expectations clear from the outset and your employees understand how they'll be evaluated, performance improves. Plus, making expectations explicit helps hold employees accountable.

CHAPTER 3

Collaborate with Your Employee to Create a Plan for Moving Forward

Once you and your employee have developed a clear set of challenging goals with specific metrics, you'll need to ensure that there's a practical plan in place for achieving them. As social psychologist Heidi Grant says, "Creating goals that teams and organizations will actually accomplish isn't just a matter of defining what needs doing; you also have to spell out the specifics of getting it done, because you can't assume that everyone involved will know how to move from concept to delivery."[1]

Goals can seem impenetrable, even overwhelming, but they become much more manageable when there's a detailed plan to reach them. An ambitious objective that will take a year to complete will be composed of many smaller parts and steps. For example, a financial services professional may set a goal of obtaining licensure for a certain specialty. It's unlikely that he'll be able to meet that goal simply by showing up for the licensure exam without any advance preparation. Instead, he'll need to break the goal down into doable components, studying for each part of the exam over a predetermined period of time.

Your employees should do the same: When people create a plan to meet a goal, they are more likely to successfully achieve it. While some such plans may be straightforward and quick to pull together, others will be more difficult to figure out. But the time you invest at the beginning of the process will pay off when your employee nimbly works through what could have been tricky steps. Remember, too, that just as goals may shift over time, plans to achieve them may need to be adjusted.

Set a Comprehensive Plan for Success

In most cases you'll want your employees to develop a plan for meeting goals that you can then review. The process of setting a plan can empower your direct report and create a sense of ownership. But in some cases, especially for challenging goals or with employees who are new to project planning, you may need to work together to complete the following steps.

Step 1: Determine the tasks needed to accomplish the goal

Break the goal down into task-based components. If one task seems overwhelming, separate it into smaller parts. Some items may be completed simultaneously (such as making tweaks to a draft marketing campaign while awaiting additional feedback), while others may need to be completed sequentially (such as getting approval for the final campaign before implementing it), so list them in the appropriate order. Determining each required task can make complex or long-term projects seem much more manageable.

Step 2: Plan the timing for each task

Set a start and finish date for each individual task, and describe the desired results or outcomes for each item. For team projects, you may be familiar with a Gantt chart or other time-scaled task diagram that illustrates an estimated schedule. A Gantt chart is an easy-to-read bar chart that clearly communicates what needs to be done in a particular time frame (see figure 3-1). The graphic shows you what tasks are upcoming and allows you to make adjustments in your plans as necessary, such as if one task takes longer than expected and subsequent ones need to be pushed forward.

Individuals can use a similar visual for their tasks by creating such a chart in an excel file or digital calendar. Mark intended milestones along the way, such as "We should have the first stage of task A completed by May 15." With your employee, create an individualized

FIGURE 3-1

Gantt chart example

Product development project

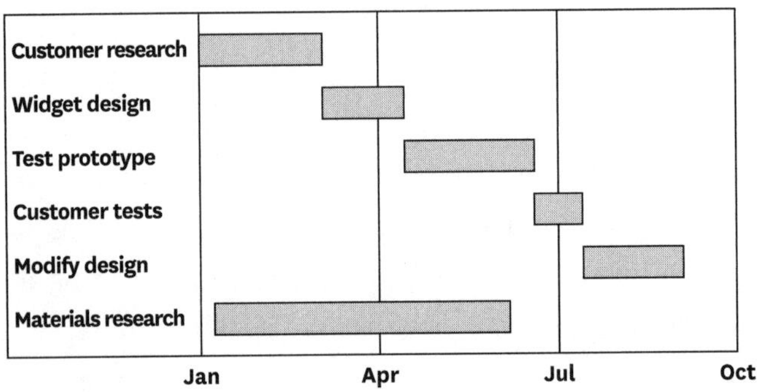

Source: Harvard Business Essentials: Manager's Toolkit: The 13 Skills Managers Need to Succeed (Boston: Harvard Business School Press, 2004), 11.

diagram that includes each of their tasks. Watch out for overloading or tight time crunches, where if one task moves, deadlines may be missed. This tool can then be updated throughout the review period as schedules and goals shift.

As you develop the chart, think through contingency plans. If something does move, how should your employee adapt? Discuss such possibilities with your direct report, so they can stay on track even when the unexpected happens.

Step 3: Gather the resources needed to fulfill each task

Many efforts fail because people underestimate the time and resources required to accomplish each task. Once you've planned how each task will be executed and assigned its individual time line, consider what the employee will need to complete it. Do they have the bandwidth and equipment to manage these tasks in addition to their ongoing responsibilities? Does your direct report have the training and knowledge to be successful?

In some cases you may be able to supply the additional resources your employee requires—a new piece of technology, access to a database, or colleagues to assist them. But in others, you may discover that the person needs to learn new skills, particularly if they're facing an especially challenging goal. When that's the case, discuss ways you can help your employee fill the gaps. (See chapter 9, "Expand Your Employee's Skill Sets," to read more on how to develop these proficiencies.)

Step 4: Get it on paper

Once you and an employee have reached agreement on goals and created a detailed plan to reach them, document your conclusions. Your organization may have a form you can use, or you can create your own using the template in table 3-1 at the end of this chapter. Either way, you'll want to include the following information:

- The date of your performance-planning meeting
- Key points brought up by both parties
- The employee's goals for the next review period
- A detailed plan of what is required to achieve them
- A description of any resources or training you have agreed to provide
- A time frame for follow-up meetings

Some organizations require that statements of goals be submitted to HR, but whether yours does or not, keep the document on file for yourself, and share it with your employee as well. You'll find this write-up helpful when it comes time to revise an employee's goals, for evaluating their performance throughout the review period, and in the instance of a formal appraisal.

Follow Up and Reassess Goals

Performance management is an ongoing process, so regularly schedule check-in conversations to keep track of your direct reports' progress toward both short- and long-term goals. If you don't know how well someone is doing, you won't know when to make adjustments in their plan to reach their objectives—or in the goals themselves. For example, GE encourages frequent conversations with employees to revisit two key questions: "What am I doing that I should keep doing? And what am I doing that I should change?"[2]

The timing of these check-ins can vary depending on how many employees you manage, how you work with your employees, or the general pace of your industry. In some instances your organization may have a particular recommendation. For instance, in their revamping of performance management practices, Deloitte implemented weekly check-ins. Some other companies suggest their managers check in monthly or quarterly.

You're the best judge of how frequently you should meet with each of your direct reports. At the end of your performance-planning meeting, discuss with your employee when it makes sense to check in. Some meetings should be event-based: when an employee completes a task, reaches a milestone, or achieves a goal. But others will be between these points, simply to discuss ongoing progress. Set a schedule of check-ins in advance, and put your next meeting date on the calendar before you conclude the performance-planning session. These regular conversations are the most effective and time-efficient way to stay up-to-date on your employees' performance.

When to change your employee's goals

It's possible that an employee may need to update their goals before the next performance appraisal comes around. Perhaps they've achieved a goal and need a new challenge, they're taking over responsibilities for a teammate who's shifted to a new role, or the organization's objectives have changed. For instance, the goal of developing an innovative new app may need to adjust if the organization has decided to prioritize its current mobile interface instead.

If an employee's goals need to be revised, meet to review previously set goals and plans. Three questions can guide you in your discussion as you reassess targets:

- Are they still *realistic*, given any changes in constraints or resources?
- Are they still *timely*? Is now the best possible moment to achieve them?
- Are they still *relevant*? Do they still align with the company's strategy?

It may be necessary to change only a single goal by replacing it with a new one, but in cases of major change, the entire plan may need to shift. If, for example, your team has been diligently working toward a merger, everyone will need a new set of goals after the merger happens.

If you're checking in with your direct reports on a regular basis about their progress, the need to change course or revise goals will come as no surprise. Additionally, every check-in will be another opportunity to monitor your employees' performance, offer feedback, or provide coaching. These elements of ongoing performance management are the topic of the next section.

NOTES

1. Heidi Grant, "Get Your Team to Do What It Says It's Going to Do," *Harvard Business Review*, May 2014 (product #R1405E).
2. Peter Cappelli and Anna Tavis, "The Performance Management Revolution," *Harvard Business Review*, October 2016 (product #R1610D).

TABLE 3-1

Goal-setting template

Describe the three primary goals the individual is to accomplish in the upcoming year with a description of how they will be measured and any expected outcomes.

Goals	Measures of achievement/expected outcomes
1.	
2.	
3.	

In the following section, describe specific tasks that need to be completed to accomplish each of the three goals above. Include specific time lines, plans for completion, resources needed, additional actions required for follow-up, and any contingency plans discussed.

Goal 1:

Tasks required:	Start date:	End date:

Plan to execute tasks:

Resources needed:

Actions required for follow-up:

Contingency plans:

Goal 2:

Tasks required:	Start date:	End date:

Plan to execute tasks:

Resources needed:

Actions required for follow-up:

Contingency plans:

Goal 3:

Tasks required:	Start date:	End date:

Plan to execute tasks:

Resources needed:

Actions required for follow-up:

Contingency plans:

Please include any additional notes about the employee's goals or plan here:

This plan is agreed to as indicated by the signatures below.

Employee	Date
Manager	Date

Source: Adapted from *20-Minute Manager: Performance Reviews* (Boston: Harvard Business Review Press, 2015), 83–85.

SECTION TWO

Ongoing Performance Management

CHAPTER 4

Assessing Performance Isn't a Onetime Event

Performance management is an ongoing process, not a one-and-done event. Circumstances and priorities can shift over time, and gaps can form if employees are unable to keep up—which why so many companies are implementing more-flexible performance cycles. So it's particularly important, especially in a fast-changing work environment, that you observe the quality of your employees' performance and respond to it in the moment. In the previous section you read about defining goals and adjusting them as needed. Now we'll focus on keeping track of performance and responding to it regularly.

Unlike a time-bound formal review session (which we'll discuss in section 4), assessing performance and providing feedback is a continual process. You and your employees will both benefit if you give feedback often.

Take advantage of your check-in sessions as opportunities to track your employees' strengths, weaknesses, interests, and ambitions while also staying apprised of their progress. You'll be able to identify where your employees may be falling short of their goals and collaborate on ways to correct course.

Periodic progress checks and ongoing observation are essential in order to help you:

- **Stay grounded in goals.** Checking in to monitor progress toward goals offers the opportunity to revise targets based on changing priorities or circumstances. You might discover that your employee is on track to meet a goal ahead of schedule—or you might need to remind them about important items that may not be the current focus of their attention.

- **Recognize and reinforce strong performance.** People always welcome positive feedback about their contributions, successes, and achievements, so be liberal with your praise. In fact, some experts suggest that to boost performance, you should provide more positive feedback than negative. (To learn more about offering recognition, see chapter 7.)

- **Become aware of performance gaps, and close them.** A performance gap is the difference between someone's current performance and what is required. As a manager, it's crucial that you identify small gaps before they snowball into bigger issues.

If you're up-to-date on your direct report's progress, you'll be well positioned to catch any problems early and work with your employee to correct course—before they veer so far off target that carefully set goals become unattainable. Ongoing observation is key to staying on top of any issues and identifying the root cause of problems, as well as finding opportunities for positive feedback and recognition.

Observe and Gather Data

To best track performance, observe your employees and how they are progressing toward their goals. Your mission should be to identify an individual's strengths and weaknesses and to understand the impact that their work and behavior has on the person's ability to achieve specific objectives, as well as their contribution to the organization as a whole. You'll also want to keep ongoing notes on their performance. (See the sidebar "Document Your Observations.")

If there are periodic milestones built into your employee's goals, you'll easily be able to spot performance gaps as they develop. For example, Nadia is worried about her employee Eileen's performance. Eileen's goal is to increase sales in her territory by 10% this calendar year, but the first-quarter results show that Eileen's sales are only 2% above last year's numbers for the same period. If this trend continues, Eileen won't meet her annual goal. Nadia would be wise to check in with Eileen—earlier rather than later—to see what can be done to close the gap before it's too late.

Perhaps someone demonstrates a behavior that is causing problems. It's important to assess whether it's an anomaly that won't cause future damage or an ongoing behavior pattern that requires your immediate feedback so your employee can change. Consider these examples:

- During a team meeting, Harriet observed that her direct report Raul frequently interrupted others, preventing them from expressing their views. This tripped up team dynamics and undermined the teamwork that Harriet's unit depended on for its success.
- Miguel noticed that Leila, an off-site member of his team, often seemed the first to pipe up in brainstorming sessions with reasons why a colleague's suggestion wouldn't work. After overhearing some heated conversations between on-site teammates, Miguel became concerned that Leila's comments might be inhibiting the group.

While your own personal observations are important, in today's environment where tasks are complex or involve a team, you may not have the ability to see the full picture. It's helpful to ask for others' thoughts as well. Feedback from other sources provides a useful reality check of your own views—and may provide you with new information about additional good or bad performance. So, when appropriate, discuss these situations with trusted colleagues—in confidence. Add their observations to your own.

For example, Harriet viewed Raul's habit of interrupting others as stifling valuable dialogue, but someone else may applaud his strenuous articulation of his views. To better understand whether Raul was indeed hurting team interactions, Harriet could go to another manager, Leo, and request that he observe Raul's participation in an upcoming meeting and report back on his impressions. (Note that she should not request that the manager look for interruptions specifically, so as not to influence his thinking.) Once she hears back from Leo, Harriet will be better able to fairly assess whether Raul's interruptions are actually a hindrance to his performance. Similarly, Miguel could ask members of his team whether Leila's critiques during their brainstorming sessions are bothering others—and if so, how—to understand the impact of her actions before jumping to conclusions.

DOCUMENT YOUR OBSERVATIONS

Keep a file (electronically or on paper) on each of your direct report's performance, and update it throughout the year. Use it to keep track of both good and bad performance, so you have a balanced view of your employee's work. Update it after check-ins, or set a calendar reminder to add new information periodically.

This document will likely be only for your own reference, so you don't need to write much—just enough so you can see progress (or lack thereof) over time and ensure that you'll remember notable successes or missteps. That said, if someone's performance is suffering to the point where you need to consider termination,

(continued)

DOCUMENT YOUR OBSERVATIONS

you should be especially careful about documenting such actions, as your personal notes could become material in a legal case. Consult with your human resources department or internal legal team for guidance.

Here are a few points to consider when keeping track of performance:

- Record the date and specifics of what happened. For instance: "Raquel's pitch to a potential new client exceeded my expectations. When the client called to confirm that I'd received the signed contract, he mentioned that he and his staff were 'blown away' by her polished delivery and ability to think on her feet when answering questions."
- Stick to facts, not judgments. For example: "Larry has missed four project deadlines in the last three months" rather than "Larry doesn't know how to manage his time."
- Make notes on the day you've given someone feedback (or soon after), while it's fresh in your mind.
- Keep a folder of emails or other correspondence highlighting your employee's accomplishments, whether they are instances you noted yourself or include praise from others.

If you aren't able to check in regularly with your employees and jot down notes yourself—perhaps they work remotely or travel often—request periodic progress reports from each of them every week, month, or quarter. These reports don't need to be formal. An email with a few bullet points will suffice to gather the necessary information, such as their key accomplishments, questions or concerns, and what the individual aims to achieve before the next report or check-in session. You'll be able to gather additional information about each person's performance based on the quality and timeliness of the reports.

These informal records will help you when annual review time rolls around, but they'll also keep you in the loop on any developing performance gaps and help you identify opportunities to offer timely feedback and coaching throughout the year.

Always ensure you have a complete picture of the situation, and continue to watch your direct report's work and behavior if you have any doubts about your perceptions. Avoid premature judgment, and recognize that, no matter someone's behavior, any assumptions about the causes are just that—assumptions. Instead, consider what might underlie an employee's disappointing work results, and make the effort to accurately assess what's causing the problem.

Notice subtle requests for help

While observation is essential to understanding performance, it's also important to perceive the indirect ways your employees may be asking for help. People don't always know what kind of help they need or exactly how to ask for it. Sales manager Rita, for example, was frustrated by the vague monthly reports she was getting from Philip, a salesperson on her team. In their check-in meetings he asked few questions, but after receiving more similarly unsatisfactory reports, Rita realized that Philip might have dropped hints that he wasn't sure what information she was looking for.

Make a practice of actively listening when discussing projects or progress with your employee, and confirm that they understand exactly what you're asking of them. Some people, reluctant to show they're not clear on something, may subtly drop hints rather than ask for clarification directly. Tune in—what you hear may help you figure out how to improve a person's work.

Identify Possible Causes of Poor Performance

If you've noticed an employee's work isn't up to par, your next step is to investigate what may be causing the issue. The underlying cause could be a skill deficiency, poor time management or personal work habits, lack of motivation, conflict with another employee, or unclear direction on your part. Or it could be something else entirely, like a misunderstanding of expectations.

Underperformance may have a nonobvious cause and have nothing to do with lack of skill or motivation. Here are a few possible reasons why people may fall short of expectations:

- **Bad processes.** W. Edwards Deming, one of the great management teachers of the past century, warned business leaders that the source of unsatisfactory performance was usually bad work processes. If you want better performance, look to the work process before you look for faults in your people. Perhaps your employee who is frustratingly late in delivering documents is being hampered by a cumbersome approval process that relies on getting sign-offs from someone who travels often or doesn't always turn requests around quickly.

- **Workplace tensions.** Workload inequities (even if temporary) or simply a visceral dislike may produce conflict that impairs performance. Perhaps two teammates have both applied for a higher-level position; when one is promoted, the other may grow resentful. Another common—and easily remedied—cause of workplace tensions is communication style differences between colleagues. If you can discover what's behind conflict or tension, you may be able to neutralize it.

- **Work overload.** Even the most-committed employee will burn out if you demand too much too fast, so beware of unreasonably ambitious goals and expectations. Don't set the bar too high. If you notice after a series of check-ins that someone has yet to make progress toward a goal, ask what's holding them back; doing so may lead you to reassess the objective. Temporary situations can also affect the quality of an employee's or even a team's work. If one team member misses a number of days of work to tend to an ill family member, for example, their colleagues may feel supportive but also overburdened from picking up the slack.

- **Personal problems.** Sometimes the root cause of poor performance may have nothing to do with work at all. A health crisis at home may be distracting your direct report, or an employee may be struggling to manage both workplace and family demands. You might be able to help mitigate these problems if you learn what they are. For example, if an employee is stretched thin between caring for young children as well as aging parents, perhaps you can offer a flexible work schedule or an option to work remotely on occasion to allow the individual to aid their family.

If you notice poor performance, remember that there may be underlying issues that you need to identify before moving forward with a plan of action. Remedies will differ depending on the cause.

Are you part of the problem?

As you consider possible reasons behind a performance gap, assess whether you've played a role in the issue. Ask yourself if you've unwittingly thrown up roadblocks by, say, reducing necessary resources, overloading your employee with responsibility, or micromanaging. Consider these questions:

- **Have I been clear in my expectations?** It's possible that your employee may not know exactly what you're looking for. If you suspect a lack of clarity is the issue, ask your direct report to explain the task or project in their own words, instead of simply asking whether or not they understand you.
- **Am I holding up my end of the bargain?** Perhaps you and your employee have agreed that they need to step up their leadership skills and take on more responsibility—but when they tried to take ownership of a recent project, you insisted on daily updates. While this might not seem like an unreasonable request, to your employee, it could appear that you distrust them and are micromanaging.
- **How often and to what extent have I intervened in the employee's area of responsibility?** If their performance doesn't measure up, maybe it is because you overruled their decisions or insisted that they follow *your* approach to completing the work. Some people learn best by doing research and preparing beforehand, but others thrive with a less cautious approach. Action-oriented individuals may need more freedom to experiment in order to master new skills.
- **Have I changed priorities and assigned tasks without employee input?** Perhaps you assigned an employee a new short-term project, underestimating

how much time it would take away from their longer-term goals. Or you might have given an assignment that was impossible to complete on time. An unexpected—and unplanned for—shift in time or resources can throw anyone off their game.

When you have identified the cause of a problem, decide if it's worth addressing. Is this a true performance gap or a temporary glitch? If it was a onetime misstep unlikely to be repeated—an error made the first time a person used a new tool or attempted a new task, perhaps—you might let it go. Avoid giving feedback, too, in situations where your employee can't change or control the outcome. If they're being held up by someone else's delayed sign-off, for example, then they may not be the appropriate target for your feedback. Something that you deem to be a problem may simply be a matter of preference. Harriet may find Raul's habit of interruption annoying, but if it has no effect on team dynamics or performance, it may make sense to overlook it.

On the other hand, if you discover a performance problem that could happen again if not addressed, plan to discuss the issue sooner rather than later. The next chapter will guide you through the process of delivering effective feedback.

CHAPTER 5

Make a Habit of Providing Feedback

Feedback can be a useful tool for addressing performance gaps and recognizing exemplary work. In the same way that periodic tests and assignments help both teachers and students gauge progress over the course of a semester before the final exam, ongoing feedback keeps both you and your employee on top of how they are performing as they work toward their goals. Even companies that have done away with traditional elements of the performance management process—goal setting or formal annual reviews—still rely on regular feedback. In fact, many organizations are asking managers to offer it more frequently, as it's one of the most flexible and effective tools available for getting results from your people.

Make giving feedback a regular part of your ongoing performance management approach as a way to recognize good work and redirect missteps in progress.

The Two Types of Regular Feedback

Ongoing feedback falls into one of two main categories. Positive feedback or praise—*Here's what you did really well*—can enhance confidence and increase an employee's sense of commitment. Constructive feedback—*Here's where you need to improve*—is informative, providing a basis for discussion and redirection. Whatever the type, feedback is most effective when it's grounded in specific details that an employee can use.

Positive feedback should pinpoint particular actions of merit: "I liked how you handled the prototype demonstration. The way you began with the underlying technical challenges, went on to describe how those obstacles were addressed, and finished with the actual demonstration helped us all understand the technology." While vague praise—"Great job with that prototype demonstration!"—may not do harm, it doesn't communicate much useful information.

Constructive feedback should target specific opportunities for improvement: "Your demonstration suffered from a lack of organization. I wasn't sure of the problem the prototype aimed to solve, and the technical challenges weren't well-defined." Clear statements help an employee understand what to work on. On the other hand, unvarnished criticism—"People in the audience were bored and confused by your demonstration"—is neither specific nor helpful and offers neither insight nor room for improvement.

Specific feedback, both positive and constructive, is effective at different times with different types of people. Positive feedback is especially helpful for employees at early stages of their career or for individuals who are trying to master new things. "When you don't really know what you are doing, encouragement helps you stay optimistic and feel more at ease with the challenges you are facing—something novices tend to need," social psychologist Heidi Grant explains in her HBR.org article "Sometimes Negative Feedback Is Best."

More-experienced employees, on the other hand, will likely find constructive criticism more helpful and informative, showing them where they should expend their efforts and how they might improve. "When you are an expert and you already know more or less what you are doing, it's constructive criticism that can help you do what it takes to get to the top of your game," says Grant. Seasoned professionals and high performers tend to be hungrier for and more appreciative of constructive feedback that helps them advance even further.

Frequent feedback is necessary for all your employees—even your top performers. Don't assume your top performers know how well they're doing or how much you appreciate them. "The higher the performer, the more frequently you should be providing feedback," says Jamie Harris, a senior consultant at Interaction Associates.[1] People may find constructive feedback easier to take in when they feel genuinely appreciated for what they've done well.

While providing input on an employee's work can be uncomfortable for many managers, it's important to make your feedback frequent and timely. "The primary reason people struggle with giving and receiving feedback is not a lack of proficiency but of frequency," notes social scientist and author Joseph Grenny in his HBR.org article "How to Make Feedback Feel Normal." Check-ins provide opportunities for you to regularly assess progress toward goals and discuss your direct report's performance, but don't hold off on giving feedback right away just because you have a meeting on the calendar set for a later date. Even a short debrief can be useful. For example, use the two minutes it takes to walk back to your office after a meeting to offer your employee feedback on their presentation—what they did well or how they could improve for next time. With constructive comments especially, it's important to give feedback as soon as possible after you've observed a behavior you want to correct or reinforce.

If you're like most managers, addressing employees about problems and pointing out their shortcomings is the least enjoyable part of your job. No one likes to deliver bad news or tell someone that their work or behavior is unacceptable. But if you avoid relaying the message, the employee's unsatisfactory work or behavior will most likely continue—or worsen.

If you feel a natural reluctance to confront poor performance, remind yourself:

- If your aim is to improve performance, giving feedback is the most effective and efficient tool for redirecting and enhancing your employees' work.
- Not giving feedback will undermine the team. Poor performers demoralize others and thwart the success of the unit as a whole.

- You're doing that person a favor. The poor performer may actually think that they are doing satisfactory work. A frank discussion will clear up the misconception and give the employee an opportunity to improve, perhaps saving their job.

- Some employees *like* getting constructive feedback. Since it's essential to improving performance—and, by extension, to career development—many people find it valuable.

When you see an issue that needs to be addressed, don't avoid confrontation. Having an honest discussion about performance problems isn't fun for either of you, but when the conversation is over you'll know that your employee is on the right track for improvement.

Conducting the Feedback Discussion

The feedback you give will most likely cover a wide range of topics, and you'll want to tailor your delivery to the particular situation you're discussing as well as the person you're talking to. But there are some general guidelines you can follow when providing feedback.

Set the stage for a productive conversation

Before you sit down with your employee, make a few notes about what you want to say. Your goal is to elicit positive change in future performance or workplace behavior, not to rake someone over the coals for past failures, so don't dwell on the past. If your direct report

Deepa had a rocky time running her first new-employee orientation session, for example, cast your comments in the light of improving her next event. Give some thought to the most important things you can help her do better next time, rather than enumerating all the flaws you saw.

Next consider the logistics of your conversation. Be thoughtful about when you offer unexpected feedback. You don't want to risk throwing your employee off balance with constructive feedback if emotions are running high or they're due to deliver an important presentation later that day. Nor do you want to minimize the effect of giving positive feedback because you're rushing back from a meeting that ran late—or cut a productive feedback conversation short to get to your next commitment. Choose a time close enough to the event that it is fresh in everyone's minds, while still taking into account other considerations. You might, for example, wait a day (or at least a few hours) before talking to Deepa about the orientation session rather than addressing it immediately, especially if she seems flustered or frustrated. Let her cool down so that when you do deliver your message, she'll be primed to hear it.

Choose a meeting place where you won't be distracted or interrupted. You'll want to conduct the conversation in a location where you both can easily hear each other and where you're free from social interactions that could inhibit your employee from being open and honest. That doesn't necessarily mean you need to meet in your office, if you think your employee might find that intimidating. An afternoon discussion over coffee in the quiet company cafeteria could work well, but meeting in the cafeteria during a busy lunch hour won't allow either of you to devote your due attention to the conversation.

Engage in a two-way dialogue

A feedback conversation gives each party an opportunity to tell their side and to hear the same from the other. If your goal in delivering feedback is to elicit change, your best tool is a two-way discussion, not a monologue. It's easy for an employee to shut down when feeling criticized, so to make progress, involve them in the conversation. Deliver your feedback, and give your employee your undivided attention. Listen to what they have to say, but also note physical cues, such as a grimace or crossed arms. What are they expressing, verbally or otherwise? (See the sidebar "Be an Active Listener.")

Open the conversation by soliciting the person's thoughts or reactions to assess if you see the problem in a similar light. Perhaps your greatest concern about Deepa's orientation session was her delivery, but she thinks the technical issues with showing her slide deck was the main problem. Don't impose your own judgment at first. Start with an evenhanded question, such as "Deepa, how do you think the orientation session went?"

Asking the right questions will help you understand the other person and their view of performance. Open-ended and closed questions will yield different types of responses. Open-ended questions invite participation and idea sharing. Use them to get the other person talking and for the following purposes:

- **To clarify causes of a problem.** "What do you think the major issues are with this project?"
- **To uncover attitudes or needs.** "How do you feel about our progress to date?"
- **To explore alternatives and feel out solutions.** "What would happen if . . . ?"

Closed questions, by contrast, lead to yes or no answers. Ask closed questions for the following purposes:

- **To focus the response.** "Is the project on schedule?"
- **To confirm what the other person has said.** "So your main issue is scheduling your time?"

Thoughtful questioning can help you uncover the other person's views and deeper thoughts on the problem, which will help you formulate an effective response.

Stick to facts, not opinion

Move on to sharing your point of view, but focus on observed behaviors, not assumptions about character traits, attitudes, or personality. A specific comment that relates to the job—for example, "I've noticed that you haven't offered any suggestions at our last few brainstorming sessions"—opens the door for your employee to explain why. But an opinion-based statement, more often than not, can shut down the conversation entirely.

For example, an opinion-based statement like "You just don't seem engaged with your work" paints the person into a corner and invites a defensive, opinion-based

BE AN ACTIVE LISTENER

If your goal is to understand what is going wrong with your employee's performance, you must listen. You might miss out on important information if you carry too much of the conversation, suggest solutions before your employee does, or busy your mind with thoughts of what you'll say next. Instead, really focus on what your employee is saying.

To learn as much as possible from discussions with your employees, practice active listening, which encourages communication and puts others at ease. Try these tactics:

- ***Give your employee your full attention.*** Maintain eye contact and a comfortable posture. Allow time for the other person to gather their thoughts before chiming in to fill the silence. Don't interrupt, and avoid distractions like checking your phone.

- ***Observe body language.*** Do the speaker's expression and tone of voice match what's being said? If not, you might want to comment on the disconnect and ask to hear more.

- ***Reflect what you see and hear.*** To acknowledge the speaker's emotions—which will encourage them to express themselves further—describe what you're observing without agreeing

(*continued*)

BE AN ACTIVE LISTENER

or disagreeing. "You seem worried about . . ." Acknowledge if they seem to be struggling; this will demonstrate your empathy and make your employee feel recognized. "I can imagine you're having a hard time with . . ."

- ***Paraphrase what you hear.*** Check to make sure you understand what the speaker is saying. "So if I hear you right, you're having trouble with . . ." "If I understand, your idea is . . . Does that sound right?"

To give feedback effectively, you need to receive and truly hear what your employee has to say. A productive conversation, especially about a possibly sensitive performance gap, is a two-way street.

reply: "You're wrong. I *am* engaged." This isn't productive for either of you. Statements about assumed motivations can quickly lead to your employee becoming guarded, which will make it nearly impossible to persuade them to change. To make any progress, you need your employee to be a receptive, active participant in this discussion.

Instead, offer a specific observation that's free of personal judgment. To Deepa, for instance, you might say, "I noticed that you looked down at the AV equipment a lot during the orientation session and missed opportunities to see when someone had a question." This is an observation you viewed that Deepa can then respond to, rather than feeling like she needs to defend herself.

Be specific about the problem and its impact on others

Your employee may not be fully aware of the consequences of their behavior, so lay it out clearly. For example, "Deepa, because you were looking down during most of your presentation, our new hires were unable to ask the questions they had and were unsure of some of the policies you presented. I heard some frustration from the group afterward, and they may be unclear as to how to proceed when issues arise in the coming weeks." The details demonstrate that this is a real problem, not a matter of your preference, and that it impacts not only you but others as well.

Managers sometimes mistakenly think they need to act tough when giving constructive feedback. But the aim of feedback should be to motivate change, not to make your employee feel attacked. When people feel threatened, they're unlikely to really hear what you're saying, let alone absorb or apply it. Take a thoughtful, nonaggressive approach to allow the receiver to take in, reflect on, and learn from your feedback. "Deepa, let's discuss how you might modify the planning process for the next orientation session. I know this last one didn't go well, but I'm confident you can improve for next time."

It can be tempting to couch constructive feedback in praise, in an attempt to soften the blow. Sweetening your message may lessen your own anxiety about delivering bad news, but it also diminishes your employees' ability to receive it. This "sandwich" approach actually undermines your ability to communicate any meaningful feedback, either positive or constructive. Employees who are struggling may lose track of where they need to change, registering only the compliment—and high achievers may dismiss positive feedback as a mere preamble to the "real" message.

Ask how your employee can address the problem

People generally feel more ownership of solutions they suggest themselves, but if your direct report has trouble coming up with a reasonable suggestion for change, offer one yourself and check for understanding. It's important that the employee leave the conversation with a concrete step for improvement. For example, "In the future, let's arrange for you to organize practice sessions in advance of orientation meetings, so you can rehearse what you plan to say, get used to the equipment, and hear some of the questions our new hires are likely to ask." Then, check for the receiver's understanding of your suggestion: "Does this sound feasible to you?" If they seem iffy or unclear on the plan for improvement, ask them to explain it in their own words so you can assess if they've truly grasped it. If your direct report can clearly explain what they should change or do next, you've curtailed the need to deliver the same feedback again—and if the message is muddled, you can clarify it on the spot.

In some instances, you may discover that a onetime feedback discussion isn't enough to close a performance gap. In those situations, you may need to consider coaching your employee, which is the topic of the next chapter.

NOTE

1. Quoted in Amy Gallo, "Giving a High Performer Productive Feedback," HBR.org, December 3, 2009, https://hbr.org/2009/12/giving-a-high-performer-produc.

CHAPTER 6

Coach Your Employees to Close Performance Gaps

Coaching is a powerful way to encourage your employees' growth and a practical approach for developing new skills. It can also be used to close performance gaps. But coaching—an ongoing learning process in which you help your direct reports build mastery—usually won't bring about a quick fix. When you need a fast turnaround or immediate results, feedback is your best bet. When an employee is driven to improve and wants your help tackling a problem or building mastery, however, coaching is a rewarding and effective option.

Coaching is a supportive rather than a directive approach that relies on asking questions. According to executive coach Ed Batista, coaching is "asking questions that help people discover the answers that are right for them."[1] As a manager, you're often in the role of expert, providing answers and guidance. But in coaching, it's important to adopt a different mindset. Rather than suggest what your employees should do or explain how to do it, you should prompt your employees with questions to help them solve problems in new ways themselves. As Candice Frankovelgia of the Center for Creative Leadership says, "If you keep providing all the answers, people will keep lining up at your door looking for them."[2]

Since coaching is an ongoing time commitment, target your coaching to situations where you will get the highest return on your time and effort. The most-productive opportunities generally arise in these situations:

- A new employee needs direction.
- A direct report is almost ready for new responsibilities and just needs a bit more help.
- A newly minted manager under your wing is still behaving as though they were an individual contributor.
- A strong performer is eager to develop a new skill or explore career development opportunities.
- A significant performance problem has arisen in an employee's work.

As indicated in this list, coaching can be an effective way to help employees learn new skills so they can reach the next level in their career. But it can also be a powerful tool when it comes to closing performance gaps. As with feedback, the goal of coaching is not to reprimand your employees for shortfalls but to catalyze their growth and improvement. Your objective is not to simply identify what they did wrong (thereby draining motivation) but to elicit positive change. Because coaching requires that your employee be an active participant in their own development, it can have a deeper impact than outside-in sources of information.

Coaching may not be a fit for every employee—and it won't succeed unless the person is willing to do it—but it is broadly applicable and can be used with everyone from high-potential standouts to underperformers. As a manager, you set the overall direction for your employees; with coaching, you can help them figure out how best they can get where they need to be.

Get Your Employee Onboard

When you've pinpointed a coaching opportunity, talk it over with your employee to make sure they agree there is indeed a problem to fix or room for growth and that they are willing to tackle it through coaching. Agreement is the foundation of successful coaching: For it to work, the person must take ownership and responsibility of the process. If you intuit that an individual isn't invested in this approach, do some digging before expending more of your time. Do the two of you see the problem or opportunity the same way? Do they seem to *want* to improve?

If there's a disconnect, discuss how they would prefer to address the problem. It could be that they are open to coaching but would prefer to work with an outside coach rather than with you, their manager. Or perhaps they'd rather try taking a class before embarking on an intense one-on-one learning experience. On the other hand, if they are open to coaching with you, identify at the start of the process exactly what they're hoping to get out of it.

Define the Purpose of Your Coaching

Encourage your employee's participation by finding out what they hope to achieve and how they think coaching can help address the performance gap. You may want to begin by asking them to share their thoughts before you offer your own. By opening with a question, explains executive coach Amy Jen Su, "you'll begin as you hope to continue: with your employee talking, you listening, and both of you then building solutions together."[3]

Identify an explicit goal to target with coaching. This should be a separate goal from the performance goals your employee identified in section 1 and should generally be focused on learning. For instance, a coaching goal may to develop a new skill, learn a new behavior, or improve in a specific area, rather than to deliver specific work results.

Perhaps the two of you determine that your employee's performance gap can be closed or minimized by, say, improving delegating skills, running meetings, or prioritizing requests with tight deadlines. Once you nail down the purpose of your coaching, you may be tempted to fix the problem right away by sharing your hard-won wisdom, giving advice, or offering your opinion on what's going wrong. Resist that temptation. Encourage your employee to find their *own* answers. Instead of offering (unsolicited) solutions, ask questions to get more information.

Understand Your Employee's Perspective

To help your direct report, you need to learn more about their point of view on the performance gap and which skills they need to master in order to close it. Getting background information is critical in assessing the root causes of their challenge—and identifying an effective response.

Skillfully worded, open-ended questions can help draw out answers. Yes-or-no questions and those that begin with "why" can make people feel defensive. Start your questions with *what*, *how*, *when*, or *tell me more*. For example, you might ask the following of someone interested in developing their comfort around presenting to senior management:

- What was different or similar about the situations in which you were effective compared with those when you were less effective?
- How would you describe your effectiveness in presenting to this audience in the past?
- When have you been more or less successful in these types of interactions?
- Tell me more about what you think holds you back in these situations.

Listen deeply to your employee's answers. When someone senses you're completely focused and actively listening to what they say, it can be a deeply validating experience that helps build rapport and trust (see the sidebar "Building Mutual Trust").

BUILDING MUTUAL TRUST

Your people need to trust you. Otherwise, they have no reason to respect your judgment, do what you ask (especially if it's difficult), or put in the extra effort that results in high-quality work. Managers must earn—not demand—their employees' commitment. Establishing trust takes conscious effort. You can develop trust with your direct reports in a few different ways.

First, demonstrate ongoing concern for other people's well-being and success. People trust those who have their best interests in mind, so show empathy for your employees. When asking someone to work extra hours on a weekend to complete a strategic project, for example, acknowledge that it's an imposition: "This is an important initiative for the company, and I know that this may be an inconvenience. Would this upset any plans you've made with friends or family?" You can also build trust over time by demonstrating a genuine interest in an employee's career. Help them find opportunities to expand their horizons and develop skills that align with their professional aspirations.

You can also show your expertise in the matter at hand. According to Linda Hill and Kent Lineback, authors of *Being the Boss*, "You need to know not just what to do and how to do it but also how to get it done in the organization and the world where you work."[4] Ultimately, people grow to trust you through your accomplishments—the savvy decisions you make, your ability to garner necessary resources to make things happen, and your mastery of the concrete details of getting things done. For example, the person you are coaching with sales techniques will trust you if you yourself have a reputation as a successful salesperson.

Finally, be true to your word. Whenever you say, "Here's the plan: I'll do *X* and you'll do *Y*," be sure to hold up your end of the bargain—every time. This includes practicing discretion where appropriate. Don't disclose information held in confidence. Discussions with an employee about a performance problem in a feedback or coaching session may inadvertently dredge up personal information that the employee would not want shared with others. Always respect their privacy.

See the Problem in New Ways

With a stronger understanding of the situation, you can open a two-way dialogue to help your direct report consider new choices, strategies, or skills they might develop. This is different than offering a solution—instead, it leads your employee closer to developing their own answers. Try these tactics to establish a productive dialogue:

- **Hold up the mirror.** Redescribe the situation they have outlined to you, paraphrased from your own perspective, and ask for their response. For example, "Based on what you've told me, it seems that two things might be creating the issue. Do those ideas resonate?"

- **Reframe the situation.** Offering another angle can help your employee see things differently. Say, "Could I offer another perspective on the situation?"

- **Rehearse.** A coaching session is a safe environment to role-play an upcoming interaction, such as how they might interact with senior management. You can also review a presentation that they delivered well to this audience and discuss what made it effective. Or you can go over how they should prepare for these kinds of meetings and fine-tune preparation techniques.

The observations, suggestions, and practice opportunities you offer are the heart of your coaching session. To be effective, they need to be tailored to your employee's particular situation—and they likely should be complemented with ongoing "homework" that will help your direct report prepare for your next meeting.

Agree on Next Steps

Near the end of your coaching session, assess whether your employee is ready to move forward by asking them to summarize what they've learned. "What are the top two or three things you're taking away from this conversation?" Inviting them to articulate their gains, rather than doing it yourself, increases their engagement in the process and also helps you gauge what they've taken in and what they might still need to learn.

To maintain momentum between coaching sessions, set a date for when you'll meet again, and identify any tasks to be completed before then. Rather than assigning tasks, build your employee's accountability by asking them to formulate and implement their plans, and establish associated deadlines for each clearly defined action. Perhaps, for example, they'll outline a forthcoming presentation for the group that the two of you will rehearse in your next meeting.

It could be that you leave the session with homework, too. For instance, you may need to provide your employee with additional resources, like potential training programs, or introduce them to a colleague who will make a great mentor (to read more about setting your direct report up with an appropriate mentor or sponsor, see chapter 9).

Keep the Relationship Going

Coaching doesn't end after the first meeting. Effective coaching to close performance gaps and encourage growth includes checking in to track progress and ensure understanding. Doing so gives you an opportunity to prevent backsliding, reinforce learning, and continue individual improvement.

Your employee may have found it motivating to set a target date for mastering a new skill, but don't wait until then to assess how things are going. In a fast-paced workplace, it's easy to lose track of longer-term plans and agreements. Hold yourself and your employee accountable by sticking to your planned check-in dates, and follow through with the resources or introductions you agreed to provide. Your employee is more likely to take your coaching efforts seriously if you keep your commitments.

Then, observe growth and communicate impact. Over time, are you seeing progress in your employee's results, behavior, or relationships? Explicitly communicate to your direct report the impact of the progress you observe—it may be hard for them to recognize it themselves. Helping them acknowledge changes and growth can increase their motivation.

It's unrealistic to expect an employee to immediately master skills they've been without for years, so expect a few stumbles in the process. Perfection isn't necessary for someone to make real progress. Remind yourself that you may not see results right away. When you do see improvement, celebrate a direct report's successes, even if they still have room to grow.

Of course, there's no one single right way to coach employees. What works for one person may be ineffective for another. Try different approaches, and make needed adjustments. And don't expect to master the practice of coaching right away, especially if you're new to it or to management. Like any new skill, it requires practice and stepping out of your comfort zone, which can feel awkward at first.

Not every manager will choose to use coaching as a performance management tool on a regular basis, but for the right employees, it can be a rewarding experience.

NOTES

1. Ed Batista, "Introduction: Why Coach?" in *HBR Guide to Coaching Employees*, Harvard Business Review Press, 2015, xii.
2. Candice Frankovelgia, "Shift Your Thinking to Coach Effectively," *HBR Guide to Coaching Employees*, Harvard Business Review Press, 2015, 4.
3. Amy Jen Su, "Holding a Coaching Session," in *HBR Guide to Coaching Employees*, Harvard Business Review Press, 2015, 41.
4. Linda Hill and Kent Lineback, "To Build Trust, Competence Is Key," HBR.org, March 22, 2012, https://hbr.org/2012/03/to-build-trust-competence-is-k.

CHAPTER 7

How to Keep Your Employees Motivated

Motivation is at the very heart of performance management—something that managers must attend to all the time. A person can understand the importance of ambitious goals but is unlikely to achieve them without being motivated to do so. Feedback or coaching efforts, no matter how extraordinary, will go unheeded by an employee who's disinterested. Hours invested on someone's annual performance appraisal and discussion will be largely wasted if the employee doesn't feel the need to improve.

By contrast, for those who are motivated, every aspect of performance management can serve as an opportunity to learn and grow. How can you inspire engagement and boost motivation on your team?

Cultivate a Culture of Respect

Motivating your people starts with being a good manager. A company can offer great pay and benefits, employee-friendly policies, and other perks, but a bad boss can neutralize these features and demotivate people. By the same token, a terrific manager can redeem an employee's experience in even dysfunctional organizational cultures.

Employees value being treated with respect—and feel it's important that their colleagues are treated well, too. For the second year running, "respectful treatment of all employees at all levels" was cited as the leading contributor to employees' job satisfaction in the Society for Human Resource Management's 2016 Employee Job Satisfaction and Engagement survey.

Unfortunately, respect isn't the norm everywhere; to the contrary, incivility and bad behavior are far too common in the workplace. Unchecked rudeness, bullying, and abusive comments create an environment where people feel threatened and fearful. When such behavior comes from bosses, in particular, it can easily spread. Fear demotivates people, spurs excessive caution, and forces people to prioritize self-protection over workplace contribution.

In their research on sustainable individual and organizational performance, business and management professors Gretchen Spreitzer and Christine Porath found that motivation and performance plummet in response to offensive behavior: "[H]alf of employees who had experienced uncivil behavior at work intentionally decreased their efforts. More than a third deliberately decreased the quality of their work. Two-thirds spent a lot of time avoiding the offender, and about the same number said their performance had declined."[1] Rudeness in the workplace costs organizations dearly and is insidiously infectious. "Those who have been the targets of bad behavior are often, in turn, uncivil themselves," Spreitzer and Porath found. Such "uncivil" behaviors include sabotaging peers, spreading gossip, and neglecting to copy colleagues on communications.

Although Spreitzer and Porath's research shows the negative effects of incivility, additional research by Porath also emphasizes the benefits of a respectful culture, as figure 7-1 indicates. Engagement rises as respectful treatment increases. And there are a few steps you can

FIGURE 7-1

When leaders treat you with respect, you're more engaged

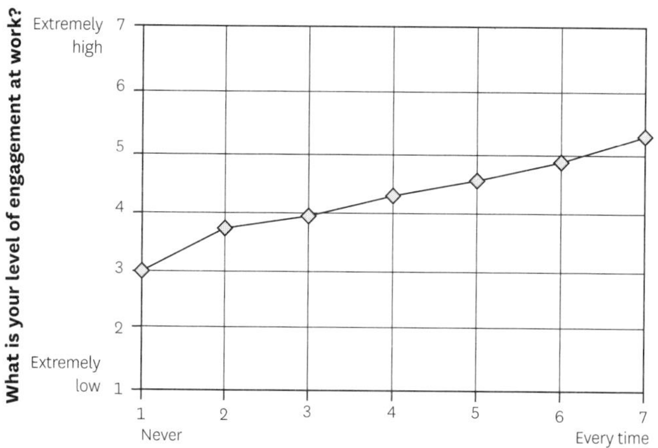

Note: Based on a study of nearly 20,000 employees around the world.

Source: Analysis of "What Is Your Quality of Life at Work?" survey data by Christine Porath. Originally published in "Half of Employees Don't Feel Respected by Their Bosses," HBR.org, November 19, 2014 (product #H0120O).

take as a manager to minimize bad behavior and foster a culture of respect, thereby boosting motivation and engagement.

- **Model good behavior.** Managers establish the tone—or lack thereof—in their workplace. A survey conducted by Porath and global leadership professor Christine Pearson found that a quarter of managers who admitted to behaving uncivilly said they did so because their own leaders and role models were rude.[2] As a manager, you have a unique opportunity to set an example of respectful treatment. Employees who see that higher-ups tolerate or embrace offensive behavior may follow suit. By contrast, when they see that a manager won't abide such behavior, they'll be less likely to engage it in themselves.
- **Respect your employee's dignity.** Discourage public criticism. A basic tenet of supervision is to praise in public and criticize in private. Being reprimanded in front of one's colleagues can have devastating effects on an employee's sense of fairness, pride, and motivation. You cannot motivate people whom you have stripped of their dignity. Some bosses inadvertently behave in ways that not only humiliate the individual target of criticism but also reduce trust among all team members who witness such incivility. Treat your employees with respect at all costs, even when you must share constructive feedback about their performance.
- **Hire respectful candidates—and stop bad behavior.** Caiman Consulting, a management consultancy

> headquartered in Redmond, Washington, boasts a 95% retention rate—which director Greg Long attributes to the firm's culture. In hiring, it conducts background checks, including "a candidate's record of civility." "People leave a trail," says Long. "You can save yourself from a corrosive culture by being careful and conscientious up front." Candidates who don't fit the culture, no matter how qualified, are not hired.[3]

Take note of the behavior of those already on your team. If you see a direct report being disrespectful, address it immediately. You may also want to reassure, in confidence, the recipient of that person's rudeness that you have responded to this issue. This will communicate that you're invested in the well-being of everyone on the team.

Once you've established a workplace where your employees are comfortable, you can increase their engagement through rewards, recognition, and challenge.

Truly Rewarding Rewards

"To many people, motivation and rewards go together like peaches and cream. They are inseparable," write Jeremy Hope and Steve Player in their book *Beyond Performance Management*. Rewards and motivation fall into two categories: extrinsic and intrinsic.

Extrinsic rewards

When people think about rewards, they often immediately think of ones that are extrinsic: external, tangible forms of recognition, such as pay hikes, promotions, bonuses, and sales prizes. On the surface, extrinsic rewards tend to be easy to execute, such as "If you make your quota, we'll pay you $5,000." In fact, most organizations' established reward systems are built around such extrinsic rewards, and in some instances, they are effective, particularly in industries like sales, where bonuses can be linked to reaching certain quantitative goals. But many managers disagree with the notion that financial incentives are necessary to boost performance. Extrinsic rewards don't necessarily make people work harder or better. As Alfie Kohn writes in his widely cited HBR article, "Why Incentive Plans Cannot Work," "rewards typically undermine the very processes they are intended to enhance."

When such motivators do succeed, the positive effects are often short-lived. Money matters, certainly, and an organization will have a tough time recruiting and keeping good employees without a competitive level of pay and benefits. But while money can be a motivator, it does not build commitment and can also encourage the wrong behaviors, such as cutting ethical corners to earn a bonus or to game the reward system. And tensions can run high when monetary prizes are awarded for the results of a team. (See the sidebar "A Fair Approach to Financial Incentives.")

The biggest problem with extrinsic rewards, by far, is that while many people believe monetary compensation is a major driver of performance, research has found little evidence to back up that assumption. In fact, bonuses and other financial incentives in some cases can do more harm than good. "When it comes to producing lasting change in attitudes and behavior," writes Kohn, "rewards, like punishment, are strikingly ineffective. Once the rewards run out, people revert to their old behaviors." Extrinsic motivators don't change the attitudes that underlie behavior.

Unless you are a senior executive, you may not have much control over the financial and extrinsic rewards you can offer, but you do have the opportunity to provide intangible options that might mean more to your employees.

A FAIR APPROACH TO FINANCIAL INCENTIVES

In theory, it's easy to dole out cash when someone performs well. But in reality, it's not that simple.

Extrinsic rewards are quantifiable, but motivation is not. How much money does it take to alter someone's behavior? Offer $100 to your sales reps if they hit their quotas, and they won't bat an eye. Offer $1 million, and you'll have their full attention, but that's not a realistic figure. No one can say for certain what the right number is—and the right number for one person may be the wrong one for someone else.

What's more, it's rarely possible to sort out individual contributions to a project or determine what they're worth. Who should be rewarded when a new car is launched, for example? Should it be the designers, the engineers, the marketing team, or the executive who oversaw the whole project? Even if it were

(*continued*)

A FAIR APPROACH TO FINANCIAL INCENTIVES

possible to pinpoint the measure of any individual's contribution, this form of financial reward can actually undermine both teamwork and performance.

Most employees' main concern about pay-related issues is fairness, so if you do want to use financial incentives, make them fair and consistent. Concerns about fairness should not arise when the criteria of rewards are standard, based on clear metrics, and obvious to all—especially when individual contributors are the ones being rewarded.

But the issue of fairness is harder to resolve when rewarding members of a team. "Everyone on the team should participate in the reward payout," suggest Jeremy Hope and Steve Player in *Beyond Performance Management*. Since it's nearly impossible to determine and quantify the exact contribution of individuals on a team, don't try.

Intrinsic rewards

The opposite of extrinsic incentives, intrinsic rewards produce nonquantifiable personal satisfaction, such as a sense of accomplishment, personal control over one's work, and a feeling that efforts are appreciated. Examples include intellectual stimulation, skill development, autonomy, or challenge. When intrinsically motivated, people do things for their own sense of achievement because they inherently want to.

Intrinsic rewards must be thoughtfully tailored to individuals. A meaningful reward to one employee may not move another. A conscientious contributor might be thrilled to be given the opportunity to attend a conference in their area of interest, while an ambitious rising star might prefer being offered face time with the CEO or an appointment to a high-level project team.

There are a variety of ways that one can encourage good work through intrinsic rewards. Here are three tactics you can incorporate into your daily work, starting with recognition.

Acknowledge good work

Recognition is one of the most powerful tools in a manager's toolbox—and a far more powerful motivator than money. "Recognition is about feeling special," explains author and motivation expert Bob Nelson, and "it is hard to feel special from a corporate program where everyone gets the same thing, like a five-year pin."[4]

Each of your employees values recognition from a different audience. One person's favorite audience might be their peers, and that individual would appreciate public praise for their achievement in front of their colleagues. Someone more concerned with developing expertise might prize a professional or technical award. A person who prioritizes customer feedback above all would treasure a letter from a customer—or a photo of the employee and customer together, framed for their office wall. For an employee who cares most about your opinion, "the most powerful recognition would be a one-on-one conversation where you tell them quietly but vividly why they are such a valuable member of the team," suggests Marcus Buckingham in his HBR article "What Great Managers Do."

When deciding how to recognize individuals, take their personalities into account. An extrovert may get a kick out of a public display, but a more introverted person might cringe at such a spectacle. Tailor your approach to what you know of their preferences—and if you aren't sure, ask. The motivation employees derive from well-tailored recognition can be significant. In his article, Buckingham describes the example of Jim Kawashima, a Walgreens manager. Jim realized that his customer service representative, Manjit, was highly competitive and measurement focused—and she thrived on public recognition. So Jim covered his office walls with charts and figures highlighting employee successes in red. Because Manjit loved to win and see her successes acknowledged, she was driven to achieve the highest sales numbers on the team. Her success galvanized the rest of the staff, and after a few months their location was ranked first out of 4,000 in a companywide selling program.

Like feedback, recognition is best delivered frequently —at least once every other week. That may seem like a lot, but if your team gathers for weekly meetings, reserving a moment every other week to acknowledge an employee's contributions will take very little time and have a big impact.

As you think about ways to recognize good work, don't overlook the value of the written word. Consider copying your employee on an email to your boss highlighting their performance—or write a sincere thank-you note for exceptional work. During his tenure as president and CEO of Campbell Soup, Doug Conant wrote more than

30,000 individualized, handwritten thank-you notes to his 20,000 employees. Such thoughtful rewards and recognition can be deeply meaningful and highly motivating to your employees. Plus, they cost nearly nothing.

Provide decision-making discretion

As any entrepreneur can tell you, people are more motivated when they feel as though they own what they do. Employees are energized when they're empowered to make decisions that affect their own work. "Showing trust, granting autonomy, and recognizing the value of individual contributions all build employees' sense of ownership of their work and pride in performing it," says Monique Valcour, executive and career coach.[5] Giving your employees control over their work as their capabilities allow and supporting their efforts to achieve meaningful goals can lead to superior performance and can also serve as rich development opportunities. (We'll explore development further in the next section.)

Granting your employees the autonomy to make decisions increases their sense of ownership and control—and boosts their motivation. For example, Home Depot grants managers decision-making discretion over their own stores' merchandise and layout, rather than insisting that each outlet operate identically. Although the practice is less efficient financially, it keeps employees feeling engaged and rewarded.

Even if your organization doesn't spearhead efforts like these to empower employees, you can do the same on a smaller scale for your direct reports. Allow opportunities for each individual to operate more independently within their own work. If a representative is eager to improve the customer service experience, allow them to decide how best to do so, perhaps by surveying customers, running a focus group, digging into an established customer database, or with another approach you might not have thought of. When granted the freedom to choose how to tackle a project, your employee will likely feel a greater sense of ownership and engagement.

Introduce challenge

People are often capable of handling tasks that are more complex and more demanding than their managers expect and than their job descriptions require. Tackling such challenges can reward, inspire, and motivate them. In researching her book *Rookie Smarts: Why Learning Beats Knowing in the New Game of Work*, management consultant Liz Wiseman found that satisfaction increases as the level of challenge grows.

Consider giving employees higher-stakes assignments that involve more-complex problems or a bigger set of stakeholders. This could be a matter of offering a new work assignment or expanding a current one. For example, you could enlarge an employee's training session in coding to include participants from the entire organization rather than offering it to only those who are in their specific department. Depending on how big or challenging the project is, you may want to revisit the goals you and your employee agreed upon to account for the new challenge.

You can also invite your employees to stretch their skills and grow their expertise by giving them projects they've never done before—tasks where they haven't yet mastered all the relevant knowledge. This tactic may not work for every employee, however. "Make sure to choose people who have core aptitude or adjacent skills, but then let them learn as they go, Wiseman explains in her HBR.org article "An Easy Way to Make Your Employees Happier." "Their comfort zones will expand, and they'll take great pride in mastering new things." Remember, though, that the learning process can be rocky—and before someone feels comfortable with a new skill, they might feel frustrated or unsure for a while.

Finally, consider redirecting a person's existing expertise by pivoting to a new problem. Many skills are transferable from one area to another; with expertise in one field, some people can quickly pick up the nuances of a related one. For example, a scientist at a pharmaceutical company shifted her research from cellular biology—her area of expertise—to oncology. She was unsure, initially, about how to do so but after a few months reported feeling invigorated, challenged, and newly creative.

Recognizing your employees' good work and challenging them to do more can motivate them to continue exemplary work and contribute more to the organization. As you consider ways to encourage, engage, and build your direct reports' skills, think about what they may aspire to and how they want to grow in the long term—a key element of performance management called development that we'll cover in the next section.

NOTES

1. Gretchen Spreitzer and Christine Porath, "Creating Sustainable Performance," *Harvard Business Review*, January–February 2012 (product #R1201F).
2. Christine Porath and Christine Pearson, "The Price of Incivility," *Harvard Business Review*, January–February 2013 (product #R1301J).
3. Quoted in Gretchen Spreitzer and Christine Porath, "Creating Sustainable Performance," *Harvard Business Review*, January–February 2012 (product #R1201F).
4. Quoted in "Employee Recognition and Reward When Times Are Tough," *Harvard Management Update*, September 2003, https://hbr.org/2008/02/employee-recognition-and-rewar-1.html.
5. Monique Valcour, "The Power of Dignity in the Workplace," HBR.org, April 28, 2014 (product #H00S6P).

SECTION THREE

Developing Employees

CHAPTER 8

Understand Your Employee's Wants and Needs

Employee development is a process for managing a person's professional growth. Learning, building new skills, and working to one's full potential is both rewarding for the individual and helpful to the organization as a whole. For your direct reports, it means getting the opportunity to focus on their upward mobility. For you, it offers a chance to boost employees' productivity, motivation, and engagement while also retaining and growing your top talent.

Development is invaluable for your employees. Frederick Herzberg, in his classic HBR article "One More Time: How Do You Motivate Employees?" argues that growth is a powerful intrinsic motivator and can increase job satisfaction. Job seekers at all levels, from recent grads to executives, are more concerned with learning and development opportunities than with any other aspect of a prospective position. And in a study of Millennials in the workplace, professional services firm PwC found that training and development were the two most-valued benefits for these workers—even more than money, which ranked third.[1]

Companies whose employees are inspired and equipped to fulfill their greatest potential yield the best business results overall. And if high-performing individuals feel that they are regularly being given chances to grow, they will be more likely to stay with the organization, even during tough times. Likewise, having strong career development opportunities in place helps your organization prepare for the future; by giving them the training and skills they need, your employees will be ready to move into key roles when the opportunities arise.

Employee development, like motivating and coaching employees, should be an ongoing part of your performance management process. Tailor development efforts—which can include training, temporary "stretch" assignments, mentoring, and coaching, among other approaches—to the individual, and work with them to determine which ones are the right fit for their skills and aims.

Your Role in Employee Development

While development was once largely considered the domain of HR, it's actually every manager's responsibility to attend to their people's growth on an ongoing basis. Managers who take employee development seriously are more likely to lead a team with good morale and high standards, maintain a spirit of continuous improvement, and achieve better results.

Yet many managers are hesitant to develop their employees. Some argue that they don't have the time, especially if there are no challenging or interesting opportunities currently available for a direct report. Others find the conversations difficult if their employee isn't ready for promotion or if the manager doesn't have a clear plan of action in mind.

But neglecting development has consequences. Your employees may feel unsupported, and their morale and motivation may decline. Even your strongest performers can begin to feel stuck in their careers, and that increases the risk of them leaving the organization (see the sidebar "Preventing Career Plateaus"). Worse are the disillusioned, weaker performers who *don't* quit, leaving you with a destructive morale problem that can infect the culture.

PREVENTING CAREER PLATEAUS

Just because someone has strong skills and impressive performance doesn't mean they're happy in their job. In fact, psychologists Timothy Butler and James Waldroop write in their HBR article "Job Sculpting: The Art of Retaining Your Best People," "managers botch career development—and retention—because they mistakenly assume people are satisfied with jobs they excel at."

(continued)

PREVENTING CAREER PLATEAUS

Don't allow good people to get stuck in career plateaus. As a manager, you have a responsibility to make sure that the people you value are progressively advancing in their career paths.

How can you tell when someone is ready for a new challenge? They usually make it clear by asking or by pursuing development opportunities. But you can also watch for a few signs:

- Everything they manage has been running smoothly—for a significant period of time.
- When faced with problems, they jump quickly to solutions.
- They spend time trying to fix other people's and other departments' problems.
- While they're still performing well, they've become increasingly but inexplicably negative.

To retain your best performers and maintain their engagement, make an effort to offer meaningful development opportunities and challenges—and to raise the topic if they don't bring it up themselves.

On the other hand, people who are challenged and engaged describe their development process as exhilarating. When people are energized by learning, it's easy for them to stay engaged and perform at their peak. Satisfaction levels rise alongside challenge.

To be sure, investing in your direct reports' development takes time and thoughtful effort devoted to discussing and thinking about each of your employees and their futures. To best help your people develop, you'll need curiosity about each individual and patience for the learning process. But your employee will have to do the hard work of development—starting with taking ownership and embracing accountability for their own growth. You can't just hand your direct report a development plan and expect them to commit and run with it. Each employee's drive to grow needs to come from within. "Highly structured, one-size-fits-all learning programs don't work anymore," explains consultant and author Keith Ferrazzi. "Individuals must own, self-direct, and control their learning futures. Yet they can't do it alone, nor do you want them to."[2]

Start with the Employee

What do your direct reports want to learn? What are their career ambitions and interests, their passions and values? These aren't questions you can answer on your own. You're best off making ongoing career development a regular part of your conversations with your employees—but start with a comprehensive discussion about where they're headed.

Identify employee aspirations

A development-focused conversation can build rapport, help you connect on a personal level, and show your commitment to helping your direct report grow while you gather useful information. Your frequent discussions about an employee's performance and progress toward goals may naturally lead to conversations about their career aspirations—but if the topic doesn't arise naturally, ask directly. Give your employee a heads-up that you'd like to talk about their career plans and future development so they can reflect beforehand.

Your goal in the discussion is to understand your employee's aspirations as well as their current state of workplace know-how and daily performance. Explore their current developmental level and goals (for example, what they are ready for, how much more work they can handle, what the next step should be in their journey), their learning style and preferences, and their motivations and values. What makes your employee tick? What is it that they're after? Recognition? A raise or promotion? Autonomy? Aim to identify what your direct report wants to achieve most both in the short term and in their long-term career.

To elicit information, ask open-ended questions rather than ones that require a simple yes or no response, and practice active listening (see the sidebar "Be an Active Listener" in chapter 5). Some sample questions you can use are:

- What do you want to be known for?
- What matters most to you?
- What do you see yourself doing a year from now that you're not currently doing?
- What does success look like for you?
- Where and when do you feel you are at your personal best?

- What's your favorite part of what you do?
- Where would you like to be in your career in three, five, or 10 years?

While you may have discussed some of these aspirations and interests in your goal-setting meeting—or even in your feedback and coaching sessions—ambitions can shift over time. When it comes to development, revisiting these topics ensures that you and your direct report will choose a productive path to meaningful growth.

By better understanding your employee's personal and learning goals, you'll both be in a stronger position to identify developmental opportunities.

Align ambitions with organizational needs

Match an individual's interests, values, and skills to growth opportunities based on their level of performance and potential. You'll want to find a development path that is meaningful to your employee to ensure their commitment, but work toward an overlap between what will bring them the most satisfaction *and* what will be best for the organization.

Erika Andersen, founding partner of the coaching, consulting, and training firm Proteus and author of *Be Bad First*, suggests focusing on three questions to help choose a direction for your employee:

- **What will drive the economic engine?** Identify capabilities that provide value to the organization. For example, someone in operations could reduce cycle and delivery times by learning how to better manage complex custom client projects, reduce expenses by learning more about sourcing materials, or boost productivity by setting and communicating clearer direction for their own direct reports. Jot down or make a mental note of all the options to choose from.

- **What is the individual best at?** Once you and your direct report have identified useful capacities that they might develop, consider whether they can excel at them by assessing their innate strengths. Are they good at performing other, similar tasks? Someone who is organized and sequential in how they approach work may easily grasp complex project management—and they could better share that thinking with their team by mastering some communication and management skills. But if they struggle with research, learning to excel at sourcing materials may be more difficult.
- **What is the individual passionate about?** After assessing where an employee's strengths overlap with valuable areas for potential development, think back to your discussion about their aspirations. Identify how interested they are in those areas. Strengths are not just things that we're good at but things that can energize us as well. Perhaps your employee perks up at the idea of managing complex projects, but the very prospect of leading a team sounds draining to them. Development efforts work best when they feel exciting, not burdensome, so capitalize on your employees' interests by helping them choose a path that energizes them.

Rethink the Traditional Promotion Track

As you think about a direction for your employee, consider their career trajectory. A traditional path of advancement may not make sense given a direct report's interests, skills, and ambitions.

A long-trusted concept in career development has been the career ladder: a logical series of stages that move a talented and promotable employee upward through progressively more challenging and responsible positions. But clear career ladders are less common in the rapidly changing, sometimes unpredictable world of contemporary work. Simple and straightforward career paths are harder to identify as hierarchical structures break down and organizations flatten. In some fields and companies, the traditional ladder model has shifted to what Deloitte vice chairman and managing principal Cathy Benko calls a "lattice." In the case of a lattice, people shift roles, responsibilities, and even business areas over the course of their careers, sometimes more than once.

"In the industrial era the corporate ladder was the standard metaphor for talent development and career paths. Its one-size-fits-all, only-way-is-up rules were clear, and incentives uniformly supported them," Benko notes in her coauthored HBR article "AT&T's Talent Overhaul." "The lattice, in contrast, represents career paths that change continually and adaptively through multidirectional, zigzag movements."

In the ladder model, career paths were clearly delineated—an editorial assistant who is promoted to assistant editor, to associate editor, and finally to editor—and headed one way: upward. But the multidirectional lattice model allows for greater flexibility: an editorial assistant who discovers an interest in video production develops those visual and technical skills, and through apprenticeships and training opportunities shifts from a text-heavy role in their organization's book-publishing division to a multimedia-focused position in its e-learning branch. With the lattice, employees can move laterally or diagonally; they can ascend or descend.

This may require a shift in thinking as you consider what your employee's direction may be in the organization. Preparing a direct report and shaping their skills to fit a traditional role in management may be a mismatch if they'd prefer another position that taps into their strengths and interests.

Instead of putting each of your employees on the same track of automatic advancement (once they've learned the appropriate skills, of course), think about their career aspirations. What does your direct report most want to do or be? Whether they hunger to become a manager, want to expand an exciting aspect of the current role they generally enjoy, or yearn to learn a new skill that overlaps with another department, identify a direction that meets your employee's personal needs as well as those of the organization, even in the long term.

Once you and your direct report have identified their wants and needs and pinpointed a specific direction or area they should develop, don't jump right into action. There are a variety of ways that they can grow their skills. For example, you might sign them up for training programs, introduce new challenges in their daily work, or let them try a temporary new assignment. Carefully consider the options available to you and what may work best with your employee. We'll explore potential development tactics in the next chapter.

NOTES

1. "Millennials Survey. Millennials at Work: Reshaping the Workplace," PwC, http://www.pwc.com/gx/en/issues/talent/future-of-work/millennials-survey.html.
2. Keith Ferrazzi, "7 Ways to Improve Employee Development Programs," HBR.org, July 31, 2015 (product #H028T9).

CHAPTER 9

Expand Your Employee's Skill Sets

Once you've decided on a direction for a motivated employee's development, you'll need to figure out how they'll acquire the skills to get them there. There are many approaches to growing your employee's capabilities, from short-term training options that help them stay up-to-date on the latest industry knowledge to encouraging them to foster career-shaping, long-term relationships. The right approach will be determined by the employee's situation and preferences. Consider the following tactics as potential options for development.

Skill-Training Programs

In many fields, learning and development have a short shelf life. In industries that are constantly changing and innovating, skills can become obsolete within mere months. Staying current in emerging technology, for example, requires a perpetual learning effort.

Some companies offer "corporate universities" as a way for their employees to learn the latest in their industry and job. These programs let a company tailor the curriculum to align training with its particular business strategy, focusing on the specific skills needed for organizational success. As a manager, you'll know whether these options are available to your employees (and if you don't, you can always ask your HR department). If you work in a particularly highly regulated field, like accounting, this traditional classroom training approach can work well.

These formal programs can be time-consuming, though, and they can take employees temporarily off the job. In some rapidly advancing fields—cloud-based computing, coding, and data science, for example—the curriculum changes so fast that traditional training methods can't keep up.

In cases like these, consider more-flexible options. Encourage your employees to pursue off-site education at local schools or universities—or through online classes, which are usually less expensive than campus-based training and require no in-person class time. Online courses, certifications, and degree and "nanodegree" programs are widely available, regardless of geographic location, through university-developed MOOCs (massive open online courses) and e-learning companies (like Coursera, Lynda.com, and Udemy). You can help your employees find such programs by looking online at reputable sources and courses that provide the skills your team members need at a pace that works for them. If price is an issue, talk to your HR department to see if your organization offers tuition assistance for employees to invest in their growth.

Task Delegation

You may discover that an employee could learn better on the job than in the classroom. Task delegation allows you to test and expand their skills by handing off specific work assignments without adding these new responsibilities to their job permanently.

In this development tactic, you hand off a task (either yours or someone else's) to your employee to gauge their ability in the project and offer more challenge. When you delegate one of your responsibilities to a direct report, you transfer not only the work but also the accountability for completing it—which builds trust. Delegating is an excellent way to communicate your confidence in your direct report's ability. In doing so, you're saying "I'm confident you can get the job done."

Every time you hand off a project or task, you're giving someone an opportunity to test their skills in mastering a new challenge. In some cases, this gives them experience with managerial work, like learning how to accept responsibility, to plan work, and to enlist the collaboration of others. In any case, it's especially important to monitor their progress, offer feedback, and coach as needed to be sure that they're learning the new skill.

Stretch Assignments

An alternative to delegation is to provide a discrete, time-limited stretch assignment. This is a particularly helpful method to assess whether an employee who has expressed interest in being promoted is truly ready for a more challenging role. Rather than handing off a task from your to-do list, design an assignment similar to what the person would handle in their potential new role. The key is for them to perform tasks they don't necessarily know how to do or that they can't yet do well.

Suitable temporary assignments for ambitious employees could include:

- Asking your direct report to develop and launch a product or head up a new initiative or project.

- Giving an employee the opportunity to fix a business or product that's in trouble, like improving the bottom line of a new service or marketing a struggling product to a new customer segment.

- Assigning a job rotation in a new work environment. For example, have a marketing manager work in the sales organization for a while, offer an employee a short-term foreign assignment, or encourage your employee to join an organization-wide committee.

- Creating distinct tours of duty, where an employee takes over a new role for a specific time period before moving on to another role. (To learn more about this option, refer to the sidebar "Tours of Duty.")

For this type of development opportunity, it's especially important to be transparent about what you're doing. Ensure that this is a short-term experiment, not a permanent change in responsibilities, and assign clear criteria for success and a time line for evaluation.

TOURS OF DUTY

Effectively a contract between a manager and an employee, a tour of duty is an arrangement in which an employee agrees to take on a new role for only a short amount of time. This tactic recognizes that lifelong employment and loyalty are no longer realistic expectations in today's work world. Few individuals will stay at any organization for the entirety of their career—but chances are good that they will stay for a few years, especially with a targeted set of goals to achieve.

A tour of duty can serve as a personalized retention plan that gives an employee concrete, compelling reasons to finish their tour and establishes a clear time frame for discussing their future at the organization. As a manager, you can construct customized tours that are mutually beneficial for the employee and your organization, with explicit terms, clear expectations, time-limited commitments, and focused goals.

When Reid Hoffman founded LinkedIn, he set the expectation for a four-year tour for each of his employees with discussions to be held after two years. If an employee produced tangible achievements for the firm during those four years, the company would

(*continued*)

TOURS OF DUTY

help them advance their career—either inside or beyond the company. One successful tour was likely to lead to another. The two- to four-year period syncs with typical product development cycles in the software business, though other industries also operate on similar schedules.

The end of the tour need not be the end of an employee's tenure with your organization, though. Instead, it can be the beginning of another tour offering another opportunity—for example, reengineering a business process, developing and launching a new product, or spearheading an organizational innovation.

As a manager, you may be assigning your employees to tours where you don't have oversight. In cases like these, you'll want to keep in regular contact with the individual to assess progress and growth and check in with their supervisor to get their point of view. This is especially important if you'd like them to return to your team in some capacity after their tour of duty.

Job Redesign

Job redesign allows a promising employee the opportunity to try their hand at a new task while changing the job permanently. Here, you make adjustments to an individual's role at the margins, reassigning rote, lower-level tasks to employees for whom the tasks are more appropriate (or eliminating the items altogether). You then replace these tasks with higher-level ones that involve challenge and learning. For example, if a direct report whose work is mainly administrative demonstrates an interest in copywriting, you may be able to shift some of their administrative duties to the department assistant, freeing up some time for them to take on introductory writing projects.

The starting point for redesign is a careful inventory of all the tasks associated with the job. You and your direct report may be able to compile a list from their formal job description, from their to-do list, or through information gathered during check-ins and ongoing performance discussions. Look for opportunities to offload low-level items, perhaps to another team member or administrative staffer. Keep in mind, though, that just because someone has always done a task doesn't mean that it is worth doing; you may identify out-of-date or unnecessary activities that can be eliminated altogether, such as pulling weekly analytics reports for the team when an automated monthly report is doing the trick. Then identify and add a more challenging assignment in its place as a regular part of the job.

Job redesign may be easiest when working within a team. Can you find your direct report a partner with complementary strengths to take on the tasks you want to hand off? It takes effort to custom fit a role to better suit an individual, but doing so will save you time in the long run. When people slave away at tasks that don't suit them, they (and by extension you) rarely get good results. People are far more energized, efficient, and effective when their responsibilities draw on their innate strengths and abilities.

If you believe that someone can contribute at a higher level, don't simply pile on new responsibilities. An "invisible" promotion that doesn't recognize a person's contributions with a corresponding raise or change in title can sap motivation. It can also lead to employee burnout. Instead, investigate how you can create a better fit between an employee's work and their best self. Consider what they do well and find intrinsically satisfying and how they can do more of it. Great managers tailor roles so that individuals can succeed in their own way, capitalizing on their strengths and neutralizing weaknesses.

For example, in his HBR article "What Great Managers Do," author and consultant Marcus Buckingham writes about Michelle, a Walgreens manager, who successfully tweaked the role of her employee, Jeffrey, to capitalize on his strengths. Not much of a people person, Jeffrey excelled when given clear, specific tasks, like stocking an aisle with new items and revising displays. In most Walgreens stores, one person is responsible for a particular aisle, including arranging the merchandise. But to capitalize on Jeffrey's gift for precision, Michelle made Jeffrey's entire job stocking and arranging products—in every aisle—while handing off his more social responsibilities to other coworkers. Jeffrey was able to spend his time on a task he excelled at and enjoyed while taking his sub-par people skills out of the spotlight. What's more, by shifting around tasks on the team, his more social colleagues were relieved of work they considered a chore and could focus more of their time on what they did best: serving customers. After the role reorganization, Michelle saw increases in the store's sales, profits, and customer satisfaction, and Jeffrey's confidence grew so much that he became interested in management roles.

Capitalizing on individual employees' unique abilities in this way can also help strengthen your team. Colleagues can recognize and better appreciate one another's strengths while their coworkers fill in to neutralize their weaknesses.

It's worth noting that it's not always realistic for someone to hand off tasks and responsibilities they don't love. If one team member drops an item from their list that doesn't bring out their very best, another team member will have to pick it up. In some instances, particularly as people are taking on more and more work, there isn't always someone who can pick up the discarded task—in which case you should consider other development options.

Mentorship and Sponsorship

Beyond course work and challenging tasks, employees can grow by tapping into the support and expertise of others around them. Mentors are individuals with experience, knowledge, skills, and perspective, who work one-on-one with employees to help them discover ways to achieve their goals. According to management consultant Tamara Erickson, "A good mentor is part diagnostician, assessing what's going on with you now, and part guide, connecting you with the advice, ideas, people, and resources you need to grow and move ahead."[1]

Mentors teach, advise, motivate, and inspire and can provide guidance, career help, and even coaching to boost professional and personal development. They can help your employees meet challenges by offering encouragement and providing valuable feedback about where to improve. Given their experience and expertise in the company and their job, they can be valuable role models who help others understand and navigate organizational politics as well as help build support networks. While you may not play an active role in the mentoring relationship for your employees, you can help them align with the right type of mentor and assist them in managing the relationship.

Mentorship is not just for ambitious early career upstarts; people at all stages of their careers can benefit from mentorship. Different types of mentors will be appropriate in different stages of a person's career.

- **Buddy or peer mentors** are suitable in the early stages of an employee's work life, when what is most helpful is a peer-based mentor who can speed up the learning curve. This type of mentor can provide assistance and information about skill development and basic organization-specific practices. Such mentoring relationships can come about somewhat informally, through social and professional networks.

- **Career mentors** serve as career advisors and advocates for employees after their initial period at an organization. This mentor helps provide context and explains how an individual's contributions fit into the bigger picture and purpose of the organization. Author and CEO Anthony Tjan explains, "When people feel that they understand their current role, its impact, and where it can take them next in a company, it leads to higher levels of satisfaction and motivation."[2] This type of mentor should be a supportive advocate and advisor within the company and should meet with their mentee semiannually or quarterly.

- **Life mentors** offer invaluable support for people in the mid- and senior stages of their careers. Tjan explains that people at this point need "someone in whom they can confide without feeling that there is any bias. This is someone who can be a periodic sounding board when one is faced with a difficult career challenge, or when they are considering changing jobs." While life mentors don't supplant career or peer mentors, they can impart significant wisdom and should be consulted annually.

- **Sponsors** are like mentors, but rather than solely focusing on support, they also advocate for an employee. As economist and author Sylvia Ann Hewlett explains, "Where a mentor might help you envision your next position, a sponsor will advocate for your promotion and lever open the door."[3] Sponsors can spur a protégé's career into corporate heights by connecting employees to senior leaders, promoting their visibility, opening up career opportunities, helping them network outside the company, and generally providing advice.

These individuals are usually two levels above the employee, with a line of sight into potential future roles.

Employees shouldn't be limited to one single mentor or sponsor. Instead, they would be better served by a "developmental network" with various areas of expertise and different perspectives. Tapping into multiple supports decreases the likelihood of wearing out one individual mentor or sponsor, or finding oneself without guidance if that person leaves the company or is unavailable. A mentoring relationship can be a long-term, even lifelong, relationship—or it can last just a few hours or weeks.

As a manager, you may be able to introduce your employee to mentors and sponsors who can turbocharge their career development. But where do you find them? Some companies offer formal programs that encourage mentorship. If your organization has no formal program in place, ask your employee what they're looking for in a mentoring relationship to see if you know anyone who might be the right fit. You might consider looking for mentors or sponsors who:

- Are able to understand and shape the employee's long-term professional goals, such as someone who has a similar background, or someone in a position the employee might like to have in the future.
- Are influential within the organization. These individuals know how things work and can help your direct report navigate the system.

- Have a broader skill set than your employee, so they can help them grow and develop in new ways.
- Possess a higher level of functional experience than your employee does. Sometimes this is a person outside your organization or outside the chain of command, like someone in a trade organization.
- Are not part of your organization and therefore may be able to offer broader perspectives and provide even better support for ambitious employees.

You may also want to discuss with your direct report some basics they should establish at the beginning of the relationship. For example, How often should they meet? What types of things should they discuss? What are their expectations for confidentiality? While you can take some steps to set your employee up for success, it is in their hands to secure and maintain the mentoring relationship once it's established.

All of these development tactics can help individuals cultivate the skills they need in order to reach their professional aspirations, but remember that your employees are unique and learn in their own ways. If you want your direct report's development efforts to be effective, you need to decide which option best meets their personal learning style and then craft a plan for paving the way to success.

NOTES

1. Tamara Erickson, "Introduction: Taking Charge of Your Career," in *HBR Guide to Getting the Mentoring You Need*, Harvard Business Review Press, 2014, 1.

2. Anthony K. Tjan, "Keeping Great People with Three Kinds of Mentors," HBR.org, August 12, 2011 (product #H007LK).

3. Sylvia Ann Hewlett, "The Right Way to Find a Career Sponsor," HBR.org, September 11, 2013, https://hbr.org/2013/09/the-right-way-to-find-a-career-sponsor.

CHAPTER 10

Craft a Development Plan

Skill training, job redesign, mentorship—your employee could take advantage of all of the development options available to them, but without a strategic plan, they still might not achieve their professional goals and aspirations. You must clearly identify a path that you both think will work best and outline the specific actions required to gain the skills they need to grow. In other words, you and your employee must define a development plan.

An individualized development plan includes specific growth objectives your employee will strive to meet over the long term, with a time line and clear steps for achieving them. Like the performance goals you developed in section 1, these targets should be challenging but achievable. After all, if the employee isn't required to stretch or push themselves, they won't grow.

Just as goals are best crafted in collaboration with an employee, so are individualized plans for development. The action steps that you identify should take into account your employee's professional aims (which you explored in chapter 8) as well as organizational needs. You'll also likely want to include some of the development tactics covered in the last chapter. In order to do so, though, you must first understand how your employee learns best. Then you can craft a plan—and implement it in a way that ensures they will follow through.

Understand Your Employee's Learning Style

Not all development options work for everyone. An effective mode of learning for one person can fall flat for another. Personality type, education, and cultural background all influence the way individuals learn, and with five generations of people in the workplace, organizations need to match training and development tools to employees' preferences. For example, digital-native Millennials may gravitate to online learning or other tech-based approaches, while employees of other generations may prefer on-the-job learning opportunities such as mentorship or stretch assignments.

In his HBR article "What Great Managers Do," author and consultant Marcus Buckingham identifies three learning styles—analyzing, doing, and watching—that are worth considering when you're planning which tactics to use for your employees' development. These styles are not mutually exclusive, and in fact, some of your direct reports may rely on a combination of two or perhaps all three.

1. **Analyzing.** An analyzer craves information. They understand a task by taking it apart into components, examining each element, and reconstructing it. An analyzer prefers to fully prepare before doing, so assigned reading, classroom experience, and role-play are effective ways for them to learn new skills.

2. **Doing.** A doer learns more during a given activity than through preparation. Trial and error is an integral part of their learning process, as they tend to enhance their skills while grappling with tasks. For a doer, it's best to pick a specific action that is simple but real, give them a brief overview of the results you want, and get out of their way. As they develop, gradually increase the degree of difficulty until they've mastered the role.

3. **Watching.** A watcher prefers to see a task or project from start to finish so they can understand what the total performance looks like. They want to see how everything fits together in a coherent whole. It's best to avoid classroom learning and how-to manuals for this type of learner. Instead, consider shadowing opportunities in which they can observe someone in the act.

Work with your employee to define how they perform best, and ask questions to get to the heart of their learning style. Once you identify their preferences, don't try to change them. Forcing your employee into a path that doesn't fit just causes frustration. Accept the uniqueness of each individual, and develop a plan that takes into account how they think and what drives them.

Craft a Plan

Outlining your employee's development plan requires time and collaborative discussion with your direct report. You may need to meet a few times before the plan is finalized to ensure agreement.

Ask your employee to draft an initial outline, and have them explain why they selected certain options. People are more engaged in plans they have some choice in creating, and allowing them to start the discussion will let them incorporate their own learning styles and preferences. If they need help pulling a plan together, ask questions like:

- Who can help and support you in learning how to become proficient at this task?
- How can I support you in figuring out how to do this on your own?
- How will we measure the success of this target?

Make suggestions if necessary, but allow your employee to choose which learning options they want to pursue.

Don't limit your employee to just one avenue for growth. For example, the 70–20-10 rule, also known as the "experience, exposure, education" framework, suggests making at least 70% of the action items on-the-job learning through stretch assignments, 20% from mentoring, and 10% from formal training or educational programs. An employee's plan might involve adding one or two challenging assignments, complemented with coaching and formal skill training. The right approach will be determined by the individual's situation and what they think they can handle.

Next, figure out what resources are needed. Perhaps your direct report needs a private work space to participate in an online course, a subscription for new software they're trying to master, or a conference registration fee paid from a corporate account. Maybe they need you to introduce them to potential mentors or sponsors. Consider the resources required for your direct report to successfully complete their development plan. If you can't afford or provide the necessary resources, reassess the plan and discuss other alternatives.

Throughout your conversations, talk with your direct report about what, if anything, their development efforts mean for their pay and position. They may have questions about what job redesign or a stretch assignment will mean in the long term. Be clear about whether this is a new job or a change in responsibilities, a promotion, or a trial assignment. Development may or may not lead to an adjustment in salary or status, but your employee should understand from the start what's in store.

Whatever options you and your direct report agree will spur their development—whether it's a one-day seminar, an online course, or a task delegated from your own to-do list—agree on a time line for completion, or highlight specific milestones if the development is an ongoing relationship, as with mentoring. Without set deadlines, your employee won't have a clear idea of the time commitment their development requires.

Document Your Decisions—and Follow Up

Get the final plan on paper. If your company has an individual development plan form, use that to make a record of your discussions. If not, create your own, using table 10-1 at the end of this chapter as a template.

As with other parts of performance management, your conversation with your employee isn't the end of the process. Schedule specific times to discuss how their development is going. Choose a date a month or so away, or fold these conversations into your regular check-ins and feedback discussions.

Don't get frustrated if your direct report isn't growing as quickly as you'd hoped. Learning is a messy process, and development doesn't always follow a straight line. As a manager, you'll need to have the patience to allow people to make mistakes. Your employees need to feel safe to explore and experiment if they are to take risks in learning and mastering new skills.

Few individuals will risk stretching to meet an ambitious target if they're not sure their manager has their back. Let your employees know you trust them to take on new challenges—and to recover from missteps. Ensure that they feel safe taking risks for growth as they do their jobs. Developing and maintaining a safe working environment requires ongoing discussion of needs and opportunities, tasks and obstacles—what is working and what is not.

Allowing your direct reports to learn and explore pays off: As individuals achieve small successes, their confidence grows, so they're less daunted by bigger challenges. Step back to allow self-sufficiency, and let your employees own their results. Once you've delegated a task or decision, don't try to take it back. Encourage each person to learn through their mistakes, and recognize and reward them when they succeed. If you do find that someone is struggling to the point of frustration or in a way that is detrimental to their performance, work with that person to make adjustments so that they can find the path that's right for them.

TABLE 10-1

Individual development plan template

List three primary development goals that the individual aims to accomplish. Include a description of how those goals will be measured or the expected outcomes.

Development goals	Measures of achievement/expected outcomes
1.	
2.	
3.	

Development goal 1:

Tactic for development:

Choose skill training, task delegation, stretch assignments, or mentoring and sponsorships.

Describe the assignment:

Tasks required for the assignment and plans to meet them:

Estimated time frame with milestones:

Development goal 2:

Tactic for development:

Choose skill training, task delegation, stretch assignments, or mentoring and sponsorships.

Describe the assignment:

Tasks required for the assignment and plans to meet them:

Estimated time frame with milestones:

TABLE 10-1 *(continued)*

Development goal 3:

Tactic for development:

Choose skill training, task delegation, stretch assignments, or mentoring and sponsorships.

Describe the assignment:

Tasks required for the assignment and plans to meet them:

Estimated time frame with milestones:

Resources needed

What additional support or resources are needed to achieve the employee's goals? How will it be provided?

Monitoring progress

How often will the employee and manager meet to discuss progress? List any upcoming dates.

Time frame

Start date of plan:	Anticipated completion date:

This plan is agreed to as indicated by the signatures below.

______________________	____________
Employee signature	Date
______________________	____________
Manager signature	Date

Source: Adapted from *Pocket Mentor: Developing Employees* (Boston: Harvard Business Press, 2009), 75–76.

CHAPTER 11

How to Develop Someone Who's Struggling

Every organization has a range of performers, from thriving stars to those who are struggling. On one end of the spectrum are the A players, the top 10% of the workforce whose contributions are exceptional. The steadily contributing B players do good work and generally form the solid backbone of units and departments. These two groups make up the vast majority of your workforce and consistently deliver strong performance.

On the bottom 10%, though, are your C players. These individuals produce work that is just barely acceptable. These aren't generally strong contributors who simply struggle with one part of their job but rather employees who consistently underdeliver and don't provide the results your team and organization need.

It's tempting to ignore this group of employees—or summarily dismiss them from the company. After all, shouldn't managers spend most of their time and energy working with the people who add the most value? Failing to develop your C players' skills outright, though, comes with its own set of downfalls. These individuals often:

- Stand in the way of advancement of more-talented employees
- Hire other C players, which lowers the performance bar across the board.
- Tend to be poor role models who encourage a low-performer mentality among their peers and direct reports
- Engender a culture of mediocrity that repels highly talented and ambitious people away from your team and organization

What's more, replacing an employee is a time-consuming task—and even a stellar new hire will need a period of training and acclimation before adding much value. So while it's true that in some cases firing a C player may be the best choice, it's rarely the place to start. You owe it to yourself and your organization—as well as the underperforming employee—to diagnose and address the underlying causes of poor performance.

Consider the three Cs of dealing with C players—converse, coach, and can—coined by John Baldoni, chair of leadership development at the global leadership advisory firm N2Growth.

Converse: Identify What's Causing the Issue

To solve the problem, you must first find the root cause. Four issues commonly underlie poor performance:

- **Lack of clarity.** Does your employee know what you expect of them?
- **Poor effort.** Is your employee investing enough time and energy into the work?
- **No sense of strategy.** Do they approach their work with an organized plan?
- **Underwhelming talent.** Do they have the skills, knowledge, and capabilities to do the job well?

To determine the cause of underperformance, collect the right information. Establish the details of the unsatisfactory work: What is the person doing or not doing? Gather your facts and observations before discussing the problem with the underperformer. Much like you would do in preparation for a feedback conversation, find out what their peers, supervisors, and direct reports have to say—but do so in confidence. Think, too, about the competencies required for the job. Does the employee have the necessary skills to perform the job effectively?

Ask yourself whether you're contributing to the problem. Were you unclear in your expectations? Did you provide your direct report the resources and freedom to complete their job? It's also worth delving into your own assumptions about the employee, which may be unduly negative. Perhaps there are certain types of tasks they do well, or maybe they contributed satisfactorily to particular projects, but you didn't see these instances because you were only focused on their flaws. What skills or qualities allowed them to perform well in these cases? If you can identify your direct report's strengths in these situations, it may be possible to replicate the conditions that made them successful in other areas of work. Even if good performance is the exception rather than the rule, the person may be worth keeping around.

Personal issues—for example, health or family problems, or even a disruptive move to a new house—can also temporarily throw someone off their game and keep them from devoting their normal level of attention to work. If you notice underperformance from someone with a history of good work, check to see if personal problems may be the cause. Such employees are worth saving, so try to find a way to work around the issue.

Consider the example of Philippe, Allie's employee who struggled to turn in complete, timely, and correct budgets. Allie had brought up the issue a few times before, but the problems persisted. To get the full picture, Allie referred to her notes about the problem from previous feedback conversations and touched base with a few of her colleagues to see if they'd had similar issues.

But Allie didn't stop there. She thought hard about her own role. She felt she had set up the right expectations for Philippe, but he still struggled to submit the budgets in a timely manner. Philippe was a team player and showed strength in other aspects of his role, but completing these regular budgets was an integral part of his job. Allie concluded that Philippe was worth taking the time to develop and change.

Once you've seen the problem from a number of angles, present the employee with the facts of what you observe, providing frank and honest feedback, and—if the person demonstrates willingness—creating a plan for improvement and development.

Coach: Work Toward Improvement

Before sitting down with your direct report, give them advance notice that you'd like to discuss their performance and development. When you meet, describe the problematic behavior and the impact it's having on the rest of the team. Review the specific details of the issue—don't just describe the problem in general terms. For example, Allie might say to Philippe, "You've been late submitting your last few budgets, and I've found some troubling errors when I reviewed them. There are some basic errors that look like a matter of attention to detail, but it takes a lot of my time to review and make sense of them. And when you don't submit them on time, it requires that my assistant figure out whose budget is missing and then track you down to find out the status. This interferes with the other work she needs to complete."

Just as you would when delivering feedback, refer to the context of the problem, if applicable. "This is not the first time we've had to talk about this. According to my records, we discussed this problem last quarter and last year. Yet the problem continues." Be explicit about how they should improve: "These budgets must be corrected and submitted by deadline for you to remain a member of this team and organization."

While this straightforward approach may be hard for your direct report to hear, assure them that you want to help. Consider these sample phrases:

- "I'm seeing issues with your performance, and I believe that you can do better. So how do we improve?"
- "What adjustments might we try that would help you achieve your goals?"
- "What can I do to help you be more effective?"

Showing your support will help your employee sidestep feelings of defensiveness and be more willing to correct course.

Assess their willingness to change

No matter how hard you try, you can't force-feed something that is ultimately the employee's responsibility. Before devoting resources to develop low performers, assess whether they're committed to their own improvement.

Once you've explained the problem at hand, listen actively to the employee's response to determine whether or not they're open to engaging on the issue. Do they get defensive, make excuses, or claim that their performance is in fact adequate? Or do they provide useful information about the causes behind the issues you've raised? Perhaps their poor work is due to inadequate resources, whether it's staff, budget, time, or managerial support, or maybe they are struggling to understand expectations or build the skills necessary for the job. Maybe they're being affected by someone else's poor performance—for example, being delayed by one of their direct reports who isn't delivering *their* complete and correct budget statements on time.

Allie took note of Philippe's tone and body language as he spoke. He didn't seem surprised by her comments, though he did seem hesitant to give her the full story. Allie pressed to get more information, and he explained that he felt uncertain about the budgets, and even if his team members submitted their information on time, the budgets were often late because he was worried he was submitting them incorrectly, based on their previous discussions. He was unable to spot the problems, but just knowing they were there made him nervous and led to his delay in sending them.

Your preparatory work and active listening will help you distinguish between responses that are true explanations and those that are defensive excuses for bad performance. Honest responses indicate that a person is open to change. When an underperformer demonstrates concern about the problem and a willingness to make an effort toward improvement, work with them to develop a specific plan. If your employee does not show an interest in change, you may need to consider other alternatives to development.

Create a plan for improvement

With a willing employee, state your firm expectations for improvement clearly, and, together, craft a concrete plan for change. Be explicit: What will each of you do differently? What measurable actions will mark progress along the way? In many cases, performance issues arise from a mismatch between a manager's expectations and those of an employee. Write a list of the employee's three most-important responsibilities, and ask them to do the same. Then compare your results. You may find that, with some alignment of expectations and continuing discussion through your ongoing check-in conversations, your direct report can soon be on the right track.

While in many aspects of performance management it's helpful for an employee to draft an initial plan for improvement in order to increase their sense of ownership, for an underperformer you should be more directive. Provide a specific request with clear timelines, and then check for understanding. For example, Allie told Philippe, "What I'd suggest is that you set a quarterly reminder a few weeks before your budget is due to ask your team members to finish the components they're responsible for, and block out a window to compile the data and go over any questions with them. Then you'll be able to submit complete and clear budgets on time, and we won't have to have another of these conversations."

This discussion provides an opportunity for you to consider the various development options available to your employee. Philippe might do well with some online training or a refresher course—on budgeting, perhaps, or in Excel. If he has a colleague who consistently delivers polished, error-free budgets, Allie might connect them to discuss best practices for preparation. Perhaps the problem is less about the budget than about Philippe's management of his own direct reports, and if so, leadership training or mentorship might be more helpful to him. Whatever you decide, keep a record of your discussions and what plan you've agreed to.

Follow up

Schedule regular meetings to talk about progress—or ask the person to check in with you periodically. (If they don't follow up on this, they may not truly be willing to work to improve.)

For example, Allie sent Philippe to a half-day course on budgeting so he could better identify errors in his budgets and those of his direct reports. She scheduled a meeting a few weeks before the next budget was due to review the information he had at that point and explain any problems with what he'd put together. They met a few times over the course of the next weeks before he was able to submit a final, error-free budget. Allie also offered Philippe some feedback and guidance about how he might address one of his employees who consistently submitted incomplete information.

It was a time-intensive intervention, but the regular meetings paid off: Philippe's next budget was complete, correct, and turned in on time. He showed clear improvement as well as motivation to continue to improve next time. "I think I have a better handle on the process now," he said, "but just in case, can we plan to review a draft of my budget in advance of next quarter's deadline?"

In addition to these follow-up meetings, provide your employee with real-time feedback. Praise positive change, and pay attention to development and improvement. Make it clear that you notice and appreciate the results of their hard work.

Cut: Know When to Let Go

It can take a while for people to change their behavior and improve their performance, so don't expect an overnight transformation. For coaching and development efforts to work, your employee must also have the capacity to get to the necessary skill level. If your employee is enthusiastic but not showing even incremental progress toward targets, find out more about why this is happening. Let them know that they're not meeting your expectations, and ask questions to get their perspective. You could say, for example, "The needle hasn't moved on these skills we've identified as important. Were the expectations we set earlier too high or unrealistic? Is there a different way that you can learn this?" You could consider bringing in a third party, perhaps even another team member, to coach in your place.

If the employee continues to underperform, you'll need to decide if they are the right person for this role, task, or responsibility. If they demonstrate willingness, you might redirect them to work that calls on the skills they do have, whether by shifting their role or changing particular assignments.

Alternatively, if they are unwilling to improve or are just meeting the base needs of the position, you'll need to take decisive action. Address issues as they arise to communicate urgency. Shift your focus from eliciting improvement through coaching and development to explaining the consequences of unchanging underperformance. Make your communication clear and straightforward. "This is the third time this has happened, and since your behavior hasn't changed, I need to explain the consequences." If you still don't see improvement after genuine efforts to boost your employee's performance, you may have to conclude that the person may not be the right fit for the organization.

Firing an employee is a painful process, but it may be the best choice for the organization and the rest of your team, which will only grow disheartened by working with an underperformer. Be sure to document progress (or lack thereof) along the way to guard against potential legal action, and consult with your legal and HR departments about how to best move forward with a dismissal.

SECTION FOUR

Formal Performance Reviews

CHAPTER 12

The Case Against (and for) Annual Appraisals

Performance appraisal is a formal method for assessing how well an individual employee is doing with respect to established goals and expectations. These reviews have traditionally been conducted annually, though some organizations do offer them semiannually or quarterly, and they often include informal follow-ups as needed. Appraisal sessions are both a confirmation and a formalization of the ongoing feedback and development discussions that should be part of every manager-employee relationship.

Performance appraisals are not widely beloved, particularly by those being evaluated. In fact, they're probably the most stressful work conversation an employee will have all year. Even star performers may approach the review process with apprehension. Opening oneself to formal judgment—particularly judgment that can define one's pay—is rarely appealing.

But busy managers are not particularly fond of performance appraisals, either. They can be extremely time-consuming, requiring individualized preparation, administration, documentation, and follow-up that's tailored to each employee. For a manager with many direct reports, an appraisal for each person is a hefty time commitment. A study by corporate research and advisory firm CEB found that the average manager spends close to five weeks doing annual appraisals.[1] And managers find the process stressful as well: Few managers enjoy telling people that they're not doing their jobs as well as they should. "What a performance appraisal requires is for one person to stand in judgment of another," says Dick Grote, author of *How to Be Good at Performance Appraisals*. "Deep down, it's uncomfortable."[2]

But, done right, formal evaluations can help you reinforce solid work and redirect poor performance. At best, a review is an opportunity to reflect on performance and potential, allowing your direct report to improve in the future rather than be lambasted for past failures. When you consider that a manager's fundamental responsibility is to get results through their people, a systematic approach to assessing the work of one's direct reports seems a natural choice. In addition to providing insights into employee performance, appraisals help managers and organizations make informed, consistent decisions about pay, development, and promotions. Well-documented performance evaluations also protect the organization against lawsuits by employees who have been terminated, demoted, or denied a merit increase.

Your company may require you to do performance reviews annually, but that practice has come under question in the past few years, especially as it relates to performance ratings. If you have flexibility in your approach to formal assessments, you may want to take these criticisms into account.

The Argument Against Annual Appraisals

The historical focus of annual performance reviews was on determining which people to reward, keep, and terminate. The roots of traditional appraisals can be traced in large part back to two sources: the "merit rating" system developed in the U.S. military during World War I and Jack Welch's forced-ranking model used at GE, in which the top 10% of people were rewarded and the bottom 10% dismissed.

But as traditional performance management comes under fire, many organizations are concluding that formal performance reviews aren't delivering on their promises—that is, to improve employees' performance. When rapid innovation is a source of competitive advantage, a system geared toward assessing past performance doesn't help propel people forward.

Organizations are also increasingly questioning the accuracy of the evaluations themselves, particularly when it comes to ratings, where standardization simply cannot be achieved. Ratings are by nature subjective; two managers may mark the same person's skills differently, resulting in ratings that reveal more about the manager than the employee being evaluated. What's more, only an employee's "official" manager is tasked with appraising their performance—but that employee may be working on multiple teams or for several managers. It's unclear if one manager's point of view can account for the full range of an employee's performance. With an overemphasis on individual contribution, traditional appraisal systems fall short in accounting for or recognizing teamwork or collaboration—which are increasingly important.

Some difficulties with the review process also stem from the fact that appraisal conversations are used to discuss more than just performance. It's tough to have an open discussion about performance problems while also delivering news about merit pay. And appraisals, often intended as a bulwark against worst-case scenarios, are especially fraught when performance problems are significant. "Traditional corporate performance reviews are driven largely by fear of litigation," writes Patty McCord, former chief talent officer at Netflix, in her HBR article "How Netflix Reinvented HR." "The theory is that if you want to get rid of someone, you need a paper trail documenting a history of poor achievement." When these discussions only exist to ensure you're covered in case of a lawsuit, the emphasis on employee improvement is lost.

The annual gap between meetings also stilts the opportunity to elicit real change from your workers. A tired metaphor likens annual reviews to a yearly check-up with your doctor. The comparison isn't completely off base, but anyone who's ever visited an emergency room knows that one physical every 12 months does not equal sufficient health care. What if you have a medical condition that needs frequent monitoring, like asthma or even pregnancy? What if you sprain your ankle or get an infection? Waiting for your annual doctor's appointment won't cut it—and when it comes to performance, neither will an annual review.

Appraisals evaluate employees on how they have or haven't met goals set a year in advance. But when an organization can't foresee needs that far out, evaluating people on how they meet shorter-term goals and priorities can make more sense than assessing them in relation to annual goals. Organizations, particularly professional services and consulting firms, are also under increasing pressure to increase their learning and development efforts. When it comes to knowledge work, structured learning opportunities, including feedback and coaching, are what transforms green college graduates into skilled professionals. Meaningful feedback and coaching from managers is better delivered through frequent check-ins than in one annual conversation.

What's more, some employees *want* their performance reviewed more than once a year, particularly those (like Millennials) who are eager for constant learning and development, and making your employees wait a year to hear feedback leads to heightened anxiety when they sit down for the conversation. Employees shouldn't be surprised by a manager's appraisal—and if they are, they can become defensive or unwilling to hear the feedback. To continue producing good work, employees need more than a yearly dose of their supervisor's attention.

It's no surprise, then, that Wharton professor Peter Cappelli proclaims, "Performance appraisals are one of the most ubiquitous, and also one of the most unpopular, protocols in the workplace."[3] But if the traditional approach is fraught, what can managers—and organizations at large—do?

Alternate Approaches to Formal Reviews

It once seemed heretical to abandon traditional performance appraisal practices, but a growing number of companies are ditching performance evaluations while attempting to create new ways to more effectively manage performance. At least 30 of the *Fortune* 500 companies had revamped their performance appraisal practices by the end of 2015.[4]

Deloitte, for example, replaced its cumbersome evaluation and rating process with a streamlined new model: "something nimbler, real time, and more individualized—something squarely focused on fueling performance in the future rather than assessing it in the past," as Marcus Buckingham and Ashley Goodall describe in their HBR article, "Reinventing Performance Management." The consulting firm replaced their complex 360-degree feedback process with a quarterly "performance snapshot." Deloitte realized that while people may rate others' skills inconsistently, they are highly consistent when rating their own feelings and intentions. So, the company discovered, rather than asking more people about their opinion of an employee, they'd get a more effective response by asking the individual's immediate team leader four key questions that focus on what they'd *do* with the individual, rather than what they *think* of them. This forward-thinking questionnaire focused on four areas: compensation, teamwork, poor performance, and promotion. Complementing the quarterly snapshot are frequent weekly check-ins.

Netflix, too, eliminated formal performance reviews, stating that they were "too ritualistic and too infrequent." They encourage regular conversations between managers and employees, but the company also implemented informal, simple 360-degree reviews that asked people to identify things their colleagues should stop, start, or continue doing. Netflix began by using a software program to elicit responses but has since shifted to signed feedback or even face-to-face conversations. According to McCord, "If you talk simply and honestly about performance on a regular basis, you can get good results—probably better ones than a company that grades everyone on a five-point scale."

Other companies choose to keep their annual appraisals but make changes to the actual event. For example, Facebook analyzed its performance management system and found that 87% of people wanted to keep performance ratings.[5] So they kept their annual reviews but revised their rating process to improve fairness and transparency and to increase their focus on development.

GE, originator of much of the traditional appraisal process, is working to replace its legacy system with a real-time approach in which managers and their employees hold frequent, informal "touchpoint" conversations to set or update priorities based on customer needs. But these forward-looking, ongoing discussions are complemented with a year-end summary conversation and document (not unlike the traditional annual review), during which both manager and employee reflect on impact achieved and look ahead. Managers base compensation, promotion, and development decisions on these summary findings—just as they did under GE's previous system. With the company's new "performance development" approach, however, the manager and employee have a richer set of data concerning the employee's contributions and impact over the course of the year, so the end-of-year discussions are both more future focused and more meaningful.[6]

Companies are also rethinking the use of time-consuming, set systems and processes in favor of allowing managers more leeway in evaluating employees. Letting people rely on logic and common sense can lead to better results than adhering to inflexible formal policies, and newer evaluation approaches generally require more discussion and less documentation, making them less cumbersome and formal, more agile and flexible.

These organizations, though, represent just a small portion of companies that are changing the way they're looking at formal appraisals. Traditional annual reviews are still widely used. According to a study by *Human Resource Executive*, "Despite all the buzz about abolishing formal performance reviews, the vast majority of organizations continue to employ traditional vehicles for sharing performance-related information."[7] In part, that's because employees do need to be evaluated. Performance inevitably must be measured and rated—and if the appraisal process is eliminated, those evaluations will be invisible to employees. Managers may draw conclusions about a direct report's performance, but without the opportunity to get input from the employee. And without rankings or numerical measures, it can be difficult to tie financial rewards to performance in a standardized way.

If organizations dismiss annual appraisals, they need to replace them with something, whether that means more-frequent formal reviews—semiannual or quarterly—or informal periodic check-in conversations.

Performance Reviews Moving Forward

So what does this mean for you as a manager? Unless you're the CEO, it's unlikely you can overhaul your entire organization's approach to appraisal, but you can control the way you manage the performance of your team. If your organization requires reviews—whether they are annual, semiannual, or quarterly—you should, of course, do them. But you can take additional steps throughout the review period to ensure that your employees are meeting goals and growing with the organization.

Make a practice of checking in with each of your direct reports on a weekly basis—or at least once a month—to ask two main questions: What are you going to get done this week (or month)? And what help do you need from me? These informal conversations don't require complex forms or burdensome documentation. Check-ins like these are your best opportunity to deliver immediate, relevant feedback—and real-time, in-the-moment course correction.

When you are faced with conducting periodic formal reviews, there are proven ways to make them easier for you and more effective for your employees—a topic that we'll explore in the coming chapters.

NOTES

1. "The Real Impact of Eliminating Performance Ratings: Insights from Employees and Managers," CEB Global, 2016.
2. Quoted in Rebecca Knight, "Delivering an Effective Performance Review," HBR.org, November 3, 2011, https://hbr.org/2011/11/delivering-an-effective-perfor.
3. Peter Cappelli, "The Common Myths About Performance Reviews, Debunked," HBR.org, July 26, 2016 (product #H030NZ).
4. Lori Goler, Janelle Gale, and Adam Grant, "Let's Not Kill Performance Evaluations Yet," *Harvard Business Review*, November 2016 (product #R1611G).
5. Ibid.
6. Peter Cappelli and Anna Tavis, "The Performance Management Revolution," *Harvard Business Review*, October 2016 (product #R1610D).
7. "Seeking Agility in Performance Management," *Human Resource Executive*, http://hr1.silkroad.com/hr-exec-agility-performance-management.

CHAPTER 13

Assess Performance, but Rethink Ratings

There is no one right way to conduct a performance appraisal, but you and your direct report will both benefit from your preparation. You must evaluate your direct report's performance in relation to the goals you defined together. You can use the same methods described in section 2 to identify gaps between goals and performance.

You'll also want to assess behaviors that may not be explicitly linked to any specific goal. Teamwork, communication skills, leadership, initiative, focus, productivity, and reliability are all competencies that affect how an employee gets work done. You may also want to consider whether or not someone has demonstrated citizenship behaviors, like helping their colleagues or making new hires feel welcome, which boost cooperation and improve the work environment.

Gather Information About Performance

Appraisals are too easily skewed by a manager's limited perspective and selective memory. One big mistake or contribution over the course of the review period may stick in a manager's mind and outweigh everything else their direct report has done during that time. And because an employee's most recent performance is fresh in their manager's mind, that behavior can weigh more heavily in the evaluation than it should. But you can help avoid these problems by drawing on different sources of information to get a fuller picture.

There are a number of resources to take under consideration when evaluating performance. If you've been keeping records on your ongoing feedback, coaching, and development conversations, you'll have plenty of material to work with. You can also gather 360-degree feedback from others to complement your own observations. But to begin, you want to solicit your employee's point of view.

Request an employee's self-assessment

About two weeks before the review session, ask your direct report to complete a self-evaluation. This document allows you to take the employee's input into account when you're preparing for the conversation, rather than potentially being surprised by it just before or during the formal review. Such self-appraisal also has the benefit of setting a tone of partnership that may help the person be more open to subsequent feedback.

Some organizations provide specific self-evaluation forms or checklists. Questions on this form may include:

- What are your most important accomplishments since your last review?
- Have you achieved the goals set for this review period?
- Have you surpassed any of your goals? Which ones? What helped you exceed them?
- Are you currently struggling with any goals? Which ones? What is inhibiting your progress toward those goals (lack of training, inadequate resources, poor direction from management)?
- Has this review period been better or worse than previous ones in the position?
- What parts of your job do you find most and least interesting or enjoyable?
- What do you most like and dislike about working for this organization?
- What do you consider to be your most important tasks and aims for the upcoming year?
- What can I as your manager, or the organization as a whole, do to help you be more successful?

Answering these questions can enhance your employee's ability to learn and reflect during your appraisal discussion. The very act of thinking them over will help the individual recognize the review not as a required drill but as a true effort toward helping them understand how they're contributing to the organization and how they might build success.

Even if you aren't required to use a formal self-appraisal form, it's still worth soliciting some information from your direct report. Ask for an informal list of your direct report's most important achievements and accomplishments—projects, tasks, relevant initiatives—over the review period to ensure you don't overlook any of your employee's successes. This can be as simple as an email with bullet points. You can also ask them for a list of people you could check with about their performance (the 360-degree feedback process). This input can give you a broader perspective on the employee's work and any related problems, since as a manager you may be seeing just a small part of what the person does or struggles with every day. It will also help refresh your memory and put a positive slant on an event that so many participants dread.

Some argue that self-appraisals don't work. For example, performance evaluation expert Dick Grote says that self-assessments give the employee the wrong impression of what an appraisal is, not to mention a false sense of collaboration, especially if someone's performance is unacceptable. Having a direct report complete a self-appraisal cues them to expect that they'll bring their evaluation, you'll bring yours, and together you'll come to an agreement on the final appraisal. But a performance evaluation is a record of your opinion of the quality of their work—not a negotiation.

In cases where there may be confusion—for example, an underperformer's work is unacceptable and requires immediate change—you may choose not to solicit a self-assessment. But if you do use self-appraisals in the review process, make it clear to your direct report that their contribution is just one piece of the data that you'll review when looking at the whole picture and that its purpose is for you to gain insight into their point of view.

Review your records

In addition to the employee's self-assessment, read over any notes you've kept on your direct report over the review period. If you've kept robust records, you won't need to rack your brain trying to remember what happened over the course of the year; you'll have the information right in front of you.

If you're preparing for a review and don't have detailed records, consider what sources you do have to jog your memory. Skim through your calendar appointments to remind yourself of specific accomplishments or problems—the sales pitch delivered flawlessly, the deadline missed, or the time your employee smoothly covered for a colleague during flu season. Look through email correspondence and meeting notes to find similar details that may have escaped you.

Solicit 360-degree feedback

You may also want to consider complementing your own observations with 360-degree feedback: feedback from colleagues and others who work closely with your direct report. For instance, an "internal customer"—someone for whom your employee provides, say, tech or design services—and a peer who works with the employee on a cross-functional team might have valuable input on dimensions of the person's work that you don't see directly. Gaining observations from the employee's larger community can expand your limited perspective.

This type of broad feedback that synthesizes others' perspectives can reduce the chance of a performance misdiagnosis. It also recognizes that many modern workplaces are multifaceted, with no one person in particular seeing all dimensions of the employee's work. Thus, several people in a position to know are asked to rate the quality of the subject's performance and their interactions with them. Some organizations present this feedback anonymously; others have colleagues participate in direct conversations about one another's work.

As a method, 360-degree feedback is not without drawbacks. First, it is time-consuming. Think for a moment about the many people whom you might be asked to rate in your organization. Your boss, four or five of your peers, the person who handles your department's expense reimbursements, and so forth. Now multiply that number by the one hour typically required to prepare an evaluation. This time adds up.

People can also be uncomfortable giving a negative report about someone else—even when that person has glaring shortcomings or you assure them their responses will remain anonymous. The reviewers know that their report might result in no raise for (or even dismissal of) their colleague. But within an organization that's committed to providing useful feedback and in which people understand the value of the 360-degree approach, soliciting others' points of view can provide much more complete information on a direct report's work than you, as an individual, possibly can. On the other hand, if an employee works with very few people or if asking for such feedback would not fit within your organization's culture, 360-degree feedback may not add much to your own evaluation.

Your organization may have a set process for facilitating 360-degree feedback, but if it doesn't, consider these tips for getting the most-useful information:

- **Diversify your pool of respondents.** Tap a number of peers, direct reports, and internal and external customers to provide input, rather than asking people from only one category or just one person from each category. Inviting a larger pool of participants means you'll get a more complete picture, the respondents will feel more comfortable sharing their feedback knowing they're not a lone identifiable voice, and your employee will be assured that you've worked to gather a broad, balanced view.

- **Clarify that your purpose is constructive, not punitive.** Explain to all involved—those giving feedback and those receiving it—that the purpose of the 360 review isn't to amass criticism but to evaluate achievements and define areas for improvement.

- **Request specific examples rather than just numeric ratings.** If you're asking about communication skills, you'll learn much more from a response like "José answers all my questions clearly and patiently" than you will from a 5 out of 5 rating in communication.

- **Ask probing questions.** Dig deeper into people's responses by asking thoughtful questions such as, How did this person contribute? What do you want this person to stop, start, and continue doing? What are their strengths as a collaborator, and what are their weaknesses?

Find additional information

Between your employee's self-assessment, your own records, and the feedback of others, you should already be forming an objective picture of an individual's performance. But consider other resources when assessing your employee's work as well, including:

- The employee's job description. You're not just evaluating the quality of your employee's work but determining how well they performed their specific job function.

- The person's goals and development plan as defined in the last review or during the review period. When assessing performance against goals, it's helpful to revisit those goals—taking into account any that may have changed over the course of the review period—to see if they've been successfully completed.

- Any documents from previous review sessions, prior evaluation forms, employment records, and other relevant material you may have on file.

After gathering your information, the next step is to pull it together into an overarching evaluation you'll later share with your employee.

Assess Performance

To synthesize the information you've gathered, sift through it and begin noting common themes. Look for patterns and recurring threads, and just as you did when preparing to give feedback, focus on things that, if addressed, will make a difference in future performance. There's no reason to rehash a onetime mistake, like the botched presentation six months ago that the employee underprepared for and that you've already discussed with them. On the other hand, if they've consistently presented poorly, and they're still not sufficiently preparing despite multiple feedback discussions, you would be wise to address it in your formal appraisal.

Give equal consideration to positive results and to shortcomings when analyzing the overall picture. Has your direct report met the goals set for the review period? (It could be that their goals have changed since you initially set them a year ago, so take that into account.) It's easiest to evaluate quantitative achievements—such as the numbers of presentations delivered, reports written, or apps developed—but to assess qualitative aspects of their work, focus on behaviors and supplement your evaluation with examples.

It can be difficult to assess performance against goals. Sure, if the goal is to assemble 150 widgets or generate mortgage loans equal to $3.5 million, it's simple to make an accurate calculation. But few jobs are that clear-cut. What if measuring someone's "output" requires evaluating how well they managed a team, influenced others, or helped people collaborate? In cases like these, assessment is more subjective. As a manager, you see only part of the employee's work activity over the course of the year. The 360-degree feedback you collected will be especially helpful in assessing how they're regarded by others and in gauging the scope and quality of their influence.

As you sift through your data, also consider how the employee has performed against behavioral expectations. Communication skills, for example, are critical for someone in a customer service role, just as coding skills are vital for a developer. Focus in on those behaviors that are most important for an employee's success in their particular role. (Looking back at the job description or competency model for the position or level in the organization can help here.) Your organization may want you to focus on key behaviors or competencies or on how company values were demonstrated. Also take into account more-general attributes like initiative, cooperation and teamwork, efficiency, dependability, and improvement that may not be specific to the role or organization.

As you begin to draw conclusions about an employee's performance, remember context. An individual's performance depends, to varying degrees, on the situation in which they work. It's not always fair or accurate to evaluate two colleagues in the same position on the same criteria, using the same scale or inflexible reference points. Consider situational factors in a call center, for example, where performance is assessed based on the dollar amount of charitable donations pledged. Different results can be caused by differences in the geographic regions or the populations of potential donors the employees are assigned. Such underlying factors may affect your direct report's performance. It's worth considering questions such as:

- What situational factors made it easier or harder for this person to achieve their goals?
- What systems, processes, structures, circumstances, or events helped or hindered this employee's performance?
- How have I contributed to this employee's success or performance problems?

Documenting the Performance Evaluation

In many organizations, you'll be required to document your impressions and feedback in a way that can be shared and saved. Your company may already have a set of questions to answer or a standard form to use. If not, you can create your own by adapting the performance evaluation form template in table 13-1 at the end of this chapter.

Record your observations about your employee's job performance as objectively as possible, and support them with examples. Provide evidence of progress (or lack thereof) by connecting accomplishments with established goals. For example: "Derek increased sales by 12%, which exceeded his goal of 10%." "Amelia reduced her error rate by 18%; her goal was 25%." Including the background data informing your conclusions will help your direct report grasp the assessment criteria and recognize the evaluation as fair.

Your organization may require you to provide ratings —a general ranking of the employee's performance or individual ratings of specific aspects of their performance. But a numeric value alone may not give your employee enough information to make improvements or continue good work. Instead, supplement your rating with qualitative examples, written and verbal observations, and comments that explain your choices. (See the sidebar "Navigating Ratings.")

NAVIGATING RATINGS

Ratings used to be an established part of many organization's performance appraisal processes. Despite movements away from this step, some organizations still require that managers rate or score their employees annually on a 5- (or sometimes 3- or 4-) point scale. And some of these require forced rankings, in which only 1 or 2 of 10 people can get the highest rating.

Some companies still find the process of rating valuable. At Facebook, for example, managers deliberate over those ratings in groups, to keep individual employees from being unduly punished or rewarded by managers who are hard or easy "graders." Ratings are also used when making decisions about compensation.

But just as performance reviews are changing, so too is the practice of using performance ratings. Companies are discovering that ratings aren't as effective as they hoped they'd be. For instance, in his HBR article "Performance Appraisal Reappraised," Dick Grote described a workplace where nearly all annual ratings of 3,200 employees were positive. Not one person was rated "unsatisfactory"; just one had been deemed "marginal." "Clearly, such uniformly glowing appraisals are useless in evaluating the relative merits of staff members," Grote writes. The result is general "performance inflation" in which nearly everyone is rated above average—a statistical impossibility.

Ratings may no longer make sense in a changing work context. Many people work in teams that their direct managers may not observe, doing cross-functional work their managers may not even understand, let alone be able to assess accurately, so an immediate manager's rating may not be correct or meaningful. As more people work in teams and as

(*continued*)

NAVIGATING RATINGS

collaboration is increasingly valued, the traditional-forced rankingapproach also leads to competition, reducing the likelihood of open collaboration and damaging overall team-based performance. In response to these arguments, more and more organizations are ditching the use of ratings and forced distribution.

If you are required to rate your direct report, certainly do as your organization dictates, but keep in mind a few caveats. A five-point scale is not analogous to A–F grades in a school context. The majority of employees will get a 3, the middle rank. Some individuals may be disappointed with a 3 rating, thinking they're merely average. In this context, a 3 means someone has hit their goal targets with solid, satisfactory performance. "In school, a C was mediocre," Grote explains, "but a 3 in the working world means they're meeting expectations. They're shooting par."[1]

In addition, combine your rating with specific comments and feedback that give the employee a clear understanding of why they got their rating and how their performance is aligning with their goals. If there isn't space on your organization's evaluation form, add a page to allow yourself room to explain the logic behind the rating, and discuss your rating during the meeting itself as well. Your employee will find your comments, observations, and qualitative examples valuable complements to a static quantitative score.

The more specific information you can provide to back up your conclusions, the more likely the employee will be to repeat and even improve on positive behaviors—and to correct negative ones. Use the most-telling examples to make your point in your written evaluation, and save the rest for your review session in case you need to support your judgment during the conversation. Examples should include:

- **Details about what you observed.** For instance, Theo, a customer service representative, has more than doubled the orders he's filled over the past year now that he's learned how to use a new customer database. Back that assessment up with detail in your write-up: "Last year Theo filled 15 orders per day. This year his average exceeded 30 per day. He also asks fewer questions now that he's effectively using the customer database."

- **Supporting data, perhaps from 360-degree feedback.** "Siobhan helped Theo learn how to use the new customer database, and she reports that he's using it on a regular basis."

- **The impact on your team and organization.** "After Theo learned how to use the new database, he no longer had to rely on colleagues to find out pertinent information. The whole team began fulfilling orders more quickly because they were answering fewer questions from him, which improved cash flow for the organization."

Expressing your observations as neutral facts rather than judgments is particularly important when it concerns subpar results. "Theo received five complaints from extremely unsatisfied customers" is objective, nonjudgmental, and specific to a particular job requirement. Contrast that with a negative characterization that doesn't describe actual behavior ("Theo doesn't seem to care about customers") or a vague judgment that fails to point to a specific skill he might improve ("Theo doesn't know how to talk to difficult customers").

When giving positive feedback, on the other hand, combine specific achievements with character-based praise. For example: "With the new accounts she generated, which delivered $1.25 million in business, Juliana exceeded the goal we set for her last July by 27%. Her creativity and perseverance drove her to look beyond the traditional client base; she researched new industries and networked at conferences to find new customers." Acknowledging the traits and behaviors that made those results possible will show your direct report that you see them as an individual and recognize their unique contributions. Such praise can generate pride and boost motivation in your employee.

Supporting your assessment with specific examples, data, and details increases the likelihood that the employee will be able to absorb and learn from your feedback, and it also mitigates any possible legal ramifications in particularly egregious situations. If a person's work is beginning to suffer, or if you suspect that you might need to dismiss someone due to poor performance, it's vital that you document the individual's behavior and the steps you've taken to correct it. As a rule of thumb, include in your evaluation only statements that you'd be comfortable testifying to in court. If you have any questions about legal ramifications, consult with your human resource manager or internal legal team.

Finally, write down the three things the employee has done best over the course of the year and the two areas that most need improvement. Distill your message down to one key idea—your overall impression of their performance, which is the single most important takeaway for your direct report. These few points will determine the overarching message that you want to convey in the review discussion, and having them documented will prevent you from forgetting any important details when you're in the conversation.

NOTE

1. Quoted in Rebecca Knight, "Delivering an Effective Performance Review," HBR.org, November 3, 2011, https://hbr.org/2011/11/delivering-an-effective-perfor.

TABLE 13-1

Performance evaluation form template

Employee information	
Review period	
Employee	
Job title	
Department	
Manager	

Scale for competencies	
Exemplary	Performance far exceeds the expectations of the position.
Excellent	Performance exceeds the expectations of the position.
Satisfactory	Performance fully meets the expectations of the position.
Fair	Performance does not meet the expectations of the position and requires some improvement.
Unsatisfactory	Performance is far below the expectations of the position and requires significant improvement.

Key accomplishments

Goals

Was each goal met?

Goal 1	Goal 2	Goal 3
☐ Yes ☐ No	☐ Yes ☐ No	☐ Yes ☐ No

Competencies: Rate the employee on all relevant competencies.

Job requirements: Fulfills required responsibilities for position
☐ Exemplary ☐ Excellent ☐ Satisfactory ☐ Fair ☐ Unsatisfactory
Comments:

Problem solving: Demonstrates ability to solve problems and execute solutions
☐ Exemplary ☐ Excellent ☐ Satisfactory ☐ Fair ☐ Unsatisfactory
Comments:

Initiative: Demonstrates ambition to succeed in the position and strives to improve processes and products
☐ Exemplary ☐ Excellent ☐ Satisfactory ☐ Fair ☐ Unsatisfactory
Comments:

Efficiency: Completes assigned tasks on time without wasting time or resources
☐ Exemplary ☐ Excellent ☐ Satisfactory ☐ Fair ☐ Unsatisfactory
Comments:

Teamwork: Works well with others and contributes to group projects
☐ Exemplary ☐ Excellent ☐ Satisfactory ☐ Fair ☐ Unsatisfactory
Comments:

Communication: Writes and speaks with clarity; interacts effectively with managers, peers, or customers
☐ Exemplary ☐ Excellent ☐ Satisfactory ☐ Fair ☐ Unsatisfactory
Comments:

Adaptability: Is receptive to new ideas or change within the team or business and makes adjustments to work as necessary
☐ Exemplary ☐ Excellent ☐ Satisfactory ☐ Fair ☐ Unsatisfactory
Comments:

(continued)

TABLE 13-1 *(continued)*

Leadership: Demonstrates ability to influence or lead others toward achieving unit, team, or firm goals
☐ Exemplary ☐ Excellent ☐ Satisfactory ☐ Fair ☐ Unsatisfactory
Comments:

Integrity: Is honest and fair and models organizational values
☐ Exemplary ☐ Excellent ☐ Satisfactory ☐ Fair ☐ Unsatisfactory
Comments:

Accountability: Accepts responsibility for failure or errors
☐ Exemplary ☐ Excellent ☐ Satisfactory ☐ Fair ☐ Unsatisfactory
Comments:

Judgment: Makes sound choices and informed decisions; able to distinguish between issues that need immediate attention and those that can wait
☐ Exemplary ☐ Excellent ☐ Satisfactory ☐ Fair ☐ Unsatisfactory
Comments:

Dependability: Elicits trust from colleagues; delivers consistently on promises and commitments
☐ Exemplary ☐ Excellent ☐ Satisfactory ☐ Fair ☐ Unsatisfactory
Comments:

Improvement: Demonstrates improved performance over the review period
☐ Exemplary ☐ Excellent ☐ Satisfactory ☐ Fair ☐ Unsatisfactory
Comments:

Areas of strength for the employee

Areas of development for the employee

Additional comments

Signatures

Manager signature and date:

Signature Date

To be signed by the employee after receipt of the performance evaluation form and discussion with the employee's manager.

Employee signature and date:

Signature Date

Source: Adapted from *HBR Guide to Delivering Effective Feedback Ebook + Tools* (Boston: Harvard Business Review Press, 2016), product #10084E.

CHAPTER 14

How to Conduct the Review Conversation

The detailed information you've captured in your performance evaluation form is a helpful guide for when you sit down with your individual team members. But simply stating what is on paper won't convince your employee to change or motivate them to continue their good work. You need to give just as much careful consideration to the discussion itself.

Much like with your ongoing feedback discussions, the logistics around your performance appraisal meeting are just as important as the points you want to communicate. Without establishing the right time, place, and tone, your message may be lost, and your direct report may not understand what to do next.

Even star performers may feel some anxiety at the prospect of a formal review conversation, so do what you can to put your employee at ease. Then, launch into a two-way discussion about performance.

Consider Logistics

Schedule the performance review session well in advance to give both of you the opportunity to prepare, and be thoughtful about choosing a meeting time. Don't infringe on personal time by proposing a meeting during lunch or after work. Set aside 45 to 60 minutes for your conversation, and make sure that neither of you has a pressing commitment immediately afterward in case the discussion takes longer than expected or your direct report needs some time to work through any emotions brought on by what might be a difficult conversation. You may want to ask when they would prefer to meet—a subtle signal that you value their time.

Choose a location that will make your employee feel comfortable, somewhere private and free from distractions and interruptions. You'll both be most at ease in a business setting—an empty office, a conference room—rather than in a cafeteria, coffee shop, or restaurant. Try to find a neutral spot, but if you do meet in your office, sit beside the person to establish a sense of partnership and open communication. Sitting behind your desk, especially in the context of delivering a judgment, can convey dominance and distance.

Explain the nature of the meeting ahead of time, even if the two of you have had review sessions in the past. Outline what you plan to discuss, which may include the employee's input or self-assessment, your completed evaluation, a rating (should your organization require it), a summary of their strengths, and areas for improvement. In most cases, you'll want to give your direct report a copy of your appraisal about an hour or so before you meet and ask them to note any questions or comments. Allow them some privacy to read the document over carefully. "When people read someone's assessment of them, they are going to have all sorts of churning emotions," says performance evaluation expert Dick Grote. "Let them have that on their own time, and give them a chance to think about it."[1]

Some employees may require special arrangements, especially if the discussion has the possibility of escalating to an uncomfortable level. For an individual whose work is unacceptable, for instance, schedule a time to meet near the end of the day, and plan to meet in your office. You may also choose not to provide your employee with their completed evaluation in advance of the meeting. These small changes will place you in a position of authority, indicate the need for improvement, and allow the employee to decompress afterward if they have an emotional reaction to the feedback.

Set the Correct Tone

To mitigate any anxiety and establish rapport, set a tone of partnership right from the start. Welcome your employee, try to put them at ease, and limit distractions. Close the door, and silence any notifications on your phone or computer. You should have already established a relationship of trust through your discussions throughout the review period, but if not, taking clear steps to demonstrate your respect for your direct report in this conversation can help. Active listening is key to making your employee feel truly heard. Resist the temptation to check your watch or your phone during the course of the conversation.

Remind the employee of the meeting's purpose: to determine how well the individual is doing with respect to assigned goals and to motivate good performance, provide constructive feedback, and understand more about what they need to do to excel in their job. Tell them explicitly that their input is necessary and valuable and that you hope the conversation will be an open dialogue so you can work together on any issues that arise. You should also mention that you'd like to take notes so that you can both remember what you've discussed.

Once you've clarified the meeting's purpose and objectives, ask questions to help you understand the employee's perspective on their performance and to keep you from controlling too much of the conversation early on. If they seem reluctant to speak up, you might probe with questions like, "How do you feel things are going on the job? What's going well, and what problems are you having?" or "Tell me some of the main points you want me to note from your self-evaluation." Focus on their point of view rather than agreeing or disagreeing.

As you would in any important conversation, practice active listening. Don't interrupt. Show that you're paying close attention by periodically paraphrasing what you've heard. You might say, "If I understand you correctly, you feel that you are meeting all goals with respect to the weekly sales reports but that you are struggling to contact all the key customers you've been assigned. Do I have that right?" This gives your direct report the opportunity to correct any misunderstandings.

It's not uncommon for an employee to request a pay increase or inquire about a promotion during appraisal discussions. These topics should not be the focus of your conversation, but if you're asked directly, be prepared to respond. The sidebar "When an Employee Asks for a Raise or Promotion" explains how to tackle these requests.

WHEN AN EMPLOYEE ASKS FOR A RAISE OR PROMOTION

Many people ask for a change in pay or title in the context of performance review meetings. If possible, keep this discussion of compensation separate by holding it at a later date. Performance and compensation are each significant enough on their own to warrant dedicated conversations, and it's seldom ideal to mix the two. Thank your direct report for bringing up the topic and promise to get back to them by a specific date. (If it's already been decided whether a raise or promotion will be granted, however, and the individual is set on discussing it as part of your review meeting, do so at the beginning of your conversation; otherwise your employee may be too distracted to take in your feedback.)

(*continued*)

WHEN AN EMPLOYEE ASKS FOR A RAISE OR PROMOTION

If your direct report is asking for an increase in pay and a decision about salary hasn't yet been made, you'll need time to fairly assess the situation and determine whether a pay increase is appropriate. And even if you think a pay increase is merited, don't grant it immediately. Word will get out that all a person needs to get a raise is to ask.

When you do meet again to discuss the request, explain that an individual's salary is determined by two factors: the value of the job itself to the organization and the quality of the individual's performance. In some cases, you may discover that someone is well deserving, but there's no opportunity for an increase in compensation. Regardless of the individual in the role, every job is worth a certain market value. If that position's pay isn't negotiable because it has reached the peak compensation your organization allows for that role, tell your employee so: Rejecting a raise request in that situation will clearly reflect only the value of the job to the organization, not the person's worth as an individual.

In other instances, your employee may be more interested in a change in title than in a raise alone. In such cases you'll need to assess their ability to take on the new job (and if that position is feasible in the organization). You may decide that your direct report isn't quite ready to take the next step. In that event, focus on what they can do to get to the next level. Joseph Weintraub, author of *The Coaching Manager*, suggests saying something along the lines of, "You're not ready today. This next level has a different set of criteria and skills. But let's talk about how you're going to get there."[2]

You'll have to explain what skills, knowledge, and experience your employee will need before a promotion is possible and assure them that you're committed to helping them succeed. Work with them to identify the gaps between their current skills and experience and where they need to be in order to step into the new role they desire. Strategize ways to fill those gaps using some of the development tactics discussed in chapter 9, including enriching and challenging stretch assignments, training, or mentoring.

Discuss Performance

Managers can feel nervous, even reluctant, about offering constructive feedback in the review session. But everyone, even your best performers, can benefit from hearing ideas for improvement—and missing out on this opportunity to deliver feedback means your time-consuming evaluation won't be of much use.

Tailor your discussion to each employee you're meeting with, and don't rely on your written assessment to dictate the agenda. Adhering to the order of an inflexible form can lock you and your direct report into an item-by-item negotiation instead of a productive discussion. Instead, use your evaluation as a reference so you remember to cover all the important points you planned to mention.

The employee's performance—not the employee themselves—should be the subject of the conversation. Focus your discussion on how agreed-upon performance goals relate to specific outcomes. For example, "We agreed that you'd bring in 10 new clients this quarter, and you exceeded that goal" or "We agreed that you'd reduce the number of production line errors by 10%, but you've only reduced them by 5%." Emphasize issues that the person can improve in the future. Be selective; you don't need to go over every shortcoming or failing you've noticed, only the most important ones.

As in your written evaluation, don't make any statements about your direct report's character, values, or intentions. Doing so can make your employee defensive and is unlikely to lead to fruitful ideas for change or improvement. Instead, use neutral language like, "I've noticed you haven't offered any suggestions at our service improvement meetings. Why is that?" Take care not to express any anger, judgment, or contempt, even with employees whose performance needs significant improvement.

Avoid any use of the stale "sandwich" technique (as discussed in chapter 5), in which you share some praise, then deliver criticism, and end with more positive feedback. It can be tempting to sugarcoat constructive comments, but couching your tough feedback in fluffy compliments will only distort what you're trying to communicate, making it less likely that your direct report will discern your real message and make needed adjustments. With the sandwich approach, you can unwittingly dishearten your best employees and misguide your poorest ones.

For most of your employees—your good, solid performers and your exceptional ones—you should focus your discussion on their successes. Highlighting what competent contributors are doing well can further motivate them. For marginal performers, you'll need to take a different approach.

Recognizing strong performance

For those employees whose results and behaviors fully meet or exceed expectations, concentrate on strengths by recognizing and celebrating what they've done well. Thank your employee for their contributions. They may not know how much you appreciate their good work. This will grab their attention and also reduce the defensiveness that they might have felt at the prospect of a performance review.

Detail specific examples where their successes and strengths were most apparent: "You've increased our social media following by 8%, you did a terrific job in organizing the quarterly marketing meetings, and your contributions at staff meetings are exemplary." By starting with their most important contributions and most noteworthy strengths, focusing on achievements and pinpointing the behaviors that led to success, you'll encourage your direct report's drive and motivation.

For star performers, introduce improvements within the context of their strengths and contributions. Your conscientious employee will likely acknowledge any missed targets or unmet goals and may initiate a discussion of opportunities for improvement. If so, they can take the lead in discussing opportunities for development, which will allow them to be more invested in the conversation and "own" improvement efforts.

If your employee doesn't volunteer any areas for change, prompt them with questions such as, How do you see the situation? What do you think worked, and what could have gone better? How might you do things differently in the future? By asking questions rather than making statements, you can establish a supportive atmosphere without devaluing any of their accomplishments. By answering your questions, the person can raise issues and explore alternative approaches.

Discussing areas for improvement (however minor) may naturally lead you to talk about development opportunities. You can also delve into achievements, both to keep the person on their successful course and to find out if the employee has learned something that can benefit others. Ask, "How did you manage to do that so well?" Identifying what made the person successful can open the topic of career aspirations and avenues for further development.

Conducting appraisals for marginal performers

Performance evaluations for employees who require serious improvement should be held last. You might be tempted to get a potentially unpleasant conversation out of the way, but your skill at conducting a review session will improve with practice. You'll gain experience with easier appraisals (with your stars, for example) before you tackle this tough conversation.

If an employee's performance—their work results, behaviors, or a combination of both—is subpar, the focus of the review session should be on immediate turnaround in order for the individual to remain employed. Open the conversation by reminding the employee of the purpose of the review and acknowledging that this sort of meeting can feel awkward. Then get right to the point: "I need to tell you that your performance is not acceptable. I want to spend our time together talking about the problems I see and hearing your ideas about what you can do to correct this situation."

After this blunt opening, explain clearly what problems you perceive and make it clear that these issues must be fixed. This three-step approach can be useful:

- **State your concern precisely:** "Your approach to customer service is of serious concern."
- **Follow with examples:** "Some customers have complained about your sarcastic and condescending tone. They've noted you seem impatient and have referred to their questions as 'dumb.'"
- **Close by requesting the employee's reaction to your perception or with a specific request for change:** "I need you to change your customer service style. If you're not willing to do that, then

customer service might not be the right career for you."

This direct confrontation of unacceptable performance will be painful for the employee to hear. Marginal performers may be used to the old sandwich technique, which enabled them to selectively focus on the few positive comments and brush off any discussion of problems. They may be surprised by your negative, one-sided approach, perhaps responding that previous years' reviews have always been good and that their work this year was no different. You might acknowledge that the employee has been done a disservice by not having the facts presented clearly in previous reviews, but that doesn't change the fact that their performance this year was not acceptable, and immediate correction must occur if they are to remain employed.

As a manager, you may find this approach uncomfortable; most of us dislike confrontation. But excessive diplomacy can be just as damaging as undue harshness. Employees can't adjust their behavior in a meaningful way if the criticism they hear is indirect or sugarcoated. Embrace an opportunity to deliver and discuss meaningful criticism. Every employee deserves an honest assessment.

Some poor performers, however, may honestly believe their work has been satisfactory. In this case, frankly correct the misconception, and give the employee an opportunity to improve. The individual's performance may get substantially better with direction and support. If not, you may determine that the person is better suited to a lower-level position or that they might not be the right fit for the organization.

Get It on the Record

Documenting the details of the review session will benefit both you and your employee in case of disagreement over what you discussed or planned during the review (and in the rarer case of legal disputes). So during your conversation, jot down the main points. Include the following information in your notes:

- The date of the meeting
- Who attended (in some cases, your boss or a human resource representative may attend)
- Key points and phrases the employee used (not necessarily verbatim)
- Any points of disagreement

Take notes with pen and paper; a computer screen can create distraction and distance between the two of you. Type up your notes right after the meeting, while your memory is still fresh.

Your organization may require you to distribute copies of this record to the employee and to HR for the employee's file. You should keep a copy as well. Some organizations request that both manager and employee sign the performance review report, and sometimes the employee has the right to append their own comments.

It's helpful to separate the review and development or performance-planning sessions over time. Review conversations and constructive criticism can rouse strong feelings, and it can be difficult to engage an emotional person in creating a plan for future development or in nailing down a new set of goals. If you are able, separate the meetings by a week or so, and let your employee know at the review session that today you'll discuss performance, and next week you'll follow up to talk about plans for development or goal setting. This gives them time to process your feedback and mull over ways they can improve and grow.

That said, if any potential goals or development opportunities do arise in your review sessions, you'll want to note those as well. Write down any performance goals for the coming year, an overview of any development plans you and your direct report talk about, and a summary of agreed-upon next steps, so you'll have it for any future discussions.

NOTES

1. Quoted in Rebecca Knight, "Delivering an Effective Performance Review," HBR.org, November 3, 2011, https://hbr.org/2011/11/delivering-an-effective-perfor.
2. Quoted in Rebecca Knight, "What to Do When Your Employee Asks for a Raise Too Soon," HBR.org, July 15, 2016 (product #H030GB).

CHAPTER 15

Define New Goals for a New Cycle

Performance management is an ongoing and continuous process, so the appraisal conversation should not serve as a hard stop. Start the cycle anew by following up with your employee for a performance-planning session after the appraisal to discuss the new goals they'll start working toward, and embrace the opportunity to evaluate your own approach to performance management by soliciting feedback from your employee.

Identify New Goals, but Be Flexible

Now that you've assessed your employee's work against past goals, what new objectives should they be pursuing in the coming months? Many of your direct reports will have grown or developed over the course of the past year, mastering new skills and taking on new challenges. Think about updated goals in the context of previous conversations. Your employee's new targets should reflect any expanded abilities, development plans, and new departmental or organizational initiatives or priorities that have arisen since they last set goals.

Closing any performance gaps and tackling lingering issues should be the focus of your C players, but your solid and star contributors can have more leeway in setting their objectives, perhaps aligning them with developmental interests. As you did when you set goals in your previous performance-planning meeting, clearly define how the employee plans to reach their new objectives and set appropriate metrics for gauging success.

The beginning of a new cycle is also a good opportunity to establish or revise an employee's development plan. Determine what coaching, training, or other support will best equip them to reach their demanding new objectives and achieve even greater success in the next year.

While goals and development plans may have changed for your employee, keep your ongoing performance management processes in place. Continue your check-ins to assess progress toward goals, adjust plans, offer feedback and coaching, recognize good performance, and head off any burgeoning performance gaps.

Evaluate Your Approach

Effectively reviewing employees' performance takes practice, so use the transition time between cycles to evaluate your own performance as a manager during this process and consider how you might make improvements. Ask for feedback from your direct reports: How did the review process go? Were the feedback sessions effective? What was useful, and what wasn't? For instance, perhaps you didn't provide enough specific examples of performance gaps or give the person enough time to change based on your feedback before you followed up. Ask for suggestions for ways to do things differently in the future. You'll build trust when an individual sees you acting on the things they mention.

You can also evaluate yourself to assess your effectiveness. Consider the following questions, and take notes on your performance:

- Did you create an open climate for communication?
- Did you listen carefully to what the employee said? Did they feel heard?
- Was your feedback clear and specific? Was it useful and future focused?
- Did you spend enough time coaching?
- Were there times when you let bad performance slip, rather than giving immediate feedback?
- Did you focus sufficiently on employees' future development, or were you more focused on the present?
- What worked well, and what could be improved upon next time?

Compare your self-evaluation with any feedback from your direct reports, and determine what changes you can make in the future. Review your notes when preparing for performance reviews and periodically throughout the year as you prepare for ongoing development and check-in conversations.

Managing performance isn't easy, but with practice and thoughtful reflection you can become more comfortable with the process—and more effective in helping your employees succeed. But as with any process, there are always issues that need special attention. These obstacles are the focus of our final section.

SECTION FIVE

Tough Topics

CHAPTER 16

Responding to the Steady Worker

Capable, solid employees rarely make waves. They get their jobs done well with little fanfare or oversight. They neither cause problems that require managerial intervention nor actively pursue the opportunity to take on more responsibility or expand their roles. In fact, these B players tend to make the fewest demands on your time, despite making up 80% of your workforce.

Because these employees may not be eager to advance in the organization or require immediate improvement, performance management for these solid B players can be confounding. Although they don't actively demand your attention, they still deserve your efforts to recognize and develop them. How can you best support your solid contributors and help them grow? It depends on what's driving them.

Who Are Your B Players?

B players tend to be reserved and averse to calling attention to themselves, even when they need to. "They are like the proverbial wheel that never squeaks—and, consequently, gets no grease," write Thomas J. DeLong and Vineeta Vijayaraghavan in their HBR article "Let's Hear It for B Players." Such reserve is alien to many A players, the lead singers and guitarists eager to solo, while B player drummers and bassists keep the band on beat. These steady contributors can work well on a team without feeling the need to stand out.

There are many reasons why these individuals choose to fly under the radar. Some B players are reformed A players who rejected the pressures of the "A" way of life. They place a high premium on work-life balance and are more interested in their day-to-day work than in their long-term careers. If they enjoy their work, they have no desire to be promoted from their roles. Others may have temporarily scaled back their ambitions to spend time with their young families or wish to devote time to meaningful pursuits and hobbies outside the workplace as they approach retirement age. Some solid performers are simply more risk averse and less entrepreneurial than their ambitious counterparts. Still others may be newly improved former C players.

B players tend to be loyal to organizations, shifting jobs less often and sticking around longer than A players. Responsible and service oriented, they bring increasing depth and stability to their work over time and accumulate valuable institutional memory. B players can quietly become go-to people thanks to their extensive organizational smarts. With strong networks and interpersonal connections, they know how to get things done.

Considering this expertise, these solid workers tend to be the backbone of many organizations. B players, like everyone else, need nurturing and recognition. Without encouragement, they can fall into the trap of seeing themselves as C players—or feel they're being taken for granted. Without some level of affirmation, they may lose their motivation and enthusiasm for their work.

No category is permanent, however. Your employee may be a solid worker at the moment, but in a year or two they could well be a rising star—or a struggling underperformer. It's important to make an explicit effort to acknowledge and foster their dedicated talent without pushing them in a direction they don't want to go. To retain them, you'll need to develop them in ways that best suit their competencies, potential, and desires.

Supporting Your Steady Workers

Managers don't always consider what they need to do to retain a good performer who demonstrates no interest in being promoted to management. Typically, management will ignore or overlook valuable B players until they get fed up and leave—or become C players.

While they may not want to stretch like their more ambitious peers, neither do they want to stagnate. To develop and motivate your solid contributors, begin the same way you would with your stars: Learn about their passions and interests, deepest work values, and strongest skills.

Understand B-player priorities, and offer growth

Psychological studies suggest we're tougher on people who differ from us than on those we identify with. Differences in ambition are a matter of temperament, a complex blend of motivation, personality, and intellect. Some managers are highly motivated, ambitious A players who may need to make a conscious effort not to undervalue B players who have different priorities. After all, some people produce solid work and prioritize getting home to family at the end of the day rather than focus on authority, influence, or power.

It's important to ask all your employees what they want from their careers, particularly when dealing with promising contributors you may feel tempted to push into new, more challenging positions. For some employees, lateral movements may be more attractive than upward promotion, and still others may not be interested in a change at all. Confirming what individuals really want out of their role in the organization can keep you from being disappointed if their ambitions don't match your plan for them. It's better to know the details of how they see their careers than to attempt to mentor an ambivalent protégé who, no matter what you do, won't be driven to pursue the same aspirations you hold dear. Some B players have reached the ceiling of their abilities, while others have made a conscious choice to stay in their current position.

Don't force an unwilling or uninterested B player to the A level, but do offer them opportunities to continue to learn, grow, and improve their skills. Stretch assignments, for example, can be invigorating opportunities to challenge your employees to acquire new skills, but choose such assignments carefully so you don't overwhelm them. Look for ways to make their jobs more interesting without burdening them with unwanted new responsibilities. Perhaps they'd appreciate training to bolster their strengths or the chance to attend a conference or seminar on a topic that excites them. Provide them with opportunities to grow within their comfort zone.

Your employee's priorities may change over time as well. If at first they tell you that they'd like to stay in their current role, check in periodically to find out if they've changed their mind, and if so, adjust their development plan accordingly.

Recognize and reward them

Strong and capable contributors can feel alienated or frustrated by a lack of attention, even if they don't seek out the spotlight. Track the frequency of your interactions with each of your direct reports. A players are rarely shy about asking for your time or stopping by to talk with you, but B players may be less likely to initiate contact. Make a point of regularly meeting with all of your employees, including the ones who never ask for it.

Acknowledge and praise B players' good work, and provide frequent affirmation. Recognition is especially important to workers who aren't gunning for a promotion. They neither expect nor receive the same financial rewards or promotions as A players, but they still crave acknowledgment of their very real contributions to the organization and want to feel appreciated and motivated. Tell them on a regular basis that they are valued, and tailor your praise to how each individual prefers to receive it. Some people appreciate public accolades, while others would prefer a simple handwritten note or a one-on-one conversation in which you thank them for their good work.

You can also show how much you trust and value your steady contributors by listening carefully to any ideas or suggestions they provide. Respond thoughtfully and respectfully. Show you recognize their contribution by giving them credit for any suggestions you act on, and demonstrate your trust by letting them be autonomous and make decisions appropriate for their skill level. You can also tap your capable contributors to mentor junior employees, demonstrating your trust in their knowledge and expertise.

All employees, not just stars, should be given opportunities for coaching, development, and—if they're interested—promotion, whether upward or lateral. Don't let your solid performers get lost in the crowd.

CHAPTER 17

Preventing Burnout on Your Team

Every once in a while, you'll encounter a poor performer who was once, according to your records, an excellent employee. This person is now just going through the motions and getting by—or worse, failing to meet expectations. What went wrong? You may be looking at a case of burnout.

Burnout is a debilitating state of work-related stress and a common danger for your best employees. People suffering from burnout will often exhibit three symptoms: exhaustion, cynicism, and inefficacy. Exhaustion includes physical, cognitive, and emotional fatigue so profound that it undermines a person's ability to work effectively and to feel good about what they're doing. Cynicism is an erosion of engagement—a way of distancing oneself psychologically from one's work. Inefficacy is a sense of incompetence and a lack of achievement and productivity.

This toxic cocktail manifests differently in each individual, but common signals include tiredness, lack of focus, expressions of anger or hopelessness, lower job performance and satisfaction, dwindling commitment to the organization, and a heightened desire to "do something different." Burnout can turn your A players into Bs and Bs into Cs. In some cases it's self-induced, but more often it's a result of heavy workloads, deadline pressures, and a nonstop workplace culture that precludes necessary rest and renewal.

As a manager, it's your job to ensure that your direct reports remain engaged and motivated in their work and performing at their highest capacity, which means helping them avoid taking on too much and encouraging them to take time to recharge.

Causes of Burnout

In a fast-paced, intense workplace where people are pressured to be perpetually on the clock, employees are more prone to anxiety, stress, and eventually burnout—especially top performers. Because it's not an official clinical term, hard data on the prevalence of burnout is elusive, but some researchers have found rates of burnout as high as 50% among medical residents and a whopping 85% among financial professionals.[1] In a 2015 Regus Group survey of more than 22,000 businesspeople across 100 countries, more than half (53%) reported being closer to burnout than they were just five years previously.[2]

Burnout occurs when an employee feels more stress than support in their work life. You risk burnout on your team if your employees are chronically overworked or under-rested. Common causes of burnout include:

- Work overload and extreme job demands, when people are given more work than can be reasonably accomplished in even a 60-hour workweek
- Streamlined staffing levels, when an individual is responsible for more work than one person can sustainably do
- The expectation of constant connectivity, when people feel pressured to work remotely (by email or phone) after work hours with little downtime
- The inability to avoid "low value-added" and monotonous tasks such as paperwork or unnecessary meetings
- Having too many projects to work on simultaneously, which creates interruptions and distractions and diminishes people's ability to focus and prioritize among projects
- High demands with low control, or conflicting demands—for example, "Think big and be creative, but don't make any mistakes"

Those most susceptible to burnout are your hardest-working, most-committed employees. They can become so involved in their jobs that they neglect other important parts of their lives, which can damage family and personal relationships as well as health. Managers can unwittingly contribute to employee burnout by relying too much on these individuals, loading all their critical projects on the same top performers—and then assigning them more important projects once they've succeeded. Don't make your employees choose between work and their mental and physical well-being. Even people who love their work shouldn't neglect everything else in their lives to take on more responsibilities.

Help Your Team Avoid Burnout

You can take steps to prevent burnout in your employees. Of course, occasional overwork may be unavoidable due to deadlines or peak work periods, but it shouldn't be constant. To keep your employees energized but not overworked, consider the following tactics.

Regularly monitor workloads, especially for your top performers

The very act of noticing an employee's overload can help them feel supported. Meet with each of your direct reports regularly to check in on how they're doing and to see if they are showing any indication that they may be overworked. (See the sidebar "Spot the Early Signs of Burnout.") If someone shows symptoms of burnout, look at their job description and their list of current tasks. It could be that they are juggling too many projects at once. Help them focus on doing one thing at a time by defining clear priorities for deliverables, ensuring that milestones don't overlap, and discerning the urgent from the important.

If the job's responsibilities are beyond the powers of even an exceptional worker, you may need to rethink their to-do list entirely. See if you can delegate some of the tasks to another team member (or even have a teammate step in temporarily to help), or consider redesigning the position.

Your employee may not want to admit to feeling overworked for fear that it will shed a negative light on them. But as a manager, you still need to see if they're able to handle everything on their plate. Get creative. For example, a major U.S. accounting firm monitored its employees' workloads by screening travel schedules. Individuals observed to be spending excessive time on the road or volunteering for too many projects were identified and counseled.

SPOT THE EARLY SIGNS OF BURNOUT

Burnout can be obvious in some people and more subtle in others. It will manifest differently in each individual. Here are some warning signs that your employee may be overworked:

- They struggle to concentrate or see the big picture.
- Routine or previously enjoyable tasks—even just getting to the office—appear difficult.

(continued)

SPOT THE EARLY SIGNS OF BURNOUT

- They seem disengaged or detached from their work, colleagues, and customers.
- They have grown increasingly negative, callous, or hostile.
- Their performance is slipping.
- They've expressed self-doubt or worry about completing tasks.

Your employee may not directly express their concern about their workload, so be a keen observer and an attentive listener. Acknowledge subtle cries for help: "I don't know how I'm going to keep up," "I'm swamped," or "It looks like I'll have to work over the weekend *again*."

If you spot any of these troubling signs, check in to gauge your employee's physical, cognitive, and emotional energy levels. If impending burnout is the problem rather than a personal issue or a temporary work upset, take corrective action before their performance suffers in the long term or they leave your company altogether.

Rein in excessive time demands

Many of us work in environments where we're expected to be accessible at all hours, even when we're on vacation. But constant connectivity costs us. Everyone needs rest and recovery time, and no one can sustain working all day, in the evening, and over the weekend. If people are available 24/7, they have no time to recharge.

With the exception of the occasional deadline, product launch, or emergency, don't require any employees to do more work than can be reasonably accomplished during a standard workweek ("standard" hours will vary across industries). Assess your team's current collective capacity, and ensure assignments and deadlines don't exceed it. Set boundaries: For example, demand that no emails are to be sent after 8 p.m. or on weekends.

Purposefully build in breaks

If you treat every day like a crisis and employees are chronically overworked, they won't have the energy, mental focus, resilience, or time to respond effectively if and when an actual crisis hits. Encourage your team to take breaks—from a simple lunch break to finally using their saved vacation time. Different fields have different busy times: Some must rush to meet end-of-year or end-of-quarter deadlines, some calendars orbit the do-or-die date of April 15, others are busiest when the school year kicks off. Identify a slow time when your employees can take a break—whether it's a short break during the day, an evening off during a crunch period, or a vacation. When individuals do take time off, build in enough teamwork and overlapping responsibilities to allow them to truly disconnect, without the need for employees to check their inbox for updates.

For example, professor Leslie Perlow and research associate Jessica Porter, both of Harvard Business School, worked with Boston Consulting Group (BCG) to see if it was possible to meet the high standards of service while still offering employees scheduled, uninterrupted time off. Each team assigned, in advance, at least one evening off per week for each team member to rest and recharge. They then adjusted the workload on the team so that others would cover for those individuals and their work wouldn't fall behind. The results were positive. According to Perlow and Porter, participants with rotating evenings off reported "higher job satisfaction, greater likelihood that they could imagine a long-term career at the firm, and higher satisfaction with work-life balance" than people on teams who didn't plan time off.[3] You can create a similar system that will let your team turn off and recharge on a regular basis, even if there's no natural break in your work cycle.

Allow for flexibility

It's not the number of hours worked but the quality of work that really matters. Instead of fretting about the time someone spends at their desk, help your employees design schedules that allow them to be more productive when they *are* working. Some folks work best in 90-minute periods followed by a 10-minute break, while others thrive on the "Pomodoro Technique" of 25-minute increments of work with 5-minute breaks. Create uninterrupted, meeting-free time for people to focus on important tasks that works with their rhythm and your needs.

Also consider the balance of priorities your employees have—not just in the office, but at home, too. People are at their most productive when they're able to adjust the time and place of their work to avoid conflicts with other responsibilities. If your top employee is struggling to get a full day of work in and arrive at home in time to deal with family demands, consider whether there are ways to allow them to get home earlier while still getting their best work from them. Your organization may have a formal program in place for you and your employees to take advantage of flextime or telecommuting arrangements, but if not, informal or ad hoc agreements can be just as or more effective. Work with your employees to design flexible arrangements that suit their job responsibilities, work styles, and personal demands.

Then, set them up for success. Advocate for the resources your people need to perform—by providing new technology or software, for example—to ensure your employees can work virtually without missing crucial communication or meetings.

Provide variety

People periodically need new challenges to stay motivated and committed, so vary your employees' tasks and responsibilities from time to time. Doing so will help your employees avoid burnout by shifting their attention to a fresh, exciting opportunity rather than feeling like they are in the same monotonous rut. You might, for example, give one person in your department responsibility for leading a team-based project for the next six months; after that time period, rotate the task to someone else. Instead of doling out responsibilities randomly, think about what might be the best options for each individual, and emphasize any professional-development benefits those opportunities might provide. Add these temporary responsibilities to the individual's performance objectives so that they're taken seriously.

While all of these steps can keep your employees from burning out, remember that they learn from you, their manager. If a direct reports sees you regularly eating at your desk, emailing late at night, or working through the weekend, they'll follow suit. Set an example, and follow these tips yourself. Not only will you show your employees it's OK to recharge, but you'll also avoid burnout yourself.

Being an attentive manager and deliberately watching for signs of burnout can help you keep your employees healthy and productive. Don't risk losing your top performers just because you're asking too much of them.

NOTES

1. "Statistics and Facts about Stress and Burnout," Statista.com, https://www.statista.com/topics/2099/stress-and-burnout.
2. Research by Regus Group, http://press.regus.com/hong-kong/majority-on-brink-of-stress.
3. Leslie A. Perlow and Jessica L. Porter, "Making Time Off Predictable—and Required," *Harvard Business Review*, October 2009 (product #R0910M).

CHAPTER 18

Managing the Performance of Remote Employees

Flexible work arrangements, telecommuting, and global offices may mean your employees aren't all sitting together in one central office. According to data from the Global Workplace Analytics, a research-based consulting organization, as of 2014, 3.7 million people worked remotely.[1] As virtual work arrangements become more common, you will likely need to apply the elements of performance management to someone you rarely, if ever, see in person.

Managing remote employees isn't fundamentally different than managing those who are physically present in your workplace, but communication challenges can easily arise when you're not colocated. Giving difficult feedback or discussing a tough performance review always requires special handling, but these tasks are further complicated when the person you're talking with isn't in the room with you to hear your tone or see subtle cues in body language. You'll need to put in extra effort to minimize the likelihood of off-site isolation, cultivate a positive team dynamic, address problems, and evaluate performance.

Whether your team members are in different time zones or simply working from home, you'll need to take a proactive approach to performance management.

Set Goals and Expectations

With remote employees, it's essential to establish a common purpose and to frame work in terms of individual team members' ambitions and needs. Clarify goals, and spell out specific guidelines for how you'll work together. Don't forget the details. Beyond identifying how projects will be divvied up, you may need to determine standards for communication that wouldn't be an issue with colocated employees, such as how the individual will collaborate with others on the team and how they'll communicate with you, their manager.

Just as you would with a direct report working in your office, schedule a performance-planning meeting, a one-on-one conversation to identify your remote employee's specific goals. Don't just trade emails; set up a video chat or, at a minimum, speak by phone. You'll have a more productive discussion, especially about professional aims and ambitions, when both of you can observe body language and hear tone and inflection. Carry the conversation much like you would with your other employees (as outlined in chapter 2), but make note of any challenges they may face because they aren't working regularly in your office. Consider if they will require additional resources to help them reach their objectives.

Once goals have been established, ask your employee to submit suggestions for meaningful performance metrics, especially for nonquantitative goals. Set clear targets—monthly, quarterly, and yearly performance milestones—to establish accountability. By collaborating with your employee in this way, they'll feel more invested in objectives, and they'll have a clear understanding about what they need to do to meet them. Finally, ensure that they know how they'll be evaluated—and assure them that you're using the same metrics you will use with the rest of your team, so they know that any future feedback or assessments will be fair.

Manage Performance and Communication

A key challenge for remote employees is isolation. Virtual workers are more prone to loneliness and loss of motivation, which can result in compromised performance. You probably won't get the opportunity to pick up visual cues or have impromptu conversations with a remote worker, so you'll need to make an extra effort to see how they're doing, keep an eye out for signs of burnout, and provide ongoing feedback. Keep the lines of communication open to prevent your remote employee from feeling truly isolated.

Just as with any other direct report, check in regularly on your remote employee's progress. You may need to be more rigorous about scheduling ongoing conversations with these workers than you would with team members you run into in the hallway or cafeteria. Even casual conversations with remote employees may need to be scheduled in advance.

When you touch base with your employee, choose communication tools carefully. Without physical cues, anyone can miss the subtleties of in-person interactions—especially during a tough conversation, such as when you're delivering constructive feedback. Face-to-face discussions are ideal, but don't hold off on having a crucial conversation or even a casual check-in just because you're waiting for an upcoming visit. Consider alternatives such as the phone, email, video, instant message, text, or group chat applications, but note that one platform won't work for every situation. Texting, IM, and team-messaging apps are lighter-touch options that carry lower emotional stakes. Information that might elicit an emotional response is better captured by phone or video, since they can allow you to project empathy, trust, concern, or firmness.

Phrase inquiries wisely when checking in. For example, when sending a quick email or IM, "Looking forward to seeing your product demo on Friday! Anything you need from me?" sounds enthusiastic and supportive. Compare this with something like "On track for Friday's deadline?" which may convey aggression and distrust.

Tracking performance from afar

When assessing work, tailor your approach to your remote employees. Take advantage of the opportunity to gather details about your direct reports' performance during team meetings. This may be the best time to assess how your remote employees work with their colleagues. Write each person's name on a pad of paper, and list their suggestions, questions, and comments. (If you find it too distracting to do this during the meeting, capture your observations immediately afterward.) When someone brings up a problem no one else has thought of, stubbornly repeats a point, or credits a colleague for doing good work, jot that down. Follow the same process as you observe conversations over discussion boards and group chats. Note who's giving helpful feedback, making smart suggestions, mediating conflict, or contributing in some other way. By capturing these details, you're creating a performance record you can refer to later.

As with any other employee, address performance issues with sensitivity. Start by gathering information. Your direct report's colleagues may have a different vantage point or more information on areas of concern. Keep in mind, though, that unless they're located in the same office as the remote worker, collaborators may not have a full picture either.

You can ask specific questions but also get more context with open-ended questions such as:

- "How's the project going with Ahkil overall?"
- "How are you finding him as a collaborator?"

- "Akhil has been doing a great job, but I'm wondering if I can do more to support his engagement. Have you observed anything that might help?"
- "You mentioned that Akhil has seemed checked out lately. When did that start? What do you think is going on?"

Handle these sensitive conversations with great care, and keep them confidential. The employee may not want a written record of any complaints or speculations, so hold these conversations by phone or video if you can't have them in person.

If you find that the situation warrants a discussion with your remote employee, prepare as you would for any feedback conversation. Consider the bigger picture: Do you know what else is going on in your employee's personal and professional life? Collect facts in advance, focus on observable behaviors, and don't speculate. Probe for root causes, so you feel fully prepared before having the conversation.

Giving feedback

When you notice something troubling in your remote employee's work that could grow into a performance gap if left unattended, address it with the same strategies you'd use in a traditional office setting. Follow up to investigate anomalies. You'll probably notice behavioral cues if someone is struggling or behind on their work. They might be uncharacteristically uncommunicative or have changed the frequency of their communications. They may seem frustrated, anxious, or even unusually relaxed before a major deadline while all their colleagues seem crunched. If you sense something is off, don't delay in reaching out to them.

When it comes to more-sensitive conversations—coaching, giving feedback, or discussing performance problems, for example—don't dictate the medium; ask your direct report what they prefer. You may well have a preference, perhaps for phone or video, but different tools can be more effective with different people. Video can provide helpful context and visual cues, but if the internet connection is poor it's more likely to be distracting than helpful. It may be worth investing in better technical gear, like a high-quality headset, to ensure you catch every nuance.

It can take special effort to give feedback effectively in a virtual setting. A written statement—say, "Your recent work contained some major problems"—seems much harsher than the same message delivered in conversation with a compassionate tone. Pay particular attention to timing. As with the employees you see regularly, you shouldn't plan to deliver tough criticism right before the person has another meeting or while they're in the last throes of a time-sensitive project. On the other hand, when it comes to recognizing strong performance, you don't need to be so careful. (Positive feedback, unlike criticism, can be delivered in writing, but your delivery will be more nuanced if you're communicating by phone or video.)

If you're using video when offering constructive feedback, position your camera at eye level; any lower will make it seem like you're looming above them. Maintain natural eye contact, and keep your body language open and relaxed. Start your conversation with the usual small talk, but make an extra effort to be warm. Because it can be difficult for people to pick up emotional cues by phone or video, be explicit about your positive feelings: "I really enjoy working with you. We've got some work to do, but I'm confident we'll get there." Express your appreciation for their work, or offer some positive feedback, if appropriate: what they are doing well or what they have made easier for you. Since your virtual employee may not have the opportunity to read your tone or body language, establishing this mutual trust and reassurance will help your message become more palatable. Keep in mind, though, that you don't want to couch your constructive comments in too much positivity, in case your request for improvement is lost. Just say enough to confirm to your employee that you're on the same team and on their side.

Limit your critical feedback to discussing a specific behavior. Offer concrete, narrowly focused comments that are free of speculation. Listen actively to their reply, and ask if anything seems wrong. If they won't meet your eyes in a video chat, for example, they could be feeling attacked, or it could just be due to camera placement.

End the conversation with an action item. Ideally, your direct report should offer a plan for fixing the problem themselves, at which point you can ask how you can help execute it. In some cases, though, you'll need to suggest a solution yourself. Thank them for the conversation before logging off, and follow up with an email summarizing how you agreed to proceed and reiterating your thanks.

Conduct the Appraisal Discussion

If your company requires a formal performance appraisal, that task can seem much harder when you're not seeing or talking to an employee on a regular basis. But if you've kept the lines of communication open throughout the review period, checked in with your employee, taken good notes, and provided feedback, you should have everything you need to help the process go smoothly.

Evaluate everyone equally

In traditional offices, it's easy to base assessments on observed face time: Who comes in early, stays late, and looks busy? But when a department allows employees to telecommute or is spread across multiple locations, management often develops a new process for evaluating remote individuals using specific metrics, while in-office workers are still assessed with the old approach. Face time unfairly becomes a factor in evaluating some but not others. While rarely a deliberate choice in the appraisal process, this disconnect in evaluation standards is especially problematic when an organization requires forced ranking. Remote employees may be "out of sight, out of mind" and overlooked for promotions or raises.

When employees work remotely, face time isn't something you can realistically assess and shouldn't be used as a performance metric. Instead, change your perspective to focus on the what and how of work. Evaluate the performance of remote employees in the same way as their office-based colleagues, and ensure that the same metrics are applied to everyone.

If you use a rating system, be sure to include context—concrete details that have contributed to the rating—in addition to a number. Remote workers are by nature somewhat isolated and may not have a good sense of how they and their colleagues are being evaluated. Receiving a numerical rating with no understanding of how it was decided does not make for a helpful or productive appraisal. Include details so the employee understands where they're falling short and how they can improve.

Avoid self-assessments

Unlike with your on-site employees, limit the use of self-assessments with your remote direct reports. Anyone who works alone much of the time can end up in a vacuum of their own perception. We all share the tendency to overrate our own abilities and take the credit for good results while denying our role in bad ones, but we're more likely to fall victim to these qualities when we're on our own. If your organization doesn't require self-assessments, don't use them. But if you must, emphasize to your virtual workers (as you would with the rest of your employees) that their self-evaluation is just one component of your performance review.

Conduct the conversation with care

Any employee can go through the motions of the appraisal process, never speaking their minds to avoid conflict—and the danger of this is greater with remote employees who may already feel disconnected. For a sensitive conversation like a performance review, ask your direct report how they'd be most comfortable meeting. Video conferencing will allow for a more-nuanced conversation, but if speaking by phone would make your employee more at ease, comply with their wishes. The more often you communicate by video during the course of the year, the more comfortable both of you will be using the medium, but if it's not something you do often, don't insist on it for an appraisal. Applying an unfamiliar technology to an already anxiety-inducing conversation may only make it more stressful for your employee. Accepting their preference will set a tone of participation and collaboration, increasing the likelihood that your remote direct report will feel comfortable being candid.

Tone of voice, facial expression, gestures, and nonverbal communication all matter in review conversations—particularly when you can't be together in person. Without contextual clues, misunderstandings can easily arise. As you did when giving feedback, be crystal clear when delivering feedback, and linger on positive messages. In the stress of an appraisal conversation, it's easy for anyone (particularly a remote worker) to focus more on constructive comments than on positive ones, so emphasize your positive feedback more than you might in an in-person meeting. After the discussion, continue the process again by setting up another meeting to establish goals and by keeping the lines of communication open.

Successfully managing your employees' performance involves a host of tasks and processes. Whether your employees are across the hall or across the globe, you should be ready to focus their efforts on the objectives that matter, work with them to move toward those goals, and ensure that they're growing, developing, and improving. Performance management may be changing rapidly, but by following the elements and best practices outlined in this guide, you can make managing performance a part of your regular routine and ensure that you get the best out of your people.

NOTE

1. GlobalWorkplaceAnalytics.com, "Latest Telecommuting Statistics," http://globalworkplaceanalytics.com/telecommuting-statistics.

Sources

General Sources

Buckingham, Marcus. "What Great Managers Do." *Harvard Business Review*, March 2005 (product #R0503D).

Buckingham, Marcus, and Ashley Goodall. "Reinventing Performance Management." *Harvard Business Review*, April 2015 (product #R1504B).

Cappelli, Peter, and Anna Tavis. "The Performance Management Revolution." *Harvard Business Review*, October 2016 (product #R1610D).

Dattner, Ben. "The Key to Performance Reviews Is Preparation." HBR.org, June 21, 2016 (product #H02WXG).

Ferrazzi, Keith. "7 Ways to Improve Employee Development Programs." HBR.org, July 31, 2015 (product #H028T9).

Goler, Lori, Janelle Gale, and Adam Grant. "Let's Not Kill Performance Evaluations Yet." *Harvard Business Review*, November 2016 (product #R1611G).

Grote, Dick. *How to Be Good at Performance Appraisals*. Boston: Harvard Business Review Press, 2011.

Harvard Business School Publishing. *Harvard Business Essentials: Performance Management*. Boston: Harvard Business School Press, 2006.

Harvard Business School Publishing. *HBR Guide to Coaching Employees*. Boston: Harvard Business Review Press, 2015.

Harvard Business School Publishing. *HBR Guide to Delivering Effective Feedback*. Boston: Harvard Business Review Press, 2016.

Harvard Business School Publishing. *Pocket Mentor: Developing Employees*. Boston: Harvard Business Press, 2009.

Harvard Business School Publishing. *Pocket Mentor: Setting Goals.* Boston: Harvard Business Press, 2009.

Harvard Business School Publishing. *20-Minute Manager: Performance Reviews.* Boston: Harvard Business Review Press, 2015.

Knight, Rebecca. "Delivering an Effective Performance Review." HBR.org, November 3, 2011. https://hbr.org/2011/11/delivering-an-effective-perfor.

Knight, Rebecca. "What to Do When Your Employee Asks for a Raise Too Soon." HBR.org, July 15, 2016 (product #H030GB).

McCord, Patty. "How Netflix Reinvented HR." *Harvard Business Review*, January–February 2014 (product #R1401E).

Wiseman, Liz. "An Easy Way to Make Your Employees Happier." HBR.org, November 13, 2014 (product #H01OZB).

Additional Chapter-by-Chapter Sources

Introduction

Cappelli, Peter. "The Annual Review Revolution." HBR.org Webinar, October 13, 2016. https://hbr.org/webinar/2016/09/the-annual-review-revolution.

Chapter 1

Grant, Heidi. "Nine Things Successful People Do Differently." *HBR Guide to Getting the Right Work Done.* Boston: Harvard Business Review Press, 2012.

Raynor, Michael E., and Derek Pankratz. "A Way to Know If Your Corporate Goals Are Too Aggressive." HBR.org, July 13, 2015 (product #H0278K).

Chapter 2

Bregman, Peter. "The Right Way to Hold People Accountable." HBR.org, January 11, 2016 (product #H02LQR).

Kirsner, Scott. "What Big Companies Get Wrong About Innovation Metrics." HBR.org, May 6, 2015 (product #H021XV).

Chapter 3

Grant, Heidi. "Get Your Team to Do What It Says It's Going to Do." *Harvard Business Review*, May 2014 (product #R1405E).

Chapter 4

Pozen, Robert C. "The Delicate Art of Giving Feedback." HBR.org, March 28, 2013. https://hbr.org/2013/03/the-delicate-art-of-giving-fee.

Zenger, Jack, and Joseph Folkman. "The Ideal Praise-to-Criticism Ratio." HBR.org, March 15, 2013. https://hbr.org/2013/03/the-ideal-praise-to-criticism.

Chapter 5

Gallo, Amy. "Giving a High Performer Productive Feedback." HBR.org, December 3, 2009. https://hbr.org/2009/12/giving-a-high-performer-produc.

Grant, Heidi. "Sometimes Negative Feedback Is Best." HBR.org, January 28, 2013. https://hbr.org/2013/01/sometimes-negative-feedback-is.

Grenny, Joseph. "How to Make Feedback Feel Normal." HBR.org, August 19, 2016 (product #H032G0).

Chapter 6

Hill, Linda, and Kent Lineback. "To Build Trust, Competence Is Key." HBR.org, March 22, 2012. https://hbr.org/2012/03/to-build-trust-competence-is-k.

Valcour, Monique. "You Can't Be a Great Manager If You're Not a Good Coach." HBR.org, July 17, 2014 (product #H00WOP).

Chapter 7

Cable, Dan, and Freek Vermeulen. "Stop Paying Executives for Performance." HBR.org, February 23, 2016 (product #H02OEX).

Harvard Business School Publishing. "Employee Recognition and Reward When Times Are Tough." *Harvard Management Update*. September 2003. https://hbr.org/2008/02/employee-recognition-and-rewar-1.html.

Hope, Jeremy, and Steve Player. *Beyond Performance Management*. Boston: Harvard Business Review Press, 2012.

Kohn, Alfie. "Why Incentive Plans Cannot Work." *Harvard Business Review*, September–October 1993 (product #93506).

Novak, David. "Recognizing Employees Is the Simplest Way to Improve Morale." HBR.org, May 9, 2016 (product #H02VEN).

Porath, Christine. "Half of Employees Don't Feel Respected by Their Bosses." HBR.org, November 19, 2014 (product #H012OO).

Porath, Christine, and Christine Pearson. "The Price of Incivility." *Harvard Business Review*, January–February 2013 (product #R1301J).

Spreitzer, Gretchen, and Christine Porath. "Creating Sustainable Performance." *Harvard Business Review*, January–February 2012 (product #R1201F).

Valcour, Monique. "The Power of Dignity in the Workplace." HBR.org, April 28, 2014 (product #H00S6P).

Chapter 8

Andersen, Erika. "How to Decide What Skill to Work On Next." HBR.org, January 25, 2016 (product #H02M5W).

Butler, Timothy, and James Waldroop. "Job Sculpting: The Art of Retaining Your Best People." *Harvard Business Review*, September–October 1999 (product #99502).

Donovan, John, and Cathy Benko. "AT&T's Talent Overhaul." *Harvard Business Review*, October 2016 (product #R1610E).

Gino, Francesca, and Bradley Staats. "Developing Employees Who Think for Themselves." HBR.org, June 3, 2015 (product #H0248M).

Herzberg, Frederick. "One More Time: How Do You Motivate Employees?" *Harvard Business Review*, January 2003 (product #R0301F).

Jen Su, Amy. "The Questions Good Coaches Ask." HBR.org, December 12, 2014 (product #H01R6J).

Valcour, Monique. "If You're Not Helping People Develop, You're Not Management Material." HBR.org, January 23, 2014 (product #H00MXT).

Chapter 9

Gallo, Amy. "Demystifying Mentoring." HBR.org, February 1, 2011 (product #H006S6).

Harvard Business School Publishing. *HBR Guide to Getting the Mentoring You Need.* Boston: Harvard Business Review Press, 2014.

Hewlett, Sylvia Ann. "The Real Benefit of Finding a Sponsor." HBR.org, January 26, 2011. https://hbr.org/2011/01/the-real-benefit-of-finding-a.

Hewlett, Sylvia Ann. "The Right Way to Find a Career Sponsor." HBR.org, September 11, 2013. https://hbr.org/2013/09/the-right-way-to-find-a-career-sponsor.

Hoffman, Reid, Ben Casnocha, and Chris Yeh. "Tours of Duty: The New Employer-Employee Compact." *Harvard Business Review*, June 2013 (product #R1306B).

Tjan, Anthony K. "Keeping Great People with Three Kinds of Mentors." HBR.org, August 12, 2011 (product #H007LK).

Chapter 10

Brendel, David. "Asking Open-Ended Questions Helps New Managers Build Trust." HBR.org, September 17, 2015 (product #H02CEG).

Goldsmith, Marshall. "Empowering Your Employees to Empower Themselves." HBR.org, April 23, 2010. https://hbr.org/2010/04/empowering-your-employees-to-e.

Petriglieri, Gianpiero. "Learning Is the Most Celebrated Neglected Activity in the Workplace." HBR.org, November 6, 2014 (product #H012ON).

Wiseman, Liz, and Greg McKeown. "Bringing Out the Best in Your People." *Harvard Business Review*, May 2010 (product #R1005K).

Chapter 11

Baldoni, John. "The Three Cs of Dealing with Under Performers." HBR.org, September 10, 2008. https://hbr.org/2008/09/underperformers.

Gallo, Amy. "Help! I'm an Underperformer." HBR.org, October 5, 2010. https://hbr.org/2010/10/help-im-an-underperformer.

Gallo, Amy. "How to Help an Underperformer." HBR.org, June 23, 2014 (product #H00VK2).

Gallo, Amy. "Making Sure Your Employees Succeed." HBR.org, February 7, 2011. https://hbr.org/2011/02/making-sure-your-employees-suc.

Hill, Linda, and Kent Lineback. "The Most Important Question a Manager Can Ask." HBR.org, April 18, 2011. https://hbr.org/2011/04/the-most-important-question-a.

Maignan Wilkins, Muriel. "Is Your Employee Coachable?" HBR.org, February 19, 2015 (product #H01VYV).

Chapter 12

Baldassarre, Leonardo, and Brian Finken. "GE's Real-Time Performance Development." HBR.org, August 12, 2015 (product #H029L8).

Buckingham, Marcus. "What If Performance Management Focused on Strengths?" HBR.org, December 3, 2013. https://hbr.org/2013/12/what-if-performance-management-focused-on-strengths.

Cappelli, Peter. "The Common Myths About Performance Reviews, Debunked." HBR.org, July 26, 2016 (product #H030NZ).

Grote, Dick. "Every Manager Needs to Practice Two Types of Coaching." HBR.org, September 30, 2016 (product #H035HV).

Rock, David. "Give Your Performance Management System a Review." HBR.org, June 14, 2013. https://hbr.org/2013/06/give-your-performance-manageme.

Chapter 13

Dattner, Ben. "In Performance Appraisals, Make Context Count." HBR.org, June 3, 2013. https://hbr.org/2013/06/in-performance-appraisals-make.

Grote, Dick. "Performance Appraisal Reappraised." *Harvard Business Review*, January–February 2000 (product #F00105).

Harvard Business School Publishing. *HBR Guide to Delivering Effective Feedback Ebook + Tools*. Boston: Harvard Business Review Press, 2016.

Chapter 16

DeLong, Thomas J., and Vineeta Vijayaraghavan. "Let's Hear It for B Players." *Harvard Business Review*, June 2003 (product #R0306F).

Chapter 17

Behson, Scott. "Don't Treat Your Career Marathon Like a Sprint." HBR.org, October 11, 2013. https://hbr.org/2013/10/dont-treat-your-career-marathon-like-a-sprint.

Behson, Scott. "Just Because You're Happy Doesn't Mean You're Not Burned Out." HBR.org, July 13, 2015 (product #H027AF).

Fernandez, Rich. "Help Your Team Manage Stress, Anxiety, and Burnout." HBR.org, January 21, 2016 (product #H02M4Z).

Perlow, Leslie A., and Jessica L. Porter. "Making Time Off Predictable—and Required." *Harvard Business Review*, October 2009 (product #R0910M).

Schwartz, Tony. "Take Back Your Attention." HBR.org, February 9, 2011. https://hbr.org/2011/02/take-back-your-attention.

Valcour, Monique. "Beating Burnout." *Harvard Business Review*, November 2016 (product #R1611H).

Wilson, H. James. "The Surprising Power of Impulse Control." HBR.org, February 25, 2014 (product #H00OSS).

Chapter 18

Batista, Ed. "Tips for Coaching Someone Remotely." HBR.org, March 18, 2015 (product #H01XI4).

Ferrazzi, Keith. "Evaluating the Employees You Can't See." HBR.org, December 20, 2012. https://hbr.org/2012/12/evaluating-the-employees-you-c.

Ferrazzi, Keith. "Getting Virtual Teams Right," *Harvard Business Review*, December 2014 (product #R1412J).

Graber, Sean. "Why Remote Work Thrives in Some Companies and Fails in Others." HBR.org, March 20, 2015 (product #H01Y22).

Harvard Business School Publishing. *20-Minute Manager: Leading Virtual Teams*. Boston: Harvard Business Review Press, 2016.

Harvard Business School Publishing. *20-Minute Manager: Virtual Collaboration*. Boston: Harvard Business Review Press, 2016.

Knight, Rebecca. "How to Manage Remote Direct Reports." HBR.org, February 10, 2015 (product #H01VI9).

Rayess, Randy. "5 Basic Needs of Virtual Workforces." HBR.org, March 17, 2015 (product #H01X2Z).

Index

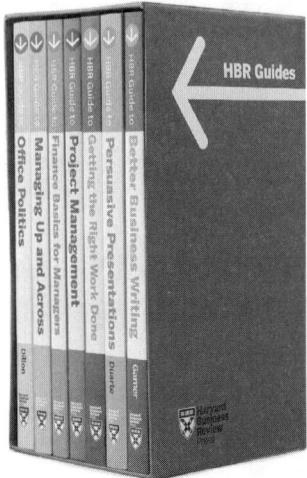

HBR Guide to
Finance Basics for Managers

Harvard Business Review Guides

Arm yourself with the advice you need to succeed on the job, from the most trusted brand in business. Packed with how-to essentials from leading experts, the HBR Guides provide smart answers to your most pressing work challenges.

The titles include:

HBR Guide to Better Business Writing

HBR Guide to Finance Basics for Managers

HBR Guide to Getting the Mentoring You Need

HBR Guide to Getting the Right Job

HBR Guide to Getting the Right Work Done

HBR Guide to Giving Effective Feedback

HBR Guide to Making Every Meeting Matter

HBR Guide to Managing Stress at Work

HBR Guide to Managing Up and Across

HBR Guide to Persuasive Presentations

HBR Guide to Project Management

HBR Guide to **Finance Basics for Managers**

HARVARD BUSINESS REVIEW PRESS

Boston, Massachusetts

Printed in the United States of America

21

Library of Congress Cataloging-in-Publication Data

HBR guide to finance basics for managers.
p. cm. — (Harvard business review guides)
ISBN 978-1-4221-8730-2 (alk. paper)
1. Business enterprises—Finance. 2. Financial statements.
I. Harvard business review.
HG4026.H435 2012
658.15—dc23

2012026162

The paper used in this publication meets the requirements of the American National Standard for Permanence of Paper for Publications and Documents in Libraries and Archives z39.48-1992.

What You'll Learn

Where do you begin if your boss asks you to prepare a breakeven analysis? Can you tell the difference between an income statement and a balance sheet? Between gross margin and revenue? Do you understand why a business that's profitable can still go belly-up? Has your grasp of your company's numbers helped—or hurt—your career?

If questions like these make you sweat, you've come to the right place. This guide will give you the tools and confidence you need to master finance basics, as *all* good managers must. You'll learn how to:

- Speak the language of finance
- Compare your firm's financials with rivals'
- Size up your vulnerability to industry downturns
- Shift your unit's focus from revenues to profits
- Use financial data to defend budget requests
- Avoid running out of cash—and going out of business

- Keep costs from killing your bottom line
- Invest smartly through cost/benefit analysis
- Sell your brilliant idea with ROI
- Avoid putting *too* much faith in the numbers

Contents

Section 1
Finance Basics: Don't Be Afraid

"What's the ROI on that software your department wants to buy?"

"The CFO says profits are great but money's tight—everyone needs to conserve cash."

"I've been studying the figures, and it looks as if your sales reps are sacrificing gross margin for revenue. Have you talked to them about that?"

"Our inventory days are creeping upward. We have to find a way to reverse that trend."

"I'm worried about our business. The financials suggest that corporate isn't investing in our future as much as it used to."

Every corporate manager hears questions and comments like these—sometimes from a boss or a finance director, other times from colleagues in water-cooler conversations. Whatever the source, they all have one thing in common: They take for granted that you understand the fundamentals of finance. The people doing the talking presume that you speak the language, that you can read the financial statements, and that you can use basic financial tools to make decisions.

But what if you're not sure of the difference between an income statement and a balance sheet, or between profit and a positive cash flow? What if you can't define inventory days or days sales outstanding, and you don't know how to use those numbers to improve financial performance? If someone asks you to prepare a return on investment (ROI) analysis, do you get a sinking feeling in the pit of your stomach because you have no idea where to begin?

Don't despair.

For one thing, you're in good company. Financial trainers Karen Berman and Joe Knight reported in "Are Your People Financially Literate?" (HBR October 2009) that when their Los Angeles–based Business Literacy Institute administered a 21-question quiz on financial basics to a representative sample of American managers, the average score was only 38%—a failing grade in any classroom. (After you read this introduction, you'll have a chance to quiz yourself with a short sample of similar questions.) At least those managers did better than the group of *Fortune* 500 officers and directors described in Andrew Ross Sorkin's *New York Times* article "Back to School, But This One Is for Top Corporate Officials" (September 3, 2002).

On another, equally basic, test of financial concepts, these executives scored an average of 32%.

But there's another reason not to feel too bad: You can easily remedy your situation. Reading this guide is a great start. The first section introduces you to the key terms and the three main financial statements. The next section shows you how to use some of the essential tools of finance. Learn these, and you'll be able to make better decisions to improve your unit's performance. The final section steps back from the numbers and emphasizes the importance of keeping your wits about you. Finance is partly science, to be sure, but it's also partly an art—and when you apply its tools, you have to be sure you understand the context for what you're doing.

Why bother with all this? The reason is simple: Every business runs on financial data. If you don't know the tools of finance, you can't put that information to work. If you can't even speak the language, you'll be left out of the larger conversation about your company, and your career may suffer as a result. When you finish this guide, you'll be well on your way to understanding and using the tools and the language. You'll also be well positioned to take a couple of advanced courses, so to speak, by turning to sources that dig deeper into the subject.

Do you worry that financial concepts will be too complex or that you won't be able to do the math? Rest assured, learning the fundamentals of finance is not the same as studying to be a numbers pro. People typically go to school for at least a couple of years to become financial experts, and then they spend a lot of time picking up specialized knowledge on the job. This guide won't give you all that—it's just about the basics. And the math involved in using financial tools is relatively simple. Most of the time it's no more complicated than the arithmetic you did in middle school; the stuff that's a little trickier can easily be done on a computer or calculator.

Ready to begin? Take the quiz on the following page. The answers are in the back of the guide, but don't peek yet. Instead, take the quiz again (on page 153) *after* you have read through all the articles, and then compare your two scores. You should be pleased with what you have learned.

Finance Quiz

Do You Know the Basics?

This 10-question quiz isn't designed to measure your entire financial IQ, but it will give you a sense of the fundamentals you should learn to become a more effective manager. When you finish reading the guide, you'll have a chance to retake the quiz and compare your scores. If you don't know an answer, just mark it "don't know" rather than guessing. That will give you a clearer indication of your progress later.

The questions here were developed with the help of the Business Literacy Institute, in Los Angeles. A more comprehensive financial IQ test is available for purchase at www.business-literacy.com.

1. **The income statement measures:**
   a. Profitability
   b. Assets and liabilities
   c. Cash
   d. All of the above

2. **A sale on credit ends up on the income statement as revenue and as what on the balance sheet?**
    a. Accounts receivable
    b. Long-term assets
    c. Short-term liability
    d. Operating cash flow

3. **What happens when a company is profitable but collection lags behind payments to vendors?**
    a. The company is OK because profits always become cash
    b. The company stands a good chance of running out of money
    c. The company needs to shift its focus to EBIT
    d. The cash flow statement will show a negative bottom line

4. **How is gross profit margin calculated?**
    a. COGS/revenue
    b. Gross profit/net profit
    c. Gross profit/revenue
    d. Sales/gross profit

5. **Which statement summarizes changes to parts of the balance sheet?**
    a. Income statement
    b. Cash flow statement
    c. Neither of the above
    d. Both of the above

6. EBIT is an important measure in companies because:

a. It is free cash flow
b. It subtracts interest and taxes from net income to get a truer picture of the business
c. It indicates the profitability of a company's operations
d. It is the key measure of earnings before indirect costs and transfers

7. Operating expenses include all of the following except:

a. Advertising costs
b. Administrative salaries
c. Expensed research and development costs
d. Delivery of raw materials

8. Owners' equity in a company increases when the company:

a. Increases its assets with debt
b. Decreases its debt by paying off loans with company cash
c. Increases its profit
d. All of the above

9. A company has more cash today when:

a. Customers pay their bills sooner
b. Accounts receivable increases
c. Profit increases
d. Retained earnings increases

10. **Which of the following is not part of working capital?**
    a. Accounts receivable
    b. Inventory
    c. Property, plant, and equipment
    d. All of the above are part of working capital

The Key Financial Statements

What does your company own, and what does it owe to others? What are its sources of revenue, and how has it spent its money? How much profit has it made? What is the state of its financial health? You can answer those questions by turning to the three main financial statements: the **balance sheet,** the **income statement,** and the **cash flow statement.**

These are the essential documents of business. Executives use them to assess performance and identify areas for action. Shareholders look at them to keep tabs on how well their capital is being managed. Outside investors use them to identify opportunities. Lenders and suppliers routinely examine them to determine the creditworthiness of the companies with which they deal.

Every manager, no matter where he or she sits in the organization, should have a solid grasp of the basic state-

---

Adapted from *Harvard Business Essentials: Finance for Managers* (product #5788BC), Harvard Business Review Press, 2002

ments. All three follow the same general format from company to company, though specific line items may vary, depending on the nature of the business. If you can, get copies of your own company's most recent financials so that you can compare them with the sample financials discussed here.

The Balance Sheet

Companies prepare balance sheets to summarize their financial position at a given point in time, usually at the end of the month, the quarter, or the fiscal year. The **balance sheet** shows what the company *owns* (its assets), what it *owes* (its liabilities), and its book value, or net worth (also called owners' equity, or shareholders' equity).

Assets comprise all the physical resources a company can put to work in the service of the business. This category includes cash and financial instruments (such as stocks and bonds), inventories of raw materials and finished goods, land, buildings, and equipment, plus the firm's **accounts receivable**—funds owed by customers for goods or services purchased.

Liabilities are debts to suppliers and other creditors. If a firm borrows money from a bank, that's a liability. If it buys $1 million worth of parts—and hasn't paid for those parts as of the date on the balance sheet—that $1 million is a liability. Funds owed to suppliers are known as **accounts payable.**

Owners' equity is what's left after you subtract total liabilities from total assets. A company with $3 million in total assets and $2 million in liabilities has $1 million in owners' equity.

That definition gives rise to what is often called the **fundamental accounting equation:**

Assets – Liabilities = Owners' Equity

or

Assets = Liabilities + Owners' Equity

The balance sheet shows assets on one side of the ledger, liabilities and owners' equity on the other. It's called a balance sheet because the two sides must always balance.

Suppose, for example, a computer company acquires $1 million worth of motherboards from an electronic parts supplier, with payment due in 30 days. The purchase increases the company's inventory assets by $1 million and its liabilities—in this case its accounts payable—by an equal amount. The equation stays in balance. Likewise, if the same company were to borrow $100,000 from a bank, the cash infusion would increase both its assets and its liabilities by $100,000.

Now suppose that this company has $4 million in owners' equity, and then $500,000 of uninsured assets burn up in a fire. Though its liabilities remain the same, its owners' equity—what's left after all claims against assets are satisfied—drops to $3.5 million.

Notice how total assets equal total liabilities plus owners' equity in the balance sheet of Amalgamated Hat Rack, an imaginary company whose finances we will consider throughout this chapter. The balance sheet (see page 14) describes not only how much the company has invested in assets but also what kinds of assets it owns, what portion comes from creditors (liabilities), and what portion comes from owners (equity). Analysis of the balance sheet can give you an idea of how efficiently a company is utilizing its assets and managing its liabilities.

Balance sheet data are most helpful when compared with the same information from one or more previous years. Amalgamated Hat Rack's balance sheet shows assets, liabilities, and owners' equity for December 31, 2010, and December 31, 2009. Compare the figures, and you'll see that Amalgamated is moving in a positive direction: It has increased its owners' equity by $397,500.

Now let's take a closer look at each section of the balance sheet.

Assets

Listed first are **current assets:** cash on hand and marketable securities, receivables, and inventory. Generally, current assets can be converted into cash within one year. Next is a tally of **fixed assets,** which are harder to turn into cash. The biggest category of fixed assets is usually **property, plant, and equipment;** for some companies, it's the only category.

Since fixed assets other than land don't last forever, the company must charge a portion of their cost against revenue over their estimated useful life. This is called depreciation, and the balance sheet shows the **accumulated depreciation** for all of the company's fixed assets. Gross property, plant, and equipment minus accumulated depreciation equals the current book value of property, plant, and equipment.

M&A can throw an additional asset category into the mix: If one company has purchased another for a price above the fair market value of its assets, the difference is known as **goodwill,** and it must be recorded. This is an accounting fiction, but goodwill often includes intangibles with real value, such as brand names, intellectual property, or the acquired company's reputation.

Liabilities and owners' equity

Now let's consider the claims against a company's assets. The category **current liabilities** represents money owed to creditors and others that typically must be paid within a year. It includes short-term loans, accrued salaries, accrued income taxes, accounts payable, and the current year's repayment obligation on a long-term loan. **Long-term liabilities** are usually bonds and mortgages—debts that the company is contractually obliged to repay over a period of time longer than a year.

As explained earlier, subtracting total liabilities from total assets leaves owners' equity. Owners' equity includes **retained earnings** (net profits that accumulate on a company's balance sheet after payment of dividends to shareholders) and **contributed capital,** or **paid-in capital** (capital received in exchange for shares).

The balance sheet shows, in effect, how its assets were paid for—from borrowed money (liabilities), the capital of the owners, or both.

Historical Cost

Balance sheet figures may not correspond to actual market values, except for items such as cash, accounts receivable, and accounts payable. This is because accountants must record most items at their historical cost. If, for example, a company's balance sheet indicated land

Amalgamated Hat Rack balance sheet as of December 31, 2010 and 2009

	2010	2009	Increase (Decrease)
Assets			
Cash and marketable securities	$ 652,500	486,500	166,000
Accounts receivable	555,000	512,000	43,000
Inventory	835,000	755,000	80,000
Prepaid expenses	123,000	98,000	25,000
Total current assets	2,165,500	1,851,500	314,000
Gross property, plant, and equipment	2,100,000	1,900,000	200,000
Less: accumulated depreciation	333,000	290,500	(42,500)
Net property, plant, and equipment	1,767,000	1,609,500	157,500
Total assets	$ 3,932,500	3,461,000	471,500
Liabilities and owners' equity			
Accounts payable	$ 450,000	430,000	20,000
Accrued expenses	98,000	77,000	21,000
Income tax payable	17,000	9,000	8,000
Short-term debt	435,000	500,000	(65,000)
Total current liabilities	1,000,000	1,016,000	(16,000)
Long-term debt	750,000	660,000	90,000
Total liabilities	1,750,000	1,676,000	74,000
Contributed capital	900,000	850,000	50,000
Retained earnings	1,282,500	935,000	347,500
Total owners' equity	2,182,500	1,785,000	397,500
Total liabilities and owners' equity	$ 3,932,500	$ 3,461,000	$ 471,500

WHERE ARE THE HUMAN ASSETS?

As people look to financial statements to gain insights about companies, many notice the traditional balance sheet's inability to reflect the value and profit potential of human capital and other intangibles. (Remember that the intangibles included in goodwill appear only when one company acquires another, and that the figure represents only the acquiree's intangibles at the time of purchase.) The absence of intangibles from the balance sheet is particularly significant for knowledge-intensive companies, whose skills, intellectual property, brand equity, and customer relationships may be their most productive assets. Indeed, a study several years ago by Baruch Lev of New York University found that 40% of the market valuation of the average company was missing from its balance sheet. For high-tech firms, the figure was over 50%. So managers and investors must look beyond the bricks and mortar, the equipment, and the cash that constitute balance sheet assets to determine the real value of a company.

worth $700,000, that figure would be what the company paid for the land way back when. If it was purchased in downtown San Francisco in 1960, you can bet that it is now worth immensely more than the value stated on the balance sheet. So why do accountants use historical instead of market values? The short answer is that it's the lesser of two evils. If market values were required, then every public company would be required to get a professional appraisal of every one of its properties, warehouse inventories, and so forth, and would have to do so every year—a logistical nightmare.

How the Balance Sheet Relates to You

Though the balance sheet is prepared by accountants, it's filled with important information for nonfinancial managers. Later in this guide you'll learn how to use balance-sheet ratios in managing your own area. For the moment, let's just look at a couple of ways in which balance-sheet figures indicate how efficiently a company is operating.

Working capital

Subtracting current liabilities from current assets gives you the company's **net working capital,** or the amount of money tied up in current operations. A quick calculation from its most recent balance sheet shows that Amalgamated had $1,165,500 in net working capital at the end of 2010.

Financial managers give substantial attention to the level of working capital, which typically expands and contracts with the level of sales. Too little working capital can put a company in a bad position: It may be unable to pay its bills or take advantage of profitable opportunities. But too much working capital reduces profitability since that capital must be financed in some way, usually through interest-bearing loans.

Inventory is a component of working capital that directly affects many nonfinancial managers. As with working capital in general, there's a tension between having too much and too little. On the one hand, plenty of inventory solves business problems. The company can fill customer orders without delay, and the inventory provides a buffer against potential production stoppages or interruptions in the flow of raw materials or parts. On the other hand, every piece of inventory must be financed, and the market value of the inventory itself may decline while it sits on the shelf.

The early years of the personal computer business provided a dramatic example of how excess inventory can wreck the bottom line. Some analysts estimated that the value of finished-goods inventory—computers that had already been built—melted away at a rate of approximately 2% *per day,* because of technical obsolescence in this fast-moving industry. Inventory meltdown really hammered Apple during the mid-1990s. Until the company could dramatically reduce its inventories through operational redesign, it had to dump its obsolete components and finished goods onto the market at huge discounts. By comparison, its rival, Dell, built computers to order—so it operated with *no* finished-goods inventory and with relatively small stocks of components. Dell's success formula was an ultrafast supply chain and assembly system that enabled the company to build PCs to customers' specifications. Finished Dell PCs didn't end up on stockroom shelves for weeks at a time, but went directly from the assembly line into waiting delivery trucks. The profit lesson to managers in this kind of situation is clear: Shape your operations to minimize inventories.

Financial leverage

The use of borrowed money to acquire an asset is called **financial leverage.** People say that a company is highly leveraged when the percentage of debt on its balance sheet is high relative to the capital invested by the owners. (**Operating leverage,** in contrast, refers to the extent to which a company's operating costs are fixed rather than variable. For example, a company that relies on heavy investments in machinery and very few workers to produce its goods has a high operating leverage.)

Financial leverage can increase returns on an investment, but it also increases risk. For example, suppose that you paid $400,000 for an asset, using $100,000 of your own money and $300,000 in borrowed funds. For simplicity, we'll ignore loan payments, taxes, and any cash flow you might get from the investment. Four years go by, and your asset has appreciated to $500,000. Now you decide to sell. After paying off the $300,000 loan, you end up with $200,000 in your pocket—your original $100,000 plus a $100,000 profit. That's a gain of 100% on your personal capital, even though the asset increased in value by only 25%. Financial leverage made this possible. If you had financed the purchase entirely with your own funds ($400,000), you would have ended up with only a 25% gain. In the United States and most other countries, tax policy makes financial leverage even more attractive by allowing businesses to treat the interest paid on loans as a deductible business expense.

But leverage can cut both ways. If the value of an asset drops, or if it fails to produce the anticipated level of revenue, then leverage works against the asset's owner. Consider what would have happened in our example if the asset's value had dropped by $100,000—that is, to $300,000. The owner would still have to repay the initial loan of $300,000 and would have nothing left over. The entire $100,000 investment would have disappeared.

Financial structure of the firm

The negative potential of financial leverage is what keeps CEOs, their financial executives, and board members from maximizing their companies' debt financing. Instead, they seek a financial structure that creates a realistic balance between debt and equity on the balance sheet. Although leverage enhances a company's potential profitability as long as things go right, managers know that every dollar of debt increases risk, both because of the danger just cited and because high debt entails high interest costs, which must be paid in good times and bad. Many companies have failed when business reversals or recessions reduced their ability to make timely payments on their loans.

When creditors and investors examine corporate balance sheets, therefore, they look carefully at the debt-to-equity ratio. They factor the riskiness of the balance sheet into the interest they charge on loans and the return they demand from a company's bonds. A highly leveraged company, for example, may have to pay two or three times the interest rate paid by a less leveraged competitor. Investors also demand a higher rate of return for their stock investments in highly leveraged companies. They will not accept high risks without expecting commensurately large returns.

The Income Statement

Unlike the balance sheet, which is a snapshot of a company's position at one point in time, the **income statement** shows cumulative business results within a defined time frame, such as a quarter or a year. It tells you whether the company is making a profit or a loss—that is, whether it has positive or negative net income (net earnings)—and how much. This is why the income statement is often referred to as the **profit-and-loss statement,** or **P&L.** The income statement also tells you the company's revenues and expenses during the time period it covers. Knowing the revenues and the profit enables you to determine the company's **profit margin.**

As we did with the balance sheet, we can represent the contents of the income statement with a simple equation:

$$\text{Revenues} - \text{Expenses} = \text{Net Income}$$

An income statement starts with the company's **sales,** or **revenues.** This is primarily the value of the goods or services delivered to customers, but you may have revenues from other sources as well. Note that revenues in most cases are not the same as cash. If a company delivers $1 million worth of goods in December 2010 and sends out an invoice at the end of the month, for example, that $1 million in sales counts as revenue for the year 2010 even though the customer hasn't yet paid the bill.

Various expenses—the costs of making and storing a company's goods, administrative costs, depreciation of plant and equipment, interest expense, and taxes—are then deducted from revenues. The bottom line—what's left over—is the **net income** (or **net profit,** or **net earnings**) for the period covered by the statement.

Let's look at the various line items on the income statement for Amalgamated Hat Rack (see below). The **cost of goods sold,** or **COGS,** represents the direct costs of manufacturing hat racks. This figure covers raw materials, such as lumber, and everything needed to turn those materials into finished goods, such as labor. Subtracting cost of goods sold from revenues gives us Amalgamated's **gross profit**—an important measure of a company's financial performance. In 2010, gross profit was $1,600,000.

Amalgamated Hat Rack income statement

	For the period ending December 31, 2010
Retail sales	$ 2,200,000
Corporate sales	1,000,000
Total sales revenue	3,200,000
Less: Cost of goods sold	1,600,000
Gross profit	1,600,000
Less: Operating expenses	800,000
Less: Depreciation expenses	42,500
Earnings before interest and taxes	757,500
Less: Interest expense	110,000
Earnings before income taxes	647,500
Less: Income taxes	300,000
Net income	$ 347,500

The next major category of cost is **operating expenses,** which include the salaries of administrative employees, office rents, sales and marketing costs, and other costs not directly related to making a product or delivering a service.

Depreciation appears on the income statement as an expense, even though it involves no out-of-pocket payment. As described earlier, it's a way of allocating the cost of an asset over the asset's estimated useful life. A truck, for example, might be expected to last five years. The company wouldn't count the full cost of the truck as an expense on the income statement in the first year; it would depreciate that amount over the full five years.

Subtracting operating expenses and depreciation from gross profit gives you a company's **operating earnings,** or **operating profit.** This is often called **earnings before interest and taxes,** or **EBIT,** as it is on Amalgamated's statement.

The last expenses on the income statement are typically taxes and any interest due on loans. If you get a positive net profit figure after subtracting all expenses, as Amalgamated does, your company is profitable.

Multiyear Comparisons

As with the balance sheet, comparing income statements over a period of years reveals much more than examining a single income statement. You can spot trends, turnarounds, and recurring problems. Many companies' annual reports show data going back five or more years.

In Amalgamated's multiperiod income statement (see page 25), you can see that annual retail sales have grown steadily, while corporate sales have declined slightly. Operating expenses have stayed about the same, however, even as total sales have expanded. That's a good sign that management is holding the line on the cost of doing business. Interest expense has also declined, perhaps because the company has paid off one of its loans. The bottom line, net income, shows healthy growth.

How the Income Statement Relates to You

Of the three main financial statements, the income statement generally has the greatest bearing on a manager's job. That's because most managers are responsible in some way for one or more of its elements:

Generating revenue

In one sense, nearly everyone in a company helps generate revenue—the people who design and produce the goods or deliver the service, those who deal directly with customers, and so on—but it's the primary responsibility of the sales and marketing departments. If same-store or same-product revenues rise faster than the competition's, you can reasonably assume that the folks in sales and marketing are doing a good job.

It's critical that managers in these departments understand the income statement so that they can balance costs against revenue. If sales reps give too many discounts, for instance, they may reduce the company's gross profit. If marketers spend too much money in pursuit of new customers, they will eat into operating profit. It's the manager's job to track these numbers as well as revenue itself.

Managing budgets

Running a department means working within the confines of a budget. If you oversee a unit in information technology or human resources, for example, you may have little influence on revenue, but you will surely be expected to watch your costs closely—and all those costs will affect the income statement. Staff departments' expenses usually show up in the operating expenses line. If you invest in any capital equipment—a complex piece of software, say—you will also add to the depreciation line.

Close study of your company's income statements over time reveals opportunities as well as constraints. Suppose you would like to get permission to hire one or two more people. If operating expense as a percentage of sales has been trending downward, you will have a stronger case than if it has been trending upward.

Managing a P&L

Many managers have P&L responsibility, which means they are accountable for an entire chunk of the income statement. This is probably the case if you're running a business unit, a store, a plant, or a branch office, or if you're overseeing a product line. The income statement you are accountable for isn't quite the same as the whole company's. For instance, it is unlikely to include interest expense and other overhead items, except as an "allocation" at the end of the year. Even so, your job is to manage revenue generation and costs so that your unit or product line contributes as much profit to the company as pos-

Amalgamated Hat Rack multiperiod income statement

	For the period ending December 31,		
	2010	**2009**	**2008**
Retail sales	$ 2,200,000	2,000,000	1,720,000
Corporate sales	1,000,000	1,000,000	1,100,000
Total sales revenue	3,200,000	3,000,000	2,820,000
Less: Cost of goods sold	1,600,000	1,550,000	1,400,000
Gross profit	1,600,000	1,450,000	1,420,000
Less: Operating expenses	800,000	810,000	812,000
Less: Depreciation expenses	42,500	44,500	45,500
Earnings before interest and taxes	757,500	595,500	562,500
Less: Interest expense	110,000	110,000	150,000
Earnings before income taxes	647,500	485,500	412,500
Less: Income taxes	300,000	194,200	165,000
Net income	$ 347,500	291,300	247,500

sible. For that you need to understand and track revenue, cost of goods sold, and operating expenses.

The Cash Flow Statement

The **cash flow statement** is the least used—and least understood—of the three essential statements. It shows in broad categories how a company acquired and spent its cash during a given span of time. As you'd expect, expenditures show up on the statement as negative figures, and sources of income figures are positive. The bottom line in each category is simply the net total of inflows and outflows, and it can be either positive or negative.

The statement has three major categories: **Operating activities,** or **operations,** refers to cash generated by, and used in, a company's ordinary business operations. It includes everything that doesn't explicitly fall into the other two categories. **Investing activities** covers cash spent on capital equipment and other investments (outgoing), and cash realized from the sale of such investments (incoming). **Financing activities** refers to cash used to reduce debt, buy back stock, or pay dividends

Amalgamated Hat Rack cash flow statement for the year ending December 31, 2010

Net income	$ 347,500
Operating activities	
Accounts receivable	(43,000)
Inventory	(80,000)
Prepaid expenses	(25,000)
Accounts payable	20,000
Accrued expenses	21,000
Income tax payable	8,000
Depreciation expense	42,500
Total changes in operating assets and liabilities	(56,500)
Cash flow from operations	291,000
Investing activities	
Sale of property, plant, and equipment	267,000*
Capital expenditures	(467,000)
Cash flow from investing activities	(200,000)
Financing activities	
Short-term debt decrease	(65,000)
Long-term borrowing	90,000
Capital stock	50,000
Cash dividends to stockholders	–
Cash flow from financing activities	75,000
Increase in cash during year	$ 166,000

* Assumes sale price was at book value; the company had yet to start depreciating this asset.

(outgoing), and cash from loans or from stock sales (incoming).

Again using the Amalgamated Hat Rack example, we see that in 2010 the company generated a total positive cash flow (increase in cash) of $166,000. This is the sum of cash flows from operations ($291,000), investing activities (minus $200,000), and financing ($75,000).

The cash flow statement shows the relationship between net profit, from the income statement, and the actual change in cash that appears in the company's bank accounts. In accounting language, it "reconciles" profit and cash through a series of adjustments to net profit. Some of these adjustments are simple. Depreciation, for instance, is a noncash expense, so you have to add depreciation to net profit if what you're interested in is the change in cash. Other adjustments are harder to grasp, though the arithmetic isn't difficult. If a company's accounts receivable are lower at the end of 2010 than they were at the end of 2009, for example, it took in "extra" cash from operations, so we would add that to net profit as well.

Let's look at each category on Amalgamated's cash flow statement for 2010.

- **Operating activities.** Net income—$347,500—appears at the top. That's the figure we want to adjust, and it comes straight from the bottom line of the income statement. Accounts receivable, inventory, prepaid expenses, accounts payable, accrued expenses, and income tax payable are all calculated from the balance sheets for 2010 and

2009. The figure appearing on the cash flow statement for each line item represents the *difference* between the two balance sheets. Again, these are all adjustments that will help translate net income into cash. As mentioned, depreciation is a non-cash expense, so it's added in. Then all the pluses and minuses are calculated to get net cash from operations.

- **Investing activities.** Amalgamated sold fixed assets—property, plant, and equipment—worth $267,000 in 2010. For simplicity's sake we're assuming that it had not yet begun to depreciate those assets. It also invested $467,000 in new fixed assets.

- **Financing activities.** Amalgamated decreased its short-term debt by $65,000, increased its long-term debt by $90,000, and sold $50,000 in stock to investors. It paid its shareholders no dividends in 2010; if it had, the amount would have shown up under financing activities.

- **Change in cash.** As noted above, the change in cash is just the total of all three categories. It corresponds exactly to the difference in the cash line items on the balance sheets for 2010 and 2009.

The cash flow statement is useful because it indicates whether your company is successfully turning its profits into cash—and that ability is ultimately what will keep the company **solvent,** or able to pay bills as they come due.

How the Cash Flow Statement Relates to You

If you're a manager in a large corporation, changes in your employer's cash flow won't typically have an impact on your day-to-day job. Nevertheless, it's a good idea to stay up to date with your company's cash situation, because it may affect your budget for the upcoming year. When cash is tight, you will probably want to be conservative in your planning. When it's plentiful, you may have an opportunity to propose a bigger budget. Note that a company can be quite profitable and still be short of cash as a result of making a lot of new investments, for example, or having trouble collecting receivables.

You may also have some influence over the items that affect the cash flow statement. Are you responsible for inventory? Keep in mind that every addition there requires a cash expenditure. Are you in sales? A sale isn't really a sale until it is paid for—so watch your receivables. There's more on tools for managing cash later in this guide.

Where to Find the Financials

Every company with shares traded in U.S. public financial markets must prepare and distribute its financial statements in an annual report to shareholders. Annual reports usually go beyond the basic disclosure requirement of the Securities and Exchange Commission and include discussion of the year's operations and the future outlook. Most public companies also issue quarterly reports.

If you are looking for even more material on your company, or on one of your competitors, obtain a copy of its annual Form 10-K. The 10-K often contains abundant and revealing information about a company's strategy, its view of the market and its customers, its products, its important risks and business challenges, and so forth. You can get 10-K reports and annual and quarterly reports directly from a company's investor relations department or online at www.sec.gov/edgar/searchedgar/webusers.htm.

Private, or closely held, companies are not required by law to share full financial statements with anybody, though prospective investors and lenders naturally expect to see all three statements. And many companies share the financials with their managers. If you work for a closely held company and have not seen its financials, ask someone in finance whether you are allowed to see them.

SUMMING UP

The balance sheet, income statement, and cash flow statement offer three perspectives on a company's financial performance. They tell three different but related stories about how well your company is doing financially:

- The **balance sheet** shows a company's financial position at a specific point in time. It provides a snapshot of its assets, liabilities, and equity on a given day.
- The **income statement** shows the bottom line. It indicates how much profit or loss was generated over a period of time—usually a month, a quarter, or a year.
- The **cash flow statement** tells where the company's cash came from and where it went. It shows the relationship between net profit and the change in cash recorded from one balance sheet to the next.

Together, these financial statements can help you understand what is going on in your company—or in any other business.

The Fundamental Laws of Business

by David Stauffer

Why was a publisher willing to pay General Electric chairman Jack Welch an eye-popping $7 million advance for a book about his career? According to Dallas-based management consultant Ram Charan, author of *What the CEO Wants You to Know* and several other books, the answer has a lot to do with Welch's ability to distill complexities—to think and talk about his sprawling global conglomerate as if it were a simple street-corner shop. An understanding of a few financial measures coupled with an enterprise-wide perspective, Charan maintains, can help you get a grip on any company, regardless of its size or location. "When you come right down to it," he says, "business is very simple. There are universal laws of

---

Adapted from *Harvard Management Update* (product #U0104A), April 2001

business that apply whether you sell fruit from a stand or are running a *Fortune* 500 company."

Understand the Measures of Moneymaking

Business acumen, writes Charan, is "the ability to understand the building blocks of how a one-person operation or a very big business makes money." Problems arise when managers don't have a precise understanding of what "making money" means. Three measures can give you a good picture of whether and how a company is making money: growth, cash generation, and return on assets.

Growth

Growth in sales is usually—but not always—a positive sign. A $16 million injection-molding company, writes Charan, "rewarded its sales representatives based on how many dollars' worth of plastic caps they sold, regardless of whether the company made a profit on the caps. Everyone was excited when the company landed $4 million in new sales from two major customers. But in the following three years, as sales rose, profit margins sank." The lesson here: "Growth for its own sake doesn't do any good. Growth has to be profitable and sustainable."

Cash generation

Cash is "a company's oxygen supply," writes Charan; it "gives you the ability to stay in business." Even if your company is growing its revenues profitably and getting a respectable return on its assets, a cash shortage—or a declining cash flow—spells trouble. "Cash generation is

BIG-PICTURE PERSPECTIVE

Consultant Ram Charan, author of *What the CEO Wants You to Know,* urges you to "get a total picture" by answering the following questions:

- What were your company's sales during the last year? Are sales growing, declining, or flat?
- What is the profit margin? Is it growing, declining, or flat?
- How does your margin compare with those of competitors? With those of other industries?
- Do you know your company's inventory velocity? Its asset velocity?
- What is its return on assets?
- Is cash generation increasing or decreasing? Why?
- Is your company gaining or losing against the competition?

the difference between all the cash that flows into the business and all the cash that flows out of the business in a given time period," Charan explains. Since most companies extend and receive credit, net cash flow and profit are seldom the same thing. Cash from operations depends largely on two factors: **accounts receiv-**

able (money owed by customers) and **accounts payable** (money owed to suppliers).

Charan recommends continually investigating where the cash is being generated, how it's being used, and whether enough is coming in. If there's not enough, of course, you'll want to find out the reasons.

Return on assets (ROA)

A company's ROA is its net profit divided by the average value of its assets during a given period of time. This measure, usually expressed as a percentage, shows you how well your company is using its assets—including cash, receivables, inventory, buildings, vehicles, and machinery—to make money. ROA gives managers a glimpse of the often-missing third element of a triad called SEA: sales, expenses, and assets. "Below the senior management level," explains Chuck Kremer, a financial trainer and coauthor of *Managing by the Numbers,* "many decision makers see only their part of the income statement," which doesn't deal with assets. Yet all employees, whether they realize it or not, are involved in managing some portion of the firm's assets.

Many people equate managing assets with watching gross profit (total sales minus all costs directly associated with creating the company's products or services). That's only half the challenge, says Charan. The other measure that needs to be monitored simultaneously is **velocity**—how fast a particular asset moves "through a business to a customer."

In times of intense price competition, for example, companies often see their gross margins shrink. Increasing asset velocity helps protect the ROA of a company in that situation, because you're doing more with fewer assets. This is the strategy that made Dell Computer so successful in the 1990s. By outsourcing much of its components manufacturing, Dell essentially became an assembler, Charan points out: Each computer was configured to meet an individual customer's specifications and delivered in less than a week. Dell cut costs by reducing inventory and increasing its **inventory turns**—the number of times in a year that its inventory turned over—to a level far higher than most manufacturers'.

"The problem with managers missing the 'A,' or assets part [of SEA], isn't usually apparent in good times," Kremer says. "It's when things are slowing down that ROA makes all the difference. And it's the companies like GE that emphasize the 'A' continuously—so that their people are always managing the receivables, the fixed assets, and the inventories—that thrive in good times and bad."

Think Like an Owner

By understanding growth, cash generation, and ROA, managers can counteract the common tendency to think and act within one's "silo" (department or unit). "None of us denies that we're members of a team comprising every department," Kremer says. "But how can I best contribute to the team if I don't understand how my actions in marketing impact engineering or production?"

Tracking these financial measures helps expand managers' thinking in three ways, says Charan: "First, we're able to think of the business as a whole. Second, we see the linkages between our unit and the business as a whole.

Third, we're better able to grasp what's happening in the outside world—such as an economic slowdown—and relate that to the company and even to our own area."

A big-picture understanding of basic financial measures has very practical benefits, says Thomas Kroeger, the executive vice president in charge of organization and people at Office Depot. "The main benefit is that it helps us cut through the clutter," he says, noting that Office Depot's fast growth necessarily created layers and distance between the CEO and store managers. Kroeger describes a telling incident that occurred during a meeting of district store managers, who had suggested that each store hire a customer greeter. At the individual store level, this didn't represent a huge financial commitment. But when the managers took a step back, they realized that their idea would cost $25 million annually to execute. "They were dumbfounded," Kroeger recalls. "But they'd experienced a critical shift, from the perspective of store manager to store *owner*."

At Alcoa Packaging Machinery in Englewood, Colorado, a financial-literacy initiative helped foster an owner's perspective among all employees. "Workers in each of about 10 manufacturing cells make the decisions that affect *them*," explains machinists' union representative Garry Harper. Should we work this Saturday? Should we buy the new tooling we need this month? The company's big picture gets factored into the decision making around such questions. What's more, all employees receive monthly updates on key financial measures of companywide performance at cell briefings and via the company's intranet. "Every cell also gets its own monthly

P&L statement," Harper adds. "I can assure you that every employee knows or has access to how well his or her cell is contributing to overall company performance."

Growth, cash generation, and return on assets—these concepts, along with a focus on customers, form the nucleus from which everything else about a business emanates, says Charan.

David Stauffer heads the corporate writing firm Stauffer Bury, in Red Lodge, Montana.

Section 2

Making Good Decisions—and Moving Those Numbers

Part of your job as a manager is to help your company reach its financial goals—in other words, to help move the key numbers in the right direction. You should now have a good idea of what those numbers are. The **income statement** shows revenue, the various costs and expenses, subtotals such as gross profit and operating profit, and of course the bottom line—net profit. The **balance sheet** shows assets and liabilities, including accounts receivable and accounts payable. The **cash flow statement** shows how well the company is turning its profits into cash and what it's doing with that cash. All three statements reflect the daily actions of managers and employees throughout the organization. The company will be financially healthy if and only if those individuals make and execute good decisions every day.

The articles in this section of the guide will help you do that. They'll enable you to see more of what the financials are telling you, where the levers and pressure points are, and what you can do to make those key numbers move. You'll learn how to help boost profits, how to use assets (such as equipment, inventory, and cash) more efficiently, how to improve your company's cash flow, and how to analyze potential investments. You'll have a better understanding of the relationship between your responsibilities and your company's financial results.

If you're a savvy manager, you always pay careful attention to the operations you oversee and to the people on your team. But you can't forget that you and your coworkers are ultimately responsible for your company's financial health—and that you must watch the numbers as closely as you watch everything else.

Using Statements to Measure Financial Health

By themselves, financial statements tell you quite a bit: how much profit the company made, where it spent its money, how large its debts are. But how do you *interpret* all the numbers these statements provide? For example, is the company's profit large or small? Is the level of debt healthy or not?

Ratio analysis allows you to dig into the information contained in the three financial statements. A financial ratio is just two key numbers expressed in relation to each other. Using ratios, you can compare your company's performance to that of its competitors, to industry averages, and to its own performance in the past. The ratios that follow are among the most common, and are used in many different industries.

Adapted from *Pocket Mentor: Understanding Finance* (product #13197), Harvard Business Review Press, 2007

Profitability Ratios

These measures gauge a company's **profitability**—its profits as a percentage of various other numbers. They'll help you determine whether your company's profits are healthy or anemic, and whether they're moving in the right direction.

- **Return on assets (ROA).** ROA indicates how well a company is using its assets to generate profit. It's a good measure for comparing companies of different sizes. To calculate it, just divide net income by total assets. For example, look back at the financials of Amalgamated Hat Rack in "The Key Financial Statements," in the opening section of this guide. The income statement shows net income of $347,500 for 2010, and the balance sheet shows total assets of $3,932,500 for December 31 of that year. Do the arithmetic, and you find that Amalgamated's ROA is 8.8%.
- **Return on equity (ROE).** ROE shows profit as a percentage of shareholders' equity. In effect, it's the owners' return on their investment—and you can bet that shareholders will be comparing it to what they could earn with alternative investments. To calculate ROE, divide net income by owners' equity. For Amalgamated, it's $347,500 divided by $2,182,500, or 15.9%.
- **Return on sales (ROS).** Also known as **net profit margin,** ROS measures how well a company is controlling its costs and turning revenue into

bottom-line profit. To calculate ROS, divide net income by revenue. Amalgamated's ROS for 2010 is 10.9%, or $347,500 divided by $3,200,000. For 2009, the calculation is $291,300 divided by $3,000,000, or 9.7%. So Amalgamated's ROS is growing—a very good sign.

- **Gross profit margin.** Gross profit margin shows how efficiently a company produces its goods or delivers its services, taking only direct costs into account. To calculate gross profit margin, divide gross profit by revenue. Amalgamated made $1,600,000 in gross profit in 2010; divide that by $3,200,000, and you get exactly 50%. That's a couple of percentage points higher than the previous year's gross profit margin—also a good sign.
- **Earnings before interest and taxes (EBIT) margin.** Many analysts use this measure, also known as **operating margin,** to see how profitable a company's overall operations are, without regard to how they are financed or what taxes the company may be liable for. To calculate it, just divide EBIT by revenue. Amalgamated's EBIT for 2010 was $757,500. Divide that by revenue, and you get 23.7%. (For an exercise, check to see whether its EBIT margin improved since 2009.)

Operating Ratios

Operating ratios help you assess a company's level of efficiency—in particular, how well it is putting its assets to work and managing its cash.

- **Asset turnover.** This ratio shows how efficiently a company uses all of its assets—cash, machinery, and so on—to generate revenue. It answers the question, *How many dollars of revenue do we bring in for each dollar of assets?* To calculate asset turnover, divide revenue by total assets. In general, the higher the number, the better—but note that you can raise the ratio either by generating more revenue with the same assets *or* by decreasing the asset base of your business, perhaps by lowering average receivables.

- **Receivable days.** This measure, also known as **days sales outstanding (DSO),** tells you how quickly a company collects funds owed by customers. A company that takes an average of 45 days to collect its receivables will need significantly more working capital than one that takes 25 days. There are a couple of different ways to calculate DSO. One common method is to divide ending accounts receivable—accounts receivable on the last day of the month or year—by revenue per day during the period just ended.

- **Days payable.** This measure, also called **days payable outstanding (DPO),** tells you how quickly a company pays its suppliers. The longer it takes, other things being equal, the more cash a company has to work with. Of course, you have to balance the advantages of more cash in your bank account against your suppliers' need to be paid—stretch DPO out too long, and you may find that suppliers don't want to do business with you. The most common way to calculate DPO is to divide ending accounts payable by cost of goods sold per day.

- **Days in inventory (DII).** This shows how quickly a company sells its inventory during a given period of time. The longer it takes, the longer the company's cash is tied up and the greater the likelihood that the inventory will not sell at full value. To calculate DII, or **inventory days,** divide average inventory by cost of goods sold per day.

Liquidity Ratios

Liquidity ratios tell you about a company's ability to meet short-term financial obligations such as debt payments, payroll, and accounts payable.

- **Current ratio.** This ratio measures a company's current assets against its current liabilities. To calculate it, divide total current assets by total current liabilities. A ratio that is close to 1 is too low: It shows that current assets are barely sufficient to cover short-term obligations. (A ratio of less than 1 is a sign of immediate trouble.) A ratio significantly higher than industry averages may indicate that the company is too "fat"—in other words, that it's holding a lot of cash that it's not putting to work or returning to shareholders in the form of dividends.

- **Quick ratio.** This ratio isn't faster to compute than any other—it simply measures a company's ability to meet its current obligations quickly. It thus ignores inventory, which can be hard to liquidate. (And if you do have to liquidate inventory quickly, you typically get less for it than you would otherwise.) This ratio is sometimes called the **acid test,** because if it is less than 1 the company may be unable to pay its bills. To calculate the quick ratio, divide current assets minus inventory by current liabilities.

Leverage Ratios

Leverage ratios tell you to what extent a company is using debt to pay for its operations and how easily it can cover the cost of that debt.

- **Interest coverage.** This ratio assesses the margin of safety on a company's debt—in other words, how its profit compares to its interest payments during a given period. To calculate interest coverage, divide earnings before interest and taxes by interest expense. For Amalgamated Hat Rack, it's $757,500 divided by $110,000, or 6.9. Bankers and other lenders look at this ratio closely; nobody likes to lend money to a company if its profits aren't substantially higher than its interest obligations.

- **Debt to equity.** This measure shows the extent to which a company is using borrowed money to enhance the return on owners' equity. Investors and lenders scrutinize the ratio to determine whether a company is too highly leveraged (usually compared to industry averages)—or whether, in contrast, management has been too conservative and isn't using enough debt to generate profits. To calculate it, divide total liabilities by owners' equity. Amalgamated's debt-to-equity ratio? It's $1,750,000 divided by $2,182,500, or 0.80.

How Ratio Analysis Relates to You

Ratios shine a powerful light on three potential areas of concern:

- **Liquidity.** The current and quick ratios can tell you whether a company will be able to pay its bills. If it can't easily do so, it's likely to cut costs abruptly. It may even need to restructure its operations.

- **Competitive advantages or disadvantages.** Comparing a company's ratios to those of competitors and to industry averages often reveals specific financial strengths and weaknesses. If your firm's debt-to-equity ratio is higher than average, for example, the company may be particularly vulnerable to a downturn in the industry. If its EBIT margin is higher than competitors', it may be more efficient than others in its operating processes.

- **Performance trends.** If ROS is shrinking, say—if costs are growing relative to sales—senior executives will probably begin looking for cuts. They'll ask managers to tighten their budgets, maybe even to delay hiring where possible. A growing ROA

> or ROS, by contrast, may put the senior team in a more expansive mood. That's the best time to consider asking for a more generous budget, a new position in your department, or a new piece of capital equipment.

It's important to understand which ratios you can influence and to talk with your team about how to have the right impact. For instance:

Profitability ratios

Most line managers are directly responsible for controlling costs in their areas. By staying under budget, for example, you can help your company's ROS. There may be other ways to improve profitability as well. If you're in engineering or product development, can you come up with new product ideas that will generate additional revenue at healthy margins? If you're in sales, are you watching the gross profit on what you and your team sell as well as your overall sales volume? If you're in marketing, can you figure out ways to get more bang from every marketing dollar? These are the kinds of efforts that make a bottom-line difference.

Operating ratios

Line managers influence operating ratios in a number of ways. Sales managers, for example, always have to make certain that their reps aren't selling to too many customers that are poor credit risks. They may need to work with their reps and the credit department to keep receivable days down to an appropriate level. Plant managers and everyone else responsible for inventory must watch inventory days relative to competitors' and to industry averages. Inventory that's higher than necessary requires more working capital, and the finance department is likely to come around asking why DII is so high.

Liquidity and leverage ratios

These ratios are mostly the responsibility of the finance department, so line managers have less influence on them. But all the other moves discussed here—generating more revenue, watching costs and profit margins, collecting on receivables, keeping inventory (and thus working capital) to a minimum—will ultimately have a positive impact on your company's liquidity and leverage ratios.

Other Financial Assessments

Other ways of evaluating a company's financial health include valuation, Economic Value Added (EVA), and productivity assessments. Like the ratios described above, all these measures are most meaningful when compared with the same ones from earlier time periods or with those for other companies in a particular industry.

Valuation

Valuation often refers to the process of determining the total value of a company for the purpose of selling it. This is an uncertain science. For example, a company considering an acquisition might estimate the prospective acquiree's future cash flows and then calculate its value accordingly. Another would-be acquirer might rely on

TIPS ON ANALYZING FINANCIAL STATEMENTS

- ***Compare companies to determine the context.*** What looks like a big (or small) number may not be once you understand what's typical for a similar-sized business in the same industry. For instance, the oil company ConocoPhillips earned close to $5 billion in 2010, which sounds like a lot of money. But the company's ROS was only 3.5%, compared with 6.4% for Chevron, which recorded only moderately higher revenue.
- ***Watch for trends.*** How have the statements changed since last year? From three years ago? Say you notice a marked increase in the level of receivables from one year to the next. To see whether it's "really" rising, calculate receivable days. If that's going up, too, then the company isn't doing as good a job at collecting its cash as it did in the past. That may be a deliberate

different data, such as the value of the acquiree's physical assets. Regardless of the method used, a company may be worth different amounts to different parties. A small high-tech firm, for instance, may be valued well beyond what its cash flow or assets would suggest if the potential acquirer wants its unique technology or engineering talent.

Valuation also refers to the process by which Wall Street investors and analysts scrutinize financial statements and stock performance to arrive at an estimate

strategy of buying market share, or it may simply reflect poor management of receivables.

- ***Translate the numbers into prose.*** Use your company's statements to write a paragraph describing how much profit it is making, how well it is managing its assets, where the money comes from, and where it goes. If you worked for Amalgamated Hat Rack, for instance, you might begin with, "We've done a pretty good job at increasing revenue over the years, and we've done a very good job of controlling our costs, particularly in 2010. That has helped boost our operating profit and our net profit as well." If you can put what you see on the statements into everyday language, you'll be able to use what the statements are telling you to make smart decisions.

of a company's value. They're interested in determining whether the market price of a share of stock is a good deal relative to the underlying value of the piece of the company that the share represents.

Wall Street uses various means of valuation—that is, of assessing a company's financial health in relation to its stock price:

- **Earnings per share (EPS)** equals net income divided by the number of shares outstanding. This is one of the most commonly watched financial indicators. If it falls, it will most likely take the stock's price down with it.

- **Price-to-earnings ratio (P/E)** is the current price of a share of stock divided by the previous 12 months' earnings per share. It is a common measure of how cheap or expensive a share is relative to the company's earnings (and relative to other companies' shares).

- **Growth indicators** are also important in Wall Street's valuations, because growth allows a company to provide increasing returns to its shareholders. The number of years over which you should measure growth depends on the industry's business cycles. For an oil company, a one-year growth figure probably wouldn't tell you much, because of the industry's long cycles. For an internet company, however, a year is a long time. Typical measures include sales growth, profitability growth, and growth in earnings per share.

Economic Value Added

This concept encourages employees and managers to think like shareholders and owners by focusing on the **net value** a company creates. EVA is the profit remaining after the company has accounted for the cost of its capital. If profit is less than the cost of capital—that is, if EVA is negative—the company is essentially destroying value.

Productivity measures

Sales per employee and net income per employee link revenue and profit-generation information to workforce data. Trend lines in these numbers help you see whether a company is becoming more or less productive over time.

Grow Your Profits by Streamlining Your Business

by Jamie Bonomo and Andy Pasternak

Managers today are under intense pressure to deliver revenue growth. But as they and their teams respond to this challenge, they may unwittingly introduce complexity that drags down overall profitability. People in design, sales, and marketing, for example, are driven to introduce new products, acquire new customers, and enter new markets—and they often add offerings, channels, brands, and customers one at a time without regard to the cumulative impact on the business.

What is this cumulative impact? As a business becomes more complex, it gets difficult to trace costs to their origins. So senior managers struggle to figure out

---

Adapted from *Harvard Management Update* (product #U0505A), May 2005

which offerings and markets are profitable. They have a hard time deciding what to sell, at what price, and to whom. Digging into the costs of individual products, brands, channels, and customers helps managers at all levels in a company better understand each link in the value chain. That knowledge will help leaders as they refine strategy and others as they execute it.

Consider the following ways companies can simplify to increase profitability:

1. Analyze profitability by offering or market

Large, complex companies often lack consistent information and systems across their many businesses and geographies. Moreover, **shared costs**—those that cannot be directly attributed to individual offerings or markets—represent a large portion of their total cost structure. But you can determine true costs by digging into the details. Profitability analysis of this sort will typically reveal large profit disparities among lines of business, brands, products, and customers.

At a consumer products company we'll call Consolidated, Inc., for instance, managers viewed a longtime large account, MacGuffin, as one of its two most important customers in a particular region. However, the prices MacGuffin paid were low, and the complexity of serving the account was staggering, given the nearly 30 product stock-keeping units (SKUs) developed specifically for this customer. Consolidated used four manufacturing facilities to produce the SKUs and operated a "mixing center" to aggregate orders across plants, primarily for MacGuffin. Those costs had not been attributed to Mac-

Guffin but rather were spread across all accounts in the region. When managers analyzed the true cost of serving MacGuffin, from the sales front end to the operations back end, they realized the account *lowered* the bottom line by $700,000 even though it generated $5 million in annual sales. To lower costs and add value, Consolidated reduced MacGuffin's SKU count by 60%, repriced certain products, and restructured supply terms.

As this example shows, decisions about product selection and pricing should not be made on the margin—that is, you shouldn't assume that the cost of infrastructure is fixed and existing excess capacity is essentially free. While appealing in the short term, this approach may accommodate unprofitable offerings.

2. *Make sure your brands and SKUs are pulling their weight*

Most complex companies have many brands or SKUs that contribute little to the bottom line. A detailed analysis by one U.S. computer maker showed managers that many of its low-volume products had only modest customer reach, low revenues, and low profits—yet those offerings added considerable complexity to the manufacturer's operations. Indeed, the company had been using up to 20% of its assets to support these marginal brands and products. By targeting profitable brands and SKUs and cutting the rest loose, it freed up significant capacity with negligible loss of revenue and volume.

This was not a purely operations-driven effort, however. The company also incorporated customers' perspectives. Through rigorous research that blended survey and

QUESTIONS FOR MANAGERS

- Do you know which of your customers, brands, and product lines bring in profits? Do you know which ones lose money?
- If a new and highly profitable opportunity came along and your company did not have enough capacity to address it, what would it do?
- Do support functions such as R&D, sales, and marketing set their own agendas, or do they collaborate closely with other groups across the enterprise?
- Are performance metrics designed to optimize overall profitability?

testing tools from psychology and economics, the computer maker estimated demand for its various brands and SKUs and learned exactly how and why customers chose those products. With the data in hand, managers could evaluate which trade-offs in volume, pricing, and systemwide costs would help profitability.

3. Consolidate production

Another way to simplify is to improve the mix of low-cost and high-cost production capacity. Eliminating or cutting back on a single account to reduce indirect costs is just the first step. If a company streamlines a sufficiently large number of accounts, it can consolidate facilities and close the highest-cost production lines or service centers. The resulting efficiencies will give managers more leeway in negotiating pricing, and will help them end relationships with accounts that still perform poorly. This approach can dramatically boost profitability through operating-margin improvements and focus resources on accounts with high growth potential.

Transforming a revenue culture into a profit culture is no small task. All functions—from sales to marketing to operations—must join in the effort. But once your firm's processes and metrics are based on an integrated perspective, you'll be one step closer to a simpler and more profitable business.

Jamie Bonomo is a managing director, and **Andy Pasternak** is a director, of New York–based Mercer Management Consulting.

Working Your Assets to Boost Your Growth

by Miles Cook, Pratap Mukharji, Lorenz Kiefer, and Marco Petruzzi

Supply chains can account for a staggering 80% of an organization's costs. And at product companies, up to 60% of net assets go toward inventory, plants, warehouses, and other supply chain assets. Yet companies seldom look at supply chain improvements as a way to boost **return on invested capital,** or **ROIC.**

Calculating ROIC can be a little complex, but here's how it's usually done:

$$\frac{\text{Earnings + Interest Expense (with an Adjustment for the Tax Benefit of Interest Costs)}}{\text{Total Assets − Cash − Non-interest-bearing Current Liabilities}}$$

Adapted from *Harvard Management Update* (product #P0503B), March 2005

Companies most often focus on growing ROIC by building up the numerator: earnings. But shrinking the less-obvious denominator by accelerating asset turns—achieving the same or better results with fewer assets—can also have a huge impact. In our experience, introducing effective customer-centric supply chain management techniques can improve ROIC by an average of nearly 30%. And as a bonus, companies that trim down assets also significantly outgrow their competitors in revenue.

Embedding Supply Chain Math in Customer-Focused Decisions

Firms looking to boost ROIC can use supply chain economics to answer three key questions involving customers:

1. **What do we sell?** Can we streamline stock-keeping units (SKUs) and eliminate complexity, costs, and assets? For instance, perhaps we can cut some low-volume or unprofitable products and reduce the number of available options on others. That will make our plants more efficient and allow us to reduce inventory.

2. **To whom do we sell?** Do we have the right marketplace focus? In other words, are we aiming our supply chain capabilities where they can make money for the company? An analysis of profitability by customer, region, and channel may turn up some areas that are relatively (or even absolutely) unprofitable.

3. **How can we best deliver our offerings?** Are our infrastructure and service policies doing the job efficiently? We typically bundle our most complex products with an extended warranty and maintenance agreement. But is that the best deal for our customers—and does it help our bottom line?

Since their jobs begin and end with the customer, supply chain leaders are increasingly focusing on customer segmentation. A better understanding of what users want creates a better understanding of which products will satisfy them. Supply chain leaders can then establish different service levels for different customers and products. Dow Corning, for instance, had originally tried to differentiate its silicone-based products by bundling them with a lot of value-added services, such as technical support. But as Bain & Company consultants Mark Gottfredson and Steve Schaubert point out in their book *The Breakthrough Imperative* (Collins, 2008), some of Dow's customers didn't need these services and didn't want to pay for them. In response, Dow introduced a standard product line that could be ordered over the internet, without any application or engineering services included. It also began to offer its value-added services on an à la carte basis, so that customers could buy only what they needed.

Supply chain leaders typically vary their forecasting and demand planning for products depending on volumes, production requirements, and lead times. They're

IMPROVING GROWTH BY "FIXING THE DENOMINATOR"

A great example of a company that used supply chain improvements to boost growth is Groupe Danone, the French food conglomerate. During a turbulent period several years ago, it lost its leadership position in yogurt sales in Brazil. Nestlé had eclipsed Danone in market share, and Danone—also under attack by Parmalat—had stopped making money. The company needed to do something fast.

Conventional wisdom held that Danone couldn't match the two giants in operational efficiency, given their vast scale advantages. The two competitors also had wider distribution networks and more power within the trade. Danone initially concluded that the only way out was to compete on quality and innovation, not the easiest thing to do in a basic food category. Yet a streamlined supply chain saved the day.

Above all else, Danone's executives realized, people wanted fresher yogurt: They didn't like buying anything that was approaching its sell-by date. Indeed, when the company surveyed consumers, about half said they based their buying decisions on expiration dates.

To figure out how to give them exactly what they wanted, Danone answered the three key customer-focused questions driving supply chain math and concluded that it could improve how it got products into customers' hands. For one thing, volumes weren't always tied to demand: To reduce production costs, manufacturing had been told it could produce only full vats of yogurt for any SKU, which led to waste. For another, Danone uncovered problems in how its product moved from the factory to retail outlets. Inventory was scattered over multiple locations across the country, yet 80% of its yogurt sales took place within a half-day travel radius of its central warehouse—meaning that a large percentage of its product was making an unnecessary second stop in a regional facility. Such logistics resulted in less-than-fresh yogurt and stockouts where demand was high. Moreover, rigid maintenance and clean-up schedules added downtime that created more deviation between store-ordered volumes and the amount of yogurt actually produced.

So Danone's team redesigned its Brazilian distribution network to serve the majority of its store customers, turning three regional warehouses into transit points without inventory. It created new rules for production, allowing manufacturing to make partial vats of yogurt when needed. The company moved most of the supply chain responsibility under a centralized logistics organization that had more oversight over the forecasting process. The result? The average number of days from factory to store fell by more than half, to four.

(*continued*)

(continued)

By fixing the denominator on ROIC, Danone liberated its numerator. There was no change other than increased freshness, but consumers responded dramatically, increasing Danone's revenue by more than 10%, as well as boosting the company's return on sales.

also constantly weeding out inefficiencies rooted in silo-based thinking. In other words, they manage the link between supply chain decisions and manufacturing operations effectively, so that their companies concentrate on items that serve their target market with the least possible complexity. In the mid-1990s, for instance, the vehicle and engine maker Navistar introduced its Diamond Spec program, through which buyers of certain trucks could choose among 16 preengineered modules rather than the thousands of possible configurations that had been available. Soon thereafter, say Gottfredson and Schaubert, Diamond Spec "accounted for 80 percent of dealer orders for that class of truck"—and Navistar's costs were significantly lower.

How Goodyear's Customer Focus Improved Sales

Consider the supply chain situation at Goodyear Tire & Rubber Company several years ago. As a new chairman and chief executive took the reins, the company's North American Tire (NAT) operations were sliding toward a significant loss. Poorly targeted attempts to reduce inventories had led to declining service levels and frequent stockouts. Customers were complaining, and the company faced a clutter of obsolescent and unprofitable inventory in its warehouses. To raise the stakes even higher, Goodyear was preparing to launch two products it hoped would be blockbusters: its Assurance passenger-car tire and its redesigned commercial steer tire, aimed at curtailing Michelin's threat in the market for outfitting trucks.

How could Goodyear turn things around and strengthen sales? With a new president on board, NAT's management reexamined a full set of assumptions around "What do we sell?" and "To whom?" NAT created a team comprising sales, marketing, manufacturing, and finance that was given a broad charter for identifying and beginning to fix structural problems that ate up cash and working capital, and for starting to optimize customer service.

When the team took a clear-eyed look at what NAT sold and why, it saw, at the core of Goodyear's culture, a manufacturing-based mind-set focused chiefly on driving down unit costs, insufficiently balanced by considerations of downstream supply chain needs and customer requirements. The team cleaned house, reducing overall stocks 15% from seasonal highs and eliminating 50% of the company's unprofitable SKUs. And it reduced complexity: One streamlining initiative consolidated low-volume products from more than a dozen warehouses around the United States to one central place.

NAT also examined its service and delivery practices for product and customer segments. New guidelines allowed for expediting high-volume products (such as the company's Eagle performance tires) in lower quantities but stipulated batching low-volume, seasonal products (such as farm tires) and delivering them with longer lead times. Such practices started to align Goodyear's product profitability with the service requirements of different customer segments.

Improving supply chain performance demanded new discipline in sales forecasting. By sharing reliable data for demand planning in a joint sales and operations planning process, NAT developed a more realistic set of sales forecasts. NAT also fine-tuned its manufacturing schedule to parse monthly quotas to weeks and days required for given shipments, which reduced the need for safety stocks.

Such moves helped NAT "attack the denominator"—and as the changes took effect, customers noticed and appreciated improvements in the company's fill rates. Goodyear substantially reduced working capital tied up in inventory and freed up cash for other initiatives. As forecasting and other processes improved, the company reduced fluctuations in inventory, reducing peak-to-trough variance from 5.3 million units to 1.4 million just three years later. As it launched its new lines of tires, Goodyear balanced efforts to meet demand and control internal costs far better than it had in the past, even though the popularity of some tires required establishing dealer quotas based on their "fair share" of the market.

How did the supply chain math add up? After implementing the changes, Goodyear reported profits of

$36.5 million on sales of $4.7 billion, versus a net loss of $119.4 million on sales of $3.9 billion for the same period in the previous year. Better earnings combined with faster asset turns also boosted ROIC. The company attributed the financial improvements and profitable growth to better operating results in all business segments, including North American Tire.

Of course, applying supply chain science has organizational implications. Chief among these is the challenge of capturing the right statistics to accurately measure progress and eliminate hunch work. This also means tracking the performance metrics of vendors, logistics partners, and distributors—and sharing appropriate forecasts and other sensitive data. Few companies do these things well. Such focus has less to do with new IT systems than it does with people.

Companies should assign star players—and give them the proper incentives—to tackle the supply chain challenge. They should reward these executives not just for having enough stock on hand but also for increasing asset turns, growth, and share price.

Based in Atlanta, **Miles Cook** and **Pratap Mukharji** are Bain & Company partners who lead the firm's Global Supply Chain practice. **Lorenz Kiefer**, a partner in Düsseldorf, leads Bain's European Supply Chain practice. **Marco Petruzzi** is a partner based in Los Angeles.

Profit ≠ Cash (and You Need Both)

by Karen Berman and Joe Knight, with John Case

Profit, shown on the income statement, is not the same as **net cash,** shown on the cash flow statement. Why should this be? Some reasons are pretty obvious: Cash may be coming in from loans or from investors, and that isn't going to show up on the income statement at all. But even **operating cash flow** is not at all the same as **net profit.**

There are three essential reasons:

- **Revenue is booked at sale.** A sale is recorded whenever a company delivers a product or service. Ace Printing Company delivers $1,000 worth of brochures to a customer; Ace Printing Company re-

---

Adapted from *Financial Intelligence* (product #4989BC), by Karen Berman and Joe Knight, with John Case, Harvard Business Review Press, 2006

cords revenue of $1,000, and theoretically it could record a profit based on subtracting its costs and expenses from that revenue. But no cash has changed hands because Ace's customer typically has 30 days or more to pay. Since profit starts with revenue, it always reflects customers' promises to pay. Cash flow, by contrast, always reflects cash transactions.

- **Expenses are matched to revenue.** The purpose of the income statement is to tote up all the costs and expenses associated with generating revenue during a given time period. However, those expenses may not be the ones that were actually paid during that time period. Some may have been paid earlier. Some will be paid later, when vendors' bills come due. So the expenses on the income statement do not reflect cash going out. The cash flow statement, however, always measures cash in and out the door during a particular time period.

- **Capital expenditures don't count against profit.** A capital expenditure doesn't appear on the income statement when it occurs; only the depreciation is charged against revenue. So a company can buy trucks, machinery, computers, and so on, and the expense will appear on the income statement only gradually, over the useful life of each item. Cash, of course, is another story: All those items are often paid for long before they have been fully depreciated, and the cash used to pay for them will be reflected in the cash flow statement.

You may be thinking that in the long run cash flow will pretty much track net profit. Accounts receivable will be collected, so sales will turn into cash. Accounts payable will be paid, so expenses will more or less even out from one time period to the next. And capital expenditures will be depreciated, so over time the charges against revenue from depreciation will more or less equal the cash being spent on new assets. All this is true to a degree, at least for a mature, well-managed company. But the difference between profit and cash can create all sorts of mischief in the meantime, especially for a growing company. Entrepreneurial businesses in particular may face periods of fluctuating sales. They may have to cope with the fact that one big customer pays its bills very slowly—or that one important vendor requires payment up front. All these can wreak havoc on an entrepreneur's cash flow, even if they don't much affect profitability.

Profit Without Cash

We'll illustrate the difference between profit and cash by comparing two simple companies with dramatically different profit and cash positions. Sweet Dreams Bakery is a new cookies-and-cakes manufacturer that supplies specialty grocery stores. The founder has lined up orders based on her unique home-style recipes, and she's ready to launch on January 1. We'll assume she has $10,000 cash in the bank, and we'll also assume that in the first three months her sales are $20,000, $30,000, and $45,000. Cost of goods sold is 60% of sales, and her monthly operating expenses are $10,000.

Just by eyeballing those numbers, you can see she'll soon be making a profit. In fact, a simplified **income statement** for the first three months looks like this:

	January	February	March
Sales	$20,000	$30,000	$45,000
COGS	12,000	18,000	27,000
Gross profit	8,000	12,000	18,000
Expenses	10,000	10,000	10,000
Net profit	($ 2,000)	$ 2,000	$ 8,000

The **cash flow,** however, tells a different story. Sweet Dreams Bakery has an agreement with its vendors to pay for the ingredients and other supplies it buys in 30 days. But those specialty grocery stores that the company sells to? They're kind of precarious, and they take 60 days to pay their bills.

So here's what happens to Sweet Dreams' cash situation:

- In *January,* Sweet Dreams collects nothing from its customers. At the end of the month, all it has is $20,000 in receivables from its sales. Luckily, it does not have to pay anything out for the ingredients it uses, since its vendors expect to be paid in 30 days. (We'll assume that the COGS figure is all for ingredients, because the owner herself does all the baking.) But the company does have to pay expenses—rent, utilities, and so on. So all the initial $10,000 in cash goes out the door to pay expenses, and Sweet Dreams is left with no cash in the bank. A simplified representation of the company's checkbook would look like this:

Beginning cash	$10,000
Expenses	(10,000)
Ending cash	$ 0

- In *February,* Sweet Dreams still hasn't collected anything. (Remember, its customers pay in 60 days.) At the end of the month, it has $50,000 in receivables—January's $20,000 plus February's $30,000—but still no cash. Meanwhile, Sweet Dreams now has to pay for the ingredients and supplies for January ($12,000), and it has another month's worth of expenses ($10,000). So it's now in the hole by $22,000. Here's the checkbook (assuming for the moment that Sweet Dreams can show a negative balance in its bank account!):

Beginning cash	$ 0
Ingredients and supplies	(12,000)
Expenses	(10,000)
Ending cash	($22,000)

Can the owner turn this around? Surely, in March those rising profits will improve the cash picture! Alas, no.

- In *March,* Sweet Dreams finally collects on its January sales, so it has $20,000 in cash coming in the door, leaving it only $2,000 short against its end-of-February cash position. But now it has to pay for February's COGS of $18,000 plus March's expenses of $10,000. So at the end of March, it ends up $30,000 in the hole—a worse position than at the end of February. Again, the checkbook:

Beginning cash	($22,000)
Collections	20,000
Ingredients and supplies	(18,000)
Expenses	(10,000)
Ending cash	($30,000)

What's going on here? The answer is that Sweet Dreams is growing. Its sales increase every month, meaning that it must pay more each month for its ingredients. Eventually, its operating expenses will increase as well because the owner will have to hire more people. The other problem is the disparity between the fact that Sweet Dreams must pay its vendors in 30 days while waiting 60 days for receipts from its customers. In effect, it has to front the cash for 30 days—and *as long as sales are increasing, it will never be able to catch up unless it finds additional sources of cash.* As fictional and oversimplified as Sweet Dreams may be, this is precisely how profitable companies go out of business. It is one reason why so many small entrepreneurial companies fail in their first year. They simply run out of cash.

Cash Without Profit

But now let's look at another sort of profit/cash disparity.

Fine Cigar Shops is a start-up that sells very expensive cigars, and it's located in a part of town frequented by businesspeople and well-to-do tourists. Its sales for the first three months are $50,000, $75,000, and $95,000—

again, a healthy growth trend. Its cost of goods is 70% of sales, and its monthly operating expenses are $30,000 (high rent!). For the sake of comparison, we'll say that it, too, begins the period with $10,000 in the bank.

So Fine Cigar's **income statement** for these months looks like this:

	January	**February**	**March**
Sales	$50,000	$75,000	$95,000
COGS	35,000	52,500	66,500
Gross profit	15,000	22,500	28,500
Expenses	30,000	30,000	30,000
Net profit	($15,000)	($ 7,500)	($ 1,500)

Fine Cigar hasn't yet turned the corner on profitability, though it is losing less money each month. Meanwhile, what does its **cash** picture look like?

As a retailer, of course, Fine Cigar collects the money on each sale immediately. And we'll assume that it was able to negotiate good terms with its vendors, paying them in 60 days.

- In *January,* it begins with $10,000 and adds $50,000 in cash sales. It doesn't have to pay for cost of goods sold yet, so the only cash out the door is that $30,000 in expenses. End-of-the-month bank balance: $30,000. Here's a simplified representation of the company's checkbook:

Beginning cash	$10,000
Cash sales	50,000
Expenses	(30,000)
Ending cash	$30,000

- In *February,* Fine Cigar adds $75,000 in cash sales and still doesn't pay anything for cost of goods sold. So the month's net cash after the $30,000 in expenses is $45,000. Now the bank balance is $75,000! The checkbook:

Beginning cash	$30,000
Cash sales	75,000
Expenses	(30,000)
Ending cash	$75,000

- In *March,* Fine Cigar adds $95,000 in cash sales and pays for January's supplies ($35,000) and March's expenses ($30,000). Net cash in for the month is $30,000, and the bank balance is now $105,000. Here's the checkbook:

Beginning cash	$75,000
Cash sales	95,000
Payment of invoices	(35,000)
Expenses	(30,000)
Ending cash	$105,000

Cash-based businesses—retailers, restaurants, and so on—can thus get an equally skewed picture of their situation. In this case Fine Cigar's bank balance is climbing every month even though the company is unprofitable. That's fine for a while, and it will continue to be fine so long as the company holds down expenses so that it can turn the corner on profitability. But the owner has to be careful: If he's lulled into thinking that his business is doing great and that he can increase those expenses, he's liable to continue on the unprofitable path. If he fails to attain profitability, *eventually he will run out of cash.*

Fine Cigar, too, has its real-world parallels. Every cash-based business, from tiny Main Street shops to giants such as Amazon.com and Dell, has the luxury of taking the customer's money before it must pay for its costs and expenses. It enjoys the float—and if it is growing, that float will grow ever larger. But ultimately, the company must be profitable by the standards of the income statement; cash flow in the long run is no protection against unprofitability. In the cigar-store example, the losses on the books will eventually lead to negative cash flow; just as profits eventually lead to cash, losses eventually use up cash. It's the timing of those cash flows that we are trying to understand here.

Understanding the difference between profit and cash is a key to increasing your financial intelligence. It opens a whole new window of opportunity to make smart decisions. For example:

- **Finding the right kind of expertise.** The two situations described above require different skills. If a company is profitable but short on cash, then it needs financial expertise—someone capable of lining up additional financing. If a company has cash but is unprofitable, it needs operational expertise, someone capable of bringing down costs or generating additional revenue without adding costs. So financial statements tell you not only what is going on in the company but also what kind of expertise you need to hire.

- **Making good decisions about timing.** Informed decisions on when to take an action can increase a company's effectiveness. Take Setpoint Systems, a company that builds factory-automation systems, as an example. Managers at the company know that the first quarter of the year, when many orders come in, is the most profitable for the business. But cash is always tight because Setpoint must pay out cash to buy components and pay contractors. The next quarter, Setpoint's cash flow typically improves because receivables from the prior quarter are collected, but profits slow down. Setpoint managers have learned that it's better to buy capital equipment for the business in the second quarter rather than the first, even though the second quarter is traditionally less profitable, just because there's more cash available to pay for it.

The ultimate lesson here is that profit and cash are different—and a healthy business, both in its early years and as it matures, requires both.

Karen Berman and **Joe Knight** are the owners of the Los Angeles–based Business Literacy Institute. Coauthor **John Case** has written several popular books on management.

Why Cash Matters

by Karen Berman and Joe Knight, with John Case

There are three big reasons for understanding the **cash flow statement.**

First, it will help you see what is going on now, where the business is headed, and what senior management's priorities are likely to be. You need to know not just whether the overall cash position is healthy but specifically where the cash is coming from. Is much of it coming from regular business operations, rather than from lenders or investors? That's a good thing—it means the business itself is generating cash. Is investing cash flow a sizable negative number? If it isn't, that may mean the company isn't investing in its future. And what about financing cash flow? If investment money is coming in, that may be reason for optimism—or it may mean that

---

Adapted from *Financial Intelligence* (product #4986BC), by Karen Berman and Joe Knight, with John Case, Harvard Business Review Press, 2006

the company is desperately selling stock to stay afloat. Looking at the cash flow statement generates a lot of questions, but they are the right ones to be asking. Are we paying off loans? Why or why not? Are we buying equipment? The answers to those questions will reveal a lot about senior management's plans for the company.

Second, you *affect* cash. Most managers focus on profit when they should be focusing on both profit and cash. Of course, their impact is usually limited to operating cash flow—but that's one of the most important measures there is. For instance:

- **Accounts receivable.** Factors such as customers' satisfaction with your service, their relationship to your salespeople, and the accuracy of your invoices all help determine how customers feel about your company, and indirectly influence how fast they are likely to pay their bills. Disgruntled customers are not known for prompt payments—they like to wait until any dispute is resolved.

- **Inventory.** If you're in engineering, do you request special products all the time? If you do, you may be creating an inventory nightmare. If you're in operations and you like to have lots in stock, just in case, you may be creating a situation in which cash is just sitting on the shelves, when it could be used for something else.

- **Expenses.** Do you defer expenses when you can? Do you consider the timing of cash flow when making purchases? Obviously, we're not saying it's always wise to defer expenses; it's just wise to take into account what the cash impact will be when you do decide to spend money.

- **Giving credit.** Do you give credit to potential customers too easily? Alternatively, do you withhold credit when you should give it? Both decisions affect the company's cash flow and sales, which is why the credit department always has to strike a careful balance.

The list goes on. Maybe you're a plant manager, and you are always recommending buying more equipment, just in case the orders come in. Perhaps you're in IT, and you feel that the company always needs the latest upgrades to its computer systems. All these decisions affect cash flow, and senior management usually understands that very well. If you want to make an effective request, you need to familiarize yourself with the numbers that they're looking at.

Third, managers who understand cash flow tend to be given more responsibilities, and thus tend to advance more quickly, than those who focus purely on the income statement. You could go to someone in finance and say, "I notice our DSO [days sales outstanding] has been heading in the wrong direction over the last few months—how can I help turn that around?" Alternatively, you might learn the precepts of lean enterprise, which focuses on (among other things) keeping inventories to a minimum. A manager who leads a company in converting to lean thereby frees up huge quantities of cash.

Our general point here is that cash flow is a key indicator of a company's financial health, along with profitability and shareholders' equity. It's the final link in the triad.

Karen Berman and **Joe Knight** are the owners of the Los Angeles–based Business Literacy Institute. Coauthor **John Case** has written several popular books on management.

Your Balance Sheet Levers

by Karen Berman and Joe Knight, with John Case

Most companies use their cash to finance customers' purchase of products or services. That's the "accounts receivable" line on the balance sheet—the amount of money customers owe at a given point in time, based on the value of what they have purchased before that date.

The key ratio that measures accounts receivable is **days sales outstanding,** or **DSO**—that is, the average number of days it takes to collect on these receivables. *The longer a company's DSO, the more working capital is required to run the business.* Customers have more of its cash in the form of products or services not yet paid for, so that cash isn't available to buy inventory, deliver more

---

Adapted from *Financial Intelligence* (product #4977BC), by Karen Berman and Joe Knight, with John Case, Harvard Business Review Press, 2006

services, and so on. Conversely, the shorter a company's DSO, the less working capital is required to run the business. It follows that the more people understand DSO and work to bring it down, the more cash the company will have at its disposal.

Managing DSO

The first step in managing DSO is to understand what it is and in which direction it has been heading. If it's higher than it ought to be, and particularly if it's trending upward (which it nearly always seems to be), managers need to begin asking questions.

Operations and R&D managers, for example, must ask themselves whether there are any problems with the products that might make customers less willing to pay their bills. Is the company selling what customers want and expect? Is there a problem with delivery? Quality problems and late deliveries often provoke late payment, just because customers are not pleased with the products they're receiving and decide that they will take their own sweet time about payment. Managers in quality assurance, market research, product development, and so on thus have an effect on receivables, as do managers in production and shipping. In a service company, people who are out delivering the service need to ask themselves the same questions. If service customers aren't satisfied with what they're getting, they too will take their time about paying.

Customer-facing managers—those in sales and customer service—have to ask a similar set of questions. Are our customers financially healthy? What is the standard in their industry for paying bills? Are they in a region of the world that pays quickly or slowly? Salespeople typically have the first contact with a customer, so it is up to them to flag any concerns about the customer's financial health. Once the sale is made, customer-service reps need to pick up the ball and learn what's going on. What's happening at the customer's shop? Are they working overtime? Laying people off? Meanwhile, salespeople need to work with the folks in credit and customer service so that everybody understands the terms up front and will notice when a customer is late. At one company we worked with, the delivery people knew the most about customers' situations because they were at their facilities every day. They would alert sales and accounting if there seemed to be issues cropping up in a customer's business.

Credit managers need to ask whether the terms offered are good for the company and whether they fit the credit histories of the customers. They need to make judgments about whether the company is giving credit too easily or whether it is too tough in its credit policies. There's always a trade-off between increasing sales on the one hand and issuing credit to poorer credit risks on the other. Credit managers need to set the precise terms they're willing to offer. Is net 30 days satisfactory—or should we allow net 60? They need to determine strategies such as offering discounts for early pay. For example, "2/10 net 30" means that customers get a discount of 2% if they pay their bill in 10 days and no discount if they wait 30 days. Sometimes a 1% or 2% discount can help a struggling company collect its receivables and thereby lower its DSO—but of course it does so by eating into profitability.

We know of a small company that has a simple, homegrown approach to the issue of giving credit to customers. It has identified the traits it wants in its customers and has even named its ideal customer Bob. Bob's qualities include the following:

- He works for a large company.
- His company is known for paying its bills on time.
- He can maintain and understand the product provided (this company makes complex technology-intensive products).
- He is looking for an ongoing relationship.

If a new customer meets these criteria, he will get credit from this small manufacturer. Otherwise he won't. As a result of this policy, the company has been able to keep its DSO quite low and to grow without additional equity investment.

All these decisions can have a huge impact on accounts receivable and thus working capital. Reducing DSO even by one day can save a large company millions of dollars per day.

Managing Inventory

Many managers (and consultants!) these days are focusing on inventory. They work to reduce it wherever possible. They use buzzwords such as **lean manufacturing,**

just-in-time inventory management, and **economic order quantity (EOQ).** The reason for all this attention is exactly what we're talking about here. Managing inventory efficiently reduces working capital requirements by freeing up large amounts of cash.

The challenge is to reduce inventory to a minimum level while still ensuring that every raw material and every part will be available when needed and every product will be ready for sale when a customer wants it. A manufacturer needs to be constantly ordering raw material, making things, and holding them for delivery to customers. Wholesalers and retailers need to replenish their stocks regularly to avoid the dreaded stockout—an item that isn't available when a customer wants it. Yet every item in inventory can be regarded as frozen cash, which is to say cash that the company cannot use for other purposes. Exactly how much inventory is required to satisfy customers while minimizing that frozen cash? Well, that's the million-dollar question (and the reason for all those consultants).

Many different kinds of managers affect a company's use of inventory—which means that all these managers can help reduce working capital requirements. For example:

- **Salespeople** love to tell customers they can have exactly what they want. ("Have it *your* way," as the old Burger King jingle put it.) Custom paint job? No problem. Bells and whistles? No problem. But every variation requires a little more inventory, meaning a little more cash. Obviously, customers must be satisfied. But that commonsense requirement has to be balanced against the fact that inventory costs money. The more that salespeople can sell standard products with limited variations, the less inventory their company will have to carry.

- **Engineers** love those same bells and whistles. In fact, they're constantly working to improve the company's products, replacing version 2.54 with version 2.55 and so on. Again, this is a laudable business objective, but one that has to be balanced against inventory requirements. A proliferation of product versions puts a burden on inventory management. When a product line is kept simple with a few easily interchangeable options, inventory declines and inventory management becomes a less taxing task.

- **Production departments** greatly affect inventory. For instance, what's the percentage of machine downtime? Frequent breakdowns require the company to carry more work-in-process inventory and more finished-goods inventory. And what's the average time between changeovers? Decisions about how much to build of a particular part have an enormous impact on inventory requirements. Even the layout of a plant affects inventory: A well-designed production flow in an efficient plant minimizes the need for inventory.

Along these lines, it's worth noting that many U.S. plants eat up tremendous amounts of working capital.

When business is slow, they nevertheless keep on churning out product in order to maintain factory efficiency. Plant managers focus on keeping unit costs down, often because that goal has been pounded into their heads for so long that they no longer question it. They have been trained to do it, told to do it, and paid (with bonuses) for achieving it.

When business is good, that goal makes perfect sense: Keeping unit costs down is simply a way of managing all the costs of production in an efficient manner. (This is the old approach of focusing only on the income statement, which is fine as far as it goes.) When demand is slow, however, the plant manager must consider the company's cash as well as its unit costs. A plant that continues to turn out product in these circumstances is just creating more inventory that will take up space on a shelf. Coming to work and reading a book might be better than building product that is not ready to be sold.

Any large company can save millions of dollars in cash, and thereby reduce working capital requirements, just by making modest improvements in its inventory management.

Karen Berman and **Joe Knight** are the owners of the Los Angeles–based Business Literacy Institute. Coauthor **John Case** has written several popular books on management.

What's Your Working Capital Model? A Case Study

by John Mullins and Randy Komisar

Imagine a working capital model where your customers pay you before your product or service is even produced, not to mention delivered. A good idea, right? Consider the subscription-based periodical publishing industry. From the bare-bones *Kiplinger Letter* (a subscription-based personal finance newsletter) to the complex workings of the *New York Times,* companies in the periodicals industry historically have had negative working capital.

Why is this? Periodicals publishers—whether they publish newsletters, newspapers, or magazines—tend to

---

Excerpted from *Getting to Plan B: Breaking Through to a Better Business Model* (product #5371BC), by John Mullins and Randy Komisar, Harvard Business Review Press, 2009

have almost no inventory, just some paper and ink. As soon as they print the current edition, out it goes. On the other hand, subscription fees are collected long before the publication is printed and shipped. That's good news if you want to drive working capital down. For the publisher, the cash the subscriber pays up front is what accountants call a **liability** (unearned subscriptions or deferred revenues, as they are often called on publishers' financial statements), since the publisher now "owes" the upcoming issues to the subscriber. The result of all this: modest **current assets** (limited mostly to accounts receivable from advertising not yet paid), large **current liabilities** (the issues due for the rest of the year, for example), and negative **working capital.**

Dow Jones & Company (Dow Jones)—known best for its newspaper, the *Wall Street Journal,* and its stock market index, the Dow Jones Industrial Average—is a case in point for negative working capital. Its business was based on this working capital model for more than a century. Then along came the digital revolution. Was it time for Plan B?

Let's start at the beginning. Founded in New York City in 1882 by Charles Henry Dow, Edward Davis Jones, and Charles Milford Bergstresser, print media was Dow Jones's bread and butter. The company started off producing daily, handwritten news bulletins called *flimsies,* delivered by messengers to subscribers in the Wall Street area of Manhattan. In 1883 the company started publishing the *Customers' Afternoon Letter,* which six years later became the *Wall Street Journal.* The four-page *Journal* could be purchased for 2 cents a copy. Advertising was sold for 20 cents per line. In 1902, Clarence Barron, who was one of Dow Jones's first employees, purchased Dow, Jones & Company for $130,000. He added a weekly financial publication, *Barron's,* in 1921. Decades later, in the 1970s, Dow Jones diversified, purchasing a number of local newspapers, increasing its circulation and reach and lessening its reliance on the financial markets.

But in the late 1980s, with the advent of digital media like the now-ubiquitous Bloomberg terminals that have sprouted on nearly every desk in the financial world, the *Wall Street Journal* started losing subscribers. Circulation dropped from a high of 2.11 million in 1983 to 1.95 million by 1989. Profits deteriorated. The publishing world was changing, the Internet had arrived, and electronic publishing became Dow Jones's Plan B. But moving from print to digital was no trivial task. That it believed it could do so was a huge leap of faith.

Let's take stock of Dow Jones's working capital model at the end of its old-economy heyday, in 1992. These were the noncash elements of its working capital at that time:

- Current assets (other than cash) = 37 days
  - Inventory: 4 days
  - Accounts receivable: 33 days (subscribers pay in advance, but advertisers pay in arrears; this figure reflects the latter)
- Current liabilities = 109 days
  - Accounts payable: 70 days

    - Unearned subscriptions: 39 days (subscriptions paid for but not yet delivered)

- Net of these elements = –72 days

That's seventy-two days' worth of customer cash, or about 20 percent (72 days out of the 365-day year = 19.7 percent) of 1992's $1.8 billion in revenue, that Dow Jones could use for other things. It's like having $360 million of free money, just sitting there, ready to use to buy printing presses, pay wages, or to develop new businesses! By paying its suppliers (of newsprint among other things) in an average of seventy days and by collecting people's subscriptions for its publications and newswires up front, Dow Jones had the ability to literally use other people's money to pay its bills. But the game was changing. Would the working capital model that was central to any publisher's success have to change as well?

Dow Jones Goes Digital

By 1992 the company had already launched DowVision, a news service customized for Dow Jones's corporate customers. DowVision delivered published text from the *Wall Street Journal, New York Times, Financial Times, Washington Post,* and *Los Angeles Times,* together with a premier version of the Dow Jones newswires, directly to corporate desktops. Pleased with its early progress, in 1995 Dow Jones's leadership went public with its new strategy. "We're taking our editorial standards to the Web, where a glut of information often makes searching for the right piece of information time-consuming and fruitless." The company saw two distinct segments for its electronic services: individuals or small companies and large enterprises, both of which it wanted to serve. Dow Jones developed new online services for individuals and small businesses, allowing them to use credit cards to purchase subscriptions or to pay for downloads of specific packages of information such as articles. Large enterprises on the other hand were expected to sign annual contracts for electronic access to Dow Jones's information, paid in advance, of course. The company's leaders had not forgotten what had gotten it this far, paid subscriptions up front!

Soon there was an online electronic supplement to the *Wall Street Journal*'s Money & Investing section, known as the "*Wall Street Journal* Interactive Edition" (known later as *WSJ Online* at WSJ.com). This electronic newspaper subscription service allowed individual users to browse articles online. Both DowVision and The Publications Library, a news archive, were made available for Web users, primarily serving large enterprises as research tools, on a subscription basis.

From 1999 through 2006, Dow Jones quickened its digital pace, developing a joint venture with Reuters to create Factiva, a Web-based source of current and archived global news—subscriptions paid up front, of course. NewsPlus, a Web-formatted enhancement of Dow Jones's newswires, and Dow Jones Financial Information Services, which gave financial professionals additional Web access to electronic media, information, and directories, were added. MarketWatch.com, which provided online business and financial news, was acquired. Dow Jones's digital Plan B was well under way.

In 2006, Dow Jones went further, getting rid of some of its paper-based products in favor of online offerings. It launched *Barron's Online* and bought Factiva outright, terminating the joint venture with Reuters. In December it sold six of the community newspapers that it had published for years. CEO Rich Zannino said, "This sale and the pending acquisition of Factiva are the latest examples of our commitment to transform Dow Jones from a company heavily dependent on print publishing revenue to a more diversified company capable of meeting the needs of its customers across all consumer and enterprise media channels, whether print, online, mobile or otherwise."

Would Its Subscription-Reliant Working Capital Model Still Work?

The Dow Jones management team consisted of veterans who understood the crucial role that the working capital model played in the publishing industry. When they adopted Plan B and its new digital revenue model, they retained a crucial element of Plan A—the company's working capital model. Take a look at the 2006 Dow Jones numbers to see what happened:

- Current assets (other than cash) = 58 days
  - Inventory: 3 days
  - Accounts receivable: 55 days
- Current liabilities = 135 days

  - Accounts payable: 88 days
  - Unearned subscriptions: 47 days

- Net of these elements = –77 days

The Dow Jones's working capital model had improved to –77 days in 2006 (compared with –72 days in 1992)! The bedrock of the model, paid subscriptions up front, was still in place. The company still charged for traditional subscriptions for the *Wall Street Journal* and its remaining local newspapers, and for *Barron's*, Factiva, and its newswires. Most components of *Barron's Online* and WSJ.com required a subscription, as did some elements of MarketWatch. The Dow Jones indexes were both subscription- and license-based. And *Dow Jones Online News* could be licensed for a fee. Only a few experiments, such as CareerJournal.com, RealEstateJournal.com and OpinionJournal.com, came subscription-free.

The business had been transformed without going hat-in-hand to investors, funded largely by its customers' cash, and its precious working capital model had remained intact. The results for Dow Jones shareholders? Net income more than tripled on virtually the same $1.8 billion in revenue, rising from $107 million in 1992 to $386 million in 2006. And, perhaps with a nod to the company's successful transition to the digital age, Rupert Murdoch's News Corporation purchased Dow Jones for $5 billion in August 2007. Notably, and probably with thanks to Dow Jones's veterans, Murdoch, who indicated before the acquisition that he would make *WSJ Online* free and ad-based, has left its subscription-based, negative working capital model in place.

Lessons from Dow Jones

Dow Jones & Company shows us that negative working capital is helpful in coping with dramatic changes, such as those it faced in the digital revolution. Such a model provides customer cash with which to develop new products and strategies to iterate toward Plan B. Equally important was its management team's ability to identify new kinds and forms of content—new products, each of which was a leap of faith until proven—that consumers and business customers would value and pay for.

By itself, a better working capital model is not enough. Indeed, this point is evidenced by the cash infusion the *New York Times* needed in January 2009 from Carlos Slim, the Mexican billionaire, in order to remain afloat. The *Times* had not been nearly as inventive as Dow Jones in developing cash-generative digital offerings to make its own digital transition. While Dow Jones largely maintained its subscription-based model as it went digital, the *New York Times* did otherwise in making the *New York Times Online* free.

Dow Jones & Company also shows how a powerful working capital model, common to an entire industry in this case, can enable changes in other parts of one's strategy and make seemingly wrenching changes appear as smooth as silk. Though sailing was not always easy for Dow Jones—there were a couple of loss-making years along the way—its transition to the digital age was, for the most part, successful. Sometimes, though, it takes innovators to bring new and different working capital models to an established industry. When they do, watch out!

John Mullins is an associate professor of management practice at London Business School. **Randy Komisar** is a partner at Kleiner Perkins Caufield & Byers and a lecturer on entrepreneurship at Stanford University.

Learn to Speak the Language of ROI

by John O'Leary

Nobody is getting approval to spend money these days unless he or she can demonstrate an economic return. And so nonfinancial professionals are having to master the mysterious lexicon of **return on investment (ROI)**, which includes terms such as **breakeven, internal rate of return**, and **discounted cash flow.**

These concepts should be second nature for anyone charged with making or contributing to financial decisions. But in too many companies, it's only the finance mavens who really understand ROI.

Say you want to spend $200,000 on a new automated call system. You're jazzed up about how reducing wait times from 60 seconds to 30 seconds will boost customer satisfaction and loyalty. As important as such improve-

Adapted from *Harvard Management Update* (product #U0210C), October 2002

ments are, they're not what the green-eyeshade types in finance care most about. For them, the key benefit is adding more money to the bottom line. Since they're the ones making the decision on your project, not only do you have to understand how the new system will increase profits, you must also be able to use the language of financial modeling to make the case for your initiative.

To get your project funded, especially when money is tight, here's what you need to learn.

Cash Flow Modeling

An ROI analysis enables you to compare the financial consequences of two (or more) business alternatives. Should we spend X dollars to do Project A or Y dollars to do Project B? Would we be better off buying or leasing? Would it be better to create this product in-house or to outsource?

To answer such questions you have to build a business case—a financial story based on facts, reasonable assumptions, and logic. At the heart of this story is a picture of the expected cash flow. A cash flow projection provides estimates of the net financial impact of a decision over a period of time. To construct such a projection, you must document not only all of the expected costs and benefits of the decision but also the time period in which they occur. Most ROI calculations seek to project three to five years out.

Here it's important to highlight a crucial difference between an ROI analysis and an income, or profit-and-loss (P&L), statement. The ROI analysis is cash-based, whereas a P&L uses standard accounting principles to spread out costs in a reasonable fashion. For example, on

BUILDING THE FINANCIAL CASE

The following ROI analysis makes projections for the launch of a fictitious new product, the RT-200. As with many cash flow analyses, this spreadsheet compares the financial consequences of investing in the launch of the RT-200 against the alternative of *not* launching the product (which carries no cost or return).

US$ in thousands	**Year 1**	**Year 2**	**Year 3**	**Year 4**	**Total**
Financial benefit (revenue or cost savings)					
Revenue	–	500	1,000	1,500	3,000
(Lost revenue)	(50)	(100)	(100)	(100)	(350)
Cost savings	–	100	120	130	350
Total benefit	(50)	500	1,020	1,530	3,000
Investments/capital expenditures:					
Hardware	600	–	100	–	700
Licenses	200	–	–	–	200
Development	500	–	–	100	600
Subtotal capital	1,300	–	100	100	1,500
Operating expenses:					
Headcount	25	25	25	25	100
Fabrication		55	90	155	300
Marketing		420	130	50	600
Subtotal operating	25	500	245	230	1,000
Total investments	1,325	500	345	330	2,500

Return on investment				**Total return = $500**	
	Year 1	**Year 2**	**Year 3**	**Year 4**	**Total**
Total cash flow	(1,375)	–	675	1,200	500
Discounted cash flow (Present value) Assumes 10% discount rate	(1,375)	–	557	902	84

(*continued*)

(continued)

The bottom-line ROI analysis on the RT-200 project:

- The project will cost $2.5 million in capital and operating expenses during the next four years but will generate $3 million in additional revenue and cost savings, for a four-year ROI of 20%.
- The project will be at breakeven during Year 4.
- The payback period for this investment is between three and four years.
- The net present value of this investment is $84,000, assuming a discount rate (or cost of capital) of 10%.
- The internal rate of return is 12.5%.

a P&L, an expenditure for a piece of equipment with a useful life of five years might be amortized on a straight-line basis over that time frame, with one-fifth of the cost hitting the P&L each year. On a cash flow statement, the charge hits in the time period that you send the check out the door.

Often an important element of building a cash flow is translating "soft" benefits into hard numbers. If you work for an airline and want to increase passenger legroom, it would be easy to calculate the hard costs of removing several rows of seats. But how would you quantify the benefits of having happier, more comfortable passengers?

One approach might be through survey data showing that, say, 10% of your passengers would be willing to pay a 15% premium for more legroom. And don't forget to estimate the financial impact of the higher customer retention you might experience because of your roomier seats, or of the new customers you might win over. You may want to build a spreadsheet to see how your estimate of the financial benefit changes as you alter your assumptions.

Once you've finished estimating all the positive and negative cash flows associated with the decision in question, summarize the cash flow by calculating the net impact for each time period. At that point, you're ready to start analyzing the results using the following methods of comparison:

- **Payback period.** This is the point at which all the costs expended have been recovered. Many companies have a benchmark of five to seven years as a maximum payback period.

- **Breakeven point.** This is the moment when costs are matched by increased revenue or cost savings for that period. The time between the breakeven point and the end of the payback period will vary according to how significantly revenues outpace costs after the breakeven point has been reached.

- **Discounted cash flow (DCF).** This is a summarized cash flow that accounts for the time value of money, which is an adjustment for the fact that

$100 received today is worth more than $20 a year for the next five years. The DCF shows the impact of your project in today's dollars. The present value of $100 in the future is calculated with the following formula:

$$\text{Present Value} = \$100 \,/\, (1+x)^n$$

where n is the number of years into the future that the benefit (or cost) will occur, and x is the interest rate expressed in hundredths.

- **Net present value (NPV).** The sum of all the present values in the discounted cash flow, the NPV gives you a sense of the absolute size of the return expected from a project. As shown in the example, the NPV of $84,000 means that the projected overall financial benefit of the project is equivalent to realizing an immediate gain of $84,000 (see "Building the Financial Case" on page 107). The NPV should be looked at in light of the size of the investment that will be made, which in this case is $2.5 million. Although any NPV above zero shows that doing the project is preferable to doing nothing, in practice the benchmark NPV to beat is not zero but how much the investment could have earned in an alternative project. (It's easy to calculate NPV on a business calculator or computer.)
- **Internal rate of return (IRR).** This is the interest rate at which the discounted cash flow yields a net present value of zero. This metric is of limited use, because it doesn't tell you how long you will enjoy

the given rate of return, nor does it show you the dollar amount of the return. Indeed, a pure IRR analysis can lead you to make poor decisions on competing investments.

Getting Your Budget Approved

Conducting the ROI analysis is just the first step. Now take it to the folks in finance. Don't bore them with talk about boosting customer satisfaction or reducing cycle times. Use the ROI analysis to spell out how your project will make the company money.

Let's return to the automated call system example: Your focus, when pitching this investment to the finance department, should be on how shorter wait times will mean fewer customers switching to competitors, which will translate into more revenue. Moreover, the new call system will require fewer customer service reps, which will also translate into lower costs.

This "dollars first" thinking will enable you to engage your audience in their passion—not yours. By describing your initiative in language that finance hears best, you're much more likely to win approval.

Boston-based business writer **John O'Leary** is the author of *Revolution at the Roots* (Free Press, 1995), a book about best practices in the public sector.

Practical Tools for Management Decisions

Finance and accounting provide a rich trove of practical tools that will help answer some of the most important management questions you'll ever face:

- What are the costs and benefits of a particular investment?
- What is its estimated return?
- How quickly will your company recoup the investment?
- How many units will it have to sell at specific prices to simply break even?
- Does your company have the right balance of fixed and variable costs?

Adapted from *Harvard Business Essentials: Finance for Managers* (product #5856BC), Harvard Business Review Press, 2002

- How can you estimate nonquantifiable costs and benefits?

Cost/Benefit Analysis

Suppose that Amalgamated Hat Rack is considering two investment options: (1) buying a new piece of machinery and (2) creating a new product line. The new machine is a smart-technology, high-temperature plastic extruder costing $100,000. Amalgamated believes that this machinery will save time and money over the long term and is safer than the current machinery. The second option, launching a line of coat racks, will require a $250,000 investment in plant, equipment, and design. How can Amalgamated decide whether either option makes economic sense? By doing a **cost/benefit analysis.** This means evaluating whether, over a given time frame, the benefits will outweigh the associated costs.

First, though, it's important to understand the cost of the status quo. You want to weigh the relative merits of each investment against the negative consequences, if any, of not making the investment at all.

Cost/benefit analysis involves the following steps:

1. **Identify the costs associated with the new business opportunity.** Consider this year's up-front costs plus those you anticipate in subsequent years.

2. **Identify the benefits of additional revenues the investment will bring.** These revenues could come from more customers or from increased purchases by existing customers. Be sure to factor

in associated new costs; ultimately, that means you'll be looking at profit.

3. **Identify the cost savings to be gained.** Some are straightforward; others are subtle and difficult to quantify. More efficient processing, for instance, could save you money because fewer people are required to do the same work, or because the process requires fewer steps, or because the time spent on each step decreases.

4. **Map out the timeline for expected costs and revenues.** When do you expect the costs to be incurred? In what increments? When do you expect to receive the benefits (additional revenues or cost savings)? In what increments?

5. **Evaluate the nonquantifiable benefits and costs.** There may be several, such as whether the investment strengthens a firm's position with distributors and whether it will add unnecessary product or process complexity to the firm's operations.

Once all that's done, you're ready to begin evaluating the investment opportunities by using one or more of the analytical tools below: accounting return on investment, payback period, or breakeven analysis.

Accounting Return on Investment

Return on investment (**ROI**)—or, to use the more technical term, **accounting return on investment**—is not always the best measure of an investment's success. But because many managers still use ROI, it pays to understand how they look at it. Accounting return on investment can take the form of cost savings, incremental profit, or value appreciation. Let's look at the simplest possible way of figuring it, although as we'll see in a moment, it isn't very realistic. You would begin by determining the net return, simply by subtracting the total cost of the investment from the total benefits received. Then, to calculate the ROI, you would divide the return by the total cost of the investment.

Suppose the new $100,000 extruder Amalgamated is considering would realize an annual $18,000 in savings for the company over the lifetime of the machine, which is estimated to be seven years. The total savings would thus be $126,000 ($18,000 × 7), making for a net return of $26,000 ($126,000 – $100,000). If you divide the net return ($26,000) by the total cost of the investment ($100,000), you get an ROI of 26%.

But that isn't the true return on investment, because it ignores the time value of money. For example, which would you rather have (assuming equal risks): an investment that gave you a 26% return in one year, or one that gave you the same return at the end of seven years? No contest there. Any rational investor would want the money sooner rather than later. Thus, true ROI calculations must always factor in the time value of money. Depending on your assumptions, you might find that the true ROI on the extruder was 5% or 10% rather than 26%.

Would any of those percentages even be a good return on the investment? In isolation, such figures have no particular meaning, since ROI calculations are a way of comparing returns on money a company invests internally with returns available to it elsewhere at the *same level of risk.* The notion of equal risk is very important here. All investors demand higher returns for higher risk. It makes no sense to compare the returns the company believes it could make from an investment in A, the relatively safe expansion of a current product line, with an investment in B, a wholly new product line for an untested market. The risk levels of the two potential investments are simply not equivalent. The higher-risk investment should have a higher potential return.

Payback Period

Companies also want to know the **payback period:** how long it will take a particular investment to pay for itself. We already know that the plastic extruder is expected to save Amalgamated $18,000 a year. To determine the payback period, divide the total amount of the investment by the annual savings expected. In this case, $100,000 divided by $18,000 equals 5.56. In other words, the extruder will pay for itself in about five-and-a-half years.

What if we assume that the extruder will wear out after four years rather than five? The investment now appears to be not particularly attractive—certainly less attractive than an investment with a similar ROI and a payback period of three years. As an analytical tool, the payback period tells you only one thing: how long it will take to recoup your investment. Although it is not useful in comparing real alternatives, some executives still rely on it.

Breakeven Analysis

Breakeven analysis tells you how much (or how much more) you need to sell in order to pay for the fixed investment—in other words, at what point you will break even on your cash flow. With that information in hand, you can look at market demand and competitors' market shares to determine whether it's realistic to expect to sell that much. Breakeven analysis can also help you think through the impact of changing price and volume relationships.

Most companies do breakeven analysis on the basis of revenue and gross profit margin. Here we will take a simplified approach and do the figuring on the basis of unit volume, so you can see the underlying reality. Our breakeven calculation will help you determine the volume level at which the total after-tax contribution from a product line or an investment covers its total fixed costs.

Before you can perform the calculation, you need to understand the components that go into it:

- **Fixed costs.** These are costs that stay mostly the same, no matter how many units of a product or service are sold—costs such as insurance, management salaries, and rent or lease payments. For example, the rent on the production facility will be the same, whether the company makes 10,000 or 20,000 units, and so will the insurance.

- **Variable costs.** Variable costs are those that change with the number of units produced and sold. Examples include labor and the costs of raw materials. The more units you make, the more you consume these items.

- **Contribution margin.** This is the amount of money that every sold unit contributes to paying for fixed costs. It is defined as net unit revenue minus variable (or direct) costs per unit.

With these concepts understood, we can do the calculation with this straightforward equation:

Breakeven Volume = Fixed Costs / Unit Contribution Margin

First, find the unit contribution margin by subtracting the variable costs per unit from the net revenue per unit. Then divide total fixed costs, or the amount of the investment, by the unit contribution margin. The quotient is the breakeven volume—that is, the number of units that must be sold for all fixed costs to be covered.

To see breakeven analysis in practice, let's look again at the plastic extruder example. Suppose that each hat rack produced by the extruder sells for $75, and that the variable cost per unit is $22:

$75 (Price per Unit) – $22 (Variable Cost per Unit) = $53 (Unit Contribution Margin)

Therefore:

$100,000 (Total Investment Required) / $53 (Unit Contribution Margin) = 1,887 Units

In other words, Amalgamated must sell 1,887 hat racks to recover its $100,000 investment. At this point,

A BREAKEVEN COMPLICATION

Our Hat Rack breakeven analysis represents a simple case. It assumes that costs are distinctly fixed or variable and that costs and unit contributions will not change if output increases or decreases. These assumptions may not hold in the real world. Rent may be fixed up to a certain level of production and then increase by 50% as you rent a secondary facility to handle expanded output. Labor costs may in reality be a hybrid of fixed and variable. And as you push more and more of your product into the market, you may find it necessary to offer price discounts—which reduce contribution per unit. You will need to adjust the breakeven calculation to accommodate these untidy realities.

the company must decide whether the breakeven volume is achievable: Is it realistic to expect to sell 1,887 additional hat racks, and if so, how quickly?

Operating Leverage

Your goal, of course, is not to break even but to make a profit. Once you've covered all your fixed costs with the contributions of many unit sales, every subsequent sale contributes directly to profits. To restate the equation used earlier in slightly different form:

$$\text{Unit Net Revenue} - \text{Unit Variable Cost} = \text{Unit Contribution to Profit}$$

You can see at a glance that the lower the unit variable cost, the greater the contribution to profits will be. In the pharmaceutical business, for example, the unit cost of producing and packaging a bottle of a new wonder drug may be a dollar or less. Yet if the company can sell each bottle for $100, it captures $99 per bottle in profit once sales have exceeded the breakeven point! Of course, the pharmaceutical company may have invested $400 million up front in fixed product development costs just to get the first bottle out the door. It will have to sell many bottles just to break even. But if it can, the profits will be extraordinary.

The relationship between fixed and variable costs is often described in terms of **operating leverage**. Companies with high fixed costs and low variable costs have high operating leverage. This is true of businesses in the software industry, for instance, where fixed product-development outlays are the bulk of a firm's costs and the variable cost of the discs on which programs are distributed represent only pennies. By contrast, companies with low operating leverage have low fixed costs relative to the total cost of producing every unit of output. A law firm, for example, has a minimal investment in equipment and fixed expenses. Most of its costs are the fees it pays its attorneys, which vary depending on the hours they bill to clients.

Operating leverage is a great thing once a company passes its breakeven point, but it can cause substantial losses if breakeven is never achieved. In other words, it's risky. This is why managers give so much thought to finding the right balance between fixed and variable costs.

Amalgamated Hat Rack, Coat Rack Division, January budget-to-actual

	Budget Jan.	Actual Jan.	Variance
Coat rack revenues	$39,000	$38,725	($275)*
Cost of goods sold	19,500	19,200	300
Gross margin	19,500	19,525	25
Marketing expense	8,500	10,100	(1,600)
Administrative expense	4,750	4,320	430
Total operating expense	13,250	14,420	(1,170)
Operating profit (EBIT)	$6,250	$5,105	($1,145)

*All parentheses indicate unfavorable variances.
Source: HMM Finance

Estimating Nonquantifiable Benefits and Costs

Because the numbers seldom tell the whole story, you'll need to look at qualitative factors too. For instance, how well does a potential investment fit the company's strategy and mission? Can the firm take it on without losing focus? How likely is it to succeed, given market conditions?

Even though such factors are not fully quantifiable, try to quantify them as much as possible. Say you're assessing the value of improved data—more comprehensive information that is easier to understand and more widely available—that a new investment would bring. You could try to come up with a dollar figure that represents the value of employees' time saved by the data, or the value of the increased customer retention that might be gleaned from your better understanding of purchase patterns. Such estimates should not necessarily be incorporated into your ROI or other quantified analyses, but they can be very persuasive nevertheless.

Weigh the quantifiable and the nonquantifiable factors together. For example, if an investment opportunity is only marginally positive according to the numbers, you may want to give equal weight to qualitative considerations (such as its likelihood to increase customer loyalty) in your final decision.

Tracking Performance

Once you've decided to undertake an investment opportunity, you should monitor its progress. Track your projections against actual revenues and expenses. It's a good idea to do this on a monthly basis, so that you can spot potential problems early on. With that in mind, let's look at projections for a new coat rack division at Amalgamated Hat Rack. The table on the previous page shows the state of affairs early in the first quarter.

The division is doing reasonably well on revenues and cost of goods sold. Its only really large negative variance is in the marketing expense line. Because the numbers are based on just the first month's figures, it is difficult to know if that variance is simply a onetime, or seasonal, variation, or if Amalgamated will have to spend more on marketing than anticipated. If your investment is not tracking according to budget, and if it looks as if the pattern of unexpectedly high costs (or unexpectedly low revenues) will hold, you may need to rethink the initiative—or even discontinue it.

Section 3
The Limits of Financial Data

This part of the *HBR Guide to Finance Basics for Managers* is a little different from the rest. In the earlier sections you learned the fundamentals. In this one you'll get some advice about how to evaluate what you know, how to use it most effectively, and how to supplement it with other kinds of information.

Why are such cautions necessary? Mainly because we tend to put too much faith in numbers. The income statement and balance sheet may seem precise, but they aren't. They reflect all sorts of assumptions, estimates, and procedural decisions, such as which depreciation method to use. Moreover, there is much about a business that the numbers—even the truly precise ones on the cash flow statement—can't capture. So when you use the financial statements, you have to exercise good judgment about what they're telling you and determine how they may be misleading you. The articles in this section will help.

What the Financial Statements Don't Tell You

by John Case

In 2006, one of the largest firms on Wall Street turned in perhaps its best performance ever. Earnings set a record for the fourth year in a row; pretax profit margin was a whopping 30.1%. "After several years of restructuring and investing in our business, all of the components came together to reflect a company capable of strong disciplined performance with tremendous potential for future success," wrote the chairman in his letter to shareholders.

The firm was Merrill Lynch. The following year it lost $8.6 billion—"the worst performance in the history of Merrill Lynch," as the (new) chairman acknowledged. In 2008 Bank of America agreed to buy Merrill in a distress sale, and in 2009 the firm ceased to exist as an independent entity.

. . .

In 2010, the chief executive of a major oil company reported a good deal of satisfaction with his company's financial results the previous year. Despite a harsh economic climate and a lower price for petroleum, return on sales had dropped only a fraction of a percentage point, and the company actually increased its dividend to shareholders by 2%. "A revitalized [company] kept up its momentum and delivered strong operating and financial results while continuing to focus on safe and reliable operations," he wrote to his shareholders on February 26.

The oil company was BP. Less than two months later, the drilling rig Deepwater Horizon *blew up, killing 11 people and unleashing the biggest offshore oil spill in history. The ultimate cost to BP—in money, in reputation, in its ability to operate around the world—wouldn't be known for years. BP's own estimates of direct costs came to roughly $40 billion.*

Grim stories such as these are cautionary tales about what you can and cannot discern just by scrutinizing a company's financials. It's true that finance is the language of business, and unless you can grasp it, you will be at a perpetual disadvantage in any kind of business career. But make no mistake: The financials describe only a fraction of a company's reality, and sometimes a misleading fraction at that.

So in this chapter we'll look not at what the financials tell you but at what they *don't* tell you. The figures themselves may be wrong or deceptive. They may be silent about a host of organizational matters that affect a company's success. They may capture a business reality that is true for the moment but that is about to be transformed by external events. Wise managers always keep one eye on the financial reports, the ultimate gauge of their performance. But they keep an equally sharp eye on all the nonfinancial or external factors that show up late, murkily, or not at all in the financial data. As we'll see, such factors fill in the rest of the picture.

Financial Sleight of Hand

One limitation of financial statements is that they can be manipulated. The usual goal, of course, is to make things look better than they really are.

The manipulation may take the form of outright fraud. The Italian company Parmalat—a multibillion-dollar food giant with operations in dozens of countries—defaulted on a bond payment in November 2003. Alarmed, auditors and lenders began scrutinizing the company's books, which seemed to show that Parmalat held nearly $5 billion in an account with Bank of America. In December, however, Bank of America reported that there was no such account. Parmalat wound up in bankruptcy, and some of its executives received prison sentences for the deception.

More often, the manipulation is subtler: A company simply alters its accounting practices. Accountants have a good deal of discretion over many items on the income statement and the balance sheet, and are free to adopt different procedures and assumptions as long as they deem the changes reasonable and apply them consistently. A company can change the way it values inventory, for example, or the amount that it sets aside for bad debt. Either move will trigger an adjustment—positive or negative—to the income statement and make the bottom line look better or worse. A company can also alter its depreciation schedule. If it owns a fleet of trucks or airplanes and decides that each one should last 12 years rather than 10, it will then record less depreciation on its income statement. Presto: The bottom line suddenly grows by a corresponding amount. In theory, any new procedure or assumption that is material to the company's results should appear in the footnotes to the financials. But the accountants get to decide whether the new way of doing things is material.

The line between fraud and a reasonable change in procedures isn't always clear. One telecommunications company got itself in trouble by taking a group of expenses that everyone else in the industry classified as operating expenses and inappropriately categorizing them as capital expenditures. Since only a part of a capital expenditure—depreciation—shows up on the income statement, the company's profits improved significantly. Some people in the company presumably believed that the change was justified. The Justice Department disagreed, characterizing the move as an "accounting trick" and issuing an indictment.

The moral here is that it pays to understand the assumptions and procedures used to calculate the financials. The statements themselves don't always tell the truth, the whole truth, and nothing but the truth.

Only One Piece of the Financial Puzzle

The three statements reveal a good deal, but not everything, about a company's financial position. For instance,

assets such as land, buildings, and equipment are recorded at historical cost on the balance sheet and depreciated accordingly—but nowhere does the balance sheet say what they might be worth on the open market today. (The continuing debate over "mark to market" accounting, in which companies use real or estimated market prices to value their assets, applies only to financial assets.) Merrill Lynch held plenty of assets, such as mortgage-backed securities. But when the housing bubble collapsed, those assets turned out to be worth far less than anybody had imagined.

Probably the most important financial fact the three major statements don't tell you is what a company as a whole is worth. The owners' equity line on the balance sheet, which you might think indicates value, really has nothing to do with what a buyer would have to pay to acquire the firm.

For publicly traded companies, the value of the entire enterprise is known as its **market capitalization,** or just **market cap.** This is the amount, in theory, that an investor would have to pay to buy all the shares of stock. To calculate market cap, you simply multiply the stock price by the total number of shares. The value changes daily, just because share prices move up and down. The price movements depend only partly on the performance reflected in financial statements. They also depend on what is happening to the market in general—that is, how interested investors are in buying stocks. General Electric's shares hit about 60 during the height of the dot-com boom in the early 2000s and plunged to about 6 during the depths of the financial crisis later in the decade. The company was performing somewhat differently during the two periods, but the gap in performance was nowhere near as great as the difference in share price and hence market cap.

Of course, it is rare for anyone to buy a publicly traded company at a figure close to its market cap on any given day. If an investor or potential acquirer announces an intention to scoop up all of a company's shares, the shares naturally rise in value. That's why prospective buyers typically have to pay a premium over the shares' value on the day of the announcement.

The value of a private company is harder to determine. A high-tech firm might be worth considerably more than its **book value,** or **owners' equity,** because a buyer would be hoping to acquire intangibles, such as engineering expertise or intellectual property. Neither of these asset categories shows up on the balance sheet. A small service company such as a marketing firm or a plumbing contractor, by contrast, might be worth considerably less than owners' equity would suggest. Its tangible assets—computers, telephone equipment, vehicles, inventory—may not yet be fully depreciated, but they may also have little value on the open market. For this kind of company, the real value lies in the experience, expertise, and contacts of the business owner. The buyer's motivations matter, too. An acquirer simply buying the business for its hard assets is likely to pay less than someone who wants to keep the enterprise as a going concern. A so-called strategic buyer—an acquirer that needs the private company to fill out its business lines, its technologies, or its geographic reach—may pay most of all.

Reaching Beyond the Financials

The financial statements are essentially backward-looking. The **income statement** and **cash flow statement** tell you how an organization performed along certain dimensions in a previous time period. The **balance sheet** gives you a snapshot of its financial health as of a given date. But a business also needs to know what is going on right now and what's likely to happen tomorrow. If its managers can do something about those factors in the present, they'll greatly improve their chances of seeing better results next quarter or next year.

Here are three key categories of information that you won't learn about from the financials:

1. The organization's nonfinancial health.

The explosion of the *Deepwater Horizon* in the Gulf of Mexico wasn't BP's first major accident in recent years. An explosion at the company's Texas City refinery in 2005 killed 15 people and injured 180 more. Later that year another BP drilling platform in the Gulf nearly sank because workers hurrying to finish it had installed a valve incorrectly. In 2006 BP's pipelines from Alaska's Prudhoe Bay field began to leak, eventually spilling 267,000 gallons—the area's worst spill ever. Somehow the company seemed unable to fix its recurrent safety problems. In 2009, reported *Fortune* magazine,

> *. . . the federal Occupational Safety and Health Administration (OSHA) proposed a record fine against BP for "failure to abate" previously cited hazards at Texas*

> *City. OSHA also cited BP for hundreds of new "willful" safety violations. (BP totaled 829 such refinery violations from June 2007 to February 2010, according to the Center for Public Integrity. The rest of the industry combined had 33.) There had been three more deaths at Texas City since the 2005 explosion.*

If a company has safety issues like these, it's probably an unhealthy organization—that is, it's likely to experience one problem after another, regardless of what the financials might say about its *fiscal* health.

Safety is just one aspect of organizational health (and one that is far more relevant in mining or manufacturing than, say, in banking). Another is the level of employee engagement. Do people enjoy working at your company? Would they recommend it to a friend? To answer these questions you need data from employee surveys, for example, and from human-resources indicators such as employee retention rates. You won't find any of this information on the financials.

Healthy organizations are also nimble: Their people can make and execute good decisions without undue time or trouble. Bain & Company consultants Marcia Blenko, Paul Rogers, and Michael Mankins, in their book *Decide & Deliver* (Harvard Business Review Press, 2010), tell the story of ABB, the big Switzerland-based power equipment and automation company. ABB was much heralded in the 1990s for its radically decentralized structure, and for a while its financial performance lived up to the accolades. But a particular kind of rot was eating away at ABB from the inside: People were fighting tooth and nail over basic business decisions such as bid-ding on big power projects. "Overall, the company was structured into a complex labyrinth, with thousands of units operating on their own," the authors write. "Many of these local entities controlled factories and thus did all they could to sell the products those factories made, even if that meant discouraging customers from patronizing other ABB units." In effect, the company was hamstrung by its own structure. "With so many decisions requiring intense negotiations, internal politics grew bitter."

There is no direct information about organizational decisiveness in the financials. Many companies gather data about it through employee surveys, interviews, and internal focus groups. As with employee engagement, the results help executives understand why and how the company's future financial performance might suffer.

2. *What customers are thinking.*

Customer attitudes—their satisfaction with a company and its products, their gripes and complaints, their intent to repurchase, and so forth—also don't appear on the financials. Yet those attitudes are critical indicators of a company's future success. After all, if a firm can't hold on to its customers and attract new ones, its prospects are likely to be dim.

Determining customer attitudes requires several different kinds of research. The periodic customer-satisfaction surveys that most large companies conduct provide a starting point. (The quality of this data is often suspect, however. For instance, a company may encourage its customers to give it high marks when the surveyor calls, as many auto dealerships do.) It is probably more helpful to scrutinize customer behavior. How long do your customers stay with you? What percentage of them buy only once and then are never heard from again? What is your "share of wallet"—that is, how much of their total spending in your categories do you get? Many companies also make a point of creating communities of customers to advise them on policies, new products, and the like. LEGO encourages and supports local hobbyists' clubs and conferences, and often creates new product kits based on ideas from the avid users who participate in such get-togethers.

3. What competitors are planning.

Every business is vulnerable to competitors, so the more you know about your rivals, the better off you are. This point is hardly original, and most companies spend a good deal of time and resources trying to anticipate competitors' next moves. Even so, they often are bested by rivals. Consider the following pitfalls:

- ***Ignoring the blind side.*** In the 1970s and 1980s, General Motors, Ford, and Chrysler competed fiercely with one another—and famously failed to notice the onslaught of lower-cost, higher-quality vehicles being imported from Japan. It took years for Detroit's Big Three to catch up with Toyota, Nissan, and Honda in cost and quality. Meanwhile the U.S. companies lost huge amounts of market share to the imports.
- ***Ignoring upstarts.*** Xerox once dominated the market for photocopiers. When Canon came along with a small, inexpensive, slow-operating copier

designed for small businesses and home offices, Xerox didn't pay much attention. As Harvard Business School professor Clayton M. Christensen points out in his work on disruptive innovation, that made perfect sense—Xerox's customers weren't interested in cheap, underperforming machines. But Canon got a toehold in the market, and it was soon able to improve its machines, move up-market, and challenge Xerox head-on.

- ***Missing the next big thing.*** Nokia, once the leader among cell phone manufacturers, found itself upstaged and outcompeted by Apple's iPhone and other smart phones. Although it had introduced a smart phone of its own, it missed the appeal of touch-screen technology. So rapid was the company's fall that by 2010 Nokia was in danger of becoming a second-tier player, particularly in the United States.

Competitors' plans don't show up in any survey. Smart companies keep a careful eye on those plans by analyzing their competitors' reports and press releases, talking to knowledgeable analysts and observers, and attending industry conferences. A business that pays little attention to the competition does so at its peril.

It makes sense for every manager to read, understand, and stay on top of the financials—not just the three key statements, which are summaries, but day-to-day data on revenues, operating costs, performance to budget, and the like. But if you put too much trust in the numbers and fail to consider factors they don't capture, you're likely to wind up in trouble. To avoid the well-chronicled missteps of Merrill Lynch, BP, and others, search *everywhere* for the information you need, and make sure you get it in a timely, useful fashion. If you wait to see the last period's financials, it will be too late.

John Case is a consulting writer to a variety of clients, including Bain & Company and the Business Literacy Institute. He is the author or coauthor of more than a dozen books on business and management.

The Five Traps of Performance Measurement

by Andrew Likierman

In an episode of *Frasier*, the television sitcom that follows the fortunes of a Seattle-based psychoanalyst, the eponymous hero's brother gloomily summarizes a task ahead: "Difficult and boring—my favorite combination." If this is your reaction to the challenge of improving the measurement of your organization's performance, you are not alone. In my experience, most senior executives find it an onerous if not threatening task. Thus they leave it to people who may not be natural judges of performance but are fluent in the language of spreadsheets. The inevitable result is a mass of numbers and comparisons that provide little insight into a company's performance and may

Reprinted from *Harvard Business Review*, October 2009 (product #R0910L)

even lead to decisions that hurt it. That's a big problem in the current recession, because the margin for error is virtually nonexistent.

So how should executives take ownership of performance assessment? They need to find measures, qualitative as well as quantitative, that look past this year's budget and previous results to determine how the company will fare against its competitors in the future. They need to move beyond a few simple, easy-to-game metrics and embrace an array of more sophisticated ones. And they need to keep people on their toes and make sure that today's measures are not about yesterday's business model.

In the following pages I present what I've found to be the five most common traps in measuring performance and illustrate how some organizations have managed to avoid them. My prescriptions aren't exhaustive, but they'll provide a good start. In any event, they can help you steal a march on rivals who are caught in the same old traps.

Trap 1: Measuring Against Yourself

The papers for the next regular performance assessment are on your desk, their thicket of numbers awaiting you. What are those numbers? Most likely, comparisons of current results with a plan or a budget. If that's the case, you're at grave risk of falling into the first trap of performance measurement: looking only at your own company. You may be doing better than the plan, but are you beating the competition? And what if the estimates you're seeing were manipulated?

To measure how well you're doing, you need information about the benchmarks that matter most—the ones outside the organization. They will help you define competitive priorities and connect executive compensation to relative rather than absolute performance—meaning you'll reward senior executives for doing better than everyone else.

The trouble is that comparisons with your competitors can't easily be made in real time—which is precisely why so many companies fall back on measurements against the previous year's plans and budgets. You have to be creative about how you find the relevant data or some proxy for them.

One way is to ask your customers. Enterprise, the car-rental company, uses the Enterprise Service Quality Index, which measures customers' repeat purchase intentions. Each branch of the company telephones a random sample of customers and asks whether they will use Enterprise again. When the index goes up, the company is gaining market share; when it falls, customers are taking their business elsewhere. The branches post results within two weeks, put them next to profitability numbers on monthly financial statements, and factor them into criteria for promotion (thus aligning sales goals and incentives).

Of course you have to make sure you don't annoy your customers as you gather data. Think about how restaurant managers seek feedback about the quality of their service: Most often they interrupt diners' conversations to ask if everything is OK; sometimes they deliver a questionnaire with the bill. Either approach can be irritating. Danny Meyer, the founder of New York's Union Square Hospitality Group, gets the information unobtrusively, through simple observation. If people dining together in one of his restaurants are looking at one another, the service is probably working. If they're all looking around the room, they may be wowed by the architecture, but it's far more likely that the service is slow.

Another way to get data is to go to professionals outside your company. When Marc Effron, the vice president of talent management for Avon Products, was trying to determine whether his company was doing a good job of finding and developing managers, he came up with the idea of creating a network of talent management professionals. Started in 2007, the New Talent Management Network has more than 1,200 members, for whom it conducts original research and provides a library of resources and best practices.

Trap 2: Looking Backward

Along with budget figures, your performance assessment package almost certainly includes comparisons between this year and last. If so, watch out for the second trap, which is to focus on the past. Beating last year's numbers is not the point; a performance measurement system needs to tell you whether the decisions you're making now are going to help you in the coming months.

Look for measures that lead rather than lag the profits in your business. The U.S. health insurer Humana, recognizing that its most expensive patients are the really sick ones (a few years back the company found that the sickest 10% accounted for 80% of its costs), offers customers incentives for early screening. If it can get more customers into early or even preemptive treatment than other companies can, it will outperform rivals in the future.

The quality of managerial decision making is another leading indicator of success. Boards must assess top executives' wisdom and willingness to listen. Qualitative, subjective judgments based on independent directors' own experience with an executive are usually more revealing than a formal analysis of the executive's track record (an unreliable predictor of success, especially for a CEO) or his or her division's financial performance. (See "Evaluating the CEO," by Stephen P. Kaufman, HBR October 2008.)

It may sound trite, but how the company presents itself in official communications often signals the management style of top executives. In August 2006 the *Economist* reported that Arijit Chatterjee and Donald Hambrick, of Pennsylvania State University, had devised a narcissism index on which to rate 105 company bosses, based on the prominence of the CEO's photo in the annual report, his or her prominence in press releases, the frequency of the first person singular in interviews with the CEO, and his or her compensation relative to that of the firm's second-highest-paid executive.

Finally, you need to look not only at what you and others are doing but also at what you aren't doing. The managers of one European investment bank told me that they measure performance by the outcomes of deals they've turned down as well as by the outcomes of deals they've won. If the ones they've rejected turn out to be lemons, those rejections count as successes. This kind of analysis seems obvious once stated, but I've noticed a persistent bias in all of us to focus on what we do over what we don't do. Good management is about making choices, so a decision not to do something should be analyzed as closely as a decision to do something.

Trap 3: Putting Your Faith in Numbers

Good or bad, the metrics in your performance assessment package all come as numbers. The problem is that numbers-driven managers often end up producing reams of low-quality data. Think about how companies collect feedback on service from their customers. It's well known to statisticians that if you want evaluation forms to tell the real story, the anonymity of the respondents must be protected. Yet out of a desire to gather as much information as possible at points of contact, companies routinely ask customers to include personal data, and in many cases the employees who provided the service watch them fill out the forms. How surprised should you be if your employees hand in consistently favorable forms that they themselves collected? Bad assessments have a tendency to mysteriously disappear.

Numbers-driven companies also gravitate toward the most popular measures. If they're looking to compare themselves with other companies, they feel they should use whatever measures others use. The question of what measure is the right one gets lost. Take Frederick Reichheld's widely used Net Promoter Score, which measures the likelihood that customers will recommend a product or service. The NPS is a useful indicator only if recommendations play the dominant role in a purchase decision; as its critics point out, customers' propensity to switch in response to recommendations varies from industry to industry, so an NPS is probably more important to, say, a baby-food manufacturer than to an electricity supplier.

Similar issues arise about the much touted link between employee satisfaction and profitability. The Employee-Customer-Profit Chain pioneered by Sears suggests that more-satisfied employees produce more-satisfied customers, who in turn deliver higher profits. If that's true, the path is clear: Keep your employees content and watch those profits soar. But employees may be satisfied mainly because they like their colleagues (think lawyers) or because they're highly paid and deferred to (think investment bankers). Or they may actually enjoy what they do, but their customers value price above the quality of service (think budget airlines).

A particular bugbear of mine is the application of financial metrics to nonfinancial activities. Anxious to justify themselves rather than be outsourced, many service functions (such as IT, HR, and legal) try to devise a return on investment number to help their cause. Indeed, ROI is often described as the holy grail of measurement—a revealing metaphor, with its implication of an almost certainly doomed search.

Suppose an HR manager undertakes to assign an ROI number to an executive training program. Typically, he or she would ask program participants to identify a benefit, assign a dollar value to it, and estimate the probability that the benefit came from the program. So a benefit that is worth $70,000 and has a 50% probability of being linked to the program means a program benefit of $35,000. If the program cost $25,000, the net benefit is $10,000—a 40% ROI.

Think about this for a minute. How on earth can the presumed causal link be justified? By a statement like "I learned a production algorithm at the program and then applied it"? Assessing any serious executive program requires a much more sophisticated and qualitative approach. First you have to specify ahead of time the needs of the program's stakeholders—participants, line managers, and sponsors—and make sure that the syllabus meets your organizational and talent management objectives. Once the program has ended, you have to look beyond immediate evaluations to at least six months after participants return to the workplace; their personal feedback should be incorporated in the next annual company performance review. At the soft drinks company Britvic, HR assesses its executive coaching program by tracking coachees for a year afterward, comparing their career trajectories with those of people who didn't get coached.

Trap 4: Gaming Your Metrics

In 2002 a leaked internal memo from associates at Clifford Chance, one of the world's largest law firms, contended that pressure to deliver billable hours had encouraged its lawyers to pad their numbers and created an incentive to allocate to senior associates work that could be done by less expensive junior associates.

Lawyers aren't the only ones: A number of prominent companies have been caught trying to manipulate their numbers. Since 2004 Royal Dutch Shell has paid $470 million to settle lawsuits relating to its overstatement of reserves. Morgan Stanley was reportedly willing to lose €20 million on a securities trade for the Finnish government just before closing its books for 2004 in order to improve its position in the league table for global equity capital market rankings.

You can't prevent people from gaming numbers, no matter how outstanding your organization. The moment you choose to manage by a metric, you invite your managers to manipulate it. Metrics are only proxies for performance. Someone who has learned how to optimize a metric without actually having to perform will often do just that. To create an effective performance measurement system, you have to work with that fact rather than resort to wishful thinking and denial.

It helps to diversify your metrics, because it's a lot harder to game several of them at once. Clifford Chance replaced its single metric of billable hours with seven criteria on which to base bonuses: respect and mentoring, quality of work, excellence in client service, integrity, contribution to the community, commitment to diversity, and contribution to the firm as an institution. Metrics should have varying sources (colleagues, bosses, customers) and time frames. Mehrdad Baghai and coauthors described in "Performance Measures: Calibrating for Growth" (*Journal of Business Strategy*, July–August 1999) how the Japanese telecommunications company SoftBank measured performance along three time horizons. Horizon 1 covered actions relevant to extending and defending core businesses, and metrics were based on current income and cash flow statements. Horizon 2 covered actions taken to build emerging businesses; metrics came from sales and marketing numbers. Horizon 3 covered creating opportunities for new businesses; success was measured through the attainment of preestablished milestones. Multiple levels like those make gaming far more complicated and far less likely to succeed.

You can also vary the boundaries of your measurement, by defining responsibility more narrowly or by broadening it. To reduce delays in gate-closing time, Southwest Airlines, which had traditionally applied a metric only to gate agents, extended it to include the whole ground team—ticketing staff, gate staff, and loaders—so that everyone had an incentive to cooperate.

Finally, you should loosen the link between meeting budgets and performance; far too many bonuses are awarded on that basis. Managers may either pad their budgets to make meeting them easier or pare them down too far to impress their bosses. Both practices can destroy value. Some companies get around the problem by giving managers leeway. The office supplier Staples, for example, lets them exceed their budgets if they can demonstrate that doing so will lead to improved service for customers. When I was a CFO, I offered scope for budget revisions during the year, usually in months three and six. Another way of providing budget flexibility is to set ranges rather than specific numbers as targets.

Trap 5: Sticking to Your Numbers Too Long

As the saying goes, you manage what you measure. Unfortunately, performance assessment systems seldom evolve as fast as businesses do. Smaller and growing companies are especially likely to fall into this trap. In the earliest stages, performance is all about survival, cash resources, and growth. Comparisons are to last week, last month, and last year. But as the business matures, the focus has to move to profit and the comparisons to competitors.

It's easy to spot the need for change after things have gone wrong, but how can you evaluate your measures before they fail you? The answer is to be very precise about what you want to assess, be explicit about what metrics are assessing it, and make sure that everyone is clear about both.

In looking for a measure of customer satisfaction, the British law firm Addleshaw Booth (now Addleshaw Goddard) discovered from a survey that its clients valued responsiveness most, followed by proactiveness and commercial-mindedness. Most firms would interpret this finding to mean they needed to be as quick as possible. Addleshaw Booth's managers dug deeper into the data to understand more exactly what "responsiveness" meant. What they found was that they needed to differentiate between clients. "One size does not fit all," an employee told me. "Being responsive for some clients means coming back to them in two hours; for others, it's 10 minutes."

The point is that if you specify the indicator precisely and loudly, everyone can more easily see when it's not fit for the purpose. The credit-rating agencies have come under attack because they gave AAA ratings to so many borrowers who turned out to be bad risks. The agencies have argued in their own defense that lenders misunderstood what the ratings meant. The AAA rating, they claim, was awarded on the basis of borrowers' credit records, and it described the likelihood of default under normal market conditions; it did not factor in what might happen in the event of a massive shock to the financial system. Reasonable as this explanation may be, it is no consolation to those who thought they knew what the magic AAA represented.

Why do organizations that excel in so many other ways fall into these traps? Because the people managing performance frameworks are generally not experts in performance measurement. Finance managers are proficient at tracking expenses, monitoring risks, and raising capital, but they seldom have a grasp of how operating realities connect with performance. They are precisely the people who strive to reduce judgments to a single ROI number. The people who understand performance are line managers—who, of course, are crippled by conflicts of interest.

A really good assessment system must bring finance and line managers into some kind of meaningful dialogue that allows the company to benefit from both the relative independence of the former and the expertise of the latter. This sounds straightforward enough, but as anyone who's ever worked in a real business knows, actually doing it is a rather tall order. Then again, who says the CEO's job is supposed to be easy?

Andrew Likierman is the dean of London Business School, a nonexecutive director of Barclays Bank, and the chairman of the UK's National Audit Office.

Finance Quiz

How Much Have You Learned?

Now it's time to retake the finance quiz that appeared in the first part of this guide. It will give you an indication of what you've learned and what you might need to study up on. The answers follow.

1. **The income statement measures:**
   a. Profitability
   b. Assets and liabilities
   c. Cash
   d. All of the above

2. **A sale on credit ends up on the income statement as revenue and as what on the balance sheet?**
   a. Accounts receivable
   b. Long-term assets
   c. Short-term liability
   d. Operating cash flow

3. **What happens when a company is profitable but collection lags behind payments to vendors?**
   a. The company is OK because profits always become cash
   b. The company stands a good chance of running out of money
   c. The company needs to shift its focus to EBIT
   d. The cash flow statement will show a negative bottom line

4. **How is gross profit margin calculated?**
   a. COGS/revenue
   b. Gross profit/net profit
   c. Gross profit/revenue
   d. Sales/gross profit

5. **Which statement summarizes changes to parts of the balance sheet?**
   a. Income statement
   b. Cash flow statement
   c. Neither of the above
   d. Both of the above

6. **EBIT is an important measure in companies because:**
   a. It is free cash flow
   b. It subtracts interest and taxes from net income to get a truer picture of the business
   c. It indicates the profitability of a company's operations
   d. It is the key measure of earnings before indirect costs and transfers

7. **Operating expenses include all of the following except:**
    a. Advertising costs
    b. Administrative salaries
    c. Expensed research and development costs
    d. Delivery of raw materials

8. **Owners' equity in a company increases when the company:**
    a. Increases its assets with debt
    b. Decreases its debt by paying off loans with company cash
    c. Increases its profit
    d. All of the above

9. **A company has more cash today when:**
    a. Customers pay their bills sooner
    b. Accounts receivable increases
    c. Profit increases
    d. Retained earnings increases

10. **Which of the following is not part of working capital?**
    a. Accounts receivable
    b. Inventory
    c. Property, plant, and equipment
    d. All of the above are part of working capital

Answers to the Finance Quiz

1. **a.** Profitability is measured by the income statement. Assets and liabilities are measured

by the balance sheet, cash by the cash flow statement.

2. **a.** A sale on credit means that the customer owes you for the amount of the purchase. That debt is an asset, and it appears under accounts receivable on the balance sheet.

3. **b.** If you're not collecting receivables as fast as you are paying vendors, you will need more and more working capital as the company grows—and if you can't find it, you will run out of money. EBIT is just another measure of profitability, which doesn't determine cash flow. And the cash flow statement's bottom line depends on many factors, not just receivables and payables.

4. **c.** Gross profit is revenue minus COGS (cost of goods sold). Gross profit margin shows gross profit as a percentage of revenue, so just divide gross profit by revenue and convert to a percent.

5. **d.** On the income statement, net profit adds to the retained earnings line on the balance sheet after dividends are paid. On the cash flow statement, the line items reflect cash-related differences between two balance sheets. Both statements thus summarize changes to the balance sheet.

6. **c.** EBIT, or operating profit, shows a company's profitability without regard to how the

company is financed (which affects interest expense) or the taxes it may owe. EBIT is not free cash flow. And it actually adds back in interest and taxes to get that picture of operating profitability. EBIT does not stand for earnings before indirect costs and transfers.

7. **d.** Delivery of raw materials is part of COGS (cost of goods sold), not operating expenses. Advertising, administrative, and expensed research and development costs are all operating expenses.

8. **c.** One element of owners' equity is retained earnings, meaning profits not distributed to shareholders as dividends. Increasing profits helps to build owners' equity through the retained earnings line. Using cash to pay debt or increasing debt and adding assets with that debt does not change equity.

9. **a.** It isn't until the customer actually pays its bill that a company's cash increases. Accounts receivable indicates future cash flows, not current ones. Neither profit nor retained earnings affects how soon a company gets its cash.

10. **c.** Working capital is current assets minus current liabilities. Property, plant, and equipment is not a current asset; rather, it represents long-term investments in the business.

Glossary

Accounts Payable. A category of balance-sheet liabilities representing funds owed by the company to suppliers and other short-term creditors.

Accounts Receivable. A category of balance-sheet assets representing funds owed to the company by customers and others.

Accrual Accounting. An accounting practice that records transactions as they occur, whether or not cash trades hands.

Allocations. See **indirect costs.**

Assets. The balance-sheet items in which a company invests so that it can conduct business. Examples include cash and financial instruments, inventories of raw materials and finished goods, land, buildings, and equipment.

Adapted from *Harvard Business Essentials: Finance for Managers* (product #8768), Harvard Business Review Press, 2002

Assets also include funds owed to the company by customers and others—an asset category referred to as **accounts receivable.**

Balance Sheet. A financial statement that describes the assets owned by the business and how those assets are financed—with the funds of creditors (liabilities), the equity of the owners, or both. Also known as the **statement of financial position.**

Book Value of Shareholder Equity. A balance-sheet valuation method that calculates value as total assets less total liabilities.

Breakeven Analysis. A form of analysis that helps determine how much (or how much more) a company needs to sell in order to pay for the fixed investment—in other words, at what point the company will break even on its cash flow.

Budget. A document that translates strategic plans into measurable quantities that express the expected resources required and anticipated returns over a certain period. It functions as an action plan and presents the estimated future financial statements of the organization.

Burden. See **indirect costs.**

Cash Flow Statement. A financial statement that details the reasons for changes in cash (and cash equivalents) during the accounting period. More specifically, it reflects all changes in cash relating to operating activities, investments, and financing.

Common Stock. A security that represents a fractional ownership interest in the corporation that issued it.

Contribution Margin. In cost accounting, the contribution by each unit of production to overhead and profits, or net revenue less direct cost per unit.

Cost/Benefit Analysis. A form of analysis that evaluates whether, over a given time frame, the benefits of a new investment or business opportunity will outweigh the associated costs.

Cost of Capital. The opportunity cost that shareholders and lenders could earn on their capital if they invested in the next-best opportunity available to them at the same level of risk, calculated as the weighted average cost of the organization's different sources of capital.

Cost of Goods Sold (COGS). On the income statement, what it costs a company to produce its goods and services. This figure at a minimum includes raw materials and direct labor costs.

Current Assets. Assets that are most easily converted to cash: cash, cash equivalents such as certificates of deposit and U.S. Treasury bills, receivables, and inventory. Under generally accepted accounting principles, current assets are those that can be converted into cash within one year.

Current Liabilities. Liabilities that must be paid in a year or less; these typically include short-term loans, salaries, income taxes, and accounts payable.

Current Ratio. Current assets divided by current liabilities. This ratio is often used as a measure of a company's ability to meet currently maturing obligations.

Days Receivables Outstanding. The average time it takes to collect on sales.

Debt Ratio. The ratio of debt to either assets or equity in a company's financial structure.

Depreciation. A noncash charge that effectively reduces the balance sheet value of an asset over its useful life.

Direct Costs. Cost incurred as a direct consequence of producing a good or service—as opposed to overhead, or indirect costs.

Discounted Cash Flow (DCF). A method based on time-value-of-money concepts that calculates value by finding the present value of a business's future cash flows.

Discount Rate. The annual rate, expressed as a percentage, at which a future payment or series of payments is reduced to its present value.

Dividend. A distribution of after-tax corporate earnings to shareholders.

Earnings Before Interest and Taxes (EBIT). See **operating earnings.**

Earnings Per Share (EPS). A company's net earnings divided by the total number of shares outstanding.

Economic Value Added (EVA). A measure of real economic profit calculated as net operating income after tax less the cost of the capital employed to obtain it.

Equity Book Value. The value of total assets less total liabilities.

Financial Leverage. The degree to which borrowed money is used in acquiring assets. A corporation is said to be highly leveraged when its balance-sheet debt is much greater than its owners' equity.

Fixed Assets. Assets that are difficult to convert to cash—for example, buildings and equipment. Sometimes called **plant assets.**

Future Value (FV). The amount to which a present value, or series of payments, will increase over a specific period at a specific compounding rate.

Generally Accepted Accounting Principles (GAAP). In the United States, a body of conventions, rules, and procedures sanctioned by the Financial Accounting Standards Board, an independent, self-regulating body. All entities must follow GAAP in accounting for transactions and representing their results in financial statements.

Goodwill. If a company has purchased another company for a price in excess of the fair market value of its assets, that "goodwill" is recorded on the balance sheet as an asset. Goodwill may represent intangible things such as the acquired company's reputation, its customer list, its brand names, and its patents.

Gross Profit Margin. Sales revenue less cost of goods sold, expressed as a percentage of revenue. The roughest measure of profitability. Also referred to as **gross margin.**

Hurdle Rate. The minimal rate of return that all investments for a particular enterprise must achieve.

Income Statement. A financial statement that indicates the cumulative financial results of operations over a specified period. Also referred to as the **profit-and-loss statement,** or **P&L.**

Indirect Costs. Costs that cannot be attributed to the production of any particular unit of output. Often referred to as **overhead, allocations,** or **burden.**

Interest Coverage Ratio. Earnings before interest and taxes divided by interest expense. Creditors use this ratio to gauge a company's ability to make future interest payments in the face of fluctuating operating results.

Internal Rate of Return (IRR). The discount rate at which the net present value of an investment equals zero.

Inventory. The supplies, raw materials, components, and so forth, that a company uses in its operations. It also includes work in process—goods in various stages of production—as well as finished goods waiting to be sold and/or shipped.

Inventory Turnover. Cost of goods sold divided by average inventory.

Liability. A claim against a company's assets.

Liquidity. The extent to which a company's assets can readily be turned into cash for meeting incoming obligations.

Net Earnings. See **net income.**

Net Income. The "bottom line" of the income statement. Net income is revenues less expenses less taxes. Also referred to as **net earnings** or **net profits.**

Net Present Value (NPV). The present value of one or more future cash flows less any initial investment costs.

Net Profits. See **net income.**

Net Working Capital. Current assets less current liabilities; the amount of money a company has tied up in short-term operating activities.

Operating Budget. A projected target for performance in revenues, expenses, and operating income.

Operating Earnings. On the income statement, gross margin less operating expenses and depreciation. Often called **earnings before interest and taxes,** or **EBIT.**

Operating Expense. On the income statement, a category that includes administrative expenses, employee salaries, rents, sales and marketing costs, and other costs of business not directly attributed to the cost of manufacturing a product.

Operating Leverage. The extent to which a company's operating costs are fixed versus variable. For example, a company that relies heavily on machinery and uses very few workers to produce its goods has a high operating leverage.

Operating Margin. A financial ratio used by many analysts to gauge the profitability of a company's operating activities. It is calculated as earnings before interest and taxes (EBIT) divided by net sales.

Overhead. See **indirect costs.**

Owners' Equity. What, if anything, is left over after total liabilities are deducted from total assets. Owners' equity is the sum of capital contributed by owners plus the company's total retained earnings over time. Also known as **shareholders' equity.**

Payback Period. The length of time it will take a particular investment to pay for itself.

Plant Assets. See **fixed assets.**

Present Value (PV). The monetary value today of a future payment discounted at some annual compound interest rate.

Profit-and-Loss Statement (P&L). See **income statement**.

Profit Margin. The percentage of every dollar of sales that makes it to the bottom line. Profit margin is net income after tax divided by net sales. Sometimes called **return on sales,** or **ROS.**

Retained Earnings. Annual net profits left after payment of dividends that accumulate on a company's balance sheet.

Return on Assets (ROA). Relates net income to the company's total asset base and is calculated as net income divided by total assets.

Return on Equity (ROE). Relates net income to the amount invested by shareholders (both initially and through retained earnings). It is a measure of the productivity of the shareholders' stake in the business and is calculated as net income divided by shareholders' equity.

Return on Sales (ROS). See **profit margin.**

Revenue. The amount of money that results from selling products or services to customers.

Shareholders' Equity. See **owners' equity**.

Solvency. A situation in which a company's assets outweigh its liabilities—that is, owners' equity is positive.

Statement of Financial Position. See **balance sheet**.

Variance. The difference between actual and expected results in the budget. A variance can be favorable, when the actual results are better than expected, or unfavorable, when the actual results are worse than expected.

Working Capital. See **net working capital**.

Index

Notes

Notes

Notes

Notes

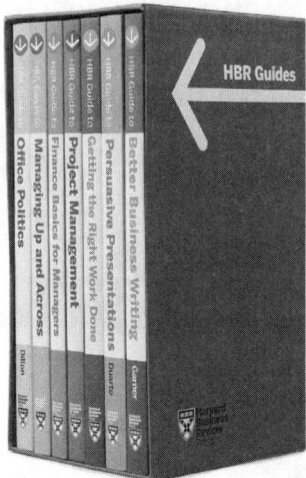

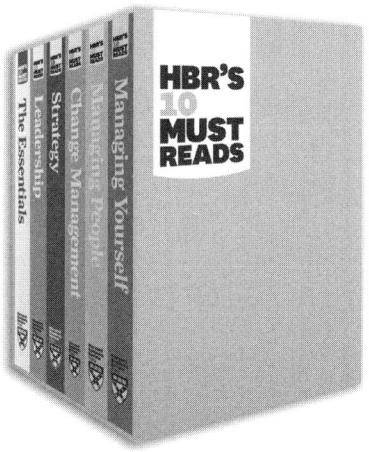

HBR Guide to **Managing Up and Across**

Harvard Business Review Guides

Arm yourself with the advice you need to succeed on the job, from the most trusted brand in business. Packed with how-to essentials from leading experts, the HBR Guides provide smart answers to your most pressing work challenges.

The titles include:

HBR Guide to Better Business Writing

HBR Guide to Finance Basics for Managers

HBR Guide to Getting the Mentoring You Need

HBR Guide to Getting the Right Job

HBR Guide to Getting the Right Work Done

HBR Guide to Giving Effective Feedback

HBR Guide to Making Every Meeting Matter

HBR Guide to Managing Stress at Work

HBR Guide to Managing Up and Across

HBR Guide to Persuasive Presentations

HBR Guide to Project Management

HBR Guide to **Managing Up and Across**

HARVARD BUSINESS REVIEW PRESS

Boston, Massachusetts

Printed in the United States of America

20 19 18 17 16 15

Library of Congress Cataloging-in-Publication Data

Guide to managing up and across.
p. cm. — (Harvard business review guides)
Includes index.
ISBN 978-1-4221-8760-9 (alk. paper)
1. Managing your boss. 2. Management—Psychological aspects.
3. Interpersonal relations.
HF5548.83.G85 2012
650.1'3—dc23

2012025301

The paper used in this publication meets the requirements of the American National Standard for Permanence of Paper for Publications and Documents in Libraries and Archives Z39.48-1992.

What You'll Learn

Does your boss make you want to scream? Do you have more than *one* boss? Do you spend your day herding cats? Working across departmental silos? Corralling contractors?

Then you know that managing up and across your company is critical to doing your job well. It's all about understanding your boss's and colleagues' priorities, pressures, and work styles. You need to manage up and across not just because you may have a problem boss, incompetent colleagues, or projects that involve stakeholders flung far and wide. You need to manage up and across, for example, to get your marketing and sales folks to see that *your* project will help them meet *their* goals, too; to establish authority with higher-ups so they'll bless your new product ideas; to secure people's time for a new team when they're already feeling overextended.

Managing up and across will help you get the information and resources you need to solve your complex problems, increase your effectiveness, and make your work more enjoyable.

You'll get better at:

- Getting what you need from people who don't report to you
- Coping with micromanaging, conflict-aversive, or generally incompetent bosses
- Discovering what drives colleagues of all ages
- Partnering with your boss—and *her* boss
- Selling your ideas up and across your company
- Making the most of your boss's influence
- Establishing a shared vision and commitment
- Juggling multiple bosses' priorities
- Tailoring your pitch to your audience
- Collaborating with remote colleagues
- Working with a new boss
- Navigating office politics

Contents

Section 2: MANAGING ACROSS

Section 1

Managing Up

Neglecting to manage up may cost you promotions or chances to put your great ideas into action. But understanding what makes your boss and his cohort tick and embracing their priorities will open doors for you.

This isn't kissing up or manipulation. You're not trying to inflate egos. You're helping the people you work for succeed, which in turn helps you succeed.

This section of the guide is about creating win-win relationships with higher-ups. You'll learn how to present problems and opportunities to them, give them feedback, connect with your boss's boss without doing an end run, and deal with a variety of difficult managers—from the micromanager to the conflict-averse.

Managing Your Boss

by Linda A. Hill and Kent Lineback

Managing *up* is important because your boss plays a pivotal role in your success—or your failure. You can leverage your boss's influence in the organization on your behalf in several ways—for example, by obtaining valuable information, winning needed resources, and securing important support for your personal development and career. When you face difficult trade-offs and must make decisions that create both beneficial and painful consequences for others, your boss's advice, insight, knowledge of the organization, and access to higher management can be invaluable. As your organization shifts and changes shape in an uncertain market, a good relationship here

---

Adapted from *Being the Boss: The 3 Imperatives for Becoming a Great Leader* (product #12285), by Linda A. Hill and Kent Lineback, Harvard Business Review Press, 2011

becomes a necessity for navigating through the turmoil. The penalties of a poor relationship are many: less influence, little information or advice, fewer resources, and limited personal development and career support. Worst case, you can find yourself isolated, ignored, pushed out—your journey stalled, your career derailed.

Why Is It Often an Uneasy Relationship?

This relationship can be problematic for two reasons. First, a boss plays conflicting roles: supporter and evaluator, which can create confusion. Second, people often bring their past experience with authority into the relationship, which can create unnecessary complications.

This is an area where being a star as an individual contributor may not have prepared you for management. As an exceptional performer, you probably had minimal interaction with your boss. If so, you most likely didn't develop the skills of managing up that you need.

Do you see your boss as coach and developer or as evaluator and judge?

You're caught in a difficult dilemma, one that can feel personally threatening. The boss is not only a potential source of great help, in both your job and your career, but also the one who evaluates your performance. To get help from her as a developer, particularly with your personal development, you must reveal your shortcomings. But if you do, she in her role as evaluator may interpret your weaknesses as serious faults. Many managers handle this dilemma by striving to appear capable and in control even when they're not. They see their boss more as threat than ally and lose the potential benefits of her help.

Are you confused by your boss's dual role? Do you tend to see your boss as primarily a judge? Does that attitude seem safer to you? That's understandable, but it's not always the most helpful point of view.

What can you do? Don't presume your boss is always one or the other, judge or coach. Instead, think of his dual roles as extremes between which he moves back and forth depending on the situation. At first, in small ways that aren't risky, test his willingness to provide support. That way, you can see when, where, and how he's likely to focus on development rather than evaluation. Learn his feelings about what's important in management—such as careful planning, decisiveness, building consensus—and make sure you develop and display those qualities.

Do you see past bosses in your current boss?

How do you feel about your current boss? How do you respond to authority in general and to those who have it? If most of your bosses have frustrated you and fallen short of your expectations, you and they may be victims of the emotional baggage you carry forward from past experience. Reflect on your own history and the feelings it's created in you. That history may lead you to perceive your current boss not as who she is but as an amalgam of past authority figures, with all the positive and negative feelings that flow from that past. Unless you're aware of these feelings, you'll be at their mercy.

On the other hand, you may respond to authority with overdependence, rather than resistance. Extreme

WHAT YOUR BOSS EXPECTS OF YOU

You and your boss agree on your annual, individual performance targets that support larger organizational goals. But what about her *undocumented* expectations? What should you be doing beyond your formal job description that will make you indispensable to your boss and your organization as a whole?

- ***Collaborate***. Overcome differences between you and others so you work together effectively—even if you don't like each other.
- ***Lead initiatives.*** Don't be reluctant to associate yourself with unproven ideas, especially those that cross functional or unit boundaries. Raise your hand, and you'll climb the ladder faster than those who don't.
- ***Develop your own people.*** Take as active an interest in your employees' development as you do in your own—if not more. Go out of your way to criticize and praise your people when they need it. And during performance reviews, supply people with specific, candid, and useful feedback.

- ***Stay current.*** Regularly read and watch the news. What happens in the world affects what happens with your team, your marketplace, and your competition. Also know what's going on with your customers—how they're changing, how their competition is changing, and how technology and world events are affecting their strategies. Your customer relationships are key assets: Bring them to the table.

- ***Drive your own growth.*** Seek perpetual education and development—not necessarily by going to school but by finding exposure to new people and ideas. Seek feedback from your boss, and accept demanding assignments.

- ***Be a player for all seasons.*** Demonstrate positive behaviors even during hard times. You'll sustain your ability to motivate and inspire your own people no matter what's going on around you.

Adapted from "What Your Leader Expects of You" (product #R0704C) by Larry Bossidy, *Harvard Business Review,* April, 2007

deference and automatic, unquestioning compliance don't work well either. Those who react this way never disagree or push back, even when they're right or it's in their best interest.

Both antagonism to authority and too much deference will keep you from seeing your boss clearly and realistically and prevent you from securing the work and personal benefits available from a good relationship.

What Should Your Relationship with Your Boss Be?

Do you realize that your relationship is actually one of *mutual* dependence? Your boss depends on you and needs your commitment and support to succeed. Just as you may wrestle with your reliance on your people, he probably struggles with his dependence on you and his other direct reports.

Think of the relationship as a partnership in which the partners depend on each other to succeed and are able to influence each other in ways that improve the performance of each. It's not a relationship of equals, certainly, but it's not entirely one-way either. You usually do have some room to negotiate and create the relationship that works for both of you.

Take Stock of Your Current Relationship

Is your current relationship a partnership? Are you and your boss able to have a normal, constructive discussion about work? If not, why not?

Don't assume you can make significant differences in how your boss thinks or operates. Most likely, the best you can do is nudge her in directions that work better for you. That's certainly worth doing. But you're unlikely to create large changes.

With that in mind, use the following questions to assess and improve your relationship. They focus on actions you can take.

Are you meeting expectations?

By far, the key factor in a good relationship is your ability to perform as expected.

Results. Performance targets create the foundation for your ongoing relationship. Unless you and your group produce the results expected, you're unlikely to enjoy much of a partnership. And it's not just the results you attain but *how* you attain them. If you hit your numbers but your boss hears complaints all day about how you railroad other groups, he probably won't consider you someone who "meets expectations."

Information. But results aren't the only expectation. Do you keep your boss informed? Reach explicit agreement about how often and in what way you will report progress. Develop a sense of what your boss wants to know. Some prefer to know a great deal; others, much less. In general, no boss likes to be surprised or seem ignorant of something she should know. If you must err, do it on the side of overinforming. Many bosses actually want more information than they say, so discover the right balance through experience. Find out as well how your boss wants information delivered: written reports via e-mail, in person if that's possible, or by video call.

Support and loyalty. Your goal is to make the relationship work for both of you, and that requires some degree of support and loyalty. Just as you want your boss to care about you, and your people want you to care about them, your boss wants your care and concern, too.

Be generous and assume the best intentions, even when you disagree. Express disagreement as your opinion offered in support of your boss's success. Some people bridle at the word *loyalty*. We don't mean blind loyalty, but loyal people earn the right to question and disagree on occasion. Those who speak up only when they disagree will usually enjoy less influence than those who have demonstrated prior support. So on those occasions when you do honestly agree with your boss, say so clearly and explicitly.

You cannot succeed in this relationship at the expense of your boss; you will rise or fall together. Your task is to make *both of you* effective. Help your boss build on her strengths, and overcome or bypass her limitations.

Does your boss trust you?

The foundation of all network relationships is trust, and the relationship with your boss is no different. Can he count on you to do the right thing? If you feel micromanaged, the reason may be that you've neglected to establish real trust. The essence of building trust is to negotiate what you both mean by "do the right thing."

Do you both see the current situation the same way? Make sure you share a common understanding of the challenges your group faces and what needs to be done. If you see the need for fundamental change and your boss wants to stay the course, you must resolve this difference right away.

Do you agree about where you and your group are going? Once again, a plan is critical. Do you have one? Have you reviewed it with your boss? Does it make clear what's to be done and when? Make sure your boss knows your goals and plans and agrees with them. Ideally, she had a hand in creating them.

Do you negotiate expectations when you're given an assignment? Don't let your relationship be one in which you simply accept whatever is passed down without discussion. If the expectations are unrealistic, you will have no one to blame but yourself when your team fails. Reach agreement on the results you're expected to produce—what will happen by when. Do this at the beginning, and update expectations periodically. Warn your boss of potential risks, and play out various scenarios of how you might handle them.

Do you see and understand your boss as a person?

It's easy to forget that beneath your boss's mantle of authority there's a person just like you. He has hopes, aspirations, frustrations, strengths, weaknesses, and fears. He's the product of his background, training, and experience. He has a personal life—a family and family history, religious beliefs, social organizations, political views, and hobbies. Do you know enough that you're able to see the world through his eyes?

Do you understand your boss as a manager?

Your boss has goals, plans, and pressures, as well as managerial strengths and weaknesses, preferences, and foibles. Do you know them? What's your boss on the line for? What's her boss telling her to do?

Do you know how your boss prefers to make decisions, and do you work within that pattern? Does he prefer lots of analysis and data? Does he need time to reach a conclusion? Does he want everyone's opinion before deciding? If you must depart from these preferences, do you first negotiate explicitly what you will do?

Do you know and respect the ways your boss prefers to work? Some bosses want written analyses before a discussion, while others prefer the discussion or presentation first, followed by a written summary. Some want lots of data; others want the highlights. Some want to be intimately involved in every detail; others prefer regular reports but nothing more unless there's a problem.

When you approach your boss, do you expect guidance or answers? We know a manager whose boss always responded to questions with questions of her own. Finally, this manager realized: "I had to come in with some ideas about how I would handle the situation, and then she would talk about them with me. She would spend all the time in the world with me."

Do you present a problem and expect your boss to solve it? Many bosses resist that approach. Instead, try going in with a problem, an analysis, alternatives, and a recommendation he can react to.

Can you identify your boss's strengths?

This stumps many managers we know. They focus on their boss's weaknesses and can talk at length about them—and often do with their peers. But they seldom look for strengths. That's a shame because your boss's strengths are what you must leverage, and you cannot leverage what you don't recognize or appreciate. Whatever your boss's weaknesses, identify what she does well. There must be something. Don't fall back on something like "She knows how to play the organizational game." There's something there. What is it, and how can you use it to learn and do your work more effectively?

Are you clear about what you need and expect?

Negotiate what you need from your boss. Don't make him guess. What can he do to help you? Provide resources, support from other groups, relief from distracting responsibilities, clearer direction?

In addition, think about the way you prefer to work and what you need from a superior, such as specific goals, help and ongoing guidance, or a certain degree of autonomy. Be sure you know where the boundaries are. Test how negotiable they are. Where your needs and your boss's way of managing diverge, talk through the differences. Where differences involve high stakes, talk sooner than later. It's easy to underestimate the risks of conflict avoidance and the cost of the passive aggression that often accompanies it. Your nonverbal communications—expression, manner, body language, tone—often reveal

CHECKLIST FOR MANAGING YOUR BOSS

Make sure you understand your boss and his or her context, including:

- ☐ Goals and objectives
- ☐ Pressures
- ☐ Strengths, weaknesses, blind spots
- ☐ Preferred work style

Assess yourself and your needs, including:

- ☐ Strengths and weaknesses
- ☐ Personal style
- ☐ Predisposition toward dependence on authority figures

Develop and maintain a relationship that:

- ☐ Fits both your needs and styles
- ☐ Is characterized by mutual expectations
- ☐ Keeps your boss informed
- ☐ Is based on dependability and honesty
- ☐ Selectively uses your boss's time and resources

Adapted from "Managing Your Boss" (product #R0501J) by John J. Gabarro and John P. Kotter, *Harvard Business Review*, January 2005 (republished from 1980)

your true feelings about your boss and can slowly corrode this critical relationship.

Have you discussed with your boss your own growth, development, and aspirations?

How can your boss help you grow and develop? She's not responsible for your career and personal development, but it's in her best interest for you to improve in ways that will help you (and her) succeed. From your boss you can get advice and guidance; feedback about your performance, strengths, and weaknesses; insight into what others think of you; developmental assignments; and access to training programs and other learning opportunities.

To obtain these, you must first communicate your desire to learn. Then, you must agree about *how* and *where* you want to grow—what competencies you need to develop, such as building a network, making a plan, managing performance, or assessing subordinates. Have reasonable expectations. Take responsibility for your own development. Besides, your boss probably has no more time and no less pressure than you, and many bosses, unfortunately, are uncomfortable in this role. The more specific the requests you make, the better—to attend a training course, for example, or advice about a specific problem.

Do you and your boss come from different cultures?

Be aware that cultures differ in their expectations and treatment of people with authority. In some, the boss is expected to be participative; in others, directive. In some, proactive and assertive; in others, humble and modest.

Compare the characteristics of both your cultures. Where your assumptions and expectations differ, be prepared to talk about them explicitly.

Work hard to build a productive relationship with your boss. Initiate the kinds of discussions we've suggested. It's difficult to succeed without his support, and impossible in the face of his opposition. Always remember that your reports face these same issues with you. Let your experience in each relationship—with your boss and with your people—guide you in the other.

Don't make the mistake, as many managers do, of ignoring such a potentially powerful source of help and support. Take responsibility for, and play an active role in, making it a partnership that benefits both of you. Avoid seeing yourself as a passive, powerless subordinate. Don't assume it cannot be a positive, mutually helpful relationship until you've tested the possibilities on several occasions. It's too important—to your ability to exercise influence and thus to your journey—to merely let it be whatever it will be.

Linda A. Hill is the Wallace Brett Donham Professor of Business Administration and faculty chair of the Leadership Initiative at Harvard Business School. Now a writer and executive coach, **Kent Lineback** spent many years as a manager and an executive in business and government. They are the coauthors of *Being the Boss: The 3 Imperatives for Becoming a Great Leader* (Harvard Business Review Press, 2011).

Winning Over Your New Boss

by Lew McCreary

Getting a new boss can be fraught with anxiety and risk, often making it hard to see the opportunities fresh leadership will bring to you and your organization. You'll have to come to terms with whatever unpredictable changes she unleashes. Don't expect the new regime to resemble the old one. Leaders are often brought in to shake up the status quo, so you'll want to make it clear right away that you're a valuable contributor.

If you get a new boss by joining another organization, you'll have no immediate worries about job security. But you will need to figure out the culture (and its politics), meet with and impress new colleagues and direct reports, and above all create a successful partnership with your new boss. You'll need to understand—quickly and in detail—exactly what you've been brought aboard to do, what key stakeholders you'll need to please, what resources you can command, and how your performance in the job will be measured.

In either new-boss scenario, uncertainties abound—but you have a role to play in taming them. As Tom Gilmore, a principal at the Center for Applied Research (CFAR), points out, you're just as responsible as your new boss for "the quality of the working alliance."

What does that responsibility involve? Establishing yourself as someone the new boss can turn to for candid opinions, insight, and support—someone she can count on to perform. Here are some tips for doing that.

Prepare to Meet the New Boss

Because your first meeting with your new boss feels like a make-or-break encounter—especially if she's the one who's new to the company and presumably looking for things to change—you may be tempted to lead with your personal agenda. If you do, you'll be part of a steady parade of petitioners, each bearing (as the leader sees it) a narrow set of demands.

Don't arrive at that initial meeting with thick stacks of documents and a PowerPoint presentation. And don't prepare an eager audition that recapitulates your LinkedIn recommendations. Instead, ask questions and listen to the answers. Find out who the new boss is, how she likes to work, what she doesn't yet know that you can help her learn. Answer her questions candidly as well, and don't be so tightly clenched that you fail to let the boss see who you are.

Gilmore, drawing on his experience and research at CFAR, offers the following advice for making crucial early encounters successful:

- **Ease into the relationship.** Think incrementally. Pick only a few vital issues to cover early on—ones that will help you lay the groundwork for an effective alliance with your new boss. For instance, initially brief her on your unit's new open-innovation initiatives. Over time, you can discuss in more depth the projects that have been green-lighted so far.
- **Observe her style.** Does your new boss prefer short or long conversations? A buffet of options or one best recommendation? Hard data or soft? Use these indicators to shape the way you present yourself and your ideas.
- **Consider others' claims on her attention.** It may be just the two of you sitting in her office, but you're not the only one who wants something from her. Take account of how other key stakeholders might affect her agenda, and highlight how your issues fit into those overall priorities.
- **Collaborate.** Help her form opinions on issues of importance to you, her, and the group. Avoid simply seeking her judgment on your ideas. If, for example, you believe the group has grown too risk-averse, begin a broader discussion about risk. Share anecdotes about how the group has dealt with it in the past, and ask about her experiences and ideas.
- **Be honest.** Most leaders understand the difficulty of speaking truth to power, and yet they must

depend at first on relative strangers for honest appraisals. Look for openings to provide helpful candor on some key aspect of the new boss's agenda. Say your boss wants to launch an initiative that would require buy-in from two unit heads who don't work well together. Diplomatically bring that dynamic to her attention and share stories of how others have been able to get the two to cooperate.

- **Accommodate her preferences.** Your new boss has inherited systems and processes tailored to her predecessor's quirks. The more you can learn about how she would like to be supported, the faster you can help develop new systems that work for her. For example, if her style is to delegate, suggest a regular weekly meeting to review assignments and workloads. Let her know what sorts of tasks you're best suited to take on and keep her apprised of your bandwidth.

Establish a sense of connection, says Gilmore, by "finding links between what you'd like to see happen and things the new boss wants to accomplish." There will be time for your agenda after you've built a solid relationship.

Be Yourself and Be Transparent

J. Bruce Harreld, who now teaches at Harvard Business School, has both been a new boss and reported to one many times—at IBM, Boston Chicken, Kraft General Foods, and elsewhere.

Whether you're getting a new boss at your current company or joining a different one, Harreld says, "The best advice I can give . . . is just to be yourself and be transparent. The more I think about 'What should I say to the boss?' the more he and I are both in trouble. I'm there for a reason—for my best opinion. And he's there for a reason, which is to guide me and help me learn, and shape what my work agenda should be. And the more I posture to him, the less effective I am." In effect, it lowers the value of the relationship.

Candor goes hand in glove with confidentiality. Don't share your boss's comments with others unless he's asked you to. And beware of carrying tales of your peers back to him. "A lot of people view their boss as someone they have to tell everything to," says Harreld. "You have to be careful with that. In a complex organization, if you view the CEO as the kingmaker, you're putting yourself at risk. If I wear my power with my boss on my sleeve, and people know I run back to him often, I've just cut out all these other relationships and made myself totally ineffective."

When Harreld worked for Lou Gerstner at IBM in the mid-1990s, they didn't always agree, but they never pulled their punches: "That's part of the process, part of being on a team. You make your recommendation as forcefully as you can. And once the decision is made, you have to snap around and say, 'OK, here we go.' And sometimes people can't [make that pivot]—they get strident. And sometimes they have to leave the team."

That's worth remembering. The agenda for change may stretch farther than you and others are willing to go. Many new leaders have transformational marching orders. Your job in the course of a leadership transition is to see how compatible the new boss's plans are with your own agenda and career goals. If they're at odds, you might have some thinking to do. And, of course, that thinking cuts both ways: If you're on the edge of disillusionment, a new boss can be a breath of fresh air, helping to rekindle your enthusiasm and optimism.

Help Your New Boss Get Up to Speed

If she's new to the organization, your boss has a lot of catching up to do. You can make it easier by:

- **Saving her some time.** Be generous with what and whom you know. Help your boss identify colleagues whose expertise will help her meet her goals.
- **Saving her some trouble.** Share shortcuts through the administrative mazes that drive every newbie crazy. This may seem like a small thing, but it's not. Let her know that Phil in the IT user-services group is the only person to call when her technology goes on the fritz. Or that Maureen in Finance has developed an idiot-proof Excel template for expense reports.
- **Saving her some work.** Being new is a job unto itself. There may be something on the boss's plate that you can take on or at least help with. If you see an opportunity, step up. Suppose your boss has been asked to honor her predecessor's speaking commitment at an industry conference, and it's clear she's not happy about going. Since you know your way around the presentation material, volunteer to fill in.

Listen for Clues to the Future

In town-hall get-acquainted sessions, new bosses often default to being politic and careful. Sometimes, however, telling comments slip out. File these away as possible clues to the mysterious future. Some of them will doubtless be worth probing later when you have one-on-one meetings with the boss.

Also bear in mind that you may end up with a new boss who isn't right for the business. Pay close attention to what she says (and how she says it). You may be able to spot trouble brewing early on. A former colleague and I, in our first joint meeting with a new boss, were surprised to hear him say, contentedly, that he really had "nothing to prove." Since just about everyone in the company was energetically focused on proving something, the comment seemed discordant. In less than a year, the new boss and the company parted ways.

Remember That the Stakes Are High

Reuben Slone has weathered—and learned from—numerous new-boss transitions in his career. He recently left OfficeMax, where he was an executive VP leading the supply-chain organization, for a comparable position at Walgreens. While at OfficeMax, he had five bosses in eight years.

Each time he's had to adapt to a new boss, Slone has reread the *Harvard Business Review* article "Surviving Your New CEO" (May 2007). He dusted it off again as he prepared for his new assignment at Walgreens, where his challenge is to take an increasingly complicated supply chain—with a growing set of channels, customers, and offerings—to the next level of sophistication.

Slone values the article's tips on how to build a strong relationship with your new leader, whether it's you or your boss who's joining the organization. But he also rereads it for a reality check: It includes sobering research on the jeopardy executives face when a new boss takes over. In some cases, turnover among top executives is 33%—nearly double the normal rate. So every opportunity to make an impression matters tremendously.

Slone's advice? "Make sure the boss knows he can count on you, what he can count on you for, and that you're there to help make the transition as easy as possible. Be explicit about that. And get in early—don't wait for him to come to you."

Lew McCreary is an editorial consultant and a contributing editor to HBR. Working as a consultant means he gets new bosses regularly. He has learned that the most valuable attribute is to be flexible—up to a point.

Steps for Presenting Problems or Opportunities to Your Boss

Did your project come in $10,000 over budget? A rival poach your star performer? Your competitor beat you to market with a new product? None of us likes to deliver a difficult message, but it can be a valuable tool for building a trusting relationship with your boss. You know that you should never bring a problem to your boss without a proposed solution. But often we forget to frame the situation in a way that helps us garner the necessary resources or approval to begin moving toward a solution.

Adapted from *Managing Up* (product #14784) from the Pocket Mentor series, Harvard Business Review Press, 2008

Here are five steps to take the next time you need to deliver bad news—or a promising opportunity.

1. **Describe the problem or opportunity to your boss.** Provide a general overview of the problem, and show the specific impact it has on your work and the company's goals. If you've identified an opportunity, show the potential benefits—not just to you or your team, but to the larger organization.

   "Stu, we've got a morale problem on our tech team. Our recent employee survey shows that 40% of our staff in Atlanta doesn't find their work rewarding or challenging. If we don't address this, we might lose some of our best talent. We can't afford that at any time, but especially now when we're trying to release the new system by Q1. I have a few ideas I'd like to try, with your help and the cooperation of HR. I think with the right approach we can keep the team focused on meeting the Q1 goal."

2. **Identify your solution or approach.** Explain how you've already tried to solve the problem and what you've learned from those attempts. Recommend a specific approach, along with alternatives, to provide your manager with options.

   Clearly define each possible option, addressing the pros and cons, and any potential risks or barriers. Explain the logic behind your recommended approach. You want your manager to be aware that you've considered several possible outcomes.

"It looks like we'd need to add two more managers to the project to meet the client's latest round of requests. When I mentioned this to Sarah during our conference call, she didn't respond. I'd like to go to Cincinnati and meet with her to discuss how we might renegotiate the contract. I think seeing her face-to-face will make a big difference. Plus if I do it the week after next, we'll have just delivered on the second phase of the project and she's likely to be pleased. We could of course take the hard line and just say no to their requests and then see what they come back with. But I'm afraid we'd be putting our future relationship at risk. We could also just expand the team and do the work and see it as a marketing investment. We'd likely win Sarah's good graces and, as you know, she's well connected with many companies in our target group. But it may be more financial risk than we're willing to take on right now."

3. **Explain the implications.** Consider the impact that your proposed solution will have on yourself and others, including your manager. Be explicit about how your idea will have far-reaching effects on the goals of the organization.

   "If we put a formal process in place to track all sales leads, I can do a better job of connecting the dots between the VPs who are meeting with potential customers. As you know, the current approach worked well when we just had two VPs doing the calls, but now we have over 20. This will increase their workload slightly, but it will be clearer to them how to share lead information. It will also give senior leadership a better view into the pipeline. It won't take a week to pull together our sales dev reports, which means you can be more responsive to requests from above."

4. **Discuss the benefits.** Focus your conversation on concrete examples of your idea's benefits. The specific features of the solution, or how it will be implemented, are less important at this stage. If you have tested your approach on a small scale with good results, share that information.

   "Delivering the product in a smaller container in the Latin American market will expand our customer base. We'll be able to serve truckers with small rigs who go on long hauls but don't have room for the 20-gallon containers. Most of these truckers haven't bought our products before, so we have the opportunity to convert them to our brand. They'll also be able to pay cash, since the smaller container will be at a lower price point. This is a real advantage in their cash-heavy economy. Carlos helped me run a quick experiment with a small set of truckers in Panama, and the response was overwhelmingly positive."

5. **Accept responsibility for the outcome.** Demonstrate your commitment to ensuring success. Work with your manager to develop a final action plan for taking advantage of the opportunity you've presented.

   "This rests squarely on my shoulders. In the unlikely event that we don't convert enough customers from this campaign, I'll quickly move on to Plan B. But to get started I'm going to reach out to Terry to get the e-mail list of current customers who have opted-in. Then I'll work with Ellen to draft the e-mail pitch. Once I've done that, I'd like to get your help running it up the flagpole. Does that sound like a sensible plan to you?"

Manage Up with Your Mentor's Guidance

by Jeanne C. Meister

Your mentors can help you build better relationships with your boss and colleagues. How? Jeanne Meister, an expert in workplace learning and development, recently shared her ideas in an IdeaCast interview with Susan Francis from HBR. Here are some highlights.

What kind of support can mentors offer as you're trying to manage up?

> Mentors can help you navigate your company's political landscape and introduce you to key people so you can branch out. And they'll get you thinking like a senior executive long before you're anointed as a member of the upper ranks—which will prepare you for that metamorphosis. One of my first mentors

shared this valuable advice with me: Know who the thought leaders are across the organization, get to know them personally, and show them how your ideas can further their business agendas.

Mentors can also help you communicate your ideas to senior executives, who juggle myriad demands and don't have time to wade through a sea of PowerPoint slides. If you want to present a complex idea to a group like this, take a first pass at boiling it down to a one-page memo that focuses on business outcomes. Then turn to one of your mentors for input: Have you crafted a message that will get executives' attention—one that clearly and succinctly shows how your idea will affect the bottom line? What details should you trim? Where do you need to add data for support?

How can mentors help you work more effectively with your boss?

They can provide insight into the high-level challenges your boss faces and suggest realistic ways of supporting his goals. Ask your boss to clarify his top priorities with you—and write up a one- or two-page summary of that conversation to share with a trusted mentor. Then think with your mentor about how you can contribute. Maybe you can volunteer to assemble sales data your boss will need for his big presentation to the executive board, for example, or tap your network to gather anecdotal feedback on a product idea he's considering.

Also try asking a mentor for help processing and incorporating feedback from your boss. Suppose you've been told you need to speak up more in large staff meetings, but you're shy. You and a mentor can practice graceful ways of jumping into the conversation or brainstorm other things you can do to show you're engaged.

Part of managing up is figuring out which organizational battles to fight and how to fight them. What can mentors do to make this easier?

They can help you develop your personal brand—which will make it clearer which battles you should take on. For instance, if you want to be known at your company for your creative product ideas, a mentor can broker opportunities for you to present them. She'll also help you develop a better sense of when to go to the mat over them. For example, you and your mentor may decide it's worth fighting to protect your vision for a new product's positioning, but not to control the timing of its introduction.

Making sure your mentor gets value out of working with you is obviously good practice for managing up. Any suggestions on how?

This is almost the same as understanding your boss's priorities. When you know what's important to her, you can find ways to work toward her objectives. Simple gestures go a long way—for instance, putting her top three subjects of interest in your Google alerts and passing along links you think she'll like. Look at her Twitter feed for insights into what she cares about: What kinds of conversations is she having—and how can you participate? Ask your mentor about her personal goals and see how you can help her achieve them. Suppose she's writing an article on pricing strategy for a marketing journal. Offer to read the manuscript and provide feedback from an execution perspective. If you find ways to give as well as receive, your mentor will take note—and become all the more invested in your development.

Jeanne C. Meister is a partner at Future Workplace, which helps organizations redefine their corporate learning and talent management strategies. She is a coauthor, with Karie Willyerd, of *The 2020 Workplace: How Innovative Companies Attract, Develop, and Keep Tomorrow's Employees Today* (HarperBusiness, 2010).

Change the Way You Persuade

A summary of the full-length HBR article by **Gary A. Williams** *and* **Robert B. Miller,** *highlighting key ideas.*

THE IDEA IN BRIEF

Your proposal was brilliant; your logic, unassailable; your argument, impassioned. So why didn't your boss buy it?

Perhaps you took a one-size-fits-all approach to persuasion. But different people use different styles when deciding to accept an idea: Each wants certain kinds of information, at specific steps in the process.

There are five common but distinct decision-making styles: charismatic, thinker, skeptic, follower, and controller. One decision-making style isn't better than another. But to tip the outcome your way, understand your listener's preferences—then tailor your persuasive efforts accordingly.

Reprint #R0205D

THE IDEA IN PRACTICE

Style	Decision-Maker's Characteristics	Prominent Examples	Persuader's Strategy	Examples of How to Approach Them
Charismatic	• Easily enthralled, but bases decisions on balanced information • Emphasizes bottom-line results	• Lee Iacocca • Herb Kelleher	• Focus on results • Make straightforward arguments • Stress proposal's benefits with visual aids	• Diagram your current organization and the problem(s), proposed solution(s), and benefits—especially improved competitiveness • Explain potential challenges and risk of inaction • Provide detailed reports for your boss to review postpresentation
Thinker	• Toughest to persuade • Cerebral, logical • Risk-averse • Needs extensive detail	• Michael Dell • Bill Gates	• Present market research, customer surveys, case studies, cost/benefit analyses • Help your boss understand all perspectives of a given situation	• Present different options in detail in a face-to-face meeting • Explain your data-gathering methods • Present case studies of similar initiatives • Use a follow-up meeting to fill argument gaps and recommend optimum plan • Wait weeks, months for your boss's decision
Skeptic	• Challenges every data point • Decides based on gut feelings	• Larry Ellison • Tom Siebel	• Establish credibility ahead of time with your expertise; draw on positive previous work experiences • Get endorsements from someone your boss trusts	• Copresent with a trusted colleague • Emphasize the credibility of your sources of information • Stroke your boss's ego ("You've probably seen this case study...") • Ground your argument in the real world

Follower	• Relies on own or others' past decisions to make current choices • Late adopter	• Carly Fiorina • Peter Coors	• Use testimonials to prove low risk • Present innovative, yet proven, solutions	• Highlight case studies from other industries, but note "We could be the first in our industry to do this." • Omit failed real-world examples (although you should have this information available should your boss request it) • Present multiple options • Tap your network for references to steer your boss toward your preferred choice; emphasize the option's affordability, etc.
Controller	• Unemotional, analytical • Abhors uncertainty • Implements only own ideas	• Martha Stewart • Ross Perot	• Present highly structured arguments • Make your boss "own" the data • Avoid aggressive advocacy	• Over several months, send your boss customer reports, marketing studies, financial projections; give him everything he needs to build your case for you • Emphasize data highlighting the company's challenge • Identify data contradictions, but let your boss analyze them • Wait for your boss to request a meeting after a significant incident (e.g., a large customer defects)

Gary A. Williams is the CEO of Miller-Williams Incorporated, a San Diego–based customer research firm. He can be reached at gaw@millwill.com. **Robert B. Miller** is the chairman of Miller-Williams Incorporated. He is the co-author of several business books, including *Strategic Selling*. He can be reached at rbm@millwill.com.

Get to Know Your Boss's Boss

by Priscilla Claman

Does your boss's boss know you well? Is she impressed with you? Does she know exactly what you do? If you can't answer these questions with a "yes," you're missing out on career opportunities.

Here's a person with a broad perspective on your organization, someone who can see what's coming down the pike—whether it's a new product or a reorg—more clearly than you or your boss can. Forming a relationship with her will help you develop a 30,000-foot view, too. But it's more than that. She has a direct say in your growth and advancement. She approves your performance reviews, raises, promotions, and major changes in duties. She also signs off on any professional development you might be offered, such as stretch assignments or formal training.

Adapted from content posted on hbr.org on November 17, 2011

To succeed in your organization, you need her to know your skills and have an idea of what your career plans are. Yes, your own boss is supposed to advocate for you, but he still has to get the approval of his boss. When you and others are competing for a promotion, it will go to someone your boss's boss thinks highly of.

But how do you get to know her? How do you earn her attention and respect? Here are some suggestions:

- **Interact with her.** It sounds basic, but smile and say "hello" when you see her. Some people duck and run when a powerful person comes into their work area. Instead, ask how you can help her. Reintroduce yourself if you see she doesn't remember you. Treat her like the very important customer she is.

- **Reach out to her.** Touch base when opportunities arise. If she gets a promotion or award, send her a congratulatory e-mail. If you find an article or book that's relevant to her interests, send her a link and ask whether she's heard about it.

- **Tap her for advice.** E-mail her to ask for input on courses you're thinking of taking, professional organizations you're considering joining, and more. First make sure it's OK with your boss, though, and use his name in your message so it's clear you're not bypassing the chain of command. Suppose your boss has asked you to research some new vendors, and you know his boss has several strong candidates in her extensive network. Send her your list of finalists to see if she has any experience with them or knows of other good options. And when you do this, make your boss look good. Preface your question with, "John thought you might have some helpful insights for us . . ." Follow up on her suggestions and thank her for them when you write to let her know which vendor you've chosen and why.

- **Extend an invitation.** Do you have an interesting guest coming in for a meeting? Are you giving a presentation? Is your manager leading a training session? Ask your boss if you should invite his boss. Whether she comes or not, it's another chance to let them both know that you're thinking of the big picture.

- **Pass along praise.** Forward complimentary e-mails from colleagues or customers to your boss. He'll most likely send them on to his boss, since your success reflects well on him, too. Customer compliments are highly regarded, whether the customers are internal or external.

- **Volunteer for a cross-functional team.** Leading or joining a cross-functional team is a great way to contribute to the larger organization. So is offering to take notes at meetings and circulate them afterward. Most people see this as drudgery, but it's an opportunity to raise your visibility. Ask team members if they'd like you to copy their managers, and see if your boss would like you to copy his boss. If they say yes, your notes—and your name—will be noticed by the senior team, including your boss's boss.

- **Fix a problem.** If you find a way to make an improvement that furthers a business objective or supports a corporate value, act on it—and share the results with your boss's boss. Here's an example: An administrative assistant at a global nonprofit found her organization's customer-tracking system inaccurate and hard to use. When she discovered that many colleagues felt the same way, she researched other systems. Some friends in accounting pulled together a cost/benefit analysis for her so she could develop a proposal for switching to a new system, which she presented to her boss and her boss's boss. She not only got funding for the project, she also earned a new leadership role: overseeing the conversion and managing the new system.

Try these tips, and your boss's boss will know—and care—who you are.

Priscilla Claman is president of Career Strategies, a Boston-based firm offering career coaching to individuals and competency development and career management services to organizations.

How to Make Your Boss Look Good—Without Becoming a Sycophant

by Michael Schrage

I find suck-ups loathsome. But I admire the managing-up technique I've seen ambitious people skillfully deploy. No fawning or flattery—they make smart use of technology to make their bosses look good.

For example, the boss's boss at one marketing firm had given a keynote speech at a major industry event. A twentysomething analyst easily found a couple of complimentary tweets referencing the talk. He e-mailed them to his fortysomething boss, who barely knew what Twitter was, but who was thrilled to bring them to his

---

Adapted from content posted on hbr.org on April 15, 2010

boss's attention. Win. Win. Win. Everyone was happy. A simple 90-second investment made his boss look good.

At another firm, a project manager found that her boss's boss had an offbeat sense of humor and liked injecting levity into boring project reviews. She made it her mission to find the appropriate *New Yorker* or Dilbert cartoon to paste into a PowerPoint slide for presentations. Of course, she didn't do this for her own presentations; she selected amusing and relevant options for her boss's talk. He was grateful, and the boss's boss liked them.

What I like about making your boss look good is that it is the mirror image of the marketing mantra about knowing the customer's customer. Understanding your boss is vital. But researching, knowing, and appreciating your boss's boss ought to give you valuable insight into what makes your boss effective—and frustrated. That shapes how to better position your boss in the mind of *his* boss.

Your Boss as a Brand

If you saw your boss as a brand, how would you sell that brand to the ultimate customer—your boss's boss? Answering this question well requires market research. What can you do that will move your project forward and make your boss look good to his boss and peers, too? It can be a worthwhile investment of your time to consider what tools and technologies may help you.

The economic and technological "barriers of entry" to figuring out appropriate approaches to making your boss look good have collapsed. Most managers are but a LinkedIn connection or a blog comment away from insights into their boss's boss that makes a win-win-win outcome a good bet. Should this occur daily? Only if you're comfortable being the teacher's pet. But there's nothing wrong with making your boss look good be a part of *your* brand.

Perhaps you think it would test the outer limits of your creativity and authenticity to make your boss look good. But give it a try. Think of it as a marketing challenge: What are the two things you could do in the next three days that would make your boss look better to his boss?

Michael Schrage, a research fellow at MIT Sloan School's Center for Digital Business, is the author of *Serious Play* (Harvard Business School Press, 1999) and the forthcoming *Getting Beyond Ideas.*

Stop Being Micromanaged

by Amy Gallo

None of us likes a boss who constantly scrutinizes our work. Micromanagers are not only annoying, their lack of faith may make you doubt yourself and stunt your professional growth. But you don't have to suffer with an overly controlling boss. If you reduce your micromanager's stress, you may be able to secure the autonomy you need.

What the Experts Say

Micromanagement can make you feel inept, but typically it has nothing to do with your performance. "It's more about your boss's level of internal anxiety and need to control situations than anything about you," says Jenny Chatman, a professor of management at Haas School of Business at UC Berkeley.

Adapted from content posted on hbr.org on September 22, 2011

You can't change the way your boss leads, but you can change the way you follow using these tactics:

Evaluate Your Boss's Behavior

Jean-François Manzoni, coauthor of *The Set-Up-to-Fail Syndrome: How Good Managers Cause Great People to Fail*, cautions that all controlling bosses are not the same. On one end of the spectrum are managers with very high standards. They may regularly have you rework something that doesn't measure up. They pay a great deal of attention to detail and exercise some degree of control, but they don't stifle you. In fact, you may learn a lot from them.

At the other end of the spectrum are people Manzoni describes as "pathological micromanagers who need to make it clear to themselves and others that they are in charge." These are the bosses who give you little to no independence, insist on being involved in every detail of your work, and are more concerned about specifics, such as font size, than the big picture. "You know you're working with [a pathological micromanager] if he gets involved in a level of detail that is way below his pay grade," says Chatman.

Don't Fight It

Railing against micromanagement isn't productive. "If you push back in one way or another—passively or aggressively—your manager may conclude you can't be trusted and get more involved," says Manzoni. It may be tempting to complain, but it will probably only make your situation worse. "If I sense disdain, I'm going to be encouraged to show you that on my forehead it says 'boss' and on yours, it doesn't," says Manzoni. Instead, try to understand what's causing your boss's behavior. Is he under immense pressure? Is this his intuitive way of managing? Does the company culture encourage and reward this kind of behavior? If you recognize the underlying reasons, you can figure out how to respond.

Increase Trust

Micromanagement is usually "based on a general view that the world's standards are not up to what they should be," says Chatman. You therefore need to make a conscious effort to earn your manager's trust by succeeding in the dimensions that he cares most about. "You absolutely, positively must deliver and deliver in a way that doesn't increase your boss's stress. In fact, identify things that reduce [it]," says Manzoni. If you meet your boss's standards—deliver work on time, make sure projects include the elements she wants—she's likely to see you as someone she can lean on. The more she trusts you, the less inclined she'll be to tell you exactly how to do something.

Make Up-front Agreements

Another tactic is to talk to your boss—before a project starts—about how he'll be involved. "Try to agree on standards and basic approach," says Manzoni. What role will each of you play? What criteria will you use to measure the project's success? Explain what you think the ideal plan of action is and then ask for his input. "Be sure you understand up front what the guiding principles are for the work—not just the tactical elements," says Chatman. For example, if you're working on an internal marketing campaign, be sure to talk about the message you want to send, not the font you should use. If the discussion becomes overly focused on detail, try to bring it back to the principles and approach you agreed on. Flattery can also work. Remind your boss that he's better off not getting involved in the minutiae because his time and effort are more valuable to the big picture.

Keep Your Boss in the Loop

Remember that micromanagers are often motivated by anxiety. "They are nervous about anyone else being able to do things as well or in the same way they would," says Chatman. Address that concern by keeping your manager informed of your project's progress. Schedule regular check-ins to help her feel part of the process. Or send unprompted e-mails that share important information. If she wants detail, get specific. Although annoying now, it may save you the effort of redoing work later on.

Give Feedback, but Only if Appropriate

Telling a micromanager that you don't appreciate his controlling behavior may only trigger more of it. But some managers may be open to hearing your input. "Try to catch your boss in a moment of openness," says Manzoni. He suggests using the time in a scheduled performance review. Focus your feedback on how his behavior affects the process. Can you tweak his involvement so that he gets the information he needs without becoming a roadblock?

Get Help or Move On

If none of these approaches work for you, ask yourself: Do I really want to work here? "If it's pathological, you should consider transferring to another part of the company or finding another job," says Manzoni. Before you throw in the towel, however, look to others inside the company. Find a trusted coworker or a reliable HR manager who can counsel you. At the very least, you'll be able to do some restorative venting, and you may uncover additional tactics that could work for you.

Principles to Remember

- Do everything you can to gain the micromanager's trust
- Know what worries your boss and try to reduce her concerns
- Provide regular and detailed updates so your boss is aware of your progress
- Don't defy the micromanager—that often triggers more of the behavior you're trying to avoid

Case Study: Be Attentive to Her Concerns

In 2006, Marcy Berke (names have been changed) worked for an insurance company with offices throughout the U.S. Her boss's boss was a woman named Barbara, who was responsible for 10 agencies in her region. Barbara was passionate about efficiency. She asked all the agents in her region to produce a time report, accounting for the number of minutes each of them spent on various tasks each day. "She was concerned with keeping her own production figures up and burnishing her image with senior management," Marcy says.

Marcy recognized what mattered most to Barbara. "If I were heading up a project, I would make certain to e-mail Barbara, early and often, with any questions I might have about what her expectations were, and give her an outline of what my team was working on and the anticipated date of completion," she says. If her team was having difficulty meeting the deadline for any reason, she would let Barbara know as soon as possible, providing both a reason and a revised end date. Marcy supplied the information Barbara needed without being asked first so that Barbara could learn to trust her.

Since Marcy knew that Barbara was so preoccupied with time, she arrived at least two or three minutes early for meetings. When Marcy needed to set up a meeting with Barbara, she would make the request by e-mail, clearly stating the reason for the meeting, listing the questions she would be asking, and indicating how long the meeting would last.

This approach worked well for Marcy. She was able to thrive at the company for four years, despite Barbara's micromanagement, before she left to start her own firm.

Amy Gallo is a contributing editor at *Harvard Business Review*. Follow her on Twitter at @amyegallo.

Dealing with Your Incompetent Boss

by Amy Gallo

We all complain about our bosses from time to time. Some of us even consider it part of our job descriptions. But there's a difference between watercooler griping and paralyzing frustration, just as there's a clear distinction between a manager with a few flaws and one who is truly incompetent. So how can you handle your bad boss?

What the Experts Say

"Most people have had experience with someone who is incompetent, or at least unhelpful," says Annie McKee, coauthor of *Becoming a Resonant Leader: Develop Your Emotional Intelligence, Renew Your Relationships, Sustain Your Effectiveness*. That's because too many companies promote people for the wrong reasons. Whether

Adapted from content posted on hbr.org on June 6, 2011

your boss lacks technical or managerial ability, says Michael Useem, author of *Leading Up*, bad bosses sap motivation, kill productivity, and can make you want to run from the job screaming.

Although leaving is sometimes an option, it's not the only one for coping with a bad boss. Consider these tactics first:

Understand Your Boss's Incompetence

Before you declare your boss useless, check your bias and better understand what you're seeing. "When you're looking at your boss, the first thing you need to do before you judge is look at yourself," says McKee. Many of us have blind spots when it comes to our bosses. Ask yourself if you're jealous of her position in the organization or if you have a natural tendency to resist authority.

Also ". . . be cautious about your judgment until you collect all the evidence," says Useem. Your boss may have stressors you don't see or fully understand. "It's very common for people to completely miss the pressures their bosses are under; partly because a good manager will buffer you from them," says McKee. By learning more about your boss and developing empathy for him, you may reevaluate his competence. Even if you still conclude that he's incapable, remember that he's human. Don't demonize him.

Ask Others for Help

Look to peers or people outside the organization for advice and a place to vent. This doesn't mean indiscriminate moaning about your boss. Instead find confidants: a trusted colleague, a spouse, a mentor, or a coach. Explain what you're seeing, how it's affecting you and your work, and ask for advice. "This is not to conspire against your boss but to check your point of view," says Useem. People outside the situation can give you a fresh perspective or offer new coping strategies.

Find a Way to Make It Work

Regardless of your boss's incompetence, you need to work together to get your job done. Be creative in collaborating with her. Figure out where she excels and then find ways to pair your strengths with her weaknesses. For example, if your boss is a competent writer but falls apart in front of an audience, suggest ways you can help with her presentation to the executive team. Can you listen to her trial run? Or present portions of it, as a development opportunity for you?

When you request something from her—whether it's input on a work plan, an introduction to a colleague, or her permission to reach out to a client—be specific about what you need. And do as much of the work for her as you can: Provide a draft e-mail or point out the three areas you'd like her to comment on. If she's unable to help, suggest an alternative: Perhaps you can ask one of her peers or superiors for input or the introduction. Your goal is to help her solve the problem, not set up more situations where she'll fail.

Step Up

Rather than give up on an ineffectual boss, focus on what *you* can do to make up the difference. If your boss fails to set priorities for the team, propose some that he can then approve or tweak. If meeting follow-up isn't his strength, offer to send out the to-dos. Without harboring resentment, do what's best for your team and the organization. Recognize that stepping up can be a growth opportunity; you may be taking on responsibilities someone at your level doesn't usually have. And in the process, you gain the respect and appreciation of other higher-ups.

Develop Yourself

Sometimes incompetence can manifest itself in a lack of communication. You may have a manager who hasn't given you a clear sense of your goals or even a concrete job description. These are essential to doing your job well and advancing your career, so take them on yourself. Write your own job description and articulate goals for the quarter or year. Send them to your boss and ask to review them together. In person, you can then confirm your priorities and understand her expectations. If she's still unresponsive, keep a record of what you've proposed and work to meet the goals you laid out. It may be that she isn't sure what you should be working on and needs you to just take action.

Take Care of Yourself

Working for an incompetent boss can be bad for your health. "There's a lot of research on the negative psychological effects," says McKee. She suggests creating boundaries that protect you from the emotional damage. We have a tendency to point to a bad boss and say, "He's ruining my life." But this ignores the fact that you have agency in the situation. "Once you become a victim, you cease to become a leader," she says. Focus on what makes you happy about your job, not miserable. "We can come to work every day and pay attention to this horrible boss, or we can choose to pay attention to the people we are happy to see every day and the work we enjoy. We can choose which emotions we lean into," says McKee.

Whenever possible, take on projects that allow you to spend time in other parts of the organization or with other leaders. Identify a mentor who can provide you with the feedback and instruction you aren't getting from your boss. Find a way to let off steam, such as taking short breaks throughout the day. Look for humor in the situation, and try not to allow one person to ruin your day, your job, or your career.

Amy Gallo is a contributing editor at *Harvard Business Review*. Follow her on Twitter at @amyegallo.

Coping with a Conflict-Averse Boss

by Anne Field

Does your boss avoid conflict at any cost? Do you find it difficult to get the resources you need because your boss won't advocate for you? Does she push your team to the brink because she fears saying no to requests from above?

Here's how to cope—and get the critical feedback and guidance you need.

Make Conflict More Comfortable

Having a defensive and conflict-averse boss doesn't mean you can never disagree with him. When an issue crops up, frame it in terms that will get the best results *for your business*. Play devil's advocate. Ask lots of "what if?" questions. "What if our printer continues to have quality-control issues? Might it be a good idea to start

---

Adapted from reprint #C0504A

investigating other options now just in case?" Use gentle lead-ins such as "I might be off base here, but . . ." or "This might sound like a crazy idea, but . . ." all the while reassuring your boss that you're working toward the same goal as he is.

Focus on Problem Solving

If you need to talk about a difficult issue with your boss, focus on the problem, not the people. This will help establish neutral ground.

Offer specific suggestions. For example, if your weekly team meeting has turned into a gripe session for your colleagues, volunteer to create and distribute agendas. "I know how busy you are preparing the Williams presentation, so why don't I poll everyone for agenda items for this week's meeting?" You'll help provide a structure for your boss to approve and then follow.

Gather Supporting Evidence

If you want your boss to use her authority on your behalf, give her everything she needs to build her case: assemble data, write drafts, zero in on how your request fits into larger unit or organizational goals.

For example, a manager in a consumer products company dragged her feet when her staff urged her to ask for a bigger budget. So, they gathered the necessary backup, specifying each team member's duties, and the resources needed to meet their goals. They highlighted how meeting their goals would contribute to the unit's overall strategy. With that ammunition in hand, the boss approached senior management with greater confidence.

Put It in Writing

If your boss dreads face-to-face conversations, especially performance reviews, send him e-mails and brief documents outlining your key accomplishments and areas of development. This will make it easier for him to engage in a productive conversation with you—rather than coming up with the documentation on his own.

Guidelines can also help your conflict-averse boss work with larger groups. If his glossing over disagreements inhibits your team's ability to air differences, check your perception with your teammates offline. If they also feel that he's squelching productive debates in favor of peaceful chats, raise the issue with your boss in a one-on-one meeting. Propose that a little debate might help stoke the team's creativity and that setting ground rules for such discussions would ensure that they're productive. Volunteer to take notes to help keep the creative ideas moving along to implementation.

Ease In

If you know that your boss will find a conversation awkward or unpleasant, don't rush into it. Instead, open with a neutral, nonthreatening icebreaker. Cite a recent newspaper article about a common interest. Ask about her child or pet. Once you sense that she's comfortable, ease into the discussion.

Anne Field is a business writer based in Pelham, New York.

How to Give Your Boss Feedback

by Amy Gallo

Have you ever wished you could tell your boss exactly what you think of her? That her obsessive mobile use during team meetings is demoralizing? That people roll their eyes about her compulsive control of the smallest details of every project?

You see your boss in a variety of settings—client and team meetings, presentations, one-on-ones, negotiations—which gives you insight into her strengths and weaknesses. But even if your observations could be helpful, is it your place to share them with her? Could frank feedback put your job or your relationship at risk?

Providing feedback to your boss, commonly called **upward feedback,** is a tricky process to master. But if you offer it correctly, your insight can not only help your boss, it can also improve your relationship with her.

Adapted from content posted on hbr.org on March 24, 2010

What the Experts Say

John Baldoni, a leadership consultant and author of *Lead Your Boss: The Subtle Art of Managing Up*, says that leadership is all about perception; if leaders don't know how others experience them, their performance suffers. And the higher up in an organization a leader sits, the harder it is to get honest feedback. Your input can help your boss see himself as others see him and help him to make critical adjustments in his behavior and approach.

Of course, giving your boss feedback requires careful thought; here are some principles to keep in mind.

The Relationship Comes First

The ability to give and receive upward feedback depends on the level of trust between you and your boss. If you know that she's unreceptive to feedback, is likely to react negatively, or if you have a rocky relationship, don't say anything. But "if your boss is open-minded and you have a good relationship," Baldoni says, "you owe her the straight talk." As with any feedback, your intentions must be good, and your desire to help your boss should supersede any issues you may have with her.

Wait to Be Invited

Even if you have a great relationship, don't launch into unsolicited feedback. Some bosses will request feedback at the end of your formal review, asking, "Is there anything else I can do to support you?" Or, when you first start working together, he may share his development areas and ask you to keep an eye out for certain behaviors that he's working on. "In a perfect world, it is a manager's responsibility to make it safe to give feedback," says Baldoni.

Of course, this is not how things usually happen. If your boss doesn't directly request feedback, ask if she would like it. This might be easiest in the context of a new project or client. You can ask something such as "Would it be useful if I occasionally check in with you about how I think the project is going?" Setting it up in advance can smooth the process, but you can also give feedback in the moment. Try asking something along the lines of "Can I tell you about something I noticed in that meeting?" Emphasize that you're trying to help her so that the client, project, or company will benefit.

Share Your Perspective

Focus your feedback on what you're actually seeing or hearing, not what *you* would do as the boss. Baldoni recommends saying things such as "I noticed that you were silent when Joe disagreed with your proposal. It can be intimidating when you don't respond to criticism." By sharing your perspective, you can help your boss see how others see him. This can be invaluable to a leader who may be disconnected from people in the lower ranks.

Focusing on your perceptions also means realizing the limitations of your standpoint—you're seeing only a partial picture of your boss's performance and all the demands he's juggling. James Detert, author of the *Harvard Business Review* articles "Why Employees Are

Afraid to Speak" and "Speaking Up to Higher-Ups," says, "Subordinates by and large don't have a full appreciation of [their bosses'] reality."

Good feedback rules still apply. Your feedback should be honest, specific, and data-driven. Open with something positive and then offer constructive comments along with suggestions for improvement. Avoid accusations.

If Your Boss Bites Back

No matter how thoughtfully you've prepared and delivered your feedback, your boss may get upset or defensive. Sometimes reframing it in terms of what your boss cares most about can help, says Detert. "Point out how specific behaviors [may be] inhibiting your boss from achieving her goals."

Gauge her reaction to determine how she prefers to receive feedback and what topics are out of bounds. Perhaps she doesn't want to receive pointers on her communication style or a certain high-pressure initiative. Rather than clamming up after a negative reaction, take the opportunity to ask her about what would be useful going forward.

When in Doubt, Hold Your Tongue

If you're not sure your boss wants feedback or if the subject in question is sensitive, it's better not to speak up. Don't risk your working relationship or your job. Instead, look for opportunities to comment anonymously, such as a 360-degree feedback process. If you feel your boss's behavior is putting the company or your unit in jeopardy, follow the appropriate channels in your company—starting with

Human Resources or your employee resource manual or wiki.

Amy Gallo is a contributing editor at *Harvard Business Review*. Follow her on Twitter at @amyegallo.

Managing Multiple Bosses

by Amy Gallo

The movie *Office Space*, a comedy about work life in a typical 1990s software company, details the saga of Peter Gibbons—a man with eight different bosses. All of them, seemingly unaware of each other, pass by his desk and tell him what to do. Although the film is most certainly a satire, for some, it's not far from the truth. Many of us report to more than one boss, so learning to handle multiple managers is essential.

What the Experts Say

"As you go to a matrixed structure, you can easily have between one and seven immediate supervisors," says Robert Sutton, the author of *Good Boss, Bad Boss*. Adam Grant, coauthor of the *Harvard Business Review* article "The Hidden Advantages of Quiet Bosses," concurs. "As com-

---

Adapted from content posted on hbr.org on August 18, 2011

panies continue to flatten, organize work around specific projects, and use temporary teams to complete projects, many employees find themselves reporting to multiple bosses," he says. Although this is more likely to happen in bigger and more complex companies, it can happen in small organizations and family-owned businesses, too. Having many bosses is complicated, and, as Grant says, "If you're not careful, you can end up letting all of them down."

Here are some guidelines to make your job, and theirs, easier.

Recognize the Challenges

Although working for more than one person can present numerous challenges, there are three common ones to watch for:

1. **Overload.** With several people assigning you work, one of the greatest risks is simply having too much to do. "If you report to multiple bosses who supervise your efforts on different tasks and projects, it's all too easy for each boss to treat you as if you have no other responsibilities," says Grant.

2. **Conflicting messages.** "The more bosses you have, the more conflicting messages you get," says Sutton. Sometimes this happens out of ignorance—your bosses aren't aware of what the others are saying—or because people are pushing their own agendas. "Different bosses often have different expectations, and what

impresses one may disappoint another," says Grant.

3. **Loyalty.** "Some bosses want to know that they're your first priority. If you have more than one boss who feels this way, it's easy to get caught in the middle," says Grant. You may need to negotiate between competing demands for your loyalty.

So, how do you make it work?

Know Who Your Ultimate Boss Is

Although you may take direction from multiple managers, most of us have one person who's ultimately responsible for our careers. Ask a lot of questions about the reporting structure. Find out who completes your reviews and who contributes to them. Who makes decisions about your compensation, promotions, and so on?

Stay Connected

Reporting to more than one person can be complicated further if your bosses are in different locations. When your bosses work remotely (or when you do), you need to overcommunicate to make up for the lack of face-to-face time. Rely on technology to help you. Make your calendar viewable to those outside the office or use a web-based tool such as Google Calendar. This will allow all your bosses to know where you are, even when they can't see you. You can use the same calendar to indicate what days you're working on which projects. To simulate the drop-by-your-desk conversations, use an instant messaging application to have brief check-ins or ask quick questions. If only one of your bosses is remote, don't inadvertently cater to the boss whom you see more often, and make sure the distant manager knows you're meeting *his* needs, too.

Be Proactive About Your Workload

Let everyone know what's on your plate. Although it may not be in your job description, it will behoove you to negotiate between your bosses. "I would err on the side of taking the initiative to coordinate between them. Most bosses prefer proactive employees," says Grant. You can create a shared document that lists all of your ongoing tasks and projects, or you can communicate these items in weekly check-in meetings.

Get Your Bosses to Communicate

Most bosses appreciate your bringing them solutions, not problems, but this is complicated when you have more than one manager. Whether you need to resolve contradictory directions, reduce your workload, or sort out inconsistent demands, the best approach is to get your bosses to talk with each other, rather than trying to represent one's agenda to the other. "Start by assuming the best. Invite them to discuss the conflicts and get them out on the table," says Sutton. Bring your bosses together in the same place—in a face-to-face meeting or on a conference call—and explain what the conflict is. Enlist them in the problem solving and push for transparency. "If you ask your bosses for advice on how to handle the disagreement, they're more likely to take your perspective and see the challenges from your point of view," says Grant.

Set Boundaries

"The most important skill for staying sane while reporting to multiple bosses is the ability to set boundaries," says Grant. He points to research done by Harvard Business School professor Leslie Perlow. She found that engineers at a *Fortune* 500 company were constantly interrupted by managers and coworkers. She helped them create norms for quiet time: Three days a week, there would be no interruptions before noon so they could focus on work. If your multiple bosses frequently come to you with questions or to check in about their projects, establish protected times. As mentioned earlier, you can block out times in your calendar for work on certain projects. Before taking on a new project, remind your bosses that you'll need to assess how it fits into your overall workload. Frame this as wanting to be sure you have enough bandwidth to do a project justice rather than putting the request off.

Get Sneaky if You Have To

The aforementioned advice works best in a *healthy* organization, but yours may not reward transparency and proactive approaches. You may find that your bosses are unresponsive or unwilling to meet with you to resolve conflicts, which requires a different approach. "If you're in a fear-based environment, you have to figure out how to protect yourself. The worse the environment, the sneakier you have to get," says Sutton. Figure out which of your bosses has the most power, and prioritize her assignments. "The smart employee doesn't ask. Instead, do your own calculation of who is more powerful and who would hurt you the least," says Sutton.

Don't Take It Personally

Sutton notes that it's easy to assume that your bosses are out to get you, but usually that's not the case. They're probably just pushing their own agendas, and you're getting caught in the middle. Try not to feel persecuted. Instead, identify the conflicts and work to resolve them.

Reap the Benefits

Despite the challenges, having more than one boss can also be an advantage. For example, you're likely to get more robust feedback. If your bosses come from different parts of the organization, you'll have access to a larger and more varied network. You probably have more autonomy because you don't have one person calling all the shots. "Like a kid playing parents off each other, ask the person who you know will give you the answer you want," says Sutton. Although this may seem underhanded, it's an effective way to align your interests with those of your bosses and the company.

Case Study: A Monday Morning To-Do List

Kim Bryant had been in the accounting industry for 15 years when she started with a new firm as a staff accountant. The company had three partners, and Kim was initially hired to work for one of them. But soon she was asked to continue her work for that partner and also help out one of the others. "The most difficult thing about working for two partners was that both had projects that they felt were urgent and it put me in an uncomfortable situation," she says. Kim had to decide which project to work on first. When she asked one of her bosses for advice, he would say he wanted his project done first. Frequently, one partner assigned her something urgent when she was working on an upcoming deadline for the other. So Kim created a to-do list every Monday morning, prioritized by due date, and shared it with the two partners. "That allowed each partner to be aware of what I had been assigned to do," she says.

She also learned to watch their schedules, often with the help of their secretary. If Kim had been told that a project was urgent, she could gauge how soon she needed to do it based on when the partner was back in the office. She knew if she got it on his desk before he returned, she would be fine.

Amy Gallo is a contributing editor at *Harvard Business Review*. Follow her on Twitter at @amyegallo.

Section 2
Managing Across

Do you depend on lots of people over whom you have no authority? Do you struggle to navigate your company's political landscape? To get your cross-functional team functioning? To collaborate across time zones? To motivate colleagues to meet *your* deadlines when they're juggling countless other projects?

Managing *across*—with peers, vendors, or consultants—is complex. You don't have a say in their reviews or decide if they get promoted. So you need to use other tactics, such as setting mutually beneficial goals, establishing your credibility, polishing your powers of persuasion, and tapping into your network. The articles in this section will give you these tools.

What Makes a Leader?

A summary of the full-length HBR article by **Daniel Goleman**, *highlighting key ideas.*

THE IDEA IN BRIEF

Are you so intent on meeting deadlines or hitting financial targets that you're neglecting working relationships? Do you often interrupt colleagues? Fail to ask them what else is on their plates?

If you nodded "yes" to any of these questions, you may have zeroed in on what's getting in the way of your ability to work well with people at all levels, across silos, and with personalities that may be very different from your own. Managing across requires *emotional intelligence*: self-awareness, self-regulation, motivation, empathy, and social skill. Developing emotional intelligence will help you better understand your own—and others'—priorities, pressures, and work styles.

Reprint #R0401H

THE IDEA IN PRACTICE

The Five Components of Emotional Intelligence

Component	Definition	Hallmarks	Example
Self-Awareness	Knowing one's emotions, strengths, weaknesses, drives, values, and goals—and their impact on others	• Self-confidence • Realistic self-assessment • Self-deprecating sense of humor • Thirst for constructive criticism	A manager knows tight deadlines bring out the worst in him. So he plans his time to get work done well in advance.
Self-Regulation	Controlling or redirecting disruptive emotions and impulses	• Trustworthiness • Integrity • Comfort with ambiguity and change	When a team botches a presentation, its leader resists the urge to scream. Instead, she considers possible reasons for the failure, explains the consequences to her team, and explores solutions with them.
Motivation	Being driven to achieve for the sake of achievement	• A passion for the work itself and for new challenges • Unflagging energy to improve • Optimism in the face of failure	A portfolio manager at an investment company sees her fund tumble for three consecutive quarters. Major clients defect. Instead of blaming external circumstances, she decides to learn from the experience—and engineers a turnaround.

Empathy	Considering others' feelings, especially when making decisions	• Expertise in attracting and retaining talent • Ability to develop others • Sensitivity to cross-cultural differences	An American consultant and her team pitch a project to a potential client in Japan. Her team interprets the client's silence as disapproval and prepares to leave. The consultant reads the client's body language and senses interest. She continues the meeting, and her team gets the job.
Social Skill	Managing relationships to move people in desired directions	• Effectiveness in leading change • Persuasiveness • Extensive networking • Expertise in building and leading teams	A manager wants his company to adopt a better Internet strategy. He finds kindred spirits and assembles a de facto team to create a prototype website. He persuades allies in other divisions to fund the company's participation in a relevant convention. His company forms an Internet division—and puts him in charge of it.

It was Daniel Goleman who first brought the term "emotional intelligence" to a wide audience with his 1995 book of that name, and it was Goleman who first applied the concept to business with his 1998 HBR article, reprinted here. In his research at nearly 200 large, global companies, Goleman found that while the qualities traditionally associated with leadership—such as intelligence, toughness, determination, and vision—are required for success, they are insufficient. Truly effective leaders are also distinguished by a high degree of emotional intelligence, which includes self-awareness, self-regulation, motivation, empathy, and social skill.

These qualities may sound "soft" and unbusiness-like, but Goleman found direct ties between emotional intelligence and measurable business results. While emotional intelligence's relevance to business has continued to spark debate over the past six years, Goleman's article remains the definitive reference on the subject, with a description of each component of emotional intelligence and a detailed discussion of how to recognize it in potential leaders, how and why it connects to performance, and how it can be learned.

Every businessperson knows a story about a highly intelligent, highly skilled executive who was promoted into a leadership position only to fail at the job. And they also know a story about someone with solid—but not extraordinary—intellectual abilities and technical skills who was promoted into a similar position and then soared.

Such anecdotes support the widespread belief that identifying individuals with the "right stuff" to be leaders is more art than science. After all, the personal styles of superb leaders vary: Some leaders are subdued and analytical; others shout their manifestos from the mountaintops. And just as important, different situations call for different types of leadership. Most mergers need a sensitive negotiator at the helm, whereas many turnarounds require a more forceful authority.

I have found, however, that the most effective leaders are alike in one crucial way: They all have a high degree of what has come to be known as *emotional intelligence.* It's not that IQ and technical skills are irrelevant. They do matter, but mainly as "threshold capabilities"; that is, they are the entry-level requirements for executive positions. But my research, along with other recent studies, clearly shows that emotional intelligence is the sine qua non of leadership. Without it, a person can have the best training in the world, an incisive, analytical mind, and an endless supply of smart ideas, but he still won't make a great leader.

In the course of the past year, my colleagues and I have focused on how emotional intelligence operates at work. We have examined the relationship between emotional intelligence and effective performance, especially in leaders. And we have observed how emotional intelligence shows itself on the job. How can you tell if someone has high emotional intelligence, for example, and how can you recognize it in yourself? In the following pages, we'll explore these questions, taking each of the components of emotional intelligence—self-awareness, self-regulation, motivation, empathy, and social skill—in turn.

Evaluating Emotional Intelligence

Most large companies today have employed trained psychologists to develop what are known as "competency models" to aid them in identifying, training, and promoting likely stars in the leadership firmament. The psychologists have also developed such models for lower-level positions. And in recent years, I have analyzed competency models from 188 companies, most of which were large and global and included the likes of Lucent Technologies, British Airways, and Credit Suisse.

In carrying out this work, my objective was to determine which personal capabilities drove outstanding performance within these organizations, and to what degree they did so. I grouped capabilities into three categories: purely technical skills like accounting and business planning; cognitive abilities like analytical reasoning; and competencies demonstrating emotional intelligence, such as the ability to work with others and effectiveness in leading change.

To create some of the competency models, psychologists asked senior managers at the companies to identify the capabilities that typified the organization's most outstanding leaders. To create other models, the psychologists used objective criteria, such as a division's profitability, to differentiate the star performers at senior levels within their organizations from the average ones. Those individuals were then extensively interviewed and tested, and their capabilities were compared. This process resulted in the creation of lists of ingredients for highly effective leaders. The lists ranged in length from seven to 15 items and included such ingredients as initiative and strategic vision.

When I analyzed all this data, I found dramatic results. To be sure, intellect was a driver of outstanding performance. Cognitive skills such as big-picture thinking and long-term vision were particularly important. But when I calculated the ratio of technical skills, IQ, and emotional intelligence as ingredients of excellent performance, emotional intelligence proved to be twice as important as the others for jobs at all levels.

Moreover, my analysis showed that emotional intelligence played an increasingly important role at the highest levels of the company, where differences in technical skills are of negligible importance. In other words, the higher the rank of a person considered to be a star performer, the more emotional intelligence capabilities showed up as the reason for his or her effectiveness. When I compared star performers with average ones in senior leadership positions, nearly 90% of the difference in their profiles was attributable to emotional intelligence factors rather than cognitive abilities.

Other researchers have confirmed that emotional intelligence not only distinguishes outstanding leaders but can also be linked to strong performance. The findings of the late David McClelland, the renowned researcher in human and organizational behavior, are a good example. In a 1996 study of a global food and beverage company, McClelland found that when senior managers had a critical mass of emotional intelligence capabilities, their divisions outperformed yearly earnings goals by 20%. Meanwhile, division leaders without that critical mass underperformed by almost the same amount. McClelland's findings, interestingly, held as true in the company's U.S. divisions as in its divisions in Asia and Europe.

In short, the numbers are beginning to tell us a persuasive story about the link between a company's success and the emotional intelligence of its leaders. And just as important, research is also demonstrating that people can, if they take the right approach, develop their emotional intelligence. (See the sidebar "Can Emotional Intelligence Be Learned?")

Self-Awareness

Self-awareness is the first component of emotional intelligence—which makes sense when one considers that the Delphic oracle gave the advice to "know thyself" thousands of years ago. Self-awareness means having a deep understanding of one's emotions, strengths, weaknesses, needs, and drives. People with strong self-awareness are neither overly critical nor unrealistically hopeful. Rather, they are honest—with themselves and with others.

People who have a high degree of self-awareness recognize how their feelings affect them, other people, and their job performance. Thus, a self-aware person who knows that tight deadlines bring out the worst in him plans his time carefully and gets his work done well in advance. Another person with high self-awareness will

The Five Components of Emotional Intelligence at Work

	Definition	Hallmarks
Self-Awareness	the ability to recognize and understand your moods, emotions, and drives, as well as their effect on others	self-confidence realistic self-assessment self-deprecating sense of humor
Self-Regulation	the ability to control or redirect disruptive impulses and moods the propensity to suspend judgment—to think before acting	trustworthiness and integrity comfort with ambiguity openness to change
Motivation	a passion to work for reasons that go beyond money or status a propensity to pursue goals with energy and persistence	strong drive to achieve optimism, even in the face of failure organizational commitment
Empathy	the ability to understand the emotional makeup of other people skill in treating people according to their emotional reactions	expertise in building and retaining talent cross-cultural sensitivity service to clients and customers
Social Skill	proficiency in managing relationships and building networks an ability to find common ground and build rapport	effectiveness in leading change persuasiveness expertise in building and leading teams

be able to work with a demanding client. She will understand the client's impact on her moods and the deeper reasons for her frustration. "Their trivial demands take us away from the real work that needs to be done," she might explain. And she will go one step further and turn her anger into something constructive.

CAN EMOTIONAL INTELLIGENCE BE LEARNED?

For ages, people have debated if leaders are born or made. So too goes the debate about emotional intelligence. Are people born with certain levels of empathy, for example, or do they acquire empathy as a result of life's experiences? The answer is both. Scientific inquiry strongly suggests that there is a genetic component to emotional intelligence. Psychological and developmental research indicates that nurture plays a role as well. How much of each perhaps will never be known, but research and practice clearly demonstrate that emotional intelligence can be learned.

One thing is certain: Emotional intelligence increases with age. There is an old-fashioned word for the phenomenon: maturity. Yet even with maturity, some people still need training to enhance their emotional intelligence. Unfortunately, far too many training programs that intend to build leadership skills—including emotional intelligence—are a waste of time and money. The problem is simple: They focus on the wrong part of the brain.

Emotional intelligence is born largely in the neurotransmitters of the brain's limbic system, which governs feelings, impulses, and drives. Research indicates that the limbic system learns best through motivation, extended practice, and feedback. Compare this with the kind of learning that goes on in the neocortex, which governs analytical and technical ability.

The neocortex grasps concepts and logic. It is the part of the brain that figures out how to use a computer or make a sales call by reading a book. Not surprisingly—but mistakenly—it is also the part of the brain targeted by most training programs aimed at enhancing emotional intelligence. When such programs take, in effect, a neocortical approach, my research with the Consortium for Research on Emotional Intelligence in Organizations has shown they can even have a *negative* impact on people's job performance.

To enhance emotional intelligence, organizations must refocus their training to include the limbic system. They must help people break old behavioral habits and establish new ones. That not only takes much more time than conventional training programs, it also requires an individualized approach.

Imagine an executive who is thought to be low on empathy by her colleagues. Part of that deficit shows itself as an inability to listen; she interrupts people and doesn't pay close attention to what they're saying. To fix the problem, the executive needs to be motivated to change, and then she needs practice and feedback from others in the company. A colleague or coach could be tapped to let the executive know when she has been observed failing to listen. She would then have to replay the incident and give a better response;

(*continued*)

(*continued*)

that is, demonstrate her ability to absorb what others are saying. And the executive could be directed to observe certain executives who listen well and to mimic their behavior.

With persistence and practice, such a process can lead to lasting results. I know one Wall Street executive who sought to improve his empathy—specifically his ability to read people's reactions and see their perspectives. Before beginning his quest, the executive's subordinates were terrified of working with him. People even went so far as to hide bad news from him. Naturally, he was shocked when finally confronted with these facts. He went home and told his family—but they only confirmed what he had heard at work. When their opinions on any given subject did not mesh with his, they, too, were frightened of him.

Enlisting the help of a coach, the executive went to work to heighten his empathy through practice and feedback. His first step was to take a vacation to a foreign country where he did not speak the language. While there, he monitored his reactions to the unfamiliar and his openness to people who were different from him. When he returned home, humbled by his week abroad, the executive asked his coach to shadow him for parts of the day, several times a week, to critique how he treated people with new or different perspectives. At the same time, he consciously used on-the-job interactions as opportunities to practice "hearing" ideas that differed from his. Finally, the executive had himself videotaped in meetings and asked those who worked for and with him to critique his ability to acknowledge and understand the feelings of others. It took several months, but the executive's emotional intelligence did ultimately rise, and the improvement was reflected in his overall performance on the job.

It's important to emphasize that building one's emotional intelligence cannot—will not—happen without sincere desire and concerted effort. A brief seminar won't help; nor can one buy a how-to manual. It is much harder to learn to empathize—to internalize empathy as a natural response to people—than it is to become adept at regression analysis. But it can be done. "Nothing great was ever achieved without enthusiasm," wrote Ralph Waldo Emerson. If your goal is to become a real leader, these words can serve as a guidepost in your efforts to develop high emotional intelligence.

Self-awareness extends to a person's understanding of his or her values and goals. Someone who is highly self-aware knows where he is headed and why; so, for example, he will be able to be firm in turning down a job offer that is tempting financially but does not fit with his principles or long-term goals. A person who lacks self-awareness is apt to make decisions that bring on inner turmoil by treading on buried values. "The money looked good so I signed on," someone might say two years into a job, "but the work means so little to me that I'm constantly bored." The decisions of self-aware people mesh with their values; consequently, they often find work to be energizing.

How can one recognize self-awareness? First and foremost, it shows itself as candor and an ability to assess oneself realistically. People with high self-awareness are able to speak accurately and openly—although not necessarily effusively or confessionally—about their emotions and the impact they have on their work. For instance, one manager I know of was skeptical about a new personal-shopper service that her company, a major department-store chain, was about to introduce. Without prompting from her team or her boss, she offered them an explanation: "It's hard for me to get behind the rollout of this service," she admitted, "because I really wanted to run the project, but I wasn't selected. Bear with me while I deal with that." The manager did indeed examine her feelings; a week later, she was supporting the project fully.

Such self-knowledge often shows itself in the hiring process. Ask a candidate to describe a time he got carried away by his feelings and did something he later regretted. Self-aware candidates will be frank in admitting to failure—and will often tell their tales with a smile. One of the hallmarks of self-awareness is a self-deprecating sense of humor.

Self-awareness can also be identified during performance reviews. Self-aware people know—and are comfortable talking about—their limitations and strengths, and they often demonstrate a thirst for constructive criticism. By contrast, people with low self-awareness interpret the message that they need to improve as a threat or a sign of failure.

Self-aware people can also be recognized by their self-confidence. They have a firm grasp of their capabilities and are less likely to set themselves up to fail by, for example, overstretching on assignments. They know, too, when to ask for help. And the risks they take on the job are calculated. They won't ask for a challenge that they know they can't handle alone. They'll play to their strengths.

Consider the actions of a midlevel employee who was invited to sit in on a strategy meeting with her company's top executives. Although she was the most junior person in the room, she did not sit there quietly, listening in awestruck or fearful silence. She knew she had a head for clear logic and the skill to present ideas persuasively, and she offered cogent suggestions about the company's strategy. At the same time, her self-awareness stopped her from wandering into territory where she knew she was weak.

Despite the value of having self-aware people in the workplace, my research indicates that senior executives don't often give self-awareness the credit it deserves when they look for potential leaders. Many executives mistake candor about feelings for "wimpiness" and fail to give due respect to employees who openly acknowledge their shortcomings. Such people are too readily dismissed as "not tough enough" to lead others.

In fact, the opposite is true. In the first place, people generally admire and respect candor. Furthermore, leaders are constantly required to make judgment calls that require a candid assessment of capabilities—their own and those of others. Do we have the management expertise to acquire a competitor? Can we launch a new product within six months? People who assess themselves honestly—that is, self-aware people—are well suited to do the same for the organizations they run.

Self-Regulation

Biological impulses drive our emotions. We cannot do away with them—but we can do much to manage them. Self-regulation, which is like an ongoing inner conversation, is the component of emotional intelligence that frees us from being prisoners of our feelings. People engaged in such a conversation feel bad moods and emotional impulses just as everyone else does, but they find ways to control them and even to channel them in useful ways.

Imagine an executive who has just watched a team of his employees present a botched analysis to the company's board of directors. In the gloom that follows, the executive might find himself tempted to pound on the table in anger or kick over a chair. He could leap up and scream at the group. Or he might maintain a grim silence, glaring at everyone before stalking off.

But if he had a gift for self-regulation, he would choose a different approach. He would pick his words carefully, acknowledging the team's poor performance without rushing to any hasty judgment. He would then step back to consider the reasons for the failure. Are they personal—a lack of effort? Are there any mitigating factors? What was his role in the debacle? After considering these questions, he would call the team together, lay out the incident's consequences, and offer his feelings about it. He would then present his analysis of the problem and a well-considered solution.

Why does self-regulation matter so much for leaders? First of all, people who are in control of their feelings and impulses—that is, people who are reasonable—are able to create an environment of trust and fairness. In such an environment, politics and infighting are sharply reduced and productivity is high. Talented people flock to the organization and aren't tempted to leave. And self-regulation has a trickle-down effect. No one wants to be known as a hothead when the boss is known for her calm approach. Fewer bad moods at the top mean fewer throughout the organization.

Second, self-regulation is important for competitive reasons. Everyone knows that business today is rife with ambiguity and change. Companies merge and break apart regularly. Technology transforms work at a dizzying pace. People who have mastered their emotions are able to roll with the changes. When a new program is announced, they don't panic; instead, they are able to suspend judgment, seek out information, and listen to the executives as they explain the new program. As the initiative moves forward, these people are able to move with it.

Sometimes they even lead the way. Consider the case of a manager at a large manufacturing company. Like her colleagues, she had used a certain software program for five years. The program drove how she collected and reported data and how she thought about the company's strategy. One day, senior executives announced that a new program was to be installed that would radically change how information was gathered and assessed within the organization. While many people in the company complained bitterly about how disruptive the change would be, the manager mulled over the reasons for the new program and was convinced of its potential to improve performance. She eagerly attended training sessions—some of her colleagues refused to do so—and was eventually promoted to run several divisions, in part because she used the new technology so effectively.

I want to push the importance of self-regulation to leadership even further and make the case that it enhances integrity, which is not only a personal virtue but also an organizational strength. Many of the bad things that happen in companies are a function of impulsive behavior. People rarely plan to exaggerate profits, pad expense accounts, dip into the till, or abuse power for selfish ends. Instead, an opportunity presents itself, and people with low impulse control just say yes.

By contrast, consider the behavior of the senior executive at a large food company. The executive was scrupulously honest in his negotiations with local distributors. He would routinely lay out his cost structure in detail, thereby giving the distributors a realistic understanding of the company's pricing. This approach meant the executive couldn't always drive a hard bargain. Now, on occasion, he felt the urge to increase profits by withholding information about the company's costs. But he challenged that impulse—he saw that it made more sense in the long run to counteract it. His emotional self-regulation paid off in strong, lasting relationships with distributors that benefited the company more than any short-term financial gains would have.

The signs of emotional self-regulation, therefore, are easy to see: a propensity for reflection and thoughtfulness; comfort with ambiguity and change; and integrity—an ability to say no to impulsive urges.

Like self-awareness, self-regulation often does not get its due. People who can master their emotions are sometimes seen as cold fish—their considered responses are taken as a lack of passion. People with fiery temperaments are frequently thought of as "classic" leaders—their outbursts are considered hallmarks of charisma and power. But when such people make it to the top, their impulsiveness often works against them. In my research, extreme displays of negative emotion have never emerged as a driver of good leadership.

Motivation

If there is one trait that virtually all effective leaders have, it is motivation. They are driven to achieve beyond expectations—their own and everyone else's. The key word here is *achieve*. Plenty of people are motivated by external factors, such as a big salary or the status that comes from having an impressive title or being part of a prestigious company. By contrast, those with leadership potential are motivated by a deeply embedded desire to achieve for the sake of achievement.

If you are looking for leaders, how can you identify people who are motivated by the drive to achieve rather than by external rewards? The first sign is a passion for the work itself—such people seek out creative challenges, love to learn, and take great pride in a job well done. They also display an unflagging energy to do things better. People with such energy often seem restless with the status quo. They are persistent with their questions about why things are done one way rather than another; they are eager to explore new approaches to their work.

A cosmetics company manager, for example, was frustrated that he had to wait two weeks to get sales results from people in the field. He finally tracked down an automated phone system that would beep each of his salespeople at 5 p.m. every day. An automated message then prompted them to punch in their numbers—how many calls and sales they had made that day. The system shortened the feedback time on sales results from weeks to hours.

That story illustrates two other common traits of people who are driven to achieve. They are forever raising the performance bar, and they like to keep score. Take the performance bar first. During performance reviews, people with high levels of motivation might ask to be "stretched" by their superiors. Of course, an employee who combines self-awareness with internal motivation will recognize her limits—but she won't settle for objectives that seem too easy to fulfill.

And it follows naturally that people who are driven to do better also want a way of tracking progress—their own, their team's, and their company's. Whereas people with low achievement motivation are often fuzzy about results, those with high achievement motivation often keep score by tracking such hard measures as profitability or market share. I know of a money manager who starts and ends his day on the Internet, gauging the performance of his stock fund against four industry-set benchmarks.

Interestingly, people with high motivation remain optimistic even when the score is against them. In such cases, self-regulation combines with achievement motivation to overcome the frustration and depression that come after a setback or failure. Take the case of an another portfolio manager at a large investment company. After several successful years, her fund tumbled for three consecutive quarters, leading three large institutional clients to shift their business elsewhere.

Some executives would have blamed the nosedive on circumstances outside their control; others might have seen the setback as evidence of personal failure. This portfolio manager, however, saw an opportunity to prove she could lead a turnaround. Two years later, when she was promoted to a very senior level in the company, she described the experience as "the best thing that ever happened to me; I learned so much from it."

Executives trying to recognize high levels of achievement motivation in their people can look for one last piece of evidence: commitment to the organization. When people love their jobs for the work itself, they often feel committed to the organizations that make that work possible. Committed employees are likely to stay with an organization even when they are pursued by headhunters waving money.

It's not difficult to understand how and why a motivation to achieve translates into strong leadership. If you set the performance bar high for yourself, you will do the same for the organization when you are in a position to do so. Likewise, a drive to surpass goals and an interest in keeping score can be contagious. Leaders with these traits can often build a team of managers around them with the same traits. And of course, optimism and organizational commitment are fundamental to leadership—just try to imagine running a company without them.

Empathy

Of all the dimensions of emotional intelligence, empathy is the most easily recognized. We have all felt the empathy of a sensitive teacher or friend; we have all been struck by its absence in an unfeeling coach or boss. But when it comes to business, we rarely hear people praised, let alone rewarded, for their empathy. The very word seems unbusinesslike, out of place amid the tough realities of the marketplace.

But empathy doesn't mean a kind of "I'm OK, you're OK" mushiness. For a leader, that is, it doesn't mean adopting other people's emotions as one's own and trying to please everybody. That would be a nightmare—it would make action impossible. Rather, empathy means thoughtfully considering employees' feelings—along with other factors—in the process of making intelligent decisions.

For an example of empathy in action, consider what happened when two giant brokerage companies merged, creating redundant jobs in all their divisions. One division manager called his people together and gave a gloomy speech that emphasized the number of people who would soon be fired. The manager of another division gave his people a different kind of speech. He was up-front about his own worry and confusion, and he promised to keep people informed and to treat everyone fairly.

The difference between these two managers was empathy. The first manager was too worried about his own fate to consider the feelings of his anxiety-stricken colleagues. The second knew intuitively what his people were feeling, and he acknowledged their fears with his words. Is it any surprise that the first manager saw his division sink as many demoralized people, especially the most talented, departed? By contrast, the second manager continued to be a strong leader, his best people stayed, and his division remained as productive as ever.

Empathy is particularly important today as a component of leadership for at least three reasons: the increasing use of teams; the rapid pace of globalization; and the growing need to retain talent.

Consider the challenge of leading a team. As anyone who has ever been a part of one can attest, teams are cauldrons of bubbling emotions. They are often charged with reaching a consensus—which is hard enough with two people and much more difficult as the numbers increase. Even in groups with as few as four or five members, alliances form and clashing agendas get set. A team's leader must be able to sense and understand the viewpoints of everyone around the table.

That's exactly what a marketing manager at a large information technology company was able to do when she was appointed to lead a troubled team. The group was in turmoil, overloaded by work and missing deadlines. Tensions were high among the members. Tinkering with procedures was not enough to bring the group together and make it an effective part of the company.

So the manager took several steps. In a series of one-on-one sessions, she took the time to listen to everyone in the group—what was frustrating them, how they rated their colleagues, whether they felt they had been ignored. And then she directed the team in a way that brought it together: She encouraged people to speak more openly about their frustrations, and she helped people raise constructive complaints during meetings. In short, her empathy allowed her to understand her team's emotional makeup. The result was not just heightened collaboration among members but also added business, as the team was called on for help by a wider range of internal clients.

Globalization is another reason for the rising importance of empathy for business leaders. Cross-cultural dialogue can easily lead to miscues and misunderstandings. Empathy is an antidote. People who have it are attuned to subtleties in body language; they can hear the message beneath the words being spoken. Beyond that, they have a deep understanding of both the existence and the importance of cultural and ethnic differences.

Consider the case of an American consultant whose team had just pitched a project to a potential Japanese client. In its dealings with Americans, the team was accustomed to being bombarded with questions after such a proposal, but this time it was greeted with a long silence. Other members of the team, taking the silence as disapproval, were ready to pack and leave. The lead consultant gestured them to stop. Although he was not particularly familiar with Japanese culture, he read the client's face and posture and sensed not rejection but interest—even deep consideration. He was right: When the client finally spoke, it was to give the consulting firm the job.

Finally, empathy plays a key role in the retention of talent, particularly in today's information economy. Leaders have always needed empathy to develop and keep good people, but today the stakes are higher. When good people leave, they take the company's knowledge with them.

That's where coaching and mentoring come in. It has repeatedly been shown that coaching and mentoring pay off not just in better performance but also in increased job satisfaction and decreased turnover. But what makes coaching and mentoring work best is the nature of the relationship. Outstanding coaches and mentors get inside the heads of the people they are helping. They sense how to give effective feedback. They know when to push for better performance and when to hold back. In the way they motivate their protégés, they demonstrate empathy in action.

In what is probably sounding like a refrain, let me repeat that empathy doesn't get much respect in business. People wonder how leaders can make hard decisions if they are "feeling" for all the people who will be affected. But leaders with empathy do more than sympathize with people around them: They use their knowledge to improve their companies in subtle but important ways.

Social Skill

The first three components of emotional intelligence are self-management skills. The last two, empathy and social skill, concern a person's ability to manage relationships with others. As a component of emotional intelligence, social skill is not as simple as it sounds. It's not just a matter of friendliness, although people with high levels of social skill are rarely mean-spirited. Social skill, rather, is friendliness with a purpose: moving people in the direction you desire, whether that's agreement on a new marketing strategy or enthusiasm about a new product.

Socially skilled people tend to have a wide circle of acquaintances, and they have a knack for finding common ground with people of all kinds—a knack for building rapport. That doesn't mean they socialize continually; it means they work according to the assumption that nothing important gets done alone. Such people have a network in place when the time for action comes.

Social skill is the culmination of the other dimensions of emotional intelligence. People tend to be very effective at managing relationships when they can understand and control their own emotions and can empathize with the feelings of others. Even motivation contributes to social skill. Remember that people who are driven to achieve tend to be optimistic, even in the face of setbacks or failure. When people are upbeat, their "glow" is cast upon conversations and other social encounters. They are popular, and for good reason.

Because it is the outcome of the other dimensions of emotional intelligence, social skill is recognizable on the job in many ways that will by now sound familiar. Socially skilled people, for instance, are adept at managing teams—that's their empathy at work. Likewise, they are expert persuaders—a manifestation of self-awareness, self-regulation, and empathy combined. Given those skills, good persuaders know when to make an emotional plea, for instance, and when an appeal to reason will work better. And motivation, when publicly visible, makes such people excellent collaborators; their passion for the work spreads to others, and they are driven to find solutions.

But sometimes social skill shows itself in ways the other emotional intelligence components do not. For instance, socially skilled people may at times appear not to be working while at work. They seem to be idly schmoozing—chatting in the hallways with colleagues or joking around with people who are not even connected to their "real" jobs. Socially skilled people, however, don't think it makes sense to arbitrarily limit the scope of their relationships. They build bonds widely because they know that in these fluid times, they may need help someday from people they are just getting to know today.

For example, consider the case of an executive in the strategy department of a global computer manufacturer.

By 1993, he was convinced that the company's future lay with the Internet. Over the course of the next year, he found kindred spirits and used his social skill to stitch together a virtual community that cut across levels, divisions, and nations. He then used this de facto team to put up a corporate website, among the first by a major company. And, on his own initiative, with no budget or formal status, he signed up the company to participate in an annual Internet industry convention. Calling on his allies and persuading various divisions to donate funds, he recruited more than 50 people from a dozen different units to represent the company at the convention.

Management took notice: Within a year of the conference, the executive's team formed the basis for the company's first Internet division, and he was formally put in charge of it. To get there, the executive had ignored conventional boundaries, forging and maintaining connections with people in every corner of the organization.

Is social skill considered a key leadership capability in most companies? The answer is yes, especially when compared with the other components of emotional intelligence. People seem to know intuitively that leaders need to manage relationships effectively; no leader is an island. After all, the leader's task is to get work done through other people, and social skill makes that possible. A leader who cannot express her empathy may as well not have it at all. And a leader's motivation will be useless if he cannot communicate his passion to the organization. Social skill allows leaders to put their emotional intelligence to work.

It would be foolish to assert that good-old-fashioned IQ and technical ability are not important ingredients in strong leadership. But the recipe would not be complete without emotional intelligence. It was once thought that the components of emotional intelligence were "nice to have" in business leaders. But now we know that, for the sake of performance, these are ingredients that leaders "need to have."

It is fortunate, then, that emotional intelligence can be learned. The process is not easy. It takes time and, most of all, commitment. But the benefits that come from having a well-developed emotional intelligence, both for the individual and for the organization, make it worth the effort.

Daniel Goleman is the author of *Emotional Intelligence* (Bantam, 1995) and a coauthor of *Primal Leadership: Realizing the Power of Emotional Intelligence* (Harvard Business School, 2002). He is the cochairman of the Consortium for Research on Emotional Intelligence in Organizations, which is based at Rutgers University's Graduate School of Applied and Professional Psychology in Piscataway, New Jersey. He can be reached at Daniel.Goleman@verizon.net.

The Discipline of Teams

A summary of the full-length HBR article by **Jon R. Katzenbach** *and* **Douglas K. Smith,** *highlighting key ideas.*

THE IDEA IN BRIEF

Managing across is especially challenging when you're leading a group of colleagues. You're not their boss, but on this project, you're their leader. How can you get them to focus on *your* team's work when they also need to tend their own small fires—or meet *their* bosses' demands?

When you instill in your group the **discipline of teams,** your struggles will diminish. You'll be helping your team create a shared vision and then realize that vision with individual and mutual accountability.

Reprint #R0507P

THE IDEA IN PRACTICE

A team's essential discipline includes these characteristics:

1. **A meaningful common purpose the team helps shape.** Most teams are responding to an initial corporate mandate. But to be successful, your team must "own" this purpose by developing its own spin on it. For example, if one of your company's strategic priorities is to increase customer retention, how might your web team translate that into its common purpose? By committing itself to becoming the online destination of choice for B2C customers in your industry.

2. **Specific performance goals that flow from the common purpose.** Developing compelling and measurable goals will inspire and challenge your team, and inject a sense of urgency. Shared goals also have a leveling effect. They require everyone to focus on their collective effort rather than on any differences in their titles or status.

   For example, your web team might set the following goals on its way to becoming the online destination of choice for its B2C customers: 1) Increase first-time visitors to the site by 50% over last year; 2) grow repeat site visitors by 25% over last year; 3) boost e-commerce sales by 15% over last year.

3. **A strong commitment to how the work gets done.** Your team must agree on who will do what jobs, how you will establish and honor schedules, and how you will make and modify decisions. On a genuine team, everyone does equivalent amounts of real work; all members—even you as leader—contribute in concrete ways to the team's collective work.

   Developing these rules of conduct at the outset will help your team achieve its purpose and goals. The most critical rules pertain to attendance (for example, "if you can't make a meeting, send notes or a representative who can speak for you"); focus ("no checking e-mail during meetings"); discussion ("no sacred cows"); confidentiality ("the only things to leave this room are what we agree on"); analytic approach ("base decisions on data, not assumptions"); end-product orientation ("everyone gets assignments and does them"); constructive confrontation ("no finger pointing"); and, often the most important, contributions ("everyone does real work").

4. **Mutual accountability.** You can't force trust and commitment. The process of creating and agreeing upon purpose and goals helps your team members forge their accountability to one another—not just to you, the leader.

   For example, as your web team makes progress toward its three goals, everyone becomes increasingly eager to contribute to the team's success. Individuals volunteer their own and others' areas of expertise: The person with the best eye for visual detail prepares the PowerPoint presentation for the next unit meeting; the one who has the strongest relationship with your IT director spearheads delicate conversations about prioritizing the team's technology needs.

Jon R. Katzenbach is a founder and senior partner of Katzenbach Partners, a strategic and organizational consulting firm, and a former director of McKinsey & Company. His most recent book is *Why Pride Matters More Than Money: The Power of the World's Greatest Motivational Force* (Crown Business, 2003). **Douglas K. Smith** is an organizational consultant and a former partner at McKinsey & Company. His most recent book is *On Value and Values: Thinking Differently About We in an Age of Me* (Financial Times Prentice Hall, 2004).

Managing Remote Relationships

by Karen Dillon

After you've dialed someone into a meeting, do you find it difficult to meaningfully involve her in the conversation—and make her *feel* involved? I've been there hundreds of times. I've even caught myself rolling my eyes as the person on the other end of that star-shaped phone breathed too loudly, spoke at the wrong time, or worst of all, didn't stop talking when everyone else was willing her to do so.

But then I began working on overseas assignments, and it was *my* voice in the dreaded "box"—so I started to see things differently. It's horrible trying to call in when people are chitchatting and making noises with their chairs. And you can never quite read the unspoken tone of the meeting. You talk too much because you want people to know you're there and at full attention. Or you talk too little because you can't figure out when it's appropriate to break in.

Though many of us work with remote colleagues and partners—or work remotely ourselves—we struggle to manage relationships with people we don't run into at the coffee station every day. That doesn't have to be the case. You *can* build strong connections. Here's what's worked in my experience.

If You're Working with Someone Remote . . .

Talk openly about the challenges

Whether you're managing a remote employee, working peer-to-peer, or partnering with someone at another company, it helps to frankly discuss the challenges as you both see them. Clarify expectations up front, and the remote worker will become more productive—and happier. When I managed a West Coast employee from an East Coast office, for example, she initially thought I expected her to immediately jump on phone calls and e-mail queries. What I actually wanted was for her to be a vibrant contributor of ideas and work; to be aware of what her East Coast colleagues were working on, helping them when possible; and to have a clear sense of how she fit into the organization. Until we directly discussed that, she slavishly sat at her desk while I imagined she was out mining her area for ideas and people. We swiftly resolved this misunderstanding with a single conversation.

Without peers in the next cubicle to informally guide them, remote employees will make basic mistakes early on, despite their good intentions, so it's also crucial to be candid with them. Perhaps they've excessively charged expenses to a corporate account, for example, or spent too much time on a low-priority project. Let them know right away. Of course, it's best practice to offer timely feedback to *all* employees, but it's especially important for remote workers. Help them correct course before a few innocent, early errors become a troublesome pattern of behavior.

Err on the side of overcommunicating

Set up regular times to catch up on the phone. As an on-site manager, I decided every two weeks felt about right for formal check-ins with my remote colleagues, with the proviso that we could talk whenever an issue arose. I was always grateful to people who came to those conversations with an agenda and a list of questions or comments (ideally sent in advance). That meant I didn't have the burden of guessing what their needs might be. It was, however, my responsibility to keep them up to date and give them information that would help them work effectively with people on-site (for example, "Joe's in meetings all day—best time to catch him is first thing in the morning"). Otherwise, they wouldn't know the right questions to ask.

Keep a running list of things to share with your remote colleagues or partners; don't assume they're copied on important announcements about your company or division. When I began working off-site, I was surprised at how much I couldn't pick up simply by keeping up with e-mail. People were hired. Projects were canceled. Desirable assignments were handed out. And I missed it all.

Sometimes even little details are critical to share—the fact that someone has had a death in the family, for example, or is under the gun for a big project deadline and won't likely be responsive this week unless it's critical. Communicate decisions large and small. E-mail, scheduled phone calls—figure out what works for your situation, and make a commitment to follow whatever protocol you mutually agree is best.

Remember time zones

It's simple, but easy to forget. Suppose you're based at your company's headquarters in New York and you have a remote colleague in Paris. You might not dive into your day until 9 a.m. your time—and that's 3 p.m. for the guy in France. So you've got about two hours of reliable overlap. If multiple people in New York want time from him, those two hours will be packed. You're sharing that window with others, so be thoughtful about what you're asking for during that time.

And respect your remote colleagues' after-hours time. When I was working in Paris for a company with a New York headquarters, I regularly fielded calls at 11 at night—5 p.m. EST. People forgot to call me until it became urgent at the end of *their* day to finish something. Set up reminders in your calendar to get in touch with remote colleagues while they're still on the clock, and don't ask them to join late calls if you can easily brief them the next day. Be clear about which meetings they can skip. They'll be much happier to take an occasional urgent call at 11 p.m. if most of your business is conducted at times that suit you both.

When you can, take *advantage* of time differences. As a manager, I loved assigning work to someone in an earlier time zone because when I came in the next morning, it would be in my inbox, ready for my attention.

Use technology to collaborate

Technology makes it easy to work with remote colleagues or partners. All it takes is a laptop to videoconference—you can bring it into any room and include someone in a meeting. With Google Docs, you and colleagues located elsewhere can simultaneously work on a file and watch one another's color-coded edits or comments appear in real time. Dropbox allows you to work on documents and then post them in a secure, cloud-based system others can easily access through the Internet.

Some companies, like Nokia, rely on instant messaging to keep remote (and local) employees in the loop. Others, like Royal Dutch Shell, host online events to get colleagues comfortable collaborating across time zones and geographical boundaries. (Shell conducted a three-day "jam" that brought together 8,200 employees from 117 countries to develop new ways to use technology to work with each other.) There's no need for someone in a satellite office to *feel* remote if you take advantage of the tools that are readily available to companies of all sizes.

If You're the Remote Colleague . . .

Make sure you're up to the challenge—and take responsibility

To integrate with a team that's located somewhere else, you have to be fearless about picking up the phone, asking to be briefed, and telling people when conference calls won't work in your time zone. You have to keep on top of a schedule when no one is around to remind you of important meetings or events. Self-starters required.

Make it clear to people that you're *present*, intellectually and physically, and dedicated to packing a lot into your day. When you speak up in a conversation, participate in a brainstorming session, or respond to an e-mail query, make sure it's a thoughtful contribution—not just a token gesture to prove that you're paying attention. Think about your colleagues and their projects and challenges, even when you're not being asked to do so. One of the most successful remote employees I've ever managed would periodically come back from an inspiring business lunch with a great connection for another colleague or send a link to a thought-provoking article that might aid a peer. She felt like a part of a team that way, not just someone covering a different territory.

Even after you've established positive relationships and earned your colleagues' trust, recognize that the burden is often on you, the remote employee, to make things work. Show your colleagues what you bring to the table. Volunteer to help with projects when you have relevant ideas or expertise. Follow social media buzz on your company or industry—and then share updates with colleagues. If you always think of yourself as part of a team, not a soloist, you'll naturally consider how your work can help others.

Partner with the home office

Work closely with the home office to establish expectations. Should you match your colleagues' hours? Is it OK to be out for appointments without telling your manager? What matters more—being available or being entrepreneurial? And so on. Actually ask those questions; don't just assume you know the answers. Without that information, you might get paranoid that you're seen as a slacker or actually not doing enough—and way, way overcompensate.

Develop and maintain your network. Justin Mass, a senior learning technologist at Adobe, volunteers for cross-functional projects that increase his exposure to his HQ colleagues. He's worked to become known as a guy who raises his hand before being asked, and that's helped him create strong connections throughout the company.

If possible, have your company occasionally fly you to HQ or other key offices. Fill your time with meetings—breakfast, lunch, and dinner—to build relationships. Ask people about themselves and their work—you can glean a lot about what's going on in the organization and where the opportunities are. (Keep it professional, of course. This isn't the time to have a few too many beers or complain about your manager.) You'll be exhausted after all these meetings, but you'll have made the most of your short amount of time onsite.

If you're a new hire, you'll need to build a foundation: Ask for a visit to the home office to put names to faces, get a sense of the culture in the building, and get face time by attending a meeting or two. But not too soon! For your first few months on the job, you'll be learning many things, so time your visit (if you can make just one) for when you're in a position of having good questions to ask, not just passively absorbing information. When you do make your trip, introduce yourself to people you'll need to interact with. Find out from team members who else you should reach out to, and ask if they'd be willing to help you connect.

It's virtually impossible to navigate a company's spoken and unspoken "rules" without a guide. You can't simply assume that the culture is casual because, say, dogs are allowed in the office on Fridays. That same company might be rigid about protocol. It takes a little digging to figure out which people in the organization get things done. Have someone in the know walk you through the org chart and explain the company's circles of influence to you. Ask pointed questions: Who is the right contact for that group? What works best here—e-mail, phone calls, or IM? Are there informal power brokers I should make contact with? That kind of thing.

Start Skyping

Adobe's Mass is the only member of his team who works entirely from a home office, yet he collaborates with colleagues in California and India every day. Videoconferencing has been critical to his success. Every chance to be seen on video, he says, is a chance to improve your visibility with your team. You become more than a disembodied voice.

While his company has installed high-end video technology in his home office, he notes that Skype, which is free to anyone, also does the job. Of course, being visible also makes you more accountable. "I think of every video meeting as an opportunity for my team to see me in action," Mass says. "I have to bring my A game."

He actually thinks like a movie director shooting a scene when he considers how he's going to be perceived by his colleagues on the other end of the camera. He dresses professionally and keeps his desk clean. He's even painted his walls the same neutral manila as those at headquarters so his workspace doesn't "look like some strange foreign office." He makes a point to sit forward in his chair, engaged, as if he were at the same conference table. He looks at the camera. Never pushes the mute button and just listens in. Never multitasks.

Mass's advice for others wanting to make videoconferencing work? Do a trial video chat with a friend. Study the thumbnail image of yourself on screen, and ask your friend for feedback. "See how your colleagues will see you," he says. "What's in the background? How are you showing yourself? Are you slumping in your chair? Are you taking notes?"

If your colleagues aren't ready for Skype, be thoughtful about the conference call. Ask your manager what's expected of you (Am I just getting briefed? Am I part of the brainstorming team? Do you need me to report on what I've been up to?). Once I was caught off guard on a conference call by a manager asking us each to "go around the horn" and give updates. What he *really* meant was, "If there's anything of burning importance, now's your chance." But absent any body language or other visual cues to put his request in context, I panicked and assumed I needed to show how productive I'd been. When I finished my monologue, a few long minutes later, it was obvious I'd gotten it wrong, and we swiftly moved on to other topics. If you don't have a chance to clarify expectations in advance, it may be better to listen quietly and then contribute follow-up thoughts by e-mail or phone. Ask your manager to occasionally put you on the agenda to discuss what you're working on, share your observations, or report on a project.

Since remote colleagues and partners are likely to be a permanent feature of any growing company, it's important to manage these relationships well. And it's worth the effort. If you're a hiring manager, who says the right person for the job you've posted lives within driving distance? And if you're a remote worker, you can get a lot of work done, in fewer hours than your HQ colleagues, if you use your time wisely.

It's possible to make off-site work relationships both productive and powerful—I've found that some of my remote colleagues over the years have been great allies and sounding boards. But the key to success, on both sides of the relationship, is utter transparency and thinking *ahead* about what your colleagues most need from you.

Karen Dillon is the former editor of *Harvard Business Review* and a coauthor, with Clayton Christensen and James Allworth, of the book *How Will You Measure Your Life?* (HarperBusiness, 2012).

A Smarter Way to Network

A summary of the full-length HBR article by **Rob Cross** *and* **Robert Thomas,** *highlighting key ideas.*

THE IDEA IN BRIEF

To maximize your and your team's performance, you need resources, information, and expertise from people across your organization. They don't report to you, but they can make—or break—your project.

So you must influence them. How? Build a better network, using these steps:

1. **Analyze:** Identify the benefits each of your existing network connections now provides. Does one person give you valuable information? Does another have expertise you need but lack?

Reprint #R1107P

2. **De-layer:** Weed out connections that aren't helping you, such as people who burn too much of your time.

3. **Diversify:** Fill the fresh openings in your network with people who can deliver the additional benefits you and your team need to accomplish your work.

Construct a strong network, and you'll have a wider, richer web of connections to draw on when the next crisis or opportunity lands on your desk.

THE IDEA IN PRACTICE

When you need help from colleagues up, down, and across the organization, every network choice you make matters. Use these steps to make your selections:

1. Analyze

Identify the individuals currently in your network.

Determine:

- **Where they're located.** Are they on your team? In your unit? Outside your organization? Are they higher-ups? Peers? Frontline workers? You want a diverse but select web of high-quality relationships with people who hail from several different spheres and levels in your organization.

- **What benefits they're providing.** Do they offer information, expertise, or best practices that can help you lead projects more effectively? Are they formally powerful people who can provide political "juice"? For instance, can they remind lazy members of a task force you're on how important their project is to the organization? Are they informally influential people who can win you needed support among the rank-and-file?

2. *De-layer*

Make tough decisions about relationships to back away from. Eliminate or minimize contact with people who sap your energy or offer benefits that others in your network already provide. By de-layering, you make room for people who can help you complete projects.

3. *Diversify*

Fill the new openings in your network with the right people, using this technique:

- Articulate three business goals you plan to achieve this year.
- List the people who could help you reach these goals—and how. Is it their expertise? Their control over resources? Their political support?
- Actively build relationships with these individuals.

  Example: Joe, an investment banker, needed to expand his global client pool. First he identified counterparts in his company's Asian and European operations who had relationships with clients he had targeted. Then he scheduled

> regular calls with his colleagues to synchronize their selling efforts. In some cases, these calls helped him identify opportunities he could pitch proactively, such as potential clients who were interested in his department's offerings. In others, the calls helped him and his peers appear more coordinated when their bank was competing against other banks for the same clients.

One of the happiest, most successful executives we know is a woman named Deb. She works at a major technology company and runs a global business unit that has more than 7,000 employees. When you ask her how she rose to the top and why she enjoys her job, her answer is simple: people. She points to her boss, the CEO, a mentor who "always has her back"; Steve, the head of a complementary business, with whom she has monthly brainstorming lunches and occasional gripe sessions; and Tom, a protégé to whom she has delegated responsibility for a large portion of her division. Outside the company, Deb's circle includes her counterparts in three strategic partnerships, who inspire her with new ideas; Sheila, a former colleague, now in a different industry, who gives her candid feedback; and her husband, Bob, an executive at a philanthropic organization. She also has close relationships with her fellow volunteers in a program for at-risk high school students and the members of her tennis group and book club.

This is Deb's social network (the real-world kind, not the virtual kind), and it has helped her career a lot. But not because the group is large or full of high-powered contacts. Her network is effective because it both supports and challenges her. Deb's relationships help her gain influence, broaden her expertise, learn new skills, and find purpose and balance. Deb values and nurtures them. "Make friends so that you have friends when you need friends" is her motto.

"My current role is really a product of a relationship I formed over a decade ago that came back to me at the right time," she explains. "People may chalk it up to luck, but I think more often than not luck happens through networks where people give first and are authentic in all they do."

Over the past 15 years, we've worked with many executives like Deb, at more than 300 companies. What began as organizational research—helping management teams understand and capitalize on the formal and informal social networks of their employees—has since metamorphosed into personal programs, which teach individual executives to increase their effectiveness by leveraging their networks.

The old adage "It's not what you know, it's who you know" is true. But it's more nuanced than that. In spite of what most self-help books say, network size doesn't usually matter. In fact, we've found that individuals who simply know a lot of people are less likely to achieve standout performance, because they're spread too thin. Political animals with lots of connections to corporate and industry leaders don't win the day, either. Yes, it's important to know powerful people, but if they account for too much of your network, your peers and subordinates often perceive you to be overly self-interested, and you may lose support as a result.

The data we've collected point to a different model

for networking. The executives who consistently rank in the top 20% of their companies in both performance and well-being have diverse but select networks like Deb's—made up of high-quality relationships with people who come from several different spheres and from up and down the corporate hierarchy. These high performers, we have found, tap into six critical kinds of connections, which enhance their careers and lives in a variety of ways.

Through our work advising individual managers, we've also identified a four-step process that will help any executive develop this kind of network. But first, let's take a look at some common networking mistakes.

Getting It Wrong

Many people take a misguided approach to networking. They go astray by building imbalanced networks, pursuing the wrong kind of relationships, or leveraging relationships ineffectively. (See the sidebar "Are You Networking Impaired?") These people might remain successful for a time, but often they will hit a plateau or see their career derailed because their networks couldn't prompt or support a critical transition.

Consider Dan, the chief information officer of one of the world's largest life-sciences organizations. He was under constant pressure to find new technologies that would spur innovation and speed the drug commercialization process at his company, and he needed a network that would help him. Unfortunately, more than 70% of his trusted advisers were in the unit he had worked in before becoming CIO. Not only did they reinforce his bias toward certain solutions and vendors, but they lacked the outside knowledge he needed. "I had started to mistake friendship, trust, and accessibility for real expertise in new domains," he told us. "This didn't mean I was going to dump these people, as they played important roles for me in other ways. But I needed to be more targeted in who I let influence my thinking."

Another overarching mistake we often see in executives' networks is an imbalance between connections that promote career advancement and those that promote engagement and satisfaction. Numerous studies have shown that happier executives are higher-performing ones.

Take Tim, the director of a large practice area at a leading professional services firm. On the surface he was doing well, but job stress had taken its toll. He was 40 pounds overweight, with alarmingly high cholesterol and blood sugar levels, and prone to extreme mood swings. When things went well at work, he was happy; when they didn't, he wasn't pleasant to be around. In fact, Tim's wife finally broke down and told him she thought he had become a career-obsessed jerk and needed to get other interests. With her encouragement, he joined Habitat for Humanity and started rowing with their daughter. As a result, his social network expanded to include people with different perspectives and values, who helped him focus on more healthful and fulfilling pursuits. "As I spent more time with different groups, what I cared about diversified," he says. "Physically, I'm in much better shape and probably staved off a heart attack. But I think I'm a better leader, too, in that I think about problems more broadly, and I'm more resilient. Our peer feedback systems are

ARE YOU NETWORKING IMPAIRED?

In our work, we have identified six common managerial types who get stuck in three kinds of network traps. Do any of the descriptions below fit you?

The wrong structure

THE FORMALIST focuses too heavily on his company's official hierarchy, missing out on the efficiencies and opportunities that come from informal connections.

THE OVERLOADED MANAGER has so much contact with colleagues and external ties that she becomes a bottleneck to progress and burns herself out.

The wrong relationships

THE DISCONNECTED EXPERT sticks with people who keep him focused on safe, existing competencies,

also clearly indicating that people are more committed to the new me."

Getting It Right

To understand more about what makes an effective network, let's look again at Deb. She has a small set of core contacts—14 people she really relies on. Effective core networks typically range in size from 12 to 18 people. But what really matters is structure: Core connections must

rather than those who push him to build new skills.

THE BIASED LEADER relies on advisers much like herself (same functional background, location, or values), who reinforce her biases, when she should instead seek outsiders to prompt more fully informed decisions.

The wrong behavior

THE SUPERFICIAL NETWORKER engages in surface-level interaction with as many people as possible, mistakenly believing that a bigger network is a better one.

THE CHAMELEON changes his interests, values, and personality to match those of whatever subgroup is his audience, and winds up being disconnected from every group.

bridge smaller, more-diverse kinds of groups and cross hierarchical, organizational, functional, and geographic lines. Core relationships should result in more learning, less bias in decision making, and greater personal growth and balance. The people in your inner circle should also model positive behaviors, because if those around you are enthusiastic, authentic, and generous, you will be, too.

More specifically, our data show that high performers have strong ties to:

1. people who offer them new information or expertise, including internal or external clients, who increase their market awareness; peers in other functions, divisions, or geographies, who share best practices; and contacts in other industries, who inspire innovation;
2. formally powerful people, who provide mentoring, sense-making, political support, and resources; and informally powerful people, who offer influence, help coordinating projects, and support among the rank and file; and
3. people who give them developmental feedback, challenge their decisions, and push them to be better. At an early career stage, an employee might get this from a boss or customers; later, it tends to come from coaches, trusted colleagues, or a spouse.

Meanwhile, the most satisfied executives have ties to:

1. people who provide personal support, such as colleagues who help them get back on track when they're having a bad day or friends with whom they can just be themselves;
2. people who add a sense of purpose or worth, such as bosses and customers who validate their work, and family members and other stakeholders who show them work has a broader meaning; and

3. people who promote their work/life balance, holding them accountable for activities that improve their physical health (such as sports), mental engagement (such as hobbies or educational classes), or spiritual well-being (music, religion, art, or volunteer work).

How does one create such a varied network? We recommend a four-point action plan: analyze, de-layer, diversify, and capitalize.

Analyze

Start by looking at the individuals in your network. Where are they located—are they within your team, your unit, or your company, or outside your organization? What benefits do your interactions with them provide? How energizing are those interactions?

The last question is an important one. Energizers bring out the best in everyone around them, and our data show that having them in your network is a strong predictor of success over time. These people aren't necessarily extroverted or charismatic. They're people who always see opportunities, even in challenging situations, and create room for others to meaningfully contribute. Good energizers are trustworthy and committed to principles larger than their self-interest, and they enjoy other people. "De-energizers," by contrast, are quick to point out obstacles, critique people rather than ideas, are inflexible in their thinking, fail to create opportunities, miss commitments, and don't show concern for others.

FOUR STEPS TO BUILDING A BETTER NETWORK

Analyze

- Identify the people in your network and what you get out of interacting with them

De-layer

- Make some hard decisions to back away from redundant and energy-sapping relationships

Diversify

- Build your network out with the right kind of people: energizers who will help you achieve your goals

Capitalize

- Make sure you're using your contacts as effectively as you can

Unfortunately, energy-sapping interactions have more impact than energizing ones—up to seven times as much, according to one study. And our own research suggests that roughly 90% of anxiety at work is created by 5% of one's network—the people who sap energy.

Next, classify your relationships by the benefits they provide. Generally, benefits fall into one of six basic categories: information, political support and influence, personal development, personal support and energy, a sense of purpose or worth, and work/life balance. It's important to have people who provide each kind of benefit in your network. Categorizing your relationships will give you a clearer idea of whether your network is extending your abilities or keeping you stuck. You'll see where you have holes and redundancies and which people you depend on too much—or not enough.

Let's use Joe, a rising star in an investment bank, as a case study. He had 24 close advisers—on the surface, a more than healthy number. But many of the people he relied on were from his own department and frequently relied on one another. If he eliminated those redundancies, his network shrank to five people. After giving it some thought and observing his peers' networks, he realized he was missing links with several important types of people: colleagues focused on financial offerings outside his own products, who could help him deliver broader financial solutions to customers; coworkers in different geographies—particularly London and Asia—who could enhance his ability to sell to global clients; and board-level relationships at key accounts, who could make client introductions and influence purchasing decisions. His insularity was limiting his options and hurting his chances of promotion to managing director. He realized he would need to focus on cultivating a network rather than allowing it to organically arise from the day-to-day demands of his work.

De-layer

Once you've analyzed your network, you need to make some hard decisions about which relationships to back away from. First, look at eliminating or minimizing contact with people who sap you of energy or promote unhealthful behaviors. You can do this by reshaping your role to avoid them, devoting less time to them, working to change their behavior, or reframing your reactions so that you don't dwell on the interactions.

John, an academic, realized that two university administrators in his network were causing him a great deal of anxiety. This had so soured his view of his school that he was considering leaving. He therefore decided to devote less time to projects and committees that would involve the negative contacts and to avoid dwelling on any sniping comments they subjected him to. Within a year he was much more productive and happy. "By shifting my role and how I reacted to the idiots, I turned a negative situation around," John says. "In hindsight it was an obvious move—rather than leave a place I loved—but emotions can spiral on you in ways you don't recognize."

The next step is to ask yourself which of the six categories have too many people in them. Early-stage leaders, for example, tend to focus too much on information and not enough on personal development and might want to shed some of the contacts who give them the former to make more time for those who give them the latter.

Beyond this, consider which individuals—and types of people as determined by function, hierarchy, or geography—have too much of you, and why. Is the cause structural, in that work procedures require you to be involved? Or is your own behavior causing the imbalance? What can you change to rectify the situation? Too often we see leaders fail because they accept or create too many collaborative demands.

Paul, the head of research in a consumer products company, had a network of almost 70 people just at work.

But he got many complaints from people who said they needed greater access to him. His productivity, and his unit's, was suffering. When he analyzed his network, he realized that he was missing "people and initiatives one or two levels out." To address this, he decided to delegate—stepping away from interactions that didn't require his presence and cultivating "go to" stand-ins in certain areas of expertise. He also changed his leadership style from extraordinarily accessible to helpful but more removed, which encouraged subordinates to solve their own problems by connecting with people around him. "As a leader you can find yourself in this bubble of activity where you feel like a lot is happening moving from meeting to meeting," Paul says. "You can actually start to thrive on this in some ways. I had to move past this for us to be effective as a unit and so that I could be more forward-thinking."

Diversify

Now that you've created room in your network, you need to fill it with the right people. Simple tools like work sheets can help you get started. For example, you might make a list of the six categories of relationships and think about colleagues who could fill the holes you have in each. Remember to focus on positive, energetic, selfless people, and be sure to ask people inside and outside your network for recommendations.

You should also think about how you could connect your network to your professional and personal goals. Here's another simple exercise: Write down three specific business results you hope to achieve over the next year (such as doubling sales or winning an Asia-based client) and then list the people (by name or general role) who could help you with them, thanks to their expertise, control over resources, or ability to provide political support. Joe, the investment banker, identified counterparts in the Asian and European operations of his company who had relationships with the clients he was focused on and then scheduled regular calls with them to coordinate efforts. "In a couple of cases this helped me identify opportunities I could pitch proactively. In others it just helped us appear more coordinated when we were competing against other banks," he says. One of the big challenges for Paul, the consumer products executive, was managing a new facility and line of innovation in China. Because none of his trusted advisers had ever even been to that country, he reached out to the head of R&D at a major life-sciences organization that had undertaken a similar effort.

Capitalize

Last, make sure you're using your contacts as effectively as you can. Are there people you rely on in one sphere, such as political support, that you could also use to fill a need in another, such as personal development? Could you get more out of some relationships if you put more energy into them? Our research shows, for instance, that high performers at all levels tend to use their information contacts to gain other benefits, such as new ideas. Reciprocal relationships also tend to be more fruitful; the most successful leaders always look for ways to give more to their contacts.

Alan, a top executive at a global insurance company, realized that although he had a good network, he was still making decisions in relative isolation. He failed to elicit insights from others and, as a result, wasn't making enough progress toward his goals. So he started inviting his more-junior contacts, who were informal opinion leaders in his company, to lunch and asking them open-ended questions. These conversations led him to streamline decision making and uncover innovation deep within the firm's hierarchy. "When I met with one lady, I was stunned at a great new product idea she had been pushing for months," Alan says. "But she hadn't been able to get the right people to listen. I was able to step in and help make things happen. To me the right way to be tapping into people is in this exploratory way—whether it is about strategic insights or just how they think I'm doing on some aspect of my job. That's how I get to new ways of thinking and doing things, and I know it makes me much more effective than people who are smarter than me."

A network constructed using this four-point model will build on itself over time. In due course, it will ensure that the best opportunities, ideas, and talent come your way.

Rob Cross (robcross@virginia.edu) is an associate professor at the University of Virginia's McIntire School of Commerce. **Robert Thomas** is the executive director of the Accenture Institute for High Performance.

How to Deal with Office Politics

by Linda A. Hill and Kent Lineback

"I don't care who they are. I won't buddy up to people I don't like and respect just because I want something from them."

These are the words of a *Fortune* 500 senior manager, but we hear similar comments from managers at all levels, in all types of companies. Perhaps you feel the same way.

Do you dismiss most of the give-and-take in organizations as "office politics"—ego-driven, manipulative, dysfunctional game playing? Do you tend to focus on your own group and deal with others only when you like them personally or the immediate work requires it? If this describes your approach, you're probably making yourself and your group less effective than you should be.

Every organization has a political environment—that is, one where human relationships matter—and yours is no exception. To obtain the resources, influence, and at-

---

Adapted from content posted on hbr.org on November 2, 2011

tention you and your group need, you must be able to function in such a setting by actively engaging others, whether you like them or not.

The good news: You can do that without succumbing to mean and self-interested tactics. The secret is to *build ongoing relationships for mutual advantage.*

Here's how to navigate your political environment positively and professionally:

- **Focus on the good of the enterprise.** A big-picture view will help you do what's best for your group. Recognize your interdependence with other units, and consider how your goals and theirs align. If customer service reps say a forthcoming product will require a lot of extra support, get their input on ways to make it more user-friendly. They'll be happier with fewer calls to answer, and you'll have a better product to sell. You'll become allies, without even a hint of schmoozing. And don't be afraid to share customers with other divisions. It shows that you're a team player—and your customers will appreciate the seamless service.

- **Keep disagreements professional.** Focus on issues, not personalities. Suppose you work at an insurance company, for example, and people in the underwriting department resist your plan to offer a new type of homeowner's policy. Assume they have legitimate concerns and try to understand and accommodate them. Accusing colleagues of "not knowing the market" or being "stuck in the last century" certainly won't win them over or allow you to find an approach that meets everyone's needs. And complaining about them behind their backs will surely come back to bite you.

- **Share information.** When it comes to information, you get what you give, and what you know depends on who you know. Say your IT director has just filled three positions that have been open for months. Alert your colleagues in product development so they can update their list of tech priorities. If you look for ways to make their lives easier, they'll probably return the favor when they get an inside scoop that affects your work.

- **Relay good news about your team members.** They'll likely appreciate the public recognition, and it'll help the rest of the organization see the value they add. Did your group finish a critical project early *and* under budget? Send an e-mail to managers you work with closely, and copy the individuals whose praises you're singing. Don't assume that everyone will automatically notice your group's success. If you don't mention it, who will?

- **Above all, focus your relationships on what's best for "us."** If you want an exception to your company's pricing policy and need a colleague's help, identify her goals and find a way you can support her and her group, too. And talk to her about what you want to achieve; perhaps there's a way to serve both your purposes simultaneously. Let "connect and collaborate" be your mantra.

We're not saying that organizations are ideal worlds where everyone always wants the best for everyone else. They're often maelstroms of conflicting goals, divergent interests, and fierce struggles for scarce resources. And organizational bullies *do* exist. They play games and pick fights. They define their success by the interpersonal battles they win, not the results they accomplish for the organization. How do you deal with them? Not by hiding.

Bullies are actually a key reason *not* to withdraw to your own corner of the organization. You can counter their tactics with the help of allies. If someone spreads half-truths about you or quotes you or your people out of context, it's much easier to set the record straight if you've developed influence through strong relationships.

Raise the bar by conducting yourself according to standards that matter to you. Be honest, courteous, and dependable—no matter how others act. If you propose an idea that someone belittles, don't retaliate by pointing out flaws in his idea. That just creates a poisonous atmosphere. Instead, try to get at what's behind the aggressive behavior. Maybe that person feels threatened by you. Look for ways to lower his defenses—ask for his advice, invite him to brainstorming sessions, and so on. You may find that he's suddenly more collaborative and less combative.

Linda A. Hill is the Wallace Brett Donham Professor of Business Administration and faculty chair of the Leadership Initiative at Harvard Business School. Now a writer and executive coach, **Kent Lineback** spent many years as a manager and an executive in business and government. They are the coauthors of *Being the Boss: The 3 Imperatives for Becoming a Great Leader* (Harvard Business Review Press, 2011).

Make Your Enemies Your Allies

by Brian Uzzi and Shannon Dunlap

John Clendenin was fresh out of business school in 1984 when he took on his first managerial position, in Xerox's parts and supply division. He was an obvious outsider: young, African-American, and a former Marine, whose pink shirts and brown suits stood out amid the traditional gray and black attire of his new colleagues. "I was strikingly different," he recalls. And yet his new role required him to lead a team including employees who had been with Xerox for decades.

One of his direct reports was Tom Gunning, a 20-year company veteran who believed Clendenin's job should have gone to him, not to a younger, nontechnical newcomer. Gunning also had a cadre of pals on the team. As a result, Clendenin's first days were filled with strained

Reprint #R1205K

smiles and behind-the-back murmurs. Though he wasn't looking for adversaries, "I knew these guys were discontented about me coming in," Clendenin remembers.

He was right to be wary. Anyone who has faced a rival at work—a colleague threatened by your skills, a superior unwilling to acknowledge your good ideas, or a subordinate who undermines you—knows such dynamics can prove catastrophic for your career, and for your group or organization. When those with formal or informal power are fighting you, you may find it impossible to accomplish—or get credit for—any meaningful work. And even if you have the upper hand, an antagonistic relationship inevitably casts a cloud over you and your team, sapping energy, stymieing progress, and distracting group members from their goals.

Because rivalries can be so destructive, it's not enough to simply ignore, sidestep, or attempt to contain them. Instead, effective leaders turn rivals into collaborators—strengthening their positions, their networks, and their careers in the process. Think of these relationships not as chronic illnesses you have to endure but as wounds that must be treated in order for you to lead a healthy work life.

Here we share a method, called the 3Rs, for efficiently and effectively turning your adversaries into your allies. If you execute each step correctly, you will develop new "connective tissue" within your organization, boosting your ability to broker knowledge and drive fresh thinking. The method is drawn from our own inductive case studies—including interviews with business leaders such as John Clendenin, who agreed to let us tell his story in this article—and from empirical research conducted by Brian and others investigating the physiology of the brain, the sociology of relationships, and the psychology of influence.

Emotions and Trust

Many well-intentioned efforts to reverse rivalries fail in large part because of the complex way trust operates in these relationships. Research shows that trust is based on both reason and emotion. If the emotional orientation toward a person is negative—typically because of a perceived threat—then reason will be twisted to align with those negative feelings. This is why feuds can stalemate trust: New facts and arguments, no matter how credible and logical, may be seen as ploys to dupe the other side. This effect is not just psychological; it is physiological. When we experience negative emotions, blood recedes from the thinking part of the brain, the cerebral cortex, and rushes to its oldest and most involuntary part, the "reptilian" stem, crippling the intake of new information.

Most executives who decide they want to reverse a rivalry will, quite understandably, turn to reason, presenting incentives for trustworthy collaboration. But in these situations, the "emotional brain" must be managed before adversaries can understand evidence and be persuaded.

When John Clendenin looked at Tom Gunning at Xerox, he immediately saw grounds for a strong partnership beyond a perfunctory subordinate-superior relationship. Gunning had 20 years' worth of organizational and technical knowledge, and contacts around the company, but he lacked the leadership skills and vision that Clendenin possessed. Conversely, Clendenin understood management but needed Gunning's expertise and connections to successfully navigate his new company. Unfortunately, Gunning's emotions were getting in the way. Clendenin needed to employ the 3Rs.

Redirection

Step 1 is to redirect your rival's negative emotions so that they are channeled away from you. Clendenin decided to have a one-on-one meeting with Gunning, but not in his office, because that would only remind Gunning of the promotion he'd lost. Instead, he found out where Gunning liked to eat and took him there for lunch. "I was letting him know that I understood his worth," Clendenin says of this contextual redirection.

He followed this with a plain statement of redirection, telling Gunning that a third entity beyond the control of both men was the root cause of their situation. "I didn't put you in this position," Clendenin said. "Xerox put us both in this position."

Many executives scoff when they first hear this story, believing Clendenin's actions to be too transparent. But redirection doesn't have to be hidden. With stage magic, for example, audience members understand that redirection is happening, but that doesn't lessen their acceptance or spoil the payoff of the technique. Other personal interactions work similarly. For instance, we accept flattery even if we recognize it as such.

Another common redirection tactic is to introduce a discussion of things you and your rival have in common, or casually portray a source of tension—a particular initiative, employee, or event—in a more favorable light. It sounds obvious. But redirection will shift negative emotions away from you and lay the groundwork for Step 2: reciprocity.

Reciprocity

The essential principle here is to *give before you ask*. Undoing a negative tie begins with giving up something of value rather than asking for a "fair trade." If you give and then ask for something right away in return, you don't establish a relationship; you carry out a transaction.

When done correctly, reciprocity is like priming the pump. In the old days, pumps required lots of exertion to produce any water. You had to repeatedly work a lever to eliminate a vacuum in the line before water could flow. But if you poured a small bucket of water into the line first, the vacuum was quickly eliminated, enabling the water to flow with less effort. Reciprocity with a rival works in much the same way.

Reflect carefully on *what* you should give and, ideally, choose something that requires little effort from the other party to reciprocate. Clendenin moved from redirection to reciprocity at the lunch by promising to support Gunning's leadership development and future advancement at Xerox. But, recognizing that mere promises of future returns wouldn't be enough to spark collaboration, he also offered Gunning something concrete: the chance to attend executive-level meetings. This was of immediate value, not a distant, murky benefit. Gunning could gain visibility, credibility, and connections.

The arrangement also ensured reciprocity. Gunning's presence at the meetings furnished Clendenin with on-hand technical expertise and organizational knowledge while giving him "reputation points" with Gunning's contacts. Thus, his offer created the purest form of reciprocity; if Gunning attended the meetings, Clendenin would never have to explicitly request a quid pro quo.

Reciprocity involves considering ways that you can immediately fulfill a rival's need or reduce a pain point. Live up to your end of the bargain first, but figure out a way to ensure a return from your rival without the person's feeling that pressure. Another example comes from Brian's colleague Adam Galinsky, who advises leaders in contentious restructurings and business closings to generate goodwill among outgoing employees by offering professional references or placements at other companies as long as the employees continue to meet or exceed expectations until their office closes. The employees see immediate value, and although they don't consciously pay back the organization, the firm nonetheless benefits by maintaining continuity in its workforce until the scheduled closure.

Similarly, a colleague who helps an adversary complete a project, or a subordinate who stays overtime to finish a task for a difficult boss, not only helps that individual but can reap rewards when other teammates or superiors benefit from that effort, too. Here the judicious giving before asking sets a foundation for reciprocity with third parties, whose buy-in can positively assist in reshaping the adversarial relationship. (See the sidebar "Rivalries Don't Exist in a Vacuum.")

Rationality

Step 3, rationality, establishes the expectations of the fledgling relationship you've built using the previous

RIVALRIES DON'T EXIST IN A VACUUM

Even when a leader executes the 3Rs flawlessly to end a rivalry, his work isn't necessarily done.

That's because the relationship is often about more than just the two individuals. We all know people who seek to play to their advantage antagonism between others; some third parties might even view a blossoming partnership with trepidation or envy, triggering new negative emotions and rivalries.

You can head off this problem, as Clendenin did, by framing your work as beneficial not just to you and your adversary but to the whole organization, which makes the reversal of rivalry in everyone's interest. When Clendenin brought Gunning into those executive-level meetings, he made it clear that Gunning was going to be a "poster child" for a new age at Xerox, in which talented, long-term employees could find new paths to leadership in a time of corporate transition. Even if the conflictmongers didn't care about Clendenin's and Gunning's success, it would be far more difficult for them to sabotage an effort that was obviously good for the company.

steps so that your efforts don't come off as dishonest or as ineffective pandering. What would have happened if Clendenin had left the lunch without explaining how he wanted to work with Gunning going forward? Gunning might have begun to second-guess his new boss's intentions and resumed his adversarial stance. If a rival is worried about the other shoe's dropping, his emotional unease can undermine the trust you've built.

To employ rationality, Clendenin told Gunning that he needed him, or someone like him, to reach his goals at Xerox. This made it clear that he saw Gunning as a valuable, but not indispensable, partner. Another, softer approach might have involved Clendenin's giving Gunning "the right of first refusal" to collaborate with him, making the offer seem special while judiciously indicating that there were others who could step in. Just to be clear, Clendenin was not asking Gunning for a specific favor in exchange for the one he'd granted in Step 2. He was simply saying that he wanted him to become an ally.

Clendenin also reinforced the connection between the three steps by making his offer time-limited, which raised the perception of the value of the deal without changing its content. He told Gunning he needed an answer before they left the restaurant. "I needed to nip this in the bud," Clendenin recalls. "He knew I didn't care if we sat in that restaurant until midnight if we had to."

When rationality follows redirection and reciprocity, it should push your adversary into considering the situation from a reasoned standpoint, fully comprehending the expectations and benefits, and recognizing that he is looking at a valued opportunity that could be lost. Most people are highly motivated to avoid a loss, which complements their desire to gain something. Rationality is like offering medicine after a spoonful of sugar: It ensures that you're getting the benefit of the shifted negative emotions, and any growing positive ones, which would otherwise diffuse over time.

And it avoids the ambiguity that clouds expectations and feedback when flattery and favors come one day, and demands the next.

Of course, Clendenin and Gunning did not walk out of the restaurant as full-blown collaborators. But both accepted that they should give each other the benefit of the doubt. Over the following weeks, this new mind-set allowed them to work as allies, a process that deepened trust and resource-sharing in a self-reinforcing cycle. So a potentially debilitating rivalry was transformed into a healthy working relationship and, in time, a strong partnership. Several years later, when Clendenin moved to another Xerox unit, he nominated Gunning as his replacement—and Gunning excelled in the position. The foundation for that remarkable shift had been established during the span of a single lunch.

Adapting the 3Rs

A key advantage of the 3Rs is that the method can work to reverse all kinds of rivalries, including those with a peer or a superior. Later in Clendenin's tenure at Xerox, he noticed an inefficiency in the company's inventory systems. At the time, Xerox was made up of semiautonomous international units that stockpiled excess inventory to avoid shortages. Clendenin proposed that the units instead share their inventories through an intrafirm network that would improve resource use and lower carrying costs for the company as a whole. Although the idea was objectively good for Xerox, it threatened the power of some unit vice presidents, so when Clendenin floated his idea, they shot it down.

WHAT IF THE 3RS FAIL?

The 3Rs are effective, but they aren't a guarantee. What should you do if the strategy isn't working?

Strive for collaboration indirectly—for example, by working well with a third party whom your rival trusts. A common ally can highlight to him the benefits of working with you.

Remember that timing matters. People in power need a reason to interact. This was certainly the case with John Clendenin's inventory-management pitch to the Xerox VPs: At first rebuffed, he was able to refloat his idea when the CEO called for a new strategy.

Recognize when to look elsewhere. Sometimes the effort needed to reverse a rivalry is so great, and the returns so low, for you and your company that you're better off deploying the same resources in another relationship.

A short time later, however, following an unexpected announcement by the CEO that the company needed better asset management, Clendenin found a way to reintroduce his proposal to the VPs. Because he knew they viewed him as an unwelcome challenger—or rival—he used the 3Rs.

His first move was to redirect their negative emotions away from him by planning a lunch for them at the regional office and serving them himself. This showed deference. He also presented himself not as an individual pushing a proposal but as someone who could expedite organizational change, shifting the reference point of his rivals' tension. "With all of those egos and personalities, I never said, 'This is my idea,'" Clendenin recalls. "I always said 'we.'"

Applying the reciprocity principle of give before you ask, he requested nothing from them at the meeting. Instead, he facilitated a discussion about the CEO-led initiative. Inventory management was, unsurprisingly, a problem cited by many of the VPs, and Clendenin's facilitation brought that to light. He then took on the luster of the person who had illuminated a generic problem, rather than someone who wanted to lessen the VPs' autonomy.

That allowed him to present the rationality of his original idea. All of a sudden, it looked like an opportunity, rather than a threat, to the formerly antagonistic group. Clendenin indicated that he would be willing to coordinate a new system more cheaply than anyone else in the market could offer, while also noting that he might not have time to do so in the future, which raised the perceived value of his offer. The VPs agreed to execute the plan in stages and put Clendenin in charge. The initiative grew in small but steady steps, eventually saving Xerox millions. Equally important, Clendenin's embrace by his rivals positioned him as a broker in the company and burnished his reputation as an institution builder.

John Clendenin understood that rivalries help no one; indeed, success often depends on not just neutralizing your foes but turning them into collaborators. By using the 3Rs to build trust in his network, Clendenin made sure everyone in his network thrived—including himself, Gunning, their team, the VPs, and Xerox—forming the basis for long-term ties and shared success. Years later, Clendenin started his own international logistics company. His partner in this new endeavor was his old rival, Tom Gunning, and the lead investors were none other than the unit VPs from Xerox who had once shot down his ideas.

Brian Uzzi is the Richard L. Thomas Professor of Leadership and Organizational Change at Northwestern's Kellogg School of Management and the codirector of the Northwestern Institute on Complex Systems (NICO). **Shannon Dunlap** is a journalist and writer based in New York City.

The authors' research was supported by grants from the National Science Foundation (OCI-0838564—VOSS) and the U.S. Army Research Laboratory's Network Science Collaborative Technology Alliance (W911NF-09-2-0053).

The Necessary Art of Persuasion

A summary of the full-length HBR article by **Jay A. Conger**, *highlighting key ideas.*

THE IDEA IN BRIEF

When you're operating outside clear reporting lines, your colleagues may not immediately see why they should collaborate with you. That's when your powers of persuasion come into play. It's not manipulation. Effective persuasion is a learning and negotiating process for leading your colleagues to a *shared solution* to a problem.

Reprint #4258

THE IDEA IN PRACTICE

The process of persuasion has four steps:

1. **Establish credibility.** Your credibility grows out of two sources: **expertise** and **relationships**. If you have a history of well-informed, sound judgment, your colleagues will trust your expertise. If you've demonstrated that you can work in the best interest of others, your peers will have confidence in your relationships.

   If you're weak on the expertise side, bolster your position by:

   - Learning more through formal and informal education—for example, conversations with in-house experts
   - Hiring recognized outside experts
   - Launching pilot projects

   Example: Two developers at Microsoft envisioned a controversial new software product, but both were technology novices. By working closely with technical experts and market testing a prototype, they persuaded management that the new product was ideally suited to the average computer user. It sold half a million units.

To fill in the relationship gap, try:

- Meeting one-on-one with key people
- Involving like-minded coworkers who have good support with your audience

2. **Frame goals on common ground.** Tangibly describe the benefits of your position. The fastest way to get a child to the grocery store is to point out the lollipops by the cash register. That's not deception—it's persuasion. When no shared advantages are apparent, adjust your position.

   Example: An ad agency executive persuaded skeptical fast-food franchisees to support headquarters' new price discounts. She cited reliable research showing how the pricing scheme improved franchisees' profits. They supported the new plan unanimously.

3. **Vividly reinforce your position.** Ordinary evidence won't do. Make numerical data more compelling with examples, stories, and metaphors that have an emotional impact.

   Example: The founder of Mary Kay Cosmetics made a speech comparing salespeople's weekly meetings to gatherings among Christians resisting Roman rule. This drove home the importance of a mutually supportive sales force and imbued the work with a sense of heroic mission.

4. **Connect emotionally.** Adjust your own emotional tone to match your audience's ability to receive your message. Learn how your colleagues have interpreted past events in the organization and sense how they will probably interpret your proposal. Test key individuals' possible reactions.

   Example: A Chrysler team leader raised the morale of employees disheartened by foreign competition when he persuaded senior management to bring a new car design in-house. He showed both groups slides of his hometown, devastated by foreign mining competition. Dramatic images of his boarded-up high school and the town's crumbling ironworks shone a sobering light on the aftereffects of outsourcing. His patriotic and emotional appeal resonated with his audiences.

Jay A. Conger is a professor of organizational behavior at the University of Southern California's Marshall School of Business in Los Angeles, where he directs the Leadership Institute. He is the author of *Winning 'Em Over: A New Model for Managing in the Age of Persuasion* (Simon & Schuster, 2001).

Three Ways *Not* to Persuade

by Jay A. Conger

In my work with managers as a researcher and as a consultant, I've had the unfortunate opportunity to see executives fail miserably at persuasion. Here are three of the most common mistakes people make:

1. **They attempt to make their case with an up-front, hard sell.** I call this the John Wayne approach. Managers strongly state their position at the outset, and then through a process of persistence, logic, and exuberance, they try to push the idea to a close. In reality, setting out a strong position at the start of a persuasion effort gives potential opponents something to grab onto—and fight against. It's far better

Excerpted from "The Necessary Art of Persuasion," by Jay A. Conger, *Harvard Business Review*, February 2000 (product #4258)

to present your position with the finesse and reserve of a lion tamer, who engages his "partner" by showing him the legs of a chair. In other words, effective persuaders don't begin the process by giving their colleagues a clear target in which to set their jaws.

2. **They resist compromise.** Too many managers see compromise as surrender, but it is essential to constructive persuasion. Before people buy into a proposal, they want to see that the persuader is flexible enough to respond to their concerns. Compromises can often lead to better, more sustainable shared solutions.

   By not compromising, ineffective persuaders unconsciously send the message that they think persuasion is a one-way street. But persuasion is a process of give-and-take. Kathleen Reardon, a professor of organizational behavior at the University of Southern California, points out that a persuader rarely changes another person's behavior or viewpoint without altering his or her own in the process. To persuade meaningfully, we must not only listen to others but also incorporate their perspectives into our own.

3. **They assume persuasion is a one-shot effort.** Persuasion is a process, not an event. Rarely, if ever, is it possible to arrive at a shared solution on the first try. More often than not, persuasion involves listening to people, testing a posi-

tion, developing a new position that reflects input from the group, more testing, incorporating compromises, and then trying again. If this sounds like a slow and difficult process, that's because it is. But the results are worth the effort.

Jay A. Conger is a professor of organizational behavior at the University of Southern California's Marshall School of Business in Los Angeles, where he directs the Leadership Institute. He is the author of *Winning 'Em Over: A New Model for Managing in the Age of Persuasion* (Simon & Schuster, 2001).

Harnessing the Science of Persuasion

A summary of the full-length HBR article by **Robert B. Cialdini,** *highlighting key ideas.*

THE IDEA IN BRIEF

Do you have it—the power to capture your audience, sway undecideds, convert opponents? In matrixed organizations, persuasion trumps formal power. It's essential to getting things done through others.

Persuasion works by appealing predictably to deeply rooted human needs. We can all learn to secure consensus, cut deals, win concessions—by artfully applying six scientific principles of winning friends and influencing people.

Reprint #R0109D

THE IDEA IN PRACTICE

Persuasion Principles

Principle	Example	Business Application
Liking: People like those like them, who like them.	At Tupperware parties, guests' fondness for their host influences purchase decisions twice as much as regard for the products.	**To influence people, win friends** through: • *Similarity*: Create *early* bonds with new peers,bosses, and direct reports by informally discovering common interests—you'll establish goodwill and trustworthiness. • *Praise*: Charm *and* disarm. Make positive remarks about others—you'll generate more willing compliance.
Reciprocity: People repay in kind.	When the Disabled American Veterans enclosed free personalized address labels in donation-request envelopes, response rate doubled.	**Give what you want to receive.** Lend a staff member to a colleague who needs help; you'll get *his* help later.
Social Proof: People follow the lead of similar others.	More New York City residents tried returning a lost wallet after learning that other New Yorkers had tried.	**Use peer power** to influence horizontally, not vertically; e.g., ask an esteemed "old timer" to support your new initiative if other veterans resist.
Consistency: People fulfill written, public, and voluntary commitments.	92% of residents of an apartment complex who signed a petition supporting a new recreation center later donated money to the cause.	**Make others' commitments active, public, and voluntary.** If you supervise an employee who should submit reports on time, get that understanding in writing (a memo); make the commitment public (note colleagues' agreement with the memo); and link the commitment to the employee's values (the impact of timely reports on team spirit).

Authority: People defer to experts who provide shortcuts to decisions requiring specialized information.	A single *New York Times* expert-opinion news story aired on TV generates a 4% shift in U.S. public opinion.	**Don't assume your expertise is self-evident.** Instead, establish your expertise *before* doing business with new colleagues or partners; e.g., in conversations before an important meeting, describe how you solved a problem similar to the one on the agenda.
Scarcity: People value what's scarce.	Wholesale beef buyers' orders jumped 600% when they alone received information on a possible beef shortage.	**Use exclusive information to persuade.** Influence and rivet key players' attention by saying, for example: "…Just got this information today. It won't be distributed until next week."

Robert B. Cialdini is the Regents' Professor of Psychology at Arizona State University and the author of *Influence: Science and Practice* (Allyn & Bacon, 2001). Further regularly updated information about the influence process can be found at http://www.influenceatwork.com/.

How to Get Your Colleagues' Attention

by Amy Gallo

Do you have to personally escort colleagues to your project meetings to make sure they show up? Does every "urgent" e-mail require phone or face-to-face follow-up to get a timely response? Do you have to hound your marketing partners to prioritize your products when they're launching new campaigns? These key tasks depend on your ability to **frame your message**—to make crystal clear what you need your colleagues to do, when, and, perhaps most important, why.

When you frame your message effectively, your audiencc will immediately understand the issue at hand and why it deserves their attention.

Here's how to frame your message to get the results you want, whether you're making a presentation, sending an e-mail, or talking in private with your boss:

- **Start with what you want.** Busy colleagues don't want to wait while you build to the punch line. Provide the most important information up front and ask for what you need.

  Example: "John, I need your advice about the product launch. I've gotten some new marketing data that may influence which message we lead with. I've come up with two alternatives, and I'd like your help deciding which to go with."

- **Set the scene.** Don't dive too deep into details, but provide enough context so your audience can follow along.

  Example: "To refresh your memory, the event we have planned is a question-and-answer panel on how to connect with today's modern moms. So far we've got five participants signed up to speak, including two CEOs of our top customers. Our goal is to reach as many marketers in the New York area as we can. We've sent out 2,500 invites and the initial response has been positive."

- **Explain the complication.** This is the specific reason for the meeting or your e-mail. What prompted you to deliver the message?

  Example: "As of today, the vendor is two weeks late with the prototypes. If there are further delays, we risk missing the deadline we set with the marketing team. We are somewhat stuck because the vendor knows we can't start over at this point with someone new. We need to figure out how to motivate the vendor and adjust our schedule so we can meet marketing's deadline."

- **Connect to the big picture.** Why should your audience care? Point out what is relevant to them and how it links to their broader goals.

  Example: "While eliminating the call checklist may seem like a small issue, it has important implications. It will encourage reps to engage with customers in a more informal way, which has been shown to increase customer satisfaction. This is a critical step toward meeting our unit's goal of 65% customer retention."

- **Make it memorable.** People hear news and information all day. Give them something to latch on to such as a metaphor, a key statistic, or a sound bite.

  Example: "Our customers feel this is an urgent issue and have told us so repeatedly. The longer we wait to respond, the more it will seem that the house is on fire and we're busy rearranging the furniture instead of calling 911."

- **Refocus your audience's attention.** It's easy for audiences to get distracted by secondary issues, so you must help them concentrate on the central objective. This is especially useful when you need to keep a large group on track or motivate people toward a common goal.

Example: "Susan, I see that you're concerned about getting the templates to design by our agreed-upon deadline. We need to make sure that happens. But let's agree on the right approach first—to be sure we're handing off a good product—and then we can work backwards to make sure we meet our deadlines."

- **End with a call to action.** Once you've set the context, reiterate what it is you need from your audience.

  Example: "Today I need to get your feedback on the presentation. I'd like to know specifically how we should tweak our high-level message to ensure it resonates with the leadership team."

Amy Gallo is a contributing editor at *Harvard Business Review*. Follow her on Twitter at @amyegallo.

Collaborating Across Generations

by Tamara Erickson

If you work with people from every generation, as many of us do these days, how do you communicate with them? And how do you get them to support and participate in your initiatives? By understanding their priorities and positioning your ideas and requests accordingly. To help with that challenge, here's a snapshot of each generation, along with tips for working effectively across the ages.

Group	Defining characteristics	How to work with them
Boomers (born between 1946 and 1960)	• Hold a deeply competitive world view; see most scenarios as win-lose • Are hardworking and driven • Value individual achievement and recognition • Question authority and hierarchy, yet feel pressure to follow established rules and procedures • Are idealistic, but have by and large put "lofty" personal goals on the back burner for the past 30 years • Are often parents of Gen Ys and inclined to enjoy members of this generation • Enjoy mentoring others and the idea of leaving a legacy	OVERALL: • **Emphasize winning:** Explain how your idea either represents a "win" or will make the organization (or individual) more competitive. For instance, if you're offering a Boomer a new position in the company, comment on how you've chosen her over numerous other candidates. Or if you're proposing a new marketing investment, discuss how it will thwart a competitor's program. • **Seek their counsel:** Appeal to their desire to pass on their knowledge. You might ask a Boomer for advice on how to get her boss's attention, for example, or for help analyzing a problem that keeps cropping up.
		IF YOU'RE A GEN XER: • **Spell out your career goals:** Clearly convey your aspirations to any Boomers with influence on your career well before you're up for a promotion or new role. Don't assume they'll automatically know where you'd like to end up long term or what kind of development path you'd prefer. Their well-intentioned ideas may be quite different from your own. • **Overcommunicate:** Be transparent in your approach to projects or problem solving. You're more likely than your Boomer colleagues to consider multiple options. Explain how and when you'll make decisions so Boomers will recognize the time

Group	Defining characteristics	How to work with them
		you're spending as due diligence, not misconstrue it as indecision or procrastination. • **Partner with them:** Tap their experience and networks. For example, invite a Boomer to join your skunkworks team. When you're ready to pitch the best ideas to your executive board, she can help socialize the top contenders with her peers, which may help speed buy-in. She can also raise potential concerns early on—helping you dodge delays at the implementation phase.
		IF YOU'RE A GEN Y: • **Ask them for mentoring:** Pair your enthusiasm for learning with a Boomer's expertise and desire to give back. For example, share your most pressing project management problems with him and discuss potential solutions. In return, offer him tutorials on social media or time-saving technologies. • **Make sure your written communication is professional:** Boomers are more likely than others to base judgments on the way you present your ideas. Express your recommendations concisely, using correct grammar and spelling. Describe the financial benefits of your suggestions when possible.
Gen Xers (born between early 1960s and late 1970s)	• Are self-reliant • Don't trust any institution (corporations,	OVERALL: • **Weigh your options:** Most Xers want to know that you've considered

(continued)

Group	Defining characteristics	How to work with them
	marriage, and so on) to take care of them forever • Like to keep their options open • Are irreverent • Think outside the box and are comfortable changing the rules as necessary • Accept the validity of diverse points of view • Have close relationships within a small group of friends (their "tribe") • Place high priority on being good parents	contingencies. Earn their respect and buy-in by including a discussion of "what if" when you present ideas to them. For instance, identify the two or three events or trends that would be most likely to disrupt your proposed course of action—and the response you would recommend taking if each one were to occur. • **Let them choose:** Whenever possible, present a menu of solutions and engage the Xer (whether she is your boss, colleague, or subordinate) in the process of choosing the best one. You might, for example, ask her what weight she would give to various decision criteria.
		IF YOU'RE A BOOMER: • **Employ their innovative thinking:** Ask an Xer to help solve a problem or reality-check your solution to make sure you're viewing the challenge from every possible angle. For example, invite him to test the validity of your strategy statement by posing a broad range of scenarios you might not have considered on your own. • **Harness their ability to integrate multiple points of view:** Invite an Xer to lead a complex group discussion—for instance, an after-action review. She's likely to ensure that everyone is heard so you'll have a fuller picture of what worked well and what needs improvement.

Group	Defining characteristics	How to work with them
		IF YOU'RE A GEN Y: • **Explore common ground:** Make the most of your shared passion for discovering new ways of working. For example, ask an Xer to help you analyze and improve your cross-functional team's processes. Or work together to find opportunities to leverage new technology in the organization. • **Respect the dues they've paid:** Most Xers have worked their way up a long career track and may feel threatened by the perception that you want to "leapfrog" past them. When you express your desire for more challenging work, be clear that you're not looking to take their seat.
Gen Ys (born between 1980 and the mid-1990s)	• Expect to live life fully each day • Are optimistic and confident • Prefer to work on their schedule, not yours • Are hungry to learn; expect regular coaching • Get things done using in-the-moment coordination rather than long-range planning • Work collaboratively • Have limited awareness of corporate hierarchy and protocol • Are comfortable expressing opinions freely and bluntly • Enjoy and respect their parents and tend to retain close relationships with them	OVERALL: • **Ramp up the challenge:** Give stretch assignments to maintain their interest. For example, ask a Gen Y to prepare a draft proposal for a client. You'll free up more of your time for other priorities, and he'll feel that he's making career progress. Or specify an outcome you need to achieve, but leave the approach to his discretion. Encourage him to find ways to do it better. Tell him, for instance, that the sales team needs to understand and get excited about a new product's features by the planned launch date, but invite him to propose the communication and training plan.

(continued)

Group	Defining characteristics	How to work with them
		• **Put their work into context:** Explain how what they do affects the larger organization. For example, invite a Gen Y to your next marketing meeting so she can see how the daily sales dashboard she's setting up will help your group accurately track the impact of different campaigns. • **Provide frequent feedback:** Take every opportunity to teach them. After a brainstorming session, for instance, pull your Gen Y direct report aside to note how useful it was for him to help facilitate. Give him a few specific suggestions on how he could do it even more effectively next time.
		IF YOU'RE A BOOMER: • **Clarify how you'll communicate with each other**: Agree on "rules" everyone feels comfortable with. For example: How frequently will you exchange e-mails or text messages? Will you share questions and thoughts as they come to mind or save them for a weekly status meeting? Work together to accommodate your different preferences. • **Tap their technological prowess:** Gen Ys are great sources of tech support, often without realizing it. Task a Gen Y with test-driving new software, for example, or looking for shortcuts in the sales-reporting process.

Group	Defining characteristics	How to work with them
		IF YOU'RE A GEN XER: • **Invite Boomers to teach them:** If you have a number of Gen Ys reporting to you, facilitate mentoring relationships between them and Boomers, who enjoy teaching and tend to click with Ys (more so than many Xers). Don't assume that all demands for coaching must be met by the Ys' managers—spread the responsibilities among other experienced colleagues. • **Clear up ambiguities:** Ys often ask their managers, typically Xers, for things in terms that can be easily misunderstood. For example, "I'd like a bigger job" may simply mean that a Y wants something more challenging, not necessarily that she's angling for a promotion. If a Y says, "I'd like to do multiple jobs this year," she's probably talking about a variety of tasks, not formal job assignments. "Feedback" often means teaching, not critique or blanket praise. If you're not 100% sure what a Y means, ask her to clarify.

Tamara Erickson wrote a trilogy of books on the generations: *Retire Retirement*, *Plugged In*, and *What's Next, Gen X?*. She was named one of the 50 leading management thinkers in 2009 and 2011 by Thinkers50.

When the Direct Approach Backfires, Try Indirect Influence

by Martha Craumer

How do you get people who don't work for you to *work for you*?

When direct management techniques don't work—especially with those over whom you have no authority—you may have better luck with these, more subtle, approaches.

1. **Talk less, listen more.** When you try to persuade people, you can spend too much time explaining your position, and not enough time asking questions, listening, and understanding other points of view.

Adapted from reprint #U0608D

Your colleagues are less likely to resist when they feel you've taken the time to acknowledge their concerns. In *The 7 Habits of Highly Effective People*, Stephen Covey says that the greatest need of human beings—after physical survival—is to be understood, affirmed, and appreciated. He explains that "empathic listening gets inside another person's frame of reference. You look out through it, you see the world the way they [do], you understand their paradigm, you understand how they feel." It's human nature to want to work with, not against, someone who "gets" us. Ask about your colleagues' challenges or people they're struggling with. This information will help you identify common goals and solutions. And you'll be building stronger working relationships.

2. **Make 'em like you.** It's hard to say no to someone you like. So how can you increase your likability? Play up similarities. We tend to like people who share our background, interests, style of dress, etc.

   We also like people who like us. We're suckers for compliments. If your colleague does a good job leading a meeting, tell him what you liked about the way he ran it. Be specific. Ask another colleague about her weekend and listen—perhaps you'll discover a shared passion for hiking or reading. Then when you need their help, your colleagues will be more likely to offer their expertise.

3. **Make 'em laugh.** Ever wonder why so many speakers open their presentations with a joke? Humor is disarming. It makes people root for us. It's hard to feel bad when you're laughing—and hard to dislike a person who makes you laugh.

   Humor makes you appear calm, approachable, and in control. It helps your audience feel more relaxed and receptive to change, new ideas, and your influence. Use humor to help soften a harsh message and make it easier to speak freely about the challenge at hand.

   But use humor with care. Inside jokes and cultural allusions can be off-putting. And, of course, humor should never be at the expense of the person you're trying to influence—nor should it make light of her issues or concerns.

4. **Do a favor—even a small one.** Doing something for someone gives you enormous power and influence over them. In his book *Influence: The Psychology of Persuasion*, Robert Cialdini discusses the unwritten rule of reciprocity and how it obligates us to repay what another person has given us.

   Cialdini cites a research study involving two groups of subjects and a "plant"—a man named Joe—who was posing as a fellow subject. Each member of the first group received a small "favor" from Joe—a Coke that he picked up for them while out of the room. The second group received no favor. Then, Joe told each group he was selling raffle tickets. The subjects who received a Coke from Joe bought twice as many tickets as the subjects who received nothing. The reciprocity rule overwhelmed all other factors—including whether they even liked Joe. The ticket buyers felt an irresistible need to repay him.

The more you raise your hand to help others, the more likely they'll do the same for you. Volunteer to take notes at a colleague's brainstorming session. Help set out lunch for a big client meeting. Offer to listen to your teammate's dry run of a big presentation.

5. **Feed 'em.** Pick up an extra coffee for the programmer who's been developing a data feed for your new website. Bring fresh fruit or candy bars to your project launch meeting. Pick one day every two weeks to take a colleague to lunch. Don't ask your buddy—invite people whom you don't often get to see outside of all-staff meetings, to help deepen your relationships and extend your network. It's simple, but true: we like to be fed.

Martha Craumer is a freelance writer based in Cambridge, Massachusetts.

Index

Notes

Notes

Notes

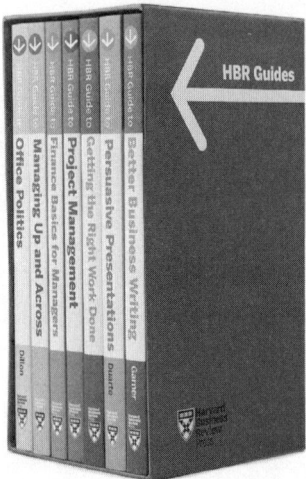

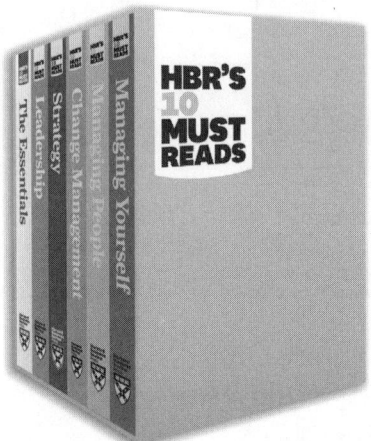

HBR Guide to
Emotional Intelligence

Harvard Business Review Guides

Arm yourself with the advice you need to succeed on the job, from the most trusted brand in business. Packed with how-to essentials from leading experts, the HBR Guides provide smart answers to your most pressing work challenges.

The titles include:

HBR Guide to Being More Productive

HBR Guide to Better Business Writing

HBR Guide to Building Your Business Case

HBR Guide to Buying a Small Business

HBR Guide to Coaching Employees

HBR Guide to Data Analytics Basics for Managers

HBR Guide to Delivering Effective Feedback

HBR Guide to Emotional Intelligence

HBR Guide to Finance Basics for Managers

HBR Guide to Getting the Right Work Done

HBR Guide to Leading Teams

HBR Guide to Making Every Meeting Matter

HBR Guide to Managing Stress at Work

HBR Guide to Managing Up and Across

HBR Guide to Negotiating

HBR Guide to Office Politics

HBR Guide to Performance Management

HBR Guide to Persuasive Presentations

HBR Guide to Project Management

HBR Guide to **Emotional Intelligence**

HARVARD BUSINESS REVIEW PRESS

Boston, Massachusetts

Printed in the United States of America
10 9 8 7 6 5 4 3 2 1

Library of Congress cataloging-in-publication data is forthcoming.

ISBN: 9781633692725
eISBN: 9781633692732

The paper used in this publication meets the requirements of the American National Standard for Permanence of Paper for Publications and Documents in Libraries and Archives Z39.48-1992.

What You'll Learn

It's been two decades since Daniel Goleman's research showed that emotional intelligence is twice as important as other skills in determining outstanding leadership. By managing your emotions and relating well to others, he explained, you can achieve higher levels of influence as well as personal well-being.

This kind of emotional intelligence is not just an innate trait: It can be learned. Becoming more finely attuned to your own emotions allows you to determine how to use those feelings more productively to make stronger decisions, overcome negative thoughts, control yourself in volatile situations, or understand others when they act in a way that surprises or angers you. Getting feedback from trusted colleagues and friends can keep you honest and aware of your areas of weakness, especially in the social sphere. And whether you're writing a difficult email, looking to keep your cool in a bitter negotiation, or managing an upset direct report, an array of frameworks and tactics can help you approach the situation in a way that takes the human element into account.

This guide will help you navigate these approaches. You'll get better at:

- Identifying and managing your own emotions
- Persuading and influencing others
- Dealing with difficult colleagues
- Responding to stress productively
- Defusing tense conversations
- Using your feelings as data to help you make smarter decisions
- Avoiding emotional pitfalls in a negotiation
- Reacting to tough situations with resilience
- Helping others on your team develop their emotional intelligence
- Developing a strong emotional culture

Contents

SECTION THREE

Manage Your Emotions

SECTION FOUR

Everyday Emotional Intelligence

SECTION EIGHT

Developing Emotional Intelligence on Your Team

SECTION ONE

What Is Emotional Intelligence?

CHAPTER 1

Leading by Feel

Like it or not, leaders need to manage the mood of their organizations. The most gifted leaders accomplish that by using a mysterious blend of psychological abilities known as *emotional intelligence*. They're self-aware and empathetic. They can read and regulate their own emotions while intuitively grasping how others feel and gauging their organization's emotional state.

But where does emotional intelligence come from? And how do leaders learn to use it? The management literature (and even common sense) suggests that both nature and nurture feed emotional intelligence. Part genetic predisposition, part life experience, and part old-fashioned training, emotional intelligence emerges in varying degrees from one leader to the next,

---

Excerpted from *Harvard Business Review*, January 2004 (product #R0401B)

and managers apply it with varying skill. Wisely and compassionately deployed, emotional intelligence spurs leaders, their people, and their organizations to superior performance; naively or maliciously applied, it can paralyze leaders or allow them to manipulate followers for personal gain.

We invited 18 leaders and scholars (including business executives, leadership researchers, psychologists, a neurologist, a cult expert, and a symphony conductor) to explore the nature and management of emotional intelligence—its sources, uses, and abuses. Their responses differed dramatically, but there were some common themes: the importance of consciously and conscientiously honing one's skills, the double-edged nature of self-awareness, and the danger of letting any one emotional intelligence skill dominate. Here are some of their perspectives.

Be Realistic

John D. Mayer *is a professor of psychology at the University of New Hampshire. He and Yale psychology professor Peter Salovey are credited with first defining the concept of emotional intelligence in the early 1990s.*

This is a time of growing realism about emotional intelligence—especially concerning what it is and what it isn't. The books and articles that have helped popularize the concept have defined it as a loose collection of personality traits, such as self-awareness, optimism, and tolerance. These popular definitions have been accompanied by exaggerated claims about the importance of emotional intelligence. But diverse personality traits, however admirable, don't necessarily add up to a single definition of emotional intelligence. In fact, such traits are difficult to collectively evaluate in a way that reveals their relationship to success in business and in life.

Even when they're viewed in isolation, the characteristics commonly associated with emotional intelligence and success may be more complicated than they seem. For example, the scientific jury is out on how important self-awareness is to successful leadership. In fact, too much self-awareness can reduce self-esteem, which is often a crucial component of great leadership.

From a scientific standpoint, emotional intelligence is the ability to accurately perceive your own and others' emotions; to understand the signals that emotions send about relationships; and to manage your own and others' emotions. It doesn't necessarily include the qualities (like optimism, initiative, and self-confidence) that some popular definitions ascribe to it.

Researchers have used performance tests to measure people's accuracy at identifying and understanding emotions; for example, asking them to identify the emotions conveyed by a face or which among several situations is most likely to bring about happiness. People who get high scores on these tests are indeed different from others. In the business world, they appear better able to deal with customers' complaints or to mediate disputes, and they may excel at making strong and positive personal connections with subordinates and customers over the long term. Of course, emotional intelligence isn't the only way to attain success as a leader: A brilliant strategist who can maximize profits may be able to hire and keep talented employees even if he or she doesn't have strong personal connections with them.

Is there value in scales that, based on popular conceptions, measure qualities like optimism and self-confidence but label them "emotional intelligence"? Certainly, these personality traits are important in business, so measuring and (sometimes) enhancing them can be useful. But recent research makes it clear that these characteristics are distinct from emotional intelligence as it is scientifically defined. A person high in emotional intelligence may be realistic rather than optimistic and insecure rather than confident. Conversely, a person may be highly self-confident and optimistic but lack emotional intelligence. The danger lies in assuming that because a person is optimistic or confident, they are also emotionally intelligent, when, in fact, the presence of those traits will tell you nothing of the sort.

Never Stop Learning

Daniel Goleman *is the cochair of the Consortium for Research on Emotional Intelligence in Organizations based at Rutgers University's Graduate School of Applied and Professional Psychology in Piscataway, New Jersey.*

You can be a successful leader without much emotional intelligence if you're extremely lucky and you've got everything else going for you: booming markets, bumbling competitors, and clueless higher-ups. If you're incredibly smart, you can cover for an absence of emotional intelligence until things get tough for the business.

But at that point, you won't have built up the social capital needed to pull the best out of people under tremendous pressure. The art of sustained leadership is getting others to produce superior work, and high IQ alone is insufficient to that task.

The good news is that emotional intelligence can be learned and improved at any age. In fact, data shows that, on average, people's emotional intelligence tends to increase as they age. But the specific leadership competencies that are based on emotional intelligence don't necessarily come through life experience. For example, one of the most common complaints I hear about leaders, particularly newly promoted ones, is that they lack empathy. The problem is that they were promoted because they were outstanding individual performers—and being a solo achiever doesn't teach you the skills necessary to understand other people's concerns.

Leaders who are motivated to improve their emotional intelligence can do so if they're given the right *information, guidance,* and *support.* The information they need is a candid assessment of their strengths and limitations from people who know them well and whose opinions they trust. The guidance they need is a specific developmental plan that uses naturally occurring workplace encounters as the laboratory for learning. The support they need is someone to talk to as they practice how to handle different situations, what to do when they've blown it, and how to learn from those setbacks. If leaders cultivate these resources and practice continually, they can develop specific emotional intelligence skills—skills that will last for years.

5 COMPONENTS OF EMOTIONAL INTELLIGENCE

In 1998, in what has become one of HBR's most enduring articles, "What Makes a Leader?" Daniel Goleman introduced a framework of five components of emotional intelligence that allow individuals to recognize, connect with, and learn from their own and other people's mental states, as well as their hallmarks. While there are many frameworks offering varying sets of EI competencies (and other models that conceive of emotional intelligence not as a set of competencies but rather as the ability to abstract and problem solve in the emotional domain), Goleman's approach, outlined in exhibit 1, can be a helpful way to start building an understanding of emotional intelligence:

EXHIBIT 1

EI Component	Definition	Hallmarks	Example
Self-awareness	Knowing one's emotions, strengths, weaknesses, drives, values, and goals—and their impacts on others	• Self-confidence • Realistic self-assessment • Self-deprecating sense of humor • Thirst for constructive criticism	A manager knows tight deadlines bring out the worst in him. So he plans his time to get work done well in advance.
Self-regulation	Controlling or redirecting disruptive emotions and impulses	• Trustworthiness • Integrity • Comfort with ambiguity and change	When a team botches a presentation, its leader resists the urge to scream. Instead, she considers possible reasons for the failure, explains the consequences to her team, and explores solutions with them.

EI Component	Definition	Hallmarks	Example
Motivation	Being driven to achieve for the sake of achievement	• A passion for the work itself and for new challenges • Unflagging energy to improve • Optimism in the face of failure	A portfolio manager at an investment company sees his fund tumble for three consecutive quarters. Major clients defect. Instead of blaming external circumstances, she decides to learn from the experience—and engineers a turnaround.
Empathy	Considering others' feelings, especially when making decisions	• Expertise in attracting and retaining talent • Ability to develop others • Sensitivity to cross-cultural differences	An American consultant and her team pitch a project to a potential client in Japan. Her team interprets the client's silence as disapproval and prepares to leave. The consultant reads the client's body language and senses interest. She continues the meeting, and her team gets the job.
Social skill	Managing relationships to move in desired directions	• Effectiveness in leading change • Persuasiveness • Extensive networking • Expertise in building and leading teams	A manager wants his company to adopt a better internet strategy. He finds kindred spirits and assembles a de facto team to create a prototype website. He persuades allies in other divisions to fund the company's participation in a relevant convention. His company forms an internet division—and puts him in charge of it.

Adapted from "What Makes a Leader" by Daniel Goleman, originally published in *Harvard Business Review*, June 2006.

Get Motivated

Richard Boyatzis *is a professor and the chair of the department of organizational behavior at Case Western Reserve University's Weatherhead School of Management in Cleveland.*

People can develop their emotional intelligence if they really want to. But many managers jump to the conclusion that their complement of emotional intelligence is predetermined. They think, "I could never be good at this, so why bother?" The central issue isn't a lack of *ability* to change; it's the lack of *motivation* to change.

Leadership development is not all that different from other areas in which people are trying to change their behaviors. Just look at the treatments for alcoholism, drug addiction, and weight loss: They all require the desire to change. More subtly, they all require a positive, rather than a negative, motivation. You have to *want* to change. If you think you'll lose your job because you're not adequately tuned in to your employees, you might become determinedly empathetic or compassionate for a time. But change driven by fear or avoidance probably isn't going to last. Change driven by hopes and aspirations, change that's pursued because it's desired, will be more enduring.

There's no such thing as having too much emotional intelligence. But there is a danger in being preoccupied with, or overusing, one aspect of it. For example, if you overemphasize the emotional intelligence competencies of initiative or achievement, you'll always be changing things at your company. Nobody would know what you were going to do next, which would be quite destabilizing for the organization. If you overuse empathy, you might never fire anybody. If you overuse teamwork, you might never build diversity or listen to a lone voice. Balance is essential.

Train the Gifted

Elkhonon Goldberg *is a clinical professor of neurology at New York University School of Medicine and the director of the Institute of Neuropsychology and Cognitive Performance in New York.*

In the past, neuropsychologists were mostly concerned with cognitive impairment. Today, they are increasingly interested in the biological underpinnings of cognitive differences in people without impairments—including differences in people's emotional intelligence.

Emotional intelligence can be learned, to a degree. It's like mathematical or musical ability. Can you become a musician if you lack natural aptitude? Yes, you can, if you take lessons and practice enough. But will you ever be a Mozart? Probably not. In the same way, emotional intelligence develops through a combination of biological endowment and training. And people who don't have that endowment probably won't become deeply emotionally intelligent just through training. Trying to drum emotional intelligence into someone with no aptitude for it is an exercise in futility. I believe the best way to get emotionally intelligent leaders is to select for people who already show the basic qualities you want. Think about it: That's how athletic coaches operate. They don't just work with anyone who wants to play a sport; they train the naturally gifted. Business managers should do the same.

How do you identify the naturally gifted? I'd say you have to look for those with a genuine, instinctive interest in other people's experiences and mental worlds. It's an absolute prerequisite for developing emotional intelligence. If a manager lacks this interest, maybe your training resources are better directed elsewhere.

Seek Frank Feedback

Andrea Jung *is the chair and CEO of Avon Products, which is based in New York.*

Emotional intelligence is in our DNA here at Avon because relationships are critical at every stage of our business. It starts with the relationships our 4.5 million independent sales reps have with their customers and goes right up through senior management to my office. So the emphasis on emotional intelligence is much greater here than it was at other companies in which I've worked. We incorporate emotional intelligence education into our development training for senior managers, and we factor in emotional intelligence competencies when we evaluate employees' performance.

Of all a leader's competencies, emotional and otherwise, self-awareness is the most important. Without it, you can't identify the impact you have on others. Self-awareness is very important for me as CEO. At my level, few people are willing to tell me the things that are hardest to hear. We have a CEO advisory counsel—ten people chosen each year from Avon offices throughout the world—and they tell me the good, the bad, and the ugly about the company. Anything can be said. It helps keep me connected to what people really think and how my actions affect them. I also rely on my children for honest appraisals. You can get a huge dose of reality by seeing yourself through your children's eyes, noticing the ways they react to and reflect what you say and do. My kids are part of my 360-degree feedback. They're the most honest of all.

I grew up in a very traditional Chinese family. My parents were concerned that the way I'd been raised—submissive, caring, and averse to conflict—would hinder my ability to succeed in the *Fortune* 500 environment. They were afraid I couldn't make the tough decisions. But I've learned how to be empathetic and still make hard decisions that are right for the company. These are not incompatible abilities. When Avon has had to close plants, for example, I've tried to act with compassion for the people involved. And I've gotten letters from some of the associates who were affected, expressing sadness but also saying thanks for the fair treatment. Leaders' use of emotional intelligence when making tough decisions is important to their success—and to the success of their organizations.

Engage Your Demons

David Gergen *directs the Center for Public Leadership at Harvard University's John F. Kennedy School of Government in Cambridge, Massachusetts. He served as an adviser to presidents Nixon, Ford, Reagan, and Clinton.*

American history suggests not only that emotional intelligence is an indispensable ingredient of political leadership but also that it can be enhanced through sustained effort. George Washington had to work hard to control his fiery temper before he became a role model for the republic, and Abraham Lincoln had to overcome deep melancholia to display the brave and warm countenance that made him a magnet for others. Franklin Delano Roosevelt provides an even more graphic example: In his early adult years, FDR seemed carefree and condescending. Then, at 39, he was stricken with polio. By most accounts, he transformed himself over the next seven years of struggle into a leader of empathy, patience, and keen self-awareness.

Richard Nixon thought he might transform himself through his own years in the wilderness, and he did make progress. But he could never fully control his demons, and they eventually brought him down. Bill Clinton, too, struggled for self-mastery and made progress, but he could not fully close the cracks in his character, and he paid a stiff price. Not all people succeed, then, in achieving self-awareness and self-control. What we have been told since the time of the Greeks is that every leader must try to control his own passions before he can hope to command the passions of others.

Best-selling author Rabbi Harold Kushner argues persuasively that the elements of selfishness and aggression that are in most of us—and our struggles to overcome them—are exactly what make for better leadership. In *Living a Life That Matters,* Kushner writes of the personal torments of leaders from Jacob, who wrestled all night with an angel, to Martin Luther King Jr., who tried to cleanse himself of weakness even as he cleansed the nation's soul. "Good people do bad things," Kushner concludes, "If they weren't mightily tempted by their *yetzer ha'ra* [will to do evil], they might not be capable of the mightily good things they do."

Find Your Voice

William George *is the former chairman and CEO of Medtronic, a medical technology company in Minneapolis.*

Authentic leadership begins with self-awareness, or knowing yourself deeply. Self-awareness is not a trait you are born with but a capacity you develop throughout your lifetime. It's your understanding of your strengths and weaknesses, your purpose in life, your values and motivations, and how and why you respond to situations in a particular way. It requires a great deal of introspection and the ability to internalize feedback from others.

No one is born a leader; we have to consciously develop into the leader we want to become. It takes many years of hard work and the ability to learn from extreme difficulties and disappointments. But in their scramble to get ahead, many would-be leaders attempt to skip this crucial developmental stage. Some of these people do get to the top of companies through sheer determination and aggressiveness. However, when they finally reach the leader's chair, they can be very destructive because they haven't focused on the hard work of personal development.

To mask their inadequacies, these leaders tend to close themselves off, cultivating an image or persona rather than opening up to others. They often adopt the styles of other leaders they have observed.

Leaders who are driven to achieve by shortcomings in their character, for example, or a desire for self-aggrandizement, may take inordinate risks on behalf of the organization. They may even come to believe they are so important that they place their interests above those of the organization.

Self-awareness and other emotional intelligence skills come naturally to some, less so to others—but these skills can be learned. One of the techniques I have found most useful in gaining deeper self-awareness is meditation. In 1975, my wife dragged me, kicking and screaming, to a weekend course in Transcendental Meditation. I have meditated 20 minutes, twice a day, ever since. Meditation makes me calmer, more focused, and better able to discern what's really important. Leaders, by the very nature of their positions, are under extreme pressure to keep up with the many voices clamoring for their attention. Indeed, many leaders lose their way. It is only through a deep self-awareness that you can find your inner voice and listen to it.

Know the Score

Michael Tilson Thomas *is the music director of the San Francisco Symphony.*

A conductor's authority rests on two things: the orchestra's confidence in the conductor's insightful knowledge of the whole score; and the orchestra's faith in the conductor's good heart, which seeks to inspire everyone to make music that is excellent, generous, and sincere.

Old-school conductors liked to hold the lead in their hands at all times. I do not. Sometimes I lead. Other times I'll say, "Violas, I'm giving you the lead. Listen to one another; and find your way with this phrase." I'm not trying to drill people, military style, to play music exactly together. I'm trying to encourage them to play as one, which is a different thing. I'm guiding the performance, but I'm aware that they're executing it. It's their sinews, their heartstrings. I'm there to help them do it in a way that is convincing and natural for them but also a part of the larger design.

My approach is to be in tune with the people with whom I'm working. If I'm conducting an ensemble for the first time, I will relate what I want them to do to the great things they've already done. If I'm conducting my own orchestra, I can see in the musicians' bodies and faces how they're feeling that day, and it becomes very clear who may need encouragement and who may need cautioning.

The objectivity and perspective I have as the only person who is just listening is a powerful thing. I try to use this perspective to help the ensemble reach its goals.

Keep It Honest

Carol Bartz *is the chairman, president, and CEO of Autodesk, a design software and digital content company in San Rafael, California.*

A friend needed to take a six-month assignment in a different part of the country. She had an ancient, ill, balding but beloved dog that she could not take with her. Her choices boiled down to boarding the poor animal, at enormous expense, or putting it out of its obvious misery. Friends said, "Board the dog," though behind my friend's back, they ridiculed that option. She asked me what I thought, and I told her, kindly but clearly, that I thought she should have the dog put to sleep rather than spend her money keeping it in an environment where it would be miserable and perhaps die anyway. My friend was furious with me for saying this. She boarded the dog and went away on her assignment. When she returned, the dog was at death's door and had to be put to sleep. Not long after that, my friend came around to say thanks. "You were the only person who told me the truth," she said. She came to appreciate that I had cared enough to tell her what I thought was best, even if what I said hurt at the time.

That event validated a hunch that has stood me in good stead as I've led my company. Empathy and compassion have to be balanced with honesty. I have pulled people into my office and told them to deal with certain issues for the sake of themselves and their teams. If they are willing to learn, they will say, "Gee, no one ever told me." If they are unwilling, they're not right for this organization. And I must let them go for the sake of the greater good.

Go for the Gemba

Hirotaka Takeuchi *is the dean of Hitotsubashi University's Graduate School of International Corporate Strategy in Tokyo.*

Self-awareness, self-control, empathy, humility, and other such emotional intelligence traits are particularly important in Asia. They are part of our Confucian emphasis on *wah*, or social harmony. When books on emotional intelligence were first translated into Japanese, people said, "We already know that. We're actually trying to get beyond that." We've been so focused on wah that we've built up a supersensitive structure of social niceties, where everyone seeks consensus. In the Japanese hierarchy, everyone knows his or her place, so no one is ever humiliated. This social supersensitivity—itself a form of emotional intelligence—can lead people to shy away from conflict. But conflict is often the only way to get to the *gemba*—the front line, where the action really is, where the truth lies.

Thus, effective management often depends not on coolly and expertly resolving conflict—or simply avoiding it—but on embracing it at the gemba. Japan's most effective leaders do both. The best example is Nissan's Carlos Ghosn. He not only had the social skills to listen to people and win them over to his ideas, but he also dared to lift the lid on the corporate hierarchy and encourage people at all levels of the organization to offer suggestions to operational, organizational, and even interpersonal problems—even if that created conflict. People were no longer suppressed, so solutions to the company's problems bubbled up.

Balance the Load

Linda Stone *is the former vice president of corporate and industry initiatives at Microsoft in Redmond, Washington.*

Emotional intelligence is powerful—which is precisely why it can be dangerous. For example, empathy is an extraordinary relationship-building tool, but it must be used skillfully or it can do serious damage to the person doing the empathizing. In my case, overdoing empathy took a physical toll. In May 2000, Steve Ballmer charged me with rebuilding Microsoft's industry relationships, a position that I sometimes referred to as "chief listening officer." The job was part ombudsperson, part new initiatives developer, part pattern recognizer, and part rapid-response person. In the first few months of the job—when criticism of the company was at an all-time high—it became clear that this position was a lightning rod. I threw myself into listening and repairing wherever I could.

Within a few months, I was exhausted from the effort. I gained a significant amount of weight, which, tests finally revealed, was probably caused by a hormone imbalance partially brought on by stress and lack of sleep. In absorbing everyone's complaints, perhaps to the extreme, I had compromised my health. This was a wake-up call: I needed to reframe the job.

I focused on connecting the people who needed to work together to resolve problems rather than taking on each repair myself. I persuaded key people inside the company to listen and work directly with important people outside the company, even in cases where the internal folks were skeptical at first about the need for this direct connection. In a sense, I tempered my empathy and ratcheted up relationship building. Ultimately, with a wiser and more balanced use of empathy, I became more effective and less stressed in my role.

Question Authority

Ronald Heifetz *is a cofounder of the Center for Public Leadership at Harvard University's John F. Kennedy School of Government in Cambridge, Massachusetts, and a partner at Cambridge Leadership Associates, a consultancy in Cambridge.*

Emotional intelligence is necessary for leadership but not sufficient. Many people have some degree of emotional intelligence and can indeed empathize with and rouse followers; a few of them can even generate great charismatic authority. But I would argue that if they are using emotional intelligence solely to gain formal or informal authority, that's not leadership at all. They are using their emotional intelligence to grasp what people want, only to pander to those desires in order to gain authority and influence. Easy answers sell.

Leadership couples emotional intelligence with the courage to raise the tough questions, challenge people's assumptions about strategy and operations—and risk losing their goodwill. It demands a commitment to serving others; skill at diagnostic, strategic, and tactical reasoning; the guts to get beneath the surface of tough realities; and the heart to take heat and grief.

For example, David Duke did an extraordinary job of convincing Ku Klux Klan members to get out of their backyards and into hotel conference rooms. He brought his considerable emotional intelligence to bear, his capacity to empathize with his followers, to pluck their heartstrings in a powerful way that mobilized them. But he avoided asking his people the tough questions: Does our program actually solve our problem? How will creating a social structure of white supremacy give us the self-esteem we lack? How will it solve the problems of poverty, alcoholism, and family violence that corrode our sense of self-worth?

Like Duke, many people with high emotional intelligence and charismatic authority aren't interested in asking the deeper questions, because they get so much emotional gain from the adoring crowd. For them, that's the end in itself. They're satisfying their own hungers and vulnerabilities: their need to be liked; their need for power and control; or their need to be needed, to feel important, which renders them vulnerable to grandiosity. But that's not primal leadership. It's primal hunger for authority.

Maintaining one's primacy or position is not in and of itself leadership, however inspiring it may seem to be. Gaining primal authority is relatively easy.

CHAPTER 2

Do You Lead with Emotional Intelligence?

by Annie McKee

Great leaders move us—they inspire, motivate, and energize us. How? They do it through emotional intelligence. Dan Goleman woke us all up when he published his groundbreaking book on the topic (in 1995). Since then we've learned a lot about EI competencies, such as self-awareness and empathy, and about what people can do to develop them. To gain a deeper understanding of your own emotional intelligence, respond to the statements in this questionnaire as honestly as possible, checking one of the columns from "Always" to "Never."

Adapted from content posted on hbr.org on June 5, 2015, as "Quiz Yourself: Do You Lead with Emotional Intelligence?"

To calculate your score, as you finish each section count the checkmarks in each column and record the number in the "Total per column" line. Multiply your total score for each column by the number in the row below it, and record it in the row below that. Add this row together to get your total score for how you perceive yourself along each of the dimensions of EI.

Reflecting on your strengths and where you can improve is important, but don't stop there. Other people's perspectives matter too. After reviewing your scores, ask one or two trusted friends to evaluate you using the same statements, to learn what others see in you.

Annie McKee is a senior fellow at the University of Pennsylvania and the director of the PennCLO Executive Doctoral Program. She is the author of *Primal Leadership* (with Daniel Goleman and Richard Boyatzis), as well as *Resonant Leadership* and *Becoming a Resonant Leader*. Her new book, *How to Be Happy at Work*, is forthcoming from Harvard Business Review Press in September 2017.

HOW WOULD YOU DESCRIBE YOURSELF?		ALWAYS	MOST OF THE TIME	FREQUENTLY	SOMETIMES	RARELY	NEVER
EMOTIONAL SELF-AWARENESS							
1	I can describe my emotions in the moment I experience them.						
2	I can describe my feelings in detail, beyond just "happy," "sad," "angry," and so on.						
3	I understand the reasons for my feelings.						
4	I understand how stress affects my mood and behavior.						
5	I understand my leadership strengths and weaknesses.						
	Total per column						
	Points per answer	x 5	x 4	x 3	x 2	x 1	x 0
	Multiply the two rows above						
	TOTAL SELF-AWARENESS SCORE *(sum of the row above)*						
POSITIVE OUTLOOK							
6	I'm optimistic in the face of challenging circumstances.						
7	I focus on opportunities rather than obstacles.						
8	I see people as good and well-intentioned.						
9	I look forward to the future.						
10	I feel hopeful.						
	Total per column						
	Points per answer	x 5	x 4	x 3	x 2	x 1	x 0
	Multiply the two rows above						
	TOTAL POSITIVE OUTLOOK SCORE *(sum of the row above)*						

HOW WOULD YOU DESCRIBE YOURSELF?		ALWAYS	MOST OF THE TIME	FREQUENTLY	SOMETIMES	RARELY	NEVER
EMOTIONAL SELF-CONTROL							
11	I manage stress well.						
12	I'm calm in the face of pressure or emotional turmoil.						
13	I control my impulses.						
14	I use strong emotions, such as anger, fear, and joy, appropriately and for the good of others.						
15	I'm patient.						
	Total per column						
	Points per answer	x 5	x 4	x 3	x 2	x 1	x 0
	Multiply the two rows above						
	TOTAL EMOTIONAL SELF-CONTROL SCORE *(sum of the row above)*						
ADAPTABILITY							
16	I'm flexible when situations change unexpectedly.						
17	I'm adept at managing multiple, conflicting demands.						
18	I can easily adjust goals when circumstances change.						
19	I can shift my priorities quickly.						
20	I adapt easily when a situation is uncertain or ever-changing.						
	Total per column						
	Points per answer	x 5	x 4	x 3	x 2	x 1	x 0
	Multiply the two rows above						
	TOTAL ADAPTABILITY SCORE *(sum of the row above)*						

EMPATHY							
21	I strive to understand people's underlying feelings.						
22	My curiosity about others drives me to listen attentively to them.						
23	I try to understand why people behave the way they do.						
24	I readily understand others' viewpoints even when they are different from my own.						
25	I understand how other people's experiences affect their feelings, thoughts, and behavior.						
	Total per column						
	Points per answer	x 5	x 4	x 3	x 2	x 1	x 0
	Multiply the two rows above						
	TOTAL EMPATHY SCORE *(sum of the row above)*						

SECTION TWO

Self-Awareness: Understand Your Emotions, Know Your Behaviors

CHAPTER 3

You Can't Manage Emotions Without Knowing What They Really Are

by Art Markman

At this point, everybody knows emotional intelligence matters in the workplace. Yet there are two aspects of emotions that make it hard for people to exercise their emotional intelligence. First, most people are still not completely clear about what emotions actually are. Second, even when we understand emotions conceptually, it can still be hard to deal with our own emotional states.

To tackle the first problem: While in everyday speech, *emotion* and *feeling* are often used interchangeably,

---

Adapted from content posted on hbr.org on December 23, 2015 (product #H02KOK)

psychologists distinguish between them. Emotions are interpretations of feelings.

The feelings you have (what psychologists call *affect*) emerge from your motivational system. You generally feel good when you're succeeding at your goals and bad when you're not. The more deeply your motivational system is engaged with a situation, the stronger your feelings.

The motivational system, however, is not that well connected to the brain regions that help you to tell stories about the world. In order to make sense of what you're feeling, you use information about what's going on around you to help you translate those feelings into emotions—emotions help to guide your actions by giving you explicit feedback on how well you are currently achieving the goals the motivational system has engaged.

Often, that interpretation is easy. If you are crossing the street and suddenly have to leap out of the way of an oncoming car, it is clear that the strong negative feeling you are having is fear from nearly getting hit by the car. If a colleague compliments you on a job well done, it is obvious that the positive feeling you are having is pride.

But things are not always so clear. You might have a bad interaction with a family member before getting to work. As the day wears on, you may interpret your negative feelings as frustration with the project you're working on rather than lingering negative affect from the events of the morning.

Many people try to power through their negative feelings rather than attempting to understand them. But this is a lost opportunity. Emotions provide valuable information about the state of your motivational system. Ignoring them is like driving around lost, not only refusing to ask for directions but refusing to consult the map or the GPS—or even to look through the windshield. You will still be moving forward, but who knows where you will end up? Conversely, paying too much attention to your feelings is also bad. That's like staring at your road atlas without ever turning on the car: You can't get anywhere that way.

When you have negative feelings, slow down and pay some attention to *what* you are feeling and *why* you are feeling the way you are.

When you find yourself stressed, anxious, or angry, take five or 10 minutes for yourself during the day. Sit alone and breathe deeply. The deep breaths help to take some of the energy or arousal out of the feelings you are having. That can help you to think more clearly.

Then start to think about some of the events of your day. Pay attention to how those thoughts influence what you are feeling. Are there particular events that increase or decrease the intensity of those feelings?

You may not completely understand the source of your feelings the first time you do this. Over time, you will become more adept at paying attention to when and where you start to feel bad.

Of course, once you have figured out what's bothering you, it's time to plan a course of action. If you keep thinking about things that bother you, you run the risk of solving nothing while getting yourself more upset. Instead, use your knowledge about the source of the bad feeling to figure out how to deal with it.

Finally, if you're really upset about something, hold off on actually executing your plan until you have given yourself a chance to calm down. Responses that seemed like a good idea in the moment may seem less ideal to a cooler head.

Being willing to understand your feelings will have two benefits in the long term. First, it will help you to discover some of the aspects of your life that trigger negative feelings. That is useful, because you don't want to misinterpret your negative feelings and attribute them to something else. For example, you would like to be able to recognize when events in your personal life are spilling over into work and are causing you to feel badly about the work you do. Second, by understanding the sources of your own emotions, you will become more expert in understanding the people around you as well. We often ignore our own feelings—and then also ignore those of our colleagues.

Once you can better understand what emotions are and where your own emotions come from, you'll have a much better ability to practice emotional intelligence.

Art Markman, PhD, is the Annabel Irion Worsham Centennial Professor of Psychology and Marketing at the University of Texas at Austin and founding director of the program in the Human Dimensions of Organizations. He has written over 150 scholarly papers on topics including reasoning, decision making, and motivation. He is the author of several books including *Smart Thinking*, *Smart Change*, and *Habits of Leadership*.

CHAPTER 4

A Vocabulary for Your Emotions

by Susan David

Dealing effectively with emotions is a key leadership skill. And naming our emotions—what psychologists call *labeling*—is an important first step in dealing with them effectively. But it's harder than it sounds: Many of us struggle to identify what exactly we are feeling, and oftentimes the most obvious label isn't actually the most accurate.

There are a variety of reasons why this is so difficult: We've been trained to believe that strong emotions should be suppressed. We have certain (sometimes unspoken) societal and organizational rules against

Adapted from content posted on hbr.org on November 10, 2016, as "3 Ways to Better Understand Your Emotions" (product #H038KF)

expressing them. Or we've never learned a language to accurately describe our emotions. Consider these two examples:

> *Neena is in a meeting with Jared, and the whole time he has been saying things that make her want to explode. In addition to interrupting her at every turn, he's reminded everyone* again *about that one project she worked on that failed. She's so angry.*

> *Mikhail gets home after a long day and sighs as he hangs up his coat. His wife asks if anything's wrong. "I'm just stressed," he says, pulling out his laptop to finish a report.*

Anger and stress are two of the emotions we see most in the workplace—or at least, those are the terms we use for them most frequently. Yet they are often masks for deeper feelings that we could and should describe in more nuanced and precise ways, so that we develop greater levels of *emotional agility*, a critical capability that enables us to interact more successfully with ourselves and the world.

Yes, Neena may be mad, but what if she is also sad—sad that her project failed, and maybe also anxious that that failure is going to haunt her and her career? With Jared interrupting her so frequently, that anxiety feels increasingly justified. Why didn't the project work? And what's going to become of her job now? All of these emotions feed into her anger, but they are also separate feelings that she should identify and address.

And what if what's behind Mikhail's stress is the fact that he's just not sure he's in the right career? Long days used to be fun—why aren't they any more? He's surely stressed, but what's going on under that?

These questions open up a world of potential inquiry and answers for Neena and Mikhail. Like them, we need a more nuanced vocabulary for emotions, not just for the sake of being more precise, but because incorrectly diagnosing our emotions makes us respond incorrectly. If we think we need to attend to anger, we'll take a different approach than if we're handling disappointment or anxiety—or we might not address them at all. It's been shown that when people don't acknowledge and address their emotions, they display a lowered sense of well-being and more physical symptoms of stress, like headaches.[1] There is a high cost to avoiding our feelings.[2] On the flip side, having the right vocabulary allows us to see the real issue at hand—to take a messy experience, understand it more clearly, and build a roadmap to address the problem.[3]

Here are three ways to get a more accurate and precise sense of your emotions:

Broaden Your Emotional Vocabulary

Words matter. If you're experiencing a strong emotion, take a moment to consider what to call it. But don't stop there: Once you've identified it, try to come up with two more words that describe how you are feeling. You might be surprised at the breadth of your emotions—or that you've unearthed a deeper emotion buried beneath the more obvious one.

EXHIBIT 2

List of emotion terms

Angry	Sad	Anxious	Hurt	Embarrassed	Happy
Grumpy	Disappointed	Afraid	Jealous	Isolated	Thankful
Frustrated	Mournful	Stressed	Betrayed	Self-conscious	Trusting
Annoyed	Regretful	Vulnerable	Isolated	Lonely	Comfortable
Defensive	Depressed	Confused	Shocked	Inferior	Content
Spiteful	Paralyzed	Bewildered	Deprived	Guilty	Excited
Impatient	Pessimistic	Skeptical	Victimized	Ashamed	Relaxed
Disgusted	Tearful	Worried	Aggrieved	Repugnant	Relieved
Offended	Dismayed	Cautious	Tormented	Pathetic	Elated
Irritated	Disillusioned	Nervous	Abandoned	Confused	Confident

Exhibit 2 shows a vocabulary list of emotion terms; you can find much more by searching Google for any one of these.

It's equally important to do this with "positive" emotions as well as "negative" ones. Being able to say that you are *excited* about a new job (not just "I'm nervous") or *trusting* of a colleague (not just "He's nice"), for example, will help you set your intentions for the role or the relationship in a way that is more likely to lead to success down the road.

Consider the Intensity of the Emotion

We're apt to leap to basic descriptors like "angry" or "stressed" even when our feelings are far less extreme. I had a client, Ed (not his real name), who was struggling in his marriage; he frequently described his wife as "angry" and often got angry in return. But as the vocabulary chart suggests, every emotion comes in a variety of flavors. When we talked about other words for his wife's emotions, Ed saw that there were times that she was perhaps just annoyed or impatient. This insight completely changed their relationship, because he could suddenly see that she wasn't just angry all the time—and so could actually respond to her specific emotion and concern without getting angry himself. Similarly, it matters in your own self-assessment whether you are angry or just grumpy, mournful or just dismayed, elated or just pleased.

As you label your emotions, also rate them on a scale of 1–10. How deeply are you feeling the emotion? How urgent is it, or how strong? Does that make you choose a different set of words?

Write It Out

James Pennebaker has done 40 years of research into the links between writing and emotional processing. His experiments revealed that people who write about emotionally charged episodes experience a marked increase in their physical and mental well-being. Moreover, in a study of recently laid-off workers, he found that those who delved into their feelings of humiliation, anger, anxiety, and relationship difficulties were three times more likely to have been reemployed than those in control groups.

These experiments also revealed that over time those who wrote about their feelings began to develop insights into what those feelings meant (or didn't mean!), using phrases such as "I have learned . . ."; "It struck me that . . ."; "The reason that . . ."; "I now realize . . ."; and "I understand . . ." The process of writing allowed them to gain a new perspective on their emotions and to understand them and their implications more clearly.

Here's an exercise you can use to reflect through writing. You could do this every day, but it's particularly important when you're going through a tough time or a big transition, or if you're feeling emotional turmoil.

- Set a timer for 20 minutes.
- Using either a notebook or computer, write about your emotional experiences from the past week, month, or year.
- Don't worry about making it perfect or readable; go where your mind takes you.
- At the end, you don't have to save the document; the point is that those thoughts are now out of you and on the page.

You can also use these three approaches—broadening your vocabulary, noting the intensity of an emotion, and writing it out—when trying to better understand *another person's* emotions. As we saw with the example of Ed and his wife, we are just as likely to mislabel someone else's emotions as our own, with similarly complicating consequences. By understanding what they are feeling more precisely, you will be better equipped to respond in a constructive way.

Once you understand *what* you are feeling, then you can better address and learn from those more accurately described emotions. If Neena addresses the sadness and regret she feels in the wake of her failed project—as well as the anxiety about what it means for her career—that is more productive than trying to figure out how to deal with her anger at Jared. And if Mikhail can recognize his own career anxiety, he can start to craft a plan to build his future more deliberately—rather than simply miring himself in more of the same work when he gets home each night.

Susan David is a founder of the Harvard/McLean Institute of Coaching and is on faculty at Harvard University. She is author of *Emotional Agility* (Avery, 2016), based on the concept named by HBR as a Management Idea of the Year. As a speaker and adviser, David has worked with the senior leadership of hundreds of major organizations, including the United Nations, Ernst & Young, and the World Economic Forum. For more information, go to www.susandavid.com or follow her on Twitter @SusanDavid_PhD.

NOTES

1. Todd B. Kashdan, "Unpacking Emotion Differentiation: Transforming Unpleasant Experience by Perceiving Distinctions in Negativity," *Current Directions in Psychological Science* 24, no. 1 (2015).
2. Tori Rodriguez, "Negative Emotions Are Key to Well-Being," *Scientific American Mind*, May 1, 2013, https://www.scientificamerican.com/article/negative-emotions-key-well-being/.
3. Lisa Feldman Barrett et al., "Knowing What You're Feeling and Knowing What to Do About It: Mapping the Difference Between Emotion Differentiation and Emotion Regulation," *Cognition and Emotion* 15, no. 6 (2001): 713–724.

CHAPTER 5

Are You Sure You Show Respect?

by Christine Porath

For the last 20 years, I've studied the costs of incivility, as well as the benefits of civility. Across the board, I've found that civility pays. It enhances your influence and performance—and is positively associated with being perceived as a leader.[1]

Being respectful doesn't just benefit you, though; it benefits everyone around you. In a study of nearly 20,000 employees around the world (conducted with HBR), I found that when it comes to garnering commitment and engagement from employees, there's one thing that leaders need to demonstrate: respect. No other leadership behavior had a bigger effect on employees

Originally published on hbr.org on May 11, 2015, as "The Leadership Behavior That's Most Important to Employees" (product #H022CI)

across the outcomes we measured. Being treated with respect was more important to employees than recognition and appreciation, communicating an inspiring vision, providing useful feedback—or even opportunities for learning, growth, and development.

However, even when leaders know that showing respect is critical, many struggle to demonstrate it. If you're one of those leaders, consider the following steps:

Ask for focused feedback on your best behaviors

This technique, originated by researcher Laura Roberts and colleagues, will help you see your most respectful self.[2] Collect feedback via email from about 10 people (coworkers, friends, family). Ask each for positive examples of your best behavior. When and how have they seen you treat people well? After compiling the feedback, try to organize the data by summarizing and categorizing it into themes. For example, create a table with columns for commonality, examples (of the behavior), and your thoughts. You might also use Wordle.net to identify themes (you'll also get a colorful picture that can serve as a reminder of you at your best, most civil self). Then look for patterns: When, where, how, with whom are you at your best? Use your insights to reinforce what you're doing well. Be mindful of additional opportunities to be your best civil self. Leverage your interpersonal strengths.

Discover your shortcomings

Gather candid feedback from your colleagues and friends not only on what you're doing that conveys respect, but also on how you can improve. Specifically, what are your shortcomings? Identify a couple of trusted colleagues who have the best intentions for you and your organization. These are folks who you believe will provide direct and honest feedback. Ask for their views about how you treat other people. What do you do well? What could you do better? Listen carefully.

Consider the actions of Lieutenant Christopher Manning, a naval intelligence officer at the Pentagon, who has systematized ways to get continuous feedback from his direct reports. He expanded the scope of anonymous feedback surveys to include not only how he could improve the organization and himself as a leader, but also his team members' personal happiness (e.g., including how supported people felt by him), and work-life balance. He also instituted an anonymous comment box and encouraged an open-door policy. He even provides incentives for the most insightful critiques, such as the chance to attend a course or conference of interest, extra time off, and public recognition. And he meets one-on-one with his direct reports frequently. The regular feedback from these sources has helped him hone his skills. The bonus: He's found that those who report to him are more engaged and respect him more.

If you don't feel comfortable soliciting the feedback of your entire team, you can also ask a trusted direct report to gather feedback within the organization about whether you (the leader) consistently demonstrate civility, and what situations may trigger uncivil behavior.

Work with a coach

Coaches can uncover potential weaknesses through surveying and interviewing those with whom you work; they can also shadow you at meetings and events to pick up on subtleties including nonverbal behavior. A skilled coach may unearth some of the underlying assumptions, experiences, and personal qualities that make one prone to uncivil behavior.

Ask, specifically, how you can improve

Once you have clarity on which behaviors you want to improve, gather information from others about *how* best to go about this. This "feedforward" method, originated by author Marshall Goldsmith, is a terrific way to gather specific ideas for improving your behavior. The process consists of five steps:

1. Describe your goal clearly and simply to anyone you know.
2. Ask for two suggestions. Encourage creative ideas.
3. Listen carefully. Write the suggestions down.
4. Respond with "thank you." Nothing more. No excuses or defensiveness.
5. Repeat by asking additional people.

Enlist your team in keeping you accountable

Choose one change that could improve your behavior and then experiment, asking your team to help you by letting you know when they see improvement. For example, after a meeting, ask your team if they saw an improvement in the behavior that you're working on. What was the impact?

Here's an example: A woman I know of—let's call her Karen—enlisted her team to help her change a specific behavior. The team had grown increasingly frustrated by her inability to listen and empower them. While she was highly intelligent, she was constantly interrupting people in meetings and taking over initial ideas before they could even be presented. Karen worked with a coach to develop a technique to avoid this pattern—in this case, tapping her toe instead of interrupting someone. (Other coaches have developed similar techniques, such as counting to 10.) She informed her team that she was working on the behavior, and after a couple of days of meetings, she checked in with them on her progress. This helped establish a norm for more open dialogue—and a shared sense that the team members could count on each other to support their own development.

Make time for reflection

Keep a journal to provide insight into when/where/why you are your best and when you are uncivil. Identify situations that cause you to lose your temper. A leader I worked with named Monica noticed that she was far more curt in the late afternoon. She began her days before 5:00 a.m. By the time late afternoon hit, she was tired and was less emotionally attuned. She was brusque in conversations and less civil in email. Before she started journaling and reflecting on her day, Monica was unaware of the effect of time of day—and her energy management—on her demeanor. Now she is much more mindful of her behavior. For challenging situations such as conflict, people who trigger her, and communication that requires tact, she waits until the following morning to respond.

Consider tracking your own energy through the day via an energy audit tool, such as "Energy Audit—Awareness and Action," which is available from the University of Michigan.[3] Reflection helps you identify strategies to maintain composure and be your best, most civil self. After adopting some of the improvement strategies, do you see a decrease in incivility, or an increase in civility? Track yourself and review progress on a regular basis (e.g., weekly or monthly).

The path toward building greater self-awareness and treating people more respectfully at work doesn't have to be walked alone. While you're working to improve your own behavior, encourage your team members to do the same. Have an open discussion with your team about what you and your teammates do or say that conveys respect. How or when are you and your teammates less than civil to each other? What could you do or say better? Discuss what the team will gain by being more respectful of each other. As the entire team develops norms, hold one another accountable for them. Consider yourselves coaches that are helping to improve both individual and team performance.

The key to mastering civility begins with improving your self-awareness. Armed with this information, you can begin tweaking your behavior to enhance your influence and effectiveness. Small acts can have big returns. Your civility will cascade throughout your organization, with benefits to you—and your organization.

Christine Porath is an associate professor of management at Georgetown University, the author of *Mastering Civility: A Manifesto for the Workplace* (Grand Central Publishing, forthcoming), and a coauthor of *The Cost of Bad Behavior* (Portfolio, 2009).

NOTES

1. Christine L. Porath et al., "The Effects of Civility on Advice, Leadership, and Performance," *Journal of Applied Psychology* 100 no. 5, (September 2015): 1527–1541.
2. Center for Positive Organizations, "Reflected Best Self Exercise," http://positiveorgs.bus.umich.edu/cpo-tools/reflected-best-self-exercise-2nd-edition/.
3. The energy audit is available at http://positiveorgs.bus.umich.edu/wp-content/uploads/GrantSpreitzer-EnergyAudit.pdf.

SECTION THREE

Manage Your Emotions

CHAPTER 6

Make Your Emotions Work for You

by Susan David

We often hear tips and tricks for helping us to "control" our emotions, but that's the wrong idea. Strong emotions aren't bad; they don't need to be pushed down or controlled; they are, in fact, data. Our emotions evolved as a signaling system, a way to help us communicate with each other and to better understand ourselves. What we need to do is learn to develop *emotional agility*, the capacity to mine even the most difficult emotions for data that can help us make better decisions.

Adapted from content posted on hbr.org on November 28, 2016, as "How to Manage Your Emotions Without Fighting Them" (product #H038NO)

What's the Function of the Emotion?

To make the most of that data, ask yourself what the *function* of your emotion is. What is it telling you? What is it trying to signal?

Consider the example of Mikhail, who found himself in a perpetual cycle of stress because of the never-ending onslaught of tasks at work. As he more precisely defined his emotions, he realized what he was feeling wasn't just stress: he felt a more general dissatisfaction with his work, disappointment in some of his career choices, and anxiety about what the future held for him. Once Mikhail recognized and accepted these emotions, he was able to see what they were signaling to him: He had started to question whether he was on the right career path.

This revelation meant that instead of tackling a productivity problem by becoming more disciplined about prioritizing his tasks or saying no to extra work, Mikhail was able to do something much more appropriate and constructive. He began working with a career coach. By examining what his emotions were telling him, rather than pushing them away or focusing on the wrong problem, he learned something new about himself and was eventually able to find a new career path where he was just as busy—but felt much less stressed.

Our emotions can teach us valuable lessons. Let them shine a light on what you want to change, how you want to act in the future, or what is valuable to you.

Is Your Reaction Aligned with Your Values?

Our emotions can also help us understand our deepest values. They can often signal what is more important to us: You feel love for your family. You feel ambition at work and appreciate achievement and self-worth. You feel fulfilled when you've been able to help a direct report achieve their goals. You feel peace and satisfaction on a mountain summit. It's far better to focus on these deeper values rather than your immediate emotions, which can spur poor decisions.

Let's say that you need to give some difficult feedback to one of your direct reports. You're anxious about the conversation and you've been putting it off (which just makes you more anxious). In examining your emotions, you realize that one of the values behind your procrastination is fairness. She's a strong employee, and you just don't want to be unfair to her. So, you ask yourself: How does having or not having the conversation either bring you toward or move you away from your value of fairness? Looking at the situation in this light, you can see that giving her the feedback and helping her to succeed is actually *more* fair to her—and to your whole team—than caving to your anxieties. You've been able to unhook yourself from the thrall of your immediate emotions and make a better choice that is true to the values that underlie them.

This kind of thinking can help you avoid situations in which you do something that makes you feel good in the short term but doesn't align with your values in the long term. Avoiding a conversation is a typical example, but there are many others: brashly telling someone off for getting on your nerves when you value compassion; sticking with a comfortable job that doesn't align with your dream of starting a business when you value growth; criticizing yourself for the smallest things when you really value self-affirmation.

Managing emotions isn't just doing away with them; it's putting strategies in place that let you use them effectively rather than letting them govern your behaviors and actions. Your emotions are your natural guidance system—and they are more effective when you don't try to fight them.

Susan David is a founder of the Harvard/McLean Institute of Coaching and is on faculty at Harvard University. She is author of *Emotional Agility* (Avery, 2016), based on the concept named by HBR as a Management Idea of the Year. As a speaker and adviser, David has worked with the senior leadership of hundreds of major organizations, including the United Nations, Ernst & Young, and the World Economic Forum. For more information, go to www.susandavid.com or follow her on Twitter @SusanDavid_PhD.

CHAPTER 7

Defuse a Challenging Interaction

Conflicts stir up many emotions, especially negative thoughts and feelings. To successfully manage these disagreements in the moment, you need to address your own emotions as well as those of the other person.

Reframe Negative Thoughts

During difficult interactions, you may begin to question your perceptions about yourself. For example, suppose a direct report says, "I didn't attend the meeting because I didn't think you valued my ideas." In response, you

---

Adapted from "Address Emotions" in the Harvard ManageMentor topic "Difficult Interactions" (Harvard Business Publishing, 2016, electronic)

wonder to yourself, "Maybe I'm not a competent manager after all."

For many people, the sense that their self-image is being challenged creates intense emotions. These feelings can become overwhelming, making it virtually impossible to converse productively about any subject. To experience—and then let go of—difficult feelings:

- **Focus on the other person's intentions and on the facts.** If you discover that your employee had legitimate reasons for not showing up at a weekly meeting, your annoyance may fade away.

- **Examine your contributions to the problem.** If you realize that you've accidentally advised an employee to focus on an unnecessary task, your frustration may dissipate.

- **Question your assumptions.** If you find your belief that a colleague doesn't value product quality is mistaken, you may feel less anger over her tendency to take shortcuts.

Your goal in reframing negative thoughts is to be able to express your complete range of emotions without judging or blaming the other person.

Neutralize Unproductive Behaviors

Although you can work to manage your own reactions, you can't control those of the other person in the conflict. Try the techniques in exhibit 3 for dealing with unproductive behaviors:

EXHIBIT 3

Tackling unproductive behaviors

If the other person . . .	Try to . . .
Is aggressive and disrespectful	• Command respect by remaining calm. • Interrupt verbal attacks by repeating the person's name. • Communicate your bottom line: "When you're ready to speak to me with respect, I will take all the time you want to discuss this."
Doesn't listen to your side	• Go into the conversation prepared to support your own perceptions and ideas. • Redirect the person to your idea or information with phrases such as "I was just wondering . . . " "Bear with me a minute," or "What do you suppose . . . ?" • Acknowledge that the person possesses valuable knowledge, too.
Has an explosive outburst	• Take a break and then continue the conversation. • Get the person's attention by waving your arms and calling their name loudly enough to be heard. • Express genuine concern for the person: "Joe, nobody should have to feel this way! I want to help."
Is uncommunicative	• Schedule plenty of time for the person to respond to your ideas and questions. • Ask open-ended questions: "What are you thinking?" "How do you want to proceed?" "Where should we go from here?" • Gaze expectantly at the person for a longer-than-usual period of time after making a comment or asking a question.
Assumes that the situation can't get better	• Give the person time to consider your plan and get back to you. • Bring up and address the negative aspects of an idea before the other person does.

CHAPTER 8

Stay Grounded in Stressful Moments

by Leah Weiss

Mindfulness should be as much a physical practice as it is a mental one. Given its name, you might think mindfulness is something you do only with your mind. In fact, lots of research, including my own, has shown that paying attention to our bodies is often an easy way into mindfulness and helps us reduce stress while it's happening.

This may seem counterintuitive because when our mind is overwhelmed, our body is often the last thing we're thinking about. If we notice our bodies at all in moments of stress, most likely it is as they interrupt our

---

Adapted from content posted on hbr.org on November 18, 2016, as "A Simple Way to Stay Grounded in Stressful Moments" (product #H039WF)

normal activities: carpal tunnel syndrome, back pain, breast pumping, dental appointments, sore feet, sick days, or simply the routine hunger that forces us to stop what we're doing multiple times a day and eat. Yet if we focus our attention on our bodies, they can be our anchor in what's happening right now, even if the sensations are unpleasant.

This is how anchoring works: We bring our attention into our bodies, noticing—rather than avoiding—the tension, circulation, pain, pleasure, or just neutral physical experience of, say, our right shoulder or the arch of our left foot. This practice helps us snap back to reality. In fact, our bodies are the quickest, surest way back to the present moment when our minds are lost in rehashing the past or rehearsing the future.

We cause ourselves a lot of unnecessary suffering when our minds aren't paying attention. The amygdala, located in the brain's medial temporal lobe, is the part of the brain that detects and processes fear. When our amygdala is activated by a situation that is interpreted as a potential threat, even if we are just reading an unpleasant email, it initiates physiological changes such as increased muscle tension and accelerated breathing. This association becomes so strong that we take the body's reaction as evidence of danger, just as Pavlov's dogs took the sound of the bell as evidence of dinner. As a result, a vicious cycle can develop wherein the increased muscle tension and rapid breathing caused by an activated amygdala further activates the amygdala. Thankfully, we can use anchoring to break out of it.

One of my students who was working on a startup business used to panic before meeting with potential venture capitalists. His mind would spin with fears of the worst outcomes: his pitch rejected, his business idea exposed as worthless. Once he learned to tune in to his body, to use a brief minute to anchor by taking a few breaths and feeling his feet on the ground, he calmed down and became poised to have much better conversations. Here are some simple, effective anchoring practices you can use:

- **Take a single breath.** It takes just one intentional breath to change our perspective. A single breath gives you a break from the mind's chatter and a chance for your body to regulate after amping up in response to a perceived threat. Most of the time, when you're in distress, you're in the middle of telling yourself a story and you fully believe it. A breath can take you out of the story, making you less gullible. You can follow the breath into your body, where you gain just enough distance to judge whether your head is with you (in line with your current intentions and greater purpose) or against you, and then consciously choose which way you want to go.
- **Pay attention to emotions.** Another reason to anchor in your body is that it's where you feel your emotions, which are important to acknowledge even if they may seem like a liability, especially at work. I've studied the downsides of

emotional suppression and I can assure you—it's not beneficial.[1]

It's paradoxical, but nonjudgmentally engaging with negative emotions *negatively* correlates with negative emotions and mood disorder. In other words, if you acknowledge and recognize unpleasant emotions, they have less power to cause you distress. In one study, participants wrote every day for four days about either a traumatic experience or a neutral event.[2] Those who wrote about trauma made fewer health center visits in the following six months than those who wrote about a neutral event. When you pay attention to your body, you can catch emotional information upstream, before it hijacks your whole system—once it does, it's too late to use it to your advantage.

- **Remember that your colleagues have bodies too.** Annoyed with your boss? Think you can't last another day with an impossible colleague? If you let it, your body can connect you to other people—even difficult ones—since the body is a major part of what we have in common. This sounds obvious, but the implications are profound. Our bodies and the pleasure and pain that come with them—their attendant aches and illnesses, their needs and indignities, the impossibility of choosing the one we want, the fear of losing it someday, and the ways we fight our bodies or pretend they don't exist—are shared experiences. When you ignore your body (or try to), you miss out on a fundamental part of what we have in common. The empathy gained from this awareness helps you to have productive professional relationships, rather than suffering from ongoing frustration and pain.

- **Magnify little pleasures.** Don't underestimate the joy of taking that first sip of afternoon coffee. It's human nature to notice pain more than pleasure, but with reminders and practice you can experience joy throughout the day in the simple, reliable pleasures of having a body. It might be from sitting when you've been standing for too long, or standing up and stretching when you've been sitting; holding a new pen with a particularly cushy, ergonomic grip; laughing hard when something's funny; eating when you're hungry; the relative quiet of the office after a morning with screaming kids; slipping out of uncomfortable shoes under your desk. Every day, no matter how lousy, affords countless opportunities like these to feel good. Recently, I had a meeting at the VA hospital in Palo Alto and came across two veterans as I was walking. They were sitting in front of the building, both in wheelchairs. One man leaned over to his companion and said, "Well, it's great that we can move our hands." The other responded, "Yes, you are right. That is great!" Their perspective provides a powerful reminder that most of us can, if we choose, find within our daily routine a small joy worthy of being celebrated.

Stress is an inevitable aspect of our lives at work, but you don't need elaborate practices or escape mechanisms to engage with it. You simply need to have the wherewithal to ground yourself in a physical sensation, to anchor and come back to reality. You need only a brief moment to tap your feet on the ground and be reminded that you have a reliable and ever-present instrument to mitigate your stress. And, it just so happens, you were born with it.

Leah Weiss is a teacher, writer, and researcher at Stanford Graduate School of Business, the Director of Education at HopeLab, and the author of the forthcoming book *Heart at Work.*

NOTES

1. Debora Cutuli, "Cognitive Reappraisal and Expressive Suppression Strategies Role in the Emotion Regulation: An Overview on Their Modulatory Effects and Neural Correlates," *Frontiers in Systems Neuroscience*, September 19, 2014; Andrea Hermann et al., "Brain Structural Basis of Cognitive Reappraisal and Expressive Suppression," *Social Cognitive and Effective Neuroscience* 9, no. 9 (September 2014): 1435–1442.; and Sally Moore et al., "Are Expressive Suppression and Cognitive Reappraisal Associated with Stress-Related Symptoms?" *Behaviour Research and Therapy* 46, no. 9 (September 2008): 993–1000
2. James J. Gross, ed., *Handbook of Emotion Regulation*, 2nd edition. New York: The Guilford Press, 2014.

CHAPTER 9

Recovering from an Emotional Outburst

by Susan David

It happens—we all get emotional at work. You might scream, or cry, or pound the table and stamp your feet. This is not ideal office behavior, of course, and there are ramifications to these outbursts, but they don't have to be career-killers either. If you take a close look at what happened, why you acted the way you did, and take steps to remedy the situation, you can turn an outburst into an opportunity.

Adapted from content posted on hbr.org on May 8, 2015, as "Recovering from an Emotional Outburst at Work" (product #H022A3)

If you tend to suppress your emotions, you're likely to just ignore your tantrum and move on. If you are prone to ruminating over your mistakes, you'll overthink your outburst and beat yourself up about it.

Neither of these strategies is productive; they don't help you solve the problem *or* promote your own well-being. Instead, treat your outburst for what it is: data. A key emotional intelligence skill is being able to manage your emotion, but you can't manage what you can't recognize and understand. So first, be open to emotions. What was I feeling here? Emotions are signals, beacons that show you that you care about something.

To *recognize* your emotions, you have to be able to differentiate between feelings—sadness, anger, frustration (see chapter 4 in this guide). In many work environments, people suffer from what psychologists call *alexithymia*—a dispositional difficulty in accurately labeling and expressing what they're feeling. These people tend to be vague about their emotions. So a manager will say to herself, for example, "Gee, I yelled because I was really stressed out." But that gives her no information about what was really going on.

Once you've recognized the emotion—fear, disappointment, anger—your next step is to *understand* what, exactly, caused it: "Why is it that I reacted in this particular way?" "What was happening in this situation that I found upsetting?" "What values of mine may have been transgressed or challenged?" For example, maybe you lost it and screamed at a colleague when you found out that your project was cut. If you dig deeper, you may find that it wasn't exactly about the project but rather how the decision was made—that you didn't feel it was made fairly.

The research on emotions shows that there are general triggers that you should be aware of.[1] When your outburst is anger—yelling, stomping your feet—it's typically because you're frustrated or feel thwarted. You've been stopped from doing something that's important to you. When you feel sadness or cry, it's usually because of a loss. Acting out on anxiety is prompted by a sense of threat. It's helpful to think about these universal triggers, and then ask, "What is it specifically that was important to me in this situation?"

Once you've recognized how you feel, and why you feel it, you can focus on what to do to make things better—to *manage* the situation. It goes without saying that you should apologize if you yelled or lost your cool, but that's not enough. Your goal isn't just to repair the relationship, but to strengthen it.

After you've calmed down and you return to your team the following day or week, instead of saying, "Gee, I'm so sorry about what I did; now let's move on," address what really happened for you. You might say something like, "I got really mad and I'm not proud of my behavior. I've been thinking long and hard about what it was that I found so upsetting and I've realized that my sense of fairness was challenged because of how the defunding decisions were made."

There's research that shows that when you appropriately disclose your emotions in this way, people are more likely to treat you with compassion and forgiveness than if you had just offered an apology.[2] From there you start a shared conversation about what's important to each of you and how you can work better together.

No one wants to earn a reputation as a crier or a screamer at work. Instead of running and hiding or wallowing in self-pity when you've lost it, bring a good dose of compassion and curiosity to the situation. To be kind and compassionate toward yourself—especially in the moments you are least proud of—is not the same as letting yourself off the hook. In fact, studies show that people who are self-compassionate are much more likely to hold themselves to high standards and work to make things right.[3] And treating yourself that way is more likely to inspire others to do the same.

Susan David is a founder of the Harvard/McLean Institute of Coaching and is on faculty at Harvard University. She is author of *Emotional Agility* (Avery, 2016), based on the concept named by HBR as a Management Idea of the Year. As a speaker and adviser, David has worked with the senior leadership of hundreds of major organizations, including the United Nations, Ernst & Young, and the World Economic Forum. For more information, go to www.susandavid.com or follow her on Twitter @SusanDavid_PhD.

NOTES

1. R. S. Lazarus, "From Psychological Stress to Emotions: A History of Changing Outlooks," *Annual Review of Psychology* 44 (1993): 1–22.
2. James J. Gross, "Emotion Regulation: Affective, Cognitive, and Social Consequences," *Psychophysiology* 39 (2002): 281–291.
3. Kristin D. Neff, "Self-Compassion, Self-Esteem, and Well-Being," *Social and Personality Psychology Compass* 5, no. 1 (2011): 1–12.

SECTION FOUR

Everyday Emotional Intelligence

CHAPTER 10

Writing Resonant Emails

by Andrew Brodsky

Imagine sending a detailed question to your boss and getting a one-word response: "No." Is she angry? Offended by your email? Or just very busy? When I conduct research with organizations on the topic of communication, one of the most common themes raised by both employees and managers is the challenge of trying to communicate emotional or sensitive issues over email. Email, of course, lacks most normal cues for relaying emotion, such as tone of voice and facial expressions.

But in many cases, using email is simply unavoidable. So how can you balance the need to communicate with

---

Adapted from content posted on hbr.org on April 23, 2013, as "The Do's and Don'ts of Work Email" (product #H020WK)

avoiding the potential pitfalls of using emotion in email? Here are three concrete, research-based recommendations:

Understand what drives how emails are interpreted

It is clear that people often misinterpret emotion in email, but what drives the direction of the misinterpretation? For one, people infuse their emotional expectations into how they read messages, regardless of the sender's actual intent.[1] Consider the email, "*Good job on the current draft, but I think we can continue to improve it.*" Coming from a peer, this email will seem very collaborative; coming from a supervisor, it may seem critical.

In addition to relative position (emails from people high in power tend to be perceived as more negative), there are other contextual factors to consider: the length of a relationship (emails from people we know well tend to be perceived as less negative), the emotional history of the relationship, and the individual's personality (negative people tend to perceive messages as more negative).

The first step in avoiding miscommunication is to try to stand in the recipient's shoes, and imagine how they are likely to interpret your message. Doing so can help you to prevent misunderstandings before they ever occur.

Mimic behaviors

What is the best way to convey emotions via email? Emoticons? Word choice? Exclamation points? There is no single correct answer; the proper cues will vary based on the context. For instance, you likely wouldn't want to send a smiley face emoticon to a client organization that is known for having a very formal culture. Alternatively, you wouldn't want to send an overly formal email to a very close colleague.

One strategy that has been found to be very effective across settings is to engage in behavioral mimicry—using emoticons, word-choice, and slang/jargon in a similar manner to the person with whom you are communicating. In a set of studies of American, Dutch, and Thai negotiators, using behavioral mimicry in the early stages of text-based chat negotiations increased individual outcomes by 30%. This process of mimicry increases trust because people tend to feel an affinity toward those who act similarly to them.[2]

State your emotions

While mimicking behaviors can be effective, it is still a rather subtle strategy that leaves the potential for emotional ambiguity. The simplest solution to avoid any confusion is to just explicitly state the emotion that you want to relay in your email.

One excellent example of how this works comes from a media organization I recently worked with. I asked employees for an email that they felt was written very poorly, and one employee provided me with the following message from a manager:

> *The intro of the commercial needs to be redone. I'm sure that's the client's doing and you will handle it :). Warm Regards, [Manager's Name].*

To me as an outsider (and I'm guessing to the manager as well), this email seemed well crafted to avoid offending the employee. However, the employee felt differently and explained: "She knows perfectly well that I made the terrible intro, and she was saying, 'Well, I'm sure the client made that segment and that you will tackle it,' and then she put a little smiley face at the end. So overall, a condescendingly nasty tone."

If the manager had avoided subtlety and stated her meaning directly, there might have been less room for interpretation. For example, what if she had written:

> *I am very happy with your work so far. I think the intro could be improved, though; would you mind giving it another shot?*

The employee would have had far less ambiguity to fill in with her own emotional expectations.

Yet people rarely state their intended emotions, even when the stakes are high. Research from NYU has shown that many people are overconfident in their ability to accurately relay emotions when it comes to email.[3] It may seem obvious to the message sender that a coworker who never takes sick days will realize a comment about them leaving early is humorous rather than serious. However, that coworker might be particularly concerned about being seen as lazy and will feel hurt or offended.

Given the constantly evolving nature of organizational communication, there is still a lot to learn about effective email use. However, there are some clear areas where we can improve. In reality, we all have the same flaw: We tend to be overly focused on ourselves and our own goals, while failing to amply account for other people's perspectives. Using these methods for bridging your and your email recipient's perspectives, by both increasing message clarity and building trust, will help you to ensure effective communication.

Andrew Brodsky is a PhD candidate in organizational behavior at Harvard Business School.

NOTES

1. Kristin Byron, "Carrying Too Heavy a Load? The Communication and Miscommunication of Emotion by Email," *Academy of Management Review* 33, no. 2 (April 2008): 309–327.
2. William W. Maddux et al., "Chameleons Bake Bigger Pies and Take Bigger Pieces: Strategy Behavioral Mimicry Facilitates Negotiation Outcomes," *Journal of Experimental Social Psychology* 44, no. 2 (March 2008): 461–468; and Roderick I. Swaab et al., "Early Words That Work: When and How Virtual Linguistic Mimicry Facilitates Negotiation Outcomes," *Journal of Experimental Psychology* 47, no. 3 (May 2011): 616–621.
3. Justin Kruger et al., "Egocentrism Over E-mail: Can We Communicate as Well as We Think?" *Journal of Personality and Social Psychology* 89, no. 6 (December 2005): 925–936.

CHAPTER 11

Running Powerful Meetings

by Annie McKee

Yes, we all hate meetings. Yes, they are usually a waste of time. And yes, they're here to stay. So it's your responsibility as a leader to make them better. This doesn't mean just making them shorter, more efficient, and more organized. People need to enjoy them and—dare I say it—have fun.

So how do we fix meetings so they are more enjoyable and produce more positive feelings? Sure, invite the right people, create better agendas, and be better prepared. Those are baseline fixes. But if you really want to improve how people work together at meetings, you'll need to rely on—and maybe develop—a couple of key

---

Adapted from content posted on hbr.org on March 23, 2015, as "Empathy Is Key to a Great Meeting" (product #H01YDY)

emotional intelligence competencies: empathy and emotional self-management.

Why empathy? Empathy is a competency that allows you to read people. Who is supporting whom? Who is pissed off, and who is coasting? Where is the resistance? This isn't as easy as it seems. Sometimes, the smartest resisters often look like supporters, but they're not supportive at all. They're smart, sneaky idea killers.

Carefully reading people will also help you understand the major and often hidden conflicts in the group. Hint: These conflicts probably have nothing to do with the topics discussed or decisions being made at the meeting. They are far more likely to be linked to very human dynamics like who is allowed to influence whom (headquarters versus the field, expats versus local nationals) and power dynamics between genders and among people of various races.

Empathy lets you see and manage these power dynamics. Many of us would like to think that these sorts of concerns—and office politics in general—are beneath us, unimportant, or just for those Machiavellian folks we all dislike. Realistically, though, power is hugely important in groups because it is the real currency in most organizations. And it plays out in meetings. Learning to read how the flow of power is moving and shifting can help you lead the meeting—and everything else.

Keep in mind that employing empathy will help you understand how people are responding to *you*. As a leader you may be the most powerful person at the meeting. Some people, the dependent types, will defer at every turn. That feels good, for a minute. Carry on that way, and you're likely to create a dependent group—or one that is polarized between those who will do anything you want and those who will not.

This is where emotional self-management comes in, for a couple of reasons. First, take a look at the dependent folks in your meetings. Again, it can feel really good to have people admire you and agree with your every word. In fact, this can be a huge relief in our conflict-ridden organizations. But again, if you don't manage your response, you will make group dynamics worse. You will also look like a fool. Others are reading the group, too, and they will rightly read that you like it when people go along with you. They will see that you are falling prey to your own ego or to those who want to please or manipulate you.

Second, strong emotions set the tone for the entire group. We take our cue from one another about how to feel about what's going on around us. Are we in danger? Is there cause for celebration? Should we be fed up and cynical or hopeful and committed? Here's why this matters in meetings: If you, as a leader, effectively project out your more positive emotions, such as hope and enthusiasm, others will "mirror" these feelings and the general tone of the group will be marked by optimism and a sense of "we're in this together, and we can do it."[1] And there is a strong neurological link between feelings and cognition. We think more clearly and more creatively when our feelings are largely positive and when we are appropriately challenged, as Mihaly Csikszentmihalyi wrote in his classic *Creativity: Flow and the Psychology of Discovery and Invention.*

The other side of the coin is obvious. Your negative emotions are also contagious, and they are almost always destructive if unchecked and unmanaged. Express anger, contempt, or disrespect, and you will definitely push people into fight mode—individually and collectively. Express disdain, and you'll alienate people far beyond the end of the meeting. And it doesn't matter who you feel this way about. All it takes is for people to see it, and they will catch it—and worry that next time your target will be them.

This is not to say that all positive emotions are good all the time or that you should never express negative emotions. The point is that the leader's emotions are highly infectious. Know this and manage your feelings accordingly to create the kind of environment where people can work together to make decisions and get things done.

It may go without saying, but you can't do any of this with your phone on. As Daniel Goleman shares in his book *Focus: The Hidden Driver of Excellence,* we are not nearly as good at multitasking as we think we are. Actually we stink at it. So turn it off and pay attention to the people you are with today.

In the end, it's your job to make sure people leave your meeting feeling pretty good about what's happened, their contributions, and you as the leader. Empathy allows you to read what's going on, and self-management helps you move the group to a mood that supports getting things done—and happiness.

Annie McKee is a senior fellow at the University of Pennsylvania and the director of the PennCLO Executive Doctoral Program. She is the author of *Primal Leadership* (with Daniel Goleman and Richard Boyatzis), as well as *Resonant Leadership* and *Becoming a Resonant Leader*. Her new book, *How to Be Happy at Work*, is forthcoming from Harvard Business Review Press in September 2017.

NOTE

1. V. Ramachandran, "The Neurons That Shaped Civilization," TED talk, November 2009, https://www.ted.com/talks/vs_ramachandran_the_neurons_that_shaped_civilization?language=en.

CHAPTER 12

Giving Difficult Feedback

by Monique Valcour

Over the years, I've asked hundreds of executive students what skills they believe are essential for leaders. "The ability to give tough feedback" comes up frequently. But what exactly is "tough feedback"? The phrase connotes bad news, like when you have to tell a team member that they've screwed up on something important. "Tough" also signifies the way we think we need to be when giving negative feedback: firm, resolute, and unyielding.

But "tough" also points to the discomfort some of us experience when giving negative feedback, and to the challenge of doing so in a way that motivates change

---

Adapted from content posted on hbr.org on August 11, 2015, as "How to Give Tough Feedback That Helps People Grow" (product #H029QB)

instead of making the other person feel defensive. Managers fall into a number of common traps when offering feedback. We might be angry at an employee and use the conversation to blow off steam rather than to coach. Or we may delay giving needed feedback because we anticipate that the employee will become argumentative and refuse to accept responsibility. We might try surrounding negative feedback with positive feedback, like disguising a bitter-tasting pill in a spoonful of honey. But this approach is misguided, because we don't want the negative feedback to slip by unnoticed in the honey. Instead, it's essential to create conditions in which the receiver can take in feedback, reflect on it, and learn from it.

To get a feel for what this looks like in practice, I juxtapose two feedback conversations that occurred following a workplace conflict. MJ Paulitz, a physical therapist in the Pacific Northwest, was treating a hospital patient one day when a fellow staff member paged her. Following procedure, she excused herself and stepped out of the treatment room to respond to the page. The colleague who sent it didn't answer her phone when MJ called, nor had she left a message describing the situation that warranted the page. This happened two more times during the same treatment session. The third time she left her patient to respond to the page, MJ lost her cool and left an angry voicemail message for her colleague. Upset upon hearing the message, the staff member reported it to their supervisor as abusive.

MJ's first feedback session took place in her supervisor's office. She recalls, "When I went into his office, he had already decided that I was the person at fault, he had all the information he needed, and he wasn't interested in hearing my side of the story. He did not address the three times she pulled me out of patient care. He did not acknowledge that that might have been the fuse that set me off." Her supervisor referred MJ to the human resources department for corrective action. She left seething with a sense of injustice.

MJ describes the subsequent feedback conversation with human resources as transformative. "The woman in HR could see that I had a lot of just-under-the-surface feelings, and she acknowledged them. The way she did it was genius: She eased into it. She didn't make me go first. Instead, she said, 'I can only imagine what you're feeling right now. Here you are in my office, in corrective action. If it were me, I might be feeling angry, frustrated, embarrassed . . . Are any of these true for you?' That made a huge difference."

With trust established, MJ was ready to take responsibility for her behavior and commit to changing it. Next the HR person said, "Now let's talk about how you reacted to those feelings in the moment." She created a space that opened up a genuine dialogue.

The subsequent conversation created powerful learning that has stuck with MJ to this day:

> *Oftentimes, when we're feeling a strong emotion, we go down what the HR person called a "cowpath," because it's well worn, very narrow, and always leads to the same place. Let's say you're angry. What do you do?*

> *You blow up. It's okay that you feel those things; it's just not okay to blow up. She asked me to think about what I could do to get on a different path.*
>
> *The feedback from the HR person helped me learn to find the space between what I'm feeling and the next thing that slides out of my mouth. She gave me the opportunity to grow internally. What made it work was establishing a safe space, trust, and rapport, and then getting down to "you need to change"—rather than starting with "you need to change," which is what my supervisor did. I did need to change; that was the whole point of the corrective action. But she couldn't start there, because I would have become defensive, shut down and not taken responsibility. I still to this day think that my coworker should have been reprimanded. But I also own my part in it. I see that I went down that cowpath, and I know that I won't do it a second time.*

The difference in the two feedback sessions illustrated above boils down to coaching, which deepens self-awareness and catalyzes growth, versus reprimanding, which sparks self-protection and avoidance of responsibility. To summarize, powerful, high-impact feedback conversations share the following elements:

1. An intention to help the employee grow, rather than to show him he was wrong. The feedback should increase, not drain, the employee's motivation and resources for change. When preparing for a feedback conversation as a manager, reflect

on what you hope to achieve and on what impact you'd like to have on the employee, perhaps by doing a short meditation just before the meeting.

2. Openness on the part of the feedback giver, which is essential to creating a high-quality connection that facilitates change. If you start off feeling uncomfortable and self-protective, your employee will match that energy, and you'll each leave the conversation frustrated with the other person.

3. Inviting the employee into the problem-solving process. You can ask questions such as: What ideas do you have? What are you taking away from this conversation? What steps will you take, by when, and how will I know?

Giving developmental feedback that sparks growth is a critical challenge to master, because it can make the difference between an employee who contributes powerfully and positively to the organization and one who feels diminished by the organization and contributes far less. A single conversation can switch an employee on—or shut her down. A true developmental leader sees the raw material for brilliance in every employee and creates the conditions to let it shine, even when the challenge is tough.

Monique Valcour is a management academic, coach, and consultant.

CHAPTER 13

Making Smart Decisions

A summary of the full-length HBR article "Why Good Leaders Make Bad Decisions" by **Andrew Campbell**, **Jo Whitehead**, *and* **Sydney Finkelstein**, *highlighting key ideas and company examples, and a checklist for putting the idea into action.*

IDEA IN BRIEF

- Leaders make decisions largely through unconscious processes that neuroscientists call pattern recognition and emotional tagging. These processes usually make for quick, effective decisions, but they can be distorted by bias.

Adapted from *Harvard Business Review*, February 2009 (product #R0902D)

- Managers need to find systematic ways to recognize the sources of bias—what the authors call "red flag conditions"—and then design safeguards that introduce more analysis, greater debate, or stronger governance. The authors identify three of these red flag conditions as the presence of:
  - Inappropriate self-interest, which, according to research, can bias even well-intentioned professionals such as doctors and auditors.
  - Distorting attachments to people, places, and things—for example, an executive's reluctance to sell a business unit they've worked in.
  - Misleading memories, which may seem relevant and comparable to the current situation but lead our thinking down the wrong path by obscuring important differentiating factors.
- By using the approach described in this article, companies will avoid many flawed decisions that are caused by the way our brains operate.

IDEA IN PRACTICE

Leaders make quick decisions by recognizing patterns in the situations they encounter, and then responding to the emotional associations attached to those patterns. Most of the time, the process works well, but it can result in serious mistakes when those emotional associations are biased.

Example: When Wang Laboratories launched its own personal computer, founder An Wang chose to create a proprietary operating system even though the IBM PC was clearly becoming the standard. This blunder was influenced by his belief that IBM had cheated him early in his career, which made him reluctant to consider using a system linked to an IBM product.

To guard against distorted decision making and strengthen the decision process, get the help of an independent person to identify which decision makers are likely to be affected by self-interest, emotional attachments, or misleading memories.

Example: The about-to-be-promoted head of the cosmetics business at one Indian company was considering whether to appoint her number-two as her successor. She recognized that her judgment might be distorted by her attachment to her colleague and by her vested interest in keeping her workload down during the transition. The executive asked a headhunter to evaluate her colleague and to determine whether better candidates could be found externally.

If the risk of distorted decision making is high, build safeguards into the decision process. Expose decision makers to additional experience and analysis, design in more debate and opportunities for challenge, add more oversight, and monitor whether the decision is generating the expected results.

Example: In helping the CEO make an important strategic decision, the chairman of one global

IDENTIFYING RED FLAGS

Red flags are useful only if they can be spotted before a decision is made. How can you recognize them in complex situations? We have developed the following seven-step process:

1. ***Lay out the range of options.*** It's never possible to list them all. But it's normally helpful to note the extremes. These provide boundaries for the decision.

2. ***List the main decision makers.*** Who is going to be influential in making the judgment calls and the final choice? There may be only one or two people involved. But there could also be 10 or more.

3. ***Choose one decision maker to focus on.*** It's usually best to start with the most influential person. Then identify red flag conditions that might distort that individual's thinking. Discuss with the individual if needed.

4. ***Check for inappropriate self-interest or distorting attachments.*** Is any option likely to be particularly attractive or unattractive to the decision maker because of personal interests or attachments to people, places, or things? Do any of these interests or attachments conflict with the objectives of the decision?

5. ***Check for misleading memories.*** What are the uncertainties in this decision? For each area of uncertainty, consider whether the decision maker might draw on potentially misleading memories. Think about past experiences that could mislead, especially ones with strong emotional associations. Think also about previous judgments that could now be unsound, given the current situation.

6. ***Repeat the analysis with the next-most-influential person.*** In a complex case, it may be necessary to consider many more people, and the process may bring to light a long list of possible red flags.

7. ***Review the list of red flags you have identified for bias.*** Determine whether the balance of red flags is likely to bias the decision in favor of or against some options. If so, put one or more safeguards in place. Biases can cancel each other out, so it is necessary to assess the balance taking account of the likely influence of each person involved in the decision.

chemical company encouraged the chief executive to seek advice from investment bankers, set up a project team to analyze options, and create a steering committee that included the chairman and the CFO to review the CEO's proposal.

Andrew Campbell is a director of the Ashridge Strategic Management Centre in England. **Jo Whitehead** (jo.whitehead@ashridge.org.uk) is a director of the Ashridge Strategic Management Centre in London. **Sydney Finkelstein** is the Steven Roth Professor of Management and Director of the Leadership Center at the Tuck School of Business at Dartmouth College. His new book is *Superbosses: How Exceptional Leaders Manage the Flow of Talent* (Portfolio/Penguin, 2016). Campbell, Whitehead, and Finkelstein are the coauthors of *Think Again: Why Good Leaders Make Bad Decisions and How to Keep It from Happening to You* (Harvard Business Review Press, 2008).

CHAPTER 14

An Emotional Strategy for Negotiations

by Alison Wood Brooks

It is, without questions, my favorite day of the semester—the day when I teach my MBA students a negotiation exercise called "Honoring the Contract."

I assign students to partners, and each reads a different account of a (fictitious) troubled relationship between a supplier (a manufacturer of computer components) and a client (a search engine startup). They learn that the two parties signed a detailed contract eight months earlier, but now they're at odds over several of

Reprinted from "Emotion and the Art of Negotiation" in *Harvard Business Review*, December 2015 (product #R1512C)

the terms (sales volume, pricing, product reliability, and energy efficiency specs). Each student assumes the role of either client or supplier and receives confidential information about company finances and politics. Then each pair is tasked with renegotiating—a process that could lead to an amended deal, termination of the contract, or expensive litigation.

What makes this simulation interesting, however, lies not in the details of the case but in the top-secret instructions given to one side of each pairing before the exercise begins: "Please start the negotiation with a display of anger. You must display anger for a minimum of 10 minutes at the beginning." The instructions go on to give specific tips for showing anger: Interrupt the other party. Call them "unfair" or "unreasonable." Blame them personally for the disagreement. Raise your voice.

Before the negotiations begin, I spread the pairs all over the building so that the students can't see how others are behaving. Then, as the pairs negotiate, I walk around and observe. Although some students struggle, many are spectacularly good at feigning anger. They wag a finger in their partner's face. They pace around. I've never seen the exercise result in a physical confrontation—but it has come close. Some of the negotiators who did not get the secret instructions react by trying to defuse the other person's anger. But some react angrily themselves—and it's amazing how quickly the emotional responses escalate. When I bring everyone back into the classroom after 30 minutes, there are always students still yelling at each other or shaking their heads in disbelief.

During the debriefing, we survey the pairs to see how angry they felt and how they fared in resolving the problem. Often, the more anger the parties showed, the more likely it was that the negotiation ended poorly—for example, in litigation or an impasse (no deal). Once I've clued the entire class in on the setup, discussion invariably makes its way to this key insight: Bringing anger to a negotiation is like throwing a bomb into the process, and it's apt to have a profound effect on the outcome.

Until 20 years ago, few researchers paid much attention to the role of emotions in negotiating—how feelings can influence the way people overcome conflict, reach agreement, and create value when dealing with another party. Instead, negotiation scholars focused primarily on strategy and tactics—particularly the ways in which parties can identify and consider alternatives, use leverage, and execute the choreography of offers and counteroffers. Scientific understanding of negotiation also tended to home in on the transactional nature of working out a deal: how to get the most money or profit from the process. Even when experts started looking at psychological influences on negotiations, they focused on diffuse and nonspecific moods—such as whether negotiators felt generally positive or negative, and how that affected their behavior.

Over the past decade, however, researchers have begun examining how specific emotions—anger, sadness, disappointment, anxiety, envy, excitement, and regret—can affect the behavior of negotiators. They've studied the differences between what happens when people simply feel these emotions and what happens when they also express them to the other party through words or actions. In negotiations that are less transactional and involve parties in long-term relationships, understanding the role of emotions is even more important than it is in transactional deal making.

This new branch of research is proving extremely useful. We all have the ability to regulate how we experience emotions, and specific strategies can help us improve tremendously in that regard. We also have some control over the extent to which we express our feelings—and again, there are specific ways to cloak (or emphasize) an expression of emotion when doing so may be advantageous. For instance, research shows that feeling or looking anxious results in suboptimal negotiation outcomes. So individuals who are prone to anxiety when brokering a deal can take certain steps both to limit their nervousness and to make it less obvious to their negotiation opponent. The same is true for other emotions.

In the pages that follow, I discuss—and share coping strategies for—many of the emotions people typically feel over the course of a negotiation. Anxiety is most likely to crop up before the process begins or during its early stages. We're prone to experience anger or excitement in the heat of the discussions. And we're most likely to feel disappointment, sadness, or regret in the aftermath.

Avoiding Anxiety

Anxiety is a state of distress in reaction to threatening stimuli—in particular, novel situations that have the potential for undesirable outcomes. In contrast to anger, which motivates people to escalate conflict (the "fight" part of the fight-or-flight response), anxiety trips the "flight" switch and makes people want to exit the scene.

Because patience and persistence are often desirable when negotiating, the urge to exit quickly is counterproductive. But the negative effects of feeling anxious while negotiating may go further. In my recent research, I wondered if anxious negotiators also develop low aspirations and expectations, which could lead them to make timid first offers—a behavior that directly predicts poor negotiating outcomes.

In work with Maurice Schweitzer in 2011, I explored how anxiety influences negotiations. First we surveyed 185 professionals about the emotions they expected to feel before negotiating with a stranger, negotiating to buy a car, and negotiating to increase their salary. When dealing with a stranger or asking for a higher salary, anxiety was the dominant emotional expectation; when negotiating for the car, anxiety was second only to excitement.

To understand how anxiety can affect negotiators, we then asked a separate group of 136 participants to negotiate a cell phone contract that required agreeing on a purchase price, a warranty period, and the length of the contract. We induced anxiety in half the participants by having them listen to continuous three-minute clips of the menacing theme music from the film *Psycho*, while the other half listened to pleasant music by Handel. (Researchers call this *incidental* emotional manipulation, and it's quite powerful. Listening to the *Psycho* music is genuinely uncomfortable: People's palms get sweaty, and some listeners become jumpy.)

In this experiment and three others, we found that anxiety had a significant effect on how people negotiated. People experiencing anxiety made weaker first offers, responded more quickly to each move the counterpart made, and were more likely to exit negotiations early (even though their instructions clearly warned that exiting early would reduce the value they received from the negotiation). Anxious negotiators made deals that were 12% less financially attractive than those made by negotiators in the neutral group. We did discover one caveat, however: People who gave themselves high ratings in a survey on negotiating aptitude were less affected by anxiety than others.

Those experiments examined what happens when people feel anxious. But what happens when they express that anxiety, making it clear to their counterparts that they're nervous (and perhaps vulnerable)? In 2012, with Francesca Gino and Maurice Schweitzer, I conducted eight experiments to explore how anxious people behaved in situations in which they could seek advice from others. We found that relative to people who did not feel anxious, they were less confident, more likely to consult others when making decisions, and less able to discriminate between good and bad advice. In the most relevant of these experiments, we found that anxious participants did not discount advice from someone with a stated conflict of interest, whereas subjects feeling neutral emotions looked upon that advice skeptically. Although this research didn't directly address how the subjects would negotiate, it suggests that people who express anxiety are more likely to be taken advantage of in a negotiation, especially if the other party senses their distress.

Excellent negotiators often make their counterparts feel anxious on purpose. For example, on the TV show *Shark Tank*, six wealthy investors ("sharks") negotiate with entrepreneurs hoping for funding. The entrepreneurs must pitch their ideas in front of a huge television audience and face questions from the investors that are often aggressive and unnerving. As this is going on, stress-inducing music fills the TV studio. This setup does more than create drama and entertainment for viewers; it also intentionally puts pressure on the entrepreneurs. The sharks are professional negotiators who want to knock the entrepreneurs off balance so that it will be easier to take ownership of their good ideas at the lowest price possible. (When multiple sharks want to invest, they often drop comments that are intended to make opposing investors anxious too.) If you watch the show closely, you'll probably notice a pattern: The entrepreneurs who seem least rattled by the environmental stressors tend to negotiate the most carefully and deliberately—and often strike the best deals.

The takeaway from both research and practice is clear: Try your utmost to avoid feeling anxious while negotiating. How can you manage that? Train, practice, rehearse, and keep sharpening your negotiating skills. Anxiety is often a response to novel stimuli, so the more familiar the stimuli, the more comfortable and the less anxious you will feel. (That's why clinicians who treat anxiety disorders often rely on exposure therapy: People who are nervous about flying on airplanes, for instance, are progressively exposed to the experience, first getting used to the sights and sounds, then sitting in airliner seats, and ultimately taking flights.) Indeed, although many people enroll in negotiation classes to learn strategies and increase skills, one of the primary benefits is the comfort that comes from repeatedly practicing deal making in simulations and exercises. Negotiation eventually feels more routine, so it's not such an anxiety-inducing experience.

Another useful strategy for reducing anxiety is to bring in an outside expert to handle the bargaining. Third-party negotiators will be less anxious because their skills are better honed, the process is routine for them, and they have a lower personal stake in the outcome. Outsourcing your negotiation may sound like a cop-out, but it's a frequent practice in many industries. Home buyers and sellers use real estate brokers partly for their negotiating experience; athletes, authors, actors, and even some business executives rely on agents to hammer out contracts. Although there are costs to this approach, they are often more than offset by the more favorable terms that can be achieved. And although anxious negotiators may have the most to gain from involving a third party (because anxiety can be a particularly difficult emotion to regulate in an uncomfortable setting), this strategy can also be useful when other negative emotions surface.

Managing Anger

Like anxiety, anger is a negative emotion, but instead of being self-focused, it's usually directed toward someone else. In most circumstances, we try to keep our tempers in check. When it comes to negotiating, however, many people believe that anger can be a productive emotion—one that will help them win a larger share of the pie.

This view stems from a tendency to view negotiations in competitive terms rather than collaborative ones. Researchers call this the *fixed-pie bias*: People, particularly those with limited experience making deals, assume that a negotiation is a zero-sum game in which their own interests conflict directly with a counterpart's. (More experienced negotiators, in contrast, look for ways to expand the pie through collaboration, rather than nakedly trying to snatch a bigger slice.) Anger, the thinking goes, makes one seem stronger, more powerful, and better able to succeed in this grab for value.

In fact, there's a body of research—much of it by Keith Allred, a former faculty member at Harvard's Kennedy School of Government—that documents the consequences of feeling angry while negotiating. This research shows that anger often harms the process by escalating conflict, biasing perceptions, and making impasses more likely. It also reduces joint gains, decreases cooperation, intensifies competitive behavior, and increases the rate at which offers are rejected. Angry negotiators are less accurate than neutral negotiators both in recalling their own interests and in judging other parties' interests. And angry negotiators may seek to harm or retaliate against their counterparts, even though a more cooperative approach might increase the value that both sides can claim from the negotiation.

Despite these findings, many people continue to see advantages to feeling or appearing angry. Some even attempt to turn up the volume on their anger, because they think it will make them more effective in a negotiation. In my own research, I have found that given a choice between feeling angry and feeling happy while negotiating, more than half the participants want to be in an angry state and view it as significantly advantageous.

There *are* cases when feeling angry can lead to better outcomes. Research by Gerben van Kleef at the University of Amsterdam demonstrates that in a one-time, transactional negotiation with few opportunities to collaborate to create value, an angry negotiator can wind up with a better deal. There may even be situations in which a negotiator decides to feign anger, because the counterpart, in an attempt to defuse that anger, is likely to give ground on terms. This might work well if you are haggling with a stranger to buy a car, for example.

But negotiators who play this card must be aware of the costs. Showing anger in a negotiation damages the long-term relationship between the parties. It reduces liking and trust. Research by Rachel Campagna at the University of New Hampshire shows that false representations of anger may generate small tactical benefits but also lead to considerable and persistent blowback. That is, faking anger can create authentic feelings of anger, which in turn diminish trust for both parties. Along the same lines, research by Jeremy Yip and Martin Schweinsberg demonstrates that people who encounter an angry negotiator are more likely to walk away, preferring to let the process end in a stalemate.

In many contexts, then, feeling or expressing anger as a negotiating tactic can backfire. So in most cases, tamping down any anger you feel—and limiting the anger you express—is a smarter strategy. This may be hard to do, but there are tactics that can help.

PREPARING YOUR EMOTIONAL STRATEGY

Preparation is key to success in negotiations. It's vital to give advance thought to the objective factors involved (Who are the parties? What are the issues? What is my best outside option if we don't reach a deal?), but it is perhaps even more important to prepare your emotional strategy. Use the following questions and tips to plan ahead for each stage of the negotiation.

	Ask yourself:	Remember:
The buildup	• How do I feel? • Should I express my emotions? • How might the people across the table feel? • Are they likely to hide or express their emotions? • Should I recruit a third party to negotiate on my behalf?	• It's normal to feel anxious and excited. • Try to avoid expressing anxiety. • Expressing forward-looking excitement may help build rapport. • In emotionally charged situations (such as a divorce), consider having a third party (such as a lawyer) negotiate on your behalf.
The main event	• What things could happen that would make me feel angry? • What things might I do that would trigger my counterparts to feel angry? • What might they do or ask that would make me feel anxious?	• Be careful about expressing anger; it may extract concessions but harm the long-term relationship. • Avoid angering your counterparts; they are likely to walk away. • Preparing answers to tough questions is critical for staying calm in the moment.
The finale	• What are the possible outcomes of the negotiation? What do I hope to achieve? What do I expect to achieve? • How would those outcomes make me feel? • Should I express those feelings? To whom? • How are my counterparts likely to feel about the possible outcomes?	• To reduce disappointment, outline clear aspirations and expectations and adjust them throughout the negotiation. • When you feel pleased about an outcome, it may be wise to keep it to yourself. • The best negotiators create value for everyone, claiming the lion's share for themselves but making their counterparts feel that they, too, won.

Building rapport before, during, and after a negotiation can reduce the odds that the other party will become angry. If you seek to frame the negotiation cooperatively—to make it clear that you're seeking a win-win solution instead of trying to get the lion's share of a fixed pie—you may limit the other party's perception that an angry grab for value will work well. If the other party does become angry, apologize. Seek to soothe. Even if you feel that his anger is unwarranted, recognize that you're almost certainly better positioned tactically if you can reduce the hostility.

Perhaps the most effective way to deal with anger in negotiations is to recognize that many negotiations don't unfold all at once but take place over multiple meetings. So if tensions are flaring, ask for a break, cool off, and regroup. This isn't easy when you're angry, because your fight-or-flight response urges you to escalate, not pull back. Resist that urge and give the anger time to dissipate. In heated negotiations, hitting the pause button can be the smartest play.

Finally, you might consider reframing anger as sadness. Though reframing one negative emotion as another sounds illogical, shared feelings of sadness can lead to cooperative concession making, whereas oppositional anger often leads to an impasse.

Handling Disappointment and Regret

It can be tempting to see negotiations in binary terms—you either win or lose. Of course, that is generally too simplistic: Most complex negotiations will end with each side having achieved some of its goals and not others—a mix of wins and losses. Still, as a negotiation winds down, it's natural to look at the nascent agreement and feel, on balance, more positive or negative about it.

Disappointment can be a powerful force when it's expressed to the other party near the end of the negotiation. There's a relationship between anger and disappointment—both typically arise when an individual feels wronged—and it's useful to understand how one can be used more constructively than the other. (Think back to how you reacted as a child if your parents said "I'm very disappointed in you" instead of "I'm very angry with you.") Although expressing anger may create defensiveness or increase the odds of a standoff, expressing disappointment can serve a more tactical purpose by encouraging the other party to look critically at her own actions and consider whether she wants to change her position to reduce the negative feelings she's caused you.

Research shows that one cause of disappointment in a negotiation is the speed of the process. When a negotiation unfolds or concludes too quickly, participants tend to feel dissatisfied. They wonder if they could or should have done more or pushed harder. Negotiation teachers see this in class exercises: Often the first students to finish up are the most disappointed by the outcome. The obvious way to lessen the likelihood of disappointment is to proceed slowly and deliberately.

Regret is slightly different from disappointment. While the latter tends to involve sadness about an outcome, someone feeling regret is looking a little more upstream, at the course of actions that led to this unhappy outcome, and thinking about the missteps or mistakes that created the disappointment.

Studies show that people are most likely to regret actions they didn't take—the missed opportunities and errors of omission, rather than errors of commission. That can be a powerful insight for negotiators, whose primary actions should be asking questions, listening, proposing solutions, and brainstorming new alternatives if the parties can't agree. Ironically, people often don't ask questions while negotiating: They may forget to raise important matters or feel reluctant to probe too deeply, deeming it invasive or rude. Those fears are often misplaced. In fact, people who ask a lot of questions tend to be better liked, and they learn more things.

In negotiations, information is king and learning should be a central goal. One way to reduce the potential for regret is to ask questions without hesitation. Aim to come away from the negotiation with the sense that every avenue was explored.

Skilled negotiators use another technique to minimize the odds of regret: the *post-settlement settlement.* This strategy recognizes that tension often dissipates when there's a deal on the table that makes everyone happy, and sometimes the best negotiating happens after that tension is released. So instead of shaking hands and ending the deal making, one party might say, "We're good. We have terms we can all live with. But now that we know we've reached an agreement, let's spend a few more minutes chatting to see if we can find anything that sweetens it for both sides." Done ineptly, this might seem as if one party is trying to renege or renegotiate. However, when handled deftly, a post-settlement settlement can open a pathway for both sides to become even more satisfied with the outcome and stave off regrets.

Tempering Happiness and Excitement

There isn't much research on how happiness and excitement affect negotiations, but intuition and experience suggest that expressing these emotions can have significant consequences. The National Football League prohibits and penalizes "excessive celebrations" after a touchdown or big play because such conduct can generate ill will. For the same reason, the "winner" in a deal should not gloat as the negotiations wrap up. Nonetheless, this happens all the time. In workshops, I routinely see students unabashedly boast and brag (sometimes to the entire class) about how they really stuck it to their opponents in a negotiation exercise. Not only do these students risk looking like jerks, but in a real-world setting, they might suffer more dire consequences: the other party might invoke a right of rescission, seek to renegotiate, or take punitive action the next time the parties need to strike a deal.

Although it's unpleasant to feel disappointed after a negotiation, it can be even worse to make your counterparts feel that way. And in certain situations, showing happiness or excitement triggers disappointment in others. The best negotiators achieve great deals for themselves but leave their opponents believing that they, too, did fabulously, even if the truth is different. In deals that involve a significant degree of future collaboration—say, when two companies agree to merge, or when an actor signs a contract with a producer to star in an upcoming movie—it can be appropriate to show excitement, but it's important to focus on the opportunities ahead rather than the favorable terms one party just gained.

Another danger of excitement is that it may increase your commitment to strategies or courses of action that you'd be better off abandoning. In my negotiation class, we do an exercise in which students must decide whether or not to send a race car driver into an important race with a faulty engine. Despite the risks, most students opt to go ahead with the race because they are excited and want to maximize their winnings. The exercise has parallels to a real-life example: the launch of the *Challenger* space shuttle. Though the engineers who designed the *Challenger*'s faulty O-ring had qualms about it, NASA managers were overly excited and determined to proceed with the launch. Their decision ultimately led to the craft's explosion and the loss of its seven crew members.

There are two lessons for negotiators here. First, be considerate: Do not let your excitement make your counterparts feel that they lost. Second, be skeptical: Do not let your excitement lead to overconfidence or an escalation of commitment with insufficient data.

Negotiating requires some of the same skills that playing poker does—a strategic focus, the imagination to see alternatives, and a knack for assessing odds, reading people, understanding others' positions, and bluffing when necessary. However, whereas the parties in a negotiation must strive for agreement, poker players make decisions unilaterally. Poker also lacks win-win outcomes or pie-sharing strategies: Any given hand is generally a zero-sum game, with one player's gains coming directly from the other players' pots.

MANAGING YOUR COUNTERPART'S EMOTIONS

Negotiating is an interpersonal process. There will always be at least one other party (and often many more) involved. In the adjoining article, I discuss how to manage your own emotions during a negotiation. But what about the other people at the table? Can you manage their emotions as well? I suggest two strategies for doing so:

1. ***Be observant.*** Perceiving how other people are feeling is a critical component of emotional intelligence, and it's particularly key in negotiations (as Adam Galinsky and his colleagues have found). So tune in to your counterpart's body language, tone of voice, and choice of words. When her verbal and nonverbal cues don't match up, ask questions. For example, "You are telling me you like this outcome, but you seem uneasy. Is something making you uncomfortable?" Or "You say you're angry, but you seem somewhat pleased. Are you truly upset about something? Or are you trying to intimidate me?"

(*continued*)

MANAGING YOUR COUNTERPART'S EMOTIONS

(*continued*)

Asking specific questions based on your perceptions of the other party's emotional expressions will make it easier for you to understand her perspective (a task people are shockingly bad at, according to research by Nicholas Epley). It will also make it difficult for a counterpart to lie to you; evidence suggests that people prefer to tell lies of omission about facts rather than lies of commission about feelings.

2. ***Don't be afraid to exert direct influence on your counterpart's emotions.*** This may sound manipulative or even unscrupulous, but you can use this influence for good. For example, if your counterpart seems anxious or angry, injecting humor or empathetic reassurance can dramatically change the tone of the interaction. By the same token, if your counterpart seems overconfident or pushy, expressing well-placed anger can inspire a healthy dose of fear.

In recent research with Elizabeth Baily Wolf, I have found that it's possible to go even further in managing others' emotions: You display an emotion, your counterpart sees it, and then you shape his interpretation of it. For example, imagine that you start crying at work. (Crying is a difficult-to-control and often embarrassing behavior.) Saying "I'm in tears because I'm passionate" rather than "I'm sorry I'm so emotional" can completely change the way others react and the way they view your self-control and competence.

Nonetheless, negotiators can learn a crucial lesson from the card table: the value of controlling the emotions we feel and especially those we reveal. In other words, good negotiators need to develop a poker face—not one that remains expressionless, always hiding true feelings, but one that displays the right emotions at the right times.

And although all human beings experience emotions, the frequency and intensity with which we do so differs from person to person. To be a better deal maker, conduct a thorough assessment of which emotions you are particularly prone to feel before, during, and after negotiations, and use techniques to minimize (or maximize) the experience and suppress (or emphasize) the expression of emotions as needed.

In one of my favorite scenes from the TV show *30 Rock*, hard-driving CEO Jack Donaghy (Alec Baldwin), who fancies himself an expert negotiator, explains to a colleague why he struck a poor deal: "I lost because of emotion, which I always thought was a weakness, but now I have learned can also be a weapon." Borrowing Jack's insightful metaphor, I urge you to wield your emotions thoughtfully. Think carefully about when to draw these weapons, when to shoot, and when to keep them safely tucked away in a hidden holster. Try to avoid feeling anxious, be careful about expressing anger, ask questions to circumvent disappointment and regret, and remember that happiness and excitement can have adverse consequences.

Just as you prepare your tactical and strategic moves before a negotiation, you should invest effort in preparing your emotional approach. It will be time well spent.

Alison Wood Brooks is an assistant professor at Harvard Business School. She teaches negotiation in the MBA and executive education curricula and is affiliated with the Behavioral Insights Group.

CHAPTER 15

Working Across Cultures

by Andy Molinsky

One of the greatest assets we have as natives of a culture is our ability to quickly "read" another person's emotions. Over time, we learn how to understand whether our colleagues are truly interested in a project or just giving it lip service by noticing the expression on their faces. We can tell when someone really likes something we've proposed by the way they react. And we can often detect motivation as well—whether someone is truly willing to put in the extra time and effort to make something happen—just by seeing the fire in their eyes or the passion in their voice.

Originally published on hbr.org on April 20, 2015, as "Emotional Intelligence Doesn't Translate Across Borders" (product #H020D6)

The problem, of course, comes when we cross cultures and venture into a completely different world of emotional expression. Emotions vary tremendously across cultures—both in terms of their expression and their meaning. Without a detailed understanding of these emotional landscapes, crossing cultures can become a communication minefield.

Take, for example, the expression of enthusiasm. In the United States, it's culturally acceptable, even admirable, to show enthusiasm in a business setting, assuming it's appropriate for the situation. When arguing for a point in a meeting, for example, it is quite appropriate to express your opinions passionately; it can help to convince those around you. Or when speaking with a potential employer at a networking event, it is often encouraged to express your interest quite enthusiastically; the employer may interpret how invested you are in a job based on your expressed eagerness.

In many other cultures, however, enthusiasm means something quite different. In Japan, for example, there are strict boundaries about when and where people are allowed to display emotion.[1] During the regular workday, Japanese individuals are not typically emotionally expressive. Even if they feel excited about their work, they will rarely show it explicitly. This often changes outside of the workplace setting, though, where Japanese people can show a great deal of emotion—for example, when drinking, having dinner with work colleagues, or singing karaoke. In China, self-control and modesty are the coin of the realm, not one's ability to outwardly express emotion.[2] In fact, expressing too much outward enthusiasm, especially in front of a boss, could be seen as showing off, which is not typically condoned in Chinese culture.

Given these differences and the importance of getting it right when communicating across cultures, what are thoughtful managers to do?

A first tip is to treat emotions like another language. If you're traveling or moving to France, you're bound to learn French, or at least some key phrases. Treat emotions in the same way. Try your best to learn the language of emotions in whatever culture you're working in. Observe whether people tend to express emotions readily or keep them to themselves, and if, as in the Japan example above, there are differences in when and where people freely express emotion. Diagnose any gaps between how you'd express emotions in your culture and how people you'll be interacting with express emotion in theirs.

In addition to learning the language of emotions, make sure you also learn how to respond constructively when you do encounter emotions different from your own. For example, if you're expecting a smile from your boss after suggesting a new idea but instead get a blank stare, don't necessarily assume she hates you or your idea. Instead, gather more information to fully understand her point of view. You might ask a follow-up question to get a better sense of her opinion: Ask if your proposal was clear or if she felt your idea addressed the concerns she had. Keep in mind that cultural norms differ in terms of how appropriate it might be to ask questions like these to your boss, but the general idea is to do what you can to collect data to help you decipher emotional expressions, rather than relying solely on your initial, knee-jerk reaction or presumption.

Andy Molinsky is a professor of international management and organizational behavior at the Brandeis International Business School. He is the author of *Global Dexterity* (Harvard Business Review Press, 2013) and the new book *Reach: A New Strategy to Help You Step Outside Your Comfort Zone, Rise to the Challenge, and Build Confidence* (Penguin Random House, 2017). Follow Andy on Twitter @andymolinsky.

NOTES

1. Fumiyo Araki and Richard L. Wiseman, Emotional Expressions in the United States and Japan," *International Communication Studies* 6, no. 2 (1996).
2. Ibid.

SECTION FIVE

Dealing with Difficult People

CHAPTER 16

Make Your Enemies Your Allies

by Brian Uzzi and Shannon Dunlap

John Clendenin was fresh out of business school in 1984 when he took on his first managerial position, in Xerox's parts and supply division. He was an obvious outsider: young, African American, and a former Marine, whose pink shirts and brown suits stood out amid the traditional gray and black attire of his new colleagues. "I was strikingly different," he recalls. And yet his new role required him to lead a team including employees who had been with Xerox for decades.

Reprinted from *Harvard Business Review*, May 2012 (product #R1205K)

One of his direct reports was Tom Gunning, a 20-year company veteran who believed Clendenin's job should have gone to him, not to a younger, nontechnical newcomer. Gunning also had a cadre of pals on the team. As a result, Clendenin's first days were filled with strained smiles and behind-the-back murmurs. Though he wasn't looking for adversaries, "I knew these guys were discontented about me coming in," Clendenin remembers.

He was right to be wary. Anyone who has faced a rival at work—a colleague threatened by your skills, a superior unwilling to acknowledge your good ideas, or a subordinate who undermines you—knows such dynamics can prove catastrophic for your career, and for your group or organization. When those with formal or informal power are fighting you, you may find it impossible to accomplish—or get credit for—any meaningful work.

And even if you have the upper hand, an antagonistic relationship inevitably casts a cloud over you and your team, sapping energy, stymieing progress, and distracting group members from their goals.

Because rivalries can be so destructive, it's not enough to simply ignore, sidestep, or attempt to contain them. Instead, effective leaders turn rivals into collaborators—strengthening their positions, their networks, and their careers in the process. Think of these relationships not as chronic illnesses you have to endure but as wounds that must be treated in order for you to lead a healthy work life.

Here we share a method, called the 3Rs (using *redirection, reciprocity,* and *rationality*), for efficiently and effectively turning your adversaries into your allies. If you execute each step correctly, you will develop new "connective tissue" within your organization, boosting your ability to broker knowledge and drive fresh thinking. The method is drawn from our own inductive case studies—including interviews with business leaders such as John Clendenin, who agreed to let us tell his story in this article—and from empirical research conducted by Brian and others investigating the physiology of the brain, the sociology of relationships, and the psychology of influence.

Emotions and Trust

Many well-intentioned efforts to reverse rivalries fail in large part because of the complex way trust operates in these relationships. Research shows that trust is based on both reason and emotion. If the emotional orientation toward a person is negative—typically because of a perceived threat—then reason will be twisted to align with those negative feelings. This is why feuds can stalemate trust: New facts and arguments, no matter how credible and logical, may be seen as ploys to dupe the other side. This effect is not just psychological; it is physiological. When we experience negative emotions, blood recedes from the thinking part of the brain, the cerebral cortex, and rushes to its oldest and most involuntary part, the "reptilian" stem, crippling the intake of new information.

Most executives who decide they want to reverse a rivalry will, quite understandably, turn to reason, presenting incentives for trustworthy collaboration. But in these situations, the "emotional brain" must be managed before adversaries can understand evidence and be persuaded.

When John Clendenin looked at Tom Gunning at Xerox, he immediately saw grounds for a strong partnership beyond a perfunctory subordinate-superior relationship. Gunning had 20 years' worth of organizational and technical knowledge, and contacts around the company, but he lacked the leadership skills and vision that Clendenin possessed. Conversely, Clendenin understood management but needed Gunning's expertise and connections to successfully navigate his new company. Unfortunately, Gunning's emotions were getting in the way. Clendenin needed to employ the 3Rs.

Redirection

Step 1 is to redirect your rival's negative emotions so that they are channeled away from you. Clendenin decided to have a one-on-one meeting with Gunning, but not in his office, because that would only remind Gunning of the promotion he'd lost. Instead, he found out where Gunning liked to eat and took him there for lunch. "I was letting him know that I understood his worth," Clendenin says of this contextual redirection.

He followed this with a plain statement of redirection, telling Gunning that a third entity beyond the control of both men was the root cause of their situation. "I didn't put you in this position," Clendenin said. "Xerox put us both in this position."

Many executives scoff when they first hear this story, believing Clendenin's actions to be too transparent. But redirection doesn't have to be hidden. With stage magic, for example, audience members understand that redirection is happening, but that doesn't lessen their acceptance or spoil the payoff of the technique. Other personal interactions work similarly. For instance, we accept flattery even if we recognize it as such.

Another common redirection tactic is to introduce a discussion of things you and your rival have in common, or casually portray a source of tension—a particular initiative, employee, or event—in a more favorable light. It sounds obvious. But redirection will shift negative emotions away from you and lay the groundwork for Step 2: reciprocity.

Reciprocity

The essential principle here is to *give before you ask*. Undoing a negative tie begins with giving up something of value rather than asking for a "fair trade." If you give and then ask for something right away in return, you don't establish a relationship; you carry out a transaction.

When done correctly, reciprocity is like priming the pump. In the old days, pumps required lots of exertion to produce any water. You had to repeatedly work a lever to eliminate a vacuum in the line before water could flow. But if you poured a small bucket of water into the line first, the vacuum was quickly eliminated, enabling the water to flow with less effort. Reciprocity with a rival works in much the same way.

Reflect carefully on *what* you should give. Ideally, choose something that requires little effort from the other party to reciprocate. Clendenin moved from redirection to reciprocity at the lunch by promising to support Gunning's leadership development and future advancement at Xerox. But, recognizing that mere promises of future returns wouldn't be enough to spark collaboration, he also offered Gunning something concrete: the chance to attend executive-level meetings. This was of immediate value, not a distant, murky benefit. Gunning could gain visibility, credibility, and connections.

The arrangement also ensured reciprocity. Gunning's presence at the meetings furnished Clendenin with on-hand technical expertise and organizational knowledge while giving him "reputation points" with Gunning's contacts. Thus, Clendenin's offer created the purest form of reciprocity; if Gunning attended the meetings, Clendenin would never have to explicitly request a quid pro quo.

Reciprocity involves considering ways that you can immediately fulfill a rival's need or reduce a pain point. Live up to your end of the bargain first, but figure out a way to ensure a return from your rival without the person's feeling that pressure. Another example comes from Brian's colleague Adam Galinsky, who advises leaders in contentious restructurings and business closings to generate goodwill among outgoing employees by offering professional references or placements at other companies as long as the employees continue to meet or exceed expectations until their office closes. The employees see immediate value, and although they don't consciously pay back the organization, the firm nonetheless benefits by maintaining continuity in its workforce until the scheduled closure.

Similarly, a colleague who helps an adversary complete a project or a subordinate who stays overtime to finish a task for a difficult boss not only help themselves but can reap rewards when other teammates or superiors benefit from that effort, too. Here the judicious giving before asking sets a foundation for reciprocity with third parties, whose buy-in can positively assist in reshaping the adversarial relationship. (See the sidebar "Rivalries Don't Exist in a Vacuum.")

Rationality

Step 3, rationality, establishes the expectations of the fledgling relationship you've built using the previous steps so that your efforts don't come off as dishonest or as ineffective pandering. What would have happened if Clendenin had left the lunch without explaining how he wanted to work with Gunning going forward? Gunning might have begun to second-guess his new boss's intentions and resumed his adversarial stance. If a rival is worried about the other shoe dropping, his emotional unease can undermine the trust you've built.

To employ rationality, Clendenin told Gunning that he needed him, or someone like him, to reach his goals at Xerox. This made it clear that he saw Gunning as a valuable, but not indispensable, partner. Another, softer approach might have involved Clendenin's giving Gunning "the right of first refusal" to collaborate with him, making the offer seem special while judiciously indicating that there were others who could step in. Just to be clear, Clendenin was not asking Gunning for a specific favor in exchange for the one he'd granted in Step 2. He was simply saying that he wanted him to become an ally.

Clendenin also reinforced the connection between the three steps by making his offer time-limited, which raised the perception of the value of the deal without changing its content. He told Gunning he needed an answer before they left the restaurant. "I needed to nip this in the bud," Clendenin recalls. "He knew I didn't care if we sat in that restaurant until midnight if we had to."

When rationality follows redirection and reciprocity, it should push your adversary into considering the situ-

RIVALRIES DON'T EXIST IN A VACUUM

Even when a leader executes the 3Rs flawlessly to end a rivalry, his work isn't necessarily done. That's because the relationship is often about more than just the two individuals. We all know people who seek to play to their advantage antagonism between others; some third parties might even view a blossoming partnership with trepidation or envy, triggering new negative emotions and rivalries.

You can head off this problem, as John Clendenin did, by framing your work as beneficial not just to you and your adversary but to the whole organization, which makes the reversal of rivalry in everyone's interest. When Clendenin brought Tom Gunning into those executive-level meetings, he made it clear that Gunning was going to be a "poster child" for a new age at Xerox, in which talented, long-term employees could find new paths to leadership in a time of corporate transition. Even if the conflictmongers didn't care about Clendenin's and Gunning's success, it would be far more difficult for them to sabotage an effort that was obviously good for the company.

ation from a reasoned standpoint, fully comprehending the expectations and benefits, and recognizing that he is looking at a valued opportunity that could be lost. Most people are highly motivated to avoid a loss, which complements their desire to gain something. Rationality is like offering medicine after a spoonful of sugar: It ensures that you're getting the benefit of the shifted negative emotions, and any growing positive ones, which would otherwise diffuse over time. And it avoids the ambiguity that clouds expectations and feedback when flattery and favors come one day, and demands the next.

Of course, Clendenin and Gunning did not walk out of the restaurant as full-blown collaborators. But both accepted that they should give each other the benefit of the doubt. Over the following weeks, this new mindset allowed them to work as allies, a process that deepened trust and resource-sharing in a self-reinforcing cycle. In this way, a potentially debilitating rivalry was transformed into a healthy working relationship and, in time, a strong partnership. Several years later, when Clendenin moved to another Xerox unit, he nominated Gunning as his replacement—and Gunning excelled in the position. The foundation for that remarkable shift had been established during the span of a single lunch.

Adapting the 3Rs

A key advantage of the 3Rs is that the method can work to reverse all kinds of rivalries, including those with a peer or a superior. Later in Clendenin's tenure at Xerox, he noticed an inefficiency in the company's inventory systems. At the time, Xerox was made up of semiautonomous international units that stockpiled excess inventory to avoid shortages. Clendenin proposed that the units instead share their inventories through an intrafirm network that would improve resource use and lower carrying costs for the company as a whole. Although the idea was objectively good for Xerox, it threatened the power of some unit vice presidents, so when Clendenin floated his idea, they shot it down.

WHAT IF THE 3RS FAIL?

The 3Rs are effective, but they aren't a guarantee of defusing resistance. What should you do if the strategy isn't working?

Strive for collaboration indirectly. For example, work well with a third party whom your rival trusts. A common ally can highlight to him the benefits of working with you.

Remember that timing matters. People in power need a reason to interact. This was certainly the case with John Clendenin's inventory-management pitch to the Xerox VPs: At first rebuffed, he was able to refloat his idea when the CEO called for a new strategy.

Recognize when to look elsewhere. Sometimes the effort needed to reverse a rivalry is so great, and the returns so low, for you and your company that you're better off deploying the same resources in another relationship.

A short time later, however, following an unexpected announcement by the CEO that the company needed better asset management, Clendenin found a way to re-introduce his proposal to the VPs. Because he knew they viewed him as an unwelcome challenger—or rival—he used the 3Rs.

His first move was to redirect their negative emotions away from him by planning a lunch for them at the regional office and serving them himself. This showed deference. He also presented himself not as an individual pushing a proposal but as someone who could expedite organizational change, shifting the reference point of his rivals' tension. "With all of those egos and personalities, I never said, 'This is my idea,'" Clendenin recalls. "I always said 'we.'"

Applying the reciprocity principle of "give before you ask," he requested nothing from them at the meeting. Instead, he facilitated a discussion about the CEO-led initiative. Inventory management was, unsurprisingly, a problem cited by many of the VPs, and Clendenin's facilitation brought that to light. He then took on the luster of the person who had illuminated a generic problem, rather than someone who wanted to lessen the VPs' autonomy.

That allowed him to present the rationality of his original idea. All of a sudden, it looked like an opportunity—rather than a threat—to the formerly antagonistic group. Clendenin indicated that he would be willing to coordinate a new system more cheaply than anyone else in the market could offer, while also noting that he might not have time to do so in the future, which raised the perceived value of his offer. The VPs agreed to execute the plan in stages and put Clendenin in charge. The initiative grew in small but steady steps, eventually saving Xerox millions. Equally important, Clendenin's embrace by his rivals positioned him as a broker in the company and burnished his reputation as an institution builder.

John Clendenin understood that rivalries help no one; indeed, success often depends on not just neutralizing your foes but turning them into collaborators. By using the 3Rs to build trust, Clendenin made sure everyone in his network thrived—including himself, Gunning, their team, the VPs, and Xerox—forming the basis for long-term ties and shared success. Years later, Clendenin started his own international logistics company. His partner in this new endeavor was his old rival, Tom Gunning, and the lead investors were none other than the unit VPs from Xerox who had once shot down his ideas.

Brian Uzzi is the Richard L. Thomas Professor of Leadership and Organizational Change at Northwestern's Kellogg School of Management and the codirector of the Northwestern Institute on Complex Systems (NICO). **Shannon Dunlap** is a journalist and writer based in New York City.

CHAPTER 17

How to Deal with a Passive-Aggressive Colleague

by Amy Gallo

Your colleague says one thing in a meeting but then does another. He passes you in the hallway without saying hello and talks over you in meetings. But when you ask to speak with him about it, he insists that everything's fine and the problem is all in your head. Argh! It's so frustrating to work with someone who is acting passive-

---

Adapted from content posted on hbr.org on January 11, 2016 (product #H02LQP)

aggressively. Do you address the behavior directly? Or try to ignore it? How can you get to the core issue when your colleague pretends that nothing's going on?

What the Experts Say

It's not uncommon for colleagues to occasionally make passive-aggressive remarks to one another over particularly sensitive issues or when they feel they can't be direct. "We're all guilty of doing it once in a while," says Amy Su, coauthor of *Own the Room: Discover Your Signature Voice to Master Your Leadership Presence.* But persistent passive-aggressive behavior is a different ball game. "These are people who will often do anything to get what they need, including lie," says Annie McKee, founder of the Teleos Leadership Institute and coauthor of *Primal Leadership: Unleashing the Power of Emotional Intelligence.* In these cases, you have to take special precautions that help you and, hopefully, your counterpart both get your jobs done. Here are some tips:

Don't Get Caught Up

When your coworker pretends nothing is going on or accuses you of overreacting, it's hard not to get angry and defensive. But, McKee says, "This is not one of those situations to fight fire with fire." Do your best to remain calm. "The person may want you to get mad so they can then blame you, which is a release of their own anxiety," Su explains. "Responding in an emotional way will likely leave you looking—and feeling—like the fool. This is your opportunity to be the bigger person."

Consider What's Motivating the Behavior

People who routinely act in a passive-aggressive way aren't necessarily complete jerks. It could be that they don't know how to communicate or are afraid of conflict. McKee says that passive-aggressive behavior is often a way for people to "get their emotional point across without having true, healthy conflict." There's also a self-centeredness to it. "They make the flawed assumption that others should know what they're feeling and that their needs and preferences are more important than others'," says Su. Understand this, but don't try to diagnose all your colleague's problems. "You just have to see it for what it is," Su adds, "an unproductive expression of emotions that they can't share constructively."

Own Your Part

Chances are that you're not blameless in the situation. Ask yourself if something you're doing is contributing to the dynamic or causing the person to be passive-aggressive. "Own your half," says Su. Also, consider whether you've dished out the same behavior. "It can happen to even the best of us, whether we're procrastinating or wanting to avoid something. We might leak emotions in a way that's hurtful to others," says Su.

Focus on the Content, Not the Delivery

It might be the last thing you want to do, but try to see the situation from your colleague's perspective. What is the underlying opinion or perspective she's attempting to convey with her snarky comment? "Analyze the position the person is trying to share with you," says McKee. Does she think that the way you're running the project isn't working? Or does she disagree about your team goals? "Not everyone likes or knows how to publicly discuss or express what they think," says Su. If you can focus on the underlying business concern or question rather than the way she's expressing herself, you can move on to addressing the actual problem.

Acknowledge the Underlying Issue

Once you're calm and able to engage in a productive conversation, go back to the person. Say something like: "You made a good point in that exchange we had the other day. Here's what I heard you saying." This will help them talk about the substance of their concerns. "By joining *with* them, you have a better chance of turning the energy around," McKee explains. Do this in a matter-of-fact way, without discussing how the sentiment was expressed. "Don't listen or give any credence to the toxic part," advises Su. "Sometimes it's that they just want their opinion heard."

Watch Your Language

Whatever you say, don't accuse the person of being passive-aggressive. "That can hurt your cause," says McKee. Su agrees: "It's such a loaded word. It would put someone who's already on the defensive into a more angry position. Don't label or judge them." Instead, McKee suggests recounting how some of your previous interactions have played out and explaining the impact it's having on you and possibly others. If feasible, show that the behavior is working against something your counterpart cares about, like achieving the team's goals.

Find Safety in Numbers

You don't have to deal with this situation alone. "It's OK to reality-check with others and have allies in place to say you're not crazy," says Su. But be sure to frame your discussions as an attempt to constructively improve the relationship, so it doesn't come across as gossiping or bad-mouthing your colleague. Su suggests you ask something like: "I was wondering how Susan's comment landed with you. How did you interpret that?"

Set Guidelines for Everyone

You might also enlist the help of others in coming up with a long-term solution. "As a team, you can build healthy norms," McKee says. Together, you can agree to be more up-front about frustrations and model the honest and direct interactions you want to happen. You can also keep one another accountable. If your problematic colleague tends to ignore agreements, you might take notes in meetings about who's supposed to do what by when, so there are clear action items. The worst offenders are likely to give in to the positive peer pressure and public accountability.

Get Help in Extreme Situations

When a colleague persistently tries to undermine you or prevent you from doing your job, and outside observers confirm your take on the situation, you might have to go further. “If you share the same manager, you may be able to ask for help,” says McKee. You might tell your boss: “A lot of us have noticed a particular behavior, and I want to talk about how it’s impacting my ability to do my work.” But she warns, “Step into those waters carefully. Your manager may be hoodwinked by the person and may not see the same behaviors, or be conflict-averse himself and not want to see it.”

Protect Yourself

“If there’s an interdependence in your work, make sure you’re meeting your commitments and deadlines,” Su says. “Copy others on important emails. Don’t let that person speak for you or represent you in meetings. After a meeting, document agreements and next steps.” McKee also suggests keeping records: “Track specific behaviors so that you have examples if needed. It’s hard to argue with the facts.” She also recommends you try to avoid working with the person and “keep contact to a minimum. If you have to work together, do it in a group setting” where your colleague is likely to be on better behavior. You might not be able to break their passive-aggressive habits, but you can control your reaction to any incidents.

Principles to Remember

Do:

- Understand why people typically act this way—their needs probably aren’t being met

- Focus on the message your colleague is trying to convey, even if their delivery is misguided
- Take a step back and ask yourself if you're contributing to the issue in some way

Don't:

- Lose your cool—address the underlying business issue in a calm, matter-of-fact way
- Accuse the person of acting passive-aggressively—that will only make them madder
- Assume you can change your colleague's behavior

Case Study #1: Make Your Coworker Publicly Accountable

One of Neda Khosla's coworkers (names and details have been changed) in the student guidance office of the public high school where she worked was making things difficult for her. "He would agree to a plan in a meeting but then sabotage it by not following through," she explains. Her colleague, Gareth, defended himself by saying things like "That's not how I remember it" or "I didn't think we had finalized the plan." She tried to talk about these "misunderstandings" with him, but he always shrugged her off: "He'd say he was busy or didn't have time to talk," she recounted.

When Neda told Jim, her and Gareth's boss, that a certain project hadn't gotten done because of this strange dynamic, Jim said that he had noticed the pattern too. Together, they devised a plan to make Gareth more accountable. "He and I agreed that he would publicly ask for a volunteer to take notes on each meeting, [documenting] who would be responsible for accomplishing each task and by when," Neda recalls. She was the first volunteer.

And the approach worked. After Neda sent around the task list, Gareth couldn't make excuses. He was accountable to everyone who attended the meetings. And Neda didn't mind the additional work: "The extra effort I put in was less than the time I was spending fuming about my coworker and running around to pick up the pieces of the things he didn't complete. It actually helped everyone in our department be more productive and was something we should have done a long time ago."

Case Study #2: Get Help Sooner Rather Than Later

James Armstrong, a digital marketing consultant for Roman Blinds Direct, used to manage an eight-person team at a digital marketing agency. He had gotten the promotion three months after one of his direct reports, Violet, joined the agency, and she clearly wasn't thrilled to suddenly have him as a new boss. But "she was a top performer and extremely competent," James recalls, and since they'd worked "fairly harmoniously together as colleagues," he was happy to have her in the group.

Unfortunately, Violet became very difficult to manage. She didn't communicate with him unless absolutely necessary; she didn't actively engage in training sessions that he offered; and she "poked holes" in his initiatives. "She took every opportunity to make it clear that she didn't value my input," he explains.

Surprised and dismayed by her attitude, he decided to address it as he would with any other team member: "directly and clearly." He started by asking her in their one-on-one meetings whether something was wrong. She said there wasn't, but the behavior persisted, so he tried taking her out to coffee and asking whether he had unknowingly offended her or if she wanted to be managed in a different way. She acknowledged that there was a "personality clash," but she ended the conversation there and continued to treat him dismissively at the office. He heard from other staff members that she had even called him "lazy and useless."

"The last thing I wanted was to pass the issue further up the chain and potentially harm Violet's career," he says. After all, she was a valuable team member and he wanted to protect her. But, he reflects, "I should have immediately approached my manager." When he eventually did, she pointed out that his failure to effectively manage a key team member amounted to poor performance on his part.

Within a year, both James and Violet voluntarily left the agency, but neither was happy with the circumstances. He says that if he could do it over again, he would have talked to his manager sooner, kept better records on Violet's "toxic attitude," and when there weren't drastic improvements, fired her "without hesitation."

Amy Gallo is a contributing editor at *Harvard Business Review* and the author of the *HBR Guide to Dealing with Conflict*. She writes and speaks about workplace dynamics. Follow her on Twitter @amyegallo.

CHAPTER 18

What to Do If You're a Toxic Handler

by Sandra L. Robinson and Kira Schabram

Divani (not her real name) is a senior analyst at a large telecommunications firm. She proudly describes herself as her department's "resident cheer-upper." As she says, "I have always been the person that people turn to for support . . . I listen really well and I like to listen, I like to help." But the year before I spoke to her, Divani's organization was going through a major change initiative: "I already had so much on my plate, and so many colleagues were leaning on me—turning to me to process,

---

Adapted from "When You're the Person Your Colleagues Always Vent To" posted on hbr.org on January 11, 2016 (product #H03A8W)

commiserate, ask for advice. It was hard to get through my own deadlines and also be there for my coworkers. I was drowning in stress and nearing burnout." She told us about feeling down on Sunday nights, feeling increasingly angry and cynical, and having trouble sleeping because she couldn't "shut my mind off." She took up smoking again after having given it up for four years and let her exercise routine falter.

Divani is what former Sauder School of Business professor Peter Frost and one of us (Sandra) have termed a *toxic handler*, someone who voluntarily shoulders the sadness, frustration, bitterness, and anger that are endemic to organizational life just as joy and success are. Toxic handlers can be found at all levels of the organization, particularly in roles that span disparate groups. And they are by no means confined to management roles. Their work is difficult and critical even if it often goes uncelebrated; it keeps organizations positive and productive even as the individuals within them necessarily clash and tussle. By carrying others' confidences, suggesting solutions to interpersonal issues, working behind the scenes to prevent pain, and reframing difficult messages in constructive ways, toxic handlers absorb the negativity in day-to-day professional life and allow employees to focus on constructive work.

This isn't easy work. And as Sandra's and Peter Frost's research of over 70 toxic handlers (or those who managed them) revealed, individuals in these roles frequently experience untenably high levels of stress and strain, which affect their physical health and career paths and often mean they have a diminished capacity to help others in the long run—a side effect that is most troubling for handlers.

But if handlers can recognize that they're playing a role that is both highly valuable *and* burdensome, they can see their own emotional competence in a new light and recognize the signs of serious strain while there's still something they can do about it.

How do you know if *you're* a toxic handler? Here are some questions to ask yourself:

- Are you working in an organizational characterized by lots of change, dysfunction, or politics?
- Are you working in a role that spans different groups or different levels?
- Do you spend a lot of time listening to and offering advice to colleagues at work?
- Do people come to you to unload their worries, emotions, secrets, or workplace problems?
- Do you have a hard time saying "no" to colleagues, especially when they need you?
- Do you spend time behind the scenes, managing politics and influencing decisions so others are protected?
- Do you tend to mediate communication between a toxic individual and others?
- Are you that person who feels compelled to stand up for the people at work that need your help?

- Do you think of yourself as a counselor, mediator, or peacemaker?

If you've answered "yes" to four or more of these questions, then you may be a toxic handler. Before you panic at that label, recognize that there are both positives and negatives to fulfilling this role. On the positive side, being a toxic handler means you have valuable emotional strengths: You're probably a good listener; you're empathetic; you're good at suggesting solutions instead of piling on problems. The people around you value the support you provide. It's important, too, to understand that this role is strategically critical to organizations: You likely defuse tough situations and reduce dysfunction.

Now for the bad news. Chances are that you're taking on more work than is covered in your formal job description (and in fact, as an unsung hero, you may not be getting any kind of formal credit from the organization for these efforts and how much you bring to them). Listening, mediating, and working behind the scenes to protect others takes important time away from your other responsibilities. More importantly, it also takes tremendous emotional energy to listen, comfort, and counsel. As you are not a trained therapist, you may also be inadvertently taking on others' pain and slowly paying a price for it. Sandra's research shows that toxic handlers tend to take on others' emotions but have no way to offload them. Quite likely, as a person who is constantly helping others, you may be unlikely to be seeking support for yourself. And lastly, this role may be part of your identity, something that brings you fulfillment and in which you take satisfaction—and so it is difficult to step away from.

Consider Sheung-Li (not his real name). His manager was a star with a great track record, but he created a lot of turmoil. He wouldn't take the time to get to know anyone on Sheung-Li's team personally and totally disregarded more junior members. He was also obsessed with lofty performance goals that seemed to come out of nowhere. "My main role became protecting my team, reassuring them, keeping them focused on our objectives and away from the tensions this guy continually created," Sheung-Li described. "I spent an inordinate amount of time massaging the message, trying to convince my boss to reconsider his decisions so as to avoid the obvious fallout they would bring, playing mediator when our team was not delivering. I felt like I was treading water all the time. And I'm not even sure I was protecting my team from the pain he was causing. I was losing sleep over what was happening to my team, I had lost weight, and I was starting to get sick with one bug after another. I don't know if that was the cause but I know this was a really tough time in my life. It was hard to concentrate on anything else."

So if Sheung-Li's and Divani's stories sound familiar, how can you continue to help to your colleagues (and your organization!) while also protecting yourself? How can you keep playing your valuable role in a *sustainable* way?

Start by assessing whether the role is indeed taking a toll. Some toxic handlers are able to naturally take on more than others; you need to know what's right for you at any given time. Look for evidence of strain and burnout: physical symptoms like insomnia, jaw pain and TMJ, heart palpitations, more sickness than usual. Do you have a shorter fuse than you used to, or an inability to concentrate? Sometimes these symptoms can sneak up on you, so it may help to check in with others to see if they've noticed a change. If you're not experiencing stress as a result, there's nothing you need to change other than being aware and keeping an eye out. Being a toxic handler only needs to be "fixed" if it's actually hurting you. Here's how:

Reduce symptoms of stress

Turn to tried-and-true methods for stress relief: meditation, exercise, enough sleep, and healthful eating. Because toxic handlers have trouble doing things just for themselves, keep in mind that you're helping your colleagues by taking care of yourself. Set your colleagues as your intention for your meditation or yoga practice.

Pick your battles

It's hard to ask yourself where you'll have the most impact if you're emotionally drawn to every problem, but it's an exercise that will allow you to be more helpful where you can actually make a difference. Who is likely to be fine without your help? In which situations have you not even made a dent, despite your best efforts? Step away from these interactions.

Learn to say "no"

It's hard to say no to things you want to do, but it's important. Here's how to do it while still being supportive:

- Convey empathy. Make it clear that you feel for your colleague in their pain—you're not denying that they are having a legitimate emotional response to a situation.
- Tell them you're currently not in a position to be most helpful to them right now and, to the extent you are comfortable, explain the reasons why.
- Consider alternative sources of support. Refer your colleague to another person in the organization, or someone having a similar experience (so they can provide mutual support to one another). Suggest an article, book, or other resource on the topic (e.g., something on managing conflict or handling office politics). Or, if you know from experience that the person is good at coming up with creative solutions themselves, you can simply offer them encouragement to do so.

Let go of the guilt

If you feel guilty that you're not stepping in to help someone, here are some things to consider:

- Recognize that conflicts are often better solved by the parties directly involved. If you're stepping in repeatedly, you're not helping people acquire the skills and tools they need to succeed.

- Question whether you are truly the only one that can help in a particular situation. Enlist trusted others in the organization to help you think through this—you may identify a way to share the load.

- Remember that there is only so much of you to go around: Saying yes to one more person necessarily means that you are agreeing to do less for those people and projects you have already committed to.

Form a community

Find other toxic handlers to turn to for support—these could be others in similar roles in your organization, or other team members whom you see dealing with the fallout from the same toxic leader. You can also identify a pal to vent to or create a more formal group that comes together regularly to share their experiences. This is a particularly good option if your whole team or organization is going through turmoil and you know there are others experiencing the same challenges. Keep these outlets from turning into repetitive venting sessions by focusing the conversation on creative problem solving and advice.

Take breaks

These can be as small or as dramatic as you need. Divani started working with her door closed, which she had never done before. "I felt terrible about this, as if I was abandoning my coworkers who needed me. But if I lost my job, I wasn't going to be much good to anybody," she explained. Consider giving yourself a mental health day off of work or planning a significant vacation. In more dramatic situations, you could also consider a temporary reassignment of your role; because jobs that require you to mediate between multiple teams or groups tend to come under particular fire, you're more likely to get the respite you need if you are able to step away from that role for a time.

These breaks don't need to be forever, though. "Things have since calmed down at work," Divani has reported, "and I find I have gravitated back to being the person people lean on for emotional support, but at this point it is totally doable."

Make a change

If nothing you are doing has resulted in a shift, your best option may be to leave. Sheung-Li explained: "After two years of this [toxic situation], and at the encouragement of my wife, I saw a therapist. It then became clear to me this work reality was not going to change, this toxic manager was not going anywhere, the stress was eating me alive, and I am the one that needed to change. I did a bunch of things, but I think the key thing I did was I ended up making a lateral move in our company to escape this role and to protect my long-term well-being. It was the best decision I ever made."

Consider therapy

It may sound dramatic, but Sheung-Li's decison to talk to a therapist is a highly useful one. A trained psychologist can help you identify burnout, manage your symptoms of stress, help you learn to say "no," and work through any guilt. Not only can they help you protect yourself from the emotional vagaries of being a toxic handler; they can also assist you in your role. Clinical psychologists themselves are trained to listen to their clients empathetically without taking on their emotions. They can help you build the skills you need to help others without absorbing as much of the emotional burden yourself.

Lastly, here are some things we suggest you avoid. While they seem like good solutions on the surface, they often aren't as helpful as you'd think.

Just venting

While it's good to unburden yourself of your emotions—catharsis *can* reduce aggression—too much venting can actually increase stress levels. You want to move forward, rather than dwelling on problems. And this is as true for those confiding in you as it is for you! When people come to you to vent, consider saying something like, "I hear you! How about we think about what we can change to make this better?"

Going to your boss or HR

Sadly, the role of toxic handler is often underrecognized and underappreciated in organizations, despite its tremendous value. This means that while your boss may want to help, it can be risky for them in many organizational cultures. Similarly, many firms are unlikely to intervene in a toxic situation on behalf of the handler.

Yet toxic handlers are critical to the emotional well-being of organizations and the people in them. If you're a toxic handler, learn to monitor yourself for signs of emotional or physical fatigue—and know how to step away when you need to—so that you can keep doing what you do best.

Sandra L. Robinson is a professor of organizational behavior at the University of British Columbia's Sauder School of Business. **Kira Schabram** is an assistant professor of organizational behavior at the University of Washington's Foster School of Business.

SECTION SIX

Understand Empathy

CHAPTER 19

What Is Empathy?

by Daniel Goleman

The word "attention" comes from the Latin *attendere*, meaning "to reach toward." This is a perfect definition of focus on others, which is the foundation of empathy and of an ability to build social relationships—the second and third pillars of emotional intelligence (the first is self-awareness).

Executives who can effectively focus on others are easy to recognize. They are the ones who find common ground, whose opinions carry the most weight, and with whom other people want to work. They emerge as natural leaders regardless of organizational or social rank.

The Empathy Triad

We talk about empathy most commonly as a single attribute. But a close look at where leaders are focusing when

---

Excerpted from "The Focused Leader" in *Harvard Business Review*, December 2013 (product #R0205B)

they exhibit it reveals three distinct kinds of empathy, each important for leadership effectiveness:

- **Cognitive empathy:** the ability to understand another person's perspective.
- **Emotional empathy:** the ability to feel what someone else feels.
- **Empathic concern:** the ability to sense what another person needs from you.

Cognitive empathy enables leaders to explain themselves in meaningful ways—a skill essential to getting the best performance from their direct reports. Contrary to what you might expect, exercising cognitive empathy requires leaders to think about feelings rather than to feel them directly.

An inquisitive nature feeds cognitive empathy. As one successful executive with this trait puts it, "I've always just wanted to learn everything, to understand anybody that I was around—why they thought what they did, why they did what they did, what worked for them and what didn't work." But cognitive empathy is also an outgrowth of self-awareness. The executive circuits that allow us to think about our own thoughts and to monitor the feelings that flow from them let us apply the same reasoning to other people's minds when we choose to direct our attention that way.

Emotional empathy is important for effective mentoring, managing clients, and reading group dynamics. It springs from ancient parts of the brain beneath the cortex—the amygdala, the hypothalamus, the hippocampus, and the orbitofrontal cortex—that allow us to feel fast without thinking deeply. They tune us in by arousing in our bodies the emotional states of others: I literally feel your pain. My brain patterns match up with yours when I listen to you tell a gripping story. As Tania Singer, the director of the social neuroscience department at the Max Planck Institute for Human Cognitive and Brain Sciences, in Leipzig, Germany, says, "You need to understand your own feelings to understand the feelings of others." Accessing your capacity for emotional empathy depends on combining two kinds of attention: a deliberate focus on your own echoes of someone else's feelings and an open awareness of that person's face, voice, and other external signs of emotion. (See the sidebar "When Empathy Needs to Be Learned.")

Empathic concern, which is closely related to emotional empathy, enables you to sense not just how people feel but what they need from you. It's what you want in your doctor, your spouse—and your boss. Empathic concern has its roots in the circuitry that compels parents' attention to their children. Watch where people's eyes go when someone brings an adorable baby into a room, and you'll see this mammalian brain center leaping into action.

Research suggests that as people rise through the ranks, their ability to maintain personal connections suffers.

One neural theory holds that the response is triggered in the amygdala by the brain's radar for sensing danger and in the prefrontal cortex by the release of oxytocin, the chemical for caring. This implies that empathic

WHEN EMPATHY NEEDS TO BE LEARNED

Emotional empathy can be developed. That's the conclusion suggested by research conducted with physicians by Helen Riess, the director of the Empathy and Relational Science Program at Boston's Massachusetts General Hospital. To help the physicians monitor themselves, Riess set up a program in which they learned to focus using deep, diaphragmatic breathing and to cultivate a certain detachment—to watch an interaction from the ceiling, as it were, rather than being lost in their own thoughts and feelings. "Suspending your own involvement to observe what's going on gives you a mindful awareness of the interaction without being completely reactive," says Riess. "You can see if your own physiology is charged up or balanced. You can notice what's transpiring in the situation." If a doctor realizes that she's feeling irritated, for instance, that may be a signal that the patient is bothered too.

Those who are utterly at a loss may be able to prime emotional empathy essentially by faking it until they make it, Riess adds. If you act in a caring way—looking people in the eye and paying attention to their expressions, even when you don't particularly want to—you may start to feel more engaged.

concern is a double-edged feeling. We intuitively experience the distress of another as our own. But in deciding whether we will meet that person's needs, we deliberately weigh how much we value his or her well-being.

Getting this intuition-deliberation mix right has great implications. Those whose sympathetic feelings become too strong may themselves suffer. In the helping professions, this can lead to compassion fatigue; in executives, it can create distracting feelings of anxiety about people and circumstances that are beyond anyone's control. But those who protect themselves by deadening their feelings may lose touch with empathy. Empathic concern requires us to manage our personal distress without numbing ourselves to the pain of others. (See the sidebar "When Empathy Needs to Be Controlled.")

Daniel Goleman is a codirector of the Consortium for Research on Emotional Intelligence in Organizations at Rutgers University, coauthor of *Primal Leadership: Leading with Emotional Intelligence* (Harvard Business Review Press, 2013), and author of *The Brain and Emotional Intelligence: New Insights* and *Leadership: Selected Writings* (More Than Sound, 2011). His latest book is *A Force for Good: The Dalai Lama's Vision for Our World* (Bantam, 2015).

WHEN EMPATHY NEEDS TO BE CONTROLLED

Getting a grip on our impulse to empathize with other people's feelings can help us make better decisions when someone's emotional flood threatens to overwhelm us.

(continued)

WHEN EMPATHY NEEDS TO BE CONTROLLED

(*continued*)

Ordinarily, when we see someone pricked with a pin, our brains emit a signal indicating that our own pain centers are echoing that distress. But physicians learn in medical school to block even such automatic responses. Their attentional anesthetic seems to be deployed by the temporal-parietal junction and regions of the prefrontal cortex, a circuit that boosts concentration by tuning out emotions. That's what is happening in your brain when you distance yourself from others in order to stay calm and help them. The same neural network kicks in when we see a problem in an emotionally overheated environment and need to focus on looking for a solution. If you're talking with someone who is upset, this system helps you understand the person's perspective intellectually by shifting from the heart-to-heart of emotional empathy to the head-to-heart of cognitive empathy.

What's more, some lab research suggests that the appropriate application of empathic concern is critical to making moral judgments. Brain scans have revealed that when volunteers listened to tales of people being subjected to physical pain, their own brain centers for experiencing such pain lit up instantly. But if the story was about psychological suffering, the higher brain centers involved in empathic concern and compassion took longer to activate. Some time is needed to grasp the psychological and moral dimensions of a situation. The more distracted we are, the less we can cultivate the subtler forms of empathy and compassion.

CHAPTER 20

Beyond Empathy: The Power of Compassion

An interview with Daniel Goleman by Andrea Ovans

Two decades before Daniel Goleman first wrote about emotional intelligence in the pages of HBR, he met the Dalai Lama at Amherst College. The Dalai Lama mentioned to the young science journalist for the *New York Times* that he was interested in meeting with scientists. Thus began a long, rich friendship as Goleman became involved over the years in arranging a series of

---

Adapted from content posted on hbr.org on May 4, 2015, as "What the Dalai Lama Taught Daniel Goleman About Emotional Intelligence" (product #H021KQ)

what he calls "extended dialogues" between the Buddhist spiritual leader and researchers in fields ranging from ecology to neuroscience. On the occasion of his friend's 80th birthday, he was asked to write a book describing the Dalai Lama's compassionate approach to addressing the world's most intractable problems. *A Force for Good: The Dalai Lama's Vision for Our World*, which draws both on Goleman's background in cognitive science and his long relationship with the Dalai Lama, is both an exploration of the science and the power of compassion and a call to action. Curious about the book and about how the Dalai Lama's views on compassion informed Goleman's thinking on emotional intelligence, I caught up with Goleman over the phone. What follows are edited excerpts from our conversation.

HBR: Let's start with some definitions here. What is compassion, as you are describing it? It sounds a lot like empathy, one of the major components of emotional intelligence. Is there a difference?

> **Goleman:** Yes, an important difference. Three kinds of empathy are important to emotional intelligence: *cognitive empathy*—the ability to understand another person's point of view, *emotional empathy*—the ability to feel what someone else feels, and *empathic concern*—the ability to sense what another person needs from you [see chapter 19, "What Is Empathy?"]. Cultivating all three kinds of empathy, which originate in different parts of the brain, is important for building social relationships.

But compassion takes empathy a step further. When you feel compassion, you feel distress when you witness someone else in distress—and because of that you want to help that person.

Why draw this distinction?

Compassion makes the difference between understanding and caring. It's the kind of love that a parent has for a child. Cultivating it more broadly means extending that to the other people in our lives and to people we encounter.

I think that in the workplace, that attitude has a hugely positive effect, whether it's in how we relate to our peers, how we are as a leader, or how we relate to clients and customers. A positive disposition toward another person creates the kind of resonance that builds trust and loyalty and makes interactions harmonious. And the opposite of that—when you do nothing to show that you care—creates distrust and disharmony and causes huge dysfunction at home and in business.

When you put it that way, it's hard to disagree that if you treat people well things would go better than if you don't or that if you cared about them they would care a lot more about you. So why do you think that doesn't just happen naturally? Is it a cultural thing? Or a misplaced confusion about when competition is appropriate?

I think too often there's a muddle in people's thinking that if I'm nice to another person or if I have their interests at heart it means that I don't have my own interests at heart. The pathology of that is, "Well, I'll just care about me and not the other person." And that, of course, is the kind of attitude that leads to lots of problems in the business realm and in the personal realm. But compassion also includes yourself. If we protect ourselves and make sure we're okay—and also make sure the other person is okay—that creates a different framework for working with and cooperating with other people.

Could you give me an example of how that might work in the business world?

There's research that was done on star salespeople and on client managers that found that the lowest level of performance was a kind of "I'm going to get the best deal I can now, and I don't care how this affects the other person" attitude, which means that you might make the sale but that you lose the relationship. But at the top end, the stars were typified by the attitude, "I am working for the client as well as myself. I'm going to be completely straight with them, and I'm going to act as their advisor. If the deal I have is not the best deal they can get I'm going to let them know because that's going to strengthen the relationship, even though I might lose this specific sale." And I think that captures the difference between the "me first" and the "let's all do well" attitude that I'm getting at.

How would we cultivate compassion if we just weren't feeling it?

Neuroscientists have been studying compassion recently, and places like Stanford, Yale, UC Berkeley, and the University of Wisconsin, Madison, among others, have been testing methodologies for increasing compassion. Right now there's a kind of a trend toward incorporating mindfulness into the workplace, and it turns out there's data from the Max Planck Institute showing that enhancing mindfulness does have an effect in brain function but that the circuitry that's affected is not the circuitry for concern or compassion. In other words, there's no automatic boost in compassion from mindfulness alone.

Still, in the traditional methods of meditation that mindfulness in the workplace is based on, the two were always linked, so that you would practice mindfulness in a context in which you'd also cultivate compassion.

Stanford, for example, has developed a program that incorporates secularized versions of methods that have originally come from religious practices. It involves a meditation in which you cultivate an attitude of loving-kindness or of concern, or of compassion, toward people. First you do this for yourself, then for people you love, then for people you just know. And finally you do it for everyone. And this has the effect of priming the circuitry responsible for compassion within the brain so that you are more inclined to act that way when the opportunity arises.

You've remarked that the Dalai Lama is a very distinctive kind of leader. Is there something we could learn as leaders ourselves from his unique form of leadership?

Observing him over the years, and then doing this book for which I interviewed him extensively, and of course being immersed in leadership literature myself, three things struck me.

The first is that he's not beholden to any organization at all. He's not in any business. He's not a party leader. He's a citizen of the world at large. And this has freed him to tackle the largest problems we face. I think that to the extent that a leader is beholden to a particular organization or outcome, that creates a kind of myopia of what's possible and what matters. Focus narrows to the next quarter's results or the next election. He's way beyond that. He thinks in terms of generations and of what's best for humanity as a whole. Because his vision is so expansive, he can take on the largest challenges, rather than small, narrowly defined ones.

So I think there's a lesson here for all of us, which is to ask ourselves if there is something that limits our vision—that limits our capacity to care. And is there a way to enlarge it?

The second thing that struck me is that he gathers information from everywhere. He meets with heads of state, and he meets with beggars. He's getting information from people at every level of society worldwide. This casting a large net lets him understand situations in a very deep way, and he can analyze them in many different ways and come up with solutions that aren't confined by anyone. And I think that's another lesson everyday leaders can take from him.

The third thing would be the scope of his compassion, which I think is an ideal that we could strive for. It's pretty unlimited. He seems to care about everybody and the world at large.

Daniel Goleman is the codirector of the Consortium for Research on Emotional Intelligence in Organizations at Rutgers University, a coauthor of *Primal Leadership: Leading with Emotional Intelligence* (Harvard Business Review Press, 2013), and the author of *The Brain and Emotional Intelligence: New Insights* (More Than Sound, 2011). His latest book is *A Force for Good: The Dalai Lama's Vision for Our World* (Bantam, 2015). **Andrea Ovans** is a former senior editor at *Harvard Business Review*.

SECTION SEVEN

Build Your Resilience

CHAPTER 21

Resilience in the Moment

During difficult interactions, you may begin to question your perceptions about yourself. For example, suppose a direct report says, "I didn't attend the meeting because I didn't think you valued my ideas." In response, you wonder to yourself, "Maybe I'm not a competent manager after all."

For many people, the sense that their self-image is being challenged creates intense emotions. These feelings can become overwhelming, making it virtually impossible to converse productively about *any* subject. For this reason, be sure to address feelings about self-image—in yourself and in the other person—during tough conversations.

Adapted from "Address Emotions" in the Harvard ManageMentor topic "Difficult Interactions" (Harvard Business Publishing, 2016, electronic).

Understand Self-Image

Your self-image comes from many different assumptions that you've made about yourself:

- "I'm an effective manager."
- "I'm a good person."
- "I care about my employees."
- "I'm committed to my organization's success."

This set of assumptions may help you meet a need for self-esteem, competence, and appreciation from others. Few people like to view themselves in a negative light—as incompetent, uncaring, or disloyal.

Why Denial Is Common

Many people view self-image from an "either/or" mindset: "I'm either loyal or disloyal" or "I'm either caring or uncaring." Unfortunately, this perspective makes it impossible for people to tolerate criticism and negative feedback from others.

For instance, if a colleague says, "I was really disappointed when you didn't support my proposal," you might conclude, "I can't possibly be a loyal person if I don't support my peer's ideas." If deciding that you're disloyal feels intolerable, you may practice *denial* and shoot back with something like, "I *did* support your proposal."

Other Reactions to Threats

Other reactions to self-image challenges include:

- **Burying the feelings, adopting a detached manner, and resorting to generalizations:** "Let's calm down and establish precise standard operating procedures here."

- **Striking back at the other person defensively:** "Are you calling me a liar?!"

- **Refusing to face the disagreement directly:** "Let's just forget about it and move on."

None of these responses enables you to listen to feedback and make the changes needed to improve the way you interact with others.

Handle Threats to Your Self-Image

Several strategies can help you effectively handle challenges to your self-image:

- **Understand your self-image.** List all the assumptions that influence your perception of yourself. By anticipating that you might experience defensiveness over threats to these particular beliefs, you may be better able to control negative feelings if they do arise.

- **Adopt a "both/and" mindset.** Instead of assuming that you can be, for example, either competent or incompetent, remind yourself that you and others are a mixture of positive and negative. You're likely competent at some things and not so skilled at others.

- **Accept imperfection.** Acknowledge that everyone makes mistakes at times. The key is to learn from them.

HOW TO RESPOND TO CRITICISM

by Peter Bregman

At one point or another, we've all been blindsided by criticism and reacted poorly. I remember once leading a project that I thought was going great—until my two colleagues took me aside to tell me I was being controlling and overbearing. I immediately became defensive. I had trouble listening to them, and I became self-conscious and awkward for the rest of the project.

Surprise criticism about an issue you haven't perceived yourself often has that effect. It emotionally overpowers you. But you can respond more productively. As you listen to the feedback and your adrenaline starts to flow, pause, take a deep breath, and then follow this game plan.

Acknowledge and set aside your feelings. We call it *constructive* criticism, and it usually is, but it can also feel painful, destabilizing, and personal. Notice and acknowledge to yourself the hurt, anger, embarrassment, or insufficiency you might feel. Recognize the feelings, label them as feelings, and then put them aside so the noise doesn't crowd out your hearing.

Also, look beyond the delivery of the criticism. Feedback is hard to give, and your critic may not be skilled at doing it well, but that doesn't mean it's not valuable and insightful. Avoid confusing the package with the message.

Next, don't agree or disagree. Just collect the data. Ask questions. Solicit examples. Recap what you're hearing, all in the spirit of understanding. Let go of the need to respond. That will reduce your defensiveness and give you space to really listen.

Criticism, especially surprise criticism, is useful information about how someone else perceives you. Following these steps will help make sure you can fully understand it and can learn from it.

Peter Bregman is CEO of Bregman Partners, Inc., a global management consulting firm that advises CEOs and their leadership teams.

CHAPTER 22

Cultivate Resilience in Tough Times

A summary of the full-length HBR article "How Resilience Works" by **Diane Coutu**, *highlighting key ideas and examples*

IDEA IN BRIEF

Resilient people possess three defining characteristics:

- They coolly accept the harsh realities facing them.
- They find meaning in terrible times.

Adapted from "How Resilience Works" in *Harvard Business Review*, May 2002 (product #R0205B)

- They have an uncanny ability to improvise, making do with whatever's at hand.

Fortunately, you can learn to be resilient. To cultivate resilience, apply these practices.

Face Down Reality

Instead of slipping into denial to cope with hardship, take a sober, down-to-earth view of the reality of your situation. You'll prepare yourself to act in ways that enable you to endure—training yourself to survive before the fact.

Example: Admiral Jim Stockdale survived being held prisoner and tortured by the Vietcong in part by accepting he could be held for a long time. (He was held for eight years.) Those who didn't make it out of the camps kept optimistically assuming they'd be released on shorter timetables—by Christmas, by Easter, by the Fourth of July. "I think they all died of broken hearts," Stockdale said.

Search for Meaning

When hard times strike, resist any impulse to view yourself as a victim and cry, "Why me?" Rather, devise constructs about your suffering to create meaning for yourself and theirs. You'll build bridges from your present-day ordeal to a fuller, better future. Those bridges will make the present manageable, by removing the sense that the present is overwhelming.

Example: Austrian psychiatrist and Auschwitz survivor Victor Frankl realized that to survive the camp, he had to find some purpose. He did so by imagining himself giving a lecture after the war on the psychology of the concentration camp to help outsiders understand what he had been through. By creating concrete goals for himself, he rose above the sufferings of the moment.

Continually Improvise

When disaster hits, be inventive. Make the most of what you have, putting resources to unfamiliar uses and imagining possibilities others don't see.

> *Example:* Mike founded a business with his friend Paul, selling educational materials to schools, businesses, and consulting firms. When a recession hit, they lost many core clients. Paul went through a bitter divorce, suffered from depression, and couldn't work. When Mike offered to buy him out, Paul slapped him with a lawsuit claiming Mike was trying to steal the business.

Mike kept the company going any way he could—going into joint ventures to sell English-language training materials to Russian and Chinese competitors, publishing newsletters for clients, and even writing video scripts for competitors. The lawsuit was eventually settled in his favor, and he had a new and much more solid business than the one he started out with.

Diane Coutu is the director of client communications at Banyan Family Business Advisors, headquartered in Cambridge, Massachusetts, and is a former senior editor at *Harvard Business Review*.

CHAPTER 23

Practice Self-Compassion

by Christopher Germer

If a good friend tells you about an ordeal they're facing or a mistake they've made, how do you typically respond? In all likelihood, you'll offer kindness and comfort, perhaps speaking in a warm and soothing tone, and maybe offering a hug to show how much you care. When your friend recovers and the conversation continues, chances are that you'll expand your support by encouraging your friend to take necessary action or try to discover how to steer clear of similar difficulties in the future.

Now reflect for a moment how you might you treat *yourself* when *you* make a big mistake or experience a

---

Adapted from content posted on hbr.org on January 5, 2017, as "To Recover from Failure, Try Some Self-Compassion" (product #H03E32)

setback. It's likely that you'd be much tougher on yourself—that you'd spring to self-criticism ("I'm such an idiot!"), hide in embarrassment or shame ("Ugggh!"), or ruminate for a long time about your perceived shortcomings or bad luck ("Why me? Why did this happen to me?"). When things go wrong in our lives, we tend to become our own worst enemy.

To recover emotionally and get back on your feet, however, there's a different approach you can take: *self-compassion.*

I've been working with mindfulness in my psychotherapy practice for over 30 years. It is a powerful resource that helps us stay present and focused on the task at hand. I've come to realize, however, that a component of mindfulness that is essential for emotional resilience is often overlooked. In particular, when we fail in a big way, we're likely to become engulfed in shame and our sense of self is dismantled. We all know what this feels like—we're unable to think straight, temporarily suspended in time and place, dislocated from our bodies, and uncertain who we really are. Shame has a way of wiping out the very observer who is needed to be mindful of our situation.

What does it take to rescue yourself and begin to address the situation in an effective manner? You need to treat yourself with the same kindness and support as you'd provide for a dear friend.

A substantial and growing body of research shows that this self-compassion is closely associated with emotional resilience, including the ability to soothe ourselves, recognize our mistakes and learn from them, and motivate ourselves to succeed. Self-compassion is also consistently correlated with a wide range of measures of emotional well-being such as optimism, life satisfaction, autonomy, and wisdom, and with reduced anxiety, depression, stress, and feelings of shame.[1]

To achieve these benefits, self-compassion must include three components, according to my colleague and pioneering self-compassion researcher, Kristin Neff:

- **Mindfulness:** Awareness of what's going on in the present moment. To be kind to ourselves, first we need to *know* that we're struggling *while* we're struggling. It also helps to name the emotions we're feeling in tricky situations and to ground ourselves in the here and now (sensations, sounds, sights). These are all skills associated with mindfulness that make space for a compassionate response.

- **Common humanity:** Knowing we're not alone. Most of us tend to hide in shame when things go really wrong in our lives, or we hide from *ourselves* through distraction or with a few stiff drinks. The antidote is recognizing our common humanity—understanding that many others would feel the same way in similar situations, and that we're not the only ones who suffer in life.

- **Self-kindness:** A kind and warm-hearted response to ourselves. This can take many forms, such as a gentle hand over the heart, validating how we feel, talking to ourselves in an encouraging manner, or by a simple act of kindness such as drinking a cup of tea or listening to music.

> When we feel threatened, our nervous system is awash in adrenaline and thus goes into overdrive. When we're in this state, showing ourselves care and kindness is usually the last thing we're inclined to do. When we experience positive, warm connections, however, our system releases oxytocin instead, a feel-good hormone that downregulates the effects of adrenaline. Taking a mindful pause and then bringing kindness to ourselves seems to activate our innate caregiving system and the calming effect of oxytocin, allowing the mind to clear and giving us a chance to take rational steps to resolve the issue.

Even though self-compassion is not the default option for most of us when things go wrong, anyone can learn to do it. Neff has developed an exercise you can use in everyday life when you need self-compassion the most—the Self-Compassion Break (see the sidebar "Self-Compassion Break")—which is based on the three components of self-compassion described above. (This is just one exercise we offer as part of our empirically supported Mindful Self-Compassion training program.)

SELF-COMPASSION BREAK

When you notice that you're under stress or are emotionally upset, see if you can locate where the emotional discomfort resides your body. Where do you feel it the most? Then say to yourself, slowly:

1. ***"This is a moment of struggle."*** That's mindfulness. See if you can find your own words, such as:
    - "This hurts."
    - "This is tough."
    - "Ouch!"
2. ***"Struggle is a part of living."*** That's common humanity. Other options include:
    - "Other people feel this way."
    - "I'm not alone."
    - "We all struggle in our lives."

Now, put your hands over your heart, or wherever it feels soothing, sensing the warmth and gentle touch of your hands, and say to yourself:

3. ***"May I be kind to myself. May I give myself what I need."*** Perhaps there are more specific words that you might need to hear right now, such as:
    - "May I accept myself as I am."
    - "May I learn to accept myself as I am."
    - "May I be safe."
    - "May I be strong."
    - "May I forgive myself."

(*continued*)

SELF-COMPASSION BREAK

(continued)

If you're having trouble finding the right language, it can help to imagine what you might say to a close friend struggling with that same difficulty. Can you say something similar to yourself, letting the words roll gently through your mind?

Consider the following example of the Self-Compassion Break in action: Your boss gave you a stretch assignment to lead a large and critical project. The project was a great success, due in large part to your skillful leadership, and you believe you demonstrated that you're ready for a promotion. But when you raise the idea with your boss, she laughs dismissively and changes the subject. Livid with anger, you retreat from the conversation, asking yourself why you bothered to work so hard in the first place, since you would never be recognized for it. *Of course* your boss wasn't going to support you, or even notice—she just wanted someone to do the heavy lifting to promote her own selfish agenda. Or maybe you're hopelessly out of touch and your performance really wasn't as good as you thought it was? When we're in the grip of strong emotions, our minds run wild.

As a savvy businessperson, you might think that this would be the perfect moment to advocate for yourself if it were only possible to make a balanced, compelling case for your promotion. But without a moment of self-compassion, your emotional reactivity is likely to stand in your way—you'd put your anger on display instead of showing off your leadership skills, or you'd let self-doubt eat at your resolve to see the discussion through to an acceptable conclusion.

How do you activate self-compassion in the heat of the moment? Begin by acknowledging how you feel; for example, recognizing that you might still feel angry ("She's terrible, and I hate her"), see yourself as the victim ("She made me go through all of that—for what?!"), or doubt yourself ("Maybe she's right—maybe I don't deserve a promotion—I didn't do that great a job after all").

Next, acknowledge that others would probably have similar feelings in this situation: requesting a promotion after you've expanded your skills and taken on more responsibility is a reasonable thing to do, and your emotional reaction to the rejection of that request is not out of line. Consider any examples you know of others in similar situations—perhaps Rob in the finance department told you last year that his promotion was also denied and you noticed how angry he was and how he doubted his own worth. You are not alone.

Finally, express kindness to yourself: What would you say to a friend in your shoes? Perhaps you'd say, "It's rough being taken for granted." "Whatever comes of it, that project *was* a huge success—look at the numbers." Also think about how you care for yourself already. Do you go for a run, pet your dog, call a friend? If you do that when you're suffering, that's self-compassion.

Once you've shifted your frame of mind from a threat state to self-compassion, you're likely find yourself calmer and in a place that you can sit down and write a thoughtful and persuasive proposal about your promotion—one that builds on your project success and exhibits your leadership potential under stress.

Lastly, a warning: Many people dismiss self-compassion because they think it flies in the face of their ambition or hard self-driving attitude—qualities that they feel have made them successful. But being self-compassionate doesn't imply that you shouldn't be ambitious or push yourself to succeed. Rather it's about *how* you motivate yourself. Instead of using a whip—motivating yourself with blame and harsh self-criticism—self-compassion motivates like a good coach, with encouragement, kindness, and support. It's a simple reversal of the Golden Rule—learning to treat *ourselves* as we naturally treat others in need—with kindness, warmth, and respect.

Christopher Germer is a clinical psychologist and part-time lecturer on psychiatry at Harvard Medical School. He is a co-developer of the Mindful Self-Compassion (MSC) program, author of *The Mindful Path to Self-Compassion*, co-editor of *Mindfulness and Psychotherapy*, and *Wisdom and Compassion in Psychotherapy*, and a founding faculty member of the Institute for Meditation and Psychotherapy and the Center for Mindfulness and Compassion, Cambridge Health Alliance/Harvard Medical School.

NOTE

1. See, for example: L. K. Barnard and J. F. Curry, "Self-Compassion: Conceptualizations, Correlates, and Interventions," *Review of General*

Psychology 15, no. 4 (2011): 289–303; K. D. Neff, S. S. Rude, and K. Kirkpatrick, "An Examination of Self-Compassion in Relation to Positive Psychological Functioning and Personality Traits," *Journal of Research in Personality* 41 (2007): 908–916; F. Raes, "The Effect of Self-Compassion on the Development of Depression Symptoms in a Non-clinical Sample," *Mindfulness* 2 (2011): 33–36; D. L. Zabelina and M. D. Robinson, "Don't Be So Hard on Yourself: Self-Compassion Facilitates Creative Originality Among Self-Judgmental Individuals," *Creativity Research Journal* 22 (2010): 288–293; E. Schanche et al., "The Relationship Between Activating Affects, Inhibitory Affects, and Self-Compassion in Patients with Cluster C Personality Disorders," *Psychotherapy* 48, no. 3 (2011): 293–303.

CHAPTER 24

Don't Endure; Recharge

by Shawn Achor and Michelle Gielan

As constant travelers and parents of a two-year-old, we sometimes fantasize about how much work we could do if we could just get on a plane, undistracted by phones, friends, or *Finding Nemo*. And so in advance of a trip, we race to get all our groundwork done: packing, going through TSA, doing a last-minute work call, calling each other, boarding. But then when we try to have that amazing in-flight work session, we find that we get nothing done. Even worse, after refreshing our email or reading the same studies over and over, we are too exhausted when we land to soldier on with the emails that have inevitably still piled up.

Adapted from content posted on hbr.org on June 24, 2016, as "Resilience Is About How You Recharge, Not How You Endure" (product #H02Z3O)

Why can't we be tougher—more resilient and determined in our work—so we can accomplish all of the goals we set for ourselves? Through our current research, we have come to realize that the problem comes from a cultural misunderstanding of what it means to be resilient, and the resulting impact of overworking.

As a society, we often associate "resilience" and "grit" with a militaristic, "tough" approach to our work. We imagine a Marine slogging through the mud, a boxer going one more round, or a football player picking himself up off the turf for one more play. We believe that the longer we tough it out, the tougher we are, and therefore the more successful we will be.

However, this entire conception is scientifically inaccurate. In fact what's holding back our ability to be resilient and successful is the lack of any kind of recovery period. Resilience is defined as the ability to quickly bounce back from stressful situations—no matter what problems are thrown at us, we continually get back up, ready for the next one. But even for the most resilient person, getting ready doesn't happen instantly. It is a process—and an important one. Research has found that there is a direct correlation between lack of recovery and increased incidence of health and safety problems. And lack of recovery—whether it disrupts our sleep with thoughts of work or keeps us in continuous cognitive arousal as we obsessively watch our phones—is costing our companies $62 billion a year (that's *billion,* not million) in lost productivity.[1]

Misconceptions about resilience as nonstop activity and energy are often bred into us from an early age.

For instance, parents might praise the resilience of their high school student who stays up until 3 a.m. to finish a science fair project. But when that exhausted student drives to school, his impaired driving poses risks for himself and others; at school, he doesn't have the cognitive resources to do well on his English test and has lower self-control with his friends; and at home, he is moody with his parents.

The bad habits we learn when we're young only magnify when we hit the workforce. In a study released last month, researchers from Norway found that 7.8% of Norwegians have become workaholics, where *workaholism* is defined as "being overly concerned about work, driven by an uncontrollable work motivation, and investing so much time and effort to work that it impairs other important life areas."[2] And in fact that drive can backfire in the very area for which we're sacrificing ourselves: In her excellent book *The Sleep Revolution: Transforming Your Life, One Night at a Time*, Arianna Huffington wrote, "We sacrifice sleep in the name of productivity, but ironically our loss of sleep, despite the extra hours we spend at work, adds up to 11 days of lost productivity per year per worker, or about $2,280."[3]

The key to resilience is *not* working really hard all the time. It is actually found in the time that we stop working and recover. Ideally, we need to create cycles for ourselves in which we work hard, then stop and recover, and then work again.

This conclusion is based on biology. *Homeostasis*, a fundamental biological concept, is the ability of the body to continuously restore and sustain its own well-being.

When the body is out of alignment and therefore in a state of stress or exhaustion from overworking, we waste a vast amount of mental and physical resources trying to return to balance before we can move forward. As Jim Loehr and Tony Schwartz have written in *The Power of Full Engagement*, the more time you spend in the performance zone, the more time you need in the recovery zone; otherwise you risk burnout.

And if, instead of taking a break, you muster your resources to continue to "try hard," you need to burn ever more energy in order to overcome your currently low arousal level, which only exacerbates your exhaustion. It's a vicious downward spiral.

But the more imbalanced we become due to overworking, the more value there is in activities that allow us to return to a state of balance.

So what are those activities that allow us to return to homeostasis and thereby increase our resilience? Most people assume that if you stop doing a task like answering emails or writing a paper, that your brain will naturally recover, so that when you start again later in the day or the next morning, you'll have your energy back. But stopping work doesn't mean you're actually recovering: If after work you lie around on the couch and check your phone and get riled up by political commentary, or get stressed thinking about decisions about how to renovate your home, your brain has not received a break from high mental arousal states. And surely everyone reading this has occasionally lain in bed for hours, unable to fall asleep because their brain is thinking about work, even if they don't have a device in hand. If you're in bed for eight hours, you may have rested, but you can still feel exhausted the next day. That's because rest and recovery are not the same thing.

If you're trying to build resilience at work, you need adequate internal and external recovery periods. As researchers F. R. H. Zijlstra, M. Cropley, and L. W. Rydstedt wrote in a 2014 paper: "Internal recovery refers to the shorter periods of relaxation that take place within the frames of the workday or the work setting in the form of short scheduled or unscheduled breaks, by shifting attention or changing to other work tasks when the mental or physical resources required for the initial task are temporarily depleted or exhausted. External recovery refers to actions that take place outside of work—e.g., in the free time between the workdays, and during weekends, holidays or vacations."[4]

There are four main researched ways to increase your resilience. First, start by deliberately opening a space for recovery to happen. We've worked with several companies that tout the benefits of investing in employee well-being, but fail to create tangible results because they don't carve out time for their workers to devote part of their workday to those rejuvenating activities. Adding more activities to an already full plate of work increases the stress load.

Second, it is crucial that you take *all* of your paid time off. As we described in a previous HBR article entitled "The Data-Driven Case for Vacation," taking your days off not only gives you recovery periods to recharge, but in fact significantly raises your productivity and the likelihood of promotion.

Third, while it might sound counterintuitive, it is possible to use technology to limit tech use while building internal recovery periods into your daily routine. The average person turns on their phone 150 times every day.[5] If every distraction took only 1 minute (which would be seriously optimistic), that would account for 2.5 hours of every day. In her upcoming book *The Future of Happiness*, based on her work at Yale Business School, Amy Blankson suggests downloading the Instant or Moment apps to see how many times *you* turn on your phone each day; using the app reminds you to make a choice in those moments when you grab your phone—and choose to stay away. You can also use apps like Offtime or Unplugged to create tech-free zones by strategically scheduling automatic airplane modes. In addition, you can take a cognitive break every 90 minutes to recharge your batteries. Try to not have lunch at your desk, but instead spend time outside or with your friends—*not* talking about work.

Fourth, now that you have carved out time for rejuvenation, it's time to engage in an activity or two that make you feel happy and replenished. Take the pressure off and just do something for the fun of it! Go on a walk or run, call and old friend, meditate by watching your breath go in and out for five minutes, try a new recipe, or do something nice for someone else. Choose to do something that makes you feel alive, gives you a mental break from work, and keeps you fully engaged the whole time. Not only does spending your time this way help you come back stronger, oftentimes these activities are more memorable in the long run.

As for us, we've started using our plane time as a work-free zone, and thus as time to dip into the recovery phase. The results have been fantastic. We are usually tired already by the time we get on a plane, and the cramped space and spotty internet connection make work more challenging. Now, instead of swimming upstream, we relax, meditate, sleep, watch movies, journal, or listen to entertaining podcasts. And when we get off the plane, instead of being depleted, we feel rejuvenated and ready to return to the performance zone.

Shawn Achor is *New York Times* best-selling author of *The Happiness Advantage* and *Before Happiness.* His TED talk is one of the most popular, with over 14 million views. He has lectured or researched at over a third of the *Fortune* 100 and in 50 countries, as well as for the NFL, NASA, and the White House. He is leading a series of courses on "21 Days to Inspire Positive Change" with the Oprah Winfrey Network. **Michelle Gielan**, a national CBS News anchor turned UPenn positive psychology researcher, is the best-selling author of *Broadcasting Happiness.* She is partnered with Arianna Huffington to research how a solution-focused mindset fuels success, and shares her research at organizations including Google, American Express, and Boston Children's Hospital. Michelle is the host of the *Inspire Happiness* program on PBS.

NOTES

1. J. K. Sluiter, "The Influence of Work Characteristics on the Need for Recovery and Experienced Health: A Study on Coach Drivers,"

Ergonomics 42, no. 4 (1999): 573–583; and American Academy of Sleep Medicine, "Insomnia Costing U.S. Workforce $63.2 Billion a Year in Lost Productivity," *ScienceDaily*, September 2, 2011.

2. C. S. Andreassen et al., "The Relationships Between Workaholism and Symptoms of Psychiatric Disorders: A Large-Scale Cross-Sectional Study," *PLoS One* 11, no. 5 (2016): e0152978.

3. Ronald C. Kessler et al., "Insomnia and the Performance of US Workers: Results from the America Insomnia Survey," *Sleep* 34, no. 9 (2011): 1161–1171.

4. F. R. H. Zijlstra et al., "From Recovery to Regulation: An Attempt to Reconceptualize 'Recovery from Work'" (special issue paper) (Hoboken, NJ: John Wiley & Sons, 2014), 244.

5. J. Stern, "Cellphone Users Check Phones 150x/Day and Other Internet Fun Facts," *Good Morning America*, May 29, 2013.

CHAPTER 25

How Resilient Are You?

by Manfred F. R. Kets de Vries

We all face setbacks from time to time, and the ability to bounce back stronger than before is something we envy in others. So how can we develop that ability in ourselves?

A large body of research shows that resilient people are generally strong in three areas: challenge, control, and commitment. They accept that change, not stability, is the norm; they believe they can influence events in their lives; and they are engaged with the world around them.

This test will help you assess your strengths and weaknesses in these areas and provide feedback on ways to improve.

Adapted from material originally published on hbr.org on January 20, 2015

Circle your reaction to each statement, then follow the instructions below to score yourself.

Challenge

1. You're told that you won't be getting the promotion you sought, because another candidate is more qualified.

    a. Although you are upset, you say nothing.
    b. You acknowledge that you are disappointed and request a fuller explanation.
    c. You ask what you need to do to improve your chances for advancement in the future.

2. You learn that your company will be opening an office in Beijing. Succeeding in that market would be difficult, but you know that you have the right experience to lead the office.

    a. You consider the risks and decide not to pursue the opportunity.
    b. You discuss the pros and cons with some of the people in your network.
    c. You throw your hat into the ring.

3. A major client tells you that a contract you worked hard to win has been given to a competitor.

    a. You tell your team that you made every effort to land the client.
    b. You put the setback out of your mind, accepting that some factors in the client's decision were beyond your control.

c. You reflect on the experience, realizing that you now have a much better understanding of how to deal with this client in the future.

Control

4. You overhear an unflattering conversation about yourself.

    a. You pretend it doesn't bother you.
    b. You remind yourself that the speakers don't know you very well.
    c. You approach the speakers calmly and express your desire to understand why they see you that way.

5. Your boss comes to you on Friday afternoon with an emergency: He wants to meet with a client on Monday morning and needs you to prepare a feasibility study first. You have a family camping trip planned for the weekend.

    a. You accept the assignment, not mentioning your weekend plans.
    b. You mention the camping trip but agree to the assignment after your boss emphasizes its importance.
    c. You tell your boss that you have made a commitment to your family and ask if he can schedule the meeting for Tuesday instead.

6. Work has become increasingly stressful. There are too many deadlines, too many requests, too many late nights.

a. You tell yourself, "This, too, shall pass."
b. You try to give some of your work to a colleague.
c. You request a vacation or a leave of absence to recharge.

Commitment

7. Your best friend says that he is worried about your health and suggests that you join his fitness club.

   a. You say, "No, thanks. I'm fine."
   b. You agree that the fitness club is a good idea and make a note in your calendar to look into it.
   c. You take his concern to heart and arrange to visit the club together.

8. Your company's subsidiary in Africa requests financial and technical support for a high school in the region. Although there would be no immediate monetary benefit to the firm, this is a valuable opportunity to build a reputation as a socially responsible employer.

   a. You decline the request on cost grounds.
   b. You agree to give the matter serious consideration.
   c. You give your consent and call a friend at the World Bank for suggestions on how to launch the initiative.

9. Early in your career you had set a goal to become general manager at a *Fortune* 1000 company by

age 50. The clock is ticking: You're 48, and you're a division head.

a. You accept your current role and decide to make the best of it.
b. You continue striving for advancement but lower your ambitions a bit.
c. You figure out a way to reach your goal.

Score Yourself

For each area, record the number of each answer below and add up your total score for that area.

Challenge

of a ____ =

# of b ____ x 2 =

# of c ____ x 3 =

Total = = Challenge Score

If you had a high challenge score (7–9):

You turn difficult events to your advantage and view setbacks as learning opportunities. You have positive relationships with others.

If you had a low challenge score (1–6):

You need to work on turning difficult events to your advantage and reframing them in a constructive light. If you experience setbacks in the process, regard them as learning opportunities, not failures. Remember the importance of positive relationships with others.

Control

of a ____ =

# of b ____ x 2 =

# of c ____ x 3 =

Total = = Control Score

If you had a high control score (7–9):

You can distinguish between things you can and can't control, and you deal with emotionally difficult problems proactively. You see things in perspective and know how to set boundaries.

If you had a low control score (1–6):

Work on distinguishing between things you can and can't control, perhaps with the help of an executive coach or a therapist. Try to deal with emotionally difficult problems proactively. Use humor to "roll with the punches." Set boundaries in both your professional life and your personal life to avoid burnout. Delegate more responsibilities to your direct reports.

Commitment

of a ____ =

# of b ____ x 2 =

# of c ____ x 3 =

Total = = Commitment Score

If you had a high commitment score (7–9):

You pursue goals that are meaningful to you and maintain positive relationships with people who matter to you. You recognize the importance of health and balance and have an active life outside of work.

If you had a low commitment score (1–6):

Clarify what is important to you and pursue those activities. Make an effort to spend time with people who are meaningful in your life. Develop healthy habits, including daily exercise, regular sleep, and relaxation techniques. Don't ignore problems.

To take this assessment online and compare your results to those of other HBR readers, visit https://hbr.org/2015/01/assessment-how-resilient-are-you.

Manfred F. R. Kets de Vries is the Distinguished Professor of Leadership Development and Organizational Change at INSEAD in France, Singapore, and Abu Dhabi. His most recent book is *Riding the Leadership Roller Coaster: An Observer's Guide* (Palgrave Macmillan, 2016).

SECTION EIGHT

Developing Emotional Intelligence on Your Team

CHAPTER 26

How to Help Someone Develop Emotional Intelligence

by Annie McKee

It's easy to point fingers at those in the office who lack basic self-awareness or social skill. Whether clueless colleagues or brutish bosses, these people make life challenging for the rest of us, ruining the dynamic of work teams and shattering productivity and morale. But in fact most of us can stand to improve our emotional intelligence. Even those of us who are adept extroverts can

Adapted from content posted on hbr.org on April 24, 2015 (product #H0216Z)

learn how to become more empathetic; those who are kind givers can learn to be more persuasive.

As a manager, it's up to you to develop the emotional intelligence of your direct reports—whether they are socially awkward, downright nasty, or simply looking to become more influential. In doing so, you'll help them grow in their careers—and make your workplace a healthier, happier, more productive place to be.

Here's the problem: Emotional intelligence is difficult to develop because it is linked to psychological development and neurological pathways created over an entire lifetime (to learn more, see Daniel Goleman's book *The Brain and Emotional Intelligence: New Insights*). It takes a lot of effort to change long-standing habits of human interaction—not to mention foundational competencies like self-awareness and emotional self-control. People need to be invested in changing their behavior and developing their emotional intelligence, or it just doesn't happen. What this means in practice is that you don't have even a remote chance of changing someone's emotional intelligence unless *they* want to change.

Most of us assume that people will change their behavior when told to do so by a person with authority (you, the manager). For complicated change and development, however, it is clear that people don't *sustain* change when promised incentives like good assignments or a better office.[1] And when threatened or punished, they get downright ornery and behave really badly. Carrot-and-stick performance management processes and the behaviorist approach on which they are based are deeply flawed; yet most of us start (and end) there, even in the most innovative organizations.

What *does* work is:

> First, helping people find a deep and very personal vision of their own future.
>
> Then, helping them see how their current ways of operating might need a bit of work if that future is to be realized.

These are the first two steps in Richard Boyatzis's *intentional change* theory—which we've been testing with leaders for years. According to Boyatzis—and backed up by our work with leaders—here's how people really can begin and sustain change on complex abilities linked to emotional intelligence:

First, find the dream

If you're coaching an employee, you must *first* help them discover what's important in life. Only then can you move on to aspects of work that are important to them. Help your employee craft a clear and compelling vision of a future that includes powerful and positive relationships with family, friends, and coworkers. Notice that I'm talking about *coaching*, not *managing*, your employee. There's a big difference.

Next, find out what's really going on

What's the current state of your employee's emotional intelligence? Once people have a powerful dream to draw strength from, they're strong enough to take the heat—to find out the truth. If you are now truly coaching, you're trusted and your employee will listen to you. Still, that's probably not enough. You will want to find a way to gather input from others, either through a 360-degree feedback instrument like the ESCI (Emotional and Social Competency Inventory), or a Leadership Self-Study process (as described in our book, *Becoming a Resonant Leader*), which gives you the chance to talk directly to trusted friends about their emotional intelligence and other skills.

Finally, craft a gap analysis and a learning plan

Note that I did not say "performance management plan," or even "development plan." A learning plan is different in that it charts a direct path from the personal vision to what must be learned over time to get there—to actual skill development.

Learning goals are *big*. Take, for example, one executive I know. Talented though he was, his distinct lack of caring about the people around him had placed him in danger of being fired. He wanted what he wanted—and watch out if you were in his way. He couldn't seem to change until it finally dawned on him that his bulldozer style was playing out at home too, with his children. That didn't fit at all with his dream of a happy, close-knit family who would live close to each other throughout their lives. So, with a dream in hand and the ugly reality rearing its head at work and at home, he decided to work on developing empathy. As a learning goal, empathy is one of the toughest and most important competencies to develop. The capacity for emotional and cognitive empathy is laid down early in life, and then reinforced over many years. This exec had a good foundation for empathy in childhood, but intense schooling and a stint at an up-or-out management consulting firm had driven it out of him. He needed to relearn how to read people and care about them. He was able to succeed—yes, it took a good while, but he did it.

This sounds like a lot of hard work for your employee, and it can be. Here's where a final important piece of the theory comes into play. They—and you—can't do it alone. People need people—kind and supportive people—when embarking on a journey of self-development. Are you there for your employees? Do you help them find other supporters, in addition to yourself, who will help when their confidence wanes or when they experience inevitable setbacks?

Developing one's emotional intelligence can make the difference between success and failure in life and in work. If you're the one responsible for people's contributions to the team and your organization, you are actually on the hook to try to help those (many) people who are emotional-intelligence-challenged, deficient, and dangerous. It's your job.

But what if you're not the boss? You can still make a difference with colleagues. All of the same rules apply to how people change. You just need to find a different entry point. In my experience, that entry begins with you creating a safe space and establishing trust. Find something to like about these people and let them know it. Give them credit where credit is due, and then some (most of these folks are pretty insecure). Be kind. In other words, use your emotional intelligence to help them get ready to work on theirs.

And finally, if none of this works, these "problem people" don't belong on your team—or maybe even in your organization. If you're a manager, that's when it's time to help them move on with dignity.

Annie McKee is a senior fellow at the University of Pennsylvania and the director of the PennCLO Executive Doctoral Program. She is the author of *Primal Leadership* (with Daniel Goleman and Richard Boyatzis), as well as *Resonant Leadership* and *Becoming a Resonant Leader*. Her new book, *How to Be Happy at Work*, is forthcoming from Harvard Business Review Press in September 2017.

NOTE

1. "What Motivates Us?" interview between Daniel Pink and Katherine Bell, *HBR Ideacast* (podcast), February 10, 2010.

CHAPTER 27

Handling Emotional Outbursts on Your Team

by Liane Davey

Do you have a crier on your team—you know, the one with tissue-thin skin who expresses frustration, sadness, or worry through tears? Maybe you have a screamer, a table pounder who is aggressively invested in every decision. These kinds of emotional outbursts are not just uncomfortable; they can hijack your team, stalling productivity and limiting innovation.

Adapted from content originally posted on hbr.org on April 24, 2015, as "Handling Emotional Outbursts on Your Team."

Don't allow an emotional person to postpone, dilute, or drag out an issue that the business needs you to resolve. Instead, take the outburst for what it is: a communication. Emotions are clues that the issue you are discussing is touching on something the person values or believes strongly in. So look at outbursts as giving you three sets of information: emotional data; factual or intellectual data; and motives, values, and beliefs.

We get stuck when we only focus on the first two—emotions and facts. It's easy to do. When someone starts yelling, for instance, you might think he's mad (emotion) because his project has just been defunded (fact). And many managers stop there, because they find feelings uncomfortable or aren't sure how to deal with them. That's why the first step is to become more self-aware by questioning your mindset around emotions. There are several myths that often get in a team leader's way:

Myth #1: There is no place for emotion in the workplace. If you have humans in the workplace, you're going to have emotions too. Ignoring, stifling, or invalidating them will only drive the toxic issues underground. This outdated notion is one reason people resort to passive-aggressive behavior: Emotions will find their outlet; the choice is whether it's out in the open or in the shadows.

Myth #2: We don't have time to talk about people's feelings. Do you have time for backroom dealings and subterfuge? Do you have time to reopen decisions? Do you have time for failed implementations? Avoiding the emotional issues at the outset will only delay their impact. And when people don't feel heard, their feelings amplify until you have something really destructive to deal with.

Myth #3: Emotions will skew our decision making. Emotions are already affecting your decision making. The choice is whether you want to be explicit about how (and how much) of a role they play or whether you want to leave them as unspoken biases.

With your beliefs in check, you'll be better able to get beyond the emotion and facts to the values the person holds that are being compromised or violated. This is critical because your criers and screamers are further triggered when they don't feel understood. The key is to have a discussion that includes facts, feelings, *and* values. People will feel heard and the emotion will usually dissipate. Then you can focus on making the best business decision possible.

Here's how.

Spot the emotion. If you wait until the emotion is in full bloom, it will be difficult to manage. Instead, watch for the telltale signs that something is causing concern. The most important signals will come from incongruence between what someone is saying and what their body language is telling you. When you notice someone is withdrawing eye contact or getting red in the face, acknowledge what you see: *"Steve, you've stopped midsentence a couple of times now. What's going on for you?"*

Listen. Listen carefully to the response, both to what is said and what you can infer about facts, feelings, and values. You will pick up emotions in language, particularly in extreme words or words that are repeated: *"We have a $2 million budget shortfall and it's our fourth meeting sitting around having a lovely intellectual discussion!"* Body language will again provide clues. Angry (leaning in, clenched jaw or fists) looks very different from discouraged (dropping eye contact, slumping) or dismissive (rolling eyes, turning away).

Ask questions. When you see or hear the emotional layer, stay calm, keep your tone level, and ask a question to draw the person out and get them talking about values: *"I get the sense you're frustrated. What's behind your frustration?"* Listen to their response and then go one layer further by testing a hypothesis: *"Is it possible that you're frustrated because we're placing too much weight on the people impact of the decision and you think we need to focus only on what's right for the business?"*

Resolve it. If your hypothesis is right, you'll probably see relief. The person might even express their pleasure: *"Yes, exactly!"* You can sum it up: *"We've talked about closing the Cleveland office for two years and you're frustrated because you believe that the right decision for the business is obvious."* You've now helped them articulate the values they think should be guiding the decision. The team will now be clear on why they are disagreeing. Three people might jump in, all talking at once: *"We* are *talking about* *people who have given their lives to this organization!" "Here we go again . . ."* Use the same process to reveal the opposing points of view.

Once everyone is working with the same three data sets—facts, emotions, and values—you will be clear what you need to solve for—in this case, *"How will we weigh the financial necessity against the impact on people?"* Although taking the time to draw out the values might seem slow at first, you'll see that issues actually get resolved faster. And ironically, as you validate emotions, over time people will tend to be less emotional because it's often the suppression of emotions or attempts to cobble together facts to justify those emotions that was causing irrational behavior.

If you're leading a high-performing team, you'd better be ready to deal with uncomfortable, messy, complex emotions. If there's a situation you have failed to address because of an emotional team member, spend some time thinking about how you will approach it and then go have the conversation. Today. You can't afford to wait any longer.

Liane Davey is the cofounder of 3COze Inc. She is the author of *You First: Inspire Your Team to Grow Up, Get Along, and Get Stuff Done* and a coauthor of *Leadership Solutions: The Pathway to Bridge the Leadership Gap.* Follow her on Twitter @LianeDavey.

CHAPTER 28

How to Manage Your Emotional Culture

by Sigal Barsade and Olivia A. O'Neill

When people talk about "corporate culture," they're typically referring to *cognitive* culture: the shared *intellectual* values, norms, artifacts, and assumptions that serve as a guide for the group to thrive. Cognitive culture sets the tone for how employees think and behave at work—for instance, how customer-focused, innovative, team-oriented, or competitive they are or should be.

Cognitive culture is undeniably important to an organization's success. But it's only part of the story. The

---

Adapted from "Manage Your Emotional Culture" in *Harvard Business Review*, January 2016 (product #R0601C)

other critical part is what we call the group's *emotional* culture: the shared *affective* values, norms, artifacts, and assumptions that govern which emotions people have and express at work and which ones they are better off suppressing. Though the key distinction here is thinking versus feeling, the two types of culture are also transmitted differently: Cognitive culture is often conveyed verbally, whereas emotional culture tends to be conveyed through nonverbal cues such as body language and facial expression.

In our research over the past decade, we have found that emotional culture influences employee satisfaction, burnout, teamwork, and even hard measures such as financial performance and absenteeism. Countless empirical studies show the significant impact of emotions on how people perform on tasks, how engaged and creative they are, how committed they are to their organizations, and how they make decisions. Positive emotions are consistently associated with better performance, quality, and customer service—this holds true across roles and industries and at various organizational levels. On the flip side (with certain short-term exceptions), negative emotions such as group anger, sadness, fear, and the like usually lead to negative outcomes, including poor performance and high turnover.

So when managers ignore emotional culture, they're glossing over a vital part of what makes people—and organizations—tick. They may understand its importance in theory but can still shy away from emotions at work. Leaders expect to influence how people think and behave on the job, but they may feel ill-equipped to understand and actively manage how employees feel and express their emotions at work. Or they may regard doing so as irrelevant, not part of their job, or unprofessional.

Emotional Cultures in Action

Nearly 30 years ago, the social psychologist Phil Shaver and his colleagues found that people can reliably distinguish among 135 emotions. But understanding the most basic ones—joy, love, anger, fear, sadness—is a good place to start for any leader trying to manage an emotional culture. Here are a few examples to illustrate how these emotions can play out in organizations.

A Culture of Joy

Let's begin with one that's often clearly articulated and actively reinforced by management—above the surface and easy to spot. Vail Resorts recognizes that cultivating joy among employees helps customers have fun too, which matters a lot in the hospitality business. It also gives the organization an edge in retaining top talent in an extremely competitive industry. "Have fun" is listed as a company value and modeled by Vail's CEO, Rob Katz—who, for instance, had ice water dumped on his head during a corporate ALS Ice Bucket Challenge and then jumped fully clothed into a pool. About 250 executives and other employees followed his lead.

This playful spirit at the top permeates Vail. Management tactics, special outings, celebrations, and rewards all support the emotional culture. Resort managers consistently model joy and prescribe it for their teams.

During the workday, they give out pins when they notice employees spontaneously having fun or helping others enjoy their jobs. Rather than asking people to follow standardized customer service scripts, they tell everyone to "go out there and have fun." Mark Gasta, the company's chief people officer, says he regularly sees ski-lift operators dancing, making jokes, doing "whatever it takes to have fun and entertain the guest" while ensuring a safe experience on the slopes. On a day-to-day basis, Vail encourages employees to collaborate because, as Gasta points out, "leaving people out is not fun." At an annual ceremony, a Have Fun award goes to whoever led that year's best initiative promoting fun at work. The resort also fosters off-the-job joy with "first tracks" (first access to the ski slopes for employees), adventure trips, and frequent social gatherings.

All this is in service to an emotional culture that makes intuitive sense. (Joy at a ski resort? Of course.) But now consider an organization where the demand for joy wasn't immediately visible. When we surveyed employees at Cisco Finance about their organization's emotional culture, it became clear to management that fostering joy should be a priority. The survey didn't ask employees how they felt at work; it asked them what emotions they saw their coworkers expressing on a regular basis. (By having employees report on colleagues' emotions, researchers could obtain a more objective bird's-eye view of the culture.) It turned out that joy was one of the strongest drivers of employee satisfaction and commitment at the company—and more of it was needed to keep up engagement.

So management made joy an explicit cultural value, calling it "Pause for Fun." This signaled that it was an important outcome to track—just like productivity, creativity, and other elements of performance. Many companies use annual employee engagement surveys to gauge joy in the abstract, often in the form of job satisfaction and commitment to the organization. But Cisco Finance measured it much more specifically and is conducting follow-up surveys to track whether it is actually increasing. In addition, leaders throughout the organization support this cultural value with their own behavior—for example, by creating humorous videos that show them pausing for fun.

A Culture of Companionate Love

Another emotion we've examined extensively—one that's common in life but rarely mentioned by name in organizations—is *companionate love.* This is the degree of affection, caring, and compassion that employees feel and express toward one another.

In a 16-month study of a large long-term-care facility on the East Coast, we found that workers in units with strong cultures of companionate love had lower absenteeism, less burnout, and greater teamwork and job satisfaction than their colleagues in other units.[1] Employees also performed their work better, as demonstrated by more-satisfied patients, better patient moods, and fewer unnecessary trips to the emergency room. (Employees whose dispositions were positive to begin with received an extra performance boost from the culture.) The families of patients in units with stronger cultures of companionate love reported higher satisfaction with the facility. These results show a powerful connection between emotional culture and business performance.

Because this study took place in a health-care setting, we wondered whether companionate love matters only in "helping" industries. So we surveyed more than 3,200 employees in 17 organizations spanning seven industries: biopharmaceutical, engineering, financial services, higher education, public utilities, real estate, and travel. In organizations where employees felt and expressed companionate love toward one another, people reported greater job satisfaction, commitment, and personal accountability for work performance.

Creating an Emotional Culture

To cultivate a particular emotional culture, you'll need to get people to feel the emotions valued by the organization or team—or at least to behave as if they do. Here are three effective methods:

Harness What People Already Feel

Some employees will experience the desired emotions quite naturally. This can happen in isolated moments of compassion or gratitude, for example. When such feelings arise regularly, that's a sign you're building the culture you want. If people have them only periodically and need help sustaining them, you can try incorporating some gentle nudges during the workday. You might schedule some time for meditation, for instance; or provide mindfulness apps on people's work devices to remind them to simply breathe, relax, or laugh; or create a kudos board, like the one in an ICU we studied, where people can post kind words about other employees.

But what can you do about emotions that are toxic to the culture you're striving for? How can you discourage them when they already exist? Expecting people to "put a lid" on those feelings is both ineffective and destructive; the emotions will just come out later in counterproductive ways. It's important to listen when employees express their concerns so that they feel they are being heard. That's not to say you should encourage venting, or just let the emotions flow without attempting to solve the root problems. Indeed, research shows that extended venting can lead to poor outcomes. You're better off helping employees think about situations in a more constructive way. For example, loneliness, which can eat away at employee attitudes and performance, is best addressed through cognitive reappraisal—getting people to reexamine their views of others' actions. Considering plausible benign motivations for their colleagues' behavior will make them less likely to fixate on negative explanations that could send them into a spiral.

Model the Emotions You Want to Cultivate

A long line of research on emotional contagion shows that people in groups "catch" feelings from others through behavioral mimicry and subsequent changes in brain function.[2] If you regularly walk into a room smiling with high energy, you're much more likely to create a culture of joy than if you wear a neutral expression. Your employees will smile back and start to mean it.

But negative feelings, too, spread like wildfire. If you frequently express frustration, that emotion will infect your team members—and their team members, and so on—throughout the organization. Before you know it, you'll have created a culture of frustration.

So consciously model the emotions you want to cultivate in your company. Some organizations go a step further and explicitly ask employees to spread certain emotions. Ubiquity Retirement + Savings says, "Inspire happiness with contagious enthusiasm. Own your joy and lend it out." Vail Resorts says, "Enjoy your work and share the contagious spirit."

Get People to Fake It 'Til They Feel It

If employees don't experience the desired emotion at a particular moment, they can still help maintain their organization's emotional culture. That's because people express emotions both spontaneously and strategically at work. Social psychology research has long shown that individuals tend to conform to group norms of emotional expression, imitating others out of a desire to be liked and accepted. So employees in a strong emotional culture who would not otherwise feel and express the valued emotion will begin to demonstrate it—even if their initial motivation is to be compliant rather than to internalize the culture.

This benefits the organization, not just the individuals trying to thrive in it. In early anthropological studies of group rituals, strategic emotional expression was found to facilitate group cohesion by overpowering individual feelings and synchronizing interpersonal behavior.

So maintaining the appropriate culture sometimes entails disregarding what you are truly feeling. Through "surface acting," employees can display the valued emotion without even wanting to feel it. Surface acting isn't a long-term solution, though. Research shows that it can eventually lead to burnout—particularly in the absence of any outlet for authentic emotions.[3]

A better way to cultivate a desired emotion is through "deep acting." With this technique, people make a focused effort to feel a certain way—and then suddenly they do. Imagine that an employee at an accounting firm has a family emergency and requests a week off work at the height of tax audit season. Although his boss's first thought is *No—not now—no!* she could engage in deep acting to change her immediate feelings of justifiable panic into genuine caring and concern for her subordinate. By trying hard to empathize, saying "Of course, you should go be with your family!" and using the facial expressions, body language, and tone of voice she would use when actually feeling those emotions, she could coax herself into the real thing. She would also be modeling a desired behavior for the subordinate and the rest of the team.

Fortunately, all these ways of creating an emotional culture—whether they involve really feeling the emotion or simply acting that way—can reinforce one another and strengthen the culture's norms. People don't have to put on an act forever. Those who begin by expressing an emotion out of a desire to conform will start to actually feel it through emotional contagion. They'll also receive positive reinforcement for following the norms, which will make them more likely to demonstrate the emotion again.

Of course, the culture will be much stronger and more likely to endure if people truly believe in the values and assumptions behind it. Someone who is uncomfortable with an organization's emotional culture and has to keep pretending in order to be successful would probably be better off moving to a different work environment. Companies often have more than one emotional culture, so another unit or department might be a good fit. But if the culture is homogeneous, the employee may want to leave the company entirely.

Implementation Matters at All Levels

Just like other aspects of organizational culture, emotional culture should be supported at all levels of the organization. The role of top management is to drive it.

Leaders are often insufficiently aware of how much influence they have in creating an emotional culture. Traci Fenton is the founder and CEO of WorldBlu, a consulting firm that tackles fear at work. She shares this example: At one *Fortune* 500 company, unbeknownst to the CEO, senior employees regularly use text message codes to describe his nonverbal expressions of anger in meetings. "RED" means he is getting red in the face. "VEIN" means his veins are popping out. "ACP," which stands for "assume the crash position," means he is about to start throwing things. This leader is very effective at creating an emotional culture—but it's probably not the one he wants.

So don't underestimate the importance of day-to-day modeling. Large, symbolic emotional gestures are powerful, but only if they are in line with daily behavior. Senior executives can also shape an emotional culture through organizational practices. Take "compassionate firing," which is common at companies that build a strong culture of companionate love. Carlos Gutierrez, the vice president of R&D systems at Lattice Semiconductor, was deeply concerned about the impact of layoffs on his employees. He recognized that the traditional HR protocol of asking terminated employees to clean out their desks immediately and leave the premises would be especially painful to people who had worked side by side for 10–20 years. Along with his partners in HR and R&D, he implemented a protocol whereby employees had an extended time to say good-bye to their colleagues and to commemorate their time together at the company. Also, although two-thirds of the R&D workforce is outside the United States, Sherif Sweha, the corporate vice president of R&D, believed it was important for the affected team members in each region to receive the news from a senior leader face-to-face. So he and members of his staff flew to the company's sites in Asia to have in-person conversations with all the employees to be laid off—and also those who would remain with the company.

Though top management sets the first example and establishes the formal rules, middle managers and front-line supervisors ensure that the emotional values are consistently practiced by others. Because one of the biggest influences on employees is their immediate boss, the suggestions that apply to senior executives also apply to those managers: They should ensure that the emotions they express at work reflect the chosen culture, and they should speak explicitly about what is expected from employees.

It's also important to link the emotional culture to operations and processes, including performance management systems. At Vail Resorts, the culture of joy has been incorporated into the annual review, which indicates how well each employee integrates fun into the work environment and rates everyone on supporting behaviors, such as being inclusive, welcoming, approachable, and positive. Someone who exceeds expectations is described as not only taking part in the fun but also offering "recommendations to improve the work environment to integrate fun."

Decades' worth of research demonstrates the importance of organizational culture, yet most of it has focused on the cognitive component. As we've shown, organizations also have an emotional pulse, and managers must track it closely to motivate their teams and reach their goals.

Emotional culture is shaped by how all employees—from the highest echelons to the front lines—comport themselves day in and day out. But it's up to senior leaders to establish which emotions will help the organization thrive, model those emotions, and reward others for doing the same. Companies in which they do this have a lot to gain.

Sigal Barsade is the Joseph Frank Bernstein Professor of Management at Wharton. **Olivia A. O'Neill** is an assistant professor of management at George Mason University and a senior scholar at the school's Center for the Advancement of Well-Being.

NOTES

1. Sigal Barsade and Olivia A. O'Neill, "What's Love Got to Do with It? A Longitudinal Study of the Culture of Companionate Love and Employee and Client Outcomes in a Long-Term Care Setting," *Administrative Science Quarterly* 59, no 4. (2014).
2. Sigal Barsade, "The Ripple Effect: Emotional Contagion and Its Influence on Group Behavior," *Administrative Science Quarterly* 47, no. 4 (2002).
3. Alicia A. Grandey, "When 'The Show Must Go On': Surface Acting and Deep Acting as Determinants of Emotional Exhaustion and Peer-Rated Service Delivery," *Academy of Management Journal* 46, no. 1 (February 2003): 86–96.

Index